For
Christine

THE CAMBRIDGE HANDBOOK OF AGE AND AGEING

The Cambridge Handbook of Age and Ageing is a state-of-the-art guide to the current body of knowledge, theory, policy and practice relevant to age researchers and gerontologists around the world. It contains almost eighty original chapters, commissioned and written by the world's leading gerontologists from sixteen countries and five continents. The broad focus of the book is on the behavioural and social sciences but it also includes important contributions from the biological and medical sciences. It provides comprehensive, accessible and authoritative accounts of all the key topics in the field ranging from theories of ageing, to demography, physical aspects of ageing, mental processes and ageing, nursing and healthcare for older people, the social context of ageing, cross-cultural perspectives, relationships, quality of life, gender, and financial and policy provision. This handbook will be a must-have resource for all researchers, students and professionals with an interest in age and ageing.

MALCOLM L. JOHNSON is Professor of Health and Social Policy (Emeritus), University of Bristol, and Director of the International Institute on Health and Ageing. From 1984 to 1995 he was Professor and Dean of the School of Health and Social Welfare at the Open University. He has published 9 books and over 150 chapters and articles reflecting the broad range of his academic interests, of which ageing, the lifespan and end-of-life issues are the most prominent. He is a former Associate Editor of *Sociology of Health and Illness*, was Secretary of the British Society of Gerontology and Founding Editor of the international journal *Ageing and Society* (1980–92). He has taught and researched widely in the UK and has been Distinguished Visiting Professor at several North American universities.

VERN L. BENGTSON is the AARP/University Chair in Gerontology and Professor of Sociology at the University of Southern California. He has published 15 books and over 220 articles. He was elected President of the Gerontological Society of America and has been granted a MERIT award from the National Institute on Aging for his 35-year Longitudinal Study of Generations.

PETER G. COLEMAN is Professor of Psychogerontology at the University of Southampton, Fellow of the British Psychological Society (FBPsS), a Chartered Health Psychologist, and Academician of the Academy of Learned Societies for the Social Sciences (AcSS). His publications include *Ageing and reminiscence processes*, *Ageing and development: theories and research* (with Ann O'Hanlon), *Life-span and change in a gerontological perspective* (co-ed.) and *Ageing in society* (co-ed.). He was Assistant Editor of *Reviews in Clinical Gerontology* from 1990 to 1993, and Editor of *Ageing and Society* from 1992 to 1996.

THOMAS B. L. KIRKWOOD is Professor of Medicine and Co-Director of the Institute for Ageing and Health at the University of Newcastle upon Tyne, and a Council Member of the UK Academy of Medical Sciences. He is Co-Editor of *Mechanisms of Ageing and Development* and his books include *Chance, development and ageing* (with Caleb Finch), the award-winning *Time of our lives: the science of human ageing* and *The end of age* based on his BBC Reith Lectures in 2001.

THE CAMBRIDGE
HANDBOOK OF
AGE AND AGEING

Edited by
MALCOLM L. JOHNSON
University of Bristol

Association with
VERN L. BENGTSON
University of Southern California

PETER G. COLEMAN
University of Southampton

THOMAS B. L. KIRKWOOD
University of Newcastle upon Tyne

CAMBRIDGE
UNIVERSITY PRESS

CAMBRIDGE UNIVERSITY PRESS
Cambridge, New York, Melbourne, Madrid, Cape Town, Singapore, São Paulo

Cambridge University Press
The Edinburgh Building, Cambridge CB2 2RU, UK

Published in the United States of America by Cambridge University Press, New York

www.cambridge.org
Information on this title: www.cambridge.org/9780521533706

First published 2005

Printed in the United Kingdom at the University Press, Cambridge

A catalogue record for this book is available from the British Library

Library of Congress Cataloguing in Publication data
The Cambridge handbook of age and ageing / general editor, Malcolm Johnson;
associate editors, Vern L. Bengtson, Peter G. Coleman, Thomas B. L. Kirkwood.
   p.   cm.
Includes bibliographical references and index.
ISBN 0-521-82632-2 – ISBN 0-521-53370-8 (paperback)
1. Gerontology.   2. Ageing.   3. Older people – Social conditions.   4. Older people – Care.
I. Johnson, Malcolm Lewis.
HQ1061.C315   2005
305.26 – dc22   2005047832

ISBN-13 978-0-521-82632-7 hardback
ISBN-10 0-521-82632-2 hardback
ISBN-13 978-0-521-53370-6 paperback
ISBN-10 0-521-53370-8 paperback

Contents

Contributors

Isabella Aboderin, Institute of Ageing, University of Oxford

W. Andrew Achenbaum, College of Liberal Arts and Social Sciences, University of Houston

Katherine R. Allen, Department of Human Development, Virginia Polytechnic Institute and State University

Toni C. Antonucci, Department of Psychology, University of Michigan

Sara Arber, Centre for Research on Ageing and Gender, Department of Sociology, University of Surrey

Claudine Attias-Donfut, CNAV, Paris

Paul B. Baltes, Max Planck Institute of Human Development, Center for Lifespan Psychology, Berlin

Sandhi Maria Barreto, Ageing and Health, World Health Organization

Vern L. Bengtson, Andrus Gerontology Center and Department of Sociology, University of Southern California

Simon Biggs, Age Concern Institute of Gerontology, King's College, University of London

Joanna Bornat, Faculty of Health and Social Care, The Open University

Julie B. Boron, College of Health and Human Development, Pennsylvania State University

Mike Boulton, School of Optometry and Vision Sciences, Cardiff University

Clive E. Bowman, Medical Director, BUPAcare Services, UK

Marjolein Broese van Groenou, Sociology and Social Gerontology, Vrije University, Amsterdam

Edna Brown, Department of Psychology, University of Michigan

Robert N. Butler, Co-Chair, Alliance for Health of the Future; Geriatrics and Adult Development, Mount Sinai School of Medicine, New York

Bill Bytheway, Faculty of Health and Social Care, The Open University

Neena L. Chappell, Centre on Ageing and Department of Sociology, University of Victoria

Neil Charness, Department of Psychology, Florida State University

Kaare Christensen, Ageing Research Centre, and Epidemiology, Institute of Public Health, University of Southern Denmark.

Peter G. Coleman, School of Psychology, University of Southampton

Ingrid Arnet Connidis, Department of Sociology, University of Western Ontario

Neal E. Cutler, Financial Gerontology, Widener University, Chester, Penn.

Sara J. Czaja, Department of Psychiatry and Behavioral Sciences, University of Miami School of Medicine

Svein Olav Daatland, Norwegian Social Research, Oslo

Lia Susana Daichman, International Network for the Prevention of Elder Abuse (INPEA), Buenos Aires, Argentina

Adam Davey, Polisher Research Institute, Philadelphia

Bleddyn Davies, Personal Social Service Research Unit at the LSE and universities of Kent and Manchester

Freya Dittmann-Kohli, Center for Psychogerontology, University of Nijmegen

Glen H. Elder, Jr, Carolina Population Center, The University of North Carolina at Chapel Hill

Carroll L. Estes, Institute for Health and Ageing, University of California, San Francisco

Mike Featherstone, Theory, Culture and Society Centre, Nottingham Trent University

Amy Fiske, University of Southern California

Alexandra Freund, School of Education and Social Policy, Northwestern University

Daphna Gans, Andrus Gerontology Center, University of Southern California

Linda K. George, Department of Sociology, Duke University

Roseann Giarrusso, California State University

Chris Gilleard, St George's Hospital Medical School, London

Jay Ginn, Centre for Research on Ageing and Gender, Department of Sociology, University of Surrey

Edlira Gjonça, Department of Epidemiology and Public Health, University College London

Elena L. Grigorenko, Department of Psychology, Yale University

Jaber F. Gubrium, Department of Sociology, University of Missouri

Sarah Harper, Oxford Institute of Ageing, University of Oxford

Jutta Heckhausen, School of Ecology, University of California – Irvine

Akiko Hashimoto, Department of Sociology, University of Pittsburgh

Jon Hendricks, Department of Sociology, Oregon State University

Mike Hepworth, Department of Sociology and Anthropology, University of Aberdeen

Charlotte Ikels, Department of Anthropology, Case Western Reserve University

James S. Jackson, Department of Psychology, University of Michigan

Yuri Jang, Gerontology Center, University of Georgia

Bernard Jeune, Ageing Research Centre, and Epidemiology, Institute of Public Health, University of Southern Denmark

Malcolm L. Johnson, International Institute on Health and Ageing and University of Bristol

Randi S. Jones, Emory University

Alexandre Kalache, Ageing and Health, World Health Organization

Robert L. Kane, Health Services Research and Policy, University of Minnesota

Rosalie A. Kane, Health Services Research and Policy, University of Minnesota

Ingrid Keller, Ageing and Health, World Health Organization

Rose Anne Kenny, Department of Geriatrics, Royal Victoria Infirmary, Newcastle upon Tyne

Thomas B. L. Kirkwood, Institute for Ageing and Health, Newcastle General Hospital, University of Newcastle upon Tyne

Kees Knipscheer, Sociology and Social Gerontology, Vrije University, Amsterdam

Martin Kohli, European University Institute, Florence

Gisela Labouvie-Vief, Department of Psychology, Wayne State University

Kristina Larsson, Stockholm Gerontology Research Center, Stockholm, Sweden

Shu-Chen Li, Max Planck Institute of Human Development, Center for Lifespan Psychology, Berlin

Charles F. Longino, Jr, Sociology Department, Wake Forest University, N.C.

Ariela Lowenstein, Centre for the Research and Study of Ageing, University of Haifa, Israel

Erick McCarthy, Gerontology Center, University of Georgia

Gerald E. McClearn, Center for Developmental and Health Genetics and Department of Biobehavioral Health, The Pennsylvania State University

Brendan McCormack, Nursing Research, University of Ulster / Royal Hospitals

Elizabeth MacKinlay, Centre for Ageing and Pastoral Studies, School of Theology, Charles Sturt University

Alfons Marcoen, Department of Psychology, Catholic University Leuven

Michael Marmot, Department of Epidemiology and Public Health, University College London

Tom Margrain, School of Optometry and Vision Sciences, Cardiff University

Victor W. Marshall, Institute of Ageing, The University of North Carolina at Chapel Hill

Elizabeth A. Maylor, Department of Psychology, University of Warwick

Ruud ter Meulen, Department of Caring Sciences, University of Maastricht

Harry R. Moody, International Longevity Center – USA, New York

Robert A. Neimeyer, Department of Psychology, University of Memphis

Demi Patsios, Centre for Health and Social Care, School for Policy Studies, University of Bristol

Margaret J. Penning, Centre on Aging and Department of Sociology, University of Victoria

Stephen A. Petrill, Center for Developmental and Health Genetics and Department of Biobehavioral Health, The Pennsylvania State University

Chris Phillipson, Institute of Ageing, Keele University

Leonard W. Poon, Gerontology Center, University of Georgia

Norella M. Putney, Andrus Gerontology Center, University of Southern California

Jill Quadagno, Pepper Institute on Aging and Public Policy, Florida State University

Pat Rabbitt, Age and Cognitive Performance Research Centre, University of Manchester

Jennifer Reid Keene, Department of Sociology, University of Nevada – Las Vegas

Sandra G. Reynolds, Gerontology Center, University of Georgia

Steven R. Sabat, Department of Psychology, Georgetown University

Clive Seale, Department of Human Sciences, Brunel University, London

Merril Silverstein, Leonard Davis School of Gerontology, University of Southern California

Hannes B. Staehelin, Geriatric University Clinic, University Hospital Basel

Ursula M. Staudinger, Institute for Educational and Developmental Psychology, Dresden University

Robert J. Sternberg, Department of Psychology, Yale University

Debra Street, Pepper Institute on Aging and Public Policy, Florida State University

Philip Taylor, Cambridge Interdisciplinary Research Centre on Ageing, University of Cambridge

Fleur Thomése, Sociology and Social Gerontology, Vrije University, Amsterdam

Mats Thorslund, Department of Social Work, Stockholm University

Jinzhou Tian, Institute of Geriatrics, Beijing University of Chinese Medicine

Theo van Tilburg, Sociology and Social Gerontology, Vrije University, Amsterdam

Fernando M. Torres-Gil, School of Public Policy, University of California, Los Angeles

Josy Ubachs-Moust, Department of Caring Sciences, University of Maastricht

Christina Victor, School of Health and Social Care, University of Reading

K. Warner Shaie, College of Health and Human Development, Pennsylvania State University

Anthony M. Warnes, Sheffield Institute for Studies on Ageing, Northern General Hospital, Sheffield

James L. Werth, Jr, Department of Psychology, The University of Akron

Sherry L. Willis, College of Health and Human Development, Pennsylvania State University

François-Charles Wolff, Faculty of Economics, University of Nantes; CNAV and INED, Paris

Bob Woods, School of Psychology, University of Wales, Bangor

Foreword

Ageing of individuals and populations of human-kind has long been studied and described out of simple academic curiosity, in search of scientific explanation, to enunciate better the social, health and economic consequences and in the quest for solutions to the imagined or real negative outcomes of the phenomena. The level of public and political attention given to the issues has recently expanded to an astonishing degree epitomised by the global response represented by the United Nations World Assemblies on ageing convened in 1982 in Vienna and again in 2002 in Madrid. At these global summits the member states of the UN convened to review the implications and necessary policy responses to the unprecedented scale and rapidity of population ageing. During the second half of the last century the UN Population Division had observed that the global population of those persons aged 60 years and over almost trebled from 205 million to 606 million, and average global human life expectancy increased by 20 years from 46 years in 1950 to 66 years by 2000. During the same period unprecedented rates of decline in fertility saw many developed countries drop close to or below replacement levels, with the developing world following similar trends and progressively showing signs of 'catching up'. While the 1982 Assembly focussed on the situation of older persons, particularly in the developed nations of the world, at the 2002 event the increasing significance of the ageing in developing countries, where more than half of the world's older (aged 60 years and over) population reside, was

recognised. The 2002 Madrid World Assembly was preceded by The Valencia Forum, an event auspiced by the International Association of Gerontology that brought together some 580 scientists, practitioners and educators in ageing to present, debate and articulate the evidence base in support of the 'political' deliberations of the Assembly. An important accompaniment to the Madrid International Plan of Action on Ageing 2002, the product of the Second World Assembly on Ageing, was the joint UN Office on Ageing and the International Association of Gerontology project report – the Research Agenda on Ageing for the Twenty-First Century, which identified priorities for policy-relevant research world wide. A series of expert group meetings had been convened during 1999–2000 which led to formulation of this global research agenda. The Valencia Forum endorsed the final version that was subsequently presented at the Second World Assembly on Ageing in Madrid. The United Nations General Assembly, in its resolution 57/177, subsequently 'welcomed the adoption in April 2002 by the Valencia Forum of research and academic professionals of the Research Agenda on Ageing for the Twenty-First Century, to support the implementation of the Madrid International Plan of Action on Ageing, 2002'.

The importance of high-quality relevant research and the continuing expansion in knowledge and understanding of ageing and all its ramifications has been acknowledged at the highest levels. Over this time and continuing into the present era there has been a commensurate growth in research, knowledge and information on human ageing from a myriad of perspectives. Anyone with an interest in the subject is now literally bombarded by a burgeoning literature on the issues at many levels, from the most fundamental evolutionary genetic, biomolecular, physiological and psychological, to social, economic and national socioeconomic developmental scenarios.

Any powerfully informed effort to marshal systematically and concisely the breadth and depth of our contemporary knowledge and understanding of the phenomena of human ageing must be applauded as timely and highly relevant in these present times.

This handbook has admirably achieved that goal, presenting as it does an impressive set of contributions from some of the world's leading scholars, educators and practitioners across the many fields, enhancing our knowledge and understanding of ageing. While the array of knowledge and information set forth is impressive, it is also important to note the call in many areas for more research and exploration of key issues and questions yet unanswered or only incompletely tapped.

The triumphs of increasing human longevity and population control, as well as the challenges posed by the need to change societal perceptions and attitudes and adjust social and economic institutions, are becoming a universally shared experience of the developed and developing countries of the world. The time frames, demographic trajectories and socioeconomic contexts vary widely but the overall trends are a collective experience. Even the many other challenges to human well-being and prosperity, such as emerging epidemics of HIV/AIDS and other infectious diseases, terrorism, war, environmental decay, sectarian strife and violence, extensive poverty and major natural disasters, have links to population ageing through the role shifts and consequences imposed on ageing persons.

Closer to home, national social institutions are variously grappling with the policy implications of increasing longevity and population ageing. Responses vary greatly from relatively scant attention to comprehensive aged care policies and programmes covering social security, health insurance, acute and chronic care, residential and community programmes, treatment, rehabilitation and long

term care services. In addition some more enlightened nations have enacted legislation to deal with such issues as age based discrimination, rights of older persons, labour force participation and so on.

The human landscape viewed from the perspective of population age structure and intergenerational roles and relationships has changed dramatically over the last century and will continue to do so at many levels. Greater knowledge and understanding of the processes shaping these changes and their inevitable consequences in polity, social, economic, health and broader humanitarian terms are critically needed.

Chapters in this book attest to the extent we have progressively uncovered the complex mechanisms underlying ageing at evolutional genetic, biomolecular and cellular levels in ways that have potential to identify positive interventions, especially where the fundamental links between ageing processes and age associated chronic diseases lie.

The realms of demography, social science, anthropology, epidemiology, psychology, mental and physical health, sexuality, quality of life, care, technology, ageism, images, attitudes, families, intergenerational relations, cultural influences, death, dying, spirituality, ethics and economics among others are explored in this extensive collection of contributions.

Moreover, the big questions concerning health and social policy are explored and lessons drawn from some of the policy initiatives of the past and current models for social security provision and health care coverage that are in place in various situations around the globe.

This is a wide-ranging tome that draws on an extraordinary multidisciplinary and erudite scholarship, which is demanded by the comprehensive study of ageing and its implications. While it is multifaceted, nonetheless the insights offered by so many informed perspectives seem to present a common thread, clear at points and faint at others but consistent throughout, that suggests some potential for the evolution of what Edmund O. Wilson defined as 'consilience', a word originally coined by William Whewell who used it in his book *The philosophy of the inductive sciences* in 1840 to describe the interlocking of explanations of cause and effect between disciplines. At least in the fields of study which provide commentary on human ageing from the vantage points of genetics, biology, medicine, sociology, psychology, anthropology, economics and social policy, as well as art, literature and philosophy, we seem to be making our way little by little towards some very fundamental and shared truths about the nature and rewards of the experience of human ageing. It may be some time before these rich and diverse understandings of the expression of ageing can be reconciled in some common and more fundamental scientific framework but the production of an authoritative multidimensional exploration of the state of the art(s) as set forth here provides a very interesting point at which such an exploration might begin.

Within a common framework or not, there is a need for all of those associated with human ageing as scientists, practitioners, educators, policy and decision makers to be better informed across a very broad range of arenas. Decisions of all kinds and policies, whether precisely targeted or broad, should be made on the basis of sound evidence. This is perhaps more

cogent in an area like ageing where myths, misconceptions and false assumptions have abounded through all of recorded history.

Certainly, in this book we are led to a more enlightened positive and proactive perspective on, and understanding of individual and population ageing. This handbook may well be heralded as marking an important turning point in how we see and respond to ageing in both personal and societal terms. With greatly improved knowledge and understanding across many realms – informed by realities, clearer in appreciation of the challenges – comes a greater confidence in our capacity to achieve maximum benefit from humankind's maturation and to deal more effectively and positively with the much chronicled real and imagined vicissitudes of ageing.

GARY R. ANDREWS
University of South Australia
Immediate past President
International Association of Gerontology

General Editor's Preface

AGEING IN THE MODERN WORLD

The invitation to design and edit a major new *Handbook* which captures the state of research and knowledge in relation to human ageing came both as a rare and exciting privilege and as a daunting prospect. Having spent a significant part of my academic career engaged in the developing field of gerontology, I felt I knew what the research and public policy agendas were around the world. But capturing the exponential growth in the body of knowledge at the beginning of the twenty-first century inevitably required a careful selection of issues and perspectives rather than a representative sample of the whole burgeoning output. Early notions that such a volume could reasonably encompass all the main disciplinary areas were soon set aside. Not only was the sheer volume of research emerging from the human and policy sciences (which I could make some claim to know) now vast and diverse, the prodigious expansion of research in the medical and biological sciences was both monumental in scale and beyond my range. So the enterprise had to become somewhat more focused and more collaborative, involving three Associate Editors of unrivalled scholarship and vision: Vern Bengtson, Peter Coleman and Tom Kirkwood.

Despite the need to acknowledge that a single comprehensive sourcebook for gerontology was no longer achievable, I wanted the *Handbook* still to represent the full range of contemporary knowledge and debate. So what the reader will find here is a very substantial representation of what is known about age and the processes of ageing across the lifespan, from the social and behavioural sciences. This is the core of the book. But in order to contextualise and connect with the social and psychological dimensions, there is a series of expert and accessible distillations of key developments in biomedicine.

These contributions are, for me, an essential part of the rationale of the Handbook. They ensure that the core readership remains in touch with areas of science which are central to the study of ageing and which will certainly transform the lived experience of it, as the human genome project provides new and previously unimagined forms of intervention which will re-write the health and illness map of later life and produce a paradigm shift in life expectation. Any future edition will find the consequences of these changes have reshaped the rest of the gerontological enterprise. They will set new and urgent agendas for families, worklife, pensions, inheritance, intergenerational relations, images of ageing, mental health, lifespan perspectives, assistive technology, long term care. They will give rise to new forms of wellbeing and a range of new stresses and maladies as relationships in every context are stretched to meet even longer duration and new sets of expectations.

Yet, much of what is to come will be an extension of familiar ground. The twentieth century saw unprecedented reductions in premature death, in the developed world, which in turn led to a spectacular increase of life expectation. As a result, the second half of the century saw similarly unanticipated changes in family patterns, gender and generational relations, the emergence of the Third Age and the beginnings of a globalisation of extended life.

To fulfil the intention of providing the reader with a comprehensive view of the subject area, in the form of 'state of the art' chapters from leading authorities, the book is organised into seven parts, which represent the major domains of debate and empirical enquiry. Within each part the selection is offered in a relatively unstructured way. No attempt has been made to sequence or link the contributions, as this would create a false construction of the way research and ideas proceed. Nonetheless, there is a multitude of points of contact which will assist readers to gain a coherent picture of the extent to which there is agreement amongst scholars and where there is unresolved contest and debate.

Part One was, nonetheless, designed to provide a panoramic introduction to the study of age and ageing. Those who choose to read all of these opening chapters should gain an authoritative perspective on the state of gerontology, in all its dynamic diversity. They will observe emerging trends as the lifespan approach gains favour, new ethical concerns, approaches to health are being re-configured, the neurologists and the psychologists struggle to establish the scientific foundations of human behaviour, and the sociologists and policy analysts debate the most effective ways of ensuring a good but affordable old age. In all of this discourse there remains a lack of over-arching concepts which provide a coherent view, a mind-map, of what ageing is and what its principal components are. This absence of an integrating framework is simply the reality in an area of enquiry which is still relatively young. It also represents the enormous complexity of age and ageing as enduring but constantly changing features of the global human landscape.

Emerging themes

For more than thirty years I have been a participant observer of the inter-disciplinary field we call gerontology. One important segment of this endeavour has been to be an editor of academic journals and of books. As founding Associate Editor of *Sociology of Health and Illness* (1978--80) and for twelve years the founding Editor of the international journal published by Cambridge University Press *Ageing and Society* (1980–92), it was a necessary task to view how this emerging field was shaping up. So, from time to time, I have attempted to assess the trends of development and, in so doing, drawn attention to areas of neglect.

In the opening editorial of *Ageing and Society* in March 1981 I raised a continuing theme about the narrowness of focus in the existing literature:

The stock of existing research on ageing is characteristically about retirement; it is also largely about 'being old' at particular chronological ages and at particular times. It has in the recent past been excessively concerned with the social characteristics, experiences, views and maladies of cohorts of retired people . . . these enquiries contained relatively little which recognized the dynamics and continuities of social ageing, nor did they use personal or group history as a tool for interpreting their snap-shots of older people. (p. 2)

A year later, after having read over a hundred submitted manuscripts, I continued the critique: 'How can we begin to create a convincing gerontology if its enquiries are confined to what the French call the third and fourth ages? So much of what has been published to date consists of sets of data offering descriptions of the performance and characteristics of older people as though they were in themselves meaningful.' Then turning to another persistent theme, the lack of theory and the parochial nature of such work as there was, I asked: 'Why is it, . . . there is no prominent debate within ageing studies of those theoretical and ideological concerns which suffuse other related fields of study?' (Johnson, 1982).

My aspiration was to make the journal a distinctive vehicle for research which, in addition to presenting the results of research, gave a good account of its methodology, set the new material in the context of existing literature and drew conceptual observations from the new contributions to the body of knowledge. I also wished to stimulate research into aspects of ageing which were under-represented or non-existent at the time. Some modest success was achieved in publishing the work of economists, but this key discipline has still to engage fully with gerontology. Contributions from the arts remained rare as did work from lawyers. But the political economy of ageing was born in the first issue, with seminal papers from Peter Townsend (1981) and Alan Walker (1981), as was the stream of work on biographical analysis initiated by Leopold Rosenmayr

(1981). In later years the journal sponsored work on the linkages between oral history and ageing, lifespan psychology, gender, the moral economy of ageing and a landmark special issue on history and ageing (4) (1984), amongst other themes. These important articles helped to establish a reputation for serious discourse, which then as now seemed so vital to a proper understanding of the lifespan of individuals, groups, institutions and societies.

The *Cambridge Handbook* is a further attempt to present the latest and most important developments in research, in a way which provides the reader with a body of concepts and ideas to shape interpretations of the ever growing resources of data and commentary. Again, the achievement is partial, reflecting the state of the field. Yet within the almost eighty chapters there is ample evidence of diversification and a developing capacity for integrating knowledge across disciplines, nation states and continents.

THE PREOCCUPATION WITH HEALTH

From its inception the core area of gerontology has been health. If the principal narrative of the past thirty years has been about apocalyptic demography, the motive force of that story is the global extension of life. As any introductory lecture in gerontology will now relate, in the developed world people, on average, have around a 50 per cent greater expectation of life at birth than their forefathers had a hundred years ago. Moreover, recent statistical studies have shown that the tide of life extension has not stopped. Oeppen and Vaupel (2002) demonstrated that there has been an annual gain in expectation of life in northern Europe of three months per year, consistently over the last 160 years. If the trend was coming to an end, the increments would show signs of tailing off. But the trend is as strong and consistent as ever. So regardless of any scientific breakthrough which might lead to further reduction in the causes of death, our collective age will continue to rise.

It is part of contemporary received wisdom, that 'having your health' is the foundation of a good old age. We equally acknowledge that there is a global gradient in health and this reflects income, wealth and education. So it is not surprising that health and its promotion has been the central arena of gerontology for the whole of its relatively short collective life. Indeed the whole field was developed originally by physicians who were concerned about the impact of chronic diseases and the pathologies of later life. As Andrew Achenbaum points out in his elegant history of gerontology, *Crossing frontiers* (1995), this interdisciplinary field has been dominated by preoccupations with oldness and its linked profile of physical decline associated with the Western world's epidemic of chronic illnesses which make up the principal causes of death – cancers and heart diseases. Despite the growing importance of research on the social features of life in the Third and Fourth Ages, which explore the positive potentialities of being an older person, these studies are overwhelmed by the sheer weight of inquiries about illnesses – physical and psychological – and the interventions which might ameliorate their consequences. An analysis of the hundreds of presentations at national and international conferences shows that their programmes are little different in structure and balance of content from those of ten, twenty or even thirty years ago.

What has changed is the nature of the focus on health, illness and its remediation. The research is more methodologically and technically proficient. It is more likely than in the past to produce data which can be translated into scales, typologies and professional procedures with their accompanying protocols for assessment and evaluation. This increasing sophistication is not to be regretted. It represents a higher degree of professional skill and a strong knowledge base, for use in addressing the requirements of the growing legions of old people worldwide. But, there is no parallel development in our conceptualising. Theoretical work remains a remarkably neglected area of gerontological work. So the oft-repeated observation that gerontology is 'data rich and theory poor' is demonstrably still the case (see Bengtson *et al.*, 1999; and in this volume, Chapter 1.1).

Research on the causal connections between health and age is activated by the push from governments and the funding for 'big science', which together have fuelled a huge drive towards: (a) the development of biologically based studies that are designed to yield interventions to halt or divert the effects of physical ageing; (b) clinical medical studies to produce drugs and surgical and technical procedures to treat age-related illnesses; and (c) research related to the roles of health professionals and those engaged in long term care and the development of techniques which enhance the capacity of older people (with the support of family carers) to live in so-called 'independence' in their own homes.

These preoccupations can be seen as the strongest domains of gerontological work, for the past fifty years. The latest manifestation is a belated recognition that prevention is both better and cheaper. So across the developed world there is what almost amounts to a tidal wave of measures to reduce smoking and obesity, promote exercise and the manifestations of what is called 'healthy living'. None of this is new of course. The evidence base has been there for decades. So too was the literature on ageing populations and the need to see pensions policy reflect demography. Nonetheless, this body of evidence and analysis has remained comparatively neglected by politicians and policy makers until market collapse with its dramatic impact on pension funds thrust the issue onto the public agenda. These observations are not new revelations to contemporary observers. We are aware of the pressures and inducements to a health and employment focus which is supported by governmental funding and leads to peer reviewed publications. So what is the purpose of drawing attention to them now?

First, because there is an emerging awareness that these strategies – both for research and for service delivery – are not sustainable. They require too much of the GNP. Projections of health and pension costs to 2030 or 2050 already show us that current health and social care systems will be undeliverable as the post- Second World War 'baby boomer' generations enter the Fourth Age. Countries like China, India and Brazil with rampantly ageing populations and unsustainable dependency ratios will quite possibly lead the way in developing new paradigms of health care. But Western nations must seriously reconsider their own strategies if a care crisis is to be avoided.

History and experience tell us that major transitions in public policy usually occur at the confluence of a real or perceived crisis along with the availability of worked-out ideas and evidence, which find that their time is come: what C. M. Cornford in his masterly essay called 'ripe time' (1908). There are many issues addressed within the *Handbook* which still await their day in the sun; but fortunately gerontol-

ogists have already seen their importance and made them the subject of serious enquiry. Amongst these issues in waiting, are: the consequences of ageing in Asia, Sub-Saharan Africa and South America; death and dying in very old age; spirituality in later life; the ethics of intergenerational tensions at the macro and micro levels; the consequences of declines in cognition, memory and self-esteem in an ever more complex world; the role of inheritance in the personal, familial and national economy. All these, and more, are to be found in this volume.

So, what are the emerging new perspectives? Drawing on the experience of creating this book, designed to benchmark the current state of gerontology, I can see a selection of developments which may provide the next generation of research and policy. Some are in the list just noted. Others will derive from the growing understanding of the changing psychology of the human lifespan, which Paul Baltes *et al.* unfold in Chapter 1.4. Their conclusions are:

that the major challenge for research is to understand, on a behavioural level, the mechanisms of adaptive resource allocation that help individuals compensate for the inevitable loss of neurobiological and psychological resources in old age and, at the same time, permit them to direct a sizeable share of their resources to maintaining functions, and addressing new tasks that are unique to the conduct and meaning of life in old age.

This intersection of psychological functioning, existential meaning and the practical realities of advanced old age represents one enormously important facet of the search for lifelong wellbeing.

Whilst the complexities of human behaviour will rise in the priority list, it seems unlikely that it will, in the near future, displace our preoccupation with physical health. That is where gerontology began and where the funds for research are likely to be most available.

Health as an individual human resource

The epidemiologists are homing into the notion of investment in personal health profiles in a way that can be seen to parallel the huge investment in education in the second half of the twentieth century. The point is not explicitly made, but the evidence that higher levels of education lead to increased longevity and higher resistance to illness and disease is leading to 'avoidance of disability' as a key element of successful ageing. This is perceived, as Christina Victor indicates in Chapter 2.2, as a mix of genetics, environment, occupational, work and individual behaviours. There is an emerging narrative which speaks of the public/private contract for health. It requires the individual to avoid or to stop smoking, taking drugs, over-consuming alcohol and over eating, and to take serious regular exercise.

Robert Butler (Chapter 6.7), drawing on his lifetime of distinguished work in gerontology, says we are still driven by the fears of Adam Smith and Thomas Malthus which indicated that more (people) means greater cost. He observes that this has led to a focus on 'shortevity' and illness reduction. This is refocusing the governmental view. Michael Marmot, a clinical epidemiologist who has turned his attention latterly to issues of ageing, argues that the principal focus must be on the quality of life. He suggests that we have gone through the first three stages of epidemiological transition and have now reached the fourth stage of delayed degenerative disease – which is dominated by cardiovascular disease and cancer. The situation is not the compression of morbidity predicted in the seminal work by Fries and Crapo (1981) but longer periods of severe disability.

Michael Marmot's impressive interpretation of the evidence is that education, plus income, plus autonomy are the keys to healthy old age. He says in *Status syndrome* (2004), and in Chapter 2.3 of this book, that the answer to the age/health nexus lies in autonomy – how much control you have over your own life is central. In particular he claims 'the opportunities for full social engagement and participation are crucial for health' and 'It is inequality in these that plays a big part in producing the social gradient in health': what he calls the 'status syndrome' (2004: 2).

It does appear that if gerontology is to serve us for our future, its health researchers need to lead the paradigm shift. The established models of disease treatment and social amelioration are only likely to compound the problems and allow them to accumulate into a mountain of disability-induced depression and its inevitable neglect through inadequate resources. A shift to a human investment model is perhaps the new phase of what we have hitherto called 'health promotion'.

Acknowledgements

There are many people who contribute to a book of this nature. All deserve acknowledgement for giving their knowledge, ideas, commitment and patient goodwill.

First must be the three Associate Editors. The task of knowing gerontology is beyond any one person. So, without the vast knowledge, experience and generosity of spirit provided by Vern Bengtson, Peter Coleman and Tom Kirkwood, this ambitious enterprise could not have been brought to fruition. Vern and Peter have been valued friends and colleagues for most of my adult life. They are both people of enormous integrity as well as scholars of the first rank internationally. They have long had my admiration. It is a privilege to have their friendship. Their active collaboration on this book has been vital for its reach across the social and behavioural sciences. Their intellectual judgement, personal support and advice have been vital to the project.

Tom dwells in another land: that of the biological sciences. Our paths first crossed through endeavours to stimulate interdisciplinary research, long ago. Then he was the rising star of British biomedical research. Today he is pre-eminent, not only in the UK but internationally – a position confirmed by his selection as the BBC's Reith Lecturer in 2001. He was the obvious choice to ensure there was an accessible and authoritative link across the worlds of knowledge that relate to age. That he agreed to be involved in the *Handbook* was a wonderful assurance that the wider vision could be achieved. My profound thanks to him.

The second, rather large group, are the authors who agreed to write and actually delivered, re-wrote and revised their chapters – more than a hundred of them. From sixteen countries and representing all five continents, these scholars of considerable note number amongst them the best in the world, and some who surely will be in the future. They include friends, colleagues and fellow academics I know only through their published work. To all of them, my genuine gratitude.

Cambridge University Press is not only one of the world's leading (and oldest) academic publishers; it continues to enhance its reputation by employing editors and technical staff of the highest calibre and intelligence. Sarah Caro (Senior Editor, Social

Sciences) supplied a highly professional combination of advice, encouragement and practical guidance. Her readiness to share good humour and personal concerns, alongside the tasks of book production, has been a real pleasure. Once the manuscripts began to appear Juliet Davis-Berry became an indispensable collaborator. Her mapping of progress, promptings to 'encourage' dilatory authors and the almost daily exchanges provided a framework of agreeable colleagueship, which was of considerable value. Leigh Mueller provided truly expert and constructive copy-editing of the whole text and Fiona Barr produced an excellent index.

Finally, the most special thanks of all, to Christine, who has shared our life and part of our house with this book over several years. She and our now-adult children, Dominic, Cressida and Simeon, have taken a real and encouraging interest in the whole venture. To Christine I dedicate this book.

MALCOLM JOHNSON

Bristol, 2005

REFERENCES

Achenbaum, A. W. (1995). *Crossing the frontiers: gerontology emerges as a science*. Cambridge: Cambridge University Press.

Bengtson, V. L., Rice, C. J., and M. L. Johnson (1999). 'Are theories of ageing important? Models and explanations in gerontology at the turn of the century'. In V. L. Bengtson and K. W. Schaie, eds., *Handbook of theories of ageing*. New York: Springer Publishing Co.

Cornford, C. M. (1908). *Microcosmographia Academica: being a guide to the young academic politician*. Cambridge: Bowes and Bowes.

Fries, J. F., and Crapo, L. M. (1981). *Vitality and ageing: implications of the rectangular curve*. San Francisco, Calif.: W. H. Freeman.

Johnson, M. L. (1981). Editorial, *Ageing and Society*, 1(1): 1–3.

(1982). 'Observations on the enterprise of ageing', *Ageing and Society*, 2(1): 1–5.

Marmot, M. (2004). *Status syndrome: how your social standing directly affects your health and life expectancy*. London: Bloomsbury.

Oeppen, J., and Vaupel, J. (2002). 'Demography enhanced: broken limits to life expectancy', *Science*, 10 May (296): 1029–31.

Rosenmayr, L. (1981). 'Age, lifespan and biography', *Ageing and Society*, 1(1): 29–50.

Townsend, P. (1981). 'The structured dependency of the elderly: creation of social policy in the twentieth century', *Ageing and Society*, 1(1): 5–28.

Walker, A. (1981). 'Towards a political economy of old age', *Ageing and Society*, 1(1): 73–94.

PART ONE

INTRODUCTION AND OVERVIEW

CHAPTER 1.1

The Problem of Theory in Gerontology Today

VERN L. BENGTSON, NORELLA M. PUTNEY AND
MALCOLM L. JOHNSON

Are theories of ageing necessary? Of course from one perspective, that of traditional science, theories of ageing help us to systematize what is known, explain the *how* and *why* behind the *what* of our data, and change the existing order to solve problems, such as age-related disabilities or memory disorders.

But from other perspectives, theories of ageing are not only unnecessary, but may be impossible. One argument is that the development of explanations is an arm-chair enterprise that may be interesting, and occasionally valuable, but is largely irrelevant to the major activity of researchers – to collect observations (data) and construct empirical generalizations. Many researchers in ageing, from geriatricians to epidemiologists to anthropologists, probably share this view. Another argument is that science and positivism are severely limiting, if not irrelevant, for understanding aspects of ageing. Social gerontologists from constructivist and critical orientations suggest that there are other ways to look at, interpret and develop knowledge about ageing, which may not entail scientific theories at all.

A third perspective is shared by many advocates, practitioners, and policymakers in ageing: we have enough research and we have enough theories about ageing. What we must focus on is application, helping older people and their families surmount the problems associated with ageing. To this, scientists, engineers and other policymakers might reply: you must have good theory in order to ameliorate problems successfully through policy and interventions! Policy without a theoretical foundation runs the risk

of causing more harm than good. A fourth argument is that there is no such thing as a theory or theories *of* ageing per se, only theories *in* ageing that explain changes in outcomes with the passage of time, outcomes such as health, memory and perception, social connectedness or loneliness, economic status, or retirement satisfaction.

In this chapter we review current theoretical developments in gerontology, with particular focus on social gerontology. By theory, we mean the construction of explicit explanations that account for empirical findings (Bengtson *et al.*, 1999). We will argue that in building theory, researchers rely on previous explanations of behavior that have been organized and ordered in some way. Whenever researchers begin a project, they are operating under some implicit theory about how a set of phenomena may be related, and these expectations or hunches are derived from previous explanations. Yet too often research agendas proceed absent any stated theory about how things work. If empirical results are not presented within the context of more general explanations or theory, the process of building, revising and interpreting how and why phenomena occur is limited. Particularly in the area of public policy applications or program interventions in gerontology, it is crucial to specify the theoretical assumptions of a research investigation or program intervention before investing large sums of money in it. If the theory is inadequate, it is unlikely the research intervention program or public policy will achieve its objectives. If the research findings are not backed by tested theoretical assumptions, then it is difficult to judge whether an intervention policy is grounded in supportable assumptions about why things happen.

THE QUEST FOR EXPLANATION IN GERONTOLOGY

The field of gerontology has accumulated vast amounts of data over the past several decades, creating a goldmine of potential theoretical knowledge. Yet explicit theory development has lagged – prompting some to observe that gerontology remains data-rich and theory-poor (Birren, 1999; Settersten and Dobransky, 2000). Several factors may have impeded theoretical progress in gerontology: (1) the inability or unwillingness to integrate theory-based knowledge within topic areas and synthesize theoretical insights in the context of existing knowledge; (2) the difficulty of crossing disciplinary boundaries in order to create multidisciplinary explanations and interpretations of phenomena of ageing; (3) the strong "problem-solving" orientation of gerontology that tends to detract from basic research programs where theory plays a central role; (4) the trend towards focusing on individuals in micro settings while ignoring wider social contexts, which tends to dampen even middle-range theory building (Hagestad and Dannefer, 2001); (5) epistemological debates over the virtues of the scientific approach to knowledge or whether human behavior can be understood at all in terms of laws, causes and prediction (mirroring theoretical disagreements within sociology since the mid 1960s).

What Do We Have to Explain? The Age-Old Problem of Ageing

Why do we age? What is the nature of senescence and can its process be altered? Why do we live long after our peak reproductive years and why has the postreproductive span of life increased so significantly over the last century? How can we live healthier and more fulfilling lives? How can we better address the needs of elderly people and unleash their potentialities? At the societal level, the rapid ageing of populations presents researchers and policymakers with new and difficult questions. In all countries of the world, population ageing is altering dependency ratios and dramatically increasing the number of elders who will need care. Gerontologists –

whether as scientists, practitioners or policymakers – concern themselves with these questions.

Gerontologists focus on three sets of issues as they attempt to analyze and understand the phenomena of ageing. The first set concerns *the aged*: the population of those who can be categorized as elderly in terms of their length of life lived or expected lifespan. Most gerontological research in recent decades has focused on the functional problems of aged populations, seen in human terms as medical disability or barriers to independent living. A second set of issues focuses on *ageing* as a developmental process. Here the principal interest is in the situations and problems, which accumulate during the lifespan and cannot be understood separate from developmental experiences and processes across a lifetime. Gerontologists examine the biological, psychological and social aspects of the ageing process as including variable rates and consequences.

A third set of issues involves the study of *age* as a dimension of structure and behavior within species. Social gerontologists are interested in how social organizations are created and changed in response to age-related patterns of birth, socialization, role transitions and retirement or death. The phenomena to be explained relate to how institutions such as labor markets, retirement and pension systems, healthcare organizations, and political institutions take into account or deal with "age." The study of age is also a concern of zoologists, primate anthropologists and evolutionary biologists who note its importance as an organizing principle in many species' behaviors and survival (Wachter and Finch, 1997). While these three emphases are quite different in focus and inquiry, they are nonetheless interrelated in gerontological research and practice. Theoretical engagement helps to distinguish among these basic categories of interest.

The New Problem of Societal Ageing

Rapid population ageing and higher dependency ratios will create major challenges for states and economies over the next half-century. Less obvious but equally important is the profound effect that population ageing will have on social institutions such as families. Who will care for the growing numbers of very old members of human societies? Will it be state governments? The aged themselves?

Their families? Private care providers? These challenges are the result of four remarkable sociodemographic changes that have occurred since the start of the twentieth century and particularly since the 1970s.

EXTENSION OF THE LIFECOURSE. Over this period, there has been a remarkable increase in life expectancy, and an astonishing change in the normal, expected lifecourse of individuals, especially in industrialized societies. Remarkably, an entire generation has been added to the average span of life over the past century.

CHANGES IN THE AGE STRUCTURES OF NATIONS. This increase in longevity has also added a generation to the social structure of societies. In many economically developed nations, those aged 80 and over are the fastest growing portion of the total population. At the same time, total fertility rates in developed nations have plummeted. Several countries in Europe (notably Germany) as well as Japan are beginning to lose population. Most nations today have many more elders, and many fewer children, than fifty years ago.

CHANGES IN FAMILY STRUCTURES AND RELATIONSHIPS. Families look different today than they did fifty years ago. We have added a whole generation to the structure of many families. Some of these differences are the consequence of the expanding lifecourse. Others are the result of trends in family structure, notably higher divorce rates and the higher incidence of childbearing to single parents. Still others are outcomes of changes in values and political expectations regarding the role of the state in the lives of individuals and families.

CHANGES IN GOVERNMENTAL EXPECTATIONS AND RESPONSIBILITIES. For most of the twentieth century, governmental states in the industrialized world increasingly assumed more responsibility for their citizens' welfare and wellbeing. Since the mid 1990s, however, this trend appears to have slowed or reversed as states make efforts to reduce welfare expenditures. The economic and social implications of ageing and the aged for societies are vast.

Problems of Theory-Building in Gerontology

The field of gerontology has accumulated many findings, and has begun to establish several important traditions of theory (Bengtson *et al.*, 1997). It seems, however, that gerontologists (especially social gerontologists) have lost sight of the essential contributions of theory. Recently published findings in ageing research suggest many researchers and practitioners are relatively unconcerned about theories of ageing. In the biology of ageing, for example, many researchers seem focused on empirical models that *describe* ageing at the cellular or molecular levels, leaving integrative theories of ageing to other investigators (for exceptions, see Cristofalo *et al.*, 1999; Finch, 1990, 1997; and Finch and Seeman, 1999). In the psychology of ageing, the pursuit of experimental models of age differences has seldom been accompanied by similar efforts to integrate findings with theory (Birren, 1999; Salthouse, 1991, 1999), although Baltes and his associates have begun to draw up broader theoretical frameworks (Baltes and Smith, 1999). In the sociology of ageing, there has been an increase in empirical analyses but a decrease in efforts at theoretical explanation concerning such critical social phenomena as the consequences of population ageing, the changing status of ageing individuals in society, and the interdependency of age groups in the generational compact (Bengtson *et al.*, 1997; O'Rand and Campbell, 1999). We suggest that, in gerontology today, the problems of theory-building and the development of a corpus of cumulative knowledge can be attributed to several factors.

THE PROBLEM OF TACIT ASSUMPTIONS. Gerontologists, whether their disciplinary focus is biological, behavioral or sociological, approach their research or study with certain assumptions and tacit theoretical orientations, even if these are not made explicit. In their eagerness to exploit new data sources and analytic techniques, and generate findings for the solution of the problems associated with ageing, many gerontologists neglect to spell out clearly their theoretical assumptions. One of the purposes that theories on ageing should achieve is to lay out these tacit assumptions and orientations in an explicit and systematic way.

THE PROBLEM OF RESTRICTING THEORY TO EMPIRICAL GENERALIZATIONS. Skepticism about the importance of theory, as well as the proliferation of single-aspect research which tends to lack theoretical grounding, has led some gerontology researchers to substitute empirical generalization for theory. Propositional statements based on empirical generalizations are about specific events in particular empirical settings rather than about more general processes that occur across a range of contexts. Often empirical generalizations are little more than summaries of research findings that require a theory to explain them (Turner, 2003). There is a need to raise these empirical generalizations to the level of explanation. Many gerontology researchers appear to have ignored theory altogether. For example, a review of articles published between 1990 and 1994 in eight major journals relevant to the sociology of ageing found that 72 percent of the publications made no mention of any theoretical tradition (Bengtson *et al.*, 1997). An unfortunate consequence is that current gerontological research may be accumulating a vast collection of empirical generalizations without the parallel development of integrated knowledge.

THE PROBLEM OF DISCIPLINARY BOUNDARIES. Is theorizing across disciplinary boundaries possible? The field of gerontology itself is in need of integration, because so many more factors are now recognized to be involved in human ageing (Birren, 1999). For the mountains of data to yield significant new insights, an integrating framework is essential. But this cannot be done without theories and concepts that are broader and more general in scope. This lack of integration in theories of ageing is also an artifact of disciplinary specialization. In the increasingly differentiated fields of inquiry that now constitute gerontology, the factors which militate against comprehensive theory development are multiplying. The various disciplines study a growing diversity of outcomes, hence there is little overlap in theoretical explanations. In the social and behavioral sciences, for example, some perspectives such as critical and postmodern theories and strains of feminist theory embrace a more "relativistic" stance towards knowledge and the study of ageing. This poses a further challenge for integrating theory and findings across the sciences when distinct areas of inquiry pursue knowledge under different epistemological assumptions.

THEORY DEVELOPMENT AS A SOCIAL ENTERPRISE. As Thomas Kuhn (1962) so forcefully argued four decades ago, science is a social endeavor that cannot be separated from social and professional considerations. Science reflects the concerns, careers and competitiveness of collective groups of practitioners. Moreover, like the ageing process itself, theoretical development processes – and the explanations that ensue – are embedded in institutional and historical contexts. Achenbaum (1995) observes how the development of gerontological theories paralleled the historical construction of gerontology around new scientific methods and medical practices. Not surprisingly, the biomedicalization of ageing remains a guiding research paradigm. We must be mindful of the connections between scientific inquiry and the social milieu at particular points in time that influence how a subject matter is conceived. In recent years, interpretive and critical social gerontologists have called attention to these connections (Hendricks and Achenbaum, 1999), cautioning researchers to be more reflective on their own values or biases as they interpret findings, develop explanations and make policy recommendations.

THE CURRENT STATE OF THEORY IN GERONTOLOGY

Gerontology in the U.S. emerged as a distinct field of study following the Second World War when a number of American scientists from the fields of biology, psychology and human development founded the Gerontology Society of America. Since its beginnings, gerontology's scholarly and scientific interests were broadly defined – because old age was considered "a problem" that was unprecedented in scope (Achenbaum, 1987). Indeed, ageing has become one of the most complex subjects facing modern science (Birren, 1999). To understand and explain the multifaceted phenomena and processes of ageing required the scientific insights of biology and biomedicine, psychology and the social sciences. Over time, the field expanded beyond these core disciplines to include anthropology, demography, economics, epidemiology, history, the humanities and arts, political science and social work, as well as the many professions that serve older persons.

Over the past several decades, gerontology has endeavored to define itself as a "science" (Achenbaum, 1995). Scientific theories are premised on the idea that the natural universe has fundamental properties and processes that explain phenomena in specific contexts, that knowledge can be value-free, that it can explain the actual workings of the empirical world, and that it can be revised by a better theory as a result of careful observations of empirical events (Turner, 2003).

The Structure of Theories in Gerontology

Contemporary theories of ageing differ in several respects: (1) their underlying assumptions (particularly about human nature – whether human behavior is essentially determined and thus predictable – or whether individuals are essentially creative and agentic); (2) their subject matter (reflecting specific disciplinary interests, or whether the focus is on macrolevel institutions or on microlevel personal encounters and interactions); (3) their epistemological approach (positivistic, interpretive or critical); (4) their methodological approach (deductive or inductive); and (5) their ultimate objectives (whether they aim largely at describing things, explaining or even predicting them, or changing the way things are). The positivistic approach continues to characterize mainstream gerontological research, as reflected for example in the *Journals of Gerontology* in its four-part publication framework – biological science, clinical science, behavioral science and social science.

The classical definition of a scientific theory is essentially a deductive one, starting with definitions of general concepts and putting forward a number of logically ordered propositions about the relationships among concepts. Concepts are linked to empirical phenomena through operational definitions, from which hypotheses are derived and then tested against empirical observations. A general theory allows investigators to deduce logically a number of quite specific statements, or explanations, about the nature and behavior of a large class of phenomena (Turner, 2003; Wallace and Wolf, 1991). Because such theories are useful in predicting

and hence manipulating our environments, they are considered essential for the design of programs aimed at ameliorating problems associated with ageing, especially by government funding agencies.

Some researchers have generated explanations of ageing phenomena using inductive or "grounded" theoretical approaches (Glaser and Strauss, 1967; Strauss and Corbin, 1990) and qualitative methods, starting with the data and leading in the final stages of analysis to the emergence of key concepts and how they relate to one another. Research using quantitative methods can also proceed inductively. For example, the relatively new subdiscipline of neuropsychology proceeds from the "bottom up," starting with data and developing theory (Woodruff-Pak and Papka, 1999), which mirrors grounded theory in sociology.

Is gerontology a science? Today, not all researchers in gerontology agree with the scientific approach to knowledge. In social gerontology, as in sociology more generally, there is controversy over the definition of theory and whether *social* theories can be scientific. Many social gerontologists – in particular those espousing social constructionist and critical perspectives – believe there are other "non-scientific" ways to look at, interpret and develop knowledge about ageing. They argue that general explanatory arguments are likely to miss so much of people's experiences that they are seriously flawed and inadequate. Researchers in these traditions focus on describing and understanding how social interactions proceed, and on the subjective meanings of age and ageing phenomena. Knowledge of the social world derives from the meanings individuals attach to their social situations. A "theory" – many social constructionists prefer the term "sensitizing scheme" – is useful to the extent it provides a deeper understanding of particular social events and settings (Gubrium and Holstein, 1999). The interpretive perspective is premised on the notion that individuals are active agents and can change the nature of their social environments. Thus there cannot be general theories of ageing reflecting "immutable laws" of human social organization (Turner, 2003).

The critical theory perspective, most often associated with the Frankfurt School of epistemology represented by Habermas (1970), questions positivism and the search for scientific natural laws as a principal source of knowledge. The understanding of meanings (which Habermas termed hermeneutic/historical knowledge) and the analysis of domination and constraints in social forces (termed critical knowledge) are equally as important as "objective knowledge" in understanding phenomena (Bengtson et al., 1997; Moody, 2001). Critical theory assumes that values cannot be separated from "facts" and that all research is value-laden. Thus social constructionist and critical perspectives in gerontology today operate under different assumptions about the subject and the purpose of ageing research. At the same time, the insights provided by these approaches about the experience of ageing, what it means to grow old and be old, and about issues of social justice for the aged, have filled a gap in the knowledge base obtained through the positivist paradigm, and we feel they have enriched the field of gerontology. An example is the extraordinary contribution of Barbara Myerhoff's (1978) classic ethnographic study of Jewish elders, *Number our days*. It should be remembered, however, that, while different in their objectives and methods, all these theoretical approaches do involve a set of concepts, which are the building blocks of any theory.

Debates over Epistemology

To understand the controversies in social gerontology surrounding forms of knowledge and the use of theory, we must concern ourselves with epistemology: *how we know what we think we know*. Is there a reality out there? Are social phenomena real facts? Or is reality itself socially constructed through the collaborative definitional and meaning-sharing activities of people who observe it (Marshall, 1999). Such concerns are "meta-theoretical," and they have been the subject of a great deal of debate in recent years among scholars in the sociology of ageing. Meta-theories (technically, theories of theories) are concerned with more fundamental epistemological and metaphysical questions addressing such things as the nature of human activity about which we must develop theory; the basic nature of human beings or the fundamental nature of society; or the appropriate way to develop theory and what kind of theory is possible (scientific theories, interpretative frameworks, general concepts that sensitize and orient, or critical approaches) (Turner, 2003). Given their incommensurability, we suggest that the way

to address these epistemological questions in social gerontology is to regard these perspectives as providing different lenses that can enrich our understanding of the multiple facets of ageing. But is there any prospect of them finding a common currency of ideas and concepts that would allow a synthesis to emerge?

Biological, Psychological and Sociological Theories of Ageing

In the next section we provide an overview of the major biological, behavioral and social theoretical perspectives in gerontology. Theory development in the biological and behavioral sciences seems to have been a less difficult process than it has been for social gerontology. In the biology and psychology of ageing there is little disagreement that science is the appropriate paradigm for building knowledge. Admittedly, these disciplines are closer to the "natural sciences" where the discoveries of science have given humankind extraordinary progress in overcoming infectious diseases, combating cancers, ameliorating the devastating symptoms of mental illness, and advancing our knowledge of cognitive processes in later life. Theoretical progress has been more challenging for social gerontology, in part because social phenomena are considerably more complex and fluid, and researchers approach their topics with different epistemological assumptions.

BIOLOGICAL THEORIES OF AGEING

Biological theories address ageing processes at the organism, molecular and cellular levels. Instead of a defining theory of biological ageing, there are a multitude of smaller theories, no doubt reflecting the fact that there is no single cause, mechanism or basis for senescence. Most of these biological theories fall into one of two general classes: stochastic theories, and programmed (developmental-genetic) theories (Cristofalo et al., 1999). Since the early 1990s, however, evolutionary senescence theory has gained prominence as an explanation of why and how ageing occurs.

Stochastic Theories

This class of theories explains ageing as resulting from the accumulation of "insults" from the environment, which eventually reach a level incompatible with life. The best-known is the *somatic mutation theory*, which came to prominence after the Second World War as a result of research on radiation exposure and damage. The theory states that mutations (genetic damage) will produce functional failure eventually resulting in death. Cristofalo (1996) notes, however, that an explanation of a shortened lifespan as a consequence of gene-altering exposure is not at all the same as explaining the normal processes of ageing. In general, experiments have not supported somatic mutation theory. Another stochastic explanation, *error catastrophe theory*, proposes that a defect in the mechanism used for protein synthesis could lead to the production of error-containing proteins, resulting in the dysregulation of numerous cellular processes that eventually results in the death of the individual. While appealing, there is no convincing evidence for error catastrophe (Cristofalo *et al.*, 1999).

Developmental-Genetic Theories

This class of biological theories of ageing proposes that the process of ageing is continuous with and probably operating through the same mechanisms as development, hence genetically controlled and programmed. Three categories of developmental-genetic theories have received empirical support (Cristofalo *et al.*, 1999). First are the *neuroendocrine theories*, which posit functional decrements in neurons and their associated hormones as central to the ageing process. One such theory proposes that the hypothalamic/pituitary/adrenal axis is the primary regulator of the ageing process, and that functional changes in this system are accompanied by or regulate functional decrements throughout the organism (Finch and Seeman, 1999). There is considerable evidence relating ageing of the organism to loss of responsiveness of the neuroendocrine tissue to various signals. A second neuroendocrine explanation, the *immunological theory of ageing* (Walford, 1969), is based on the observation that the functional capacity and fidelity of the immune system declines with age, as indicated by the strong age-associated increase in autoimmune disease. A third neuroendocrine explanation, *free radical theory* (Harman, 1956), proposes that most ageing changes are due to damage caused by free radicals. Free radicals are highly chemically reactive agents that are generated in single electron transfer reactions

to metabolism. This theory is more general in that it provides a mechanism applicable to all aerobic tissues (Cristofalo, 1996). Another explanation that relates differential rates of metabolism and lifespan expectancy is that of *caloric restriction* (Cristofalo *et al.*, 1999).

Theories of Cellular Ageing

While most well-known theories deal with the organism and its integrative functioning, the idea of ageing as a cell-based phenomenon is relatively recent (Cristofalo, 1996). Three cellular-level research directions have emerged. The first focuses on a genetic analysis of senescence primarily based on cell–cell hybridization. A second strand relates to analyzing steps in the growth factor signal transduction. More recently, a third area of cellular-level research focuses on DNA replication and telomere shortening as a mechanism, which eventually curtails replication.

Evolutionary Theories

Martin (2003) argues that the single most important shift in biology-of-ageing paradigmatic thinking since the 1980s has been the widespread acceptance of evolutionary senescence theory as an explanation for why ageing happens. Challenging the developmental-genetic approach is the idea of the "selection" of ageing mechanisms through evolution. This has been accompanied by growing skepticism that the diverse scenarios and trajectories of ageing can be controlled by a process whose mechanisms regulate the precise processes of development (Cristofalo, 1996). Evolutionary theories attempt to explain the origin of ageing as well as the divergence of species lifespans (Kirkwood, 2001). Evolutionary explanations of ageing are based on three major theories. First is *mutation accumulation theory* (Medawar, 1952) which states that ageing is an inevitable result of the declining force of natural selection with age (that is, the expression of deleterious genes associated with senescence may be delayed until the postreproductive period). Mutation accumulation theory claims the accumulation of heritable, late-acting deleterious constitutional mutations, as distinct from the accumulation of somatic mutations. The second evolutionary theory of ageing, *antagonistic pleiotropy theory* (Williams, 1957), states further that late-acting deleterious genes might even be favored by selection and actively accumulated if they have any beneficial effects early in life. Simply put, the theory posits there are genes that have good effects early in life and bad effects later in life. The third evolutionary theory is *disposable soma theory* (Kirkwood, 2001). This refers to a process whereby there is limited investment in soma cell durability because such cells have a short expected duration of use. Soma are those parts of the body which are distinct from the "germ-line" that produces the reproductive cells. From this perspective, an increased rate of ageing occurs through optimizing the investment in reproductive function as opposed to somatic maintenance functions. (See Kirkwood, this volume, for a detailed discussion of disposable soma theory.)

A General Theory of Biological Ageing

To address the need to organize the diverse findings of biological ageing research into a comprehensive body of knowledge, Gavrilov and Gavrilova (2003) recently proposed the application of a general theory of systems failure known as *reliability theory* to explain ageing processes in humans. Their holistic approach complements the evolutionary perspective on ageing and longevity. Reliability theory predicts that a system may deteriorate with age even if it is built from nonageing elements. The theory postulates that it is the system's redundancy for irreplaceable elements which is responsible for the ageing phenomenon. Gavrilov and Gavrilova note that the human species displays considerable system redundancy, and that the positive effect of system redundancy is damage tolerance (which decreases mortality and increases lifespan). This makes it possible for damage to be accumulated over time, thus producing the ageing phenomenon. Gavrilov and Gavrilova's research demonstrates that systems that have higher redundancy show a higher ageing rate or expression of ageing. This helps explain the cases of negligible senescence observed in the wild and at extreme old ages.

Neuropsychological Theories of Ageing

Drawing from the fields of neurology, physiology and psychology, the neuropsychology of ageing is a relatively new discipline that scientifically investigates, clinically assesses, and develops treatments for age-related and neurodegenerative changes in brain function and behavior. Theorizing proceeds inductively from empirical observations to models and theoretical explanations – a "bottom up" approach. In a sense, the diagnosis is the theory (Woodruff-Pak and Papka, 1999). Contemporary theories of neuropsychology and ageing differentiate between normal age-related changes in brain function, and neurodegenerative changes.

"THEORIES" OF NORMAL AGE-RELATED CHANGE. There are two major configurations of change in cognitive functioning related to ageing: (1) change in the prefrontal cortex, and (2) change in the ability to form declarative memory. The prefrontal cortex is involved in executive function, attention, and working memory (Woodruff-Pak and Papka, 1999). Based on the principle that neural structures and related abilities laid down last should be the most vulnerable to processes of ageing, evidence indicates that the frontal lobes (the last structure to develop) are the part of the brain affected earliest by normal ageing. Declarative memory, which is dependent on circuitry in the medial temporal lobe or mammilary body, is involved in the manipulation and organization of memory; for example, "trying to learn" a task as opposed to performing a task (Woodruff-Pak and Papka, 1999). While memory resides in a constellation of interacting brain areas, the medial temporal lobe circuitry for declarative memory appears to be most affected by processes of both normal and neuropathological ageing.

"THEORIES" OF NEURODEGENERATIVE CHANGE. There are several age-linked neuropathological changes of the brain which produce observable degenerative deficits in cognitive functioning (the most prominent being Alzheimer's, but also Lewy body, Parkinson's, Huntington's, epilepsy, and Creutzfeldt-Jakob disease). Theories of Alzheimer's Disease relate to its neuropathological mechanisms (amyloid plaques and tangles associated with neuronal death); its genetic predisposition (presence of e4 allele within the ApoE genotypes and other factors modulating its expression; Woodruff-Pak and Papka, 1999); and various existing and potentially new biochemical therapies (theories): manipulating the cholinergic system (acetylcholine), manipulating brain excitation or signaling (blocking glutamate's ability to activate NMDA receptors, controlling the effect of calcium on NMDA receptors), blocking the formation of beta amyloid (secretase inhibitors), and reducing brain inflammation (NSAIDs, Statins) (Walsh, 2004).

PSYCHOLOGICAL THEORIES OF AGEING

The psychology of ageing is a complex field with several subfields (cognitive development, personality development, social development) and topic areas (memory, learning, sensation and perception, psycholinguistics, social psychology, motor skills, psychometrics and developmental psychology) (see Baltes *et al.*, this volume). Disciplinary boundaries can be amorphous. Schroots (1996) observes that sometimes psychological theories of ageing are labeled as psychosocial; at other times they are conceived as biobehavioral, behavioral genetic or neuropsychological. Theories in the psychology of ageing seek to explain the multiple changes in individual behavior, across these domains, in the middle and later years of the lifespan. As with biological and sociological theories of ageing, there is no defining psychology-of-ageing theory.

Lifespan Development Theory

One of the most widely cited explanatory frameworks in the psychology of ageing, lifespan development theory conceptualizes ontogenetic development as biologically and socially constituted and as manifesting both developmental universals (homogeneity) and inter-individual variability (for example, differences in genetics and in social class). This perspective also proposes that the second half of life is characterized by significant individual differentiation, multidirectionality and intraindividual plasticity. Using the lifespan development perspective, Baltes and Smith (1999) identify three principles regulating the dynamics between biology and culture across the ontogenetic life span: first, evolutionary selection benefits decrease with age; second, the need for culture increases with age; and third, the efficacy of culture decreases with age. Their focus is on how these dynamics contribute to the

optimal expression of human development and the production of outcomes of adaptive fitness. Drawing from evolutionary theory and ontogenetic theories of learning, Baltes and Smith (1999) also postulate that a condition of loss, limitation or deficit could play a catalytic role for positive change.

Selective Optimization with Compensation Theory

Lifespan development theory has produced one overall theory to explain how individuals manage adaptive (successful) development in later life (Baltes and Smith, 1999). The theory identifies three fundamental mechanisms or strategies: selection, optimization and compensation (Baltes and Carstensen, 1996, 1999). This is a model of psychological and behavior adaptation where the central focus is on managing the dynamics between gains and losses as one ages. Selection refers to the increasing restriction of an individual's life to fewer domains of functioning because of age-related loss in the range of adaptive potential. Optimization reflects the idea that people engage in behaviors which augment or enrich their general reserves and maximize their chosen lifecourses. Like selection, compensation results from restriction of the range of adaptive potential, and becomes operative when specific behavioral capacities are lost or are reduced below a standard required for adequate functioning. This life-long process of selective optimization with compensation enables people to age successfully (Schroots, 1996).

Socioemotional Selectivity Theory

In this theory, Carstensen (1992) combines insights from developmental psychology – particularly the selective optimization with compensation model developed by Baltes and Baltes (1990) – with social exchange theory, to explain why the social exchange and interaction networks of older persons are reduced over time (a phenomenon which disengagement theory tried to explain). Through mechanisms of socioemotional selectivity, individuals reduce interactions with some people as they age while increasing emotional closeness with significant others, such as an adult child or an ageing sibling. Carstensen's (1992) theory provides a concise development-behavioral explanation for selective interaction in old age. This theory explains the change in social contact by the self-interested need for emotional closeness with significant others, which leads to increasingly selective interactions with others in advancing age. Such chosen interactions reflect the levels of reward these exchanges of emotional support achieve for older persons.

Cognition and Ageing Theories

Researchers of cognition differentiate between types of cognitive abilities: *fluid* intelligence, reflecting genetic-biological determinants; and *crystallized* abilities, representing social–cultural influences on general world knowledge. The primary phenomenon to be explained by a theory of cognition is the age-related decline in *fluid* cognitive performance (the efficiency or effectiveness of performing tasks of learning, memory, reasoning and spatial abilities) (Salthouse, 1999). Fluid abilities have been shown to decline with age, while crystallized abilities are more stable across the lifespan and may even display some growth with age. Salthouse (1999) suggests there are apparently no theoretical accounts of the stability of crystallized cognition.

Most theories of fluid cognition and ageing can be categorized by whether the primary determinants are distal or proximal in nature (Salthouse, 1999). *Distal determinant explanations* postulate factors that exert their influence over time and are responsible for age-related differences evident in the level of cognitive performance. One type of distal explanation emphasizes changes in the social and cultural environment as opposed to changes within the individual. For example, changes in educational patterns may explain age-related declines in cognitive functioning (although these differences in education probably account for only a small proportion of age-related differences in cognitive functioning). Another distal explanation is the disuse or "use it or lose it" perspective. While popular among the public and some researchers, this perspective has had little empirical support (Salthouse, 1999).

Proximal determinant explanations of age-related differences in fluid cognition tend to incorporate specific mechanisms linking theoretical constructs to cognitive performance. First, there are

strategy-based explanations, of which there are two types: a production deficiency version which posits older people have capacities similar to younger people but use less than optimal strategies, and a processing deficiency version which posits that differences in strategy are less important than differences in more fundamental abilities. Empirical results tend to support the processing deficiency explanation (Salthouse, 1999). Second, there are *specific-deficit explanations*, which postulate age-related differences in the efficiency of "particular" information processing stages or components. A third category are *reduced processing resource explanations*, which postulate there are age-related declines in the efficiency or effectiveness of "elementary" cognitive operations or processing resources. These theories hold that ageing leads to a reduction in the quantity of one or more processing resources, such as attentional capacity, working memory capacity, or speed of processing. Experimental studies have shown processing speed to be a fundamental construct in human cognition, linked to explicit changes in neural structure and functioning as well as to higher-order cognitive processes like reasoning and abstraction (Salthouse, 1991). Because the key constructs of reduced processing resources theory are broader than in the specific-deficit model and presumably affect a wide variety of tasks, this theoretical approach has proven to be more useful and found wide support (Salthouse, 1999; Schroots, 1996).

Personality and Ageing Theories

Theories of personality and ageing focus on the extent and nature of personality stability and change over the lifespan. There are two categories of explanation of age-related changes in personality. First are the *developmental explanations* as represented by Erikson's (1950) stages of development (in adulthood and old age, the stages of generativity vs stagnation, and integration vs despair), and Levinson's (1978) stage theory of personality development. "Stage" theories of personality have fallen out of favor in recent years. Second are the *personality trait explanations*, based on the "big five" factors of personality (neuroticism, extroversion, openness to experience, agreeableness and conscientiousness). These personality theories postulate that people show a high degree of stability in basic dispositions and personality, particularly during the latter half of their lifecourse. There is growing consensus that personality traits tend to be stable with age whereas key aspects of self such as goals, values, coping styles and control beliefs are more amenable to change (Baltes and Smith, 1999). In research on the self and personality in old age, the current emphasis is on understanding the mechanisms that promote the maintenance of personal integrity and wellbeing in the face of social loss and health constraints (Baltes and Baltes, 1990; Baltes and Smith, 1999).

Gerotranscendence Theory

Tornstam's (1989, 1996) critical theory of wisdom, or "gerotranscendence," postulates that human ageing encompasses a general shift from a materialistic and rational metaphysical stance to a more cosmic and transcendent one, and that this leads to greater life satisfaction. Studies suggest that gerotranscendence may occur at three levels of age-related ontological change: a cosmic level (changes in perception of time and space, changes in perception of life and a disappearing fear of death, and increase of affinity with past and coming generations); the level of self; and a social and individual relations level. Schroots (1996) contrasts gerotranscendence theory with disengagement theory, with the former implying a "redefinition of reality," connection to "social activity" and a need for solitary "philosophizing," while the latter reflects a "turning inwards," defensive coping strategies and social breakdown.

SOCIOLOGICAL THEORIES OF AGEING

In contrast to the biological and behavioral sciences, theoretical progress in social gerontology has been more problematic. We have already discussed reasons for this lack of theoretical development. Nevertheless, we suggest several theoretical traditions which should be exploited in developing explanations and understandings of empirical phenomena.

Historical Foundations of Explanations in Social Gerontology

Scholars in gerontology have invested much intellectual effort in theory building. Early researchers on ageing, such as Hall (1922), Cowdry (1939), Linton (1942), Parsons (1942) and Havighurst (1943) integrated empirical findings into theoretical insights and established the foundations of gerontology. Out of these pioneering efforts grew four theories, representing a first generation of social gerontology theories (Bengtson et al., 1997): *disengagement theory* (Cumming and Henry, 1961); *activity theory* (Lemon et al., 1972); *modernization theory* (Cowgill and Holmes, 1974); and *subculture theory* (Rose, 1965). The most explicitly developed of these, disengagement theory (Cumming and Henry, 1961) attempted to explain human ageing as an inevitable process of individuals and social structures mutually disengaging and adaptively withdrawing from each other in anticipation of the person's inevitable death. Drawn from structural-functionalism, this general theory of ageing was elegant, multidisciplinary, parsimonious and intuitively provocative (Achenbaum and Bengtson, 1994). However, its ambitious propositions were roundly criticized (Hochschild, 1975). The theory had attempted to explain both macro- and micro-level changes with one "grand theory," but, when tested against the cited data, its validity and generalizability claims could not be supported. While many older people do appear to be "disengageing" or withdrawing from their social connections and activities, many do not.

In a second period of theoretical development, from about 1970 to 1985, several new theoretical perspectives emerged: *continuity theory* (Atchley, 1993); *social breakdown/competence theory* (Kuypers and Bengtson, 1973); *exchange theory* (Dowd, 1975); the *age stratification perspective* (Riley et al., 1972); and the *political economy of aging perspective* (Estes et al., 1984). Since the late 1980s many of these theories have been refined and reformulated, and new theoretical perspectives have emerged. Hendricks (1992) suggests many of these more recent theoretical developments reflect an effort to synthesize the distinct micro- or macro-level approaches of earlier theorizing. Following is an overview of contemporary theoretical perspectives in social gerontology.

The Lifecourse Perspective

This perspective is perhaps the most widely cited theoretical framework in social gerontology today. Its proponents argue that to understand the present circumstances of elderly people we must take into account the major social and psychological forces that have operated throughout the course of their lives (George, 1996). While there is debate as to whether the lifecourse is a "theory" or an orienting perspective, it represents a convergence of thinking in sociology and psychology about processes at both macro- and micro-social levels of analysis and for both populations and individuals over time. Researchers using this perspective are attempting to explain: (1) the dynamic, contextual and processual nature of ageing; (2) age-related transitions and life trajectories; (3) how ageing is related to and shaped by social contexts, cultural meanings and social structural location; and (4) how time, period and cohort shape the ageing process for individuals as well as for social groups (Bengtson and Allen, 1993; Elder, 1992; Elder and Johnson, 2002). This approach is multidisciplinary, drawing content and methods from sociology, psychology, anthropology and history. The lifecourse approach is also explicitly dynamic, focusing on the life cycle in its entirety while allowing for deviations in trajectories (Dannefer and Sell, 1988). Although studies so far have not incorporated all four of these lifecourse perspective dimensions in their empirical analyses, new methodological advances suggest such a multilevel, cross-time model in the future (Alwin and Campbell, 2001).

The Age Stratification (Age and Society) Perspective

This perspective represents one of the oldest traditions of macro-level theorizing in social gerontology. Riley *et al.* (1988) trace this perspective's intellectual roots to structural functionalism, particularly the works of sociologists Sorokin (1947), Mannheim (1928/1952) and later, and Parsons (1942). There are three components to this "paradigm": (1) studying the movement of age cohorts across time in order to identify similarities and differences between them; (2) examining the asynchrony between structural and individual change over time; and (3) exploring the interdependence of age cohorts and social structures. A major concept is that of structural lag (Riley *et al.*, 1994), which occurs when social structures cannot keep pace with the changes in population dynamics and individual lives. Using this theoretical perspective, Riley and Loscocco (1994) argue that a more age-integrated society, brought about by policy changes, can compensate for structural lag. Restructuring the social institutions of work, education and the family through such things as extended time off for education or family, can bring social structures in balance with individuals' lives.

Social Exchange Theory

This micro-level theory has been useful in many recent studies in the sociology of ageing, particularly those focusing on intergenerational social support and transfers. Developed and extended by Dowd (1975), the social exchange theory of ageing draws from sociological formulations by Homans (1961) and Blau (1964) and work in economics that assumes a *rational choice* model of decision making behavior. Applied to ageing, this perspective attempts to account for exchange behavior between individuals of different ages as a result of the shift in roles, skills and resources that accompany advancing age (Hendricks, 1995). It explicitly incorporates the concept of power differentials. A central assumption is that the various actors (such as parent and child or elder and youth) each bring resources to the interaction or exchange and that resources need not be material and will most likely be unequal. A second assumption is that the actors will only continue to engage in the exchanges for as long as the benefits are greater than the costs and while there are no better alternatives. This theoretical approach also assumes that exchanges are governed by norms of reciprocity; that when we give something, we trust that something of equal value will be reciprocated.

Social Constructionist Perspectives

Social constructionist theories draw from a long tradition of micro-level analysis in the social sciences: *symbolic interactionism* (Mead, 1934), *phenomenology* (Berger and Luckmann, 1966) and *ethnomethodology* (Garfinkel, 1967). Using hermeneutic or interpretive methods, social constructionism focuses on individual agency and social behavior within larger structures of society, and particularly on the subjective meanings of age and the ageing experience. Researchers working in this tradition emphasize their interest in understanding, if not explaining, individual processes of ageing as influenced by social definitions and social structures. Examples include Gubrium's (1993) study of the subjective meanings of quality of care and quality of life for residents of nursing homes, and how each resident constructs meanings from her or his own experiences. These meanings emerge from analyses of life narratives, but cannot be measured by predefined measurement scales, such as those used by most survey researchers.

Feminist Theories of Ageing

Feminist gerontology gives priority to gender as an organizing principle for social life across the lifespan that significantly alters the experience of ageing, often in inequitable ways (Calasanti, 1999; McMullen, 1995). This theoretical perspective also challenges what counts as knowledge and how it functions in the lives of older women and men. Current theories and models of ageing are regarded as insufficient because they fail to address gender relations, the experience of women in the context of ageing and caregiving demands, or issues of race, ethnicity or class (Blieszner, 1993; Calasanti, 1999; Ray, 1996). At the macro-level of analyses, feminist theories of ageing combine with political economy and critical perspectives to examine differential access to the key material, health and caring resources which substantially alters the experience of ageing for women and men (Arber and Ginn, 1995). For example, feminist researchers seek to explain the comparatively high rates of poverty among older women, and to propose changes in the ideologies and institutions that perpetuate it. From a feminist perspective, family caregiving can be understood as an experience of obligation, structured by the gender-based division of domestic labor and the devaluing of unpaid work (Stroller, 1993). At the micro-level, feminist perspectives hold that gender should be examined in the context of social meanings, reflecting the influence of the social constructionist approach.

Political Economy of Ageing Perspective

These theories, which draw originally from Marxism (Marx, 1967[1867–95]), conflict theory (Simmel, 1966[1904]) and critical theory (Habermas, 1971), attempt to explain how the interaction of economic and political forces determines how social resources are allocated, and how variations in the treatment and status of the elderly can be understood by examining public policies, economic trends, and social structural factors (Estes, 2001). Political economy perspectives applied to ageing maintain that socioeconomic and political constraints shape the experience of ageing, resulting in the loss of power, autonomy and influence of older persons. Life experiences are seen as being patterned not only by age, but also by class, gender, and race and ethnicity. These structural factors, often institutionalized or reinforced by economic and public policy, constrain opportunities, choices and experiences in later life. Another focus of the political economy of ageing perspective is how ageism is constructed and reproduced through social practices and policies, and how it negatively affects the wellbeing of older people (Bytheway, 1995).

Critical Perspectives of Ageing

Critical perspectives are reflected in several theoretical trends in contemporary social gerontology including the political economy of ageing, feminist theories, theories of diversity, and humanistic gerontology. Coming primarily out of the Frankfurt School of Critical Theory (Horkheimer and Adorno, 1944; Habermas, 1971), and poststructuralism (Foucault, 1977), these perspectives share a common focus on criticizing "the process of power" (Baars, 1991) as well as traditional positivistic approaches to knowledge. Critical gerontology has developed two distinct patterns, one which focuses on humanistic dimensions of ageing, and the other on structural components. Moody (1993) postulates four goals of the humanistic strand of critical theory: (1) to theorize subjective and interpretive dimensions of ageing; (2) to focus on praxis (involvement in practical change) instead of technical advancement; (3) to link academics and practitioners through praxis; and (4) to produce "emancipatory knowledge." A second strand emphasizes that critical gerontology should create positive models of ageing focusing on the strengths and diversity of age, in addition to critiquing positivist knowledge (Bengtson et al., 1997). To reach the goals of critical gerontology, researchers focus on the key concepts of power, social action and social meanings in examining the social aspects of age and ageing.

Social constructionism, feminist theories, and critical perspectives have gained prominence in social gerontology theorizing, mirroring recent theoretical developments in sociology and the humanities. Not uncommonly, gerontologists will combine insights from all three perspectives to guide their research and interpret findings. At the same time, these theoretical perspectives pose a challenge to the scientific assumptions that have traditionally guided gerontological research.

Postmodernism

This perspective can also be referred to as a post-positivist or post-Enlightenment perspective, following the work of Foucault (1977), Lyotard (1984), and Rorty (1994). While there are various strands of postmodernism (economic, cultural, deconstructionist), all postmodernists challenge the Enlightenment's emphasis on individual freedom, rationality, progress, and the power of science to better the human condition. They see science and knowledge as inexorably linked to social control and power. Postmodernists reject outright the canons of science, the assumption that reason can provide an objective, reliable, and universal foundation for knowledge, or the idea that reality has a unitary nature that can be definitively observed and understood. This position of extreme relativity towards "truth" causes postmodernists to challenge the relevance or possibility of any theory. Postmodernism has been strongly attacked for its anti-theoretical stance and for having provided a great deal of criticism of existing theory but offering little that can actually replace it. What postmodernism has contributed is to make social theorists aware of the limits of using a "modern" metaphor to understand contemporary circumstances, and the limits of methodological approaches developed under the modernist metaphor (Pescosolido and Rubin, 2000).

CONCLUSION

Our goal in this chapter was, first, to examine the state of theory and knowledge building in the field of gerontology and gauge its prospects for future development; and second, to present an overview of the major theories in each of its core disciplines: the biology of ageing, the psychology of ageing, and the sociology of ageing.

We began by asking whether theories of ageing are still useful, or necessary, for the advancement of knowledge in the field of gerontology. While theory development remains crucial from the perspective of science, many in our field, especially within social gerontology, seem to question the importance, or even the validity, of theory. Others may see theorizing as an impediment to getting on with the practical matters of solving the problems of older people and their families. At the beginning of the twenty-first century, are theories of ageing an anachronism, a remnant of the once reigning paradigm of positivism?

In the quest to understand the diverse phenomena of ageing, gerontologists focus on three sets of issues: biological and social processes of ageing; the aged themselves; and age as a dimension of structure and social organization. Societal ageing poses new problems for gerontologists. We suggested that developing knowledge that informs policies that can effectively deal with the challenges posed by growing numbers of elders will be crucial in the coming decades. There are good practical reasons for theory development in the field of gerontology.

Yet theory development has lagged. We offered several reasons why we believe this has occurred: the difficulty of integrating theory-based knowledge across topic areas and disciplines; the strong problem-solving focus of gerontology that detracts from theorizing, which has played such an important role in the advancement of basic research; the excessive focus on individuals and micro settings while ignoring wider social contexts; and probably most important in social gerontology, the seemingly endless epistemological debates that detract from the work of developing and applying theoretically based knowledge.

We then identified specific problems that impede the development of theory and cumulative knowledge building. First, researchers need to make explicit their assumptions and theoretical orientations when presenting their results and interpretations. Second, there has been a proliferation of single aspect research findings – too frequently generated by overly narrow research inquiries – that lack theoretical grounding and explanation. There is a need to raise these "empirical generalizations" to an explanatory level, and integrate explanations and understandings with previous knowledge and explanations. Third, there is the need to cross disciplinary boundaries and develop multidisciplinary and interdisciplinary causal explanations of broader theoretical scope. Fourth, researchers need to be more sensitive to the social dimensions of scholarly research and values that imbue paradigmatic frameworks, affecting the kinds of questions asked, the analytic approaches and methods chosen, and the interpretations put forth.

We posed a crucial question: is gerontology a science? Certainly gerontology throughout its history has endeavored to be scientific. For most in gerontology – biologists, psychologists and a majority of social gerontologists – science remains the reigning paradigm. But since the mid 1980s, science has come under serious critique from those who espouse social constructionist or critical approaches to knowledge. They argue that general explanatory laws cannot account for people's day-to-day experience and meanings, and such laws are rendered impossible because of individual choice making. More fundamentally, critical and postmodernist perspectives reject the Enlightenment ideals of reason and progress; they critique science as an approach to knowledge, or, worse, as a source of subordination. Within social gerontology, controversies over epistemology and the virtues or limitations of science and positivism continue.

Yet there is a way that these seemingly incommensurate epistemological positions can be accommodated. We suggest that explanation and understanding in the complex field of gerontology should draw from a range of theories and theoretical perspectives developed by its constitutive disciplines. It builds knowledge not only through the methods of formal theory development that characterize science, but from the understandings developed by interpretivists and critical theorists. This diversity of theoretical perspectives can offer complementary insights. But, in order for this to happen, it is important that researchers pay more attention to the accumulated knowledge of the field, and to being explicit in their theoretical perspectives and insights.

Future Trends in Social Gerontological Thinking

- In our review of theoretical development in gerontology, it is obvious that positivism is still with us. Yet changes are on the horizon. Perhaps in response to political economy and critical theorists' critiques, there appears to be increasing concern over the "microfication" of theories of social gerontology (Hagestad and Dannefer, 2001). This refers to the over-emphasis on micro-level analysis, agency, and the individual subject. Related to this is a critique of methodological individualism, a key element of the positivistic paradigm.

- In future theorizing we expect to see greater emphasis being placed on macro-level phenomena and the structural contexts of ageing. This is because there is increased awareness of structures as having effects on processes of ageing independent of individual actions, and because of the recognition that structures and institutions are not socially constructed but have a certain facticity (O'Rand and Campbell, 1999; Turner, 2003). This shift in awareness may promote renewed interest in theory-building and social gerontology's development as a science.

- Theory development in social gerontology may be promoted by trends within sociology. The epistemological wars in sociological theorizing continue, but interest in postmodernist approaches may be waning (Turner, 2003). Although postmodern perspectives have severely critiqued modernist assumptions and positivist approaches to knowledge, they have failed to offer alternatives for bringing about greater understanding of social processes or organization.

- Shifting the emphasis from theories *of* ageing to theories *in* ageing opens up a novel strategy for developing cross-disciplinary explanations and understanding in gerontology (Turner, 2003). The process starts with the collective identification of the major problems in ageing research by practitioners of various disciplines and theoretical perspectives. The process then inquires what discipline-specific theoretical knowledge can be brought to bear on illuminating and/or resolving these problems. Engaging in such a process holds the potential for forging a cross-disciplinary fertilization of ideas and possibly new approaches. Such a process tests the usefulness of theories in gerontology in a very practical way. It also becomes possible to evaluate whether theoretical integration across disciplines is needed.

REFERENCES

Achenbaum, W. A. (1987). "Can gerontology become a science?" *Journal of Aging Studies*, 1: 3–15.

(1995). *Crossing frontiers: gerontology as a science*. New York: Cambridge University Press.

Achenbaum, W. A., and V. L. Bengtson (1994). "Re-engaging the disengagement theory of aging: on the history and assessment of theory development in gerontology," *Gerontologist*, 34: 756–63.

Alwin, D., and R. T. Campbell (2001). "Quantitative approaches." In R. H. Binstock and L. K. George, eds., *Handbook of aging and the social sciences*, 5th edn. San Diego, Calif.: Academic Press, pp. 22–43.

Arber, S., and J. Ginn, eds. (1995). *Connecting gender and aging: a sociological approach*. Philadelphia: Open University Press.

Atchley, R. C. (1993). "Critical perspectives on retirement." In T. R. Cole, W. A. Achenbaum, P. L. Jakobi, and R. Kastenbaum, eds., *Voices and visions: towards a critical gerontology*. New York: Springer.

Baars, J. (1991). "The challenge of critical theory: the problem of social construction," *Journal of Aging Studies*, 5: 219–43.

Baltes, P. B., and M. M. Baltes (1990). "Psychological perspectives on successful aging. The model of selective optimization with compensation." In P. B. Baltes and M. M. Baltes, eds., *Successful aging: perspectives from the behavioral sciences*. New York: Cambridge University Press, pp. 1–34.

Baltes, M. M., and L. L. Carstensen (1996). "The process of successful ageing," *Ageing and Society*, 16: 397–422.

(1999). "Social-psychological theories and their applications to aging: from individual to collective." In V. L. Bengtson and K. W. Schaie, eds., *Handbook of theories of aging*. New York: Springer, pp. 209–26.

Baltes, P. B. and J. Smith (1999). "Multilevel and systemic analyses of old age: theoretical and empirical evidence for a fourth age." In V. L. Bengtson and K. W. Schaie, eds., *Handbook of theories of aging*. New York: Springer, pp. 153–73.

Bengtson, V. L., and K. R. Athen (1993). "The lifecourse perspective applied to families over time." In P. Boss, W. Doherty, R. LaRossa, W. Schumm, and S. Steinmets, eds., *Sourcebook of family theories and methods: a contextual approach*. Boston: Allyn & Bacon, pp. 452–75.

Bengtson, V. L., Burgess, E. O., and T. M. Parrott (1997). "Theory, explanation, and a third generaton of theoretical development in social gerontology," *Journal of Gerontology*, 52B: S72-S88.

Bengtson, V. L., Rice, C. J., and M. L. Johnson (1999). "Are theories of aging important? Models and explanations in gerontology at the turn of the century." In V. L. Bengtson and K. W. Schaie, eds., *Handbook of theories of aging*. New York: Springer, pp. 3–20.

Berger, P. L., and T. Luckmann (1966). *The social construction of reality*. New York: Doubleday.

Birren, J. E. (1999). "Theories of aging: a personal perspective." In V. L. Bengtson and K. W. Schaie, eds., *Handbook of theories of aging*. New York: Springer, pp. 459–71.

Blau, P. M. (1964). *Exchange and power in social life*. New York: Wiley.

Blieszner, R. (1993). "A socialist – feminist perspective on widowhood," *Journal of Aging Studies*, 7: 171–82.

Bytheway, B. (1995). *Ageism*. Buckingham: Open University Press.

Calasanti, T. M. (1999). "Feminism and gerontology: not just for women," *Hallym International Journal of Aging*, 1: 44–55.

Carstensen, L. (1992). "Social and emotional patterns in adulthood: support for socioemotional selectivity theory," *Psychology and Aging*, 7: 331–8.

Cowdry, E. V., ed. (1939). *Problems of aging*. Baltimore, Md.: Williams and Wilkins.

Cowgill, D. A., and L. D. Holmes (1974). "Aging and modernization. A revision of theory." In J. Gubrium, ed., *Laterlife: community and environmental policies*. New York: Basic Books, pp. 305–23.

Cristofalo, V. J. (1996). "Ten years later: what have we learned about human aging from studies of cell cultures?" *Gerontologist*, 36: 737–41.

Cristofalo, V. J., Tresini, J., Francis, M. K., and C. Volker (1999). "Biological theories of senescence." In V. L. Bengtson and K. W. Schaie, eds., *Handbook of theories of aging*. New York: Springer, pp. 98–112.

Cumming, E. and W. Henry (1961). *Growing old: the process of disengagement*. New York: Basic Books.

Dannefer, W. D., and R. R. Sell (1988). "Age structure, the lifecourse and aged heterogeneity: prospects for research and theory," *Comprehensive Gerontology*, 2: 1–10.

Dowd, J. J. (1975). "Aging as exchange: a preface to theory," *Journal of Gerontology*, 30: 584–94.

Elder, G. H., Jr. (1992). "Models of the lifecourse," *Contemporary Sociology: A Journal of Reviews*, 21: 632–5.

Elder, G. H., Jr., and M. K. Johnson (2002). "The life course and aging: challenges, lessons, and new directions." In R. A. Settersten, ed., *Invitation to the lifecourse: towards new understandings of later life*. Amityville, N. Y.: Baywood, pp. 49–81.

Erikson, E. H. (1950). *Childhood and society*. New York: W. W. Norton.

Estes, C. L. (2001). "Political economy of aging: a theoretical framework." In C. L. Estes and Associates, *Social policy and aging: a critical perspective*. Thousand Oaks, Calif.: Sage.

Estes, C. L., Gerard, L. E., Jones, J. S., and J. H. Swan (1984). *Political economy, health, and aging*. Boston, Mass.: Little, Brown.

Finch. C. (1990). *Longevity, senescence, and the genome.* Chicago: University of Chicago Press.

—— (1997). "Comparative perspectives on plasticity in human aging and life spans." In K. W. Wachter and C. E. Finch, eds., *Between Zeus and the salmon: the biodemography of longevity.* New York: National Academy Press.

Finch, C. E., and T. E. Seeman (1999). "Stress theories of aging." In V. L. Bengtson and K. W. Schaie, eds., *Handbook of theories of aging.* New York: Springer, pp. 81–97.

Foucault, M. (1977). *Discipline and punish: the birth of a prison.* Trans. A. Sheridan. New York: Vintage / Random House.

Garfinkel, H. (1967). *Studies in ethnomethodology.* Englewood, N. J.: Prentice-Hall.

Gavrilov, L. A., and N. S. Gavrilova (2003). "The quest for a general theory of aging and longevity," *Science.* Retrieved July 2003 from: http://sageke.sciencemag.org/cgi/content/full/sageke;2003/28/re5.

George, L. K. (1996). "Missing links: the case for a social psychology of the lifecourse," *Gerontologist,* 36: 248–55.

Glaser, B. G., and A. L. Strauss, (1967). *The discovery of grounded theory: strategies for qualitative research.* New York: Aldine.

Gubrium, J. F. (1993). *Speaking of life: horizons of meaning for nursing home residents.* New York: Aldine de Gruyter.

Gubrium, J. F., and J. A. Holstein (1999). "Constructionist perspectives on aging." In V. L. Bengtson and K. W. Schaie, eds., *Handbook of theories of aging.* New York: Springer, pp. 287–305.

Habermas, J. (1970). *Science and technology as ideology. Towards a rational society.* Boston: Beacon Press.

—— (1971). *Knowledge and human interests.* Trans. J. J. Shapiro. Boston: Beacon Press.

Hagestad, G. O., and D. Dannefer (2001). "Concepts and theories of aging: beyond microfication in social science approaches." In R. H. Binstock and L. K. George, eds., *Handbook of aging and the social sciences,* 5th edn. San Diego, Calif.: Academic Press, pp. 3–21.

Hall, G. S. (1922). *Senescence.* New York: Appleton.

Harman, D. (1956). "Aging: a theory based on free radical and radiation chemistry," *Journal of Gerontology,* 11: 298–300.

Havighurst, R. J. (1943). *Human development and education.* New York: Longman.

Hendricks, J. (1992). "Generations and the generation of theory in social gerontology," *International Journal of Aging and Human Development,* 35: 31–47.

—— (1995). "Exchange theory in aging." In G. Maddox, ed., *The encyclopedia of aging,* 2nd edn. New York: Springer.

Hendricks, J., and A. Achenbaum (1999). "Historical development of theories of aging." In V. L. Bengtson and K. W. Schaie, eds., *Handbook of theories of aging.* New York: Springer, pp. 21–39.

Hochschild, A. R. (1975). "Disengagement theory: a critique and a proposal," *American Sociological Review,* 40: 553–69.

Homans, G. C. (1961). *Social behavior: its elementary forms.* New York: Harcourt Brace Jovanovich.

Horkheimer, M., and T. W. Adorno (1944). "The cultural industry: enlightenment as mass deception." In M. Horkheimer and T. W. Adorno, eds., *Dialectic of enlightenment.* Trans. J. Cumming. New York: Continuum Publishing.

Kirkwood, T. B. L. (2001). "Why does aging occur?" In V. J. Cristofalo, R. Adelman, and K. W. Schaie, eds., *Annual review of gerontology and geriatrics,* Vol XXI. New York: Springer, pp. 41–55.

Kuhn, T. (1962). *The structure of scientific revolutions.* New York: Norton.

Kuypers, J. A., and V. L. Bengtson (1973). "Social breakdown and competence: a model of normal aging." *Human Development,* 16: 181–201.

Lemon, B. W., Bengtson, V. L., and J. A. Peterson (1972). "An exploration of the activity theory of aging," *Journal of Gerontology,* 27: 511–23.

Levinson, D. J. (1978). *The seasons of a man's life.* New York: Knopf.

Linton, R. (1942). "Age and sex categories," *American Sociological Review,* 7: 589–603.

Lyotard, J. F. (1984). *The postmodern condition.* Minneapolis, Minn.: University of Minnesota Press.

McMullen, J. (1995). "Theorizing age and gender relations." In S. Arber and J. Ginn, eds., *Connecting gender and aging: a sociological approach.* Philadelphia: Open University Press.

Mannheim, K. (1952[1928]). "The problem of generations." In P. Kecskmeri, ed., *Essays in sociology of knowledge.* London: Routledge and Kegan Paul.

Marshall, V. W. (1999). "Analyzing social theories of aging." In V. L. Bengtson and K. W. Schaie, eds., *Handbook of theories of aging.* New York: Springer, pp. 434–55.

Martin, G. M. (2003). "Biology of aging: the state of the art," *Gerontologist,* 43: 272–4.

Marx, K. (1967[1867–95]). *Capital: a critique of political economy.* New York: International Publishers.

Mead, G. H. (1934). *Mind, self, and society.* Chicago: University of Chicago Press.

Medawar, P. B. (1952). *An unsolved problem of biology.* London: H. K. Lewis.

Moody, H. R. (1993). "Overview: what is critical gerontology and why is it important?" In T. R. Cole, W. A. Achenbaum, P. L. Jakobi, and R. Kastenbaum, eds., *Voices and visions: towards a critical gerontology.* New York: Springer.

—— (2001). "The humanities and aging: a millennial perspective," *Gerontologist,* 41: 411–15.

Myerhoff, B. (1978). *Number our days*. New York: Dutton.

O'Rand, A. M., and R. T. Campbell (1999). "On reestablishing the phenomenon and specifying ignorance: theory development and research design in aging." In V. L. Bengtson and K. W. Schaie, eds., *Handbook of theories of aging*. New York: Springer, pp. 59–78.

Parsons, T. (1942). "Age and sex in the social structure of the United States," *American Sociological Review*, 7: 604–16.

Pescosolido, B. A., and B. A. Rubin (2000). "The web of group affiliations revisited: social life, postmodernism, and sociology," *American Sociological Review*, 65: 52–76.

Ray, R. E. (1996). "A postmodern perspective on feminist gerontology," *Gerontologist*, 36: 674–80.

Riley, M. W., and K. A. Loscocco (1994). "The changing structure of work opportunities: towards an age-integrated society." In R. P. Abeles, H. C. Gift, and M. G. Ory, eds., *Aging and quality of life*. New York: Springer.

Riley, M. W., Johnson, M., and A. Foner (1972). *Aging and society*. Vol. III: *A sociology of age stratification*. New York: Russell Sage Foundation.

Riley, M. W., Foner, A., and J. Waring (1988). "Sociology of age." In N. J. Smelser, ed., *Handbook of sociology*. Beverly Hills, Calif.: Sage.

Riley, M. W., Kahn, R. L., and E. Foner, eds. (1994). *Age and structural lag: society's failure to provide meaningful opportunities in work, family and leisure*. New York: John Wiley.

Rorty, R. (1994). "Method, social science, and social hope." In S. Seidman, ed., *The postmodern turn: new perspectives on social theory*. Cambridge: Cambridge University Press.

Rose, A. (1965). "A current theoretical issue in social gerontology," *Gerontologist*, 4: 46–50.

Salthouse, T. A. (1991). *Theoretical perspectives on cognitive aging*. Hillsdale, N. Y.: Lawrence Erlbaum Associates.

(1999). "Theories of cognition." In V. L. Bengtson and K. W. Schaie, eds., *Handbook of theories of aging*. New York: Springer, pp. 196–208.

Schroots, J. J. F. (1996). "Theoretical developments in the psychology of aging," *Gerontologist*, 36: 742–8.

Settersten, R. A., Jr., and L. M. Dobransky (2000). "On the unbearable lightness of theory in gerontology," *Gerontologist*, 40: 367–73.

Simmel, G. (1966[1904]). *Conflict*. Trans. K. H. Wolff. Glencoe, Ill.: Free Press.

Sorokin, P. A. (1947). *Society, culture and personality*. New York: Harper and Brothers.

Strauss, A., and J. Corbin (1990). *Basics of qualitative research: grounded theory procedures and techniques*. Newbury Park, Calif.: Sage.

Stroller, E. P. (1993). "Gender and the organization of lay healthcare: a socialist-feminist perspective," *Journal of Aging Studies*, 7: 151–70.

Tornstam, L. (1989). "Gerotranscendence; a reformulation of the disengagement theory," *Aging*, 1: 53–63.

(1996). "Gerontranscendence – a theory about maturing in old age," *Journal of Aging and Identity*, 1: 37–50.

Turner, J. H. (2003). *The structure of sociological theory*. Belmont, Calif.: Wadsworth / Thomson Learning.

Wachter, K. W., and C. E. Finch, eds. (1997). *Between Zeus and the salmon: the biodemography of longevity*. Washington, D.C.: National Academy Press.

Walford, R. (1969). *The immunologic theory of aging*. Copenhagen: Munksgaard.

Wallace, R. A., and A. Wolf (1991). *Contemporary sociological theory: continuing the classical tradition*, 3rd edn. Englewood Cliffs, N.J.: Prentice Hall.

Walsh, J. P. (2004). "Drug therapy in Alzheimer's Disease." Andrus Gerontology Center's Research Roundtables presentation, University of Southern California, December.

Williams, G. C. (1957). "Pleiotropy, natural selection and the evolution of senescence," *Evolution*, 11: 398–411.

Woodruff-Pak, D. S., and M. Papka (1999). "Theories of neuropsychology and aging." In V. L. Bengtson and K. W. Schaie, eds., *Handbook of theories of aging*. New York: Springer, pp. 113–32.

Ageing and Changing: International Historical Perspectives on Ageing

W. ANDREW ACHENBAUM

THE DECLINE OF THE AGEING BODY: THE FOUNDATION FOR PERSPECTIVES ON AGEING

Old age is an age-old, universal phenomenon. Every culture past and present has employed terms or phrases that demarcate the beginning and end phases of the human life course. Nonetheless, how people describe the last stage of life (as well as how they delineate intervals within the period of old age) varies enormously from place to place over historical time. Different societies attribute divergent meanings to the same features of senescence, including aspects of physical ageing.

'Old age', like other dimensions of the human condition, is a social construct. Men and women everywhere throughout recorded history have ascribed to ageing a plethora of positive, negative, contradictory, ambiguous and ambivalent images and ideas. Attitudes, traits and behaviours in ageing-related constructs typically correlate with the processes, problems, challenges and opportunities of growing older. Yet international historical perspectives on ageing do not always mirror senescence's realities. Often they arise from political, social, economic, cultural and demographic factors that shape a particular society at a specific historical moment (Sokolovsky, 1997: xxv).

Let us begin with the physical signs of ageing and old age, starting with the oldest known document – a description by the philosopher and poet Ptah-hotep, writing in Egypt in 2500 BCE:

How hard and painful are the last days of an aged man! He grows weaker every day; his eyes become dim, his ears deaf; his strength fades; his heart knows peace no longer; his mouth falls silent and he speaks no word. The power of his mind lessens and today he cannot remember what yesterday was like. All his bones hurt. Those things which not long ago were done with pleasure are painful now; and taste vanishes . . . His nose is blocked, and he can smell nothing any more. (Quoted in de Beauvoir, 1972: 92)

This characterization challenges notions that the elderly in primordial times lived healthily and happily. Ptah-hotep characterized physical ageing as bodily decline. This became a universally recurring theme – but not everywhere (Achenbaum, 1985).

The aged thrived in the East during ancient times. Confucianism laid out relations between superiors and inferiors in terms beneficial to the elderly. Confucius described moral development in chronological terms: 'At fifteen, I applied myself to wisdom; at thirty, I grew stronger at it; at forty I no longer had doubts; at sixty there was nothing on earth that could shake me; at seventy I could follow the dictates of my heart without disobeying the moral law.' In the family, which the Chinese viewed as a microcosm of society, all members owed strict obedience to the oldest man. A man's fiftieth birthday in ancient China and for centuries thereafter was marked with great ritual and reverence. Maturity, declared the sages, deepened an elder's affinity to family ancestors. Because age was critical in the Confucian world view, older women prevailed over their sons and daughters (Thang, 2000: 196).

Similar conditions existed elsewhere in the region. In the Taoist tradition, old age was unattainable through physical practices, but attaining extreme longevity was proof of sainthood ('Taoism', *Encyclopaedia Britannica* (henceforth *EB*): XXVIII, 398). According to Brahamic canons, a few elderly hermits attained so much wisdom that their bodies were transubstantiated into immortality (Hall, 1922: 82; Cremin, 1970–88).

Such veneration of grey hairs was not common in early Western civilization. Following Aristotle's lead, as well as findings by physicians in the fifth century BC, the ancient Greeks hypothesized that the physiological characteristics of old age explained its lamentable nature. Unlike a child's body, which was said to be hot and moist, the aged's body was deemed abnormally cold and dry. In the schematization of humours that conformed to the Greek typology of the four stages of human development, elders' bile was black, thus making death the natural consequence of ageing (Gruman, 1966: 15).

The ancient Greeks also believed that specific diseases afflicted certain stages of life. Hippocrates catalogued old-age maladies in his *Aphorisms* (400 BC): 'To old people, dyspnoea, catarrhs accompanied with coughs, dysuria, pains of the joints, nephritis, vertigo, apoplexy, cachexia, pruritus of the whole body, insomnolency, defluxions of the bowels, of the eyes, and of the nose, dimness of sight, cataracts.' Hippocrates' list established a precedent for the observation by Seneca (4 BC–AD 65) that *senectus morbidus est* – 'Old age is a disease.'

Greek images of old age were not resolutely negative. Sparta, beginning in the seventh century BC, was ruled by a *gerousia*, a council of men who were at least 60 years old. Elderly leaders, selected for their wisdom, were expected to exercise authority conservatively. Yet some Greeks, such as Aristophanes in the fifth century, satirized abuses by the *gerousia*.

Like the Greeks, Roman interpretations of the decrements that accompanied age varied considerably. Virgil (70–19 BC) in the *Georgics* (iii.66) bemoaned how 'all the best days of life slip away from us poor mortals first: illnesses and dreary old age and pain sneak up, and the fierceness of harsh death snatches away'. Juvenal (60–130) fiercely mocked the elderly's physical ailments in his *Satires*:

What a train of woes – and such woes – come with a prolonged age. To begin with, this deformed, hideous, unrecognizable face; this vile leather instead of skin; these pendulous cheeks; these wrinkles like those around the mouth of an old she-ape as she sits scratching . . . Old men are all the same; their voices tremble, so do their limbs; no hair left on their shining scalps; they run at the nose like little children. To chew his bread, the poor ancient has nothing but toothless gums . . . A perpetual train of losses, incessant mourning and old age dressed in black, surrounded by everlasting sadness – that is the price of a long life. (Quoted in de Beauvoir, 1972: 121–2)

Cicero (106–43 BC) acknowledged, but did not accentuate, the negative consequences of ageing. He argued in *De senectute* that years of experience more than compensated for the physical decline that came with advancing age: 'It is not by muscle, speed, or physical dexterity that great things are achieved, but by reflection, force of character, and judgment; in these qualities old age is usually not poorer, but is even richer . . . old age, so far from being feeble and inactive, is ever busy and doing and effecting something' (Falconer, 1923: 27, 35).

Hebrew scripture provides another variegated treasure trove of late-life images. 'A hoary head is a crown of glory; it is gained in a righteous life', according to Proverbs (16:31). The Fifth Commandment not only demanded respect for elders, but implied that children would be punished if they disobeyed their parents (Deuteronomy 5:16). In addition, the author of Deuteronomy stipulated (4:40, 5:33) that longevity was the Lord's reward for faithful service. Accounts of Noah (Genesis 7:6, 9:29), Abraham (Genesis 25:8), Moses (Deuteronomy 34:7), Caleb (Joshua 14:10–11) and Gideon (Judges 8:32) all attest to the longevitousness of their 'good old age'. The fruits of ripeness were not limited to Hebrew males. Jews celebrate Sarah's ability to conceive a son long after she had reached menopause (Genesis 24:36) as proof of God's graciousness. Ruth (4:13–17) in her later years was rewarded for her loyalty to her mother-in-law.

Yet certain passages in Hebrew scripture resemble other ancient texts in their gruesome depiction of physical decline with advancing years. Ecclesiastes 12:1–8 metaphorically details the trembling arms, stooping legs, missing and worn-down teeth, failing vision, swollen stomachs and diminished libido. The Psalmist (71:9) poignantly conveys the elderly's fear of rejection: 'Do not cast me off in the time of old age; forsake me not when my strength is gone.'

Psalm 90:10 draws a distinction between the relative healthfulness of septuagenarians and the inevitable vulnerability of those over eighty. (This verse anticipates contrasts between a 'green' old age and second childhood, as well as the more recent distinction that Bernice Neugarten (1974) posited between the young-old and old-old.) Living too long was lamentable. Hence a young virgin gave King David warmth but no sexual satisfaction in his declining days (1 Kings 1:2–3). Prophets urged the children of Israel to care for helpless, decrepit widows.

This modest set of texts suffices to establish an important generalization: the physical aspects of senescence, sometimes linked to chronological age, lay the foundation for a perception, both international and historical, that people who attained old age declined in the process. In the Quran, this 'fact' meant 'neither more nor less than one more sign' of Allah's power (Thursby, 2000: 159). In most traditions, however, diminished capacity degenerated into a diseased state, ending in death. Subsequent generations of writers and artists incorporated such ideas about 'decline' into their work. Shakespeare in *As You Like It* mocks the 'second childishness and mere oblivion, sans teeth, sans eyes, sans tastes, sans everything'. In *Hamlet* the Bard has a 'satirical rogue' declaim 'that old men have grey beards, that their faces are wrinkled, their eyes purging thick amber and plum-tree gum, and that they have a plentiful lack of wit, together with most weak hams'. Jonathan Swift observed that 'every man desires to live; but no man would be old'.

Folk artists between the fourteenth and eighteenth centuries designed graphic renditions of the 'steps of ages' wherein toddlers traversed up stairs and then descended another set of stairs to death. The progression varied in steps: sometimes artists crafted as few as four scenes, others as many as thirteen, but their images became iconic. Children played with toys. Boys carried books while girls learned to spin. Men in their prime were soldiers; women, mothers. Artists made their aged subjects stooped; the elderly were assigned sedentary duties. At 70 or 80 the old ones were confined to their beds, dependent on others, awaiting Father Time to turn his sickle (a symbol of fertility) into an instrument of destruction (Achenbaum, 1985: 137–8).

Diverse depictions of the physical manifestations of old age have passed down to the contemporary era, filtered through broader cultural and historical lenses. There has been no dramatic or sudden shift in old-age imagery, although revolutionary situations tend to undermine prevailing images of old age (Troyansky, 1989). For instance, young Chinese intellectuals in the early twentieth century assaulted the centuries-old respect for age as part of their sweeping attack on Confucianism. 'Youth is like the early spring, like the rising sun . . . like a newly sharpened blade. It is the most valuable period of life', wrote a leader of the May 4th Movement. 'The function of youth in society is the same as that of a fresh and vital cell in a human body. In the processes of metabolism the old and rotten are incessantly eliminated to be replaced by the fresh and living. What is the struggle [of youth]? It is to exert one's intellect, discard resolutely the old and the rotten' (quoted in Ganschow, 1978: 308–9). Modern Chinese revolutionaries no longer felt bound to defer to their elders on account of their advanced age.

Sometimes shifts in physicians' clinical gaze altered perceptions of the elderly. Edward J. Steiglitz, MD, who headed the US government's first gerontological research centre, was aware of the animus against old age expressed by medical professionals. Physicians and researchers earlier in the twentieth century generally accepted Nobel Laureate Elie Metchnikoff's diagnosis that 'old age . . . is an infectious, chronic disease which is manifested by a degeneration, or an enfeebling of the noble elements' (1905: 48). Steiglitz partly acknowledged this characterization in *The second forty years* when he noted that 'old organs are scarred organs' (1946: 36). Yet he contended that the potentialities of age outweighed its deficiencies:

Senescence is not all decline. Some functions and capacities do insidiously but persistently decline, but certain other faculties may actually increase. With planned cultivation of these compensatory capacities, the increments can very nearly balance the decrements. The hair may stop growing and the pate become a polished dome fringed with silver, but the mind below this shining cupola can continue to grow in understanding, wisdom, and appreciation of life. Which is more important? (1946: 2–3)

Geriatric interventions, added Steiglitz, compensated for the loss of certain functions by cultivating the elderly's cognitive capacities.

Although not always articulated fully in the historical literature, a gender bias persists over time and across space in characterizing senescence, which is more detrimental to women than to men. To wit: the derogatory term 'hag' comes from 'hagia', Greek for a holy woman; and this description of Gloria Steinem at 50:

Wallace Stevens has written that 'death is the mother of beauty,' but certainly in Western culture youth is the prized gift, and ageing, the deprivation of youth, is viewed as a cruel loss. First comes the despair at the ageing body, and particularly the ageing face, a despair whose alleviation can be sought either by impersonating youth with the aid of drugs, surgery, or makeup, or by abandoning all hope of a youthful appearance and accepting with wry humor the inevitable expanding and sagging. (Heilbrun, 1995: 355)

Now over 60 Steinem remains a beautiful woman, actively engaged in gender politics. But Steinem lives in a culture that marginalizes older women. How ironic, since females represent the majority of ageing populations in both developing and advanced-industrial societies.

DEMOGRAPHIC PATTERNS IN INTERNATIONAL HISTORICAL PERSPECTIVE

Just as the physical attributes of old age represent salient traits of the last stage of life, so too the demographic realities of human longevity put numbers to its dimensions. Anthropological and historical research suggests three generalizations about demographic patterns of ageing (Simmons, 1945; Cole, 1992):

1. Old people have existed throughout most of recorded history, but they constituted a very small percentage of the total population in any given time or place – less than 2 per cent of the total, usually far smaller than that (Hauser, 1976: 66). Reaching old age was a rare event, where the odds of surviving to the age of 1 were poor. Only one in three babies survived their first birthday in Bombay at the beginning of the twentieth century (Robinson, 1989: 119). If a person reached the age of 20, then his or her chances of surviving to the age of 40 and beyond were much improved.

2. At least since 1700, written records in Europe and North America (such as laws, diaries and encyclopaedias) have loosely placed the onset of old age chronologically at around 65, give or take 15 years either way (Harris, 1988: 129). There is no evidence obtained from ancient times or primitive cultures that the chronological onset of old age was thought to occur before the age of 40. Men and women who controlled physical and economic resources, and who gained favourable status through the tasks that they performed, were considered to be in their prime. The Chimu kingdom in Peru at the time of the Spanish conquest, for instance, considered warriors between the ages of 50 and 60 to be 'half old'. After 60, individuals paid no tribute and were exempt from military service (Collier *et al.*, 1992: 183).

3. The greatest increases in life expectancy at birth and in life expectancy at age 40 have occurred in the twentieth century. Since 1950 there have been modest gains in life expectancy at the age of 60. Three-quarters of all gains in longevity have been attained since 1900 (Riley and Riley, 1985). Declines in mortality and increases in life expectancy, however, have been less pertinent in population ageing since the end of the Second World War than sharp declines in fertility rates. Thus Japan, which, as late as 1950, had only 5 per cent of its population over 65 now has the greatest percentage of elders in its midst, surpassing even Sweden (Myers, 1990: 26). Life expectancy for men rose from 50 to 78, and from 55 to 83 for women, from 1947 to 1995 (Thang, 2000: 193).

These generalizations affect in at least two ways how people around the world have perceived ageing.

Consider first that, until recently, few human beings attained old age. The paucity of elders consigned them the role of 'strangers' in the land of the young – and even to themselves (Gutmann, 1987). 'Old age is the most unexpected of all things that happen to a man', declared Lev Trotsky, aged 56, in 1935. Strangers get by if people are hospitable and helpful. Indeed, sometimes the elderly were venerated simply because they had lived so long: a healthful, virtuous manner of living presumably made a 'ripe' old age attainable. Some elders put a spin on this idea: Thomas Jefferson, arguably America's greatest sage, and Maggie Kuhn, the founder of the Gray Lobby 150 years later, both exulted in their eighties about the pleasure of out-living their opponents. They enjoyed having the last word in revising the history of their days.

Viewing the aged as strangers lends itself to a less sanguine interpretation of ageing – one of wariness, even fear. People sometimes treat aliens with sus-picion, and heap contempt on those who speak our language with a heavy accent. Those unfamiliar with the vicissitudes of age do not need to justify pro-jecting their fears onto the spectre of senescence. Indeed, the picture drawn by eye-witnesses can be as gloomy as younger people imagine. Here is an account by John Burroughs writing in his journal in 1920, shortly before his death at the age of 84:

One of the drawbacks of old age is that one outlives his generation and feels alone in the world. The new gen-erations have interests of their own, and are no more in sympathy with you than you are with them. The octo-genarian has no alternative but to live in the past. He lives with the dead, and they pull him down.

Survivorship without the requisite support network brings the risk of rejection and dependency.

Second, ponder that old age's prescribed span of years has always been perceived to be longer than any other stage of life. Infancy lasts no more than two years, adolescence nowadays rarely stretches more than a decade. But one can qualify for some old-age privileges at 50 or deny being old indefi-nitely. Bernard Baruch after 80 persistently claimed that old age began at his current age plus 15 years (Achenbaum *et al.*, 1996: 61). Elastic boundaries make old age the most heterogeneous stage of life. Today's generation of elders varies enormously in physical, mental, psychological and social capabil-ities. Two people the same age may share no other common attribute. Such diversity has always existed across cohorts. Some people mature fruitfully as they grow older, while some decline slowly – or suddenly because of an unexpected mishap. Many older people try to maintain lifestyles that they adapted in middle age. Others opt, by choice or cir-cumstance, for radical changes in what they think, feel, live or do. Some move on; others become stuck.

The heterogeneity that inheres in late life may have grown more rich in recent decades. A subtle revolution is in the making, which results from soci-etal ageing. When the aged were few in numbers,

their 'problems' were manageable. It mattered little if the aged's potential contributions were squan-dered. Now an increasingly larger subset of the pop-ulation, the elderly's wants, desires and needs can no longer be discounted. They represent a potent voting bloc, one entitled to governmental support. Aged consumers buy luxuries; they avail themselves of (medical) services they can ill afford. People dur-ing the past century came to believe that they would reach 65. This demographic reality alone justifies hypothesizing that the great watershed in the his-tory of ageing, particularly in developed countries, occurred during the twentieth century.

Perceptions of ageing remain in transition. Older persons today, and increasingly in the twenty-first century, will have added years to fill that their par-ents and grandparents did not have. This extension of the 'average' lifecourse permits greater individual differentiation than ever before. Only death causes a convergence of attitudes or behaviour among the aged.

FAMILY TIES

Regardless of historical moment or geographic location, family members have always been the pri-mary line of defence in situations of old-age depen-dency. Structures vary enormously over time and by setting. In Western European nations and North America, the elderly (usually men) have traditionally wished to remain heads of their own household as long as possible. This generalization requires at least two qualifications. First, in the early modern period, some domestic units became 'stem families' – rela-tives young or old would move into a middle-aged householder's residence – an arrangement that typ-ically lasted for only a few years. Second, a greater emphasis has been placed lately on the 'autonomy' than on the 'dependence' of a family elder. Nuclear families typify the Western model: older people maintain their own residences until they must go somewhere else.

Elsewhere, very different arrangements obtain. In Africa and parts of Asia, elderly women often headed the family unit (Humphrey with Oron, 1996: 26). Daughters-in-law either resided in mother-in-law's abode or they lived in such proximity that they were able to conform to her domestic plans; women who lived in their husband's village viewed the arrangement as a temporary enclave (*EB*, XV: 645–6). Deference to elders animated pre-industrial Japanese families, where permanent members ranked before temporary ones, men before women (Bowring and Kornicki, 1993: 236). Aborigines in Australia opted for more 'open' arrangements, so 'fathers' might not be kin, and 'elders' might not be aged, but they controlled local matters energetically (*EB*, XIV: 425–6).

Regardless of domestic arrangements, women have been more likely than men in virtually every historical setting around the world to be the primary caregivers. In some places the responsibility falls to the youngest daughter. Sometimes aunts or female cousins fulfil the tasks of cooking food, bathing or caring for an infirm elder. Men typically get involved only when there is no other alternative.

Some safety nets have holes. Estrangements and divorce disrupt caregiving plans. Designated caregivers can move with their spouse out of their community to a place too far away to be able to serve. Death breaks bonds. In such situations, neighbours and friends take over on an informal basis. In modern times, compensatory arrangements exist. New modes of transportation and communication enable siblings and children to remain in touch with their elder kin even if not in physical contact daily.

Societal ageing nevertheless has disrupted traditional familial patterns in at least three ways. In the East, skyrocketing real estate prices has made it impossible for family members to cohabit in commodious space. Elders in Japan and China now make hard choices about residency like their contemporaries in the West. Second, many women are unwilling or unable to serve as primary caregivers for elders because they are gainfully employed outside the household. Finally, the traditional pyramidal family structure has, with multigenerational survivors come to resemble a 'bean-pole'. More older persons can assist with caring for the chronically impaired or very old, but because of divorce, geographical mobility and deaths, unlikely folk may assume caregiving roles.

ECONOMIC PATTERNS

Agricultural pursuits, which have been the most prevalent mode of economic activity everywhere throughout recorded history, generally provide favourable opportunities for elderly men and women. Farming is hard work, especially at harvest time. Yet there are many tasks entailed in keeping a farm running, which can be accomplished by people with diminished capacities – if they know what they are doing. The aged can supervise the work of others and keep records. The experiences accrued over a lifetime of observing Nature's bounty and brutality have solidified the perception of the elderly as veterans of productivity.

Control of the land, moreover, assured older people a measure of economic security. Children worked the land for their parents or grandparents with the expectation that in due course they would gain title to the family property. Elders wisely transferred property only after making due provisions for themselves in their declining years or for their spouse's widowhood. Healing powers and the magic of Shamanistic rituals associated with the land, moreover, accorded the aged additional control in Native American tribes and in other primitive cultures (Simmons, 1945: 162–3).

After the Industrial Revolution the economic status of older people changed, especially insofar as new modes of production and consumption altered prevailing ways of doing business. Economies of scale made hand-made goods a luxury. Machines displaced traditional means of craft making. 'Scientific management' ushered in new modalities for measuring job performance. Efficiency standards were tracked by the clock; older people (who rarely perform well under time pressures) found their expertise less and less a valued commodity. In a world dominated by bureaucratic procedures rather than personal/familial connections, it became more difficult for elders to adapt to the changing marketplace (Haber and Gratton, 1994). Old workers were obsolescent.

In the initial phases of industrialization the aged were treated as if they were disabled. Like the lame and blind they begged for money at the factory gate or at the saloon. By the middle of the nineteenth century, progressive banks in Britain and transportation companies in the United States began to offer pensions based on a candidate's age and years of service. 'Retirement' became a reward for faithful service and an effective tool for getting rid of worn-out workers. Corporate pensions were deemed gratuities in the board room; only after the government established its own social-security measures did the financing of corporate and union pensions become regularized (Hannah, 1985).

It has always been possible for older people to retrain themselves for new positions in a changing marketplace. Various private organizations, beginning in the mid eighteenth century, established lyceums and adult education programmes to teach older people new skills or to enrich their lives with learning opportunities they did not have earlier in life. Such programmes may become increasingly significant in the future, but their success in reintegrating older workers into the marketplace thus far has been modest.

A dramatic change in the elderly's economic patterns since the mid twentieth century has been a consequence of women's growing participation in the paid work force. Traditionally, young women worked before they married; widows became bartenders or inn keepers or laundresses to make ends meet. Career women, like men, now seek part-time or seasonal employment in their later years. Continuing to work is not always volitional: women live longer on average than men, and sex discrimination still impedes their career opportunities and salary history.

Indeed, the plight of older women workers is simply the latest phase of a general economic late-life pattern. People have always expected the aged to make provisions for their old age. Generally, this has meant that the old had to work until they were disabled or dead. Pensions, public and private, have made it possible for people to look forward to a sunny 'retirement'; but for most humans internationally and historically, the dream of genuine economic security has not been realized. The aged usually have lived at subsistence levels, rarely confident that they could survive once their resources were exhausted.

POLITICAL DEVELOPMENTS

We have already noted that the elderly everywhere throughout history have held many important leadership positions: in African and Southeast Asian tribes, in the papacy and episcopacy, and in democratically elected offices. The aged putatively have the requisite experience, having risen through the ranks, and the wisdom, having dealt with all sorts of conditions and personalities. Despite the gradual ageing of most populations, however, there has no apparent preference given to older rulers (the aged leaders of the old Soviet Union and Communist China notwithstanding). That fresh faces enliven political campaigns does not mean that age discrimination is rampant in heated contests.

The most important political old-age development has been in the area of social welfare. States provide for those aged considered deserving and/or needy. 'Public' intervention on behalf of the old typically began in the local community. Institutions such as a religious organization or charity set aside funds (thereby supplementing resources provided by family, friends and neighbours) to shelter, feed, or provide medical care to elderly indigents. Over time, local entities – the country, a city, a state, a district – regularized allocations, sometimes also erecting facilities to house the old. State governments or regional polities provided a third layer of non-familial support: they granted pensions to their employees and gave assistance to the elderly poor who met stringent eligibility requirements.

Military or veterans' pensions have been the most important sources of old-age relief. The precedent for giving loyal bureaucrats retainers so that they might become superannuated dates back to twelfth-century China and fifteenth-century France. By the 1800s, ageing veterans began to qualify for stipends or land grants comparable to those awarded to wounded soldiers and sailors. Allocations were not insignificant: by 1913, for instance, pensions to northern Civil War veterans represented 18 per cent of the US federal budget (Achenbaum, 1978: 84).

In the twentieth century, virtually every nation has enacted some sort of old-age assistance programme to deal with the aged poor's immediate needs and an old-age insurance plan to enable workers to prepare for their later years. The historical timing and scope of such schemes depended on the country's population structure, the ideology of the ruling party willing to enact such provisions, and the Treasury's current and anticipated funds. The growth of old-age interest groups ensured the liberalization of public benefits (Binstock and Day, 1995: 369). Until very recently, social security measures enjoyed widespread popularity. With population ageing and the staggering cost of elder care, however, many nations (rich and poor) are rethinking the 'entitlements' that their citizens can claim and that they feel that they can afford to offer.

CULTURAL ASPECTS

This chapter began by emphasizing how images of bodily decline generated unfavourable perceptions of old age; it ends with a brief overview of cultural traditions that have influenced the aged's status historically and internationally. Traditions often accentuate positive elements associated with growing older. We have already seen that 'wisdom' and 'experience' count in agricultural settings, certain political milieux, and in religious institutions. The elderly, especially men, retain and increase their power as long as they remain vital. Some, like the Ayatollah Khomeini, dominate revolutions (Robinson, 1996: 119).

The young have always respected the old's capacity to mentor. They count on the stories that elderly men and women tell to help them to clarify options, and to identify pitfalls that lie ahead. The historical record suggests that 'veterans' have sometimes been considered a special, if relatively minor, subset of mentors.

Postmodern cultures of consumption have attempted to manufacture perceptions of a 'good old age' in order to capitalize on the growing numbers of older men and women in ageing societies. Attempts have been made by confectioners and card makers to commercialize 'grandparents' day' as successfully as Mother's Day or Father's Day. So far the efforts have not borne fruit. Advertisers do not know how to reach the grey market. The most memorable media images, in fact, are those depicting 'greedy geezers': well-off, narcissistic, elders squandering resources that rightly should go to rising generations. Robert Butler (1975) coined the term 'ageism' to identify a prejudice comparable to sexism and racism. Contemporary ageism is not the same as Ptah-hotep's, but it serves to remind us that humans tend to honour those who are vitally contributing to other people's wellbeing, and that they tend to disesteem those whose vulnerabilities cannot be masked by a sunny disposition, good health and economic wellbeing. We are entering a new phase in the history of ageing, shaped by a long past.

FURTHER READING

Achenbaum, W. Andrew (1995). *Crossing frontiers: gerontology emerges as a science*. Cambridge: Cambridge University Press.

Cole, Thomas R. (1992). *The journey of life: a cultural history of Aging in America*. Cambridge: Cambridge University Press.

Gullette, Margaret Morganroth (2004). *Aged by culture*, Chicago: University of Chicago Press.

REFERENCES

Achenbaum, W. A. (1978). *Old age in the new land*. Baltimore: Johns Hopkins University Press.

— (1985). 'Societal perceptions of Aging and the aged'. In R. Binstock and E. Shanas, eds., *Handbook of Aging and the social sciences*, 2nd edn. New York: Van Nostrand Reinhold.

Achenbaum, W. A., Weiland, S., and C. Haber (1996). *Keywords in sociocultural gerontology*. New York: Springer Publishing Co.

Binstock, R. H., and C. L. Day (1995). 'Aging and politics'. In R. H. Binstock and L. George, eds., *Handbook of Aging and the social sciences*, 4th edn. San Diego: Academic Press.

Bowring, R., and P. Kornicki, eds. (1993). *The Cambridge encyclopedia of Japan*. Cambridge: Cambridge University Press.

Butler, R. N. (1975). *Why survive?* New York: Harper and Row.

Cole, T. R. (1992). *Journey of life*. New York: Cambridge University Press.

Collier, S., Skidmore, T. E., and H. Blakemore, eds. (1992). *The Cambridge encyclopedia of Latin America and the Caribbean*, 2nd. edn. Cambridge: Cambridge University Press.

Cremin, Laurence A. (1970–88). *American education*, 3 vols. New York: Harper Terchbooks.

de Beauvoir, S. (1972). *The coming of age*. New York: G. P. Putnam.

Encyclopaedia Brittanica (1985). 15th edn. Chicago: University of Chicago Press. XIV: 'Australia'; XV: 'Central Africa'; XVIII: 'History of Education'; XXVIII: 'Taoism'.

Falconer, W. A. (1923). *Cicero: De senectute, de amicitia, de divinatione*. Cambridge, Mass.: Harvard University Press.

Ganschow, T. (1978). 'The aged in a revolutionary milieu: China'. In S. F. Spicker, K. M. Woodward and D. D. VanTassel, eds., *Aging and the elderly: humanistic perspectives in gerontology*. Atlantic Highlands, N.J.: Humanities Press, Inc.

Gruman, G. (1966). 'A history of ideas about the prolongation of life', *Transactions of the American Philosophical Society*, vol. 56.

Gutmann, D. (1987). *Reclaimed powers*. New York: Basic Books.

Haber, C., and B. Gratton (1994). *Old age and the search for security*. Bloomington: Indiana University Press.

Hall, G. S. (1922). *Senescence*. New York: D. Appleton & Sons.

Hannah, L. (1985). *The invention of retirement*. Cambridge: Cambridge University Press.

Harris, D. K. (1988). *Dictionary of gerontology*. New York: Greenwood Press.

Hauser, P. (1976). 'Aging and world-wide population change'. In R. Binstock and E. Shanas, eds., *Handbook of Aging and the social sciences*. New York: Van Nostrand Reinhold.

Heilbrun, C. (1995). *The education of a woman: the life of Gloria Steinem*. New York: Dial Press.

Humphrey, C., with U. Oron (1996). *Shamans and elders*. Oxford: Clarendon Press.

Metchnikoff, E. (1905). 'Old Age'. In *Smithsonian Institution Annual Report, 1903–4*. Washington, D.C.: Government Printing Office.

Myers, G. C. (1990). 'Demography of aging'. In R. H. Binstock and L. George, eds., *Handbook of aging and the social sciences*, 3rd edn. San Diego: Academic Press.

Neugarten, B. L. (1974). 'Age groups in America and the rise of the young-old', *Annals of the American Society of Political and Social Science*, 415: 187–98.

Riley, M. W. and J. R. Riley (1985). 'Longevity and social structure: the potential of the added years'. In A. Pifer and L. Bronte, eds., *Our aging society*. New York: W. W. Norton.

Robinson, F., ed. (1989). *The Cambridge encyclopedia of India, Pakistan, Bangladesh, Sri Lanka, Nepal, Bhutan and the Maldives*. Cambridge: Cambridge University Press.

(1996). *The Cambridge illustrated history of the Islamic world*. Cambridge: Cambridge University Press.

Simmons, L. W. (1945). *The role of the aged in primitive society*. New Haven: Yale University Press.

Sokolovsky, J., ed. (1997). *The cultural context of aging*, 2nd edn. Westport, Conn.: Bergen & Garvey.

Steiglitz, E. (1946). *The second forty years*. Philadelphia: J. B. Lippincott.

Thang, L. L. (2000). 'Aging in the East: comparative and historical reflections'. In T. R. Cole, R. Kastenbaum and R. E. Ray, eds., *Handbook of aging and the humanities*, 2nd edn. New York: Springer.

Thursby, G. R. (2000). 'Aging in eastern religious traditions'. In T. R. Cole, R. Kastenbaum and R. E. Ray eds., *Handbook of aging and the humanities*, 2nd edn. New York: Springer.

Troyansky, D. (1989). *Old age in the old regime*. Ithaca: Cornell University Press.

Global Ageing: The Demographic Revolution in All Cultures and Societies

ALEXANDRE KALACHE, SANDHI MARIA BARRETO
AND INGRID KELLER

INTRODUCTION

The world's total number of older people (defined as 60 years of age and over) is expected almost to double within the next 25 years – from 606 million in 2000 to over 1.2 billion by the year 2025 – and to reach the 2 billion mark by around 2050 (Table 1). Rapid increases in the absolute and relative numbers of older people in both developing and developed countries will be observed. While the global population will increase from around 6 billion in 2000 to 9 billion in 2050 – a 50% increase – the world's elderly population will experience within the same period a 300% increase; the increase in the elderly population of developing countries will be even more substantial at 400% (Table 1). In 2000 for the first time there were more people aged 60 and older than children under 5 in a number of developing countries (United Nations Population Division, 2003). Population ageing could be compared to a silent revolution that will impact on all aspects of society. It is imperative to prepare ourselves in the way most appropriate to it: the opportunities and the challenges are multiple.

AGEING IN THE TWENTY-FIRST CENTURY

The demographic transition

The process of population ageing is driven by two major factors: increased life expectancy and declining fertility rates. This process is commonly referred to as the 'demographic transition'.

Developing countries will experience the steepest increase in the older population segment within the foreseeable future. Already today over 60% of the aged population live in developing countries increasing to around 75% in 2025 and 85% in 2050 (United Nations Population Division, 2002). Countries such as China, Brazil and Nigeria will double their absolute number of older persons from now to 2025. In China for example the population aged 60 years and over will increase from 128 million in 2000 to 286 million in 2025. Respective figures for Brazil are 13 and 34 million and for Nigeria 5.5 and 11.5 million (United Nations Population Division, 2003). In other countries, such as Indonesia, Colombia, Kenya and Thailand, increases will be even higher – between 300 and 400% – i.e. up to eight times higher than the increases in already aged societies such as western European countries, where population ageing occurred over a much longer period of time. For example, it took 114 years in France for the aged population to increase from 7% to 14% (from 1865 to 1979), and 82 years in Sweden (from 1890 to 1972) (JARC, 1998). The same doubling will occur in China in less than 30 years from 2000 to 2027 (US Department of Commerce, 1993). Brazil and Republic of Korea are two other examples: the proportions of older persons in the population are expected to increase from, respectively, 7.8% and 11% in 2000 to 15.2% and 24% in 2025 (United Nations Population Division, 2002).

In addition to the increases in absolute numbers, important increases in the proportion of older people within the general population are expected in virtually all countries of the world, the exception

TABLE 1. Number of older persons (60+, in millions) by world region today and projections

	2000	2025	2050
More developed countries	232	344	394
Less developed countries	375	836	1514
World (million)	606	1180	1908

Source: United Nations Population Division (2003).

being sub-Saharan Africa. By the year 2025 Japan and Switzerland will lead the list of 'oldest countries' with 35% of their population aged 60 years or over, followed by Italy (34%), Germany and Slovenia (each 31%). Table 2 shows the total number and the proportion of older persons (60+) in the eleven most populous countries in the world (more than 100 million inhabitants in the year 2000), as well as France as one example of a large European country as a reference for the first continent to have aged.

Figures 1 and 2 show the population pyramids for Japan and Brazil, illustrating ageing trends world wide in the first decades of the twenty-first century. Brazil will experience a steady decline in the proportions of youth and children while Japan's population structure will show further and substantial ageing of its population.

Table 3 shows life expectancy at birth for men and women in the ten most populous countries and France. As a reflection of world wide trends, in all of the selected countries substantial increases in life expectancy at birth for both sexes have been registered over recent years and are likely to continue. By and large the overall trend towards women outliving men will be consolidated.

In most of the world, fertility rates have experienced important declines over the last 25 years, and by 2025 most countries will show total fertility rates[1] close to or below the 2.1 replacement-level[2] as shown in Table 4. By 2025 only in Bangladesh, Pakistan and Nigeria will total fertility rates be

[1] Definition: the average number of births each woman between 15 and 49 years would have if her lifetime fertility summed the fertility of women of successive ages measured at the same time (WHO, 1995).

[2] Replacement-level fertility is the total fertility rate of 2.1 children per woman.

higher than replacement-level (but considerably lower than now). Indeed, it is estimated that by 2025, 103 countries will have reached, or will have rates below, replacement level, a substantial increase compared to 19 countries in 1975 (United Nations Population Division, 2003).

Chile offers a clear example of the demographic transition. Only 63% of the cohort born in 1909 reached their fifth birthday and only 13% expected to live beyond the eighty-fifth birthday. In comparison, of the 1999 cohort, only 2% will have died before their fifth birthday and virtually half is expected to reach 85 years of age (WHO, 1999a).

With increasing numbers of older persons (60+), by 2025 the ratio between the aged and the working age population (15–59 years) will substantially increase (Table 5). The ratio is expected to more than double from 2000 to 2025 in Brazil (8 to 19), China (11 to 25) and Mexico (7 to 16); Nigeria (5 to 6) and Pakistan (6 to 8) will show the smallest increases in the old-age dependency ratio. In the other selected countries the ratio is estimated to increase by more than 50% in the same period. The Russian Federation, France and Japan will have much higher ratios in 2025 (37, 40 and 55, respectively). This means that Japan, for example, already now one of the oldest countries in the world, will experience a more than four-fold increase in the old-age dependency ratio between 1975 and 2025 (13 to 55) (United Nations Population Division, 2003).

CONSEQUENCES OF AGEING

The epidemiological transition

Population ageing brings substantial challenges to healthcare policy-makers. A major challenge relates to the 'epidemiological transition', a term coined to describe the increasing importance of disease and death attributable to non-communicable diseases (NCDs) in comparison with those caused by infectious diseases. In developed countries the epidemiological transition was a relatively long process starting at the end of the nineteenth century; in developing countries it is occurring now at a much faster pace.

For example, the main causes of deaths for the 1909 birth-cohort in Chile were respiratory infections (20%), other infectious diseases (13%) and

TABLE 2. Percentage of older persons (60 years and older) among the total population and total number of older persons (in millions) in the eleven most populous countries and France in 1975, 2000 and projections for 2025

	Bangladesh	Brazil	China	France	India	Indonesia	Japan	Mexico	Nigeria	Pakistan	Russ.Fed.	USA
Total number of older persons (millions)												
1975	4.2	6.5	64.3	9.6	38.5	7.3	13.0	3.3	2.6	3.9	18.2	32.6
2000	6.9	13.4	128.7	12.2	76.8	16.2	29.5	6.9	5.4	8.1	27.0	45.9
2025	17.6	33.8	285.9	18.2	167.3	34.6	43.7	17.7	11.5	18.2	33.5	84.7
Percentage of older persons (60+)												
1975	6%	6%	7%	18%	6%	5%	12%	6%	5%	6%	14%	15%
2000	5%	8%	10%	21%	8%	8%	23%	7%	5%	6%	19%	16%
2025	9%	16%	20%	28%	12%	13%	35%	14%	6%	7%	27%	24%

Source: United Nations Population Division (2003).

cardiovascular diseases (12%) – whereas for the 1999 birth-cohort they are projected to be replaced by cardiovascular diseases (31%) and cancers (23%) (WHO, 1999a). While the shift away from infectious diseases towards non-communicable diseases is itself a societal achievement, it will pose a different sort of challenge for developing countries. In 1990 about 40% of all deaths in developing countries were attributable to communicable diseases, around 50% to non-communicable diseases, the remaining attributable to external causes of death (mostly accidents). By 2020 a very different picture will have emerged and non-communicable diseases are projected to be responsible for over three-quarters of the deaths in developing countries (WHO, 1999a). That is not to say, however, that infectious diseases will have disappeared in the foreseeable future. Many developing countries will continue to face a double burden of disease, i.e., the upsurge of NCD will co-exist with the burden from the 'old' agenda, with infectious diseases, such as malaria and tuberculosis, still at devastating proportions. Adding to that

Figure 1. Population pyramid for Japan in 2000 (grey) and 2025.

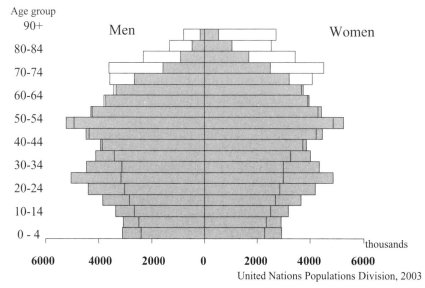

United Nations Populations Division, 2003

TABLE 3. Life expectancy at birth for men and women in selected countries

	1975–1980		2000–2005		2025–2030	
	Male	Female	Male	Female	Male	Female
Bangladesh	47	47	61	62	69	72
Brazil	59	64	64	73	70	78
China	64	66	69	73	71	77
France	70	78	75	83	79	85
India	53	52	63	65	67	71
Indonesia	52	54	65	69	71	75
Japan	73	78	78	85	81	90
Mexico	62	69	70	76	74	80
Nigeria	45	47	51	52	58	58
Russian Federation	63	74	61	73	67	75
USA	70	77	74	80	76	82

Source: United Nations Population Division (2003).

there is the problem of new infectious diseases, particularly AIDS. The most affected countries, e.g. Botswana in sub-Saharan Africa, are now experiencing the paradox of seeing life expectancy at birth rapidly declining (reflecting premature death of children and young adults), while the percentage of older people remains the same or even increases (as they are at much lower risk of being infected by HIV). All in all, resources will continue to be required for infectious diseases, either for their treatment or for their prevention, in parallel to increasing demands related to non-communicable diseases.

The challenge for health systems

With increasing proportions of older persons in the population, the demands on healthcare systems in developing countries will gradually change.

Figure 2. Population pyramid for Brazil in 2000 (grey) and 2025.

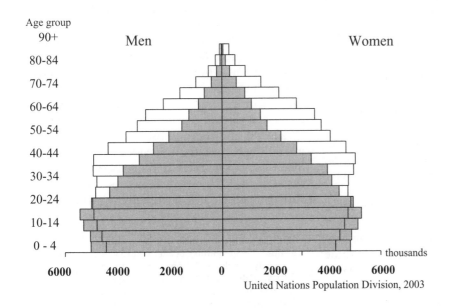

United Nations Population Division, 2003

TABLE 4. Total fertility rate for selected countries over time

	1970–1975	2000–2005	2020–2025
Bangladesh	6.6	3.5	2.3
Brazil	4.7	2.2	1.9
China	4.9	1.8	1.9
France	2.6	1.9	1.9
India	5.4	3.0	2.1
Indonesia	5.6	2.4	1.9
Japan	2.1	1.3	1.5
Mexico	6.8	2.5	1.9
Nigeria	6.9	5.4	3.3
Pakistan	6.3	5.1	3.1
Russian Federation	2.0	1.1	1.4
USA	2.0	2.1	2.0

Source: United Nations Population Division (2003).

TABLE 5. Number of persons aged 60 or older per 100 persons aged 15 to 59 years

Country	1975	2000	2025
Bangladesh	06	05	09
Brazil	06	08	19
China	07	11	25
France	22	26	40
India	07	08	14
Indonesia	06	08	15
Japan	13	30	55
Mexico	06	07	16
Nigeria	05	05	06
Pakistan	06	06	08
Russian Federation	16	23	37
USA	17	19	31

Source: United Nations Population Division (2003).

Health care systems will be expected to accommodate care of older adults alongside with, for example, child and maternal care. Also, more advanced healthcare systems in the developed world will have to adapt to the shifting needs due to further population ageing. This does not imply that ageing is in itself a disease, and old age should not be seen as equal to frailty, sickness and a high demand for healthcare services. Recent evidence coming from developed countries is encouraging. As data from the US Long Term Care Survey (Manton and Gu, 2001) in Figure 3 show, the disability rates of people aged 65 and over in 1999 were considerably lower than predicted. The rate of decline is impressive. If recent trends continue, the total numbers of disabled elderly people in the USA within the next few decades may stabilize or even diminish, as seen in Figure 7.

In the literature, discussions on how ageing influences healthcare expenditure have received increasing attention, particularly regarding expenditures on acute healthcare. In 1980 Fries published the 'compression of morbidity' hypothesis, suggesting that chronic disease would occupy only a small part of the entire lifespan – 'compressed' into the very end of life – while life expectancy would continue to rise to a set, biological limit of around 85 years (Kalache *et al.*, 2002). According to Fries' hypothesis the number of very old persons would not increase

beyond such a limit and the period of physical disability would decrease, mainly due to improved public health measures and health promotion translated into lifestyle changes. While some of his views were subsequently challenged, a series of studies on healthcare expenditures in old age seem to support his hypothesis of the 'compression of morbidity' (McCall, 1984; Spector and Mor, 1984; Riley *et al.*, 1987; Roos *et al.*, 1987; Temkin-Greener *et al.*, 1992; Lubitz and Riley, 1993; Busse *et al.*, 1996; Zweifel *et al.*, 1996). Several authors relate the higher acute healthcare expenditures / acute health service utilization in old age not to age per se, but to closeness to death, which is independent of an individual's age (Ginzberg, 1980; Fuchs, 1984). This hypothesis is also supported by data from a study using German sickness fund records, showing that the number of days spent in hospital in the last year of life was greatest at ages 55–64 and lowest among individuals aged 85 and above (Busse *et al.*, 2002). Another interesting perspective is provided by an analysis of Medicare[3] expenditures (not covering nursing home costs) in the USA, which shows that costs decline with increasing age at death. This may indicate that

---

[3] Medicare is the public insurance programme covering certain healthcare expenditures of the aged (65 and over), the permanently disabled and people with end-stage renal disease in the US. Medicare is the single largest payer in the US medical care system and is financed through mandatory payroll taxes and premiums paid by the aged (Iglehart, 1992).

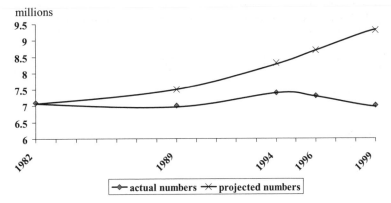

Figure 3. Numbers of chronically disabled Americans aged 65 and over (millions) 1982 to 1999. Actual and projected numbers.

Total number of older people in the USA;
1982: **26.9**; 1994: **33.1**; 1999: **35.3**

Source: Manton and Gu (2001: 6354-9)

the very old (80 years and over) are not treated with the highest technology available – rather with palliative care.

Another study from Germany (Breyer, 1999) indicated that the contribution of advances in medical care to the increased healthcare expenditures is highly underestimated, whereas the contribution of population ageing is being overestimated. The author suggested that ageing is not the only factor (it may even be one of the smallest factors) which affects the rising healthcare expenditures in the developed world.

Population ageing also modifies the demand for informal and formal long-term care. Although, world wide, the bulk of care for frail elderly people is still provided by the family, changes in family structure and increasing participation of women in the paid work force are gradually eroding the capacity of the family to provide care (World Health Organization / Millbank Memorial Fund, 1999). Accordingly, new models of home care, provided by professionals to support the family, but avoiding costly stays in nursing homes are being explored in most developed countries (Geneva Association and Geneva International Network on Ageing (GINA), 2002).

In the developing world, where healthcare systems are struggling with the double burden of diseases, the issues are even more complex. There is a strong need for training primary healthcare personnel in prevention and treatment of noncommunicable diseases as well as for adapting healthcare systems in order to prepare them for an

aged population. This is particularly important in areas where no health insurance or pension schemes exist. Innovative schemes of community healthcare and long term care for the aged are urgently required to counteract factors such as disrupted family ties due to, for example, the trend towards nuclear families, migration to cities by young people and, particularly in sub-Saharan Africa, the HIV/AIDS epidemics leaving orphaned children to be looked after by their grandparents (WHO, 2002a).

Socio-economic consequences

Where available, public and private pension schemes are major contributors to protecting old people from poverty. Many developing countries do not have pension schemes, but the number of countries implementing them is growing. Traditionally, funding resources for post-retirement come from three sources: a compulsory state pension, a (supplementary) occupational pension and individual savings. A fourth source is gradually emerging: a combination of public pension and continued (part-time) work – as trends in some Western countries indicate (The Geneva Association, 1997). The future financing of pension schemes places economic burdens on virtually all countries even when considering the most optimistic forecasts. By and large pension schemes were set up at times of low unemployment and low old-age dependency ratios. With changes in age and employment structures, there is an urgent need for adaptation in these systems. In this respect it is particularly important to note that

TABLE 6. Life expectancy at age 60 in selected countries

	1990–1995		2000–2005		2010–2015	
	Male	Female	Male	Female	Male	Female
Bangladesh	14.5	15.7	15.3	16.6	15.9	17.2
Brazil	15.9	18.6	17.2	20.7	18.2	22.1
China	15.3	18.5	16.3	20.1	17.2	21.2
France	19.5	24.6	20.0	25.5	20.9	26.2
India	15.0	16.5	16.1	17.9	17.1	19.1
Indonesia	15.2	16.9	15.9	17.8	16.6	18.4
Japan	20.2	25.1	21.5	27.2	22.6	29.0
Mexico	19.1	21.2	20.0	22.7	20.6	23.6
Nigeria	15.1	15.9	16.0	16.9	16.6	17.5
Pakistan	15.2	15.7	16.1	16.7	17.0	17.6
Russian Fed.	13.4	19.5	14.0	19.2	15.1	20.2
USA	18.7	22.3	20.2	23.8	21.2	24.9

Source: United Nations Population Division (2003).

life expectancy in old age has experienced substantial increases over the past 15 years and is expected to continue to increase as shown in Table 6. The table shows also that in relatively poor countries – such as Brazil and Mexico – life expectancy in old age is very close to much richer countries such as the USA.

Most western countries have been undertaking substantial reforms in their public pension systems, especially taking into consideration that the 'baby-boom' generations are now approaching retirement age. Main features of these reforms are the following.

1. Increase of retirement age: for example, in 1983, in the USA, it was agreed to increase retirement age gradually from 65 to 67 years within the period 2001–27. Further, in Japan, retirement age will be raised from 60 to 65 years between 2001 and 2013 and in France it was recently raised to 67 years.
2. Increasing flexibility of retirement age and promotion of gradual retirement. Belgium was the first European country to introduce such a scheme, where retirement can be flexible between 60 and 65 years of age.
3. Increased contribution period and freedom to combine pension with work income. The number of contribution years was recently increased in several European countries – from 37.5 to 40 years. The combination of limited work income in addition to the public pension is now possible in all EU countries.

This is one of the newest characteristics of public pension schemes: (particularly part-time) work continues for some years after the 'official' retirement age, thus wage and public pension supplement each other. This system makes a significant contribution to reducing the constraints on publicly financed pension schemes.

4. Curtailing early retirement as a mediating feature between programmes to decrease occupational life and social policies to increase retirement age. Employees will not necessarily leave work earlier, but the costs of early retirement are then borne by the individual or the firm and not the state any more. In France and Germany such a feature is visible in current reforms, where costs are shared between the state, the employer and the employee.
5. Reduced levels of pension benefits were introduced in, for example, Denmark through taxation of pensions or through linking pensions to prices not to wages, as adopted by France, Sweden, Portugal and the United Kingdom.
6. Changing the funding of public pension schemes, so that they depend less on contributions rather than on taxes, as the examples of Sweden, Spain and Finland show. The advantage of such schemes is a reduction of costs of labour at a time of high unemployment (The Geneva Association, 1997).

In many developing countries 'retirement age' is mostly non-existent for the majority of the population. The aged continue to work in small-scale farming, the informal sector or artisan undertakings, where they frequently play a crucial role in teaching their skills to younger generations, ensuring them employment opportunities. Old persons becoming too frail to work largely rely on their family to care for them, especially daughters or daughters-in-law (Hoskins, 1993).

While population ageing is certainly a challenge for healthcare and social security systems in developed countries, developing countries remain largely unprepared for the ageing of their populations. In essence it should be said that industrialized countries became rich before they became old, while developing countries will become old before they become rich.

ISSUES ASSOCIATED WITH HEALTH AND AGEING

Gender and ageing

Being male or female affects health and illness throughout the life course. Understanding the role of sex and gender in health and disease is thus essential at all ages, not only during the reproductive years. The term sex is used when differences in health are primarily biological in origin and may be genetic or phenotypic, i.e. genetic or physiological characteristics of being a man or woman (Wizemann and Pardue, 2001). Gender refers to socially constructed roles and socially learned behaviours and expectations associated with femininity and masculinity. It is a social category that largely establishes one's life chances and, compounded with economic and cultural factors, shapes men's and women's physical and mental health (Bird and Rieker, 1999; Doyal, 2001; Moynihan, 1998).

Men and women have different patterns of diseases and different life expectancies. A higher life expectancy at birth for females compared with males is virtually universal, although negligible differences (less than a year) are found in countries such as Bangladesh, Nepal, Nigeria and Pakistan (Table 3). In the year 2000 the overall world gap in longevity was 4.2 years, being lowest in the African continent (1.6 years) and highest in Europe (8.3 years) (United

Nations Population Division, 2002). The widest female advantage in longevity, around 12 years, is observed in some Eastern European countries, such as the Russian Federation, Kazakhstan and Latvia. At the age of 60, the female–male gap in life expectancy remains the same as the 'at birth' gap (4.1 years), but shows narrower variation among continents (from 2 years in Africa to 4.6 years in Europe) (United Nations Population Division, 2002).

While women live longer than men, they often spend more years in poor health. For instance, the gap between life expectancy and healthy life expectancy, which measures the number of years of life to be lived in good health, is larger for women than men. At age 60, the overall female–male gap in healthy life expectancy is two years lower than the gap in life expectancy at 60. In eastern Mediterranean countries and Africa, healthy life expectancies are even lower for females than males (Mathers et al., 2002).

The survival advantage of women is present at all ages (Kraemer, 2000). Part of this advantage is biological and includes genetic, hormonal and metabolic factors (Wizemann and Pardue, 2001). For instance, women's stronger and somewhat different immune system is an important feature that allows them to pass on a substantial level of protective antibodies to their infants during breast-feeding (Pinn, 2003). In addition, pre-menopausal women benefit from the important cardiovascular protective effects of estrogen on serum lipid concentrations, blood vessel dilatation and response to injuries (Mendelsohn and Karas, 1999). However, knowledge and research on these matters are as yet insufficient to understand fully the role of biological differences in relation to disease pattern and susceptibility (Mendelsohn and Karas, 1999; Kraemer, 2000; Wizemann and Pardue, 2001; Pinn, 2003).

Many diseases that affect both sexes often have different frequencies and presentations in males and females. Men suffer earlier onset of many life-threatening chronic diseases, including cardiovascular diseases, cancer, emphysema, cirrhosis of the liver and kidney disease (Bird and Rieker, 1999). Coronary heart disease, for instance, tends to manifest 10 to 20 years earlier in men than in women. Age-specific incidence rates of stroke are generally higher in men than in women, but women have higher stroke case-fatality rates (Goldstein *et al.*, 2001). A number of autoimmune diseases, such as Hashimoto thyroiditis, systemic lupus erythomatosus and rheumatoid arthritis, are strikingly predominant in females (Wizemann and Pardue, 2001). Type 2 diabetes is also more common in women than men, especially after 65 years of age (Pinn, 2003). Women seem to have a lower pain threshold and to respond differently to pain therapy (Wizemann and Pardue, 2001). The lifetime risk of osteoporosis in women is over threefold that in men (Lips, 1997).

While some disparities in disease frequencies and presentation are attributed to sex-related factors (Wizemann and Pardue, 2001), others are more significantly linked to gender-related inequalities in determining whether men and women are able to realize their potential for a long and healthy life (Doyal, 2000). Further, differences in the living and working conditions of men and women, in the nature of their social responsibilities and in their access to resources put them at differential risks of developing health problems or, conversely, being protected from them. For example, beliefs about masculinity are deeply rooted in culture and supported by social institutions. They play a major role in shaping the behavioural patterns of men in ways that have consequences for health (Courtenay, 2000; Moynihan, 1998). Lifestyle factors, such as smoking and drinking as well as other risk-taking behaviours, combined with occupational risks, all contribute to greater numbers of premature deaths from cardiovascular diseases, cancer and injuries among men (Doyal, 2000).

Misconceptions and stereotypes of men's and women's health seem also to influence disease outcome. For instance, socially constructed beliefs and chronic illness may influence the perception of older women as habitual complainers and lead to a devaluation of older women's symptoms. For example, after the age of 65, women are at equal risk of suffering from heart disease and stroke, commonly perceived as a male problem; consequently, older women tend to receive less effective care than men with the same need (Clarke *et al.*, 1994; Raine *et al.*, 2000; Hetemaa *et al.*, 2003; Di Carlo *et al.*, 2003). On the other hand, research in developed countries suggests that men may experience more diffi-culties in talking about their health problems and postpone seeking healthcare until they reach more advanced stages of disease (Kaplan, 1995; Bird and Rieker, 1999).

Women's traditional disadvantages in access to and control of resources, in educational and economic opportunities and in political decision-making are well documented. Older women are less likely to have received formal education than younger women or men of the same age, especially in developing countries (Sennanayake, 2001). As a result of shorter working careers and lower earnings, older women's pensions are generally much lower than those of men. Once older women become widows, they are more likely to be affected by poverty, lower social support and even social isolation, all of which are associated with declining health and loss of functional capacity (Kalache, 2002).

Gender-related health problems in later life are still under-researched. The reality of being male and female varies significantly across cultures and across the life cycle. Hence the impact of gender on health and well-being will vary too. In some societies, older women lose status as they leave behind childbearing potential and the sexual allure of youth (Doyal, 2000). Men's social status, largely rooted in their work and earnings, may be severely affected by retirement and the perceived loss of status, with devastating effects on men's health (WHO, 2001). More systematic and interdisciplinary research is required to understand the complex mechanisms by which social and biological processes interact during the lifecourse (Doyal, 2000; Wizemann and Pardue, 2001; Moynihan, 2002; Bird and Rieker, 1999).

Contributions of older persons

It is often argued that: 'older people have nothing to contribute and are an economic burden to society'. In reality older persons make innumerable contributions to their families, their communities and to societies at large. Substantial contributions are made for instance within the informal sector and the unpaid labour force or as volunteers (as carers, community leaders or by teaching). In the United States, for example, there are over 3 million persons aged 65 and over actively involved in volunteer activities in health and political organizations, schools and religious bodies – in addition to many more millions of older persons providing 'informal' care in the community (WHO, 1999a). All these contributions to society remain (mostly) neglected in national macroeconomic indicators. The group contributing the most are older women, through their significant role as carers for their spouses and grandchildren and for sick relatives in general. In Spain, for example, caring for dependent and sick individuals (of all ages) is mostly done by older people (particularly older women); the average number of minutes per day they spend in providing such care increases exponentially with the carer's age: 201 minutes if the carer is in the age group 65–74 and 318 minutes if aged 75–84 – compared to only 50 minutes if the carer is in the age group 30–49 (Durán, 2002). The universal trend towards women joining the paid work force reinforces the role of older women as family caregivers and community workers, throughout the world.

The extent to which older persons are involved in the care sector is illustrated by their role within the context of the AIDS epidemics in Africa. Out of the thirty-four countries hardest hit by HIV and AIDS, twenty-nine are in sub-Saharan Africa, three in Asia and two in Latin America and the Caribbean (United Nations Population Division, 1999). In these countries the spread of HIV/AIDS infection is devastating the adult population, leaving their orphaned children behind. Current figures estimate that, globally, 16 million children under 15 have already lost either one or both parents to AIDS (HelpAge International, 2003). This is a critical developmental issue for Africa and other similarly severely HIV-affected developing countries, with significant implications for future human capital. The trauma of losing one or both parents is often magnified by relocation, possibly from an urban to a rural living environment, within the extended family structure. The burden of care and support falls mostly on only slightly older brothers and sisters and on the grandparents (Drew *et al.*, 1998). In Zambia, Uganda and Tanzania, grandparents make up the single largest category of carers for orphans (HelpAge International, 2003). Information and support for those older people providing care is essential to prevent an over-extension of family capacities to care for family members with AIDS, and subsequently to care for their orphaned children (Kamali *et al.*, 1996; Seely *et al.*, 1993). As a 65-year-old man caring for three school-age orphans in

Zimbabwe explains: 'Looking after orphans is like starting life all over again, because I have to work on the farm, clean the house, feed the children, and buy school uniforms. I thought I would no longer do these things again. I am not sure if I have the energy to cope' (WHO, 2002a).

Urbanization, migration and ageing

Urbanization is another major recent global phenomenon. While in 1960 only 30% of the world's population were living in urban areas, it is now nearly 50%. By 2030 it is likely that more than 80% of the population of North America, Europe, Australia and Latin America, and more than 50% of Asia and Africa, will be living in urban areas (Montgomery *et al.*, 2003).

Urbanization is a major reason behind the split of three-generation households. Together with migration between countries, urbanization often leads to the need for grandparents to act as carers for their grandchildren left behind by their parents when they move to the city in search of employment. Most of the latter are unskilled workers and find it difficult to compete in the job market. Consequently, financial support to their families is usually low, leaving to the old relatives the difficult task of providing nourishment for themselves and their grandchildren. Care policies and care programmes on national and local levels need to reflect this global trend and include steps to support these aged carers, mainly women. Furthermore, the ageing process of previous migrants is often a particular challenge for individuals who have not fully been integrated into the 'host' community – but who will feel particularly 'up-rooted' once the changes common to ageing occur and the longing for more remote experiences becomes more acute.

In addition, urbanization can also result in very frail older persons being left isolated in rural areas as younger generations move to cities. As social security schemes providing adequate pensions are rare, elderly persons left in rural areas often depend on financial support from their children living in the city – which may never reach them.

Adjustment to all these factors combined with loosening family ties and erosion of cultural and traditional values is often difficult for older persons as they are themselves not being supported by their children in the same way they used to assist their own parents.

FACING THE CHALLENGE: THE WHO AGEING AND HEALTH PROGRAMME

In April 1995 the World Health Organization launched the Ageing and Health Programme (AHE), replacing the former 'Health of the Elderly' Programme. In developing its response to global ageing AHE has incorporated the following perspectives:

- a lifecourse perspective focused on 'ageing' rather than compartmentalizing the healthcare of 'the elderly';
- health promotion, focusing on Active Ageing – physically, socially and mentally, since, whether early or later in life, people have multiple opportunities to improve their health status as they age; provided they are properly supported by the environment (physical and social) where they live;
- a socio-economic and cultural perspective, paying tribute to the fact that the settings in which individuals age play an important part in their health and wellbeing;
- a gender perspective – recognizing the important differences in men's and women's health and way of life, which become more pronounced in later life;
- an intergenerational perspective – emphasizing strategies for maintaining cohesion and solidarity between the generations. Above all, a culture of ageing is a culture of solidarity – between young and old; rich and poor; developed and developing nations.
- an ethical perspective – enhancing the understanding of ethical issues such as human rights, elder abuse, long-term care, as well as undue prolongation or hastening of death; and
- a community-oriented perspective, since throughout the world, even in rich societies, the majority of older persons live in the community and it is at the community level that most of their problems will have to be dealt with.

AHE activities are concentrated into four major programme components: information dissemination; capacity building through research and training; advocacy; and policy development. Each of the programme components incorporates the perspectives previously mentioned. Through the development of these four programme components AHE expects a global strategy on Active Ageing to become increasingly focused and effective.

THE WHO ACTIVE AGEING POLICY FRAMEWORK

On the occasion of the Second UN World Assembly on Ageing in April 2002, which endorsed the Madrid International Plan of Action on Ageing, WHO launched its Policy Framework on Active Ageing. This followed a period of in-depth reflections, literature reviews and consultations with governments, civil society and some of the world's leading experts on health and ageing. Through this process and by developing a consensus among the experts, the challenges posed by global population ageing were identified, the determinants of Active Ageing described and a definition of Active Ageing established. The Policy Framework approaches health from a broad perspective and acknowledges the fact that health can only be created and sustained through the participation of multiple sectors (WHO, 2002b).

Active Ageing is therefore defined as: 'the process of optimising opportunities for health, participation and security in order to enhance quality of life as people age'.

Active Ageing policies apply to both individuals and population groups. Policy action is necessary on the three basic pillars of Active Ageing: Participation, Health and Security. In line with the Madrid International Plan of Action on Ageing, clear recognition needs to be given to the fact that Active Ageing policies should be based on the rights, needs, preferences and capacities of older people.

Central to the rationale behind Active Ageing is the concept of maintaining functional capacity throughout the lifecourse (Figure 4).

Our capacity in relation to a number of functions (such as ventilatory capacity, muscular strength, cardiovascular output) increases in childhood and peaks in early adulthood. Such a peak is eventually followed by a decline. How fast the decline is, however, is largely determined by factors related to adult life style – such as smoking, alcohol consumption and diet; and the environment where one lives. The natural decline in cardiac function, for example, can be accelerated by smoking, leaving the individual with a functional capacity level lower than would

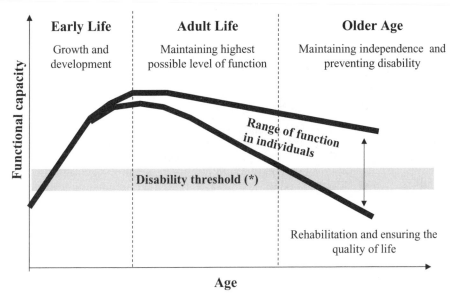

Figure 4. Maintaining functional capacity over the life-course. (*Source*: Kalache and Kickbusch, 1997).

normally be expected for his/her age. The gradient of decline may become so steep as to result in premature disability. However, the slope of the decline can be influenced in any stage of life through individual as well as policy measures. For example, smoking cessation at the age of 50 reduces the risk of dying within the next 15 years by 50% (WHO/AHE, 1999a).

In addition to these factors others, conditioned by social class, also affect functional capacity. Poor education, poverty and harmful living and working conditions all make reduced functional capacity more likely in later life. In some countries, people with poor functional ability are more likely to become institutionalized, which in itself can lead to dependence, particularly for the small minority of older people who suffer from loss of mental function and/or confusion.

For those who become disabled, provision of rehabilitation and adaptation of the physical environment can greatly reduce the level of disability. Furthermore, specific interventions can help them to improve their functional capacity and thus quality of life. For example cataracts, causing nearly 50% of all blindness world wide, can be treated through a fairly simple surgical procedure, increasingly available in developing countries (WHO, 1999b).

Quality of life should be a major consideration throughout the lifecourse, particularly for those whose functional capacity can no longer be maintained. For example, changes in the living environment can vastly improve quality of life. However, most of the gains are obtained by acting on the 'care unit' – in most cases, the family and close friends. It is often by supporting the informed carer (frequently an older women, in many cases in poor health herself) that the quality of life of the dependent older person can be most improved.

Finally, through appropriate environmental changes – such as adequate public transport, the availability of lifts in apartment or office blocks, ramps, adapted kitchenware or a toilet seat with rails – the disability threshold can be lowered. Such changes – not only in the physical, but also in the social environment – can ensure a more independent life well into very old age and one of the major challenges is to ensure access to them for all older persons – including the poor and those who live in remote areas. In practice this means lowering the disability threshold, and, in doing so, freeing from disability individuals who while living with impairments, can now have independent lives in their own community.

THE DETERMINANTS OF ACTIVE AGEING

Active Ageing depends on a variety of influences or 'determinants' that surround individuals, families

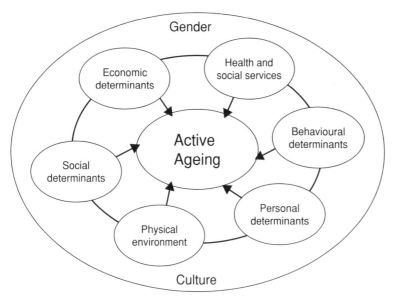

Figure 5. Determinants of Active Ageing.

and nations (Figure 5). Understanding the evidence we have about these determinants helps us design policies and programmes that work.

These determinants apply to the health of all age groups and become particularly important as individuals age. At this point, it is not possible to attribute direct causation to any one determinant; however, the substantial body of evidence on what determines health suggests that all of these factors (and the interplay between them) are good predictors of how well both individuals and populations age. More research is needed to clarify and specify the role of each determinant, as well as the interaction between determinants, in the active ageing process. We also need to understand better the pathways that explain how these broad determinants actually affect health and wellbeing.

Moreover, it is helpful to consider the influence of various determinants over the life course so as to take advantage of transitions and 'windows of opportunity' for enhancing health.

- **Behavioural determinants:** the adoption of healthy lifestyles is important at all stages of the life course. For instance, smoking is a major modifiable risk factor for non-communicable diseases and an important preventable cause of death. Diet and physical activity are of paramount importance. Excess energy intake combined with physical inactiv-

ity greatly increases the risk of obesity, chronic diseases and disabilities as people grow older.
- **Determinants related to physical environment:** physical environments that are age-appropriate can make the difference between independence and dependence for all individuals but are of particular importance for those growing older. For example, older persons who live in unsafe environments or areas with multiple physical barriers are more prone to isolation and increased mobility problems.
- **Determinants related to the social environment:** social support, freedom from violence and abuse, and access to life-long learning are key factors in the social environment that enhance health, participation and security as people age.
- **Economic determinants:** three aspects of the economic environment have a particularly significant effect on Active Ageing: income security and access to work throughout the lifecourse as well as social protection.
- **Health and social services** should be available throughout the lifecourse. They need to be integrated, coordinated, cost-effective and based on the principle of universal access. A continuum of care from preventive, curative, rehabilitative, long-term to palliative should be available. Community-based approaches and community-based care are of paramount importance for managing disease and promoting wellbeing. Basic training in geriatrics and

Figure 6. The three pillars of a policy framework for Active Ageing.

gerontology for community-based healthcare workers, as well as practical support for formal and informal carers, should be provided.

All these determinants need to be approached while paying close attention to two critical dimensions: the cultural context where one lives (as culture shapes the way in which individuals age as it influences all of the other determinants of active ageing) and gender, also of paramount importance to the ageing process as previously discussed.

The framework for policy development on Active Ageing is shown in Figure 6. It is guided by the *United Nations principles for older people* (the outer circle). These are independence, participation, care, self-fulfilment and dignity. In addition a clear understanding of how the determinants of Active Ageing influence the way that individuals and populations age is needed.

The policy framework requires action on three basic pillars:

Health When the risk factors (both environmental and behavioural) for chronic diseases and functional decline are kept low while the protective factors are kept high, people will enjoy both a longer quantity and higher quality of life; they will remain healthy and able to manage their own lives as they grow older; fewer older adults will need costly medical treatment and care services.

For those who do need care, they should have access to the entire range of health and social services that address the needs and rights of women and men as they age.

Participation When labour market, employment, education, health and social policies and programmes support their full participation in socioeconomic, cultural and spiritual activities, according to their basic human rights, capacities, needs and preferences, people will continue to make a productive contribution to society in both paid and unpaid activities as they age.

Security When policies and programmes address the social, financial and physical security needs and rights of people as they age, older people are ensured of protection, dignity and care in the event that they are no longer able to support and protect themselves. Families and communities are supported in efforts to care for their older members.

The Active Ageing Policy Framework is a call to action for policymakers. Together with the newly adopted UN International Plan of Action on Ageing (UN, 2002b), this framework provides a roadmap for designing multisectoral *Active Ageing* policies which will enhance health and participation among ageing populations while ensuring that older people have adequate security, protection and care when they require assistance.

The WHO recognizes that public health involves a wide range of actions to improve the health of the population and that health goes beyond the provision of basic health services. Therefore, it is committed to working in co-operation with other international agencies and the United Nations itself to encourage the implementation of Active Ageing policies at global, regional and national levels. Due to the specialist nature of its work, the WHO will provide technical advice and play a catalytic role in health development. However, this can only be done as a joint effort. Together, we (international organizations, governments, NGOs, academic institutions and other stakeholders) must provide the evidence and demonstrate the effectiveness of the various proposed courses of action. Ultimately, however, it will be up to nations and local communities to develop culturally sensitive, gender-specific, realistic goals and targets, and to implement policies and programmes tailored to their unique circumstances.

Active Ageing provides a framework for the development of global, national and local strategies on population ageing. By pulling together the three pillars for action of health, participation and security, it offers a platform for consensus building that addresses the concerns of multiple sectors and all regions. Policy proposals and recommendations are of little use unless follow-up actions are put in place. The time to act is now.

FURTHER READING

Kalache, A. (1996). 'Ageing world-wide'. In S. Ebrahim and A. Kalache, eds., *Epidemiology in old age*. London: *BMJ*, pp. 22–32.

(1998). 'Future prospects for Geriatrics Medicine in the developing countries'. In Raymond Tallis, ed., *Brocklehust's textbook of geriatric medicine and gerontology*, 5th edn. Edinburgh: Churchill Livingstone, pp. 1513–21.

Kalache, A., and I. Keller (2000). 'The graying world: a challenge for the 21st century', *Science Progress*, 83 (1): 33–54.

World Health Organization (2002). *Active ageing – a policy framework*. Geneva: WHO, available from: www.who.int/hpr/ageing/publications.htm.

REFERENCES

Banks, I. (2001). 'No man's land: men, illness, and the NHS', *British Medical Journal*, 323: 1058–61.

Bird, C. E., and P. P. Rieker (1999). 'Gender matters: an integrated model for understanding men's and women's health', *Social Science & Medicine*, 48: 745–55.

Breyer, F. (1999). Paper prepared for the 2nd World Conference of the IHEA on Private and Public Choices in Health and Health Care, Rotterdam, June 1999.

Busse, R., Schwartz, F. W., Schwenburg, M. v. d., *et al.* (1996). *Leistungen und Kosten der Medizinischan Versorgung im Retzten Lebensjahr*, Norddeutscher Forschungsverbund Public Health – Project D3. Hanover: Abschlußbericht.

Busse, R., Krauth, C., and F. W. Schwartz (2002). 'Use of acute hospital beds does not increase as the population ages: results from a seven year cohort study in Germany', *Journal of Epidemiology of Community Health*, 56: 289–93.

Clarke, K. W., Gray, D., Keating, N. A., and J. R. Hampton (1994). 'Do women with acute myocardial infarction receive the same treatment as men?' *British Medical Journal*, 309: 563–6.

Courtenay, W. H. (2002). 'Constructions of masculinity and their influence on men's well-being: a theory of gender and health', *Social Science & Medicine*, 50: 1385–401.

Di Carlo, A., Lamassa, M., Baldereschi, M., Pracucci, G., Basile, A. M., Wolfe, C. D., Giroud, M., Rudd, A., Ghetti, A., Inzitari, D., and European BIOMED Study of Stroke Care Group (2003). 'Sex differences in the clinical presentation, resource use, and 3-month outcome of acute stroke in Europe: data from a multicenter multinational hospital-based registry', *Stroke*, 34: 1114–19.

Doyal, L. (2000). 'Gender equity in health: debates and dilemmas', *Social Science & Medicine*: 931–9.

(2001). 'Sex, gender, and health: the need for a new approach'. *British Medical Journal*, 323: 1061–3.

Drew, R. S., Makufa, C., and G. Foster (1998). 'Strategies for providing care and support to children orphaned by AIDS', *AIDS Care*, 10 (Suppl. 1): S9–11.

Durán H. M. A. (2002). *Los costes invisibles de la enfermedad*. Madrid: Fundación Banco Bilbao Vizcaya Argentina.

European Institute of Women's Health (1996). 'Women in Europe towards healthy ageing, a review of the health status of mid-life and older women', Dublin: European Institute of Women's Health.

Fries, J. F. (1980). 'Aging, natural death, and the compression of morbidity', *New England Journal of Medicine*, 303: 130–5.

Fuchs, V. R. (1984). '"Though much is taken": reflections on aging, health, and medical care', *Milbank Memorial Fund Quarterly: Health & Society*, 62: 143–66.

Geneva Association (1997). 'The future of retirement in Europe, a summary of recent reforms of public (1st pillar) pensions', Research Programme on Social Security, Insurance and Saving and Employment, 21bis. Geneva: Geneva Association.

Geneva Association and Geneva International Network on Ageing (GINA) (2002). *The future of pensions and retirement, 10 key questions*. Geneva: Geneva Association and Gina.

Ginzberg, E. (1980). 'The high cost of dying', *Inquiry*, 17: 293–5.

Goldstein, L. B., Adams, R., Becker, K., Furberg, C. D., Gorelick, P. B., Hademenos, G., Hill, M., Howard, G., Howard, V. J., Jacobs, B., Levine, S. R., Mosca, L., Sacco, R. L., Sherman, D. G., Wolf, P. A., and G. J. del Zoppo (2001). 'Primary prevention of ischemic stroke: a statement for healthcare professionals from the Stroke Council of the American Heart Association', *Stroke*, 32: 280–99.

HelpAge International (2003). 'Forgotten families, older people as carer of orphans and vulnerable children', available from: www.helpage.org/publications/.

Hetemaa, T., Jeskinmatk, I., Mandebacka, K., Leyland, A., and S. Kioskinen (2003). 'How did the recent increase in the supply of coronary operations in Finland affect soceoeconomic and gender equity in their use?'

Journal of Epidemiology & Community Health, 57: 178–85.

Hoskins, I. (1993). 'Combining work and care for the aged: an overview of the issues', *International Labour Review*, 123 (3): 347.

Iglehart, J. K. (1992). 'The American health system – Medicare', *New England Journal of Medicine* 327: 1467–72.

International Society for the Study of the Aging Male (1998). *The Weimar initiative, appendix, The aging male 1*, p. 7

Japan Aging Research Centre (JARC) (1998). 'Aging in Japan 1998'. Tokyo.

Kalache, A. (1998). 'Health and the ageing male', *World Health*, 51st year (5).

 (2002). 'Gender-specific healthcare in the 21st century: a focus in developing countries', *The Aging Male*, 5: 129–38.

Kalache, A., and I. Kickbusch (1997). 'A global strategy for healthy ageing', *World Health*, 4 (July–August): 4–5.

Kalache, A., and I. Keller (2000). 'The graying world: a challenge for the 21st century', *Science Progress*, 83 (1): 33–54.

Kalache, A., Aboderin, I., and I. Hoskins (2002). 'Compression of morbidity and active ageing: key priorities for public health policy in the 21st century', *Bull World Health Organ.* 80: 243–4.

Kamali, A., Seely, J. A., Nunn, A. J., Kengeya-Kayondo, J. F., Ruberantwari, A., and D. W. Mulder (1996). 'The orphan problem: experience of a sub-Saharan Africa rural population in the AIDS epidemic', *AIDS Care*, 8 (5): 509–15.

Kraemer, S. (2000). 'The fragile male', *British Medical Journal*, 321: 1609–12.

Lips, P. (1997). 'Epidemiology and predictors of fractures associated with osteoporosis', *American Journal of Medicine*, 18 (103): 3S–8S; discussion 8S–11S.

Lubitz, J. D., and G. F. Riley (1993). 'Trends in Medicare payments in the last year of life,' *New England Journal of Medicine*, 328: 1092–6.

Manton, K., and X. Gu (2001). 'Changes in the prevalence of chronic disability in the United States, black and nonblack population above age 65 from 1982 to 1999', *Proceedings of the National Academy of Sciences*, 22: 6354–9.

Mathers, C. D., Murray, C. J., Lopez, A. D., Sadana, R., and J. A. Salomon (2002). 'Global patterns of healthy life expectancy for older women', *Journal of Women & Aging*, 14: 99–117.

McCall, N. (1984). 'Utilization and costs of Medicare services by beneficiaries in their last year of life', *Medical Care*, 22: 329–42.

Mendelsohn, M. E., and R. H. Karas (1999). 'The protective effects of estrogen on the cardiovasuclar system', *New England Journal of Medicine*, 340: 1801–11.

Moynihan, C. (1998). 'Theories of masculinity', *British Medical Journal*, 317: 1072–5.

 (2002). 'Men, women, gender and cancer', *European Journal of Cancer Care*, 11: 166–72.

Montgomery, M. R., Stren, R., Cohen, B., H. E. Reed, eds. (2003). 'Looking ahead'. In Committee on Population, Division of Behavioral and Social Sciences and Education, *Panel on urban population dynamics*. Washington, D.C.: National Research Council of the National Academies.

Murray, C., and A. Lopez (1996). *The global burden of disease*. Cambridge, Mass.: Harvard University Press.

OECD (1998). Health Data, databank, OECD.

Pinn, V. W. (2003). 'Sex and gender factors in medical studies', *Journal of the American Medical Association*, 289: 397–400.

Raine, R. A., Black, N. A., Bowker, T. J., and D. A. Wood (2002). 'Gender differences in management and outcome of patients with acute coronary artery disease', *Journal of Epidemiol Community Health*, 56: 791–7.

Riley, G., Lubitz, J., Prihoda, R., and E. Rabey (1987). 'The use and costs of Medicare services by cause of death', *Inquiry*, 24: 233–44.

Roos, N. P., Montgomery, P., and L. L. Roos (1987). 'Health care utilization in the years prior to death', *Milbank Memorial Fund Quarterly: Health & Society*, 65: 231–54.

Seely, J., Kajura, E., Bachengana, C., Okongo, M., Wagner, U., and D. Mulder (1993). 'The extended family and support for people with AIDS in a rural population in South West Uganda: a safety net with holes?' *AIDS Care*, 5 (1): 117–22.

Spector, W. D., and V. Mor (1984). 'Utilisation and charges for terminal cancer patients in Rhode Island', *Inquiry*, 21: 328–37.

Temkin-Greener, H., Meiners, M. R., Petty, E. A., and J. S. Szydlowski (1992). 'The use and cost of health services prior to death: a comparison of the Medicare-only and the Medicare–Medicaid elderly populations', *Milbank Memorial Fund Quarterly: Health & Society*, 70: 679–701.

The Economist (1999). 'Ageing workers – A full life', 4 Sept., pp. 75ff.

United Nations (2002). 'International plan of action on ageing', adopted at the Second UN World Assembly on Ageing, Madrid, available from www.un.org/esa/socdev/ageing/waa/.

United Nations Population Division (1998). *Human development report 1998*. New York: Oxford University Press.

 (1999). *World population prospects – the 1998 revision*. New York: United Nations.

 (2002). *World population prospects – the 2000 revision*. New York: United Nations.

 (2003). *World population prospects – the 2002 revision*. New York: United Nations.

US Department of Commerce (1993). *An aging world II*, International Population Reports P95/92–3. Washington D.C.: USDC.

US Long Term Care Survey (1996), available from www.cds.duke.edu/NLTCS_INTRO:html

WHO (World Health Organization) (1995). *World health statistics*. Geneva: WHO.

(1998a). *Health promotion glossary*, WHO/HPR/HEP/98.1. Geneva: WHO.

(1998b). *World health report 1998*. Geneva: WHO.

(1999a). *World health report 1999*. Geneva: WHO.

(1999d). *Ageing-exploding the myths*, WHO/HSC/AHE 99.1. Geneva: WHO.

(2001). *Men, ageing and health, achieving health across the lifespan*. Geneva: WHO.

(2002a). *Impact of AIDS on older people in Africa. Zimbabwe case study*. Geneva: WHO.

(2002b). *Active ageing, a policy framework*. Geneva: WHO.

WHO/AHE (1999a). *Fact sheet on ageing and tobacco*, published for World Health Day, available on request from AHE through http://activeageing@who.ch.

(1999b). *Fact sheet on ageing and visual disability*, published for World Health Day, available on request from AHE through http://activeageing@who.ch.

Wizemann, T. M., and M. L. Pardue, eds. (2001) 'Exploring the biological contributions to human health: does sex matter?' In Institute of Medicine (US), *Committee on understanding the biology of sex and gender differences*. Washington: National Academy Press.

World Health Organization / Millbank Memorial Fund (1999). 'Consensus approaches on long term care', unpublished, World Bank 1998, World Development Indicators.

Zweifel, P., Felder, S., and M. Meier (1996). 'Demographische Alterung und Gesundheitskosten: Eine Fehlinterpretation'. In P. Oberender, ed., *Alter und Gesundheit*, Gesundheitsökonomische Beiträge 26. Baden-Baden: Nomos, pp. 29–46.

The Psychological Science of Human Ageing

PAUL B. BALTES, ALEXANDRA M. FREUND AND SHU-CHEN LI

OVERVIEW

As is true for other scientific disciplines of ageing, the task of summarizing psychological research on ageing is a daunting one. Even within a given field, such as psychology, ageing is a complex and diversified field. The science of psychological ageing varies not only by such dimensions as methodology (e.g. subjective vs. objective methods), but also by substantive categories (e.g. memory, intelligence, personality), generality (universalism vs. cultural specification), or objectives of study (e.g. descriptive vs. explanatory vs. optimizing analysis). It is also a field in which rather different perspectives reign even within a given domain, such as cognitive functioning.

Moreover, as far as its methodological and theoretical bases are concerned, the field of psychology is inherently an "interdiscipline." Psychological research spans the biological, behavioral, and social sciences (Schönpflug, 2001; Smelser and Baltes, 2001). Not surprisingly, therefore, a summary will vary dramatically depending on the substantive, methodological, and discipline predilections of the authors in charge. For instance, a neuroscientist would emphasize the interplay between the functional architecture of the brain and behavior, a cultural psychologist the role of culture-based experiences and related cultural skills. Any condensed review of psychological approaches to human ageing, therefore, will suffer from selectivity and author bias.

To deal with this diversity and complexity, we have chosen to provide first a rather general metaframe that in our view applies to any approach. This metaframe is aimed at (a) showing how the psychological study of ageing is closely connected with theories of evolution and ontogenesis, (b) making explicit why psychological ageing is better understood if viewed within a lifespan conception of human development, and (c) summarizing the kinds of general (universal) theoretical scripts that researchers have articulated to understand age-related changes in the zone (plasticity) of psychological ageing. We then apply these general observations to two areas of research that are particularly familiar to us.

FROM AGEING AS DECLINE TO AGEING AS A DYNAMIC OF GAINS AND LOSSES

We begin with some historical observations. Historically, the psychological study of human ageing evolved in the twentieth century. Publications that mark this evolution are, for instance, Eisdorfer and Lawton (1973) and the first major handbook on the psychology of ageing edited by Birren and Schaie (1977). Closely connected with the emergence of a psychology of ageing was the evolution of the field of lifespan psychology (P. B. Baltes, 1983; P. B. Baltes et al., 1998; P. B. Baltes and Goulet, 1970; Neugarten, 1969; Staudinger and Lindenberger, 2003; Thomae, 1979). Among the earlier classics of lifespan psychology, the monumental work of Tetens (1777) and the intellectually rich early work by Pressey et al. (1939) are especially noteworthy.

TABLE 1. Theories of psychological ageing: four levels of analyses and their coordination

Level 1:   Biological and cultural evolutionary perspectives: on the incomplete architecture of human ontogenesis and the fact that ageing is the most incomplete

Level 2:   Lifespan changes in the relative allocation of resources from functions of growth to maintenance (resilience) and regulation of loss

Level 3:   An example of a systemic and overall theory of successful (adaptive) psychological ageing: selective optimization with compensation (SOC)

Level 4:   Theories of psychological ageing in specific functions and domains: e.g. intelligence, cognition, personality, and self

---

This historical evolution of the psychological science of ageing was guided not only by the process of articulating a psychological line of inquiry differentiating itself from the larger multidisciplinary field of gerontology (Birren, 1959), but also by a movement from sheer description to more theory-guided efforts. Another important historical change was a movement that rejected the conventional – largely biologically inspired – definition of ageing as a phenomenon of decline (or loss of function) in favor of a multidimensional and multidirectional conception of ageing that included, besides decline, the possibility of growth or other forms of advance (Aspinwall and Staudinger, 2003; P. B. Baltes, 1987; Commons *et al.*, 1989; Erikson, 1959; Labouvie-Vief, 1982). It actually took quite some time before conceptions of human ageing freed themselves from the exclusive connection to loss in function.

Aside from the philosophical inquiry into human functioning which had always included positive aspects of ageing, the lifespan approach to adult development and ageing was especially instrumental in generating this movement. The lifespan approach emerged from a childhood-based conception of development that defined development as a process of increasing levels of functioning (P. B. Baltes, 1987; Harris, 1957; Lerner, 2002). This approach could therefore be extended to elevate the older ages of the lifecourse to a conceptual platform upon which development in the sense of adaptive progress was part of the intellectual agenda, although the sum score of all age-related changes may signal an increasing component of decline. For contemporary researchers of psychological ageing, therefore, the nature of ageing includes gains and losses in adaptive capacities.

PSYCHOLOGICAL THEORIES OF HUMAN DEVELOPMENT: INTEGRATING LEVELS OF ANALYSIS

In the following, we place psychological theories of ageing in a framework of human development that includes four levels (or perspectives) of analysis. Considering these levels together facilitates the understanding of the biocultural and psychological constraints as well as opportunities that shape human ageing. As shown in Table 1, in terms of principles of causality or developmental determinants, we move from the distal and general conditions of human ageing to the more proximal and specific. This movement also implies a movement from the metatheoretical to more and more specific psychological factors and mechanisms (see P. B. Baltes *et al.*, 1998 and P. B. Baltes *et al.*, 1999 for more detail and references). Each subsequent level of analysis uses the former level(s) as a prefiguring framework. In concert, they represent a fabric of interconnecting propositions, theoretical specifications, and empirical facts.

Level 1, the most distal and general, makes explicit the fundamental cornerstone of the biocultural territory in which psychological ageing unfolds. It is akin to what developmental biologists have called the "norms of reaction" or "potentialities." Our own preferred term is that of the "fundamental biocultural architecture of the lifecourse." By considering Level 1, we obtain information on what we can expect about the most general scope and shape of human ageing.

Level 2 applies this information to the case of human ontogenesis. Level 3 specifies, within these previous frames, one general theory of development and ageing, the theory of selective optimization with compensation. Couched within the previous levels of analyses, Level 4, finally, takes a deeper look at the factors and mechanisms that regulate specific developmental functions. It would be possible to add a Level 5 to deal with what developmental psychologists have come to call microgenesis, that is, the operation of developmental mechanisms in micro-time and microspace.

We have chosen to proceed from a broad and pre-figuring macro level of analysis to more and more specific and micro levels of psychological analysis because it demonstrates the conceptual importance of interdisciplinary and multilevel thinking (Magnusson, 1996). Furthermore, the approach illustrates one of the central premises of theories of human development, namely, that ontogenetic development is embedded in larger evolutionary, historical, and cultural contexts (P. B. Baltes *et al.*, 1998; Cole, 1996; Lerner, 2002; Staudinger and Lindenberger, 2003). Behavioral dispositions developed in the past have major influences on human behavior in modern times (e.g. Barkow *et al.*, 1992; Durham, 1991; Gigerenzer, 1996; Gottlieb, 1998; Kirkwood, 2003; Klix, 1993; S.-C. Li, 2003). Note that we are not arguing that the evolutionary and cultural past is the entire prologue to human ageing. Rather, our argument is that ontogenesis can be better understood if the interaction between the evolutionary past and the ontogenetic present is considered.

The term we use to capture the dynamical exchanges between biology and culture which unfold across different time scales of human development is *"developmental biocultural co-constructivism"* (P. B. Baltes & Singer, 2001; S.-C. Li, 2003). Recognizing the powerful conditioning of human behavior and human development by biological and cultural evolution and their co-evolution has an additional advantage. It emphasizes that the future is not predetermined and that ageing includes features of an open system. In this spirit, gerontologists like to argue that their field has a paradoxical feature. Historically,

old age is young and, therefore, still rather underdeveloped.

LEVEL 1: THE OVERALL BIOCULTURAL ARCHITECTURE OF LIFESPAN DEVELOPMENT

Let us now turn to the overall biocultural architecture of lifespan development, Level 1, in Table 1. What is the role of cultural and biological factors in ontogenesis; how do they interact and condition each other; how does their dynamic likely change with age (P. B. Baltes, 1997; P. B. Baltes and Graf, 1996)? What is the "zone of development," the "norm of reaction" (Lerner, 2002) that we can expect to operate during ontogenesis? Despite the sizable plasticity of homo sapiens, not everything is possible in ontogenetic development.

With a view to the future and future societal changes, we need to recognize first that the overall biocultural architecture of human development is not only incomplete in general, but that its relative incompleteness increases with age. The earlier age periods of the lifecourse have a longer history of fine-tuning through biological and cultural co-evolution (P. B. Baltes *et al.*, 1998; Durham, 1991). Figure 1 illustrates the main lines of argument. Note first that the specific form (level, shape) of the functions characterizing the overall lifespan dynamics between biology and culture is not critical. What is critical is the overall direction and reciprocal relationship between these functions.

Evolutionary selection benefits decrease with age

Dating back to the early work of Medawar (1946), and later quantified especially by Charlesworth (1994), the central argument depicted in the left part of Figure 1 is that the benefits resulting from evolutionary selection display a negative age correlation. As a result, biological plasticity decreases with age. During evolution, the older the organism, the less the genome benefited from the genetic advantages associated with evolutionary selection. This assertion is in line with the idea that evolutionary selection was tied to the process of reproductive fitness and its midlife location in the

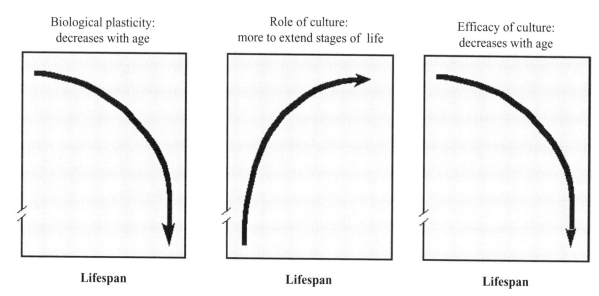

Biological plasticity: decreases with age

Role of culture: more to extend stages of life

Efficacy of culture: decreases with age

Lifespan

Lifespan

Lifespan

Figure 1. Schematic representation of basic facts about the average dynamics between biology and culture across the lifespan (after Baltes, 1995). Three meta-principles co-regulate human ontogeny: on the growing incompleteness of the life course. There can be much debate about the specific forms of the functions, but less about directionality.

lifecourse. During evolution, this age-associated diminution of evolutionary selection benefits was further enhanced by the fact that in earlier historical times only few people reached old age. Thus, evolutionary selection could not operate as frequently to begin with when it came to older individuals.

As a consequence, with age the expressions and mechanisms of the genome lose in functional quality and fidelity (Finch, 1990; Hayflick, 1987; Kirkwood, 2003; Martin *et al.*, 1996). The fact that the genome evinces less late-age selection pressure is also the primary reason why many molecular biologists argue that there is no strong genetic program for ageing. Moreover, there are other aspects of ageing that imply an age-associated loss in biological functioning, for instance, associated with the costs involved in creating and maintaining life (Finch, 1990, 1996; Martin *et al.*, 1996; Osiewacz, 1995; Yates and Benton, 1995). Together, they add up to the conclusion that biological plasticity and fidelity decline with age.

Age-related increase in need for culture

The middle part of Figure 1 adds a general perspective on the role of culture. By culture, we mean the entirety of psychological, social, material, and symbolic (knowledge-based) resources which humans have developed over millennia, and which, as they are transmitted across generations, make human development as we know it possible (Cole, 1996; Durham, 1991; S.-C. Li, 2003). These cultural resources include cognitive skills, motivational dispositions, socialization strategies, physical structures, and the world of economics as well as that of medical and physical technology.

Three arguments support an age-related increase in the "need" for more advanced levels of culture as human development extended itself into longer lifetimes and higher levels of functioning. First, for human ontogenesis to have reached higher and higher levels of functioning, whether in physical (e.g. sports) or cultural (e.g. reading and writing) domains, there had to be a conjoint evolutionary increase in the richness and dissemination of culture. In line with this view, the further we expect human ontogenesis to extend itself into adult life and old age, the more it will be necessary for particular cultural factors and resources to emerge to make this possible. Second, there is the issue of negative acceleration of experience-based learning curves and their possible asymptotes. The higher the functioning, the more difficult it will become to obtain further gains.

Third, the need for culture increases with age, because of the conditions shown in the left part of Figure 1, the age-associated biological weakening of the system as a whole. That is, the older individuals are, the more they are in need of culture-based resources (material, social, economic, psychological) to generate and maintain high levels of functioning.

Figure 1, however, does not mean that children require little cultural input and support. Early in ontogenetic life, because the human organism is still underdeveloped biologically, infants and children need a wide variety of psycho-social–material–cultural support. In terms of overall resource structure, this support in childhood is focused on basic levels of functioning, such as environmental sensory stimulation, nutrition, language, and social contact. Subsequent age stages, however, require increasingly more and more differentiated cultural resources.

Age-related decrease in the efficiency of culture

The right panel of Figure 1 depicts the third cornerstone of the overall biocultural architecture of the lifecourse and deals with the relative efficacy of cultural influences. During the second half of life, we submit that there is an age-associated reduction in the efficiency of cultural factors. With age, and conditioned primarily by the negative biological trajectory of the life course, the relative power (effectiveness) of psychological, social, material, and cultural interventions becomes weaker and weaker, even though large interindividual differences in the onset and rate of these decreases in effectiveness are likely (P. B. Baltes and Smith, 2003; Nelson and Dannefer, 1992).

Take the cognitive system in old age as an example (S.-C. Li, 2002; Salthouse, 1991, 1996; Singer et al., 2003a,b). The older the adult person, the larger the loss in cognitive capacity, the more practice and cognitive support it takes to attain the same learning gains. Moreover, at least in some domains of information processing, older adults may never be able to reach the same levels of functioning as younger adults, even after extensive training.

We argue that the three conditions and trajectories outlined form a robust biocultural fabric (architecture) of the lifespan dynamics between biology and culture. With age, this architecture becomes more and more incomplete and evinces lesser potential. We submit that this fabric represents a first tier of lifespan theory that guides, in a prefigurative sense, our understanding of psychological ageing.

LEVEL 2: LIFESPAN CHANGES IN THE ALLOCATION OF RESOURCES TO DISTINCT FUNCTIONS – GROWTH VS. MAINTENANCE VS. LOSS

One of the consequences of the lifespan architectural script outlined is a lifespan change in the allocation of resources to different developmental functions (Level 2 perspective in Table 1). Developmental psychologists distinguish between three outcomes or goals that guide developmental investments: growth (advances), maintenance, and the regulation of loss (e.g. Freund and Ebner, 2005; Baltes, 1987; Staudinger et al., 1995). By resources, we mean the entirety of physical, mental, social, and external resources and behaviors that individuals command in the pursuit of personal goals (see also Freund and Riediger, 2001; Hobfoll, 2001).

By the adaptive tasks of growth, we mean behaviors and related investments aimed at reaching higher levels of functioning or adaptive capacity. Under the heading of maintenance, we group behaviors which are aimed at maintaining levels of functioning in the face of new adaptive challenges or returning to previous levels after a loss. With the adaptive tasks of regulating loss, we identify those behaviors which organize adequate functioning at lower overall levels when maintenance or recovery is no longer possible.

The incomplete biocultural architecture of the lifecourse suggests the following general pattern. In childhood, the primary allocation of resources is directed toward growth; during adulthood, the predominant allocation is towards maintenance and recovery. In old age, more and more resources are directed towards regulation (management) of loss. Such a characterization, of course, is an oversimplification. Individual, domain, and contextual differences need to be taken into account. Thus, the

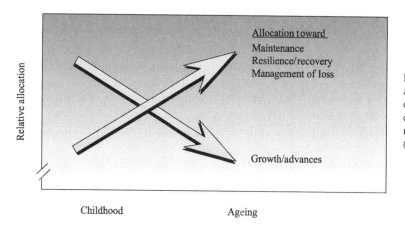

Figure 2. Lifespan changes in the allocation of resources into distinct functions (objectives) of development: Growth, maintenance, and regulation (management) of loss.

characterization is one about relative probability. In our view, the lifespan shift in the relative allocation of biology- and culture-based resources to the functions of growth, maintenance, and the management of loss is a major issue for any theory of lifespan development (e.g. P. B. Baltes, 1987, 1991, 1997; Staudinger *et al.*, 1995; for related arguments, see also Brandtstädter and Greve, 1994; Labouvie-Vief, 1982).

The lifespan trajectories outlined in Figure 2 for the functions of growth, maintenance, and regulation of loss also emphasize the significance of the dynamics between these functions. Thus, the mastery of life often involves conflicts and competition among the three functions and objectives of human development. In old age, the dynamic tilts more and more in the direction of managing vulnerability and loss (P. B. Baltes & Baltes, 1990). As to current-day research, one telling example of the dynamics among the functions of growth, maintenance, and regulation of loss is the lifespan comparative study of the interplay between autonomy and dependency in children and older adults. In old age, to deal effectively with age-based losses and to retain some independence, the productive and creative use of dependent behaviors becomes critical. By invoking dependency and support from others, resources are freed up for use in other domains involving personal efficacy and growth (M. M. Baltes, 1996).

In sum, we submit that a further step in developing lifespan and psychological ageing theory is to recognize and specify the nature of the dynamics of resource allocation for growth, maintenance, and regulation of loss. Of particular importance is the nature of the shift in this systemic interplay and its orchestration over the life course.

Deficits as Catalysts for Adaptive Progress

The Level 1 and Level 2 perspectives draw attention to the important role of compensatory strategies in shaping the nature of psychological ageing. Because the notion of loss is typically associated with negative expectations, we highlight the positive role of deficit in biological and cultural evolution (P. B. Baltes, 1987; Brandtstädter and Wentura, 1995; Dixon and Bäckman, 1995; Gehlen, 1956; Marsiske *et al.*, 1995; Uttal and Perlmutter, 1989). Following anthropological and evolutionary arguments, contemporary behavioral scientists have increasingly maintained that suboptimal biological states or imperfections are catalysts for the evolution of culture and for the advanced states achieved in human ontogeny. In this line of thinking, the human organism is by nature a "being of deficits" (*Mängelwesen*; Gehlen, 1956) and social culture has developed or emerged in part to deal specifically with biological deficits.

This "deficits-breed-progress" view also plays a role in ontogenesis. Thus, throughout life, but especially during old age, it is possible for individuals, when they reach states of increased vulnerability, to invest more and more heavily in efforts that are oriented explicitly towards regulating and compensating such losses and deficits. They thereby counteract losses (e.g. through a hearing aid when loss in hearing makes following conversations or detecting sounds in the environment difficult) and in

---

TABLE 2. A theory of adaptive development: selection optimization and compensation (SOC)

Definition
SOC involves the orchestration of three processes: selection (contexts, goals), optimization (means/resources), and compensation (substitutive means/resources)

Selection: elective and loss-based
Concerns directionality (goals) of development including selection of alternative contexts, outcomes, and goal structures

Optimization
Concerns the acquisition and refinement of means for achieving desired outcomes and attaining higher levels of functioning

Compensation
Concerns activation or acquisition of new substitutive means for counteracting loss/decline in previously operative means that threatens maintenance of a given level of functioning

- SOC behaviors are universal processes of adaptive development
- SOC behaviors are relativistic in that their phenotype depends on person- and context-specific features

Source: Freund and Baltes (2000); P. B. Baltes and Baltes (1990)

---

addition, under certain conditions, may be able to acquire a broad range of novel behaviors, new bodies of knowledge and values, and new environmental features, such as household technology (Freund *et al.*, 1999). The acquisition of wisdom, for instance, seems critically linked to understanding not only the gains, but also the losses of life (P. B. Baltes and Staudinger, 2000).

LEVEL 3: AN OVERALL THEORY OF SUCCESSFUL (ADAPTIVE) PSYCHOLOGICAL AGEING – ORCHESTRATING SELECTION, OPTIMIZATION, AND COMPENSATION

In the next step, we move to an example of Level 3 analysis and present one general theory of psychological ageing that reflects the framing conditions prefigured by the perspectives described as Level 1 and Level 2. This is not the only theory that would fit this overall frame; however, it is a theory that was explicitly developed to suit this purpose.

The theory, originally called "selective optimization with compensation" (M. M. Baltes, 1996; P. B. Baltes, 1987, 1997; P. B. Baltes and Baltes, 1980, 1990; Freund and Baltes, 2000, 2002a), is based on the operation and coordination of three components: *selection* of goals or behavior outcomes, *optimization* of the means to reach these goals, and *compensation*, that is, the use of substitutive means

to maintain functioning when previously available means are lost or blocked (see summary in Table 2). There are other similar approaches (see Freund and Riediger, 2003, for a more detailed comparative discussion), most notable are those of Brandtstädter (1984; Brandtstädter and Greve, 1994), Carstensen (1995), and Heckhausen (1999; Heckhausen and Schulz, 1995).

On the most general level of definition (P. B. Baltes, 1997; Freund and Baltes, 2000, 2002a), *selection* refers to the process of specifying a particular pathway or set of pathways of development. This selective specification includes the narrowing down of a range of alternatives that the scope of biocultural plasticity would in principle permit. In this sense, selection is a general-purpose mechanism to generate new resources and higher developmental states. At the same time, because of limited resources such as time and energy, this advance in some domains implies a reduction of advances in others. Only by concentrating time and energy on delineated domains of functioning can certain skills and abilities evolve.

Recently, we have distinguished within selection between two forms of selection: elective selection, where selection is primarily driven by goals, and loss-based selection, where selection is a response to a loss in the potential to reach desirable goals and a reorganization of goals is indicated (Freund and Baltes, 2002a). Both elective and loss-based selection imply the structuring and continuing reorganization of goals.

Optimization in the general sense refers to the acquisition, application, coordination, and refinement of internal and external means involved in attaining higher levels of functioning. The relevant means are many, ranging from genetic expressions (including epigenesis) to health behavior, practice, cognitive skills, social support, educational learning, and personality dimensions such as maintaining a sense of control. A large amount of deliberate practice of skills, for instance, has been shown to be a key for any kind of expertise – be it physical, such as in sports and health, or cognitive, such as in work and education (e.g. Ericsson *et al.*, 1993; Krampe and Baltes, 2003).

Compensation, like optimization, refers to means. Compensation is defined as counteracting losses in means previously operative in goal attainment by using alternative (substitutive) means to maintain functioning. One example of compensation is the use of hearing aids to counteract hearing loss and the greater reliance on visual cues to compensate for declining speed of language processing in old age (Thompson, 1995).

Let us return to SOC as a theory and its role as a general theory of development. The SOC theory was developed (1) to account for the realization of development in general and, in addition, (2) to specify how individuals can effectively manage the overall lifespan changes in biological, psychological, and social conditions that form opportunities and constraints on level and trajectories of development. The biogenetic and cultural contexts provide constraints and affordances, including interindividual differences in such constraints and affordances. Plasticity and age-related changes in biological and environmental plasticity are the cornerstones for this view (M. M. Baltes, 1996; P. B. Baltes and Schaie, 1976; P. B. Baltes *et al.*, 1998; Lerner, 2002).

In the theory of SOC, successful development is defined as the process of the simultaneous maximization of gains and minimization of losses over the life course. As to gains in development, by engaging in SOC, individuals develop their potentialities. Thus, SOC is a development-producing set of processes resulting in increasingly higher levels of functioning. Regarding the management of life, as is evidenced in the task of triangulating

aspects of growth, maintenance, and loss, SOC is an effective way to reallocate resources between these three functions. Another way to communicate the rationale of SOC is to label it as the most general-purpose mechanism of development and adaptive functioning.

In principle, the SOC theory can be realized from many different theoretical perspectives, including social, behavioral-learning, cognitive, and neuropsychological (M. M. Baltes and Carstensen, 1996; P. B. Baltes and Singer, 2001; Marsiske *et al.*, 1995). One of the theoretical frameworks within which we have articulated the theory in more detail is psychological action theory (Freund and Baltes, 2000; Freund *et al.*, 1999). Action theories in psychology proceed from the assumption that human behavior and human development can be understood by considering behaviors as actions and their structuring in terms of goals and means (Boesch, 1991; Brandtstädter and Lerner, 1999; Eckensberger, 2001; von Cranach and Tschan, 2001). The SOC theory is intended to translate this action-theoretical perspective into a "systemic" process of developmental regulation.

Furthermore, SOC processes can vary along the dimensions active – passive, conscious – nonconscious, and internal – external. This reflects the many levels of consciousness and automaticity as well as external constraints that human development entails (see also Freund and Baltes, 2002a; Heckhausen, 1999; Wilson, 2002). An example of passive selection, for instance, is being born into a particular cultural, historical context, to parents of a specific socioeconomic background and personality. An example of a highly automatized and therefore largely non-conscious SOC process, described in ageing research, is the preference of older adults to allocate their resources primarily to motor behavior (such as keeping one's balance) rather than to solving a memory problem. Moreover, they effectively use compensatory help, such as a handrail (an external means of compensation), when experiencing difficulty in maintaining balance (K. Z. H. Li *et al.*, 2001). As these examples show, the behavioral expressions of selection, optimization, and compensation can vary greatly, depending upon the domain and the stage of life under consideration. The processes and their functions, however, are assumed to be universal.

Finally, note that SOC-related behaviors, although universal in their occurrence, have the potential for a high degree of individual "phenotypic" specificity (P. B. Baltes and Baltes, 1990). A recent study by Gignac *et al.* (2002) demonstrates this simultaneous occurrence of SOC as a general process and SOC as an individualized strategy of life-management. Observational methods were used to study older patients afflicted with osteoarthritis and their strategies of management. Results showed that virtually all older adults made at least one adaptation that reflected either selection (e.g., restrict activity), optimization (e.g., practice movement), or compensation (use assistive devices). That is the universal aspect of SOC. The results also demonstrated large interindividual variability in the specific SOC behaviors expressed. This finding underscores the many variations that individuals can pursue as they produce their special ways of identifying and orchestrating ways of selecting, optimizing, and compensating. Similar evidence can be found in a work by de Frias *et al.* (2003) in the area of memory compensation.

Further explication of SOC processes

The further explication of the components of SOC and their coordination is central to future work. This can be accomplished, for instance, by linking SOC to more specific psychological theories associated with selection, optimization, and compensation.

One such theory is the theory of expertise and other learning-attainments (Ericsson, 2003; Ericsson and Smith, 1991; Krampe and Baltes, 2003). Expertise and expertise-related theories offer general explanations for acquiring and maintaining high levels of functioning and can be applied to most domains of psychological ageing. Thus, for SOC to be realized effectively, factors of expertise acquisition and maintenance are critical. Another theoretical model that has much relevance for understanding the specifics of SOC is motivational psychology and, especially, the developmental theories of personal goals. Personal goals are defined as states a person wishes to attain or avoid (Emmons, 1996) that motivate and organize behavior over time and across situations into action sequences (e.g. Freund and Baltes, 2000; Heckhausen, 1999; Oettingen, 1997; Riediger, 2001).

SOC: EMPIRICAL EVIDENCE IN ADULT DEVELOPMENT AND AGEING

What are some of the major findings from studies that addressed specifically the role of SOC in the description, explanation, and modification of psychological ageing? First, there is evidence that the relative prevalence of the employment and coordination of the components of SOC themselves change with age. Second, there is evidence that people who engage in SOC behaviors show more adaptive outcomes. Third, there is increasing evidence that SOC-related behaviors can be discerned with several methods of investigation: self-report, observation, and experimental studies (Freund and Baltes, 2002a).

Self-report data on SOC use

Age differences. As shown in Figure 3, the reported use of SOC exhibits age gradients. When asked – by means of a self-report instrument developed for assessing SOC – whether they engage in SOC-related behaviors, people of different adult ages report distinct levels of expression.

We highlight two aspects of the age gradients obtained. First, it is during adulthood that we observe the highest level of reporting of SOC. Such a finding is consistent with the notion that SOC is a developmental construct with a peak in middle adulthood. Second, in old age the effective use of SOC becomes less prevalent. Only elective selection continues to increase. The positive side of this finding is the self-reports of older adults that they are selective as motivational agents. The less positive side of the findings is that they report lesser use of optimization and compensation. This is not due to a lack of effectiveness of SOC in old age (Freund and Baltes, 1998). Nor is it due to a lack of knowledge about the effectiveness of SOC in old age. Using a choice reaction approach, for instance, Freund and Baltes (2002b) found that older adults have a preference for proverbs reflecting SOC content when these are compared to alternative proverbs. The primary reason for a weakening of the OC part of the behavioral repertoire in old age is more probably that optimizing and compensating are effortful and therefore increasingly exceeding the resources available. This is especially true when people suffer from severe

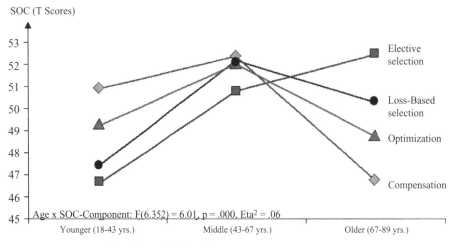

SOC (T Scores)

Elective selection

Loss-Based selection

Optimization

Compensation

Age x SOC-Component: F(6.352) = 6.01, p = .000, Eta² = .06

Younger (18-43 yrs.)   Middle (43-67 yrs.)   Older (67-89 yrs.)

Age Groups (Adulthood)

Figure 3. Age-related mean differences in SOC: Middle-aged adults show the highest and most convergent endorsement of SOC. SOC = selection, optimization, and compensation; yrs = years (after Freund and Baltes, 2002a).

illnesses or enter the oldest-ages, the Fourth Age (M. M. Baltes, 1998; P. B. Baltes and Smith, 2003; Jopp, 2002).

Outcomes Associated with Self-Report SOC

The research on the connection between self-reported use of SOC and outcomes shows that, throughout life, people who report using SOC are functioning at a higher level when outcomes of subjective and objective functional status are considered. Table 3 summarizes some of the relevant findings. In samples ranging in age from 14 to 100+ years, adults who report engaging in selection, optimization, and compensation when pursuing personal goals also report higher wellbeing as reflected in measures such as frequency of experiencing positive emotions, having a purpose in life, or life satisfaction (Freund and Baltes, 1998, 2002; Wiese *et al.*, 2000, 2002).

The pattern of correlations is stable across adulthood into old and very old age. Moreover, it is robust even when a number of rival predictors of positive development such as personality (e.g. "Big Five") and motivational constructs (e.g. tenacious goal pursuit and flexible goal adjustment; Brandtstädter and

Wentura, 1995) are controlled for. Similar findings in support of the adaptive use of SOC have been reported by Lang *et al.* (2002; see also M. M. Baltes and Lang, 1997). Similar findings were obtained with younger age groups, for instance, in the area of the planning and management of dual careers (B. B. Baltes and Heydens-Gahir, 2003; Wiese and Freund,

TABLE 3. Summary of findings on the correlations of self-reported SOC and subjective indicators of positive development

Subjective indicators of positive development	Correlation with overall SOC score
Freund and Baltes, 2002a (N = 395; 14–89 years)	
Positive emotions	.33**
Everyday competence	.35**
Personal growth	.37**
Meaning in life	.44**
Freund and Baltes, 1998 (N = 200; 72–102 years)	
Satisfaction with ageing	.33**
Positive emotions	.47**
Emotional loneliness	−.30**
Freund et al. 2000 (N = 206; 25–36 years)	
Life satisfaction	.49**
Emotional balance	.37**
Self-acceptance	.21**

Note: ** p < = .01.

2001; Wiese *et al.*, 2002). Such findings are important for our understanding of ageing as well, since they suggest the life-history role of SOC in the production of successful ageing.

As already mentioned, in future research it will be important to decompose the SOC factors and processes at a more fine-grained level. One concept, for instance, that has turned out to be relevant for understanding the microprocesses of SOC in the selection domain, is "adaptive goal selection" (Freund and Baltes, 2000; Marsiske *et al.*, 1995). Riediger *et al.* (2003) found, for instance, that compared to younger adults, older adults report more mutually facilitative and less conflicting personal goals. In addition, due to this more "integrated" goal system, adults and older persons also worked more intensely on their goals. A movement from more interfering goals to more mutually facilitating goals therefore seems to be a hallmark of successful ageing.

Behavioral expression of SOC in dual-task research

Another – and for some researchers more powerful – approach is to demonstrate the operation of SOC at the behavioral-performance level. Indeed, there is such evidence, and the evidence is pretty good. Much of this research was conducted in the context of dual-task paradigms.

One key issue of adaptive ageing is how to manage multitasking. Performing several tasks concurrently is typical for everyday life. Concurrent performances – such as driving a car while talking with a companion – are more difficult than engaging in each of the tasks separately. Thus, it is not surprising that, because of the general losses in reserves and resources that occur with age, dual or multitasks become more and more difficult with age (for a review, see Craik and Salthouse, 2000).

Given age-associated decrements or increases in dual-task costs, an interesting question is whether older adults suffer in their performance under dual-task conditions in both tasks equally, or whether they show preferential behavior, for instance, by differential (asymmetric) allocation of their resources to one task over another. As a result of such a differential allocation of attentional resources, they would lose less in the task they favor.

The SOC model offers predictive specificity in the direction of asymmetry. Thus, goal-related selection would involve a selective focus on the task that has higher significance. For instance, when the dual task is to memorize a word list while walking fast or on difficult ground, the expectation is that older adults prioritize walking because falling would be a more serious problem than not remembering a word in a list.

Such prioritizations, of course, can be expected in all age groups, but in old age they are assumed to be more frequent, and more often involve a prioritization for bodily functioning because the body is the primary domain where ageing losses occur and serious risks exist. In this vein, K. Z. H. Li *et al.* (2001; see also Lindenberger *et al.*, 2000) investigated behavioral expressions of SOC in the context of a dual-task study involving memorizing and walking. A similar study was conducted by Rapp *et al.* (in press) with cognitive information processing and motor balance as competing tasks.

First, and consistent with other work, older adults showed greater dual-task costs. When performing two tasks, each of the tasks was, relatively speaking, less well executed than in younger individuals. Second, however, the dual-task costs were not equal or symmetrical between the two tasks. Older adults in each study showed less costs for the sensori-motor task compared to the cognitive task. This finding suggests a differential resource allocation. Third, older adults were rather effective in using this procedure of differential resource allocation. For sensori-motor behavior, they showed much resilience, occasionally even no increase in dual-task costs. This even applied to Alzheimer patients (see also Baddeley *et al.*, 2001). Moreover, older adults were able to use compensatory skills to maintain a higher level of performance. Each of these ageing-associated effects of the differential use of SOC in favor of motor over cognitive task behavior was stronger when the behavioral system was tested at its limits, such as by making the tasks more and more difficult.

Another relevant study was conducted by Krampe, Rapp, Bondar and Baltes (2003). Its focus was on the effectiveness of the instruction to allocate differentially. On the one hand, this study demonstrated that young as well as older adults can be taught to allocate resources to different task requirements. At the same time, however, older adults seemed to be unable to do so for a motor-behavior situation that entailed the risk of falling. In this case, the differential allocation system of older adults was robust, if not set in place. In light of the significance of maintaining motor function and balance, this asymmetric allocation seems adaptive despite its seeming rigidity.

Differential allocation of resources can take many forms. Consider a different combination of tasks, namely "talking while walking." Kemper *et al.* (2003) were able to demonstrate that older and younger adults differ regarding their compensatory strategies when task demands exceeded their resources. Whereas young adults reduced the length and grammatical complexity of their spoken sentences, older adults reduced the rate of speech when they simultaneously had to walk. By speaking more slowly, then, older adults were able to preserve their speaking even under taxing dual-task conditions.

Taken together, self-report, observational, as well as experimental studies lend support to the perspective of the SOC theory of adaptive development including ageing. The replicated pattern of results suggests that older people direct their resources to those domains of functioning that have high priority for them: for instance, that are either important to them in the sense of personal goals, or are vital to their maintenance of functioning and protecting themselves from losses such as falling. Thus, as SOC theory predicts, their resource allocation is not symmetrical, but selective and guided by individual patterns of resources and efficacy.

LEVEL 4: PSYCHOLOGICAL AGEING IN SPECIFIC DOMAINS – THE EXAMPLE OF COGNITIVE AGEING

We finally move to Level 4 and focus on one specific functional area, namely, intelligence and cognition, and their development in adulthood and old age. As we review theories and findings specific to cognitive ageing, it will become clear that the previous levels of analyses apply at this level as well. The field of cognitive or intellectual ageing has many facets. Thus far, four main research approaches have been developed, two of which (the psychometric and the functional approaches) have traditions

that date back to the dawn of intelligence research in the late nineteenth century, and the other two (the information-processing and the neurocognitive approaches) evolved in the second half of the twentieth century with the advent of computer- and brain-based methods and metaphors.

Ageing and Two Broad Domains of Psychometric Intelligence

Beginning with the Cattell-Horn theory of intelligence (Cattell, 1971; Horn, 1970), the key concepts of intellectual ageing have been multidimensionality, multidirectionality, and adaptive multifunctionality (e.g. P. B. Baltes and Labouvie, 1973; Botwinick, 1967; Dixon and Baltes, 1986). Broad categories of intelligence were identified, such as fluid and crystallized intelligence, and they showed different trajectories with respect to the directions, onsets, and rates of change across life. Recent work has added more precision and theoretical rigor to this general impression of differential age trajectories. Specifically, dual-component theories of intellectual development, which integrate psychometric intelligence research with developmental theories of learning and expertise as well as with insights into the biocultural dynamics of the lifecourse, have resulted in a more comprehensive view of intellectual ageing that is both theoretically and empirically supported.

DIFFERENTIAL TRAJECTORIES OF BIOLOGY- AND CULTURE-BASED FACETS OF INTELLIGENCE. Dual-component theories of intelligence (e.g. P. B. Baltes *et al.*, 1999; Horn, 1982) distinguish between *fluid cognitive mechanics*, which reflect the operations of the relatively more neurobiology-based basic information-processing mechanisms, and *crystallized cognitive pragmatics*, which are the outgrowth of experience- and culture-based knowledge. Cross-sectional age gradients (e.g. Horn, 1970; Jones and Conrad, 1933) and longitudinal age trajectories (e.g. McArdle *et al.*, 2002) of these two domains of intellectual abilities generally show a lead–lag pattern across the life course: the relatively more biology-based fluid cognitive mechanics develop and decline earlier than the more culture-based crystallized cognitive pragmatics. Note that

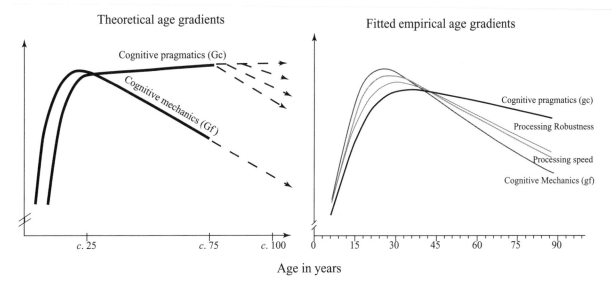

Figure 4. Dual-component theory of intellectual development. Theoretical expectations and empirical findings regarding the fluid cognitive mechanics vs. crystallized cognitive pragmatics. Theoretical age gradients are plotted in the left panel. Fitted empirical age gradients of these two categories of intelligence along with basic processing speed and processing robustness are presented on the right (see S.-C. Li *et al.*, 2004, for more details about the empirical curves).

this pattern is consistent with the lifespan architecture presented in Figure 1.

As an illustration, Figure 4 shows the hypothetical lifespan age gradients predicted by the dual-component theories and the empirical cross-sectional age gradients covering the age range from 6 to 89 years reported in a recent study (S.-C. Li *et al.*, 2004; see also Park *et al.*, 1996). The maximum performances of cognitive mechanics were achieved by individuals in their mid-20s, and decrements were already visible by age 30; the maximum performances of cognitive pragmatics were achieved by individuals in their mid-40s and remained stable until 70 years of age, at which point they also declined. Longitudinal findings from the Berlin Ageing Study showed an even sharper contrast between the trajectories of these two broad categories of intelligence: longitudinal decline in some facets of the crystallized pragmatics (i.e., verbal knowledge) was not observed until the individuals reached the late 80s (Singer *et al.*, 2003b).

In addition to differential age gradients, the neurobiology vs. acculturation distinction between these two aspects of intelligence has been supported by findings showing that the cognitive mechanics correlated more with basic sensory processing, whereas cognitive pragmatics correlated more with sociobiographical predictors (e.g. Lindenberger and Baltes, 1997). Furthermore, on the biology–culture continuum, lifespan age gradients of basic information-processing mechanisms (e.g., processing speed) corresponded very closely to the gradient of cognitive mechanics but less to the cognitive pragmatics (see Figure 4, right panel).

DYNAMIC TRANSFORMATION IN THE ORGANIZATION OF INTELLIGENCE. Although traditionally the organization of mental abilities and their underlying cognitive processes are viewed as static, dual-component theories of intellectual development consider the functional organization of intellectual abilities as dynamic – developing and transforming throughout life. Specifically, the relative contributions of biology and culture are postulated to vary across life periods and ability domains.

During life periods in which there are strong biological constraints on the information-processing mechanisms underlying knowledge acquisition and expression, stronger coupling between different facets of intelligence and their constituent cognitive

Degree of integration/covariation

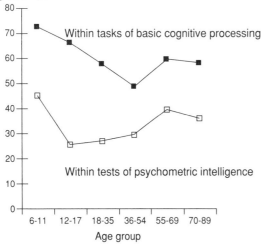

Covariation with basic processing speed

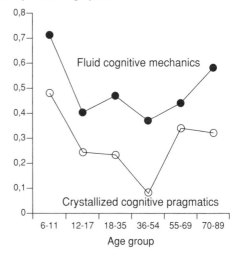

Figure 5. Differentiation and dedifferentiation of intellectual abilities and basic information processing across the lifespan. The left panel shows age-related differences in ability integration. The degree of integration/covariation is indicated by the percent of variance accounted by the first principal component within the domain of basic cognitive processing and within the domain of psychometric intelligence, separately. The right panel shows age differences in the associations of the major components of intelligence with basic information processing speed, an elementary aspect of the fluid cognitive mechanics. Two general findings are noteworthy. First, the association is highest at both ends of the lifespan. Second, the association between knowledge-based individual differences and basic information processing is rather low in adulthood, pointing to a relatively large independence of knowledge-based individual differences from basic intelligence during adulthood.

processes are expected. This prediction is supported by recent findings (S.-C. Li *et al.*, 2004) showing that the amount of variance shared among different aspects of intellectual abilities (memory, reasoning, perceptual speed, verbal knowledge and fluency) and the processing speed of a wide range of basic cognitive processes (e.g., visual and memory search, response competition, choice reactions) were higher at both ends of the lifespan (left panel in Figure 5). The correlations between the two aspects of intelligence and basic processing speed showed a similar pattern of higher correlations in the child developmental and ageing portion of the lifespan (right panel in Figure 5). Together, these findings suggest

that the structure of mental abilities is dedifferentiated in old age.

Other earlier ageing studies also indicated that the correlations associated with subscales of intelligence tests (e.g. P. B. Baltes and Lindenberger, 1997) and among measures of perceptual speed (Babcock *et al.*, 1997) were higher in old than in young adults. Longitudinal data supporting ability dedifferentiation in old age are much more rare. Recently, latent dynamic models applied to longitudinal data from the Berlin Ageing Study yielded first direct longitudinal evidence of coupled age-related changes in the two broad domains of intelligence. More interestingly, the influence of change in fluid cognitive mechanics on change in crystallized pragmatics is greater than vice versa (Ghisletta and Lindenberger, 2003). This suggests that in old age, when the level of cognitive mechanics reaches a lower-bound threshold, the relatively more biology-based cognitive mechanics constrains the operation of the knowledge-based cognitive pragmatics. In addition, there is evidence for increased correlation between cognitive abilities and simple sensory processing in old age (e.g. P. B. Baltes and Lindenberger, 1997; Salthouse *et al.*, 1996), suggesting that the phenomenon of ability dedifferentiation goes beyond the cognitive domain. However, it should be noted that some studies found relatively weaker and less consistent evidence for such cross-domain ability dedifferentiation (e.g., Anstey *et al.*, 2003).

Ageing and Selective Positive Development in Cognitive Pragmatics

Declines in basic information-processing mechanisms are dealt with later in the chapter; here we highlight some positive aspects of intellectual ageing that are mostly associated with the role of culture, knowledge, and associated practice. Not all aspects of the crystallized pragmatics evince a positive age trend: only those in which an as yet unspecifiable level of cognitive mechanics is maintained, and in which there is opportunity for practice. Thus, the broader zone of positive development in the pragmatic component of intelligence reflects the support from contextual and cultural resources gained through a lifetime of acquiring and utilizing culturally transmitted bodies of declarative and procedural knowledge (P. B. Baltes *et al.*, 1999).

Besides general normative cultural knowledge (such as language competency and other within- and cross-cultural norms), cognitive pragmatics also include person-specific bodies of knowledge that result from person-specific combinations of social experiences, personal conditions, personality characteristics, emotional and motivational constellations (e.g. P. B. Baltes and Staudinger, 2000; Carstensen *et al.*, 1999; Kunzmann and Baltes, 2003; Marsiske *et al.*, 1995), as well as expertise associated with the occupational, leisure, and cultural dimensions of life (e.g. Blanchard-Fields and Hess, 1996; Schooler and Mulatu, 2001; Schooler *et al.*, 1999). One of the most general bodies of such knowledge is *wisdom*, the expert knowledge about the fundamental pragmatics of life and human affairs, and about the meaning and conduct of life. To some degree all individuals acquire such a body of knowledge, although very few if any reach true levels of expertise. Because wisdom-demanding situations continue to exist through life and are probably highly practiced, such wisdom-related knowledge, as is true for language competence, can remain stable into the older ages (P. B. Baltes and Staudinger, 2000).

There are many other factual and procedural bodies of knowledge that can be considered as part of the crystallized pragmatics, ranging from occupational skills to skills in personal functioning, to lifestyles and artistic creativities. Individuals vary considerably in how far these skills are developed.

Reaching a certain level of expertise in some of these skills is generally considered desirable. The acquisition of a given expertise can be considered as a life-long resource investment in mastering a particular domain of knowledge and associated skills (Ericsson and Smith, 1991). Studies comparing young and old typists (Salthouse, 1988), chess players (Charness, 1981; Reingold *et al.*, 2001), and pianists (Krampe and Ericsson, 1996) all indicate that high levels of performance, if not expert performance, can be maintained in old age although the details of possible compensatory mechanisms used by old experts to keep up their level await further investigations. Analogous examples have also been found regarding other bodies of factual and procedural knowledge that characterize the practical intelligence(s) of ageing individuals in their everyday life contexts. The finding that older individuals exhibit good skills of emotional regulation and social intelligence is a telling example (Carstensen *et al.*, 1999; Kunzmann and Baltes, 2003).

In summary, extant findings from cross-sectional, longitudinal, and cohort-sequential studies indicate that different aspects of intellectual abilities change differently, by age and by cohort (see Schaie, 1996, 2001, for reviews). Through the psychometric approach, we have begun to understand the seemingly intractable mixture of confounding effects that result from cohort differences, lack of measurement equivalence, selection effects associated with experimental and population mortality, practice effects of longitudinal designs, mixture effects of interindividual differences with intraindividual change, or the questionable assumption of generalizing from group data to individual change trajectories (see Hertzog and Nesselroade, 2003, for review). Other recent work also gives ample testimony to the methodological fallacies that most ageing research is exposed to and remedies for treating these confounds (Hofer *et al.*, 2003; Lövden *et al.*, 2003; McArdle *et al.*, 2002; Singer *et al.*, 2003a; Singer *et al.*, 2003b).

Ageing and basic information processing

Cognitive psychologists interested in human ageing have been exploring the influence of ageing on basic information-processing mechanisms. In the process of ageing, people's abilities to keep information in mind, attend to relevant information, coordinate different information, and process information promptly all are compromised. The specific details of age-related declines, however, depend on task types, demands, and the processes involved. In general, the less practiced, the more difficult or complex the tasks are, the greater the costs of making errors, and the more "new learning" is involved, the larger the negative age difference is (see, for review, Craik and Salthouse, 2000; Park and Schwarz, 2000; Perfect and Maylor, 2000).

WORKING MEMORY. People's ability to hold information in immediate memory while simultaneously operating on the same or other information has been termed working memory (WM) (Baddeley, 1986). Age-related decline in working memory has been obtained on a variety of tasks, including backward digit span, sentence span, and several types of computational span (e.g. Park et al., 1996). Age-related decline in WM capacity plays a role in many other cognitive activities, ranging from long-term memory encoding and retrieval, syntactic processing, language complexity and comprehension, and reasoning (e.g. Kemper and Sumner, 2001; see Zacks et al., 2000, for review).

ATTENTIONAL AND INHIBITORY MECHANISMS. There is much evidence showing that old people have more problems in attending to relevant information and inhibiting irrelevant information. Negative age differences have been found in various selective and focused attention tasks as well as with the Stroop and proactive interference tasks. Age-related declines in attentional and inhibitory mechanisms have functional consequences for language comprehension, memory, problem solving, and other daily activities, such as driving (see McDown and Shaw, 2000, for review).

EXECUTIVE CONTROL. Baddeley's (1986) working memory model distinguishes between storage and executive control components. In addition to earlier work examining the mnemonic, maintenance aspect of working memory, lately much attention has been directed to the effect of ageing on executive control processes. Currently, a general consensus about what executive control entails is still lacking. Nonetheless, one proposal is that executive control involves the online modulation of attentional and response processes by maintaining information about the task context (Cohen et al., 2000). Various dual-task and task-switching paradigms involving divided or selective attention (i.e., individuals are asked to coordinate or switch their performance between multiple tasks) have been applied to study the effect of ageing on executive control (e.g. Glass et al., 2000; Kray and Lindenberger, 2000). Thus far, the evidence suggests that adult age differences in executive control functions are modulated by the extent to which the mental representations of multiple task sets need to be activated (see Mayr et al., 2001, for review).

PROCESSING SPEED AND PROCESSING ROBUSTNESS. Speed is a ubiquitous aspect of information processing. All processes take time, however brief. There is abundant evidence showing that older people are slower than younger adults in their responses in a great variety of cognitive tasks. Many correlational analyses showed that the observed age differences in fluid intelligence are greatly reduced or eliminated after individual differences in processing speed are controlled for (see Birren and Fisher, 1995; Salthouse, 1996, for review).

In studies of adult age differences in psychometric intelligence, there is evidence for age-related increases in within-person short-term performance variations (e.g. Hultsch et al., 2000; S.-C. Li et al., 2001a) and between-individual differences (e.g. Morse, 1993; Nelson and Dannefer, 1992), in addition to age-related decline in performance level. With respect to basic information processing, recent findings (e.g. Hultsch et al., 2000; S.-C. Li et al., 2004; Rabbitt et al., 2001) also show age-related decline in processing robustness (i.e., an increase in within-person processing fluctuation). Although individual differences in processing speed and robustness were highly correlated and their age gradients parallel each other closely across the lifespan (see right panel of Figure 4), in old-age processing *robustness* accounted for as much variance in cognitive mechanics as did processing *speed*. Moreover, processing robustness accounted for more variance in chronological age than did processing speed (S.-C. Li et al., 2004). Given that processing robustness seems to be more sensitive than speed in differentially predicting the relatively more biology-based cognitive mechanics, reduced processing robustness in old people might be a "purer" indicator of the attenuated functional status of the ageing brain, for example, lower neuronal information-processing fidelity (e.g. Welford, 1965).

Ageing and adaptive resource allocation

Our treatment of the theory of SOC as the general strategy of behavioral management has already identified the processes of resource allocation (growth vs. maintenance vs. regulation of loss; as well as selection of goals, optimization, and compensation) as key components of adaptive ageing. In a similar vein, since the mid 1980s, theoretical and empirical efforts have been devoted to expanding psychometric intelligence research by explicitly considering both the functional and contextual aspects of intelligence (e.g. Ackerman, 1988, 1996; Krampe and Baltes, 2003). A special emphasis of the resource allocation approach is its inquiry into how cognitive processes are coordinated and how they can be improved. Cognitive plasticity is one of the leading concepts in this regard, often studied by means of cognitive training research and work on multitasking.

Regarding cognitive plasticity, it has been demonstrated that older people, especially during the Third Age (60s to 80s), hold sizable latent potential (Willis, 1990). They are quite capable of improving their levels of performance. It is equally true, however, that such training effects evince little transfer and at limits (asymptotes) of performance, the levels of performance in older adults decline in comparison with those of younger adults (P. B. Baltes and Kliegl, 1992; Singer et al., 2003a). What is not clear is whether cognitive training results in improvement in the cognitive mechanics or whether such improvements are bound to the crystallized-pragmatic components. The existing evidence points to continual decline in cognitive mechanics that are, as argued above, predominately driven by brain ageing, and therefore leave the ageing individuals a smaller and smaller pool of information-processing resources for the maintenance and further refinement of culture-based cognitive pragmatics. Thus, eventually, in very old age the cognitive mechanics may fall below the limit required for the cognitive pragmatics to function well. The loss of cognitive plasticity in

old age is intensified by geriatric pathology (e.g. Camp, 1998). In sum, to understand the conditions of the ageing mind, it is important to maintain a dual-faced view: potential and limits (P. B. Baltes, 1993).

The resource allocation approach offers a view that permits linking the two sides, loss in overall cognitive resources and targeted focus on improvement in select domains. For instance, recent studies have taken the functionalist approach to understanding how old adults allocate their resources across different domains of daily functioning. Thus far, the evidence suggests that old adults allocate resources in ways that are adaptive to the physical, cognitive, and motivational constraints of old age (e.g. Kemper et al., 2003; Krampe and Baltes, 2003; S.-C. Li, et al., 2001a; Lindenberger et al., 2000). We expect future research to pursue this line of reasoning – for instance, by linking it to conceptions of executive control.

The Ageing Brain of The Ageing Mind

At the neurobiological level, brain ageing involves both neuroanatomical and neurochemical changes. Anatomically, there are structural losses in neurons and synaptic connections (see Raz, 2000, for review). Neurochemically, there is evidence for deterioration in various neurotransmitter systems (Schneider and Rowe, 1996, for review). Neuroanatomical and neurochemical declines notwithstanding, recent evidence indicates that the ageing brain still shows functional and structural plasticity.

ATTENUATED NEUROMODULATION. Among different neurotransmitter systems, the catecholamines, including dopamine (DA) and norepinephrine (NE), are important neurochemical underpinnings of age-related cognitive impairments. Across the adult lifespan, dopaminergic function in the basal ganglia and various regions of the frontal cortex decreases by 5–10 percent each decade (e.g. Kaasinen et al., 2000). Furthermore, research since the mid 1980s suggests that catecholamines modulate the prefrontal cortex's working memory functions in utilizing briefly activated cortical representations of external stimuli to regulate attention (see Arnsten, 1998, for review). Recent computational theories have aimed at exploring principles for relating age-related declines in dopaminergic modulation with different aspects of cognitive ageing, such as deficits in error processing (Nieuwenhuis, 2002), context memory (Braver *et al.*, 2001), and neural information-processing fidelity along with the ensuing consequences for cortical representational distinctiveness and cognitive plasticity (S.-C. Li *et al.*, 2001b).

FUNCTIONAL AND STRUCTURAL PLASTIC-ITY. Recent neuroimaging studies provide evidence for functional reorganization in the ageing brain. In comparison to the more lateralized cortical information processing in young adults, people in their 60s and beyond showed bilateralized (bihemispheric) activity during retrieval and during both verbal and spatial working memory tasks. These findings of cortical functional reorganization in old age suggest that the ageing brain still has functional plasticity that enables it to adapt to reduced brain integrity, on the one hand, and to benefit from neurocognitive and behavioral compensatory mechanisms, on the other (for reviews, see Cabeza, 2002; Reuter-Lorenz, 2002). Furthermore, there is new evidence for neurogenesis (growth of new neurons) in adulthood and old age. Recent findings indicate that broader experiences gained in complex environments stimulate the growth of new hippocampal neurons in the adult brain of various species, including humans (see Gross, 2000, for review).

OUTLOOKS: INTEGRATING THE MULTIPLE FACETS AND LEVELS OF PSYCHOLOGICAL AGEING

The various subfields of psychological ageing research are increasingly in need of overarching frameworks for integration (cf. S.-C. Li, 2001, 2002; Staudinger and Lindenberger, 2003; Stern and Carstensen, 2000). The multilevel analyses discussed in the opening sections could serve as a framework for integration. A major challenge for future research is to understand, on a behavioral level, the mechanisms of adaptive resource allocation that help individuals compensate for the inevitable loss of neurobiological and psychological resources in old age and, at the same time, permit them to direct a sizable share of their resources to maintaining functions and addressing new tasks that are unique to the conduct and meaning of life in old age.

Some integrative research undertakings have gradually commenced. For instance, to integrate better the larger contexts of human–environment exchange and evolutionary–ontogenetic dynamics, some researchers have started to examine human ageing through the lens of *developmental biocultural co-constructivism* (e.g. P. B. Baltes and Singer, 2001; S.-C. Li, 2003) and begun to explore cultural influences on psychological ageing at a microlevel of analysis (e.g. Lachman, 2001; Park *et al.*, 1999). While the benefits of evolutionary selection and the efficacy of neurobiological implementations of the mind decrease with ageing, the need for environmental and cultural support increases. Given the growing evidence showing that even in old age, there is still development plasticity at the behavioral, cognitive, and neuronal levels, future research efforts should be devoted towards strengthening our understanding of the reciprocal, biogenetic, and experiential–environmental influences on human ageing.

As for relating the biocultural architecture of ageing to mechanisms of adaptive resource allocation that involve selection, optimization, and compensation (e.g. P. B. Baltes and Baltes, 1990; Freund and Baltes, 1998), it is important for future research to investigate how declines in psychological resources may be compensated by neural compensatory mechanisms, by the individual's more selective allocation of these resources to different task domains at the behavioral level, and by contextual supports such as cognitive (e.g. Dixon and Bäckman, 1995; K. Z. H. Li *et al.*, 2001) or physical training (e.g. Kramer, 1999). Better environmental stimulus and contextual supports are helpful in overcoming age-related deficits in the effortful, self-initiated processes implicated in various memory and attentional tasks (e.g. Craik, 1986), thereby creating better societal conditions for productive ageing (Willis *et al.*, 1997). Furthermore, also of much interest are issues on how a lifetime of expertise in specific skill domains (e.g. Krampe and Ericsson, 1996; Salthouse, 1988), as well as the expertise in general life pragmatics (e.g. P. B. Baltes and Staudinger, 2000), may buffer age-related losses in different domains.

If there is a conundrum left, it is the context and resource status of the oldest-old. Although this topic has not been prominent in the present chapter, we need to point out that there is reason for more attention to the oldest-old (P. B. Baltes and Smith, 2003). First systematic and longitudinal evidence on the psychological functioning of the oldest-old (aged 85+), the Fourth Age, is worrying. The greater the size and generality of the losses and the seemingly much reduced malleability in the last period of life (P. B. Baltes and Mayer, 1999; Singer *et al.*, 2003b), the more important it is that we make the Fourth Age a new focus of research activities.

FURTHER READING

Baltes, M. M. (1996). *The many faces of dependency in old age*. New York: Cambridge University Press.

Baltes, P. B., and K. U. Mayer, eds. (1999). *The Berlin Aging Study: aging from 70 to 100*. New York: Cambridge University Press.

Baltes, P. B., and J. Smith (2003). "New frontiers in the future of aging: from successful aging of the young old to the dilemmas of the fourth age," *Gerontology*, 49: 123–35.

Birren, J. E., and K. W. Schaie, eds. (2001). *Handbook of the psychology of aging*, 5th edn. San Diego, Calif.: Academic Press.

Craik, F. I. M., and T. A. Salthouse, eds. (2000). *The handbook of aging and cognition*, 2nd edn. Hillsdale, N.J.: Erlbaum.

Hedden, T., and J. D. E. Gabrieli (2004). "Insights into the aging mind: a view from cognitive neuroscience," *Nature Reviews Neuroscience*, 5: 87–96.

Li, S.-C. (2003). "Biocultural orchestration of developmental plasticity across levels: the interplay of biology and culture in shaping the mind and behavior across the lifespan," *Psychological Bulletin*, 129: 171–94.

Staudinger, U. M., and U. Lindenberger, eds. (2003). *Understanding human development: dialogues with lifespan psychology*. Dordrecht, Netherlands: Kluwer.

REFERENCES

Ackerman, P. L. (1988). "Determinants of individual differences during skill acquisition: cognitive abilities and information processing," *Journal of Experimental Psychology: General*, 117: 288–318.

(1996). "A theory of adult intellectual development: process, personality, interests, and knowledge," *Intelligence*, 22 (2): 227–57.

Anstey, K. J., Hofer, S. M., and M. A. Luszcz, (2003). "Cross-sectional and longitudinal patterns of dedifferentiation in late-life cognitive and sensory functions: the effects of age, ability, attrition, and occasion of measurement," *Journal of Experimental Psychology: General*, 132: 470–87.

Arnsten, A. F. T. (1998). "Catecholamine modulation of prefrontal cortical cognitive function," *Trends in Cognitive Sciences*, 2: 436–47.

Aspinwall, L. G., and U. M. Staudinger, eds. (2003). *A psychology of human strengths: fundamental questions and future directions for a positive psychology*. Washington, D.C.: American Psychological Association.

Babcock, R. L., Laguna, K. D., and S. C. Roesch (1997). "A comparison of the factor structure of processing speed for younger and older adults: testing the assumption of measurement equivalence across age groups," *Psychology and Aging*, 12: 268–76.

Baddeley, A. D. (1986). *Working memory*. Oxford: Clarendon Press.

Baddeley, A. D., Baddeley, H. A., Bucks, R. S., and G. K. Wilcock (2001). "Attentional control in Alzheimer's disease," *Brain*, 124: 1492–1508.

Baltes, B. B., and H. A. Heydens-Gahir (2003). "Reduction of work–family conflict through the use of selection," *Journal of Applied Psychology*, 188: 1005–18.

Baltes, M. M. (1996). *The many faces of dependency in old age*. New York: Cambridge University Press.

(1998). "The psychiatry of the oldest-old: the fourth age," *Current Opinion in Psychology*, 11: 411–15.

Baltes, M. M., and L. L. Carstensen (1996). "The process of successful aging," *Aging and Society*, 16: 397–422.

Baltes, M. M., and F. R. Lang (1997). "Everyday functioning and successful aging: the impact of resources," *Psychology and Aging*, 12: 433–43.

Baltes, P. B. (1983). "Life-span developmental psychology: observations on history and theory revisited." In R. M. Lerner, ed., *Developmental psychology: historical and philosophical perspectives*. Hillsdale, N.J.: Erlbaum, pp. 79–111.

(1987). "Theoretical propositions of life-span developmental psychology: on the dynamics between growth and decline," *Developmental Psychology*, 23: 611–26.

(1991). "The many faces of human ageing: toward a psychological culture of old age," *Psychological Medicine*, 21: 837–54.

(1993). "The aging mind: potential and limits," *Gerontologist*, 33: 580–94.

(1997). "On the incomplete architecture of human ontogeny: selection, optimization, and compensation as foundation of developmental theory," *American Psychologist*, 52: 366–80.

Baltes, P. B., and M. M. Baltes (1980). "Plasticity and variability in psychological aging: methodological and theoretical issues." In G. E. Gurski, ed., *Determining the effects of aging on the central nervous system*. Berlin: Schering, pp. 41–66.

(1990). "Psychological perspectives on successful aging: the model of selective optimization with compensation." In P. B. Baltes and M. M. Baltes, eds., *Successful aging: perspectives from the behavioral sciences*. New York: Cambridge University Press, pp. 1–34.

Baltes, P. B., and L. R. Goulet (1970). "Status and issues of a life-span developmental psychology." In L. R. Goulet and P. B. Baltes, eds., *Life-span developmental psychology: research and theory*. New York: Academic Press, pp. 4–21.

Baltes, P. B., and P. Graf (1996). "Psychological aspects of aging: facts and frontiers." In D. Magnusson, ed., *The life-span development of individuals: behavioural, neurobiological and psychosocial perspectives*. Cambridge: Cambridge University Press, pp. 427–59.

Baltes, P. B., and R. Kliegl (1992). "Further testing of limits of cognitive plasticity: negative age differences in a mnemonic skill are robust," *Developmental Psychology*, 28: 121–5.

Baltes, P. B., and G. V. Labouvie (1973). "Adult development of intellectual performance: description, explanation, modification." In C. Eisdorfer and M. P. Lawton, eds., *The psychology of adult development and aging*. Washington, D.C.: American Psychological Association, pp. 157–219.

Baltes, P. B., and U. Lindenberger (1997). "Emergence of a powerful connection between sensory and cognitive functions across the adult life span: a new window at the study of cognitive aging?" *Psychology and Aging*, 12: 12–21.

Baltes, P. B., and K. U. Mayer, eds. (1999). *The Berlin Aging Study: aging from 70 to 100*. New York: Cambridge University Press.

Baltes, P. B., and K. W. Schaie (1976). "On the plasticity of intelligence in adulthood and old age: where Horn and Donaldson fail," *American Psychologist*, 31: 720–5.

Baltes, P. B., and T. Singer (2001). "Plasticity and the aging mind: an exemplar of the biocultural orchestration of brain and behaviour," *European Review: Interdisciplinary Journal of the Academia Europaea*, 9: 59–76.

Baltes, P. B., and J. Smith (2003). "New frontiers in the future of aging: from successful aging of the young old to the dilemmas of the fourth age," *Gerontology*, 49: 123–35.

Baltes, P. B., and U. M. Staudinger (2000). "Wisdom: a metaheuristic (pragmatic) to orchestrate mind and virtue toward excellence," *American Psychologist*, 55: 122–36.

Baltes, P. B., Lindenberger, U., and U. M. Staudinger (1998). "Life-span theory in developmental psychology." In R. M. Lerner, ed., *Handbook of child psychology*, Vol. I: *Theoretical models of human development*, 5th edn. New York: Wiley, pp. 1029–143.

Baltes, P. B., Staudinger, U. M., and U. Lindenberger (1999). "Lifespan psychology: theory and application to intellectual functioning," *Annual Review of Psychology*, 50: 471–507.

Barkow, J. H., Cosmides, L., and J. Tooby (1992). *The adapted mind: evolutionary psychology and the generation of culture*. New York: Oxford University Press.

Birren, J. E., ed. (1959). *Handbook of aging and the individual: psychological and biological aspects*. Chicago, Ill.: University of Chicago Press.

Birren, J. E., and L. M. Fisher (1995). "Aging and speed of behavior: possible consequences for psychological functioning," *Annual Review of Psychology*, 46: 329–53.

Birren, J. E., and K. W. Schaie, eds. (1977). *Handbook of the psychology of aging*. New York: Van Nostrand Reinhold.

Blanchard-Fields, F., and T. M. Hess, eds. (1996). *Perspectives on cognitive change in adulthood and aging*. New York: McGraw-Hill.

Boesch, E. E. (1991). *Symbolic action theory and cultural psychology*. Heidelberg: Springer.

Botwinick, J. (1967). *Cognitive processes in maturity and old age*. New York: Springer.

Brandtstädter, J. (1984). "Personal and social control over development: some implications of an action perspective in life-span developmental psychology." In P. B. Baltes and O. G. Brim, Jr., eds., *Life-span development and behavior*, vol. VI. New York: Academic Press, pp. 1–32.

Brandtstädter, J., and W. Greve (1994). "Explaining the resilience of the aging self: reply to Carstensen and Freund," *Developmental Review*, 14: 93–102.

Brandtstädter, J., and R. M. Lerner, eds. (1999). *Action and self development: theory and research through the life span*. Thousand Oaks, Calif.: Sage.

Brandtstädter, J., and D. Wentura (1995). "Adjustment to shifting possibility frontiers in later life: complementary adaptive modes." In R. A. Dixon and L. Bäckman eds., *Compensating for psychological deficits and declines: managing losses and promoting gains*. Hillsdale, N.J.: Erlbaum, pp. 83–106.

Braver, T. S., Barch, D. M., Keys, B. A., Carter, C. S., Cohen, J. D., Kaye, J. A., *et al*. (2001). "Context processing in older adults: evidence for a theory relating cognitive control to neurobiology in healthy aging," *Journal of Experimental Psychology: General*, 130: 746–63.

Cabeza, R. (2002). "Hemispheric asymmetry reduction in older adults: the Harold model," *Psychology and Aging*, 17: 85–100.

Camp, C. J. (1998). "Memory intervention for normal and pathological old adults," *Annual Review of Gerontology and Geriatrics*, 18: 155–89.

Carstensen, L. L. (1995). "Evidence for a life-span theory of socioemotional selectivity," *Current Directions in Psychological Science*, 4: 151–6.

Carstensen, L. L., Isaacowitz, D. M., and S. T. Charles (1999). "Taking time seriously: a theory of socioemotional selectivity," *American Psychologist*, 54: 165–81.

Cattell, R. B. (1971). *Abilities: their structure, growth, and action*. Boston, Mass.: Houghton Mifflin.

Charlesworth, B. (1994). *Evolution in age-structured populations*, 2nd edn. Cambridge: Cambridge University Press.

Charness, N. (1981). "Search in chess: age and skill differences," *Journal of Experimental Psychology: Human Perception and Performance*, 7: 467–76.

Cohen, J. D., Botvinick, M., and C. S. Carter (2000). "Anterior cingulate and prefrontal cortex: who's in control?" *Nature Neuroscience*, 3: 421–3.

Cole, M. (1996). "Interacting minds in a life-span perspective: a cultural/historical approach to culture and cognitive development." In P. B. Baltes and U. M. Staudinger, eds., *Interactive minds: life-span perspectives on the social foundation of cognition*. New York: Cambridge University Press, pp. 59–87.

Commons, M. L., Sinnott, J. D., Richards, F. A., and C. Armon, eds. (1989). *Adult development: comparisons and applications of developmental models*, Vol. I. New York: Praeger.

Craik, F. I. M. (1986). "A functional account of age differences in memory." In F. Klix and H. Hagendorf, eds., *Human memory and cognitive capabilities, mechanisms, and performance*. Amsterdam: North-Holland, pp. 409–22.

Craik, F. I. M., and T. A. Salthouse, eds. (2000). *The handbook of aging and cognition*, 2nd edn. Hillsdale, N.J.: Erlbaum.

de Frias, C. M., Dixon, R. A., and L. Bäckman (2003). "Use of memory compensation strategies is related to psychosocial and health indicators," *Journal of Gerontology: Psychological Sciences*, 58B: 12–22.

Dixon, R. A., and L. Bäckman, eds. (1995). *Compensating for psychological deficits and declines: managing losses and promoting gains*. Mahwah, N.J.: Erlbaum.

Dixon, R. A., and P. B. Baltes (1986). 'Toward life-span research on the functions and pragmatics of intelligence.' In R. J. Sternberg and R. K. Wagner, eds., *Practical intelligence: nature and origins of competence in the everyday world*. New York: Cambridge University Press, pp. 203–34.

Durham, W. H. (1991). *Coevolution: genes, culture and human diversity*. Stanford, Calif.: Stanford University Press.

Eckensberger, L. H. (2001). "Action theory: psychological." In N.J. Smelser and P. B. Baltes, eds., *International encyclopedia of the social and behavioral sciences*. Oxford: Elsevier Science, pp. 45–9.

Eisdorfer, C., and G. V. Lawton, eds. (1973). *The psychology of adult development and aging*. Washington, D.C.: American Psychological Association.

Emmons, R. A. (1996). "Striving and feeling: personal goals and subjective well-being." In P. M. Gollwitzer and J. A. Bargh, eds., *The psychology of action: linking cognition and motivation to behavior*. New York: Guilford Press, pp. 313–37.

Ericsson, K. A. (2003). "The search for general abilities and basic capacities: theoretical implications from the modifiability and complexity of mechanisms mediating expert performance." In R. J. Sternberg and E. L. Grigorenko, eds., *Perspectives on the psychology of abilities, competencies, and expertise*. New York: Cambridge University Press, pp. 93–125.

Ericsson, K. A., and J. Smith, eds. (1991). *Towards a general theory of expertise: prospects and limits*. New York: Cambridge University Press.

Ericsson, K. A., Krampe, R. T., and C. Tesch-Römer (1993). "The role of deliberate practice in the acquisition of expert performance," *Psychology Review*, 100 (3): 363–406.

Erikson, E. H. (1959). *Identity and the life cycle*. New York: International University Press.

Finch, C. E. (1990). *Longevity, senescence, and the genome*. Chicago, Ill.: University of Chicago Press.

Finch, C. E. (1996). "Biological bases for plasticity during aging of individual life histories." In D. Magnusson, ed., *The life-span development of individuals: behavioral, neurobiological and psychosocial perspective*. Cambridge: Cambridge University Press, pp. 488–511.

Freund, A. M., and P. B. Baltes (1998). "Selection, optimization, and compensation as strategies of life-management: correlations with subjective indicators of successful aging," *Psychology and Aging*, 13: 531–43.

(2000). "The orchestration of selection, optimization, and compensation: an action-theoretical conceptualization of a theory of developmental regulation." In W. J. Perrig and A. Grob, eds., *Control of human behavior, mental processes, and consciousness*. Mahwah, N.J.: Erlbaum, pp. 35–58.

(2002a). "Life-management strategies of selection, optimization, and compensation: measurement by self-report and construct validity," *Journal of Personality and Social Psychology*, 82: 642–62.

(2002b). "The adaptiveness of selection, optimization, and compensation as strategies of life management: evidence from a preference study on proverbs," *Journal of Gerontology: Psychological Sciences*, 57B: 426–34.

Freund, A. M., and N. C. Ebner (2005). "The aging self: shifting from promoting gains to balancing losses." In W. Greve, K. Rothermund and D. Wentura, eds., *The adaptive self: personal continuity and intentional self-development*. Ashland, Ohio: Hogrefe & Huber, pp. 185–202.

Freund, A. M., and M. Riediger (2001). "What I have and what I do: the role of resource loss and gain throughout life," *Applied Psychology: An International Review*, 50: 370–80.

(2003). "Successful aging." In R. M. Lerner, M. A. Easterbrooks, and J. Mistry, eds., *Comprehensive handbook of psychology*, Vol. VI: *Developmental psychology*. New York: Wiley, pp. 601–28.

Freund, A. M., Li, K. Z. H., and P. B. Baltes (1999). "Successful development and aging: the role of selection, optimization, and compensation." In J. Brandtstädter and R. M. Lerner, eds., *Action and self development: theory and research through the life span*. Thousand Oaks, Calif.: Sage Publications, pp. 401–34.

Gehlen, A. (1956). *Urmensch und Spätkultur*. Bonn: Athenäum.

Ghisletta, P., and U. Lindenberger (2003). "Age-based structural dynamics between perceptual speed and knowledge in the Berlin Aging Study: direct evidence for ability dedifferentiation in old age," *Psychology and Aging*, 18: 696–713.

Gigerenzer, G. (1996). "Rationality: why social context matters." In P. B. Baltes and U. M. Staudinger, eds., *Interactive minds: life-span perspectives on the social foundation of cognition*. New York: Cambridge University Press, pp. 317–46.

Gignac, M. A. M., Cott, C., and E. M. Badley (2002). "Adaptation to disability: applying selective optimization with compensation to the behaviors of older adults with osteoarthritis," *Psychology and Aging*, 17: 520–4.

Glass, J. M., Schumacher, E. H., Lauber, E. J., Zurbriggen, E. L., Gmeindl, L., Kieras, D. E., *et al.* (2000). "Aging and the psychological refractory period: task-coordination strategies in young and old adults," *Psychology and Aging*, 15: 571–95.

Gottlieb, G. (1998). "Normally occurring environmental and behavioral influences on gene activity: from central dogma to probabilistic epigenesis," *Psychological Review*, 105: 792–802.

Gross, C. G. (2000). "Neurogenesis in the adult brain: death of a dogma," *Nature Reviews Neuroscience*, 1: 67–73.

Harris, D. B., ed. (1957). *The concept of development*. Minneapolis, Minn.: University of Minnesota Press.

Hayflick, L. (1987). "Biological aging theories." In G. L. Maddox, ed., *The encyclopedia of aging*. New York: Springer, pp. 64–8.

Heckhausen, J. (1999). *Developmental regulation in adulthood: age-normative and sociostructural constraints as adaptive challenges*. New York: Cambridge University Press.

Heckhausen, J., and R. Schulz (1995). "A life-span theory of control," *Psychological Review*, 102: 284–304.

Hertzog, C., and J. R. Nesselroade (2003). "Change in adulthood: an overview of methodological issues," *Psychology and Aging*, 18: 639–57.

Hobfoll, S. E. (2001). "The influence of culture, community, and the nested-self in the stress process: advancing conservation of resources theory," *Applied Psychology: An International Review*, 50: 337–421.

Hofer, S. M., Berg, S., and P. Era (2003). "Evaluating the interdependence of aging-related changes in visual and auditory acuity, balance, and cognitive functioning," *Psychology and Aging*, 18: 285–305.

Horn, J. L. (1970). "Organization of data on life-span development of human abilities." In L. R. Goulet and P. B. Baltes, eds., *Life-span developmental psychology: research and theory*. New York: Academic Press, pp. 423–66.

(1982). "The theory of fluid and crystallized intelligence in relation to concepts of cognitive psychology and aging in adulthood." In F. I. M. Craik and G. E. Trehub, eds., *Aging and cognitive processes: advances in the study of communication and affect*, Vol. VIII. New York: Plenum Press, pp. 237–78.

Hultsch, D. F., MacDonald, S. W. S., Hunter, M. A., Levy-Bencheton, J., and E. Strauss (2000). "Intraindividual variability in cognitive performance in older adults: comparison of adults with mild dementia, adults with arthritis, and healthy adults," *Neuropsychology*, 14: 588–98.

Jones, H. E., and H. Conrad (1933). "The growth and decline of intelligence: a study of a homogeneous group between the ages of ten and sixty," *Genetic Psychological Monographs*, 13: 223–98.

Jopp, D. (2002). "Erfolgreiches Altern: Zum funktionalen Zusammenspiel von personalen Ressourcen und adaptiven Strategien des Lebensmanagements." Doctoral Dissertation, Freie Universität Berlin. http://darwin.inf.fu-berlin.de/2003/50/Titel.pdf.

Kaasinen, V., Vilkman, H., Hietala, J., Någren, K., Helenius, H., Olsson, H., *et al.* (2000). "Age-related dopamine D2/D3 receptor loss in extrastriatal regions of the human brain," *Neurobiology of Aging*, 21: 683–8.

Kemper, S., and A. Sumner (2001). "The structure of verbal abilities in young and old adults," *Psychology and Aging*, 16: 312–22.

Kemper, S., Herman, R. E., and C. H. T. Lian (2003). "The costs of doing two things at once for young and older adults: talking while walking, finger tapping, and ignoring speech or noise," *Psychology and Aging*, 18: 181–92.

Kirkwood, T. B. L., ed. (2003). *Understanding human development: dialogues with lifespan psychology*. Dordrecht, Netherlands: Kluwer.

Klix, F. (1993). *Erwachendes Denken: Geistige Leistungen aus evolutionspsychologischer Sicht*. Heidelberg: Spektrum Akademischer Verlag.

Kramer, A. F. (1999). "Aging, fitness, and neurocognitive function," *Nature*, 400: 418–19.

Krampe, R. T., and P. B. Baltes (2003). "Intelligence as adaptive resource development and resource allocation: a new look through the lenses of SOC and expertise." In R. J. Sternberg and E. L. Grigorenko, eds., *Perspectives on the psychology of abilities, competencies, and expertise*. New York: Cambridge University Press, pp. 31–69.

Krampe, R. T., and K. A. Ericsson (1996). "Maintaining excellence: deliberate practice and elite performance in young and older pianists," *Journal of Experimental Psychology: General*, 125 (4): 331–59.

Krampe, R. T., Rapp, M. A., Bondar, A., and P. B. Baltes (2003). "Selektion, Optimierüng und Kompensation in Doppelaufgaben," *Nervenarzt*, 74: 211–18.

Kray, J., and U. Lindenberger (2000). "Adult age differences in task switching," *Psychology and Aging*, 15: 126–47.

Kunzmann, U., and P. B. Baltes (2003). "Beyond the traditional scope of intelligence: wisdom in action." In R. J. Sternberg, J. Lautrey, and T. I. Lubart, eds., *Models of intelligence: international perspectives*. Washington, D.C.: American Psychological Association, pp. 329–43.

Labouvie-Vief, G. (1982). "Dynamic development and mature autonomy: a theoretical prologue," *Human Development*, 25: 161–91.

Lachman, M. E. (2001). *Handbook of midlife development*. New York: Wiley.

Lang, F. R., Rieckmann, N., and M. M. Baltes (2002). "Adapting to aging losses: do resources facilitate strategies of selection, compensation, and optimization in everyday functioning?" *Journal of Gerontology: Psychological Sciences*, 57B: 501–09.

Lerner, R. M. (2002). *Concepts and theories of human development*. Mahwah, N.J.: Erlbaum.

Li, K. Z. H., Lindenberger, U., Freund, A. M., and P. B. Baltes (2001). "Walking while memorizing: age-related differences in compensatory behavior," *Psychological Science*, 12: 230–7.

Li, S.-C. (2001). "Aging mind: facets and levels of analysis." In N.J. Smelser and P. B. Baltes, eds., *International encyclopedia of the social and behavioral sciences*, Vol. I. Oxford: Elsevier Science, pp. 310–17.

(2002). "Connecting the many levels and facets of cognitive aging," *Current Directions in Psychological Science*, 11: 38–43.

(2003). "Biocultural orchestration of developmental plasticity across levels: the interplay of biology and culture in shaping the mind and behavior across the lifespan," *Psychological Bulletin*, 129 (2): 171–94.

Li, S.-C., Aggen, S. H., Nesselroade, J. R., and P. B. Baltes (2001a). "Short-term fluctuations in elderly people's sensorimotor functioning predict text and spatial memory performance: the MacArthur successful aging studies," *Gerontology*, 47: 100–16.

Li, S.-C., Lindenberger, U., and S. Sikström (2001b). "Aging cognition. From neuromodulation to representation," *Trends in Cognitive Sciences*, 5: 479–86.

Li, S.-C., Lindenberger, U., Hommel, B., Aschersleben, G., Prinz, W., and P. B. Baltes (2004). "Lifespan transformations in the couplings of mental abilities and underlying cognitive processes," *Psychological Science*, 15: 155–63.

Lindenberger, U., and P. B. Baltes (1997). "Intellectual functioning in old and very old age: cross-sectional results from the Berlin Aging Study," *Psychology and Aging*, 12: 410–432.

Lindenberger, U., Marsiske, M., and P. B. Baltes (2000). "Memorizing while walking: increase in dual-task costs from young adulthood to old age," *Psychology and Aging*, 15: 417–36.

Lövden, M., Ghisletta, P., and U. Lindenberger (in press). "Cognition in the Berlin Aging Study (BASE): the first ten years," *Aging, Neuropsychology, and Cognition*.

Magnusson, D., ed. (1996). *The life-span development of individuals: behavioural, neurobiological, and psychosocial perspectives. A synthesis*. Cambridge: Cambridge University Press.

Marsiske, M., Lang, F. R., Baltes, M. M., and P. B. Baltes (1995). "Selective optimization with compensation: life-span perspectives on successful human development." In R. A. Dixon and L. Bäckman, eds., *Compensation for psychological defects and declines: managing losses and promoting gains*. Hillsdale, N.J.: Erlbaum, pp. 35–79.

Martin, G. M., Austad, S. N., and T. E. Johnson (1996). "Genetic analysis of aging: role of oxidative damage and environmental stresses," *Nature Genetics*, 13: 25–34.

Mayr, U., Spieler, D., and R. Kliegl (2001). *Aging and executive control*. Howe: Psychology Press.

McArdle, J. J., Ferrer-Caja, E., Hamagami, F., and R. W. Woodcock (2002). "Comparative longitudinal structural analyses of the growth and decline of multiple intellectual abilities over the life span," *Developmental Psychology*, 38: 115–42.

McDown, J. M., and R. J. Shaw (2000). "Attention and aging: a functional perspective." In F. I. M. Craik and T. A. Salthouse, eds., *The handbook of aging and cognition*. Mahwah, N.J.: Erlbaum, pp. 221–91.

Medawar, P. B. (1946). "Old age and natural death," *Modern Quarterly*, 1: 30–56.

Morse, C. K. (1993). "Does variability incease with age? An archival study of cognitive measures," *Psychology and Aging*, 8: 156–64.

Nelson, A. E., and D. Dannefer (1992). "Aged heterogeneity: fact or fiction? The fate of diversity in gerontological research," *Gerontologist*, 32: 17–23.

Neugarten, B. L. (1969). "Continuities and discontinuities of psychological issues into adult life," *Human Development*, 12: 121–30.

Nieuwenhuis, S. (2002). "A computational account of altered error processing in older age: dopamine and error-related processing," *Cognitive, Affective, and Behavioral Neuroscience*, 2: 19–36.

Oettingen, G. (1997). *Psychologie des Zukunftsdenkens*. Göttingen: Hogrefe.

Osiewacz, H. D. (1995). "Molekulare Mechanismen biologischen Alterns," *Biologie in unserer Zeit*, 25: 336–44.

Park, D. C., and N. Schwarz, eds. (2000). *Cognitive aging: a primer*. Philadelphia (u.a.): Psychology Press.

Park, D. C., Smith, A. D., Lautenschlager, G., Earles, J. L., Frieske, D., Zwahr, M., *et al.* (1996). "Mediators of long-term memory performance across the life span," *Psychology and Aging*, 11 (4): 621–37.

Park, D. C., Nisbett, R. E., and T. Hedden (1999). "Aging, culture, and cognition," *Journal of Gerontology: Psychological Sciences*, 54B: 75–84.

Perfect, T. J., and E. A. Maylor (2000). *Models of cognitive aging*. New York: Oxford University Press.

Pressey, S. L., Janney, J. E., and R. G. Kuhlen (1939). *Life: a psychological survey*. New York: Harper.

Rabbitt, P., Osman, P., Moore, B., and B. Stollery (2001). "There are stable individual differences in performance variability, both from moment to moment and from day to day," *Quarterly Journal of Experimental Psychology: Section A*, 54: 981–1003.

Rapp, M., Krampe, R. T., and P. B. Baltes (in press). "Preservation of skills in Alzheimers disease: the case of postural control." *American Journal of Geriatrics*.

Raz, N. (2000). "Aging of the brain and its impact on cognitive performance: integration of structural and functional findings." In F. I. M. Craik and T. A. Salthouse, eds., *The handbook of aging and cognition*. Mahwah, N.J.: Erlbaum, pp. 1–90.

Reingold, E. M., Charness, N., Pomplun, M., and D. M. Stampe (2001). "Visual span in expert chess players: evidence from eye movements," *Psychological Science*, 12: 48–55.

Reuter-Lorenz, P. A. (2002). "New visions of the aging mind and brain," *Trends in Cognitive Sciences*, 6: 394–400.

Riediger, M. (2001). "On the dynamic relations among multiple goals: intergoal conflict and intergoal facilitation in younger and older adulthood." Doctoral dissertation, Freie Universität Berlin. www.diss.fu-berlin.de/2001/266.

Riediger, M., Freund, A. M., and P. B. Baltes (2003). "Managing life through personal goals – a strength of later adulthood? Goal integration and persistent pursuit in younger and older adults." Unpublished manuscript, Max Planck Institute for Human Development, Berlin.

Salthouse, T. A. (1988). "Resource-reduction interpretations of cognitive aging," *Developmental Review*, 8: 238–72.

(1991). *Theoretical perspectives on cognitive aging*. Hilldale, N.J.: Erlbaum.

(1996). "The processing-speed theory of adult age differences in cognition," *Psychological Review*, 103: 403–28.

Salthouse, T. A., Hancock, H. E., Meinz, E. J., and D. Z. Hambrick (1996). "Interrelations of age, visual acuity, and cognitive functioning," *Journal of Gerontology: Pychological Sciences*, 51B (6): 317–30.

Schaie, K. W. (1996). *Adult intellectual development: the Seattle Longitudinal Study*. New York: Cambridge University Press.

(2001). "Cognitive aging." In N.J. Smelser and P. B. Baltes, eds., *International encyclopedia of the social and behavioral sciences*. Oxford: Elsevier Science, pp. 2072–5.

Schneider, E. L., and J. W. Rowe (1996). *Handbook of the biology of aging*, 4th edn. San Diego, Calif.: Academic Press.

Schönpflug, W. (2001). "Psychology: overview." In N.J. Smelser and P. B. Baltes, eds., *International encyclopedia of the social and behavioral sciences*. Oxford: Elsevier Science, pp. 12409–16.

Schooler, C., and M. S. Mulatu (2001). "The reciprocal effects of leisure time activities and intellectual functioning in older people: a longitudinal analysis," *Psychology and Aging*, 16: 466–82.

Schooler, C., Mulatu, M. S., and G. Oates (1999). "The continuing effects of substantively complex work on the intellectual functioning of older workers," *Psychology and Aging*, 14: 483–506.

Singer, T., Lindenberger, U., and P. B. Baltes (2003a). "Plasticity of memory for new learning in very old age: a story of major loss?" *Psychology and Aging*, 18: 306–17.

Singer, T., Verhaeghen, P., Ghisletta, P., Lindenberger, U., and P. B. Baltes (2003b). "The fate of cognition in very old age: six-year longitudinal findings in the Berlin Aging Study (BASE)," *Psychology and Aging*, 18: 318–31.

Smelser, N.J., and P. B. Baltes, eds. (2001). *International encyclopedia of the social and behavioral sciences*. Oxford: Elsevier Science.

Staudinger, U. M., and U. Lindenberger, eds. (2003). *Understanding human development: dialogues with lifespan psychology*. Dordrecht, Netherlands: Kluwer Academic Publishers.

Staudinger, U. M., Marsiske, M., and P. B. Baltes (1995). "Resilience and reserve capacity in later adulthood: potentials and limits of development across the life span." In D. Cicchetti and D. Cohen, eds., *Developmental psychopathology*, Vol. II: *Risk, disorder, and adaptation*. New York: Wiley, pp. 801–47.

Stern, P. C., and L. L. Carstensen (2000). *The aging mind*. Washingtons, D.C.: National Academy Press.

Tetens, J. N. (1777). *Philosophische Versuche über die menschliche Natur und ihre Entwicklung*. Leipzig: Weidmanns Erben und Reich.

Thomae, H., ed. (1979). *The concept of development and life-span developmental psychology*, Vol. II. New York: Academic Press.

Thompson, L. A. (1995). "Encoding and memory for visible speech and gestures: a comparison between young and older adults," *Psychology and Aging*, 10: 215–28.

Uttal, D. H., and M. Perlmutter (1989). "Toward a broader conceptualization of development: the role of gains and losses across the life span," *Developmental Review*, 9: 101–32.

von Cranach, M., and F. Tschan (2001). "Psychology of action planning." In N.J. Smelser and P. B. Baltes, eds., *International encyclopedia of the social and behavioral sciences*. Oxford: Elsevier Science, pp. 41–5.

Welford, A. T. (1958). *Aging and human skill*. London: Oxford University Press.

(1965). "Performance, biological mechanisms, and age: a theoretical sketch." In A. T. Welford and J. E. Birren, eds., *Behavior, aging, and the nervous system*. Springfield, Ill.: Thomas, pp. 3–20.

Wiese, B. S., and A. M. Freund (2001). "Zum Einfluss persönlicher Prioritätensetzungen auf Maße der Stimuluspräferenz," *Zeitschrift für Experimentelle Psychologie*, 48: 57–73.

Wiese, B. S., Freund, A. M., and P. B. Baltes (2000). "Selection, optimization, and compensation: an action-related approach to work and partnership," *Journal of Vocational Behavior*, 57: 273–300.

Wiese, B. S., Freund, A. M., and P. B. Baltes (2002). "Subjective career success and emotional well-being: longitudinal predictive power of selection, optimization, and compensation," *Journal of Vocational Behaviour*, 60: 321–35.

Willis, S. L. (1990). "Contributions of cognitive training research to understanding late life potential." In M. Perlmutter, ed., *Late-life potential*. Washington, D.C.: The Gerontological Society of America, pp. 25–42.

Willis, S. L., Schaie, K. W., and M. Hayward, eds. (1997). *Societal mechanisms for maintaining competence in old age*. New York: Springer.

Wilson, T. (2002). *Strangers to ourselves*. Cambridge, Mass.: Harvard University Press.

Yates, E., and L. A. Benton (1995). "Biological senescence: loss of integration and resilience," *Canadian Journal on Aging*, 14: 106–20.

Zacks, R. T., Hasher, L., and K. Z. H. Li (2000). "Human memory." In F. I. M. Craik and T. A. Salthouse, eds., *Handbook of aging and cognition*. Hillsdale, N.J.: Erlbaum, pp. 293–357.

The Biological Science of Human Ageing

THOMAS B. L. KIRKWOOD

Over the last few decades, important advances have been made in understanding the biological basis of human ageing. Once dismissed as simply too complex for serious study, we now have insight into the nature of the genetic factors influencing longevity, the molecular and cellular mechanisms underlying the ageing process, and the environmental and lifestyle factors that can modulate individual health trajectories through later life. This knowledge is far from complete. Nevertheless, what is known already provides a sound basis for beginning to construct interdisciplinary links between biological, clinical and social gerontology. This chapter briefly surveys the current state of the biological science of human ageing, while indicating the potential for exciting new links with other branches of the field.

WHY AGEING OCCURS

One of the key questions addressed by biological gerontologists is the nature of the genetic contribution to longevity. How has it evolved? How does it work? It is clear on several grounds that ageing and longevity are influenced by genes (Finch and Tanzi, 1997). First, there are significant lifespan differences between different inbred strains of laboratory animals. Second, lifespans of human monozygotic twin pairs are statistically more similar to each other than lifespans of dizygotic twins. Third, studies of simple organisms like fruit flies, nematode worms and yeast have identified gene mutations that affect duration of life. However, it is also clear that genes account for only about 25 per cent of what determines human longevity (Finch and Tanzi,

1997; Cournil and Kirkwood, 2001). So what is the nature of the genetic control of ageing and how has it evolved?

We need to begin by remarking that most animals in the natural world die young. Out of a population of newborn wild mice, for example, nine out of ten of them will be dead before 10 months even though half of the same animals reared in captivity would still be alive at 2 years (Austad, 1997). Animals survive much longer when protected from natural hazards like predators, starvation and cold. But even if we protect them from such hazards all the mice will die within a few years, having spent their last months in the state of increasing frailty that we call senescence. Thus, ageing is in one sense an artifact of protected environments, but it is also an intrinsic biological process from which there appears to be no escape, except in species that do not exhibit senescence at all (see, for example, Martinez, 1997).

The fact that ageing is rarely seen in natural animal populations speaks tellingly against the first (and still popular) explanation of ageing, namely, that ageing is a genetically programmed means to limit population size and avoid overcrowding. A related idea is that ageing helps to facilitate the turnover of generations and thereby aid the adaptation of organisms to changing environments. The flaws in these arguments have been recognised by biological gerontologists for many years (see review by Kirkwood and Cremer, 1982). First, because ageing has a negligible impact on organisms in their natural environment it clearly cannot serve to control population size (Medawar, 1952). Animals die young, as previously remarked. They do not, for the most part, live long enough for ageing to exert any effect on their survival. Therefore, a basic premise of the ageing gene hypothesis can be discounted. Second, because animals die young, natural selection cannot exert a *direct* influence over the process of senescence. It is hard to identify any process through which an ageing gene might have evolved. Indeed, the failure of natural selection to control tightly the late stages of the life history is at the heart of the evolutionary theory of ageing, as discussed below. Third, even if neither of the above objections applied, the ageing gene concept has a major logical fault. Since ageing is clearly deleterious to the individual organism, any individual in whom the hypothetical ageing gene was inactivated by mutation would enjoy an advantage within the population, so freedom from ageing should spread. The only way this could be prevented is by an advantage to the species or group that outweighs the disadvantage for the individual. Such arguments are very hard to construct. No one has yet been able to suggest a plausible basis for such 'group selection' to operate in the broad context of ageing.

Instead of being programmed to die, as the ageing gene concept suggests, organisms are genetically programmed to survive. However, in spite of a formidable array of survival mechanisms, most species appear not to be programmed well enough to last indefinitely. The key to understanding why this should be so, and what governs how long a survival period should be catered for, comes from looking once more at the data from survival patterns in wild populations. If 90 per cent of wild mice are dead by the age of 10 months, any investment in programming for survival much beyond this point can benefit at most 10 per cent of the population. This immediately suggests that there will be little evolutionary advantage in programming long-term survival capacity into a mouse. The argument is further strengthened when we observe that nearly all of the survival mechanisms required by the mouse to combat intrinsic deterioration (DNA damage, protein oxidation, etc.) require metabolic resources. Metabolic resources are scarce, as is evidenced by the fact that the major cause of mortality for wild mice is cold, due to insufficient energy to maintain body temperature. From a Darwinian point of view, the mouse will benefit more from investing any spare resource into heat production

or reproduction than into better DNA repair capacity than it needs.

This concept, with its explicit focus on evolution of optimal levels of cell maintenance, is termed the disposable soma theory (Kirkwood, 1977, 1997). In essence, the investments in durability and maintenance of somatic (non-reproductive) tissues are predicted to be sufficient to keep the body in good repair through the normal expectation of life in the wild environment, with some measure of reserve capacity. Thus, it makes sense that mice (with 90 per cent mortality by 10 months) have intrinsic lifespans of around 3 years, while humans (who probably experienced something like 90% mortality by age 50 in our ancestral environment) have intrinsic lifespans limited to about 100 years. The distinction between somatic and reproductive tissues is important because the reproductive cell lineage, or germ line, must be maintained at a level that preserves viability across the generations, whereas the soma needs to serve only a single generation. As far as is known, all species that have a clear distinction between soma and germ line undergo somatic senescence while animals that do not show senescence have germ cells distributed throughout their structure (Bell, 1984).

The above argument clearly identifies the level of extrinsic mortality as the principal driver in the evolution of longevity. If the level of extrinsic mortality is high, the average survival period is short and there is little selection for a high level of maintenance. Any spare resources should go instead toward reproduction. Consequently, the organism is not long-lived even in a protected environment. Conversely, if the level of extrinsic mortality is low, selection is likely to direct a higher investment in building and maintaining a durable soma. Comparative studies bear this prediction out at both the ecological and molecular level. Adaptations that reduce extrinsic mortality (wings, protective shells, large brains) are linked with increased longevity (bats, birds, turtles, humans). Cells from long-lived organisms exhibit greater capacity to repair molecular damage and withstand biochemical stresses than cells from short-lived species (Kapahi *et al.*, 1999; Ogburn *et al.*, 2001).

To this analysis, we can bring two earlier perspectives drawn from evolution theory. Medawar (1952) suggested that, because organisms die young, there is little force of selection to oppose the accumulation within the genome of mutations with late-acting deleterious effects. Under this hypothesis, many different mutations could accumulate, which may vary from individual to individual within the population. Attempts to identify a contribution to ageing from such mutations have had mixed success but it would be surprising if they were entirely absent.

In a second perspective, Williams (1957) suggested that genes with beneficial effects would be favoured by selection even if these genes had adverse effects at later ages. This is known as the theory of 'antagonistic pleiotropy', the term pleiotropy meaning that the same gene can have different effects in different circumstances. Again, the plausibility of this hypothesis rests on the fact that there is negligible survival to older ages in the wild. There is some overlap between some of the predictions from the pleiotropy theory and the disposable soma theory, particularly as regards the idea that evolution may trade longer life for other benefits such as reproduction. However, there are differences. The disposable soma concept is not restricted to trade-offs resulting from pleiotropic characteristics of single genes, whereas there may be pleiotropic gene actions unconnected with maintenance of the soma (Kirkwood and Rose, 1991).

In summary, the evolutionary theories of ageing thus make the following predictions about the genetic factors involved in ageing:

1. There are no specific genes for ageing.
2. Genes of particular importance for ageing and longevity are those governing durability and maintenance of the soma.
3. There may exist other genetically determined trade-offs between benefits to young organisms and their viability at older ages.
4. There may exist a variety of gene mutations with late deleterious effects that contribute to the senescent phenotype.

It is clear that multiple genes probably contribute to the ageing phenotype and a major challenge is therefore to identify how many of each category exist, and which are the most important. A number of ongoing studies are attempting to answer exactly these questions.

Finally, an aspect of the evolutionary understanding of ageing that has not yet received the attention it merits is the extensive evidence that, in addition to genetic and environmental impacts on ageing, intrinsic chance plays an important part (Finch and Kirkwood, 2000). This is directly compatible with the disposable soma concept, which suggests that ageing results from an accumulation of random damage at the cell and molecular level as a consequence of evolved limitations in somatic maintenance and repair. Individuals such as monozygotic twins having identical genetic specification of their somatic maintenance systems will nevertheless, through the actions of chance, experience different accumulations of damage within their various organs. They may also, through intrinsic variations in development, begin life with somatic structures that differ in durability. For example, monozygotic twins show important variations in brain development (Finch and Kirkwood, 2000).

A striking instance of how chance variation affects ageing is found in the nematode worm *Caenorhabditis elegans*, which has been extensively studied as a model for genetic effects on longevity. This tiny animal (1mm long) reproduces mainly as a self-fertilising hermaphrodite, so the production of pure genetic strains is easy. It grows in the laboratory in highly uniform culture conditions, where each worm experiences the same environment. It develops from egg to adult according to a strict developmental programme, so that adult worms contain exactly 959 somatic cells. Yet, when populations of worms are allowed to age, there is marked individual variation in how their tissues deteriorate and a three-fold variation in individual lifespans (Herndon *et al.*, 2002; Kirkwood and Finch, 2002).

HOW AGEING AFFECTS TISSUES

In terms of the mechanisms that lead eventually to age-related frailty, disability and disease (and eventually to increasing mortality), the predictions from the evolutionary theory are clear. Ageing is neither more nor less than the progressive accumulation through life of a variety of random molecular defects that build up within cells and tissues (Figure 1). These defects start to arise very early in life, probably even in utero, but in the early years both the fraction of affected cells and the average burden of damage per affected cell are low. However, over time the faults increase, resulting eventually

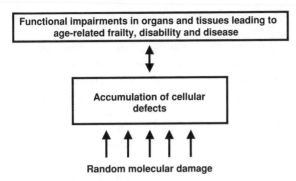

Figure 1. The ageing process is driven by a lifelong accumulation of molecular damage, resulting in gradual increase in the fraction of cells carrying defects. After sufficient time has passed, the increasing levels of these defects interfere with both the performance and functional reserves of tissues and organs, resulting in age-related frailty, disability and disease.

in age-related functional impairment of tissues and organs.

This view of the ageing process makes clear the life-course nature of the underlying mechanisms. Ageing is a continuous process, starting early and developing gradually, instead of being a distinct phase that begins in middle to late life. The view also helps us to re-examine the sometimes controversial relationship between 'normal ageing' and age-related disease. In an extreme version of this view, the term 'normal ageing' is reserved for individuals in whom identifiable pathology is absent, whereas specific age-related diseases, such as Alzheimer's disease, are seen as distinct entities. An obvious difficulty that arises, however, when any attempt is made to draw a line between normal ageing and age-related disease is that as a cohort ages, the fraction of individuals who can be said to be ageing 'normally' declines to very low levels. Whether the word 'normal' can be meaningfully applied to such an atypical subset is debatable.

Although drawing a distinction between normal ageing and disease can have practical relevance, particularly where clinical decisions must be made, its final clarification is likely to have to await further elucidation of the underlying biological mechanisms. The majority of the chronic, degenerative conditions, such as dementia, osteoporosis and osteoarthritis, involve the progressive accumulation of specific types of cellular and molecular lesions. Since the general ageing process, as we have seen, is caused by the accumulation of such lesions, there may be much greater overlap between the causative pathways leading to normal ageing and age-related diseases than has hitherto been generally recognised. In the case of osteoporosis, for example, progressive bone loss from the late 20s onwards is the norm. Whether an individual reaches a critically low bone density, making him or her highly susceptible to fracture, is governed by how much bone mass they had to start with and by their individual rate of bone loss. The process that leads eventually to osteoporosis is thus entirely 'normal', but what distinguishes whether or not this process results in an overtly pathological outcome is a range of moderating factors. In the case of Alzheimer's disease, most people above age 70 have extensive cortical amyloid plaques and neurofibrillary tangles (the so-called 'hallmarks' of classic Alzheimer's disease) even though they may show no evidence of major cognitive decline (Esiri *et al.*, 2001). In this instance, what determines whether or not the diagnosis of Alzheimer's disease is called for may be not so much the presence of lesions as which specific targets are affected.

MECHANISMS OF CELLULAR DAMAGE

Ageing is highly complex, involving multiple mechanisms at different levels. Nevertheless, recent evidence suggests that several of the most important mechanisms are linked via endogenous stress-induced DNA damage caused by reactive oxygen species (ROS; also known as 'free radicals') (Martin *et al.*, 1996; von Zglinicki *et al.*, 2001). Understanding how such damage contributes to age-related changes requires that we explain how these different mechanisms relate to each other and potentially interact. Of particular significance are the contributions of stress-induced damage to cellular DNA through (i) damage to nuclear DNA and its repair, (ii) damage to telomeric DNA and its contribution to telomere-driven cell senescence, and (iii) damage to and the accumulation of mutations in mitochondrial DNA.

DNA damage and repair

One of the most important targets of oxidative damage within cells is DNA, particularly since damage to DNA can readily accumulate, whereas damage to other targets such as proteins and membranes can be removed when these components of the cell are turned over. Numerous studies have reported age-related increases in somatic mutation and other forms of DNA damage, suggesting that an important determinant of the rate of ageing at the cell and molecular level is the capacity for DNA repair (Promislow 1994; Bürkle *et al.*, 2002).

Although DNA damage may take many forms, it is estimated that oxidative damage is among the most important, accounting for large numbers of oxidative hits per cell per day. A key player in the immediate cellular response to ROS-induced DNA damage is the enzyme poly(ADP-ribose) polymerase-1 (PARP-1; Bürkle *et al.*, 2002). Grube and Bürkle (1992) assessed poly(ADP-ribosyl)ation capacity of mononuclear leukocytes from mammalian species and discovered a strong, positive correlation with the species-specific lifespan. In a similar vein, it was found that human centenarians, who have often maintained remarkably good general health, have a significantly greater poly(ADP-ribosyl)ation capacity than the general population (Muiras *et al.*, 1998). Overall, the picture is emerging that PARP-1, which functions as a negative regulator of DNA-damage induced genomic instability (Meyer *et al.*, 2000), tunes the vulnerability to constant attack by endogenous and exogenous DNA-damaging agents and may therefore play a role in determining the rate of ageing.

Telomeres and replicative senescence

In many human somatic tissues a decline in cellular division capacity with age appears to be linked to the fact that the telomeres, which protect the ends of chromosomes, get progressively shorter as cells divide (Kim *et al.*, 2002). This is due to the absence of the enzyme telomerase, which is normally expressed only in germ cells (in testis and ovary) and in certain adult stem cells. Some have suggested that in dividing somatic cells telomeres act as an intrinsic 'division counter', perhaps to protect us against runaway cell division as happens in cancer but causing ageing as the price for this protection (Campisi, 1997). Erosion of telomeres below a critical length appears to trigger activation of the same kinds of cell cycle checkpoint, especially the p53/p21/pRb system, as

are involved in the more general cellular response to DNA damage.

While the loss of telomeric DNA is often attributed mainly to the so-called 'end-replication' problem – the inability of the normal DNA copying machinery to copy right to the very end of the strand in the absence of telomerase – it has been found that stress, especially oxidative stress, has an even bigger effect on the rate of telomere loss (von Zglinicki, 2002). Telomere shortening is greatly accelerated (or slowed) in cells with increased (or reduced) levels of stress. The clinical relevance of understanding telomere maintenance and its interaction with stress is considerable. A growing body of evidence suggests that telomere length is linked with ageing and mortality (e.g. Cawthon *et al.*, 2003). Not only do telomeres shorten with normal ageing in several tissues (e.g. lymphocytes, vascular endothelial cells, kidney, liver), but also their reduction is more marked in certain disease states. For example, there appears to be a hundredfold higher incidence of vascular dementia in people with prematurely short telomeres (von Zglinicki *et al.*, 2000). Viewed together with the observation that oxidative stress accelerates telomere loss, the intriguing possibility arises that prematurely short telomeres in vivo are an indicator of previous exposure to stress and may therefore serve as a prognostic indicator for disease conditions in which oxidative stress plays a causative role (von Zglinicki, 2002).

Mitochondria and stress

An important connection between oxidative stress and ageing is suggested by the accumulation of mitochondrial DNA (mtDNA) deletions and point mutations with age (Wallace, 1992). Mitochondria are intracellular organelles, each carrying its own small DNA genome, which are responsible for generating cellular energy. As a by-product of energy generation, mitochondria are also the major source of ROS within the cell, and they are therefore both responsible for, and a major target of, oxidative stress. Any age-related increase in mutation of mtDNA is likely to contribute to a progressive decline in the cell and tissue capacity for energy production. Age-related increases in frequency of cytochrome c oxidase (COX)-deficient cells have been reported in human muscle (Müller-Höcker, 1989; Müller-Hocker *et al.*, 1993; Brierley *et al.*, 1998) and brain (Cottrell *et al.*, 2000), associated with increased frequency of mutated mtDNA.

One of the intriguing questions about the accumulation of defective mitochondria with age is why selection within the mitochondrial population does not act to prevent it. Several energy-dependent steps are needed for mitochondrial replication, and it is therefore hard to see how a defective mitochondrion can achieve an accelerated division rate. Nevertheless, several studies have shown that muscle fibres with abnormalities of the electron transport system are apparently taken over by mitochondria of a single mutant mtDNA genotype (Müller-Höcker *et al.*, 1993; Brierley *et al.*, 1998), suggesting that defective mitochondria somehow overgrow the wild-type.

Until recently, the evidence for age-related accumulation of mtDNA mutations came mainly from tissues such as brain and muscle where cell division in the adult, if it occurs at all, is rare. This led to the idea that accumulation of mtDNA mutation was driven mainly by the dynamics of mitochondrial multiplication and turnover within non-dividing cells (Kowald and Kirkwood, 2000). However, recent work has revealed a strongly age-dependent accumulation of mtDNA mutations in human gut epithelium, which has the highest cell division rate of any tissue in the body (Taylor *et al.*, 2003). Thus, it appears that mtDNA mutation accumulation may be a widespread phenomenon.

METABOLIC FACTORS INFLUENCING RATE OF AGEING

From the comparative perspective, numerous opportunities exist to test the evolutionary prediction that in safe environments (those with low extrinsic mortality) ageing will evolve to be retarded, whereas ageing should evolve to be more rapid in hazardous environments. Field observations comparing a mainland population of opossums subject to significant predation by mammals with an island population not subject to mammalian predation found the predicted slower ageing in the island population (Austad, 1993). What is interesting from the metabolic perspective is to understand how these ecologically driven effects are mediated at the level of cellular and molecular mechanisms.

The disposable soma theory predicts that the proportional effort devoted to cellular maintenance and repair processes will vary directly with longevity. Numerous studies support this idea. For instance, the long-lived rodent species *Peromyscus leucopus* exhibits lower generation of reactive oxygen species (ROS), higher cellular concentrations of some antioxidant enzymes, and overall lower levels of protein oxidative damage than the shorter-lived species *Mus musculus* (Sohal *et al.*, 1993). A similar relationship between mammals and similar-sized but much longer-lived birds (Herrero and Barja, 1999), has also been found, as has a direct relation between species longevity and rate of mitochondrial ROS production in captive mammals (Ku *et al.*, 1993; Barja and Herrero, 2000). Markers of glycoxidation, the non-enzymatic modification of reducing sugars, are also found to accumulate more slowly in long-lived, as opposed to short-lived, mammals (Sell *et al.*, 1996).

The quality of maintenance and repair mechanisms may be revealed by the capacity to cope with external stress. The prediction that cells from long-lived species are better protected by somatic maintenance and repair has been tested in a comparative study of stress resistance in primary cultures of skin fibroblasts from eight different mammalian species (Kapahi *et al.*, 1999). To minimise potentially confounding variables, cells were derived using a carefully standardised protocol. Replicate cultures were exposed to a dose of one of the following stressors (period of stress shown in brackets): hydrogen peroxide (2 h), paraquat (24 h), tert-butyl hydroperoxide (2 h), sodium arsenite (6 h) or sodium hydroxide (6 h). For each stressor, a range of doses was used to establish a dose-response relationship plotting per cent cell survival against the dose (concentration) of the stressor that was used. It was found that cell stress resistance, expressed in terms of the dose of the stressor required to kill 90 per cent of the cell population, correlated positively with species lifespans. The fact that similar correlations were obtained for a variety of cellular stresses that damage cells in different ways supports the idea that multiple stress response mechanisms are involved in the determination of species-specific lifespans.

Of particular significance in terms of metabolic factors influencing ageing rates has been the discovery that insulin signalling pathways appear to have effects on ageing that may be strongly conserved across the species range (Gems and Partridge, 2001). Insulin signalling regulates responses to varying nutrient levels and so the discovery of the major role for these pathways in ageing fits well with the central concept of the disposable soma theory, namely that ageing results from and is controlled by the allocation of the organism's metabolic resources to maintenance and repair.

One of the clearest examples of how metabolic signalling affects ageing and longevity comes from a study on genes of the insulin signalling pathway in *C. elegans* (Murphy *et al.*, 2003; see also Kirkwood, 2003). When threatened with overcrowding, which the larval worm detects by the concentration of a pheromone, it diverts its development from the normal succession of larval moults into a long-lived, dispersal form called the dauer larva (Larsen *et al.*, 1995). Dauers show increased resistance to stress and can survive an extended period of time, reverting to complete their development into the adult form should more favourable conditions be detected. An insulin/IGF-1-like gene, *daf-2*, heads the gene regulatory pathway that controls the switch into the dauer form, and mutations in *daf-2* produce animals that develop into adults with substantially increased lifespans (Kenyon *et al.*, 1993). In common with other members of the evolutionarily conserved insulin/IGF-1 signalling pathway, *daf-2* also regulates lipid metabolism and reproduction. The *daf-2* gene product exerts its effects by influencing downstream signalling, in particular via the actions of another gene belonging to the dauer-formation gene family, *daf-16*, which it inhibits (Kimura *et al.*, 1997).

It was shown by Murphy *et al.* (2003) that more than 300 genes appeared to have their expression levels altered by *daf-16* regulation. This large number suggests that, as predicted by the evolutionary theory, many genes are involved in determining longevity. The genes modulated by *daf-16* turned out to be a heterogeneous group although several broad categories could be discerned. The first category comprised a variety of stress-response genes, including players like antioxidant enzymes. Given the evidence that stress is a major player in ageing across the species range, and that long-lived *C. elegans* mutants generally show enhanced stress resistance, this might have been expected. A second group of

genes encoded antimicrobial proteins. These have special relevance for *C. elegans* ageing because in this organism death is commonly caused by proliferation of bacteria in the gut. A miscellaneous third group included genes involved in protein turnover, which is an important cellular maintenance system.

By this point, it will be seen that, from a range of studies at the genetic, cellular and molecular levels, both in humans and a variety of other organisms, a picture is clearly emerging of the main elements of the biological science of human ageing. The main elements in this picture are the relentless role of biochemical *stresses*, such as exposure to ROS, driving a gradual but progressive accumulation of *damage* to cells, tissues and organs. The process is not entirely passive, since the rate of accumulation is strongly resisted by maintenance and repair processes, which are controlled by *genes*. Furthermore, the regulation of these genes may, at least in some organisms, be influenced by metabolic factors, e.g. responding to levels of nutrition. This picture is one that readily accommodates the role of at least five major elements contributing to the individuality of the human ageing process: genes, nutrition, lifestyle (e.g. exercise), environment and chance. The recognition of this interplay of factors is likely to be crucial for integrating biological, clinical and social gerontology. For example, environment is often defined by social factors such as housing, transport and income. Poor environments may adversely affect an individual's opportunities to do the optimal things for healthy ageing in terms of nutrition, lifestyle, etc. In particular, a poor environment can reinforce a tendency for the older person to suffer social isolation, which in turn can exacerbate psychological and physical deterioration. On the positive side, the understanding that we now have of the biological science of human ageing supports the idea that the ageing process is much more malleable than has hitherto been recognised. This opens the way to a range of interventions that may improve health in old age and extend quality of life.

MENOPAUSE – THE BIOLOGICAL VALUE OF OLD AGE?

This chapter concludes with a brief discussion of the biology of menopause, not only because menopause is a unique feature of the human life history but also because it probably reflects that during the recent evolution of our species, old age achieved a biological value in its own right, probably for the first time.

Menopause – the universal cessation of human female fertility at around age 50 – presents an intriguing evolutionary puzzle. Why should a woman cease reproducing at a much earlier age relative to her biological lifespan potential than occurs in other mammals? Although life expectancy in earlier times was much shorter than it is today, the evidence suggests that a woman who escaped the hazards of juvenile mortality had a reasonable chance of surviving past menopausal age (Hill and Hurtado, 1996). This means that ceasing reproduction early would, if other things were equal, have an adverse effect on evolutionary fitness.

The explanation for the evolution of the menopause appears to be found in the unique circumstances affecting the human life history (see Kirkwood, 1997, for review). The pressure to evolve increased lifespans was probably driven by the increase in human brain size, leading to advanced intelligence, tool use and social living, all of which will have reduced the level of extrinsic mortality and favoured increased investments in somatic maintenance. Increased neonatal brain size, however, makes giving birth riskier. The result appears to have been a compromise whereby, in comparison with other mammals, the human infant is born unusually altricial (i.e. requiring extended postnatal development before gaining independence from the mother) while still possessing an unusually large head. This has led to the suggestion that the menopause protects older mothers from the risks of late childbearing, when senescence may make pregnancy and childbearing less safe, and favours the survival of the mother to raise her existing children to independence. An alternative is that post-reproductive females may gain more by contributing to the reproductive success of their offspring, through helping to care for and provision their offspring, than they would gain from attempting further reproduction of their own. The latter 'grandmother' has attracted powerful empirical support from anthropological studies (Hawkes *et al.*, 1998; Lahdenpera *et al.*, 2004).

In order to test the alternative ideas about a possible evolutionary basis for menopause, it is important to establish whether the hypotheses are quantitatively supported by a sufficiently large effect on Darwinian fitness. In other words, it is not enough simply to suggest they might occur for this or that reason; it has to be shown that the benefit in terms of an increased genetic contribution to future generations is sufficient to outweigh any costs. Recent theoretical modelling indicates that neither of the two hypotheses outlined above – the 'maternal mortality' and 'grandmother' hypotheses – is in fact adequate on its own. However, when both are taken together in a combined model, they show that menopause does indeed confer an evolutionary advantage (Shanley and Kirkwood, 2001). This is important because it may explain why menopause is essentially unique to our species, in which this combination of factors has occurred. In essence, it is this combination, representing a convergence of biological and cultural evolution, that conferred sufficient biological value on older women that menopause evolved as an adaptation to reflect this value in evolving human social groups.

FURTHER READING

Austad, S. N. (1997). *Why we age: what science is discovering about the body's journey through life*. New York: John Wiley & Sons.

Hayflick, L. (1994). *How and why we age*. New York: Ballantine Books.

Holliday, R. (1995). *Understanding ageing*. Cambridge University Press.

Kirkwood, T. B. L. (1999). *Time of our lives: the science of human ageing*. London: Weidenfeld and Nicolson.

REFERENCES

Austad, S. N. (1993). 'Retarded senescence in an insular population of opossums', *J. Zool.*, 229: 695–708.

(1997). 'Comparative aging and life histories in mammals', Exp. Gerontol., 32: 23–38.

Barja, G., and A. Herrero (2000). 'Oxidative damage to mitochondrial DNA is inversely related to maximum life span in the heart and brain of mammals', *FASEB J.*, 14: 312–18.

Bell, G. (1984). 'Evolutionary and nonevolutionary theories of senescence', *Am. Nat.*, 124: 600–3.

Brierley, E. J., Johnson, M. A., Lightowlers, R. N., *et al.* (1998). 'Role of mitochondrial DNA mutations in human aging: implications for the central nervous system and muscle', *Ann. Neurol.*, 43: 217–23.

Bürkle, A., Beneke, S., Brabeck, C., Leake, A., Meyer, R., Muiras, M. L., and R. Pfeiffer (2002). 'Poly(ADP-ribose) polymerase-1, DNA repair and mammalian longevity', *Exp. Gerontol.*, 37: 1203–5.

Campisi, J. (1997). 'Aging and cancer: the double-edged sword of replicative senescence', *J. Am. Geriatric Soc.*, 45: 482–8.

Cavallone, L., Bonafe, M., Olivieri, F., Cardelli, M., Marchegiani, F., Giovagnetti, S., Di Stasio, G., Giampieri, C., Mugianesi, E., Stecconi, R., Sciacca, F., Grimaldi, L. M., De Benedictis, G., Lio, D., Caruso, C., and C. Franceschi (2003). 'The role of IL-1 gene cluster in longevity: a study in Italian population', *Mech. Ageing Dev.*, 124: 533–8.

Cawthon, R. M., Smith, K. R., O'Brien, E., Sivatchenko, A., and R. A. Kerber (2003). 'Association between telomere length in blood and mortality in people aged 60 years or older', *Lancet*, 361: 393–5.

Cottrell, D. A., Blakely, E. L., Johnson, M. A., Ince, P. G., Borthwick, G. M., and D. M. Turnbull (2000). 'Cytochrome c oxidase deficient cells accumulate in the hippocampus and choroid plexus with age', *Neurobiol. Ageing*, 22: 265–72.

Cournil, A., and T. B. L. Kirkwood (2001). 'If you would live long, choose your parents well', *Trends Genet.*, 17: 233–5.

Esiri, M. M., Matthews, F., Brayne, C., Ince, P. G., Matthews, F. E., Xuereb, J. H., Broome, J. C., McKenzie, J., Rossi, M., McKeith, I. G., Lowe, J., and J. H. Morris (2001). 'Pathological correlates of late-onset dementia in a multicentre, community-based population in England and Wales', *Lancet*, 357: 169–75.

Finch, C. E., and R. Tanzi (1997). 'The genetics of aging', *Science*, 278: 407–11.

Finch and Kirkwood (2000).

Gems, D., and L. Partridge (2001). 'Insulin/IGF signalling and ageing: seeing the bigger picture'. *Curr. Opin. Genet. Dev.*, 11: 287–92.

Grube, K., and A. Bürkle (1992). 'Poly(ADP-ribose) polymerase activity in mononuclear leukocytes of 13 mammalian species correlates with species-specific life span', *Proc. Natl. Acad. Sci. USA*, 89: 11759–63.

Hawkes, K., O'Connell, J. F., Jones, N. G. B., Alvarez, H., and E. L. Charnov (1998). *Proc. Natl. Acad. Sci. USA*, 95: 1336–9.

Herndon, L. A., Schmeissner, P. J., Dudaronek, J. M., Brown, P. A., Listner, K. M., Sakano, Y., Paupard, M. C., Hall, D. H., and M. Driscoll (2002). 'Stochastic and genetic factors influence tissue-specific decline in ageing *C. elegans*', *Nature*, 419: 808–14.

Herrero, A., and G. Barja (1999). '8-oxo-deoxyguanosine levels in heart and brain mitochondrial and nuclear DNA of two mammals and three birds in relation to their different rates of aging', *Aging Clin. Exp. Res.*, 11: 294–300.

Hill, K., and A. M. Hurtado (1996). *Ache life history: the ecology and demography of a foraging people*. New York: Walter de Gruyter Inc.

Kapahi, P., Boulton, M. E., and T. B. L. Kirkwood (1999). 'Positive correlation between mammalian life span and cellular resistance to stress', *Free Radic. Biol. Med.*, 26: 495–500.

Kenyon, C., *et al.* (1993). 'A *C. elegans* mutant that lives twice as long as wild-type'. *Nature*, 366: 461–4.

Kim, S., Kaminker, P., and J. Campisi (2002). 'Telomeres, aging and cancer: in search of a happy ending', *Oncogene*, 21: 503–11.

Kimura, K. D., *et al.* (1997). '*daf-2*, an insulin receptor-like gene that regulates longevity and diapause in *Caenorhabditis elegans*', *Science*, 277: 942–6.

Kirkwood, T. B. L. (1977). 'Evolution of ageing', *Nature*, 270: 301–4.

—— (1997). 'The origins of human ageing', *Phil. Trans. R. Soc. Lond. B*, 352: 1765–72.

—— (2003). 'Genes that shape the course of ageing', *Trends Endocrinol. Metab.*, 14 (8): 345–7 (October).

Kirkwood, T. B. L., and S. N. Austad (2000). 'Why do we age?' *Nature*, 408: 233–8.

Kirkwood, T. B. L., and T. Cremer (1982). 'Cytogerontology since 1881: a reappraisal of August Weismann and a review of modern progress', *Hum. Genet.*, 60: 101–21.

Kirkwood, T. B. L., and C. E. Finch (2002). 'The old worm turns more slowly', *Nature*, 419: 794–5.

Kirkwood, T. B. L., and M. R. Rose (1991). 'Evolution of senescence – late survival sacrificed for reproduction', *Phil. Trans. R. Soc. Lond. B*, 332: 15–24.

Kowald, A., and T. B. L. Kirkwood (2000). 'Accumulation of defective mitochondria through delayed degradation of damaged organelles and its possible role in the ageing of post-mitotic and dividing cells', *J. Theor. Biol.*, 202: 145–60.

Ku, H.-H., Brunk, U. T., and R. S. Sohal (1993). 'Relationship between mitochondrial superoxide and hydrogen-peroxide production and longevity of mammalian-species', *Free Rad. Biol. Med.*, 15: 621–7.

Lahdenpera, M., Lummaa, V., Helle, S., Tremblay, M., and A. F. Russell (2004). 'Fitness benefits of prolonged post-reproductive lifespan in women', *Nature*, 428: 178–81.

Larsen, P. L., *et al.* (1995). 'Genes that regulate both development and longevity in *Caenorhabditis elegans*', *Genetics*, 139: 1567–83.

Martin, G. M., Austad, S. N., and T. E. Johnson (1996). 'Genetic analysis of ageing: role of oxidative damage and environmental stresses', *Nat. Genet.*, 13: 25–34.

Martinez, D. E. (1997). 'Mortality patterns suggest lack of senescence in hydra', *Exp. Gerontol.*, 33: 217–25.

Medawar, P. B. (1952). *An unsolved problem of biology*. London: Lewis.

Meyer, R., Müller, M., Beneke, S., Küpper, J. H., and A. Bürkle (2000). 'Negative regulation of alkylation-induced sister-chromatid exchanges by poly(ADP-ribose) polymerase-1 activity', *Int. J. Cancer*, 88: 351–5.

Muiras, M. L., Müller, M., Schächter, F., and A. Bürkle (1998). 'Increased poly(ADP-ribose) polymerase activity in lymphoblastoid cell lines from centenarians', *J. Mol. Med.*, 76: 346–54.

Müller-Höcker, J. (1989). 'Cytochrome-c-oxidase deficient cardiomyocytes in the human heart – an age-related phenomenon. A histochemical ultracytochemical study', *Am. J. Pathol.*, 134, 1167–73.

Müller-Höcker, J., Seibel, P., Schneiderbanger, K., *et al.* (1993). 'Different *in situ* hybridization patterns of mitochondrial DNA in cytochrome c oxidase-deficient extraocular muscle fibres in the elderly', *Virchows Archives A*, 422: 7–15.

Murphy, C. T., McCarroll, S. A., Bargmann, C. I., Fraser, A., Kamath, R. S., Ahringer, J., Li, H., and C. Kenyon (2003). 'Genes that act downstream of DAF-16 to influence the lifespan of *Caenorhabditis elegans*', *Nature*, 424: 277–84.

Ogburn, C. E., Carlberg, K., Ottinger, M. A., Holmes, D. J., Martin, G. M., and S. N. Austad (2001). 'Exceptional cellular resistance to oxidative damage in long-lived birds requires active gene expression', *J. Gerontol. Series A*, 56: B468–B474.

Puca, A. A., Daly, M. J., Brewster, S. J., Matise, T. C., Barrett, J., Shea-Drinkwater, M., Kang, S., Joyce, E., Nicoli, J., Benson, E., Kunkel, L. M., and T. Perls (2001). 'Genome-wide scan for linkage to human exceptional longevity identifies a locus on chromosome 4', *Proc. Natl. Acad. Sci. USA*, 98: 10505–8.

Promislow, D. E. L. (1994). 'DNA-repair and the evolution of longevity – a critical analysis', *J. Theoret. Biol.*, 170: 291–300.

Sell, D. R., Lane, M. A., Johnson, W. A., Masoro, E. J., Mock, O. B., Reiser, K. M., Fogarty, J. F., Cutler, R. G., Ingram, D. K., Roth, G. S., and V. M. Monnier (1996). 'Longevity and the genetic determination of collagen glycoxidation kinetics in mammalian senescence', *Proc. Natl. Acad. Sci. USA*, 93: 485–90.

Shanley, D. P., and T. B. L. Kirkwood (2001). 'Evolution of the human menopause', *BioEssays*, 23: 282–7.

Sohal, R. S., Ku, H.-H., and S. Agarwal (1993). 'Biochemical correlates of longevity in two closely-related rodent species', *Biochem. Biophys. Res. Comm.*, 196: 7–11.

Taylor, R. W., Barron, M. J., Borthwick, G. M., Gospel, A., Chinnery, P. F., Samuels, D. C., Taylor, G. A., Plusa, S. M., Needham, S. J., Greaves, L. C., Kirkwood, T. B. L., and D. M. Turnbull (2003). 'Mitochondrial DNA mutations in human colonic crypt stem cells', *J. Clin. Invest.*, 112: 1351–60.

von Zglinicki, T. (2002). 'Oxidative stress shortens telomeres', *Trends Biochem. Sci.*, 27: 339–44.

von Zglinicki, T., Serra, V., Lorenz, M., Saretzki, G., Lenzen-Großimlighaus, R., Geßner, R., Risch, A., & Steinhagen-Thiessen, E (2000). 'Short telomeres in patients with vascular dementia: an indicator of low antioxidative capacity and a possible prognostic factor?' *Lab. Invest.*, 80: 1739–47.

von Zglinicki, T., Bürkle, A., and T. B. L. Kirkwood (2001). 'Stress, DNA damage and ageing – an integrative approach', *Exp. Gerontol.*, 36: 1049–62.

Wallace, D. C. (1992). 'Mitochondrial genetics: a paradigm for aging and degenerative diseases?' *Science*, 256: 628–32.

Williams, G. C. (1957). 'Pleiotropy, natural selection and the evolution of senescence', *Evolution*, 11: 398–411.

PART TWO

THE AGEING BODY

Biodemography and Epidemiology of Longevity

BERNARD JEUNE AND KAARE CHRISTENSEN

Within the last decades a new paradigm about ageing processes has emerged. Previously ageing was regarded as a very mechanistic process with little room for external factors to influence it. However, evidence ranging from population level to individuals to model organisms and genetic studies suggests that ageing processes are plastic and modifiable.

Demographic studies from a variety of Western countries with reliable mortality statistics as well as biodemographic experiments on very large populations of model organisms such as flies, nematodes, and yeast led to the discovery that mortality does not continue to increase exponentially throughout adult life (Vaupel *et al.*, 1998). At extreme ages mortality levelled off, reached a plateau, or even decreased.

Recent demographic research has documented that mortality in low-mortality countries had declined even among the oldest-old leading to a proliferation of centenarians since 1950 (Kannisto, 1996) and to the emergence of genuine long-livers during the 1990s (Jeune and Vaupel, 1999; Robine and Vaupel, 2001), such as Jeanne Calment who with her 122 years is in all probability the human being who has lived the longest, and Chris Mortensen who with his 115 years is probably the man who has lived the longest.

In multiple biological experiments on different living organisms it has been shown that caloric restriction led to a substantial increase in longevity (Masoro, 2001). Subsequent experiments with mutations of very few genes on organisms like the little roundworm *C. elegans*, the yeast cell, and the fruit fly showed that longevity could be doubled (Guarante and Kenyon, 2000). By combining caloric restrictions or other changes of stress factors with gene mutations, longevity could be increased even more. Thus, these experiments showed that ageing is extremely plastic and that longevity can be extended substantially.

Today many researchers into ageing think that prolongation of human life is possible, although they do not agree if it is also desirable. Most demographers agree that we are living longer and will live even longer in the future. However, we have little good evidence to help us answer the major question: will the longer life also be a better life? But that is what people and society want to know. If prolongation of life will result in an increasing number of years with comorbidity, disability, and frailty, nobody will find it attractive, and the whole community of researchers in ageing will be damned and attacked for not recognizing the warnings of the ancient myths that it is not possible both to live longer and to stay young (Jeune, 2002).

In this chapter we will address a number of biodemographic and epidemiological questions related to longevity: first of all, whether there is a limit to lifespan. We also discuss reasons why we are living longer, the characteristics of those living long, and whether longevity runs in families. Central underlying questions for all the biodemographic and epidemiological studies of longevity are not just whether we are living longer but also whether we are living better.

IS THERE A LIMIT?

Since the beginning of the 1900s, demographers have stated that life expectancy is approaching its limits. However, evidence suggests otherwise (Oeppen and Vaupel, 2002). All estimations of a limit have been broken, on average five years after publication. The female life expectancy in the record-holding countries has risen for 160 years at a steady pace of almost three months per year. In 1840 the record was held by Swedish women, who lived on average a little more than 45 years. Today the longest expectation of life, 85 years, is enjoyed by Japanese women. If life expectancy was close to a maximum, then the increase in record expectation of life should be slowing down, but it is not.

Several authors have stated that in spite of the increasing life expectancy, the maximum human lifespan has been constant (Fries, 1980; Olshansky et al., 1990; Hayflick, 1994). However, when these statements were written, the extension of the maximum human lifespan was already in progress. During the last decades of the twentieth century, a remarkable increase in longevity took place in the human species (Kannisto, 1996; Thatcher, 1999; Wilmoth et al., 2000). In the course of the 1990s alone, more than ten individuals reached 115 years or more (Robine and Vaupel, 2001).

At the beginning of modern times it was unlikely that anyone had lived to 110, and it is even questionable whether it was possible to reach 100 years before 1800 (Jeune and Vaupel, 1995). The existence of centenarians was not certain until the mid 1800s (Jeune and Vaupel, 1999). The proportion was almost constant in the second half of the 1800s with only one centenarian per million inhabitants in countries with reliable statistics. The number of centenarians only grew very slowly in the first half of the 1900s and they were extremely rare before 1950, but the number has increased markedly since (Kannisto, 1996). In countries with low mortality the number of centenarians has more than doubled every 10 years in the last 50. In Denmark the proportion has risen from 5 to more than 100 per million inhabitants today (Jeune and Skytthe, 2001).

Women outnumber men at age 100 by five to one, and at still higher ages even more. There are more centenarians today than ever, and they also live longer. The probability of reaching 105 years for 100-year-old women has doubled since the 1950s and survival from 100 to 110 years has even increased fourfold. As a result, more persons are now living to such high ages as 105 and 110, and women outnumber men at age 110 by ten to one (Kannisto, 1996).

In around 1900, the maximum lifespan probably did not exceed 105 years in most countries, but it seems that several centenarians reached the age of 110 in the 1960s in the larger European countries (Robine and Vaupel, 2001). During the 1970s they constituted such a number that it is possible to identify the rate of increase in the following years. Their number increased fivefold from 1975 to 1995 in countries with reliable and complete observations.

Wilmoth et al. (2000) have demonstrated that the maximum lifespan in Sweden has increased since 1860, first very slowly – up to half a year per decade until 1970 – and thereafter more quickly with one year per decade. In Europe the maximum lifespan increased from 112 years in 1980 to 122 in 1997 (Robine and Vaupel, 2001). Recent demographic research thus indicates that the highest attained age has increased by about twenty years since the beginning of the nineteenth century, with a particularly high rate of increase during recent decades. If there is a limit to the maximum human lifespan it is far beyond the 115 years stated by Hayflick (1994).

WHY ARE WE LIVING LONGER?

The reasons for this increase in the maximum lifespan and the proliferation of long-livers are not well understood. It is important to distinguish between two different questions which are often confused: (1) Why are we living longer? (2) Who lives very long? It seems unlikely that a major change in the genetic makeup of the population has occurred in just a few generations. However, even though genetic factors cannot explain the increasing growth rate in the numbers of the oldest-old, it is highly probable that interactions between genes and environmental factors have a substantial influence on who lives very long. Kannisto (1996) suggests that the increase of the oldest-old is mainly a period effect, i.e. due to improvements of environmental factors affecting all age groups, and not a cohort effect, i.e. due to the "accumulated" exposure of cohorts, but this is still being discussed.

Possible cohort effects

Obviously, the birth cohorts born around 1900 have experienced huge changes in socioeconomic conditions, hygiene, lifestyle, and medical care, which led to the dramatic decline in infant mortality and the most important causes of death such as infectious diseases and respiratory diseases. These improved conditions were probably mainly socioeconomic, such as improvements of living and sanitary conditions, education, and personal hygiene, and much less related to medical improvements (McKeown, 1965), although better nutrition, including vitamins, and vaccinations probably also played a role.

The improved nutrition in the beginning of the 1900s may have contributed to the mortality decline several decades later, if reduced growth in utero and early in life, as stated in the fetal-origin hypothesis, is related to adverse health outcomes later in life, such as higher mortality from cardiovascular diseases (Barker, 1998). Doblhammer (1999) found that the season of birth influences longevity, as those who were born during late autumn and early winter in Austria and Denmark lived almost half a year longer than those who were born in the spring, which may be due to an easier access to fruit and vegetables throughout most of the pregnancy. However, other studies do not support the fetal-origin hypothesis (Christensen *et al.*, 1995).

In Denmark, women gave birth to about four to five children before 1900 but only to two to three children in the 1920s. If there was a cost of reproduction at that time, the decreasing birthrate may have had an impact. We have shown (Christensen *et al.*, 1998) that women of low social status lost about one additional tooth per child, thereby confirming the proverb "A child, a tooth," whereas women of high social status only lost one additional tooth per two children, indicating that the cost of reproduction probably does not have the same impact on wealthier cohorts born later.

Analyzing historical data in the genealogy of the British peerage, Westendorp and Kirkwood (1998) found an inverse correlation between fertility and longevity. Controlling for the effects of differences in mortality selection during childbearing ages in the same data, a significant trade-off was found among females, but not for males (Doblhammer and Oeppen, 2003). It is not clear whether this relationship may be a trade-off between reproduction and somatic maintenance going on over generations, may be due to a more direct impact of a reduced cost of reproduction, or may be mediated by a delay of the menopause due to fewer and later-born children (cf. Jeune, 2002).

Several epidemiological studies have tried to identify relative impact of parents' social class, childhood, and adult conditions on later mortality. According to the Whitehall study (Marmot *et al.*, 2001), the adult socioeconomic status was a more important predictor of coronary disease and chronic bronchitis than social status early in life.

Probable period effects

Due to the societal improvements in the first half of the 1900s, a much higher proportion of the early twentieth century cohorts survived to middle age. Of those who were born in Denmark in 1850, only about 50 percent survived to the age of 50 years in 1900, while more than 90 percent of those who were born in 1900 survived to the age of 50. Those who made it from 50 to 80 had to survive the modern epidemic of cardiovascular diseases (CVD) which peaked in the 1960s. The oldest-old of today have experienced the beginning of the improvements which led to the decline of CVD mortality when they were younger elderly. However, the growth of centenarians in recent decades is mainly due to the dramatic decline in mortality *among the oldest-old* (Jeune and Vaupel, 1995; Kannisto, 1996; Vaupel *et al.*, 1998).

Thus, the increase in centenarians is connected with the factors which have determined the drastic fall in mortality among the elderly, especially the oldest-old, but also among other groups, and therefore it is a period effect and not a cohort effect. These improvements are probably mainly related to factors which have lowered the incidence of potentially fatal diseases, diminished their severity, and reduced the case fatality of such diseases, i.e. factors associated with improvement of life conditions and lifestyle causing a reduction in risk factors (primary prevention) and with improvement of treatments, including risk reduction in patients (secondary prevention). However, it is also possible that a slowing down of the rate of physiological ageing has occurred which results in an improved resistance to age-related diseases and an improved long-term survival.

The most important causes of death among the oldest-old are cardiovascular diseases, cancer, and pneumonia. The main explanation may be found in the epidemiology of CVD, as CVD is the only major group of diseases which has shown a remarkable decline in recent decades, and in spite of that is still the major cause of hospitalization and death among the elderly. Cardiovascular diseases share some common risk factors with cancer, diabetes, and osteoporosis – such as smoking, nutrition, and physical activity – which have changed during recent decades. Furthermore, new diagnostic methods based on high technology, and new treatments, often based on randomized controlled trials, have been implemented during recent decades. Improvement of survival to high ages is therefore to be expected as a result of changes in incidence, severity, and case fatality of these very common, age-related diseases. However, it seems that coronary heart disease and stroke, especially, respond more rapidly to changes in lifestyle or environment than cancer, and new research indicates that the lag time is shorter than previously assumed.

A consistent finding in the epidemiological literature on CVD (see Jeune, 2002) is that both incidence and case fatality have declined in recent decades. Declining trends in cardiovascular risk factors have been observed in most low-mortality countries. Classical risk factors such as diet, smoking, and physical activity still seem to be important risk factors for the younger elderly. However, it is not evident whether these declining trends were similar above the age of 80 years, and it is very controversial how important they are among the oldest-old. There is more evidence supporting the view that the oldest-old have benefitted from the improvement of diagnostics and more effective treatments. In the latest decades there seems to be a tendency in clinical practice to treat an increasing number of elderly, including the oldest-old, with the new technologies and drugs. This is also suggested by some studies of past diseases that centenarians have survived.

WHO LIVES VERY LONG?

Centenarian studies may provide some indications of how humans are living when they are living longer. However, knowledge of how the oldest-old have survived to the age of 100 years is very scanty. In spite of that, it has been claimed that centenarians are survivors who have avoided major diseases (Candore et al., 1997; Hitt et al., 1999). This claim has never been examined in longitudinal studies of octogenarians or nonagenarians. We only have very few retrospective studies of previous morbidity among centenarians.

In a study of Danish centenarians, about three-quarters had been treated for and survived pneumonias, myocardial infarcts, strokes, malignant neoplasms, and/or hip fractures (Andersen-Ranberg et al., 2001). This high proportion of past diseases has been found in other large, representative studies of Finnish and Japanese centenarians (Louhija, 1994; Tauchi et al., 1999). A high proportion of "survivors" and "delayers" has also been found in selected centenarians from the US, although a minor proportion were "escapers," i.e. had escaped major age-related diseases before the age of 100 (Evert et al., 2003).

If these centenarians had been born about 1850 instead of about 1900, most of them would not have survived to 100. They would then have been octogenarians or nonagenarians in a period without antibiotics, vaccination against influenza, effective cardiovascular drugs, anti-diabetics, etc., and without modern anaesthetics and surgery. Only 1 in 5,000 of the Danish cohorts born in the 1840s became centenarians, while 1 in 250 of those born in the 1890s did so.

Most centenarians have not only survived age-related diseases but some of them continued to live several years with many age-related diseases. Among Danish centenarians, three-quarters had one or more cardiovascular diseases, more than half had manifest osteoarthritis, about half were demented, and one-third of the men had diagnosed prostate hypertrophy. A considerable comorbidity was present with, on average, more than four chronic conditions. The same high prevalence of diseases and comorbidity was found among the unselected Finnish and Japanese centenarians (Louhija, 1994; Tauchi et al., 1999).

However, it is possible that the diseases that centenarians have survived were less serious than those among their contemporaries, or that some specific diseases are no more frequent in centenarians than in younger elderly (Andersen-Ranberg et al., 2001a). A levelling-off either of the prevalence of specific diseases or of the severity of these diseases might be expected as the mortality rates decelerate with advancing age (Vaupel *et al.*, 1998), e.g. a levelling-off of the exponential increase in the prevalence of dementia (Ritchie and Kildea, 1995).

It should be stressed that at least one-third of the centenarians in most studies had no sign of dementia (Allard and Robine, 2000; Andersen-Ranberg *et al.*, 2001; Beregi, 1990; Hagberg *et al.*, 2001; Louhija, 1994; Silver *et al.*, 2001). Clinical dementia is thus not obligatory even at extremely high ages, and it may be that centenarians have had better-preserved cognitive functions than their generation fellows. Perhaps other psychological factors such as certain personality traits and strategies of coping may have helped centenarians to survive age-related diseases, disability, or frailty (Martin *et al.*, 1992).

A number of basic biological mechanisms may be well preserved in centenarians, which may explain why they have survived age-related diseases and why they are still living in spite of a high level of comorbidity. It seems that, e.g., immunologic functions, cytokine production, apoptosis, haematopoiesis, hormonal, and metabolic functions are preserved in many centenarians (see Jeune, 2002). However, some findings are intriguing and have therefore been called *centenarian paradoxes* (Robine *et al.*, 1999a, 1999b), i.e. the finding of high values of a number of risk markers in apparently well-functioning centenarians. High values of biomarkers may be a result of a remodelling adaptation with age (Franceschi *et al.*, 1995) or may reflect immune activation due to chronic inflammation (Bruunsgaard *et al.*, 2002), possibly as part of frailty (Morley *et al.*, 2002).

Only results from longitudinal studies of younger elderly may properly elucidate the question of who the oldest-old are and how they survive to 100 years or more. However, as only one or two of 80-year-old people survive to 100 years, an examination of huge cohorts of younger elderly is required to give enough prediction power. At our Ageing Research Centre we are following more than 2,000 Danes born in 1905. Those who were not disabled, were cognitively intact, had high BMI, high self-rated health, and the strongest handgrip at the baseline had a significantly higher survival in the follow-up (Nybo *et al.*, 2003). No association was found with marital status, education, smoking, use of alcohol, or the number of self-reported diseases, which all are associated with survival at younger ages.

The above results indicate that centenarians are able to maintain a number of biological, cognitive, and psychological functions, although they are not healthy. This preservation of maintenance functions may explain why the extreme tail of elderly individuals have aged later or are inflicted later by chronic diseases and by a milder kind than their contemporaries.

DOES LONGEVITY RUN IN FAMILIES?

In accordance with evolutionary theories, and in contrast to growth and sexual maturity, ageing is not programmed but a byproduct of the trade-off between reproduction and maintenance (Kirkwood and Austad, 2000). It is therefore unthinkable that genes "cause" ageing or that special "death genes" exist (Austad, 1997; Kirkwood, 1999; Miller, 1999). However, the different lifespans of the species are genetically controlled, and within the species, genetic variation may influence the rate of ageing and the lifespan (Butler *et al.*, 2003; Finch, 1990; Finch and Tanzi, 1997; Schächter *et al.*, 1993). Probably thousands of genes are involved in multiple aspects of ageing and age-related diseases, and in important maintenance mechanisms which interact with several environmental factors (Butler *et al.*, 2003; Martin *et al.*, 1996). The inheritance of these thousands of genes which have been accumulated over thousands of years may explain why "longevity runs in families."

Since Beeton and Pearson, 100 years ago, first compared the lifespans of parents and children in the genealogy of the British peerage, several studies on this subject have been carried out (see Gavrilov and Gavrilova, 2001). Most of the studies show a significant though modest relation explaining only a few percent of the variation in lifespan. Danish twin studies (Herskind *et al.*, 1996) have shown a somewhat larger, moderate genetic influence on lifespan explaining approximately 25 percent of the variation with an average difference in lifespan of 14 years for monozygotic twins versus about 19 years for dizygotic twins. Increasing parental lifespan appeared to be positively associated with the cognitive and physical abilities of the elderly children (Frederiksen *et al.*, 2002).

A moderate familial clustering of extreme longevity has been observed in the few studies published in this area. Perls *et al.* (1998) found a fourfold higher probability of survival to 91 years for siblings of centenarians than for siblings of "controls" who died at the age of 73 years. Kerber *et al.* (2001) also found, based on Mormon genealogies, an increased recurrence probability for siblings of surviving to extreme ages, although the estimate was somewhat lower than Perls'. Gudmundsson *et al.* (2001), using the population-based genealogy in Iceland, found that first-degree relatives of probands who live to an extreme old age are twice as likely as the controls to survive to the same age.

In an attempt to test whether variations in specific candidate genes are affecting longevity, a comparison of gene variant frequencies between centenarians and younger cohorts has been widely used. This "classical centenarian association study" is one of the most debated study designs within gerontology (Olshansky *et al.*, 2001; Yashin *et al.*, 2000). Opponents of the approach argue that centenarian studies are of little interest because centenarians are just outliers and that survival is dependent on so many genetic and non-genetic factors that identifying them is impossible. Supporters of the design point to the fact that centenarian studies have been able to reveal the effect of some genetic and non-genetic factors and that these findings have been repeated also when using other study designs. A reason for the limited success of centenarian studies in identifying genetic, environmental, or behavioral factors of importance for survival until extreme ages may be the lack of an appropriate control group as cohort specific characteristics may confound the comparison between centenarians and younger cohorts.

More than thirty candidate genes which were either known to be risk genes for major diseases or genes involved in fundamental mechanisms have been examined. The findings from the published studies of these genes have recently been reviewed by DeBenedictis *et al.* (2001). The only consistent finding is the lower frequency among centenarians of the e4-allele in the APOE-genotype, since this result has been reproduced in seven countries. Irrespective of considerable differences in frequencies among these countries, the e4-allele frequency has almost been halved in centenarians, indicating a lower survival in carriers of the e4-allele which increases the risk of cardiac diseases and of Alzheimer's disease (Gerdes *et al.*, 2000).

Apart from this consistent finding on the ApoE-gene, the allele frequencies of several other gene polymorphisms have been found to deviate between centenarians and adults in general in at least one examined population. Most of these gene polymorphisms are involved in fundamental mechanisms, such as Apo-B (cholesterol homeostasis), HLA (immune response), MTHFR (homocysteine methylation), mitochondrial DNA (oxidation and phosphorylation), CYP2D6 (metabolism), TH (catecholamine synthesis), and SOD2 (anti-oxidative defense). The effects have been small but together, and with advancing age and increasing mortality, such small risks may have a substantial effect on survival to 100 years.

One approach in localizing genetic regions of importance for longevity is to examine long-living families with several siblings who have lived to the age of 90 or 100 years (sib-pair method). Puca *et al.* (2001) have identified 137 American families with a minimum age of 98 years for at least one member of the family (the proband) and with siblings of 90 years or more, comprising 308 individuals. By using genome-wide scan and non-parametric analysis, they found significant evidence for linkage for chromosome 4 at D4S1564. The authors stress that this linkage "indicates the likelihood that there exists a gene, or genes, that exerts a substantial influence on the ability to achieve exceptional old age."

Although it is unlikely that human longevity is determined by a few genes on one chromosome, studies on the genetic makeup of long-livers may contribute to the understanding of important interactions between genes and environmental factors and sex which influence the trajectories of different pathways of survival to exceptional longevity.

LIVING LONGER, BUT BETTER?

The most reasonable explanations of the increasing number of long-livers are multifactorial. Cohort effects, including reproduction and early childhood, may explain a minor part, while periodic effects such as improvements of life conditions, education, lifestyle, and medical care seem to explain the major part of the increase. However, within a given cohort, genetic variation as well as environmental factors and chance may explain why some individuals and not others from the same generation become centenarians. Human beings end their life among worms, but until then they do not share the same environment as worms and experience other gene–environment interactions (Austad, 1997).

In spite of our genetic makeup, humans are living longer in most parts of the world, and very probably we will live even longer in the future. The major question is therefore whether the added years will be good years or will just lead to more years with comorbidity, disability, and frailty, i.e. whether the so-called "disability-free" or healthy life expectancy is increasing by the same number of years as – or by even more than – the life expectancy, as suggested by Fries' compression of morbidity hypothesis (Fries, 1980). American studies seem to confirm this hypothesis, although only a few studies were of fair or good quality (Freedmann *et al.*, 2002). In the National Long-Term Care Survey (Manton and Gu, 2001), the prevalence of chronic disability among the elderly (over 65 years) declined from 26.2% in 1982 to 19.7% in 1999, i.e. a relative decline of 25% over 17 years. The prevalence of disability even declined among the oldest-old, and the rates of decline accelerated during this period. Reasons for this decline in disability in the US are less clear, but seem to be multifactorial (Fries, 2002).

However, recent European studies, which have examined disability, self-reported health, and morbidity, have come to contradictory conclusions (cf. Wilhelmson, 2003). According to the results of the Göteborg longitudinal studies of 70-year-olds it seems that health among younger elderly has improved in recent years, i.e. later born cohorts have better self-reported health, fewer symptoms, and better physical functioning than earlier born cohorts, although they seem to live longer with diseases. In a recent Danish study (Brønnum-Hansen, 2003), the number of "good years" (i.e. without functional limitations) among 65-year-old men increased from 8.9 years in 1987 to 11.3 years in 2000, i.e. by 2.4 years, while their life expectancy increased only by 0.9 years (from 14.1 to 15.0 years). Among women the disability-free life expectancy increased from 9.9 to 11.0 years, i.e. by 1.1 years, while their life expectancy increased by only 0.2 years (from 17.9 to 18.1 years). Although the expected lifetime in self-rated health had improved,

the trend in life expectancy with longstanding illness had also increased in the same period, confirming the finding from the Göteborg studies.

Health expectancy trends seem to depend on the choice of the population and subpopulation, the design of the study, the health indicator, and the measurement of this, and the method used to calculate the disability-free expectancy or the health expectancy (Robine *et al.*, 1999; Crimmins and Saito, 2001; Brønnum-Hansen, 2003). Further, well-designed cohort studies of different populations, also including the oldest-old, using different health indicators, have to be carried out before we can conclude that all aspects of healthy life expectancy are improving, thereby confirming Fries' hypothesis of the compression of morbidity.

In this new century the number of oldest-old, including centenarians, in low-mortality countries will increase. It may even be possible that girls born today will on an average live to the age of 100 if the oldest-old mortality continues to decline as it has done in recent decades (Vaupel and Gowan, 1986). However, it will probably never be possible to become long-livers without comorbidity, disability, and frailty, regardless of the improvement of treatments, although these will certainly attenuate the severity and complications of the diseases, e.g. the treatment of hypertension and heart diseases which may prevent dementia and stroke. Therefore, it is very important to know if it is possible to reach the advanced age of 100 or more and still be able to be autonomous and independent of help, regardless of increasing morbidity.

Centenarian studies (see Jeune, 2002) show that more than one third live in their own home, even if their cognitive and physical capacities, especially walking, were reduced. However, not all of these can be considered totally autonomous as most of them cannot manage without at least a little help from home helpers or family members to carry out different daily activities, especially Activities of Daily Living (ADLs) like shopping. Defining autonomy as living at home, being relatively ADL-independent (Katz Index A–C), and being cognitively intact (non-demented), we found a proportion of at least 10 percent among Danish centenarians (Andersen-Ranberg *et al.*, 2001a), though some of these centenarians needed help, e.g., to do shopping and housecleaning. It is our personal impression that a larger proportion of centenarians could carry out more IADL-tasks if they were encouraged and physically trained.

We may conclude that it is possible to preserve a relative autonomy up to a very high age in spite of different diseases and disabilities. We may also expect that the small proportion of relatively autonomous centenarians will increase in the future due to better treatment, better cognitive and physical training, and a more active lifestyle. It is therefore important to know more about the engagement and mood of centenarians and how they look at their own future. All who have interviewed centenarians have met some who think that they have been forgotten by God and would like to die, but they have also met some who are still looking forward to their next birthday. It therefore seems possible to preserve good spirits up to very high ages, Jeanne Calment being an excellent example. She thought that God knew her too well and therefore did not want her.

As already pointed out by Buffon in an interesting chapter on "Le bonheur de l'âge avancé" ("The happiness of advanced age") in his book *De l'homme* (1971 [1749]), there is no reason to become sad when life is nearing its end. No matter what age a person has reached, there are always a certain amount of days left. From the vital statistics of his time, Buffon was able to make the estimations that at the age of 70 you had 6 years left, at 75 you still had 4 years, and at 80 still 3 years. Today at the age of 90 you have more than 3 years left, at the age of 100 more than 2 years left, even at the age of 110 you still have about 1 year left, and Jeanne Calment lived 7 more years after having had a hip fracture at the age of 115.

We are moving from the large, horizontal family of 100 years ago with two or three generations and a lot of siblings and cousins, to the smaller, vertical family with four generations and two generations of elderly people. In the future it will be very important to know more about the relation between these two elderly generations. The oldest generation will still be very frail and often dependent on help from the family or the social service system. However, they will also be very present in the family as the reparitory of longest memories. The younger generation of grandparents who still have living parents seem to be healthier and fitter than earlier generations of elderly people. In the future, these generations of younger elderly people have to be in even better health and at least well-functioning, as they will have both downward and upward obligations regarding family networks and care. The improvement of trends in the health and the dependency on help in these two generations, and the relation between them, is the challenge of the future.

FURTHER READING

Jeune, B., and J. W. Vaupel, eds. (1999). *Validation of exceptional longevity*, Odense Monographs on Population Ageing 6. Odense University Press.

Kannisto, V. (1996). *The advancing frontier of survival*, Odense Monographs on Population Ageing 3. Odense University Press.

National Research Council (2000). "Cells and surveys. should biological measures be included in social science research?" In C. E. Finch, J. W. Vaupel, and K. Kinsella, eds., *Commission on behavioral and social sciences and education*, Report of the Committee on Population. Washington D.C.: National Academy Press.

Vaupel, J. W., Carey, J., Christensen, K., Johnson, T., Yashin, A. I., Holm, N. V., Iachine, I. A., Kannisto, V., Khazaeli, A., Liedo, P., Longo, V., Yi, Z., Manton, K., and J. Curtsinger (1998). "Biodemographic trajectories of longevity," *Science*, 280: 855–60.

REFERENCES

Allard, M., and J. M. Robine (2000). *Les centenaires français*. Paris: Serdi Edition.

Andersen-Ranberg, K., Schroll, M., and B. Jeune (2001a). "Healthy centenarians do not exist, but autonomous centenarians do: a population-based study of morbidity among Danish centenarians," *Journal of the American Geriatrics Society*, 49: 900–8.

Andersen-Ranberg, K., Vasegaard, L., and B. Jeune (2001b). "Dementia is not inevitable: a population-based study of Danish centenarians," *Journal of Gerontology: Psychological Sciences*, 56P: 152–9.

Austad, S. (1997). *Why we age*. New York: John Wiley & Sons, Inc.

Barker, D. J. (1998). *Mothers, babies and health in later life*. Edinburg: Churchill Livingstone.

Beregi, E., ed. (1990). *Centenarians in Hungary: a sociomedical and demographic study*. Basel: Karger.

Brønnum-Hansen, H. (2003). "Health expectancy in Denmark, 1897–2000," *European Journal of Public Health*.

Bruunsgaard, H., Østergaard, L., Andersen-Ranberg, K., Jeune, B., and B. K. Pedersen (2002). "Proinflammatory cytokines, antibodies to Chlamydia pneumonia and age-associated diseases in Danish centenarians: is there a link?" *Scandinavian Journal of Infectious Diseases*, 34: 493–9.

Buffon (1971[1749]). *De l'homme*. Paris: Edition François Maspero.

Butler, R. N., Austad, S. N., Barzilai, N., Braun, A., Helfland, S., Larsen, P. L., McCormick, A. M., Perls, T. T., Shuldiner, A. R., Sprott, R. L. and H. R. Warner (2003). "Longevity genes: from primitive organisms to humans," *Journal of Gerontology: Biological Sciences*, 58A: B581–B584.

Candore, G., Di Lorenzo, G., Mansueto, P., Melluso, M., Fradà, G., Li Vecchi, M., Pellitteri, M. E., Drago, A., Di Salvo, A., and C. Caruso (1997). "Prevalence of organ-specific and non organ-specific autoantibodies in healthy centenarians," *Mechanisms of Ageing and Development*, 94: 183–90.

Christensen, K., Vaupel, J. W., Holm, N. V., and A. I. Yashin (1995). "Mortality among twins after age 6: fetal origins hypothesis versus twin method," *British Medical Journal*, 310: 432–6.

Christensen, K., Gaist, D., Jeune, B., and J. W. Vaupel (1998). "A tooth per child?" [Letter]. *Lancet*, 352: 204.

Crimmins, E. M., and Y. Saito (2001). "Trends in healthy life expectancy in the United States, 1970–1990: gender, racial and educational differences," *Social Science & Medicine*, 52: 1629–41.

De Benedictis, G., Tan, Q., Jeune, B., Christesen, K., Ukrantseva, S. V., Bonafé, M., Fransceschi, C., Vaupel, J. W., and A. I. Yashin (2001). "Recent advances in human gene-longevity association studies," *Mechanisms of Ageing and Development*, 122: 909–20.

Doblhammer, G. (1999). "Longevity and month of birth: evidence from Austria and Denmark," *Demographic Research*, 1/3: www.demographic-research.org.

Doblhammer, G., and J. Oeppen (2003). "Reproduction and longevity among the British peerage: the effect of frailty and health selection," *Proceedings of the Royal Society of London*, B/270: 1541–7.

Evert, J., Lawler, E., Bogan, H., and T. Perls (2003). "Morbidity profiles of centenarians: survivors, delayers and escapers," *Journal of Gerontology: Medical Sciences*, 58A: 232–7.

Finch, C. E. (1990). *Longevity, senescence and the genome*. Chicago: University of Chicago Press.

Finch, C. E., and R. E. Tanzi (1997). "Genetics of ageing," *Science*, 278: 407–11.

Franceschi, C., Monti, D., Sansoni, P., and A. Cossarizza (1995). "The immunology of exceptional individuals: the lesson of centenarians," *Immunology Today*, 16: 12–16.

Frederiksen, H., McGue, M., Jeune, B., Gaist, D., Nybo, H., Skythe, A., Vaupel, J. W., and K. Christensen (2002). "Do children of long-lived parents age more successfully?" *Epidemiology*, 13: 334–9.

Freedman, V. A., Martin, L. G., and R. F. Schoeni (2002). "Recent trends in disability and functioning among older adults in the United States. A systematic review," *Journal of the American Medical Association*, 288: 3137–46.

Fries, J. F. (1980). "Aging, natural death, and the compression of morbidity," *New England Journal of Medicine*, 303: 130–5.

(2002). "Reducing disability in older age" [Editorial], *JAMA*, 288: 3164–6.

Gavrilov, L. A., and N. S. Gavrilova (2001). "Biodemographic study of familial determinants of human longevity," *Population: An English Selection*, 13: 197–222.

Gerdes, L. U., Jeune, B., Andersen-Ranberg, K., Nybo, H., and J. W. Vaupel (2000). "Estimation of apolipoprotein E genotype-specific relative mortality from the distribution of genotypes in centenarians and middle-aged men: apolipoprotein E gene is a 'frailty gene,' not a 'longevity gene,'" *Genetic Epidemiology*, 19: 202–10.

Guarante, L., and C. Kenyon (2000). Genetic pathways that regulate ageing in model organisms, *Nature 2000*, 408: 255–62.

Gudmundson, H., Gudbjartsson, D. F., Frigge, M., Gulcher, J. R., and K. Stefanson (2001). "Inheritance of human longevity in Iceland," *European Journal of Human Genetics*, 8: 743–9.

Hagberg, B., Alfredson, B. B., Poon, L. W., and A. Homma (2001). "Cognitive funtioning in centenarians: a coordinated analysis of results from three countries," *Journal of Gerontology: Psychological Sciences*, 56P: 141–51.

Hayflick, L. (1994). *How and why we age*. New York: Ballantine Books.

Herskind, A. A., McGue, M., Holm, N., Harvald, B., and J. W. Vaupel (1996). "The heritability of human longevity: a population-based study of 2,872 Danish twin pairs born 1870–1900," *Human Genetics*, 97: 319–23.

Hitt, R., Young-Xu, Y., Silver, M., and T. T. Perls (1999). "Centenarians: the older you get, the healthier you have been" [Letter], *Lancet*, 354: 652.

Jeune, B. (2002). "Living longer – but better?" *Ageing Clinical and Experimental Research*, 14: 72–93.

Jeune, B., and A. Skytthe (2001). "Centenarians in Denmark in the past and the present," *Population: An English Selection*, 13: 75–94.

Jeune, B., and J. W. Vaupel, eds. (1995). *Exceptional longevity: from prehistory to the present*, Monographs on Population Ageing 2. Odense University Press.

(1999). *Validation of exceptional longevity*, Odense Monographs on Population Ageing 6. Odense University Press.

Kannisto, V. (1996). *The advancing frontier of survival*, Odense Monographs on Population Ageing 3. Odense University Press.

Kerber, R. A., O'Brien, E., Smith, K. R., and R. M. Cawthorn (2001). "Familial excess longevity in Utah genealogies," *Journal of Gerontology: Biological Sciences*, 56B: 130–9.

Kirkwood, T. B. L. (1999). *Time of our lives*. London: Weidenfeld & Nicolson.

Kirkwood, T. B. L., and S. N. Austad (2000). "Why do we age?" *Nature*, 408: 233–7.

Louhija, J. (1994). "Finnish centenarians. A clinical epidemiological study." Academic dissertation, University of Helsinki, Helsinki.

Manton, K. G., and X. Gu (2001). "Changes in the prevalence of chronic disability in the United States black and nonblack population above age 65 from 1982 to 1999," *Proc Natl Acad Sci USA*, 98: 6354–9.

Marmot, M., Shipley, M., Brunner, E., and H. Hemingway (2001). "Relative contribution of early life and adult socioeconomic factors to adult morbidity in the Whitehall II study," *Journal of Epidemiology and Community Health*, 55: 301–7.

Martin, P., Poon, L. W., Clayton, G. M., Lee, H. S., Fulks, J. S., and M. A. Johnson (1992). "Personality, life events and coping in the oldest," *International Journal of Aging & Human Development*, 34: 19–30.

Martin, G. M., Austad, S. N., and T. E. Johnson (1996). "Genetic analysis of aging: role of oxidative damage and environmental stresses," *Nature Genetics*, 13: 25–34.

Masoro, J. E., ed. (2001). "Caloric restriction's effect on aging: opportunities for research on human implications," *Journal of Gerontology: Biological Sciences*, 56A: Special issue I.

McKeown, T. (1965). *Medicine in modern society. Medical planning based on evaluation of medical achievement.* New York: Hafner Publishing Company.

Miller, R. A. (1999). "Kleemeier award lecture: are there genes for aging?" *Journal of Gerontology: Biological Sciences*, 54A: B297–B307.

Morley, J. E., Perry, H. M., and D. K. Miller (2002). "Something about frailty," *Journal of Gerontology: Medical Sciences*, 57A: 698–704.

Nybo, H., Pedersen, H. C., Gaist, D., Jeune, B., Andersen, K., McGue, M., Vaupel, J. W., and K. Christensen (2003). "Predictors of mortality among 2,249 nonagenarians – the Danish 1905-Cohort Survey," *JAGS (in press)*.

Oeppen, J., and J. W. Vaupel (2002). "Broken limit to life expectancy," *Science*, 10: 1029–31.

Olshansky, S. J., Carnes, B. A., and C. Cassel (1990). "In search of Methuselah: estimating the upper limits to human longevity," *Science*, 250: 634–40.

Olshansky, S. J., Carnes, B. A., and A. Désquelles (2001). "Prospects for human longevity," *Science*, 291: 1491–2.

Perls, T., Wager, C., Bubrick, E., Vijg, J., and L. Kruglyak (1998). "Siblings of centenarians live longer" [Letter], *Lancet*, 351: 1560.

Puca, A. A., Daly, M. J., Brewster, S. J., Matise, T. C., Barrett, J., Shea-Drinkwater, M., Kang, S., Joyce, E.,

Benson, E., Kunkel, L. M., and T. Perls (2001). "A genome-wide scan for linkage to human exceptional longevity identifies a locus on chromosome 4," *PNAS*, 98: 10505–8.

Ritchie, K., and D. Kildea (1995). "Is senile dementia 'age-related' or 'ageing-related?' – evidence from a meta-analysis of dementia prevalence in the oldest-old," *Lancet*, 46: 931–4.

Robine, J. M., and J. W. Vaupel (2001). "Supercentenarians: slower ageing individuals or senile elderly?" *Experimental Gerontology*, 36: 915–30.

Robine, J. M., Forette, B., Franceschi, C., and M. Allard, eds. (1999a). *The paradox of longevity.* Berlin and Heidelberg: Fondation Ipsen, Springer-Verlag.

Robine, J. M., Romieu, I., and E. Cambois (1999b). "Health expectancy indicators," *Bull WHO*, 77: 181–5.

Schächter, F., Cohen, D., and T. Kirkwood (1993). "Prospects for the genetics of human longevity," *Hum Genet*, 91: 519–638.

Silver, M. H., Jilinskaia, E., and T. T. Perls (2001). "Cognitive functional status of age-confirmed centenarians in a population-based study," *Journal of Gerontology: Psychological Sciences*, 56P: 134–40.

Tauchi, H., Sato, T., and T. Watanaba, eds. (1999). *Japanese centenarians – medical research for final stages of human aging.* Aichi Medical University, Aichi.

Thatcher, R. (1999). "The long-term pattern of adult mortality and the highest attained age," *Journal of Royal Statistical Society A*, 162 (1): 5–43.

Vaupel, J. W., and A. E. Gowan (1986). "Passage to Methuselah: some demographic consequences of continued progress against mortality," *American Journal of Public Health*, 76: 430–3.

Vaupel, J. W., Carey, J. R., Christensen, K., Johnson, T. E., Yashin, A. I., Holm, N. V., Iachine, I. A., Kannisto, V., Khazaeli, A. A., Liedo, P., Longo, V. D., Zeng, Y., Manton, K. G., and J. W. Curtsinger (1998). "Biodemographic trajectories of longevity," *Science*, 280: 855–60.

Westendorp, R. G. J., and T. B. L. Kirkwood (1998). "Human longevity at the cost of reproductive success," *Nature*, 396: 743–6.

Wilhelmson, K. (2003). "Longer life – better life? Studies on mortality, morbidity and quality of life among elderly people." Ph.D. thesis, Göteborg University, Göteborg.

Wilmoth, J. R., Deegan, L. J., Lundström, H., and S. Horiuchi (2000). "Increase of maximum life-span in Sweden," *Science*, 289: 2366–8.

Yashin, A. I., De Benedictis, G., Vaupel, J. W., *et al.* (2000). "Genes and longevity: lessons from studies on centenarians," *Journal of Gerontology: Biological Sciences*, 55A: 319–28.

The Epidemiology of Ageing

CHRISTINA VICTOR

We may distinguish three major approaches towards the study of age and ageing: ageing as an individual experience (a micro-level perspective), understanding the experiences of older people within society and the societal implication of population ageing; both of these latter two approaches focus upon a macro-level view of the issues of ageing and later life. Epidemiology is concerned with describing and understanding the patterns and determinants of health at a population level. Consequently this is an approach towards the study of age and ageing which operates at the macro level. Rather than examining the individual experience of ageing, the epidemiological perspective is concerned with aggregate or group experiences of health and with the search for the determinants of patterns of ill health identified. As such it forms one element of the broader tradition of public health which is concerned with the organized efforts of society to improve health at the population level – again an approach towards health improvement that operates at the group rather than individual level. It is also an approach which is concerned with biological, social and environmental determinants of ill health and disease.

The importance of health is a key feature of many studies of the experience of age and ageing, and health is seen as central to the experience and maintenance of quality of life in old age. Arber and Ginn (1991) argue that health is one of the key sets of 'resources' that older people bring to the experience of ageing. Indeed, health and the maintenance of physical and mental health, and the avoidance of disability, are central to the concept of successful ageing developed by Rowe and Kahn

(1997). Hence, the discussion of health and illness is basic to any consideration of the experience of ageing and this is reflected in the contents of this book. The health status of any specific older person reflects the interaction of numerous factors including genetic makeup, individual behaviours (such as diet, exercise or smoking), exposure to environmental and occupational hazards and the availability and quality of health care. Social factors such as gender, ethnicity and social class also have an important impact upon the experience of health status, health behaviour and access to health care. Hence health in old age, or indeed other phases of the life cycle, can be viewed as a result of a complex interaction between both individual-level and macro-level social and environmental factors. In this chapter we employ an epidemiological approach to examine the health status of older people and consider how the experience of health in later life is shaped by macro-social factors such as gender, class and ethnicity. We summarize the key debates concerning health in later life and conclude the chapter with a brief consideration of issues concerned with the provision of health care for older people.

DESCRIBING THE HEALTH OF OLDER PEOPLE

Health remains a difficult entity to define. We can distinguish three main approaches: health as the absence of disease (a medical model approach); health as the absence of illness (a sociological perspective); health as an ideal or 'optimal state' (the World Health Organization model); and health as a pragmatically defined entity. Each of these perspectives derives from different theoretical conceptualizations of health and generates different types of research questions and different types of 'knowledge' about the epidemiology of ageing. However, when we attempt to describe and analyze the health status of populations, or of particular groups within defined populations, we are usually forced to use more limited disease-orientated measures. This largely reflects the dominance of the medical model within the areas of routine health information collection, health surveys such as The Health Survey for England and epidemiological investigations.

Measuring health: mortality and morbidity

In attempting to describe the health status of populations and their constituent elements we ideally need measures that allow comparisons between individuals, groups, places or different points in time (or indeed some combination of these). This latter requirement is especially important if we are to test empirically the two propositions outlined below concerning the likely health experience of future cohorts of elders. The measure that comes closest to fulfilling the technical requirements of being accurate, complete and routinely available for populations over a fairly long historical time span is mortality data or information concerning the distribution of patterns of death within the population. Mortality is probably the oldest and most widely used index of health status, especially as the end state or outcome is unambiguous, although establishing the cause is often more problematic. As early as the sixteenth century, mortality statistics relating to epidemics of the plague were published in London. However, by using this approach we are making certain assumptions. We are enumerating patterns of deaths within populations and presuming that these mirror the distribution of health and illness of survivors of the same ages and that the major causes of death are the principal causes of ill health amongst survivors.

Morbidity measures are concerned with the patterns of non-morbidity health status. There are a number of different approaches to the development of morbidity indicators and it is only possible to summarize the major approaches. Four main types

of perspectives on the measures of morbidity may be identified: studies of specific conditions such as heart disease or dementia; studies of 'generic' health status or self-rated health; studies of disability and chronic disease; and indirect indices that are based upon the secondary analysis of routine clinical or health service activity data, such as the use of data for hip fractures to establish the prevalence of osteoporosis. Researchers concerned with the health status of older people are usually less interested in acute illnesses as these do not demonstrate the 'age-related' increases illustrated by the measures noted above (see Victor, 2004a). Another way of examining this issue is to use combinations of mortality and morbidity data to calculate measures of 'healthy' or 'disability-free' life expectancy. These types of measures express a related, and rather fundamental, concept, especially if we are concerned with examining both quality and quantity of life. How many years of the expected duration of life will be healthy or free from disability, dementia or dependency? What is both the duration and quality of life?

Measuring the extent of disability, impairment and handicap within populations is both methodologically and conceptually problematic as there is no universally accepted method for assessing this. One approach is that exemplified by the national studies of the prevalence of disability within Britain (Martin et al., 1988) which examined the severity of the nine major areas of disabilities identified by WHO. Perhaps the measures most frequently used to determine the extent of disability within older populations are the measures of functional ability; that is, how well can people undertake a range of activities considered essential for the maintenance of an independent life in the community (see Melzer et al., 1999). There are many scales and measures which classify individual abilities to undertake activities in three major aspects of daily life: self-care, mobility, and instrumental activities such as shopping and cleaning. Inevitably such measures have been developed from the 'top down'. The items measured reflect the concerns of policymakers with estimating the need for different types of services and enumerating the factors which place older people 'at risk' of entering institutional care or requiring state services, rather than reflecting the concerns of older people.

KEY DEBATES CONCERNING HEALTH IN OLD AGE

Health status is clearly of great concern to older people both as individuals and more collectively (as is the case for individuals of any age group). However, the health of older people is also an area of concern for governments throughout the developed world because older people are the main users of health services and the main consumer group for the expenditure of health funds (Seshamani and Gray, 2002). Consequently the increase in the number of older people within the population is seen as posing a considerable challenge for governments in terms both of pension provision and of provision of health and social care services. Hence there has been considerable interest in looking at trends in the health status of older people and considering how patterns of health status may change, either for better or for worse, in future decades. There are several theories concerning such trends and what is likely to happen in the future. In this section we outline these differing theoretical positions and consider the empirical data.

The rectangularization of mortality

Whilst there may be debates as to why these changes have happened, there is no doubt as to the reality of the very profound changes in the scale and pattern of deaths within the population of developed countries. Using Great Britain as an exemplar the crude mortality rate, deaths per 1,000 population, for England in 1541 was approximately 30 per 1,000 (Grundy, 1997) (although it was subject to violent fluctuations as a result of epidemics of infectious diseases) compared with approximately 10 per 1,000 in 2002. The decrease in mortality rates is illustrated most dramatically for infant mortality, deaths within the first year of life. In England and Wales in the mid nineteenth century, approximately 15 per cent of babies died in the first year of life compared with less than 1 per cent (5.8 per 1,000) in 2002.

The pattern of deaths within the population of most developed countries shows a J-shaped distribution. Mortality is (relatively) high in the first year of life, at 5.8 per 1,000, and then remains at under this level until the seventh decade of life. There-

after mortality rates increase from 20 per 1,000 for those aged 65–74 years to 170 per 1,000 at age 85+. This age-related increase in mortality is used as evidence to support the notion that ill health and disease are not simple factors associated with old age but that they are 'caused' by old age. One of the key challenges for gerontologists remains in distinguishing between pathology and disease and 'normal' ageing. It remains the case that many still do not differentiate these related but distinct concepts. Manton (1991) suggests that the pattern of mortality in later life is influenced by two interacting sets of factors: senescence (or the rate of 'natural ageing') and the distribution of risk factors for specific diseases within populations such as the prevalence of smoking, obesity or environmental/occupational hazards. Perhaps we should also add in social factors and the availability and quality of health care when considering key influences upon the health status of older people. Manipulations or interventions which change either (or both) of these factors would, in theory at least, result in changes in the pattern of mortality within populations.

One result of the major reduction in mortality, especially in infancy and childhood, has been the 'redistribution' of death from the young to the old. There are approximately 556,000 deaths each year in England and Wales, of which the majority, 80%, is accounted for by people aged 65+, and 64% by those aged 75+. This contrasts with the situation in 1841 when approximately 37% of all deaths were accounted for by those aged under 14. Hence, over the course of the last century and a half, the shape of the distribution of mortality has changed significantly. This has been described as the regtangularization of mortality and can be seen in most developed countries. That mortality has become increasingly concentrated into the later phases of life, in most developed countries, is not disputed. Rather, it is the consequences of this 'compression' of mortality into the later phases of life which are contested.

Compression of morbidity

The optimistic perspective argues that, as a result of the constriction of mortality into later life, morbidity will also demonstrate a similar trend because of the link between mortality and morbidity. Fries (1980) started from the assumption there is a 'fixed' biological limit to expectation of life of 85 years and a 'skewed' distribution of 'natural' mortality; under 'ideal' conditions 95% of deaths would occur between the ages of 77 and 95 years. We are, therefore, advancing rapidly towards this state whereby premature death has been largely eradicated and mortality in later life is as a result of the body 'wearing out' at the end of its 'natural' lifespan rather than because of disease per se. His thesis is that morbidity, as well as mortality, would also be 'compressed' into the later phases of life as a result of advances in medicine and living standards because the causes of morbidity and mortality are the same (or at least are influenced by the same risk factors). Fries (1980) argues both that there will be more people surviving into 'old age' and that those who do survive will be fitter because the factors that have delayed mortality will also have delayed morbidity. Hence those people surviving to old age will be fitter for longer with significant levels of morbidity being limited to a short period at the very end of life. This theory has very obvious policy implications. If the compression of morbidity thesis is correct, then expenditure on health care could, in theory at least, be reduced (or perhaps contained) and the 'ageing' of the population does not imply any great challenge to the provision of health services and social welfare.

Expansion of morbidity

It is no surprise to note that this concept of the compression of morbidity in later life has not gone unchallenged, and the counter argument to this is much less optimistic and suggests that the result of the compression of mortality will be an increase in morbidity. This position argues that the observed decline in mortality is the result of a decrease in fatality rates for many diseases such as stroke or cancer rather than as a result of any improvements in population health status. It is further proposed that neither the incidence of chronic diseases nor the rate of progression for these conditions has changed as a result of changes in mortality. Hence, as a result of decreased death rates, there will be an increase in the morbidity of the population because, although more people will survive into old age, they will do

so with much poorer health. Rather than morbidity being compressed into a short period at the end of life it will be extended across a longer period. This scenario has been variously termed the 'survival of the unfittest', a pandemic of mental disorder, chronic disease and disability, and the 'expansion of morbidity hypothesis'. Olshansky et al. (1990, 1991) share the assumption of a fixed maximum average life expectancy of 85 years with Fries (1980). However, they do not maintain the concept of skewed mortality distribution. Rather they presume that the distribution of age at death will continually shift towards the highest age groups, resulting in an increase in numbers of the oldest old with a consequent increase in the number of people with (multiple) chronic diseases within the population. This is obviously a pessimistic view as to the implications of more people surviving to older age groups: the implication is that there will be a massive increase in the numbers of disabled people (Olshansky and Carnes, 2002; Verbrugge, 1984).

To date, the debate concerning the validity of these two opposing propositions has been conducted at the population level. There has been remarkably little research examining the veracity of the compression/expansion of morbidity theses within subgroups of the total populations. Sidell (1997) argues that the compression of morbidity hypothesis may hold for men but not for women. However, this is a neglected area and there is clearly a large research agenda to examine morbidity trends both within populations and in terms of entire populations. Given our knowledge that the experience of morbidity is not distributed equally within societies – with rates of morbidity elevated amongst certain groups such as women, those from less privileged backgrounds and from minority communities – it seems unlikely that any changes in morbidity would be equitably distributed throughout the population. On the basis of current evidence it seems likely that if patterns of morbidity are changing amongst the older populations then some groups will be benefiting from such changes more than others do. Hence we need to examine these hypotheses both in terms of entire populations and in terms of the subgroups within these populations. Only focusing at the population level may mask the complex variations experienced within the 'big picture'.

Changes in mortality and morbidity rates over time

Another way of illustrating changes in mortality rates and survival over time is to examine variations in life expectancy and the probability of survival to old age. Olshansky and Rudberg (1997) report that, for the United States, 52% of those born in 1900 would live to age 65 and 18% to age 85, compared with 85% and 45% respectively for those born in 1990. On average, 75% of us will live to be aged 75 years. So profound has this social and cultural change been that we now all expect to live to experience 'old age'. Very few of us in western societies will die before we get old! In future decades this maxim will become increasingly true for the 'Third World' as population ageing spreads.

It is, of course, extremely difficult to test many of the propositions in the mortality/morbidity debates in human populations. However, one way is to look at patterns of mortality in populations with very low rates. If death rates amongst the 'oldest-old' and other members of the older population were approaching a biological limit then we would expect that mortality improvements in countries with low rates would be slower than in countries with higher rates.

Vaupel (1997) suggests that there is little evidence to support this proposition and countries with low late age mortality rates continue to show improvements. Mortality rates in later life are by no means static and do not yet seem to have reached a threshold. Taking 1911 as the index point, Vaupel (1997) demonstrates that mortality rates for females aged 85 have halved over the course of the twentieth century in England and Wales, a trend displayed by many western industrial societies including France, Sweden, Japan and the Nordic countries. For female octogenarians and nonagenarians in the same countries, death rates for these populations have decreased from about 165–85 per 1,000 in 1950 to 90–5 per 1,000 in the mid 1990s: an approximate halving in four decades. As well as changes in overall mortality rates, there have been significant changes in mortality from specific diseases. For both males and females aged 65 years and over, mortality from heart disease in the USA decreased by about 15% in the years 1980–6. Similarly, we can look at gender differences. Females have lower mortality rates than

men in late old age and it is females who have shown the greatest improvements in late age mortality. That there is scope for further reductions in late age mortality is suggested by comparing rates between countries. For example, at age 90, death rates in western Europe and Japan are about 50% higher (0.19% versus 0.13%) than in the Mid-Western region of the USA (Vaupel, 1997). Hence, it is unlikely that we have, as yet, reached the biological limit on decreasing mortality rates in later life.

In order to test the compression/expansion of morbidity thesis we need detailed data on secular trends in morbidity, which are rarely available. Data from routine community-based British surveys, collected over almost thirty years, hint that the latest cohorts studied illustrated some small decreases in disability that were not due to changes in the supply of long-stay care. Overall there is considerable stability in the responses obtained over time and no evidence, from these data, of marked changes in functional ability over the previous two decades (Victor, 2004a). Recently, Manton *et al.* (1997) and Manton and Gu (2001) have examined trends in chronic disability in the United States between 1982 and 1994. They conclude that disability prevalence declined by 0.34% per year or by 4.3% for the period 1982–96. Such decreases are not trivial. These authors observe that there were 1.4 million fewer disabled people aged 65+ in 1994 than if the 1982 rates had been maintained. This provides some tentative evidence that there might be some reduction in severe disability but no change in the 'less severe' categories. Fries (2003) has also produced evidence suggestive of decreasing rates of chronic disability within the older American population. He suggests that disability has been decreasing at 2% per year for the period 1982–99. His thesis is supported by the work of Freedman *et al.* (2002). Fries (2003) suggests that a decrease in disability of 1.5% per annum would be sufficient to contain health care expenditure within budgetary limits for at least seventy years. By combining overall life expectancy and 'healthy' life expectancy we can determine the number of years or percentage of the lifespan that individuals can expect to live, on average, free from disability. We can also use these measures to look at changes over time, although these measures are only as 'good' as the initial morbidity data upon which they are based. For the UK, both life expectancy and 'healthy' life expectancy have increased, although the increase has been greatest for the latter. Hence there has been a marginal increase in the percentage of life spent in poor health or disability (Kelly *et al.*, 2000).

A 'fixed' expectation of life?

The hypothesis of Fries (1980) rests upon a central assumption of a 'maximum' average life expectancy of 85 years. In the United Kingdom, expectation of life at birth is 80 for women and 75 for men, and in fifteen countries expectation of life at birth is 80+ years. Examining data for the United States, Olshansky *et al.* (1990) indicate that mortality rates need to decline by approximately 50% (40% for women and 60% for men) for this goal to be achieved. However, in the UK late age mortality has declined by this amount over the course of the last century and Robine *et al.* (1996) suggest that some countries will achieve an average life expectancy at birth of 85 years in the next two decades (assuming current trends continue). Furthermore, Manton (1991) has proposed that, for women, if the population demonstrated 'ideal' risk factor profiles, mortality would be reduced such that life expectancy at birth increased to 106 years. To date there is no clear evidence to suggest that we have reached a limit to average life expectancy, although the example of Russia always serves to remind us that increases in life expectancy are neither inevitable nor natural (Shkolnikov *et al.*, 2001).

INEQUALITIES IN HEALTH

Most debates about the 'compression of mortality/morbidity' hypothesis have been undertaken at the general population level. However, it is also pertinent to investigate whether some subgroups of the older population are experiencing decreases in morbidity/mortality that are not shared by the whole population of older people. For older people in Britain this debate takes place within the context of well-established general variations in mortality (and health more broadly defined) in terms of class, gender, ethnicity, geography or time of year. The empirical data available make it difficult to test all these potentially differing hypotheses. However, we can examine variations in health status within the older age groups and consider the degree to which these well-characterized health variations persist into later life and tentatively consider which groups appear to have benefited most from recent changes in mortality and morbidity.

Age and gender

Both mortality and chronic morbidity rates, as measured by a variety of indices, increase with age. Overall mortality rates for men are 7–10% higher than for women but after the age of 65 years the differential ranges from 6 to 25%. Furthermore, the gender difference in mortality seems to have increased from about 10% male excess in 1850 to 25–60% at the turn of the millennium. However, the pattern is reversed for chronic illness/disability where community surveys consistently show that women report more chronic illness than men, with a differential of about 10%. This differential is at its most extreme amongst the 85+ age group, where there is an 'excess' of morbidity of about 25%. It is the severe disability category which demonstrates both the largest age-related increase and the biggest gender differential, especially for those aged 80+. However, how much of this difference reflects a 'true' difference in morbidity and how much is a reflection of the social definition of gender roles and the tasks considered appropriate to those roles remains unclear (see the chapter by Arber and Ginn for further discussion of this point).

Ethnicity

Comparative mortality differentials between the different ethnic minority groups and the White population in later life are complex, largely because of the complexity of the ethnicity groups within developed countries. However, there is a consistent body of evidence indicating that, in Western Europe and the USA, some major diseases and conditions such as stroke, diabetes, hypertension and circulatory diseases are higher amongst minority communities than the 'host' population. Bone *et al.* (1995) have produced estimates of mortality amongst the differing ethnic populations. For men aged 65–74, mortality rates range from 439 per 10,000 for Black elders; 340 for those from the Indian subcontinent and 374 for the White population. It is almost certainly the case that the distribution of mortality in later life is not equally spread throughout the different ethnic minority populations, with Black African populations especially vulnerable. Evandrou (2000) reports elevated morbidity rates amongst elders from the Indian subcontinent or with Caribbean origins. However, current levels of analysis fail to disaggregate the 'Black' and 'Indian subcontinent' into their various constituent groups and rarely look at communities such as the Irish or Chinese. It seems probable that variation between ethnic minority communities is as great as between them in aggregate and the White population. Clearly there is a significant research agenda in carefully researching the variations in mortality and morbidity within and between the varying subgroups within our population.

Social class

Within most developed countries both mortality and morbidity amongst those of working age is strongly associated with socioeconomic position. For example, in Britain there is an almost 6-year difference in expectation of life at birth observed for boys, and 3.4 years for girls, according to social position (Khaw, 1999). It is only comparatively recently that this analysis has been extended to the retired population. It was presumed that socioeconomic differences were rendered irrelevant once individuals had entered old age because of the perceived 'universal' experience of chronic illness and disability. There is now a growing body of evidence pointing to the continuation into later life of these socioeconomic mortality differentials, expectation of life at ages 65 and over and the prevalence of chronic illness (Khaw, 1999; Marmot and Shipley, 1996; Breeze et al., 1999, 2001). For example, Victor (1991) has reported, overall, a 60 per cent mortality differential for males aged 65+ according to their social class position. There is a class-based mortality gradient amongst older women, although it may not be as strong as that for males (Victor, 1991; Khaw, 1999). Such differentials are not trivial. In Britain, at age 65 years, a man from the professional social groups could expect to live for another 15 years whilst his contemporary from an unskilled occupation would live for another 12 years (Hattersley, 1997). Reductions in the class-based mortality differentials would

clearly have an impact upon overall mortality and this, again, hints that mortality rates have not yet 'bottomed out'. Melzer et al. (2000) demonstrate the existence of socioeconomic differentials in the overall distributions both of disability and of severe disability, which are evident for all age/sex groups, and claims that the achievement of the disability prevalence of the most privileged groups by all older people would result in an absolute fall in the numbers of disabled elders, despite projected increases in both population and longevity.

Overall, this evidence suggests that increases in life expectancy, resulting from decreases in mortality, have not been equally shared throughout the population of older people. Women appear to have benefited more than men have and those from professional occupations have benefited at the expense of those from manual occupations. Whilst there are no comparable data on ethnicity, it seems highly improbable that increases in life expectancy, improved mortality and probability of surviving to reach 'old age' will have been shared equally across the major ethnic groups.

ESTABLISHING HEALTH NEEDS: CAUSES OF MORTALITY AND MORBIDITY

A central assumption of the use of mortality data to describe the health status of populations is that they accurately reflect the distribution of disease and disability within those populations. There are two distinct aspects to this assumption: demographic (i.e. the age and sex distribution of health problems) and the type of health problems identified. By comparing mortality and morbidity data we can test the veracity of these assumptions. We have already noted the similarity of patterns of mortality and morbidity for age, class and ethnicity and the reverse patterns for gender. In terms of mortality the most important causes of death for older adults are circulatory disease (accounting for 40% of deaths), respiratory disease (accounting for 19% of deaths) and cancers (23% of deaths), which account for 82% of all deaths amongst those aged 65+. Data from England report that of those with chronic illness approximately 30% have heart/circulatory disease, 30% have musculo-skeletal disorders, 10% respiratory problems, and less than 1% have cancers. Hence the patterns of mortality and morbidity in later life are not identical and we can distinguish three distinct categories of condition:

- High mortality and high morbidity (e.g. heart and circulatory diseases)
- High morbidity but low mortality (musculo-skeletal disease and dementia)
- High mortality and low morbidity (cancer)

The majority of older people can undertake the main 'activities of daily living' without difficulty. For example, for the task which presented the most difficulty to people elderly – cutting toenails – 30% were unable to undertake this alone and 70% were totally independent. Yet the fact that 30% of approximately 9 million people experience problems with this activity indicates that, in absolute terms, there are substantial numbers of people within the population who may have compromised independence. Melzer *et al.* (1999) suggest that 15.7% of people aged 65+ in England and Wales are disabled; a total of 1.3 million people. Whilst we may not wish to ascribe to the notion that all older people experience ill health and disability, there remain significant needs within this group which require a service response in order to help older people remain at home.

HEALTH BEHAVIOUR IN LATER LIFE

Across the developed world older people constitute the major consumer group for the services provided by health care systems (Seshamani and Gray, 2002). Yet even with these high levels of utilization, the vast majority of illness is not presented for consideration by the health care services. Only an estimated quarter to a third of all illness episodes result in a medical consultation as the decision to seek medical aid is only one illness behaviour strategy out of a whole range of possible options. One of the enduring stereotypes about old age is that treatable illnesses are mis-ascribed by older people to the process of ageing rather than being the manifestation of 'disease' (we return to this point in the section concerned with ageism). Consequently, it is argued, older people do not seek appropriate treatment. In support of this view a variety of studies have demonstrated that there are a large number of previously unidentified medical conditions to

be found amongst the older people living at home. Researchers have not undertaken such 'case finding' exercises comprehensively with younger populations and so it is not clear that these levels of 'unreported' health care problems are higher or lower than other groups within the population. The focus of attention is upon enumerating the number of previously undiagnosed medical conditions rather than identifying if this problem was seen as important by the older person or was causing them some inconvenience or disability. They may well not have drawn it to the attention of their GP because it was not a problem for them and not because they ascribed it to the inevitability of ageing. R. Williams (1990) in his study of ageing in Aberdeen argues that older people do not ignore symptoms and are equally as likely to seek treatment for these health problems as any other age group, representing a continuation of patterns of behaviour established earlier in the life cycle. Older people are every bit as diverse in their illness behaviour as other age groups and that illness behaviour in later life represents a continuation of previously established patterns.

Rowe and Kahn (1997) argue that promoting optimal physical and mental health remains a priority for successful ageing. This suggests that individuals need to minimize 'lifestyle' threats such as smoking, excess alcohol consumption and obesity, and to maintain an active way of life, combined with the uptake of preventive health measures such as screening, management of hypertension, etc. However, there is comparatively little attention paid to the promotion of health of older people and only a very limited research base as to what interventions are effective (see Victor and Howse, 1999, for a review).

CONCLUSION

Clearly, one of the key debates in gerontology is that concerning possible changes in the prevalence of ill health in later life. Exploration of this issue is methodologically complex, especially given our over-reliance upon cross-sectional survey data. There is clear and unambiguous evidence across the developed world for the continuing decline of mortality rates. However, the evidence concerning disability-free life expectancy, chronic illness and functional ability was inconsistent. On the basis of current data there is no evidence to support the view that there will be massive changes in morbidity amongst older people in the near future. However, within this broad generalization we also need to examine the different subsets of the older population. It is entirely possible that different elements of the older population will benefit disproportionately from changes in overall patterns of morbidity. There is evidence that women and those of high socioeconomic status have gained most from improvements in both expectation of life and disability-free life expectancy. Even if there is only a relatively small overall improvement in health status this may be differentially 'gained' by some groups at the expense of others. Indeed there is some evidence to suggest that it is the most 'advantaged' groups who are gaining from these changes and that differentials may be increasing rather than decreasing.

It remains the case that older people are the major consumers of health care services across the developed world and that this reflects the overall distribution of health problems within the population. Each of the different health care systems is challenged by specific nationally based problems concerning the care of older people. However, we can identify several common problems (see Victor, 2004b). First there is the issue of what is the most appropriate model of care for older people. Those in favour of the specialist approach argue that, given the difficulties the health/welfare system has dealing with those with complex needs or difficult circumstances, such groups are best served by specialist, expert services. The generic argument holds that, however complex or difficult the needs presented by a specific client group, the general system should be of such a good standard in terms of administration and quality that we should be able to care for all groups within the mainstream. The generic argument implies, if not specifically articulates, that to deal with groups outside of the mainstream both marginalizes, stigmatizes and ghettoizes such groups and those who work with them. Should services be specialist and 'age based' with care to people above a threshold age provided by specialist services (variously called medicine for old age, health care for older people, geriatric medicine, etc.) or are older people best served by the generic services? Perhaps

it is within the realm of the specialist services for older people that we can see elements of the 'ageing enterprise' thesis advanced by Estes (1979). Are older peoples' needs best met by services where age is the criteria for entry or do such services serve to detach older people from 'the mainstream' and thereby isolate and stigmatize them and provide an implicit justification for the delivery of substandard care?

In the current configuration of the welfare state in most developed countries, a variety of different agencies are involved in the provision of health care to older people, including primary and secondary care sectors, long-term care agencies, social care agencies and a mixture of public, private and voluntary contractors. So, even considering only the most basic aspects of the health service response to older people, it is immediately obvious that this variety of agencies all have varying professional objectives and differing modes of working. Such dislocations in care pathways are most evident at specific transition points such as admission and discharge from hospital or arranging assessment and admission to long-term care. We can also distinguish between the locations where services for older people are provided, and again there are vigorous debates at different levels as to the most appropriate locations for the provision of care. One key debate concerns the boundaries between primary and secondary care. Hospital services have been extended beyond the hospital buildings with the development of 'hospital at home' schemes. Perhaps the most influential and important debate within the post Second World War welfare state surrounds the respective merits of institutional versus community-based responses for groups such as older people. Academic research and sociological theory, combined with the revelation of systematic and sustained abuse in various British long-stay hospitals, merged to create a powerful perception that institutional care was inherently a 'bad thing'. Irrespective of the resources and funds involved, institutional care solutions were seen as being inherently ineffective and inhumane. Hence the concept of community care is imbued with both positive attributes (the cosy and comforting image of the 'caring community' as personified by some radio and television soap operas) and important negative ones (i.e., it is not institutional care!). This is an example of policies being defined in terms of negative outcomes (what they are not or are seeking to avoid) rather than being based upon a more positive goal.

Perhaps the greatest challenge faced by older people when using health services relates to the concepts of ageism, age discrimination and age-based rationing. These are three interrelated but distinct concepts. Ageism is concerned with implicit/explicit 'negative' attitudes towards older people. Age-discrimination involves either positive (or negative) treatment of individuals/groups on the basis of chronological age. At the most negative extreme is the concept of age-based rationing – access to health resources are restricted at the institutional level solely upon the basis of chronological age. There are essentially two positions in terms of the attitudes towards 'age'-based rationing of health care. A. Williams (1997) argues for the 'fair innings' thesis, in that once a certain age has been achieved then priority for treatment should be given to other age groups. Grimley Evans (1997) advances the view that age is a very imprecise mechanism by which to allocate care and that we should treat older people on their 'merits'. The National Service Framework for Older People for England and Wales (Department of Health, 2001, 2002) has taken the battle against 'ageism' and 'age discrimination' as its first challenge and is an exemplar of the institutional response to the identified challenges. However, this is a complex issue with several different elements which include both 'simple' access to services (can older people get the care they need?) and the quality of care (are older people treated to the same quality of care as other groups?). The debate is further complicated by differences in how the varying subgroups of the older population are treated. Are older men more likely to receive care than older women are? Do issues of class and race matter? How do the characteristics of the health professionals influence such attitudes? It remains a challenge for developed countries to ensure that older people have equal access to care of equal quality to that provided for other age groups.

FURTHER READING

Bowling, A. (1999). 'Ageism in cardiology', *British Medical Journal*, 319: 1353–5.
Ebrahim, S., and A. Kalache (1996). *The epidemiology of ageing*. London: BMJ Books.

Marmot, M., Banks, J., Blundell, R., *et al.* (2003). *Health, wellbeing and lifestyles of the older population in England: the 2002 English Longitudinal Study of Ageing*. London: Institute for Fiscal Studies.

REFERENCES

Arber, S., and J. Ginn (1991). *Gender and later life*. London: Sage.
Bone, M., Bebbington, A., Jagger, C., *et al.* (1995). *Health expectancy and its uses*. London: HMSO.
Breeze, E., Fletcher, A., and D. Leon (2001). 'Socio-economic differentials persist in old age', *American Journal of Public Health*, 9192: 277–83.
Breeze, E., Sloggett, A., and A. Fletcher (1999). 'Socio-economic status and transitions in status in old age in relation to limiting longstanding illness measured at the 1991 Census', *European Journal of Public Health*, 9 (4): 205–40.
Department of Health (DoH) (2001). *National service framework for older people*. London: Stationery Office. Available from www.doh.gov.uk/nsf/olderpeople.htm.
   (2002). *National service framework for older people: interim report on age discrimination*. Available only from www.doh.gov.uk/nsf/olderpeople.htm/. April.
Estes, C. L. (1979). *The aging enterprise*. San Francisco: Jossey-Bass.
Evandrou, M. (2000). 'Ethnic inequalities in health in later life', *Health Statistics Quarterly*, 8: 20–8.
Freedman, V., Martin, L., and R. Schoeni (2002). 'Recent trends in disability and functioning among older adults in the United States: a systematic review', *Journal of the American Medical Association*, 288 (24): 3137–46.
Fries, J. F. (1980). 'Aging, natural death and the compression of morbidity', *New England Journal of Medicine*, 303: 130–5.
   (2003). 'Measuring and monitoring success in compressing morbidity', *Annals of Internal Medicine*, 139 (5): 455–63.
Grimley Evans, J. (1997). 'The rationing debate: rationing health care by age – the case against', *British Medical Journal*, 314: 822.
Grundy, E. M. (1997). 'The health and health care of older adults in England and Wales, 1841–1994'. In J. Charlton and M. Murphy, eds. *The health of adult Britain 1841–1994, Vol. II*. London: The Stationery Office.
Hattersely, L. (1997). 'Expectation of life by social class'. In M. Whitehead, and F. Driver, eds. *Health inequalities*. London: Stationery Office.
Kelly, S., Baker, A., and S. Gupta (2000). 'Healthy life expectancy in Great Britain 1980–1996', *Health Statistics Quarterly*, 7: 16–24.

Khaw, K. T. (1999). 'Inequalities and health: older people'. In D. Gordon, M. Shaw, D. Dorling, and G. Davey-Smith, *Inequalities in health: the evidence*. Bristol: The Policy Press.

Manton, K. (1991). 'New biotechnologies and limits to life expectancy'. In W. Lutz, ed. *Future demographic trends in Europe and North America*. New York: Academic Press.

Manton, K., and X. Gu (2001). 'Changes in the prevalence of chronic disability in the United States black and non-black population above age 65 from 1982 to 1999', *Proceedings National Academy of Science USA*, 98: 6354–9.

Manton, K., Cordes, L., and E. Stallard (1997). 'Chronic disability trends in elderly United States populations: 1982–1984', *Proceedings National Academy of Science USA*, 94: 2593–8.

Marmot, M., and M. Shipley (1996). 'Do socio-economic differences in mortality persist after retirement?' *British Medical Journal*, 313: 1177–80.

Martin, J., Meltzer, H., and D. Elliot (1988). *The prevalence of disability amongst adults*. London: HMSO.

Melzer, D., McWilliams, B., Brayne, C., Johnson, T., and J. Bond (1999). 'Profile of disability in elderly people: estimates from a longitudinal study', *British Medical Journal*, 318: 1108–11.

(2000). 'Socio-economic status and the expectation of disability in old age: estimates for England', *Journal of Epidemiology and Community Health*, 54: 286–92.

Olshansky, S. J., and B. A. Carnes (2002). *The quest for immortality*. New York: H. H. Norton.

Olshansky, S. J., and M. A. Rudberg (1997). 'Postponing disability: identifying points of decline and potential intervention'. In T. Mickey, M. Speers and T. Protraska, eds., *Public health and aging*. Baltimore, Md: Johns Hopkins University Press.

Olshansky, S. J., Carnes, B., and C. Cassel (1990). 'In search of Methuselah: estimating the upper limits to human longevity', *Science*, 250: 634–40.

Olshansky, S. J., Rudberg, M. A., Cassel, B. A., and J. A. Brady (1991). 'Trading off longer life for worsening health: the expansion of morbidity hypothesis', *Journal of Aging and Health*, 312: 194–216.

Robine, J. M., Mathers, C., and N. Brooard (1996). 'Trends and differentials in disability free life expectancy, concepts, methods and findings'. In G. Caselli and A. D. Lopez, eds., *Health and mortality among elderly populations*. Oxford: Clarendon Press.

Rowe, J. W., and R. L. Kahn (1997). 'Successful aging', *Gerontologist*, 37 (4): 433–40.

Seshamani, M. and A. Gray (2002). 'The impact of ageing on expenditures in the National Health Service', *Age and Ageing*, 31 (4): 287–94.

Shkolnikov, V., McKee, M., and D. Leon (2001). 'Changes in life expectancy in Russia in the mid 1990s', *Lancet*, 357: 917–21.

Sidell, M. (1997). *Health in old age*. Buckingham: Open University Press.

Vaupel, J. W. (1997). 'The remarkable improvements in survival at older ages', *Royal Society: Philosophical transactions – biological sciences*, 352: 1761–1920.

Verbrugge, L. M. (1984). 'Longer life but worsening health', *Millbank Memorial Fund Quarterly*, 62: 475–519.

Victor, C. R. (1991). 'Continuity or change: inequalities in health in later life', *Ageing and Society*, 11: 23–39.

(2004a). *The social context of ageing*. London: Routledge.

(2004b). 'Services for older people'. In J. Healy and M. McKee, eds., *Accessing health care: responding to diversity*. Oxford: Oxford University Press.

Victor, C. R., and K. Howse (1999). *Effective health promotion interventions for older people*. London: Health Education Authority.

Williams, A. (1997). 'The rationing debate: rationing health care by age – the case for', *British Medical Journal*, 314: 820–5.

Williams, R. (1990). *A protestant legacy*. Oxford: Clarendon Press.

Patterns of Illness and Mortality Across the Adult Lifespan

EDLIRA GJONÇA AND MICHAEL MARMOT

INTRODUCTION

Health is commonly considered one of the most important factors relevant to the quality of life. Health can become related to, and can even determine, lifespan through different pathways. For the purpose of this discussion we are going to analyze mortality changes as well as health ones. In general, mortality data are more readily available and reliable than morbidity data. Moreover, without longitudinal data it is difficult to give a picture of the patterns of illness. However, the two concepts are closely related and will be discussed later in this chapter. Knowledge about health conditions of different groups in society in different countries is very fragmented (Marmot and Nazroo, 2001). On the other hand, reliable information on deaths by cause is available for most countries and provides an important source of information for this work. In this chapter we are focusing only on adult ages, more specifically ages over 40. We are also discussing this topic in the context of both developed and developing countries. One of the reasons why we are focusing on both types of societies is that, despite the fact that developed countries have relatively high proportions of people aged 65 and over, the most rapid increases in the elderly population are in the developing world. We are also including countries in transition in the discussion as they portray an interesting picture of societies that are at the crossroads between developed and developing stages.

PATTERNS OF ILLNESS AND MORTALITY IN DEVELOPED COUNTRIES

Doubling life expectancy at birth

Over the past two centuries the average expectation of life at birth in developed countries has doubled from about 40 to 80 years. For instance, in England and Wales the life expectancy at birth (both sexes combined) improved from 44.8 years at the beginning of 1800 (Wrigley *et al.*, 1997) to 77 years in 2000. The spectacular increases in human life expectancy that began in the mid-1800s and continued during the following century are not simply the result of the development of medicine. A growing research consensus attributes the gain in human longevity to a number of complex factors: the advancement of medicine; sanitation; changes in familial, social, economic and political organization (Moore, 1993). Improvements in life expectancy have taken place at different ages and have been associated with changing patterns of causes of death. While the early stages of demographic transition saw the improvement of mortality mainly at very young ages, a different situation is seen today where most of the improvement in mortality is occurring at old age, even among the oldest-old (Thatcher, 1999; Kannisto *et al.*, 1994; Gjonça *et al.*, 2000). Figure 1 shows the changes in mortality for ages above 40 since 1950 in England and Wales.

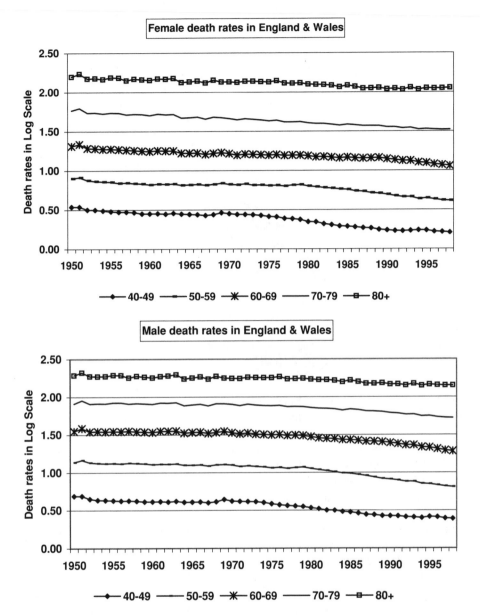

Figure 1. Death rates for ages 40–9, 50–9, 60–9, 70–9, 80+, 1950–2000, for England and Wales (male, female).

It is clear that since the mid twentieth century mortality has improved at all ages of the adult lifespan. This extends to the two oldest age groups. There is some evidence that female improvement has preceded male improvement.

In some developing countries, the proportional increase in life expectancy at older ages is approaching or has even surpassed the relative increase in life expectancy at birth (Kinsella, 1994). At present, over half of all deaths happen at ages 75 and over in devel-

oped societies (Figure 2), while mortality at younger ages is low. Further life expectancy gains will depend mainly on reduction of mortality over the age of 65. The size of the elderly population has increased continuously in the last century. In 2000 there were 600 million people worldwide aged 60 and over, and by 2050 there will be more than 2 billion (WHO, 1998).

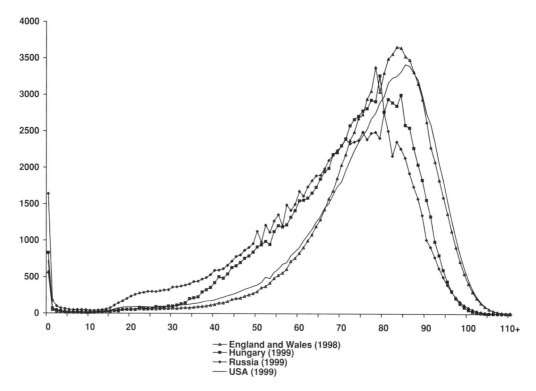

Figure 2. Distribution of life table deaths by age in developed and developing countries in 2000.

In the UK between 1971 and 1994 the population aged 60 and over increased by 13 per cent. People over 60 currently constitute a fifth of the British population. By 2030 they are expected to reach one third of the population (Greengross *et al.*, 1997). In Europe, every seventh person is aged 65 years or more and this proportion is growing while the proportion of children is declining (WHO, 2002). As baby boomers grow old, the elderly population is expected to grow rapidly in the years to come. The continued reduced fertility level (below replacement level of 2.1 children per woman) in developed countries and increased survival at the very old ages are main determinants of this proportional increase in size of the elderly population in developed countries today. Advanced industrial societies now have an 'aged' as well as an 'ageing' population. The proportion of elderly people in such societies was high even at the beginning of the last century and has continued to increase.

Another central feature of the increase in life expectancy is the existing sex differential. In 1900,

in Europe and North America, women typically outlived men by 2–3 years. Today, the average gap between the sexes is about 7 years. Underlying this differential is the fact that in most countries females have lower mortality than males in every age group and for most causes of death. The gender differential is smaller in developing countries and in some cases it is even reversed in favour of males (Kinsella and Velkoff, 2001). Female mortality between ages 35 and 84 has fallen more than male mortality (Gjonça *et al.*, 1999).

The improvements in mortality at the very old ages since the early 1970s have called into question the commonly accepted assumption that human life expectancy is close to its biological limits in today's developed societies. The assumption of a fixed lifespan, possibly with a maximum life expectancy at birth of about 85 years, is no longer tenable (Wilmoth *et al.*, 2000; Oeppen and Vaupel, 2002). Previous research had shown that death rates increase exponentially with age, especially at old ages. More recently researchers have documented that, at the very old ages, this rate tends to slow down. Kannisto *et al.* (1994), Vaupel (1997) and, later, Wilmoth and colleagues

(2000) have confirmed this finding in independent research.

Chronic diseases have surpassed acute diseases

The increase in survival in part reflects the shift in the main causes of death from infectious diseases to chronic degenerative diseases. Olshansky and Ault (1986) showed that we are living in what they called the 'fourth stage of epidemiological transition', in a time when degenerative diseases are the main killers of human life. Today, cardiovascular diseases and cancers combined constitute more than half of deaths among people of age 40 and above. Of all deaths for the female population aged 60 and over, 60 per cent were attributable to CVD in 1990, while the figure for males was 50 per cent (Murray and Lopez, 1996).

A major disparity in health and mortality exists between countries of western and northern Europe and those of central and eastern Europe. A gap in life expectancy at birth between these two regions has always existed. However, prior to the 1970s the gap was closing, mainly due to the improvements in infant and child mortality in eastern Europe (Mesle, 1996). Later the gap increased due to both worsening mortality among adult males in eastern Europe and continuous improvement in survival at old age in Western societies. A large number of factors have been linked to this disparity, with particular focus on material deprivation and psychosocial stress, as well as diet and lifestyle (Bobak and Marmot, 1996).

The trend in cardiovascular disease mortality has followed the pattern of overall mortality at all ages over 40 (Figure 3). This is understandable if one takes into account the fact that CVD accounts for more than 50 per cent of deaths at these ages. Figure 3 shows that all ages have seen a gradual improvement in mortality from CVD, but the improvement is most noticeable for ages 45–54 and 55–64. Trends in cancer are less clear (Figure 3), partly as a result of different trends for different cancer sites. In Britain, stomach cancer mortality rates have declined markedly. The decline in cancer mortality at younger ages has much to do with a cohort effect in smoking patterns. Younger cohorts are smoking less than older cohorts. Hence there has been a decline in lung cancer rates at younger ages.

Since Olshanky's definition of the four stages of epidemiological transition there have been efforts to try and explain the present changes in the disease pattern of adults in contemporary societies and to portray them in a theoretical context. Horiuchi (1999) divides the last stage of Olshansky's 'age of delayed degenerative diseases' into one that is dominated by CVD and is characteristic of industrial societies, and one dominated by cancers when mortality from CVD goes down dramatically and cancers replace them as the major killers. This stage is associated with a move from industrial to highly technological societies. He believes that the present situation in most Western societies is one of a transition between these two stages.

PATTERNS OF ILLNESS AND MORTALITY IN DEVELOPING AND TRANSITIONAL SOCIETIES

Large differences still in place

Historically there have been marked differences in mortality between the more developed societies and the least developed ones (Figure 4). Despite major improvements in the last 50 years in developing countries, the differences in the levels of life expectancy at birth today are still dramatic. The difference in life expectancy in the 1950s was about 31 years; it was still about 23 years in 2000.

Infant and child mortality are major contributors to the differences in overall mortality between developed and developing regions. The differences in adult mortality are less dramatic. This may be due to the high levels of adult mortality in some developed countries. In some parts of the developing world (Latin America and the Middle East) the levels of adult mortality are similar to those found in eastern European countries.

Figure 4 shows some narrowing of the mortality gap between developed and developing countries. This was reversed in the 1980s as the mortality improvement in the least developed countries slowed down – a result of the spread of the HIV/AIDS epidemic in most of the sub-Saharan countries of Africa.

Ageing is of concern not only in developed societies, but in a large number of developing countries.

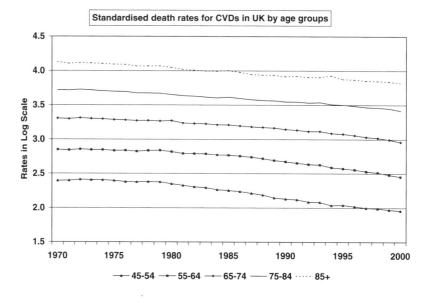

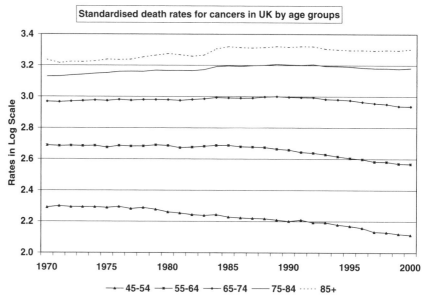

Figure 3. Standardized death rates for CVD and cancers in the UK by age, 1970–2000.

China, Brazil and India, three large developing countries, are showing the signs of ageing populations. In percentages the population over 60 by 2025 will be respectively at 20%, 16% and 12%. Generally, in developing societies the percentage of population over 60 has increased from 6.4% in 1950 to 7.7%, and is projected to be at 20.6% in 2045 (UN, 2001).

HIV/AIDS and the emerging new threats

In eastern Africa since the 1980s life expectancy at birth has decreased as a result of increased mortality from HIV/AIDS (Figure 4). By the end of 1999, 18.8 million people had died of AIDS worldwide. AIDS deaths in 2002 amounted to 3.1 million, of which 2.5 million were adults. In most of sub-Saharan Africa, adults and children are acquiring HIV at a higher rate than ever before. In Africa there are sixteen countries where more than one

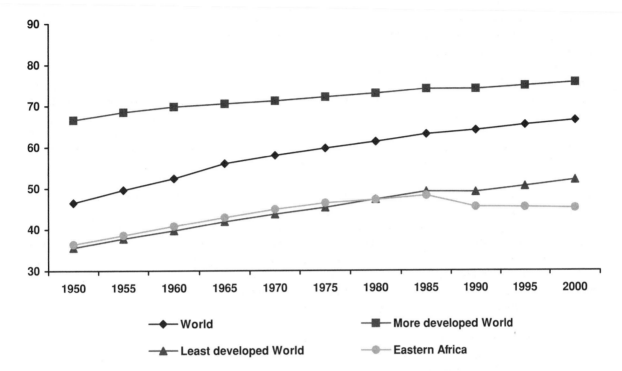

Figure 4. Life expectancy at birth in different regions of the world.

tenth of the adult population is infected with HIV (UNAIDS/WHO, 2000). More than 60 per cent of deaths in developing countries are due to communicable and maternal diseases. Malaria is still a major killer in most African countries. Even in countries where improvements were significant with regards to infectious and parasitic diseases in the past, we are facing the emergence of particular infectious diseases such as tuberculosis (e.g. countries of Central Asia). The percentage of these deaths is higher among females compared to males in these countries. While infectious and parasitic diseases are still major killers in developing societies, cancers and CVD have started to emerge. Most common cancers are cervix, stomach, mouth–pharynx and oesophagus.

A large number of developing countries (e.g. Latin American countries and Central Asian republics) are experiencing high incidence and prevalence of both communicable and non-communicable diseases at the same time: what is called 'the double burden of diseases'. This phenomenon is creating massive problems for their health systems, which have both to face a fight against infectious and parasitic diseases, and to cope with expensive treatment of non-communicable diseases.

THE COMPRESSION OF MORBIDITY AND THE PROSPECTS FOR HEALTH AND MORTALITY IMPROVEMENT

Increase of illness with age

The increase of life expectancy has been accompanied by discussions on whether this increase brings a compression of morbidity or is characterized by an increase in disability. Often the process of ageing is viewed as a result of disease whose effect becomes increasingly obvious with the passage of time. In extreme form, this point of view holds that what we see with advancing age is solely the product of disease. This becomes clearer when looking especially at diseases that occur in older persons such as dementia or Alzheimer's disease.

Thirty years ago, Dilman (1976) stated that 'normal ageing is accompanied by the gradually developing imbalance of the internal environment of the body, e.g., increased body weight and serum cholesterol, decreased glucose tolerance, climacteric, etc. These changes characterise ageing as a derangement of homeostasis.' There are two contradicting notions about the changes in illness patterns in older populations. One is that the older populations are now healthier as they have higher living standards, education and better medical treatments than previously. The other view holds that the health of the older population is deteriorating. Because of better medical treatments more people are surviving to old ages and, as such, it is possible even for frail people to survive longer (Gruenberg, 1977).

Later, Fries (1980) argued that continuing improvements in health and life expectancy will increasingly 'compress' morbidity and disability into a brief period in the last years of life. He states that the ageing population will not need an increase in the provision of health and other services, as changes in health-related behaviour will mean that the onset of morbidity is delayed while age at death will remain the same. When raising this hypothesis, Fries assumed that death rates at old ages were not changing. This was not true even when Fries wrote about it, as the death rates for the elderly populations in the USA and other developed countries had started to decline in the mid-1970s and decelerated more noticeably in the 1990s (Vaupel, 1997).

Moreover, a continuous strong association between health and mortality at old ages has been observed (Warren and Night, 1982). Death in old age is generally preceded by long periods of serious disability, and the duration of pre-death disability rises with age and may be increasing overall (Gruenberg, 1977). As the person grows old, new diseases become clinically evident. A number of scholars argue that increasing life expectancy may be producing 'longer life and worsening health' by adding years to life in which people are increasingly ill and disabled (Gruenberg, 1977; Manton, 1982; Schneider and Brody, 1983).

Research from the USA (Pope and Tarlov, 1991) has shown that 'more than half of the 4-year increase in life expectancy between 1970 and 1987 was accounted for by time spent with activity limitations'. Also Robine (1991) concluded from a comparison of time series that, whatever the period, country or study used, life expectancy at birth free of light or moderate disability favoured the expansion hypothesis, whereas there were no significant trends in the evolution of life expectancy without very severe disability.

However, recent evidence (Manton *et al.*, 1997; Manton and Gu, 2001; Bobak *et al.*, 2004) shows that the prevalence of chronic disability has declined faster in recent periods compared to previous periods. This implies that health is improving alongside mortality and the implications for health and social welfare costs will be different.

Lastly, research into patterns of change in mortality, sickness and disability suggest that these factors do not necessarily evolve in a similar fashion. Self-reported morbidity as a subjective assessment of own health is widely used in social statistics and policymaking nowadays. Self-reported health is determined by personal characteristics as well as characteristics of the environment where the person lives. In many instances, in countries where life expectancy is high and disability is low, self-reported ill health is also high. As such this measure of health and disability should be used in conjunction with other measures (Sen, 2002).

Rectangularization of survival curve and death distribution by age

Many societies worldwide have experienced both the demographic and epidemiological transition. Improvements in mortality from premature deaths lead to 'rectangularization' of mortality, with low mortality at young and early adult ages followed by a sharp increase around the age of the natural lifespan (Figure 5). If the human lifespan were assumed to be fixed, the improvement of mortality at young and adult ages would cause a further rectangularization of survival curves. This hypothesis is based on the assumption that mortality rates after the age of 30 increase in a Gompertz curve (exponentially). Consequently, an exponential increase of mortality rates ensures a finite lifespan.

However, it has been proven that mortality rates do not exactly follow a Gompertz curve at old and very old ages. There is a plateau in the curve of mortality rates at very old ages. Mortality at old ages has improved dramatically since the early 1970s and this has brought an increasing number of centenarians

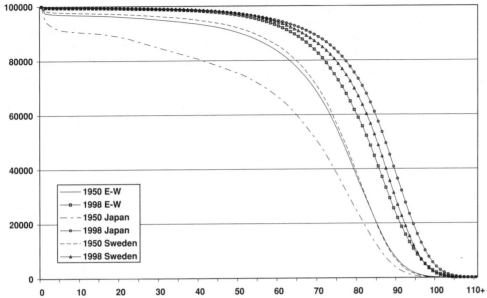

(Ahlburg and Vaupel, 1990; Vaupel and Gowan, 1986).

Figure 5. Number of survivors among females in England and Wales (E+W), Japan and Sweden.

DETERMINANTS OF DISEASE ACROSS THE ADULT LIFESPAN IN DEVELOPED SOCIETIES

In order to understand the process behind changes in patterns of morbidity and mortality, one should study the determinants of health and mortality. It is important to look at both earlier life and current effects, and their interaction with genetic predisposition. Ageing results in biological degeneration that in turn increases vulnerability to disease.

Most chronic conditions have a very strong environmental or lifestyle link. For example, it has been estimated that around a third of all cancers are related to smoking and a further third to diet. As a person ages, their cumulative exposure to these environmental and lifestyle risks increases, resulting in a higher probability of succumbing to chronic diseases such as cancer and heart disease. As the population ages, so these chronic diseases account for an ever increasing share of the burden of disease.

Modern medicine has converted previously life-threatening conditions into chronic conditions; hence there is concern that this could result in higher numbers of older people with chronic age-related conditions such as arthritis and dementia.

Prevailing risk factors, medical advance and the quality of the healthcare system also have an impact on the level and type of disease that will occur, but before considering their impact on the current disease profile (i.e. those diseases that constitute the major burden to society) it is important to examine influences associated with demography.

Demographic factors

Age has the strongest association with mortality. Age itself is important because of the strong relationship between age and individual characteristics and circumstances. The main biological characteristic of ageing is the gradual decline of the homeostatic mechanism. Ageing is associated with many biological changes such as musculo-skeletal and sensory changes. It is not just the biological aspect of human lifespan that changes with age, other factors such as socioeconomic and behavioural ones are also determined by the age of the individual.

Sex is the other key demographic factor associated with mortality. On average, women in developed countries live 5 years longer than men (Gjonça et al., 1999). Several explanations have been suggested (Verbrugge, 1989). Biological differences by sex (e.g. genetic, hormonal differences and reproduction differences) may have an impact, which could be cumulative and persist even at old age. Women are thought to be in more frequent contact with health services and to be more health-aware. Certainly women are more likely than men to report their health as less than good and to be more frequent reporters of health problems. It has also been suggested that the mortality differences between sexes may be linked with behaviour differences such as smoking or alcohol consumption as well as with occupational hazards (Waldron, 1987).

As indicated in the previous paragraph, females might live longer than males but they do not live in 'better health'. Research suggests that women reaching 65 years of age can expect to spend a slightly greater proportion of their remaining years in a severely disabled state relative to elderly men, thus negating some of the potential benefit of their life expectancy. A number of studies of gender differences in the incidence of disabling conditions at older ages support this argument (Heikkinen et al., 1996; Dunlop et al., 1997; Robine and Romieu, 1998).

A third demographic factor is marital status. Married individuals have significantly lower risk of mortality than their single counterparts (Kitagawa and Hauser, 1973; Makuc et al., 1990; Smith and Zick, 1994; Sorlie et al., 1996); these results are particularly strong for men (Lillard and Panis, 1996). Rogers (1995) reported that widowed and divorced persons were twice as likely to die as married persons, while never-married individuals were about three times as likely to die in a given year. The difference between the married and the unmarried could arise through both *protection* and *selection* processes. Selection must exist – that is, people liable to ill health being less likely to be in the married state. It is unlikely that this is the only mechanism. Protection could operate because being married is also thought to encourage healthier behaviour. Marriage may, of course, provide the benefit of social support and thereby lower mortality risk.

Socioeconomic factors

Being in a higher social or occupational class is associated with better health and lower mortality (Marmot, 2004; J. Smith, 1998). A diverse and long-standing literature, especially from the developed countries, has identified a number of socioeconomic factors that affect health and mortality, such as education, social and occupational class, wealth and income. People with higher educational attainment tend to live longer (Kitagawa and Hauser, 1973; Elo and Preston, 1996). A study by Wray and colleagues (Wray et al., 1998) showed that people with a higher educational attainment were more likely to have a healthy behaviour or to change their behaviour positively after a health event like, for example, a heart attack.

Research has also focused on possible pathways by which socioeconomic status affects health (Power and Hertzman, 1997; Brunner et al., 1999; Marmot et al., 2000). As results from the Whitehall study have shown, psychosocial factors such as work-related stress and social support networks strongly affect health, both directly and indirectly (Marmot et al., 1997).

Although socioeconomic position has been shown to affect health and mortality, most studies have traditionally focused at younger ages, typically the ages below retirement, and less so at the older ages. There are a few reasons that justify this.

- Socioeconomic differences are thought to diminish with age, perhaps as a result of selection (Fox and Goldblatt, 1982; Arber and Ginn, 1993).
- As studies such as the Whitehall study have shown, it is difficult to measure socioeconomic position after retirement. However, results from the Whitehall study (Breeze et al., 2001) and, more recently, preliminary results from the English Longitudinal Study of Ageing (Marmot et al., 2003), show that socioeconomic factors affect health even at old ages.

Studies have shown that the effect of socioeconomic factors on health and mortality varies by country and region (Kunst et al., 1999; Houweling, 2001).

Genetic factors

Individuals are endowed at birth with different genetic inheritances. Studies of twins have suggested that part of the variation in adult lifespans is of genetic origin (McGue *et al.*, 1995; Herskind *et al.*, 1996; Christensen and Vaupel, 1996; Yashin *et al.*, 2000). Although genetics might explain some of the variation in longevity, it is important to emphasize that environmental and socioeconomic factors can account for much of the variation in mortality among populations (Yashin *et al.*, 2000; Tan *et al.*, 2001).

Behavioural

There are clear associations between life expectancy and health behaviours (Breslow and Breslow, 1993). Yet, it has often been observed that behavioural risk factors predict mortality less well in the elderly than at younger ages. There is good reason to believe, however, that the effects of exposure to adverse health behaviours accumulates throughout life (Heikkinen, 1987). That said, it has been found that short-term changes in behaviour and lifestyle affect mortality (Gjonça *et al.*, 2000).

DETERMINANTS OF DISEASE ACROSS THE ADULT LIFESPAN IN DEVELOPING COUNTRIES

The differing pattern of morbidity and mortality in developing countries is associated with a different pattern of determinants. If there were the political will, these should be readily amenable to intervention.

Poverty

Poverty is still a major hazard in developing countries. Poverty is associated with lack of many basic necessities such as drinking water, food, housing, sanitation; malnutrition; chronic parasitic infections as well as the lack of adequate health services. Although data are sparse, it is likely that the association between income and mortality is greater in developing than in developed countries. The greatest reduction of mortality with higher incomes in poor countries will come from infectious diseases (Kjellstrom *et al.*, 1992).

Medical Care

Medical service access and provision is an important determinant of health. Many deaths occurring in developed countries could be avoided with appropriate medical treatment. In many cases (e.g. tuberculosis or malaria), the treatment of sick people is important in controlling and stopping the spread of disease.

Housing and Malnutrition

Crowded and poor housing conditions increase the incidence of infectious diseases such as tuberculosis. Poor housing conditions are also associated with pollution through cooking with unsuitable materials and fuels. Poor sanitary conditions in the household also affect the spread of infectious diseases.

Malnutrition is an important determinant of disease and mortality in developing countries as it causes diseases of deficiency. Deficient diets affect children as well as adults. Malnutrition affects many developing countries but the worst situation is in Africa where almost a quarter of the population is undernourished. The major hazards are protein and energy malnutrition as well as vitamin A, iodine and iron deficiencies. The situation is quite often worse for women than for men (Feachem *et al.*, 1992; WHO, 2002; Ezzati *et al.*, 2002).

High fertility and unhealthy childhood

Giving birth is still hazardous in developing countries. High levels of fertility are associated with high adult (female) mortality. The lifetime risk of dying of maternity-related causes is 1 in 20 in Africa while it is only 1 in 10,000 in northern Europe (Kjellstrom *et al.*, 1992).

Unhealthy childhood is associated with unhealthy adulthood. Many negative health conditions in adulthood may stem from risks established early in life (Elo and Preston, 1992). Barker (1995) argued that adult health has a fetal origin, wherein nourishment in utero and during infancy has a direct bearing on the development of risk factors for adulthood diseases (especially cardiovascular diseases). Childhood infections may have long-term effects on adult mortality.

Behavioural

Other hazards, and especially environmental hazards such as pollution, workplace hazards and injuries, are also common in developing countries. Attention should be paid also to emerging new threats – modern hazards – such as smoking, drinking, violence and adoption of unhealthy diets and lifestyle.

In other words, developing countries are now having to cope with long-term hazards associated with poverty and, at the same time, the problems of alcohol and tobacco (Shkolnikov et al., 1996; WHO, 2002; Ezzati et al., 2002; Bobak et al., 2003).

Smoking is becoming a problem in developing countries. Unfortunately, data on this are very scarce, especially since the smoking epidemic in these countries is a more recent phenomenon. For some developing countries (for example, China), in which smoking rates are high, smoking is likely to have a major effect on adult mortality. While in many developed countries tobacco consumption per capita has decreased due to anti-smoking campaigns, in developing countries this consumption has increased (Kjellstrom et al., 1992).

LIVING LONGER AND HEALTHIER? HEALTHY LIFE EXPECTANCY (HLE)

Given the growth in the numbers of older people in the population, emphasis is shifting from simply measuring the quantity or length of life lived to monitoring both the quality and quantity of remaining life. This has led to the idea of healthy life expectancy: expectancy without limitation of function that may be the consequence of disease. It was first proposed in the 1960s (Sanders, 1964) with the first method of calculation in the following decade (Sullivan, 1971). Since then, healthy expectancies have been increasingly used in contemporary developed societies (Robine et al., 2003). The calculation of healthy life expectancies combines information on both mortality and morbidity. Healthy life expectancies, in

particular disability-free life expectancy, were first developed to address the question of whether or not the longer life expectancy experienced by most developed countries is being accompanied by an increase in the time lived in better health (compression of morbidity) or in poorer health (expansion of morbidity). Recent studies in the UK and USA suggest that the years gained have not been years free of disability, but the level of severity appears to have diminished (Grundy et al., 1994; Waidmann and Manton, 1998).

Healthy life expectancies (HLE) can aid in understanding the effect of interventions on the public health. Suppression of certain causes of morbidity, cancer for example, has been shown to increase life expectancy without increasing disability-free life expectancy to the same degree. By contrast, treatment of arthritis tends to extend disability-free life expectancy without changing total life expectancy. A condition such as diabetes decreases both life expectancy and disability-free life expectancy (Jagger et al., 2003).

Since 1998, forty-nine nations have estimated healthy life expectancies, attempting to integrate mortality and morbidity conditions of a population into a single index (Robine et al., 1999). In 1999, for the first time, the WHO estimated disability-adjusted life expectancy (DALE) for 191 countries (Mathers et al., 2001). However, international comparisons are still difficult because of the varying definitions of disability used.

CONCLUSIONS

There is evidence that not only are people living longer but they are living healthier as well. As Mathers and colleagues (2001) point out, as average levels of health expenditure per capita are increasing, healthy life expectancy is increasing too and at a greater rate than total life expectancy.

Although people throughout the developed world live longer, the developing countries are facing new emerging threats and a double burden of disease. In developing countries, communicable and non-communicable diseases each make up more than 40 per cent of deaths. These populations already face many of the same risks as industrialized countries, for example tobacco use and high blood pressure, while also having to contend with major remaining problems of under-nutrition and communicable diseases.

The WHO report on 'Reducing risks, promoting healthier life' (2002) suggests strategies for reducing risks to health, especially focusing on developing countries. Such strategies involve improving children's environment and nutrition, water disinfection, treatment of diarrhoea and pneumonia, and preventive interventions to reduce the incidence of HIV infections. Investment in health also means stimulating economic growth, reducing poverty and inequality. Almost all the risk factors assessed in the WHO report occur more commonly in the poor countries, which typically also have less autonomy and fewer resources to reduce risks. Tackling these major risks has the potential to substantially reduce inequalities worldwide.

One of the conclusions of this chapter has to be that there is little possibility of comparing morbidity information across ages and countries. It is even harder comparing it by different socioeconomic factors. Disease can be observed or self-perceived. This also poses a problem in defining disease and collecting data on disease patterns. Morbidity data are of greater importance than mortality data, yet most countries record morbidity less rigorously. Especially lacking are longitudinal data. Knowing the lifelong history of health and illness could clearly demonstrate the difference among social groups as well as predict likely future trends. Conducting longitudinal surveys would not only help us to understand adult health patterns, transitions to and from different health statuses, and how to differentiate between morbidity and ageing per se, but it would also aid more comprehensive comparisons between countries and in policymaking.

As the demographic and epidemiological pictures change, we might expect to see related changes in the nature and prevalence of various disabilities. The fact that the number of older people is increasing and disability is declining has long-term implications for policy. The complex determinants, from socioeconomic factors through environmental and community conditions to individual behaviour, offer many different options for prevention.

FURTHER READING

Feachem, R., *et al.*, eds. (1992). *The health of adults in the developing world*. Oxford: Oxford University Press, 1992.

Manton, K. and XiLiang Gu (2001). 'Changes in the prevalence of chronic disability in the United States black and non-black population above age 65 from 1982 to 1999', *PNAS*, 98 (11): 6354–9.

Oeppen, J., and J. W. Vaupel (2002). 'Broken limits to life expectancy', *Science*, 296 (10 May): 1029–31.

World Health Organization (2002). *World Health Report. Reducing risks, promoting healthy life*. Geneva: WHO.

REFERENCES

Ahlburg, D. A., and J. W. Vaupel (1990). 'Alternative projections of the U.S. population', *Demography*, 27 (4): 639–52.

Arber S., and J. Ginn (1993). 'Gender and inequalities in health in later life', *Social Science and Medicine*, 36 (1): 33–46.

Barker, D. J. P. (1995). 'Fetal origins of coronary heart disease', *British Medical Journal*, 311: 171–4.

Bobak, M., and M. G. Marmot (1996). 'East–West mortality divide and its potential explanations: proposed research agenda', *British Medical Journal*, 312: 421–5.

Bobak, M., Kristenson, H., Pikhart, H., and M. G. Marmot (2004). 'Life span and disability: a cross-sectional comparison of Russian and Swedish community-based data', *BMJ* 329: 767.

Breeze, E., Fletcher, A. E., Leon, D., Marmot, M. G., Clarke, R. J., and M. J. Shipley (2001). 'Do socioeconomic disadvantages persist into old age? Self-reported morbidity in a 29-year follow-up of the Whitehall study', *American Journal of Public Health*, 91: 277–83.

Breslow, L., and N. Breslow (1993). 'Health practices and disability: some evidence from Alameda County', *Preventive Medicine*, 22 (1): 86–95.

Brunner, E. J., Shipley, M. J., Blane, D., Davey Smith, G., and M. G. Marmot (1999). 'When does cardiovascular risk start? Past and present socioeconomic circumstances and risk factors in adulthood'. *Journal of Epidemiology and Community Health*, 53: 757–64.

Christensen K., and J. Vaupel (1996). 'Determinants of longevity: genetic, environmental and medical factors', *Journal of Internal Medicine*, 240 (6): 333–41.

Dilman, V. M. (1976). 'The hypothalamic control of ageing and age-associated pathology. The elevation mechanism of ageing'. In A. V. Everitt and J. A. Burgess, eds., *Hypothalamus, pituitary, and ageing*. Springfield, Ill.: Charles C. Thomas, pp. 634–7.

Dunlop, D., Hughes, S. L, and L. M. Manheim (1997). 'Disability in activities of daily living: patterns of change and a hierarchy of disability', *American Journal of Public Health*, 87 (3): 378–83.

Elo, I., and S. Preston (1992). 'Effects of early-life conditions on adult mortality: a review', *Population Index*, 58 (2): 186–212.

(1996). 'Educational differentials in mortality in the United States, 1979–1985', *Social Science and Medicine*, 42 (1): 47–57.

Ezzati, M., Lopez, A. D., Rodgers, A., Hoorn, S. V., Murray, C. J. L., and Comparative Risk Assessment Collaborating Group (2002). 'Selected major risk factors and global and regional burden of disease', *Lancet*, 360: 1347–60.

Feachem, R., Kjellstrom, T., Murray, C. J. L., Over, M., and M. A. Phillips, eds. (1992). *The health of adults in the developing world*. Oxford: Oxford University Press.

Fox, A. J., and P. O. Goldblatt (1982). *Longitudinal study: socio-demographic mortality differentials*. London: HMSO.

Fries, J. F. (1980). 'Ageing, natural death and the compression of morbidity'. *New England Journal of Medicine*, 303 (3): 130–5.

Gjonça, A., Tomassini, C., and J. W. Vaupel (1999). 'Pourquoi les femmes survivent aux hommes?' In *La Recherche*, special issue: To live 120 years, 322 (juillet/août): 96–9.

Gjonça, A., Brockmann, H., and H. Maier (2000). 'Old-age mortality in Germany prior to and after reunification', *Demographic Research*, 3 (1).

Greengross, S., Murphy, E., Quam, L., Rochon, P., and R. Smith (1997). 'Ageing: a subject that must be at the top of world agendas' [editorial], *BMJ*, 315: 1029–30.

Gruenberg, E. M. (1977). 'The failures of success'. *Millbank Memorial Fund Quarterly*, 55: 3–24.

Grundy, E., Ahlburg, D., Ali, M., Breeze, E., and A. Sloggett (1994). *Disability in Great Britain*. DSS Research Report No. 94. London: DSS.

Heikkinen, E. (1987). 'Health implications of population aging in Europe', *WHO, World Health Statistical Quarterly*, 40: 22–40.

Heikkinen, E., Jokela, J., and M. Jylha (1996). 'Dissability and functional status among elderly people: cross-national comparisons'. In G. Caselli and D. Alan, eds., *Health and mortality among elderly populations*. Oxford: Oxford University Press, pp. 202–20.

Herskind, A. M., McGue, M., Holm, N. V., Sørensen, T. A., Harvald, B., and J. W. Vaupel (1996). 'The heritability of human longevity: a population-based study of 2872 Danish twin pairs born 1870–1900', *Human Genetics*, 97: 319–23.

Horiuchi, S. (1999). 'Epidemiological transitions in developed countries: past, present and future'. In United Nations, *Health and Mortality – Issues of Global Concern*. New York: United Nations, pp. 54–71.

Houweling, T., Kunst, A., and J. P. Mackenbach (2001). 'World Health Report 2000: inequality index and socioeconomic inequalities in mortality', *Lancet*, 357: 1671–2.

Jagger, C., Goyder, E., Clarke, M., Brouard, N., and A. Arthur (2003). 'Active life expectancy in people with and without diabetes', *Journal of Public Health Medicine*, 25: 42–6.

Kannisto, V., Lauritsen, J., Thatcher, R. A., and J. W. Vaupel (1994). 'Reductions in mortality at advanced ages: several decades of evidence from 27 countries', *Population Development Review*, 20 (4): 793–810.

Kinsella, K. (1994). 'Dimensiones demográficas y de salud en America Latina y el Caribe'. In E. Anzola Perez, D. Galinsky, F. Morales Martinez, A. R. Salas, and M. Sanchez Ayendez, eds., *La atención de los ancianos: un desafio para los años noventas*. Washington, D.C.: Pan American Health Organization.

Kinsella, K., and V. A. Velkoff (2001). *An Ageing World: 2001*, US Census Bureau.

Kitagawa, E., and P. Hauser (1973). *Differential mortality in the United States: a study in socioeconomic epidemiology*. Cambridge, Mass.: Harvard University Press.

Kjellstrom, T., Koplan, J. P., and R. B. Rothenberg (1992). 'Current and future determinants of adult ill-health'. In R. Feachem, T. Kjellstrom, C. J. L. Murray, M. Over, and M. A. Phillips, eds., *The health of adults in the developing world*. Oxford: Oxford University Press.

Kunst, A. E., Groenhof, F., Andersen, O., Borgan, J. K., Costa, G., Desplanques, G., Filakti, H., Giraldes, M. D., Faggiano, F., Harding, S., Junker, C., Martikainen, P., Minder, C., Nolan, B., Pagnanelli, F., Regidor, E., Vagero, D., Valkonen, T., and J. P. Mackenbach (1999). 'Occupational class and ischaemic heart disease mortality in the United States and 11 European countries'. *Am. Journal of Public Health*, 89 (1): 47–53.

Lillard, L. A., and C. W. A. Panis (1996). 'Marital status and mortality: the role of health', *Demography* 33: 313–27.

Makuc, D., *et al.* (1990). 'Sociodemographic differentials in mortality'. In *Health status and wellbeing of the elderly*. Oxford: Oxford University Press, pp. 155–71.

Manton, K. (1982). 'Changing concepts of morbidity and mortality in the elderly population', *Millbank Memorial Fund Quarterly*, 60: 183–244.

Manton, K., and XiLiang Gu (2001). 'Changes in the prevalence of chronic disability in the United states black and non-black population above age 65 from 1982 to 1999', *PNAS*, 98 (11): 6354–9.

Manton, K., Corder, L., and E. Stallard (1997). 'Chronic disability trends in elderly United States populations: 1982–1994', *Proceedings of National Academy of Sciences*, 94: 2593–8.

Marmot, M. (2004). *Status syndrome*. London: Bloomsbury.

Marmot, M. G., and J. Y. Nazroo (2001). 'Social inequalities in health in an ageing population', *European Review*, 9 (4): 445–60.

Marmot, M., Bosma, H., Hemingway, H., Brunner, E. J., and S. A. Sansfeld (1997). 'Contribution of job control and other risk factors to social variations in coronary heart disease incidence', *Lancet*, 350 (9073): 235–9.

Marmot, M. G., Shipley, M. J., Brunner, E. J., and H. Hemingway (2000). 'Relative contribution of early life and adult socioeconomic factors to adult mortality in the Whitehall II study', *Journal of Epidemiology and Community Health*, 55: 301–7.

Marmot, M. G., Banks, J., Blundell, R., Lessof, C., and J. Nazroo (2003). *Health, wealth and lifestyles of the older population in England. The 2002 English Longitudinal Study of Ageing*. London: The Institute of Fiscal Studies.

Mathers, C., Sadana, R., Salomon, J. A., Murray, C. L., and A. D. Lopez (2001). 'Healthy life expectancy in 191 countries, 1999', *Lancet*, 357: 1685–91.

McGue, M., *et al.* (1995). 'Longevity is moderately heritable in a sample of Danish twins born 1870–1880', *Journal of Gerontology*, 48: B237–B244.

Mesle, F. (1996). 'Mortality in eastern and western Europe: a widening gap'. In David Coleman, ed., *Europe's Population in the 1990s*. Oxford: Oxford University Press.

Moore, T. J. (1993). *Lifespan*. New York: Simon and Schuster.

Murray, C. J. L., and A. D. Lopez (1996). *The global burden of disease: a comprehensive assessment of mortality and disability from diseases, injuries, and risk factors in 1990 and projected to 2020*. Published by Harvard School of Public Health on behalf of the World Health Organization and the World Bank. Cambridge, Mass.: Harvard University Press.

Oeppen, J., and J. W. Vaupel (2002). 'Broken limits to life expectancy', *Science*, 296 (10 May): 1029–31.

Olshansky, S. J., and A. B. Ault (1986). 'The fourth stage of the epidemiologic transition: the age of delayed degenerative diseases', *Milbank Memorial Fund Quarterly*, 65: 355–91.

Pope, A. M., and A. R. Tarlov, eds. (1991). *Disability in America, towards a national agenda for prevention. Summary and recommendations*. Institute of Medicine.

Power, C., and C. Hertzman (1997). 'Social and biological pathways linking early life and adult disease', *British Medical Bulletin*, 53: 210–21.

Robine, J. M. (1991). 'Changes in health conditions over time'. Paper presented to the 4th International Meeting of the Network on Health Expectancy (REVES), Leuven.

Robine, J. M., and I. Romieu (1998). 'Healthy active ageing: health expectancies at age 65 in the different parts of the world'. Paper prepared for the Meeting of the WHO Expert Committee on Determinants of Healthy Ageing, Geneva, 1–7 December.

Robine, J. M., Romieu, I., and E. Cambois (1999). 'Health expectancy indicators', *Bulletin World Health Organization*, 77 (2): 181–5.

Robine, J. M, Romieu, I., and J. P. Michel (2003). 'Trends in health expectancies'. In J. M. Robine, C. Jagger, C. D. Mathers, E. M. Crimmins, and R. M. Suzman, eds., *Determining health expectancies*. Chichester: Wiley.

Rogers, R. G. (1995). 'Sociodemographic characteristics of long-lived and healthy individuals', *Population and Development Review*, 21 (1): 33–58.

Sanders, B. S. (1964). 'Measuring community health levels', *American Journal of Public Health*, 54: 1063–70.

Schneider, E. A., and J. A. Brody (1983). 'Aging, natural death and the compression of morbidity: another view', *New England Journal of Medicine*, 309 (14): 854–5.

Sen, A. (2002). 'Health: perception versus observation', *BMJ*, 324: 860–1.

Shkolnikov, V., Mesle, F., and J. Vallin (1996). 'Health crisis in Russia. Recent trends in life expectancy and causes of death from 1970 to 1993', *Population (An English Selection)*.

Smith, J. (1998). 'Socioeconomic status and health', *American Economic Review*.

Smith, K. R., and C. D. Zick (1994). 'Linked lives, dependent demise? Survival analysis of husbands and wives', *Demography*, 31: 81–93.

Sorlie, P., *et al.* (1996). 'US mortality by economic, demographic and social characteristics: the National Longitudinal Mortality Study', *American Journal of Public Health*, 85 (7): 949–56.

Sullivan, D. F. (1971). 'A single index of mortality and morbidity', *HSMHA Health Report*, 86: 347–54.

Tan, Q., *et al.* (2001). 'Measuring the genetic influence in modulating human life span: gene–environment interaction and the sex specific genetic effect', *Biogerontology*, 2: 141–53.

Thatcher, A. R. (1999). 'The Demography of Centenarians in England and Wales', *Population Trends*, 84 (Summer). London: HMSO.

UN (2001). *World population prospects: the 2000 revisions*. New York: United Nations Department of Economic and Social Affairs, Population Division.

UNAIDS / World Health Organization (UNAIDS/WHO) (2000). *Report on the global HIV/AIDS epidemic*. Geneva: WHO.

Vaupel, J. W. (1997). 'The remarkable improvements in survival at older ages', *Philosophical Transactions of the Royal Society of London – Series B: Biological Sciences*, 352 (1363): 1799–1804.

Vaupel, J. W., and A. E. Gowan (1986). 'Passage to Methuselah: some demographic consequences of continued progress against mortality', *American Journal of Public Health*, 76: 430–22.

Verbrugge, L. M. (1989). 'The Twain meet: empirical explanations of sex differences in health and mortality', *Journal of Human Resources*, 30: S158–83.

Waidmann, T. A., and K. G. Manton (1998). 'International evidence on disability trends among the elderly', Paper prepared for the Office of Disability, Aging, and Long-Term Care Policy, US Department of Health and Human Services, Washington, D.C.

Waldron, I. (1987). 'Why do women live longer than men?' *Social Science and Medicine*, 24.

WHO (1998). *Population ageing – a public health challenge*, Fact Sheet No. 135. Accessed from www.who.int/inf-fs/en/fact135.html.

—— (2002). *World health report: reducing risks, promoting healthy life*. Geneva: WHO.

—— (2003). *The European health report 2002*. Geneva: WHO.

Wilmoth, J. R., Deegan, L. J., Lundström, H., and S. Horiuchi (2000). 'Increase of maximum life-span in Sweden, 1861–1999', *Science*, 289: 2366–8.

Wray, L., R. Herzog, R. Wallace, R. Willis, L. Wray (1998). 'The impact of education and heart attack on smoking cessation among middle-aged adults', *Journal of Health and Social Behavior*, 39 (4): 271–94.

Wrigley, E. A., Davies, R. S., Oeppen, J. E., and R. S. Schofield (1997). *English population history from family reconstruction 1580–1837*, Cambridge: Cambridge University Press.

Yashin, A. I., *et al.* (2000). 'Genes and longevity: lessons from studies of centenarians', *Journal of Gerontology: Biological Sciences*, 55A: B319–B328.

CHAPTER 2.4

Sensory Impairment

TOM H. MARGRAIN AND MIKE BOULTON

INTRODUCTION

Sensory impairment is arguably the characteristic feature of old age and represents one of the greatest challenges to modern society. Unfortunately, age itself is the biggest risk factor for all forms of sensory impairment and therefore the longer people live the greater their sensory loss. For example, current estimates suggest that, of the 4.3 million people in Britain over the age of 75 years, 873,000 have impaired vision (acuity of 6/12 or less) and 1.1 million have difficulty hearing (failure of the whisper test). The relationship between age and sensory impairment is exemplified in Figure 1 which shows the results of hearing and vision tests in a sample of more than 14,000 elderly adults.

This chapter examines the effect of age on the senses of vision, hearing, taste, smell and touch. The emphasis of this brief account is on normal age-related changes rather than the effects of environmental insult or age-related disease.

VISION

In this section we discuss the ageing of our most remarkable sense, that of vision. From an evolutionary perspective it is this sense more than any other that has contributed to our success as a species. The scale of our investment in vision is perhaps best reflected in the fact that approximately 45 per cent of the cortical surface of the brain is involved in the processing of visual information.

Structurally, vision is dependent on the optical properties of the cornea, the pupil and the crystalline lens, and on the neurosensory characteristics of the retina and visual cortex. Before looking at the effect of ageing on each of these structures in turn, we examine the effects of ageing on vision from a functional point of view. That is, we shall examine age-related changes in the visual system's refractive status, its ability to resolve spatial, temporal and chromatic information, as well as changes in its absolute sensitivity. These changes are exemplified in Figure 2 which shows the same scene through the eyes of people of different ages.

The eye's static refractive status is measured in dioptres and varies systematically with age. Caucasian eyes tend to be optically underpowered (hypermetropic) both in childhood and in old age (mid-70s) but are almost perfectly focused for distant objects (emmetropia) in the mid-30s. In childhood the optical defocus that would result from uncorrected hypermetropia is overcome by the ability of the ciliary muscle to deform the crystalline lens thereby increasing the eye's refractive power. However, this ability, known as accommodation, diminishes steadily with age and this, combined with the general shift to hypermetropia in later life, leads to the earliest sign of sensory ageing, presbyopia.

Presbyopia, literally 'old eye', manifests itself as the inability to read small print at around the age of 45 and affects the entire population. Fortunately, the optical defocus resulting from uncorrected hypermetropia and presbyopia may be overcome with spectacles. Without such correction, vision in old age would be poor. Distance vision would be blurred to the extent that it would be difficult to see the top of the optometrist's chart and reading would be

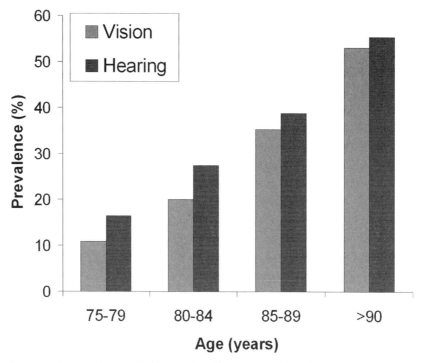

Figure 1. Effect of age on the prevalence of vision and hearing impairment in the British population. Vision impairment is defined as a visual acuity of <6/12 and hearing impairment as failure of the 'whisper test'. (Based on results from the MRC trial of assessment and management of older people reported by Evans *et al.*, 2002 and Smeeth *et al.*, 2002.)

impossible. When the eye is fully optically corrected, the measure of the visual system's ability to resolve high-contrast spatial detail is known as visual acuity. Following an initial increase in visual acuity during childhood it remains stable until the age of 60 years when a gradual decline becomes apparent. Although visual acuity is a relatively poor measure of the visual system's ability to respond to spatial information, its preservation, in comparison with other sensory faculties, is remarkable.

A more complete measure of the visual system's ability to respond to spatial information is provided by the 'contrast sensitivity function' which is a plot of sensitivity to contrast as a function of spatial frequency. Contrast sensitivity declines with age but the effect is spatial frequency-dependent, being greatest for intermediate spatial frequencies i.e. ~ 4 cycles/degree. From the third to ninth decade of life, contrast sensitivity to this spatial

frequency drops by almost 2 log units. The age-related decline in contrast sensitivity is only partly explained by changes in optical factors such as changes in pupil size and increased intraocular light scatter, i.e. retinal and cortical changes are also required to explain the decline (McGrath and Morrison, 1981).

The ability of the eye to resolve temporal events also declines with age. For example, the frequency at which a flickering light is perceived to be steady reduces from about 40 Hz in the fifth decade to 30 Hz in the eighth.

Colour perception, which is based on the presence of three types of cone photoreceptors which preferentially absorb long, medium or short wavelength light, also changes with age. Data from colour vision tests such as the Farnsworth Munsell 100 Hue test suggest that colour perception peaks at the age of 20 and declines steadily there after. The decline is particularly evident in the short wavelength (blue) range and this reflects the combined effects of lens yellowing and the selective loss of short-wavelength-sensitive cones. There is some evidence to suggest that the loss of short wavelength cones is dependent on exposure to short wavelength radiation. Consequently, it is not clear how much of the decline in

20 year old

40 year old

60 year old

80 year old

colour perception is due to ageing and how much to environmental insult.

The visual system's absolute sensitivity to light also declines with age, reducing approximately threefold over the course of a lifetime. This change is largely due to an age-related reduction in pupil size known as 'senile miosis' (pupil diameter in the dark reduces from about 8 mm in the second decade of life to just 5 mm in the eighth) and to increased lens absorbance. Experiments correcting for these optical changes suggest that absolute sensitivity (determined by rod photoreceptors) decreases slowly at a rate of 0.08 log units per decade (Jackson and Owsley, 2000).

The time taken for the eye to attain its maximum sensitivity, described by the dark adaptation function (a plot of sensitivity in the dark as a function of time), increases with age at a rate of approximately 3 min per decade. This increased sluggishness is attributed to delayed photopigment regeneration and may contribute to some of the night vision

Figure 2. Looking at the Norwegian church in Cardiff Bay through ageing eyes. The same scene observed by a 20-, 40-, 60- and 80-year-old. The original scene has been adjusted for changes in pupil size, lenticular absorption of blue light, optical defocus and contrast sensitivity.

problems experienced by the elderly (Jackson *et al.*, 1999).

The functional changes described in the preceding paragraphs, and reviewed in great depth by Weale (1992), may be attributed to organic changes in the eye's optical and neurosensory capabilities and these are discussed below.

The cornea is the most powerful refractive surface in the eye and changes relatively little with age. Therefore, its contribution to functional age-related changes is minimal. There is a modest age-related reduction in the cornea's touch sensitivity, a small decrease in its radius of curvature but no significant change in its ability to transmit visible light.

Unlike the cornea, the crystalline lens undergoes a number of age-related changes which have a profound effect on visual performance. For example, the refractive power of the lens declines by 2 dioptres over a 50-year period. This reduction is mainly due to a decrease in the lens's refractive index and contributes to the age-related development of hypermetropia observed after the age of 30 (Koretz and Cook, 2001).

Changes in the mechanical properties of the lens also contribute to the development of presbyopia. Many theories have been proposed to explain presbyopia but it seems most likely that a hardening of the lens matrix, a loss in its basement membrane's elasticity and a change in ciliary muscle shape, which reduces its mechanical efficiency, are the main reasons for the development of presbyopia.

The ageing lens is also responsible for increased intraocular light scatter which contributes to the reduction in spatial contrast sensitivity, increased glare sensitivity and photophobia. These changes, combined with a reduction in the ability of the lens to transmit short wavelength light, gives the senescent lens its characteristic murky yellow appearance. Cataract, which is just an extension of these age-related changes, is the major cause of 'blindness' in the world.

Many of the age-related changes in visual function cannot be attributed to optical factors and must therefore be due to retinal or central visual pathways. Intriguingly, it appears that some neurons are more susceptible to ageing than others. For example, unlike cone photoreceptors, rods appear to be particularly vulnerable and, by the ninth decade, 30 per cent of these cells are lost (Curcio *et al.*, 2000). Ganglion cell density also declines with age at a rate of approximately 0.5 per cent per year (Harman *et al.*, 2000) but the pattern of ganglion cell loss is dependent on retinal location.

The limited number of anatomical studies of the visual cortex suggest that ageing has only minor effects on the retino-geniculo-striate pathway. For example, there are only minimal age-related changes in the number, density and soma size of neurons in the visual cortex (see Spear, 1993, for a review of the neural bases of age-related visual deficits). However, electrophysiological and functional imaging studies suggest more profound changes. For example, the latency of the principal component of the visual evoked potential, elicited in response to a patterned stimulus presented at a low temporal frequency, increases from 108 msec to 153 msec in elderly

observers (Polidori *et al.*, 1993). Further, Functional Magnetic Resonance Imaging (fMRI) studies show a substantial age-related decline in light-triggered functional activation (Ross *et al.*, 1997). The visual system is known to process information in a number of parallel pathways, i.e. information about colour, motion and spatial contrast are processed simultaneously but routed through different cortical areas. The observation that age-related changes in the latency and amplitude of visual evoked potentials are dependent on the luminance, colour, contrast, check size and motion characteristics of the stimulus suggests that age differentially affects distinct cortical areas.

Visual impairment is a well-established cause of depression, personal injury and social isolation. Thankfully, at least for those of us lucky enough to live in the developed world, many of the age-related changes in visual function are of an optical nature and are therefore amenable to treatment, i.e. with the use of spectacles and the surgical removal of cataract. Despite these benefits epidemiological evidence from Britain suggest that one in five over the age of 75 has impaired vision (binocular acuity less than 6/12) (Evans *et al.*, 2002). The greatest threat to vision for this age group is from 'age-related macular degeneration' a condition that affects the photoreceptors and their supporting cells in the central retina and currently accounts for half of all blind registrations in the UK. Although its aetiology remains unclear many consider it to be an accelerated form of retinal senescence best avoided by eating a healthy diet, the avoidance of cigarette smoke and a fortunate genetic predisposition (Evans, 2001).

HEARING

Hearing loss is one of the most prevalent chronic health conditions encountered in the elderly but the magnitude and rate of loss vary considerably. Epidemiological evidence suggests that approximately 17 per cent of the UK population aged 61–80 years are unable to hear sounds that equate to a moderate whisper (45dB) and less substantial degrees of hearing loss are evident in 35 per cent of those over 50.

Hearing loss has a number of psychosocial consequences. People may avoid going out, paranoid tendencies may be accentuated and relationships with family and friends may become strained. Hearing loss may also jeopardize independent living when the loss prevents individuals from hearing doorbells, smoke alarms and sirens. Hearing loss also leads to social isolation, depression, loss of self-esteem and has been implicated as a cofactor in senile dementia. However, the main deleterious effect of hearing loss is its effect on communication (Fook and Morgan, 2000).

Typically, people with hearing loss do not complain of difficulty hearing per se but rather they report difficulty in understanding speech, i.e. words are confused or misinterpreted. For example the word 'gate' may be confused with 'goat'. Such communication difficulties occur because although ordinary speech is carried out in the range of frequencies 250–6,000 Hz certain consonants which are critical to understanding speech occupy the higher frequency range and it is this range of frequencies that are selectively impaired in age-related hearing loss. Figure 3 shows the pure tone audiogram for people of different ages.

There are two main types of hearing loss: conductive and neurosensory. Conductive hearing loss results from a physical impediment to the transmission of sound waves from the external ear canal through to the footplate of the stapes, e.g. fixation of the ossicular chain or a perforated ear drum. Neurosensory hearing loss results from a deficit in the cochlea or associated neural pathways. Age-related hearing loss is usually referred to as presbycusis, literally 'elder hearing', and is of neurosensory origin. More specifically, presbycusis is defined as hearing impairment associated with various types of auditory system dysfunction, peripheral or central, that accompany ageing and cannot be accounted for by extraordinary ototraumatic, genetic or pathological conditions. Four distinct types of presbycusis have been described. These are: degeneration of the sensory hair cells in the cochlea (sensory loss), loss of spiral ganglia and associated nerve fibres (neural loss), strial atrophy (metabolic changes), and a degeneration of the inner ear support components (mechanical changes). Of these, sensory loss is the commonest type affecting approximately 75 per cent of those with age-related hearing loss but it is unclear how much of this loss is due to genuine age-related changes and how much to excessive noise exposure.

Clearly, hearing steadily worsens with age but the association of hearing loss with age alone is weak. This is exemplified by the findings of the Framing-

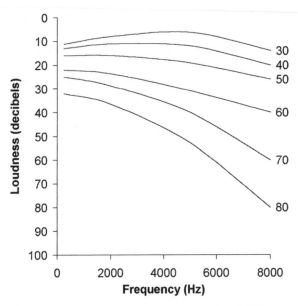

Figure 3. Pure tone audiogram for people of different ages.

ham Heart Study which found that only 10 per cent of the variance in hearing thresholds was accounted for solely by age (Gates *et al.*, 2002). Much of the variance in presbycusis is likely to be due to accumulated noise-induced hearing damage. Of course, distinguishing lifetime noise-related hearing losses from genuine age-related loss is extremely difficult in humans. Indeed, animal studies suggest that strial atrophy rather than sensory hair cell loss is the mechanism underlying true age-related hearing loss. For example, sensory hair cell loss (the main finding in people with presbycusis) is only found in gerbils raised in noisy environments. Animals raised in quiet environments have minimal hair cell loss but they do show signs of strial atrophy suggesting that this rather than hair cell loss is the main cause of age-related hearing loss (Willott *et al.*, 2001).

In addition to environmental noise, age-related hearing loss has been attributed to oxidative mechanisms, mitochondrial damage, neurotrophic and genetic factors (for a review, see Willott *et al.*, 2001).

Although there is no pharmacological treatment for presbycusis, the onset of age-related hearing loss may be delayed by manipulation of several environmental risk factors. For example, unlike smoking which is associated with an increased risk of hearing loss, moderate alcohol consumption has been shown to have a protective effect. However, perhaps the single most important step that may be taken to delay the onset of presbycusis is avoidance of, or protection from, excessive environmental noise (90 dB).

Unlike hearing loss of a conductive origin, which may be treated medically by surgical intervention, the unwanted effects of presbycusis are best overcome by using a hearing aid. Unfortunately, although hearing aids are extremely effective, they are only used by a fraction (10–20 per cent) of those who might benefit. This is regrettable because the use of hearing aids has been demonstrated to improve individuals' quality of life. There are numerous factors which may account for the low usage rate, for example low expectations of hearing aid performance, fear of stigmatization or the belief that hearing loss is an inevitable part of ageing (Gates and Rees, 1997).

TASTE AND SMELL

A decrease in sensitivity or distortion of the chemical senses of taste and smell is a common feature of ageing and can place the elderly at risk from impaired nutrition, the inability to adequately discriminate potentially dangerous chemicals (e.g. rotten food and poisonous gases) and loss of pleasure through association (e.g. odour-evoked memories) (reviewed in Schiffman, 1997; Winkler et al., 1999). It can also be detrimental for an individual whose livelihood is dependent on acute taste and/or smell (e.g. chef, wine taster, perfumier).

Gustatory dysfunction in the elderly is associated with an increase in the taste threshold sensitivity and a difficulty in discriminating between the intensity of substances (hypogensia). Healthy elderly individuals demonstrate a moderate threshold increase for the common tastes (i.e. sweet, salty, sour, bitter). However, this threshold is markedly increased in relatively healthy individuals taking one or more medications. For instance, Schiffman and Graham (2000) report that, compared to young individuals, the average detection level for elderly subjects can be greater than 11 and 7 times higher for salt and bitter respectively. Interestingly, highly medicated patients in hospitals and nursing homes showed an even greater loss of sensitivity. In addition to medication, other age-related trends may contribute to the loss of taste (e.g. use of dentures and cumu-

lative smoking damage). Suprathreshold taste perception is also affected with the elderly sensing a broad range of tastes as being less intense than their younger counterparts. Furthermore, the elderly have a decreased ability to discriminate intensity differences and are less likely to identify the flavours of food in a mixture.

The reason for the decline in taste sensitivity is equivocal but it is generally ascribed to anatomical changes in the peripheral components of the gustatory system. Bradley (1988) reported a steady decline of up to 50 per cent in papillae / taste buds throughout life. However, this was not confirmed by Mistretta (1984) who proposed that taste loss in the elderly is due to the altered function of ion channels and receptors in taste cell membranes. Marked age-related changes in regional taste sensitivity have also been reported for different regions of the tongue. Other anatomical changes which may be important in the age-related increase in taste thresholds could include: changes in tongue structure, a reduction in innervation of the taste receptors, and cell loss/dysfunction in the nucleus of the Solitary tract which processes signals from the taste receptors.

Olfaction or smell is the sensation arising from the nasal cavity following stimulation of the olfactory epithelium by volatile chemicals. Surveys and psychophysical tests have revealed that there are age-related losses in smell perception at both the threshold and suprathreshold levels (hyposmia). The classic National Geographic Smell Survey which involved a 'scratch and sniff' test assessed 1.42 million people worldwide for their ability to detect six different odours (Wysocki and Pelchat, 1993). Analysis of the data revealed a decline in intensity ratings of ~20 per cent from the second to the tenth decade of life (see Figure 4). For natural and common odours (e.g. banana/pear, clove oil and rose) the decrease in olfactory sensitivity became most pronounced in the seventh decade with females being more resistant to loss of smell than their male counterparts (see Figure 5). The study also noted that there was considerable heterogeneity in the rates of change with age for different odours, suggesting that olfactory deficits across odours are not uniform. Furthermore, the ability to discriminate between different odours and their concentration appears to decline with age with more than three-quarters of persons older than 80 having major difficulty in perceiving and identifying odour. Most subsequent studies, using a variety of measurement criteria, have supported these observations and suggest anywhere between a two- and fifteenfold decline in olfactory sensitivity in the aged population compared to the young. Stevens and Cain (1993) found higher absolute thresholds for odorants in the elderly compared to a young group. The differences varied depending on the odorant but, in the elderly, thresholds were increased nine, three and two times for lemon, almond and fruity odours respectively. Odour memory is greatly reduced in the normal aged population with the ability to recall previously presented odours significantly decreased compared to their young counterparts. Most studies support the observation that the sense of smell is even more impaired in ageing than the sense of taste.

The cause of olfactory loss in the elderly could include normal ageing, medication or exposure to a variety of environmental toxins during life. Whatever the cause, there are noted anatomical and physical changes in the olfactory epithelium, olfactory bulb and associated nerves. In the elderly the olfactory epithelium shows loss of zonal organization, there is reduced innervation of the olfactory bulbs and loss of basal and supporting cells. A study by Bhatnagar and colleagues (1987) identified a significant loss of neurons in the human olfactory bulb, decreasing from 50,000 at age 25 to 15,000 by 90 years. Most of this decline occurred from the sixth decade onwards. This degeneration of the olfactory receptor system can become such that in some aged humans there is complete loss of smell. In addition, an age-related loss of neurons has been reported for the higher nerve centres associated with smell, indicating that there may be some dysfunction in processing olfactory responses. This is partly supported by the observation that olfactory threshold measures are not strongly affected by cognitive losses while suprathreshold performance is severely impaired.

Nutrition is highly dependent on both taste and smell since these senses initiate, sustain and terminate ingestion. Smell may well be more important than taste in regulating humans' appetite and food choices. Clearly, a reduction in these sensory functions as occurs in the elderly will reduce their ability to identify foods and can lead to nutritional

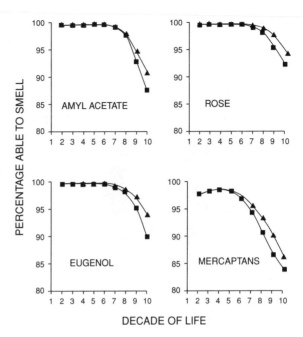

Figure 4. Graphs depicting the percentage of subjects at different decades of life able to detect four of the odours tested in the National Geographic Smell Survey. (Modified from the data presented in Wysocki and Gilbert, 1989.)

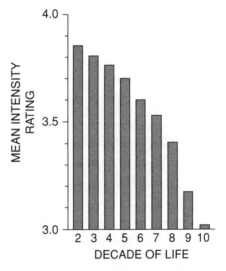

Figure 5. Graph demonstrating an age-related decline in the ability of the male population to distinguish different intensities of odour. (Modified from the data presented in Wysocki and Gilbert, 1989.)

deficiencies thus making individuals more susceptible to other age-related conditions (see Schiffman, 1997). Furthermore, suprathreshold perception of sweet and salt can have health consequences for

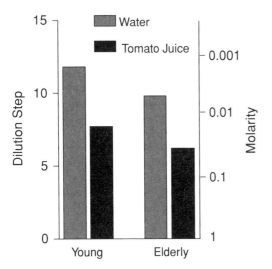

Figure 6. Average detection threshold of NaCl in deionized water and in tomato juice for young (18–30 yr) and elderly (69–87 yr). (Modified from the data presented in Stevens and Cain, 1993.)

Surface	Elderly/young ratio
Hand palm[1]	1.24
Thumb pad[1]	1.7
Little finger pad[1]	3
Index finger pad[2]	1.2
Great toe pad[2]	2.1

TABLE 1. Comparison of somatic sensation between the young (20–30 yrs) and elderly (60–80 yrs). The higher the elderly/young ratio above 1 the less the sensitivity in the elderly group. Data taken from Meisami *et al.* (1994)

[1]Two-point linen data;
[2]Vibrotactile thresholds measured at 100 Hz

the elderly who may be tempted to consume excess sugar or salt, which has implications for diabetes and hypertension respectively (see Figure 6). It is also important to note that both smell and taste are severely impaired in age-related disease such as Alzheimer's disease and Parkinson's disease, both of which affect the central nervous system. While there is no treatment for the neurosensory decline in taste and/or smell sensitivities, provided loss is not complete, the effect on nutrition can be addressed at least in part by flavour enhancement of foods, thus making them more appealing to the elderly.

TOUCH

Reduced cutaneous sensitivity to tactile and vibrotactile stimuli is common in the elderly and is associated with a higher threshold for pain (reviewed in Meisami, 1994) (see Table 1). Tactile sensitivity varies by body location with detection thresholds being lowest at the finger-tips, lips and tip of the tongue and relatively high on the back of the hands and feet. Tactile thresholds on the palmar surface of the finger are elevated between two- and threefold between the young and old, with evidence that the rate of increase in threshold detection is greatest over the age of 40 (Bruce, 1980). The

decline in vibrotactile sensation with age appears to be frequency-dependent (Verrillo, 1980). At least a threefold increase in threshold sensitivity between childhood and old age ($\geq$ 90 years) has been reported at 100 Hz while age-related changes appear to be negligible for low frequency stimuli (25–40 Hz).

The sensation of touch is mediated through two types of mechanoreceptor: the Meissner end organs respond to the sensation of fine touch and the Pacinian corpuscles respond to pressure and vibration (see Meisami, 1994). The numbers of both receptor types decrease with increasing age (e.g., Bolton *et al.*, 1966), demonstrated a threefold decrease in Meissner corpuscles in the little finger from 25 per mm^2 at 20 years to 8 at 80 years), possibly due to a decrease in receptor renewal rate. In addition, significant morphological changes are noted in the remaining mechanoreceptors in the elderly. Meissner corpuscles demonstrate a loss of anchorage and changes in cell structure while Pacinian corpuscles show an increase in size and a distortion in shape. What causes the loss and dysfunction of these receptors is unclear and may be an inherent component of the ageing process or, at least in part, as a result of environmental insults to the external body surface or age-related changes in skin structure. Furthermore, loss of touch sensation may also reflect an age-related decrease in sensory innervation and a decline in neuronal processing.

CONCLUSION

Although sensory impairment has always been a feature of old age, contributing to depression, loss of self-esteem and social isolation, its socioeconomic impact has grown dramatically because medical advances in the treatment of sensory impairment are progressing more slowly than those leading to increased life expectancy. Perceptual deficits with a neurosensory origin are proving particularly problematic. For example, there is no treatment for the vast majority of people with age-related macular degeneration (the main cause of visual impairment in the developed world) which has been estimated to affect 12.7 million people in Europe and North America.

There is, however, a growing body of evidence which suggests that individuals can help themselves. By eating a healthy diet high in antioxidants, avoiding cigarette smoke, excessive noise and short wavelength light it seems that we can all enjoy our senses for longer (Evans, 2001; Fook and Morgan, 2000).

FURTHER READING

Fook, L., and R. Morgan (2000). 'Hearing impairment in older people: a review', *Postgrad Med J*, 76: 537–41.

Meisami, E. (1994). 'Aging of the sensory system'. In P. S. Timiras, ed., *Physiological basis of aging and geriatrics*. Boca Raton, Fla.: CRC Press Inc., pp. 115–31.

Schiffman, S. (1997). 'Taste and smell losses in normal aging and disease', *JAMA*, 278: 1357–62.

Weale, R. A. (1992). *The senescence of human vision*. New York: Oxford University Press.

REFERENCES

Bhatnagar, K. P., Kennedy, R. C., Baron, G., and R. A. Greenberg (1987). 'Number of mitral cells and the bulb volume in the aging human olfactory bulb: a quantitative morphological study', *Anat Rec*, 218: 73–87.

Bolton, C. F., Winkelman, R. K., and P. J. Dyck (1966). 'A quantitative study of Meissner's corpuscles in man', *Neurology*, 16: 1–9.

Bradley, R. M. (1988). 'Effects of aging on the anatomy and neurophysiology of taste', *Gerodontics*, 4: 244–8.

Bruce, M. F. (1980). 'The relation of tactile thresholds to histology in the fingers of the elderly', *J Neurol Neurosurg Psychiatry*, 43: 730–4.

Curcio, C. A., Owsley, C., and G. R. Jackson (2000). 'Spare the rods, save the cones in aging and age-related maculopathy', *Invest Ophthalmol Vis Sci*, 41: 2015–18.

Evans, J. R. (2001). 'Risk factors for age-related macular degeneration', *Prog Ret Eye Res*, 20: 227–53.

Evans, J. R., Fletcher, A. E., Wormald, R . P . L., Siu-Woon, Ng E., Stirling, S., Smeeth, L., Breeze, E., Bulpitt, C. J., Nunes, M., Jones, D., and A. Tulloch (2002). 'Prevalence of visual impairment in people aged 75 years and older in Britain: results fom the MRC trial of assessment and management of older people in the community', *Br J Ophthalmol*, 86: 795–800.

Fook, L., and R. Morgan (2000). 'Hearing impairment in older people: a review', *Postgrad Med J*, 76: 537–41.

Gates, G. A., and Rees, T. S. (1997). 'Hear ye? Hear ye? Successful auditory aging', *Western Journal of Medicine*, 167: 247.

Gates, G. A., Mills, D., Nam, B., D'Agostino, R., and Rubel, E. W. (2002). 'Effects of age on the distortion product otoacustic emission growth functions', *Hearing Research*, 163: 53–60.

Harman, A., Abrahams, B., Moore, S., and R. Hoskins (2000). 'Neuronal density in the human retinal ganglion cell layer from 16–77 years', *Anatomical Rev*, 260: 124–31.

Jackson, G. R., and Owsley, C. (2000). 'Scotopic sensitivity during adulthood', *Vision Res*, 40: 2467–73.

Jackson, G. R., Owsley, C., and G. McGwin, Jr (1999). 'Aging and dark adaptation', *Vision Res*, 39: 3975–82.

Koretz, J. F., and C. A. Cook (2001). 'Aging of the optics of the human eye: lens refraction models and principal plane locations', *Optometry Vision Sci*, 78: 396–404.

McGrath, C., and J. D. Morrison, (1981). 'The effects of age on spatial frequency perception in human subjects', *Quart J Exp Physiol*, 66: 253–61.

Meisami, E. (1994). 'Aging of the sensory system'. In P. S. Timiras, ed., *Physiological basis of aging and geriatrics*. Boca Raton, Fla.: CRC Press Inc., pp. 115–31.

Mistretta, C. M. (1984). 'Aging effects on anatomy and neurophysiology of taste and smell', *Gerontology*, 3: 131–6.

Polidori, C., Zeng, Y. C., Zaccheo, D., and F. Amenta (1993). 'Age-related changes in the visual cortex – a review', *Arch Gerontol Geriat*, 17: 145–64.

Ross, M. H., Yurgelun Todd, D. A., Renshaw, P. F., Maas, L. C., Mendelson, J. H., Mello, N. K., Cohen, B. M., and J. M. Levin (1997). 'Age-related reduction in functional MRI response to photic stimulation', *Neurology*, 48: 173–6.

Schiffman, S. (1997). 'Taste and smell losses in normal aging and disease', *JAMA*, 278: 1357–62.

Schiffman, S., and B. G. Graham (2000). 'Taste and smell perception affect appetite and immunity in the elderly', *Eur J Clin Nutr*, 54: S54–S63.

Smeeth, L., Fletcher, A. E., Ng, E. S. W., Stirling, S., Nunes, M., Breeze, E., Bulpitt, C. J., Jones, D., and A. Tulloch (2002). 'Reduced hearing, ownership, and use of hearing aids in elderly people in the UK – the MRC Trial of the Assessment and Management of Older People in the Community: a cross-sectional survey', *Lancet*, 359: 1466–70.

Spear, P. D. (1993). 'Neural bases of visual deficits during aging', *Vision Res*, 33: 2589–2609.

Stevens, J. C., and W. S. Cain (1993). 'Changes in taste and flavor in aging', *Crit Rev Food Sci Nutr*, 33: 27–37.

Verrillo, R. T. (1980). 'Age-related changes in the sensitivity to vibration', *J Gerontol*, 35: 185–93.

Weale, R. A. (1992). *The senescence of human vision*. New York: Oxford University Press.

Willott, J. F., Chisolm, T. H., and J. J. Lister (2001). 'Modulation of presbycusis: current status and future directions', *Audiol Neuroontol*, 6: 231–49.

Winkler, S., Garg, A., Mekayarajjananonth, T., Bakaeen, L., and E. Khan (1999). 'Depressed taste and smell in geriatric patients', *JADA*, 130: 1759–65.

Wysocki, J., and Gilbert (1989). 'National Geographic Smell Survey-effects of age are heterogenous', *Annals of the New York Academy of Sciences*, 561: 12–28.

Wysocki, C. J., and M. L. Pelchat (1993). 'The effects of aging on the human sense of smell and its relationship to food choice', *Crit Rev Food Sci Nutr*, 33: 63–82.

Mobility and Falls

ROSE ANNE KENNY

INTRODUCTION

Falls are among the most common and serious problems facing older people. Falling is associated with considerable mortality, morbidity, reduced functioning and premature nursing home admission. Falls generally result from an interaction of multiple and diverse risk factors and situations, many of which can be corrected. This interaction is modified by age, disease and the presence of hazards in the environment. Frequently older people are not aware of their risk of falling and neither recognize risk factors nor report these issues to their physicians. Consequently, opportunities for prevention of falls or of falling are often overlooked, with risks becoming evident only after injury and disability have already occurred.

DEFINITION OF A FALL

A fall is defined as an event, reported either by the faller or a witness, resulting in a person inadvertently coming to rest on the ground or another lower level with or without loss of consciousness. This definition takes account of amnesia for loss of consciousness, frequently demonstrated in cardiovascular disorders, and the limited recall of falls by patients with cognitive impairment and dementia (Kenny *et al.*, 2001a).

SCOPE OF THE PROBLEM

Prospective studies have reported that 30–60% of community-dwelling older adults aged over 65 fall each year, with approximately half of them experiencing multiple falls. Fall incidence rates for community-dwelling older populations range from 0.2 to 1.6 falls per year, per person, with a mean of approximately 0.7. The incidence rises steadily after middle age and tends to be highest among individuals 80 years of age and older. These incidence rates are based on self-reported data which may underestimate the true incidence of falls and over-represent the proportion of individuals who report multiple falls.

The incidence amongst institutionalized elderly populations is considerably higher than among community-dwelling populations. Both the frailer nature of institutionalized populations and the more accurate reporting of falls cause this difference. In surveys of nursing home populations, the percentage of residents who fall each year averages 43%. The annual incidence of falls in long-term care facilities averages approximately 1.6 falls per bed ranging from 0.2 to 3.6.

Incidence rates from hospital-based surveys are somewhat lower, with a mean of 1.4 falls per bed, per year, and a range of 0.5 to 2.7. This variation most likely reflects differences in case mix, ambulation levels and fall prevention policies.

Falls are a major cause of morbidity and mortality in older people who have cognitive impairment and dementia. Their fall risks are double those seen in cognitively normal older people. The estimated annual incidence is up to 85%. The incidence is up to five times higher than in cognitively normal people in general (Rubenstein and Josephson, 2002).

FALL-RELATED MORBIDITY

A key issue of concern is not simply the high incidence of falls in older persons – because young people and athletes have an even higher incidence of falls – but rather the combination of this high incidence and high susceptibility to injury. The propensity for fall-related injuries in elderly persons is caused by a high prevalence of clinical disease, such as osteoporosis and age-related physiological changes such as slow protective reflexes, that make even a relatively mild fall dangerous. Half of falls result in injuries which are usually minor. Of community-dwelling older people who fall, 5–10% do sustain a serious injury such as a fracture, head injury or laceration. Among community-dwelling individuals with fall-related hip fractures, studies have shown that between 25% and 75% do not recover their pre-fracture level of ambulation or activities of daily living (Rubenstein and Josephson, 2002).

Patients who have cognitive impairment and dementia are at increased risk for sustaining a serious injury. The annual incidence of fractures is three times the rate reported in cognitively normal fallers. More worryingly, half the fractures are fractures to the femoral neck. This is three times greater than the rate experienced by cognitively normal older people. The prognosis after a fall is poor in people with dementia. They are even less likely to make a good functional recovery after an injury and are five times more likely to be institutionalized than patients with dementia who do not fall. In one series, the one year mortality from a femoral neck fracture was more than three times higher for patients with dementia than that for cognitively normal patients – 71% versus 19% respectively.

In addition to physical injuries, falls can also have psychological and social consequences. Repeated falls are a common reason for the admission of previously independent older persons to long-term care. In one study, 50% of fall-related injuries that required hospital admission resulted in older people being discharged to a nursing home. The risk of nursing home placement for individuals who sustain at least one fall with a serious injury is three times greater than for individuals with only one minor injurious fall. Fear of falling has been recognized as a negative consequence of falls. Surveys have reported 30–73% of persons aged over 65 years who have fallen acknowledge a fear of falling. This post-fall anxiety syndrome can result in self-imposed activity restrictions among both home-living and institutionalized older individuals who have experienced a fall. Loss of confidence in the ability to ambulate safely can result in further functional decline, in depression, feelings of helplessness and social isolation (Rubenstein and Josephson, 2002).

FALL-RELATED MORTALITY

Accidents are among the fifth leading cause of death in older adults after cardiovascular, cancer, stroke and pulmonary causes. Falls constitute two-thirds of accidental death. Three-quarters of deaths caused by falls in the United States occur in the 13% of the population aged 65 years and older. Fall-related mortality increases dramatically with advancing age, especially in people over 70. Older men have a higher mortality rate from falls than do women and nursing home residents aged 85 years and older account for 1 in 5 fatal falls. Of people who fall and sustain a hip fracture, the one year mortality rate is 20–30%. Mortality rates are even higher in fallers with dementia (Health Promotion England, 1999).

POSTURAL INSTABILITY

The human body is mechanically unstable, with its small base of support in relation to height. Even during ordinary activities such as standing up or walking, complex regulatory mechanisms are required to maintain stability and prevent falls. As illustrated in Figure 1, the maintenance of stability requires sensory input from visual, vestibular and proprioceptive receptors in addition to central processing by structures in the brain stem cerebellum, vasoganglia and sensory motor cortex. Efferent control is via the spinal cord and peripheral innervation of muscles. Impairment of any component of these mechanisms occurs with normal ageing. Older people display great instability and an abnormal gait pattern compared with younger people. This decline probably starts at 50 years of age. Data suggests that impaired visual acuity, proprioception and vestibular function, as well as a slowing of reaction time, contribute

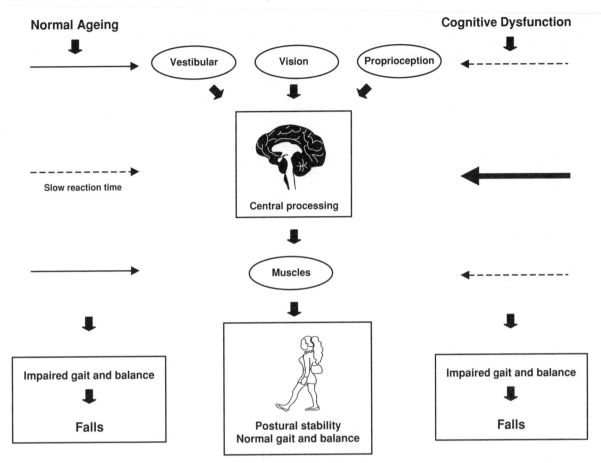

Figure 1. Postural control: effects of normal ageing and cognitive dysfunction.

to these abnormalities. The related problems of gait and balance disorders are extremely prevalent among older persons and can have a very profound effect on physical health, quality of life and capacity for independent living. Detectable gait abnormalities affect 20–40% of persons aged 65 years of age and older, approximately half of whom have a grossly abnormal gait. Gait problems are even more common in older subgroups, for example 40–50% of those over 85 years of age are affected. In a larger study of community-dwelling persons of 75 years of age and older, 10% needed assistance to walk across a room, 20% were unable to climb a flight of stairs without help and 40% were unable to walk half a mile (Shaw and Kenny, 2001; Shaw, 2002).

Patients with cognitive impairment and dementia experience even greater impairment of gait and balance. Compared with age- and sex-matched controls, patients with Alzheimer's disease have signifi-

cantly shorter step length, slower gait speed, slower step frequency, increased step to step variability and a greater sway path. The most likely explanation for the observed higher frequency of falls and higher prevalence of gait and balance instability in dementia is impaired central processing and integration of perceptual information.

Patients with dementia have particular difficulty in maintaining balance under conditions where central integration of information is stressed – for example, in situations where suppression of incongruous information, particularly visual information, is necessary to maintain balance. Neuropathologic degeneration in the areas of the brain that control postural stability are evident in Alzheimer's disease (Shaw et al., 2003).

TABLE 1. Results of univariate analysis of most common risk factors for falls identified in sixteen studies that examined risk factors

Risk factor	Significant/ Total +	Mean RR-OR #	Range
Muscle weakness	10/11	4.4	1.5–10.3
History of falls	12/13	3.0	1.7–7.0
Gait deficit	10/12	2.9	1.3–5.6
Balance deficit	8/11	2.9	1.6–5.4
Use assistive device	8/8	2.6	1.2–4.6
Visual deficit	6/12	2.5	1.6–3.5
Arthritis	3/7	2.4	1.9–2.9
Impaired ADL	8/9	2.3	1.5–3.1
Depression	3/6	2.2	1.7–2.5
Cognitive impairment	4/11	1.8	1.0–2.3
Age > 80 years	5/8	1.7	1.1–2.5

Source: (Kenny *et al.* 2001a)

RISK FACTORS FOR FALLING

A number of studies have identified risk factors for falling; these can be classified as either intrinsic (lower limb extremity weakness, poor grip, lack of strength, balance disorders, functional and cognitive impairment, visual deficits) or extrinsic (polypharmacy (four or more medications), and environmental factors such as poor lighting, loose carpets and lack of bathroom safety equipment). Although investigators have not used consistent classifications, a recent review of fall risk factor studies from Rubenstein's group ranked the risk factors and summarized relative risk of falls for persons with each risk factor (Table 1; Rubenstein and Josephson, 2002). In addition, a meta-analysis that studied the relationship between falls and medications, found a significantly increased risk from psychotropic medication (odds ratio 1.7), Class 1 anti-arrhythmics (odds ratio 1.6), digoxin (odds ratio 1.2) and diuretics (odds ratio 1.1) (Leipzig *et al.*, 1999). Perhaps as important as identifying underlying risk factors is appreciating the interaction and probable synergism between multiple risk factors. Several studies have shown that the risk of falling increases dramatically as the number of risk factors increases. Tinetti *et al.* (1988) surveyed community-dwelling older persons

and reported that the percentage of persons falling increased from 27% for those with no or one risk factor to 78% for those with four or more risk factors. Similar results were found among the institutionalized population. In another study, Nevitt *et al.* (1989) reported that the percentage of community-living persons with recurrent falls increased from 10 to 69% as the number of risk factors increased from one to four or more. Robbins *et al.* (1989) used multivariant analysis to simplify risk factors so that the maximum predictive accuracy could be obtained by using only three risk factors (i.e., hip weakness, unstable balance, taking more than four medications) in an algorithm format. With this model, the predicted one year risk of falling ranged from 12% for persons with none of the three risk factors to 100% for persons with all three.

In addition to the risk factors outlined in Table 1, other risk factors are reported as significant in single studies. The most prominent of these are visual deficit, impaired mental state, functional independence, incontinence, depression, generalized pain, reduced activity, fear as illustrated by scores from the falls efficacy scale, high alcohol consumption, Parkinson's disease, arthritis, diabetes, stroke and low body mass.

ASSESSMENT FOR RISK

The intensity of assessment varies by target populations, for example fall risk assessment as part of a routine primary health care visit with relatively low-risk senior populations would involve a brief assessment. In contrast, high-risk persons such as those with recurrent falls or those living in the nursing home, or persons prone to injurious falls or persons presenting after a fall, should require a more comprehensive and detailed assessment. An algorithm detailing the assessment and management of falls is outlined in Figure 2. The essential elements of any fall-related assessment include details about the circumstances of the fall, including a witness account, identification of the subject's risk factors for falls, any medical comorbidity, functional status and environmental risk. A comprehensive assessment may necessitate referral to a specialist, i.e., a geriatrician. Risk factors identified in the assessment may be modifiable (such as muscle weakness, medication side-effects, slow heart rates, fast heart

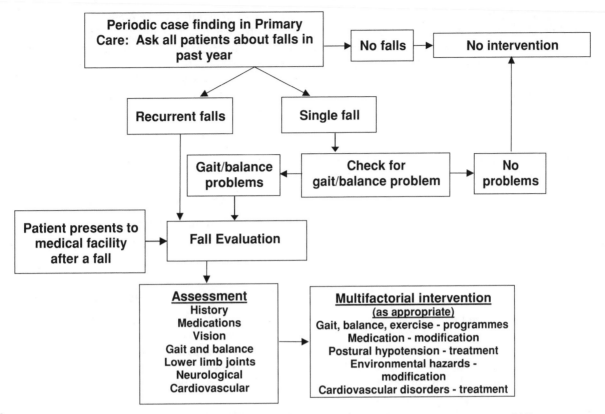

Figure 2. Assessment and management of falls.

rates or low blood pressure) or non-modifiable (such as hemiplegia or blindness). However, knowledge of all risk factors is important for treatment planning. Falls are usually multifactorial in origin and thus require a comprehensive assessment of key risk factors suggested from the history and other components of the assessment.

RISK FACTORS FOR INJURIOUS FALLS

More important than identifying risk factors for falling is arguably identifying risk factors for injurious falls, because most falls do not result in injury. Several research groups have identified risk factors associated with injurious falls. Among nursing home residents, lower extremity weakness, female gender, poor vision and hearing, disorientation, number of falls, impaired balance, dizziness, low body mass and use of mechanical restraints have been identified as factors that increase the risk of an injurious fall. Surprisingly, patients who are functionally independent and not depressed also have a greater

risk of injury, probably because they are more active. Among community-dwelling individuals, falls, previous injurious falls, impaired cognitive function and impaired balance increase the risk of injurious falls. The risk of hip fracture increases twofold for both nursing home residents and community-dwelling older persons who are taking psychotropic medications.

OVERLAP BETWEEN FALLS AND SYNCOPE

Syncope is defined as transient loss of consciousness due to low blood pressure. Falls have traditionally been treated as separate clinical conditions with different causes. More recently, accumulated evidence indicates that these symptoms overlap. The separation of falls and syncope into two distinct entities relies on an accurate history of the event and/or a witness account. However, for almost half of older people who experience syncope, such information is not available. In one study of 354 community-dwelling older fallers, over one-third did not recall having fallen three months after a documented event. Similarly, witness accounts of syncopal events are available in only 40–60% of cases.

The overlap for falls and syncope can be demonstrated in young and old subjects alike – although less common in younger persons with syncope. In one study, syncope was induced in 56 of 59 young healthy volunteers (in their early 20s) by a sequence of over-breathing, rapid change in posture from squatting to standing, and breath-holding. One-quarter fell but had preserved consciousness whereas the remainder fell with loss of consciousness. Even in this younger age group, 12% were unable to recall loss of consciousness.

Amnesia for loss of consciousness can particularly be demonstrated in patients with a disorder of the carotid sinus gland which results in pauses in heart rate and drops in blood pressure: carotid sinus syndrome. During a test which stimulates the carotid sinus and slows the heart rate dramatically, a majority of patients lose consciousness but only half recall loss of consciousness – despite this being clearly witnessed by laboratory staff. The clinical presentation in most of these patients is falls and not syncope (Kenny *et al.*, 2001b, 2002; Kenny, 2003). Cardiac pacemakers can reduce falls and injurious events by 75% in such patients – more than any other single intervention for falls (Kenny *et al.*, 2001b; McAnulty, 2001).

Two-thirds of older patients with significant blood pressure drops when they stand up (orthostatic hypotension) also present with falls or falls and dizziness. Orthostatic hypotension is a well-recognized risk factor for falls. Other disorders which are associated with slow heart rhythms are also recognized as a cause of falls.

In addition to amnesia for loss of consciousness, cardiovascular disorders can present as falls because loss of balance during slow heart rates or sudden drops in blood pressure can cause an older person to fall, without necessarily losing consciousness. This is particularly so in older persons who have postural instability. Treatment of the underlying cardiovascular condition can reduce falls in these people.

Falls are five times more common in people with cognitive impairment and dementia. Cardiovascular diagnoses, such as orthostatic hypotension and carotid sinus syndrome, are present in 70% of fallers with dementia (Kenny *et al.*, 2002). Identifying cardiovascular events as an attributable cause of falls/syncope is particularly difficult in older people with dementia because of the absence of witness accounts and inaccurate patient recall. However, it is important to determine whether cardiovascular events are responsible for symptoms because the majority can be successfully treated (Kenny *et al.*, 2001a).

QUALITY INDICATORS FOR FALLS

Rubenstein's group (2001) have recently published quality indicators for falls which recommend the following.

Quality Indicator 1. *Enquiring about falls*

All vulnerable elders should have documentation that they were asked at least annually about the occurrence of recent falls BECAUSE falls are common, often preventable, frequently unreported, and often the cause of injury and unnecessary restriction of activity, which results in a reduction in overall health and quality of life. In addition, a recent history of falls is a strong predictor of future falls.

Quality Indicator 2. *Detecting gait and balance disturbances*

All vulnerable elders should have documentation that they were asked about or examined for the presence of balance or gait disturbances at least once a year BECAUSE normal balance and mobility are important to health and quality of life and underlying treatable problems often go undetected.

Quality Indicator 3. *Basic fall evaluation*

IF a vulnerable elder reported two or more falls in the previous year or a single fall with injury requiring treatment, THEN there should be documentation that a basic fall evaluation was performed that resulted in specific diagnostic and therapeutic recommendations BECAUSE many causes of falls can be detected and treated, and detection and treatment will reduce the likelihood of future falls and their associated complications.

Quality Indicator 4. *Gait, mobility and balance evaluation*

IF a vulnerable elder person reports or is found to have new or worsening difficulty with ambulation, balance or mobility, THEN there should be documentation that a basic gait, mobility and balance evaluation was performed, within six months, that resulted in specific diagnostic and therapeutic recommendations BECAUSE many causes of gait and mobility disturbances can be detected and treated, often by prescribing specific assistive devices and exercises that will reduce the likelihood of future falls and their associated complications.

Quality Indicator 5. *Exercise and assistive device prescription for balance problems*

IF any vulnerable elder demonstrated decreased balance or proprioception or increased postural sway THEN an appropriate exercise programme should be offered and an evaluation for an assistive device performed BECAUSE impaired balance or proprioception and increased postural sway can contribute to instability, and appropriate treatment will reduce the likelihood of falls and their complications.

Quality Indicator 6. *Exercise prescription for gait problems and weakness*

IF a vulnerable elder is found to have problems with gait, strength or endurance, THEN an exercise programme should be offered BECAUSE these problems can contribute to falls and mobility dysfunction, and exercise intervention can improve or ameliorate them and reduce the likelihood of falls and their complications.

INTERVENTIONS TO PREVENT FALLS

The American Geriatrics Society/British Geriatrics Society (AGS/BGS) guidelines have made further, more specific recommendations for intervention incorporating medical assessments. The recommendations refer to populations in three settings – community-based, long-term care facilities and acute hospital inpatient settings. The interventions are described as multifactorial or single, based on

the study designs from which the recommendations were derived (Kenny *et al.*, 2001a).

MULTIFACTORIAL INTERVENTIONS

Community-Based Studies

The elements of the multifactorial interventions in community-dwelling older adults include advice about medication use (with or without subsequent modification of medications), exercise, medical assessment, management of cardiovascular disorders (such as postural hypotension and carotid sinus syndrome), home environment modifications, education programmes and self-management programmes.

Reduction in the number and dosage of prescribed medications is associated with benefit in most studies that included this intervention. However, medication review without subsequent direct efforts to modify medications is of no benefit. Exercise programmes are also associated with benefit in most studies. Medical assessment followed by specific interventions for any medical problems that were identified (including cardiovascular disorders and visual problems) was also beneficial. The management of postural hypotension was part of the effective intervention in two studies. Evidence of benefit from modification of home environmental hazards was equivocal or of no benefit. Staff education programmes were not effective in reducing falls. Self-management programmes were not beneficial in the five studies in which they are reported. Advice alone about fall risk factor modification (without measures to implement recommended changes) is of equivocal or no benefit.

LONG-TERM-CARE-BASED STUDIES. Randomized controlled studies in long term care settings show overall benefit from multifactorial interventions, and significant reductions in subsequent falls. The effective components are comprehensive assessment, staff education (in contrast to community settings), assistive devices, and reduction of medications.

IN-HOSPITAL-BASED STUDIES. Although falls prevention strategies are widely implemented, there are no adequate randomized controlled trials of multifactorial intervention studies to reduce falls among hospital inpatients.

SINGLE INTERVENTION

Exercise

Although exercise has many proven benefits, the optimal type, duration and intensity of exercise for falls prevention remains unclear. Older people who have had recurrent falls should be offered long-term exercise and balance training. Tai Chi C'uan is a promising type of balance exercise, although it requires further evaluation before it can be recommended as the preferred balance training.

Successful exercise programmes have consistently been over ten weeks' duration. Exercise needs to be sustained for sustained benefit.

In the Frailty and Injuries Cooperative Studies of Intervention Techniques (FICSIT) (Province *et al.*, 1995), the meta-analysis of seven studies that featured exercise as a prominent part of multifactorial interventions demonstrated an overall significant reduction in falls among intervention subjects, although only three of the seven individual trials showed significant reductions.

Environmental Modification

When older patients at increased risk of falls are discharged from the hospital, a facilitated environmental home assessment should be considered. A facilitated home modification programme after hospital discharge is effective in reducing falls. Otherwise, modification of home environment without other components of multifactorial intervention is not beneficial.

Medications

Patients who have fallen should have their medications reviewed and altered or stopped as appropriate in light of their risk of future falls. Particular attention to medication reduction should be given to older persons taking four or more medications and to those taking psychotropic medications. For all settings (i.e., community, long-term care, hospital, and rehabilitation), there is a consistent association between psychotropic medication use (i.e.,

neuroleptics, benzodiazepines and anti-depressants) and falls. Although there are no randomized controlled studies of manipulation of medication as a sole intervention, reduction of medications is a prominent component of effective interventions in community-based and long-term care multifactorial studies. Multifactorial studies suggest that a reduction in the number of medications in patients who are taking more than four preparations is beneficial.

Behavioural and Educational Programmes

Although studies of multifactorial interventions that have included behavioural and educational programmes have demonstrated benefit, when used as an isolated intervention, health or behavioural education does not reduce falls and should not be carried out in isolation.

Assistive Devices

Studies of multifactorial interventions that have included assistive devices (including bed alarms, canes, walkers (Zimmer frames) and hip protectors) have demonstrated benefit. However, there is no direct evidence that the use of assistive devices alone will prevent falls. Among hospitalized patients there is insufficient evidence for or against the use of bed alarms. Hip protectors do not appear to affect the risk of falling. However, there are a number of studies that strongly support the use of hip protectors for prevention of hip fractures in high-risk individuals.

Bone Strengthening Medications

A number of medications used widely to prevent or treat osteoporosis (e.g., hormone replacement therapy (HRT), calcium, vitamin D, anti-resorptive agents) reduce fracture rates. However, these agents do not reduce rates of falls per se. Given the wealth of information concerning HRT and vitamin D in osteoporotic fractures, including ample prior analyses and practice guidelines, bone strengthening should be considered in those at risk of injurious falls.

Cardiovascular Intervention

There is evidence that some falls have a cardiovascular cause that may be amenable to intervention strategies often directed to syncope, such as medication change or cardiac pacing. In particular, up to 30% of older patients with carotid sinus syndrome present with falls and have amnesia for loss of consciousness when bradyarrhythmia is induced experimentally. Patients with recurrent unexplained falls and a bradycardic response to carotid sinus stimulation experience fewer falls after implantation of a permanent cardiac pacemaker (Kenny *et al.*, 2001b).

Visual Intervention

Patients should be asked about their vision and, if they report problems, their vision should be formally assessed, and any remediable visual abnormalities should be treated. There are no randomized controlled studies of interventions for individual visual problems despite a significant relationship between falls, fractures and visual acuity.

Footwear Interventions

There are no experimental studies of footwear which examine falls as an outcome.

Restraints

There is no evidence to support restraint use for falls prevention. Restraints have been traditionally used as a falls prevention approach. However, they have major, serious drawbacks and can contribute to serious injuries. There is no experimental evidence that widespread use of restraints or, conversely, the removal of restraints, will reduce falls.

CONCLUSION

Falls and mobility problems are generally the result of multiple diverse and interacting causes. Falls and gait disorders represent an underlying pathological condition that may be amenable to treatment but may herald clinical demise if left unrecognized. Improvement in processes of care for falls in high-risk populations may lead to substantial improvements in patient outcomes.

Assessment of those at risk of falls and targeted single or multifactorial interventions for risk factors will reduce further falls and their consequences – injuries, loss of confidence, institutionalization and death. Awareness that cardiovascular syncope can present as falls has facilitated further successful interventions. The diagnosis of the attributable cause of falls continues to present a challenge – this is particularly so for fallers who have dementia.

FURTHER READING

Armstrong, V. L., and R. A. Kenny (2004). 'Syncope related falls in the older person'. In A. M. Bronstein, T. Brandt, M. Woolacott, and J. G. Nutt, eds., *Clinical disorders of balance, posture and gait.* London: Arnold Publishers, Chapter 22, pp. 422–37.

Petterson, T., and R. A. Kenny (2002). 'General medical causes of disequilibrium'. In L. M. Luxon, J. M. Furman, A. Martini, and D. Stephens, eds., *Textbook of audiological medicine: clinical aspects of hearing and balance.* London: Martin Dunitz Publishing, pp. 841–61.

Kenny, R. A., and D. O'Shea, eds. (2002). *Clinics in geriatric medicine – syncope and falls in the elderly.* Philadelphia: W. B. Saunders & Co.

REFERENCES

Health Promotion England (1999). *Older people and accidents: factsheet 2.* London: Health Promotion England.

Kenny, R. A. (2003). 'Syncope'. In W. R. Hazzard, J. P. Blass, J. B. Halter, J. G. Ouslander, and M. Tinetti, eds., *Principles of geriatric medicine and gerontology*, 5th edn. New York: McGraw-Hill Professional, pp. 1553–62.

Kenny, R. A., Rubenstein, L. Z., Martin, F. C., and M. E. Tinetti (2001a). 'Guideline for the prevention of falls in older persons. American Geriatrics Society, British Geriatrics Society, and American Academy of Orthopaedic Surgeons Panel on Falls Prevention', *J Am Geriatr Soc*, 49 (5): 664–72.

Kenny, R. A., Richardson, D. A., Steen, N., Bexton, R. S., Shaw, F. E., and J. Bond (2001b). 'Carotid sinus syndrome: a modifiable risk factor for nonaccidental falls in older adults (SAFE PACE)', *J Am Coll Cardiol*, 38 (5): 1491–6.

Kenny, R. A., Kalaria, R., and C. Ballard (2002). 'Neurocardiovascular instability in cognitive impairment and dementia', *Ann N Y Acad Sci*, 977: 183–95.

Leipzig, R. M., Cumming, R. G., and M. E. Tinetti (1999). 'Drugs and falls in older people: a systematic review and meta-analysis – cardiac and analgesic drugs', *J Am Ger Soc*, 47 (Part 11): 40–50.

McAnulty, J. H. (2001). 'Carotid sinus massage in patients who fall: will it define the role of pacing?' *J Am Coll Cardiol*, 38 (5): 1497.

Nevitt, M. C., Cummings, S. R., Kidd, S., and D. Black (1989). 'Risk factors for recurrent nonsyncopal falls. A prospective study', *JAMA*, 261 (18): 2663–8.

Province, M. A., Hadley, E. C., Hornbrook, M. C., Lipsitz, L. A., Miller, J. P., Mulrow, C. D., Ory, M. G., Sattin, R. W., Tinetti, M. E., and S. L. Wolf (1995). 'The effects of exercise on falls in elderly patients. A preplanned meta-analysis of the FIC-SIT Trials. Frailty and Injuries: Cooperative Studies of Intervention Techniques', *JAMA*, 273 (17): 1341–7.

Robbins, A. S., Rubenstein, L. Z., Josephson, K. R., Schulman, B. L., Osterweil, D., and G. Fine (1989). 'Predictors of falls among elderly people. Results of two population-based studies', *Arch Intern Med*, 149 (7): 1628–33.

Rubenstein, L. Z., and K. R. Josephson (2002). 'The epidemiology of falls and syncope', *Clin Geriatr Med*, 18 (2): 141–58.

Rubenstein, L. Z., Powers, C. M., and C. H. MacLean (2001). 'Quality indicators for the management and prevention of falls and mobility problems in vulnerable elders', *Ann Intern Med*, 135 (8 Pt 2): 686–93.

Shaw, F. E. (2002). 'Falls in cognitive impairment and dementia', *Clin Geriatr Med*, 18 (2): 159–73.

Shaw, F. E., and R. A. Kenny (2001). 'Science of risk factors in fallers: impact of cognitive dysfunction', *Rev Clin Gerontol*, 11 (4): 299–309.

Shaw, F. E., Bond, J., Richardson, D. A., Dawson, P., Steen, I. N., McKeith, I. G., and R. A. Kenny (2003). 'Multifactorial intervention after a fall in older people with cognitive impairment and dementia presenting to the accident and emergency department: randomised controlled trial', *BMJ*, 326 (7380): 73.

Tinetti, M. E., Speechley, M., and S. F. Ginter (1988). 'Risk factors for falls among elderly persons living in the community', *N Engl J Med*, 319 (26): 1701–7.

The Genetics of Behavioural Ageing

GERALD E. McCLEARN AND STEPHEN A. PETRILL

The topic of genetics of behavioural ageing implies that genes are involved in ageing processes, that there are behavioural changes as a function of age, and that genes influence behaviour. The first two propositions are, of course, well documented, and substantial bodies of theory and empirical data exist in each case. The latter proposition, that genes might influence behaviour, has been plagued by controversy, usually expressed in terms of *nature versus nurture*. This mellifluous phrasing has regrettably encouraged thinking about influences of heredity and environment on behaviour in alternative, either-or, adversarial terms: differences among individuals in a particular behaviour may be attributed to hereditary factors, or environmental factors, but not both.

Indeed, some of the most ardent scholars in behavioural and social sciences simplified the issue even further, from 'nature versus nurture' to 'nurture alone', by denying the possibility that heredity could have any effect on any behaviour. A particularly flamboyant expression of this view was that of Watson, founder of the influential school of psychological thought called *Behaviourism* (Watson, 1924). He acknowledged the influence of genes on structure, but denied that this had any implications for function, and rhetorically claimed that a healthy child could be made to develop any prescribed behavioural attributes – good or bad – solely on the basis of rearing environment. The anti-heredity view was certainly reinforced by revulsion at the excesses of eugenics programmes that were being promoted in that era, and most particularly after the Second World War by profound horror at revelations

of the Holocaust. Because justification or rationalization for these programmes had engaged notions of genetic 'inferiority', with particular emphasis on intellectual functioning, condemnation of the programmes appeared to many people to require rejection of the genetic rationale, as distorted and convoluted as it had been, and of genetics in general.

In spite of this negative atmosphere, explicit empirical evidence of genes influencing behaviour gradually accumulated so that, in the mid-twentieth century, a prominent publication, *The handbook of experimental psychology*, included a summary chapter on 'The genetics of Behavior' (Hall, 1951). The summarized studies had involved rats and mice mostly, and the range of behavioural attributes for which genetic influence had been described was quite broad. This publication was followed by the appearance of a textbook on the subject by Fuller and Thompson (1960). The field of *behavioural genetics* had achieved an identity, and research in the area increased exponentially. Animal research showed genetic influence on activity, aggression, alcohol-related behaviour, audiogenic seizures, communication, emotionality, feeding, learning, maternal behaviour, memory, psychomotor responses, reproduction, sensory processes and social behaviour. In human beings, the domains for which genetic influence was demonstrated included personality, temperament, attitudes, interests, mental illness, sensory and perceptual processing, cognitive and intellectual functioning, alcoholism, creativity and criminality. To be sure, there were relative emphases with some phenotypes more popular than others, but the widespread array of topics suggests that in respect to behavioural phenotypes, as in any biological domain, some role of heredity may be expected.

Although single gene influence was sought for some behavioural phenotypes, it became obvious early on that the appropriate model for dealing with complex behaviours was usually the *quantitative genetic model* that considered the influence of many anonymous genes and of environmental factors. Twin and adoption studies in human beings, and selective breeding studies and comparisons of inbred strains and derived generations in animal models, have been featured in this enterprise. Currently, the database from these 'classical' approaches is being complemented, supplemented and extended through vigorous exploitation of the tools provided by molecular genetics (Plomin *et al.*, 2001a).

An important general outcome of behavioural genetic research has been the demonstration of the speciousness of the nature/nurture formulation. Firstly, instead of all-or-nothing assignment to one or the other category, variation in behavioural phenotypes can be assigned fractionally, attributing some of the variance to heredity and some to environment. Secondly, genes and environment interact and co-act in many and subtle ways. Thus, it is not an issue of nature versus nurture; it is nature in harmonious conjunction with nurture.

We shall thus emphasize data concerning these interrelationships in respect to ageing of complex behavioural phenotypes. It has not been possible, at the same time, to provide a comprehensive account of the data describing genetic influence in behavioural ageing in general. A number of recent reviews collectively provide a broader summary of this abundant literature (Goodrick, 1978; Kallman and Jarvik, 1959; McClearn, 2001, 2002; McClearn and Foch, 1985; McClearn and Vogler, 2001; McClearn *et al.*, 2001; Omenn, 1977; Pedersen, 1996; Plomin and McClearn, 1990).

AGE DIFFERENCES IN GENETIC AND ENVIRONMENTAL INFLUENCES ON BEHAVIOUR

The target phenomena of gerontological genetics are phenotypes that have changed since youth or midlife (aerobic capacity, short term memory, for examples), or that newly appear in older populations (e.g. senile dementia, cataracts). In the former case, we may inquire about changes in the genetic and environmental underpinnings; in the latter case, we may seek to discover if a genetic basis can be identified for the emergent attribute. Both cases invoke the concept of change in gene expression as a function of age. This general idea has been long accepted, particularly in the realm of developmental genetics, and the database concerning both Mendelian genes and polygenic systems in early development is extensive. Further, the striking advances in the molecular genetics of developmental processes have provided powerful tools, both conceptual and operational, for elucidation of the mechanisms involved.

EARLY AND MIDLIFE EVIDENCE

Reflecting the importance of the domain in developmental psychology, developmental behavioural genetics has emphasized *cognitive functioning*, and the past 30 years of quantitative genetic research have raised fundamentally important issues concerning development from early childhood through old age (see Loehlin *et al.*, 1989; McGue *et al.*, 1993). Behavioural genetic studies have examined development using three broad approaches. First, the *age-related differences* approach has examined differences in the magnitude of genetic, shared environmental, and non-shared environmental influences at different ages. Genetic influences increase in importance with the age of the sample when examining cognitive development (Boomsma, 1993; McCartney *et al.*, 1990; McGue *et al.*, 1993; Plomin, 1986; Plomin *et al.*, 1997; Wilson, 1983) and appear to be centrally important to questionnaire-rated and observationally rated measures of *temperament* and *personality* throughout the lifespan (see Petrill and Brody, 2002, for a review). With respect to social–emotional adjustment and the development of psychopathology, *heritability* emerges in childhood for anti-social behaviours, problems in attention regulation and hyperkinesis, as well as emotional disturbances involving anxiety and depressive symptoms – and there is evidence that these genetic influences increase with age for some behavioural and emotional disorders (Eley and Stevenson, 1999; Feigon *et al.*, 2001; Rhee and Waldman, 2002; Thapar and McGuffin, 1996). Shared environmental estimates are significant in early childhood but approach zero in adolescent and adult samples for most behavioural outcomes (see Plomin *et al.*, 2001b) and the non-shared environment (including error) remains significant throughout the lifespan.

Second, the *stability/instability approach* has examined whether the genetic, shared environmental, and non-shared environmental influences at one age are related to the genetic, shared environmental, and non-shared environmental influences at later ages. These studies have suggested that the genetic covariance among cognitive skills across age becomes increasingly important (Bartels *et al.*, 2002; Bishop *et al.*, in press; Cherny *et al.*, 1994; Fulker *et al.*, 1993). Shared environmental covariance across age is also important in early childhood but is ultimately non-significant by adolescence. In addition, genetic overlap across age exists between many dimensions of normal personality and psychopathology, such as between earlier anxiety and later depression in girls (e.g. Silberg *et al.*, 2001). Important examples of this kind of research in children and adolescents include the Louisville Twin Study (Wilson, 1983) and NEAD (e.g., Neiderhiser *et al.*, 1996).

Whereas the stability/instability approach examines the magnitude of the covariance of genetic and environmental influences at different ages, the *change-as-phenotype* approach has also examined the genetic, shared environmental, and non-shared environmental influences upon the rate and trajectory of change across age. In his classic 'developmental synchronies' paper, Wilson (1983) found that the trajectories of development in identical twins are more similar than in fraternal twins, suggesting genetic influences on growth. More recently, behavioural genetic studies have utilized latent growth curve and multilevel modelling procedures to test more explicitly genetic and environmental influences upon change (e.g. McArdle, 1986; McArdle *et al.*, 1998; McGue and Christensen, 2002; Neale and McArdle, 2000; Reynolds *et al.*, 2002). These studies have indicated that genetic influences are primarily responsible for the intercept while non-genetic influences are implicated in change. However, it is important to note that these studies have typically examined very young children (e.g. McArdle, 1986) or older adults (e.g. McGue and Christensen, 2002; Reynolds *et al.*, 2002). The magnitude of genetic influences upon change has not been systematically examined in intermediate ages. Thus, it is unclear whether genetic influences are important to change in later childhood, adolescence and early adulthood.

The general message that cuts across each of the three approaches to development described above is that genes are important and may become more – not less – important with age, that the shared environment is less important after childhood, and that the *non-shared environment* (including error) is significant. These results have begun to influence developmental theory. For example, because shared environmental variance is negligible by adolescence for many phenotypes, some have argued that early experiences are ultimately unimportant to the study of individual differences in development (e.g. Harris, 1998). Others have argued that what is necessary is a more systematic examination of the child-specific environments (see Plomin *et al.*, 2001a). This approach has led to mixed results for family environment (Reiss *et al.*, 2000) and much controversy about the efficacy of examining the non-shared environment as a useful predictor of developmental outcomes (e.g. Plomin *et al.*, 2001a; Turkheimer and Waldron, 2000). Understanding how environmental influences impact development in the context of increasingly large and stable genetic factors is one of the central issues in current behavioural genetic research.

LATER LIFE EVIDENCE

It has been assumed that genetic influences become less important with age, as the 'slings and arrows of outrageous fortune' accumulate across a lifetime of experience. (Perhaps more apt in the gerontological context would be 'the whips and scorns of time' (Hamlet III).) However, behavioural genetic studies suggest that genetic influences remain important throughout the lifespan. The heritability of general cognitive ability is around .60 in old age (McClearn and Heller, 2000; McClearn *et al.*, 1997) which is attenuated slightly from younger adult estimates of around $h^2 = .80$ (Finkel *et al.*, 1995, 1998). However, as in studies of younger adults, the shared environmental variance is essentially zero in old age.

A more important gerontological question is how genes and environments influence the relationship among cognitive abilities in old age. For example, cognitive abilities *de-differentiate*, or become more highly correlated, as a function of old age. An important question is the extent to which genes and environments influence de-differentiation. In general, studies indicate that genetic influences are primarily responsible for de-differentiation (Finkel *et al.*, 1995; Pedersen *et al.*, 1994). These studies have shown that genes accounted for the correlation among verbal ability, spatial ability, perceptual speed, and memory. This pattern of results was still more pronounced in even older samples (Petrill *et al.*, 1998). Furthermore, genetic influences accounted for 75% of the covariance between measures of intelligence and educational attainment in old age (Lichtenstein and Pedersen, 1997). Finally, studies have shown that the correlation among measures of cognitive ability across age are influenced largely by genetic factors (Finkel *et al.*, 1995). In general, the correlation among cognitive skills increases with age, and genes are mainly responsible for this correlation. Non-shared environmental influences are primarily responsible for independence among cognitive skills.

The studies described above examine the stability of individual differences across age and across measures of cognitive ability. Other studies have examined intra-individual change across age: examining the extent to which change in cognitive skills across time is influenced by genetic or environmental factors. These studies indicate that, while genetic factors influence the average level or intercept, non-genetic influences account for change, or, in the case of old age, decline, in cognitive skills (McArdle, 1986; McArdle *et al.*, 1998; McGue and Christensen, 2002; Neale and McArdle, 2000; Reynolds *et al.*, 2002). Again, for many phenotypes, genetic influences appear to foster stability while non-genetic influences appear to foster instability and change.

The animal literature on genetics of behavioural ageing unsurprisingly features studies of inbred strains, with an emphasis on mice. A popular basic design has been to characterize two or more strains of mouse on some behavioural phenotype at two or more ages. An inference of genetic influence on rate of ageing emerges from strain differences in the change or difference between the two ages. Also, given the salience of the topic to the enterprise of psychology, it is unsurprising that much attention has been focused on aspects of learning and cognition. An early programme of research

in this area addressed avoidance learning, a topic of widespread interest in investigations of animal learning phenomena. Sprott (1972) tested C57BL/6 and DBA/2 mice and their F_1 hybrid at 5 weeks and at 4–5 months of age in a passive avoidance situation, where the animals had to learn to avoid stepping from a platform to a grid floor which administered a foot shock. The DBA/2 improved with age; the C57BL/6 performance deteriorated; and the F_1 performance closely resembled that of their C57BL/6 parent, implying average dominance of the presumably polygenic influence on the phenotype.

A wide range of other, non-learning, phenotypes has also been examined in inbred strains at different ages. Goodrick (1975) compared mice of two inbred strains (the C57BL/6 and A strains) on a variety of phenotypes at 5 months and at 23 or 26 months of age. Interactions of age with strain were found for exploratory activity, open field activity, wheel-running activity, bar-pressing for light, quinine discrimination, sucrose discrimination and alcohol preference. This latter phenotype was further explored by Wood (1976). C57BL/6 and BALB/c mice were assessed for alcohol consumption in a choice situation at 7–9 months, 14–16 months and 22–4 months of age. The BALB/c mice exhibited relatively low intake at all ages. The youngest C57BL/6 mice displayed the high preference typical for the strain, and a gradual decline ensued at both older ages; even at the older age, the strain difference was substantial. The result was an interaction reflecting differences both in level and in changes with age.

INTERACTIONS IN GENETICS OF BEHAVIOURAL AGEING

Warren (1986) explored many parameters of maze learning with the popular C57BL/6 and DBA/2 strains, at 100, 200, 400, 600 and 700 days of age. The results emphasized task-specificity. In a latent learning situation, young DBA/2 animals were superior to old ones; young C57BL/6 mice were inferior to their older strain-mates. In a visual discrimination problem, the performance of C57BL/6 deteriorated with age, but that of DBA/2 animals did not. This particularity of outcome dependent upon circumstances of measurement can, of course, be considered to be an example of gene–environment interaction such as those discussed previously, but here in the context of age-change. A further example of genetic influence on age differences in the context of apparatus-specific environments is provided by McGaugh and Cole (1965). A focal topic of the lively area of learning theory in psychology concerned the role of inter-trial interval in maze-learning situations. There was a theoretical basis for expecting longer intervals (within limits) to result in quicker learning. McGaugh and Cole examined the issue in two lines of rats selectively bred by Tryon (1940) for good performance and poor performance, respectively, in a complicated maze. The performance of young (29–33 days) and young adult (142–54 days) 'Brights' and 'Dulls' were compared under conditions of 30-second or 30-minute intervals between trials in a somewhat simpler maze. In females, the younger Brights showed the expected result, with fewer errors being committed under the distributed condition. The Dulls, however, showed no effect whatsoever of distribution of practice, and in neither condition did they commit more errors than the Brights. In the adults, both Dulls and Brights showed strong effects of the inter-trial interval, but in neither condition was the performance of the Dulls inferior to that of the Brights. In the case of the younger males, a distribution-of-practice effect was evident in the Brights, but not the Dulls, and the Dulls committed more errors only in the distributed condition. Only in the adult males were expectations met with respect to both the distribution of practice and strain: in each condition, Dulls made more errors, and in each strain, a distribution effect was present.

These results, rather intricate in their detail, display the interdependence of genotype, environmental circumstance, sex and age in a phenotype operationally defined as an assessment of rodent cognitive abilities. They serve well to illustrate the types of complexities that can be encountered in apparently straightforward measurement situations.

An animal study with possible relevance to Alzheimer's disease (AD) was conducted by Fosmire and associates (1993). These investigators conjectured that the inconsistent evidence concerning aluminium exposure as a risk factor for AD might arise from population differences in allelic frequency at loci that influence individual differences in susceptibility to aluminium. To test the reasonableness of this proposition in an animal model, they

exposed mice of five inbred strains (A, BALB/c, C3H/2, C57BL/6 and DBA/2) to a diet with elevated aluminium levels. Brain aluminium levels of these animals were compared to those on a control diet. Briefly stated, three strains (A, BALB/c, C57BL/6) showed no elevation of brain aluminium levels whatsoever as a consequence of the dietary exposure; one (C3H/2) showed a mild elevation; and one (DBA/2) showed a nearly fourfold increase. Generalizing broadly, we might expect that there will be genetically influenced individual differences in susceptibility to many or most risk factors that are identified in epidemiological investigations. Similarly, we might expect that there will be individual differences, genetically influenced, in susceptibility to preventive interventions or remedial treatments.

SUMMARY AND CONCLUSIONS

A concise summary of the body of research we have cited is that:

- age-related change occurs in many behavioural phenotypes
- the pattern and magnitude of change differs among phenotypes
- genetic influence is demonstrable in many of the age-related behavioural changes
- the extent of genetic influence varies from phenotype to phenotype
- the extent of genetic influence varies from age to age
- the interaction of genetic and environmental influences can be substantial

In many ways, this summary is unremarkable. Much the same could be said for any biological phenotypic domain into which gerontologists have delved. But this ordinariness of outcome is important in locating the behavioural domain comfortably within biogerontology. The nature versus nurture formulation, which would have it that behaviour is somehow insulated from genetic influence (and, therefore, from all of the biological mechanisms through which genetic influence is mediated), is clearly vacuous in this, as in other contexts.

It is quite apparent that the scope for complexities in the causal nexus onto which genetic and environmental factors impinge is great, both in subtlety and in the magnitude of their effects. (We note, incidentally, that many of the examples cited were published many years ago. The phenomena are not recently discovered revelations.) If the magnitude of effect of an allelic substitution at one locus depends upon the environmental circumstances, or if the impact of an environmental risk factor or the efficacy of a preventive or therapeutic intervention depends upon the genotype of the individual, or if a causal route proceeds from genes to behaviour that affects environmental exposure, and that environment has behavioural consequences, and may perhaps also change expression of genes that have a function related to that environment, then simple unidirectional concepts of causality are clearly limited in explanatory and descriptive power.

The extent to which such interactions and correlations pervade our subject matter is not yet apparent, however. A major problem is that most of the research designs that have been employed have not looked for them. We have cited considerable positive evidence for their existence, but over the entire spectrum of age-relevant behaviours, the evidence is sparse. Clearly there are main effects of some genes; clearly there are main effects of some environments. These may be 'sledge-hammer' effects. What needs to be illuminated is the extent to which the interactions influence the great middle range of effect sizes of causal agencies.

It seems clear that future research should be encouraged to incorporate measured environments in a genetically informative context. Behavioural genetic research in child development has suggested that there may be a shift from passive to active/evocative *gene–environment processes*. There may be shifts either towards or away from these processes as a function of ageing. To the best of our knowledge, these kinds of questions have yet to be addressed empirically. Furthermore, understanding the environments through which genes operate may help to explain why heritability estimates are so high for cognitive functioning in adulthood. Heritability is estimated by comparing identical vs fraternal twin resemblance. If identical twins are more likely to come into contact with more similar environments, and these environments make identical twins more similar, then heritability estimates will reflect these indirect influences.

If we are to understand gene–environment process in the gerontological context, it is essential to examine the relationship between measured environments and outcomes using both parent–offspring and sibling designs across age-related differences, stability/instability, and change-as-phenotype perspectives of development. Quantifying the connections between gene–environment process and development will provide a more complete picture of the mechanisms that yield individual differences in important developmental outcomes such as *cognitive ability, academic achievement, psychopathology* and *family/peer relations*.

In animal model investigations, the particularity of results depending upon the configuration of controlled and manipulated variables offers both methodological and conceptual challenge. The first lesson is the importance of humility in regards to the generalizability of results of any one study, and this argues for the advantages of multivariate approaches. It would appear that generalizations must be established empirically, and not assumed *ab initio*.

If we can refer to Saxe's useful allegory of the blind men and the elephant, our understanding of ageing will depend on how much of the elephant we can stroke. And perhaps what we thought were broad sweeps of the hand are best thought of as taps with a finger. It may take much tapping to get a useful image of the genetics of behavioural ageing. And the tapping must include both environmental and genetic taps. The complexities of *gene X environment interactions* and correlations not only complicate the logistics and pragmatics of research, however. They also offer perhaps the most propitious areas for concentrated research. Our understanding of the dynamics of the complex systems of ageing will certainly be furthered by tackling these issues directly; in the process, there are attractive prospects of identifying promising avenues of prevention and intervention.

FURTHER READING

Petrill, S. A., Saudino, K. S., Wilkerson, B., and R. Plomin (2001). 'Genetic and environmental molarity and modularity of cognitive functioning in 2-year-old twins', *Intelligence*, 31–43.

McClearn, G. E. (2001). 'The genetics of behavioral aging'. In V. J. Cristofalo, and R. Adelman, eds., *Annual Review of Gerontology and Geriatrics*. New York: Springer Publishing Company, pp. 237–71.

REFERENCES

Bartels, M., Rietveld, M. J. H., Van Baal, G. C. M., and D. I. Boomsma (2002). 'Genetic and environmental influences on the development of intelligence', *Behavior Genetics*, 32 (3): 237–49.

Bishop, E. G., Cherny, S. S., and J. K. Hewitt (2003). 'Developmental analysis of IQ'. In S. A. Petrill, R. Plomin, J. C. DeFries and J. K. Hewitt, eds., *Nature, nurture, and the transition to early adolescence*. New York: Oxford University Press, pp. 13–77.

Boomsma, D. I. (1993). 'Current status and future prospects in twin studies of the development of cognitive abilities: infancy to old age'. In T. J. Bouchard, Jr, and P. Propping, ed., *Twins as a tool of behavioral genetics*. Chichester: Wiley, pp. 67–82.

Cherny, S. S., Fulker, D. W., Emde, R. N., Robinson, J., Corley, R. P., Reznick, J. S., *et al.* (1994). 'A developmental genetic analysis of continuity and change in the Bayley Mental Development Index from 14 to 24 months: the MacArthur Longitudinal Twin Study', *Psychological Science*, 5 (6): 354–60.

Eley, T. C., and J. Stevenson (1999). 'Exploring the covariation between anxiety and depression symptoms: a genetic analysis of the effects of age and sex', *Journal of Child Psychology and Psychiatry and Allied Disciplines*, 40 (8): 1273–82.

Feigon, S. A., Waldman, I. D., Levy, F., and D. A. Hay (2001). 'Genetic and environmental influences on separation anxiety disorder symptoms and their moderation by age and sex', *Behavior Genetics*, 31 (5): 403–11.

Finkel, D., Pedersen, N. L., McGue, M., and G. E. McClearn (1995). 'Heritability of cognitive abilities in adult twins: comparison of Minnesota and Swedish data', *Behavior Genetics*, 25 (5): 421–31.

Finkel, D., Pedersen, N. L., Plomin, R., and G. E. McClearn (1998). 'Longitudinal and cross-sectional twin data on cognitive abilities in adulthood: the Swedish Adoption/Twin Study of Ageing', *Developmental Psychology*, 34: 1400–13.

Fosmire, G. J., Focht, S. J., and G. E. McClearn (1993). 'Genetic influences on tissue deposition of aluminum in mice', *Biological Trace Element Research*, 37: 115–21.

Fulker, D. W., Cherny, S. S., and L. R. Cardon (1993). 'Continuity and change in cognitive development'. In R. Plomin and G. E. McClearn, eds., *Nature, nurture and psychology*. Washington, D.C.: American Psychological Association, pp. 77–97.

Fuller, J. L., and W. R. Thompson (1960). *Behaviour genetics*. New York: Wiley.

Goodrick, C. L. (1975). 'Behavioural differences in young and aged mice: strain differences for activity measures, operant learning, sensory discrimination, and alcohol preference', *Experimental Ageing Research*, 1: 191–207.

(1978). 'Behaviour genetics and ageing'. In E. L. Schneider, ed., *The genetics of aging*. New York: Plenum Press, pp. 403–15.

Hall, C. S. (1951). 'The genetics of behavior'. In S. S. Stevens, ed., *Handbook of experimental psychology*. New York: John Wiley and Sons, pp. 301–29.

Harris, J. R. (1998). *The nurture assumption: why children turn out the way they do*. New York: Free Press.

Kallman, F. J., and L. Jarvik (1959). 'Individual differences in constitution in genetic background'. In J. E. Birren, ed., *Handbook of aging in the individual*. Chicago: University of Chicago Press, pp. 216–75.

Lichtenstein, P., and N. L. Pedersen (1997). 'Does genetic variance for cognitive abilities account for genetic variance in educational achievement and occupational status? A study of twins reared apart and twins reared together', *Social Biology*, 44: 77–90.

Loehlin, J. C., Horn, J. M., and L. Willerman (1989). 'Modeling IQ change: evidence from the Texas Adoption Project', *Child Development*, 60: 993–1004.

McArdle, J. J. (1986). 'Latent variable growth within behavior genetic models', *Behavior Genetics*, 16 (1): 163–200.

McArdle, J. J., Prescott, C. A., Hamagami, F., and J. L. Horn (1998). 'A contemporary method for developmental-genetic analyses of age changes in intellectual abilities', *Developmental Neuropsychology*, 14 (1): 69–114.

McCartney, K., Harris, M. J., and F. Berneiri (1990). 'Growing up and growing apart: a developmental meta-analysis of twin studies', *Psychological Bulletin*, 107: 226–37.

McClearn, G. E. (2001). 'The genetics of behavioral aging'. In V. J. Cristofalo and R. Adelman, eds., *Annual review of gerontology and geriatrics*, Vol. XXI. New York: Springer Publishing Company, pp. 237–71.

(2002). 'Genetics of behavioral ageing: animal models and the human condition', *Experimental Aging Research*, 28: 453–76.

McClearn, G. E, and T. T. Foch (1985). 'Behavioral genetics'. In J. E. Birren and K. W. Schaie, eds., *Handbook of the psychology of aging*, 2nd edn. New York: Van Nostrand Reinhold, pp. 113–43.

McClearn, G. E., and D. A. Heller (2000). 'Genetics and aging. In S. B. Manuck, R. Jennings, B. S. Rabin and A. Baum, eds., *Behavior, health, and aging*. Mahwah, N.J.: Lawrence Erlbaum Associates, pp. 1–14.

McClearn, G. E., and G. P. Vogler (2001). 'The genetics of behavioral ageing'. In J. E. Birren and K. W. Schaie, eds., *Handbook of the psychology of aging*, 5th edn. San Diego, Calif.: Academic Press, pp. 108–31.

McClearn, G. E., Johansson, B., Berg, S., Pedersen, N. L., Ahern, F., Petrill, S. A., and R. Plomin (1997). 'Substantial genetic influence on cognitive abilities in twins 80 or more years old', *Science*, 276: 1560–3.

McClearn, G. E, Vogler, G. P., and S. M. Hofer (2001). 'Environment–gene and gene–gene interactions'. In E. J. Masoro and S. N. Austad, eds., *Handbook of the biology of aging*, 5th edn. San Diego, Calif.: Academic Press, pp. 423–44.

McGaugh, J. L., and J. M. Cole (1965). 'Age and strain differences in the effect of distribution of practice on maze learning', *Psychonomic Science*, 2: 253–4.

McGue, M., and K. Christensen (2002). 'The heritability of level and rate-of-change in cognitive functioning in Danish twins aged 70 years and older', *Experimental Aging Research*, 28 (4): 435–51.

McGue, M., Bouchard, T. J., Jr, Iacono, W. G., and D. T. Lykken (1993). 'Behavioral genetics of cognitive ability: a lifespan perspective'. In R. Plomin and G. E. McClearn, eds., *Nature, nurture, and psychology*. Washington, D.C.: American Psychological Association, pp. 59–76.

Neale, M. C., and J. J. McArdle (2000). 'Structured latent growth curves for twin data', *Twin Research*, 3: 165–77.

Neiderhiser, J. M., Reiss, D., and E. M. Hetherington (1996). 'Genetically informative designs for distinguishing developmental pathways during adolescence: responsible and antisocial behavior', *Development and Psychopathology*, 8 (4): 779–91.

Omenn, G. S. (1977). 'Behavior genetics'. In J. E. Birren and K. W. Schaie, eds., *Handbook of the psychology of aging*. New York: Van Nostrand Reinhold, pp. 190–218.

Pedersen, N. (1996). 'Gerontological behavior genetics'. In J. E. Birren and K. W. Schaie, eds., *Handbook of the psychology of aging*, 4th edn. San Diego, Calif.: Academic Press, pp. 59–77.

Pedersen, N. L., Plomin, R., and G. E. McClearn (1994). 'Is there G beyond g? (Is there genetic influence on specific cognitive abilities independent of genetic influences on general cognitive ability?)', *Intelligence*, 18: 133–43.

Petrill, S. A., and N. Brody (2002). 'Methodological issues in the study of personality and individual differences'. In H. Pashler and J. Wixted, eds., *Stevens' handbook of experimental psychology*, 3rd edn. New York: John Wiley and Sons, pp. 563–600.

Petrill, S. A., Plomin, R., Berg, S., Johansson, B., Pedersen, N., Ahern, F., and G. E. McClearn (1998). 'The genetic and environmental relationship between general and specific cognitive abilities in twins 80 years and older', *Psychological Science*, 9 (3): 183–9.

Plomin, R. (1986). *Development, genetics, and personality*. Hillsdale, N.J.: Lawrence Erlbaum Associates.

Plomin, R., and G. E. McClearn (1990). 'Human behavioural genetics of ageing'. In J. E. Birren and K. W. Schaie, eds., *Handbook of the psychology of aging*, 3rd edn. New York: Academic Press, pp. 66–77.

Plomin, R., Fulker, D. W., Corley, R., and J. C. DeFries (1997). 'Nature, nurture, and cognitive development

from 1 to 16 years: a parent–offspring adoption study', *Psychological Science*, 8 (6): 442–7.

Plomin, R., Asbury, K., and J. Dunn (2001a). 'Why are children in the same family so different? Nonshared environment a decade later', *Canadian Journal of Psychiatry*, 46: 225–33.

Plomin, R., DeFries, J. C., McClearn, G. E., and P. McGuffin (2001b). *Behavioral genetics*, 4th edn. New York: Worth Publishers.

Reiss, D., Neiderhiser, J., Hetherington, E. M., and R. Plomin (2000). *The relationship code: deciphering genetic and social influences on adolescent development*. Cambridge, Mass.: Harvard University Press.

Reynolds, C. A., Finkel, D., Gatz, M., and N. L. Pedersen (2002). 'Sources of influence on rate of cognitive change over time in Swedish twins: an application of latent growth', *Experimental Aging Research*, 28 (4): 407–33.

Rhee, S. H., and I. D. Waldman (2002). 'Genetic and environmental influences on antisocial behavior: a meta-analysis of twin and adoption studies', *Psychological Bulletin*, 128 (3): 490–529.

Silberg, J. L., Rutter, M., and L. Eaves (2001). 'Genetic and environmental influences on the temporal association between earlier anxiety and later depression in girls', *Biological Psychiatry*, 49 (12): 1040–9.

Sprott, R. (1972). 'Passive-avoidance conditioning in inbred mice: effects of shock intensity, age, and genotype', *Journal of Comparative and Physiological Psychology*, 80: 327–34.

Thapar, A., and P. McGuffin (1996). 'A twin study of antisocial and neurotic symptoms in childhood', *Psychological Medicine*, 26 (6): 1111–18.

Tryon, R. C. (1940). 'Genetic differences in maze-learning ability in rats', 39th *Yearbook of the National Society for the Study of Education*. Bloomington, Ill.: Public School, Part I, pp. 111–19.

Turkheimer, E., and M. Waldron (2000). 'Nonshared environment: a theoretical, methological, and quantitative review', *Psychological Bulletin*, 126 (1): 78–108.

Warren, J. M. (1986). 'Appetitive learning by old mice', *Experimental Aging Research*, 12: 99–105.

Watson, J. B. (1924). *Behaviorism*. New York: Norton and Co. (Rev. edn. 1930.)

Wilson, R. S. (1983). 'The Louisville Twin Study: developmental synchronies in behavior', *Child Development*, 54: 298–316.

Wood, W. G. (1976). 'Ethanol preference in C57BL/6 and BALBc mice at three ages and eight ethanol concentrations', *Experimental Aging Research*, 2: 425–34.

Psychodynamic Approaches to the Lifecourse and Ageing

SIMON BIGGS

INTRODUCTION

Psychoanalytic thinking has held a key position in shaping how identity is conceived and contemporary notions of what it is to be an adult. Such cultural embeddedness means that it often forms a tacit backdrop to the way we interpret our experience of the everyday social world, as well as lending shape to ways that health and welfare practitioners make sense of issues in their day-to-day work.

When Freud (1956[1930]) wrote 'Civilization and its discontents' he believed he was demonstrating that the psychoanalytic method could be used to explain social phenomena. And to this day psychodynamic approaches share properties arising from the western Enlightenment, including a belief in progress, faith in the power of rationality and the positive value of individual autonomy. As Frosh (1991) points out, these approaches involve a focus on change and a critical stance towards past events.

For ageing, psychoanalysis is particularly important, because it is primarily a developmental theory that exerts a moral as well as a scientific force. It is assumed that much of the behaviour and identity occurring in adulthood can be explained through childhood experience, resulting in a developed understanding of the early lifecourse but underdevelopment of later phases. The past is generally seen as being problematic, and especially so when relationships between generations are considered.

A second issue concerns the relationship between hidden and surface meanings. Difference between internal and external experience of age has been noted by a number of writers (Featherstone and Hepworth, 1989; Thompson, 1992). A multiplicity of inner meanings might adhere to any one event and, whilst these may not be immediately available to consciousness, psychoanalysis supplies a method to uncover them.

These two themes, arising from psychodynamic ideas, inform the rest of this chapter.

CLASSICAL PSYCHOANALYSIS

Freud's own statements on the prospect of development in mature adulthood are few, and are dispersed amongst papers largely concerned with other issues.

'Sexual aetiology of neuroses' (1956[1897]) contains a speculative account (there is little evidence that Freud had worked with older patients) suggesting that psychoanalytic therapy might be unsuitable for the young, the 'feeble minded' and people who are 'very advanced in years'. In the case of older people, the amount of material accrued over a lifecourse would take too long to analyse, whilst a lack of value attached to 'nervous health' in the later stages of adulthood affects motivation.

In his essay 'On psychotherapy', Freud famously claimed that:

Psychotherapy is not possible near or above the age of 50, the elasticity of the mental processes, on which treatment depends, is as a rule lacking – old people are not educable – and, on the other hand, the mass of material to be dealt with would prolong the duration of treatment indefinitely. (1956[1905])

A third reference supplies further explanation of what this might mean. In 'Types of onset of neuroses' (1956[1912]), neurotic breakdowns are linked to puberty and the menopause, which occasion 'more or less sudden increases of libido'. Libidinal energy is seen as providing the motive for psychological change and is thenceforth relatively absent, which leads to a pessimistic prognosis for intervention.

Whilst Freud's position appears unfortunate from the perspective of later life, there are reasons to believe that they were provisional and not central to his ideas.

Freud was himself 48 when he gave his paper, falls within his own 'near or above' age-range and was yet to recast his own theory of mind (Hildebrand, 1982). Melanie Klein was 41 when she began a personal analysis with Karl Abraham, and Wilfred Bion was 48 when he started with Klein. Abraham concluded that prognosis depended on age at onset, with earlier onset making the chances of cure less likely: 'In other words the age at which the neurosis breaks out is of greater importance to the success of psychoanalysis than the age at which treatment is begun' (1919: 316).

Freud's arguments are focused on technique rather than adult subjectivity. There may be less energy available for psychic change, but the mature psyche is still subject to the same processes and mechanisms as in any other part of life. Rechtschaffen (1959) notes that 'there is no reason to discuss geriatric psychotherapy as distinct from any other psychotherapy'.

If the unconscious is essentially without time and chaotic in character, then unconscious material is not in itself age-related. If personal identity is determined in early childhood, and adult conflicts and tensions are simply neurotic repetitions of early experiences, then it should show the same patterns however many times they are re-enacted. The 'mass of material' argument does not hold water, following this logic, because the underlying processes determine the validity of material and not vice versa.

These points may explain the absence of reference to patients' age in Freud's own mature work.

However marginal the argument against work with older people appears to be, it quickly gained credence within analytic circles. By 1952, Hollender notes that 'Perhaps the best explanation for the fact that analysis is not a procedure for people in their fifties and over is that there is not enough hope in the future to provide the motivation needed to endure the tensions mobilised by analysis' (1952: 342).

By the 1960s, it became accepted wisdom that those over 40 should be dissuaded from analytic training as well as therapy. However, King (1974) argued that 'particularly between the ages of 40 and 65' older patients can benefit greatly from analysis, but because of prevailing beliefs within psychoanalysis, very few older people actually found their way into the consulting-room. King, her analysand Hildebrand (1982), and a small number of other analysts including Terry (1997) and Davenhill (1998) have maintained an interest in work with older people.

EGO PSYCHOLOGY

The work of Erik Erikson has been described as holding pride of place when the whole lifecourse is considered (Sugarman, 2001). Erikson (1982) developed ideas within psychoanalysis, expanding the role of the conscious ego and linking identity to the social world. In so doing he moved psychoanalytic attention beyond libidinal development to questions of psychosocial adaptation. In *The life-cycle completed*, Erikson describes his age-stage model as enumerating the 'basic qualities that "qualify" a young person to enter the generational cycle – and an adult to conclude it' (1982: 55).

This life cycle is seen to consist of eight agestages, two of which address Adulthood and Old Age, each with its own special conflict to be negotiated. Adulthood, for example, centres on tension between generativity and stagnation, which establishes an attitude towards caring, and the core task of raising the next generation. Whichever stage a person is currently experiencing lends coherence to preceding and subsequent ones.

Erikson has, then, given much greater emphasis to current experience. Indeed, elders interviewed in Erikson *et al.*'s (1986) longitudinal study gave little emphasis to earlier events that at the time were seen as important and potentially traumatic.

The tasks of Old Age are centred on personal development as an acceptance of one's own and only life cycle and of the people who have become significant to it (Erikson, 1963). In Old Age, integrity competes with disgust and despair, which, depending upon its resolution, influences the achievement of wisdom. According to this view, the challenge of a late life consists of maintaining a sense of personal 'integrality', which has been defined as 'a tendency to keep things together' (Erikson, 1982), in the sense both of maintaining identity in the face of bodily ageing and the loss of contemporaries and of the development of a coherent life story.

A number of Ego Psychologists have elaborated Erikson's original stages of adult development. Vaillant (1993), for example, adds 'career consolidation', and a 'keeper of meaning' role, between adulthood and old age. Colarusso and Nemiroff (1985) have attempted to specify four stages of mid-life. Kivnick (1988) has proposed periods of 'post maintenance generativity' or 'grand-generativity', which are closely related to grandparenthood.

Vaillant suggests that postgenerative age-stages involve a shift from 'taking care of one's children to preserving one's culture' (1993: 151).

This abstract, sublimated means of caring passes accumulated knowledge on to the next generation and invests in forms of meaning that outlive the self.

Ego Psychology is open to the criticism that it sees old age as a grand wrapping-up of the lifecourse with few intrinsic issues and largely second-hand meanings arising from its functional value to other generations (Biggs, 1993). This impression is not helped by Erikson's remark that: 'Having now reviewed the end of the lifecycle as much as my context permitted, I do feel the urgency to enlarge on a "real" stage – that is, one that mediates between two stages of life – and on the generational cycle itself' (Erikson et al., 1986: 66).

A second problem with the model is its uncritical relation towards social context. For Erikson, social structure lends that necessary coherence to the lifecourse, it 'lifts the known facts into a context apt to make us realise their nature' (1982: 90).

This trend has been exacerbated by the work of Vaillant (1993) and Kivnick (1988), which have drained Ego Psychology of its conflictual tensions. Woodward (2002) argues that 'wisdom' simply confers legitimacy to social conformity that is both ageist and gendered. Within the eight stages of

development exists a 'fordist' or production-line model of the lifecourse, closely related to the needs of contemporary capital, such that old age becomes a hang-over from the 'real business' of generating a stable career and family and loses meaning once this 'productive' part of the life cycle is over (Biggs, 1999). Thus, whilst partially freeing mature adulthood from the determining power of childhood, Ego Psychology throws it onto the mercy of social conformity.

JUNGIAN PSYCHOLOGY

Whereas Erikson and his followers explored the relationship between the ego and the social world, Jung's Analytical Psychology focused on the inner world of the imagination, where mature adulthood is seen as having little in common with earlier parts of the lifecourse. His acrimonious split with Freud allowed Jung to formulate a new model for the 'second half of life' that addressed adult psychology within its own terms of reference.

Jung (1967[1930]) maintained that psychoanalysis helps clear away the unfinished business of childhood but that new possibilities made available by the resulting release of psychological energy leave classical psychoanalysis with nothing to say. In Jung's approach, early adulthood up until middle age consists of a time of consolidation around the personal will as one attempts to 'win . . . a place in society and to transform one's nature so that it is more or less fitted in to this kind of existence' (1967[1930]: IX,771).

However, in the second half of life, thought to begin in mid-life, the mature adult increasingly divests the 'false wrappings' of social conformity. Attempts to maintain the priorities of the first half of life into the second are an indication of poor lifecourse adjustment, which he describes as a delusion. Instead, the individual begins a journey towards personal knowledge, a process that Jung called 'individuation'. Individuation is seen as occurring naturally as successively greater parts of the self become available to consciousness and the individual becomes 'whole, indivisible and distinct from others' (Samuels et al., 1986). Thus, 'A person in the second half of life . . . to understand the meaning of his individual life needs to experience his own inner being. Social usefulness is no longer an aim for him, although he does not deny its desirability' (Jung, 1967[1930]: XVI,110). Tasks associated with this second period involve the discovery of potential that had been repressed during the earlier search for conformity, increased sensitivity to an inner psychological life, and an increasing awareness of finitude and mortality (Biggs, 1993).

Unlike Freud, 'fully two thirds' of Jung's cases were mature adults. As the priorities of the first half of life cease to provide meaning, patients are encouraged to use the unconscious in their everyday experience and achieve a dialogue between the two (Chodorow, 1997). Stevens (2000) points out that, as a result, one can take in the complexity of diverse lifecourse positions. There is an increased awareness of age-based identities arising from the unconscious, and figures, such as the wise old woman and man, act as psychological mentors indicating the possibility of an alternative state of being. Resistance to the influence of wise elders arises because they intimate personal change rather than the properties of old age itself.

Contemporary gerontologists such as Tornstam (1996) have drawn on Jungian and Eriksonian ideas in identifying 'gerotranscendence': 'Gerotranscendence is related to higher degrees of both social activity and life satisfaction simultaneously as the degree of social activity becomes less important in attaining satisfaction' (1996: 38).

Later life can be connected with social activity and solitary philosophizing, marked by 'positive solitude' and an increased broad-mindedness. Schroots (1996) notes that such processes are connected to more active and complex coping patterns in social situations, as analytic psychology would predict.

Whilst Jung saw mid-life as a period in which the social mask is dissolved, allowing a more authentic expression of a more complete self, more recent writing has attempted to reconcile the individuation process with the continued existence of ageism. This has given rise to the observation that older adults often deploy a masquerade, in order to protect the emerging self from negative environments (Woodward, 1991; Biggs, 1993). The protective function of the persona is something which has been traditionally underplayed within this approach.

Jung leaves us with an understanding of the subjectivity of mature adulthood that emphasizes self-exploration but is underdeveloped in examining social influence.

MCADAMS AND NARRATIVE TURN

At the turn of the millennium, an increasing awareness of diversity and the influence of consumerism on identity have produced a more fluid notion of the adult lifecourse (Featherstone and Hepworth, 1989). An 'ageless' extension of mid-lifestyles leads to continual re-invention of the self, which depends on a capacity to keep a particular narrative going. Under these conditions, talking therapies are used to maintain a chosen story line about what one is or wants to be, and one's relationship to past events (Biggs, 1999). There is considerable pressure to deny the effects of adult ageing as 'There are no rules now, only choices' (Blaikie, 1999: 104).

Psychotherapy that focuses on the construction of personal narratives has become increasingly popular. McAdams (1993, 2001) has taken an interest in mid- and later-life issues and the view that, from mid-life onwards, individuals should 'story' their lifecourse from their own resources: 'Defining the self through myth may be seen as an ongoing act of psychological and social responsibility. Because our world can no longer tell us who we are and how we should live, we must figure it out on our own' (McAdams, 1993: 35). As such, narrative therapies aim to provide techniques whereby a multiplicity of possibilities for identity can be negotiated in the absence of binding cultural guidelines.

For McAdams, mid-life is a time of 'putting it together . . . integrating and making peace among conflicting imagoes in one's personal myth'. By their early 40s, people will have collected a number of alternative identities, and from the 40s to the late 60s a key task consists of sorting out these accumulated aspects of self, marking a rejection of absolutes and a 'Growing realisation that good lives, like good stories, require good endings' (1993: 202).

A narrative re-organization of life's material does not, however, require Freud's painstaking reconstruction of past events, Eriksonian conformity with an age-stage or Jungian discovery of changed existential priorities. Rather, it takes place in the service of the present in situationally specific solutions, linked to particular contexts. The ageing adult is not faced with fixed stages to work through, but rather flexible 'scripts'. Here, a 'Generativity script', for example, 'functions to address the narrative need for a sense of an ending, a satisfying vision or plan concerning how, even though one's life will eventually end, some aspect of the self will live on' (1993: 240).

The popularity of narrative therapy rests on recognition that age-stages are stories that clients tell about themselves rather than an underlying state of reality. In mid-life and beyond, a need arises to make sense of the multiple stories created during earlier phases of adulthood, and create a workable narrative which better fits the social indeterminacy of contemporary ageing. However, a focus on maintaining an ageless lifestyle may create false expectations of what is possible and fail to take into account the need for resilience to losses and adaptation to forms of decline (Heckhausen, 2001).

Inner Worlds, Outer Worlds and Ageing

An analysis of historical trends indicates successive phases of accommodation to the practice of psychotherapy with mature adults, moving from a view that older people made unsuitable analysands to one that outlined the possibility of such work and finally a rejection of traditional frameworks as in themselves inappropriate. However, insight into the unique psychological experience of ageing and the relationship between inner and outer worlds may prove a valuable inheritance for gerontology and prefigure contemporary debates within the discipline. This brief review of the development of psychodynamic ideas on adult ageing raises a number of questions and areas in which the tradition could make a significant contribution but, for reasons of history, has had little impact to date.

King (1974) noted a 'new dynamic and sense of urgency' that mature adults brought to therapy, driven by a keener awareness of the finite nature of existence. The lessening of nervous energy 'reduces the need for the maintenance of the rigidity of their defence systems, . . . and they begin to experience a *new sense of their own identity* and the value of their own achievement and worth' (1974: 33, King's italics).

Older people also exhibited a capacity to delay gratification, allow problems to resolve and take the long view, and often have much greater self-reliance than do younger people (Hildebrand, 1982; Knight, 1996; Gaudie, 2002).

A second re-alignment concerns associations that patients make towards therapists (transference) and vice versa (counter-transference). Rechtschaffen (1959) and Hildebrand (1982) both noted the existence of 'reverse-transference' when a therapist is younger than an analysand, the opposite of the common age-relationship.

Hillman (1970) has developed notions of archetypal figures from analytical psychology that are said to mediate relationships with significant others. Being age-related, they also populate the inner life of the individual with a series of imagined identities.

King points out that: 'middle aged and elderly clients may be functioning within a number of different timescales. These may include a chronological time scale, a psychological one and a biological one, or unconscious processes which are paradoxically timeless' (1980: 154). The implication of this is that the other, in terms of transference, the analyst, 'can be experienced as any significant figure from the elderly patient's past, sometimes covering a span of five generations, and for any of these transference figures the roles may be reversed' (1980: 154).

Knight (1996) indicates that therapists and others may be responded to as if they were the child, grandchild, parent, spouse or lover of an older person, depending upon the quality of their emerging relationship. Further, this may also affect younger adult's associations; so that those working with older people may themselves experience countertransference and act out unconscious associations arising from their own unresolved conflicts with figures from across the lifecourse. These tacit influences, if left unexplored, may explain the resistance of many helping professionals to work with older people (Sprung, 1989; Woolfe and Biggs, 1997). The observation that first and second halves of life provoke different perspectives, and the expression of personal potential that may be suppressed during early adulthood, also raise the question of intergenerational projection, resentment and rivalry (Biggs, 1989).

These insights have clear implications for the study of age, identity and intergenerational relations. A historical re-alignment of the psychotherapies, away from a preoccupation with childhood and towards issues in the here and now, aids this process. The distinction between inner and outer worlds allows chronological age to be peeled off from psychological age. One might be classified by others, looking from the outside, as 24, 48 or 96, whilst the internal experience of self could be at any of these ages at any one point in time. If, as psychoanalysis maintains, we are all to some extent talking by association to figures 'who are not there', then perhaps the view that older adults 'live in the past' is not such an age-specified experience as some would like to think. Further, the notion that intergenerational relationships might be subject to misunderstanding, avoidance and even rivalry, suggested by transference relations, may significantly deepen gerontological understanding. We are, perhaps, witnessing the end of the beginning of a relationship between gerontology and psychotherapy.

FURTHER READING

Biggs, S. (1999). *The mature imagination: dynamics of identity in midlife and beyond*. Buckingham: Open University Press.
'Counselling and psychotherapy with older people' (1998). Special issue of *Journal of Social Work Practice*, 12 (2): 135–239.
Knight, B. (1992). *Older adults in psychotherapy*. Beverley Hills: Sage.
Terry, P. (1997). *Counselling the elderly and their carers*. London: Macmillan.

REFERENCES

Abraham, K. (1919). *Selected papers in psychoanalysis*. London: Hogarth.
Biggs, S. (1989). 'Professional helpers and resistances to work with older people', *Ageing & Society*, 9 (1): 43–60.
  (1993). *Understanding ageing*. Buckingham: Open University Press.
  (1999). *The mature imagination: the dynamics of identity in midlife and beyond*. Buckingham: Open University Press.
Blaikie, A. (1999). *Ageing and popular culture*. Cambridge: Cambridge University press.
Chodorow, N. (1997). *Jung on active imagination*. London: Routledge.
Colarusso, C. A., and Nemiroff, R. A. (1985). *The race against time: psychotherapy and psychoanalysis in the second half of life*. New York: Plenum.
Davenhill, R. (1998). 'No truce with the furies', *Journal of Social Work Practice*, 12 (2): 149–58.
Erikson, E. (1963). *Childhood and society*. New York: Norton.
  (1982). *The life-cycle completed*. New York: Norton.
Erikson, E., Erikson, J., and H. Kivnick (1986). *Vital involvement in old age*. New York: Norton.
Featherstone, M., and M. Hepworth (1989). 'Ageing and old age, reflections on the post-modern lifecourse'. In B. Byetheway, ed., *Becoming and being old*. London: Sage, pp. 143–57.
Freud, S. (1956). *Collected works*. London: Hogarth.
Frosh, S. (1991). *Identity crisis*. London: Macmillan.
Gaudie, F. (2002). 'Psychological therapy with older adults'. In R. Woolfe, W. Dryden and S. Strawbridge, eds., *Handbook of counselling psychology*. London: Sage.
Heckhausen, J. (2001). 'Adaptation and resilience in midlife'. In M. Lachman, ed., *Handbook of midlife development*. New York: Wiley.
Hildebrand, P. (1982). 'Psychotherapy with older patients', *British Journal of Medical Psychology*, 55: 19–28.
Hillman, J. (1970). *The myth of analysis*. Evanston, Ill.: Northwestern.
Hollender, M. (1952). 'Individualising the aged', *Social Casework*, 33: 337–42.
Jung, C. G. (1967[1930]). *Collected works*. London: Routledge.
King, P. (1974). 'Notes on the psychoanalysis of older patients,' *Journal of Analytical Psychology*, 19: 22–37.
  (1980). 'The lifecycle as indicated by the nature of the transference of the middle-aged and elderly', *International Journal of Psychoanalysis*, 61: 153–60.
Kivnick, H. (1988). 'Grandparenthood, life-review and psychosocial development', *Journal of Gerontological Social Work*, 12 (3/4): 63–82.
Knight, B. (1996). *Psychotherapy with older adults*. Beverley Hills: Sage.
McAdams, D. (1993). *The stories we live by*. New York: Morrow.
  (2001). 'Generativity in midlife'. In M. Lachman, ed., *Handbook of midlife development*. New York: Wiley, pp. 395–447.
Rechtschaffen, A. (1959). 'Psychotherapy with geriatric patients', *Journal of Gerontology*, 14: 73–84.
Samuels, A, Shorter, B., and F. Plaut (1986). *A critical dictionary of Jungian analysis*. London: Routledge.
Schroots, J. (1996). 'Theoretical developments in the psychology of aging,' *Gerontologist*, 36 (6): 742–8.
Sprung, G. (1989). 'Transferential issues in working with older adults,' *Social Casework*, 70 (10): 597–602.
Stevens, A. (2000). *On Jung*. London: Penguin.
Sugarman, L. (2001). *Lifespan development*. London: Routledge.
Terry, P. (1997). *Counselling the elderly and their carers*. London: Macmillan.

Thompson, P. (1992). 'I don't feel old', *Ageing & Society*, 12 (1): 23–48.

Tornstam, L. (1996). 'Gerotranscendence: a theory about maturing into old age', *Journal of Aging & Identity*, 1 (1): 37–50.

Vaillant, G. (1993). *The wisdom of the ego*. Cambridge, Mass.: Harvard University Press.

Woodward, K. (1991). *Aging and its discontents*. Bloomington: Indiana University Press.

—— (2002). 'Against wisdom: the social politics of anger and aging', *Journal of Aging Studies,* 17 (1): 55–67.

Woolfe, R., and S. Biggs (1997). 'Counselling older adults: issues and awareness', *Counselling Psychology Quarterly*, 10: 189–95.

Cultural Approaches to the Ageing Body

CHRIS GILLEARD

There is, in the UK, a common road sign that shows two black silhouetted figures, backs bent, resting on sticks, preparing, it would seem, to shuffle heedlessly across the road to the consternation of the passing motorist. Below the sign was written 'Elderly People Crossing'. Like the signs with silhouettes of leaping deer, such images rarely come to life. But they serve to remind us how readily old age is symbolized by the body. Weakness and infirmity are inscribed in the sign's outline; the words were there to eliminate any lingering ambiguity. They are no longer needed: the sign is universal. Such are 'old people'.

Symbolic portrayals of old age and the ageing body go back well before the era of the motorist. Most of the medieval depictions of the life cycle or 'ages of man' include a bent back and sticks or crutches, often with long white hair and a white beard added for good measure. These representations of 'senectus' are predominantly those of old men (Sears, 1986). Although the clothing they wear is typically sombre, it is not threadbare. The images are not those of poor old men but of an elite. Similar portrayals of generic agedness continued into the early modern period with two notable changes. In the first place, women appeared, often accompanying 'their' man, though women's agedness was less demarcated compared with that of the man's. His status served as age's true exemplar. The second change was the replacement of the cycle or wheel of life by the idea of 'life as a career', the various figures placed upon steps which rise in power and influence until reaching a peak in mid-life, eventually falling back towards a second infancy and death (Cole, 1992: 18–19). Despite the limited

life expectancy of the time, these *degrés des âges* would typically cover a 100-year lifespan with only the very latter stages intimating decrepitude and dependency (Troyansky, 1989: 20–2). The *degrés des âges* motifs began to die out during the course of the nineteenth century, as a result of industrialization and the growing problems of unemployment and poverty that bore down heavily upon older people.

The new restless urban-industrial society challenged the symbolic unity of life that was portrayed in the traditional iconography of the human life cycle. Relatively early in the twentieth century, a cultural divide between the generations began to open up. 'Youth' was evolving its own 'culture', defined by what was new and what was 'modern'. Age was its antithesis. The United States of America provided the lead. From the end of the nineteenth century, the novelties of urban life were introduced at a rate and to a degree that had not been matched before. The cinema, the automobile, the gramophone, dancehalls and music halls, amusement parks and sports stadia, new music and new fashions and, above all, the gradual appearance of mass affluence fuelled a nascent youth culture (Fass, 1979). Between 1918 and 1926, twenty-five films appeared in the USA which all had the word 'youth' in their title (Hine, 2000: 178–9). Although youth traditionally has been associated with radical politics, youth in 1920s America found a voice principally 'in cultural matters, or rather in matters of style. They conceived of themselves as modern in dress, manners and interests, and they were proud of it. They opposed all attempts to return American life to an impossible past that would condemn their new liberties' (Fass, 1979: 376).

This new culture valorized the distinctiveness of youth, its look. Between 1914 and 1925, US cosmetics sales increased from $17 million to $141 million. The number of beauty salons increased by over 800 per cent. Clothing and cosmetics manufacturers extended their sales by appealing to their power to grant youth. One advert for corsets promised that they would 'not only provide a youthful silhouette but would also improve the strength of the wearer's internal organs so that she is younger in fact as well as in appearance' (Dumenil, 1995: 141). Whereas in Victorian and Edwardian times, young women had sought to make themselves look more mature by having their hair swept up and out, that trend was reversed after the First World War, when the 'bob' and the 'Eton crop' appeared (Cox, 1999: 38).

THE CULTIVATION OF YOUTH AND THE GHETTOIZATION OF AGE

Parallel with the twentieth century's cultivation of youth has been the ghettoization of old age. Reviewing this modern representation of gender and age/generation, Laura Hirshbein suggests that 'in the decades after the 1920s, the most lasting consequence of the contest between the generations was the gradual marginalisation of older men from cultural power' (Hirshbein, 2001: 128). At the start of the twentieth century, the majority of men aged 65 and over were working and the majority of women aged 65 and over were living with their families. By the end of the century, men over the age of 65 were no longer in paid employment (at least 90 per cent of them: Kinsella and Velkoff, 2001: 96) and older women no longer lived with their children (Ruggles, 1993). Those over 65 had been removed or removed themselves from the settings of work and home which had once been the principal sites of intergenerational exchange. Beyond these two spheres the ghettoization of age has continued more forcefully. Retired people less often frequent shopping malls; they less often eat at fast-food restaurants. They are less often to be found in pubs, bars and cafes, or amongst cinema audiences. They rarely go to major sports events or visit amusement parks. Compared with working people they are less likely to go to the

Figure 1. UK road sign indicating that elderly pedestrians may cross the road ahead.
Source: www.highwaycode.gov.uk.signs_index shtml_signlog

gym, or join health clubs or attend leisure centres.[1] Whilst they watch TV, listen to music and read books and magazines as much as any other age group, these are private, individualized and essentially passive leisure activities. They call for no expression of social identity nor do they possess cultural agency. Being old seems just a sign by the roadside that increasingly is passed, unnoticed.

Youth culture meanwhile has grown and expanded within each 'post-war' period. By far the most significant development took place in the 1960s, the era when a now ageing Roger Daltrey first sang 'I hope I die before I get old' and the now deceased Timothy Leary advised campus youth to ignore anyone over 30. If the 'youth culture' of the twenties and thirties chose not to 'diss' old age completely, the more democratic youth culture of the sixties made no bones about it. Age stank. Youth subcultures proliferated, united in their considered dismissal of everything that was old and out-dated. Youth acquired ever greater cultural salience, while old age languished on the edges of society, cloaked by an increasingly unfashionable and out-dated poverty.

Throughout the fifties and sixties, older people were heavily over-represented amongst the poor. Even during the affluent sixties, poverty rates amongst those aged 65 and over in the

[1] For a broad review of age-related 'leisure' activities, see the various tables in US Census Bureau (2001).

USA remained high. In contrast, the number of poor young people virtually halved (Iceland, 2003: 39–43). By 1969, over a quarter of those over 65 were still living below the official US poverty rate; of those aged 18 and under, fewer than 15 per cent were. Youth, not age, was the first to benefit from the affluence of post-war society; youth was the focus and symbol of change. Youth subcultures and youth-oriented counter-cultural movements dominated the media. New 'sites' devoted to youth culture rose to prominence, overshadowing the neighbourhood pubs, bars or cafés where previously the generations had mixed and maintained a common popular culture. Economically, culturally and socially, old age was becoming a fast disappearing social world.

THE NEW, YOUTHFUL AGEING

By the time the 'cultural revolution' of the sixties had begun to die down, many of those who had exemplified youth and revolution were no longer feeling so young. As adults seeing middle age approaching, they had a much stronger stake in a continuously expanding mass consumer society. Ageing – or rather resisting ageing – began to emerge as a new theme within contemporary culture. By the early 1980s, middle age had become the new cultural battlefield as a 'post-youth' transformation of consumer culture began to gather momentum. Those who had been young in the 1960s were reluctant to forfeit the benefits of youth and its freedoms now they were reaching mid-life. There were several interlinked aspects to this culture shift. In the first place was the continuing individualization of everyday life, amplified if not created by the political emphasis on individual choice and individual responsibility both by the Reagan government in the USA and by Thatcher's in Britain. Second was the broadening appeal of 'fitness' as a key lifestyle element, whereby dress and demeanour were no longer sufficient to achieve social differentiation and esteem. Third was the 'maturing' of the women's movement and its persisting challenge to cultural stereotypes, including the stereotype of age. Finally, the marketization and commodification of the 'lifeworld' expanded significantly as people turned increasingly to self-help literature, self-medication and the promotion of lifestyle advice from magazines and TV.

The problem of identity was moving beyond the boundaries of youth. The search for a place within this 'subject-centred universe' became a concern to an ever widening age group across increasingly differentiated communities (see Schulze, 1997).

Whereas, in the sixties and through much of the seventies, later life had been largely an irrelevancy to cultural life and old age a source of anathema, by the 1980s, there was an increasing acknowledgement that a 'market' existed in and for later life (Schewe, 1985). The concept of the Third Age first made its appearance (Laslett, 1987) and generational marketing established a firm foothold in the world of advertising (Lumpkin, 1985). Cultural exhibitions began to display images of a newly aestheticized old age (Blaikie, 1999: 131–49). Radical feminists started addressing the 'double jeopardy' facing women growing old in America (see Sontag, 1978). Meantime 'youth culture' was starting to acquire a history with the inauguration of the Rock and Roll Hall of Fame Foundation in 1985 (Strausbaugh, 2002).

INDIVIDUALIZATION AND THE FRAGMENTATION OF LATER LIFE

From the late seventies onwards, age began to emerge from the shadows of youth culture, not so much in its traditional form as a marginalized category distinguished by 'poverty', 'lack' and 'decrepitude', but as individualized experience. Research into ageing began to focus on the individual lifecourse. There was a growth of magazines directed towards older consumers and a wider range of financial and non-financial products that were explicitly geared towards retired people. Despite this recognition of the individual ageing person, the presentation in the media of 'ageing bodies' was quite limited. Images of later life tended to be confined to particular magazines and selected radio and TV channels. They figured less often on prime-time TV or in major cultural media (Zhou and Chen, 1992). In such segmented settings, older people were often portrayed in positive ways, usually by emphasizing their relative fitness, wealth and power/masculinity (Roberts and Zhou, 1997).

The consequence of the individualization of society is that 'ageing' has become less of a collective experience and the lifecourse a less invariant sequence of experiences and expectations. Older people are less evident as a 'collective' presence in society. Old age possesses a marginal, often derisory status, which is reinforced through various indirect means such as in newspaper cartoons and birthday cards (Demos and Jache, 1981). But this collective other – this body species – does not represent the older individual consumer. When individual older characters appear in films, on the TV and in advertisements, they are often presented in a positive light. But though the images are more positive, overall there are much fewer portrayals of older people (Roy and Harwood, 1997).

What is true for the media is true for advertisements. To appeal to the older individual, advertisers increasingly avoid stereotypically 'older persons' since they, no doubt accurately, assume that the potential retiree has little wish to be stereotyped as an 'old' consumer. Hence the absence of the ageing body in much advertising media. Where it is evident that older persons are looking at or listening to something that is clearly oriented towards their identity as older, retired people (e.g. magazines or programmes specifically for retirees), then aspirational images of later life predominate. These images privilege male gender, white European ethnicity, high social class and positive health status. If these images diverge from the actuality of the potential consumer, a common bond still links the attractiveness of the character with the position of the viewer.

Within an individualized society, the best way to avoid confronting uncomfortable collective realities is to make them disappear. There is no wish for a collective representation of each stage of life, no motivation to present the virtue of sagacity or the vice of senility that once were used to polarize old age and agedness. The cultural representation of later life is now textual not physical: more is written about financial self-management and bodily self-management than is ever portrayed about the ageing body. Retirement exists almost in ignorance of bodily ageing, as each individual is expected to form (and increasingly fund) his or her own idea of retirement. The focus is on keeping fit, maintaining a regime of self-care through exercise and diet, without being distracted by any collective representations of the ageing body. This focus upon fitness emphasizes leisure work that can be carried out at home – and 'working from home' defines the situation of most retired people. While this process of individual negotiation over ageing encourages the exercise of individual agency, it also limits the scope for collective action and collective representation.

FITNESS AND THE POSTMODERNIZATION OF MATURITY

The neo-liberal politics of the Reagan–Thatcher era signalled the demise of sixties-style 'communal' youth culture. The emphasis remained upon 'freedom' but it was a freedom defined as individual choice and responsibility. This change in tone permeated many aspects of contemporary culture, stressing what Foucault (1988) called 'the technologies of the self', the active contemplation, management and maintenance of the self. Mid-life became a key site for this 'self generativity' with its emphasis upon staying young and keeping 'fit'. The body was fast becoming a template against which to judge individual 'moral worth'. Mid-life celebrities such as Jane Fonda and Joan Collins became the 'empowering' voice for older women, echoing Sartre's comment that 'after a certain age you get the face you deserve' (Blaikie, 1999: 104).

As the turn towards fitness increased, magazines targeting older audiences became increasingly enthusiastic about the possibilities of age-makeovers. *Modern Maturity*, the mass-circulation magazine of the American Association of Retired Persons, proved an exemplary leader, with a series of articles about the possibilities of a fitter, younger and more prosperous 'age'. Even relatively staid British 'retirement' magazines joined the rush towards 'choice' and 'opportunity' (see Featherstone and Hepworth, 1995). It was no coincidence that, around this time, the media began to present a new image of older people: WOOPIES, well-off older people – not just physically, but financially, fitter than ever before (see Falkingham and Victor, 1991).

Old age has become an outcome acknowledged primarily through actions designed to refute its presence. Body technologies – jogging, workouts, tanning salons, facials, anti-wrinkling and anti-ageing creams – focus upon the polarity between fitness and agedness, a polarity that seems now to maintain its intensity despite increasing chronological age.[2] Those most active in negotiating this passage between youth and age were, and still are, a distinct generation. John Strausbaugh (who includes himself in this generation) has described it as the 'Me Generation' who 'eat better than our parents did, work smarter, live longer. We are healthier and more active and we have more time and money to spend in the pursuit of fun. We want to keep on rockin'. For us it was never enough just to work eat sleep procreate and die. We wanted life to have meaning' (Strausbaugh, 2002: 241).

In 1980, James Fries published his seminal paper on the rectangularization of the lifespan (Fries, 1980) in which he proposed that, while increasing numbers of people can anticipate living to the chronological limit of human life, this will be accompanied by an ever shortening period of morbid 'old age'. His thesis reflected the desire-turned-expectation of ever more 'fitness' and the personal promotion of health in later life. His hypothesis has been tested many times, and the findings more or less support the thesis (Hessler *et al.*, 2003). Lifelong fitness is a cultural ideal supported by science and sustained by personal as well as commercial interests. People of nearly all ages have increased their level and frequency of exercise. Walking, jogging, swimming and running have become a central form of leisure-work, before and after retirement. Most 'leisure'-oriented magazines target 'health and fitness' as essential goals for both men and women, and in the process signal the message that 'fitness seems to be the key to better living' (Scafidi, 2003: 38). But the cost of this focus on fitness has begun to be questioned, particularly by some feminist writers.

WOMEN AGEING AND THE BODY

Many of the key figures in the move towards 'restoring' the ageing body are women working in the area of cultural studies. During the eighties, feminism became increasingly conscious of age as an issue. As a topic it initially divided the movement between those who focused upon the structural and personal difficulties facing women as carers of others' ageing bodies and minds (e.g. Finch and Groves, 1983) and those who instead focused upon the cultural denial of old age, both outside and within the movement itself (e.g. MacDonald, 1986). Such divisions are creating a new focus upon the ageing body, with the consequence that 'it is by women and within communities of women that questions of old age have begun to be raised' (Chivers, 2003: xv).

That the ageing body has become a focus for feminist writing has had two consequences. First, there is a small but growing literature based upon women's accounts of bodily ageing (e.g. Furman, 1997). These accounts, supplemented by recent fictional narratives and photographic exhibitions of bodily ageing, promote a broader understanding of the contradiction that seems to lie at the heart of the experience of ageing, namely the externality and otherness of age while it slowly, and at times quite swiftly, comes to lodge itself within one's body and one's self, fuelling pre-existing anxieties that surround what Wolf termed 'the beauty myth' (Wolf, 1990). This contradiction reflects the difficulty for women of owning their 'agedness' and retaining a sense of confidence and empowerment as one's body ages (Morell, 2003).

The ageing body in both contemporary literature and the visual arts is presented very much as the ageing female body. Attempts to explore and represent men's experience of bodily ageing are quite rare, and even those few books devoted to men's ageing steer clear of the ageing male body (see Thompson, 1994). Whilst it is popularly assumed that women fare less well than men in terms of the cultural value attributed to ageing and agedness, there is no strong evidence to support this. What does seem to be the case is that men traditionally have expressed less concern, in public, over their bodily appearance, focusing instead upon issues of potency and performance. But though the market remains very gendered in its approach to bodily ageing, and women are very much the target audience for and principal consumers of anti-ageing products, the success of Viagra shows that men are not unconcerned with bodily ageing and eagerly pursue their own strategies of age-resistance (see Marshall and Katz, 2002). While survey research suggests that older men and women neither view their bodies with greater distaste, nor feel they are less attractive, than do younger men and women (Oberg and Thornstam, 1999), these findings need to be set

---

[2] Whilst one might anticipate some upper age limit to this process, examples of 80- and 90-year-old 'super-athletes' increasingly occur in the media.

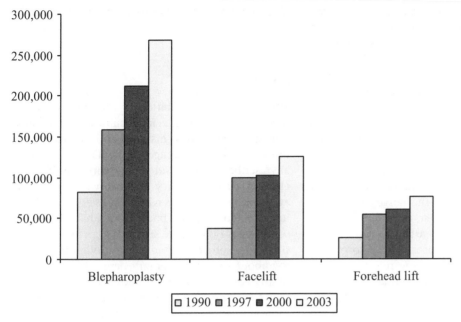

Figure 2. Number of anti-ageing cosmetic surgery procedures performed in the US, 1990–2003.
Source: ASAPS (2001, 2002a, 2002b, 2004)

beside more qualitative, intimate accounts which suggest that many women feel 'a sense of profound loss . . . [and] dissatisfaction with their own bodies [that] translates into negative evaluations of other aging women's bodies as well' (Hurd, 1999: 432). Such 'close up' studies are mostly confined to older women: we lack similar accounts for men. Are markets more aware of and more responsive to such personal sensitive feelings than academia?

AGEING BODIES AND THE MARKET

The changing demographics of societies in the West are not just the concerns of governments. The market has become equally interested in the 'greying' of the population. This is reflected both in the importance of pension funds in global financial markets and in the importance of the retired population as a new 'age group' with significant disposable income (Smith and Clurman, 1997). Current cohorts of retired people are more likely than their predecessors to use credit cards, purchase leisure goods and services, take holidays, and invest. Their consumption focuses upon leisure, not their bodies. The body remains the province of younger cohorts. Whether future cohorts of retired people will show more interest in resisting age through the consumption of age-resisting products and services remains to be seen. Some recent trends suggest they will.

Surveys by the American Society for Aesthetic Plastic Surgery (ASAPS) indicate that about half of the US population approves of cosmetic surgery, while over a quarter would actively consider such surgery for themselves. Just over 15% of those over 65 would consider surgery, but twice that number of 40-year-olds would (ASAPS, 2002a). These findings confirm an earlier survey by the American Association of Retired People (AARP) that had as its banner headline: 'We have seen the future of cosmetic surgery – and it is us.' The AARP survey found high levels of acceptance of cosmetic surgery, particularly among those aged between 55 and 64 (69%), with slightly lower acceptance rates amongst the over 65s (58%). This level of acceptance itself reflects the increasing amount of anti-ageing surgery performed, as Figure 2 illustrates[3].

Over and above these dramatic increases in anti-ageing surgical procedures, there has been an even

---

[3] Forehead lifts, facelifts and blepharoplasty (removing the bags under the eyes) have been chosen because they are the procedures most commonly performed on older people (AACS, 2004). The data are a compilation from a number of reports produced by ASAPS and AACS – see list of References.

greater rise in non-invasive anti-ageing resurfacing techniques such as chemical skin peels (up from 481,227 in 1997 to 722,248 in 2003) and botox injections (up from 65,157 in 1997 to 2,272,080 in 2003). The use of anti-ageing surgical and non-surgical procedures by those aged 65 and over increased by over 350% from 1997 to 2002 (ASAPS, 2002b).

Turning to less momentous age-resisting practices supported by the market, there has been a similar rise in the sales of various dietary supplements, herbal products and related 'nutraceuticals' (AARP, 2002), all of which form a central element in popular anti-ageing regimes. As the range of products expands to meet the number of potentially preventable targets that emerge (arthritis, Alzheimer's, cancer, heart disease, skin diseases and so on), so the market acquires an increasing role in shaping the cultural images of both age and age resistance. This is particularly evident in the promotion of anti-ageing cosmetic products (cosmaceuticals) that offer the promise of preventing or masking the signs of ageing.

In another AARP survey, nearly half of US 35–44-year-olds said they used or will use in the future skin products to reduce or prevent ageing while over two-thirds would use cosmetics to cover up age spots and nearly three-quarters hair dyes to hide grey hair (AARP, 2001). While those over 65 were less likely to endorse the use of such anti-ageing strategies, future cohorts of retirees may prove less reticent in actively choosing to mask or minimize the physical markers of their ageing, having begun the habit earlier. While this may seem to have no discernible effect upon their mortality and morbidity, the use of 'anti-ageing' products raises interesting questions about the impact of such 'colonization of the lifeworld' by the market. Research consistently indicates that personal identification with agedness and old age offers risks to health and wellbeing (Bultena and Powers, 1978; Levy et al., 2002). If this is so, choosing not to be old – i.e., not to have an old-looking body – seems likely to prove life enhancing rather than life limiting (Jolanki et al., 2000). Rather than berating age-resistance as a refusal to confront deep old age, perhaps we need to acknowledge that few seek to 'acquire' the dubious identity of being 'old'. If a market exists for 'deep old age', it is primarily a market for long-term care insurance. Like life insurance,

we pay the premiums but we do not really want the payoff.

CONCLUSION

The cultural representation of the life cycle has a history that goes back as far as culture itself. Distinctions between youth, maturity and old age appear universal. The various ages of life have their culturally ascribed virtues and vices – with youth pirouetting between vibrancy and callowness while old age stumbles between sagacity and senility. Cultural images of the ageing body always have been presented in ways that are stylized, sometimes sympathetically, sometimes sadistically. What is interesting about the contemporary period is the absence of any coherent image of agedness or old age. Our own ageing and the agedness of others have become more ambiguous phenomena. Images of ageing bodies are presented in ways that either deny their age or attempt to aestheticize it. Every voice raised against the ageism of society is accompanied by an image of how old age should be represented that either applauds a long life that has escaped the signs of agedness (see Hurd, 1999) or seeks to honour bodies that have 'properly' matured/aged (see Tornstam, 1996). The various champions of agedness have much to combat, whether it is the impoverished quality of life that some older people endure or the impoverished quality of services that some older people receive. But this sympathetic 'othering' of agedness masks and makes mute the complexities and contradictions that individuals confront with their individually ageing bodies. Despite the fact that there is so much of it about, agedness and the ageing body continue to be a cultural absence. It is this absence of the body that matters most. Generations of gerontologists, geriatricians and other well-intentioned agents of care and control have filled this space by demands for more resources for a needy but disembodied 'old age'. But after all the extra beds and benefits have been delivered, the body still ages. It is unclear where we are to find the confidence to voice our despair that this should be so, as well as our hope that it may not be so, not at least for our own, particular, individualized bodies.

FURTHER READING

Gilleard, C., and P. Higgs (2000). *Cultures of ageing: self, citizen and the body*. Harlow: Prentice Hall.

Gullette, M. M. (2004). *Aged by culture*. Chicago: University of Chicago Press.

Walker, Margaret Urban, ed. (2000). *Mother Time: women, aging and ethics*. Lanham, Md.: Rowman & Littlefield Publishers.

Wolf, N. (1990). *The beauty myth*. London: Vintage.

REFERENCES

American Academy of Cosmetic Surgery (2000). 'Statistics of cosmetic procedures: 2000 statistics summary'. www.cosmeticsurgery.org/Media_Center/stats/2000statistics/00statsummary.html (accessed 29 June 2002).

—— (2004). *2003 procedural census*. Chicago, Ill.: Leeveresearch.

AARP (American Association of Retired Persons) (2001). *Public attitudes toward aging, beauty and cosmetic surgery*. Washington, D.C: AARP.

—— (2002). *Dietary supplements and older consumers*. Washington, D.C: AARP.

ASAPS (American Society for Aesthetic Plastic Surgery) (2001). 'Cosmetic Surgery National Data Bank: 2001 statistics. 5 year comparisons for nearly 30 cosmetic procedures'. www.surgery.org.

—— (2002a). 'Consumer attitudes survey'. www.surgery.org.

—— (2002b). 'News release: older patients benefit from modified cosmetic plastic surgery techniques'. www.surgery.org/news_releases/feb0102age65.html (accessed 27 June 2002).

—— (2004). 'Cosmetic Surgery National Data Bank: 2003 statistics'. www.surgery.org (accessed 29 January 2004).

Blaikie, A. (1999). *Ageing and popular culture*. Cambridge: Cambridge University Press.

Bultena, G. L., and E. A. Powers (1978). 'Denial of aging: age identification and reference group orientations,' *Journal of Gerontology*, 52: 125–34.

Chivers, S. (2003). *From old woman to older women: contemporary culture and women's narratives*. Columbus: Ohio State University Press.

Cole, T. R. (1992). *The journey of life: a cultural history of aging in America*. Cambridge: Cambridge University Press.

Cox, C. (1999). *Good hair days: a history of British hairstyling*. London: Quartet Books.

Demos, V., and A. Jache (1981). 'When you care enough: an analysis of attitudes towards aging in humorous birthday cards', *Gerontologist*, 21: 209–15.

Dumenil, L. (1995). *Modern temper: American culture and society in the 1920s*. New York: Hill and Wang.

Ekerdt, D. J. (1986). 'The busy ethic: moral continuity between work and retirement,' *Gerontologist*, 26: 239–44.

Falkingham, J., and C. R. Victor (1991). The myth of the Woopie: incomes, the elderly and targeting welfare, *Ageing & Society*, 11: 471–93.

Fass, P. (1979). *The Damned and the Beautiful: American youth in the 1920s*. New York: Oxford University Press.

Featherstone, M., and M. Hepworth (1995). 'Images of positive aging: a case study of *Retirement Choice* magazine'. In M. Featherstone and A. Wernick, eds., *Images of aging: cultural representations of later life*. London: Routledge, pp. 29–47.

Finch, J., and D. Groves, eds. (1983). *A labour of love: women, work and caring*. London: Routledge and Kegan Paul.

Foucault, M. (1988). 'Technologies of the self'. In L. H. Martin, H. Gutman and P. H. Hutton, eds., *Technologies of the self: a seminar with Michel Foucault*. London: Tavistock Publications, pp. 16–49.

Fries, J. F. (1980). 'Aging, natural death and the compression of morbidity', *New England Journal of Medicine*, 303: 130–5.

Furman, F. K. (1997). *Facing the mirror: older women and beauty shop culture*. London: Routledge.

Hessler, R. M., Eriksson, B. G., Dey, D., Steen, G., Sundh, V. and B. Steen (2003). 'The compression of morbidity debate in aging: a set of empirical tests using the gerontological and geriatric population studies in Goteborg, Sweden, (H70)', *Archives of Gerontology and Geriatrics*, 37: 213–22.

Hine, T. (2000). *The rise and fall of the American teenager: a new history of the American adolescent experience*. New York: Perennial / HarperCollins.

Hirshbein, L. D. (2001). 'The flapper and the fogy: representations of gender and age in the 1920s', *Journal of Family History*, 26: 112–37.

Hurd, L. C. (1999). '"We're not old!": older women's negotiation of aging and oldness', *Journal of Aging Studies*, 13: 419–39.

Iceland, J. (2003). *Poverty in America: a handbook*. Los Angeles: University of California Press.

Jolanki, O., Jylha, M., and A. Hervonen (2000). 'Old age as a choice and as a necessity: two interpretive repertoires', *Journal of Aging Studies*, 14: 359–72.

Kinsella, K., and V. A. Velkoff (2001). *An aging world*, US Census Bureau, Series P95/01-1. Washington, D.C.: Government Printing Office.

Laslett, P. (1987). 'The emergence of the Third Age', *Ageing & Society*, 7: 113–60.

Levy, B. R., Slade, M. D., Kunkel, S. R., and S. V. Kasl (2002). 'Longevity increased by positive self-perceptions of aging', *Journal of Personality and Social Psychology*, 82: 261–70.

Lumpkin, J. R. (1985). 'Shopping orientation segmentation of the older consumer', *Journal of the Academy of Marketing Science*, 13: 271–89.

MacDonald, B. (1986). 'Outside the sisterhood: ageism in Women's Studies'. In J. Alexander, D. Berrow, L. Domitrovich, M. Donnelly and C. McLean, eds., *Women and aging: an anthology by women*. Corvallis: Calyx.

Marshall, B., and S. Katz (2002). 'Forever functional: sexual fitness and the aging male body', *Body & Society*, 8: 43–70.

Morell, C. M. (2003). 'Empowerment and long-living women: return to the rejected body', *Journal of Aging Studies*, 17: 69–85.

Oberg, P., and L. Thornstam (1999). 'Body images among men and women of different ages', *Ageing & Society*, 19: 629–44.

Roberts, S. D., and N. Zhou (1997). 'The 50 and older characters in the advertisements of *Modern Maturity*', *Journal of Applied Gerontology*, 16: 208–20.

Roy, A., and J. Harwood (1997). 'Underrepresented, positively portrayed; older adults in television commercials', *Journal of Applied Communication Research*, 25: 39–56.

Ruggles, S. (1993). 'The transformation of American family structure', *American Historical Review*, 99: 103–28.

Scafidi, G. (2003). 'Young at heart', *USC Trojan Family Magazine*, 35: 36–41.

Schewe, C. D. (1985). 'Gray America goes to market', *Business*, 35: 3–9.

Schulze, G. (1997). 'From situations to subjects: moral discourse in transition'. In P. Sulkunen, J. Holmwood, H. Radner and G. Schulze, eds., *Constructing the new consumer society*. London: Macmillan Press, pp. 38–57.

Sears, E. (1986). *The ages of man: medieval interpretations of the life cycle*. Princeton, N.J.: Princeton University Press.

Smith, J. W., and A. Clurman (1997). *Rocking the ages: the Yankelovich report on generational marketing*. New York: HarperBusiness.

Sontag, S. (1978). 'The double standard of ageing'. In V. Carver and P. Liddiard, eds., *An ageing population*, Sevenoaks, Kent: Hodder and Stoughton, pp. 72–80.

Strausbaugh, J. (2002). *Rock till you drop*. London: Verso.

Thompson, E. H., ed. (1994). *Older men's lives: research on men and masculinities*. London: Sage.

Tornstam, L. (1996). 'Gerotranscendence: a theory about maturing in old age', *Journal of Aging and Identity*, 1: 37–50.

Troyansky, D. (1989). *Old age in the Ancien Regime: image and experience in eighteenth century France*. Ithaca: Cornell University Press.

US Census Bureau (2001). *Statistical abstract of the United States: 2000, Section 7. Parks, recreation and travel*. Washington, D.C.: US Census Bureau.

Wolf, N. (1990). *The beauty myth*. London: Vintage.

Zhou, N., and M. Chen (1992). 'Marginal life after 49: a preliminary study of the portrayal of older people in Canadian consumer magazine advertising', *International Journal of Advertising*, 11: 343–54.

CHAPTER 2.9

Promoting Health and Wellbeing in Later Life

HANNES B. STAEHELIN

CONCEPTUAL ASPECTS

One of the striking changes in industrialized nations is the rapid increase in life expectancy experienced since the Second World War. Japan, which had a low proportion of people aged 65 or more in 1950, is rapidly becoming the nation with the highest proportion of elderly. In western countries, low birth rates accentuate the demographic shift by reducing the number of new individuals entering the younger age groups. In Switzerland the number of persons above 85 increased in the period from 1950 to 2000 by 450 per cent, whereas over the same period the total population increased by only 53 per cent. These examples show that life expectancy critically depends on living conditions. There is no question that the maximal lifespan is strongly influenced by genetic factors. Human mortality increases exponentially with advancing age. This was first described by Benjamin Gompertz in a paper published in 1825, *On the nature of the function expressive of the law of human mortality* (Fries and Crapo, 1981). Other species seem to obey similar laws. However, the recent increases in life expectancy are not explained by genetic shifts but by external factors, thus raising the possibility of influencing morbidity and mortality during the human lifespan. Baltes (Baltes, 1997) suggests that the human lifespan is only incompletely determined by biological evolution, and depends particularly in later life on cultural co-evolution. In a similar vein, Kirkwood postulates that natural selection is of lesser importance with advancing age and the investment in somatic maintenance becomes less significant with

age (Kirkwood, 2002). Cultural factors may therefore determine to a large extent the possibility of growing old and maintaining health and wellbeing in later life. It is mainly by selection and optimization, and compensation of deficits, that we are able to maintain an independent and satisfactory life.

Schematically, one may visualize the interaction between ageing, genes, lifestyle, and the physical and sociocultural environment as in Figure 1, which demonstrates three facts. (1) First, ageing and thus passing time exposes the organism to an intrinsic and extrinsic allostatic load (sustained perturbation from the optimum state), which, depending on the balance of noxious and/or protective elements (genes, environment, nutrition, lifestyle, socioeconomic factors), may trigger individually different specific diseases. Hence, in one subject smoking might lead to lung cancer, but in another individual to obstructive lung disease or coronary artery disease. (2) The intrinsic ability to maintain homeostasis, largely determined genetically during the first part of life, diminishes with time, and nutrition, physical and mental exercise, lifestyle, and physical and sociocultural factors become increasingly important in maintaining homeostasis and function. (3) Factors characterizing our living conditions (Figure 2), which are to a large extent contingent, and the faculties of the person together determine the individual fate.

In order to conserve and maintain health and wellbeing during ageing, we have to identify the factors contributing to or endangering health. In a dialectic sense, health is the opposite of illness. This is not necessarily the same for wellbeing. Wellbeing

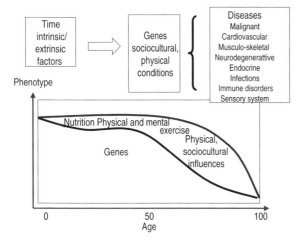

Figure 1. Interaction of nature and nurture.

is subjective and functionally defined, whereas an illness may or may not impact on wellbeing. Thus, frailty due to sarcopenia, and other age-associated physiological changes such as presbyacusis or presbyopia, may not qualify as illness but lead to disability and loss of autonomy. In industrialized societies the burden of diseases is dominated by chronic illnesses leading to impairment, disability, frailty and eventually death. The question of whether ageing is associated with diseases or whether the ageing process leads to diseases (*senectus ipsa est morbus*) is not

a real one. The issue is how we operationalize the observed disability. If it can be tracked to a distinct pathology, e.g. cancer, atherosclerosis, osteoporosis, heart failure or another illness, we may be very successful in preventing the process and its sequelae and at the same time maintain function, health and wellbeing.

In this chapter we focus mainly on this medical approach, which improved the life expectancy and the autonomy of the elderly during the past century. Empirically, we can identify a group of very old persons with little disability whom we may call 'optimally aged' (Rowe and Katzman, 1992), and a much larger group whom we can describe as 'typically aged' (Rowe and Kahn, 1987), characterized by suffering from medical conditions and cognitive dysfunctions. The aim, therefore, is to find ways and means to allow a large proportion of persons to age optimally.

Conceptually, we may thus promote health and wellbeing by:

- slowing the ageing process at the level of cells, organs and body
- by anti-ageing compounds
- by preventing age-associated illnesses
- by optimizing living conditions
- by compensating for loss of function.

All the different approaches have the same value.

In view of the age-associated increase in morbidity, the concept of health as complete physical, mental and social wellbeing, as put forward by the WHO, has to be questioned. Despite the fact that functional decline is present, the quality of life of free-living elderly persons seems to be as good as, or even superior to, younger age groups. This observation led Baltes and co-workers to postulate the concept of optimization by selection and compensation (Baltes, 1997). Whereas optimization by selection of tasks and goals can be applied universally with ageing, compensation of loss of function depends heavily on external resources. It is obvious that educational and socioeconomic resources and technical options heavily influence the potential to optimize by selection and compensation.

Figure 2. Showing the various dimensions that impact on health and wellbeing in later life.

Optimal Ageing

Biomedical Science

Ageing mechanisms
Gene–nutrients/environment
Chronic diseases:
CNS, Metabolic disorders, Cardiovascular disease, Muscle and bone disorders, Oral health

Information Technology
Prostheses
Transportation
Household support

Technology

By Selective Optimization And Compensation

Social Science

Lifestyle
Social condition and
   mental disease
Role in society
Gender issues
Health and social services
Coping/education

Income
Health services
Public service
Employment

Economy

Healthy old age is the result of a large number of factors. The prevention of diseases is one important factor which definitely contributed to the reduced mortality in industrialized regions. Interestingly, the older the individual, the larger the discrepancy between subjective health assessment and objective health (Borchelt *et al.*, 1999). Thus, wellbeing may be perceived differently, and there are substantial differences between different populations, e.g. rather high subjective wellbeing in the UK and a much lower percentage of older persons reporting wellbeing in Germany (Eurostat yearbook, 2004).

SLOWING THE AGEING PROCESS

Evidence suggests that the gain in life expectancy is associated with longer healthy life expectancy. This and animal experiments allow the conclusion that, if ageing were slowed down, the number of healthy centenarians could increase. Indeed, based on theoretical considerations, slowing down ageing might lead to the biggest gain so far in health and wellbeing in later life (Martin *et al.*, 2003). The biology of ageing revealed amazing analogies, from yeast, worms, flies, mice to humans, of how energy metabolism and growth and development are coupled (Longo and Finch, 2003). Caloric restriction is one way of slowing down ageing and it may well be that the cohort presently aged 80+ did in general experience a relatively frugal diet throughout their life. Whether this already contributes via similar mechanisms to the life expectancy observed today remains questionable. The demographic changes in Japan since the Second World War suggest that sufficient but appropriate food leads to longer life in humans. The analysis of mechanisms responsible for the burden of disease (Ezzati *et al.*, 2002) clearly indicates that being underweight and various nutritional deficiencies increase the risk of infections and thus of early mortality. However, the mechanisms protecting against infectious diseases, favourable during childhood, may increase the risk of chronic degenerative diseases later on. Thus, the preventive strategies have to be seen differently according to age and environmental as well as sociocultural contingencies.

The Third and the Fourth Age

The observed gain in individual life expectancy is not only seen as a success but also as a challenge, namely, to cope with the functional decline associated with the 'Fourth Age'. Thus the concept of the Third and Fourth Age, which is somewhat similar to the concept 'young-old' and 'old-old' but less functionally oriented, is in dynamic evolution. One population-based definition could be the chronological age at which 50 per cent of the population who reached the age of 50 or 60 have died. This puts the beginning of the Fourth Age at 80–5 years. Another approach relies on a person-based definition. This definition takes into consideration that the individual maximum life expectancy (probably mostly genetically determined when free of specific illnesses) bringing life to an end varies between 80 and 120 years. Accordingly the individual transition from Third to Fourth Age varies substantially (Baltes and Smith, 2003). As a criticism of this view one might cite the rectangularization of morbidity and mortality that has been observed over the last decades. Functional decline occurs later in life today than during previous periods.

Anti-ageing

The idea of finding a drug that interferes with the ageing process and thus slows ageing is an old human dream depicted in fountains of youth turning frail old women into charming young girls. Interestingly, these miracles were reserved for women, an attitude that did not change too much until today, since the clients for cosmetic interventions are still mainly women. The observation of age-associated declines in hormones led to the idea of supplementing these hormones, particularly estrogen, dehydroepiandrosterone and melatonin. Likewise, there is a growing trend towards ingesting large amounts of anti-oxidants. To date these approaches have proved to be, at best, harmless, and may increase the risk of certain diseases (Olshansky *et al.*, 2002). The notion that the older individual suffers from deficiencies (e.g. postmenopausal women are said to be estrogen deficient) is not substantiated by intervention studies (Shumaker *et al.*, 1998, 2003). On the other hand, in animal models, correction of lifespan in genetically vulnerable organisms with

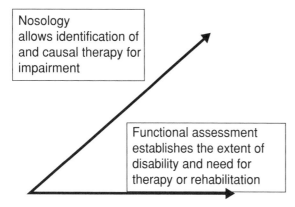

Figure 3. Depicts the two main approaches in dealing with illnesses.

TABLE 1. Impact of medical conditions on activities of daily living

Condition	Disability as measured by ADL dimensions	Odds Ratio (95% CI)
Heart failure	2.4	(0.98–5.8)
Stroke	8.7	(3.9–19.3)
Parkinson's disease	18.7	(1.3–276.0)
Hip fracture	2.6	(0.9–7.4)
Visual impairment	2.0	(0.98–4.1)
Fall(s) within 12 months	3.4	(1.6–7.4)
Body Mass Index		
<20	2.8	(1.2–6.4)
20–29	1.0	
>29	0.3	(0.04–2.7)
Age:		
65–74	1.0	
75–84	2.5	(0.5–13.1)
85+	5.9	(1.1–30.2)

a shorter lifespan, or extension of the lifespan of the wild type, seem to work (Melov *et al.*, 2000). This, however, is contended by others (McCulloch and Gems, 2003). In principle, it may well be that, for example, modulating the handling of reactive oxygen species in mitochondria might generally influence the ageing process. Indeed, oxidative stress shortens telomeres (Serra *et al.*, 2003) and could be an indicator of 'biological ageing' reflecting endogenous and exogenous factors (Cawthon *et al.*, 2003).

PREVENTION OF AGE-ASSOCIATED ILLNESSES AND DISABILITIES

Recent studies including the Berlin Ageing Study (Baltes and Mayer, 2001) have addressed the issue of health and wellbeing in old age. Physiological changes with ageing require adaptive capacities to compensate for losses. In general, subjects adapt efficiently to these declines in functions by selective optimization and by compensation (i.e. glasses for reading, hearing aids, teeth prostheses, walking aids, etc.). It is important to appreciate that even if functions decline linearly, the activities of daily living require in most cases threshold capacities. If functions are below the required threshold, a handicap results, e.g. the person is no longer able to climb stairs, which can be sufficient to force a move from a house into a more adapted apartment.

This loss of function is often unspecific and the result of different causes. The mere loss of function does not say anything about the causes leading to

it. Functional capabilities and underlying morbidity are strongly related but conceptually independent constructs. The identification of a large number of illnesses that lead to a loss of function, as well as of risk factors increasing the occurrence of diseases, allowed the development of a rational approach to preventing or curing these conditions and thus maintaining function. The fact that many primary preventive steps are very similar for a wide variety of illnesses (Figure 1), such as coronary heart disease, stroke, diabetes mellitus, cancer and Alzheimer's disease, can be easily integrated into a concept of salutogenesis or self-coherence (Forbes, 2001). On the other hand, the concept of disease proved extremely successful for finding therapies for illnesses leading to disabilities. This led Peto and Doll (1997) to the statement that 'There is no such thing as aging: Old age is associated with disease, but does not cause it.' A study by Langlois *et al.* (1999) demonstrates the impact of distinct common medical conditions on the functional ability to perform activities of daily living (ADL) (Katz *et al.*, 1963). Table 1 shows clearly the association of common medical conditions with ADL but also indicates the wide functional variability observed at a given age and the wide variability in impact on function of a number of diagnoses. Interestingly, overweight appears to be an indicator of functional health in the elderly whereas underweight (BMI < 20) indicates poor functional performance.

PREVENTION AND POSTPONING OF CHRONIC DISEASES

Cardiovascular diseases and atherosclerosis

Epidemiological studies allowed the identification of risk factors predisposing to diabetes mellitus, ischemic heart disease, stroke, cancer and, in more recent years, also to degenerative brain diseases, particularly dementia. Based upon the concept that avoiding or treating risk factors diminishes the emergence of organ-related pathological changes, powerful treatments were developed to lower raised blood pressure, to decrease the low-density lipoprotein concentration in blood, to modulate coagulation and to protect the organs from free-radical damage, etc. Careful intervention studies documented a lower morbidity and also mortality by treating risk factors.

Treatment of cardiovascular risk factors is today one of the prime pharmaceutical targets and hence of enormous economic importance. External factors influenced by the individual genetic makeup lead to large differences in morbidity (for CHD up to a factor of 10, comparing Japan with Scotland). The fact that similar risk factors predispose to a wide variety of chronic conditions, such as, e.g., atherosclerosis, cancer, dementia, suggests that more general basic cellular mechanisms such as inflammation, oxygen free radicals and DNA repair are targets of the risk factors and that it is the individual genetic makeup that decides which organ is most vulnerable. Different coping styles and dietary habits could explain, in addition to biological factors, why cardiovascular diseases occur later in women than men. The gender-specific approach to illness probably explains why women are less aggressively treated in the case of CHD and why the fact that women outnumber men with heart disease (not necessarily classified as coronary artery disease, but congestive heart failure as a result of hypertension, diabetes, etc.) has only recently been appreciated. Nevertheless, conceptually we may divide the preventive actions into public health measures, those targeted at individuals

and, among them, even those targeted at high-risk individuals.

Table 2 gives an example of this approach for CVD and women. Modern drug treatment of cardiac diseases and also of heart failure by diuretics, antihypertensive drugs, aspirin and particularly statins has greatly improved the situation of these patients. In summary, the impact on health of cardiovascular disease has declined and is postponed to later age.

Cancer

Cancer incidence increases with age. In industrialized societies cancer is the second most frequent cause of morbidity and mortality. The observation that stomach cancer, which was frequently seen in the first half of the twentieth century, is now much less common, whereas lung cancer in smokers and colon cancer in westernized societies became much more frequent, tells us that the type and incidence of cancer is the result of interactions, as illustrated schematically in Figure 1. Hence cancer prevention, early detection and therapy are important in promoting health and wellbeing in the elderly.

On the population level the identification of carcinogenic substances in the environment and in foods, the elimination of certain infectious agents (e.g. *Helicobacter pylori*), the substitution of iodine (goitre and thyroid cancer) contributed to the decline of certain types of cancer, whereas other lifestyle elements such as cigarette smoking and excessive alcohol consumption and a hypercaloric diet still convey a risk for malignant diseases in many.

Screening for pre-malignant growths (e.g. adenomas of the colon) or still locally isolated malignant conditions (skin, breast, prostate cancers) demonstrates how epidemiological knowledge and modern medical technologies, made possible by new material and information processing, have transformed the prospect of cancer. Improved surgical and medical treatment of a large number of different cancers have changed the outlook for patients and maintained wellbeing and independence over a prolonged period of time. Again, it is the synergistic use of medical, technical and social structures that determine outcome in cancer. At the population level, changes in nutritional habits by

TABLE 2. Cardiovascular diseases risk reduction objectives and strategies for women

Risk factor	Population strategy (whole population)	Population strategy (directed at women)	High risk strategy at individual women
Hypertension	Inter-sectorial collaboration with food manufacturers, industry, advertisers; e.g. salt reduction in manufactured food; promotion of a heart-healthy diet	Promotion of relevant and realistic physical activity/movement programs; promote low intake of alcohol in older women	Lifestyle advice; to high absolute risk established evidence e.g.: 10–15% risk if a CVD event over ensuing 5 years as a starting point for discussion concerning treatment
Cholesterol	As above; increased physical activity; weight control	As above; as for total population (modified)	Dietary counseling at high absolute risk determined guidelines
Current smoker	Comprehensive policies; tobacco control legislation	As for total population	Subsidized smoking programs
Physically inactive	Information and education; accessible activity programs; discouragement of individualized transport	Promotion of community based exercise programs, e.g. walking groups	Counseling by primary care physicians; women's health initiatives
Obesity	Nutrition and exercise programs (modified)	As for total population and fitness programs	Dietary counseling; exercise

Source: From Bonita (1998).

better food processing, and increasing the amount of antioxidants and micronutrients in the diet have had an important effect (Key *et al.*, 2002). This is strongly dependent on individual behaviour and thus on education, which again demonstrates the sociocultural influence.

Muscle and bones

With age, muscle strength and bone density decrease and connective tissue is transformed becoming less elastic. This leads to increased vulnerability, to falls, fractures and frailty (Carmeli *et al.*, 2000). Muscle function and, to some extent, bone density are best maintained by physical exercise (Roubenoff, 2000; Foldvari *et al.*, 2000). Modern life does not necessarily favour physical exercise at work or during leisure time. The age-associated decline in physical fitness may be aggravated by illnesses affecting bones and joints. Strain and trauma on the joints are risk factors for osteoarthritis limiting mobility by pain and impeding function. Lighter work and better

protection from injuries have resulted in diminished stress on the musculo-skeletal system during the last decades. Today hip or knee replacements are effective means of securing mobility and independence in old age: a paradigmatic example of selective optimization and compensation.

Next to physical exercise nutrition is paramount in the prevention of osteoporosis. Vitamin D and calcium and also vitamin K (important for the carboxylation of osteocalcin) are needed in sufficient quantities. Since, with age, the capacity of the skin to synthesize vitamin D precursors diminishes by over 50 per cent, the risk of vitamin D deficiency becomes substantial and supplementation is warranted particularly in inpatients (Bischoff *et al.*, 2003). Vitamin D not only helps to maintain bone density but also has a positive effect on muscle strength. Sarcopenia, osteopenia, longer reaction time, reduced vision, together with a wide number of pathological conditions, put the elderly and particularly the older woman at a high risk of falling (Tinetti *et al.*, 1988).

To protect against falls and subsequent fractures it is important to adapt the environment by eliminating obstacles, providing bright light and avoiding high-risk behaviour during in- and outdoor activities. For people at high risk, wearing hip protectors can be very effective. Medical conditions requiring drug therapy have to be evaluated carefully and medication (e.g. sedating drugs or drugs inducing orthostatic hypotension) kept to a minimum. Since the fear of falling is an important factor restricting independence in the elderly, devices that facilitate calling for help may restore self-confidence and mobility and allow the old person to maintain autonomy longer.

Endocrine and metabolic disorders

In recent years in industrialized societies an epidemic of obesity has developed. Obesity is associated with a number of pathological conditions that interfere with health and wellbeing. The most serious complication is the metabolic syndrome (obesity, hypertension, hyperlipidemia, impaired glucose tolerance and hyperuricemia) with all the related illnesses (Ginsberg, 2003). The metabolic consequences can be traced back to insulin resistance as the pathophysiological mechanism.

Since the mid 1990s, the number of obese persons in the US has increased dramatically (Mokdad et al., 2003) and there has been a parallel increase in the number of patients with type II diabetes mellitus. Diabetes is a condition that accelerates ageing, e.g. by advanced glycation changing not only metabolism but also proteins. The risk of age-associated illnesses such as myocardial infarction, stroke, end-stage renal disease, cataract, neuropathy, etc., doubles in the presence of diabetes. This phenomenon will have an impact on the cohorts that are now ageing. Recent clinical studies clearly demonstrate that intensive diabetes therapy is able to prevent, diminish and postpone the metabolic consequences of diabetes and thus of accelerated ageing.

Obesity is also associated with a higher cancer incidence (Key et al., 2002), probably by the growth-promoting effect of insulin and other obesity-related stimulation of pro-inflammatory and pro-oncogenic cytokines. On the other hand, there is a clear relation between weight and morbidity and mortality in old age (Langlois et al., 1999). Thus, in the old, a high body mass index is associated with a lower mortality, in stark contrast to low BMI which, in general in the old, indicates presence of somatic or psychic illness or malnutrition. Energy intake diminishes with age and thus body fat and lean body mass decreases, in part due to a diminished sensory control of appetite (Roberts et al., 1994).

The intensive search for a pharmacological cure for obesity is unlikely to be successful – certainly not on an economic scale – since the multicausal origin will not be effectively dealt with by this approach and the related illnesses will need multiple therapies and lead to substantial medical interventions. The present-day older population experienced a very different adult life with less obesity than those who will become old in the future. Thus the projections based on the mortality of today may prove wrong.

In old age, clinical symptoms of some nutritional deficiencies are often difficult to detect. Hypothyroidism, vitamin D deficiency, vitamin B12 and folic acid deficiency are very common. As a consequence, hyperhomocysteinemia is very prevalent in the elderly population (Bostom et al., 1999; Johnson et al., 2003), increasing the risk of vascular and neurodegenerative diseases. This warrants food fortification for the population and supplementation for high-risk persons such as pregnant women (neural tube defects) and the elderly.

Immune response, inflammation and infections

Ageing is associated with an increase of lymphokines that mediate the inflammatory response of the body. The clinical benefits of aspirin in coronary heart disease, stroke and colon cancer are probably related to the interference of aspirin with the inflammatory response. Polyunsaturated fatty acids, especially n-3 fatty acids from marine sources, may act in a similar way.

Conditions leading to stimulation of the immune response also accelerate ageing. Today's better sanitation, nutrition and housing have meant that infectious disorders during early life have become less frequent. This has led to a shift in lymphocyte helper cell population from Th1 to Th2 helper cells in the young and to an increase in allergic reactions in the population. To what extent this will affect health in later life is unclear. Nevertheless, the recently observed reluctance to vaccinate children against certain viral and bacterial diseases may also impact on health and wellbeing in late life by shifting certain illnesses into an age range where the natural course of the infection is more severe.

Two hundred years ago, about 50 per cent of children died before the age of 10, and even in 1900 almost 20 per cent died before 10. These mortality rates are still found today in countries where poor nutrition, unsafe water, poor sanitation and hygiene and unsafe sex continue to lead to high morbidity through infectious diseases (Ezzati *et al.*, 2002). In industrialized societies infections remain of great importance in the frail elderly. The age-related changes in organs, e.g. sarcopenia, osteopenia, changes in renal function, etc., diminish the functional reserve. The immune system responds less vigorously and less precisely to challenges.

Infections trigger catabolic processes that may reduce physical activity, promote malnutrition and rapidly exhaust the functional reserve of aged organs. In the old, undernutrition may be a very serious problem that increases vulnerability to infections. Thus pneumonias tend to be more serious in older people, requiring hospitalization and vigorous medical treatment. Vaccination against influenza is thus highly effective in reducing not only influenza-related morbidity and mortality but also other morbid conditions (Nichol *et al.*, 2003), in spite of the fact that the immune response is less effectively stimulated in the old than in the young.

Sensory system

For health and wellbeing, the faculty of communication is paramount. Thus the widespread decline in hearing severely affects the ability of many older people to socialize and participate in family life, the community and in cultural life. Impairment or loss of vision is another common factor that impedes physical functioning and is an important source of disability.

Hearing loss may be due to genetic factors but is accelerated by ear trauma. Today the exposure to very loud noise during leisure time may have serious consequences in later life. In the presently old cohort, protective devices were less in use and

loud noise during work contributed extensively to hearing impairment. Hearing aids can compensate increasingly well for these conditions. Preventing acoustic trauma is today an important public health issue at work but much less appreciated during leisure-time activities.

Similarly, the age-associated loss of visual accommodation is compensated by glasses and thus function is maintained. Cataract surgery has enormously improved with excellent functional results. Again co-morbid conditions such as diabetes accelerate ageing by glycation and induce retinal changes. By treating diabetes mellitus vigorously, it is possible to ward off diabetic microangiopathy. Screening for glaucoma allows early detection and treatment in incipient cases. These developments show how progress in medicine and technical sciences may contribute to maintaining function and autonomy in the old.

Nutrition

The German word 'alt', meaning 'old', derives from the Latin words 'alere' meaning 'well-fed' and 'altus' ('grown-up'). The link of ageing to nutrition is also found in the French expression 'aliment, alimenter'. That nutrition influences lifespan may be seen not only in the phenomenon of life extension through caloric reduction in animal models but also in the modification of the disease pattern during advancing age. In addition to providing the necessary nutrients for maintaining body functions, eating serves important social functions and is regulated by sociocultural mechanisms. Thus physical and economic and social resources that give access to a large variety of food are important in maintaining health in the elderly. This is well illustrated by the EURONUT Seneca Study (Schroll *et al.*, 1996). Lower average levels of physical exercise today contribute more to obesity than the age-associated lower energy intake in the adult will compensate for. In the old, many factors (see below) lead to a lower caloric intake and consequently also to a loss in body mass and, if not compensated by supplements, to a low micronutrient intake (Bates *et al.*, 2002). Thus, in order to promote health and wellbeing in the old it is important to prevent weight loss or aid the regaining of weight. Since the capacity of the body to control fluid and salt diminishes with age (Phillips *et al.*,

1984), intake should be monitored by the individual and eventually by the caregiver.

Since risk of malnutrition in the elderly population is substantial – the most serious cause being depression – and since malnutrition is a major cause of frailty, diet is important, particularly in elderly persons with chronic illnesses, in persons living alone, and in institutions. In general the following diet, usually characterized as 'Mediterranean', seems to be associated with longer survival (Trichopoulou and Vasilopoulou, 2000; de Groot *et al.*, 1996):

- high monounsaturated to saturated fat ratio (<1.6)
- moderate ethanol consumption (men < 10 g/day)
- high consumption of legumes (men > 60 g/day, women > 49 g/day)
- high consumption of cereals (men > 291 g/day, women > 248 g/day)
- high consumption of fruits (men > 249 g/day, women > 216 g/day)
- high consumption of vegetables (men > 303 g/day, women > 248 g/day)
- low consumption of meat and meat products (men *c.* 109 g/day, women < 91 g/day)
- low consumption of milk and dairy products (men < 201 g/day, women < 194 g/day)

In summary the composition of the diet is probably more important than the single ingredients.

With ageing, the perception of thirst and hunger diminishes (Phillips *et al.*, 1984; Roberts *et al.*, 1994). As a consequence the endogenously controlled intake of fluids and nutrients is insufficient to maintain or restore homeostasis after a challenge. This requires more deliberate control by the individual or the societal mechanism.

Good oral health is required for health and wellbeing. This is a life-long task but prevention and treatment of medical conditions that interfere with appetite or induce catabolic states are also important. Progress in dentistry, e.g. by implants, has helped not only to sustain function but also to provide aesthetic improvements that maintain self-esteem and self-confidence and thus wellbeing.

Sexuality

Human sexuality is an important component of wellbeing and health that changes with age but does not stop. Physiological change in sex hor-

mones for women and men lead to transformation of the body with loss of lean body mass and gain of body fat, decreasing libido and potency and thus impact on sexuality. Sexuality in the old has been affected by many factors such as demography (with a longer lifespan for women compared to men), social transformation with less stable families, higher divorce rates, greater permissiveness towards extramarital sex, and changing cultural practices and attitudes.

Sexual dysfunction in men and women is increasingly seen as a medical problem. Male erectile dysfunction needs a medical work-up (Seftel, 2003). The availability of effective drugs and, if indicated, of testosterone to treat erectile dysfunction in the young-old male, and somewhat less effectively in the old male, contributes to wellness by increasing self-confidence and diminishing anxiety. The future will show whether the now widely promoted use of testosterone will ultimately improve wellness and quality of life in the old man and also woman, or whether it will suffer from the same fate as hormonal therapy with estrogen and progestin. Large randomized trials funded by public sources largely disproved the anti-ageing claims and the disease-specific preventive effectiveness (Shumaker *et al.*, 2003). In women, psychosocial factors, strongly influenced by cultural stereotypes, lead to wide differences in the use of hormonal therapy after menopause and these also affect the mechanisms for coping with sexual dysfunction and sexuality as a whole. Epidemiological studies demonstrate that the better-educated women have different coping styles with better outcomes than the less educated. Hence, education of the public seems to be also effective in improving sexuality in old age.

Mental health

Probably the greatest fear and challenge of ageing is the loss of mental capacities with age. In the young-old, however, affective disorders are much more common than neurodegenerative disorders. In the old-old, dementia becomes the paramount challenge to the individual and to society. So the question is, what are the options for maintaining mental health and wellbeing by prevention or therapy?

Late-onset depression is common, characterized by an increased mortality. The rate of suicide which increases with age is the most serious problem. Depression is also a powerful risk factor for cardiovascular mortality (Frasure-Smith, 1986) but not for cancer (Whooley and Browner, 1998). Depression is very common as a sequela of major, disabling illnesses such as stroke, Parkinson's disease and early stages of dementia. Psychosocial factors such as loneliness, loss of significant others, loss of work or a meaningful perspective in life, disability, economic strain, etc., are important triggers. This demonstrates that anti-depressant therapy should not only be pharmacological but focus on the psychosocial conditions of the elderly. By identifying factors triggering depression and appropriate counter measures, combined with effective psycho- and pharmacotherapy, it is possible to lower significantly the burden of depression in the older population.

The prevalence of dementia doubles, from a low rate in the under-60-year-old, for every additional five years of life (Ritchie and Kildea, 1995; Jorm and Jolley, 1998), to affect one-third of the 85-year-old population, Alzheimer's disease (AD) being the single most important cause of dementia in western societies. The exponential increase with age is best explained by a multicausal mechanism. Analysis of the Canadian data (2000) show an almost identical incidence for men and women, men running a higher risk between 70 and 80. But probably more important is the levelling off at age 90, suggesting that selective survival favours individuals with less susceptibility to become demented.

Several studies clearly show the close connection between cardiovascular risk and the development of Alzheimer's disease and dementia (Forette *et al.*, 1998). This link is even stronger in carriers of the $\epsilon 4$ allele of the polymorphic Apolipoprotein E, gene. This allele is associated with higher risk for AD (Hofman *et al.*, 1997). Effective treatment of cardiovascular risk factors is therefore thought to be an important preventive strategy against dementia. Consequently, numerous studies looked at factors known from prevention strategies against cardiovascular diseases to see whether they have an impact on the development of cognitive disorders in late life. There is good evidence that reactive oxygen radicals play an important role in triggering the pathological changes leading ultimately to deposits of β-amyloid, fibrillary tangles and neuronal death, or other protein deposits such as

TABLE 3. Subjective Health and Nutritional Intake judged by participants. SENECA Results (2,586 Europeans aged 70–75)

	Health		
	poor	good	p(D)
Cal/day	1540	1800	<.0001
Fat g/day	54	79	<.0001
Calcium mg/day	691	906	<.0001
Vit. B1 mg/day	0.83	0.98	<.0001
Vit. C mg/day	84	110	<.001
Low budget	29.4%	7%	<.0001
All meals at home	91%	75%	<.001

α-synuclein in Parkinson's disease. Indeed, observational studies show that a diet rich in fruits and vegetables (Engelhart *et al.*, 2002) and hence natural anti-oxidants (Perrig *et al.*, 1997; Haller *et al.*, 1996) (some vitamins, some bioactive compounds such as cartenoids or flavonoids), but also rich in folate and vitamin B12, are correlated with lower incidence of dementia. High blood levels of homocysteine were found to be a risk factor for AD (Seshadri *et al.*, 2002). Thus, dietary factors play a role in preserving cognitive function and decreasing the susceptibility to neurodegenerative diseases.

Caloric intake correlates inversely with cognitive function (Luchsinger *et al.*, 2002) if susceptibility for Alzheimer's disease exists. This is not necessarily the case for the depressed and frail old individuals where malnutrition aggravates the clinical situation of the patient (Table 3).

For alcohol intake, epidemiological studies point to a U-shaped association with cognitive function in the old (Kalmijn *et al.*, 2002). The protective effects seen in recent studies are confined to men with low to moderate, disciplined use of alcohol and thus reflect life- and coping-styles which are associated with better cognitive function (Leroi *et al.*, 2002).

In Alzheimer's disease, the neurotransmitter acetylcholine is reduced in the brain. Acetylcholine is important for memory, vigilance, and has neurotrophic properties. By stimulating acetylcholine receptors, symptoms of dementia and delirium

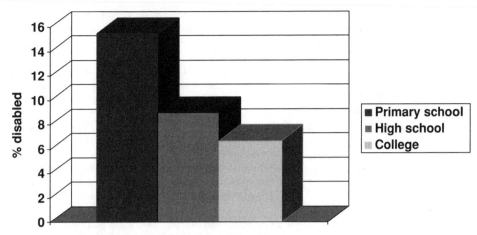

Figure 4. Education and disability in the US.

may be ameliorated. Acetylcholine receptors occur as nicotinic or muscarinic receptors. Smoking stimulates nicotinic receptors. The question now is whether smoking is preventing neurodegenerative disorders by stimulating nicotinic receptors in the brain. In Parkinson's disease (PD), there was an inverse relationship between smoking and incidence of PD (Doll *et al.*, 1994). In AD, current evidence suggests that the possible preventive effects of smoking are far outweighed by the negative effects on the cardiovascular system. Smoking is clearly a risk factor for vascular dementia.

The most important prevention of cognitive decline is education and the continuing use of intellectual faculties. This is not only explained by a greater neuronal functional reserve but by a much more general phenomenon relating education to better coping styles, less cardiovascular risk, better nutrition and more control over life.

SOCIAL AND ECONOMIC FACTORS

The importance of education is clearly demonstrated by the findings of Manton (Manton *et al.*, 1997), where the rate of chronic disability is less than half in individuals with a college or university degree compared to those with less schooling. A meta-analysis (Stuck, in preparation) confirms this relation also for other developed societies. Thus, promoting health and wellbeing in old age depends crucially on the educational opportunities in a population which should be of paramount political concern also from a public health point of view. Based on this, the

positive effects of educational programmes for the older population will substantially contribute to health and wellbeing in late life. Probably the most important benefit is that elderly citizens will find it easier to find meaning in their life.

Increasingly, more responsibility for health and wellbeing is placed with the individual through education and 'patient empowerment'. This development runs the risk of endangering the solidarity concept that is based on the notion that ill health is largely contingent and not under one's own control. On the other hand, the highly valued patient autonomy places limits on public health approaches (e.g. food fortification, enforcing safety measures, etc.). The responsibility for health may increasingly shift to the individual and thereby weaken the highly effective public health approach. Each society has to find a reasonable and fair balance in this dynamic field.

The recent decline in the percentage living in nursing homes is an indicator that alternative care is available or that individuals with disability can effectively compensate for or treat the disability. Modern technology facilitates housing, shopping, commuting and communicating. These technologies extend the autonomy of formerly handicapped persons. It is obvious that these developments are not independent of the general economy, and affluent societies – usually better educated – will profit disproportionately.

Thus, promotion of health and wellbeing by preventing and treating of diseases, which also provides a safe social and physical environment, will promote economic growth of the nation optimally and increase healthy life expectancy. There is evidence that the economic benefits of medical research may far exceed anything wrought by information technology. Thus Murphy and Topel (2000) estimated that the gain in life expectancy of 6 years in the US over a 20-year period from 1970 to 1990 yielded a remarkable US$ 57 trillion, in 1992 dollars.

Therefore the biomedically oriented approach to promoting health and wellbeing in late life is worthwhile.

FURTHER READING

Baltes, P. B., and K. U. E. Mayer (2001). *The Berlin Aging Study*. Cambridge: Cambridge University Press.

Felsenthal, G., Garrison, S. J., and F. U. Steinberg, eds. (1994). *Rehabilitation of the aging and elderly patient*. Philadelphia: Lippincott Williams & Wilkins.

Grimley Evans, J., Williams, T. F., Beattie, B. L., and J-P. Michel (2000). *Oxford textbook of geriatric medicine*, 2nd edn. Oxford: Oxford University Press.

Kirkwood, T., ed. (2001). *Aging vulnerability: causes and interventions*. New York: John Wiley & Sons, Inc.

REFERENCES

Baltes, P. B. (1997). 'On the incomplete architecture of human ontogeny. Selection, optimization, and compensation as foundation of developmental theory', *Am Psychol*, 52 (4): 366–80.

Baltes, P. B., and K. U. Mayer, eds. (2001). *The Berlin Aging Study*. Cambridge: Cambridge University Press.

Baltes, P. B., and J. Smith (2003). 'New frontiers in the future of aging: from successful aging of the young old to the dilemmas of the fourth age', *Gerontology*, 49 (2): 123–35.

Bates, C. J., Benton, D., *et al.* (2002). 'Nutrition and aging: a consensus statement', *J Nutr Health Aging*, 6 (2): 103–16.

Bischoff, H. A., Stahelin, H. B., *et al.* (2003). 'Effects of vitamin D and calcium supplementation on falls: a randomized controlled trial.' *J Bone Miner Res* 18 (2): 343–51.

Bonita, R. (1998). 'Women, menopause and the primary prevention of cardiovascular disease'. In E. G. Lakatta, *Vascular diseases in older persons*. New York: The Parthenon Publishing Group, pp. 73–90.

Borchelt, M., Gilberg, R., *et al.* (1999). 'On the significance of morbidity and disability in old age'. In P. B. Baltes and K. U. Mayer, eds., *The Berlin aging Study: aging from 70 to 100*. New York: Cambridge University Press, pp. 403–29.

Bostom, A. G., Rosenberg, I. H., *et al.* (1999). 'Nonfasting plasma total homocysteine levels and stroke incidence in elderly persons: the Framingham Study', *Ann Intern Med* 131 (5): 352–5.

Canadian Study of Health and Aging Working Group (2000). 'The incidence of dementia in Canada. The Canadian Study of Health and Aging Working Group', *Neurology*, 55 (1): 66–73.

Carmeli, E., Reznick, A. Z., *et al.* (2000). 'Muscle strength and mass of lower extremities in relation to functional abilities in elderly adults, *Gerontology*', 46 (5): 249–57.

Cawthon, R. M., Smith, K. R., *et al.* (2003). 'Association between telomere length in blood and mortality in people aged 60 years or older', *Lancet*, 361 (9355): 393–5.

de Groot, L., van Staveren, W. R., *et al.* (1996). 'Survival beyond age 70 in relation to diet', *Nutrition Review*, 54: 211–12.

Doll, R., Peto, R., *et al.* (1994). 'Mortality in relation to smoking: 40 years' observations on male British doctors', *BMJ*, 309 (6959): 901–11.

Engelhart, M. J., Geerlings, M. I., *et al.* (2002). 'Dietary intake of antioxidants and risk of Alzheimer disease', *JAMA*, 287 (24): 3223–9.

Eurostat yearbook (2004). *The statistical guide to Europe – Data 1992–2002*. Brussels: Statistical Office of the European Commission.

Ezzati, M., Lopez, A. D., *et al.* (2002). 'Selected major risk factors and global and regional burden of disease', *Lancet*, 360 (9343): 1347–60.

Foldvari, M., Clark, M., *et al.* (2000). 'Association of muscle power with functional status in community-dwelling elderly women', *J Gerontol: A Biol Sci Med Sci* 55(4): M192–9.

Forbes, D. A. (2001). 'Enhancing mastery and sense of coherence: important determinants of health in older adults', *Geriatr Nurs* 22 (1): 29–32.

Forette, F., Seux, M. L., *et al.* (1998). 'Prevention of dementia in randomised double-blind placebo-controlled Systolic Hypertension in Europe (Syst-Eur) trial', *Lancet*, 352 (9137): 1347–51.

Fries, J. F., and L. M. Crapo (1981). *Vitality and aging*. San Francisco: W. H. Freeman & Co.

Ginsberg, H. N. (2003). 'Treatment for patients with the metabolic syndrome', *Am J Cardiol*, 91(7A): 29E–39E.

Haller, J., Weggemans, R. M., *et al.* (1996). 'Mental health: Minimental State examination and geriatric depression score of elderly Europeans in the SENECA study of 1993', *Eur J Clin Nutr*, 50. (Suppl. 2): S112–16.

Hofman, A., Ott, A., *et al.* (1997). 'Atherosclerosis, apolipoprotein E, and prevalence of dementia and Alzheimer's disease in the Rotterdam Study', *Lancet*, 349 (9046): 151–4.

Johnson, M. A., Hawthorne, N. A., *et al.* (2003). 'Hyperhomocysteinemia and vitamin B-12 deficiency in elderly using Title IIIc nutrition services', *Am J Clin Nutr*, 77 (1): 211–20.

Jorm, A. F., and Jolley, D. (1998). 'The incidence of dementia: a meta-analysis', *Neurology*, 51 (3): 728–33.

Kalmijn, S., van Boxtel, M. P., *et al.* (2002). 'Cigarette smoking and alcohol consumption in relation to cognitive performance in middle age', *Am J Epidemiol*, 156 (10): 936–44.

Katz, S., Amasa, B. F., *et al.* (1963). 'Studies of illness in the aged. The index of ADL: a standardized measure of biological and psychological function', *J Amer Med Assoc*, 185: 914–19.

Key, T. J., Allen, N. E., *et al.* (2002). 'The effect of diet on risk of cancer', *Lancet*, 360: 861–8.

Kirkwood, T. B. (2002). 'Evolution of ageing', *Mech Ageing Dev*, 123 (7): 737–45.

Langlois, J. A., Norton, R., *et al.* (1999). 'Characteristics and behaviours associated with difficulty in performing activities of daily living among older New Zealand women', *Disabil Rehabil*, 21 (8): 365–71.

Leroi, I., Sheppard, J. M., *et al.* (2002). 'Cognitive function after 11.5 years of alcohol use: relation to alcohol use', *Am J Epidemiol*, 156 (8): 747–52.

Longo, V. D., and C. E. Finch (2003). 'Evolutionary medicine: from dwarf model systems to healthy centenarians?' *Science*, 299 (5611): 1342–6.

Luchsinger, J. A., Tang, M. X., *et al.* (2002). 'Caloric intake and the risk of Alzheimer's disease', *Arch Neurol*, 59 (8): 1258–63.

Manton, K. G., Stallard, E., *et al.* (1997). 'Education-specific estimates of life expectancy and age-specific disability in the US elderly population: 1982 to 1991', *J Aging Health*, 9 (4): 419–50.

Martin, G. M., LaMarco, K., *et al.* (2003). 'Research on aging: the end of the beginning', *Science*, 299 (5611): 1339–41.

McCulloch, D., and D. Gems (2003). 'Body size, insulin/IGF signaling and aging in the nematode Caenorhabditis elegans', *Exp Gerontol*, 38: 129–36.

Melov, S., Ravenscroft, J., *et al.* (2000). 'Extension of lifespan with superoxide dismutase/catalase mimetics', *Science*, 289 (5484): 1567–9.

Mokdad, A. H., Ford, E. S., *et al.* (2003). 'Prevalence of obesity, diabetes, and obesity-related health risk factors, 2001', *JAMA*, 289 (1): 76–9.

Murphy, K., and R. Topel (2000). *Exceptional returns: the economic value of America's investment in medical research.* Chicago: University of Chicago Press.

Nichol, K. L., Nordin, J., *et al.* (2003). 'Influenza vaccination and reduction in hospitalizations for cardiac disease and stroke among the elderly', *N Engl J Med*, 348 (14): 1322–32.

Olshansky, S. J., Hayflick, L., *et al.* (2002). 'No truth to the fountain of youth', *Sci Am*, 286 (6): 92–5.

Perrig, W. J., Perrig, P., *et al.* (1997). 'The relation between antioxidants and memory performance in the old and very old', *J Am Geriatr Soc*, 45 (6): 718–24.

Peto, R., and R. Doll (1997). 'There is no such thing as aging', *BMJ*, 315 (7115): 1030–2.

Phillips, P. A., Rolls, B. J., *et al.* (1984). 'Reduced thirst after water deprivation in healthy elderly men', *N Engl J Med*, 311 (12): 753–9.

Ritchie, K., and D. Kildea (1995). 'Is senile dementia "age-related" or "ageing-related"? – evidence from meta-analysis of dementia prevalence in the oldest old', *Lancet*, 346 (8980): 931–4.

Roberts, S. B., Fuss, P., *et al.* (1994). 'Control of food intake in older men (published erratum appears in *JAMA* 1995 Mar 1; 273(9):702)', *JAMA* 272 (20): 1601–6.

Roubenoff, R. (2000). 'Sarcopenia and its implications for the elderly', *Eur J Clin Nutr*, 54 (S3): S40–S47.

Rowe, J. W., and R. L. Kahn (1987). 'Human aging: usual and successful', *Science*, 237 (4811): 143–9.

Rowe, J. W., and R. Katzman (1992). 'Principles of geriatrics as applied to neurology'. In R. Katzman and J. W. Rowe, *Principles of geriatric neurology*. Philadelphia: F. A. David Company, pp. 3–17.

Schroll, M., Carbacjal, D., *et al.* (1996). 'Food patterns of elderly Europeans', *Eur J Clin Nutr*, 50 (Suppl. 2): 86–100.

Seftel, A. D. (2003). 'Erectile dysfunction in the elderly: epidemiology, etiology and approaches to treatment', *J Urol*, 169 (6): 1999–2007.

Serra, V., von Zglinicki, T., *et al.* (2003). 'Extracellular superoxide dismutase is a major antioxidant in human fibroblasts and slows telomere shortening', *J Biol Chem*, 278 (9): 6824–30.

Seshadri, S., Beiser, A., *et al.* (2002). 'Plasma homocysteine as a risk factor for dementia and Alzheimer's disease', *N Engl J Med*, 346 (7): 476–83.

Shumaker, S. A., Reboussin, B. A., *et al.* (1998). 'The Women's Health Initiative Memory Study (WHIMS): a trial of the effect of estrogen therapy in preventing and slowing the progression of dementia.' *Control Clin Trials*, 19 (6): 604–21.

Shumaker, S. A., Legault, C., *et al.* (2003). 'Estrogen plus progestin and the incidence of dementia and mild cognitive impairment in postmenopausal women: the Women's Health Initiative Memory Study – a randomized controlled trial', *JAMA* 289 (20): 2651–62.

Tinetti, M. E., Speechley, M., *et al.* (1988). 'Risk factors for falls among elderly persons living in the community', *N Engl J Med*, 319 (26): 1701–7.

Trichopoulou, A., and E. Vasilopoulou (2000). 'Mediterranean diet and longevity', *Br J Nutr*, 84 (Suppl. 2): S205–9.

Whooley, M. A., and W. S. Browner (1998). 'Association between depressive symptoms and mortality in older women. Study of Osteoporotic Fractures Research Group', *Arch Intern Med*, 158 (19): 2129-35.

PART THREE

THE AGEING MIND

Psychological Approaches To Human Development

JUTTA HECKHAUSEN

Psychological research can greatly profit from investigating the developmental emergence and change of behavior and experience across the lifespan, because it reveals not only the potential, unfolding, and construction, but also the limits, decline, and undoing, of psychological functions. Therefore, from the earliest interest of psychology in human development, select and visionary psychologists, especially in Europe, have proposed a lifespan-encompassing view of human development (Bühler, 1933; Werner, 1926; Wundt, 1893; see review in Baltes *et al.*, 1998). However, it took several decades for lifespan developmental psychology to become internationally established and accepted as a mainstream field of psychological research. Today, lifespan developmental psychology is institutionalized in graduate programs, textbooks, scientific conferences, journals, and societies.

The upsurge of psychological research in lifespan development since the 1970s started with metatheoretical and methodological propositions that opened up a huge new field for interdisciplinary research (Baltes *et al.*, 1998). Even though more recent developments in lifespan developmental psychology have outgrown the lack in specificity and testability of these initial grand conceptions, it is useful to keep in mind some key principles when studying developmental processes across the lifespan. They provided the hatching and initial thriving context for many productive lines of research, and still provide a unifying framework for otherwise diverse scientific approaches and networks, and will be discussed briefly next.

KEY PROPOSITIONS OF LIFESPAN DEVELOPMENTAL PSYCHOLOGY

Development As Lifelong Interface of Gains and Losses

First, of course, development is conceptualized as a lifelong process, starting at conception and continuing into old age and until death. This implies that lifespan developmental psychology not only encompasses one direction of change, namely growth, but also involves decline and loss. Neither phase of development is exclusively characterized by growth or decline. Instead development is multidirectional throughout the lifespan with a shifting ratio of gains and losses along the age axis. During childhood and adolescence, gains in functioning dominate, although certain capacities (e.g., the light adaptation of the pupils) already begin to decline in adolescence. During later midlife and old age, in contrast, developmental losses increase. This shifting balance between gains and losses across the lifespan is well reflected in lay conceptions about psychological development in adulthood. In a study of normative conceptions about age-related psychological change (Heckhausen *et al.*, 1989), adults at different ages were asked to indicate psychological dimensions showing decline and growth across the adult lifespan (i.e., 20 to 90 years). As shown in Figure 1, gains in psychological functioning were viewed to dominate most of adulthood up until old age. However, with increasing age, more and more losses were expected, which in

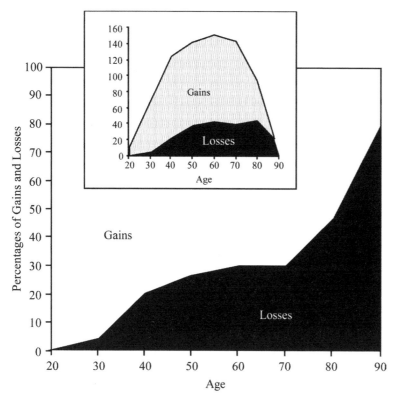

Figure 1. Quantitative Relation of Gains and Losses across the Adult Life Span: Percentages and Absolute Numbers (insert) (adapted from J. Heckhausen, Dixon, & Balte, 1989).

characteristic of lifespan development, namely its selectivity, will be addressed below.

Potential and Limits of Plasticity

A major line of inquiry in lifespan developmental psychology is directed at the nature and limits of change and plasticity (Baltes *et al.*, 1998; Finch, 1996; see review in Heckhausen and Singer, 2001). Behavioral plasticity can refer to variability of lifecourse patterns (*ontogenetic plasticity*) or to the variability of a performance in a specific moment in time (*concurrent plasticity*). Human behavioral plasticity has its roots in the phylogeny of mammals, a biological strata characterized by open behavioral programs (Mayr, 1974). For the most part, human behavior is not regulated by preprogrammed stimulus–response patterns, but entails the potential to adapt to a variety of ecologies and stimulus constellations, and to acquire new behavioral patterns. As to the latter, the capacity to instruct, learn from instruction, and thus create and perpetuate culture is a hallmark of human ontogenetic potential (Tomasello *et al.*, 1993).

Psychological plasticity extends across the lifespan and is based on learning, self-regulation, and the goal striving of individuals to expand existing or regain lost functional capacities. In the domain of intellectual functioning, the phenomenon of plasticity has been studied in terms of developmental reserve capacity at the respective age and domain of functioning (Kliegl and Baltes, 1987). The concept of developmental reserve capacity implies that there are constraints or limits to plasticity, which may have high diagnostic value for the developmental status of the individual (Kliegl and Baltes, 1987). In infancy and childhood, developmental reserve achievements are typically facilitated by social interaction with more able individuals and indicate upper limits of potential performance (Brown, 1982), and they are captured by the concept

advanced old age eventually were perceived to overpower one's growth potential. Thus, during most of the lifespan, gains and losses in biological and psychological functioning co-exist and, what is more, they mutually condition each other (Baltes *et al.*, 1998). Specifically, the process of selective investment has the consequence that gains in one domain lead to simultaneous losses in another domain of functioning. For example, in infants' language learning, focusing on the phonemes of the native language implies not practicing phonemes of other languages. This leads to active speech acquisition in one language at the expense of the vast repertoire of sounds prelanguage infants are able to produce. Similar processes constitute the mutual conditioning of gains and losses in career choice and investment, so that chosen paths are optimized and rejected paths move further and further out of reach. This

of "zone of proximal development" (Vygotsky, 1978). In adulthood and old age, potential and limits of plasticity have been empirically demonstrated in cognitive training research (Baltes *et al.*, 1998).

In the domain of personality and coping, plasticity has been addressed in terms of adaptations to ageing (e.g. Brandtstädter and Rothermund, 2002), resilience to developmental stress (Staudinger *et al.*, 1993), and coping with adverse events in the lifecourse (e.g. Hultsch and Plemons, 1979; Schulz and Rau, 1985). The whole array of these and related phenomena is captured by the concept of developmental regulation, a topic discussed later (p. 185). It is the degree of intra-individual variability and plasticity that sets the limits and thereby the stage for the individual to influence and manage his or her own development. This leads to another major dimension in lifespan psychological research, differences between individuals.

Interindividual Differences in Developmental Change

Interindividual differences in developmental change can pertain to the mean level attained in a given domain of functioning, the rate or slope of change in a given period of the lifespan, or the timing of growth and decline along the age axis. Interindividual differences can be based on many factors of influence, including genetic endowment, gender, social class, ethnicity, specific characteristics of the socialization context, and individual agency and investment (e.g. in a career as a world-class-level performer or expert). A prime example is research in peak performance across the lifespan, which revealed that many supportive conditions have to come together, including a long-term and extremely intense investment during childhood, adolescence, and/or early adulthood (Ericsson *et al.*, 1993).

Development as a Multifactorial System of Influences

Another characteristic of modern psychological theories of development is that they are systemic rather than uni-factorial in their conceptions about relevant influences and causes of development

(Lerner, 1998). Such approaches have outgrown old dichotomies of "nature versus nurture" or "individual versus society." Instead, development is viewed as a product of phylogenetic heritage and universal biological change, genetic endowment, cultural, societal, and social network context, and the individual's own actions and other regulatory efforts. These factors can be grouped into three broad classes of influences: biological, societal, and individual. Action-theoretical approaches to developmental regulation provide a prime example of how modern lifespan developmental research has moved beyond the mere proposition of complex intersystemic influences by specifying the relationships between these grand systems of influence and putting them to the empirical test. Five major models in this field will be discussed in greater detail below.

Systemic and contextualist accounts of human development emphasize the causal role of various systems of influence that are based, for instance, on historical–cultural differences, social strata, and other characteristics of the developmental ecology (Baltes *et al.*, 1998). At any given point in the lifespan the individual's behavior is influenced by these different systems as they interact synchronically as well as diachronically with earlier or even anticipated future experiences and events. These contextual influences can be classified into three broad groups: age-graded influences, history-graded influences, and non-normative influences (Baltes *et al.*, 1998). It is noteworthy that each of these classes of influences is also reflected in older adults' retrospective accounts of their biographies. Thomae and Lehr (1986) report that, among the subjective turning points in biographical narratives of their subjects, about one-third referred to age-normative events, about one-half involved non-normative events (personal experiences unrelated to age structure of the lifecourse or historical events), and the bulk of the remaining turning points related to historical events (e.g., the Second World War).

AGE-NORMATIVE INFLUENCES. Age-normative influences comprise biological and social influences on development that hold a substantial relation to chronological age. Genetic–biological age-gradedness includes processes of maturation, ageing, and age-differential evolutionary selection effects (Finch, 1996). Society-related age-gradedness can be differentiated into objectified social institutions of age stratification (Hagestad, 1990; Riley, 1985), on the one hand, and their psychological complements in age-normative conceptions that are internalized and shared by the individual members of a given society (Heckhausen, 1999), on the other.

In this context, two constructs are most relevant, "developmental tasks" and "critical life events." Developmental tasks (Havighurst, 1952) represent age-specific goals and developmental challenges, which result from biological changes (e.g. in fertility), transitions into new social roles (e.g. from student to worker; see reviews in Clausen, 1986; Riley, 1985), and age-normative expectations about psychological change (e.g. autonomy in value judgments expected in adolescence; see review in Heckhausen, 1999).

The other class of potentially age-graded influences to be mentioned here consists of critical life events (Brim and Ryff, 1980; Dohrenwend and Dohrenwend, 1974; Hultsch and Plemons, 1979; Lowenthal et al., 1977). Critical life events are major changes in an individual's developmental ecology that present a substantial stress to the individual's wellbeing and therefore involve major coping responses (e.g., Brim and Ryff, 1980). Critical life events may instigate life crises that present a danger to developmental regulation, but they also present the opportunity for psychological growth that would otherwise not have occurred (e.g., Olbrich, 1981). Critical life events can be classified according to different components of age normativity (Brim and Ryff, 1980; see also Schulz and Rau, 1985): the correlation with age, the commonness within a population, and the probability of occurrence (Brim and Ryff, 1980). Prototypical age-normative critical life events, such as the first steps in childhood and the transition to retirement, are highly age-determined and happen to almost everybody with a very high probability. At the other end of the continuum are events that are non-normative, such as the loss of a limb or winning a lottery.

NON-NORMATIVE INFLUENCES. Events that can be described as non-age-related, happening to few and occurring with low probability (Brim and Ryff, 1980), are examples of non-normative influences on lifespan development (Baltes et al., 1998). They include positive (e.g. winning the lottery) as well as negative (e.g. being injured in an accident) events (Bandura, 1982). The characteristic of non-normative influences on development is that they cannot be anticipated by the individual, that social models for coping with them are hardly available, and that social support systems are not set up (Hultsch and Plemons, 1979; Schulz and Rau, 1985). Because of these characteristics, non-normative influences are particularly challenging to the individual's potential for developmental plasticity (resilience; Staudinger et al., 1993), and can have particularly extreme effects on the individual's development.

HISTORY-GRADED INFLUENCES. Finally, history-graded influences on lifespan development are associated with historical events or transitions that affect everybody alive at the given point in time. When these influences are differential for individuals at different ages, they are referred to as "cohort effects" (Ryder, 1965). History-graded influences are manifold in their characteristics and causes. They encompass sudden and hardly predictable events such as natural catastrophes, outcomes of more continuous processes such as economic crises, and non-spectacular and gradual social change or technological development (e.g. in medical treatment). History-graded influences in themselves can affect changes in the system of age-graded influences and even in the probability and occurrence of non-normative events (Elder, 1985). Depending on how social change and historical events interact with the social and personality resources an individual brings to bear in the given situation, very different and even contrasting lifecourse outcomes may result (e.g. Caspi and Elder, 1986; Elder and Caspi, 1990). Entering military service, for instance, turned many young men's lifecourses in a favorable direction (e.g. receiving vocational training), although it, of course, led to injury or death for many others. Another example for differential historical effects are the social hardships related to the Great Depression, which ultimately had a positive effect on life satisfaction of middle-class women, but a negative effect on long-range satisfaction for working-class women (Caspi and Elder, 1986).

Individuals as Agents in Their Own Development

Researchers in lifespan developmental psychology soon realized the great potential of individuals as active co-producers of their own development and lifecourse (Brandtstädter and Lerner, 1999). From an action-theoretical perspective, the lifecourse is an action field that provides an age-graded structure of opportunities and constraints to influence one's course of development (Brandtstädter, 1998; Heckhausen, 1999). On the most general level, this structure of opportunities affords a gradual shift in the allocation of resources from striving for developmental growth to striving for maintaining functioning and avoiding decline (Baltes *et al.*, 1998). Empirical research about adults' developmental goals has indicated that across adulthood more and more goals are directed towards avoiding loss and fewer and fewer goals aim at maximizing growth (Heckhausen, 1997).

AGE-GRADED OPPORTUNITIES CALL FOR AGE-GRADED GOAL ENGAGEMENT. At a more differentiated level, opportunities for important developmental goals (e.g. graduating from high

school, finding a partner, having a child) also exhibit an age-graded structure, which prescribes certain age spans as windows of opportunity to reach the goals. Figure 2 displays hypothetical trajectories of waxing and waning opportunities for a set of common developmental goals such as graduating from school, getting married, establishing a career, retiring. In order to achieve successful development, the individual should select developmental goals on-time, when the opportunities are at their peak, and disengage from these goals when opportunities wane away below a certain minimum level. Therefore, individual agents need to take into account shifts in relevant opportunities when deciding which developmental goal to invest in at a given time. They can take an active role in their development by seizing opportunities as they evolve across the lifespan and engage with and invest in the relevant on-time developmental goal.

MODELS OF DEVELOPMENTAL REGULA-TION. In recent years, several groups of researchers have proposed models and conducted empirical research addressing the psychological processes and strategies involved in individuals' regulation of development. Specifically, these models are the Baltes and Baltes model of selection, optimization, and compensation (Baltes *et al.*, 1998), Carver and Scheier's self-regulation model (Carver and Scheier,

Figure 2. Hypothetical age-related trajectories of opportunities for attaining developmental goals (adopted from Heckhausen, 2000).

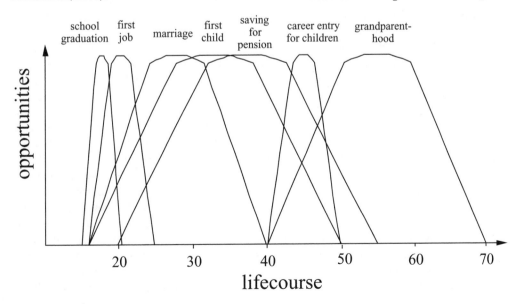

1998), the lifespan theory of control with its model of developmental optimization in primary and secondary control (Heckhausen, 1999; Heckhausen and Schulz, 1995; Schulz and Heckhausen, 1996), Brandtstädter's dual-process model of development (Brandtstädter, 1998; Brandtstädter and Rothermund, 2002), and Lindenberg's social production function theory (Lindenberg, 1996; Steverink *et al.*, 1998).

All these models address behavior and cognition directed at long term goals that encompass significant segments of the lifespan and thus have developmental implications. All these models in one way or another center around two basic processes in developmental regulation, the selective investment in attaining some specific chosen goals over other goals and the efforts to compensate for goal-discrepancy, loss, and decline.

Selection, optimization, and compensation (Baltes and Baltes). The most general and least process-specific of these models is the model of selection, optimization, and compensation (SOC model), which assumes the three components (S, O, and C) of successful development to be operating throughout life and in all domains of functioning (Baltes *et al.*, 1998). Essentially, the SOC model proposes that successful development requires that the individual selects specific domains of functioning for investing resources, invests effort in optimizing their functioning in those domains, and resorts to compensatory means when encountering function loss in the respective domain. Empirical evidence shows that the use of selection, optimization, and compensation predicts psychological wellbeing (Freund and Baltes, 1998) and subjective career success (Wiese *et al.*, 2002). However, the SOC model does not address the specific motivational and executive functions that lead to the selection of domains or goals, govern the optimization of functioning in the selected domains, or activate compensatory strategies when encountering loss. The three component processes are assumed to operate in parallel, so that neither a higher-level executive nor lower-level specific processes are conceptualized in this model, thus restricting its usefulness for investigating processes involved in mastering developmental challenges. It is noteworthy that the SOC model does not commit to a criterion of successful development that is accessible to common standards of functioning, because it defines successful development "as the maximization and attainment of positive (desired) outcomes and the minimization and avoidance of negative (undesired) outcomes" (Freund and Baltes, 1998: 531). What is desired or undesired is a function of the individual's subjective preferences.

Self-regulation (Carver and Scheier). At the other end of the continuum in terms of specificity of processes is Carver and Scheier's self-regulation model (Carver and Scheier, 1998). Based on principles of cybernetics, this model specifies an elaborate system of feedback processes that play a role in the regulation of goal-related behavior. Carver and Scheier account for a rich arsenal of processes and regulatory feedback loops that propel the individual's behavior either closer to or away from goals. Their self-regulation model has been criticized as mechanistic (Locke and Latham, 1990) and lacking a sense of human self-determination (Deci and Ryan, 1991), and when reading their elaborate descriptions of feedback processes, one cannot help but envision the individual as a pawn in the complex interface of external and internal forces that push the individual towards or away from certain behaviors and thoughts. However, Carver and Scheier's selective focus on feedback processes provides important insights into how goal-directed behavior is regulated once the individual has chosen a goal. Which goal is selected and why it is selected constitutes a different set of questions that the self-regulation model does not claim to answer (Carver and Scheier, 1998).

Lifespan theory of control (Heckhausen and Schulz). The lifespan theory of control (Heckhausen and Schulz, 1995; Schulz and Heckhausen, 1996) and its model of developmental regulation, the optimization in primary and secondary control model (Heckhausen, 1999), proposes that human motivation is guided by a fundamental and universal striving for primary control. Primary control striving is directed at producing effects in the environment that are contingent on one's own behavior. Secondary control, in contrast, addresses the internal world of the individual and serves to protect and expand motivational resources that are needed for primary control. The ultimate criterion for adaptive development is thus the overall potential for primary control attained across the lifespan. When trying to regulate their own development, individuals get engaged with and disengage from developmental goals (e.g. to start a career, have a child, move to a retirement community), ideally in synchrony with waxing and waning opportunities for these goals. Individuals differ, however, with regard to the regulatory capacity in matching their goal selections to the opportunities provided in their respective developmental ecologies. Moreover, individuals vary in their ability to orchestrate their control strategies of primary control striving and secondary control support for volitional commitment, or alternatively, in the case of lacking opportunities, in their disengagement and motivation-protective secondary control strategies. These individual differences in regulatory capacity of control strategies are good predictors of developmental outcomes, mental health, and affective wellbeing (Heckhausen *et al.*, 2001; Wrosch and Heckhausen, 1999; Wrosch *et al.*, 2002). These comprise important motivational resources for primary control striving across the lifespan. The empirical research on the lifespan theory of control utilizes both self-report measures of conscious regulatory processes and experimental methods to assess non-conscious biases in information processing. However, the model does not really address these two components of motivational functioning separately.

Dual-process model (Brandtstädter). Brandtstädter's dual-process model of coping proposes two types of mechanism by which the person can preserve self-consistency in the face of adversity, ageing-related decline, and loss. These are assimilation and accommodation (Brandtstädter, 1998; Brandtstädter and Rothermund, 2002). The construct of assimilation refers to active attempts "to change an unsatisfying situation so that it becomes congruent or compatible with desired self-definitions or identity goals" (Brandtstädter, 1998). Thus, assimilation is similar to primary control in the sense that it refers to active efforts to change the situation. However, unlike primary control, the criterion for successful assimilation is not maximizing control potential, but consistent self-definitions and identity goals. In accommodative modes of coping, by contrast, "the individual eliminates aversive discrepancies by adjusting personal goals and preferences" (Brandtstädter, 1998). This construct is akin to secondary control, except that it is restricted to changes in goals, and does not include other pro-

cesses involved in protecting motivational resources. This is, of course, consistent with the overall model being directed at maintaining consistency of self-definitions and enriching identity – very different from the ultimate function of maximizing primary control behavior that guides regulatory behavior according to the lifespan theory of control. Moreover, the processes involved in accommodation are typically non-conscious or as Brandtstädter calls it "subpersonal." Brandtstädter's argument for this is that changes in goal priorities cannot be willed, but can only come about by implicit processes (Brandtstädter, 1998).

Social production function theory (Lindenberg). Lindenberg's social production function theory addresses individuals' sequential commitment to goal pursuits that reflect two basic needs, physical wellbeing and social wellbeing (Lindenberg, 1996; Steverink *et al.*, 1998). These needs can be satisfied by pursuing five instrumental goals: stimulation, comfort, status, behavioral confirmation, affection. The key proposition of social production function theory is that people choose and substitute instrumental goals so as to optimize the production of their wellbeing, subject to constraints in available means of production. As individuals get closer to or further away from satisfying their need in a given need domain or attaining their goal in a given goal domain, their commitment to invest in this domain increases or decreases. For example, when having accomplished a lot in attaining social status, any further gain in status becomes less significant. Thus goal engagement is likely to shift to another domain, for instance to affection. Moreover, within a given domain, subgoals can substitute each other as long as they serve the same higher-level goal or need. For example, when seeking intimacy, one particular person might prove out of reach, but another person can take their place. Thus, within goal domains, goals are substitutable, especially when the production function in this domain is deficient. Once the production function becomes plentiful, the system may shift to another domain that is in need of investment. Lindenberg's model can account for shifts in goals not only in terms of when disengagement occurs but also which goal is chosen instead of the abandoned one, thus furnishing a model of sequential goal engagement. A limitation of the model is that it is constrained to physical and social needs, thus ignoring the domain of control and mastery. Moreover, processes of reorientation, whether conscious or unconscious, are not themselves addressed in this theory.

In sum, several models of developmental regulation contribute unique insights to the study of lifespan development. The next step in this area of research is to try and integrate these models, incorporating their respective strengths and avoiding their limitations.

FURTHER READING

Baltes, P. B., Staudinger, U. M., and U. Lindenberger (1999). "Lifespan psychology: theory and application to intellectual functioning," *Annual Review of Psychology*, 50: 471–507.

Heckhausen, J. (2003). "The future of life-span developmental psychology: perspectives from control theory." In U. M. Staudinger and U. Lindenberger, eds., *Understanding human development: lifespan psychology in exchange with other disciplines*. Dordrecht, Netherlands: Kluwer, pp. 383–400.

REFERENCES

Baltes, P. B., Lindenberger, U., and U. M. Staudinger (1998). "Life-span theory in developmental psychology." In R. M. Lerner, ed., *Handbook of child psychology*, Vol. I: *Theoretical models of human development*, 5th edn. New York: Wiley, pp. 1029–143.

Bandura, A. (1982). "The psychology of chance encounters and life paths," *American Psychologist*, 37: 747–55.

Brandtstädter, J. (1998). "Action perspectives on human development." In R. M. Lerner, ed, *Handbook of child psychology*, Vol. I: *Theoretical models of human development*, 5th edn. New York: Wiley, pp. 807–63.

Brandtstädter, J., and R. Lerner, eds. (1999). *Action and self-development: theory and research through the life-span*. London: Sage Publications.

Brandtstädter, J., and K. Rothermund (2002). "The life-course dynamics of goal pursuit and goal adjustment: a two-process framework," *Psychological Review*, 22: 117–50.

Brim, O. G., Jr., and C. D. Ryff (1980). "On the properties of life events." In P. B. Baltes and O. G. Brim, Jr., eds., *Life-span development and behavior*, Vol. III. New York: Academic Press, pp. 367–88.

Brown, A. (1982). "Learning and development: the problem of compatibility, access, and induction," *Human Development*, 25: 89–115.

Bühler, C. (1933). *Der menschliche Lebenslauf als psychologisches Problem*. Göttingen: Hogrefe.

Carver, C. C., and M. Scheier (1998). *On the self-regulation of behavior*. New York: Cambridge University Press.

Caspi, A., and G. H. Elder (1986). "Life satisfaction in old age: linking social psychology and history," *Psychology and Aging*, 1: 18–26.

Clausen, J. A. (1986). *The life course: a sociological perspective*. Englewood Cliffs, N.J.: Prentice-Hall.

Deci, E. L., and R. M. Ryan (1991). *Intrinsic motivation and self-determination in human behavior*. New York: Plenum Press.

Dohrenwend, B. S., and B. P. Dohrenwend (1974). *Stressful life events: their nature and effects*. New York: Wiley.

Elder, G. H., Jr. (1985). *Life course dynamics: trajectories and transitions, 1968–1980*. Ithaca, N.Y.: Cornell University Press.

Elder, G. H., Jr., and A. Caspi (1990). Studying lives in a changing society: sociological and personological explorations. In A. Rabin, R. Zucker, R. Emmons, and S. Frank, eds., *Studying persons and lives*. New York: Springer, pp. 201–47.

Ericsson, K. A., Krampe, R. T., and C. Tesch-Römer (1993). "The role of deliberate practice in the acquisition of expert performance," *Psychology Review*, 100 (3): 363–406.

Finch, C. E. (1996). "Biological bases for plasticity during aging of individual life histories." In D. Magnusson, ed., *The life-span development of individuals: behavioral, neurobiological and psychosocial perspective*. Cambridge: Cambridge University Press, pp. 488–511.

Freund, A. M., and P. B. Baltes (1998). "Selection, optimization, and compensation as strategies of life management: correlations with subjective indicators of successful aging," *Psychology and Aging*, 13: 531–43.

Hagestad, G. O. (1990). "Social perspectives on the life course." In R. Binstock and L. George, eds., *Handbook of aging and the social sciences*, 3rd edn. New York: Academic Press, pp. 151–68.

Havighurst, R. J. (1952). *Developmental tasks and education*. New York: McKay.

Heckhausen, J. (1997). "Developmental regulation across adulthood: primary and secondary control of age-related challenges," *Developmental Psychology*, 33: 176–87.

(1999). *Developmental regulation in adulthood: age-normative and sociostructural constraints as adaptive challenges*. New York: Cambridge University Press.

(2000). "Developmental regulation across the life span: an action-phase model of engagement and disengagement with developmental goals." In J. Heckhausen, ed., *Motivational psychology of human development. Developing motivation and motivating development*. Oxford: Elsevier, pp. 213–31.

Heckhausen, J., and R. Schulz (1995). "A life-span theory of control," *Psychological Review*, 102: 284–304.

(1999). "Biological and societal canalizations and individuals' developmental goals." In J. Brandtstädter and

R. Lerner, eds., *Action and self-development: theory and research through the life-span*. London: Sage Publications, pp. 67–103.

Heckhausen, J., and T. Singer (2001). "Plasticity in human behavior across the lifespan." In N. J. Smelser and P. B. Baltes, eds.-in-chief, *International Encyclopedia of the Social and Behavioral Sciences*, Vol. XVII. Oxford: Elsevier Science, pp. 11497–501.

Heckhausen, J., Dixon, R. A., and P. B. Baltes (1989). "Gains and losses in development throughout adulthood as perceived by different adult age groups," *Developmental Psychology*, 25: 109–21.

Heckhausen, J., Wrosch, C., and W. Fleeson (2001). "Developmental regulation before and after a developmental deadline: the sample case of 'biological clock' for child-bearing," *Psychology and Aging*, 16: 400–13.

Hultsch, D. F., and J. K. Plemons (1979). "Life events and life-span development." In P. B. Baltes and O. G. Brim, Jr., eds., *Life-span development and behavior*, Vol. II. New York: Academic Press, pp. 1–37.

Kliegl, R., and P. B. Baltes (1987). "Theory-guided analysis of mechanisms of development and aging through testing-the-limits and research on expertise." In C. Schooler and K. W. Schaie, eds., *Cognitive functioning and social structure over the life course*. Norwood, N.J.: Ablex, pp. 95–119.

Lerner, R. M. (1998). "Theories of human development: contemporary perspectives." In R. M. Lerner, ed., *Handbook of child psychology*, Vol. I: *Theoretical models of human development*. New York: Wiley, pp. 1–24.

Lindenberg, S. M. (1996). "Continuities in the theory of social production functions." In S. M. Lindenberg and H. B. G. Ganzeboom, eds., *Verklarende sociologie: opstellen voor Reinhard Wippler [Explanatory sociology: essays for Reinhard Wippler]*. Amsterdam: Thesis Publishers, pp. 169–84.

Locke, E. A., and G. P. Latham (1990). *A theory of goal setting and task performance*. Englewood Cliffs, N.J.: Prentice-Hall.

Lowenthal, M. F., Thurnher, M., and D. Chiriboga (1977). *Four stages of life. A comparative study of women and men facing transition*, 3rd edn. San Francisco, Calif.: Jossey-Bass.

Mayr, E. (1974). "Behavior programs and evolutionary strategies," *American Scientist*, 62: 650–9.

Riley, M. W. (1985). "Age strata in social systems." In R. H. Binstock and E. Shanas, eds., *Handbook of aging and the social sciences*, 2nd edn. New York: Van Nostrand Reinhold, pp. 369–411.

Ryder, N. B. (1965). "The cohort as a concept in the study of social change," *American Sociological Review*, 30: 843–61.

Schulz, R., and J. Heckhausen (1996). "A life-span model of successful aging," *American Psychologist*, 51: 702–14.

Schulz, R., and M. T. Rau (1985). "Social support through the life course." In S. Cohen and L. Syme, eds., *Social support and health*. New York: Academic Press, pp. 129–49.

Staudinger, U. M., Marsiske, M., and P. B. Baltes (1993). "Resilience and levels of reserve capacity in later adulthood: perspectives from life-span theory," *Development and Psychopathology*, 5: 541–66.

Steverink, N., Lindenberg, S., and J. Ormel (1998). "Towards understanding successful ageing: patterned change in resources and goals," *Ageing and Society*, 18: 441–67.

Thomae, H., and U. Lehr (1986). "Stages, crises, conflicts, and life-span development." In A. B. Sørensen, F. E. Weinert, and L. R. Sherrod, eds., *Human development and the life course: multidisciplinary perspectives*. Hillsdale, N.J.: Erlbaum, pp. 343–75.

Tomasello, M., Kruger, A. C., and H. H. Ratner (1993). "Cultural learning," *Behavioral and Brain Sciences*, 16: 495–552.

Vygotsky, L. S. (1978). *Mind in society*. Cambridge, Mass.: Harvard University Press.

Werner, H. (1926). *Einführung in die Entwicklungspsychologie*. Leipzig: Barth.

Wiese, B. S., Freund, A. M., and P. B. Baltes (2002). "Subjective career success and emotional well-being: longitudinal predictive power of selection, optimization and compensation," *Journal of Vocational Behavior*, 60: 321–35.

Wrosch, C., and J. Heckhausen (1999). "Control processes before and after passing a developmental deadline: activation and deactivation of intimate relationship goals," *Journal of Personality and Social Psychology*, 77: 415–27.

Wrosch, C., Schulz, R., and J. Heckhausen (2002). "Health stresses and depressive symptomatology in the elderly: the importance of health engagement control strategies," *Health Psychology*, 21: 340–8.

Wundt, W. (1893). *Grundzüge der physiologischen Psychologie*. Leipzig: Engelmann.

Cognitive Changes Across the Lifespan

PAT RABBITT

Cognitive gerontology is the attempt to understand how biological changes, particularly in the brain and central nervous system, alter mental abilities and behaviour in old age. The basic questions are: when changes in mental abilities first appear, how rapidly they then proceed, whether all mental abilities change at the same rate or some change earlier and more markedly than others, and whether all individuals experience the same, or different, rates and patterns of change. As a population ages, so mental and physical differences between its most and least able members markedly increase. The main reason for this is that individuals' trajectories of change are determined by complex interactions between a great variety of factors including genetic inheritance, uterine and infant environments, levels of socioeconomic advantage and lifestyle, exposure to diseases, toxicity and stress, and access to health education and medical aid. Because these factors affect individuals to different extents, their calendar ages are uninformative indices of the changes they have experienced. A main task for cognitive gerontologists is to understand the reasons for this diversity of rates of ageing so as to learn how more of us can avoid factors that lead to accelerated decline and maintain competence and wellbeing to the ends of our lives.

To study human ageing we can carry out cross-sectional studies in which people are compared against others of different ages, longitudinal studies in which people are repeatedly tested and compared against themselves at different ages, or use a combination of these methodologies in which groups of people of different ages are compared both with each other and themselves at different times in their lives. The advantages and limitations of these methodologies tell us much about the nature of the processes we hope to study. They are all prone to participant self-selection because people who volunteer to take part in laboratory investigations are seldom representative members of their generations and tend to be much more healthy, socioeconomically advantaged, intellectually able, well-educated, confident and highly motivated than most of their peers. Cross-sectional comparisons have the additional problem that groups of people of different ages differ in many important ways other than their birthdays, such as the quality of their childhood and lifetime nutrition, exposure to industrial toxicity and other health hazards, access to medical care and lifetime general health and also their average levels of education, the work and lifestyles that they have experienced, the societies in which they grew up and their experiences of dramatically life-altering historical events. When these and other factors are considered separately they all strikingly affect both individuals' levels of performance at any age and also the rate at which their performance changes as they grow older. For these reasons, investigators usually decide that the best that they can do is to document their volunteers as thoroughly as possible and use retrospective statistical analyses to identify and take into consideration the effects of factors that obscure the effects of differences in calendar age. Longitudinal comparisons have the advantage that changes in individuals of the same generational cohort and level of socioeconomic advantage can be monitored as they age. However, the problem that volunteers are unrepresentative because they are self-selected is compounded by selective dropout because frail, older and least able volunteers withdraw early leaving elite subgroups of atypically healthy, able and highly motivated individuals. Paradoxically, this methodological disadvantage focuses attention on the basic issue in human ageing. The discovery that, during longitudinal studies, individuals' rates of decline in mental abilities accelerate for up to eight years before they die or withdraw because of frailty and worsening health, emphasizes that trajectories of change are driven as powerfully by the increased incidence of pathologies in later life as by whatever other factors contribute to the 'normal' or 'usual' processes of biological change that affect us all.

This means that, while we can accurately and confidently measure the changes that occur during our lifespans, and determine what factors most strongly accelerate or retard the overall rate of change, we are much less certain whether all changes are caused by the same or different factors, whether different factors cause different kinds, as well as amounts, of change, and so also whether individuals with different life-histories experience different patterns, as well as amounts, of change. Given these uncertainties the general picture emerging from current data is that as individuals grow older, or less well and less able, their mental performance becomes increasingly more variable. This variability increases not only from moment to moment during brief tasks but also in terms of average levels of performance from day to day or over periods of weeks and months. This increase in variability not only is a salient feature of changes that occur in all kinds of mental performance but also affects the accuracy with which we can attribute differences in individuals' trajectories of change to the effects of particular factors: because older people vary more with respect to themselves from occasion to occasion, it necessarily follows that they will also vary more with respect to each other when compared on any particular occasion. As we have seen, differences in variability between individuals also reflect the fact that they change at very different rates as they grow older. Current analyses have not yet come to terms with the need to separate the effects of increases in variability within individuals from increases in variability between individuals due to differences in underlying rates of change.

The divergences in individual trajectories of ageing are a basic topic of research for gerontologists. They indicate that 'calendar age' tells us nothing about the biological processes that cause changes over time and which are brought about, slowed and speeded by a great variety of different factors. Some processes of biological change, such as telemerization, seem to occur in all individuals and not to be linked to any specific pathology. In contrast, the rates of other biological changes are related to factors that differ markedly between individuals, such as adequacy of uterine environment and so of birthweight, nutrition and thriving in infancy, lifetime exposure to health hazards and especially to the cumulative burden of pathologies experienced throughout the lifespan. All of these factors, in turn, are influenced by demographic variables such as geographical and social environments and levels of socioeconomic advantage. For instance, in a large sample of residents of Manchester and Newcastle upon Tyne, individual differences in longevity and mortality and so also in rates of cognitive change have been more strongly influenced by differences in socioeconomic advantage than by any other factor. Nevertheless, although a distinction between individuals' 'calendar ages' and their 'biological ages' is a helpful reminder that trajectories of ageing are determined by complex interactions between biological systems and the total environments they inhabit, this is only the beginning of the story. Attempts to derive indices of 'biological age' from complex combinations of markers of general health and of physiological change have been unsuccessful because we still know little about the nature of, and the complex interactions between, the biological factors that determine rates of changes. The concept of biological age remains useful only in so far as it forces us to recognize that it is always more interesting to explore factors that contribute to age-related variability between individuals than simply to study declines in average performance.

A different distinction is that between 'normal' or 'usual' and 'pathological' ageing. There is ample evidence that pathologies accelerate the rate of cognitive decline in later life. Very many studies have shown that older people who suffer from particular pathologies such as diabetes or cardiovascular problems perform more poorly than age-matched healthy controls. Older individuals' levels of cognitive performance vary inversely with the number of different pathologies, including minor pathologies, from which they suffer. Cognitive decline accelerates as death approaches, and significant losses in performance are apparent up to 11 years before death from a variety of different pathologies. In contrast, within samples of people who are selected for exceptionally high levels of general health, differences in age have little or no measurable effect on cognitive performance. However, the distinction between 'normal' and 'pathological' changes remains unhelpful in practice because the nature of allegedly inevitable 'normal' changes is as yet poorly understood, because it is by no means clear how distinct they may be from some changes that are also associated with pathologies, and because strong interactions between putatively 'normal' and 'pathological' processes undoubtedly occur. At present, it seems more useful to regard the progress of ageing in an individual in terms of the entire range of changes that she has, so far, experienced, whatever their individual causes. This 'holistic' definition has the obvious disadvantage of vagueness but the compensating advantage of allowing us to consider the effects, on rate of change over time, of any number and any combination of the manifold factors that are known, individually, to affect our biological and intellectual integrity. It also provides a useful reminder that biological changes are not the sole determinants of cognitive status in later life and that models for cognitive ageing are inadequate unless they also include demographic, social, and lifestyle factors. For example, prolonged education, lengthy marriage to an intelligent spouse, complexity of workplace environment, higher income, and personality factors have all been shown to affect maintenance of cognitive functioning in old age in addition to, and independent of, their effects on health or general biological wellbeing (e.g. Arbuckle *et al.*, 1986; Hayslip, 1988; Schaie, 1990). Similarly, individuals' cognitive status is known to decline with increases in the levels of depression, or even of mild unhappiness, that they suffer, and with the levels of stress imposed on them by life events that they cannot control.

Many problems can be avoided by investigating one variable at a time and statistically controlling for as many others as possible, but the issues of functional causality remain formidably complex. An illustration is the interdependence between changes in the sense organs and in mental abilities. Among the most obvious effects of age are losses in the efficiency of all our sense organs, including touch, taste, smell, and vestibular perception of balance, but perhaps most inconveniently of vision and hearing. Losses of visual acuity are compounded by increasing narrowing of the visual field, by some degradation of colour vision, and by some loss of acuity of movement perception, among other changes. Losses of hearing are earliest and most marked in frequencies above 2,500 Hz, but also extend below this point to impair speech perception. In fact, since correlations between loss of hearing at high frequencies and calendar age are as high as .8, high-frequency deafness is, possibly, the best available marker of years of survival. These sensory losses are partly due to peripheral factors such as increasing opacity of the corneas and the aqueous and vitreous humours in our eyes, deposition of yellow pigment over the fovea, increasing rigidity of our lenses causing difficulties with focusing, and damage to the hair cells in the cochleae of our ears due to the cumulative effects of noise over our lifetimes. Although these particular changes are causally unrelated to changes in our brains and central nervous systems, they nevertheless affect our mental efficiency because they degrade the information that our brains need to interpret the world and so oblige us to make more effort to recognize complex inputs such as spoken and written language. This added cost on processing capacity reduces the speed and accuracy with which we can interpret, store in memory, and make correct inferences from what we see and hear (Rabbitt, 1968, 1991; Dickenson and Rabbitt, 1991). Further, the efficiency of our eyes and ears is also degraded by losses of receptor cells and neurons in our auditory and visual pathways and in the representation areas of our brains. Consequently, differences in individuals' auditory and visual acuity are also good markers for central losses, and predict much of that particular proportion of the variance in general intelligence and memory between them that is associated with differences in their ages (Lindenberger and Baltes, 1994). For similar reasons, in older populations, individual differences in balance and gait are not only affected by arthritis and other problems of the muscles and joints but also by changes in the brain and central nervous system and, to this extent, also serve as effective markers for age-related differences in mental competence. Thus, changes in our sense organs and bodies not only bring about secondary 'knock-on' effects in our mental competence but are also good markers for changes in our brains and central nervous systems (CNSs) that directly affect our general mental efficiency.

An obvious next question is whether we can discover which particular mental tests are the most sensitive indices of changes in our brains and CNSs. This also addresses the interesting questions of whether all our mental abilities decline at the same rate or, if not, which of our mental abilities are first, and most severely, affected by age, and whether different kinds of tests can reveal different patterns of changes in abilities from which we can infer patterns of neurophysiological changes in ageing brains. An exhaustive and brilliant analysis of studies published up to the mid 1980s by Cerella (1985) and further studies by Salthouse (1985, 1991) suggest that, on nearly all cognitive tasks, most of the variance in performance between individuals that is associated with differences in their ages can be accounted for by differences in the speed with which they can make simple decisions. These findings suggest a 'global' model for age-related changes in mental abilities that implies that all our cognitive skills decline at similar rates because they all strongly depend on the maximum speed with which we can process information, and this markedly declines in old age. It is also the case that most of the variance in performance between individuals on most tasks can be correlated with by differences in their performance in pencil-and-paper intelligence tests, so that the 'general fluid mental ability' (gf) that such tests are held to measure can also be taken as a particularly sensitive index of the overall progress of mental ageing (Deary, 2000). It then becomes an interesting question when these 'master' indices of cognitive ageing, gf and information processing speed, first begin to decline and how swiftly they change thereafter. Declines in tasks that strongly depend on speed of performance, such as video games, and in scores on intelligence tests are detectable by the age of 30 and thereafter very gradually accelerate. However, this apparently grim prospect is mitigated by considering details of the

kinds of statistics on which such conclusions are based.

This can be illustrated by the performance of 2,190 residents of Greater Manchester, aged between 40 and 92 years, on the Alice Heim (1970) AH4-1 intelligence test. For successive decades samples from 40 through 92, average scores were 49, 36, 33, 29, 23 and 20 points. This overall decline of about 41 per cent seems dire, especially in view of the fact that it is less than the real value for the population at large because, naturally, only the most exceptional and elite members of the oldest groups volunteered themselves for assessment. However, a different way to evaluate these differences is to consider that the total variance in performance between individuals can be attributed to a great variety of factors including genetics, education, lifestyle and differences in health. Differences in performance that are associated with differences in calendar ages are most meaningful if considered in relation to this total variance. The percentages of variance between individuals, for example in AH4-1 intelligence test scores, that is associated with their ages are given by the square of the correlation between individuals' calendar ages and their AH4-1 scores. For the sample described above, this correlation was only $r = .366$, for which the square gives approximately 13.4. So we can conclude that, if we consider the total variance in intelligence test scores between individuals as 100%, only 13.4% of this can be attributed to differences in their ages between 40 and 92 years. These estimates are typical for scores on all of a very large number of different mental tasks that this group and other large groups of individuals have undertaken. The point is that while differences in performance between people of any age are indeed substantial, compared to other factors differences in age contribute surprisingly little to differences between people.

To interpret what these differences mean in terms of the success with which people manage their everyday lives it is important to bear in mind that the kinds of achievements that most of us greatly respect, such as outstanding performance in graphic arts, music, literature, painting, the management of people and comprehension of very complex issues in science, politics or business, do not necessarily depend on speed of decision so much as on the possession and appropriate use of very large bodies of relevant information and of complex problem-solving skills. Both the information and the skills take many years to acquire. Even on simple laboratory tasks, slowing of decision speed, and of the ability to solve novel problems rapidly contrasts with stability, and even with increased mastery of acquired information. For example, peoples' vocabularies can continue to increase well into and beyond their 70s. This distinction between losses of speed and problem-solving ability and retention of acquired data and skills has been characterized by Horn and his associates (Horn, 1982, 1987; Horn *et al.*, 1981) as a contrast between 'fluid' and 'crystallised' intelligence. A metaphor for this might be the difference between the 'benchmark' power of a computer, defined in terms of the maximum speed and capacity of its processor and the amount of memory immediately available to it, the amount of data that it can permanently store on its hard disk, and the economy and efficiency of the programs that it has been 'taught'. Powerful and economical stored programs can allow even relatively slow computers to solve very complex problems efficiently. The passage of time can bring benefits as well as costs.

The contrast between stability of performance on tests of crystallized intelligence, such as vocabulary tests, and declines in performance on tests of fluid mental abilities, such as 'tests of fluid general intelligence' (gf) offers a methodology for checking that the groups of older people that we now study were, when they were young, similar in mental ability to the young adults against whom we may compare them. When people are young, their scores on vocabulary tests are also good proxy measures for their scores on tests of gf. As they grow older this strong correlation declines because their intelligence test scores (gf) steadily fall but their vocabulary scores do not change. Thus an older person's current vocabulary test score remains a good index of her youthful intelligence test score. Consequently, we can safely assume that if a group of elderly people are matched to a group of younger people on their current vocabulary test scores, the older have, since they themselves were young, declined from very similar levels of gf. Pending availability of time machines that allow us to go back and assess our older volunteers when they were young, matching on vocabulary test scores is the best way to ensure comparability of our older and younger groups. The fact that elderly individuals' vocabulary test scores are good proxies for their youthful scores on tests of fluid intelligence also means that we can compare their current, empirically measured, scores against their youthful estimated scores, on tests of gf. This gives us a way to estimate the declines in gf that individuals have suffered as they have grown old and allows us to ask interesting questions, such as whether people of high and low levels of general intelligence decline at the same rate. The answer seems to be that there is a natural justice in the sense that individuals of high, medium and low mental ability show closely similar losses in intelligence test scores over time. There is, however, less pleasure in the inevitable corollary that while a loss of 10 score points may be hardly noticeable to an individual who originally had a score of 150, it may severely disable someone who had a young adult score of 70.

In this context, it is also important to bear in mind that practice greatly reduces age differences. This is true even on simple laboratory tests of the speed with which people can make elementary decisions, such as which of a set of lights has come on. This does not mean that age can abolish differences in information processing speed since, if all individuals are practised to the point at which they can no longer improve, the young will continue to respond much faster than the old. Moreover, because age slows improvement with practice, the older people are the longer they will have to practice to achieve the same gain as their juniors. Nevertheless, on nearly all tasks, the benefits that older people can attain by practice are much greater, in both absolute and relative terms, than the losses that their increasing ages have brought about. Highly practised older people can be markedly more capable than unpractised younger people, and the advantages gained by practice can persist, without intervening training, over many years.

Given the logical and methodological difficulties of making quantitative behavioural comparisons, it might seem that the best way to learn about mental ageing would be simply to ask people what changes they have noticed as they have grown older. In principle this is a good idea because people are often accurate and insightful monitors of their own abilities but, in practice, there are logical problems. A Canadian national survey of problems faced by older people found that complaints of losses of memory efficiency came second only to complaints of arthritis. However, in striking contrast, when people are given questionnaires that probe how often they have experienced particular, specified, kinds of memory failures and cognitive lapses, elderly people often report no more, or even fewer, problems than young adults. This is because we have no way to judge the levels of our own abilities except by comparing ourselves to others or by evaluating how well we cope with the particular demands that our lives make of us. As people grow old so their environments also change and may become increasingly lenient. They no longer can evaluate their performance at difficult workplace tasks or against able young colleagues. Thus, although their abilities have objectively declined they can quite realistically believe that they are seldom inconvenienced by cognitive lapses. A similar issue is that because their lifestyles may have changed even more radically than their abilities, older people begin to experience different kinds of lapses that are not described on questionnaires based on the lifestyles of the young.

Older peoples' self-reports of their own states of health also require similar reinterpretation. When asked to rate their current states of health on a scale from 'Good' to 'Poor', people aged over 80 who, objectively, are being treated for several different medical conditions often give as favourable reports as healthy young adults. This is not because they are confused or unaware of their condition but because their context of comparison is, inevitably, against their own age group who may indeed, on average, be much worse off. If asked to compare their health against that of younger people, or against their own state 5 or 10 years previously, older people then give realistic and accurate answers.

Perhaps the main goal of cognitive gerontology is to discover tasks on which age effects appear especially early, or are especially marked. This would allow us to detect whether age affects some mental abilities earlier than others. The discovery of such patterned, or local, age deficits would be of practical benefit in predicting the particular situations which older adults would find most inconvenient and in which they would need any help that good design, engineering or the development of better systems can offer them. Equally importantly, it would allow theoretical advances, linking neurophysiological to

behavioural changes by allowing early changes in mental abilities to be related to correspondingly early or more severe age-related changes in particular brain areas. The problem of deciding whether ageing has general and equal effects on all mental abilities or patterned effects, causing some to decline earlier than others, has been the main preoccupation of cognitive gerontology since the 1980s. The difficulty of resolving the issue partly stems from a problem with the limitations of the measurements that we can make to compare peoples' performance on mental tests of any kind. In behavioural tasks the main, and usually the only, quantifiable measurements we can make are the speed with which people can do things and how many errors they make while doing them. These two measurements are usually related because the faster people try to perform, the more errors they are likely to make. Consequently, most functional models for cognitive processes against changes are derived solely from measures of speed and accuracy of task performance. So we might hope to conclude that if older people perform disproportionately more slowly or make disproportionately more errors on some kinds of tasks than on others the particular brain areas, or brain functions, that support these particular demands are especially sensitive to the ageing process. In practice it has proved very difficult to show that old age affects performance on some tasks disproportionately more than on others. The key to the difficulty is contained in the concept of 'disproportionate' change. Figure 1 shows a hypothetical comparison of the average decision times of older and younger groups of people on an easy and on a much more difficult task. We might conclude that because the older people show a greater absolute increase in decision times between tasks the harder task must be more 'age sensitive' than the easier task. However, because the older group are slower on both tasks the necessary question is whether or not their decision speeds are disproportionately slowed on this task, or whether they are simply scaled up by a constant amount. This issue was first realized, and tested, by Joseph Brinley (1965), using data from many different tasks to plot the mean decision times of older against those of younger groups of people. His striking finding, extended and discussed by Cerella (1985), was that, whatever might be the nature, and so the particular qualitative demands, of the tasks

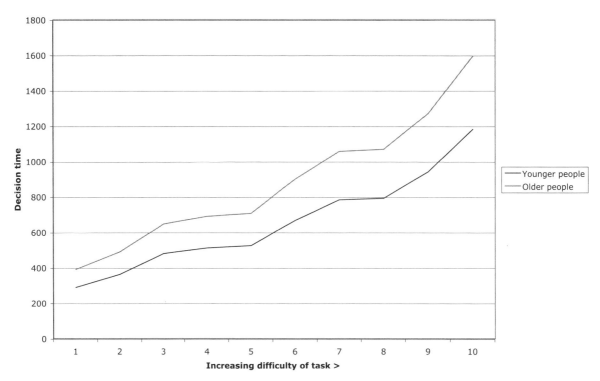

Figure 1. Dummy data showing how absolute differences in decision time between groups of older and younger people increase with the difficulty of the tasks on which they are compared.

from which the data were obtained, average decision times could be fitted by the same straight line. The implication is that for most or all tasks, including those that we might suppose to be more and less age-sensitive, average decision times for the elderly can be very accurately estimated simply by multiplying those for the young by the same simple constant, in the range 1.2 to 1.4. Figure 2 illustrates this situation with data from an experiment in which the average decision speeds of the same groups of older and younger people were compared across fifteen different kinds of tasks, for some of which there was a good theoretical reason to suppose that the older would be disproportionately slower than the young. In fact data points were fitted by the same straight line, indicating that age-related slowing was proportionately equal for all cases.

A very large number of experiments have shown that these findings can be replicated for decision times on nearly all tasks, whatever the specific demands they make. This is highly convenient

for applied psychologists because, if they have measured the times that young adults take to make particular decisions, including quite complex ones, they can obtain a reasonably accurate estimate of how long older people will require simply by multiplying the decision times of the young by a constant in the range 1.2 to 1.4. It is much less convenient for investigators who attempt to relate behavioural to brain changes. For example, it has been known since the mid 1970s that individuals steadily lose brain mass as they age, and that these losses are most severe in the frontal cortex of the brain which is known to support performance on particular categories of so-called 'executive' tasks that make demands such as the planning of sequences of choices and selection of critical from distracting information. Thus, an obvious speculation is that age differences would appear earlier and be more marked on tasks that are, than on those that are not, supported by frontal and prefrontal cortical systems. While the balance of the evidence suggests that this may, in general, be the case, the evidence is not yet compelling because meta-analyses of results from many different studies suggest that age differences in performance of these 'frontal' tasks can be almost entirely explained in terms of age differences

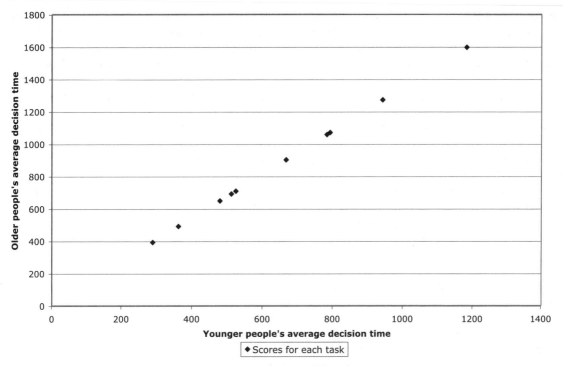

Figure 2. Data in Figure 1 replotted. For each task the average time for the older group is plotted against that for the younger group. All data points fall on the same straight line. These typical data illustrate that, irrespective of qualitative task demands, age brings about the same proportionate increase in decision times.

in information processing speed. In other words that they are, proportionally, slowed no more than other, nonexecutive tasks. This ambiguity is partly due to methodological problems with the particular tasks that are supposed to be sensitive measures of frontal function. This continues to frustrate attempts to make connections between changes in patterns of performance on behavioural measures and neuroanatomical and neurophysiological changes in the brain. This invariance of proportional effect also has theoretical implications. Findings that changes in performance of a wide range of tasks are strongly associated with changes in decision times have been interpreted as evidence that age-related changes in information processing speed must be the sole functional determinants of all other changes in cognitive performance, such as in efficiency of memory, in perceptual processes and in problem solving (see Salthouse, 1985, 1991).

This problem of interpretation extends to tasks in which the units of measurement used are numbers of errors rather than speed. Objective research on changes in memory efficiency in old age is described by Elizabeth Maylor in this *Handbook*, Chapter 3.3, but it is helpful here to note that comparisons of memory efficiency between older and younger

people also illustrate the general difficulty in discovering whether old age affects our ability to meet particular kinds of demands on memory earlier and more severely than others. Recent analyses of published data have plotted percentages of errors made by older and younger people in over 100 memory tasks that made very different qualitative demands. We might reasonably infer that the tasks on which both young and old people made more errors were harder. However, 'Brinley plots' of these data suggest that the proportional difference between young and old groups remains similar across tasks of all levels of difficulty, and across a great variety of different task demands. This suggests that the particular kinds of qualitative demands that tasks make may have much less effect than does task difficulty on the sizes of the differences between young and older people that we observe. This is methodologically inconvenient because the main goal of cognitive gerontology is to relate differential age sensitivity to specific behavioural tasks as evidence of unequal rates of change in the different parts of the brain that support performance on them.

This hypothesis that age-related changes need not be patterned and differentiated, affecting some abilities more than others, but are, rather, 'global' and proportionally uniform across all abilities has strong consequences for our understanding of cognitive ageing. One is that, within any group of individuals, differences in performance on all, or most, cognitive tasks that are associated with differences in their ages can be accounted for by differences in their information processing speeds. For many tasks, including memory tests, in which the index of performance is errors rather than speed, this does usually seem to be the case. However, it is equally the case that age-related differences in performance on many tasks, including tests of frontal lobe function, can be accounted for by individual differences in intelligence test scores (gf). This is true even for tests, such as the Raven's Matrices, in which participants are allowed to take as long as they need to complete as many problems as they can, so that differences in scores cannot be determined by speed of performance alone (Deary, 2000).

Whether information processing speed or intelligence test performance is the most comprehensive index of changes in cognitive performance on all tasks, the theoretical issue remains the same. The simplest explanation is that either of these behavioural measures is a good index of gross biological changes that affect all functional systems in the brain, and so also affect behavioural measures of performance on most cognitive tasks – except, as we have seen, tasks on which performance depends on acquired information and highly practised problem-solving routines. A further assumption is that the effects of these gross biological changes are sufficiently large to mask the effects of lesser changes in performance that are associated with early changes in anatomically localized systems, such as the frontal lobes, that support particular kinds of cognitive functions.

To check these assumptions, we need evidence of strong links between measures of gross neurophysiological or neuroanatomical changes and age-related differences in information processing speed and in gf. Promising recent studies find that differences caused by age-associated atrophy of the entire brain can account for up to 90% of age-related changes in information processing speed on simple tasks. On the same tasks, changes in information processing speed account for most of age-related changes in scores on tests of memory, of frontal lobe function and of the reliability with which information can be briefly held and processed in short term memory – that is in the efficiency and capacity of 'working memory'.

Such findings do not yet amount to a specification of the ways in which ageing of the brain is expressed in terms of changes in cognitive performance. They only illustrate one approach to the problem and suggest a framework within which useful further work can be done. Age-associated brain atrophy is an extremely gross index of the progress of a very wide range of changes in the brain. Many of these more particular changes might prove to have specific effects on particular cognitive processes if we had accurate means to measure them. What we have at present is only an indication that some behaviourally measurable indices such as information processing speed and gf are excellent predictors of age-related variance in performance across a wide range of different kinds of tasks; also that these 'global' measures of cognitive efficiency are strongly correlated with some measures of diffuse changes in brain integrity. This is a starting point, but hardly a conclusion to discussions of how and why our mental abilities alter as we grow old.

FURTHER READING

Rabbitt, Patrick, ed. (1997). *Methodology of the frontal and executive function*. Hove: Psychology Press.

Salthouse, T. A. (1991). *Theoretical perspectives in cognitive ageing*. Hillsdale, N.J.: Erlbaum.

Schaie, K. W. (1990). 'Intellectual development in adulthood'. In J. E. Birren and K. W. Schaie, eds., *Handbook of the psychology of aging*, 3rd edn. San Diego, Calif.: Academic Press.

REFERENCES

Arbuckle, T. Y., Gold, D., and D. Andres (1986). 'Cognitive functioning of older people in relation to social and personality variables', *Psychology and Aging*, 1: 55–62.

Brinley, J. F. (1965). 'Cognitive sets, speed and accuracy of performance in the elderly'. In A. T. Wellford and J. E. Birren, eds., *Behaviour, aging and the nervous system*. Springfield, Ill.: Charles C. Thomas, pp. 114–49.

Deary, I. J. (2000). *Looking down on human intelligence*. Oxford: Oxford University Press.

Dickenson, C. M. and P. M. A. Rabbitt (1991). 'Simulated visual impairment: effects on text comprehension and reading speed', *Clinical Vision Science*, 6: 301–8.

Hayslip, B. Jr (1988). 'Personality–ability relationships in aged adults', *Journal of Gerontology*, 45: 116–27.

Horn, J. (1982). 'The theory of fluid and crystallised intelligence in relation to concepts of cognitive psychology and aging in adulthood'. In F. I. M. Craik and S. Trehub, eds., *Aging and cognitive processes*. New York: Plenum Press, pp. 237–78.

Horn, J. L. (1987). 'A context for understanding information processing studies of human abilities'. In P. A. Vernon, ed., *Speed of information processing and intelligence*. Norwood, N.J.: Ablex, pp. 201–38.

Horn, J. L., Donaldson, G., and R. Engstrom (1981). 'Application, memory and fluid intelligence decline in adulthood', *Research on Aging*, 3: 33–84.

Lindenberger, U., and P. Baltes (1994). 'Sensory functioning and intelligence in old age. A strong connection', *Psychology and Aging*, 9: 339–55.

Rabbitt, P. M. A. (1968). 'Channel-capacity, intelligibility and immediate memory', *Quarterly Journal of Experimental Psychology*, 20: 241–40.

(1991). 'Mild Hearing Loss can cause apparent memory failures which increase with age and reduce with IQ', *Otolaryngologica* (Stockholm), 476 (Suppl.): 167–76.

(1997). 'Methodologies and models in the study of executive function'. In Patrick Rabbitt, ed., *Methodology of frontal and executive function*. Hove: Psychology Press, pp. 1–38.

Rabbitt, P., Diggle, P., Holland, F. and L. McInnes (2004). 'Practice and drop-out effects during a 17 year longitudinal study of cognitive aging', *J. Gerontol. B. Psych.Sci. Soc. Sci.* 59: P84–P97.

Salthouse, T. A. (1985). *A cognitive theory of aging*. Berlin: Springer-Verlag.

(1991). *Theoretical perspectives in cognitive aging*. Hillsdale, N.J.: Erlbaum.

(1996). 'The processing speed theory of adult age differences in cognition', *Psychological Review*, 103: 403–28.

Schaie, K. W. (1990). 'Intellectual development in adulthood'. In J. E. Birren and K. W. Schaie, eds., *Handbook of the psychology of aging*, 3rd edn. San Diego, Calif.: Academic Press.

CHAPTER 3.3

Age-Related Changes in Memory

ELIZABETH A. MAYLOR

It is commonly believed that memory declines in old age. This chapter examines evidence from laboratory-controlled studies of ageing memory and asks whether changes are universal (i.e., associated with all types of memory) or whether certain types are more affected than others. Before describing the data, it is useful to begin with a brief outline of some recent theoretical approaches to ageing memory, followed by a summary of the ways in which memory has been subdivided in the literature.

THEORETICAL OVERVIEW

Effects of old age on memory have been interpreted in terms of three main theoretical frameworks, namely, limited processing resources, reduced processing speed and impaired inhibitory functioning. The limited processing resources approach (e.g. Craik, 1986) supposes that older people are limited in the resources they have available for encoding information into memory and then for retrieving information from memory. Thus they are less able to carry out resource-demanding operations such as linking items together on a list or organizing retrieval in a systematic way. This self-initiated processing is particularly required when the environment itself does not provide many cues at either encoding or retrieval. Evidence consistent with this general view comes, for example, from the finding that age deficits are greater in memory tasks that are more demanding of processing resources, such as recalling an item rather than simply recognizing it as having been encountered earlier (Craik and McDowd, 1987).

The reduced processing speed hypothesis stems from the ubiquitous observation of mental slowing in old age. Salthouse (1996: 403) proposed two mechanisms that underlie the relationship between processing speed and age differences in cognition. The *limited time mechanism* suggests that 'cognitive performance is degraded when processing is slow because relevant operations cannot be successfully executed'; the *simultaneity mechanism* proposes that 'products of early processing may no longer be available when later processing is complete'. Thus, even when allowed unlimited time, older adults' performance in a memory task may not match that of young adults. Support for the processing speed theory comes, in part, from studies in which the age-related deficit in memory is greatly attenuated when a simple measure of perceptual motor speed is statistically taken into account (see Salthouse, 1996).

On the impaired inhibitory functioning view (Hasher and Zacks, 1988), the claim is that older adults have less inhibitory control over the contents of their memory than do young adults. Inhibition is required both to prevent distracting or goal-irrelevant information from entering memory, and to prevent information remaining in memory when no longer relevant. With impaired inhibitory functioning in old age, memory is assumed to be cluttered up with distracting information during both encoding and retrieval of goal-relevant information. The inhibition deficit hypothesis has created much debate (see discussion papers in the *Journal of Gerontology: Psychological Sciences*, 1997, 52B: P253–83) but also supportive evidence from a variety of paradigms as summarized by Hasher *et al.* (1999).

TYPES OF MEMORY

The vast literature on ageing memory is best understood by considering effects on different types of memory as traditionally categorized by memory researchers. First, there is the distinction between *short-* and *long-term memory* (STM and LTM). STM refers to the retention of information for just a few seconds, whereas LTM refers to the retention of information over longer periods, from seconds or minutes to many years. STM can be further subdivided into *primary memory* (associated with the passive retention of information) and *working memory* (where stored information is actively manipulated in some way).

Several distinctions have been drawn within LTM. For example, *episodic memory* refers to memory for specific autobiographical events, such as recalling what you did on holiday in Paris last year or what you had for breakfast this morning, whereas *semantic memory* refers to the store of general knowledge about the world, such as knowing that Paris is the capital of France or that breakfast is the first meal of the day. Also relevant to an understanding of ageing memory is the distinction between *explicit memory* (which requires the conscious recollection of a particular prior event) and *implicit memory* (as revealed by enhanced performance on a task as a result of an earlier encounter with the stimulus). Finally, the recall or recognition of information from the past is termed *retrospective memory*, whereas remembering to perform some action in the future without any external prompting is termed *prospective memory*. As we shall see, at least some of these distinctions have revealed striking dissociations in terms of the effects of normal ageing.

STM: (1) PRIMARY MEMORY

The capacity of primary memory is commonly assessed by memory span, which is the longest sequence of unrelated items (digits, letters or words) that can be reproduced in the correct order immediately after presentation on at least 50 per cent of occasions. Some early studies claimed that memory span was largely unaffected by increased age. But more recently, small to moderate age-related declines have been observed in memory span. For example, Salthouse (1991) showed that adults in

their 60s–70s performed approximately one standard deviation below the level of those in their 20s, with decline slightly greater for word span than for digit span.

Maylor *et al.* (1999) presented young and older adults (mean ages of 20 and 65, respectively) with lists of seven letters at a rate of one letter per second. Participants were required to recall each list immediately in serial order by writing their responses in seven boxes from left to right. Figure 1 shows correct responding as a function of serial position for both auditory and visual presentation. The young group outperformed the older group in both modalities (75% and 63% correct overall for young and older adults, respectively). Typical serial position curves were evident in both age groups, with early and late serial positions better recalled than middle positions and a more pronounced increase in recall of the final item for auditory presentation than for visual presentation. Finally, the age-related deficit was greater in the early and middle serial positions than in the later serial positions for auditory presentation, whereas the reverse was true for visual presentation.

Clearly, primary memory declines with age. But to what extent can this be attributed to decline in a single factor such as processing speed? In Maylor *et al.*'s (1999) study, the correlation between age and STM performance was −.43. When a standard measure of perceptual motor speed was partialled out, the correlation dropped to zero, consistent with the reduced processing speed hypothesis. However, this general hypothesis is unable to predict the precise pattern of age differences in both correct and erroneous responses by serial position. For this, Maylor *et al.* applied a computational model of memory for serial order and found that, by altering two parameters, which could be construed as corresponding to slower encoding and slower output, they could simulate the detailed pattern of age deficits in performance.

Other STM data consistent with a generalized slowing account come from a study by Multhaup *et al.* (1996). A widely accepted view of memory span is that items are entered into a passive phonological store that holds speech-based information for approximately 1.5–2.0 seconds before it decays. An active articulatory rehearsal process based on inner speech can refresh the memory trace so that memory span corresponds to the number of items that can

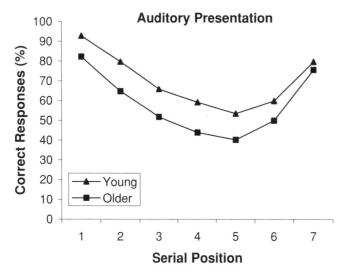

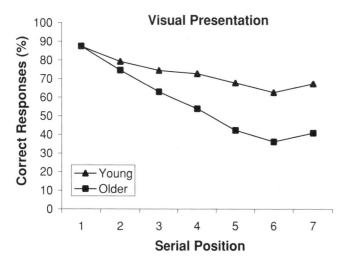

Figure 1. Immediate serial recall of sequences of seven letters presented auditorially (upper panel) and visually (lower panel): mean percentages of correct responses as a function of serial position for young and older adults. Data from Figure 1 of Maylor *et al.* (1999).

be articulated in 1.5–2.0 seconds. Older adults are known to have slower articulation rates than young adults and therefore we would expect their memory spans to be correspondingly lower. Multhaup *et al.* examined the relationship between memory span and speech rate in young and older adults (mean ages of 22 and 68, respectively). The stimuli were words and nonwords of three different lengths – short, medium and long – and items were presented

at a rate of one per second. Speech rate was measured by asking participants to repeat pairs of items ten times. The results confirmed a linear relationship between memory span and speech rate (see Figure 2) and, as expected, young adults had larger spans and faster speech rates than older adults. Crucially, the functions for the two age groups were collinear – in other words, the reduction in memory span for older adults was predictable on the basis of their slower speech (and therefore rehearsal) rate. To conclude, there is small to moderate age decline in memory span that is at least consistent with the generalized slowing account of ageing (see Maylor *et al.*, 1999, for further discussion).

STM: (2) WORKING MEMORY

In contrast to primary memory, working memory involves both the storage and the processing of information, such as would be required in a mental arithmetic task. Craik (1986), for example, examined age differences on a primary memory task (digit span) and a working memory task (alpha span) in which the to-be-remembered list of words had to be rearranged into alphabetical order before recall. The age deficit was found to be greater for alpha span than for digit span. On the other hand, researchers have not always observed greater age deficits for backwards span (where items must be recalled in reverse order to that of presentation) than standard forwards span (see Salthouse, 1991, and Verhaeghen *et al.*, 1993, for examples of similar age deficits for forwards and backwards span).

More traditional (and more resource-demanding) measures of working memory usually involve the sequential presentation of a series of problems that require processing (e.g., *Cows eat grass – true or false? Spoons are made of paper – true or false?*). At the end of the series, the task would be to recall the last word of each statement (*grass, paper*, etc.) in the correct order. Working memory span is the longest series that can be remembered reliably, assuming also that the problems were processed correctly (in this case, the true/false responses). Results from many studies consistently show substantial age-related decline in working memory span (see Salthouse, 1992).

The general conclusion on STM is that age-related decline is less striking in tasks in which lists of items simply have to be reproduced in the presented order (primary memory) than in more demanding tasks requiring the simultaneous storage and processing of information (working memory). This pattern can therefore be readily interpreted in terms of the limited processing resources view. On the reduced processing speed hypothesis, the correlations with age either drop to zero (primary memory; Maylor et al., 1999) or are considerably attenuated (working memory; Salthouse, 1996) when speed is taken into account. In other words, there is evidence that slower processing is a fundamental underlying mediator of age differences in STM.

Recently, May et al. (1999) observed that memory span procedures typically start with short lists and then gradually increase in length until a participant fails consistently at a particular length. To perform well, participants must focus on the current list and suppress previous lists; otherwise proactive interference (PI) occurs. If older adults are less able to avoid PI (as suggested by the inhibition deficit hypothesis), then as the lists increase in length, performance will suffer earlier as a result of accumulating interference from previous items.

May et al. (1999) employed a reading span task in which participants read printed sentences aloud while remembering the final word in each sentence for recall at the end of the list. In the *standard* condition, trials were presented in the usual ascending order (2-, 3-, then 4-sentence lists); in the *descending* condition, trials were presented in the reverse order (4-, 3-, then 2-sentence lists). Table 1 shows the mean list lengths reliably recalled (i.e., reading span) by young and older adults (mean ages of 19 and 67, respectively) under these two conditions. There was a significant age deficit under the standard condition. However, there was no age difference under the descending condition where PI was minimized at the longest list length. This provides support for the view that at least some age-related

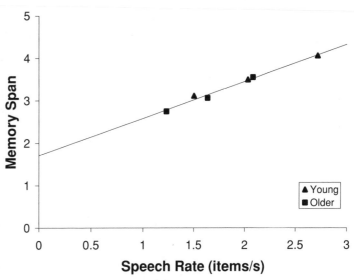

Figure 2. Memory span as a function of speech rate for young and older adults. For each age group, long items are represented by the leftmost point, medium items by the middle point, and short items by the rightmost point. Data from Table 1 of Multhaup et al. (1996), averaged across words and nonwords. The linear regression function shown is $y = 0.87x + 1.71$ ($R^2 = 0.98$).

TABLE 1. Reading span for young and older adults in which lists either increased in length (standard condition) or decreased in length (descending condition). Data from Experiment 1 of May et al. (1999)

Condition	Young	Older
Standard	3.1	2.6
Descending	2.9	3.0

deficits in working memory may be attributable to failures in clearing working memory of information that is no longer relevant to the current task.

LTM: (1) SEMANTIC VS EPISODIC MEMORY

As mentioned earlier, the semantic memory system can be considered as analogous to the contents of a combined dictionary and encyclopaedia, whereas the episodic memory system is more similar to a personal diary. This is an important distinction with

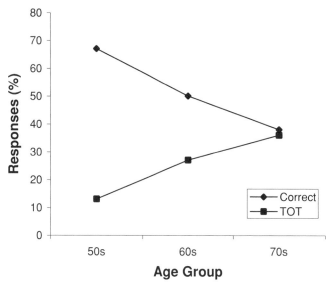

Figure 3. Percentages of faces recognized as familiar that were correctly named or received a tip-of-the-tongue (TOT) response for 50-, 60- and 70-year-olds. Data from Figure 1 of Maylor (1990c).

respect to ageing because it is often claimed that, in contrast to episodic memory, semantic memory shows little or no age-related decline. For example, there are few systematic age effects on measures of general knowledge as included in various IQ tests (see Salthouse, 1991). Similarly, scores on vocabulary tests remain relatively stable in old age. However, this may depend to some extent on the demands of the particular test employed. Thus, Maylor (1990b) observed the usual result of no significant decline with age on a vocabulary test requiring the selection of a synonym for the target word; in contrast, older adults performed more poorly than younger adults when required to identify a word from its definition (see Table 2 for examples). This finding within semantic memory mirrors the observation noted earlier that tests of recognition are less affected by ageing than are tests of recall because of their differing processing demands.

Consistent with their subjective complaints, older people are more susceptible to the experience of finding themselves temporarily unable to retrieve a familiar name or word – the well-known 'tip-of-the-tongue' (TOT) state (e.g. Burke *et al.*, 1991). This is illustrated in Figure 3 by data from a study by Maylor (1990c) in which participants were shown photographs of famous people and were asked to name each person within 50 seconds. Clearly, while the numbers of correct names decreased with increasing age, the numbers of TOT states correspondingly increased. It is important to note that almost all TOT states are eventually resolved in both younger and older people, suggesting that the semantic knowledge base remains intact but speeded access to it is impaired by ageing. Moreover, these temporary retrieval failures from semantic memory in old age are not unique to proper names. However, TOT states associated with people's names may be particularly noticeable because there are no synonyms available. Name retrieval failures may also be more frustrating because of their obvious social significance and therefore may be more memorable.

TABLE 2. Examples of items from two vocabulary tests used by Maylor (1990b), with correct answers shown in italics. Age-related decline from 50- to 70-year-olds was absent for the multiple-choice test but present for the word identification test

Multiple-choice vocabulary test
Choose the word that is closest in meaning to:
                    FECUND
esculent profound sublime optative *prolific* salic
                    ABNEGATE
contradict *renounce* belie decry execute assemble

Identifying words from definitions
What is the word meaning:
'Something out of keeping with the times in which it exists' (*anachronism*)
'House of rest for travellers or for the terminally ill, often kept by a religious order' (*hospice*)

There is considerable evidence that episodic memory declines markedly with age as revealed, for example, by the common laboratory task of free recall in which a long list of unrelated items is presented for subsequent recall in any order (see Verhaeghen *et al.*, 1993). Moreover, older adults are not only less able to recall items that were presented, they are also more likely to recall items that were not presented. For example, Norman and Schacter (1997) elicited high rates of false remembering by presenting lists of words (e.g., *door, glass, pane, shade, ledge, sill.* . . .) that were each thematically related to a word that was not presented (in this case, *window*). Figure 4 shows that recall of presented words was much higher than recall of nonpresented theme words for young adults (mean age of 19), whereas recall was approximately equally likely for presented and nonpresented words for older adults (mean age of 68). Thus, it seems that older adults are more susceptible to this false memory effect. One explanation assumes that, during initial presentation, the theme word is automatically activated through semantic priming. At recall, this nonpresented theme word may be retrieved, but, perhaps because of limited processing resources, older adults are less likely or able to carry out strategic retrieval or monitoring processes that are required to evaluate its source (i.e., internally rather than externally generated). This would be consistent with the general view that age-related deficits are particularly striking for contextual details of events (see Spencer and Raz, 1995).

Older people themselves often report that, while their memory is poor for what happened yesterday, they have very clear recollections of events that happened a long time ago, perhaps in childhood or during the war. In fact, older people's own perceptions of their memories seem to follow Ribot's law, which states that recent memories are forgotten but remote memories are preserved. However, there are obvious problems is assessing such reports: (1) personal memories recalled from the distant past are often highly selective events that are personally salient – in other words, they are typically not the routine daily occurrences of the sort that are currently being forgotten; (2) the remote events are more likely to have been frequently rehearsed and recounted; (3)

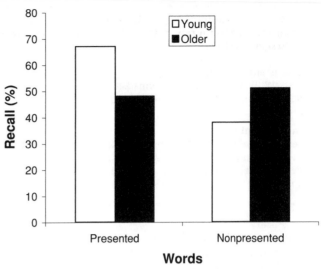

Figure 4. Free recall of lists of thematically related words in young and older adults: percentages of presented words correctly recalled and nonpresented theme words falsely recalled. Data from Table 1 of Norman and Schacter (1997).

remote memories are probably liable to unconscious distortion and embellishment.

Cohen *et al.* (1994) investigated ageing episodic memory dating back a year by examining people's recall of their personal circumstances associated with a notable public event, namely, the resignation of Margaret Thatcher as Prime Minister. Young and older volunteers (mean ages of 22 and 72, respectively) were asked to give detailed accounts of how they first heard the news that Margaret Thatcher had resigned. They were initially tested within 10–14 days of the resignation and were subsequently retested approximately one year later. The question of interest was whether the two accounts were consistent or inconsistent (see Table 3 for an example of each). The results revealed that, whereas 90 per cent of young participants were highly consistent in their accounts, only 42 per cent of older participants were highly consistent. Thus, it seems that older people are indeed mistaken in their impressions of generally preserved remote memories.

LTM: (2) IMPLICIT VS EXPLICIT MEMORY

The memory tasks considered so far explicitly asked participants to recall or recognize information

TABLE 3. Examples of people's accounts of how they heard the news of Margaret Thatcher's resignation after a few days (test) and after approximately a year (retest). Data from Cohen _et al._ (1994)

Consistent example
Test: 'While waiting in the supermarket till queue, a supervisor spread the news to the till operators.'
Retest: 'While waiting in the till queue in Sainsbury's Oxford store, a supervisor informed the till operators of the resignation.'

Inconsistent example
Test: 'I was at the school in which I work, and I entered the Bursar's office to see her put down the telephone and then announce very excitedly "she's resigned" . . .'
Retest: 'I was in the office of the school in which I work when a colleague burst in and in a very loud voice announced that Mrs Thatcher's resigned . . .'

encountered earlier. In contrast, consider an experiment in which participants are asked to read some words (e.g., _mechanism_), perhaps in a passage of text. Later in the session, they may be presented with a word stem (_mec------_) or fragment (_-e-h-n-s-_) and asked to complete it with the first word that comes to mind – note that there is no reference to the prior study period. Implicit memory is revealed by an increased likelihood of completion for studied words (_mechanism_) relative to unstudied words. Several studies have shown striking dissociations between no significant age differences on implicit memory tests and significant age differences on explicit memory tests (see Light _et al._, 2000, for examples).

Age differences on implicit memory tests may not reach significance but they usually favour the young, at least numerically. This raises the possibility that there is some decline in implicit memory with increasing age, which individual studies are unable to detect because of insufficient power. Combining multiple studies together in a meta-analysis reveals slight, but nevertheless significant, age-related decline for implicit memory (Light _et al._, 2000). This pattern of impaired explicit memory but relatively spared implicit memory can be interpreted in terms of the view that explicit and implicit forms of memory depend on different memory systems that are associated with distinct regions of the brain and that these different brain areas are differentially impaired by ageing. An alternative view is that different processing resources are involved, with explicit memory tasks requiring consciously controlled recollective processes that are effortful and

demanding, and implicit memory tasks relying on automatic processing. For further discussion and evidence that ageing impairs conscious recollection but not automatic retrieval or familiarity, see Light _et al._ (2000).

LTM: (3) RETROSPECTIVE VS PROSPECTIVE MEMORY

Compare the task of describing what happened in a television soap opera last night to a friend who missed it, with remembering to set the video-recorder to tape tonight's episode. These are tests of retrospective and prospective memory, respectively. We have already seen examples of age-related deficits in laboratory tests of retrospective memory. In recent years, there has been increasing interest in prospective memory, which can be defined as remembering at the appropriate point in the future that something has to be done, without any prompting in the form of explicit instructions to recall. Craik (1986) suggested that age-related deficits should be particularly evident in such tasks because prospective remembering by definition places heavy demands on self-initiated retrieval processes.

Early naturalistic studies of prospective memory, in which volunteers were asked to make telephone calls or mail postcards at particular times over the course of several days, revealed that older people can perform at least as well as young people provided that they employ efficient cues (e.g. Maylor, 1990a). These probably work well for important appointments, but alarm clocks, memos and so on are impractical for many everyday tasks. Thus, it is significant that older people perform less well in prospective memory tasks conducted in the laboratory. However, not all of these studies have observed age-related decline – it appears that prospective memory tasks, like retrospective memory tasks, vary both in their processing demands and in the salience of the cues provided by the environment at retrieval (see, for examples, Einstein *et al.*, 1995; Maylor *et al.*, 2002). Age-related deficits in prospective memory tasks are therefore most pronounced in situations where participants are engaged in demanding activities and self-initiated processing is required to recognize the appropriate conditions for action.

CONCLUSIONS

There is clearly some variation in the effects of normal ageing on memory, depending on the type of memory in question:

- For short-term memory, there are small to moderate age deficits for primary memory but larger age deficits for working memory. In both cases, the data are consistent with the reduced processing speed hypothesis, although there is also evidence that impaired inhibitory functioning may play a role in the working memory deficit.
- For long-term memory, although semantic memory is considerably less affected by ageing than episodic memory, it is not completely spared – for example, speeded access is impaired, resulting in noticeable and frustrating temporary retrieval failures. Episodic memory decline is well documented and includes an increased susceptibility to false memories and inaccurate remote memories (contrary to subjective reports).
- The implicit–explicit memory distinction shows the most striking difference with respect to ageing, with little or no decline for implicit memory in contrast to robust decline for explicit memory.
- Prospective memory in old age is a relatively new area of research but the evidence so far indicates that qualitatively similar principles probably apply to the impact of ageing on remembering things from the past and on remembering to do things in the future.

Finally, in addition to variation in age-related changes across different types of memory, there is considerable variability across individuals such that some older people are less adversely affected than others (Morse, 1993). It is also worth repeating Verhaeghen *et al.*'s (1993) cautionary note that age-related deficits in the laboratory 'do not necessarily imply the breaking down of everyday memory functioning in old age' (p. 168). They suggest that the memory system of young adults 'functions at a level much higher than is needed for survival. Even though a decrease in functioning can be irritating, depressing, or upsetting for the older person who experiences it, the consequences of the decrease for daily life performance may be rather trivial, precisely because the culminating point of functioning in young adulthood is situated way above survival level' (p. 168).

FURTHER READING

Backman, L., Small, B. J., and A. Wahlin (2001). 'Aging and memory: cognitive and biological perspectives'. In J. E. Birren and K. W. Schaie, eds., *Handbook of the psychology of aging*, 5th edn. San Diego: Academic Press, pp. 349–77.

Kausler, D. H. (1994). *Learning and memory in normal aging*. San Diego: Academic Press.

Naveh-Benjamin, M., Moscovitch, M., and H. L. Roediger, eds. (2001). *Perspectives on human memory and cognitive aging: essays in honour of Fergus Craik*. Hove: Psychology Press.

Zacks, R. T., Hasher, L., and K. Z. H. Li (2000). 'Human memory'. In F. I. M. Craik and T. A. Salthouse, eds., *The handbook of aging and cognition*, 2nd edn. Mahwah, N.J.: Erlbaum, pp. 293–357.

REFERENCES

Burke, D. M., MacKay, D. G., Worthley, J. S., and E. Wade (1991). 'On the tip of the tongue: what causes word finding failures in young and older adults?' *Journal of Memory and Language*, 30: 542–79.

Cohen, G., Conway, M. A., and E. A. Maylor (1994). 'Flashbulb memories in older adults', *Psychology and Aging*, 9: 454–63.

Craik, F. I. M. (1986). 'A functional account of age differences in memory'. In F. Klix and H. Hagendorf, eds., *Human memory and cognitive capabilities: mechanisms and performances*. Amsterdam: Elsevier Science Publishers, North-Holland, pp. 409–22.

Craik, F. I. M., and J. M. McDowd (1987). 'Age differences in recall and recognition', *Journal of Experimental Psychology: Learning, Memory, and Cognition*, 13: 474–9.

Einstein, G. O., McDaniel, M. A., Richardson, S. L., Guynn, M. J., and A. R. Cunfer (1995). 'Aging and prospective memory: examining the influences of self-initiated retrieval processes', *Journal of Experimental Psychology: Learning, Memory, and Cognition*, 21: 996–1007.

Hasher, L., and R. T. Zacks (1988). 'Working memory, comprehension, and aging: a review and a new view'. In G. H. Bower, ed., *The psychology of learning and motivation*, Vol. XXII. New York: Academic Press, pp. 193–225.

Hasher, L., Zacks, R. T., and C. P. May (1999). 'Inhibitory control, circadian arousal, and age'. In D. Gopher and A. Koriat, eds., *Attention and performance. Cognitive regulation and performance: interaction of theory and application*, Cambridge, Mass.: MIT Press, pp. 653–75.

Light, L. L., Prull, M. W., La Voie, D. J., and M. R. Healy (2000). 'Dual-process theories of memory in old age'. In T. J. Perfect and E. A. Maylor, eds., *Models of cognitive aging*. Oxford: Oxford University Press, pp. 238–300.

May, C. P., Hasher, L., and M. J. Kane (1999). 'The role of interference in memory span', *Memory & Cognition*, 27: 759–67.

Maylor, E. A. (1990a). 'Age and prospective memory', *Quarterly Journal of Experimental Psychology*, 42A: 471–93.

—— (1990b). 'Age, blocking and the tip of the tongue state', *British Journal of Psychology*, 81: 123–34.

—— (1990c). 'Recognizing and naming faces: aging, memory retrieval, and the tip of the tongue state', *Journal of Gerontology: Psychological Sciences*, 45: P215–P226.

Maylor, E. A., Vousden, J. I., and G. D. A. Brown (1999). 'Adult age differences in short-term memory for serial order: data and a model', *Psychology and Aging*, 14: 572–94.

Maylor, E. A., Darby, R. J., Logie, R. H., Della Sala, S., and G. Smith (2002). 'Prospective memory across the lifespan'. In P. Graf and N. Ohta, eds., *Lifespan development of human memory*. Cambridge, Mass.: MIT Press, pp. 235–56.

Morse, C. K. (1993). 'Does variability increase with age? An archival study of cognitive measures', *Psychology and Aging*, 8: 156–64.

Multhaup, K. S., Balota, D. A., and N. Cowan (1996). 'Implications of aging, lexicality, and item length for the mechanisms underlying memory span', *Psychonomic Bulletin & Review*, 3: 112–20.

Norman, K. A., and D. L. Schacter (1997). 'False recognition in younger and older adults: exploring the characteristics of illusory memories', *Memory & Cognition*, 25: 838–48.

Salthouse, T. A. (1991). *Theoretical perspectives on cognitive aging*. Hillsdale, N.J.: Erlbaum.

—— (1992). *Mechanisms of age–cognition relations in adulthood*. Hillsdale, N.J.: Erlbaum.

—— (1996). 'The processing-speed theory of adult age differences in cognition', *Psychological Review*, 103: 403–28.

Spencer, W. D., and N. Raz (1995). 'Differential effects of aging on memory for content and context: a meta-analysis', *Psychology and Aging*, 10: 527–39.

Verhaeghen, P., Marcoen, A., and L. Goossens (1993). 'Facts and fictions about memory aging: a quantitative integration of research findings', *Journal of Gerontology: Psychological Sciences*, 48: P57–P71.

CHAPTER 3.4

Intelligence and Wisdom

ROBERT J. STERNBERG AND ELENA L. GRIGORENKO

In this chapter, we discuss the trajectory of development during adulthood of intelligence and wisdom. We begin with intelligence, then discuss wisdom.

INTELLIGENCE

Loosely speaking, intelligence is the ability to adapt to the environment. Many intellectual functions (mostly those contributing to the so-called general or g-factor of intelligence – for a review, see Berg, 2000) have been found to be associated with age across the lifespan. Many of these associations are rather complex and of a curvilinear nature, reflecting rapid growth during the years of formal schooling and slow decline thereafter (Salthouse, 1998). However, the results of research also suggest somewhat different developmental functions for changes in performance on various *kinds* of intellectual tasks across the adult lifespan. In particular, data from Williams, Denney, and Schadler show that older adults commonly report growth in practical abilities over the years, even though their academic abilities decline.

Author's note: preparation of this chapter was supported by Grant REC-9979843 from the National Science Foundation, by a grant from the W. T. Grant Foundation, and by a government grant under the Javits Act Program (Grant No. R206R00001) as administered by the Institute of Education Sciences (formerly the Office of Educational Research and Improvement), US Department of Education. Grantees undertaking such projects are encouraged to express freely their professional judgment. This chapter, therefore, does not necessarily represent the positions or the policies of the US government or the W. T. Grant Foundation, and no official endorsement should be inferred.

In general, intelligence during adulthood is characterized, on one hand, by losses in the speed of mental processes, abstract reasoning, and specific characteristics of memory performance and, on the other hand, by gains in the metacognitive ability to integrate cognitive, interpersonal, and emotional thinking in a synthetic understanding of the world, self, and others.

The most commonly used theoretical framework for the interpretation of findings on age-related changes in intellectual performance is that of fluid and crystallized abilities (Horn, 1994). *Fluid* abilities are those more associated with the creative and flexible thinking required to deal with novelty, such as in the immediate testing situation (e.g. discovering the pattern in a figure sequence). *Crystallized* abilities are represented by accumulated knowledge (e.g. finding a synonym of a low-frequency word). Utilizing this distinction, various researchers have demonstrated that fluid abilities are relatively susceptible to age-related decline, whereas crystallized abilities are relatively resistant to ageing (Dixon and Baltes, 1986), except near the end of one's life.

The majority of these findings, however, were obtained in the framework of cross-sectional methodologies, that is, by comparing different groups of individuals of various ages. When the same individuals are followed across time in the framework of longitudinal design, the findings show that, with respect to fluid intelligence, decline does not generally begin until the 60s and loss of crystallized intelligence occurs almost a decade later, in the 70s (Schaie, 1996).

In addition, even when there are age-based group differences in intellectual performance, there is extensive interindividual variability for specific cognitive abilities within age groups. For instance, Schaie (1996), although consistently reporting mean cross-sectional differences in overall intellectual performance, pointed out impressive variability within age groups. To quantify this variability, Schaie investigated the overlap in distributions of intellectual performance among young adults and the elderly. Even in the group of individuals of 80 years and older the overlap was about 53 percent. In other words, slightly more than half of individuals in the later age groups perform comparably to a group of young adults on measures of both crystallized and fluid intelligence.

The idea that practical and academic–analytical abilities might have different developmental trajectories has been supported in a number of studies. Denney and Palmer (1981) were among the first research teams to demonstrate this discrepancy. They compared the performance of adults (aged 20 through 79) on traditional analytical reasoning problems (e.g. a "twenty questions" task) and a problem-solving task involving real-life situations (e.g., "If you were traveling by car and got stranded out on an interstate highway during a blizzard, what would you do?"). One of the many interesting results obtained in this study was a difference in the shape of the developmental function for performance on the two types of problems. Performance on the *traditional* problem-solving task or cognitive measure declined almost linearly from age 20 onward. Performance on the *practical* problem-solving task increased to a peak in the 40- and 50-year-old groups, declining thereafter. Expanding on this line of research, Jackie Smith and her colleagues compared responses to life-planning dilemmas in a group of younger (mean age 32) and older (mean age 70) adults. Unlike the results of studies of ageing and academic abilities, which demonstrated the superior performance of younger adults over the elderly, in this study young and older adults did not differ. In addition, each age-cohort group received the highest ratings when responding to a dilemma matched to their own life phase.

Similar results were obtained in a study by Cornelius and Caspi (1987). They studied adults between the ages of 20 and 78. These researchers examined relationships between performance on tasks measuring fluid intelligence (letter series), crystallized intelligence (verbal meanings), and everyday problem solving (e.g., dealing with a landlord who won't make repairs, filling out a complicated form, responding to criticism from a parent or child). Performance on the measure of fluid ability increased from ages 20 to 30, remained stable from ages 30 to 50, and then declined. Performance on the everyday problem-solving task and the measures of crystallized ability increased through age 70.

Likewise, the neofunctionalist position, advanced by Baltes and his associates (Baltes and Staudinger, in press), suggests that although some aspects of intellectual functioning estimated via traditional tests may decline with age, stability and growth also exist, if to a lesser extent. The approach of Baltes and his colleagues also utilizes the constructs of fluid and crystallized intelligence, although a different emphasis is placed on the relative roles and meanings of these two kinds of intelligence. Here, both aspects of intelligence are considered as coequals in defining the developmental course of intelligence. In general, Baltes argues that crystallized intelligence has been too narrowly defined, and that its importance increases as one moves into adulthood and old age. In this sense, it may be inappropriate to associate a decrease in fluid intelligence with an average decline in intellectual competence.

Baltes and his associates see adult cognitive competence in terms of a dual-process model. The first process, called the *mechanics* of intelligence, is concerned with developmental change in basic information processing that is genetically driven and assumed to be knowledge-free. With ageing, there is a biologically based reduction in reserve capacity. The second process, *pragmatic* intelligence, relates the basic cognitive skills and resources of the first process to everyday cognitive performance and adaptation. Measures of pragmatic intelligence within select domains are viewed as tapping abilities more characteristic of adult intellectual life than are traditional psychometric measures of cognitive abilities. Similarly to empirical findings on the distinction between fluid and crystallized intelligence, Baltes (1993) and his colleagues showed that the mechanics of intelligence tend to decline with age almost linearly, whereas the pragmatics of intelligence tend to maintain relative stability throughout adulthood. For example, whereas linear declines were found in the speed of comparing information in short-term memory (i.e., aspects of intellectual mechanics), no age differences were registered for measures of reasoning about life planning (i.e., aspects of intellectual pragmatics).

Cognitive abilities are assumed to operate on content domains involving factual and procedural knowledge; they are regulated by higher-level, trans-situational, procedural skills and by higher-order reflective thinking (metacognition), all of which define the "action space" in which problem solving occurs within a given individual. According to this approach, successful ageing entails limiting one's tasks and avoiding excessive demands. Baltes used the concept of selection to refer to a self-imposed restriction in one's life to fewer domains of functioning as a means to adapt to age-related losses. It is assumed that by concentrating on high-priority domains and devising new operational strategies, individuals can optimize their general reserves (Baltes, 1993). By relating adult intelligence to successful cognitive performance in one's environment, this position acknowledges that not all tasks are equally relevant for measuring intelligence at different ages.

Specific manifestations of pragmatic intelligence are said to differ from person to person as people proceed through selection, optimization, or compensation (Baltes, 1993). Selection refers simply to diminishing the scope of one's activities to things that one is still able to accomplish well, despite a diminution in reserve capacity. Optimization refers to the fact that older people can maintain high levels of performance in some domains by practice, greater effort, and the development of new bodies of knowledge. Compensation comes into play when one requires a level of capacity beyond remaining performance potential. For example, Salthouse was able to show that older typists, although slower on several simple speeded reaction-time tasks, were able to compensate for this deficit and maintain their speed by reading further ahead in the text and planning ahead. According to Salthouse and Somberg, age-related decrements at the "molecular" level (e.g. in speed of execution of the elementary components of typing skill) produce no observable effects at the "molar" level (i.e., the speed and accuracy with which work is completed).

Neil Charness showed similar effects with older chess players, who exhibited poorer recall in general, but were better able to plan ahead than younger, less experienced players. In related studies, older adults have been found to compensate for declines in memory by relying more on external memory aids than do younger adults. Older adults must often transfer the emphasis of a particular task to abilities that have not declined in order to compensate for those that have. In other words, when a task depends heavily on knowledge, and speed of processing is not a significant constraint, peak performance may not be constrained in early to middle adulthood (Charness and Bieman-Copland, 1994). As an example, consider chess competitions by correspondence. In these "chess-by-mail" competitions, players are permitted 3 days to deliberate each move. The mean age of the first-time winners of one postal world championship is 46. In contrast, the peak age for tournament chess, where deliberation averages 3 minutes per move, is about 30, according to Charness and Bosman (1990). A series of studies on the relationship between ageing and cognitive efficiency in skilled performers has attested to the compensatory and stabilizing role of practical intelligence.

The developmental trajectory of everyday intelligence has been examined by a number of researchers (for reviews, see Berg, 2000; Berg and Klaczynski, 1996). The summary of the field today is that the pattern of age differences in practical intelligence differs dramatically depending on how problems to be solved are defined and what criteria are used for optimal problem solving. For example, Berg and her colleagues, studying participants' own ratings of how effective they were in solving their own everyday problems, did not find any age differences. Denney and her colleagues (Denney and Palmer, 1981) utilized the number of "safe and effective solutions" as the criterion of optimal problem solving and found that the highest number of such solutions was generated by middle-aged adults, with both younger and older adults offering fewer solutions. Cornelius and Caspi (1987), using the closeness between participants' ratings of strategy effectiveness and a "prototype" of the optimal everyday problem solver as the criterion, found an increase in everyday problem-solving ability with adult age.

A number of studies have examined everyday problem solving with a neo-Piagetian approach to intellectual development in adulthood (Labouvie-Vief, 1990). According to this paradigm, in middle and late adulthood, the formal-operational reasoning of late adolescents and young adults, with its focus on logic, is replaced by more sophisticated mental structures distinguished by relativistic reasoning based on synthesizing the irrational, emotive, and personal. Specifically, Blanchard-Fields stated that, when dealing with social dilemmas, older adults are superior to younger adults in their integrative attributional reasoning (i.e., reasoning based on the integration of dispositional and situational components).

WISDOM

There are two major approaches that have been taken to understanding wisdom and its development: implicit-theoretical and explicit-theoretical.

Implicit-Theoretical Approaches

Implicit-theoretical approaches to wisdom have in common the search for an understanding of people's folk conceptions of what wisdom is. Thus, the goal is not to provide a "psychologically true" account of wisdom, but rather an account that is true with respect to people's beliefs, whether these beliefs are right or wrong.

Some of the earliest work of this kind was done by Clayton (1975), who multidimensionally scaled ratings of pairs of words potentially related to wisdom for three samples of adults differing in age (younger, middle-aged, older). In her earliest study, the terms that were scaled were ones such as *experienced*, *pragmatic*, *understanding*, and *knowledgeable*. In each study, participants were asked to rate similarities between all possible pairs of words. The main similarity in the results for the age cohorts for which the scalings were done was the elicitation of two consistent dimensions of wisdom, which Clayton referred to as an affective dimension and a reflective dimension. The reflective dimension seems to be the one of these two that more overlaps with intelligence. There was also a suggestion of a dimension relating to age. The greatest difference among the age cohorts was that mental representations of

wisdom seemed to become more differentiated (i.e., to increase in dimensionality) with increases in the ages of the participants.

Holliday and Chandler (1986) also used an implicit-theories approach to understanding wisdom. Approximately 500 participants were studied across a series of experiments. The investigators were interested in determining whether the concept of wisdom could be understood as a prototype, or central concept. Principal-components analysis of one of Holliday and Chandler's studies revealed five underlying factors: exceptional understanding, judgment and communication skills, general competence, interpersonal skills, and social unobtrusiveness.

Sternberg (1985) has reported a series of studies investigating implicit theories of wisdom. In one study, 200 professors each of art, business, philosophy, and physics were asked to rate the characteristicness of each of the behaviors obtained in a prestudy from the corresponding population with respect to the professors' ideal conception of each of an ideally wise, intelligent, or creative individual in their occupation. Laypersons were also asked to provide these ratings but for a hypothetical ideal individual without regard to occupation. Correlations were computed across the three ratings. In each group except philosophy, the highest correlation was between wisdom and intelligence; in philosophy, the highest correlation was between intelligence and creativity. The correlations between wisdom and intelligence ratings ranged from .42 to .78 with a median of .68. For all groups, the lowest correlation was between wisdom and creativity (which ranged from − .24 to .48 with a median of .27).

In a second study, 40 college students were asked to sort three sets of 40 behaviors each into as many or as few piles as they wished. The 40 behaviors in each set were the top-rated wisdom, intelligence, and creativity behaviors from the previous study. The sortings then each were subjected to nonmetric multidimensional scaling. For wisdom, six components emerged: *reasoning ability*, *sagacity*, *learning from ideas and environment*, *judgment*, *expeditious use of information*, and *perspicacity*. These components can be compared with those that emerged from a similar scaling of people's implicit theories of intelligence, which were *practical problem-solving ability*, *verbal ability*, *intellectual balance and integration*, *goal orientation and attainment, contextual intelligence,* and *fluid thought.* In both cases, cognitive abilities and their use are important. In wisdom, however, some kind of balance appears to emerge as important that does not emerge as important in intelligence, in general.

In a third study, 50 adults were asked to rate descriptions of hypothetical individuals for wisdom, intelligence, and creativity. Correlations were computed between pairs of ratings of the hypothetical individuals' levels of the three traits. Correlations between the ratings were .94 for wisdom and intelligence, .62 for wisdom and creativity, and .69 for intelligence and creativity, again suggesting that wisdom and intelligence are highly correlated in people's implicit theories, at least in the US.

Explicit-Theoretical Approaches

Explicit theories are constructions of (supposedly) expert theorists and researchers rather than of laypeople. In the study of wisdom, most explicit-theoretical approaches are based on constructs from the psychology of human development.

The most extensive program of research has been that conducted by Baltes and his colleagues. This program of research is related to Baltes' longstanding program of research on intellectual abilities and ageing. For example, Baltes and Smith (1990) gave adult participants life-management problems, such as "A fourteen-year-old girl is pregnant. What should she, what should one, consider and do?" and "A fifteen-year-old girl wants to marry soon. What should she, what should one, consider and do?" These same problems might be used to measure the pragmatics of intelligence, about which Baltes has written at length. Baltes and Smith tested a five-component model of wisdom on participants' protocols in answering these and other questions, based on a notion of wisdom as expert knowledge about fundamental life matters or of wisdom as good judgment and advice in important but uncertain matters of life.

Three kinds of factors – general personal factors, expertise-specific factors, and facilitative experiential contexts – were proposed to facilitate wise judgments. These factors are used in life planning, life management, and life review. Wisdom is in turn then reflected in five components: (a) rich factual knowledge (general and specific knowledge about the conditions of life and its variations); (b) rich procedural knowledge (general and specific knowledge about strategies of judgment and advice concerning matters of life); (c) lifespan contextualism (knowledge about the contexts of life and their temporal [developmental] relationships); (d) relativism (knowledge about differences in values, goals, and priorities); and (e) uncertainty (knowledge about the relative indeterminacy and unpredictability of life and ways to manage). An expert answer should reflect more of these components, whereas a novice answer should reflect fewer of them. The data collected to date generally have been supportive of the model. These factors seem to reflect the pragmatic aspect of intelligence but to go beyond it, for example in the inclusion of factors of relativism and uncertainty.

Over time, Baltes and his colleagues (see Baltes and Staudinger, in press) have collected a wide range of data showing the empirical utility of the proposed theoretical and measurement approaches to wisdom. For example, Staudinger *et al.* (1997) found that measures of intelligence (as well as personality) overlap with but are nonidentical to measures of wisdom in terms of constructs measured, and Staudinger *et al.* (1992) showed that human-services professionals outperformed a control group on wisdom-related tasks. They also showed that older adults performed as well on such tasks as did younger adults, and that older adults did better on such tasks if there was a match between their age and the age of the fictitious characters about whom they made judgments. Baltes *et al.* (1995) found that older individuals nominated for their wisdom performed as well as did clinical psychologists on wisdom-related tasks. They also showed that, up to the age of 80, older adults performed as well on such tasks as did younger adults. In a further set of studies, Staudinger and Baltes (1996) found that performance settings that were ecologically relevant to the lives of their participants and that provided for actual or "virtual" interaction of minds increased wisdom-related performance substantially. Thus, wisdom seems to behave more like crystallized than like fluid intelligence in its development over the lifecourse (see Horn, 1994).

Some theorists have viewed wisdom in terms of postformal-operational thinking, thereby viewing wisdom as a form of intellectual functioning that extends the development of thinking beyond the Piagetian stages of intelligence. These theorists seem to view wisdom in a way that is similar or even identical to the way they perceive the development of intelligence past the Piagetian stage of formal operations. For example, some authors have argued that wise individuals are those who can think reflectively or dialectically, in the latter case with the individuals' realizing that truth is not always absolute but rather evolves in a historical context of theses, antitheses, and syntheses (e.g., Labouvie-Vief, 1990). Consider a very brief review of some specific dialectical approaches.

Kitchener and Brenner (1990) suggested that wisdom requires a synthesis of knowledge from opposing points of view. Similarly, Labouvie-Vief has emphasized the importance of a smooth and balanced dialogue between logical forms of processing and more subjective forms of processing. Juan Pascual-Leone (1990) has argued for the importance of the dialectical integration of all aspects of a person's affect, cognition, conation (motivation), and life experience. Similarly, Orwoll and Perlmutter (1990) have emphasized the importance to wisdom of an integration of cognition with affect. Deirdre Kramer (1990) has suggested the importance of the integration of relativistic and dialectical modes of thinking, affect, and reflection. And Birren and Fisher (1990), putting together a number of views of wisdom, have suggested as well the importance of the integration of cognitive, conative, and affective aspects of human abilities. A common feature of these models is the balancing of different aspects of the mind – what Baltes and Staudinger (in press) refer to as the "orchestration of mind and virtue."

Other theorists have suggested the importance of knowing the limits of one's own extant knowledge and of then trying to go beyond them. For example, Meacham (1983) has suggested that an important aspect of wisdom is a kind of metacognition – an awareness of one's own fallibility and a knowledge of what one does and does not know. Kitchener and Brenner similarly have also emphasized the importance of knowing the limitations of one's own knowledge. Patricia Arlin (1990) has linked wisdom to problem finding, the first step of which is the recognition that how one currently defines a problem may be inadequate. Arlin views

problem finding as a possible stage of postformal-operational thinking. Such a view is not necessarily inconsistent with the view of dialectical thinking as such a postformal-operational stage. Dialectical thinking and problem finding could represent distinct postformal-operational stages, or two manifestations of the same postformal-operational stage.

Although most developmental approaches to wisdom are ontogenetic, Mihalyi Csikszentmihalyi and Kevin Rathunde (1990) have taken a philogenetic or evolutionary approach, arguing that constructs such as wisdom must have been selected for over time, at least in a cultural sense. Intelligence, too, has been understood by some in a cultural-evolutionary sense. In other words, wise ideas should survive better over time in a culture than unwise ideas. The theorists define wisdom as having three basic dimensions of meaning: (a) that of a cognitive process, or a particular way of obtaining and processing information; (b) that of a virtue, or socially valued pattern of behavior; and (c) that of a good or a personally desirable state or condition. The first of these dimensions seems to be primarily intellectual, whereas the latter two are not.

Wisdom according to another theory, the balance theory of wisdom (Sternberg, 1998), is the application of intelligence and experience as mediated by values towards the achievement of a common good through a balance among (a) intrapersonal, (b) interpersonal, and (c) extrapersonal interests, over the (a) short and (b) long terms, in order to achieve a balance among (a) adaptation to existing environments, (b) shaping of existing environments, and (c) selection of new environments.

FURTHER READING

Sternberg, R. J., ed. (1990). *Wisdom: its nature, origins, and development*. New York: Cambridge University Press.
    (2000). *Handbook of intelligence*. New York: Cambridge University Press.
Sternberg, R. J., and C. A. Berg, eds. (1992). *Intellectual development*. New York: Cambridge University Press.

REFERENCES

Arlin, P. K. (1990). "Wisdom: the art of problem finding." In R. J. Sternberg, ed., *Wisdom: its nature, origins, and development*. New York: Cambridge University Press, pp. 230–43.

Baltes, P. B. (1993). "The aging mind: potentials and limits," *Gerontologist*, 33: 580–94.

Baltes, P. B., and J. Smith (1990). "Toward a psychology of wisdom and its ontogenesis." In R. J. Sternberg, ed., *Wisdom: its nature, origins, and development*. New York: Cambridge University Press, pp. 87–120.

Baltes, P. B., and U. Staudinger (in press). *Wisdom: the orchestration of mind and virtue*. Boston: Blackwell.

Baltes, P. B., Staudinger, U. M., Maercker, A., and J. Smith (1995). "People nominated as wise: a comparative study of wisdom-related knowledge," *Psychology and Aging*, 10: 155–66.

Berg, C. A. (2000). "The intellectual development in adulthood." In R. J. Sternberg, ed., *Handbook of intelligence*. New York: Cambridge University Press, pp. 117–37.

Berg, C. A., and P. Klaczynski (1996). "Practical intelligence and problem solving: searching for perspective." In F. Blanchard-Fields and T. M. Hess, eds., *Perspectives on cognitive change in adulthood and aging*. New York: McGraw-Hill, pp. 323–57.

Birren, J. E., and L. M. Fisher (1990). "The elements of wisdom: overview and integration." In R. J. Sternberg, ed., *Wisdom: its nature, origins, and development*. New York: Cambridge University Press, pp. 317–32.

Charness, N., and S. Bieman-Copland (1994). "The learning prospective: adulthood." In R. J. Sternberg and C. A. Berg, eds., *Intellectual development*. New York: Cambridge University Press, pp. 301–27.

Charness, N., and E. A. Bosman (1990). "Expertise and ageing: life in the lab." In T. M. Hess, ed., *Aging and cognition: knowledge organization and utilization*. Amsterdam: Elsevier Science, pp. 343–85.

Clayton, V. (1975). "Erickson's theory of human development as it applies to the aged: wisdom as contradictory cognition," *Human Development*, 18: 119–28.

Cornelius, S. W., and A. Caspi (1987). "Everyday problem solving in adulthood and old age," *Psychology and Aging*, 2: 144–53.

Csikszentmihalyi, M., and K. Rathunde (1990). "The psychology of wisdom: an evolutionary interpretation." In R. J. Sternberg, ed., *Wisdom: its nature, origins, and development*. New York: Cambridge University Press, pp. 25–51.

Denney, N. W., and A. M. Palmer (1981). "Adult age differences on traditional and practical problem-solving measures," *Journal of Gerontology*, 36: 323–8.

Dixon, R. A., and P. B. Baltes (1986). "Toward life-span research on the functions and pragmatics of intelligence." In R. J. Sternberg and R. K. Wagner, eds., *Practical intelligence: nature and origins of competence in the everyday world*. New York: Cambridge University Press, pp. 203–35.

Holliday, S. G., and M. J. Chandler (1986). *Wisdom: explorations in adult competence*. Basel: Karger.

Horn, J. L. (1994). "Theory of fluid and crystallized intelligence." In R. J. Sternberg, ed., *The encyclopedia of human intelligence*, Vol. I. New York: Macmillan, pp. 443–51.

Kitchener, K. S., and H. G. Brenner (1990). "Wisdom and reflective judgment: knowing in the face of uncertainty." In R. J. Sternberg, ed., *Wisdom: its nature, origins, and development*. New York: Cambridge University Press, pp. 212–29.

Kramer, D. A. (1990). "Conceptualizing wisdom: the primacy of affect–cognition relations." In R. J. Sternberg, ed., *Wisdom: its nature, origins, and development*. New York: Cambridge University Press, pp. 279–313.

Labouvie-Vief, G. (1990). "Wisdom as integrated thought: historical and developmental perspectives." In R. J. Sternberg, ed., *Wisdom: its nature, origins, and development*. New York: Cambridge University Press, pp. 52–83.

Meacham, J. (1983). "Wisdom and the context of knowledge: knowing that one doesn't know." In D. Kuhn and J. A. Meacham, eds., *On the development of developmental psychology*. Basel, Switzerland: Karger, pp. 111–34.

Orwoll, L., and M. Perlmutter (1990). "The study of wise persons: integrating a personality perspective." In R. J. Sternberg, ed., *Wisdom: its nature, origins, and development*. New York: Cambridge University Press, pp. 160–77.

Pascual-Leone, J. (1990). "An essay on wisdom: toward organismic processes that make it possible." In R. J. Sternberg, ed., *Wisdom: its nature, origins, and development*. New York: Cambridge University Press, pp. 244–78.

Salthouse, T. A. (1998). "Relation of successive percentiles of reaction time distributions to cognitive variables and adult age," *Intelligence*, 26: 153–66.

Schaie, K. W. (1996). *Intellectual development in adulthood: the Seattle Longitudinal Study*. New York: Cambridge University Press.

Staudinger, U. M., and P. M. Baltes (1996). "Interactive minds: a facilitative setting for wisdom-related performance?" *Journal of Personality and Social Psychology*, 71: 746–62.

Staudinger, U. M., Smith, J., and P. B. Baltes (1992). "Wisdom-related knowledge in life review task: age differences and the role of professional specialization," *Psychology and Aging*, 7: 271–81.

Staudinger, U. M., Lopez, D. F., and P. B. Baltes (1997). "The psychometric location of wisdom-related performance: intelligence, personality, and more?" *Personality & Social Psychology Bulletin*, 23: 1200–14.

Sternberg, R. J. (1985). "Implicit theories of intelligence, creativity, and wisdom," *Journal of Personality and Social Psychology*, 49 (3): 607–27.

(1998). "A balance theory of wisdom," *Review of General Psychology*, 2: 347–65.

CHAPTER 3.5

Everyday Competence in Older Adults

K. WARNER SCHAIE, JULIE B. BORON, AND
SHERRY L. WILLIS

One of the prevailing concerns as individuals enter older adulthood is the ability to maintain an independent lifestyle. Maintaining independence requires possessing the abilities to care for the self and to manage one's property. The term "everyday competence" refers to the ability to solve problems associated with everyday life. While this definition is brief and simple, daily problems are often complex and multidimensional. At the heart of everyday competence is the ability to solve problems. Problem solving involves assessing the current state, defining the desired state, and finding ways or strategies to transform the current state into the desired state. In solving a problem, the individual often needs to make decisions. One may need to decide what is the problem, what is the desired outcome, and what are the alternative solutions that might lead to the desired outcome. The process of decision making involves the evaluation of these possible solutions and the selection of one to implement in order to attain the goal (Reese and Rodeheaver, 1985). Moreover, everyday problem solving is dynamic. As one ages the nature of the problems changes as well as the appropriateness and desirability of alternative solutions. Expectations regarding everyday competence often vary for the young-old versus the old-old, as well as solution options. The tasks associated with everyday competence also vary culturally and contextually. The context, in part, defines the tasks or problems associated with everyday competence for the elderly. Expectations regarding everyday competence vary dramatically within Western cultures as well as in third-world countries.

This chapter addresses four major issues. First, we consider various theoretical approaches to the study of everyday competence. Second, the literature on antecedents of everyday competence is reviewed. Third, alternative procedures for the measurement of everyday competence are considered. Finally, issues related to the maintenance of everyday competence are discussed.

While this chapter will consider everyday competence primarily from a social science perspective, the corollaries to legal definitions of competence are useful to acknowledge. Legal definitions of competence often include two domains – care of the self and care of one's property. Guardianship is concerned with the care, safety, and wellbeing of the self. Conservatorship is concerned with management of one's property. In social science terminology, the Activities of Daily Living (ADLs; Katz et al., 1963) usually comprise the activities assessed to determine competence to care for oneself. ADLs include the ability to toilet, bathe, feed, clothe, and transport oneself. The Instrumental Activities of Daily Living (IADLs; Lawton and Brody, 1969) constitute the activities assessed to decide whether a person is competent to manage property. IADLs consist of the ability to manage finances, prepare meals, manage medications, shop, use the telephone, clean the home, and use transportation. The IADLs are the types of activities more commonly incorporated in the assessment of everyday competence. Although psychological definitions are typically framed in terms of a person's competence, legal definitions often focus on impairment or incompetence. Legal and psychological definitions do converge with respect to four common themes (Grisso, 1994; Sabatino, 1996; Willis, 1996). In defining and assessing functioning, both perspectives take into account: (1) assignment of status or disabling condition, (2) emphasis given to cognitive functioning, (3) focus on a functional or behavioral impairment, not just a disease diagnosis, and (4) competence, seen as including the congruence of both the person's abilities and the demands and supports of the environment. Utilizing preventative measures, as well as modifications or interventions, can extend maintenance of everyday competence. Decreasing environmental demands, changing the social environment, appropriate health behaviors, and increasing skill, possibly through various training programs, serve as means to prolong everyday competence.

THEORETICAL APPROACHES TO EVERYDAY COMPETENCE

In recent years a number of alternative approaches have been taken to the study of everyday competence. The approaches vary in terms of whether the focus is almost solely on the characteristics of the individual or whether contexts, as well as the individual, are considered. Even in approaches focusing extensively on individual characteristics, there is variation in the degree to which noncognitive as well as cognitive factors are considered. The approaches also vary in whether competence is considered as a global phenomenon or whether a domain-specific perspective of competence (e.g. financial management, medication adherence) is taken.

Three different approaches to the study of everyday competence are considered in this section. It should be acknowledged that these approaches give greater attention to cognitive factors than when considering broader constructs, such as functional competence (Fillenbaum, 1987; Lawton and Brody, 1969), which are defined in terms of physical and social as well as cognitive components. The first perspective views everyday competence in terms of a hierarchical model in which subsets of basic cognitive abilities and skills serve as the "building blocks" for more cognitively complex everyday activities. In the second approach, everyday cognitive competence is conceptualized as involving

domain-specific knowledge bases. The focus in the third approach is on the fit, or congruence, between the individual's cognitive competency and the environmental demands faced by the individual. Willis (1996) presented a model for the study of everyday problem solving that was based on four assumptions: (1) antecedent characteristics of the problem solver and the sociocultural context; (2) the elderly are active problem solvers who construct a representation of the problem and its solution; (3) characteristics of the task (problem) interact with antecedent characteristics of the individual, and they influence the problem-solving process; and (4) the elderly's competence to solve a given problem reflects a match between the individual's problem-solving skills and the demands and resources of the immediate environment.

Componental and Hierarchical Models

In this section we consider several models that view cognition (including everyday problem solving) as involving multiple components (P. B. Baltes *et al.*, 1984; Labouvie-Vief, 1992; see also Park, 1992). Moreover, many models include a hierarchical perspective of cognition, extending from basic, factorially distinct abilities and skills to higher, more complex levels of cognition that are derived in part from these more basic abilities and skills. Everyday competence is represented as a higher-order complex form of cognition.

TRIARCHIC THEORY OF ADULT INTELLIGENCE. Sternberg (1985) has proposed a triarchic theory of adult intellectual development involving three components: metacomponential processes, experiential and contextual components. The first component, metacomponential processes, consists of processes such as encoding, allocation of mental resources, and monitoring of thought processes. The metacomponential components operate at different levels of experience with a task. Whether the components operate in a novel fashion or are in the process of becoming automatized determines how competent the person is at the task, with eventual automaticity signifying competency in the task. In addition, adjusting to environmental changes requires the capability to apply metacomponents at different levels of experience. The components most relevant to everyday competence are the experiential and contextual components. Both experience and environmental/contextual conditions impact performance or problem-solving ability.

PRAGMATICS AND MECHANICS OF INTELLIGENCE. Baltes and colleagues (P. B. Baltes *et al.*, 1984) proposed a componential model with two dimensions. In their approach the mechanisms of cognition are considered in terms of psychometric abilities, rather than the information processing model employed by Sternberg in describing metacomponents. Mechanics, the first component of the model, includes basic cognitive operations and structures associated with perceiving relationships, classification, and logical reasoning. "Pragmatics of intelligence" refers to the second component of the model, which encompasses function and application of intelligence, specifically the application of intelligence dependent upon the context. The second component involves generalized systems of knowledge, specialized dimensions of knowledge, and knowledge about factors of performance. This model suggests that everyday competence is more closely associated with the pragmatics of intelligence. The environmental context is critical to the particular form or manifestation in which pragmatic intelligence is shown. Baltes posits that although mechanisms of intelligence decline with age, there is enhancement in the pragmatic component through much of adulthood. This pragmatic component is developed throughout one's life in the form of declarative and procedural knowledge.

"BUILDING BLOCKS" OF COMPETENCE. Hierarchical relationships between basic cognition and everyday competence have been conceptualized by Willis and Schaie (Willis, 1987; Willis and Schaie, 1986, 1993). Basic cognition has been represented by domains of psychometric intelligence, such as the second-order constructs of fluid and crystallized intelligence and the primary mental abilities associated with each higher-order construct. Willis and Schaie suggest that everyday competences, as represented in activities of daily living, are phenotypic expressions of intelligence that are context- or age-specific. The particular activities and behaviors that serve as phenotypic expressions of intelligence vary with the age of the individual, that person's social roles, and the environmental context. Due to the complexity of problem solving in everyday activities, multiple basic cognitive abilities are involved in the process of solving a problem. The specific combination of basic cognitive processes varies for specific task demands and situational constraints. Allaire and Marsiske (1999) have also found that several basic cognitive abilities are involved in everyday cognitive performance. Their research supports the claim that everyday cognition is composed of a set of underlying, basic cognitive abilities, all of which may be drawn upon to solve novel or familiar tasks of daily living.

POSTFORMAL REASONING. Labouvie-Vief (1992) and colleagues (Labouvie-Vief and Hakim-Larson, 1989) have proposed the development in middle and later adulthood of a more pragmatic, concrete, and subjective approach to reality that focuses on inner, personal experiences. These age-related changes refer to the shift from bottom-up to top-down reasoning, meaning that older adults tend to focus on the end result or goal when solving a problem. Hence, they pay less attention to many details and are less likely to check their steps in solving a problem since the emphasis is on the end result. Older adults are believed to selectively use postformal-operational reasoning in everyday problems that are emotionally salient and pertinent to their lives. They rely heavily on prior experiences in solving problems and sometimes have difficulty judging whether prior experiences are relevant to the current tasks. In more recent work, Labouvie-Vief and colleagues (Diehl *et al.*, 1996; Labouvie-Vief, 2000) report that older adults use greater impulse control when applying coping and defense strategies. Labouvie-Vief (2000) found that coping was positively related to crystallized intelligence and reflective cognition, while defense coping was negatively related to these factors.

Domain-specific Models of Competence

This approach maintains that competence involves the development and organization of an increasingly complex and well-integrated body of knowledge that is domain-specific (Salthouse, 1990). The focus is on the manner in which a problem is represented by the problem solver and the increasingly complex manner in which domain-specific knowledge becomes integrated and organized. In this approach competence is specific to a particular domain or type of task, rather than being a global characteristic of the individual that is reflected in multiple content domains.

An example of domain-specific approach is provided by the work of Hershey and colleagues (1990) on financial decision-making. Through investigation of the different approaches novices and experts employ in solving financial problems, Hershey *et al.* found that experts utilize different information and work faster and more efficiently and accurately, compared to novices. In addition, experts tend to use problem-solving scripts to reach a solution. Through continued exposure and experience with a task, experts evolve sets of rules/scripts/algorithms that guide the identification of important facts and ways to organize these facts to reach a solution. The scripts serve as a template for the experts to use to solve problems encountered in a content domain, ranging from simple to extremely complex problems.

In another approach to study domain-specific knowledge, Sternberg and colleagues (Sternberg, 2002; Sternberg and Grigorenko, 2000) have studied what they call "tacit knowledge," the knowledge gained through the day-to-day experiences of life. They have examined the tacit knowledge acquired by those in a specific profession such as a salesman, engineer, or pharmacist. Tacit knowledge includes not only the factual information regarding chemistry and medications that a pharmacist may acquire, but also an understanding of how a pharmacist should interact and communicate with customers and how they progress professionally throughout their careers. Tacit knowledge is accumulated when individuals learn from their experiences and subsequently are able to achieve goals they consider personally relevant (Sternberg, 2002); Hershey's participants who had a wealth of knowledge regarding finances would be considered "experts" in tacit knowledge. Tacit knowledge would be relevant to everyday competence in the instances when individuals are able to draw upon prior experience, knowledge, and skills to solve encountered problems.

In study of domain-specific problem solving, a distinction is made between well-structured problems and ill-structured problems; ill-structured problems are often the novel experiences where effective problem solving is most pertinent since there is often more than one possible solution. Allaire

and Marsiske (2002) investigated well- and ill-structured approaches to measuring everyday cognition. They found that both well- and ill-defined measures of everyday cognition are predictive of real-world outcomes, hence suggesting that utilizing both approaches would be most advantageous in assessing everyday cognition. The domain-specific approach is nondevelopmental; competence arises out of automatization, prior experience, and the development of expertise in specific activities. According to Salthouse (1990), a lack of competence implies a mismatch of demands and skill.

Person–Environment Fit Models

The third approach to everyday competence emphasizes the degree of congruence between the abilities of the individual and the demands and resources available in the environment (Lawton, 1987; Willis, 1996). Competent behaviors occur when there is a match between individual capabilities and environmental demands and resources. For example, an older adult with some cognitive limitations may appear competent with respect to everyday activities when functioning in a supportive environment with many resources. In this perspective, a loss of competence can result from a decrease in individual ability, change in the environmental demands and/or resources, or a combination of the two. Models of person–environment fit emphasize that competence does not solely reside in the individual or the environment, but rather in the fit between the individual and the environment.

ANTECEDENTS OF EVERYDAY COMPETENCE

Everyday competence is a multidimensional concept. Although all of the perspectives addressed above focus specifically on the cognitive aspects of everyday competence, social support, health, personality, belief systems, and environmental demands may also impact everyday competence. Each individual comes to a problem with his/her own unique developmental history, which influences how the adult defines the problem and selects and utilizes strategies for resolving the problem. Many of these antecedent variables are intertwined. Medication compliance, for example, involves not only cognitive processes such as memory and reasoning but also the sensory ability to read the label, manual dexterity to open the bottle and measure the dosage, and social support.

Cognitive Abilities

Cattell (1987) differentiated between two broad domains of mental abilities: crystallized and fluid abilities. Crystallized abilities tend to remain relatively stable throughout old age, and are said to reflect acculturation influences, such as level of education. In contrast, fluid abilities involve abstract reasoning and speeded responding, and exhibit patterns of decline beginning, on average, in the mid-60s. Hence, depending on whether the tasks are more closely related to underlying fluid or crystallized abilities, older adults' performance on everyday tasks would be expected to show different patterns of developmental change. In an investigation on concurrent relationships between mental abilities and everyday tasks, Willis and colleagues (Willis and Marsiske, 1991; Willis and Schaie, 1986) found that over half of the variance in older adults' performance on everyday tasks could be accounted for by mental ability performance. Additionally, both fluid and crystallized abilities accounted for everyday task performance, with a somewhat greater portion of the variance accounted for by fluid abilities. Through a series of structural equation analyses, Willis et al. (1992) found that fluid ability at the first assessment occasion predicted everyday task performance seven years later. In contrast, everyday task performance at the first occasion predicted basic abilities at the second occasion less well (Willis et al., 1992). Overall, the findings supported their hypothesis that level of functioning on basic mental abilities is a significant antecedent of performance on everyday tasks involving printed materials. Allaire and Marsiske (1999) also found that everyday cognition represents "compiled cognition" in that cognitive abilities develop into cognitive competencies that manifest in adult life as everyday cognition. Each everyday task encountered involves multiple basic abilities, thus everyday tasks are cognitively complex because they involve more than one ability. Hence, individuals who experience decline in one or more cognitive abilities may experience increasing difficulty performing the tasks essential in daily life.

While Willis, Marsiske, and Allaire have examined the association between specific abilities and objective everyday task performance, Wolinsky and colleagues (Fitzgerald et al., 1993; Wolinsky et al., 1992) have investigated the relationship between global measures of cognitive functioning, the performance of Activities of Daily Living (ADLs) and Instrumental Activities of Daily Living (IADLs), and self-reports of everyday competence. Wolinsky and colleagues proposed three unidimensional scales termed "basic ADL," "household ADL," and "advanced or cognitive ADL." The basic ADL activities include personal activities such as bathing, dressing, walking, and toileting. The household ADL consists of household chores, meal preparation, and shopping. Managing money, using the telephone, and eating comprise the advanced or cognitive ADL. The advanced ADL was directly associated with global measures of cognitive functioning. Wolinsky's work lends further confirmation to the link between cognitive ability and everyday competence in specifically showing that IADLs in general require more cognitive capabilities than ADLs.

Park and colleagues have examined the association of various aspects of memory to a complex and important everyday task, adherence to a medication regimen (Park, 1992). Based on prior research in the field, Park suggested that both comprehension and retrospective aspects of memory should be problematic for adherence to a medication regimen in older adults. Morrell et al. (1989) found significantly more older adults (21 percent) to make errors on comprehension of prescription drug labels than young adults (14 percent). Morrell et al. (1989) also found that older adults had considerable difficulty with long-term recall of medication information when it was presented in an experimental setting. When given organizational devices that supported the cognitive demands of the task, the adherence behaviors of older adults improved significantly (Park et al., 1992).

Health

The individual's health impacts not only physical ability to carry out everyday tasks but also the cognitive aspects. Sensory impairment is a major aspect of health that affects everyday problem solving. Branch, Horowitz, and Carr (1989) investigated the relationship between ability to perform tasks of daily living and visual impairment. Self-reported interviews were compared between those consistently reporting good vision and those reporting a decline in vision over a 5-year period. Results indicated that those reporting a decline in vision were more likely to need assistance with shopping and paying bills, were 1.5 times less likely to leave their residence, and only half as likely to travel by car. Fincham (1988) found that elderly persons with multiple disease pathologies who were taking multiple drugs with complicated regimens were less compliant in taking their medications. Health also has implications for everyday competence when reviewed in terms of social support.

Social Support

As people age, everyday competence involves the ability to adapt to changing situations in one's health and the environment. Antonucci and Jackson (1987) have proposed the Support/Efficacy Model of social relations to explain the processes and mechanisms through which social relations might have an observed positive effect on health and wellbeing. This model predicts that supportive others help older people set and meet goals that maximize adaptation to the challenges of ageing or illnesses. For older adults, this model has been applied most directly to the health/disease continuum.

Researchers have demonstrated the effect of supportive others on maintaining effective lifestyles and health behaviors at the predisease level (Rakowski *et al.*, 1988; Umberson, 1987). At the point of a specific health crisis, supportive others can help with treatment choices, or simply reassurance. Finally, supportive others can provide psychological support in the rehabilitation period; this is an especially critical time when social relations with others are essential in providing motivation to recover. Aside from strictly health-related social support, Antonucci and Akiyama (1997) state that social support for older adults includes confiding, reassurance, respect, talking about problems, and talking about health. In a study of older African Americans, Whitfield and Wiggins (2003) found that social support is a predictor of everyday problem solving. Whitfield and Wiggins noted that both giving and receiving social sup-

port are important contributors to everyday competence, and that those who gave social support had higher levels of everyday problem solving. Their research also contributed support to the view that physical limitations partially mediate the relationship between social support and everyday problem solving.

Personality

Personality traits display remarkable stability throughout the adult lifecourse (McCrae and Costa, 1990). Hence, personality or cognitive-style variables can provide important information on individual differences associated with how problems are represented, coped with, or resolved. Cox (1967) investigated the association between personality characteristics, cognitive style, and willingness to try innovative products. Those tolerant of ambiguity engaged in more extensive information searches, particularly when ambiguous or discrepant information about products was involved (Schaninger and Schiglimpaglia, 1981). Those intolerant of ambiguity or high in trait anxiety were less likely to be attracted to or to buy products that were novel, complex, or innovative. When examining the cognitive styles of simplifiers versus clarifiers in relation to problem solving in the consumer context, Cox (1967) found that simplifiers tended to react to uncertain or inconsistent product information by avoiding the incongruent information. By contrast, clarifiers actively sought new and additional information in order to reduce the ambiguity or inconsistencies.

Leventhal and colleagues (1993) noted the salience of personality characteristics, such as tolerance for ambiguity, in medical decision-making. When compared to middle-aged adults, older patients made quicker decisions when they were ill and also sought medical care sooner when they judged the condition to be serious. Quicker decision-making was interpreted as being due to less tolerance of ambiguity and the need to reduce uncertainty on the part of the older adults. Meyer and colleagues (1995) also found that, in making decisions about treatment for breast cancer, older women made quicker decisions and were more likely to seek less information about treatment than younger women. Evidence from this research suggests that personality characteristics may impact not only the desired outcome, but also the strategy chosen to achieve that outcome.

Belief Systems about Knowledge

Kuhn (1992) has suggested that individuals' beliefs about knowledge and ways of knowing influence their approaches to problem solving. Three types of belief systems were identified based on the certainty of knowledge and the process by which knowledge is acquired. The absolutists believe that knowledge is certain and cumulative; even complex questions can be answered with complete certainty. Multiplists or relativists hold that no knowledge is absolutely certain, and that all opinions are of equal validity. The third type, evaluative, viewed knowing as a process rather than a certainty, and the focus was on use of thinking, evaluation, and argument in order to examine the relative merits of various types of information. The work of Kuhn and others (Kramer and Woodruff, 1986) suggest that individuals' beliefs about the certainty of knowledge and ways of knowing may be more salient in their approach to the problem than the characteristics of the problem as defined by the investigator.

Berg and colleagues (1998) have examined the impact of individual characteristics on everyday problem solving. They found that how the individuals defined the problem was reflected through interpersonal characteristics or competence components or both. Strategies used reflected altering cognitions, actions, or regulating and including others. Age differences were also observed in how the problem was defined. These results demonstrate the importance of individuals' definition of the problem for addressing the effects of age and context on strategy use. Hence individual differences emerge in defining the problem, strategy used to solve the problem, and context of the problem, all of which impact everyday problem solving.

MEASUREMENT OF EVERYDAY COMPETENCE

Everyday competence is defined in terms of ability to maintain an autonomous lifestyle. Measures of competence then focus on activities involved in living independently. In the field of gerontol-ogy and geriatrics, requirements for maintaining independent living have generally focused on the ability to complete certain common activities of daily living. Katz and colleagues (1963) devised one set of criteria termed the Activities of Daily Living (ADLs). ADLs include tasks that are primarily concerned with self-care, such as feeding, bathing, toileting, and basic mobility. Lawton and Brody (1969) also have a set of criteria associated with more complex tasks of independent living. These tasks are known as the Instrumental Activities of Daily Living (IADLs). Seven domains comprise the IADLs including managing medications, shopping for necessities, managing one's finances, using transportation, using the telephone, maintaining one's household (housekeeping), and meal preparation and nutrition (Fillenbaum, 1985; Lawton and Brody, 1969). The ADLs and IADLs are generally included when appraising everyday competence. ADL and IADL serve as phenotypic expressions of everyday intelligence that vary with age, social roles, and environmental context (Schaie and Willis, 1999). Three approaches to assessment of everyday competence have been studied: objective measures, subjective measures, and behavioral observation. There are benefits and limitations to each type of assessment, hence using more than one type of measure when assessing everyday competence is optimal.

Subjective Assessments of Everyday Competence

The traditional and most common assessment approach involves subjective ratings of everyday competence. This type of measure reflects the individual's perception of his/her own skills and abilities. One commonly used measure is the Instrumental Activities of Daily Living (IADL; Lawton and Brody, 1969), in which individuals report the degree of help needed with these activities. Usually self-report measures also contain descriptions of tasks primarily concerned with self-care, such as feeding, bathing, toileting, and basic mobility, for which individuals must also report the degree of help needed. Often subjective measures require the individual to report how well he/she performs tasks relative to others in their same age group or cohort. Although self-reports may not be completely accurate, use of a subjective measure may dissipate anxiety, fatigue, unfamiliarity, and other biases imposed by objective measures.

In an attempt to capture multiple levels of self-reported competence, and hence a more complete representation of everyday competence, in the Berlin Aging Study M. M. Baltes and colleagues (1999) differentiated between a basic level of competence and an expanded level of competence. A basic level of competence included the ability to perform activities necessary to maintain health and independence, such as bathing, eating, dressing, and shopping. An expanded level of competence was composed of activities based on individual preferences, skills, motivations, and interests. Results indicated that there was a direct relationship between basic and expanded levels of competence.

Objective Assessments of Everyday Competence

In objective assessment of everyday competence the elder is presented with a description or stimulus material (e.g. prescription label) related to an everyday task and then asked to solve one or more problems related to the task. The measures vary in types of everyday tasks included and how the accuracy of elders' responses are evaluated or scored.

Willis and her colleagues (Marsiske and Willis, 1995; Willis and Marsiske, 1991; Willis and Schaie, 1993) developed an instrument designed to assess skills associated with the IADL domains. Some of the categories are similar to those evaluated in the Basic Skills Test. The Everyday Problems Test (EPT) consists of seven scales including food preparation, medication use, telephone use, shopping and consumerism, financial management, housekeeping, and transportation. Reliability estimates for the EPT have been in the moderate to high range (Marsiske and Willis, 1995). Although the Basic Skills Test and the EPT reflect an individual's competency level in certain domains, as opposed to the single index score produced by the Minimental State Examination (MMSE) and the Dementia Severity Rating Scale (DRS), the content of these measures constrains the definition of competence to the domains assessed. In addition, even though the tasks assessed are relevant to daily life, the method in which participants must respond to the tasks differs from daily life, responding as a paper-and-pencil task as opposed to actively doing the task.

Cornelius and Caspi (1987) took a different approach to assessing everyday competence. Using Goldfried and D'Zurilla's (1969) behavior-analytic model for assessing competence, Cornelius and Caspi devised the Everyday Problem Solving Inventory (EPSI; 1987). This measure consisted of six content domains described as problems that an adult might experience: (a) as an economic consumer, (b) in dealing with complex or technical information, (c) in managing a home, (d) in resolving interpersonal conflicts with one's family members, (e) in resolving conflicts with friends, and (f) in conflict resolution with co-workers. Two characteristics of the various situations were of particular importance, the age relevance of the situations and the person who caused the problem. This inventory considers four possible responses based on the literature on coping with real-life stressors (Lazarus and Folkman, 1984). The four possible response modes were: (1) problem-focused action, (2) cognitive problem analysis, (3) passive-dependent behavior, and (4) avoidant thinking and denial. Judges evaluated the adequacy of each response mode for a given problem.

In a third approach to objective assessment, Denney and her colleagues (Denney and Palmer, 1981; Denney et al., 1982) have also done research on practical problem solving. Denney's work is primarily based upon open-ended responses to hypothetical problems (Denney and Pearce, 1989).

Although many objective instruments measuring everyday competence exist, not much research on convergence among these instruments has been explored. Marsiske and Willis (1995) investigated the relationships among the Practical Problems Test (Denney and Pearce, 1989), the Everyday Problem Solving Inventory: Situational decision making (Cornelius and Caspi, 1987), and the Everyday Problems Test (Willis and Marsiske, 1991). Results indicated that, although there was little relation between the instruments, content domains within each of the instruments could be identified. Marsiske and Willis (1995) noted that these findings may be because the three instruments assess different tasks, and possibly even distinct aspects of everyday cognition. In addition, the various measures employed may have required the use of different combinations of cognitive abilities. Results from this study simply reiterate that everyday competence is a multidimensional construct involving many cognitive abilities.

Behavioral Observation of Everyday Competence

A third type of measure of everyday competence is behavioral observation. When behavioral observation methods are used, an individual is observed when completing a subset of tasks, usually IADLs such as counting change, telling the time, and looking up a number in the phone book. One behavioral observation measure is the Observational Tasks of Daily Living (OTDL; Diehl *et al.*, 1995). This measure evaluates food preparation, medication intake, and telephone use. Individuals are required to read material and then perform the appropriate actions to complete a task. A second type of behavioral observation measure is The Direct Assessment of Functional Status (DAFS; Loewenstein *et al.*, 1989) that measures time orientation, communication, finances, shopping, eating, and dressing. The DAFS was developed for use with cognitively challenged elders, while the OTDL was developed for use with nondemented, community-dwelling elders. An obvious limitation of behavioral observation is that ratings are based on observers, which presents the possibility of bias. Additionally, although actively performing the task is a more realistic assessment than a paper-and-pencil one, there is still the possibility that the individual must perform the task out of context.

Researchers have reported only modest correlations between self-reports and objective or behavioral measures of functional competence (Fillenbaum, 1978; Willis, 1996). The association between objective and behavioral measures is much higher than between objective/behavioral measures and self-report measures. The antecedents found to be related to objective versus subjective assessments often differ. For example, cognitive ability has been found to show a higher association with objective and behavioral assessments. In contrast, health status, report of disease and disability, use of health services, and social support have been found to exhibit a stronger relation to subjective assessments than to some objective/behavioral measures. Health-related values show a significant but more modest association with objective/behavioral measures.

Due in part to the influence of different antecedent variables for objective versus subjective measurements, the two types of assessment would not be expected to have a high association.

MAINTAINING EVERYDAY COMPETENCE

It is obvious that everyday competence is a dynamic process involving characteristics of the individual and of the environment that change quantitatively and qualitatively throughout adulthood. Thus, theoretical models and measures of everyday functioning need to include not only the level of functioning of the individual, but also quantitative and qualitative changes and rate of change in functioning. Since maintaining an independent lifestyle is so important to older adults, strategies or methods to facilitate maintenance of everyday competence is of concern to both the individual and society. Competence in everyday problem solving occurs when the abilities of the problem solver are congruent with the demands of the environment. Throughout adult development, the shifts in individual ability and situational demands require older adults constantly to familiarize and adapt to novel circumstances. One of the most noticeable declines that older adults face as tasks take on increasing complexity is in their reaction time. Additionally, fluid and visualization abilities tend to experience decline with increasing age. Maintenance of everyday competence can be facilitated in at least three ways: through social or institutional support, environmental modifications, and behavioral interventions.

The Support/Efficacy model of social relations proposed by Antonucci and Jackson (1987) describes how supportive social relationships can have a positive effect on health and wellbeing. Since changes in physical health or health status often accompany the ageing process, the assistance of supportive others can help older adults cope and adjust to the challenges of ageing, especially functional/behavioral impairments. Thus, the support of others can not only aid older adults at the time of health crisis and recovery, but can also help older adults adopt/maintain appropriate preventative health measures, such as proper nutrition, seatbelt use, and medication compliance, contributing to the person–environment fit. Social support is most commonly provided by family and friends. However, there is also formal, institutional support from community, state, and federal agencies. Programs such as Share a Ride, Meals on Wheels, and Fuel Subsidies are examples of formal institutional support.

Modifying the environment, and thus decreasing environmental demands, is a second method that can prolong independent living for older adults. There are many environmental modifications that can be instituted to increase an individual's capability to live independently. An individual's home environment could be physically modified to make it easier to bathe and cook by adding devices to assist the older adult with these tasks. In addition, older adults could receive assistance with shopping by utilizing a grocery delivery service. Social services, such as meals on wheels, transportation, and medical care professionals, could also be employed to facilitate independent living. Family members and/or friends could also help contribute to the older adult's independence by assisting with ADLs and/or IADLs.

Another way to promote everyday competence in older adults is through interventions. Interventions differ from modifications in that interventions focus on increasing the individual's skill level, rather than decreasing the environmental demands. Most research on increasing individual skill has focused on cognitive training programs. Cognitive training programs can serve as a preventative measure for those individuals who have not yet experienced decline, or as an intervention for those who have begun to show slight decline. The purpose of cognitive training programs is to help prevent further decline and possibly remedy any decline already experienced. The targeted abilities for most training programs include fluid abilities such as inductive reasoning, processing speed, spatial orientation, and verbal memory. To date, cognitive training programs have focused on a single ability. Much research has demonstrated that the cognitive training programs were able to improve individual skill level on the single ability trained. However, since everyday competence is a multidimensional construct involving multiple abilities, future behavioral interventions may need to develop programs training individuals on multiple abilities. Training on

these abilities can affect the cognitive abilities associated with daily functioning.

The overarching purpose of training programs is to improve skill on cognitive ability in addition to improving quality of life for older adults in terms of health and mobility. One of the most recent training programs, A Cognitive Intervention Trial to Promote Independence in Older Adults (ACTIVE; Jobe et al., 2001), attempts to produce primary and secondary outcomes through training older adults on the abilities of memory, reasoning, and speed of processing. Hence, the researchers are attempting to enhance everyday functioning and secondarily to influence health-related quality of life, mobility, and health service utilization, by training individuals on cognitive abilities.

Prior research on everyday problem solving has focused primarily on elders in young-old and old-old age. Thus, the tasks of everyday problem solving most intensively studied have been those encountered by those 60 to 75 years of age. However, most adults live independently into their 80s and increasingly into their 90s. Thus, the study of everyday functioning must increasingly consider changes in everyday functioning occurring in the oldest-old. Cross-sectional and the more limited longitudinal research available suggests that decline in everyday functioning occurs somewhat later than for the fluid basic abilities. Poon et al. (1992) found negative age effects on all cognitive measures, with the exception of a practical problem-solving measure by Denney and colleagues (Denney et al., 1982). However, after age 75 or 80, the rate of decline in everyday tasks increases markedly. Thus, the oldest-old are most vulnerable to notable decline in the tasks required to live independently (Marsiske and Willis, 1995).

Maintaining the ability to solve problems encountered in daily life effectively is essential for older adults to retain their ability to live independently. Although cognitive factors are extremely important to everyday problem solving, other factors such as health, personality, social support, belief systems, and environmental context must be considered as well. Due to the variety of tasks encountered in daily life, all of the abilities are important to everyday competence. Individuals must attempt to prevent any cognitive abilities from experiencing decline if maintaining competence to live independently is desired. All of the individual factors involved in everyday problem solving can impact one's ability to maintain an independent lifestyle. Hence, all of these individual factors must also be considered when employing preventative measures, environmental modifications, and/or interventions.

FURTHER READING

Baltes, M. M., Maas, I., Wilms, H.-U., Borchelt, M., and T. D. Little (1999). "Everyday competence in old and very old age: theoretical considerations and empirical findings." In P. B. Baltes and K. U. Mayer, eds., *The Berlin Aging Study: aging from 70 to 100*. New York: Cambridge University Press, pp. 384–402.

Berg, C. A., Strough, J., Calderone, K. S., Sansone, C., and C. Weir (1998). "The role of problem definitions in understanding age and context effects on strategies for solving everyday problems," *Psychology and Aging*, 13: 29–44.

Schaie, K. W., and S. L. Willis (1999). "Theories of everyday competence and aging." In V. L. Bengtson and K. W. Schaie, eds., *Handbook of theories of aging*. New York: Springer Publishing Co., pp. 174–95.

Sternberg, R. J., and E. L. Grigorenko (2000). "Practical intelligence and its development." In R. Bar-Oh and J. D. A. Parker, eds., *The handbook of emotional intelligence: theory, development, assessment, and application at home, school, and in the workplace*. San Francisco, Calif.: Jossey-Bass/Pfeiffer, pp. 215–43.

REFERENCES

Allaire, J. C., and M. Marsiske (1999). "Everyday cognition: age and intellectual ability correlates," *Psychology and Aging*, 14 (4): 627–44.

(2002). "Well- and ill-defined measures of everyday cognition: relationship to older adults' intellectual ability and functional status," *Psychology and Aging*, 17: 101–15.

Antonucci, T. C., and H. Akiyama (1997). "Social support and the maintenance of competence." In S. L. Willis, K. W. Schaie, and M. Hayward, eds., *Societal mechanisms for maintaining competence in old age*. New York: Springer Publishing Co., pp. 182–206.

Antonucci, T. C., and J. S. Jackson (1987). "Social support, interpersonal efficacy, and health: a life course perspective." In L. L. Carstensen and B. A. Edelstein, eds., *Handbook of clinical gerontology*. New York: Pergamon Press.

Baltes, P. B., Dittman-Kohli, F., and R. Dixon (1984). "New perspective on the development of intelligence in adulthood: toward a dual-process conception and a model of selective optimization with compensation."

In P. B. Baltes and O. G. Brim, Jr., eds., *Life-span development and behavior*, Vol. VI. New York: Academic Press, pp. 33–76.

Baltes, M. M., Maas, I., Wilms, H.-U., Borchelt, M., and T. D. Little (1999). "Everyday competence in old and very old age: theoretical considerations and empirical findings." In P. B. Baltes and K. U. Mayer, eds., *The Berlin Aging Study: Aging from 70 to 100*. New York: Cambridge University Press, pp. 384–402.

Berg, C. A., Strough, J., Calderone, K. S., Sanson, C., and C. Weir (1998). "The role of problem definitions in understanding age and context effects on strategies for solving everyday problems," *Psychology and Aging*, 13: 29–44.

Branch, L. G., Horowitz, A., and C. Carr (1989). "The implications for everyday life of incidents of self-reported visual decline among people over age 65 living in the community," *Gerontologist*, 29: 359–65.

Cattell, R. B., ed. (1987). *Intelligence: its structure, growth and action*. Amsterdam: North-Holland.

Cornelius, S. W., and A. Caspi (1987). "Everyday problem solving in adulthood and old age," *Psychology and Aging*, 2: 144–53.

Cox, D. F., ed. (1967). *Risk taking and information handling in consumer behavior*. Boston, Mass.: Harvard University Press.

Denney, N. W., and A. M. Palmer (1981). "Adult age difference on traditional practical problem-solving measures," *Journal of Gerontology*, 36: 323–8.

Denney, N. W., and K. A. Pearce (1989). "A developmental study of practical problem solving in adults," *Psychology and Aging*, 4: 438–442.

Denney, N. W., Pearce, K. A., and A. M. Palmer (1982). "A developmental study of adults' performance on traditional and practical problem-solving tasks," *Experimental Aging Research*, 8: 115–18.

Diehl, M., Willis, S. L., and K. W. Schaie (1995). "Practical problem solving in older adults: observational assessment and cognitive correlates," *Psychology and Aging*, 10: 478–91.

Diehl, M., Coyle, N., and G. Labouvie-Vief (1996). "Age and sex differences in strategies of coping and defense across the life span," *Psychology and Aging*, 11: 127–39.

Educational Testing Service (1977). *Basic skills assessment test: reading*. Princeton, N.J.: Educational Testing Service.

Fillenbaum, G. G. (1978). "Reliability and validity of the OARS multidimensional functional assessment questionnaire." In Duke University Center for the Study of Aging, *Multidimensional functional assessment: the OARS methodology*, 2nd edn. Durham, N.C.: Duke University.

(1985). "Screening the elderly: a brief instrumental activities of daily living measure," *Journal of the American Geriatrics Society*, 33: 698–706.

(1987). "Multidimensional functional assessment." In G. L. Maddox, ed., *The encyclopedia of aging.* New York: Springer Publishing Co., pp. 460–4.

Fincham, J. E. (1988). "Patient compliance in the ambulatory elderly: a review of the literature," *Journal of Geriatric Drug Therapy,* 2: 31–52.

Fitzgerald, J. F., Smith, D. M., Martin, D. K., Freedman, J. A., and F. D. Wolinsky (1993). "Replication of the multidimensionality of activities of daily living," *Journal of Gerontology: Social Sciences,* 48: S28–S31.

Goldfried, M. R., and T. J. D'Zurilla (1969). "A behavioral-analytic model for assessing competence." In C. D. Spielberger, ed., *Current topics in clinical and community psychology,* Vol. I. New York: Academic Press, pp. 151–96.

Grisso, T. (1994). "Clinical assessment for legal competency of older adults." In M. Storandt and G. R. Vanden Bos, eds., *Neuropsychological assessment of dementia and depression in older adults: a clinician's guide.* Washington, D.C.: American Psychological Association, pp. 119–39.

Hershey, D. A., Walsh, D. A., Read, S. J., and A. S. Chulef (1990). "The effects of expertise on financial problem solving: evidence for goal-directed, problem-solving scripts," *Organizational Behavior and Human Decision Processes,* 46: 77–101.

Jobe, J. B., Smith, D. M., Ball, K., Tennstedt, S. L., Marsiske, M., Willis, S. L., Rebok, G. W., Morris, J. N., Helmers, K. F., Leveck, M. D., and K. Kleinman (2001). "ACTIVE: a cognitive intervention trial to promote independence in older adults," *Controlled Clinical Trials,* 22: 453–79.

Katz, S., Ford, A. Moskowitz, R., Jackson, B., and M. Jaffee (1963). "Studies of illness in the aged: the Index of ADL, a standardized measure of biological and psychological function." *JAMA,* 185: 94–9.

Krammer, D., and D. Woodruff (1986). "Relativistic and dialectical thought in three adult age groups," *Human Development,* 29: 280–90.

Kuhn, D. (1992). "Thinking as argument," *Harvard Educational Review,* 62: 155–78.

Labouvie-Vief, G. (1992). "A neo-Piagetian perspective on adult cognitive development." In R. J. Sternberg and C. A. Berg, eds., *Intellectual development.* New York: Cambridge University Press, pp. 197–228.

(2000). "Cognitive complexity and cognitive-affective integration: related or separate domains of adult development?" *Psychology and Aging,* 15 (3): 490–504.

Labouvie-Vief, G., and J. Hakim-Larson (1989). "Developmental shifts in adult thought." In S. Hunter and M. Sundel, eds., *Midlife myths.* Newbury Park: Sage.

Lawton, M. P. (1987). "Contextual perspectives: psychosocial influences." In L. W. Poon, ed., *Handbook for clinical memory assessment of older adults.* Washington, D.C.: American Psychological Association.

Lawton, M. P., and E. M. Brody (1969). "Assessment of older people: self-maintaining and instrumental activities of daily living," *Gerontologist,* 9: 179–85.

Lazarus, R. S., and S. Folkman (1984). *Stress, appraisal, and coping.* New York: Springer.

Leventhal, E. A., Leventhal, H., Schaefer, P. M., and D. Easterling (1993). "Conservation of energy, uncertainty reduction, and swift utilization of medical care among the elderly," *Journal of Gerontology: Psychological Sciences,* 48: 78–86.

Loewenstein, D. A., Amigo, E., Duara, R., Guterman, A., Hurwitz, D., Berkowitz, N., Wilkie, F., Weinberg, G., Black, B., Gittelman, B., and C. Eisdorfer (1989). "A new scale for the assessment of functional status in Alzheimer's Disease and related disorders," *Journal of Gerontology: Psychological Sciences,* 44: 114–21.

Marsiske, M., and S. L. Willis (1995). "Dimensionality of everyday problem solving in older adults," *Psychology and Aging,* 10: 269–83.

McCrae, R. R., and P. T. Costa (1990). *Personality in adulthood.* New York: Guiford.

Meyer, B. J. F., Russo, C., and A. Talbot (1995). "Discourse comprehension and problem solving: decisions about the treatment of breast cancer by women across the life span," *Psychology and Aging,* 10: 84–103.

Morrell, R. W., Park, D. C., and L. W. Poon (1989). "Quality of instructions on prescription drug labels: effects on memory and comprehension in young and old adults," *Gerontologist,* 29: 345–54.

Park, D. C. (1992). "Applied cognitive aging research." In F. I. M. Craik and T. A. Salthouse, eds., *Handbook of cognition and aging.* Hillsdale, N.J.: Erlbaum, pp. 449–93.

Park, D. C., Morrell, R. W., Frieske, D., and D. Kincaid (1992). "Medication adherence behaviors in older adults: effects of external cognitive supports," *Psychology and Aging,* 7: 252–6.

Poon, L. W., Martin, P., Clayton, G. M., Messner, S., Noble, C. A., and M. A. Johnson (1992). "The influences of cognitive resources on adaptation and old age," *International Journal of Aging and Human Development,* 34: 31–46.

Rakowski, W., Julius, M., Hickey, T., Verbrugge, L. M., and J. B. Halter (1988). "Daily symptoms and behavioral responses results of a health diary with older adults," *Medical Care,* 26 (3): 278–97.

Reese, H. W., and D. Rodeheaver (1985). "Problem solving and complex decision making." In J. E. Birren and K. W. Schaie, eds., *Handbook of the psychology of aging,* 2nd edn. New York: Van Nostrand-Reinhold, pp. 474–99.

Sabatino, C. P. (1996). "Competency: refining our legal fictions." In M. Smyer, K. W. Schaie, and M. Kapp, eds., *Older adults' decision-making and the law.* New York: Springer Publishing Co., pp. 1–28.

Salthouse, T. A. (1990). "Cognitive competence and expertise in the aging." In J. E. Birren and K. W. Schaie, eds., *Handbook of the psychology of aging*, 3rd edn. San Diego, Calif.: Academic Press, pp. 311–19.

Schaie, K. W., and S. L. Willis (1999). "Theories of everyday competence and aging." In V. L. Bengtston and K. W. Schaie, eds., *Handbook of theories of aging*. New York: Springer Publishing Co., pp. 174–95.

Schaninger, D. M., and D. Schiglimpaglia (1981). "The influence of cognitive personality traits and demographics on consumer information acquisition," *Journal of Consumer Research*, 8: 208–16.

Sternberg, R. J. (1985). *Beyond IQ: A triarchic theory of human intelligence*. New York: Cambridge University Press.

(2002). "Smart people are not stupid, but they sure can be foolish: the imbalance theory of foolishness." In R. J. Sternberg, ed., *Why smart people can be so stupid*. New Haven: Yale University Press, pp. 232–42.

Sternberg, R. J., and E. L. Grigorenko (2000). "Practical intelligence and its development." In R. Bar-Oh and J. D. A. Parker, eds., *The handbook of emotional intelligence: theory, development, assessment, and application at home, school, and in the workplace*. San Francisco, Calif.: Jossey-Bass/Pfeiffer, pp. 215–43.

Umberson, D. (1987). "Family status and health behaviors: social control as a dimension of social integration," *Journal of Health and Social Behavior*, 38: 306–19.

Whitfield, K. E., and S. Wiggins (2003). "The influence of social support and health on everyday problem solving in adult African Americans," *Experimental Aging Research*, 29: 1–13.

Willis, S. L. (1987). "Cognitive interventions in the elderly," *Annual Review of Gerontology and Geriatrics*, 11: 159–88.

(1996). "Everyday problem solving." In J. E. Birren and K. W. Schaie, eds., *Handbook of the psychology of aging*, 4th edn. San Diego: Academic Press, pp. 287–307.

Willis, S. L., and M. Marsiske (1991). "A life-span perspective on practical intelligence." In D. Tupper and K. Cicerone, eds., *The neuropsychology of everyday life*. Boston: Kluwer Academic Publishers, pp. 183–98.

Willis, S. L., and K. W. Schaie (1986). "Practical intelligence in later adulthood." In R. Sternberg and R. Wagner, eds., *Practical intelligence*. New York: Cambridge University Press, pp. 236–70.

(1993). "Everyday cognition: taxonomic and methodological considerations." In J. M. Puckett and H. W. Reese, eds., *Mechanisms of everyday cognition*. Hillsdale, N.J.: Erlbaum, pp. 33–54.

Willis, S. L., Jay, G. M., Diehl, M., and M. Marsiske (1992). "Longitudinal change and prediction of everyday task competence in the elderly," *Research on Aging*, 14: 68–91.

Wolinsky, F. D., Johnson, R. J., and J. F. Fitzgerald (1992). "Falling, health status, and the use of health services by older adults: a prospective study," *Medical Care*, 30: 587–97.

The Psychology of Emotions and Ageing

GISELA LABOUVIE-VIEF

How individuals adjust to adversity and difficult life experiences by maintaining positive levels of affect and wellbeing has presented a paradox to researchers into ageing. As we grow older, we are faced with a decline of adaptive reserves of various kinds; we experience a shrinking of the temporal horizon and begin to experience ourselves as mortal; we increasingly experience bereavement and loss, failing health, and the restriction of more youthful roles, dreams, and ideals. From such evidence one might expect a picture of lowered self-esteem and positive affect in old age. Yet, quite to the contrary, older individuals maintain a good sense of wellbeing (e.g. Carstensen *et al.*, 2003; Mroczek and Kolarz, 1998; Staudinger *et al.*, 1995).

Such evidence has suggested a remarkable adaptive "resiliency" (Staudinger *et al.*, 1995) in older individuals who, in the face of loss or of the temporal limits of the lifespan, arrange their environments so as to maximize positive and dampen negative affect. Yet maintenance of positivity is not *always* a sign of "good" emotional development, but also may indicate restrictions in individuals' ability to coordinate positive and negative affect into flexible and differentiated views of reality. How to negotiate these two goals of emotion regulation – maintaining overall positive affect on one hand, and securing an overall objective representation of reality on the other – constitutes a second criterion of "good" emotional development. To maintain such a balance is a challenge at any stage of life, but may be particularly so in later life. Which criterion one adopts in evaluating the extant literature is, in part, a matter of the theory of emotion regulation which researchers

adopt. Below, I distinguish between two primary theoretical strands and review the literature associated with each.

AGEING AND "PRIMARY" EMOTIONS

A major body of research on ageing and emotions has been derived in one way or another from differential emotions theory, which is based on the notion that there are a limited number of basic, hard-wired emotion systems that have evolved to deal with emergency situations in a highly automated, safe, and reliable way (Darwin, 1955; Ekman, 1984; Izard, 1997). These primary emotion systems involve specific programs for such "negative" emotions as anger, fear, sadness, and disgust, and "positive" emotions such as joy/happiness, love, and interest/surprise. These programs are thought to be quite invariant with respect to age, although individuals can learn to link them to specific situations (e.g. anger at the malfunctioning of a car) as a result of their individual learning history. A large body of research has examined whether these primary emotional systems appear to remain intact with age, and whether individuals are able to regulate the arousal/activation associated with them.

Positive Affect Balance in Later Life

As already noted, many researchers who compared younger and older adults by means of self-report assessments of emotions have been impressed with the positive emotional balance of older individuals (Charles *et al.*, 2001; Labouvie-Vief and Medler,

2002; Mroczek and Kolarz, 1998). Such positive balance reflects a systematic decline in negative emotions throughout the adult lifespan, while positive emotions appear to remain fairly constant. This work is also supported by a series of studies suggesting that older individuals are less likely to use immature defenses than younger adults, and more likely to use such defenses as giving an abstract meaning to an event or reversing that meaning (Diehl *et al.*, 1996). Older individuals also indicate they are better able to control their emotions than are younger individuals, and instead rely on such mechanisms as principalization and reversal. Overall, they indicate better levels of self-control (Gross, 1998; Gross *et al.*, 1997), suggesting that they display high levels of "expertise" in regulating their emotions.

Studies examining age differences in primary emotions from a physiological perspective also have tended to show that older individuals show less reactivity when inducted into a variety of negative emotions. For example, one set of studies required younger and older adults to enact emotions facially and examined the resulting pattern of physiological activity (Levenson *et al.*, 1990, 1991). The researchers concluded that, while the pattern of arousal was comparable in the young and old, it appeared to be more difficult to produce this pattern in older individuals. Overall, the level of arousal was lower in the elderly. The conclusion that older individuals exhibit less physiological reactivity in a variety of emotion inductions (ranging from the presentation of short films to recalling autobiographical memories) has been upheld in other studies since, giving support to the conclusion that, overall, elderly individuals are adept at regulating emotional arousal (Tsai *et al.*, 2000). Even so, the heart rate changes in these studies are extremely variable, from nearly 8 beats per minute to only 1 for the younger, and from about 5 to nearly 0 for the elders. This variability suggests that attention needs to be focused on the kinds of factors that influence the degree of variability, as indicated below.

Finally, a series of recent studies by Carstensen and her collaborators (Carstensen *et al.*, 2003) indicates that older individuals appear to selectively process positive emotions to a greater degree than negative emotions, in contrast to younger individuals who process similar levels of positive and negative emotions. For example, they recall relatively fewer nega-

tive images compared to positive or neutral images, a bias also shown by recognition memory. Further, the age differences for recall and recognition memory in terms of accuracy are also greatest for negative images (Charles *et al.*, 2003).

One major current theory addressing the above findings is Carstensen's Socioemotional Selectivity Theory (Carstensen *et al.*, 2003). This theory suggests that, faced with limited time to live, older individuals reorganize their goals so as to place greater emphasis on emotions and their regulation. By rearranging their environments so as to optimize emotional functioning and meaning, they are able to maintain positive and decrease negative affect, resulting in overall improved emotion regulation. This position, as indicated, has garnered a good bit of evidence, but not all studies have concurred. For example, a recent study by Labouvie-Vief *et al.* (2003) reported that the usual pattern of reduced emotional reactivity with ageing did not hold for the men in their sample, but for women only – and in the women it appeared to be due to the inordinately high levels of reactivity of younger women. This may reflect the fact that younger women tend to judge their inner states more by the reactions of others than their own feelings, while older women come to be more confident in their judgment of their inner states. In contrast, no such age differences appeared to exist for men.

More recently, Kunzmann and her colleagues (e.g. Kunzmann and Grün, 2003) reported a number of studies showing that, in some situations, older individuals are actually *more* reactive than younger individuals. Many of the physiological studies cited earlier used stimuli that involve either self-selection of the types of emotional event, or events that are not necessarily personally meaningful, such as short scenes from films, isolated pictures, and so forth. In contrast, Kunzmann's team developed shortened versions of commercial films that showed highly coherent, integrated narratives of event sequences that individuals could easily identify with. One of those sequences, for example, told of a middle-aged woman who learned that she had been diagnosed with an early stage of Alzheimer's disease. Another film told of how a family deals with a mother's death from cancer, and the third about a middle-aged woman whose husband and daughter were killed in a car accident. These personally meaningful events produced higher levels of reactivity in the oldest group, who felt higher levels of sadness than the younger and whose autonomic reactivity was not different from that of the younger adults. This suggests that levels of reactivity in the elderly may be highly dependent on the nature of the situation. Most importantly, it is likely to depend on whether older individuals can rely on well-rehearsed, well-integrated schemas that provide ready-made solutions to emotion regulation situations. Such well-integrated schemas not only minimize the processing load involved in many emotion regulation situations, but also make possible anticipatory control of emotion-related arousal situations (Gross, 1998).

But what of situations in which individuals cannot readily rely on already available schemas, or ones (as in Kunzmann's work) that tap age-relevant emotion systems in a highly meaningful way, or even ones in which the schemas they have available actually hinder task perfomance? In such novel and high-arousal situations, the demands of reflective and executive control are likely to create problems with emotion regulation. Such situations will be considered next.

AGEING OF "SECONDARY" AFFECTS

A second general theoretical framework of emotion regulation suggests that emotions not be studied as isolated systems, but in interaction with other systems, in particular cognitive processes. This is because throughout the process of development, "primary" emotions, which are based in limbic structures, become embedded into more complex cognitive networks mediated by higher-order cortical processes (see Labouvie-Vief et al., 2003; Labouvie-Vief and Marquez, 2004; Metcalfe and Mischel, 1999). Much recent interest has focused on such limbic-cortical networks and how the growth or decline in cognitive capacities alters the dynamics of emotion regulation, resulting in "secondary emotions."

For example, early in development, as children develop complex (especially linguistic) forms of representation, emotions become less tied to the here-and-now, and more to an inner world of mental states shared with others. This supports not only the ability to plan, evaluate, and delay emotions; it even gives rise to *new* emotions – such as embarrassment, pride, or guilt – that signal awareness that our feelings and thoughts link us to those of others (Harris, 2000; Lewis, 2000). By adolescence, individuals are able to invest emotions in abstract ideals and norms and to guide their behavior through complex plans that project their identity across wide segments of time and context. Even so, adolescents' representational skills remain limited (Labouvie-Vief, 1994), relying on the presence of already well-structured societal and cultural systems such as political and religious ideologies.

Adults, in turn, develop more complex representations. For example, Labouvie-Vief and collaborators investigated such transformations in individuals aged 10 to 80+ (Labouvie-Vief et al., 1989; Labouvie-Vief et al., 1995). Their descriptions of their emotions and their selves were coded into qualitative levels of differing *cognitive–affective complexity*. Findings showed that from adolescence to middle adulthood, individuals became more flexible in coordinating nonconscious and conscious aspects of emotions, gained clearer differentiation of self from others, and blended distinct emotions, especially ones involving positive and negative contrasts. These differentiations allowed many (but not all) adults to carve out a renewed sense of self that is complex, historically situated, and more individuated.

These results confirmed the expectation that significant growth in affective complexity continues through middle adulthood. But they also indicated that growth not only abates in late middle adulthood, but there is significant decline thereafter (see Figure 1). Specifically, even though (as predicted from the primary emotion framework) the elderly used very low levels of negative affect words to represent their emotions as well as to describe self and others, these lowered levels were related to less conceptual complexity. Other researchers, too, have commented on the lowered levels of conceptual complexity of elderly individuals. For example, Porter and Suedfeld (1981) also concluded that increases in complexity characterize the earlier part of the adult lifespan, while older adults tend to be less complex. Similarly, Blanchard-Fields (1999) has observed that the elderly often are less likely to think dialectically about emotional issues, and to give relatively undifferentiated "snap judgments."

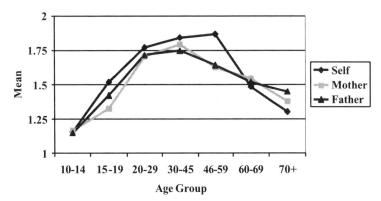

Figure 1. Levels of cognitive–affective differentiation of self and parents.

Although these findings are disappointing in some sense, they would be expected from what we know about the ageing of the types of cognitive functions that appear to be related to self-regulation in complex and/or novel situations. Older individuals typically demonstrate a variety of cognitive declines including decreased executive control and inhibitory functioning (Dempster, 1992; Hasher and Zacks, 1988; McDowd and Oseas-Kreger, 1991; Stoltzfus *et al.*, 1996; Zacks and Hasher, 1994); these behavioral problems are related, as well, to neuroanatomical (Cabeza, 2002; Raz, 2000) and neuromodulatory (Li *et al.*, 2001) changes in structures that are thought to support these processes. Such declines should lead to difficulty in emotion regulation in resource-demanding situations – that is, in situations that do not permit reliance on already well-structured schemas but that require conscious attention and regulation.

Much available research does, in fact, attest to such regulatory failures. For example, the research of Labouvie-Vief (see Labouvie-Vief and Marquez, 2004) and Blanchard-Fields (1999) has consistently shown that, compared to middle-aged adults, older individuals represent emotions in simplified terms, often relying on descriptions that are less reflective and that are primarily positive rather than integrating positive and negative statements. Similarly, a host of experimental studies has found that, in comparison to younger adults, older adults (a) distort information in a positive direction (Labouvie-Vief and Medler, 2002; Mather and Johnson, 2000); (b) are less resistant to stereotypes

(Mather *et al.*, 1999; von Hippel *et al.*, 2000) and tend to give "snap" judgments (Blanchard-Fields, 1999); (c) are, in terms of their performance levels, more dependent on contexts that are personally relevant – e.g. when the emphasis is on personally vital dimensions such as safety, truth, and moral character (Rahhal *et al.*, 2002), as well as personal identification with targets (Hess *et al.*, 2001) – while suffering performance decreases in ones that are less so; and (d) limit their behavior to a more restricted range of physical (Lawton and Nahemow, 1973) and social (Carstensen *et al.*, 2003) environments, and to a narrower range of goals (Baltes and Baltes, 1990). All of these findings suggest that, as individuals experience reductions in cognitive–affective complexity, they can maintain sufficiently positive hedonic tone only as long as they reduce the demands made on them by their external environment (Labouvie-Vief and Marquez, 2004).

These general findings can be explained in terms of theories that emphasize the interaction of two different ways of processing emotional information (Metcalfe and Mischel, 1999). One is based on relatively automatic processes that tend to restore a sufficiently positive balance by gating out negative affect. The other is based on evaluating and elaborating on emotional information with the aim of representing information in a way that is objective and complex. Labouvie-Vief and her collaborators (Labouvie-Vief and Marquez, 2004; Labouvie-Vief and Medler, 2002) coin these different core strategies "affect optimization" and "affect complexity." An emerging theoretical perspective integrates these two positions by proposing that the emotional and the cognitive system dynamically interact in such a way that lowered cognitive resources lead to a selective bias towards information that has high salience for self-preservation. Thus, many apparently positive changes reflect an adaptive response to the restriction of resources – yet one that implies a restriction of the complexity of affective processing. For example, it is well known from the clinical literature that such patterns of affective positivity can be indicative of one-sided idealizations that can go along with certain pathological states. In a similar fashion, the social-psychological literature indicates that an idealizing pattern of positivity bias can reflect a simplification of representations (e.g. Paulhus and Lim, 1994). Finally, individuals attempt to retreat to "safe havens" by reducing the range of action and/or seeking refuge in close social networks. Note that all of these responses reflect a self-protective process by which concern for complexity is traded for concern for personal safety. Labouvie-Vief and Marquez (2004) have referred to this process as "dynamic integration."

Ideally, dynamic integration works in a dynamic, flexible, and integrated way, but two major conditions can reduce flexible integration. First, normative changes in cognitive resources can alter vulnerability to degradation. As these resources grow or decline, individuals become less or more vulnerable to the degrading effects of over-activation (Labouvie-Vief and Marquez, 2004; Metcalfe and Mischel, 1999). Second, if development does not proceed in a context of relatively low and well-regulated arousal or activation, individuals are likely to develop poor strategies of affect regulation; these, in turn, should render individuals particularly vulnerable to the degrading affects of over-activation. As a consequence, regulation difficulties would be expected not only in older individuals who have reduced cognitive resources, but also in younger adults who display habitually poor coping and emotion regulation strategies. What is the evidence for such an interaction between age and regulation strategy?

Age and Individual Differences in Emotion Regulation

Labouvie-Vief and Medler (2002) recently examined the relationship between age, emotion regulation strategies, and the dynamic trade-offs discussed in the previous section in the context of an ongoing longitudinal-sequential study involving individuals from all stages of the adult lifespan. Two regulation modes, *affect-optimization* and *affect-differentiation*, were defined. As predicted, individuals who emphasized positive hedonic tone displayed an optimization strategy, while those favoring cognitive–affective complexity adopted differentiation strategies. High optimizers minimize negative feelings; they do not engage in rich exploration of feelings and nonrational processes, tend to ignore unpleasant facts, but also are low in self-doubt. High differentiators tend to analyze their emotions; they are also high in tolerance of ambiguity and low in repression. Further results indicated that the two dimensions also show different relations to age: optimization tends to increase linearly with age, while complexity shows the curvilinear growth-and-decline pattern already discussed in the previous section.

Optimizers and differentiators also report different life events (Labouvie-Vief and Marquez, 2004). Optimizers describe their lives as free from major negative life events and turning points, such as emotional problems, loss of friends, experience with severe punishment and/or discrimination, and identity crises. In contrast, those high in cognitive–affective complexity describe their lives as containing major negative experiences such as severe punishment and discrimination, and turning points such as changes in self-concept or spiritual belief.

These results suggest that quite different pathways of development may exist in adulthood – one characterized by optimization, the other by differentiation. Do individuals develop unique styles of coordinating these modes? Four such styles were identified, following Werner (1975). Individuals who score high on both dimensions were identified as *integrated*. These individuals display the most positive development: they score high in positive but low in negative affect and report high well-being, empathy, and self-rated health, and attachment security. In contrast, the *dysregulated* score lowest on all of these variables, except on negative affect, on which they score highest. The *self-protective* (low differentiation, high optimization) and the *complex* (high differentiation, low optimization) display more mixed patterns that are nevertheless fairly coherent. Compared to the complex, the self-protective score low in negative affect but are similar in positive affect, attachment security, and self-rated health. The self-protective also place less emphasis on personal growth but more on environmental mastery; they score higher on good impression and conformance but lower on empathy, compared to the complex. This suggests that the self-protective tend to *dampen* negative affect, while the complex *amplify* it. The diverging affective patterns

	Integrated	Complex	Self-Protective	Dysregulated
Young adult	23 (30%)	24 (31%)*	13 (17%)	17 (22%)
Adult	40 (39%)	18 (18%)	24 (23%)	21 (20%)
Middle-aged	38 (40%)	21 (22%)	21 (22%)	14 (15%)
Older adult	52 (41%)	13 (10%)*	52 (42%) *	8 (6%) *
Total	155	76	111	60

Figure 2. Distribution of four regulation styles by age group.

appear to indicate different identity styles, each reflecting characteristic variations in how they integrate positive and negative affect (see Helson and Srivastava, 2001). As can be seen from Figure 2, the different groups are widely distributed over the adult age spectrum, which underscores the need to examine individual differences in affect regulation along with age, per se. The dynamic integration principle also predicts that, especially among individuals such as the elderly who suffer from resource restrictions, the two strategies are related in a compensatory fashion. Indeed, when comparing young, middle-aged, and old adults, results indicate that, among the oldest age group, a significantly smaller-than-expected number of individuals falls into the complex group, while a disproportionately high number falls into the self-protective group. About 20% of the young adult to middle-aged adults (ages younger than 60) fall each into the complex and self-protective groups, while for the older adults (ages above 60) only 10% are classified as complex, but 42% as self-protective. Thus, as individuals grow older and experience declines in cognitive–affective complexity, they tend to rely more strongly on optimization strategies. This pattern is confirmed by longitudinal evidence, as well: over a 6-year interval, *declines* in differentiation predict *increases* in optimization.

Figure 2 also shows, however, that, even though the percentage of self-protective individuals significantly increases from middle to old age, the percentage of integrated individuals is about equal at nearly 40%. This finding underscores the importance of differentiating different groups of elderly individuals. It would be particularly interesting to find out more about those individuals who are able to resist the tendency to trade-off complexity for optimization. For example, are those who maintain high levels of integration those who are initially better-functioning cognitively? Are they distinguished by a previous life history of good affect regulation? Does their positive emotional ageing result from a long life history of good cognitive, emotional, and physical health? Such questions will be important to answer for future research.

Summary and Conclusions

In sum, changes in emotion regulation in later life indicate a pattern that is somewhat mixed. On one hand, when older individuals report on their own emotions, or when situations permit them to select emotions such as in autobiographical accounts, or when situations can draw in well-rehearsed and well-integrated patterns of regulation, evidence suggests that they may do well in many emotion regulation situations. In fact, by relying on a self-protective pattern of optimization, they can maintain high levels of positive affect by a compensatory trade-off of complexity of self and environment (see also Baltes and Baltes, 1990; Brandstädter and Greve, 1994). On the other hand, when emotion regulation requires considerable cognitive effort, much evidence suggests that the well-known cognitive changes brought with ageing bring with them also reductions in the ability to regulate affect. These reductions are not necessarily evident when focusing on positive affect about the self, but rather come to the fore when one examines how negative affect is dealt with. Thus an increase in optimization combined with a reduction in complexity encourages a more self-protective attitude in which positive affect is maintained by narrowing the range of social and physical environments to those in which one can maintain emotional stability.

FURTHER READING

Carstensen, L. L., Fung, H. H., and S. T. Charles (2003). "Socioemotional selectivity theory and the regulation of emotion in the second half of life," *Motivation and Emotion*, 27: 103–23.

Labouvie-Vief, G. (2003). "Dynamic integration: affect, cognition, and the self in adulthood," *Current Directions in Psychological Science*, 12: 201–6.

Labouvie-Vief, G., and M. Marquez (2004). "Dynamic integration: affect optimization and differentiation in development." In D. Y. Dai and R. J. Sternberg, eds., *Motivation, emotion, and cognition: integrative perspectives on intellectual functioning and development.* Mahwah, N.J.: Lawrence Erlbaum Associates, pp. 237–72.

REFERENCES

Baltes, P. B., and M. M. Baltes (1990). "Psychological perspectives on successful aging: the model of selective optimization with compensation." In P. B. Baltes and M. M. Baltes, eds., *Successful aging: perspectives from the behavioral sciences.* New York: Cambridge University Press, pp. 1–34.

Blanchard-Fields, F. (1999). "Social schemacity and causal attributions." In T. M. Hess and F. Blanchard-Fields, eds., *Social cognition and aging.* San Diego, Calif.: Academic Press, pp. 219–36.

Brandstädter, J., and W. Greve (1994). "The aging self: stabilizing and protective processes," *Developmental Review*, 14: 52–80.

Cabeza, R. (2002). "Hemispheric asymmetry reduction in older adults: the HAROLD model," *Psychology and Aging*, 17: 85–100.

Carstensen, L. L., Fung, H. H., and S. T. Charles (2003). "Socioemotional selectivity theory and the regulation of emotion in the second half of life," *Motivation and Emotion*, 27: 103–23.

Charles, S. T., Reynolds, C. A., and M. Gatz (2001). "Age-related differences and change in positive and negative affect over 23 years," *Journal of Personality and Social Psychology*, 80: 136–51.

Charles, S. T., Mather, M., and L. L. Carstensen (2003). "Aging and emotional memories: the forgettable nature of negative images for older adults," *Journal of Experimental Psychology*, 132: 310–24.

Darwin, C. (1955). *The expression of the emotions in man and animals.* Oxford: England Philosophical Library.

Dempster, F. N. (1992). "The rise and fall of the inhibitory mechanism: towards a unified theory of cognitive development and aging," *Developmental Review*, 12: 45–75.

Diehl, M., Coyle, N., and G. Labouvie-Vief (1996). "Age and sex differences in strategies of coping and defense across the life span," *Psychology and Aging*, 11: 127–39.

Ekman, P. (1984). "Expression and the nature of emotion." In K. R. Scherer and P. Ekman, eds., *Approaches to emotion.* Hillsdale, N.J.: Erlbaum, pp. 319–43.

Gross, J. J. (1998). "Antecedent- and response-focused emotion regulation: divergent consequences for experience, expression, and physiology," *Journal of Personality and Social Psychology*, 74: 224–37.

Gross, J., Carstensen, L., Pasupathi, M., Tsai, J., Gotestam Skorpen, C., and A. Hsu (1997). "Emotion and aging: experience, expression, and control," *Psychology and Aging*, 12: 590–9.

Harris, P. L. (2000). "Understanding emotion." In M. Lewis and J. Haviland-Jones, eds., *Handbook of emotions*, 2nd edn. New York: Guilford Press, pp. 281–92.

Hasher, L., and R. T. Zacks (1988). "Working memory, comprehension, and aging: a review and a new view." In G. Bower, ed., *The psychology of learning and motivation.* San Diego, Calif.: Academic Press, pp. 193–225.

Helson, R., and S. Srivastava (2001). "Three paths of adult development: conservers, seekers, and achievers," *Journal of Personality and Social Psychology*, 80: 995–1010.

Hess, T. M., Rosenberg, D. C., and S. J. Waters (2001). "Motivation and representational processes in adulthood: the effects of social accountability and information relevance," *Psychology and Aging*, 16: 629–42.

Izard, C. E. (1997). *Human emotions.* New York: Plenum Press.

Kunzmann, U., and D. Grün (2003). "Emotional reactions to sad film clips: evidence for greater reactivity in old age." Paper presented at the 2003 Annual Meeting of the American Psychological Association, Toronto, August.

Labouvie-Vief, G. (1994). *Psyche and Eros: mind and gender in the life course.* New York: Cambridge University Press.

Labouvie-Vief, G., and M. Marquez (2004). "Dynamic integration: affect optimization and differentiation in development." In D. Y. Dai and R. J. Sternberg, eds., *Motivation, emotion, and cognition: integrative perspectives on intellectual functioning and development.* Mahwah, N.J.: Lawrence Erlbaum Associates, pp. 237–72.

Labouvie-Vief, G., and M. Medler (2002). "Affect optimization and affect complexity: modes and styles of regulation in adulthood," *Psychology and Aging*, 17: 571–87.

Labouvie-Vief, G., DeVoe, M., and D. Bulka (1989). "Speaking about feelings: conceptions of emotion across the life span," *Psychology and Aging*, 4: 425–37.

Labouvie-Vief, G., Chiodo, L. M., Goguen, L. A., Diehl, M., and L. Orwoll (1995). "Representations of self across the life span," *Psychology and Aging*, 10: 404–15.

Labouvie-Vief, G., Lumley, M. A., Jain, E., and H. Heinze (2003). "Age and gender differences in cardiac reactivity and subjective emotion responses to emotional autobiographical memories," *Emotion*, 3: 115–26.

Lawton, M. P., and L. Nahemow (1973). "Ecology and the aging process." In C. Eisdorfer and M. P. Lawton, eds., *The psychology of adult development and aging.* Washington, D.C.: American Psychological Association.

Levenson, R., Ekman, P., and W. Friesen (1990). "Voluntary facial action generates emotion-specific autonomic nervous system activity," *Psychophysiology*, 27: 363–84.

Levenson, R., Carstensen, L., Friesen, W., and P. Ekman (1991). "Emotion, physiology, and expression in old age," *Psychology and Aging*, 6: 28–35.

Lewis, M. D. (2000). "Emotional self-organization at three time scales." In M. D. Lewis and I. Granic, eds., *Emotion, development, and self-organization: dynamic systems approaches to emotional development*. New York: Cambridge University Press.

Li, S.-C., Lindenberger, U., and S. Sikstroem (2001). "Aging cognition: from neuromodulation to representation," *Trends in Cognitive Sciences*, 5: 479–86.

Mather, M. J., and M. K. Johnson (2000). "Choice-supportive source monitoring: do our decisions seem better to us as we age?" *Psychology and Aging*, 15: 596–606.

Mather, M., Johnson, M. K., and D. M. De Leonardis (1999). "Stereotype reliance in source monitoring: age differences and neuropsychological test correlates," in *Cognitive Neuropsychology*, special issue: "The cognitive neuropsychology of false memories," 16: 437–58.

McDowd, J. M., and D. M. Oseas-Kreger (1991). "Aging, inhibitory processes, and negative priming," *Journal of Gerontology*, 46: 340–5.

Metcalfe, J., and W. Mischel (1999). "A hot/cool-system analysis of delay of gratification: dynamics of willpower," *Psychological Review*, 106: 3–19.

Mroczek, D. K., and C. M. Kolarz (1998). "The effect of age on positive and negative affect: a developmental perspective on happiness," *Journal of Personality and Social Psychology*, 75: 1333–49.

Paulhus, D. L., and D. T. K. Lim (1994). "Arousal and evaluative extremity in social judgments: a dynamic complexity model," *European Journal of Social Psychology*, 24: 89–99.

Porter, C. A., and P. Suedfeld (1981). "Integrative complexity in the corresponding of literary figures: effects of personal and societal stress," *Journal of Personality and Social Psychology*, 40: 321–30.

Rahhal, T. A., May, C. P., and L. Hasher (2002). "Truth and character: sources that older adults can remember," *Psychological Science*, 13: 101–5.

Raz, N. (2000). *Aging of the brain and its impact on cognitive performance: and clinical analyses*. New York: Academic Press.

Staudinger, U. M., Marsiske, M., and P. B. Baltes (1995). "Resilience and reserve capacity in later adulthood: potentials and limits of development across the life span," In D. Cicchetti and D. Cohen, eds., *Developmental psychopathology*. Vol. II: *Risk, disorder, and adaptation*. New York: Wiley, pp. 801–47.

Stoltzfus, E. R., Hasher, L., and R. T. Zacks (1996). "Working memory and aging: current status of the inhibitory view." In J. T. E. Richardson, R. W. Engle, L. Hasher, R. H. Logie, E. R. Stolzfus, and R. T. Zacks, eds., *Working memory and human cognition*. New York: Oxford University Press.

Tsai, J., Levenson, R., and L. Carstensen (2000). "Autonomic, subjective, and expressive responses to emotional films in older and younger Chinese Americans and European Americans," *Journal of Personality and Social Psychology*.

Von Hippel, W., Silver, L. A., and M. E. Lynch (2000). "Stereotyping against your will: the role of inhibitory ability in stereotyping and prejudice among the elderly," *Personality and Social Psychology Bulletin*, 26: 523–32.

Werner, H. (1975). *Comparative psychology of mental development*. New York: International Universities Press.

Zacks, R. T., and L. Hasher (1994). "Directed ignoring: inhibitory regulation of working memory." In D. Dagenback and T. H. Carr, eds., *Inhibitory processes in attention, memory, and language*. San Diego, Calif.: Academic Press, pp. 241–64.

Personality and Ageing

URSULA M. STAUDINGER

A frequent distinction drawn in reviews of personality and ageing (Kogan, 1990) is the one between trait and growth models of personality development. Trait models equate personality with personality traits, that is, dispositional behaviors and attributes, and argue that personality is "set like plaster" after age 30 (Costa and McCrae, 1994). Growth models, like the most influential one by Erik Erikson, contend that we continuously adapt to changing internal and external requirements and thereby grow. If all requirements are successfully met, at the end of an ideal trajectory Erikson envisions a person full of hope, will power, purpose in life, competence, fidelity, love, care, and wisdom. Clearly, this outcome is not the rule but rather the exception.

More and more empirical evidence based on either of the two models, however, has demonstrated that *both* stability *and* change characterize personality development in adulthood and old age. Thus, the focus of this overview will be on presenting this evidence and suggesting ways to understand better the dialectic between stability and change in personality development.

There are three longstanding concerns of personality research – structure/content, dynamics, and development of personality – that historically have been approached by very different research traditions. Personality structure and content have been the focus of attention in trait models of personality. The "Big Five" dimensions of neuroticism, extraversion, openness to experience, agreeableness, and conscientiousness (Costa and McCrae, 1994) have been consistently identified across samples and measurement instruments as comprehensive descriptors

of personality differences (John, 1990). Content and structure have also been of primary interest in a self-system approach to the study of personality. The latter, in stark contrast to the former, however, has also been very much interested in understanding the dynamics of personality (Markus and Wurf, 1987). Focusing on personality dynamics or the processes underlying microgenetic personality change is yet a third tradition, the study of self-regulation (Carver and Scheier, 1998). Recently, a number of efforts have been made to integrate these rather disconnected fields of research (Cloninger, 2003; Hooker, 2002; McAdams, 1996; McCrae *et al.*, 2000; Roberts and Caspi, 2003; Staudinger and Pasupathi, 2000). Finally, investigating the ontogenetic change of personality structure as comprising content and dynamics is a focus of lifespan psychology (Baltes *et al.*, 1998). Lifespan psychology conceives of development as a continuous sequence of interactions between biological and sociocultural influences and the developing person. Lifespan research has demonstrated that with increasing age we encounter more and more losses with regard to physical functioning and health but also social status (Baltes *et al.*, 1998), and has examined how personality development in old age is aimed at mastering this challenge (Staudinger *et al.*, 1995).

In the following, two central questions related to the lifespan perspective will be pursued: (i) does personality change during adulthood and old age and, if so, to which degree, and in which way?; and (ii) which are the basic sources and mechanisms underlying this stability and/or change?

PERSONALITY STABILITY AND CHANGE DURING ADULTHOOD AND OLD AGE

Do Personality Traits Stay Stable or Change?

When asking about stability or change of personality traits, this implies three questions rather than one, that is, stability or change of (i) mean levels within a group of individuals, (ii) interindividual differences between individuals (variance), and (iii) the measurement dimensions of personality (covariances). To start, a meaningful comparison between different age groups is solely possible if personality dimensions measure the same characteristics at different ages. For the Big Five factorial model of personality, cross-sectional as well as longitudinal information on structural invariance is available (Costa and McCrae, 1994; Small *et al.*, 2003). Such studies have demonstrated high structural invariance during adulthood and into old age.

Similarly, many longitudinal and cross-sectional studies are available to analyze stability or change of interindividual differences in the Big Five. Stability coefficients get smaller with longer measurement intervals, ranging between .46 and .83 (Baltes *et al.*, 1998: 1096). With an average interval of approximately 7 years, interindividual consistency is ascending until around age 50 (.75) and slightly declines thereafter (.72) (Roberts and DelVecchio, 2000). Comparison among the five dimensions showed that extraversion and agreeableness had slightly higher consistencies than the other three dimensions. Consistency varied neither by assessment method (i.e., self-report, other-report, projective test) nor by gender. Controlling for sample attrition did not alter results in this meta-analysis. The findings from this meta-analysis are confirmed with regard to old and very old age by recent publications from two longitudinal ageing studies (Mroczek and Spiro, 2003; Small *et al.*, 2003). In both studies, consistencies across 12 and 6 years, respectively, were around .7. No evidence has been found for cohort differences in consistency. Personality consistency peaking at age 50 contradicts earlier arguments that the consistency of personality traits should plateau after age 30 (Costa and McCrae, 1994). We will return to this finding and possible explanations when discussing the possible sources of stability and

change. In the same vein, please note that, even though a consistency of .75 at age 50 is high, it is not perfect (1.0), and leaves room for individual change. In this vein, recent studies using latent growth modeling found that, with increasing age, individual differences in personality change also increase (Pedersen and Reynolds, 1998; Small *et al.*, 2003). As no age-graded increase in genetic influences has been found, this increasing interindividual variability of change most likely is related to non-normative life events (see below).

Finally, what happens with the mean levels of personality traits? Do we become less extravert and less open, but also less neurotic, as we move through adulthood and old age? Taking into account cross-sectional and longitudinal evidence, it seems that neuroticism decreases across adulthood (Mroczek and Spiro, 2003) and may show some increase again very late in life (Small *et al.*, 2003). Some decrease is also found for openness to experience and extraversion (Field and Millsap, 1991). In contrast, agreeableness and conscientiousness slightly increase (Helson and Kwan, 2000). McCrae and others (e.g. 2000) lately offered an interesting proxy of a longitudinal study. Comparing samples between ages 14 and 83 years from Korea, Portugal, Italy, Germany, Czech Republic, and Turkey, they found exactly the pattern of mean-level changes described above. The authors argue that the observed similarity across cultures makes it unlikely – given the very different historical and cultural circumstances in these different countries – that such age differences are indeed cohort differences. The pattern of mean-level changes across adulthood and into old age may be described as an increase in social adjustment, in the sense of becoming emotionally less volatile and more attuned to social demands (Whitbourne and Waterman, 1979). Some authors even speculate whether this developmental pattern may have been selected for by evolution (McCrae *et al.*, 2000).

Using a psychometric approach to the study of growth-aspects of personality replicates and extends this finding. Measuring dimensions such as "environmental mastery," "autonomy," or "personal growth" and "purpose in life," Ryff and Keyes (1995) find that the first two dimensions increase with age during adulthood and old age and the latter two level off after midlife. The increases in environmental mastery and autonomy again can be described as being highly functional and adaptive for mastering life in a community (replication). Personal growth and purpose in life level off in midlife. Together with the decline in openness to new experiences in old age, this finding may indicate that, in contrast to social adjustment, personal growth is less likely to come normatively with age (extension). And, indeed, studies of wisdom (Staudinger, 1999) and of ego development (Labouvie-Vief & Medler, 2002) find no normative increase with age during adulthood.

Do Self-Conceptions Change with Age?

People's self-conceptions vary substantially over time but structural features of people's self-organization (e.g. self-discrepancy, positivity) are more stable (Strauman, 1996). Stability of self-conceptions also depends on the measurement instrument. When using open self-descriptions there is more change than when using prefixed lists (Freund and Smith, 1999). There is, for instance, substantial stability in the content of self-definitions across different age groups when it comes to central domains of life (e.g. health, social relations; George and Okun, 1985). With increasing age, however, people define themselves more and more in terms of health and physical functioning, life experiences, and hobbies (Dittmann-Kohli, 1991). Another aspect of that adaptation to ageing seems that, as activity and agency are no longer self-evident, they become important parts of one's self-definition in old age (Herzog *et al.*, 1998).

Developmental trajectories in the structure of self-definitions depend on the structural characteristic under investigation. Labouvie-Vief and her colleagues (1995) have shown that self-definitions move from little differentiation between self and other, and heavy influence from social conventions early in life, towards definitions that emphasize contextual, process-related, and idiosyncratic features of selfhood later. Complexity of self-thought, in that sense, peaks in midlife and declines thereafter. At the same time, similarity of self-conceptions across different situations, another structural feature of the self – in line with age-graded societal demands for consistency – was highest in midlife and lower in early and late adulthood (Diehl *et al.*, 2001).

In sum, then, people's self-conceptions do possess stable and changing elements. The evidence, though, is pointing somewhat more strongly towards the change side than findings based on personality trait questionnaires. (Note, however, that trait questionnaires were constructed to measure the stable aspects of personality.) How can we understand this coexistence of continuity and change?

SOURCES AND MECHANISMS UNDERLYING PERSONALITY STABILITY AND CHANGE

In the following, taking a lifespan perspective, three major sources of personality stability and change will be discussed. The interacting sources are biology, sociocultural context, and last but by no means least the developing person (Lerner and Busch-Rossnagel, 1981). Each of these three sources provides opportunities for change as well as constrains personality development into continuity.

The Person: Self-Regulatory Mechanisms as Sources of Stability and Change

Self-regulation may be defined as the organized abilities and skills that a person brings to bear on monitoring experiences and behavior. Viewing personality as a self-organizing system suggests that individuals are striving towards consistency, and self-regulatory mechanisms, thus, are very important in the pursuit of dynamic homeostasis (Baltes *et al.*, 1998). Therefore, personality stability observed on the trait or self-concept level of measurement does not imply that nothing has been changing. Rather, as research on subjective wellbeing and resilience has demonstrated, the stability observed on one level of personality functioning (i.e., structure/content) is to some degree already the product of self-regulation at work (Brandtstädter and Greve, 1994; Staudinger *et al.*, 1995). Among the most important means of self-regulation in the ageing context are processes of self-evaluation, emotion-regulation, and goal setting.

ADJUSTING SELF-EVALUATIONS. By means of self-evaluation we reinterpret reality such that we can perceive ourselves consistently even though our behavior and experiences may have changed.

Rich evidence is available on how comparison processes help us to do so by selecting the appropriate social or temporal comparison that makes our experience and behavior less different from earlier times (Filipp, 1996). And it has been found that as we grow older we use those compensatory mechanisms more often and do so successfully (Staudinger *et al.*, 1995). There is also evidence that, with increasing age, perceptions of ourselves in the past, the present, and the future become more closely linked, which may contribute to perceiving fewer changes (Staudinger *et al.*, 2003).

CHANGING LIFE GOALS. Selection of life priorities and also of shorter-range goals has been shown to be of crucial importance for effective developmental regulation (Freund *et al.*, 1999). We can, for instance, maintain our self-concept of having a good memory, even though objectively memory performance has declined, by selecting new goals in the memory domain. Instead of being indicated by memorizing phone numbers, "having a good memory" is now achieved by not forgetting any item on the shopping list (Greve and Wentura, 2003). We adapt to the normative requirements of the lifecourse by adjusting our life priorities. In young adulthood, we invest most time and effort in work, friends, family, and independence. In middle adulthood highest investment is found in the domains of family, work, friends, and cognitive fitness. The young-olds invest most in family, health, friends, and cognitive fitness, and finally, in very old age, most is invested in health, family, thinking about life, and cognitive fitness. For the domain of social relations it has been shown that as we grow older the prime motivation changes from information seeking to emotion regulation (Carstensen *et al.*, 1999). Thus, someone may consider himself still to be extraverted by having close emotional relations rather than seeking out many new acquaintances.

EMOTION-REGULATION. Given the higher frequency and degree of losses that we are facing with increasing age, the lack of bigger personality changes becomes all the more puzzling. One further piece in solving this puzzle is the experience and regulation of emotions in old age. No age differences in physiological patterns have emerged but negative age differences in magnitude of physiological response have been found (Levenson *et al.*, 1991). Findings concerning the subjective experience of emotions are less consistent (Magai, 2001). Overall there seems to be no decline (or even slight increases) in the frequency of positive emotions until very late in life, and negative emotions stay stable (e.g. Diener and Suh, 1998) or decline (e.g. Carstensen *et al.*, 2000). In addition, greater co-occurrence of positive and negative emotions has been found for older as compared to younger samples (Carstensen *et al.*, 2000). Older adults also report that they feel better able to control their emotions. And there are first indications that this control works towards minimizing negative and optimizing positive emotions. These findings support the contention that emotion-regulation is one contributing factor supporting stability in the face of adversity.

Biology

What role do biological influences play in interindividual differences in personality structure and process as well as their age-related changes? To answer this question, it may be useful to consider the two-component model of the mechanics and pragmatics of life (Baltes *et al.*, 1998; Staudinger and Pasupathi, 2000). In this model the mechanics of life reflect individual differences in biology-based basic patterns of perception, information processing, emotionality, and motivational expression. Thus, life mechanics include basic indicators of information processing (cognitive mechanics) but also basic dimensions of temperament (e.g. activity, reactivity, emotionality, sociability), comprising basic emotional (positive vs. negative tone) and motivational tendencies (approach vs. avoidance). These biological building blocks of personality feed into the lifespan development of personality structure (i.e., Big Five, self-concept) by means of interacting with cultural contexts and the developing person (i.e., self-regulation). So, the question becomes: to which degree are changes in personality structure and process influenced by the biological mechanics? In contrast, advocates of the trait approach have argued that the Big Five themselves are highly heritable, and that also age-related mean-level differences are the result of age-graded changes in gene expression (McCrae *et al.*, 2000).

Consulting evidence from behavior-genetic research, which is mostly available for the Big Five, demonstrates that the extent to which genetic influences account for phenotypic variability in personality measures is smaller than for intelligence measures, with heritability coefficients between .3 and .5 depending on the study, the dimension and the age of assessment. The importance of genetic influences seems to stay stable or decrease slightly with increasing age. And finally, there is initial evidence for a quite high overlap in the genetic effects operating on personality expression at different ages (Pedersen and Reynolds, 1998). These results are consistent with the interpretation that personality stability and change are partially related to genetic information and its expression. By no means, however, can personality traits and their development be reduced to these influences. These results, combined with the finding that, well into old age, no major declines in personality-related functioning are observed (Staudinger et al., 1995), can be taken to imply that the mechanical building blocks of personality functioning may be less prone to age-related declines than the cognitive mechanics. But more research on the biological basis of personality and how it interacts with context and the person is needed. For instance, we need to know more about how much of the age-related differences in emotion-regulation are based on changes in the mechanics (biology) of emotions and how much are due to differences in the pragmatics (experience).

Contextual (Experiential) Influences on Stability and Change in Personality Development

The third element underlying personality functioning concerns the pragmatics of life. They reveal the power of human agency and culture (Valsiner and Lawrence, 1997). In continuous transactions with life contexts, which we also select and modify, we accumulate and construct (declarative *and* procedural, "hot" and "cold") knowledge about the *world* (i.e., knowledge about other people, events, circumstances, rules, places, and objects relevant for leading our lives), and about our *selves*, as well as about transactions between the world and ourselves.

Life mechanics provide the necessary "hardware" enabling these transactions.

When considering contextual (pragmatic) influences on stability and change in personality functioning, we need to consider that stable contexts constrain us to staying the same just as much as changing contexts may provide the opportunity for change (Roberts and Caspi, 2003). The picture is further complicated by the fact that contexts vary according to historical time, age, and individual life histories (e.g. Baltes et al., 1998).

HISTORICAL EXPERIENCES. Many studies have documented the influences of historical contexts on personality development. Such influences can be transient or lasting (e.g. Elder, 1998). In a recent cross-sequential study, for instance, interesting cohort differences emerged with regard to the trajectories of extraversion and neuroticism (Mroczek and Spiro, 2003). For both dimensions, the cohorts born around the turn of the last century (1897–1919) had a "harder" time growing old than the younger cohorts (1920–9; 1930–45). The authors speculate that the younger cohorts accumulated "hardiness" while growing up during the Depression (Elder, 1998). Another possible interpretation is that the older cohorts may experience a more challenging "old age" than younger cohorts because they age in poorer health due to less healthy lifestyles (mechanics), and they may have grown up with different images of old age, which they then make come true (pragmatics).

AGE-GRADED EXPERIENCES. Experiences differ depending on chronological age. This basic idea is captured in the notion of developmental tasks that are central to growth models of personality like the one proposed by Erikson. Thus, the age-graded experiential pattern of increasing commitment and responsibility contributes to the personality change towards social adjustment reported above. Age-graded experiences in old age also include a number of losses (e.g. of health, of social status, of close friends). Thus, in old age, personality processes often focus on repair, maintenance, or even management of losses in order to maintain stability – rather than on further growth – and do so successfully (Staudinger et al., 1995).

NON-NORMATIVE EXPERIENCES. Embedded in historical and age-graded contexts, there are also highly idiosyncratic experiences that influence personality development in adulthood and old age. Idiosyncratic experiences can be elicited or encountered by the individual. On the one hand, personality contributes to a certain degree to the occurrence of life experiences and, on the other hand, events happen and produce personality change. The older we get, the more likely it is that events are encountered rather than elicited (e.g. health events, loss of close friends). Nevertheless, older people on average maintain their sense of control and agency (Smith and Baltes, 1999). Again, this stability should not be taken as a sign of standstill but rather as the result of successful self-regulation.

CONCLUSION AND FUTURE DIRECTIONS

Considering the evidence on the development of personality structure presents only half of the picture. Without the investigation of personality processes, we may be led to think that personality and ageing is about stability *and* social adjustment. Taking self-regulation and developmental regulation into account, however, "complicates" the story. Yes, there is stability and we need that consistency to be able to have a sense of enduring self. This stability, however, is indicative of resilience rather than standstill. Considerable regulatory processes "produce" that stability. Change on the structural level of personality occurs when self-regulation cannot withstand the pressure for modification any longer. In the future, we need to understand better the biological underpinnings of personality functioning and how they change with age and interact with contextual features and individual choices.

FURTHER READING

Baltes, P. B., Lindenberger, U., and U. M. Staudinger (1998). "Life-span theory in developmental psychology." In R. M. Lerner, ed., *Handbook of child psychology*, Vol. I: *Theoretical models of human development*. 5th edn. New York: Wiley, pp. 1029–143.

Lachman, M. E., ed. (2001). *Handbook of midlife development*. New York: Wiley.

Roberts, B. W., and A. Caspi (2003). "The cumulative continuity model of personality development: striking a balance between continuity and change in personality traits across the life course." In U. M. Staudinger and U. Lindenberger, eds., *Understanding human development: dialogues with lifespan psychology*. New York: Kluwer Academic Publishers, pp. 183–214.

REFERENCES

Baltes, P. B., Lindenberger, U., and U. M. Staudinger (1998). "Life-span theory in developmental psychology." In R. M. Lerner, ed., *Handbook of child psychology*, Vol. I: *Theoretical models of human development*. 5th edn. New York: Wiley, pp. 1029–143.

Brandtstädter, J., and W. Greve (1994). "The aging self: stabilizing and protective processes," *Developmental Review*, 14: 52–80.

Carstensen, L. L., Isaacowitz, D. M., and S. T. Charles (1999). "Taking time seriously: a theory of socioemotional selectivity," *American Psychologist*, 54: 165–81.

Carstensen, L. L., Pasupathi, M., Mayr, U., and J. R. Nesselroade (2000). "Emotional experience in everyday life across the adult life span," *Journal of Personality and Social Psychology*, 79: 644–55.

Carver, C. S., and M. F. Scheier (1998). *On the self-regulation of behavior*. New York: Cambridge University Press.

Cloninger, C. R. (2003). "Completing the psychobiological architecture of human personality development: temperament, character, and coherence." In U. M. Staudinger and U. Lindenberger, eds., *Understanding human development: dialogues with lifespan psychology*. New York: Kluwer Academic Publishers, pp. 159–81.

Costa, P. T., and R. R. McCrae (1994). "Set like plaster? Evidence for the stability of adult personality." In T. F. Heatherton and J. L. Weinberger, eds., *Can personality change?* Washington, D.C.: American Psychological Association, pp. 21–40.

Diehl, M., Hastings, C. T., and J. M. Stanton (2001). "Self-concept differentiation across the adult life span," *Psychology and Aging*, 16: 643–54.

Diener, E., and E. Suh (1998). "Subjective well-being and age: an international analysis," *Annual Review of Gerontology and Geriatrics*, 17: 304–24.

Dittmann-Kohli, F. (1991). "Meaning and personality change from early to late adulthood," *European Journal of Personality*, 1: 98–103.

Elder, G. H., Jr. (1998). "The lifecourse and human development." In R. M. Lerner, ed., *Handbook of child psychology*, Vol. I: *Theoretical models of human development*, 5th edn. New York: Wiley, pp. 939–91.

Field, D., and R. E. Millsap (1991). "Personality in advanced old age: continuity or change?" *Journals of Gerontology: Psychological Science*, 46: 299–308.

Filipp, S.-H. (1996). "Motivation and emotion." In J. E. Birren and K. W. Schaie, eds., *Handbook of the psychology of aging*. San Diego, Calif.: Academic Press, pp. 218–35.

Freund, A., and J. Smith (1999). "Content and function of the self-definition in old and very old age," *Journals of Gerontology*, B54: P55–P67.

Freund, A., Li, K., and P. Baltes (1999). "Successful development and aging: the role of selection, optimization, and compensation." In J. Brandtstädter and R. M. Lerner, eds., *Action and self-development: theory and research through the life-span*. Thousand Oaks, Calif.: Sage, pp. 401–34.

George, L. K., and M. A. Okun (1985). "Self-concept content." In E. Palmore, E. W. Busse, G. L. Maddox, J. B. Nowlin, and I. C. Siegler, eds., *Normal aging III: reports from the Duke Longitudinal Studies, 1975–1984*. Durham, N.C.: Duke University Press, pp. 267–82.

Greve, W., and D. Wentura (2003). "Immunizing the self: self-concept stabilization through reality-adaptive self-definitions," *Personality and Social Psychology Bulletin*, 29: 39–50.

Helson, R., and V. S. Y. Kwan (2000). "Personality development in adulthood: the broad picture and processes in one longitudinal sample." In S. Hampson, ed., *Advances in personality psychology*, Vol. I. London: Routledge, pp. 77–106.

Herzog, A. R., Franks, M. M., Markus, H. R., and D. Holmberg (1998). "Activities and well-being in older age: effects of self-concept and educational attainment," *Psychology and Aging*, 13: 179–85.

Hooker, K. (2002). "New directions for research in personality and aging: a comprehensive model for linking level, structure, and processes," *Journal of Research in Personality*, 36: 318–34.

John, O. P. (1990). "The 'big five' factor taxonomy: dimensions of personality in the natural language and in questionnaires." In L. A. Pervin, ed., *Handbook of personality: theory and research*. New York: Guilford Press, pp. 66–100.

Kogan, N. (1990). "Personality and aging." In J. E. Birren and K. W. Schaie, eds., *Handbook of Psychology of Aging*, 3rd edn. New York: Academic Press, pp. 330–46.

Labouvie-Vief, G., and M. Medler (2002). "Affect optimization and affect complexity as adaptive strategies," *Psychology and Aging*, 17: 571–87.

Labouvie-Vief, G., Chiodo, L. M., Goguen, L. A., Diehl, M., and L. Orwoll (1995). "Representations of self across the life span," *Psychology and Aging*, 10: 404–15.

Lerner, R. M., and N. A. Busch-Rossnagel (1981). "Individuals as producers of their development: conceptual and empirical bases." In R. M. Lerner and N. A. Busch-Rossnagel, eds., *Individuals as producers of their development: a life-span perspective*. New York: Academic Press, pp. 1–36.

Levenson, R. W., Carstensen, L. L., Friesen, W. V., and P. Ekman (1991). "Emotion, physiology, and expression in old age," *Psychology and Aging*, 6: 28–35.

Magai, C. (2001). "Adulthood: emotional development." In N. Smelser and P. B. Baltes, eds., *International encyclopedia of the social and behavioral sciences*, Vol. I. New York: Elsevier, pp. 156–9.

Markus, H., and E. Wurf (1987). "The dynamic self-concept: a social psychological perspective," *Annual Review of Psychology*, 38: 299–337.

McAdams, D. P. (1996). "Personality, modernity, and the storied self: a contemporary framework for studying persons," *Psychological Inquiry*, 7: 295–321.

McCrae, R. R., Costa, P. T., Ostendorf, F., Angleitner, A., Hrebickova, M., Avia, M. D., Sanz, J., and M. L. Sanchez-Bernados (2000). "Nature over nurture: temperament, personality, and life span development," *Journal of Personality and Social Psychology*, 78: 173–86.

Mroczek, D. K., and R. A. Spiro III (2003). "Modeling intraindividual change in personality traits: findings from the Normative Aging Study," *Journals of Gerontology*, 58B: P153–P165.

Pedersen, N. L., and C. A. Reynolds (1998). "Stability and change in adult personality: genetic and environmental components," *European Journal of Personality*, 12: 365–86.

Roberts, B., and A. Caspi (2003). "The cumulative continuity model of personality development: striking a balance between continuity and change in personality traits across the lifecourse." In U. M. Staudinger and U. Lindenberger, eds., *Understanding human development: dialogues with lifespan psychology*. New York: Kluwer Academic Publishers, pp. 183–214.

Roberts, B. W., and W. F. DelVecchio (2000). "The rank-order consistency of personality traits from childhood to old age: a quantitative review of longitudinal studies," *Psychological Bulletin*, 126: 3–25.

Ryff, C. D., and C. L. M. Keyes (1995). "The structure of psychological well-being revisited," *Journal of Personality and Social Psychology*, 69 (4): 719–27.

Small, B. J., Hertzog, C., Hultsch, D. F., and R. A. Dixon (2003). "Stability and change in adult personality over 6 years: Findings from the Victoria Longitudinal Study," *Journals of Gerontology*, 58B: P166–P176.

Smith, J., and P. B. Baltes (1999). "Trends and profiles of psychological functioning in very old age." In P. B. Baltes and K. U. Mayer, eds., *The Berlin Aging Study: aging from 70 to 100*. New York: Cambridge University Press, pp. 197–226.

Staudinger, U. M. (1999). "Older and wiser? Integrating results on the relationship between age and wisdom-related performance," *International Journal of Behavioral Development*, 23 (3): 641–64.

Staudinger, U. M., and M. Pasupathi (2000). "Life-span perspectives on self, personality and social cognition." In T. Salthouse and F. Craik, eds., *Handbook of cognition and aging*. Hillsdale, N.J.: Erlbaum, pp. 633–88.

Staudinger, U. M., Marsiske, M., and P. B. Baltes (1995). "Resilience and reserve capacity in later adulthood: potentials and limits of development across the life span." In D. Cicchetti and D. Cohen, eds., *Developmental psychopathology*, Vol. II: *Risk, disorder, and adaptation*. New York: Wiley, pp. 801–47.

Staudinger, U. M., Bluck, S., and P. Y. Herzberg (2003). "Looking back and looking ahead: adult age differences in consistency of diachronous ratings of subjective well-being," *Psychology and Aging*, 18: 13–24.

Strauman, T. J. (1996). "Stability within the self: a longitudinal study of the structural implications of self-discrepancy theory," *Journal of Personality and Social Psychology*, 71: 1142–53.

Valsiner, J., and J. A. Lawrence (1997). "Human development in culture across the life-span." In J. W. Berry, P. R. Dasen, and T. S. Saraswathi, eds., *Handbook of cross-cultural psychology*, Vol. II. Boston, Mass.: Allyn & Bacon.

Whitbourne, S. K., and A. S. Waterman (1979). "Psychosocial development during the adult years: age and cohort comparisons," *Developmental Psychology*, 15: 373–8.

Depression

AMY FISKE AND RANDI S. JONES

INTRODUCTION

Late-life depression differs in many respects from depression in adults generally. Its aetiology, risk factors and clinical presentation may all differ from those for younger individuals, making it likely that health professionals without specialized training in gerontology or geriatric medicine may overlook the disorder in their patients. It is not a normal part of ageing, and failure to diagnose and treat it can result in impaired functioning and increased suffering and mortality.

DEFINITION

Several categories of depression have been defined in both the Diagnostic and Statistical Manual for Mental Disorders (DSM-IV; American Psychiatric Association, 1994) and the International Classification of Diseases (ICD-10; World Health Organization, 1993), including major depressive disorder and dysthymia. Major depressive disorder is defined as depressed mood or loss of interest or pleasure lasting at least two weeks, plus five or more of nine other symptoms including significant weight loss or appetite change, physical agitation or psychomotor retardation, difficulty concentrating or making decisions, and feelings of worthlessness or guilt. Dysthymia is characterized by depressive symptoms that may be less severe than in major depression but endure for at least 2 years. Major depressive disorder and dysthymia may occur together as 'double depression'. (A related set of disorders including bipolar disorder and cyclothymia involves alternating episodes of depression and mania. Because these disorders differ significantly from unipolar depression and are rare in late life, they will not be discussed in depth here.)

Depression may be marked by different symptoms in older and younger adults, with the emotional and cognitive features most often associated with depression, such as sadness and negative self-attitudes, more common in youth and middle age (Powers *et al.*, 2002). Somatic symptoms such as fatigue, insomnia, and appetite disturbance, as well as feelings of apathy and hopelessness and thoughts about death, are more typical of the elderly.

Although depressive disorder is less common in the elderly than in any other group of adults, presence of symptoms that do not meet diagnostic criteria (sometimes referred to as subsyndromal depression) is more common (Lavretsky and Kumar, 2002), suggesting that older adults' experience of depression fits poorly into existing diagnostic rubrics. A category of minor depression provisionally included in DSM-IV is characterized by dysphoria or anhedonia with one or more additional symptoms, closely resembling the criteria for mild depressive episode in ICD-10. Family history of depression is more closely associated with major depressive disorder, while stressful life events more often predict minor depression (Chen *et al.*, 2000). Subsyndromal depression is particularly common in medical settings, where it may be overlooked for treatment because it is often interpreted as a normal reaction to illness or its treatment.

Late onset depression, where the disorder occurs for the first time in old age rather than continuing or recurring from earlier episodes, is often linked to cognitive impairment and may presage the appearance of Alzheimer's disease or vascular dementia. Co-morbidity with other physical and mental disorders is common.

EPIDEMIOLOGY

Major depressive disorder is present in 1–2% of adults over 65. Dysthymia affects approximately 2%. One older adult in 1,000 has bipolar disorder. Minor depression is present in 3–13% of older adults. Using a cutoff on a symptom checklist without applying syndromal criteria, epidemiologic studies find between 15% and 25% of adults aged 65 and older are affected by clinically significant levels of symptoms (Jeste *et al.*, 1999). Prevalence of depressive disorders in late life may be higher in certain ethnic minority populations, including Mexican Americans, with socioeconomic status a likely explanation for differential rates. The preponderance of depression among women compared to men at midlife and earlier may be lessened in old age, although evidence is still inconclusive.

CONCEPTUAL FRAMEWORK

Late-life depression can be conceptualized as resulting from the interplay among biological, psychological, and social influences that change over the lifecourse. Gatz and colleagues have proposed a developmental diathesis–stress model in which stressful life events interact with a diathesis dimension that includes genetic susceptibility, biological vulnerability, and psychological attributes (Figure 1; Gatz *et al.*, 1996). The model posits that genetic propensity for depression may be more important early than late in life, whereas biological risk factors such as neuroanatomical changes and certain physical illnesses may increase in frequency in old age. Moreover, psychological vulnerability to depression may decrease with age as individuals learn to cope with stressors and adjust expectations.

Empirical literature confirms that an accumulation of negative life events is associated with depression in older adults, as in younger individuals. Specific events that have been examined in regard to late-life depression include bereavement, caregiving, and the onset of illness. Social support and

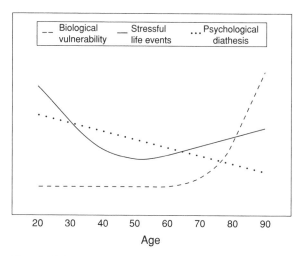

Figure 1. Depiction of developmental changes in the magnitude of influence on depressive symptomatology exerted by biological vulnerability (dashed line), psychological diathesis (dotted line), and stressful life events (solid line). Reprinted from: Gatz *et al.* (1996: 370), copyright 1996, with permission from Elsevier.

spirituality have been studied for their potential to buffer the effects of these stressors. We will consider in turn genetic and biological vulnerability to depression, as well as selected psychosocial risk and protective factors.

BIOLOGICAL FACTORS

One form of biological vulnerability to depression is genetic risk. Among older adults, both depressive disorder and clinically significant depressive symptoms are genetically influenced. As to depressive disorder, most evidence comes from mixed age samples, which show heritability (proportion of variation in the population attributable to genetic influences) in the range of 31–42% (Sullivan *et al.*, 2000). Depressive symptoms are slightly less heritable. Family studies, which compare the prevalence of a disorder among relatives of affected vs unaffected individuals, suggest that genetic influences on depression may wane in late life.

Another risk factor for depression that may reflect biological or other vulnerability is a previous history of depression, with at least half of depression in older adults occurring in individuals who were previously depressed. A major depressive episode is associated with an 80% risk that another will follow (Judd, 1997). Minor depression and depressed mood are also predictors of major depressive disorder.

Organic changes in the brain secondary to disease or, perhaps, to normal ageing constitute another form of biological vulnerability. Depression after stroke is well established, as is depression associated with Parkinson's disease. Although little evidence directly links late-life depression to the neuroanatomical or neurochemical changes that occur in normal ageing, recent work implicates disease-related brain changes in depression for this age group. Alexopoulos and colleagues (1997) use the term 'vascular depression' to describe a proposed subtype of depression in older adults characterized by late onset, an association with cerebrovascular risk factors, and the presence of white matter abnormalities on neuroimaging. Mechanisms that have been suggested include a model in which microvessel disease leads to an accumulation of lesions in the brain, as well as a cytokine-mediated model. Vascular depression is associated with a unique symptom profile, including psychomotor retardation, executive functioning deficits, and impaired insight, and is less likely to include agitation and guilt. Early research indicated that vascular depression may respond less well to antidepressant medications than depression with other aetiologies; however, more recent work has not found this difference. To our knowledge, no studies to date have examined response of vascular depression to psychotherapy.

PSYCHOSOCIAL RISK AND PROTECTIVE FACTORS

Health Status

In addition to biological mechanisms discussed above, psychological and social factors also appear to play a role in the relationship between health status and depression. Restriction of normal activities mediates the relationship between illness severity and depressive symptoms. Activity restriction can result from illness-related disability or pain, but can also be associated with other factors such as financial resources and social support (Williamson and Shaffer, 2000). Pain is also directly related to depression, independent of the effects of disability.

Relationships between health status and depression appear to be reciprocal, with poor health leading to depression but depression also leading to increased morbidity and even mortality. Depressive disorders, and even elevated levels of depressive symptoms, have been shown in prospective studies to lead to increasing difficulty performing activities of daily living. In middle-aged to older adults, depression is also associated with occurrence of a first heart attack, worsened prognosis following a heart attack, and mortality from stroke and other cardiovascular causes. The reciprocal relationship between health status and depression may result in a downward spiral of declining health and increasing depression.

Bereavement

Bereavement, especially the loss of a spouse, is among the most stressful events likely to occur late in life. Depressive symptoms are pervasive among surviving spouses within the first year after bereavement (Oakley et al., 2002), although symptom levels may actually be higher in the period before the loss, possibly due to effects of anticipatory grieving or caregiving (Lichtenstein et al., 1996). For widows, depressive symptoms are triggered primarily by concerns about income, consistent with findings that lower socioeconomic status predicts higher rates of depression in adults generally (e.g. Wilson et al., 1999). The most important mediator of depressive symptoms for widowers is loss of emotional support. Widowers are at greater risk than widows with respect to a variety of indicators of distress.

Complicated grief, although not a separate diagnostic category in DSM-IV or ICD-10, has been defined as a reaction to the death of a loved one that continues for at least six months with daily experience of three of four listed symptoms (intrusive thoughts about, and yearning, searching, and excessive loneliness for, the deceased), together with four of eight additional symptoms such as feelings of purposelessness or futility, numbness, disbelief, anger, and emptiness, which together cause significant impairment in functioning (Prigerson and Jacobs, 2001). Some, although not all, researchers have distinguished complicated grief from major depressive disorder on the basis of the longer duration, greater intensity, and differing nature of its symptoms. Complicated grief is typically resistant to some forms of treatment that have been effective in the treatment of older individuals with major depressive disorder (interpersonal psychotherapy and tricyclic antidepressants).

Caregiving

Caring for a family member with physical illness or dementia represents a risk factor for depression with particular significance for older women. Caregiving responsibilities, which are associated with elevated levels of depression, are more likely to fall to women than to men. Women generally have been found to be at higher risk for depression than are men, and this differential applies in the context of caregiving as well, both because male caregivers may be less likely to recognize and report distress and because the 'escape–avoidance' coping style more typically employed by women may be less effective at alleviating distress (Lutzky and Knight, 1994).

Other factors associated with caregiver depression include perceived levels of external support and behaviour disturbance, memory loss, depression, and functional impairment of the care recipient, all of which are associated with extent of caregiving needs. African American caregivers are less likely to endorse depressive symptoms than are Caucasians, possibly due to culture-specific mechanisms for managing stress, while Latina caregivers report distress levels similar to those of Anglo caregivers.

Social Support

As noted above, the presence of social support has been associated with lower levels of depressive symptoms and may buffer the effects of ill health, disability, bereavement, and other stressors, at least where the recipient appraises such support as positive (Wallsten et al., 1999). Loneliness and isolation are themselves risk factors for depression among both community-dwelling and hospitalized older adults. Structural variables, such as size and composition of the support network, and its actual effectiveness have less impact on depression than do more subjective dimensions such as perceived level of support. Paradoxically, overly intensive social support may increase depressive symptoms, perhaps by eroding the individual's sense of personal control and self-efficacy. Reciprocity may also be relevant, as Wallsten and colleagues found that offering support to another was associated with a lower level of depressive symptoms in the offerer.

Spirituality

Spirituality and religiosity have shown varying effects on depression, depending upon exactly what is being studied. Different dimensions of religiosity – public displays, private behaviours and religious coping – may have differing effects. For instance, 'intrinsic' or private religiousness has been found to reduce time to remission of depression significantly among older individuals; 'extrinsic' religious behaviours such as church attendance had no such effect (Koenig et al., 1998). Religious coping is also associated with lower levels of depressive symptoms, but at least one study found religiousness to worsen the effect of some family stressors (for a review, see Van Ness and Larson, 2002).

SUICIDE AND DEPRESSION

A serious consequence of late-life depression is an increased risk of suicide, which is more prevalent among older adults than any other age group (Conwell and Duberstein, 2001). Rates of completed suicide vary considerably by gender and ethnicity, with the most dramatic age-related increases seen in older Caucasian men. Suicidal behaviour in late life is characterized by high lethality and fewer non-lethal attempts than in younger age groups.

While depression is the most common risk factor for suicide in all age groups, the association is strongest in late life. Older adults who commit suicide are more likely than younger or middle-aged adults to have physical health problems, although the relationship is largely mediated by depression. Even among terminally ill individuals, suicide is uncommon outside the context of depression.

Primary care may offer a valuable opportunity to reach older adults at risk of suicide, as more than half of those who commit suicide visit a physician in the month before death. Training physicians to assess and respond to depression can be an effective way to reduce suicide rates (Rutz et al., 1992).

ASSESSMENT

The depression screening instruments most often used with adults in general, the Beck Depression Inventory (BDI; Beck *et al.*, 1961) and the Center for Epidemiologic Studies Depression Scale (CES-D; Radloff, 1977), are reliable and valid for use with the elderly as well. The Geriatric Depression Scale (GDS; Yesavage *et al.*, 1983) has been adopted by many health professionals because it was designed to exclude somatic symptoms and contains only items relevant to older adults. It should be noted, however, that certain somatic symptoms, such as sleep disturbance and lack of energy, are prognostic (Norris *et al.*, 1995) and may, in fact, be more likely to be endorsed by older adults who would be reluctant to endorse more obviously psychiatric symptoms. In-depth structured interviews such as the Structured Clinical Interview for the DSM-IV Axis I disorders (SCID; Spitzer *et al.*, 1988) and the Schedule for Affective Disorder and Schizophrenia, geared towards DSM-III criteria (SADS; Spitzer and Endicott, 1978), also have been shown to work well with the elderly (see Powers *et al.*, 2002).

Diagnosis of depression in individuals who are seriously or terminally ill may be especially difficult. Risk factors among these patients include advanced disease (especially pancreatic cancer), pain, and use of specific medications such as corticosteroids and interferon (Block, 2000). In addition to the criteria listed in DSM-IV and ICD-10, indicators of depression in this group may include excessive preoccupation with somatic symptoms, disability that is disproportionate to actual physical condition, and lack of co-operation with or refusal of treatment. While almost all terminally ill patients experience grief, full-blown affective disorders appear only in a minority; however, patients whose personal or family histories include substance abuse, depression or bipolar disorder are at greater risk for depression (Block, 2000).

TREATMENT

A range of effective treatment options exists for late-life depression, including psychotherapy, pharmacotherapy and electroconvulsive therapy. The effects of psychotherapy and pharmacotherapy appear to be equivalent, although few studies have compared these treatments directly. Combining pharma-cotherapy and psychotherapy is frequently recommended, despite lack of empirical evidence of incremental efficacy, particularly in the acute phase of treatment.

Psychotherapy is generally as effective in treating depression in older adults as in other groups. Cognitive-behavioural, behavioural, cognitive and brief psychodynamic therapies have been shown to be effective with patients in the acute phase of depression, whereas maintenance with interpersonal therapy reduces rates of recurrence (reviewed by Gatz *et al.*, 1998). Problem-solving therapy and modified dialectical behaviour therapy both show promise, but require additional research.

Both selective serotonin reuptake inhibitors (SSRIs) and tricyclic antidepressants (TCAs) are effective in treating depression in older adults (Salzman, 2001). Efficacy is comparable for these drugs in this population. While SSRIs may have slightly better tolerability, differences appear to be minimal. TCAs pose a greater risk of lethal overdose.

Electroconvulsive therapy (ECT) is an effective, rapidly acting treatment for late-life depression (Kelly and Zisselman, 2000), although risk of cardiac complications and delirium suggest that it should be used cautiously. ECT has been recommended particularly for treatment-resistant depression.

Much attention has been focused recently on improving identification and treatment of depressed older adults in primary care, in part because older adults are more likely to seek mental health care from physicians than from mental health specialists. Undertreatment of depression in this setting may be due to the difficulty of diagnosing depression in the context of co-morbid physical illness, lack of time during the primary care visit, and patient preferences, which may reflect stigma and other barriers to treatment. Rates of treatment among older adults diagnosed with depression have increased in recent years, although rates of diagnosis remain unchanged. A multi-site investigation showed that treatment of depression in older adults by a depression specialist within the primary care setting was more effective than providing a psychiatric referral (Unutzer *et al.*, 2002).

PREVENTION

Research findings related to risk and protective factors suggest several strategies that may be effective in preventing depression in late life. Broad health promotion initiatives, with particular emphasis on reducing the risk of cardiovascular disease, as well as enhancing opportunities for older adults to receive and provide social support and encouraging intrinsic religiousness, could reduce rates of depression. Subgroups of older adults at particular risk of depression, such as those with disabling or painful medical conditions, a family history of depression, or caregiving responsibilities, could be targeted for depression screening and specific preventive interventions. Stress inoculation and relaxation training have been shown to reduce symptoms of depression in normal older populations and may protect against the onset of depression in vulnerable groups. Finally, because depression is a recurrent disorder, individuals with a history of depression should be targeted for psychotherapeutic or pharmacological maintenance therapy, both of which have been shown to prevent recurrence of depressive episodes.

CONCLUSIONS

Depression in late life is a heterogeneous disorder that differs in many ways from depression in other age groups. Effective assessment methods, treatment options, and preventive strategies already exist, and interest in developing new techniques is increasing. It is hoped that additional research focusing on types of depression that may be more likely in late life, such as vascular and subsyndromal depressions, will help future cohorts and their doctors become better aware of both the signs and costs of this most disabling of late-life mental disorders.

FURTHER READING

Blazer, D. (2002). *Depression in late life*, 3rd edn. New York: Springer Publishing.

Karel, M. J., Ogland-Hand, S., and M. Gatz, eds. (2002). *Assessing and treating late-life depression: a casebook and resource guide*. New York: Basic Books.

Williamson, G. M., Shaffer, D. R., and P. A. Parmelee, eds. (2000). *Physical illness and depression in older adults: a handbook of theory, research, and practice*. New York: Kluwer Academic / Plenum.

REFERENCES

Alexopoulos, G. S., Meyers, B. S., Young, R. C., Campbell, S., Silbersweig, D., and M. Charlson (1997). '"Vascular depression" hypothesis', *Archives of General Psychiatry*, 54: 915–22.

American Psychiatric Association (1994). *Diagnostic and statistical manual of mental disorders*, 4th edn. Washington, D.C.: American Psychiatric Association.

Beck, A. T., Ward, C. H., Mendelson, M., Mock, J., and J. Erbaugh (1961). 'An inventory for measuring depression', *Archives of General Psychiatry*, 4: 53–63.

Block, S. D. (2000). 'Assessing and managing depression in the terminally ill patient', *Annals of Internal Medicine*, 132: 209–18.

Chen, L., Eaton, W. W., Gallo, J. J., Nestadt, G., and R. M. Crum (2000). 'Empirical examination of current depression categories in a population-based study: symptoms, course, and risk factors', *American Journal of Psychiatry*, 157: 573–80.

Conwell, Y., and P. R. Duberstein (2001). 'Suicide in elders', *Annals of the New York Academy of Sciences*, 932: 132–50.

Gatz, M., Kasl-Godley, J. E., and M. J. Karel (1996). 'Aging and mental disorders'. In J. E. Birren and K. W. Schaie, eds., *Handbook of the psychology of aging*, 4th edn. San Diego, Calif.: Academic Press, pp. 365–82.

Gatz, M., Fiske, A., Fox, L., Kaskie, B., Kasl-Godley, J. E., McCallum, T. J., and J. Wetherell (1998). 'Empirically-validated psychological treatments for older adults', *Journal of Mental Health and Aging*, 4: 9–46.

Jeste, D. V., Alexopoulos, G. S., Bartels, S. J., Cummings, J. L., Gallo, J. J., Gottlieb, G. L., Halpain, M. C., Palmer, B. W., Patterson, T. L., Reynolds, C. F., III, and B. D. Lebowitz (1999). 'Consensus statement on the upcoming crisis in geriatric mental health: research agenda for the next 2 decades', *Archives of General Psychiatry*, 56: 848–53.

Judd, L. L. (1997). 'The clinical course of unipolar major depressive disorders', *Archives of General Psychiatry*, 54: 989–91.

Kelly, K. G., and M. Zisselman (2000). 'Update on electroconvulsive therapy (ECT) in older adults', *Journal of the American Geriatrics Society*, 48: 560–6.

Koenig, H. G., George, L. K., and B. L. Peterson (1998). 'Religiosity and remission of depression in medically ill older patients', *American Journal of Psychiatry*, 155: 536–42.

Lavretsky, H., and A. Kumar (2002). 'Clinically significant non-major depression: old concepts, new insights', *American Journal of Geriatric Psychiatry*, 10: 239–55.

Lichtenstein, P., Gatz, M., Pedersen, N. L., Berg, S., and G. E. McClearn (1996). 'A cotwin-control study of response to widowhood', *Journal of Gerontology: Psychological Sciences*, 51B: P279–89.

Lutzky, S. M., and B. G. Knight (1994). 'Explaining gender differences in caregiver distress: the roles of emotional attentiveness and coping styles', *Psychology and Aging*, 9: 513–19.

Norris, M. P., Snow-Turek, A. L., and L. Blankenship (1995). 'Somatic depressive symptoms in the elderly:

contribution or confound?' *Journal of Clinical Geropsychology*, 1: 5–17.

Oakley, F., Khin, N. A., Parks, R., Bauer, L., and T. Sunderland (2002). 'Improvement in activities of daily living in elderly following treatment for post-bereavement depression', *Acta Psychiatrica Scandinavica*, 105: 231–4.

Powers, D. V., Thompson, L., Futterman, A., and D. Gallagher-Thompson (2002). 'Depression in later life: epidemiology, assessment, impact, and treatment'. In I. H. Gotlib and C. L. Hammen, eds., *Handbook of depression*. New York: Guilford Press.

Prigerson, H. G., and S. C. Jacobs (2001). 'Caring for bereaved patients: "All the doctors just suddenly go"', *JAMA*, 286: 1369–76.

Radloff, L. S. (1977). 'The CES-D scale: a self-report depression scale for research in the general population', *Applied Psychological Measurement*, 1: 385–401.

Rutz, W., von Knorring, L., and J. Wålinder (1992). 'Long-term effects of an educational program for general practitioners given by the Swedish Committee for the Prevention and Treatment of Depression', *Acta Psychiatrica Scandinavica*, 85: 83–8.

Salzman, C. (2001). *Psychiatric medications for older adults: the concise guide*. New York: Guilford Press.

Spitzer, R. L., and J. Endicott (1978). *NIMH Clinical Research Branch collaborative program on the psychobiology of depression: schedule for affective disorders and schizophrenia (SADS)*. New York: Biometrics Division, New York State Psychiatric Institute.

Spitzer, R. L., Williams, J. B. W., Gibbon, M., and M. B. First (1988). *Structured clinical interview for DSM-IIIR: patient version (SCID-P, 6/1/88)*. New York: Biometrics Research Department, New York State Psychiatric Institute.

Sullivan, P. F., Neale, M. C., and K. S. Kendler (2000). 'Genetic epidemiology of major depression: review and meta-analysis', *American Journal of Psychiatry*, 157: 1552–62.

Unutzer, J., Katon, W., Callahan, C. M., Williams, J. W., Jr, Hunkeler, E., Harpole, L., Hoffing, M., Della Penna, R. D., Noel, P. H., Lin, E. H. B., Arean, P. A., Hegel, M. T., Tang, L., Belin, T. R., Oishi, S., Langston, C., and IMPACT Investigators (2002). 'Collaborative care management of late-life depression in the primary care setting: a randomized controlled trial', *JAMA*, 288: 2836–45.

Van Ness, P. H., and D. B. Larson (2002). 'Religion, senescence, and mental health: the end of life is not the end of hope', *American Journal of Geriatric Psychiatry*, 10: 386–97.

Wallsten, S. M., Tweed, D. L., Blazer, D. G., and L. K. George (1999). 'Disability and depressive symptoms in the elderly: the effects of instrumental support and its subjective appraisal', *International Journal of Aging and Human Development*, 48: 145–59.

Williamson, G. M., and D. R. Shaffer (2000). 'The activity restriction model of depressed affect: antecedents and consequences of restricted normal activity'. In G. M. Williamson, D. R. Shaffer and P. A. Parmelee, eds., *Physical illness and depression in older adults: a handbook of theory, research, and practice*. New York: Kluwer Academic / Plenum, pp. 173–200.

Wilson, K. C. M., Chen, R., Taylor, S., McCracken, C. F. M., and J. R. M. Copeland (1999). 'Socio-economic deprivation and the prevalence and prediction of depression in older community residents: The MRC-ALPHA study', *British Journal of Psychiatry*, 175: 549–53.

World Health Organization (1993). *The ICD-10 classification of mental and behavioural disorders: diagnostic criteria for research*. Geneva: WHO.

Yesavage, J. A., Brink, T. L., Rose, T. L., Lum, O., Huang, V., Adey, M., and V. O. Leirer (1983). 'Development and validation of a geriatric screening scale: a preliminary report', *Journal of Psychiatric Research*, 17: 37–49.

CHAPTER 3.9

Dementia

BOB WOODS

The relationship between dementia and ageing – which justifies the inclusion of several chapters on dementia in this handbook – was the subject of much examination and re-evaluation in the second half of the twentieth century. On the one hand, the prevalence of the dementias increases sharply with age, and many of those experiencing such a condition attribute it to the effects of ageing. On the other hand, the biomedical research community has sought to make a clear distinction between a dementia, reflecting one or more specific disease processes, and 'normal ageing'. It is evident that a significant number of people in their 40s and 50s develop a dementia, and that these are not conditions which only occur in late life. They are viewed as diseases, which have their own distinct pattern of brain changes, which can potentially be treated, even cured, and possibly prevented. A number of medications are already available which have been shown in rigorous research studies to slow down the rate of progression of impairments in a significant number of people with particular types of dementia. The emphasis on Alzheimer's *disease* as the flagship dementia can be justified in terms of it being the most frequently occurring of the family of dementia disorders, but it has certainly also served to reinforce the disease model of dementia.

However, it is increasingly clear from those epidemiological studies which are able to go on to study the brains of participants at post-mortem that dementia in those aged 75+ is less straightforward than the simple disease paradigm suggests. A number of questions arise regarding dementia in advanced old age. How accurate are our diagnoses

of dementia? Would we all develop dementia if we lived long enough? Are the characteristic brain changes of Alzheimer's and vascular dementias always associated with a clinical dementia? What role does the person's environment play in protecting from or accelerating a dementia process? How important are genetic factors in the development of a dementia?

This chapter will attempt to address these issues which illuminate our understanding of ageing and its interface with dementia.

DEFINING AND DIAGNOSING DEMENTIA

According to the two major internationally accepted diagnostic classification systems, dementia is defined as an acquired global impairment of cognitive function, sufficient to impinge on everyday activities, occurring in clear consciousness (ICD-10: World Health Organization, 1993; DSM-IV: American Psychiatric Association, 1994). Both systems have a rather limited view of globality, essentially requiring at least one area of ability to be impaired in addition to memory – memory impairment being an essential component of the diagnosis of dementia. Change from a previous level is a key part of the definition, and dementias are usually expected to show progressive deterioration. At one time, the definition would specify that the condition is usually irreversible, but, with increased optimism regarding therapeutic strategies, this aspect has tended to be dropped.

Although cognitive changes are universal in dementia, other features, whilst not present in every case, are common enough to merit attention. Indeed, it is likely that it is these features which contribute more than cognitive deficits to carer strain (Donaldson *et al.*, 1998) and placement decisions. These 'non-cognitive' features (often described as BPSD – Behavioural and Psychological Symptoms of Dementia) include depression, anxiety, hallucinations, delusions and challenging behaviours of various types (Burns *et al.*, 1990a, 1990b, 1990c). For example, delusions – often concerning theft – were reported by Burns *et al.* in about a sixth of their sample of people with Alzheimer's disease, with another fifth having shown some ideas of persecution since their dementia began. Thirty per cent had misidentification syndromes, for instance mistaking TV pictures or images in a picture or mirror for real people. Visual and auditory hallucinations were each noted in around a tenth of the sample.

A number of different types and variants of dementia have been identified. Amongst older people, three main disorders need to be considered. The most common form is Alzheimer's disease, associated with the presence of neurofibrillary tangles and amyloid plaques in the cortex of the brain at postmortem. Blessed *et al.* (1968) showed that what had until then been thought of as 'senile dementia' was characterized by these brain changes in older people; Alzheimer's had previously been considered as a disorder primarily occurring in younger individuals. Vascular dementia is also relatively common. In the past it has been referred to as arteriosclerotic dementia or multi-infarct dementia; vascular dementia is preferred, as it reflects the range of ways in which damage to the blood supply to different areas of the brain can be impaired, not just through mini-strokes, although these are an important component of the pathology. More recently, Lewy body dementia (LBD) has been identified. Lewy bodies are found in the basal ganglia in people with Parkinson's disease; in LBD they are found in other areas of the brain also. In order to be certain of the type of dementia present, a post-mortem examination of the brain is required, and this has often been taken as the gold standard of diagnosis, although, as we shall see later, this is not always straightforward. During life, there are some differences in presentation between the dementias; in LBD hallucinations often occur early, there are fluctuations in performance, and memory does not stand out as

the primary impairment; Alzheimer's has an insidious onset and gradual progression, with memory and learning especially impaired; vascular dementia shows a more step-wise decline, with periods of stability and recovery before further decline, and a patchy picture of impairment. However, these textbook presentations are sometimes difficult to discern in real life, and the likelihood of mixed presentations may make diagnosis of dementia type during life a hit and miss exercise.

Although the diagnosis of a dementia syndrome (as opposed to a specific type) is generally thought to be relatively clear-cut, this applies more to the moderate/severe cases. Diagnostic uncertainty is frequent in older people, particularly where there is low mood and depression, or where cognitive impairment is mild.

DEPRESSION AND DEMENTIA

There have been numerous attempts to develop cognitive tests which will distinguish older people with dementia from those with depression. These attempts were perhaps doomed to failure, firstly because the two diagnoses are not mutually exclusive, and secondly because some people with depression, while not having a dementia as such, may show cognitive impairments. This patient group has been variously described as having the 'reversible dementia of depression' or a 'pseudodementia'. Neither label is really satisfactory, in that the extent of their reversibility has been questioned (Abas *et al.*, 1990) and the impairments may not much resemble dementia (Poon, 1992). It has proved difficult to identify clearly the nature of cognitive impairments in depression. There are clear indications of heterogeneity amongst older people with depression; some show no cognitive impairment, whilst others do perform poorly (Speedie *et al.*, 1990). The cognitively impaired also have more subjective cognitive complaints, particularly on recent memory and concentration (O'Boyle *et al.*, 1990). Some efforts have been made to identify a neuropathological basis in those patients showing impairment (Nussbaum, 1994), and subcortical dysfunction has been proposed as a possible model (Massman *et al.*, 1992). Several studies have shown depressed patients to occupy a mid-way position between normal controls and people with dementia on a variety of indices of brain function and structure; for example, Pearlson *et al.* (1989) demonstrated that, on CT scanning, depressed patients with cognitive impairment fall between people with dementia and depressed patients without cognitive impairment.

The co-occurrence of dementia and depression is beginning to be more widely recognized, with figures of around 30 per cent of people with dementia showing symptoms of depression being reported (Ballard *et al.*, 1996). Although it might be thought that depression might occur early in dementia, reflecting awareness of impairment, those people with dementia who show greater awareness are not reliably more likely to be depressed (e.g. Verhey *et al.*, 1993). Psychological therapies for depression, including cognitive behavioural therapy, have been successfully adapted to the context of mild dementia impairment (Teri *et al.*, 1997; Scholey and Woods, 2003). Treating depression in dementia may, arguably, make more of a difference to quality of life, for both the person affected and their supporters, than improving cognitive function.

MILD COGNITIVE IMPAIRMENT

Epidemiological studies typically include a category reflecting the hinterland between 'normality' and 'dementia'. A number of such diagnostic terms synonymous with mild memory impairment have been utilized: these include benign senescent forgetfulness (BSF); mild dementia; very mild cognitive decline; questionable dementia; limited cognitive disturbance; minimal dementia; age-associated memory impairment (AAMI) (Dawe *et al.*, 1992); age-associated cognitive decline (AACD) (Cullum *et al.*, 2000); and mild cognitive impairment (MCI) (Tuokko and Zarit, 2003).

BSF was described initially by Kral (1962) as a static memory difficulty, in contrast to malignant memory problems, which developed into a dementia. BSF was thought to reflect 'normal' age-related changes in memory. These cognitive changes, deemed insufficient to be classed as a dementia, have become the focus of a new diagnostic category – age-associated memory impairment (AAMI). The definition of AAMI has been very broad, taking as a comparative standard the memory performance of younger age groups, and it is likely that a large proportion of those over 50 could be included. The

definition also requires the person to complain of poor memory, although subjective complaints have generally proved to have little relationship with objective performance, and may have a greater association with anxiety and depression (Dawe *et al.*, 1992).

The whole concept of AAMI has generated much controversy, raising issues of what is meant by 'normal'. Should we be searching for a treatment for 'normal ageing'? The perceived interest of the pharmaceutical industry in this area has led to calls for the costs and potential side-effects of treating a condition which is not disabling to be carefully considered (Deary, 1995). It is perhaps significant that psychological memory retraining techniques have been given little attention (Yesavage *et al.*, 1989; Scogin, 1992). Although the power of such approaches may be relatively weak, they are not associated with troublesome side-effects.

Clearly, if AAMI or whatever were a precursor of dementia, the balance of cost and benefit would be different. If early treatment of such a condition could prevent a dementia developing, then identification might well be worthwhile. O'Brien and Levy (1993) argue that follow-up studies are required, using age-standardized norms, to identify those declining in relation to their peers. Generally such follow-up studies show that only a small proportion of those with mild memory impairment progress to dementia (less than 10 per cent) where the complaints are mainly subjective. For example, O'Brien *et al.* (1992) report that 8.8 per cent of those attending a memory clinic and initially diagnosed as 'normal' or having 'memory loss associated with normal ageing' went on to develop a clear-cut dementia – slightly more than would have been expected from general population incidence figures. Where there is objective evidence of memory loss, the proportion having dementia at follow-up is much greater (O'Brien and Levy, 1993).

DEMENTIA AND NORMAL AGEING

The central diagnostic problem in older people is of identifying a decline in cognitive function against a backdrop of some decline being expected in any event. The literature on the psychology of ageing is replete with examples – from longitudinal and cross-sequential studies – of age changes in cognitive function in groups of older people (e.g. Cullum *et al.*, 2000). Whilst it can be argued that the extent of change has been over-stated at times, that changes occur cannot be refuted. There is individual variation, and a range of possible factors contributing to cognitive decline – most notably physical health problems (Holland and Rabbitt, 1991; Elwood *et al.*, 2002). What is it that marks out the changes of dementia from those experienced by many (perhaps most) older people?

Conventionally, dementia has been seen as qualitatively as well as quantitatively distinct from normal ageing. However, it is possible to envisage normal ageing and dementia on a continuum, separated only by a necessarily arbitrary cut-off point (Huppert, 1994; Cohen, 1996). The essential distinction could perhaps be in the *rate*, rather than simply the absolute amount, of change. The argument against such a model is usually based on the qualitative differences observed in cognitive changes between Alzheimer's and normal ageing. However, such differences are less where the Alzheimer's cases are mildly impaired (Dawe *et al.*, 1992), suggesting there may be a continuum of change. Such a model does suggest that distinguishing cases of early dementia may be a very difficult task, and may ultimately become a matter of definition, of setting a threshold of rate of change, as in effect is often the case in epidemiological studies.

The rate-of-change concept would account for the appearance (perhaps in smaller numbers) of neuropathological features, such as those associated with Alzheimer's, in the brains of older people who died without dementia. It also accounts for the decline in cognitive function reported in normal ageing. For example Xuereb *et al.* (2000) report post-mortem findings on a number of participants from a longitudinal population study of over 2,000 over-75-year-olds. The 101 brains studied came from older people who had been examined thoroughly on one or more occasions prior to their death; some were diagnosed as having dementia whilst alive, others appeared to be ageing normally. Two main findings emerged; firstly, there were often present the pathologies of several forms of dementia; thus the characteristic Alzheimer changes might co-occur with widespread vascular changes. Secondly, there was considerable overlap in the pathologies found in the people with dementia and those with-

out. Similar findings are emerging from the Cognitive Function and Ageing Study in the UK, which is following up in total over 17,500 older people. Ince (2003) concludes from these findings that: 'the medical model of dementia which seeks to allocate people to distinct "diseases" becomes increasingly untenable in the face of this type of data'. Evidently, some older people show dementia during life, with no obvious brain pathology at postmortem, whilst others have significant pathology, but have been apparently unimpaired during life. In older people, the link between clinical picture and pathology appears less certain than has conventionally been claimed. Snowdon (2003) commenting on the Nun Study, a longitudinal study of a population of older nuns, who have all agreed to regular examinations and to an eventual post-mortem, describes a sister who died at the age of 85 without apparent cognitive impairment on testing, but whose brain showed large amounts of Alzheimer-type pathology. He concludes: 'Given nearly the same location, type and amount of neuropathologic lesions, participants in our study show an incredible range of clinical manifestations, from no symptoms to severe symptoms' (p. 453). Clearly other factors also need to be considered.

DEMENTIA AND EDUCATION

It has been shown in a number of studies that those with lower levels of education are at greater risk of developing dementia (although there are some inconsistent findings), and it has been argued that education protects against dementia (Orrell and Sahakian, 1995). One of the most dramatic and fascinating findings comes from the Nun Study (Snowdon *et al.*, 2000). The research team were able to analyze handwritten autobiographies written by the nuns at an average age of 23, some 62 years previously, and compare linguistic ability at that time with pathological brain changes observed at postmortem. The measure of linguistic ability reflected the density of ideas within the autobiography. There was a remarkably strong association with the severity of Alzheimer-type pathology in different brain regions. However, in a larger sample from the same study, low education was not related to a diagnosis of Alzheimer's disease at post-mortem (Mortimer *et al.*, 2003). Letenneur *et al.* (2000) report from four

European follow-up studies (the EURODEM project) that the increased risk of developing dementia associated with fewer years of schooling was evident in women, but not in men. Women who had 7 or fewer years of education were more than four times as likely to develop dementia during the study as women with 12 or more years.

The issue is a complex one (Gilleard, 1997). Educational level is often seen as a proxy for intellectual ability (although this varies greatly across cultures and cohorts). One possibility is that a person with greater intelligence can decline for a longer time-period before reaching a point where impairment is evident. Psychologists and psychometricians struggle to assess change of function over time satisfactorily, and are often left relying on measures of memory and cognition which instead offer a threshold of impairment: simplistically, above-threshold scores are viewed as normal, those below are 'in the dementia range'. Clearly, those with a lifelong relatively low intellectual and educational level require only a small degree of change to enter the range of impairment. Those with high intellectual function and education have, it would appear, more resources in reserve to maintain their function. Certainly, those with low intellectual level are amongst those most often misdiagnosed as having a dementia. This may be attributable in part to the high educational loading of many of the screening tests available, such as the Mini-Mental State Examination (Orrell *et al.*, 1992). The practice in many epidemiological studies of assessing fully only those who screen positive on such a test is likely to mean that well-educated, intelligent people with dementia are excluded from the study at the outset, as they may score above the cut-off point, despite having clear impairment on more detailed neuropsychological assessment. On the other hand, in a clinical context, those around a highly intelligent person in a very demanding environment might become aware of signs of incipient dementia earlier than those supporting a person with a low intellectual level who is subject to few cognitive demands outside a well-established routine.

There is increasing interest in considering models of the relationship between pathology and function which account for individual differences, the effect of education, etc. Tuokko *et al.* (2003) describe three models which might account for the differences

in incidence of dementia between those with high education / high IQ / high occupational attainment and those with low achievement in these areas. The brain reserve capacity model suggests some individuals have greater brain reserve, i.e. they can afford to lose more neurons, have a higher amount of pathological changes, before reaching a threshold for clinical symptoms. Education could lead to greater brain reserve capacity, with more synaptic connectivity, and brain size might be a marker of this reserve. For example, in the Nun Study, head circumference (a crude index of brain size) was related to the clinical diagnosis of dementia (Mortimer *et al.*, 2003), although not to the presence of Alzheimer pathology. Those nuns with low education and small head circumference were four times as likely to show dementia as the rest of the sample.

The cognitive reserve model concerns itself with how effectively the remaining neural tissue is used. Intelligent, educated people have available to them the facility to use alternative cognitive strategies, which again can result in a delay in expression of clinical and functional impairments associated with underlying brain pathology. They are more likely to continue to exercise their cognitive processes, and build their reserve further. The third possibility relates to the ascertainment bias described earlier; are markers of reserve confounded with measures of outcome, i.e. the measures of impairment are not sensitive enough to pick up changes in this high functioning group. From their analyses of data on the incidence of dementia from the Canadian Study on Health and Ageing, a study of over 10,000 older people, Tuokko *et al.* (2003) conclude that the lower incidence of dementia for high functioning people primarily results from ascertainment bias; the high functioning people who developed dementia were scoring less well on tests of memory initially than those who did not develop dementia, but not within the 'impaired' range. The problem is that one threshold does not fit all, and there is a clear need for tests with normative data broken down by both age and education (Tuokko *et al.*, 2003).

PREVALENCE OF THE DEMENTIAS

The prevalence of the dementias has been the subject of numerous epidemiological studies internationally (e.g. Hofman *et al.*, 1991). There are a number of differences between studies, but there is a broad consensus that the prevalence doubles for each increase of 5.1 years; 5% of the over-65s and 20% of the over-80s are widely accepted figures (Livingston and Hinchliffe, 1993). However, there is less certainty regarding prevalence in the over-90s and amongst centenarians. If everyone who lived long enough developed a dementia, this would reinforce the concept of a continuum between normal ageing and dementia. On the other hand, survival to a certain age may mark a crossover effect, where the probability of dementia lessens, reflecting the general robust status of such survivors.

Howieson *et al.* (2003) report a longitudinal study of ninety-five healthy community-dwelling older people who had an average age of 84 at the commencement of the study, which followed participants up for up to 13 years. Almost exactly half of the sample remained cognitively intact over the whole period or until death. Several studies have conducted population-based evaluations of centenarians. Andersen-Ranberg *et al.* (2001) attempted to interview every person in Denmark who reached 100 years old over a 13-month period. They report that 37% had no signs of dementia, which was diagnosable in 51% of the sample. A smaller study in the USA (Silver *et al.*, 2001) reports 21% having no dementia and broadly similar findings are emerging across countries (Antonucci, 2001). Silver *et al.* (2002) have examined the brains of fourteen centenarians from their study at post-mortem; in ten cases the clinical picture during life and the post-mortem findings were consistent; in two cases, there were significant Alzheimer changes despite no apparent impairments on neuropsychological tests; and in two cases, there had been apparent dementia during life, but no obvious neuropathological changes. It appears that the inconsistency observed in younger samples continues into extreme old age.

RISK FACTORS FOR DEMENTIA IN LATE LIFE

The greatest risk factor for developing dementia appears to be increasing age. However, a number of other possible factors have emerged. Launer *et al.* (1999) report factors associated with the incidence of dementia from four European population-based studies. In addition to low levels of education

(especially in women), female gender and current smoking (especially in men) increased the risk of dementia. History of head injury did not emerge as a factor, and there was no evidence for smoking history being a protective factor. Vascular risk factors such as history of heart attacks have also been shown to predict the incidence of dementia (Brayne *et al.*, 1998).

Specific genetic abnormalities have attracted much attention in younger people with Alzheimer's disease. In older people, it is the presence of a particular genetic marker ApoE4 (the E4 variant of apolipoprotein E) which has been associated with increased risk of Alzheimer's disease. For example, using data from the Nun Study, Riley *et al.* (2000) indicate that the absence of ApoE4 was related to maintenance of high levels of cognitive function, and Howieson *et al.* (2003) report similar results. Snowdon (2003) describes a sister from the Nun Study who had two copies of the ApoE4 (the strongest version of this risk factor), and who had extensive indications of Alzheimer changes in her brain at post-mortem, but who remained cognitively intact throughout her life. Increasingly, when risk factors are considered, two aspects must be taken into account: which are risk factors for pathological changes, and which are risk factors for the expression of dementia during life. Thus, for example, Mortimer *et al.* (2003) suggest that low education and head circumference are risk factors for expression, but not for pathology.

CONCLUSIONS

This chapter has attempted to address some of the complexity surrounding dementia in late life. It has shown clearly that the simple disease model of dementia is untenable in late life, that brain changes are not always congruent with the clinical presentation, and that multiple pathologies are more common than single disease processes.

These conclusions are a remarkably good fit with the arguments propounded by the British social psychologist, the late Tom Kitwood, who argued that the clinical presentation of dementia was not simply a manifestation of the neuropathological impairment, the damaged brain. He argued that other factors, the person's health, life history and personality, were also important, along with their social environment. Kitwood (1993) expressed this understanding of the variety of influences on the presentation of dementia in a simple equation –

$$D = P + B + H + NI + SP$$

– where:

D = Dementia presentation
P = Personality
B = Biography
H = Physical Health
NI = Neurological Impairment
SP = Social Psychology

From the above discussion, we would need to include education and occupational attainment under Biography, and genetic risk factors under Health. It is perhaps the social environment that has yet to receive full attention. Kitwood highlighted the impact of the social environment surrounding the person, suggesting that often it constituted a 'malignant social psychology', devaluing, diminishing, dehumanizing, depersonalizing the person, leading to greater disability and dysfunction. Examples of a malignant social psychology would include infantilization, disempowerment and objectification. His suggestion that the person with dementia may well appear more impaired, or to have a more severe level of dementia than is necessitated by the actual neuropathological damage that has been sustained, now appears well supported. His assertion that someone may appear to have dementia without evident neuropathological impairment also finds support, although this conclusion is diluted by the possibility that there is a form of pathology we have yet to recognize.

These considerations emphasize the need for a wide-ranging, holistic response to dementia. While the first wave of pharmacological interventions are available, acting on one of the impaired neurotransmitter systems, psychosocial interventions have been relatively overlooked. However, there is an increasingly strong evidence-base on interventions with family caregivers (e.g. Brodaty *et al.*, 2003) and on approaches such as cognitive stimulation of people with dementia, which has been shown to have an effect of the same order as the first wave of medications (Spector *et al.*, 2003).

Many challenges remain. Both pharmacological and psychosocial responses to some of the non-cognitive features of dementia, such as agitation and aggression, have limited effectiveness (e.g. Teri *et al.*, 2000), although the latter are much less harmful. People with dementia have proved especially difficult to maintain at home with packages of community care, in view of their need for monitoring over long time periods, the unpredictability of their needs and their frequent lack of awareness of their need for support and care. Predictions of a future epidemic of dementia remain cataclysmic. According to the Alzheimer's Association in the USA (2003): 'If left unchecked . . . Alzheimer's disease will destroy the health care system'. By 2030 half of those people with Alzheimer's will be 85 years and older. There are calls for more research to prevent the disease and delay its onset; this chapter indicates that further understanding of why some people can function well despite the presence of pathological brain changes would also be important; modifiable factors such as health, activity, stimulation, mood and social environment would be a good starting point.

FURTHER READING

Kitwood, T. (1997). *Dementia reconsidered: the person comes first.* Buckingham: Open University Press.
Snowdon, D. (2001). *Aging with grace. The Nun study and the science of old age: how we can all live longer, healthier and more vital lives.* London: Fourth Estate.

REFERENCES

Abas, M. A., Sahakian, B. J., and R. Levy (1990). 'Neuropsychological deficits and CT scan changes in elderly depressives', *Psychological Medicine*, 20: 507–20.
Alzheimer's Association (2003). *New Alzheimer projections add urgency to search for prevention, cure* [press release]. Chicago: Alzheimer's-Association.
American Psychiatric Association (1994). *Diagnostic and statistical manual of mental disorders*, 4th edn. Washington, D.C.: American Psychiatric Association.
Andersen-Ranberg, K., Vasegaard, L., and B. Jeune (2001). 'Dementia is not inevitable: a population-based study of Danish centenarians', *Journal of Gerontology: Psychological Sciences*, 56B: P152–P159.
Antonucci, T. C. (2001). 'Introduction to special section on centenarians and dementia', *Journal of Gerontology: Psychological Sciences*, 56B: P133.
Ballard, C. G., Bannister, C., and F. Oyebode (1996). 'Depression in dementia sufferers', *International Journal of Geriatric Psychiatry*, 11 (6): 507–15.

Blessed, G., Tomlinson, B. E., and M. Roth (1968). 'The association between quantitative measures of dementia and of senile change in the cerebral grey matter of elderly subjects', *British Journal of Psychiatry*, 114: 797–811.

Brayne, C., Gill, C., Huppert, F., Barkley, C., Gehlhaar, E., Girling, D. M., O'Connor, D. W., and E. S. Paykel (1998). 'Vascular risks and incident dementia: results from a cohort study of the very old', *Dementia, Geriatric Cognitive Disorders*, 9: 175–80.

Brodaty, H., Green, A., and A. Koschera (2003). 'Meta-analysis of psychosocial interventions for caregivers of people with dementia', *Journal of American Geriatrics Society*, 51: 657–64.

Burns, A., Jacoby, R., and R. Levy (1990a). 'Psychiatric phenomena in Alzheimer's disease. I: Disorders of thought content', *British Journal of Psychiatry*, 157: 72–6.

—— (1990b). 'Psychiatric phenomena in Alzheimer's disease. II: Disorders of perception', *British Journal of Psychiatry*, 157: 76–81.

—— (1990c). 'Psychiatric phenomena in Alzheimer's disease. IV: Disorders of behaviour', *British Journal of Psychiatry*, 157: 86–94.

Cohen, G. (1996). 'Memory and learning in normal ageing'. In R. T. Woods, ed., *Handbook of the clinical psychology of ageing*. Chichester: Wiley, pp. 43–58.

Cullum, S., Huppert, F., McGee, M., Dening, T., Ahmed, A., Paykel, E. S., and C. Brayne (2000). 'Decline across different domains of cognitive function in normal ageing: results of a longitudinal population-based study using CAMCOG', *International Journal of Geriatric Psychiatry*, 15: 853–62.

Dawe, B., Procter, A., and M. Philpot (1992). 'Concepts of mild memory impairment in the elderly and their relationship to dementia – a review', *International Journal of Geriatric Psychiatry*, 7: 473–9.

Deary, I. J. (1995). 'Age-associated memory impairment: a suitable case for treatment?' *Ageing & Society*, 15: 393–406.

Donaldson, C., Tarrier, N., and A. Burns (1998). 'Determinants of carer stress in Alzheimer's disease', *International Journal of Geriatric Psychiatry*, 13 (4): 248–56.

Elwood, P. C., Pickering, J., Bayer, A., and J. E. J. Gallacher (2002). 'Vascular disease and cognitive function in older men in the Caerphilly cohort', *Age & Ageing*, 31: 43–8.

Gilleard, C. J. (1997). 'Education and Alzheimer's disease: a review of recent international epidemiological studies', *Aging & Mental Health*, 1 (1): 33–46.

Hofman, A., Rocca, W. A., Brayne, C., *et al.* (1991). 'The prevalence of dementia in Europe: a collaborative study of the 1980–1990 findings', *International Journal of Epidemiology*, 20: 736–48.

Holland, C. A., and P. Rabbitt (1991). 'The course and causes of cognitive change with advancing age', *Reviews in Clinical Gerontology*, 1: 81–96.

Howieson, D. B., Camicioli, R., Quinn, J., Silbert, L. C., Care, B., Moore, M. M., Dame, A., Sexton, G., and J. A. Kaye (2003). 'Natural history of cognitive decline in the old old', *Neurology*, 60: 1489–94.

Huppert, F. A. (1994). 'Memory function in dementia and normal ageing – dimension or dichotomy?' In F. A. Huppert, C. Brayne and D. O'Connor, eds., *Dementia and normal ageing*. Cambridge: Cambridge University Press.

Ince, P. G. (2003). 'Concepts of Alzheimer's disease', *Alzheimer's Disease International: Global Perspective*, March: 6.

Kitwood, T. (1993). 'Towards a theory of dementia care: the interpersonal process', *Ageing & Society*, 13: 51–67.

Kral, V. A. (1962). 'Senescent forgetfulness, benign and malignant', *Journal of the Canadian Medical Association*, 86: 257–60.

Launer, L. J., Andersen, K., Dewey, M. E., Letenneur, L., Ott, A., Amaducci, L. A., Brayne, C., Copeland, J. R., Dartigues, J. F., Kragh-Sorensen, P., Lobo, A., Martinez-Lage, J. M., Stijnen, T., and A. Hofman (1999). 'Rates and risk factors for dementia and Alzheimer's disease: results from EURODEM pooled analyses', *Neurology*, 52: 78–84.

Letenneur, L., Launer, L. J., Andersen, K., Dewey, M. E., Ott, A., Copeland, J. R., Dartigues, J. F., Kragh-Sorensen, P., Baldereschi, M., Brayne, C., Lobo, A., Martinez-Lage, J. M., Stijnen, T. and A. Hofman (2000). 'Education and the risk for Alzheimer's disease: sex makes a difference – EURODEM pooled analyses', *American Journal of Epidemiology*, 151: 1064–71.

Livingston, G., and A. C. Hinchliffe (1993). 'The epidemiology of psychiatric disorders in the elderly', *International Review of Psychiatry*, 5: 317–26.

Massman, P. J., Delis, D. C., Butters, N., and R. M. Dupont (1992). 'The subcortical dysfunction hypothesis of memory deficits in depression: neuropsychological validation in a subgroup of patients', *Journal of Clinical & Experimental Neuropsychology*, 14: 687–706.

Mortimer, J. A., Snowdon, D. A., and W. R. Markesbery (2003). 'Head circumference, education and risk of dementia: findings from the Nun study', *Journal of Clinical & Experimental Neuropsychology*, 25: 671–9.

Nussbaum, P. D. (1994). 'Pseudodementia: a slow death', *Neuropsychology Review*, 4: 71–90.

O'Boyle, M., Amadeo, M., and D. Self (1990). 'Cognitive complaints in elderly depressed and pseudodemented patients', *Psychology & Aging*, 5: 467–8.

O'Brien, J. T., and R. Levy (1993). 'Age-associated memory impairment', *International Journal of Geriatric Psychiatry*, 8: 779–80.

O'Brien, J. T., Beats, B., Hill, K., Howard, R., Sahakian, B., and R. Levy (1992). 'Do subjective memory complaints precede dementia? A three-year follow-up of patients with supposed "benign senescent forgetfulness"', *International Journal of Geriatric Psychiatry*, 7: 481–6.

Orrell, M. W., and B. J. Sahakian (1995). 'Use it or lose it: does education protect against dementia?' *British Medical Journal*, 310: 951–2.

Orrell, M., Howard, R., Payne, A., Bergmann, K., Woods, R., Everitt, B. S., and R. Levy (1992). 'Differentiation between organic and functional psychiatric illness in the elderly: an evaluation of four cognitive tests', *International Journal of Geriatric Psychiatry*, 7: 263–75.

Pearlson, G. D., Rabins, P. V., Kim, W. S., and L. J. Speedie (1989). 'Structural brain CT changes and cognitive deficits in elderly depressives with and without reversible dementia ("pseudodementia")', *Psychological Medicine*, 19: 573–84.

Poon, L. W. (1992). 'Towards an understanding of cognitive functioning in geriatric depression', *International Psychogeriatrics*, 4 (Suppl. 2): 241–66.

Riley, K. P., Snowdon, D. A., Saunders, A. M., Roses, A. D., Mortimer, J. A., and N. Nanayakkara (2000). 'Cognitive function and apolipoprotein E in very old adults', *Journal of Gerontology: Psychological Sciences and Social Sciences*, 55B: S69–S75.

Scholey, K. A., and B. T. Woods (2003). 'A series of brief cognitive therapy interventions with people experiencing both dementia and depression: a description of techniques and common themes', *Clinical Psychology & Psychotherapy*, 10: 175–85.

Scogin, F. (1992). 'Memory training for older adults'. In G. Jones and B. Miesen, eds., *Care-giving in dementia*. London: Routledge, pp. 260–71.

Silver, M. H., Jilinskaia, E., and T. T. Perls (2001). 'Cognitive functional status of age-confirmed centenarians in a population-based study', *Journal of Gerontology: Psychological Sciences*, 56B: P134–P140.

Silver, M. H., Newell, K., Brady, C., Hedley-White, E. T., and T. T. Perls (2002). 'Distinguishing between neurodegenerative disease and disease-free ageing: correlating neuropsychological evaluations and neuropathological studies in centenarians', *Psychosomatic Medicine*, 64: 493–501.

Snowdon, D. A. (2003). 'Healthy aging and dementia: findings from the Nun study', *Annals of Internal Medicine*, 139: 450–4.

Snowdon, D. A., Greiner, L. H., and W. R. Markesbery (2000). 'Linguistic ability in early life and the neuropathology of Alzheimer's disease and cerebrovascular disease: findings from the Nun study', *Annals of the New York Academy of Sciences*, 903: 34–8.

Spector, A., Thorgrimsen, L., Woods, B., Royan, L., Davies, S., Butterworth, M., and M. Orrell (2003). 'Efficacy of an evidence-based cognitive stimulation therapy programme for people with dementia: randomised controlled trial', *British Journal of Psychiatry*, 183: 248–54.

Speedie, L., Rabins, P. V., Pearlson, G. D., and P. J. Moberg (1990). 'Confrontation naming deficit in dementia of depression', *Journal of Neuropsychiatry & Clinical Neurosciences*, 2: 59–63.

Teri, L., Logsdon, R. G., Uomoto, J., and S. M. McCurry (1997). 'Behavioral treatment of depression in dementia patients: a controlled clinical trial', *Journal of Gerontology*, 52B: P159–P166.

Teri, L., Logsdon, R. G., Peskind, E., Raskind, M., Weiner, M. F., Tractenberg, R. E., Foster, N. L., Schneider, L. S., Sano, M., Whitehouse, P., Tariot, P., Mellow, A. M., Auchus, A. P., Grundman, M., Thomas, R. G., Schafer, K., and L. J. Thal (2000). 'Treatment of agitation in AD: a randomized, placebo-controlled clinical trial', *Neurology*, 55: 1271–8.

Tuokko, H., and S. H. Zarit (2003). 'Mild cognitive impairment', *Aging & Mental Health*, 7 (4): 235–7.

Tuokko, H., Garrett, D. D., McDowell, I., Silverberg, N., and B. Kristjansson (2003). 'Cognitive decline in high-functioning older adults: reserve or ascertainment bias?' *Aging & Mental Health*, 7 (4): 259–70.

Verhey, F. R. J., Rozendaal, N., Ponds, R. W. H. M., and J. Jolles (1993). 'Dementia, awareness and depression', *International Journal of Geriatric Psychiatry*, 8: 851–6.

World Health Organization (1993). *The ICD-10 classification of mental and behavioural disorders: diagnostic criteria for research*. Geneva: WHO.

Xuereb, J. H., Brayne, C., Dufouil, C., Gertz, H., Wischik, C., Harrington, C., Mukaetova-Ladinska, E., McGee, M. A., O'Sullivan, A., O'Connor, D., Paykel, E. S., and F. Huppert (2000). 'Neuropathological findings in the very old: results from the first 101 brains of a population-based longitudinal study of dementing disorders', *Annals of the New York Academy of Sciences*, 903: 490–6.

Yesavage, J. A., Lapp, D., and J. I. Sheikh (1989). 'Mnemonics as modified for use by the elderly'. In L. W. Poon, D. C. Rubin and B. A. Wilson, eds., *Everyday cognition in adulthood and late life*. Cambridge: Cambridge University, Press, pp. 598–611.

Dementia in an Asian Context

JINZHOU TIAN

INTRODUCTION

Alzheimer's disease and other dementias are already a major public health problem among the elderly in Western countries. These dementias could also have a devastating impact on Asian countries, especially those whose populations are ageing the most rapidly. By the year 2020, approximately 70% of the world's population aged ≥ 60 will be located in developing countries like China and India, the two most populated countries in the world. Reviewing what is known about the current burden of the disorder, the principal contributing factors, and the outcome of treatment strategies and care services for dementia in Asian countries is important for better understanding of the disorder and for better provision of care for the demented patients, depending on the level of resources available.

PREVALENCE AND INCIDENCE OF DEMENTIA

There is little information available in international literature on the prevalence and incidence of dementia in Asian countries. Population samples studied have been composed mostly of people over 65 years of age, although some studies have included younger populations, especially in those countries where the expected lifespan is shorter (for example, India). The reported average prevalence of dementia between Asian countries varies (Table 1). The standardized prevalence of dementia in people aged 65 and older has been reported to be 1.8% to 7.8% in China (M. R. Zhang *et al.*, 1990; Z. X. Zhang *et al.*, 1999) and 3.7% to 6.7% in Japan (Yamada *et al.*, 1999) since the mid-1980s. The prevalence of dementia in Korea varies from 8.2% to 10.8% (Woo *et al.*, 1998). This is somewhat higher than that in other Asian countries, similar to the 6.3% to 11.9% in Western developed countries (Fratigilioni *et al.*, 1991). However, the prevalence of dementia in India may be the lowest among Asian countries, ranging from 1.4 to 3.4%.

The wide range of prevalence figures (1.4–10.8%) between these studies is partly explained by the different age samples, diagnostic criteria and threshold for establishing cases. The rate of dementia in Japanese American men in Hawaii is reported to be 7.6%, which is rather higher than the 3.4% to 6.7% rate found in Japan (Yamada *et al.*, 1999), but this includes very mild dementia (CDR (Clinical Dementia Rating) = 0.5) when defining cases. If only cases of mild or greater severity (CDR ≥ 1) are considered, the estimates of dementia in Japanese American men are about 5.5%, closer to those of the Japanese studies, with a 4.7% prevalence considering only mild or greater severity cases (CDR ≥ 1) for older urban Japanese. A similar estimate (5.3%) in a Korean population aged over 65 years excluded very mild cases (CDR = 0.5), and a higher prevalence (7.8%) of dementia than those of other Chinese studies (MMSE ≤ 23) included very mild cases (MMSE ≤ 26) for elderly northern Chinese (Lin *et al.*, 1998; Lee *et al.*, 2002). In addition, the high mortality (25.2% within 1 year) from onset of dementia as compared to the mortality (4.3%) for the general population aged 65 or above in Taiwan (China) may also explain the lower prevalences

TABLE 1. Reported prevalence of dementia in Asian countries

Year	Survey site	Overall (%)	AD* (%)	VaD** (%)	Other (%)	VaD/AD
China		**4.7**	**2.8**	**1.4**	**0.5**	**0.7**
1981	Wuhan	0.5	0.1	0.4	0	5.6
1989	Beijing	1.2	0.4	0.8	0	2.0
1990	Shanghai	4.6	3.0	1.2	0.4	0.4
1996	Taiwan	4.4	2.2	1.1	1.1	0.5
1998	Taiwan	4.0	2.3	0.9	0.8	0.4
1998	Hong Kong	6.1	4.0	1.8	0.3	0.5
1999	Beijing	7.8	4.8	2.7	0.3	0.6
Japan		**6.1**	**2.4**	**2.2**	**1.2**	**1.1**
1982	Tokyo	4.8	1.2	2.0	1.6	1.7
1986	Aichi	5.8	2.4	2.8	0.6	1.2
1992	Hisayama	6.7	1.7	3.8	1.2	2.2
1995	Okinawa	6.7	3.1	2.1	1.5	0.7
1999	Hiroshima	7.2	Male 2.0	2.0	NA	1.0
			Female 3.8	1.8		0.5
Korea		**9.5**	**5.5**	**1.9**	**2.75**	**0.4**
1994	Young-II	10.8	6.5	1.3	3.0	0.2
1998	Yonchon	9.5	4.5	2.5	2.5	0.6
1998	Yonchon	6.8	4.2	2.4	0.2	0.6
2002	Seoul	8.2	5.4	2.0	NA	0.4
India		**2.4**	**1.25**	**2.0**	**0.5**	**0.7**
1996	Kerala	3.4	1.4	2.0	0.0	1.4
1998	Ballabgarh	1.4	1.1	–	–	–a

* AD – Alzheimer's disease; ** VaD – vascular dementia. a – Although authors did not report the prevalence of VaD, it is definite that AD was at least 3–4 times more prevalent than VaD.
Adapted from Suh and Shah (2001).

TABLE 2. The reported incidence of dementia in population aged ≥65 in China, Japan and India

Survey year	Author	Site	Overall (‰)	Males/Females	AD* (‰)	VaD** (‰)	Other (‰)
1998	Zhang et al. (1998)	Shanghai (China)	11.5	9.8 / 12.7	7.4	3.3	0.8
1995	Yoshitake et al. (1995)	Hisayama (Japan)	20.1	19.3 / 20.9	8.9	10.6	
1998	Liu et al. (1998)	Taiwan (China)	12.8		5.4	4.1	
2001	Chandra et al. (2001)	Ballagarh (India)		2.5 / 3.7	4.7		

* AD – Alzheimer's disease; ** VaD – vascular dementia. a – Although authors did not report the prevalence of VaD, it is definite that AD was at least 3–4 times more prevalent than VaD.

(4.0%) (Lin et al., 1998). Although differences in study design, case finding procedure, and population characteristics between studies should be carefully considered, dementia prevalence discrepancies within Asian populations including Japanese, Korean and Chinese may not really be as great as seemingly reported. However, the prevalence of dementia in India may be the lowest among Asian populations, even though case finding criteria already included very mild dementia (CDR ≥ 0.5).

There are very few Asian incidence studies of dementia: one from Japan, one from Taiwan, and

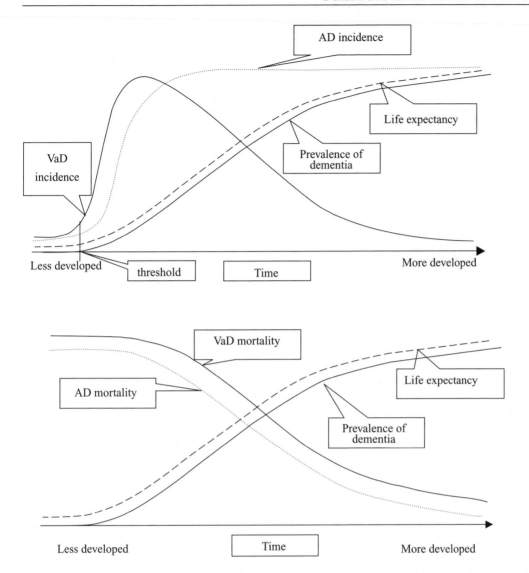

Figure 1. A hypothetical model about temporal change in the incidence and mortality of dementia compared with life expectancy. Every society started as a low incident – high mortality society. As the average life expectancy increases and begins to reach the threshold age of risk for dementia, there is a gradual transition from low incidence – high mortality society to a high incidence – high mortality society. If known risk factors of AD are difficult to modify, incidence of AD may not decline after increase. If those of VaD can be modified, VaD will decline with the improved survival. Ultimately, every society reaches low-incidence and low-mortality state. Reprinted from Suh and Shah (2001).

one from Shanghai in China, and one from India (Table 2) (Guh and Shah, 2001). The reported rates of incidence range from 5.4 to 20.1 per 1,000 person-years among those aged ≥65 years. Rates for China are from 11.5 to 12.8 per 1,000 person-years among those aged ≥65 years, with 5.4 to 7.4 for AD and 3.3 to 4.1 for VaD. The incidence rate of dementia in Japan is the highest among Asian studies, 20.1 per 1,000 person-years among those aged ≥65 years, with incidence rates of 8.9 for AD and 10.6 for VaD. The overall AD incidence rate among those aged ≥65 years in India is 4.7 per 1,000 person-years, also lower than that in China and Japan, and considerably lower than the 17.5 found by using

similar methods and criteria in largely White reference American populations. Such findings imply

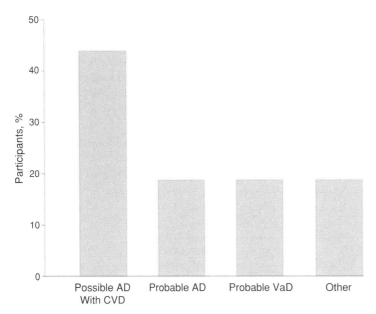

Figure 2. Reprinted from Brust (1983). The most common dementing disease in Tajiri, Japan, was possible Alzheimer disease (AD) with cerebrovascular disease (CVD) (by means of the National Institute of Neurological Disorders and Stroke and the Association Internationale pour la Recherche et l'Enseignement en Neurosciences criteria), followed by probable AD (by means of the National Institute of Neurological and Communicative Disorders and Stroke and the Alzheimer's Disease and Related Disorders Association criteria). It seemed that vascular dementia (VaD) tends to be overdiagnosed if possible AD with CVD is thought to be VaD.

that there are substantial geographical differences in incidence of AD within the heterogeneous populations of Asia. Low incidence rates may be associated with the low average life expectancy in India, with fewer persons living into age of risk, especially if there is selectively earlier mortality in those at increased risk (Figure 1). Low incidence rates may also suggest the presence of underlying protective factors, or the absence of underlying risk factors.

The prevalence rate of dementia in Asian countries increases with age, somewhat similar to that found in Western countries (Guh and Shah, 2001). This age-dependent increase in prevalence is more prominent for AD than for VaD in Taiwan. Consistent with studies in Western countries, for every 5-year increase in age in those elderly aged 65 and over, the risk of dementia increases nearly one-fold (74%). The prevalence rate of dementia increases from 1.3% in people aged 65–9 years to 16.5% in the older Chinese populations aged 80–5. The Korean population contains a somewhat lower proportion of older people aged 80 and over (14.3%) (Lee *et al.*, 2002) than those of developed countries such as the US (24.7%) and Japan (19.7%) (United Nations, 1999). However, age is a significant risk factor for the increased incidence of both VaD and AD in people aged over 65 years in Japan. There is no evidence of any sex difference in incidence, however: Malay women suffer more frequently from VaD (4.4%)

than Chinese women (0.9%) in Singapore (Kua and Ko, 1995). In addition, low education is associated with increased risk of dementia ranging from 0.1 to 1.0 for school education ≥7 years to 0 years in China (Lee *et al.*, 2002; Guh and Shah, 2001). Older age and lower education levels contribute to higher CDR scale scores, which in turn correlate with higher total Neuropsychiatric Inventory (NPI) scores in AD cohorts from Taiwan and Hong Kong, similar to Caucasian subjects in Los Angeles, California.

Almost all evidence agrees on the proportions of AD (50 to 60%) and VaD (25 to 30%) in Western countries. However, the relative frequencies of these subtypes of dementia in Asian populations are still controversial. Guh and Shah (2001) claim a temporal change in the ratio of the prevalence of VaD to AD in Korea, China and Japan (Table 1). Before 1989, VaD was markedly more common than AD, 1.2 to 2.2 ratios of AD to VaD in Japan, 2.0 to 5.6 in China. Since 1990, VaD has generally been less prevalent than AD, ratios of VaD to AD are 0.7 to 0.5 in Japan, 0.2 to 0.6 in Korea, 0.4 to 0.6 in China. Two surveys of Japanese Americans also show the dominance of AD over VaD. Therefore, it is believed that VaD is currently the second most common dementia in most Asian countries, although several recent studies conducted in Japan have reported more VaD than AD. One possible explanation for this discrepancy is that the incidence of cerebral vascular disease has recently decreased in Japan. Another explanation for the variation in research findings includes the diagnostic criteria used for VaD. Almost all surveys conducted in Japan use the Hachinski ischaemic score (HIS) to distinguish VaD and AD. A high 'ischaemic score' can identify patients who have had a stroke, but prior stroke does not necessarily ensure that vascular disease caused or even contributed to the dementia, so VaD is almost certainly overdiagnosed clinically (Figure 2). However, considering the high stroke prevalence in Taiwan and North China, the relative lower prevalence rates for VaD in these regions deserves further investigation.

PRINCIPAL RISK FACTORS FOR DEMENTIA

The exact biological cause of dementia remains unknown, although as in Western countries a number of similar risk factors have been suggested in Asian studies. These include disturbances in the metabolism and regulation of amyloid precursor protein (APP), other plaque-related proteins, tau proteins, genetic risk factors such as Apolipoprotein E (ApoE), and family history of dementia, as well as psychosocial factors.

Apolipoprotein E gene

ApoE, a major component of plasma lipoproteins, participates in the transport and redistribution of lipids in the body. The ApoE gene is polymorphic, with three major alleles ($\varepsilon2$, $\varepsilon3$, $\varepsilon4$) according to Apo E2, E3 and E4 isoforms at a single gene locus on chromosome 19. Consequently there are six genotypes, including three homozygous genotypes (Apo E2/2, E3/3, and E4/4) and three heterozygous genotypes (Apo E3/2, E4/3 and E4/2). The emergence of the APOE $\varepsilon4$ allele as a major risk factor for AD, especially in late-onset AD (LOAD), has been confirmed in more than 100 studies worldwide (Farrer et al., 1997). The APOE $\varepsilon4$ allele represents a major risk factor for AD in many ethnic groups studies, across all ages between 40 and 90 years, and in both men and women. The $\varepsilon2/\varepsilon3$ genotype appears equally protective across ethnic groups. However, the strength of the association between ApoE genotype and AD or VaD varies with ethnic group, particularly with

TABLE 3. Frequency of the $\varepsilon4$ allele in reported studies of AD

Year ethnicity	$\varepsilon2$	$\varepsilon3$	$\varepsilon4$
Worldwide			
Saunders et al. (1993)			0.36
Kuusisto et al. (1994)	0.022	0.620	0.359
Tsuda et al. (1994)	0.02	0.63	0.35
Hendrie et al. (1995)	0.048	0.548	0.403
Japan			
Ueki et al. (1993)	0.02	0.67	0.31
Noguchi et al. (1993)	0.013	0.711	0.276
Yoshizawa et al. (1994)	0.02	0.64	0.34
Nakayama et al. (1999)	0.02	0.63	0.35
Korea			
H. C. Kim et al. (2001)	0.183	0.583	0.233
K. W. Kim et al. (1999)	0.041	0.736	0.223
China			
Chen et al. (1999)			0.221
Katzman et al. (1997)			0.254
Hong et al. (1996)			0.232
Yang et al. (2001)			0.301
India			
Ganguli et al. (2000)			0.073– 0.11

regard to the relative proportions of APOE $\varepsilon2$ allele and APOE $\varepsilon4$ allele.

The APOE$\varepsilon4$–AD association in Japanese subjects is stronger than that in Caucasian subjects ($\varepsilon3/\varepsilon4$: OR (Odds Ratio) = 5.6, 95% CI (Confidence Interval) = 3.9–8.0; $\varepsilon4/\varepsilon4$: OR = 33.1, 95% CI = 13.6–80.5). However, the frequency (0.32) of APOE $\varepsilon4$ allele in AD Japanese subjects, and the frequency (0.24 to 0.35) in LOAD Japanese subjects, is slightly lower than that in other ethnic groups (0.36 to 0.50) in Western studies (Ueki et al., 1993; Saunders et al., 1993), but rather higher than that in other Asian studies (Ganguli et al., 2000; Katzman et al., 1997; K. W. Kim et al., 1999): 0.22 to 0.30 in China, and 0.22 to 0.23 in Korean patients, as well as 0.073 to 0.11 in Indian patients. Apparently, the association between the APOE $\varepsilon4$ allele and AD is strongest in Japanese subjects, followed by Chinese, and Korean, and is seemingly weaker among Indian subjects (Table 3); Farrer et al., 1997. The influence of APOE $\varepsilon4$ allele on age-at-onset of AD is evident in Japanese, while it has no effect in Chinese (Tsuda et al., 1994).

The findings of early Western studies on the association between early-onset Alzheimer's disease (EOAD) and allele ε4 were controversial, but later studies have shown that allele ε4 is a risk for EOAD. The frequency of EOAD subjects with at least one ε4 allele is 44.0 to 58.3% in China (Katzman *et al.*, 1997). However, the distribution of APOE genotypes and the frequency of the ε4 allele are not significantly different between LOAD and EOAD (0.28 to 0.44) subjects in Japan (Dai *et al.*, 1994). Several factors may explain this strong APOE ε4–AD association in Japanese. First, differences in the distribution of ages of subjects within ethnic groups may affect the risk for AD associated with the APOE ε4 allele, since the patterns of risk are different among East Asians. In Japanese, for example, ORs for AD associated with the APOE ε4 allele increase steadily between ages 40 and 60 years and then decline with age thereafter. However, in Chinese, ORs increase between ages 60 and 84 years but then decline with age thereafter. In Korea, ORs increase between ages 50 and 69 years, then decline with age. Thus the odds of AD would be higher if more subjects at high-risk age are included in the population studied. Second, gender differences between the AD patients and controls might also contribute to the high ORs in Japanese. Japanese AD patients and the Japanese controls pooled by Farrer *et al.* (1997) significantly differed by gender; the proportion of women was 70.5% in the AD group and 27.6% in the control group (p < 0.01 by χ^2 test). Considering that the OR for AD associated with the APOE ε4 allele is higher in women than in men in Korea and in a meta-analysis by Farrer *et al.* (1997), this gender difference might also have contributed to the high ORs in Japanese, at least in part. Finally, some as yet unknown ethnic differences present in Japanese might have contributed to the strong APOE ε4–AD association. The report of APOE ε4 allele and AD from the Indian subcontinent shows, although the prevalence of AD in Ballagarh, India is very low, the association of APOE ε4 with AD in Indians is similar to that in US populations (Ganguli *et al.*, 2000).

The association between APOE ε4 allele and VaD is also still controversial in Asian studies. Apo E4 may increase plasma cholesterol and accelerate the development of atherosclerosis. However, there are no definitive studies on whether APOE ε4 allele has any effect on the pathogenesis of VaD (Higuchi *et al.*, 1996). The association between APOE ε4 allele and VaD is weak, being 0.12 in Japanese patients,

and 0.11 to 0.22 in Chinese. Hence, any association between APOE ε4 allele and VaD is still uncertain partly because of the scant international literature on the frequency of APOE ε4 allele associated with VaD, and the heterogeneous nature of vascular lesions which may have influenced the frequency of ε4 allele in the Asian studies.

In summary, therefore, the APOE ε4 allele is more prevalent in Japanese AD subjects than in other Asian AD populations. However, the APOE ε2 allele is less prevalent in Japanese than in Chinese and Korean populations. In Caucasian populations, a protective effect of the APOE ε2 allele for AD has been reported. Although a number of Asian studies have confirmed the lowered APOE ε2 allele frequency in AD patients versus controls, others have not found such an association. H. C. Kim *et al.* (2001) showed an increase in the frequency of the APOE ε2 allele in Korean AD patients ($\chi^2 = 1.30$, d.f. = 2, p = 0.523), suggesting the APOE ε4 allele plays a role as a risk factor for AD in Koreans though the APOE ε2 allele may not play a protective role. However, the frequency of the APOE ε2 allele in controls, in another Korean study, was significantly higher than reported by H. C. Kim *et al.* ($\chi^2 = 25.79$, d.f. = 2, p = 0.000). This may be due to differences in population characteristics. APOE ε2 allele may not have a protective role against AD in Japanese and Chinese people.

Other molecular causes

Recently, several other candidate genes, such as alpha-1 antichymotrypsin (ACT) and alpha-2 macroglobulin (A2M), have been reported to be associated with LOAD in Caucasians. Such findings were not confirmed in a Korean population. However, the A2M I/V genotype might be a risk factor for both AD and Parkinson's disease in a Chinese Han population (Tang *et al.*, 2002), even though its contribution is relatively moderate (in AD: AF = 13.65%; in PD: AF = 16.51%). In a Japanese study (Sodeyama *et al.*, 2000), there was no association of the A2M polymorphism with AD, age at onset, or duration of illness in AD. The A2M polymorphism was not associated with the extent of senile plaques (SPs), SPs with dystrophic neurites (NPs), or neurofibrillary tangles (NFTs) in AD or non-demented patients. An Hpal restriction polymorphism in the apolipoprotein C-I gene (APOC 1), which forms part of a cluster with APOE and APOC2 genes on the long arm of chromosome 19, has been associated with LOAD. In Korea (Ki *et al.*, 2002), the frequency of APOC1 insertion allele (H2) was significantly increased in LOAD compared to age-matched controls (healthy volunteers), giving an odds ratio of 3.3 (95% Cl 2.0–5.5, $p < 0.0001$). Logistic regression analysis revealed that the interaction model between APOE ε4 and APOC1 H2 yielded a larger odds ratio than other models including either APOE ε4 or APOC1 H2 alone. In addition, the association between APOC1 H2 and LOAD remained significant after adjustment of the effect of APOE ε4 ($p = 0.036$). The result suggests that the APOC1 polymorphism may be an additional susceptibility gene for LOAD in Korean populations.

Tauopathy may occur as a primary event in frontotemporal dementia (FTD) and Parkinsonism linked to chromosome 17 (FTDP-17), and as a secondary event after amyloid β protein (Aβ) amyloidosis in AD. Increased levels of CSF tau have been proposed as a biomarker of AD. In a Japanese study (Shoji *et al.*, 2002) on total CSF tau, the cut-off value of tau, 375 pg/ml, showed 59.1% sensitivity and 89.5% specificity for diagnosis of AD compared with other groups. Tau levels were increased from early to late stages of AD. Thus, measurement of CSF tau is useful as a supplementary biomarker for early and differential diagnosis of AD in Japan. Although a Chinese study (Hu and Wang, 2001) also reported that the levels of total tau and pathological tau in CSF specimens of AD patients were significantly higher than those in CSF of patients with VaD and non-dementia neurological disorders, and in age-matched non-neurological normal controls, unfortunately these latter cerebrospinal fluid specimens came from different ethnic groups in China and the Netherlands, making interpretation difficult. Some epidemiological studies have shown that anti-inflammatory drugs delay the onset or progression of AD. The genotype and allelic variations in the IL4+33C/T gene may influence the degree of inflammation in the brain. Association between the IL4+33C/T polymorphism and AD in Japanese was declared but another Japanese study obtained an adverse conclusion with no association between the IL4+33C/T polymorphism and AD, nor was any association demonstrated between the IL4+33C/T polymorphism and the plasma IL4 concentration. Another inflammatory cytokine,

IL-6, might be involved in the pathophysiology of AD. The G/C allele of IL-6 gene promoter region (IL-6prom) G allele, which may affect plasma IL-6 concentration, may be a risk factor for sporadic AD in Japanese (Shibata *et al.*, 2002).

THE BURDEN OF CARING FOR DEMENTIA

The burden of caring for elderly people with dementia is an increasing problem in Asian countries. The patients' functional impairment and the behavioural and psychological symptoms of dementia (BPSD) are the main factors increasing the caregiver's burden. Patients with AD progressively lose cognition and ability to carry out activities of daily living, simultaneously developing BPSD such as delusions, hallucinations, agitation, anxiety, euphoria, disinhibition, aberrant motor behaviours, sleep disturbance and poor appetite. BPSD are a source of distress to both family caregivers and the elderly persons, and have an economic impact on societies and on the quality of life of individuals and families with dementia.

Caregiver distress accumulates and can result in physical illness, psychological illness, substance abuse, and other maladaptive behaviours during the adjustment process. Asian American caregivers have shown distress levels mostly similar to Caucasian Americans though differences between ethnic groups were noted in relationship to depression and apathy towards AD patients. Chinese caregivers were less likely to have depression-related caregiver distress than US caregivers, and were less sensitive to apathy symptoms in AD patients than US caregivers (Pang *et al.*, 2002). These differences in the level of burden of depression between Asian caregivers and US caregivers might suggest cultural influences towards caregiving. Chinese or Korean people traditionally emphasize peace and moderation, so apathy may not be viewed as problematic by caregivers, although some studies have denied such cultural differences at the level of the feelings of caregivers (Arai and Washio, 1999).

ECONOMIC COST OF DEMENTIA PATIENTS

The economic cost of dementia to society is already massive in Western developed countries and will continue to increase. In Taiwan, it is estimated that cost of home care per patient per month is

TABLE 4. Monthly private direct cost; Mean (SD)

	Total	BPSD
Paid help	$281.00(361.00)	$78.70[1]
Payment for physicians' visits	$2.20(12.00)	$0.15(0.30)
Payment for cholinesterase inhibitors	$30.20(61.20)	$30.20(61.20)[2]
Payment for other psychotropics	$11.60(48.70)	$11.60(15.60)
Total	$325.00(460.00)	$120.70

[1] Assuming that the needs of the patient are the same regardless of who provides the care (paid help or indirect caregivers), it can be hypothesized that the same 28% of the caregiving effect is devoted to BPSD.
[2] Assuming that BPSD benefit from cholinesterase inhibitors.
Reproduced from Beeri et al. (2002).

NT$85,256 for patients with AD and NT$74,152 for patients with VaD. For patients receiving nursing-home care, costs per month per patient were estimated to be NT$28,972 for patients with AD and NT$31,576 for those with VaD. Nursing-home fees were the major component of costs incurred by families (at least 78% of total family costs). For both AD and VaD, payment for nursing-home services amounted to approximately one-third of the labour costs of home care. Nursing-home care is also a better choice when patients have great need for multiple health services. Moreover, higher costs are encountered for caregiving at home when patients have severe dependence. This tendency is more evident for patients with AD than for patients with VaD (Chiu et al., 1999).

In Israel, the total annual cost of AD per patient is US$14,420. The indirect cost for management of BPSD in an AD patient was approximately US$2,665 – over 25% of the total annual indirect cost of care (US$10,520). The annual direct cost of BPSD of an AD patient is approximately $1,450 – over 35% of the total annual direct cost of care (US$3,900). Approximately 30% (US$4,115) of the total annual cost of AD is invested in the direct management of BPSD. Of this, 65% is indi-

rect cost (see Table 4). Moreover, the mean monthly hours of indirect care provided by primary caregivers and by secondary caregivers are 210 hours and 55 hours, respectively. Income is found to be negatively related to indirect cost of BPSD and positively related to the direct cost (Beeri et al., 2002). Not surprisingly, this indicates that patients and caregivers with higher income choose to use paid help to manage this demanding problem while caregivers with low income most probably do not have this alternative, thus treating the patients themselves. This tendency has been confirmed by data from Taiwan showing that the amount of monthly family income was strongly associated with the willingness to pay (WTP) for nursing-home care in dollars. The WTP for nursing-home care ranged from US$185 to US$2,407 per month, and 37.5% of the family caregivers interviewed indicated a WTP at least 50% of the monthly family income for nursing-home placement (Chiu et al., 1998).

REDUCING THE BURDEN OF CARING FOR DEMENTIA

Drug therapy has been suggested to be an effective way of reducing the burden of caring for dementia. The administration of cholinesterase inhibitors such as donepezil may significantly improve cognitive function in patients with dementia. Meanwhile, neuroleptics such as risperidone and haloperidol may reduce the burden of care on caregivers through eliminating BPSD including 'delusions of theft' in Japanese patients (Shigenobu et al., 2002). Low-dose haloperidol and risperidone are well tolerated and reduce significantly the severity and frequency of behavioural symptoms in Chinese patients with dementia (Chan et al., 2001). However, polypharmacy may lead to the high incidence of adverse drug reactions (ADRs) in older people with dementia in Japan. Therefore, it has been recommended in that country that the number of drugs be limited to three in patients with severe cognitive dysfunction. The use of complementary medicines, such as plant extracts, in dementia therapy varies according to the different regional cultural traditions in Asian countries. In orthodox Western medicine, contrasting with that in China and the Far East, for example, pharmacological properties of traditional cognitive- or memory-enhancing plants have not been widely investigated in the context of current models of AD. An exception is Huperzine A, an alkaloid from the Chinese herbal medicine Qian Ceng Ta, prepared from the moss Huperzia serrata, which has been used in China for centuries to treat fever and inflammation. Huperzine A is a strong inhibitor of cholinesterases with high selectivity to acetylcholinesterase and in China has been developed as therapeutic against AD (Z. Zhang *et al.*, 2002). Huperzine A may be better than other centrally active anticholinesterases in treating AD. It appears to have pharmacological properties that make it an attractive candidate therapy for clinical trials. Another exception is Ginkgo biloba (Figure 3) in which the gingkolides have antioxidant, neuroprotective and cholinergic activities relevant to AD mechanisms. The therapeutic efficacy of Ginkgo extracts for treating AD or VaD in placebo-controlled clinical trials has been reportedly similar to currently prescribed drugs such as tacrine or donepezil and, importantly, undesirable side effects of Ginkgo are minimal (LeBars *et al.*, 1997). In Germany, and now in the USA and China, it has been developed as a therapeutic agent against dementia. In addition, Ginseng has also been used in China for centuries to treat 'insufficient syndrome' (as defined by Chinese medicine) and to postpone ageing. Ginseng saponins are extracted from Chinese ginseng roots (Figure 4). Ginsenosides Rb1 and Rg3 exert significant neuroprotective effects on cultured cortical cells against glutamate-induced neurodegeneration, and are efficacious in protecting neurons from oxidative damage related to VaD or AD mechanisms. The therapeutic effects of Chinese ginseng compound in mild to moderate cognitive impairment of VaD are reportedly similar to the prescribed drug, Duxil, and, importantly, undesirable side effects of Chinese ginseng compound are few (Tian *et al.*, 2003).

A new public long term care insurance system was launched in Japan in April 2000. The first national survey on special units of psychiatric hospitals for dementia patients showed that care level and cog-

Figure 3. Leaves of ginkgo tree, from Western mountains in Beijing, China.

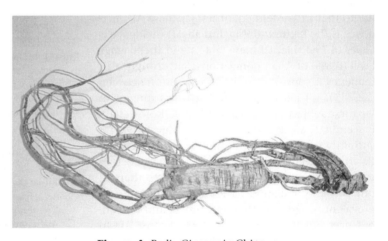

Figure 4. Radix Ginseng in China.

nitive impairment are generally correlated in the primary assessment, but some adjustment measure for cognitive impairment is needed in mildly or moderately physically disabled patients (Ito *et al.*, 2001). *The mutual support group* was found to improve distress levels and quality of life in families of dementia sufferers in Hong Kong, suggesting the importance of psychosocial support beyond the conventional services generally offered to family caregivers in dementia care (Fung and Chien, 2002).

Day-care programmes may be an effective way to maintain the stability of cognitive function in elderly Koreans with mild-to-moderate-stage dementia (Chou *et al.*, 1999). However, reducing the burden on carers, whilst maintaining the requirement of filial obligation, had positive effects on the caring relationship. Caregiving involvement and emotion-focused coping had direct positive effects on the caregiving burden. Filial obligation, caregiving self-efficacy, and problem-focused coping had no direct positive effects on the caregiving burden (N. C. Kim *et al.*, 2002).

SUMMARY

The average prevalence of dementia in Asian countries is 5.4%, ranging from 1.4–10.8%. Among Asian populations, the average prevalence of dementia in Koreans is the highest (9.5%), followed by Japanese (6.1%) and Chinese (4.7%), and is lowest in Indians (2.4%). However, the prevalence of dementia in Asian countries increases with age, somewhat similar to that in Western countries. Japanese AD incidence is the highest (8.9%); Indian AD incidence is lower (4.7%) than Chinese (5.4%) and the average level (6.6%) of Asian populations. Surprisingly, this tendency is consistent with the association between the APOE ε4 allele and AD, that it is strongest in Japanese subjects, followed by Chinese/Korean, and is seemingly weaker among Indian subjects. VaD is currently the second most common type of dementia in most Asian countries. The APOE ε4 allele is more prevalent in Japanese AD subjects than in other Asian populations. The APOE ε2 allele is less prevalent in Japanese than in Chinese and Korean, but may not have a protective role against AD in Japanese and Chinese people. The patients' function impairment and BPSD are the main factors increasing the caregiver's burden in Asian countries. Nursing home fees are the major component of costs incurred by families, and more evident for patients with AD than for patients with VaD. Drug therapeutics is to be an effective way of reducing the burden of caring for dementia. The use of complementary medicine such as Chinese herbal medicine in dementia therapy has potential prospects. However, care for dementia patients in Asian countries, including community care, long term care policies, and provision of information on dementia care, is rather weak compared to that in Western developed countries.

FURTHER READING

Chiu, L., and W. C. Shyu (2001). 'Estimation of the family cost of private nursing home care versus home care for patients with dementia in Taiwan', *Chang Guang Medical Journal*, 24: 608–14.

Tian, J. Z., Zhu, A. H., Gu, X. H., Shi, J., Zhong, J., Peng, S. L., Liu, X. F., and Y. Y. Wang (2003). 'A double-blind, randomized controlled clinical trial of compound of Gastrodine in treatment of mild and moderate vascular dementia in Beijing, China', *Circulation*, 107: 177–8.

Suh, G. H., and A. Shah (2001). 'A review of epidemiological transition in dementia – cross-national comparisons of the indices related to Alzheimer's disease and vascular dementia', *Acta Psychiatrica Scandinavica*, 104: 4–11.

REFERENCES

Arai, Y., and M. Washio (1999). 'Feelings of burden of family members caring for the disabled elderly in southern Japan', *Ageing and Mental Health*, 3: 158–64.

Beeri, M. S., Werner, P., Davidson, M., *et al.* (2002). 'The cost of behavioural and psychological symptoms of dementia (BPSD) in community dwelling Alzheimer's disease patients', *Int J Geriatr Psychiatry*, 17: 403–8.

Brust, J. M. M. (1983). 'Vascular dementia – still overdiagnosed', *Stroke*, 14: 298–300.

Chan, W. C., Lam, L. C., Choy, C. N., *et al.* (2001). 'A double-blind randomized comparison of Risperidone and Haloperidol in the treatment of behavioural and psychological symptoms in Chinese dementia patients', *Int J Geriatr Psychiatry*, 16: 1156–62.

Chandra, V., Pandav, R., Dodge, H. H., *et al.* (2001). 'Incidence of Alzheimer's disease in a rural community in India: the Indo-US Study', *Neurology*, 57: 985–9.

Chen, L., Baum, L., Ng, H. K., *et al.* (1999). 'Apolipoprotein E genotype and its pathological correlation in Chinese Alzheimer's disease with late onset', *Hum Pathol* 30: 1125–7.

Chiu, L., Tang, K. Y., Liu, Y. H., *et al.* (1998). 'Willingness of families caring for victims of dementia to pay for nursing home care: results of a pilot study in Taiwan', *J Manag Med*, 17: 349–60.

(1999). 'Cost comparisons between family-based care and nursing home care for dementia', *J Adv Nurs*, 29: 1005–12.

Chou, K. R., LaMontagne, L. L., and J. T. Hepworth (1999). 'Burden experienced by caregivers of relatives with dementia in Taiwan', *Nurs Res*, 48: 206–14.

Dai, X. Y., Nanko, S., Hattori, M., *et al.* (1994). 'Association of apolipoprotein E4 with sporadic Alzheimer's disease is more pronounced in early onset type', *Neurosci Lett*, 175: 74–6.

Farrer, L. A., Cupples, L. A., Haines, J. L., *et al.* (1997). 'Effects of age, sex, and ethnicity on the association between apolipoprotein E genotype and Alzheimer's disease: a meta analysis', *JAMA*, 278: 1349–56.

Fratigilioni, L., Grut, M., Forsell, Y., *et al.* (1991). 'Prevalence of Alzheimer's disease and other dementias in an elderly urban population: relationship with age, sex, and education', *Neurology*, 41: 1886–92.

Fung, W. Y., and W. T. Chien (2002). 'The effectiveness of a mutual support group for family caregivers of a relative with dementia', *Arch Psychiatr Nurs*, 16: 134–44.

Ganguli, M., Dodge, H. H., Chen, P., *et al.* (2000). 'Ten year incidence of dementia in a rural elderly US community population: the MoVIES Project', *Neurology*, 54: 1109–16.

Guh, H. S., and A. Shah (2001). 'A review of the epidemiological transition in dementia – cross-national comparisons of the indices related to Alzheimer's disease and vascular dementia', *Acta Psychiatrica Scandinavica*, 104: 4–11.

Hendrie, H. C., Hall, K. S., Hui, S., *et al.* (1995). 'Apolipoprotein genotypes and Alzheimer's disease in a community study of elderly African Americans', *Ann Neurol*, 37: 118–20.

Higuchi, S., Arai, H., Nakagawa, T., *et al.* (1996). 'The apolipoprotein E gene in Binswangger's disease and vascular dementia', *Clin Genet*, 50: 459–61.

Hong, C. J., Liu, T. Y., Liu, H. C., *et al.* (1996). 'Epsilon 4 allele of apolipoprotein E increases risk of Alzheimer's disease in a Chinese population', *Neurology*, 46: 1749–51.

Hu, Y., and J. Wang (2001). 'Diagnostic value of tau in cerebrospinal fluid in Alzheimer disease', *Zhonghua Yi Xue Za Zhi*, 81 (22): 1377–9.

Ito, H., Tachimori, H., Miyamoto, Y., *et al.* (2001). 'Are the care levels of people with dementia correctly assessed for eligibility of the Japanese long-term care insurance?' *Int J Geriatr Psychiatry*, 16: 1078–84.

Katzman, R., Zhang, M. Y., Chen, P. J., *et al.* (1997). 'Effects of apolipoprotein E on dementia and aging in the Shanghai Survey of dementia', *Neurology*, 49: 779–85.

Ki, C. S., Na, D. L., Kim, D. K., *et al.* (2002). 'Genetic association of an apolipoprotein C-I (APOC1) gene polymorphism with late-onset Alzheimer's disease', *Neuroscience Letters*, 319: 75–8.

Kim, H. C., Kim, D. K., Chol, I. J., *et al.* (2001). 'Relationship of apolipoprotein E polymorphism to clinically diagnosed Alzheimer's disease in the Korean population', *Psychiatr Clin Neurosci*, 55: 115–20.

Kim, K. W., Jhoo, J. H., Lee, K. U., *et al.* (1999). 'Association between apolipoprotein E polymorphism and Alzheimer's disease in Koreans', *Neurosci Lett*, 277: 145–8.

Kim, N. C., Kim, H. S., Yoo, Y. S., *et al.* (2002). 'Outcomes of day-care: a pilot study on changes in cognitive function and agitated behaviours of demented elderly in Korea', *Nurs Health Sci*, 4: 3–7.

Kua, E. H., and S. M. Ko (1995). 'Prevalence of dementia among elderly Chinese and Malay residents of Singapore', *Int Psychogeriatr*, 7: 439–46.

Kuusisto, J., Koivisto, K., Kervinen, K., *et al.* (1994). 'Association of apolipoprotein phenotypes with late onset Alzheimer's disease: population based study', *BMJ*, 309: 636–8.

LeBars, P. L., Katz, M. M., Berman, N., *et al.* (1997). 'A placebo-controlled, double-blind, randomised trial of an extract of ginkgo biloba for dementia', *JAMA*, 278: 1327–32.

Lee, D. Y., Lee, J. H., Ju, Y. S., *et al.* (2002). 'The prevalence of dementia in older people in an urban population of Korea: the Seoul Study', *JAGS*, 50: 1233–9.

Lin, R. T., Lai, C. L., Tai, C. T., *et al.* (1998). 'Prevalence and subtypes of dementia in southern Taiwan: impact of age, sex, education, and urbanization', *J Neurol Sci*, 160: 67–75.

Liu, C. K., Lai, C. L., Tai, C. T., *et al.* (1998). 'Incidence and subtypes of dementia in southern Taiwan: impact of socio-demographic factors', *Neurology*, 50: 1572–9.

Nakayama, S., and S. Kuzuhara (1999). 'Apolipoprotein E phenotypes in healthy normal controls and demented subjects with Alzheimer's disease and vascular dementia in Mie Prefecture of Japan', *Psychiatr Clin Neurosci*, 53: 643–8.

Noguchi, S., Murakami, K., Yamada, N., *et al.* (1993). 'Apolipoprotein E genotype and Alzheimer's disease', *Lancet*, 342: 737.

Pang, F. C., Chow, T. W., Cummings, J. L., *et al.* (2002). 'Effect of neuropsychiatric symptoms of Alzheimer's disease on Chinese and American caregivers', *Int J Geriatr Psychiatry*, 17: 29–34.

Saunders, A. M., Strittmatter, W. J., Schmechel, D., *et al.* (1993). 'Association of apolipoprotein E allele e4 with late-onset familial and sporadic Alzheimer's disease', *Neurology*, 43: 1467–72.

Shibata, N., Ohnuma, T., Takahashi, T. H., *et al.* (2002). 'Effect of IL-6 polymorphism on risk of Alzheimer disease: genotype–phenotype association study in Japanese cases', *Am J Med Genet*, 114: 436–9.

Shigenobu, K., Ikeda, M., Fukuhara, R., *et al.* (2002). 'Reducing the burden of caring for Alzheimer's disease through the amelioration of delusions of theft by drug therapy', *Int J Geriatr Psychiatry*, 17: 211–17.

Shoji, M., Matsubara, E., Murakami, T., *et al.* (2002). 'Cerebrospinal fluid tau in dementia disorders: a large scale multicenter study by a Japanese study group', *Neurobiology of Aging*, 23: 363–70.

Sodeyama, N., Yamada, M., Itoh, Y., *et al.* (2000). 'Alpha 2-macroglobulin polymorphism is not associated with AD or AD-type neuropathology in the Japanese', *Neurology*, 54 (2): 443–6.

Suh, Guk-Hee, and Ajit Shah (2001). 'A review of the epidemiological transition in dementia', *Act Psychiatrica Scandinavica*, 104: 4–11.

Tang, G. T., Zhang, M. Z., Xie, H. J., *et al.* (2002). 'Alpha-2 macroglobulin I1000V polymorphism in Chinese sporadic Alzheimer's disease and Parkinson's disease', *Neurosci Lett*, 328: 195–7.

Tian, J., Yin, J. X., Yang, C. Z., *et al.* (2003). 'A randomized pilot study of compound of Chinese ginseng treatment of memory impairment in patients with mild and moderate dementia after ischemic stroke', *Stroke* (suppl.): 327.

Tsuda, T., Lippez, R., Rogaeva, E. A., *et al.* (1994). 'Are the associations between Alzheimer's disease and polymorphisms in the apolipoprotein E and the apolipoprotein CII genes due to linkage disequilibrium?' *Ann Neurol*, 36: 97–100.

Ueki, A., Kawano, M., Namba, Y., *et al.* (1993). 'A high frequency of apolipoprotein E4 isoprotein in Japanese patients with late-onset nonfamilial Alzheimer's disease', *Neurosci Lett*, 163: 166–8.

United Nations (1999). *Demographic Yearbook*. New York: United Nations Publications Board.

Woo, J. I., Lee, J. H., Yoo, K. Y., *et al.* (1998). 'Prevalence estimation of dementia in a rural area of Korea', *J Am Geriatr Soc*, 46: 983–7.

Yamada, M., Sasaki, H., Mimori, Y., *et al.* (1999). 'Prevalence of and risk of dementia in the Japanese population: RERF's adult health study Hiroshima subjects. Radiation Effects Research Foundation', *J Am Geriatr Soc*, 47: 189–95.x

Yang, J., Feng, G., Zhang, J., *et al.* (2001). 'Is ApoE gene a risk factor for vascular dementia in Han Chinese?' *Int J Med*, 7 (2): 217–19.

Yoshitake, T., Kiyohara, Y., Kato, I., *et al.* (1995). 'Incidence and risk factors of vascular dementia and Alzheimer's disease in a defined elderly Japanese population: the Hisayama Study', *Neurol*, 45: 1161–8.

Yoshizawa, T., Yamakawa-Kobayashi, K., Komatsuzaki, Y., *et al.* (1994). 'Dose-dependent association of apolipoprotein E allele e4 with late-onset, sporadic Alzheimer's disease', *Ann Neurol*, 36: 656–9.

Zhang, M. R., Katzman, D., Salmon, D., *et al.* (1990). 'The prevalence of dementia and Alzheimer's disease in Shanghai, China: impact of age, gender, and education', *Ann Neurol*, 27: 428–37.

Zhang, M., Katzman, R., Yu, E., *et al.* (1998). 'A preliminary analysis of incidence of dementia in Shanghai, China', *Psychiatry Clin Neurosci* 52 (Suppl.): S291–4.

Zhang, Z., Wang, X., Chen, Q., *et al.* (2002). 'Clinical efficacy and safety of huperzine-A in treatment of mild to moderate Alzheimer disease, a placebo-controlled, double-blind, randomised trial', *Zhonghua Yi Xue Za Zhi*, 82: 941–4. (Chinese.)

Zhang, Z. X., Wei, J., Hong, X., *et al.* (1999). 'Is China a low risk area for dementia?' Presented at the Symposium of IPA Beijing Joint Meeting, Beijing, 12 April.

PART FOUR

THE AGEING SELF

CHAPTER 4.1

Self and Identity

FREYA DITTMANN-KOHLI

PART ONE

INTRODUCTION

The self is perhaps the most exciting knowledge structure and processing system of the human species, and is at least as amazing as human intelligence directed to understanding and control of the world. Self-awareness and self-construction have caught the attention of philosophers and writers over centuries, even two millennia. Nevertheless, and unfortunately, and in spite of more than a hundred years of reflection and writing, the field of psychological research on self and identity is still marked by fuzzy terms and concepts among different researchers, authors and research traditions. Within articles, chapters or books, however, the terms and concepts are usually used in a consistent way. During the last hundred years since James' publication (1890), psychologists and lifespan researchers have most often used the terms "self" and "self-concept," but the term "identity" is gaining popularity and has always been the favourite in sociology. Studies on self and identity are carried out in developmental, personality and social psychology, but also in educational and occupational psychology. There has been a vast number of studies on the self (-concept and identity), but their sheer number has not by itself contributed to integration of empirical results from different approaches and (sub)disciplines. In spite of some integrative work (see below), an increasing number of terms and overlapping, ill-defined concepts continue to haunt the field (see Joplin, 1997); separate research on childhood and late life have increased theoretical ambiguity. The fuzziness of the field also hampers a lucid overview; the following can only be a sketchy report. Questions of definition and overlap between identity and self will be treated first because these terms are sometimes used interchangeably for the same referent, sometimes they seem to be overlapping concepts, and sometimes they seem to have different meanings. Different psychological approaches will be mentioned to clarify the point. My own preferred approach is a contextual model of the individual as an organism that forms contextual, culturally dependent concepts and identity constructions of the self and its personal life.

Regarding this model, the question of the relation between self and personality is important to consider. Also, the issue of universal versus specific structures (and content) of self and identity is discussed, looking at biology, evolution and history, at cultural regions as well as at ontological development, life stages and intra-cultural differences. Another critical issue will be measurement problems of traditional instruments and the role of language in self-concept construction and measurement, which is related to narrative self-report (self- and life writing).

The framework of the contextual self and narrative self-report has been used for (and was corroborated by) most of the empirical studies presented in the second part of this text. In agreement with the concepts on narrative identity, I selected studies using open methods that together point to systematic differences between age groups. These are apparently in line with our scientific and everyday knowledge about the changing ecology and organism over the lifespan. Open-ended, narrative data with a broad range of self-knowledge, in contrast to single variables, have been selected to demonstrate that fargoing age-related differences in self (-concept) and identity are the rule.

A contextual model of the self also implies that sociocultural context is reflected in self and identity. In order to balance the dominance of North American data used in most publications, the focus will here be on material gathered in Germany, with some references to other European and American studies. The scientific accretion of presenting data from two German studies derives from their being representative for the second half of life and from their differentiation on the very old age group, which renders them ecologically valid.

The conclusions will take up (shortly, because of space) the question of whether self and identity can and must change over the lifespan, according to available scientific concepts. Such concepts help to explain the observed age-related differences in terms of developmental changes in self-conceptualizations, and not only as cohort differences. My conclusion will be that there are several suitable psychological concepts of change in cognitive–affective organization to suggest genuine individual development. The final point of the chapter will be an outlook to the future (of self and society) and remarks about making use of research on self–concept and identity to benefit older individuals.

Scientific approaches to self and identity

Identity in the sense of personal identity is a concept often used in psychology and sociology in the study of motivational–cognitive problems with and commitments of the self. Originally, Erikson (1968) saw adolescence as the time to solve the psychosocial task of identity construction. Because of multiple changes in society and in the organism in middle adulthood and old age, identity (re-)construction has now emerged as a major task for the second half of life (Biggs, 1999; van Halen, 2002). Identity construction is a life-long developmental task comparable to the (sociological) constructivist task of adapting one's concept of the life-course to the changing social environment, and of continuing to adapt one's life story to the growing

number of events and experiences in the course of life (Holstein and Gubrium, 2000). Adult identity development and the individual lifespan construct have been proposed by Whitbourne as important scientific constructs for long-term changes in personality and self. Extreme adaptation to external changes, and exaggerated rigidity or avoidance of ageing-related changes in self-concept have been proposed, respectively, as accommodative and assimilative styles of identity change (Whitbourne and Conolly, 1999).

Identity is also studied in the sense of the collective self, i.e. identification with small (face to face) and large (demographic) groups (e.g. nationality, ethnicity, gender, age group; see Kohli, 2000). In social psychology within psychology, identity is often used for identification with (and competition between) local (face to face) groups, as well as with demographic ethnic groups, and around other types of the collective self, such as gender, age, nationality.

In gerontological and lifespan psychological research, age identity has been a frequent topic. The point about age identity is whether one feels younger, older or the same as one's true age. A gap is related to wellbeing, health and other psychological and demographic variables (Steverink *et al.*, 2001; Teuscher, 2003). Feeling younger than one's true age is connected to characteristics of younger persons, such as being healthy, entrepreneurial and energetic.

Role identity is a topic that stresses the sharing of and identification with certain characteristics of activities and obligations within social structures, known as roles (Breytspraak, 1984). Role identity in later life has been studied in relation to occupation and retirement (Teuscher, 2003). During the last occupational years and in retirement, role change and the transition to another lifestyle and social environment are reflected in identity change, i.e. a different self-concept. The old occupational identity cannot be retained without a serious rupture in mental health. Westerhof (2001a) and Westerhof and Dittmann-Kohli (2000) found in a nationwide representative study on the second half of life that the change from work to the retirement role is seen as an acceptable change in identity status; it is not generally accompanied by feelings of rejection and low self-esteem as in the state of unemployment.

In contrast to social or collective identity, "personal identity" is a term that overlaps and is often interchangeable with "self" or "self-concept." Personal identity is then understood as "who I am," in the sense of what kind of person I am, and this may include psychological characteristics and psychological traits, perceived interpersonal relations and motives, and group identities. Becoming the person "who one really is" or might be has been seen as a virtue within (humanistic) psychology, when individualization and self-reflection became a positive goal for personal growth. With the advent of the consumer and knowledge society, the emergence of the real self became less a consequence of working through limiting social norms and social controls than was the case in earlier centuries and generations. At present, the real self tends to be lost in the multitude of possibilities and the lack of clear guidelines, with the danger of endless flexibility and a loss of meaningfulness (Biggs, 1999; Taylor, 1989; van Selm and Dittmann-Kohli, 1998).

Narrative identity and life writing (Brockmeier, 2001; Freeman, 2001) are constructs in a new psychological approach to the self. Here, linguistic aspects, process character, active construction, situational dependence and temporality are stressed as important aspects of identity (see below).

SELF, SELF-CONCEPT AND IDENTITY. These three terms are often overlapping. In many cases, the terms "identity," "self" and "self-concept" are used interchangeably, in other cases not. For instance, the social psychologists Sedikides and Brewer (2001) refer to individual self, interpersonal self and collective self, where the latter covers group identity. "Identity as story" (McAdams, 1996) as a theoretical framework was tested by Coleman et al. (1998), in an investigation of the overall unity and purpose of elderly person's lives, by means of interviews and narratives. Self-esteem served as an indicator of psychological wellbeing; late life changes in fulfillment of important motivations and values were observed to be connected to self-concept and identity.

While "self-concept" is usually understood as a cognitive, especially a dynamic cognitive–affective structure, the term "self" is being used in a multiplicity of ways. On the one hand it can mean the personality of an individual as experienced, known and regulated from the inside. This seems to meet the term "selfhood" (Joplin, 1997; M. B. Smith, 2003): individuals construct their special type of selfhood using

the cultural models of "personhood" as well as their own observations and understanding of themselves and their lives. "The self" without a further term is also used to stress that human beings are conscious subjects which experience themselves and the world from an inner, personal perspective. If "the self" is combined with other terms like "(dynamic) system," or "ways" (see Joplin, 1997), a personality-like meaning is often being designated.

The concept of "possible selves" (i.e. future feared and hoped-for selves) has been introduced by Hazel Markus and has stimulated many empirical studies using student populations, but has also inspired studies covering the lifespan and those about adulthood and ageing (Cross and Markus, 1991; Ryff, 1991). Lachman and Bertrand (2001) consider the changing personal hopes and fears that constitute the possible self as part of identity development.

In many psychological studies, particular aspects of self are investigated and connected with specific terms referring to behaviors, traits or beliefs. Here, the self is the object of the belief, trait or behavior, e.g. self-reliance. An example of a belief which is of interest in research into ageing is perceived intellectual self-efficacy as an assumption about one's cognitive competency in intelligence test tasks (Dittmann-Kohli et al., 1991). Very frequently investigated variables are self-esteem, self-evaluation, self-assessment, self-regard which refer to processes and products with a focus on (e)valuation of the self. Self-regulation refers to agency but seems to include both intentional and unintentional behaviors with an ordering purpose or function. Some combinations of terms stress consciousness and reflexivity as a marker, like self-awareness, self-consciousness, self-reflection, self-understanding, self-definition, self-construction. There are also terms around stability and change, like self-development, personal growth, self-maintenance, continuity of the self, reorganization of the life story or the self-concept. The concepts designated by those terms are alternatively seen as belonging to the self (e.g. Brown, 1998) or to personality, in the sense of personality traits (with interindividual differences) or as (strategic) behavioral processes.

THE SELF AS MIDDLE LEVEL OF PERSONALITY. In some personality research traditions like that on the BIG FIVE, personality research is defined exclusively as research on interindividual differences in (universal, decontextualized) personality traits (Costa and McCrae, 1998). Self-schemata or self-beliefs are thus seen as personality traits, not as meaning variables. Many researchers simply disregard the problem, others have made suggestions to integrate theoretical approaches (Hooker, 2002; McAdams, 1996; Staudinger & Pasupathi, 2000). For instance, traits and life stories are considered as being located at the highest (or first) and lowest (third) out of three layers of the personality system. The self is placed at the middle level, comprising cognitive–affective representations ("I am healthy and advantaged") and motivational cognitions (goals, desires, plans).

The life story, residing at the third level of Hooker and McAdams' (2003) classification, is determined by person and environment. The tripartite and the structure–process classification of these authors is not so convincing as a theoretical model, but it is a heuristically useful and necessary scheme for structuring and grouping different research traditions and analytical approaches. Different scientific constructs and forms of verbal data are used to study the self (i.e. closed, open and storied self-accounts). These provide different findings and need to be ordered according to the authors' tripartite model to be seen in combination.

One problem with the theoretical definition of the authors is that the self and identity are seen not just as belief–motivation–action constructions but as a broad knowledge system, the "Me" (James, 1890), created by the "I" as agent and knower. The self as "I" is then an observing, interpreting process doing the "selfing" and producing the "Me." The latter is composed of beliefs and other mental representations of the person interacting with its body and its spatial, social and temporal context. These mental representations can in their turn be used in decision-making and self-regulation (agency). Narrative psychologists and other psychological researchers treat autobiography and life stories as a product of the process of self-construction and part of (narrative) identity. The self-concept as assessed at one point of time can be seen as a cross-sectional account of the present self, casting some glimpses into the past and future, while the narrative is the construction of the temporally sequenced chain of life events around the self as an "I" defined as author. The biographical view of the self in a temporal dimension is the narrative identity (Brockmeier, 2001; McAdams, 1996).

BOUNDARIES BETWEEN SELF AND PERSONALITY VARIABLES. The conceptual boundaries between self and personality variables are often treated inconsistently between different studies. Thus, any frequently studied aspects of self and identity are treated as behavioral and not as meaning variables, for example psychological well-being, self-efficacy beliefs, control beliefs, future expectations, goals, plans, self-management strategies, subjective health, subjective age, etc. Measures of life satisfaction, psychological and physical wellbeing, are among the most frequently studied variables in research into ageing. Psychological well-being (as a summary term) is usually used as an output variable and marker of successful ageing in the sense of mental health (analogous to school grades for student achievement), instead of as self-knowledge or an aspect of personal identity. When treated as meaning structure, psychological wellbeing or life satisfaction (Westerhof, 2001b; Westerhof *et al.*, 2001a, 2003) and self-esteem (Coleman *et al.*, 1998) appear to be based on judgements of age-related changes in sources of wellbeing. The ageing paradox lies in the observation that wellbeing is stable while resources supposedly diminish. The ageing paradox is explained through processes of adaptation, such as selection and compensation, lowering of aspirations and redefinition of values and goals, shifting areas of activity and finding new means and resources (see other chapters in this volume). Narrative self-accounts of reasons for and views of life satisfaction provide the perceptual and judgemental basis of these adaptations as occuring in Western cultural areas (Westerhof *et al.*, 2003).

UNIVERSAL AND SPECIFIC STRUCTURE AND CONTENT OF SELF-CONCEPTS. The issue of universal versus specific structures (and content) of self and identity is of importance in a contextual model of self and life. Biology, evolution, history, and culture are influencing factors. Ontological development and life stages are of particular interest because the contextual model will predict changes in person and ecology over the lifespan. James' concept of the self-as-object (the "Me") is a type of knowledge or conceptualization that covers important sections of perceived reality to which the self is seen and felt as being related. Such knowledge is designed to help the individual to interact meaningfully with the world, to grow into and act as a member of society, and to chart development and ageing. In so far as ecology, culture, social structure, etc., in our worlds are different and produce different personalities, self-concepts will differ, too.

Studies using spontaneous, open-ended self-reports and inductive content analyses have brought forth repeatedly certain clusters of meanings (Dittmann-Kohli, 1995; Dittmann-Kohli *et al.*, 2001; Nuttin, 1984; Nuttin and Lens, 1985) within such self-knowledge. These content-based configurations (clusters of meanings) seem to reflect universal as well as socioculturally specific aspects of existence, confirming the utility of the self as a working model or subjective self-theory (Epstein, 1973, 1980). Thus, we find certain domains of meaning such as body, appearance to others, ideas about close persons and the relations to them, work, and activities of leisure and subsistence which recur in different parts of the world in different configurations, according to individual culture and ecology. In line with social structure and ecology, we find variations in meaning domains correlating with measures of family status, work status, cultural region and gender. Cross-cultural studies have shown regular variations in line with ecological, cultural and institutional differences (Westerhof *et al.*, 2001b).

Cultural comparisons can be made between different continents (involving large cultural differences) or between countries and groups with relatively small, (sub)cultural differences, such as those between East and West Germany or those between Germany and the Netherlands. Spontaneous verbal self-reports are useful in comparative studies of self-concepts and lifespan constructs between distant cultures and close, overlapping civilizations, such as those in Europe or North America (see Bode, 2003). Only systematic comparisons can pin down the role of nature and nurture, and the corresponding convergence and divergence of self- and life concepts, and of lifespan mechanisms and strategies of adaptation to ageing.

Research from a wide range of scientific inquiry helps us to understand the factors determining the content and structure of the self-concept. There appears to exist a biological predisposition for body feedback and mental representations of social interaction and activities, the historical emergence and evolution of coherent self-understanding (Vroon, 1978) and, finally, of modern, individualized personhood (e.g. Taylor, 1989). All of these factors, in addition to individual variations of genetic and developmental determinants, contribute to human self-construction as a process of making sense of (self-)experience.

THE CONTEXTUAL MODEL OF THE SELF AND LIFESPAN CONSTRUCT. In the present context, "identity" and "self-concept" (or self- and life concept) will be used as terms for a broad view of self-understanding and self-interpretation, leading to more or less structured self-knowledge in the sense of a subjective theory that can function as a cognitive map (with goal markers) to orientate and motivate behavior (Dittmann-Kohli, 1995). As indicated, this approach represents a contextual model of the individual as a developing and ageing organism that forms contextual, culturally dependent self-concepts and identities of the self and its personal life.

Process and product of self-understanding are rooted in brain structures, resulting especially from the interaction between the frontal lobes and the limbic system (Roth, 2001). The preformed brain structures are thoroughly molded by use and input, however. Cultural and historical evolution and the sociocultural features of broad cultural areas (such as Western industrial countries, Asia, Africa; see Markus *et al.*, 1997) contribute in shaping the common structures of the self- and life concept of peoples with common contexts. Ontological development, life stages, and subcultural as well as inter-individual differences are also important aspects of the contextual model of self- and life concept.

McAdams (1996: 302–3) has given an intelligible description of how the "I" produces the "Me" through a process he calls "selfing." This mental process of selfing fits nicely with the neuro-physiological and the contextual model of the self. In later childhood, adolescence and adulthood, a temporally and spatially contextualized Me emerges out of the activities of the I as agent, as knower, and as author. In this process, salient features of the personal environment are stored in a cognitive map of activities, roles, social interactions, positively and negatively valued sensations (e.g. aesthetic pleasure, irritation, stress), etc. These will be remembered in a form of "Me" as interacting with my daily context in my world, getting on with my life. This map marks the difference between the world at a distance (represented by media, for instance) and the immediate "life space" where action occurs, for example through interacting with my computer. Experiences are being marked and linked as being "mine," my sensations and perceptions of my body are known to me as mine. My emotions, intentions, desires, habits, stable dispositions and changing moods are, if remembered, marked and stored, and become part of my identity. Research on neural plasticity shows that perceptions and experiences leave traces in the hardware of the brain and can be empirically traced after repetitions (Rösler, 2004). At another "level," meta-knowledge about self and world is "stored" and used to reflect about the self; thought processes and lifestyle can be used to develop higher states of awareness and distance from the given or "worldly" self, as practiced in Buddhism.

Events and spatial context of past and future are interconnected in perspective to construct biographical identity comprising the present, the former, and the future Me. The Me is thus a multidimensional cognitive–affective map with possible areal enlargements, as well as a multi-line story that represents what is important for producing personal memories, present self and visions of my future. Social interaction and cultural input are necessary in the process of learning and storing what is the content of the Me, while interacting with the world and myself. The narrative Me is a story of myself within the general structure of personhood typical for my cultural context. Though the particular, individual aspect of my selfhood is indispensable in our present-day Western world, this appears to be less salient and important in (more traditional) Asian and African societies. The major structure and content of self and identity differs according to ecology and culture, but common features and problems of human existence also emerge. We all share a human biology and live on the same planet; civilizations discover how to satisfy common needs and take into account changing biosociocultural dispositions over the lifecycle. In this way, we share similarities and differences in the make-up of the self-concept. The process of selfing produces a Me according to biological heritage, individual experiences, and the features of micro- and macro-contexts.

LANGUAGE AND OPEN MEASUREMENT INSTRUMENTS. The development of language and communication skills, as well as intellectual development, renders the young child capable of narrating elements of self-experience in overt or covert speech (Bruner, 2001). Much later, the older child and adolescent is able to tell others who s/he thinks s/he is as a particular individual (among others), and how to understand and tell others his/her life as a story. Proceeding through life, the story gets longer with more experiences stored in the Me. Various forms of communicating about self and identity to others, including researchers, become available: everyday interactions often contain questions and answers about how we feel, what has happened lately, or over all these years. Researchers also use life-story-telling, as well as other forms of data gathering, for their particular purposes; with instructions and questions to answer, they specify aspects of the self they want to focus on.

Measurement problems are produced by treating self-concept dimensions as behavioral traits instead of as domains of meaning or aspects of a life story, and language as a means of interpersonal and intra-personal communication is seldom included in traditional measurement concepts. Self-concept research has originated in studies on the first two decades of life, mostly using closed response format with pre-chosen items representing several dimensions of clearly structured self-knowledge familiar from the researchers' own context. In the last century, social, developmental and educational psychology accumulated many consistent findings about the features of the modern Western self, especially that of the United States and on the first third of life. However, experimental and questionnaire research on the dimensions and functions of the self were simply transferred to later life, far too often without considering ecological validity. Because the dimensions (the domains) of the self-concept are shaped by culture, history, personality and ecology, the dimensions and findings cannot be shifted to old age without consideration of ecological validity, and integration of findings from different stages of the lifecourse collected with closed instruments is dangerous. Unfortunately, studies using open instruments are still considered some-how unscientific by traditional researchers. Never-theless, narrative methods become more known and gain a little ground.

Narrative psychology has been established, among other reasons, to study identity within the medium in which it is suggested to exist. Brockmeier (1991) emphasized that development of personal time and identity cannot occur without language, since, as also in general, knowledge is based on language and communication (Brockmeier and Carbaugh, 2001). The product of discourse over the self is a self-report or life story. Social constructivist approaches to the lifecourse are also using the life narrative (see Holstein and Gubrium, 2000), while Hermans (1996), for instance, stresses the dialogue between different self positions as the major characteristic of the self. These self posi-tions are subject to change during the lifespan. Studies using open answers and natural language in research on the ageing self have provided data that are mindful of content and language while using quantification procedures when possible. Early longitudinal interview studies (e.g. Thomae, 1992) have brought rich findings on the self- and life perspectives of elderly persons in Western Germany and have also demonstrated the extent of interindividual differences, life themes and coping. For Great Britain, Coleman *et al.* (1998) have reported about their 15-year longitudinal study with repeated interviews and multiple other assessments. Different forms of communication and feeback have been used to ensure depth and veridi-cality of the elderly's self-understanding and life story.

A more restricted and easy-to-quantify method is the possible selves approach used in a cross-sectional study covering the whole adult lifespan (Cross and Markus, 1991). Smith and Freund (2002) also used this method in a longitudinal project of the Berlin Ageing Study. The possible selves approach provides verbal accounts of desired and feared expectations and images of the future self that are transformed into frequency data using content analysis. Overall, the findings show similar lines of content change in self-reports elicited with incomplete sentences (see below). The self-definition method used by Freund (Freund and Smith, 1999) is a Who-am-

I technique with open answers producing a wide range of answers from social status to personality and motivational cognitions; they are also quanti-fied by content analysis.

A study by Pennebaker and Stone (2003) is an example of linguistic attention and automatic word counting. For instance, for the use of emotional terms and phrases (used by participants in dis-cussions), two words were employed in order to test predictions derived from socioemotional selec-tivity theory. Coupland and Coupland (1995), on the other hand, investigated discussions between young and elderly adults to study emerging iden-tity formation in the aged; their method of anal-ysis was discourse analysis. Lakoff (1997) provides examples from studying English language terms and phrases in detail, charting out domains and layers of the linguistic building blocks used for self-accounts and in constructing individual self-concepts and life stories.

The sentence completion method has been applied to self-concept research on young and elderly adults by L'Ecuyer (1981) and Dittmann-Kohli (see 1990, 1995). The potential of this method resides in being open as well as structured enough to apply small-scale as well as large-scale content anal-ysis (providing quantitative and qualitative results in national surveys; Dittmann-Kohli *et al.*, 2001). Sentence completions have been used in clin-ical personality psychology, but Nuttin (1984) and Nuttin and Lens (1985) have provided the funda-mental research on this method. They used sentence stems representing motivational cognitions (MIM method) in various cultures and in connection with achievement motivation, investigating mostly stu-dents and young adults. Its extension to the sec-ond half of life by Dittmann-Kohli (1995) required a modification of the set of sentence stems and the coding system, in order to do justice to age groups over the whole lifespan. An important characteris-tic of this method is to use "inductors" (i.e. sen-tence stems) that are very open and general, in order to allow any kind of response, simulating everyday language in talking about the self. Earlier, L'Ecuyer (1981) used sentence stems cross-sectionally to study the self-concept over the lifespan, mapping them onto a system of categories close to personality traits and developmental stages.

PART TWO

EMPIRICAL FINDINGS ON SELF AND IDENTITY IN RESEARCH INTO AGEING

Changes in self- and life concepts over the lifespan

The conceptual framework of the contextual self and the narrative self-report method presented in the above sections have been used in most of the empirical studies presented below. These studies capture a wide range of self-knowledge variables derived from the similarities of content units, not from pre-designed variables or dimensions, as is the case in the traditional "closed self-report instruments." A series of findings on self and identity will be presented that compare age groups over the second half of the lifespan. With one exception (Smith and Freund, 2002), the data are cross-sectional. Most findings are from the psychological part of the German Aging Survey (Dittmann-Kohli et al., 2001), where somewhat fewer than 3,000 adults between 40 and 85 years of age were interviewed and produced written self-statements as responses to simple, everyday-like sentence beginnings using the "I" as author. The data were collected in a large representative survey in East and West Germany. The study assembled sociodemographic and other sociological data as well as psychological data about the self, about psychological and physical wellbeing, etc. The project covered sociological as well as psychological perspectives and data. The participants of the study were divided into three (and sometimes five) age groups; the three age groups will be referred to as middle-aged adults, young old, and old old. An earlier study (Dittmann-Kohli, 1990, 1995) produced the same kind of open verbal data with a shorter list of sentence stems. That study compared 300 young (apprentices and students) and 300 elderly (60–90 years, average 74 years) adults. In both studies, the findings being reported below emerged from spontaneous self-reports and extensive content analyses. The categories were derived inductively, that is, following the similarities and differences in semantic content emerging from the informed reading of the participants' answers.

Additional findings from the Berlin Aging Study on the old and very old will be reported, focusing here on open-ended instruments assessing possible selves and self-definitions. Another questionnaire-type study will be reported because it sharpens our results on the physical self. Because of space limitations, it is not possible to review more empirical findings from other important ageing research, such as the BOLSA (Thomae 1992), the ILSE study (see Martin et al., 2001), LASA (e.g. Comijs et al., 2002), and several American projects with cross-sectional or longitudinal designs. (A systematic integration of the results of all the major ageing studies with qualitative and quantitative data is highly desirable; this would require a special large-scale scientific effort, however.)

People and interpersonal relations

In this section, the interpersonal or social self in later life is of interest; responses referring to the collective self (referring to society or humanity) are included. As in many other studies, our narrative self-reports provide consistent evidence of the significance of other people and interpersonal relations over the lifespan (Bode, 2001a, 2003; Dittmann-Kohli, 1995). Social contact appears to be meaningful and central throughout life, to men and women, and across social classes and cultures. There are gender differences in the importance (centrality, frequency) of other individuals for the self, for instance in connection with broad cognitive–motivational orientations known as "independent" and "interdependent" selves (see Bode, 2003).

In self-reports to incomplete sentences, the spontaneous naming of other persons can be easily coded. In two studies it appeared that members of the family or the family in general is by far the most frequently coded category. In contrast to expectation, even in inner cities, elderly friends do not occupy a more important place in the inner space of the "Me," though the childless do name them more often. As expected, and in line with findings on interdependence and gender, women mention more often than men the partner and children in their self-accounts; this applies to young adults as well as to middle-aged and older adults. In the German Aging Survey, women have also a higher frequency regarding all categories of the social self, i.e. naming others, referring to relations and to social personality characteristics. It is an important finding, however, that this more extended social self of women is accounted for by the negative responses, that is, more negative and ambivalent ideas and feelings are being expressed in regard to social contact, social competence, and interactions. This is true for the whole group of participants between 40 and 85 years.

In stating that the social self is of similar importance to young adults and over the second half of life, qualifications must be made. First, how extended (central) the social self categories are to a person depends on the type of categories included. In the German Aging Survey, social self categories included responses about loss of autonomy and fears of becoming dependent. This type of negative social meaning did not occur in young adults and much less often in middle age. In old age, important concerns and goals related to dependency are related to life conditions associated with biological decline. In young adults, exactly the opposite concern of gaining independence is part of the social self; their self-accounts on independence are semantically related with the desire for personal growth and success in education and work. It is thus a matter of definition of the boundaries (the set of categories) of the social self that determines whether socially related self-reports become less central (i.e. frequent) from early to middle and late adulthood. If fears and concerns around becoming dependent on other persons are not considered as belonging to the social self (but rather, for instance, as a personal, psychological characteristic) then the social self is less central in old age.

Leaving the quantitative decision in this matter apart, it can be said that the social self is qualitatively different over the lifespan. On the one hand, this is a matter of social ecology. Since individuals in different age groups are necessarily oriented towards and interacting with persons of their own age, the elderly's interaction partners will have characteristics and environments of elderly persons. The elderly's interactions with partners and reference groups older and younger than they will also have different characteristics than those of younger adults, and will activate other needs and behaviors, which are a reflection of biological lifecycles of respondents, their family and other persons of their social environment. For instance, while vocational school students (apprentices) dream of being with a partner in a romantic situation on an island, middle-aged and older parents may be worried about their children's development or marriage. Older

persons are concerned about being alone, about the illness of their partner, or about becoming dependent on their children. The content of the social self varies thus with the stage of life. In addition, gender and family status are important demographic variables.

Based on Markus *et al.*'s (1997) conceptions about cultural orientations producing person-oriented versus social-collective selves, Bode (2003) has studied age differences in the centrality and content of dependent and interdependent selves by using a range of subcategories within these basic motivational orientations. Here, too, regular downward changes over the second half of the lifespan were observed in data from our nationwide cross-sectional survey. The major concerns (themes) within the interdependent (social) self showed significant age-related decreases in centrality (concerns about societal and national issues, interpersonal and social traits, concerns about the life and wellbeing of other family members, social behavior of the other towards respondent, common experiences of projects and events, quality of interpersonal relationships). The exception to these decreases was the component "social contact and relations": it did not show significant differences with age.

Work and leisure

Institutional structures, type of work status, stage of life and biological status are clearly visible in the type and number of answers in the domains of work identity and of leisure activities (Dittmann-Kohli, 1995; Westerhof 2001a, 2001b; Westerhof & Dittmann-Kohli, 2000). The transition to retirement, as well as being a retiree for some time, is clearly reflected in the narrative self-reports. This is evident for middle-aged employed and "transitional" men and women, but not for housewives. In respect to retirement, both positive and negative perspectives transpire. There is partly regret that one is (or will be) no longer working, but in general people look forward to stopping or enjoy their freedom and rest. The findings show that only during retirement can the status of not working be wholeheartedly appreciated, while identification with one's former occupation may persist. During working age, those who have paid work perceive their status as positive; having work is considered as valuable. Statements on work include possible improvements in self and work environment, as well as (deficits in) competencies, work motivation, and feelings.

Self-statements differ between persons according to work status (employee, unemployed, retiree and housewife); work identity differs in line with the widespread desirability of paid work. Housework is accepted by women, but paid work is hoped for in the future. In the youngest age group of the sample (i.e. the middle-aged adults), both housewives and unemployed persons would like to have (at least part-time) paid work.

Sociocultural (regional) differences are reflected in the data of East and West Germans. Within the unemployed and persons in transition to retirement, East Germans see unemployment in a more negative way and want to take up paid work more often. This regional effect, however, is not evident in retired people, who seem to accept the socially defined non-work status as retiree as much as those in West Germany. Speaking to a different work identity in Eastern Germany, however, is that women there do not define themselves as being pure housewives. (But, in both East and West Germany, there are practically no men who consider themselves as being "house husbands," while in the groups of the unemployed, the retirees and the group in transition to retirement, women mention the topic of housework much more often than men.)

References to the domain of leisure are more frequent than those to work, however: the evidence points to a continuity of the leisure-time self in terms of type of activities. Thus, radically new designs for life after work are not common. A significant reduction of the most popular leisure between the young old and the old old emerged in the age-comparative study (Dittmann-Kohli, 1995). The old old (75–90 years) mentioned self-related thoughts in the category "travel" much less often than the young old. Travel was the most frequent preference in hobbies and (future) leisure plans. This decline in frequency is presumably a reflection of lowered expectations in respect to physical fitness in the old old.

The existential self: time, health, death

Self-concept and identity during adulthood reflect ageing in the strongest way in the area defined as "existential self." The existential self combines several meaning domains directly connected to the (biological) ageing of the organism: statements on the passing of lifetime, its effect on stability and decline, the experience of ageing, and body-related statements such as appearance, health, illness and dying, physiological functioning and competency are classified together as belonging to the existential self. The most remarkable finding of the studies using the SELE (SELf and LifE) instrument is that the existential self becomes more strongly salient (frequently cited) with increasing age, while the social (the interdependent) self and the independent self decrease in frequency. The independent self (individualistic orientation) comprises six major themes or concerns (psychological wellbeing and restful life, control, individual achievements and goals, autonomy, self-reflection, personal projects and activities). Of these components, only the first category, psychological wellbeing and restful life, did not reach significance in age-related decreases of centrality.

THE PHYSICAL SELF: BODY, HEALTH AND FUNCTIONING. The human self-concept appears to reflect the biological aspects of existence as understood in present-day Western culture. At a youthful age, men and women put forth bodily concerns associated with sexual and interpersonal attractiveness in a positive and in a critical sense (e.g. romance, weight, beauty). As elderly adults, and in line with other findings about the existential self, the complaints and hopes of late life become central: general psychophysical functioning, health, illness, frailty, work circumstances related to decline in everyday competencies are reported. Death and dying is referred to more often by elderly than by young adults. The qualitative aspect in such statements is more impressive than differences in frequencies. For instance, only elderly referred to death in a positive sense (wanting it, waiting for it); and only the elderly were concerned about the quality of the process of dying (Dittmann-Kohli, 1995).

Categories for sportive activities, physical anxieties and being tired (from work and school) do not show very large age differences in frequency, but again the content of statements is age-typical, reflecting different concerns, self-evaluations, feelings and ideas in young versus elderly adults. Overall, the physical self is dominated by statements about health (in opposition to illness) and about psychophysical functioning. These include concerns about fitness, hopes for good health, lack of energy, mobility and competence. The German Aging Survey (Kuin *et al.*, 2001; Westerhof *et al.*, 1998) provided the possibility to test whether the physical self increased in centrality in the middle age group, the young Old and the old Old. As expected, this was the case. Gender did not show differences, but it became evident that "physical integrity" (i.e. health, illness and psychophysical functioning) becomes a more and more central part of the self. Physical integrity was strongly related to other variables such as well-being, age identity, attitude to ageing, etc.

Franzoi and Koehler (1998) investigated age and gender differences in body attitudes of young (mean age 19 years) and elderly adults (mean age 74 years) on a wide range of (closed) items. As expected, women had much stronger critical evaluations of bodily appearance, and the affective evaluation of thirty-five different bodily parts or aspects showed the expected age differences in women. In contrast to the older men and women, young subjects were more positive about their bodies, except weight. Older women were more negative about their bodies than older men. The findings reflect the circumstance that in Western (and other) societies the body image of women is much more critically evaluated in terms of beauty.

THE TEMPORAL SELF. The temporal framework of identity is one of the very interesting evolving constituents of the self over the lifecourse. The position of an individual on a (chronologically structured) life line seems to be reflected in self narratives. Life stage and temporal frame of reference become manifest through a whole array of semantic elements in the SELE responses (Dittmann-Kohli, 1995). First, the temporal extension of the self into the past and future show the typical signs of the individual's position on the life line in terms of frequency and content. Spontaneous references to past self and life were rare in young adults, but were made (often repeatedly) by nearly all of the elderly adults. References to the future, on the other hand, were uttered twenty times as often by the young as by the elderly adults. Complementing the past and future autobiographical perspective, however, additional types of temporal references appeared with great frequency. These included statements on "sub-

jective age," such as wanting to be younger, being already old, being too old, being of retirement age, living at the dawn of life, etc. Young adults (students) are much less time-conscious in their self-statements, showing a different type of lifespan construct. An additional class of categories refers to change, transition and development. Whereas thoughts about personal growth were more typical for young adulthood, references to maintenance, to reduction/decline, to limited continuation and to the finitude of life were ten times as often proffered in the elderly's spontaneous self-reports.

Complementing the above studies, an investigation of all the temporal adverbs used in all of the sentence completions in the German Aging Study showed that there is a steady increase of such terms from one to the other age group in the second half of life. These adverbs refer to cognitive representations of (hoped-for) preservation, limited continuation and decline/loss (Dittmann-Kohli, in press) and are in line with the results of Timmer *et al.* (2003).

Timmer *et al.* (2003) and Timmer *et al.* (2002) analyzed expectations of gains in personal projects under the perspective of enrichment strategies in the second half of life, as well as the content of cognitive representations (anticipations) of gains, maintenance and losses, using the representative data of the German Aging Study collected with the SELE instrument. The most frequently mentioned gains (future-related themes of possible enrichment) were lifestyle and leisure activities, such as traveling. Future-oriented themes on generativity, caring for others, societal commitment and vocational ambitions, for instance, showed substantial decreases around 50 years of age. The analysis of personal projects and anticipations on the motivational dimension of maintenance (continuation, desired stability) demonstrated very different content than those of expected gains, namely reference to physical and behavioral resources and to lifestyle. Anticipated losses, on the other hand, are related to concerns about external living conditions and physical decline.

The conclusion from these findings is that identity changes over the lifespan are strongly linked to temporal self-location in the various domains of self and life. It is evident that the awareness of having a temporary, transitional existence, and therefore a transitory I and Me, is much more intense as well as prominent in self-narratives of the older adults, compared to the younger ones.

Possible selves

Possible selves are statements made upon request about future hopes and fears regarding one's own person. In a cross-sectional study, Cross and Markus (1991) showed regular changes in feared and desired possible (future) selves over the adult lifespan, for instance in respect to health-related hopes and fears. Their main findings have been corroborated by the corresponding (future-oriented) statements with the SELE instrument, and by many other researchers. In another, longitudinal, study of old and very old persons (70–100+ years; Berlin Aging Study), assumptions about future orientations were tested, also using open-ended questions about hopes and fears (Smith and Freund, 2002). Content categories about personal characteristics, health and social relationships predominated. Motivational cognitions about gain, maintenance and avoiding loss were also coded, showing that gain motives were mentioned most often. After four years, around three-quarters of the participants introduced new domains of hopes and about half added new domains of fears, demonstrating that change in possible selves occurs even in very late life. The findings also showed that a decline in life satisfaction occurred in those men and women who mentioned new concerns about health and maintenance. In general, however, only a small number of new hopes were mentioned after a period of four years.

Psychological self

The psychological self is a domain defined by categories overlapping strongly with the item content of traditional self-concept measures, that is, personality traits, feelings, thought processes, self-evaluation and self-esteem. Our findings (Gerritsen et al., 2001) indicate that even character traits and psychological processes are not stable elements in identity and self-concept over the second half of life. In contrast to measurements with traditional self-concept instruments, our results demonstrate that the overall frequency of spontaneous self-statements within this domain is significantly lower in the old Old group, except for the number (not the content) of emotions.

The features reported as characterizing the self seem to differ according to the requirements of the self's context. In comparing early and late adulthood, the character traits, abilities, skills and motivations mentioned by apprentices and students favored education and training, and the social self contained content related to the world of peers and parents/teachers. Also, the middle-aged group (40–54) in the German Aging Survey was relatively more tuned to competencies in dealing with self and life. Our results indicate that personality traits become less important in old age, while the physical self becomes more so.

Positive and negative self-evaluation was also investigated in the German Aging Survey and in the earlier age-comparative study using the SELE method. In both studies it turned out that different criteria were used to derive positive self-regard. A comparison between young and elderly adults on the reactions to the sentence stem "When I compare myself with others . . ." showed the different criteria for positive self-evaluation used by young and elderly individuals (Dittmann-Kohli, 1989, 1995) The typical themes of late life identity, especially psychophysical integrity, were used to assess the value of the own person; and downward comparisons were applied in statements with positive self- and life evaluation.

Gerritsen et al. (2001) reported that the old old do not generally assess themselves more negatively, but that the content of self-evaluations is different from those of the young old and the middle aged. The old old used the term "being satisfied" as well as "being lonely" or "unhappy" more often to characterize themselves. Also, expressions in the category of emotional balance/imbalance were used less often. On the other hand, the middle-aged adults referred more often to categories of inter- and intrapersonal competence. Here again, choosing aspects of the psychological self seems to be a matter of relevance for everyday life.

Overall self-definition

Freund and Smith (1999) report the findings of a "who am I" investigation in old and very old age, on persons 70–103 years (from the Berlin Aging Study), in order to study the content and function of self-definition in relation to age.

Very old individuals (85–103 years) with more health-related problems and constraints described themselves using fewer and less rich self-defining content categories; those who were relatively younger (70–84 years) and had better psychophysical and health status showed a more multifaceted self-definition. Those who reported self-defining characteristics, like interests, activities and events in richer and more different content categories also reported more positive emotional wellbeing. In the Berlin Aging Study, being 85 and older meant personality traits were less often mentioned, categories around family and interaction became less frequent, and around outdoor interests and habits as well, but health, daily living routine and everyday competence more frequent, and emotions stayed the same. Men and women in this study generated more positive than negative evaluations in their self-definitions, but the group of the very old produced relatively more negative and fewer positive self-evaluations. That health was associated with more negative aspects of the self-concept supports findings from the German Aging Survey. Age differences in the frequencies of content categories of self-definitions also demonstrated a similar trend as observed in the German Aging Survey.

In Coleman's longitudinal study on old and very old people (Coleman *et al.*, 1998) a broad range of data were collected with different instruments and procedures, including self-esteem, life themes, life-story conceptualizations, and longitudinal case studies producing a rich network of findings. Among other things, the authors found that the central sources of identity did partly shift with higher age, while the most continuing themes were family, own home and independence.

Competence loss and substitution

Bode (2001) analyzed an aspect of the interface between physical and psychological self related to adaptation theories of compensation and substitution. Completions to the sentence stem "When I cannot do something anymore . . ." showed that the most frequently used category contained acceptance of (contentment with) or substitutions for declining abilities. These frequencies declined in number with higher age. The second largest category contained asking other persons for help; the old old (especially the women) had higher frequencies (depend more often on others) than the middle-aged adults. The young old expressed more negative feelings

and evaluations to loss of competence than both the middle aged and the old old group, indicating that young old age is the main life stage for coming to terms with functional decline. Approaches to the self-perception of responses to ageing such as the above may be seen in combination with other studies on coping with ageing and with critical life events, and with the theories of lifespan adaption mentioned earlier (see also below).

CONCLUSIONS

Change mechanisms for self-conceptions

Are cross-sectional differences such as the above an effect of cohort differences? In traditional social psychology, changes in the "working self" are recognized as being short-term accommodations to different daily roles and actions, while far-going reorganizations of self-concept and personality were (and still are) not considered to be the rule over the adulthood lifespan (see Dittmann-Kohli, 1991). However, approaches (smaller studies and large-scale, cross-sectional and longitudinal) using open-ended methodology and case studies suggest that far-reaching personality change on the "middle level" can in fact be demonstrated. Furthermore, as mentioned earlier, self-concept research (on adolescence) was usually based on the implicit assumption of a quasi-universal structure of dimensions and average scores. Though cultural psychology (Markus *et al.*, 1997) has contributed to refuting universality, age-changes in dimensions are only hesitantly attributed to ontogenetic change in the cognitive–affective structures of self-concept and identity.

The dominant lifespan developmental theories (see review in Diehl, 1999) understand development as adaption over the human lifecourse in the area of goals and aspirations, substitution of internal and external resources, primary and secondary control strategies of coping and life management, and keeping up illusionary self-perceptions as defenses against loss. However, these theories do not look at the content of self-reports as relevant for the theory and scientific understanding of persons in different life stages. This lack could be filled by using cognitive developmental approaches (see Lautrey, 2004). I think it is useful for this purpose to revive Piagetian perspectives of concept development (such as the conservation of volume) to include the cognitive–affective structures of the self, and to investigate their change in later life. For instance, by paying attention to clashes between different dimensions (categories) of defining the self as being young or old, oscillations between both might be observed in a time of health crisis leading to a transitional stage. We might find a perception of the self as biologically ageing but as reviving earlier self-conceptions as risk-taking and independent. Finally, an integration of two dimensions may lead to definition of self in the sense of "conservation of personhood" that combines aspects of both stages and redefines the self as a more complex human being with an expanding mind and higher states of consciousness, able to supersede the boundaries found in social (and scientific) categorizations of earlier life stages.

Within social psychological self-concept research, the use of the term "self-schemata" could suggest a similar mechanism. But that is not the case: the change of self-schemata was seen as limited to the effects of behavioral change being absorbed into the self-concept by self-observation (Stein and Markus, 1996; see overview in Onorato and Turner, 2001). This should occur insofar as behavioral change is required when body and environment change over the lifespan. Another concept of change was proposed in educational research and knowledge theory, focusing on "deep changes" in central concepts of subjective theories, as opposed to peripheral ones (Carey, 1985). This concept of a change mechanism in turn fits well with the assumption that self-concept changes derive from re-arranging response hierarchies in chronic availabilities (Dittmann-Kohli, 1995).

However, more molar, reflective and conscious strategies of change for the self are also evident. Beliefs, deliberate decision-making and adoption of self-development strategies can be observed. Open methods tend to show very clearly that individuals do not passively adapt to their ageing organisms. Rather, they anticipate the future and devise personal projects, reflect about decisions and the choice of possible selves, and try to shape themselves and their environments in a way to build a meaningful, fulfilling life and sense of self. Critical life events will be circumvented as much as possible in an effort to conserve energy in a time of biological decline, while trying to develop wisdom in understanding the present and future of self and society

in order to make informed choices (Aldwin and Levenson, 2001). Contemporary ageing women particularly, in the West and in other parts of the world, are also aware of the importance of, and potentials for, communicating about present and future selves, and of finding further information and support (e.g. in friends, in the media). They also begin to understand how to give advice to others and to facilitate self-understanding in the process of coping with transitions and self-transformation.

Future outlook and further applications

Belief in and readiness to accept change and growth may be an important aspect of ageing for all persons, at least in Western societies. In fact, these beliefs and motivations are called for as our responsibility and major virtue within our graying societies. Both young, middle-aged and eldely adults will probably become more aware of the need for continued, informed "selfing" processes in a globalized world that puts the responsibility to create selfhood on the individual, while parents, schools and neighbourhoods lose their power to socialize.

The aspects of self-concept and identity presented in the empirical part above provide access to the private world of adults in their second half of life in Germany. However, the basic structures of identity in the various age groups can be recognized in other European and industrialized Western countries, while differences in living conditions can be accounted for. Understanding their age-related perspectives on self and life is a first step in designing strategies and interventions aiming to enhance personal growth and competent functioning in an ageing and quickly changing society. Societal responses to ageing must build on the mental preconditions and representations of society's members in various stages of life. To increase positive self-concepts and positive identity in all periods of life is a question of human dignity and life fulfillment, while at the same time also being a constituent for improving the person–environment fit of ageing.

The central role of the self-conception and self development for societal futures derives of course from demographic increases in the ageing population. Societal economic resources have become a problem because the ratio of young versus older workers has changed and will continue to become worse. Demands for the prolongation of work life call for detailed knowledge of what the concerned groups understand to be their identity, competencies, commitments and concerns. For instance, the design of training schemes and other interventions to prevent obsolescence of vocational knowledge and to facilitate the maintenance of skills, work motivation and stress resistance must rely on thorough knowledge of the outlook of middle-aged adults and the young old. Even after retirement, identities should contain the role of creativity and productivity as part of realizing a fulfilled life, and the search for respective goals and means should be assisted. Creativity and skills in social interactions should also be targets of training designs for the later stages of life, as well as other aspects of coping with the difficulties and possibilities of later life. Common to these interventions is the attempt to specify and develop positive facets of the self; learning through training focuses directly on changing and increasing self-knowledge with the purpose of changing self-related dispositions to stimulate successful ageing. These include possible selves, goals, efficacy expectations, self-evaluation criteria, etc. (see overview in Dittmann-Kohli and Jopp, in press). In the realms of psychotherapy for the aged, negative concerns within the self- and life conceptions (Takkinen *et al.*, in press) are of central importance for those who want to understand what disturbs and motivates men and women in the second half of life.

FURTHER READING

Coleman, P., Ivani-Chalian, C., and M. Robinson (1998). "The story continues: persistence of life themes in old age," *Ageing and Society*, 18: 389–419.

Cross, S., and H. R. Markus (1991). "Possible selves across the life span," *Human Development*, 34: 230–55.

Herzog, A. R., and H. R. Markus (1999). "The self-concept in life span and aging research." In V. L. Bengtson and K. W. Schaie, eds., *Handbook of theories of aging*. New York: Springer, pp. 227–52.

McAdams, D. P. (1996). "Personality, modernity, and the storied self: a contemporary framework for studying persons," *Psychological Inquiry*, 7: 295–321.

REFERENCES

Aldwin, C. M., and M. R. Levenson (2001). "Stress, coping, and health at midlife: a developmental perspective." In M. E. Lachman, ed., *Handbook of midlife development*. New York: Wiley, pp. 188–214.

Biggs, S. (1999). *The mature imagination*. Buckingham: Open University Press.

Bode, C. (2001a). "Das soziale Selbst." In F., Dittmann-Kohli, C. Bode and G. J. Westerhof, eds., *Die zweite Lebenshälfte: Psychologische Perspektiven – Ergebnisse des Alters-Survey*. Stuttgart: Kohlhammer, pp. 279–339.

(2001b). "'Wenn ich bestimmte Dinge nicht mehr kann. . .': der antizipierte Umgang mit Einbußen im Kompetenz- und Fähigkeitsbereich." In F. Dittmann-Kohli, C. Bode and G. J. Westerhof, eds., *Die zweite Lebenshälfte: Psychologische Perspektiven – Ergebnisse des Alters-Survey*. Stuttgart: Kohlhammer, pp. 169–91.

(2003). *Individuality and relatedness in middle and late adulthood. A study of women and men in the Netherlands, East and West Germany*. Enschede: PrintPartners Ipskamp.

Breytspraak, L. (1984). *The development of self in later life*. Boston: Little, Brown & Co.

Brockmeier, J. (1991). "The construction of time, language, and the self," *Quarterly Newsletter of the Laboratory of Comparative Human Cognition*, 13: 42–52.

(2001). "Identity." In *Encyclopedia of life writing, autobiographical and biographical forms*, Vol. I. London and Chicago: Fitzroy Dearborn.

Brockmeier, J., and D. Carbaugh (2001). *Narrative and identity. Studies in autobiography, self and culture*. Amsterdam: John Benjamins.

Brown, J. D. (1998). *The self*. Boston, Mass.: McGraw Hill.

Bruner, J. (2001). "Self-making and word-making." In J. Brockmeier and D. Carbaugh (2001). *Narrative and identity. Studies in autobiography, self and culture*. Amsterdam: John Benjamins, pp. 25–37.

Carey, S. (1985). *Conceptual change in childhood*. Cambridge: Cambridge University Press.

Coleman, P., Ivani-Chalian, C., and M. Robinson (1998). "The story continues: persistence of life themes in old age," *Aging and Society*, 18: 389–419.

Comijs, H. C., Deeg, D. J. H., Dik, M. G., Twisk, J. W. R., and C. Jonker (2002). "Memory complaints: the association with psycho-affective and health problems and the role of personality characteristics. A six-year follow-up study," *Journal of Affective Disorders*, 72: 157–65.

Costa, P. T., Jr., and R. R. McCrae (1988). "Personality in adulthood: a six-year longitudinal study of self-reports and spouse ratings on the NEO personality inventory," *Journal of Personality and Social Psychology*, 54: 853–63.

Coupland, N., and J. Coupland (1995). "Discourse, identity, and aging." In J. F. Nussbaum and J. Coupland, eds., *Handbook of communication and aging*. Mahwah, N.J.: Lawrence Erlbaum, pp. 79–103.

Cross, S., and H. R. Markus (1991). "Possible selves across the life span," *Human Development*, 34: 230–55.

Diehl, M. (1999). "Self development in adulthood and aging: the role of critical life events." In C. D. Ryff and V. W. Marshall, eds., *The self and society in aging processes*. New York: Springer, pp. 150–83.

Dittmann-Kohli, F. (1989). "Erfolgreiches Altern in subjektiver Sicht," *Zeitschrift für Gerontopsychologie und Geriatrie*, 2: 301–7.

(1990). "The construction of meaning in old age: possibilities and constraints," *Ageing and Society*, 10: 270–94.

(1991). "Meaning and personality change from early to late adulthood," *European Journal of Gerontology*, 1: 98–103.

(1995). *Persönliche Sinngebung im frühen und späten Erwachsenenalter*. Göttingen: Hogrefe.

(in press). "Temporal references in the construction of self-identity: a life span approach." In J. Baars and H. Visser, eds., *Concepts of time in the study of aging*. Amityville: Baywood Publishers.

Dittmann-Kohli, F., and D. Jopp (in press). "Self- and life management." In J. Bond, F. Dittmann-Kohli, S. Peace, and G. Westerhof, eds., *Ageing in society*, 3rd edn. London: Sage Publications.

Dittmann-Kohli, F., Lachman, M., Kliegl, R., and P. B. Baltes (1991). "Effect of cognitive training and testing on intellectual efficacy beliefs in elderly adults," *Journal of Gerontology, Psychological Sciences*, 46: 162–4.

Dittmann-Kohli, F., Bode, C., and G. Westerhof, eds. (2001). *Die zweite Lebenshälfte: Psychologische Perspektiven – Ergebnisse des Alters-Survey*. Stuttgart: Kohlhammer.

Epstein, S. (1973). "The self-concept revisited: or a theory of a theory," *American Psychologist*, 28: 404–16.

(1980). "The self-concept: a review and a proposal of an integration of personality." In E. Staub, ed., *Personality: basic aspects and current research*. Englewood Cliffs, N.J.: Prentice Hall, pp. 81–132.

Erikson, E. H. (1968). *Identity: youth and crisis*. New York: Norton.

Franzoi, S. L., and V. Koehler (1998). "Age and gender differences in body attitudes: a comparison of young and elderly adults," *International Journal of Aging and Human Development*, 47 (1): 1–10.

Freeman, M. (2001). "From substance to story: narrative, identity, and the reconstruction of the self." In J. Brockmeier and D. Carbaugh, eds., *Narrative and identity. Studies in autobiography, self and culture*. Amsterdam: John Benjamins, pp. 283–9.

Freund, A. M., and J. Smith (1999). "Content and function of self-definition in old and very old age," *Journals of Gerontology*, 54 (1): 55–67.

Gerritsen, D., Bode, C., and F. Dittmann-Kohli (2001). "Das psychische Selbst." In F. Dittmann-Kohli, C. Bode and G. Westerhof, eds., *Die zweite Lebenshälfte: Psychologische Perspektiven – Ergebnisse des Alters-Survey*. Stuttgart: Kohlhammer, pp. 401–47.

Hermans, H. J. M. (1996). "Voicing the self: from information processing to dialogical interchange," *American Psychologist*, 119: 31–50.

Holstein, J. A., and J. F. Gubrium (2000). *Constructing the life course*, 2nd edn. New York: General Hall, Inc.

Hooker, K. (2002). "New directions for research in personality and aging: a comprehensive model for linking models, structures and processes," *Journal of Research in Personality*, 36: 318–34.

Hooker, K., and D. P. McAdams (2003). "Personality reconsidered: a new agenda for ageing research," *Journal of Gerontology: Psychological Sciences*, 58B (6): 296–304.

James, W. (1890). *The principles of psychology*, Vol. I. New York: Holt.

Joplin, D. A. (1997). "A 'Self of selves'?" In U. Neisser and D. A. Joplin, eds., *The conceptual self in context*. Cambridge, Mass.: Cambridge University Press, pp. 249–67.

Kohli, M. (2000). "The battle-grounds of European identity," *European Identities*, 2: 113–37.

Kuin, Y., Westerhof, G. J., Dittmann-Kohli, F., and D. Gerritsen (2001). "Psychophysische Integrität und Gesundheitserleben." In F. Dittmann-Kohli, C. Bode and G. Westerhof eds., *Die zweite Lebenshälfte: Psychologische Perspektiven – Ergebnisse des Alters-Survey*. Stuttgart: Kohlhammer, pp. 343–99.

Lachman, M .E., and R. M. Bertnand (2001). "Personality and self in midlife." In M. E. Lachman, ed., *Handbook of midlife development*. New York: Wiley, pp. 279–309.

Lakoff, G. (1997). "The internal structure of the self." In U. Neisser and D. A. Joplin, eds., *The conceptual self in context*. Cambridge: Cambridge University Press, pp. 92–113.

Lautrey, J. (2004). "Through which conceptual glasses and where should we look to understand the dynamics of cognitive development?" Paper presented at "The future of developmental psychology" symposium, Harnack House Dahlem, Berlin, 1 July.

L'Ecuyer, R. (1981). "The development of the self-concept through the life span." In M. D. Lynch, A. A. Norem-Hebeisen and K. Gergen, eds., *Self-concept: advances in theory and research*. Cambridge, Mass.: Ballinger, pp. 203–18.

Markus, H. R., Mullally, P. R., and S. Kitayama (1997). "Self-ways: diversity in modes of cultural participation." In U. Neisser and D. A. Joplin, eds., *The conceptual self in context*. Cambridge, Mass.: Cambridge University Press, pp. 13–61.

Martin, M., Grünendahl, M., and P. Martin (2001). "Age differences in stress, social resources and well-being in middle and older age," *Journal of Gerontology. Psychological Sciences*, 56: 214–22.

McAdams, D. P. (1996). "Personality, modernity, and the storied self: a contemporary framework for studying persons," *Psychological Inquiry*, 7: 295–321.

Nuttin, J. (1984). *Motivation, planning, and action: a relational theory of behaviour dynamics*. Leuven: Leuven University Press / Hillsdale, N.J.: Erlbaum.

Nuttin, J., and W. Lens (1985). *Future time perspective and motivation.* Leuven: Leuven University Press / Hillsdale, N.J.: Erlbaum.

Onorato, R. S., and J. C. Turner (2001). "The 'I,' the 'Me' and the 'Us.' The psychological group and self-concept maintenance and change." In C. Sedikides and M. B. Brewer, eds., *Individual self, relational self, collective self.* Philadelphia: Psychology Press, pp. 147–70.

Pennebaker, J. W., and L. D. Stone (2003). "Words of wisdom: language use over the life span," *Journal of Personality and Social Psychology*, 85 (2): 291–301.

Rösler, F. (2004). "Neural plasticity: a clue to understanding human development and learning." Paper presented at "The future of developmental psychology," symposium, Harnack House Dahlem, Berlin, July 1.

Roth, G. (2001). *Fühlen, Denken, Handeln.* Frankfurt am Main: Suhrkamp.

Ryff, C. D. (1991). "Possible selves in adulthood and old age: a tale of shifting horizons," *Psychology and Aging*, 66: 286–95.

Sedikides, C., and M. B. Brewer, eds. (2001). *Individual self, relational self, collective self.* Philadelphia: Psychology Press.

Smith, J., and A. M. Freund (2002). "The dynamics of possible selves in old age," *Journals of Gerontology Series B: Psychological Sciences*, 57 (6): 492–500.

Smith, M. B. (2003). *For a Significant Social Psychology: the collected writings of M. Brewster Smith.* New York: New York University Press.

Staudinger, U. M., and M. Pasupathi (2000). "Life span perspectives on the self, personality and social cognition." In F. I. Craik and T. A. Salthouse, eds., *The handbook of aging and cognition,* (2nd edn. Mahwah, N.J.: Lawrence Erlbaum Associates, pp. 633–88.

Stein, K. F., and H. R. Markus (1996). "The role of self in behavioral change," *Journal of Psychotherapy Integration*, 6 (4): 349–84.

Steverink, N., Westerhof, G. J., Bode, C., and F. Dittmann-Kohli (2001). "The personal experience of aging, individual resources, and subjective well-being," *Journals of Gerontology: Series B: Psychological Sciences and Social Sciences*, 56: 364–73.

Takkinen, S., Westerhof, G. J., and F. Dittmann-Kohli (in press). "Degree and content of negative meaning in four different age groups in Germany," *International Journal of Aging and Human Development.*

Taylor, C. (1989). *The making of the self: sources of modern identity.* Cambridge, Mass.: Harvard University Press.

Teuscher, U. (2003). Transition to retirement and aging. Change and persistence of personal identities. Dissertational thesis, Fribourg, Switzerland.

Thomae, H. (1992). "Contributions to longitudinal research to a cognitive theory of adjustment to aging," *European Journal of Personality*, 6: 157–75.

Timmer, E., Steverink, N., and F. Dittmann-Kohli (2002). "Cognitive representations of future gains, maintenance, and losses in the second half of life," *International Journal of Aging and Human Development*, 55 (4): 321–39.

Timmer, E., Bode, C., and F. Dittmann-Kohli (2003). "Expectations of gains in the second half of life: a study of personal conceptions of enrichment in a life span perspective," *Ageing and Society*, 23: 3–24.

Van Halen, C. (2002). *The uncertainties of self and identity.* Groningen: Jan Noorman.

Van Selm, M., and F. Dittmann-Kohli (1998). "Meaninglessness in the second half of life: the development of a construct," *International Journal of Aging and Human Development*, 47 (2): 81–104.

Vroon, P. (1978). *Stemmen van vroeger. Ontstaan en ontwikkeling van het zelfbewustzijn.* Baarn: Ambo.

Westerhof, G. J. (2001a). "Arbeit und Beruf im persönlichen Sinnsystem." In F. Dittmann-Kohli, C. Bode and G. J. Westerhof, eds., *Die zweite Lebenshälfte: Psychologische Perspektiven – Ergebnisse des Alters-Survey.* Stuttgart: Kohlhammer, pp. 195–245.

Westerhof, G. J. (2001b). "Freizeittätigkeiten im persönlichen Sinnsystem." In F. Dittmann-Kohli, C. Bode and G. J. Westerhof, eds., *Die zweite Lebenshälfte: Psychologische Perspektiven – Ergebnisse des Alters-Survey.* Stuttgart: Kohlhammer, pp. 247–77.

Westerhof, G. J., and F. Dittmann-Kohli (2000). "Work status and the construction of work-related selves." In K. W. Schaie and J. Hendricks, eds., *Evolution of the ageing self.* New York: Springer, pp. 123–57.

Westerhof, G. J., Kuin, Y., and F. Dittmann-Kohli (1998). "Gesundheit als Lebensthema," *Zeitschrift f. Klinische Psychologie*, 27: 136–42.

Westerhof, G. J., Dittmann-Kohli, F., and T. Thissen (2001a). "Beyond life satisfaction: lay conceptions of well-being among middle-aged and elderly adults," *Social indicators research*, 56 (2): 179–203.

Westerhof, G. J., Katzko, M. W., Dittmann-Kohli, F., and B. Hayslip (2001b). "Life contexts and health-related selves in old age: perspectives from the United States, India and Zaire," *Journal of Aging Studies*, 15: 105–26.

Westerhof, G. J., Bode, C., and F. Dittmann-Kohli (2003). "The aging paradox: towards personal meaning in gerontological theory." In S. Biggs, A. Lowenstein and J. Hendricks, eds., *The need for theory: social gerontology for the 21st century.* Amityville, N.Y.: Baywood, pp. 127–43.

Whitbourne, S. K., and L. A. Conolly (1999). "The developing self in midlife." In S. L. Willis and J. D. Reid, eds., *Life in the middle: psychological and social development in middle age.* San Diego, Calif.: Academic Press, pp. 25–45.

CHAPTER 4.2

Stress and Coping

LINDA K. GEORGE

The proposition that stress is a risk factor for a wide variety of health outcomes is now widely accepted by both researchers and the larger public. Although the relationships between stress and both morbidity and mortality are broadly recognized, a half-century of research demonstrates that they are neither simple nor straightforward. Indeed, it is now clear that understanding the links between stress and health requires detailed information about individuals' personal and social characteristics, as well as the context within which stress is experienced and coping efforts are made. The theoretical, empirical, and statistical complexity of stress research now, as compared to initial efforts, has resulted in a richer, more fine-grained understanding of the links between stress and illness, although important issues remain unresolved.

The purpose of this chapter is to summarize what is known about stress, health, and ageing. The first section describes not only the stress process model, the general conceptual paradigm that frames the vast majority of stress research, but also the elements of the model and their relationships with age. The second section reviews the state-of-the-science with regard to the effects of stress on health during later life. Finally, emerging issues are examined.

THE STRESS PROCESS MODEL

Although there have been many seminal stress studies both before and after it, Pearlin and colleagues' depiction of the stress process became the primary conceptual model in stress research (Pearlin *et al.*, 1981). This simple but elegant model proved equally

useful in synthesizing results across studies and providing a guiding conceptual framework for subsequent studies. The stress process model focuses on three classes of factors as they develop dynamically over time: stressors, resources, and health outcomes. Stressors are the primary independent variables of interest, and are hypothesized to increase the risk of negative health outcomes. Resources are the personal and social factors that mediate the effects of stressors on health. Although Pearlin *et al.* focused on the mediating role of resources, subsequent research has appropriately incorporated the moderating or buffering effects of resources as well. Each class of variables merits examination in terms of their conceptual and operational definitions and their relationships to age.

Stressors

In general, stressors are defined as conditions that challenge or threaten individuals' capacities to respond in ways that preserve and protect personal wellbeing. Stressors are commonly viewed as falling into two primary categories: acute and chronic. Acute stressors, or life events, are discrete changes in life patterns (e.g., becoming divorced or widowed, entering the labor force). The onset of an acute stressor is assumed to be identifiable and, although duration varies, length of exposure and impact are time-limited. Chronic stressors are long-term conditions that threaten wellbeing (e.g. role strain, financial deprivation). It is interesting to note that although chronic stressors are expected to persist over time, virtually no attention has been paid to the duration of chronic stressors or the extent to which duration affects their consequences.

Two other distinctions have received considerable attention in stress research. One distinction is between objective and subjective stressors. Stress is measured objectively (although externally might be a more accurate label) when investigators define the stressors under investigation (e.g. studies of the health effects of widowhood). Stress is measured subjectively when investigators limit their investigations to events and conditions that study participants view as stressful or negative. There is now considerable evidence that (a) there is no event or condition that study participants uniformly view as stressful (Hughes *et al.*, 1988), and (b) the relationships between stressors and health outcomes are stronger when stress is subjectively defined (George, 1989). As a result, the majority of recent and current stress research relies on subjective perceptions of stressful events and conditions.

Another distinction is between aggregated and disaggregated measures of stress. Aggregated stress is measured when investigators sum the total number of stressors to which study participants have been exposed. This is the usual approach, for example, for scoring life event checklists. Disaggregated measurement strategies include both relatively narrow categories (e.g. family stressors, work stressors) and investigations of single stressors. Both approaches have advantages and disadvantages. Aggregated stress measures are appropriately criticized because the antecedents, mediators, and moderators of specific stressors undoubtedly vary – and these distinctive patterns cannot be observed using aggregated measures. Disaggregated measures are appropriately criticized for failing to take into account the total amount of stress to which study participants are exposed.

One of the long-term debates in stress research is the relative importance of stress exposure versus vulnerability to stress. This is an especially prominent theme in research designed to explain status differences in health. For example, are rates of depression higher among women than men because women are exposed to greater stress, because they are more vulnerable to depression than men at equal levels of stress, or both? In these studies, stress is examined as a mediator of the relationships between achieved or ascribed statuses and health outcomes. When stress is operationalized using traditional life event checklists, results consistently suggest that status differences in health are a function of differential vulnerability to stress rather than differential exposure to stress (McLeod and Kessler, 1990).

During the past few years, the stress exposure versus stress vulnerability issue has been revisited, with several investigators arguing that previously used measures of stress exposure failed to tap the universe of stressful experiences (Wheaton, 1996). This critique led to multiple attempts to measure stress more completely. One trend is to acknowledge that the stressful experiences of significant others can be experienced as personally stressful (Thoits, 1995). For example, one reason that women exhibit higher levels of depressive symptoms than men is because they are more likely than men to report distress resulting from events and conditions in their friends' and relatives' lives. Another method of more accurately capturing stress exposure is to operationalize operant stress (Turner and Avison, 1992). Operant stress includes not only recent and current stressors, but also more temporally distant stressors that respondents report have ongoing effects. Yet a third way in which investigators have broadened the scope of stress assessment has been to include traumatic stressors, regardless of how long ago they occurred. Much of this research has focused on childhood traumas such as parental loss, severe deprivations, and child abuse (Harris *et al.*, 1990). Other traumas can occur at any age (e.g., sexual assault, criminal victimization, combat exposure) (Bryer *et al.*, 1987). As the critics who spurred efforts to expand the measurement of stress exposure posited, when more broadly defined and measured, stress exposure accounts, in part or in whole, for status differences in health (Turner and Lloyd, 1999).

One method of addressing the question of what is distinctive about the links between stress and health in late life is to determine whether there are age differences in stress exposure. A compelling body of literature demonstrates that late life is distinctive in both the quantity of stressors experienced and their nature. It is well documented that, on average, older adults experience significantly fewer acute stressors than their younger peers (Hughes *et al.*, 1988). Over a one-year interval, persons aged 65 and older report, on average, 2.3 life events. Over the same time period, individuals aged 18–34 report an average of 4.5 life events.

But the number of stressors is not the whole story. The most distinctive aspect of the age distribution of stressors is that, compared to their younger peers, older adults are more likely to experience stressors that signal the loss of resources, roles, and relationships (Lynch and George, 2002). Evidence suggests that approximately 80 percent of the events reported by older adults represent the loss of roles or resources; the corresponding percentage for young adults is 15 percent. If loss events are more difficult to cope with than other types of events, older adults are likely to be at greater risk of compromised health and wellbeing than other age groups.

Evidence is less available with regard to chronic stressors, but it seems clear that older adults are certainly no worse off than young and middle-aged adults. Moreover, the distribution of chronic stressors varies by age. Older adults are less likely to experience sustained marital conflict, job stress, and financial strain than their younger peers. In contrast, older adults are more likely to experience chronic illness and the loss of significant others. Even less is known about age differences in exposure to traumatic stress. It is clear, however, that there are cohort differences in exposure to historical events that are accompanied by high rates of traumatic stress (e.g. severe financial deprivation in childhood, combat exposure).

Resources

A myriad of factors constitute the context within which stressors are experienced and confronted. Three types of resources are considered here: social support, psychological resources (e.g. self-esteem, self-efficacy), and coping efforts.

SOCIAL SUPPORT. Social support consists of the tangible and intangible rewards and assistance provided by significant others. Conceptually and operationally, social support is multidimensional. Although consensus is lacking concerning the specific dimensions of social support, most investigators acknowledge that it has both structural and functional components (Lin and Ensel, 1999). The structural characteristics of social support include the size of the network available, the density of the network, and the distribution of the network (e.g. proportion non-kin). Functional facets of social support include the receipt of instrumental assistance (e.g., help with housework or meals), receipt of emotional support, and perceptions of social support adequacy. As these examples illustrate, social support dimensions also differ in the extent to which they are objective versus subjective.

Two hypotheses about the role of social support in the relationships between stress and health have received substantial attention. The mediating hypothesis posits that social support plays an intervening role – that stressors mobilize support networks and the assistance provided by the network decreases the probability of negative health outcomes. The stress-buffering hypothesis focuses on the interaction between stressors and social support. This hypothesis suggests that social support is relevant to health only under conditions of high stress.

Although the major hypotheses focus squarely on the expected benefits of social support for health and wellbeing, a more minor theme in the stress and coping literature concerns the possible negative consequences of social support (Rook, 1984). Some scholars note that long-term or intense receipt of assistance can undermine self-esteem and/or generate resentment. And intense social support can undermine recovery from illness or injury if the recipient is prevented from taking on as much autonomy as possible.

Although social support is an important resource at all ages, its nature and availability change across the adult lifecourse. In structural terms, the most dramatic change is the shrinking of the size of the social network during late life, as friends and relatives die or become unavailable as a result of illness or disability. The most devastating loss common in late life is widowhood. Widowhood involves many forms of loss, including the loss of what has typically been one's major source of social support. The forms of assistance received from support networks also differ across adulthood (Hogan et al., 1993). The major forms of assistance received during young adulthood are financial transfers and assistance with childcare. During late life, assistance with household tasks and personal care are the most common. Perceptions of the availability and quality of social support, however, differ little across adulthood.

PSYCHOLOGICAL RESOURCES. In addition to social resources, individuals bring a variety of psychological assets (or deficits) to stressful experiences. Although a wide range of psychological characteristics have been examined in the context of stress and illness, two dimensions of self-perception have received most empirical attention. Self-esteem is the evaluative component of the self and refers to the individual's general sense of self-worth. Self-efficacy refers to perceptions of the self as competent to handle life's challenges and is closely related to concepts such as mastery and sense of control.

The general hypothesis is that individuals who view themselves as competent and worthy will tolerate and respond to stressful situations better, reducing the probability of negative health outcomes. Thus, psychological resources are expected to mediate the relationship between stress and illness. Some scholars also suggest a relationship between psychological resources and social support (Ross and Mirowsky, 1989). Specifically, individuals who view themselves as worthy and competent may be more likely to handle stressors on their own whereas those with lower levels of self-esteem and self-efficacy may rely more upon others.

Longitudinal studies of self-esteem and self-efficacy across the adult lifecourse are lacking. Both short-term longitudinal and cross-sectional studies, however, report few age changes or differences in levels of these psychological resources.

COPING EFFORTS. Intuitively, coping plays an obvious role in the links between stress and health. The general hypothesis is that individuals who effectively cope with stressors will be less likely to experience negative consequences. Unfortunately, the concept of coping has proven to be a conundrum for social and behavioral scientists. An initial problem is understanding the boundaries of coping. Not all responses to stressful circumstances are coping responses. Moreover, a variety of questions complicate the task of defining the boundaries of coping. For example, is coping restricted to efforts to handle the stressor per se – or do efforts to contain its sequelae also count? Are efforts directed towards distracting one's attention from the stressor coping responses? Defining and measuring coping effectiveness has been equally elusive. The coping responses that are effective for one stressor may be ineffective for another. Some stressors can be reversed (e.g. unemployment can be "cured" by obtaining another job); others cannot (e.g. the death of a loved one). Moreover, what should be the gold standard against which coping responses are measured – the evaluation of the researcher or the individual's perceptions about the effectiveness of his or her coping? These conceptual issues have proven to be relatively intractable and have delayed progress in the scientific study of coping.

One component of coping, however, can be clearly defined, reliably measured, and demonstrably related to stress outcomes: the distinction between active or problem-focused and palliative or emotion-focused coping (Lazarus and Folkman, 1984). Active coping refers to efforts to alter the stressor or its consequences. Palliative coping refers to efforts, both intrapsychic and behavioral, to alleviate the emotional distress caused by stressors. In short, active coping tackles the stressor and palliative coping is designed to make oneself feel better despite the stressor.

The distinction between active and palliative coping has proven useful in several ways. First, and most obvious, researchers have investigated the extent to which active and palliative coping mediate the links between stress and negative health outcomes. The general hypothesis is that active, problem-focused coping will be superior to palliative coping efforts in short-circuiting the harmful effects of stress. In addition, this distinction has permitted examination of the extent to which individuals exhibit consistency across stressors in their coping preferences and the extent to which different stressors elicit different or distinctive patterns of coping.

The volume of studies examining age differences in the use of active and passive coping strategies has been exceedingly small – and there have been no longitudinal studies of age changes in coping efforts. Moreover, the limited findings available are contradictory, with some investigators observing no age differences in choice of coping efforts and others reporting that older adults are slightly more likely than their younger peers to use palliative coping strategies (Folkman *et al.*, 1987).

Note that social support and psychological resources also can be viewed as components of coping. When confronting stressors, individuals mobilize a variety of resources, including not only their specific coping strategies, but also their own psychological resources and assistance from others. Thus, at a more abstract level, all of the hypothesized mediators of the stress–health relationship can be considered coping resources.

THE STRESS PROCESS MODEL: EMPIRICAL EVIDENCE

Literally hundreds of studies fall under the general rubric of the stress process model. This review focuses on (a) general patterns that can be stated with confidence as a result of replication and (b) longitudinal studies in which the measurement of stressors precedes that of health outcomes. Overall, the major tenets of the stress process model receive very strong support.

The Links Between Stress and Health in Later Life

In general, the relationships between stressors and health outcomes are significant, but of modest strength. This pattern is observed for aggregate measures of stress as well as for investigations of specific stressors, and for both acute and chronic stressors. This does not imply that all stress effects are of equal strength. In general, chronic stressors are stronger predictors of negative health outcomes than acute stressors (McGonagle and Kessler, 1990). Similarly, the broader the measurement of stress, the stronger the effects on health (Turner and Lloyd, 1995).

Some stressors occur most frequently in old age and thus contribute more to the illness burden in late life than at other life stages. Widowhood occurs primarily in late life and although most widowed persons experience only temporary associated health deficits, a minority exhibits more long-term and/or severe health consequences (Lee *et al.*, 2001). The stresses associated with caregiving for an older adult have been studied extensively and have documented negative health consequences (Pinquart and Soerensen, 2003). Obviously, not all caregivers are older adults, but many are – especially spouse caregivers, but also young-old children caring for their old-old parents. Physical illness and disability are not only more prevalent in late life than earlier in the lifecourse, they are also chronic stressors with

the capacity to jeopardize other health outcomes, such as depression (Hays *et al.*, 1994).

Unfortunately, recent efforts to broaden the measurement of stress have not yet found their way into research on the stress process in late life. A recent study by Ensel and Lin (2000) is an exception, however, and demonstrates the impact of distal stressors on physical health in late life. This is clearly a priority issue for future research.

The strength of the observed relationships between stress and health also vary across illness outcomes. In general, the most negative effects of stressors are observed for depression and psychological distress, followed by physical health and disability, and then by mortality. The health dynamics captured by research to date vary as well. Most research examines changes in levels of symptoms or impairments. In these studies, statistical analyses estimate the extent to which stressors generate changes in number of symptoms or impairments. Studies that estimate the effects of stress in the onset of or recovery from illness, however, are rare. More studies of transitions in and out of illness are needed, as they provide important information about the role of stress in the course of illness.

The Mediating and Moderating Effects of Resources

SOCIAL SUPPORT. There is compelling evidence that social support plays a strong role in the links between stress and health. Not all dimensions of social support, however, are equally strong. Subjective perceptions of social support are more strongly associated with health outcomes than other dimensions (Wethington and Kessler, 1986). With regard to mental health outcomes, critics have suggested that depressed persons will rate their social support more negatively than non-depressed persons, thus contaminating tests of the effects of perceived support on depression. Time-series analysis of the relationships between perceived support and depression, however, indicate that the dominant direction of influence is from support to depression rather than the reverse (Mitchell and Moos, 1984). However, there are weaker, but statistically significant, links between depression and subsequent declines in social support. This pattern suggests that depression can eventually drive away supporters.

Although limited in volume, some evidence suggests that instrumental support may be more strongly related to health in later life than earlier in the adult lifecourse. Unlike perceived social support, instrumental support is more important for physical health outcomes than for depression and psychological distress (Lin *et al.*, 1979). Careful examination of dynamics has been important in elucidating the complex relationships between instrumental support and health outcomes. In cross-sectional studies, instrumental support is often related to negative, rather than positive, health outcomes. This pattern probably reflects the link between need for and receipt of instrumental assistance rather than detrimental effects of instrumental support on health. Longitudinal studies indicate that this is largely the case – poor health elicits instrumental assistance from significant others. But there also is evidence that long-term need for instrumental assistance can exhaust the good will or capacities of support networks, leading to decreases in instrumental support and poorer health outcomes (Silverstein and Litwak, 1993). The stress-buffering hypothesis has been tested extensively in both older and age-heterogeneous samples. Results are inconsistent, although a majority of studies find support for this hypothesis. Review of available studies suggests that support for the stress-buffering hypothesis is strongest for perceived support buffering the effects of stress on depression. Perceived social support may be especially important for depression because a sense of being valued, esteemed, listened to, understood, and cared for is especially valuable in preventing or ameliorating depression. Investigators should routinely test the stress-buffering hypothesis because evidence of stress-buffering helps to put in perspective the rather modest relationships typically observed between stressors and health outcomes. If stress jeopardizes health primarily among persons with low levels of social support, estimating only the direct effects of stress will conceal the most powerful effects of stress on health.

PSYCHOLOGICAL RESOURCES. The volume of research testing the mediating effects of psychological resources in the stress process is smaller than that for social support. The limited evidence available suggests that self-efficacy and self-esteem play a modest role in mediating the effects of stress on health (Holahan and Holahan, 1987). Almost all of this research, however, has been limited to examination of depression and psychological distress. Some investigators suggest that psychological resources mediate not only the relationship between stress and health, but also that between social support and health. That is, either receipt of social support or the perception that it is available if needed may bolster individuals' feelings of self-worth and competence, facilitating better health outcomes. There is limited evidence for this hypothesis (Krause, 1987).

It is important to examine stress, psychological resources, and health on multiple occasions over significant periods of time to capture better the dynamic interplay among them. As noted above, short-term longitudinal studies indicate that psychological resources partially mediate the effects of stress on health. But there also is evidence that long-term exposure to stress can erode an individual's sense of self-worth and/or competence (Krause, 1987).

COPING EFFORTS. The research base in which coping efforts are tested as mediators of the stress–illness relationship is even smaller than that for psychological resources and, unfortunately, empirical attention has decreased during the past two decades. To date, this research has focused on only one health outcome: psychological distress. Moreover, in contrast to investigations of other potential mediators of the links between stress and illness, studies of coping are based exclusively on cross-sectional data. Consequently, conclusions about the mediating role of coping efforts must be viewed as tentative.

Recall that the general hypothesis is that active coping will be associated with better health outcomes than palliative coping. Available evidence suggests that this hypothesis is overly simplistic. It appears true that the exclusive use of active coping is associated with both perceptions of more effective coping and lower psychological distress than the exclusive use of palliative coping. Only small minorities of individuals, however, report exclusive use of one type of coping effort. Most people report using a combination of active and palliative coping efforts when confronting threat or challenge. And this combination is associated with the highest levels of perceptions of coping effectiveness and the lowest levels of psychological distress (O'Rourke and Cappeliez, 2002).

A Note on Cultural Generalizability

Evidence about the stress process in later life that has been reviewed here is based on research in England and, especially, the United States. It is important to determine whether the stress process model and the pattern of findings reported to date apply to non-Western societies. Studies of older adults living in non-Western societies are relatively rare. Results of those studies are generally compatible with findings based on samples of older adults in the US and UK (Ferraro and Su, 1999; Krause *et al.*, 1995; Krause and Liang, 1993). Other investigators report, however, that the distribution of stressors varies somewhat across cultures (Wheatley *et al.*, 1995).

NEW DIRECTIONS AND EMERGING ISSUES

With the exception of attention to coping efforts, the stress process model remains an active and growing research focus. Some recent trends, such as increasing the boundaries of stress measurement, have received sufficient attention that they were included in the above summary of available evidence. Others, however, have emerged only recently – and while results thus far are suggestive, the volume of studies remains too small for inclusion in a review of the state-of-the science. In this final section, two such issues are briefly discussed: social integration and an alternate method of depicting the dynamics of the stress–illness relationship.

Social Integration

Social integration is typically defined as the extent to which individuals maintain meaningful ties to social structure via social roles and a variety of forms of civic participation. Social support networks consist of primary ties, defined by intimacy and, typically, expectations that relationships will be sustained over time. The bonds generated by social integration are secondary ties, characterized by more limited obligations and expectations that the duration of relationships is contingent on role occupancy. One of the potential limitations of support networks is that individuals typically develop intimate ties with persons who are socially similar to them. Consequently, network members often bring little in the way of new knowledge, new contacts, or unfamiliar resources to those who depend on them for support. Social integration, in contrast, is characterized by what Granovetter (1973) termed "the strength of weak ties." Those weak ties will not cook our meals or care for us when we are ill, but they can provide information about and introductions to resources of which we are unaware. One of the emerging research topics of the last decade or so has been increased attention to the role of social integration in health, as evidenced by a growing body of research on the health benefits of participation in voluntary organizations, religious participation, and volunteering.

Thus far, social integration has had limited impact on research investigating the stress process. But suggestions of its potential relevance are beginning to appear. For example, religious participation buffers the effects of stress in much the same way that social support does (Ellison *et al.*, 2001). The time is ripe for a systematic examination of the role of social integration in mediating and/or moderating the effects of stress on health.

A Dynamic View of Stress Exposure

As described previously, a recent addition to stress research is broadening measures of stress exposure. A more recent area of exploration is modeling the rate at which stress changes over time and the impact of those changes on changes in depression. (This technique is equally applicable to changes in physical health, but no studies have examined physical health outcomes.) Using this approach, stress exposure is examined as the waxing and waning of stress growth over time. The increased availability of latent growth curve analysis (LGCA) techniques, as well as longitudinal data that involve multiple time points over an extended period of time, set the stage for this research. In regression-based studies, stress exposure is operationalized as the number of stressors to which individuals are exposed; in LGCA, stress exposure is operationalized as the rate of stress growth. The general hypothesis is that the more rapidly one acquires stressors, the greater the threat to health.

Two studies examine the rate of growth of loss-events during later life and its impact on depression. The first study showed that, in a representative sample of community-dwelling older adults, growth in the number and rate of loss-events is the typical trajectory over six years and increasing growth of loss-events predicts increased growth in depressive symptoms (Lynch and George, 2002). In the second study, differential rates of stress growth were used to explain race differences in the growth of depressive symptoms over time. The results indicated that, as hypothesized, older African Americans experienced greater growth in loss-events than older whites and that this largely accounted for the greater growth in depression symptoms reported by the African Americans (George and Lynch, 2003).

Obviously, much more research will be required before the potential of LGCA for understanding the stress process can be assessed. But its emergence reminds us that, as the tools available for modeling processes over time expand, so does our capacity to reframe and refine our conceptual and empirical understanding of the stress process.

In summary, research on the links between stress and health has been flourishing for nearly half a century. It remains a vigorous field because investigators persistently seek out conceptual, measurement, and statistical opportunities to refine what is known. Substantively, research on the stress process is appealing because it forces us to look at the challenges life offers, the very real effects of those challenges on health and longevity, and the complex ways that personal and social characteristics generate distinctive pathways between stressors and health.

FURTHER READING

Ferraro, K., and Y. Su (1999). "Financial strain, social relations, and psychological distress among older people: a cross-cultural analysis," *Journal of Gerontology: Social Sciences,* 54B: S3–S15.

Folkman, S., Lazarus, R. S., Pimley, S., and J. Novacek (1987). "Age differences in stress and coping processes," *Psychology and Aging,* 2: 171–84.

Lin, N., and W. M. Ensel (1999). "Social support and depressed mood: a structural analysis," *Journal of Health and Social Behavior,* 40: 344–59.

Pearlin, L. I., Lieberman, M. A., Menaghan, E. G., and J. T. Mullin (1981). "The stress process," *Journal of Health and Social Behavior,* 22: 337–56.

REFERENCES

Bryer, J. B., Nelson, B. A., Miller, J. B., and P. A. Krol (1987). "Childhood sexual and physical abuse as factors in adult psychiatric illness," *American Journal of Psychiatry,* 144: 1426–30.

Ellison, E. G., Boardman, J. D., Williams, D. R., and J. S. Jackson (2001). "Religious involvement, stress, and mental health: findings from the 1995 Detroit Area Study," *Social Forces,* 80: 215–49.

Ensel, W. M., and N. Lin (2000). "Age, the stress process and physical distress: the role of distal stressors," *Journal of Aging and Health,* 12: 139–68.

Ferraro, K., and Y. Su (1999). "Financial strain, social relations, and psychological distress among older people: a cross-cultural analysis," *Journal of Gerontology: Social Sciences,* 54B: S3–S15.

Folkman, S., Lazarus, R. S., Pimley, S., and J. Novacek (1987). "Age differences in stress and coping processes," *Psychology and Aging* 2: 171–84.

George, L. K. (1989). "Stress, social support, and depression over the life course." In K. S. Markides and C. L. Cooper, eds., *Aging, stress, and health.* Chichester: John Wiley, pp. 241–68.

(2000). "Well-being and sense of self: what we know and what we need to know." In K. W. Schaie and J. Hendricks, eds., *The evolution of the aging self.* New York: Springer, pp. 1–36.

George, L. K., and S. M. Lynch (2003). "Race differences in depressive symptoms: a dynamic perspective on stress exposure," *Journal of health and social behavior,* 44: 353–69.

Granovetter, M. S. (1973). "The strength of weak ties," *American Journal of Sociology,* 78: 1360–80.

Harris, T., Brown, G. W., and A. Bifulco (1990). "Loss of parent in childhood and adult psychiatric disorder: a tentative overall model," *Development and Psychopathology,* 2: 311–28.

Hays, R. D., Marshall, G. N., Yu, E. L., and C. D. Sherbourne (1994). "Four-year cross-lagged associations between physical and mental health in the medical outcomes study," *Journal of Consulting and Clinical Psychology,* 62: 441–9.

Hogan, D. P., Eggebeen, D. J., and C. C. Clogg (1993). "The structure of intergenerational exchanges in American families," *American Journal of Sociology,* 98: 1428–58.

Holahan, C. K., and C. J. Holahan (1987). "Self-efficacy, social support, and depression in aging: a longitudinal analysis," *Journal of Gerontology,* 42: 65–8.

Hughes, D. C., George, L. K., and D. G. Blazer (1988). "Age differences in life event qualities: controlled analyses," *Journal of Community Psychology,* 16: 161–74.

Krause, N. (1987). "Life stress, social support, and self-esteem in an elderly population," *Psychology and Aging*, 2: 349–56.

Krause, N., and J. Liang (1993). "Stress, social support, and psychological distress among the Chinese elderly," *Journal of Gerontology: Psychological Sciences*, 48B: P282–P291.

Krause, N., Dowler, D., Liang, J., Gu, S., Yatomi, N., and Y. Chuang (1995). "Sex, marital status, and psychological distress in later life: a comparative analysis," *Archives of Gerontology and Geriatrics*, 21: 127–46.

Lazarus, R. S., and S. Folkman (1984). *Stress, appraisal, and coping*. New York: Springer.

Lee, G. R., DeMaris, A., Bavin, S., and R. Sullivan (2001). "Gender differences in the depressive effect of widowhood in later life," *Journal of Gerontology: Social Sciences*, 56B: S56–S61.

Lin, N., and W. M. Ensel (1999). "Social support and depressed mood: a structural analysis," *Journal of Health and Social Behavior*, 40: 344–59.

Lin, N., Simeone, R. S., Ensel, W. M., and W. Kuo (1979). "Depression-mobility and its social etiology: a model and an empirical test," *Journal of Health and Social Behavior*, 20: 108–19.

Lynch, S. M., and L. K. George (2002). "Interlocking trajectories of loss-related events and depressive symptoms among elders," *Journal of Gerontology: Social Sciences*, 57B: S117–S123.

McGonagle, K. A., and R. C. Kessler (1990). "Chronic stress, acute stress, and depressive symptoms," *American Journal of Community Psychology*, 18: 681–706.

McLeod, J. D., and R. C. Kessler (1990). "Socioeconomic differences in vulnerability to undesirable life events," *Journal of Health and Social Behavior*, 31: 162–72.

Mitchell, R. E., and R. H. Moos (1984). "Deficiencies in social support among depressed patients: antecedents or consequences of stress?" *Journal of Health and Social Behavior*, 25: 438–52.

O'Rourke, N., and P. Cappeliez (2002). "Perceived control, coping, and expressed burden among spouses of suspected dementia patients," *Canadian Journal on Aging*, 21: 385–92.

Pearlin, L. I., Lieberman, M. A., Menaghan, E. G., and J. T. Mullin (1981). "The stress process," *Journal of Health and Social Behavior*, 22: 337–56.

Pinquart, M., and S. Soerensen (2003). "Differences between caregivers and noncaregivers in psychological health and physical health," *Psychology and Aging*, 18: 250–67.

Rook, K. S. (1984). "The negative side of social interaction: impact on psychological well-being," *Journal of Personality and Social Psychology*, 46: 1097–1108.

Ross, C. E., and J. Mirowsky (1989). "Explaining the social patterns of depression: control and problem-solving – or support and talking?" *Journal of Health and Social Behavior*, 30: 206–19.

Silverstein, M., and E. Litwak (1993). "A task-specific typology of intergenerational family structure in late life," *The Gerontologist*, 33: 258–64.

Thoits, P. A. (1995). "Stress, coping, and social support processes: where are we? What next?," *Journal of Health and Social Behavior*, 37 (extra issue): 53–79.

Turner, R. J., and W. R. Avison (1992). "Innovation in the measurement of life stress: crisis theory and the significance of event resolution," *Journal of Health and Social Behavior*, 33: 36–50.

Turner, R. J., and D. A. Lloyd (1995). "Lifetime traumas and mental health: the significance of cumulative adversity," *Journal of Health and Social Behavior*, 36: 360–76.

(1999). "The stress process and the social distribution of depression," *Journal of Health and Social Behavior*, 40: 374–404.

Wethington, E., and R. C. Kessler (1986). "Perceived support, received support, and adjustment to stressful life events," *Journal of Health and Social Behavior*, 27: 78–89.

Wheatley, D., Golden, L., and J. Jainlin (1995). "Stress across three cultures: Great Britain, the United States, and China." In G. P. Chrousos and R. McCarty, eds., *Stress: basic mechanisms and clinical implications*. New York: Annals of the New York Academy of Sciences, pp. 609–16.

Wheaton, B. (1996). "The domains and boundaries of stress concepts." In H. B. Kaplan, ed., *Psychosocial stress: perspectives on structure, theory, the life course, and methods*. New York: Academic Press, pp. 29–70.

Reminiscence: Developmental, Social and Clinical Perspectives

PETER G. COLEMAN

The study of the functions of reminiscence, the process of recalling past events and experiences, has established itself as a major topic in both theoretical and applied psychogerontology. This is a relatively recent development. Encouraging older people to reminisce is seen as a natural activity nowadays, and very much part of care work. Thirty years ago this was not the case. Although there has also been a general cultural shift in favour of remembering the past, much of the impetus has come from gerontological theory, research and practice.

Interest in the reminiscences of older people owes a particular debt to Erikson's definition of integrity as 'the acceptance of one's one and only life cycle as something that had to be and that, by necessity, permitted of no substitutions' (Erikson, 1963 [1950]: 260), but even more to Robert Butler's concept of 'life review' (Butler, 1963). Writing from his experience as a practising therapist in a psychiatric journal, Butler put forward the view that life review is a normative process which all people undergo as they realise that their life is coming to an end. This article had a considerable impact, containing many literary references to illustrate its points, while being rooted in the author's own clinical observations.

The connection with the humanities has been an important feature of subsequent developments in reminiscence theory and application. Both Butler in his original article and Erikson in later writings (Erikson, 1978) refer with approval to Ingmar Bergmann's film *Wild strawberries* as depicting well the late life processes they refer to. This film depicts an egocentric professor who, through a process of disturbing dreams and later more conscious recollections, comes to appreciate his personal shortcomings and to show greater sensitivity to his family. Its positive ending indicates the healing value of the life review. However, despite the attention given to Butler's concept in the literature on reminiscence, relatively few commentators refer to the negative elements of life review that he also highlighted. Where no resolution can be found for troublesome memories, feelings of despair may result. Butler cites Samuel Beckett's *Krapp's last tape* to illustrate this point, revealing a man who has kept a fastidious record of his memories but now only feels disgust at their recall.

During the 1970s a positive, somewhat naive and sentimental image of reminiscence was projected, which is strongly evident today in the sale of reproduction artifacts and mementoes of the past. The new-found passion for reminiscence was understandable as a reaction to the previous decades' dismissal of the past, well captured in the words attributed to Henry Ford, 'history is bunk'. This is a good example of how fashions can change quickly. Up to and including the 1960s reminiscence was associated with senility, was even seen to cause dementia – of which at the time there was only a rudimentary understanding – and was actively discouraged in residential care work. By the 1980s it was viewed quite differently as important for the affirmation of personal identity and self-esteem.

However, as reminiscence came to be promoted in practice in the 1980s, a major credibility gap emerged, in that, despite plenty of anecdotal accounts of the benefits of reminiscence, controlled studies of its efficacy did not produce significant results (Thornton and Brotchie, 1987). This issue could not begin to be resolved until researchers started making distinctions between different functions of reminiscence. Because of the continuing importance of this issue this chapter will first review research on the differential functions and effects of reminiscence, before focusing on the concept of life review, consideration of one's life as a whole. It will then examine the different types of reminiscence and life review interventions and evidence for their efficacy, and end with a consideration of the value of truth as a criterion of healthy reminiscence.

TYPES AND FUNCTIONS OF REMINISCENCE

The study of reminiscence preceded the move towards narrative understanding in social science research, and it is important that it maintains its distinctiveness as the study of the personal use of the past (Webster, 2001). Developing an accurate and fruitful typology of uses of reminiscence is vital to defining the area. This is a first stage in much psychological research, but in the case of reminiscence important distinctions appear to have been neglected in the rush to demonstrate practical benefits.

This neglect is the more surprising since the basis for a typology of functions was already present in the earliest literature (McMahon and Rhudick, 1967). By the late 1960s there were at least three quite distinct sets of theoretical frameworks proposed for understanding the benefits that reminiscence brought to older people. The first was identity maintenance. This was supported by experiments that showed that older people resorted more to the past in defending their opinions from criticism (Lewis, 1971), but was mainly based on observation of older people's behaviour in threatening situations, particularly in the demeaning circumstances of American nursing homes in the 1960s and '70s. It was this conception of reminiscence that was seized on by those wanting to enliven elderly care settings. By promoting the natural defence of reminiscence they hoped to combat apathy and depression in institutionalised and otherwise neglected older people.

A quite different notion was that of life review. The idea of re-integration of the self following the midlife crisis was strongly present in Jung's writings, but it was Butler's discussion of the topic that was seized upon as a means of justifying and giving dignity to older people's reminiscences. However, whereas the identity maintenance function of reminiscence concerned the role of the past in promoting stability of the self, the life review function pointed to possibilities for change and development. These differences in function were minimised in subsequent studies of the frequency and benefits of reminiscence, and it is likely that the full implications of the concept of life review were not properly considered by most of those who promoted reminiscence in care settings.

A third, more social, aspect of reminiscence was also present in the early literature and should not be neglected. It existed in two completely different forms, both in the disengagement theory of ageing and in the contrasting theory of social and cultural re-engagement which developed partly in response to reflection on older people's disengagement in Western societies. In disengagement theory terms, reminiscence was seen as part of natural withdrawal from social responsibilities with age. It was a way of obtaining solace for the self while ceasing to have an impact on society. But at the same time anthropologists were noting the ways in which older people in traditional societies invested themselves with authority in drawing out teaching from their life's experience.

Interestingly the strongest objections to the normative nature of disengagement with ageing came to be raised by one of the psychologists who worked on the original project. David Gutmann pointed out that most societies the world has known have been gerontocracies, whereas the tendency towards disengagement with age was a characteristic of modern Western societies. From the standpoint of traditional societies which Gutmann went on to research, also in longitudinal studies – which included members of Native American tribes and Islamic people such as the Druze of the Middle East – older men especially did disengage from daily practical concerns but only in order to engage more fully at the cultural and spiritual level, in acting as voicepieces of the culture, morality, and the traditions of their society. By contrast, in societies with failing traditions and culture, the elderly lost their roles and functions, and became prey to psychopathology (Gutmann, 1987).

Gutmann still expresses these radically conservative views. But his message is a hard one to take – because, as he says himself, the loss of cultures of shared meanings and the resulting intergenerational disintegration is the price the West seems willing to pay for the liberal and egalitarian values it prizes so much. Nevertheless, some researchers have provided evidence consistent with Gutmann's view from an evolutionary consideration of older people's reminiscences. For example, older people do appear to be more effective communicators about past events, speaking about them in a more digestible mode, and in a voice that will draw the attention of their listeners (Mergler and Goldstein, 1983).

One of the first attempts to define and operationalise measures for distinct types of reminiscence was made in a study of naturally occurring reminiscence in older people living in London sheltered housing schemes (Coleman, 1974). This study developed criteria to assess different categories of reminiscence and quantify their presence in transcripts of conversation collected on multiple occasions. Using these methods the study was able to demonstrate that life review reminiscence had beneficial associations. It was related to higher levels of wellbeing in those who had more negative views of their past. Culturally informative or transmissive reminiscence was significantly associated with wellbeing in the men, but not the women, interviewed. In subsequent studies following up the same sample, Coleman (1986) illustrated how, by contrast, other types of reminiscence might be maladaptive. For example, rumination reflected guilt and regret over past events, and memories which were nostalgic to the point of pain were associated with extended grief reactions to bereavement and loss.

This differential approach to reminiscence was expanded by others. In a study also based on systematic observation of older people's reminiscence at home, Wong and Watt (1991) showed that 'integrative' reminiscence – corresponding to Butler's life review – was related to independently assessed markers of ageing well in a large sample of community- and institution-living elders. They developed a coding manual for classifying each successive 'paragraph', i.e. self-contained idea, into predefined types of reminiscence. Their observations on the negative associations of obsessive reminiscence have proved

particularly influential. People can get caught in a vicious cycle of repetition, continually revisiting painful memories but without achieving resolution.

As Brewin has noted, there are links between the study of persistent intrusive memories in Post Traumatic Stress Disorder (PTSD) and in depressed states (Brewin, 1998). PTSD is characterised by uncontrolled recall of memory with many features of sensory immediacy and without any form of reworking. Problems arising in later life as a result of the recall of earlier traumatic events have become a major area for research in the field of older people's mental health (L. Hunt et al., 1997).

Deliberate avoidance of painful memories, a common form of coping with stress but also in itself a sign of PTSD, appears a less successful strategy in the long run. Avoidance has the paradoxical effect of increasing that memory's power to disturb. Research on older British war veterans (N. Hunt and Robbins, 2001) highlights well the different consequences of avoidance as a coping strategy, which tends to break down in late life, as compared with narrative mastery which brings the memory under control in the form of story. This is not a simple process and seems to develop in stages, as the traumatic memory comes under control, then remains captured in all its detail, before becoming open to processes of development and ageing. Hunt demonstrates how the memories of very old veterans still appear to preserve much of the sensory detail of the original traumatic memory, a quality to which he applies the term 'consummate'.

In recent years there has been a healthy influx of new ideas into this field of research from outside gerontology, especially from the study of autobiographical memory (Webster and Cappeliez, 1993; Bluck and Levine, 1998; Bluck and Habermas, 2000). If the functions of reminiscence are regarded as particular uses of autobiographical memory, a number of interesting questions arise, such as the development of reminiscence behaviour in early childhood and in adolescence and the consequences for reminiscence in later life (Habermas and Bluck, 2000). In learning to reminisce, what is it precisely that is learned? How do the experiences and skills acquired in early life influence the type of reminiscence that occurs in adulthood and ageing? How do the positive and negative components in nostalgic recall interact and alter over the lifespan?

The most notable recent contribution to delineating reminiscence types comes from the attempt to produce more sophisticated and psychometrically sound self-report instruments. Whereas the method of rating conversation transcripts has led to many fresh insights, it is costly in time. The development of valid questionnaires allows for large-scale studies which can test more sophisticated hypotheses. The best-known example is Jeff Webster's 'Reminiscence Functions Scale' (RFS) (Webster, 1993). This is a 43-item questionnaire in which subjects indicate on a 6-point scale how often they reminisce for different purposes.

As well as functions of 'identity', 'teaching/informing', 'problem-solving', 'intimacy maintenance' and 'conversation', the measure assesses some hitherto little-studied functions of reminiscence: 'boredom reduction', 'bitterness revival' and 'death preparation'. 'Bitterness revival' assesses the extent to which memories are used to affectively charge recalled episodes in which the reminiscer perceives him- or herself as having been unjustly treated. Webster (2001) suggests that it may provide a justification to maintain negative thoughts and emotions towards others. It has a clear function, in preparing people to seize the moment of revenge. But it is negatively correlated with measures of personal wellbeing (Webster, 1998).

Work using the RFS illustrates how a multidimensional instrument brings us closer to more fine-grained hypotheses as more precise definitions accrue and the opportunity to build conceptually sophisticated models of reminiscence increases (Merriam, 1993). It is also significant that Webster and colleagues' research is not restricted to older people, and this is a further reason, perhaps, why it points to a number of functions of reminiscence which have not been discussed before. For example, the use of reminiscence for 'boredom reduction' is commoner among the young, and has negative associations.

Consistent gender differences have emerged for the identity function of reminiscence; women score higher than men. Webster (2002) has also considered the issue of racial differences in reminiscence function; African Americans, Chinese Canadians and Native Americans used reminiscence more. Further research needs to examine to what extent this finding reflects a stronger oral tradition among these groups and/or a greater need to use reminiscence to promote self-understanding, preserve identity, and teach younger generations.

Use of the RFS scale has also made it possible to study reminiscence function in relation to other psychological concepts. Attachment theory provides a good example. In a Canadian study, Webster (1998) showed that securely attached individuals scored significantly higher on the teaching/informing factor, and significantly lower on the bitterness revival, identity and problem-solving factors than insecure groups. Other studies in Canada have shown connections between reminiscence frequency and measures of personal meaning in older adults (Cappeliez and O'Rourke, 2002). Negative correlations with variables such as purpose in life, life control and will to meaning suggest that a struggle to find meaning may underlie much reminiscence in later life. A high level of reminiscence activity may not necessarily be a positive sign. It could indicate a person caught in negative ruminations and needing therapeutic assistance.

THE CONCEPT OF LIFE REVIEW

Despite the proliferation of different reminiscence functions, 'life review' still remains the foremost concept in the reminiscence literature. It suggests a distinct task for later life in achieving a rounded evaluation of the life that has been lived. However, life review's universal character as originally proposed by Butler has been questioned by interview studies which suggest that wellbeing in later life is not dependent on reminiscence (Coleman, 1986; Sherman, 1991), also by evidence that life review demands high levels of inner skills and is therefore not necessarily characteristic of most older people, and even by theoretical considerations of the self's bias towards continuity (Bluck and Levine, 1998; Parker, 1995). Reminiscence, in adulthood, appears to be more often used to re-assert previous patterns of self-understanding, for example in response to threat or challenge, than to create the new understanding arising from life review.

Nevertheless, life review in the radical sense enunciated by Butler remains a fascinating concept, perhaps especially because of its emergent character. It implies a search for meaning through reflection on one's life's experience and cannot be achieved without effort (Randall and Kenyon, 2001). It may lead to transformation of goals and changed values (Freeman, 1997).

Susan Bluck, in arguing for greater interaction between the study of reminiscence and that of auto-biographical memory, has pointed to the reconstructive role of memory throughout life in addition to its stabilising role (Bluck and Levine, 1998; Bluck and Habermas, 2000). The self is largely constant over time – and reminiscence certainly often serves this function – but it is also being constantly revised through the selective accession and modification of memories. It is important to recognise and respect both functions, especially in intervening in people's lives. There are times for re-assuring those we seek to help but times also for helping them to move on in their level of self-understanding.

Life review, like other emergent features of ageing, should be placed in a lifespan perspective. We need to identify systematically the developmental precursors and antecedent conditions which foster its expression. Placing it in this context also encourages attention to the different facets of reminiscence. A very interesting example of such a study of the life review has been published by Wink and Schiff (2002). It is based on the Berkeley (California) longitudinal study whose original samples of new-born babies and pre-adolescents were collected in 1928–9 and 1931 respectively. Having been studied intensively in childhood and adolescence they have been interviewed in depth on four occasions in adulthood.

Wink and Schiff were able to base their analysis on 172 participants of the Berkeley study while they were in their late 60s and mid 70s. These constituted 90% of the cohort still available (neither dead nor lost). They derived an assessment of life review activity from the interviews conducted at that time and related it to ratings of personality collected earlier in life. Two independent judges rated the material for signs of life review using a five-point scale adapted from the work of Sherman (1991). Only 22% of the sample showed clear evidence of striving for a new level of self-understanding (ratings of 4 or 5), 20% were unclear, and the remaining 58% showed no signs at all of striving for new understanding or integration.

Although life review was not associated with self-ratings of life satisfaction, it was positively linked to ratings of other characteristics, notably creativity, spirituality and generativity. As one might expect, life review was also related to ratings of openness to experience, personal growth and to using reminiscence (on the Webster RFS) for identity exploration and problem solving. Most interesting are the links found with psychological characteristics assessed earlier in life, such as observer-based indices of introspection and insight. Life review was also related to a global measure of past negative life events, such as a major off-time bereavement, other personal crisis or illness. Wink and Schiff's thesis, consistent with that of previous commentators (Coleman, 1986; Parker, 1995), is that life review is an adaptive response to ageing in those who have encountered marked difficulties in life, but that for the majority of ageing individuals it is not a necessary adaptation.

REMINISCENCE AND LIFE REVIEW INTERVENTIONS AND THEIR EVALUATION

From its beginning the study of reminiscence has been closely tied to practice. This reinforces the importance of identifying which types of reminiscence should be encouraged and which avoided, for example the integrative approach focusing on a constructive reappraisal of the older person's past and the instrumental approach centred on past problem-solving abilities and coping activities. The subject has certainly developed from the position 20 years ago when unsuspecting residents of homes or attenders at day centres might be confronted with disturbing images, for example from the First World War, as part of a reminiscence activation programme.

There has been much debate about the strengths and limitations of both group reminiscence and one-to-one interaction. The former, if used sensitively with due regard for individual differences in needs including vulnerabilities, remains the most popular and most effective practice. Its aims are different from dyadic reminiscence, and reflect the support and camaraderie that can develop especially in reminiscence group practice.

Unfortunately, most of the early evaluative studies had serious methodological flaws. Aside from the issue of inadequate definition and absence of differentiation of distinct types of definition, studies suffered from the lack of adequate controls, limited samples, and poor measurement. Indices of reminiscence activity were often subjective ratings of limited validity. The failings were such that, even by the late 1980s, critical reviews could be published pointing out the lack of convincing evidence for the benefits of stimulating reminiscence activity (Thornton and Brotchie, 1987).

In certain areas of work, for example with demented elderly people, there are still few rigorous evaluations to back up descriptive reports of the benefits of reminiscence work (Gibson, 1994; Woods and McKiernan, 1995). This is frustrating for practitioners who feel as a consequence that their efforts are not sufficiently appreciated. Nevertheless, overall there have been noticeable improvements in methods employed, particularly in the development of standardised instruments and provision of comparative control samples undertaking alternative activities to reminiscence. More attention has also been given to consolidating findings by providing systematic reviews.

Barbara Haight has been a pioneer researcher–practitioner in this field in the US, producing rigorous evaluations of the time-limited life review interventions she has developed for use by community nurse practitioners (Haight, 1988, 1992). She has also provided regular reviews of the reminiscence literature (Haight and Hendrix, 1995; Hendrix and Haight, 2002) and helped launch the International Institute for Reminiscence and Life Review as a centre for communicating ideas, practice and research findings.

A good early example of the more rigorous style of research on reminiscence interventions is Fielden's (1990) report of a project conducted in a sheltered housing complex in England. This was a small but well-controlled study, conducted by a clinical psychologist, in two sheltered housing complexes four miles apart. A reminiscence package of pictures and slides was used over nine weekly sessions in the communal lounge of one scheme, whereas in the other a 'here and now' group looked at pictures and slides of present activities and holidays. In both cases residents were encouraged to bring in their own pictures and memorabilia.

In contrast to the present-centred activities, the reminiscence group showed marked improvement in wellbeing over the course of the programme. Significant changes occurred also in patterns of socialisation and intimacy. It is not possible to assess whether these social changes accounted for the change in wellbeing or vice versa, or whether both were independent effects, but it is a plausible explanation that the reminiscence-based activity was more successful in creating relationships. It gave something more significant to talk about. Of course it is important to replicate studies such as this. There may have been special circumstances in one or both of the sheltered housing schemes that accounted for the significant effect.

The field of reminiscence interventions is now so large that it has become necessary to examine more critically the nature of the various interventions employed, and to assess their benefits for different client groups. There are already a number of different procedures in use. The method of life review advocated by Haight, for example, is a one-to-one approach, but also a time-limited series of six sessions covering the whole lifecourse, including a final integrative session. Both positive and negative themes are addressed. The design of this programme explicitly takes into account the time constraints operating on health and social welfare workers as well as the needs of their clients.

By contrast the 'guided autobiography' groups, pioneered by Birren and colleagues (Birren and Deutchman, 1991; Randall and Kenyon, 2001) are much more extensive in the time and social skills (such as written composition and creative listening) required. Participants are typically people who are from the outset well-motivated to explore the major themes of their lives in company with others (Ruth et al., 1996).

Thanks to recent advances in research we can now see more clearly how the specific outcomes of reminiscence will depend on the type of memories recalled (Bluck and Levine, 1998). Accessing some memories will encourage self-acceptance, accessing others will actually stimulate self-change. Much then depends on the aims of the intervention and the techniques used. Life review in the sense in which Butler originally described it is more concerned with the possibility of self-change than with maintaining present self-conception. It would be possible to change one's sense of self by drawing on a different, often forgotten, set of memories to the ones on which the present self is based. But this is a difficult and anxiety-raising task as Butler realised, and as he showed by means of the literary illustrations with which he accompanied his original description (Butler, 1963). It is more possible when someone is already dissatisfied with life or is already seeking self-growth, but for most people it is hard to give up a theory of the self in which they have long been invested. Life review techniques to encourage this process have understandably not been tried with older people.

REMINISCENCE AND TRUTH

Healthy psychological functions are those which are beneficial not only to the individual but also to the society around and to future generations. It is therefore appropriate to close with a focus on the witness to past truths and future values that older people provide in their reminiscing. Objective truth is an important element in establishing the story of one's life (Coleman, 1999), and the incorporation of techniques that do loosen the hold of the 'totalitarian ego' (Greenwald, 1980) would be important additions to methods of reminiscence work. Persons are potentially much more than the current stories they tell of themselves.

What for example makes a good life story? It is important to devise criteria for judging the quality of reminiscence in its own terms, and not only through the consequences for the individual's subjective sense of wellbeing. Coleman (1999) as well as Habermas and Bluck (2000) have emphasised the importance of coherence as an essential characteristic of an integrated and satisfying life story. Habermas and Bluck proposed four types of global coherence: temporal, cultural, causal and thematic.

Temporal coherence describes the manner in which remembered experiences are temporally related to one another and to external historical events. Cultural coherence refers to the normative cultural facts and events that define conventional life phases (e.g. births, marriages and deaths). Causal and thematic coherence on the other hand refer to the evaluative and meaning-making components of the life story. For example, when causal links are not established, life appears to have been determined by chance and will be experienced as meaningless.

However, it is possible to work with people on 'restorying' their lives so that negative experiences become opportunities for development and acquisition of wisdom (Randall and Kenyon, 2001). Even emotionally disturbing events can become an occasion for transformation. Tedeschi and Calhoun (1995) have gone so far as to coin the term 'post-traumatic growth'. This is consistent with what we know of human potential from biographical studies, and appears, as we have seen, to lie at the basis of the attitude-changing reminiscence that has come to be called life review.

Recent studies on lives disrupted by the historical events of the Second World War and the recent collapse of the Soviet empire, itself a product of that war (Keller, 2002; Coleman *et al.*, 2002), illustrate how such historical events interfere with normal identity processes, but also the potential resulting from such experience for appreciating and communicating new insights and values.

FURTHER READING

Birren, J. E., Kenyon, G. M., Ruth, J.-E., Schroots, J. J. F., and T. Svensson, eds. (1996). *Aging and biography. Explorations in adult development.* New York: Springer.

Garland, J., and C. Garland (2001). *Life review in health and social care.* Hove, East Sussex: Brunner-Routledge.

Gibson, F. (2004). *The past in the present: using reminiscence in health and social care.* Baltimore, Md.: Health Professions Press.

Webster, J. D., and B. K. Haight, eds. (2002). *Critical advances in reminiscence work: from theory to application.* New York: Springer.

REFERENCES

Birren, J. E., and D. E. Deutchman (1991). *Guiding autobiography groups for older adults: exploring the fabric of life.* Baltimore, Md.: Johns Hopkins University Press.

Bluck, S., and T. Habermas (2000). 'The life story schema', *Motivation and Emotion*: 121–47.

Bluck, S., and L. Levine (1998). 'Reminiscence as autobiographical memory: a catalyst for reminiscence theory development', *Ageing and Society*, 18: 185–208.

Brewin, C. (1998). 'Intrusive memories, depression and PTSD', *Psychologist*, 11: 281–3.

Butler, R. N. (1963). 'The Life Review: an interpretation of reminiscence in the aged', *Psychiatry*, 26: 65–76.

Cappeliez, P., and N. O'Rourke (2002). 'Personality traits and existential concerns as predictors of the functions of reminiscence in older adults', *Journal of Gerontology: Psychological Sciences*, 57B: P116–P123.

Coleman, P. G. (1974). 'Measuring reminiscence characteristics from conversation as adaptive features of old age', *International Journal of Aging and Human Development*, 5: 281–94.

——— (1986). *Ageing and reminiscence processes: social and clinical implications*. Chichester: Wiley.

——— (1999). 'Creating a life story: the task of reconciliation', *Gerontologist*, 39: 133–9.

Coleman, P. G., Hautamaki, A., and A. Podolskij (2002). 'Trauma, reconciliation and generativity: the stories told by European war veterans'. In J. D. Webster and B. K. Haight, eds., *Critical advances in reminiscence work: from theory to application*. New York: Springer, pp. 218–32.

Erikson, E. H. (1963[1950]) *Childhood and society*. New York: Norton (rev. edn 1963, Harmondsworth: Penguin).

——— (1978). 'Reflections on Dr. Borg's life cycle'. In E. H. Erikson, ed., *Adulthood*. New York: Norton.

Fielden, M. A. (1990). 'Reminiscence as a therapeutic intervention with sheltered housing residents: a comparative study', *British Journal of Social Work*, 20: 21–44.

Freeman, M. (1997). 'Death, narrative integrity and the radical challenge of self-understanding: a reading of Tolstoy's "Death of Ivan Ilych"', *Ageing and Society*, 17: 373–98.

Gibson, F. (1994). 'What can reminiscence contribute to people with dementia?' In J. Bornat, ed., *Reminiscence reviewed: perspectives, evaluations and achievements*. Buckingham: Open University Press, pp. 46–60.

Greenwald, A. (1980). 'The totalitarian ego: fabrication and revision of personal history', *American Psychologist*, 35: 603–18.

Gutmann, D. (1987). *Reclaimed powers: towards a new psychology of men and women in later life*. New York: Basic Books (2nd edn 1994).

Habermas, T., and S. Bluck (2000). 'Getting a life: the emergence of the life story in adolescence', *Psychological Bulletin*, 126: 748–69.

Haight, B. K. (1988). 'The therapeutic role of a structured life review process in homebound elderly subjects', *Journal of Gerontology*, 43: 40–4.

——— (1992). 'Long-term effects of a structured life review process', *Journal of Gerontology*, 47: 312–15.

Haight, B. K., and S. Hendrix (1995). 'An integrated review of reminiscence'. In B. K. Haight and J. D. Webster, eds., *The art and science of reminiscing. Theory, research, methods, and applications*. Washington, D.C.: Taylor & Francis, pp. 3–21.

Hendrix, S., and B. K. Haight (2002). 'A continued review of reminiscence'. In J. D. Webster and B. K. Haight, eds., *Critical advances in reminiscence work: from theory to application*. New York: Springer, pp. 3–29.

Hunt, L., Marshall, M., and C. Rowlings, eds. (1997). *Past trauma in late life: European perspectives on therapeutic work with older people*. London: Jessica Kingsley.

Hunt, N., and I. Robbins (2001). 'The long-term consequences of war: the experience of World War II', *Aging & Mental Health*, 5: 183–90.

Keller, B. (2002). 'Personal identity and social discontinuity: on memories of the "war generation" in former West Germany'. In J. D. Webster and B. K. Haight, eds., *Critical advances in reminiscence work: from theory to application*. New York: Springer, pp. 165–79.

Lewis, C. N. (1971). 'Reminiscing and self-concept in old age', *Journal of Gerontology*, 26: 240–3.

McMahon, A. W., and P. J. Rhudick (1967). 'Reminiscing: adaptational significance in the aged'. In S. Levin and R. J. Kahana, eds., *Psychodynamic studies on aging. Creativity, reminiscence and dying*. New York: International Universities Press, pp. 64–78.

Mergler, N. L., and M. D. Goldstein (1983). 'Why are there old people? Senescence as biological and cultural preparedness for the transmission of information', *Human Development*, 26: 72–90.

Parker, R. G. (1995). 'Reminiscence: a continuity theory framework', *Gerontologist*, 35: 515–25.

Randall, W. L., and G. M. Kenyon (2001). *Ordinary wisdom. Biographical aging and the journey of life*. Westport, Conn.: Praeger.

Ruth, J.-E., Birren, J. E., and D. E. Polkinghorne (1996). 'The projects of life reflected in autobiographies of old age', *Ageing and Society*, 16: 677–99.

Sherman, E. (1991). *Reminiscence and the self in old age*. New York: Springer.

Tedeschi, R. G., and L. G. Calhoun (1995). *Trauma and transformation: growing in the aftermath of suffering*. Thousand Oaks, Calif.: Sage.

Thornton, S., and J. Brotchie (1987). 'Reminiscence: a critical review of the empirical literature', *British Journal of Clinical Psychology*, 26: 93–111.

Webster, J. D. (1993). 'Construction and validation of the Reminiscence Functions Scale', *Journal of Gerontology: Psychological Sciences*, 48: 256–62.

——— (1998). 'Attachment styles, reminiscence function, and happiness in young and elderly adults', *Journal of Aging Studies*, 12: 315–30.

——— (2001). 'The future of the past: continuing challenges for reminiscence research'. In G. Kenyon, P. Clark and B. De Vries, eds., *Narrative gerontology: theory, research and practice*. New York: Springer, pp. 159–85.

——— (2002). 'Reminiscence functions in adulthood: age, race, and family dynamics correlates'. In J. D. Webster and B. K. Haight, eds., *Critical advances in reminiscence work: from theory to application*. New York: Springer, pp. 140–52.

Webster, J. D., and P. Cappeliez (1993). 'Reminiscence and autobiographical memory: complementary contexts for cognitive aging research', *Developmental Review*, 13: 54–91.

Wink, P., and B. Schiff (2002). 'To review or not to review? The role of personality and life events in life review and adaptation to older age'. In J. D. Webster and B. K. Haight, eds., *Critical advances in reminiscence work: from theory to applications*. New York: Springer, pp. 44–60.

Wong, P. T. P., and L. M. Watt (1991). 'What types of reminiscence are associated with successful aging?' *Psychology and Aging*, 6: 272–9.

Woods, B., and F. McKiernan (1995). 'Evaluating the impact of reminiscence on older people with dementia'. In B. K. Haight and J. D. Webster, eds., *The art and science of reminiscing: theory, research, methods and application*. Washington D.C.: Taylor & Francis, pp. 233–42.

CHAPTER 4.4

The Social Worlds of Old Age

JABER F. GUBRIUM

Decades ago, sociologist Herbert Blumer (1969 [1930]) presented a paper to the Institute of Social Research at the University of Chicago, entitled "Science without concepts." The title wasn't his choice. As Blumer noted, "To speak of science without concepts suggests all sorts of analogies – a carver without tools, a railroad without tracks, a mammal without bones, a love story without love" (p. 153). A science without concepts was inconceivable to him. Still, Blumer cautioned, concepts in science could become mere labels, "without yielding anything but the label." For Blumer, it was a leading principle of science that concepts sensitize us to the contours of the empirical world and not be left to perfunctory usage.

I wish to draw attention to a similar issue in gerontology, in particular how the social is conceptualized as a way of understanding everyday life in old age. The leading set of concepts in this area is comprised of an analytic vocabulary whose central concern is "society," a term of reference borrowed from sociology. Associated concepts include social structure, status, and role. Such concepts are used by gerontologists to explain the actions of older people, just as the concepts in sociology help to explain the conduct of people in general. For example, gerontologists commonly refer to the place of older people in society or their particular status in a social structure as explanations for older people seeing their lives in a particular way or feeling the way they do. Gerontologists also speak of the role of the older person in society, or in some part of society, such as the role of the aged in the community or in the family, providing additional understanding.

While this vocabulary has been enormously helpful in focusing attention on social influences, at the same time the vocabulary is perniciously abstract. For instance, what does it mean in practice for particular social roles to influence one's sense of self in old age? Are these roles all-pervasive in their influence, acting upon older people seven days a week, twenty-four hours per day? Do they continuously influence them in specific ways, leaving them no nooks and crannies to think or feel otherwise? Does the status of old age present itself whenever an elderly individual appears in public? If older people have a status in society, does it constantly mediate their experience? We might ask, in each instance, when and where do such social influences work their particular effects on the lives of older people?

Such questions call for a more grounded terminology, concepts that direct us to the everyday experiences of ageing, not labels that reference themselves. We might well ask how the social operates in practice? Rather than putting this in terms of society's influence on the elderly, a focus on practice behooves us to inquire how, when, and where society works its influence on the elderly? When does society do the specific things it does? Always? Now-and-then? And where? Most places? Some in particular? By asking practical questions, we stand to bring on board a more variegated sense of society than the abstract label "society" commonly conveys. Instead of asking what the status of being old does to elderly persons' life satisfaction, or what influence old age has on one's sense of the future, we might ask how age-related statuses or roles operate in particular theatres of life. An empirically grounded approach to status and role, among related concepts, sensitizes us to the working circumstances of the social in everyday life.

THE CONCEPT OF SOCIAL WORLDS

In researching the everyday experience of ageing, I have found the concept "social worlds" to be tremendously helpful in understanding the way the social actually figures in experience (Holstein and Gubrium, 2003). I've sought to research how the vocabulary of the social can help us to untangle life's complex operation in practice. "Social worlds" is plural, which highlights the perspective that the social is organized fragments, not spun out of whole cloth (see Sarbin and Kitsuse, 1994). The social spreads itself about life in different ways, and with greater or lesser force, here and there, so to speak. Social worlds turn us to the possibility that one world, such as one's immediate family, might structure our status as older persons in a different way from how another world, such as a group of longtime friends, structures it. They turn us to the likelihood that the role of being old in one world, such as in an amusement park, scripts the older individual's conduct as that of the bystander, for example, while the role of being old in another world, such as a senior center, scripts it more actively and positively, or not at all (see Hazan, 1980). The variegation offered by the concept is clear, as the social becomes a complex landscape of experiential occasions and diverse encounters with others.

I have also found the concept helpful because, in contrast to the more experientially distant concept of society, "social worlds" doesn't present individual lives as if they were "caught" in a web of totalized effects, as if society and its associated parts – social structure, status, and role, among others – were forces that imposed their wills on the elderly. Rather than thinking of the social as a set of conditions that determine what older people think, feel, and do, it is useful to approach social life in relation to the different contexts available for encountering and contending with others. This opens to view the panorama of social opportunities for older people to present themselves and come to grips with who and what they are as social beings (see Gergen and Gergen, 2003). Indeed, from this perspective, there may be social worlds where old age just doesn't "come up," altering in kind, not just degree, older people's identities in later life.

I did not invent the concept of social worlds; I have only brought it forward to understand the lived details of old age. Years ago, sociologist Anselm Strauss (1978, 1997[1959]) used it as a sensitizing rubric for delineating the social complexity of identity. Along with his colleague Barney Glaser, Strauss took inspiration from the concept to document the situated character of dying, death, and related professional work in institutional settings (Glaser and Strauss, 1965, 1968). Later, sociologist David Unruh (1983) presented the "invisible lives" of the aged, whose diverse life experiences were otherwise commonly characterized in abstract terms such as "the" elderly and "their" world, as if these were homogeneous social forms. The groundwork laid by these sociologists harkens to Blumer's plea to apply concepts sensitive to the actual practice of everyday life.

APPLICATIONS

Consider how two researchers have applied the concept of social worlds to make complexity visible in the everyday lives of older people. One of them, Sarah Matthews, works in relation to the social organization of women's ageing. The other application centers on my own research, which deals in part with differences in the meaning of self and body in dementia.

Women's Ageing Bodies

Sarah Matthews' (1979) study of self-identity among older women shows how they actively influence the everyday visibility of their bodies, and thereby their identities, by managing their social worlds. Matthews argues that ageing and being old are subjectively discerned; the visibility of the ageing body is not simply a fact of the later years. It is a consequence, rather, of the situated presentation of self, both the social and the physical.

In introducing her research, Matthews directs us to the priority of the social over the biological meaning of age for the women she interviewed.

The research . . . stands as a challenge to the notion of the "naturalness" of old as a social category defined in biology. By putting aside taken-for-granted assumptions about old age, the social worlds of old widows in American society can be seen not as dictated by physical and mental decline, but as shaped by social and historical forces. The informants for this research are social actors defined as old by the society in which they live and forced to deal with the social meaning of their chronological age. (pp. 20–1)

Matthews goes on to describe an "everyday-life" perspective (p. 21), setting the stage for presenting her empirical material in more complex terms. She observed and carried out in-depth interviews with elderly respondents who attended a local senior center along with others who lived in a housing project for older persons, extending this to interviewing and participant observation in the surrounding community. An important set of questions centered on the meaning of the ageing body in relation to different social worlds: how do these older women experience others' reactions to their physical presence? How do they respond to the reactions? Her answers to these questions tellingly show how situated the meaning of the ageing body is in practice, how differentially distributed meaning is across the social landscape.

One of Matthews' arguments is that others' reactions to older women are significantly related to how well acquainted they are. In interview after interview, the women refer to how old they feel in new surroundings, in interacting with strangers, or in public settings where "all everyone seems to see is an old woman." In contrast, the women say that, among friends and in familiar surroundings, others see the person behind physical appearances. For these older women, the ageing body is visible as a first set of clues to who they are in situations where nothing else is known about them.

In meeting someone for the first time or when they are out in public, the women have a distinct sense of being viewed as old. The mere appearance of their bodies suggests to others that they are, in fact, aged. Two respondents poignantly recount incidents that go to the heart of the matter. Passing a group of children on the way to the grocery story, one woman recounts:

I grinned at them because I like children, and one of them looked up and she said, "You're ugly, ugly, ugly." And I said, "Well, so are you." And one of them was going to hit me with a stick . . . I was surprised to death. I must have had a long face because I didn't feel very

good and it takes all of me to get there and all of me to get back. (p. 79)

Another woman reports the reactions she occasionally receives from other drivers, who figure that, as an old woman, she shouldn't be on the road.

There have been a few occasions with younger people. Well, when I say younger I don't mean in the middle twenties, I mean in the teens. I had the feeling they were saying, "The poor old soul," especially when I used to drive a car. They had the attitude, the look on their face, "What the devil are you doing in a car? You belong home in a rocking chair." (p. 79)

Not just young strangers use the ageing body as an initial set of identifiers. Older people themselves also use the body to assign identities to one another. The "newcomers" who had moved to the settings in which Matthews did her research, for example, were commonly viewed as old. In contrast, "residents" who had become familiar faces were known to others in more biographically specific terms, playing out roles not exclusive to being old. Their bodies were less visible as a result. Residents were likely to be referenced as, say, "John the successful lawyer's mother," or "the woman who has always been active in politics," or "the woman whose husband left her and for good reason" (p. 97). The ageing body, in other words, is what initially was on display for newcomers in these settings. It's all that was available to categorize them, according to Matthews.

The resident has a reputation; the newcomer is not so lucky. She arrives on the scene already old. Her move to the setting was probably precipitated by a negatively evaluated status passage. Recent retirement, either for herself or her husband, widowhood, or decreased physical capacity are the most likely explanations . . . The most salient characteristic of newcomers, then, is their oldness and their imputed, and often accepted, devalued status as no longer independent, financially, emotionally, or physically. (pp. 97–8)

At first blush, it would seem that the objective body is paramount in assigning identity in these circumstances. These old women, however, do not respond passively to others and their social situations. They actively manage their bodies' visibility by reducing the number of situations in which they are likely to encounter individuals unfamiliar to them. They avoid social worlds where their ageing bodies might be the only salient signs of their identities. In support of this, these women suppress other evidence of being old, such as not telling their age and cosmetically trying to appear younger than their years. These efforts work to control their bodies' intrusions into everyday life, with the lowered social status that implies. The aim is to reduce the salience and significance of their physical presence for designating who and what they are to others.

None of the women Matthews studied believed they were old, even while their bodies sometimes led others to view them that way. Indeed, as Matthews explains, "Each old person considers herself to be just an ordinary person and forgets whenever possible that she has the trappings of oldness. But when she must attend to the trappings, she explains that she is not what she seems" (p. 76). Some actually express surprise when they view themselves in a mirror, seeing striking evidence of what they could be were it not for the management of their social worlds. "I don't feel like I'm seventy-two. I'm surprised when I look in the mirror. I went down to get my hair cut the other day and I'm always surprised when I look down and see all that gray hair, because I don't feel gray-headed" (p. 76).

It is evident for these women that the ageing body is continuously unfinished business, not uniformly determined across social space. While there are times and places when their bodies give them away, so to speak, there are other times and places when and where this is not so. For these women, the ageing body's visibility is "occasioned." It is a complex, hyphenated reality, visible-sometimes but not at other times, visible-for-some, but not-visible-for-others. As Charles Horton Cooley (1964[1902]) pointed out a century ago, the self is like a reflection in a social looking glass. An actual physical mirror held up to one's face can make this abundantly obvious (see Furman, 1997). But, while they view themselves through social looking glasses, the women Matthews studied are not trapped in such mirrors. What is reflected are older persons in the process of actively presenting their ageing bodies, not simply responding to social reflections of them.

Self and Identity in Dementia

On some occasions, the "obvious" presence of ageing is denied. This is a significant feature of

perceptions of the ageing body by some caregivers of the elderly. My fieldwork on the everyday experience of caring for Alzheimer's disease (AD) sufferers illustrates this point (Gubrium 1986, 1992). The following examples, drawn from interviews with caregivers and participant observation in caregiver support groups, show that, even for so-called "vegetables," selfhood can be preserved when bodily evidence suggests that there is virtually nothing left of the person behind the disease.

While the term "vegetable" is repugnant, it is nonetheless a common way of referring to those whose cognitive impairment has progressed to the point where existence consists of vegetative bodies without selves. Because such individuals appear to just breathe, eat, and eliminate, and barely respond to external stimuli, they are sometimes said to be "empty shells," the barren result of a "disease that dims bright minds." Of course, not all AD sufferers become vegetative and, indeed, some may appear surprisingly fit despite their impairments. Still, for some sufferers who become vegetative – who not only have failed minds, but whose postures in some cases have regressed to near-fetal positions – a "hidden" self or mind can be socially preserved against ageing and death through the interpretive efforts of caregivers and significant others.

With remarkable resolve, some of the AD caregivers in my study actively worked to sustain a semblance of self in an otherwise vegetative loved one. They accomplished this through a combination of existential doubt about the death of the self, belief in the sufferer's personhood, and selective attention to what they took to be bodily signs of continued presence in life. Such caregivers created social worlds sustained by their "self preserving" efforts, evident in discussions about the persistent existence of minds under the circumstances.

A conversation between two support group participants, Jack, a sufferer's spouse, and Sara, another caregiver, is instructive. In the following heart-wrenching exchange, note how Sara pointedly questions caregiver Jack's ruminations about his wife's "living death," casting existential doubt on her absence of self. When Jack wonders what to think about his wife's very demented condition, Sara raises the distinct possibility that a mind really exists behind what the body hides. Even AD's infamous neurological markers – amyloid plaques and neurofibrillary tangles – are challenged as evidence of the dementia and loss of the personhood within.

Jack: That's why I'm looking for a nursing home for her. I loved her dearly but she's just not Mary anymore. No matter how hard I try, I can't get myself to believe that she's there anymore. I know how that can keep you going, but there comes a point where all the evidence points the other way. Even at those times (which is not very often) when she's momentarily lucid, I just know that's not her speaking to me but some knee-jerk reaction. You just can't let that sort of thing get your hopes up because then you won't be able to make the kind of decision that's best for everyone all around, you know what I mean?

Sara: Well, I know what you've gone through, and I admire your courage, Jack. But you can't be too sure. How do you *really* know that what Mary says at times is not one of those few times she's been able to really reach out to you? You don't *really* know for sure, do you? You don't really know if those little plaques and tangles are in there, do you? I hate to make it hard on you, Jack, but I face the same thing day in and day out with Richard [her husband]. Can I ever finally close him out of my life and say, "Well, it's done. It's over. He's gone"? How do I really know that the poor man isn't hidden somewhere, behind all that confusion, trying to reach out and say, "I love you, Sara"? [She weeps]

Certain evidence – words spoken in putatively "lucid" moments – is viewed as a positive marker of self. At the same time, neurological signs that all is lost are dismissed – "You don't really know if those little plaques and tangles are in there" – as Sara defies physical evidence to sustain what she believes remains within.

In another group meeting, Sara casts direct aspersions on the significance of the ageing body for the existence of the self. Her response suggests that what is somatically evident or otherwise in place need not be existentially conclusive. In the process, she virtually tells Rita – a group participant whose husband is very demented – that the body is only a visible indicator of a mind if one treats it as such, placing the

responsibility for being minded on those who have a choice in preserving it.

Rita: I just don't know what to think or feel. It's like he's not even there anymore, and it distresses me something awful. He doesn't know me. He thinks I'm a strange woman in the house. He shouts and tries to slap me away from him. It's not like him at all. Most of the time he makes sounds but they sound more like an animal than a person. Do you think he has a mind left? I wish I could just get in there into his head and see what's going on. Sometimes I get so upset that I just pound on him and yell at him to come out to me. Am I being stupid? I feel that if I don't do something quick to get at him that he'll be taken away from me altogether.

Sara: We all have gone through it. I know the feeling. Like you just know in your heart of hearts that he's in there and that if *you* let go, that's it. So you keep on trying and trying and trying. You've got to keep the faith, that it's him and just work at him, 'cause if you don't . . . well, I'm afraid we've lost them. That's Alzheimer's. It's up to the ones who care because they can't do for themselves.

For readers who are clinically oriented, Sara's beliefs and statements might seem to be a form of psychological denial. But a clinical view is not the only way to interpret such exchanges. These conversations are also part of the mundane philosophical considerations of everyday life. At times, we all wonder about our selves and the selves of others. In the process, we make decisions and act upon what we convince ourselves is real or relevant in our own and others' experience. We continually make judgments about existence and the operating status of our minds, thoughts, and feelings. As George Herbert Mead (1934) instructed us, selves and minds arise out of, and are part of, talk, interaction, and particular life worlds. They are social objects, in effect, and, as such, can be separated from what in this case is the ageing body and its activities. As Sara would seem to argue, we are morally implicated in the continued existence of others' minds and selves: "if *you* let go, that's it." The specific social worlds in tow – one having given up on a self, the other sustaining it – construct the self and the body in antithetical ways, abrogating the uniformity of social life.

LESSONS LEARNED

What do this perspective and these illustrations teach us about ageing and old age? Conceptually, we learn that we can fruitfully study the complexity of the later years when we direct our eyes to the many workings of the social. Emphasis is placed on the concrete rather than on the abstract, featuring the varied ways ageing comes to the fore and recedes in practice. Old age is not always there for those concerned, even while chronological age and frailty are objectively in place. Whether it is the visibility of the ageing body or perceptions of mental lucidity, social worlds such as friendship circles and caregiving groups intervene to have their say. The lesson of this is to look for the ways circumstances articulate the social, and from there document the effects of society, status, roles, and their related identities in everyday life.

A second lesson is that particular methods of procedure favor the documentation of social worlds. Large-scale social surveys, while useful for describing epidemiological matters, are not very helpful in examining the local and particular. Instead, the methods of choice are qualitative interviewing and participant observation. Qualitative interviewing encourages respondents to report on varied facets of the social in everyday life, whose variegations can be captured from the subject positions prompted in the interview process (see Holstein and Gubrium, 1995). Participant observation is especially useful for locating the boundaries and organization of social worlds, for specifying the times and places when and where society, social structure, status, roles, and identities operate as they do. The strength of these methods is unparalleled in this regard, as the researcher seeks to document how the plurality of social worlds organizes the meaning of old age.

A third and final lesson is moral. The concept of social worlds opens to view the diverse ways that old age can be constructed. Avoiding homogenizing labels, it showcases the options for everyday life that can be assembled in the later years, alerting us as much to possibilities as to facts. This offers a landscape alive with differences and choices, indicating the many directions that ageing can take in concrete experience (Gubrium and Holstein, 2003).

FURTHER READING

Furman, F. K. (1997). *Facing the mirror*. New York: Routledge.

Gubrium, J. F., and J. A. Holstein, eds. (2003). *Ways of aging*. Malden, Mass.: Blackwell.

Holstein, J. A., and J. F. Gubrium, eds. (2003). *Inner lives and social worlds*. New York: Oxford University Press.

Matthews, S. (1979). *The social world of old women*. Beverly Hills, Calif.: Sage.

Rosenfeld, D. (2003). *The changing of the guard: lesbian and gay elders, identity, and social change*. Philadelphia: Temple University Press.

REFERENCES

Blumer, H. (1969[1930]). "Science without concepts." In H. Blumer, ed., *Symbolic interactionism*. Englewood Cliffs, N.J.: Prentice-Hall, pp. 153–70.

Cooley, C. H. (1964[1902]). *Human nature and the social order*. New York: Shocken Books.

Furman, F. K. (1997). *Facing the mirror*. New York: Routledge.

Gergen, M., and K. J. Gergen (2003). "Positive aging." In J. F. Gubrium and J. A. Holstein, eds., *Ways of aging*. Malden, Mass.: Blackwell, pp. 203–24.

Glaser, B. G., and A. L. Strauss (1965). *Awareness of dying*. Chicago: Aldine.

(1968). *Time for dying*. Chicago: Aldine.

Gubrium, J. F. (1986). *Oldtimers and Alzheimer's: the descriptive organization of senility*. Greenwich, Conn.: JAI Press.

(1992). "The social preservation of mind: the Alzheimer's disease experience," *Symbolic Interaction*, 9: 13–28.

Gubrium, J. F. and J. A. Holstein, eds. (2003). *Ways of aging*. Malden, Mass.: Blackwell.

Hazan, H. (1980). *The limbo people*. London: Routledge & Kegan Paul.

Holstein, J. A. and J. F. Gubrium (1995). *The active interview*. Thousand Oaks, Calif.: Sage.

eds. (2003). *Inner lives and social worlds*. New York: Oxford University Press.

Matthews, S. (1979). *The social world of old women*. Beverly Hills, Calif.: Sage.

Mead, G. H. (1934). *Mind, self and society*. Chicago: University of Chicago Press.

Sarbin, T. R. and J. I. Kitsuse, eds. (1994). *Constructing the social*. London: Sage.

Strauss, A. L. (1978). "A social world perspective." In N. K. Denzin, ed., *Studies in symbolic interaction*. Greenwich, Conn.: JAI Press, pp. 119–28.

(1997[1959]). *Mirrors and masks: the search for identity*. New Brunswick, N.J.: Transaction.

Unruh, D. R. (1983). *Invisible lives: social worlds of the aged*. Beverly Hills, Calif.: Sage.

Listening to the Past: Reminiscence and Oral History

JOANNA BORNAT

Reminiscence and oral history have, in the UK at least, shared common goals and in many respects have a shared heritage. Since the 1960s, many of those involved in the development of these two areas of activity have been similarly motivated to challenge orthodoxies, to reverse roles and to empower people living, actually and metaphorically, on the margins of society. There are also enduring differences which offer each an alternative methodological and interpretive arena and the possibility of rich and creative explorations of late life experience.

This chapter begins with a look at the differences between oral history and reminiscence and then goes on, with examples, to look at how the practice of each can inform the other.

DEFINING DIFFERENCE

Oral history in the UK and elsewhere draws on the disciplines of history and sociology. However, as Thompson argues, the origins of oral history lie in a particular understanding of what history is. His argument that 'All history depends ultimately upon its social purpose' (2000: 1) points to an instrumental role, for history and its making.

Frisch, writing in a US context, offers a way of pinpointing the particular social role of oral history in distinguishing between what he calls the two poles of 'more history' and 'anti-history' (Frisch, 1990: 187). What he means by the 'more history' approach is the contribution which oral history makes to revealing aspects of the past which are not available through more conventional documentary sources. By means of the interview, oral historians are able to access personal experience, eye-witness accounts and the memories of people whose perspectives might otherwise be ignored or neglected. In this way we are able to add information to the historical record. So, for example, histories of major industries are altered by accounts from the workshop floor, from women and migrant workers, in relation to unemployment or struggles over hours and wages (Friedlander, 1975; Messenger, 1980; Hareven, 1982). The history of health and welfare is extended beyond administrative and organizational structures to include accounts from recipients of welfare, experiences of disability, histories of illness and of the development of professional expertise (Bornat et al., 2000).

The 'anti-history' approach, Frisch argues, takes a stronger line, challenging orthodoxy by identifying the unique quality of the oral history process. Talking about the past with those who participated in it, even created it, is a means of by-passing the control of academic scholarship, and being able to 'touch the "real" history . . . by communicating with it directly' (Frisch, 1990: 187).

Evidence from around the world indicates how the distinction which Frisch draws continues to be understood and used in a variety of ways. So, for example, research which seeks to amplify voices which might otherwise not be heard motivates not only those projects located amongst people without a literary tradition, such as the San people of Botswana (Bennett, 1999a, 1999b), but also nationally funded projects in countries where at an official level oral history methods are a new and sometimes politically innovative undertaking, as, for example, recent developments in China and Japan (Xiangyin, 2001; Yamamoto, 2003).

Where oral history tends to focus on the content of memory, what is perhaps more characteristic of reminiscence and life review is attention given to process and outcomes for participants. Groups of older people, with or without leaders, whose main concern is the retrieval of past experience and its recording and preservation can be said to be taking part in oral history. When those same group members share and communicate memories with a view to understanding each other or a shared situation, or with the aim of bringing about change in their current lives, they are involved in reminiscence. In the same way, the interviewer who focuses on a life history with a view to finding out about the past and an individual's life in that past, is working as an oral historian. The interviewer who encourages reflection on those same experiences, but with a view to encouraging greater self-awareness and personal reflection by that older person, is engaging in reminiscence and life review.

What care workers identify as reminiscence comes in a wide variety of forms. In a study of reminiscence-based activities in nursing and residential homes in England, five types have been identified, ranging from the formally planned to the informal impromptu (Bornat and Chamberlayne, 1999: 284–6). Each type is likely to have a range of possible outcomes including word-of-mouth accounts, life story books, discussions, displays, websites, outings, contributions to individual care plans, themed days, intergenerational contacts, inputs to the educational curricula of local schools and colleges, and, of course, drama. For all parties, older people and those who facilitate the process, the impact of reminiscence is an issue for evaluation and comment.

Those who work with children and young people facing troubling issues of identity and attachment have also seized on the way in which remembering may be used supportively and therapeutically. Denis and Makiwane talk about making 'memory boxes' for South African children who have lost a parent to HIV/AIDS. By sharing memories of a deceased or sick person, recording these and storing them in a box, families are helped to talk about difficult issues and children are helped to cope with loss (2003). In India, an oral history approach has been used to understand the history of leprosy and how treat-

ment policies were shaped, and continue to be influenced, by the colonial era (Kakar, 1999).

In what was to prove a seminal paper, Robert Butler argued that reminiscence and life review are a normal and essential part of ageing (Butler, 1963). He was contesting the then more prevalent view that these activities were symptoms of pathological and progressive cognitive deterioration. What is important about his contribution is that he legitimized an intervention which nurses and care workers had previously felt was natural and appropriate, but which they had been discouraged from promoting. Dobrof, for example, tells the story of her own epiphany (Dobrof, 1984), and there are others who had similar experiences once they felt free to encourage older people to talk about what they were expert in, their own life stories. Indeed, such moments of realization still occur as successive generations of care workers make their own discoveries. Rather like the powerful effect of 'anti-history', the voices of older people, talking about their childhoods, work and life experiences, have a way of cutting through professional practice, revealing the person, the individual behind the case notes, the condition or the diagnosis (Gibson, 2004; Atkinson, 1997; Bruce et al., 1999; Bornat, 2004)[1].

How oral history and reminiscence inform one another or take advantage of each other's practice will be illustrated in the next two sections.

REMINISCENCE IN ORAL HISTORY

An example from research into family change is used here to show how a reminiscence and life review perspective can be helpful in the interpretation of oral history interviews. Recent research into family change, using oral history interviews with people of all ages, focused on the impact of family break-up and reconstitution – through divorce, death, separation and remarriage/cohabitation – on the lives of older people (Bornat et al., 1999).

The aim was to hear how people talk and make sense of family change. The use of an oral history perspective enabled the people interviewed

---

[1] The enduring popularity of the poem 'Kate' or 'Crabbit Old Woman' with its balladic life story and mythic origin is indicative of the power of the voice of personal experience to stimulate a mix of emotions (Bornat and Gibson, 2004).

to reflect on their own lives over time and it was clear, as the interviews accumulated, that for many this was a first opportunity to make sense of past experience. Sixty people from families in two areas of one medium-sized English town were interviewed. Looking at the transcripts it soon became clear that people were searching for the right words and language to explain family change and decision-making relating to partnering. The results are narratives which include moral, as much as social and political, explanations for behaviour and which showed how action recorded in larger data sets is explained and justified at an interpersonal level.

For example, Wilma Waldon (a pseudonym) spoke about her experience of divorce in three generations of her family, her own, her daughter's and her granddaughter's. Her account of changing relationships between men and women in marriage was illuminating but framed within a broader narrative which depicted the children from her two marriages as a united group of caring and supportive people. In reflecting on her life, divorces appeared simply as short-term hiatuses, difficult episodes but without long-lasting effects.

This might be considered in different ways. She could be concealing more difficult and traumatic experiences. However, there is another possible structuring to her account. Her own divorce was acrimonious, and the separation which preceded it meant that she was left with three young children and the need to earn a living for them all during the Second World War. Her daughter's divorce followed years of physical abuse, whilst her granddaughter, 'married too young' and 'they no sooner married than they're divorced sort of thing'. Her account mirrors accurately the social history of family change in the UK. As she explains:

Years ago, where the woman was, she hadn't got money and that, to have a divorce. And they were the underdogs, weren't they? Because, I mean, not a lot of them went out to work in them days, did they? Not the women. There was a time when bringing up big families all the while. And I think that they, you know, well – they used to get good hidings and everything else. Well, they were round this way, they was awful. The men just go drinking and coming home, and they'll beat the women up and that. It just used to be awful. And, I mean, if anyone done that, you'll up and leave them

straight away, wouldn't you? Say to the children, 'Come on, put your coat on, we're going', you know. But there you are. That's how things were in them days.

Awareness of the historical and social context validates her account. Attitudes towards divorce and separation have changed dramatically since the mid twentieth century in the UK and her account of these experiences matches well with what is known from demography and the sociology of the family. But, as well as that, what we hear from her interview is someone who feels that she can give a good account of herself, her decisions and the actions of her children. An aim of the research was to hear how people explain events in their lives, how they reflect on changing attitudes towards divorce and separation, but there were no graphic accounts of tensions, problems and difficulties in this account.

Familiarity with an alternative possible explanation for her rather relaxed and composed account of family change over the last sixty years comes from reminiscence and life review research. Coleman's identification of the four characteristics of 'a successful life story' – 'coherence, assimilation, structure and truth value' (Coleman, 1999: 135) – are apparent in her account. Awareness of the psychological tasks facing older people opens the dialogue generated by oral history to an analysis which allows for age-related factors, as well as those which relate to gender and sociohistorical structural factors. Indeed Coleman's analysis fits Wilma Waldon rather well, as he also identifies ways in which older women often report having more control over their lives as they acquire a sense of greater financial and personal freedom.

An account such as Wilma Waldon's demonstrates how, within one interview, a narrator draws on present and past to explain experiences of family change within the private sphere, while referring out to more public, structural, determinants of opportunity for working-class women over three generations. The richness of such oral testimony notwithstanding, there are still historians, and more quantitatively disposed social scientists, who question the reliability and validity of memory as a source of evidence. Thompson in his third edition of *The voice of the past*, approaching 30 years on, still feels the need to rise to this debate. His response to critics is to point out the blurring of boundaries between different approaches, arguing that historians as far back as Boswell have typically relied on memory as a source and demonstrating that informed approaches to sampling and to the use of a variety of corroborating sources can help to contextualize testimony (Thompson, 2000; see also, for a useful discussion of these issues, Roberts, 2002: ch. 6).

Plummer discusses 'Six ways to tell a "true story"?' (2001: 240), ranging from the positivist urge to cross-check to what he describes as the *'pragmatic function'*, judging an account in terms of its value to a particular audience, or more generally in relation 'to society, to history' (p. 242).

ORAL HISTORY IN REMINISCENCE

Within oral history circles, a burning issue persists. This is the question of how a method whose purpose is to *give voice* to people out of the mainstream of history can ensure that its practice matches this ideal. Is it possible to work in partnership so that the narrators are not alienated from their own story by the analytical skills of the researcher? Early on in oral history little attention was paid to this issue. For some researchers, their own purpose and political stance seemed good enough as a guarantee of shared objectives. People's willingness to be interviewed, to make their story available to others, setting records straight, providing a challenge to the status quo, meant that issues of partnership felt irrelevant. And it is still the case that to hand back a transcript so that someone might alter or change their words is still more a feature of archive work than of research or publication. Oral history's origins within the discipline of sociology pull it in the direction of academic research and the norms of academic life tend not to recognize partnership with subjects as a necessary part of the research process.

Models of partnership in oral history projects range from handing back transcripts for checking to full-blown collaboration. In some cases, collaboration stems from inequality. So, for example, colleagues at the Open University, working with people with learning disability in the production of oral histories, have developed collaborative strategies which enable people without written communication skills to produce narrative accounts

(Atkinson, 1997; Walmsley and Atkinson, 2000; Qualidata, 2003). This more 'bottom-up' model of production has also become commonly practised in community projects, where the idea of 'shared authority' (Frisch, 1990) has been embodied within oral history practice.

Sharing the process of production has been a focus for oral history work in development contexts. For example, in Lesotho, Olivia Bennett of the Panos Institute worked with members of communities who lost their homes following resettlement during the construction of a reservoir (Bennett, 1999), and, in Nicaragua, Padmini Broomfield and Cynara Davies were funded by the University of the Caribbean Coast to develop discussion-based and interactive approaches with local people, to document local heritage through oral history interviews (Broomfield and Davies, 1999).

Feminist oral historians had earlier faced the dilemma of being both subject and researcher, noting the uncomfortable reality that the interview may be both a positive and a negative force, with subsequent analysis driving a wedge between those who should have been experiencing solidarity (Gluck and Patai, 1991; see also Armitage *et al.*, 2002).

The question of who exercises interpretive powers is at the nub of this ethical dilemma. Borland, whose grandmother challenged the feminist interpretation she drew from her interview, concludes: 'we might open up the exchange of ideas so that we do not simply gather data on others to fit into our own paradigms once we are safely ensconced in our university libraries ready to do interpretation' (Borland, 1991: 73). Ethical issues raised by oral historians concerning partnership in the process have also exercised reminiscence workers. Concern over the content of sessions, and the question of the extent to which it is representative and therefore equally inclusive of people from different backgrounds persists (Harris and Hopkins, 1994). Partnership is perhaps most easily guaranteed and sustained where older people are able to take part in the shaping of the process with a view to agreed outcomes.

To what extent such approaches are socially, politically and culturally inclusive is debatable and, indeed, awareness of diversity amongst groups of older reminiscers is an issue which reminiscence research has tended to neglect up to now. In this respect it is interesting to reflect on the comments of an older African Caribbean man:

People cannot reminisce here in Britain which is very important . . . by the time I reach 60 I will revert back to talk about family history and importance of childhood in the Caribbean, you cannot have those reminiscences in old people's home in this country. The people in these homes never talk to you. People are not going to listen to you. (Plaza, 1996: 16)

An oral history of the Polish community in the UK encountered a similar silencing, where Michelle Winslow encountered a number of depressed older people whose fluency in English was diminishing with few opportunities to express their feelings about loss and uprootedness as they dealt with 'a traumatic past and . . . present difficulties' (Winslow, 1999: 63).

An informed awareness of the past, through oral history and a developed sense of the content of a recognized history, should be an essential part of reminiscence activities. While this can, at a basic level, contribute to reminiscence which is sensitively and accurately supported through historically and contextually appropriate stimuli, more significantly such awareness can also help to point up and identify differences and continuing discrimination and oppression in late life.

ORAL HISTORY AND REMINISCENCE – SHARED CONCERNS

How people's words are used and the extent to which they are able to determine their further use is an issue which has been subjected to much debate within oral history. The idea of 'shared authority' in relation to community-based projects and publications has already been mentioned (Frisch, 1990). This type of approach is more likely to be followed where questions of witness and authenticity are highly politicized, as, for example, in contests over land rights (Goodall, 1994) and refugees (Westerman, 1998). Amongst archivists, academics, museum staff, radio and television researchers, community workers and educationalists, different strategies tend to be adopted and much critical attention has been given to ethical practice. Signing off ownership or imposing restrictions as to who may have access to tapes and transcripts and when;

adopting a protocol for sharing the production process; abiding by such basic rules as naming interviewees as authors or editors; all these are approaches which have been taken up. However, practice is variable and standards can often leave much to be desired (see www.oralhistory.org.uk for a recommended approach).

Within reminiscence and life review, appropriation and control are equally possible, despite the fact that the role of the facilitator is likely to be more personal, ongoing and immediate. Indeed the very informality of some reminiscence exchanges opens up possibilities of misrepresentation, mishandling or inaccurate reporting of personal accounts and the details of private disclosures. Here again, existing protocols relating to client and service user privacy, disclosure and confidentiality should guard against bad practice. However, given the vulnerability and high dependency of many of those involved in reminiscence activities, there is a certain element of risk involved, particularly where facilitators or group leaders have not had access to basic training in communication skills.

For example, questioning care staff about their experiences of reminiscence work in residential and nursing settings, two separate examples were obtained where it seemed reminiscence and individual past histories were being used inappropriately to explain behaviour (Bornat and Chamberlayne, 1999). Care staff explained that a man disliked having cot sides on his bed due to his Second World War experiences, and that a woman had difficulties about bathing because of her personal history. While not wanting to deny that these people had endured genuinely traumatic and abusive experiences, evoking uncontrollable emotions in their recall, there is a possibility that, by ascribing these episodes solely to past trauma, present abusive or insensitive care practices and interpersonal actions are ignored. So, for example, it might be proper to ask if anyone, whether or not they had been a prisoner of war, should be placed in a cot bed against their wishes, and to recognize that, if someone is expressing fears about bathing, then this might be an outcome of insensitive handling of intimate care. Incidents such as these not only point to a need for care workers and those interacting with older people to have an informed understanding of the history of the last eight or so decades, they also suggest a need to locate reminiscence within the present and to enable this process to highlight the quality of such interactions (Adams *et al.*, 1998).

CONCLUSION

This chapter began with a discussion of the differences between oral history and reminiscence and went on to consider examples of how each can profitably contribute to the other's area of activity. It ended with examples of shared concern, ways to achieve the accurate and acceptable representation of personal experience in situations where power inequalities may prevail. Oral history and reminiscence-based approaches to understanding how remembering contributes to knowledge of the past are both now recognized and accepted methods in research and practice settings. For each, the interconnectedness of past and present is a necessary dimension enhancing interpretation and contributing to more meaningful and helpful analyses of individual and social experience.

FURTHER READING

Bornat, J. (1994). *Reminiscence reviewed: perspectives, evaluations, achievements*. Buckingham: Open University Press.

Gibson, F. (2004). *The past in the present*. Baltimore: Health Professions Press.

Perks, R., and A. Thomson (1998). *The oral history reader*. London: Routledge.

Thompson, P. (2000). *The voice of the past*, 3rd edn. Oxford: Oxford University Press.

Webster, J. D., and B. K. Haight (2002). *Critical advances in reminiscence work: from theory to application*. New York: Springer.

REFERENCES

Adams, J., Bornat, J., and M. Prickett (1998). 'Discussing the present in stories about the past'. In A. Brechin, J. Katz, S. Peace and J. Walmsley, eds., *Care matters: concepts, practice and research*. London: Sage.

Armitage, S. H., Hart, P., and K. Weatherman, eds., *Women's oral history: the frontiers reader*. Lincoln and London: University of Nebraska Press.

Atkinson, D. (1997). *An auto/biographical approach to learning disability research*. Aldershot: Ashgate.

Bennett, O. (1999a). 'Botswana', *Oral History*, 27 (2): 22–3.

(1999b). 'Breaking the threads: the real cost of forced resettlement', *Oral History*, 27 (1): 38–46.

Borland, K. (1991). '"That's not what I said": interpretive conflict in oral narrative research'. In S. B. Gluck and D. Patai, eds., *Women's words: the feminist practice of oral history*. New York and London: Routledge, pp. 63–75.

Bornat, J. (1989). 'Oral history as a social movement: reminiscence and older people', *Oral History*, 17 (2): 16–24.

(2004). 'Finding "Kate": a poem which survives through constant discovery'. In J. Johnson, ed., *Writing old age*. London: Centre for Policy on Ageing.

Bornat, J. and P. Chamberlayne (1999). 'Reminiscence in care Settings: implications for training', *Adult Education*, 14 (3): 277–95.

Bornat, J., Dimmock, B., Jones, D., and S. Peace (1999). 'The impact of family change on older people: the case of stepfamilies'. In S., McRae ed., *Changing Britain: families and households in the 1990s*. Oxford: Oxford University Press, pp. 248–62.

Bornat, J., Perks, R., Thompson, P., and J. Walmsley (2000). *Oral history: health and welfare*. London: Routledge.

Broomfield, P., and C. Davies (1999). 'Costeño voices: oral history on Nicaragua's Caribbean coast', *Oral History*, 2003 (1): 85–94.

Bruce, E., Hodgson, S., and P. Schweitzer (1999). *Reminiscence with people with dementia: a handbook for carers*. London: Age Exchange.

Butler, R. (1963). 'The life review: an interpretation of reminiscence in the aged', *Psychiatry*, 26: 65–76.

Coleman, P. G. (1999). 'Creating a life story: the task of reconciliation', *Gerontologist*, 39 (2): 133–9.

Denis, P. and N. Makiwane (2003). 'Stories of love, pain and courage: AIDS orphans and memory boxes', *Oral History*, 31 (2): 66–74.

Dobrof, M. (1984). 'Introduction: a time for reclaiming the past', *Journal of Gerontological Social Work*, 7 (1/2): xvii–xviii.

Friedlander, P. (1975). *The emergence of a UAW local, 1936–1939: a study in class and culture*. Pittsburgh: University of Pittsburgh Press.

Frisch, M. (1990). *A shared authority: essays on the craft and meaning of oral and public history*. Albany, N.Y.: State University of New York Press.

Gibson, F. (1993). 'What can reminiscence contribute to people with dementia?' In J. Bornat, ed., *Reminiscence reviewed: perspectives, evaluations, achievements*. Buckingham: Open University Press, pp. 46–60.

Gluck, S. B., and D. Patai (1991). *Women's words: the feminist practice of oral history*. New York and London: Routledge.

Goodall, H. (1994). 'Colonialism and catastrophe: contested memories of nuclear testing and measles epidemics at Ernabella'. In K. Darian-Smith and P. Hamilton, eds., *Memory and history in twentieth century Australia*. Melbourne: Oxford University Press.

Hareven, T. (1982). *Family time and industrial time: the relationship between the family and work in a New England industrial community*. Cambridge: Cambridge University Press.

Harris, J., and T. Hopkins (1994). 'Beyond anti-ageism: reminiscence groups and the development of anti-discriminatory social work education'. In J. Bornat, ed., *Reminiscence reviewed: perspectives, evaluations, achievements*. Buckingham: Open University Press, pp. 75–83.

Kakar, S. (1999). 'Leprosy in India: the intervention of oral history'. In R. Perks and A. Thomson, eds., *The oral history reader*. London: Routledge, pp 258–68.

Messenger, B. (1980). *Picking up the linen threads: a study in industrial folklore*. Belfast: Blackstaffe.

Plaza, D. (1996). 'Family structure and social change of Caribbeans in Britain: an exploratory study of elderly Caribbean males'. Paper prepared for the Caribbean Studies Association XXI Annual Conference.

Plummer, K. (2001). *Documents of Life 2*. London: Sage.

Qualidata (2003). *Legal and ethical issues in interviewing people with learning difficulties*, www.qualidata.essex.ac.uk/creatingdata/guidelineslearningdifficulty.asp, accessed 7 July 2003.

Roberts, B. (2002). *Biographical research*. Buckingham: Open University Press.

Thompson, P. (2000). *The voice of the past*, 3rd edn., Oxford: Oxford University Press.

Walmsley, J., and D. Atkinson (2000). 'Oral history and the history of learning disability'. In J. Bornat, R. Perks, P. Thompson and J. Walmsley, eds., *Oral history, health and welfare*. London: Routledge, pp. 180–202.

Westerman, W. (1998). 'Central American refugee testimonies and performed life histories in the Sanctuary movement'. In R. Perks and A. S. Thomson, eds., *The oral history reader*. London: Routledge, pp. 224–34.

Winslow, M. (1999). 'Polish migration to Britain: war, exile and mental health', *Oral History*, 29 (1): 57–64.

Xiangyin, Y. (2001). 'China', *Oral History*, 29 (1): 21–2.

Yamamoto, E. (2003). News item in *International Oral History Newsletter*, accessed at www.ioha.fgv.br.

CHAPTER 4.6

Elder Abuse in Developing Nations

LIA SUSANA DAICHMAN

The demographic revolution under way in many regions of the world has been remarkable. This is a global phenomenon and one of the striking achievements of the twentieth century. In 2002, almost 400 million people aged 60 and over lived in the developing world. By 2025, this will have increased to approximately 840 million representing 70% of all older people worldwide, due to better nutrition and hygiene, improved medical science and services and preventive medicine (UN, 2001).

The life expectancy of females in most countries will continue to exceed that of males; today 58% of older women live in the developing world and, by the year 2025, this percentage will increase to 75%.

Most of these elderly women are in not very good health and quite vulnerable as they are particularly poor and more likely than men to be on their own. Older women are also disproportionately represented among the very old and the most disadvantaged as they also constitute the 'inevitable' caregivers. They have more chance of being widowed, to have a poor education, and be in a poor nutritional state. Restricted access to health services and to the labour market in earlier life often leaves them with very few resources in their old age (Daichman, 2002).

For elders in the developing world, the risk of communicable diseases still exists and environmental hazards present yet another threat. At the same time they will be subject to the long-term, chronic and often disabling diseases associated with old age in the developed countries.

Structural inequalities in both the developed and developing countries, which have resulted in low wages, high unemployment, poor health services, gender discrimination and lack of educational opportunities, have contributed to the vulnerability of older people.

Ageing affects men and women in different ways, reflecting their roles throughout their lives, leading also to different experiences and needs into old age. Many of these differences are related to unequal power relationships. Gender-related issues vary between different societies and cultures. However, in many societies, women experience lower status than men, leading to a poorer diet, less access to education, risk of sexual violence and physical abuse, and exclusion from decision-making.

If success is measured in numbers, population ageing must be considered a remarkable achievement. Less successful may be the impact this demographic change will have on the social and healthcare structures in each country, and many are already struggling to deliver and meet the costs of even the basic components of health and welfare which are needed. The process of industrialization has eroded long-standing patterns of interdependence between the generations, producing material and emotional hardships for elders (Apt, 1997). This demographic reality is taking place in developing countries alongside increases in mobility, emigration, economic recession, and changing family characteristics.

Family and community networks that formerly provided support to their older generation are being undermined by social and economic changes. Traditional forms of family and community support are being weakened as a consequence of the global modernization process. As a result, demographic changes

323

could mean that more and more older people will be at risk.

NATURE AND SCOPE OF THE PROBLEM

Violence is a social phenomenon with far-reaching effects on personal and public health worldwide. It crosses legal, ethical and healthcare domains and society's major institutions, making it a complex issue with moral, social, cultural, political and personal ramifications. Elder abuse, the mistreatment of older people, though a manifestation of the timeless phenomenon of interpersonal violence, is now achieving due recognition.

Prevalence studies concerning the abuse of older persons have so far been restricted to a few developed nations. In developing countries, though, there is no systematic collection of statistics or prevalence studies, crime records, journalistic reports or social welfare records. Only small-scale studies provide evidence that abuse, neglect and financial exploitation of elders are widely prevalent.

A random sample study of older people's perceptions of elder abuse was carried out in South America, primarily in Buenos Aires DC (Aguas *et al.*, 1996) and then in three other Argentinean areas (Aguas *et al.*, 1997). A similar study was conducted in three Brazilian towns and results obtained at that time confirmed the emerging picture (Machado *et al.*, 1997). Almost half (45%) of the elders admitted that they had been mistreated. The highest incidence was of psychological abuse. Using a matching protocol, residents were sampled in four Chilean cities. The proportion of mistreatment ranged from 25% to 36%. Psychological abuse occurred in 31–64% of the four city samples; physical abuse, in 14–35% (Quiroga *et al.*, 2002; García, 2001).

The National Ministry of Health and the School of Medicine of the Universidad de Concepción, Chile, has a more comprehensive picture of prevalence and incidence now with the completion of an ongoing national survey of primary-care consultants in the public health system (Quiroga *et al.*, 2002).

To determine the level of knowledge and understanding of elder abuse in South Africa, focus groups were convened with older persons from three historically 'Black' townships. They cited acts of physical, verbal, financial and sexual abuse and neglect but, in addition, they included loss of respect for elders, which they paired with neglect, accusations of witchcraft, consequences of being a witch, and systematic abuse. They also described 'the dehumanizing treatment given to older persons at health clinics and pension offices and the marginalization of elders by the government'. These lay definitions (as classified by the researchers) were the first attempt to elicit information directly from older persons in South Africa (Keikelame and Ferreira, 2000).

Accusations of witchcraft are in general directed at isolated older women, often connected with unexplained events in the locality and need to be considered in the broad context of elder abuse (WHO/INPEA, 2002b). It has been reported that an estimated 500 women accused of witchcraft are murdered every year in northern Tanzania, where the murders represent 40 per cent of all homicides. Many more are driven from their homes and communities. Research by HelpAge International cites social and economic problems including poverty, pressure on land, inadequate or inaccessible health services, and poor education as underlying causes. Unable to explain illnesses, crop failures or dried-up wells, the people look for a scapegoat.

Although men are sometimes accused of witchcraft, the situation of women and their low status in society has made them more vulnerable to these accusations. (Gorman and Peterson, 1999). In the Latin American region the present economic downturn, mainly in Argentina, Uruguay and Brazil, is resulting in a 'boomerang effect' whereby, paradoxically, adult children, squeezed by the rising cost of living and lack of chances, are moving back to their parents' houses with their own children.

Not only does this mean increased stress for older people and additional claims on their resources but also often results in them being more 'relegated'. This socioeconomical breakdown has created an unexpected and inadequate way of living within a family, which promotes conflict when facing the new intergenerational exchange. These new forced living arrangements have generated a reversal of roles between family members that were culturally defined, structured and programmed (WHO/INPEA, 2001a, 2001b).

Even in countries where the family has been the central institution and filial obligations have been strong, elders are being displaced as heads of households and deprived of their autonomy. As described in a Costa Rican study, this 'overprotection', or 'infantilization', has left the older person feeling depressed and demoralized (Gilliand and Picado, 2000).

THEORETICAL EXPLANATION

Interpersonal violence has, in the latter part of the twentieth century, been framed within age-specific compartments. Child and partner (mostly female) abuse were the first to emerge and both were seen as family violence issues. Eventually, the problem of elder abuse was revealed. The growing worldwide focus on the abuse of older people has sought to parallel the focus upon human rights, gender, equality and population ageing.

Approaching the subject from a variety of conceptual perspectives, researchers in the developed countries have viewed elder abuse as a problem of an overburdened caregiver (situational model), a dependent elder (exchange theory), a mentally disturbed abuser (intra-individual dynamics), or as learned behaviour (social learning theory) (Bennett et al., 1997). Others have used the imbalance of power within relationships (feminist theory) and the marginalization of elders (political economic theory) to explore this issue (Whittaker, 1997). Early on, elder-abuse researchers realized that a single theory could not accommodate such a complex, multifaceted phenomenon. For child abuse, and more recently domestic violence, a similar realization has led to the adoption of the ecological model as a means of explaining interactions across systems.

Most recently, the lack of fit between the organism and the environment, ecological theory (Schaumburg and Gans, 1999), has been used to explain why elder abuse occurs. In its initial formulation, the ecological model was conceived as a nested arrangement of four levels of environments. According to this conceptualization, violence results from individual, interpersonal, social-contextual and societal factors. This framework for elder abuse may be helpful not only in understanding the causes of the problem, but also in promoting interventions that address all levels of the environment.

RISK FACTORS

With so little reliable data to support the theories, the emphasis so far has been on empirical research, whilst practitioners have focused on risk factors, attributes or characteristics that increase the probability of victimization – even if these variables are not yet demonstrable as causal agents. While the developed countries have emphasized individual and family attributes as predictors of elder mistreatment, the developing nations have given more weight to societal and cultural factors such as the inheritance systems, land rights that affect the political economy of relationships, the social construction of gender that places older women at risk, rural–urban migration, and a loss of tradition ritual and arbitration roles of elders within the family through the modernization process (Daichman et al., 2002).

DEFINITIONS

Attempts to define elder abuse and neglect adequately have been fraught with difficulty, and for a long time there has not been any agreement as to a standardized definition in either Europe or North America. The principal difficulty seems to revolve around what should be included in, or excluded from, the definition of elder abuse and neglect. Despite these difficulties, a number of definitions of elder abuse have emerged.

The UK's Action on Elder Abuse, a voluntary organization, developed a definition, following consultation with its membership, which the International Network for the Prevention of Elder Abuse (INPEA)[1] has subsequently adopted. The agreed version is: 'Elder abuse is a single or repeated act or lack of appropriate action occurring within any relationship where there is an expectation of trust, which causes harm or distress to an older person' (Action

---

[1] International Network for the Prevention of Elder Abuse (INPEA), www.inpea.net. Aims: to increase society's ability to recognize and respond to the mistreatment of older people. The Network's objectives are to increase public awareness of elder abuse; promote education and training of professionals in identifying, treating and preventing elder abuse; support advocacy on behalf of abused and neglected elders; and stimulate research into the causes, consequences, treatments and prevention of elder abuse and neglect.

on Elder Abuse, 1995; INPEA, 1997). What can be seen in the above definition are notions concerning the frequency of abuse (single or repeated act); that abuse (or neglect) might consist of a lack of necessary action (omission as well as commission); that there is some relationship between the parties consisting of at least an expectation of trust; and that the action causes some harm or distress to the elder.

This kind of behaviour can be intentional or unintentional and of one or more types: physical, psychological (emotional), financial, sexual and neglectful. Whether it is labeled abusive, neglectful or exploitative may depend on its frequency, duration, intensity, severity and consequences. Encompassed within the definition is the importance of the elder's perception of the relationship, also the action (or lack of action) and whether this causes the older person distress or harm. Questions have been raised about the usefulness of statutory and professional definitions, since the older person's perception of abuse and the cultural context may be the salient factors in identification and intervention.

The mistreatment of older people is no longer considered 'a new issue' in the developing countries. However, the concept of elder abuse as such is only now gaining recognition, markedly influenced by the rapidity of socioeconomic change, weakening of the extended family, rising elderly populations and growing concern for human rights, equality and justice. Although there is not yet systematic data collection on abuse, prevalence surveys in the developing world, journalistic and crime reports, social welfare records and small-scale studies contain evidence that abuse, neglect and financial exploitation are occurring.

Definitions require a cultural context, and other issues need to be included within the total framework. For example, in some traditional societies older widows are subject to abandonment and 'property grabbing'. Mourning rites of passage for widows in most of Africa and some areas of South Asia can include cruel practices, such as sexual violence, forced marriages and evacuation from their homes.

The WHO/INPEA (2001a, 2001b) ongoing study on 'A Global Response to Elder Abuse', recently carried out in five developing countries (Argentina, Brazil, Kenya, Lebanon and India) as well as Sweden, Canada and Austria, which is now in its third phase, was presented and launched as a landmark report, *Missing Voices*, at the Valencia Forum and the NGO Forum on Ageing in Madrid, May 2002 (WHO/INPEA, 2002b).

An exploratory attempt was made to examine a sample population of six elders' focus groups and two focus groups of health professionals working with the elderly, and their perception of elder abuse, during the year 2001 in the already mentioned countries. The majority of elderly people that had been interviewed 'affirm that societal or as we also define it structural abuse' is the most frequent type of abuse, at least in most Latin American countries (WHO/INPEA, 2001a, 2001b).

The elders' focus groups which were part of the research identified other risk factors as:

- Being old
- Being ill
- Living alone
- Isolation
- Family history of mistreatment
- Lack of a social network
- Lack of information about available resources
- Poor contact with peers
- Intergenerational conflict

(WHO/INPEA, 2002b)

Some saw 'freedom deprivation' as worse than losing their personal belongings.

This was perceived as a 'psychological punishment'. Relatively independent elders found that a 'paternalistic approach' by their own children may have the effect at times of being a sort of disqualification of their own capacities. Adult children's overprotective behaviours might be resented, especially regarding relevant and sometimes vital information, withheld under the excuse that they didn't want to create anxiety or wanted to avoid causing their parent worry and anguish (WHO/INPEA, 2001a).

The final analysis of the major themes which arose in the different countries revealed remarkable similarities and indeed were virtually universal across the participating nations, with older people perceiving abuse under three broad headings:

- Neglect – isolation, abandonment and social exclusion.
- Violation – of human, legal and medical rights.

- Deprivation – of choices, decisions, status, finances and RESPECT.

(WHO/INPEA, 2002b)

THE EFFECTS AND CONSEQUENCES OF ELDER ABUSE

Elder abuse is a violation of Human Rights and a significant cause of injury, illness, loss of productivity, isolation and despair. (WHO/INPEA 2002a)

Clinical and case-study data from some developed and developing countries have documented the severe emotional distress experienced by older persons as a result of mistreatment, but empirical evidence is often lacking. Several studies have reported a higher proportion of older victims with depression / psychological distress in an abuse sample than in a non-abuse sample. Since these were cross-sectional in design, there is no way of knowing whether the condition was an antecedent or a consequence of the abuse. Other suggested symptomatology includes feelings of learned helplessness, alienation, guilt, shame, fear, anxiety, denial and post-traumatic stress disorder (PTSD); research on these conditions still remains to be done (Wolf et al., 2003). Emotional effects, along with health problems, were also cited by elders' focus groups in developing countries (WHO/INPEA, 2001a, 2001b) and in Chile and by the South African focus-group participants. One member called these 'illnesses of the heart.'

In a seminal study in the United States, Lachs and colleagues (1998) combined data from an annual health survey of 2,812 elders with reports of elder abuse and neglect made to the local adult-abuse agency over a nine-year period. When they compared the mortality rates of the non-abused and the abused, they found that, by the thirteenth year following the study's initiation, 40 per cent of the non-reported (i.e., non-abused, non-neglected) group were still alive and only 9 per cent of the physically abused or neglected elders. After controlling for all the possible factors that might affect mortality (e.g., age, gender, income, functional status, cognitive status, diagnosis, social supports, etc.) and finding no significant relationships, the researchers speculated that mistreatment causes extreme interpersonal stress that may confer an additional death risk.

INSTITUTIONAL ABUSE

Although the emphasis in the past quarter of a century has been on interpersonal abuse within the family setting, ethnographic studies, media exposés, licence reports and anecdotal information since the 1960s have consistently confirmed the existence of abuse, neglect and exploitation in nursing and residential-care homes. Unfortunately, elder mistreatment has been identified in residential care and institutional facilities in almost all countries in which they are used. About 4% to 7% of elders in developed nations reside in long term care facilities. Older persons in developing countries such as Africa can be found in long-stay hospital wards and homes for the destitute and disabled.

The current rate for nursing-home utilization in South Africa is about 5%. In the Latin-American regions, 1–4% of the older population is in institutional settings, which are no longer viewed as unacceptable places, as they were before, but are now being seen as a possible alternative and a necessity by some elders and their families. The government-sponsored 'asilos' in Latin America, originally large institutions resembling English workhouses, have been converted, refurbished and provided with professional staff representing many disciplines. Other smaller homes are sponsored by religious and immigrant organizations or just run as private nursing homes. The social, economic and cultural changes mean families will be less able to provide care for frail elders, thus promoting an increase in residential care. Abusive and neglectful behaviour towards elders in institutions has been attributed to the marginal place assigned to elders in society (structural factors), the lack of properly trained staff, inadequate facilities and management expertise (environmental), and staff who are ill-suited by temperament or history to be caregivers to dependent elders (individual) (Clough, 1999).

In the developing world, institutional abuse is said to be perpetuated by staff through unquestioning regimentation (in the name of discipline or imposed protective care) and exploitation of the elder's dependence, exacerbated by the lack of professionally trained management. Despite the amount of research and investigation that has centred on institutional facilities, little is known about the incidence of abuse. In interviews with a sample of nursing-home personnel from one state in the United States, 36% of the staff reported having seen at least one incident of physical abuse in the preceding year by other staff members, and 10% having committed at least one act of physical abuse themselves. A total of 81% of the sample had observed at least one incident of psychological abuse against a resident in the preceding year, and 40% admitted to having committed such an act themselves (Pillemer and Moore, 1989). Staff-to-resident abuse is most prevalent, but mistreatment can also occur at the hands of visiting family members and other residents. Reports from Sweden, Israel, South Africa and Brazil provide clear evidence that mistreatment in long-term-care institutions, whether narrowly or broadly defined, is a worldwide reality.

PREVENTION

The prevention of mistreatment and neglect of vulnerable adults and their carers might be achieved by taking the context and the circumstances in which abuse occurs, by eliminating the causes of abuse, and by providing a properly managed and monitored environment for care and adequate support for carers and care workers. Much more attention must be given to primary prevention beginning with a commitment to help bring about a world in which older persons are allowed to live out their lives in dignity with adequate food, shelter, healthcare, and opportunities for self-fulfilment. For some developing countries that are facing increasing impoverishment, the challenge is enormous. Perhaps the most insidious form of abuse against elders, however, lies in the negative attitudes that prevail about older persons and the ageing process, whether expressed as myths, stereotypes, intergenerational conflict or the glorification of youth. As long as older people are devalued and marginalized by society, they risk being subjected to discrimination by others and robbed of their personhood and self-esteem.

WHO's Recommended Prevention Measures are:

- To inform and educate elderly people in good time about their rights and to let them know about easy ways to access services and adequate places in case of need.
- To provide information about other relevant available possibilities.

- Information should not be denied to elders, so they can have the possibility of making their own personal choices.
- Shared decision-making is also highly valuable for an old person and very often underestimated even by significant others.
- To provide learning about remaining capacities but at the same time help them 'to be able to come to terms that they might have to resign to some things in life; that they won't be able to get all they want, and that they should have to adapt themselves to new situations in the future'.
- To include information about ageing throughout the educational process, starting in primary school, into the university curricula.
- That more comprehensive knowledge about elder abuse should reach potential caregivers and other professionals working with old people, as well as the elderly and their families.
- To encourage the media to promote positive images of ageing and provide responsible coverage of the issues surrounding elder abuse and neglect.
- To create new agencies to deal specifically with elder abuse and promote collaboration between other agencies to prevent duplication and wasting of resources.

(WHO/INPEA, 2002b)

CONCLUSIONS AND RECOMMENDED STRATEGIES

The majority of elders nowadays are able to define elder abuse and describe abusive situations even if they might use different ways to present stories and facts to do so. Therefore, it is necessary to examine elder abuse and neglect from different perspectives in order to understand the meaning of these phenomena. It might also help to ensure that societal descriptions, norms and laws are sensitive to the various groups they are intended to serve. Equally important is to consider a gender perspective, as the complex social constructs related to it help identify the form of any particular community in which it occurs. Policies and programmes that do not address gender issues are bound to promote inequality.

In any society some population subgroups are particularly vulnerable to elder abuse, such as the very old, those with limited functional capacity, women and the poor (*Toronto Declaration on the Global Prevention of Elder Abuse*, 2002). Abuse of older people is a complex phenomenon, which in some instances will require complex prevention and management strategies. It cannot be addressed without at the same time ensuring that the basic needs of all people for food, shelter, economic security and access to healthcare are met and, additionally, for older persons, the opportunity provided to continue in roles that are not only beneficial to society but crucial to communities and family relationships.

Insensitivity to these issues could block culturally sensitive detection of elder mistreatment and could also inhibit help from being offered and accepted (Hudson *et al.*, 1998). Elder abuse prevention can only be successful in a culture that nurtures solidarity and rejects violence. Acts of violence occur in any socioeconomic class, any racial group, either sex, at any educational level and at any developmental state. The hidden nature of elder abuse allows some people not to acknowledge, see, hear or talk about behaviours which are absolutely contradictory to their value systems of compassion and support.

Today, concern about elder abuse has driven a worldwide effort to increase awareness of the problem and encourage development of treatment and prevention programmes. Raising awareness is a major factor in health and social education. It can be achieved by the publication of booklets and handbooks on elder abuse prevention, by regular publicity in the media, by developing appropriate curricula content at all educational levels and by directing information to older people. Education and training are key issues for the future, facilitating raised awareness across the community. Education is still considered the most effective method of preventing elder abuse. Information is knowledge, knowledge is power and power enables. The media can be a powerful means of promoting positive images of ageing and provide responsible coverage of the issues surrounding elder abuse and neglect. They can be influential in calling attention to the problem and in disseminating information about what to do and where to go in case of mistreatment (*INPEA Newsletter*, Feb. 2002).

Developing countries should try to design public policies to prevent abuse by meeting basic needs for food, shelter, economic security and healthcare; outlawing abusive customs; initiating community programmes to stimulate social interaction; creating other social networks to promote solidarity and social support; and working with older people to create 'self-help' programmes.

The development of creative strategies which reflect national and ethnic variations will help the development of effective community-based programmes. Legal frameworks are still inadequate, not taking personal abuse into account or just missing out any reference to it. Many cases of elder abuse, when identified, are not acted upon, as they should be, for lack of proper legal instruments to respond to them, negligence, or ignorance about how to use the instruments available. Confronting and reducing elder abuse requires a multisectoral and multidisciplinary approach. Responsible agencies need to collaborate and form partnerships ensuring less duplication and wastage of resources, enhanced trust and the promotion of reliable and adequate services.

One of the crucial commitments embodied in the Second Assembly of Ageing (2002) Plan of Action promotes recognition that the ageing process is not simply a plain issue of social security and welfare, but an overall development of new and creative economic policies. Article no. 5 from the Political Declaration reaffirms the need to spare no effort to promote democracy, the protection of human rights and the fundamental freedoms, without any violence, abuse and neglect. Living with dignity should be enhanced in all human beings, without negative stereotypes: 'Government representatives have committed themselves to eliminate all forms of discrimination, and to create enough support services to face and deal with elder abuse and mistreatment cases'; 'Governments are also being encouraged to develop and fund a National comprehensive strategy and Agenda to prevent, detect and intervene in elder abuse.'

The INPEA strongly recommend that the United Nations Commission of Human Rights should appoint a Special Rapporteur on the question of mistreatment of older people (Valencia Forum, 2002).

Recognizing the human rights of older people as human beings as stipulated in the international covenants of civil, political, economic, social and cultural rights, and acknowledging the diversity of the world population, there is an obligation for society to recognize the contribution and strengths of older people and address the violation of their rights, including abuse, in whatever settings they occur, so that the later years of life will be productive, enriching and free from mistreatment and discrimination. It is hoped that, in the developing world, elder abuse will also be recognized not only as a social but also as a health problem by both governments and society.

FURTHER READING

Bennett, G., Kingston, P., and B. Penhale (1997). *The dimensions of elder abuse*: *perspectives for the practitioner*. London: Macmillan Press.

Daichman, L. (2004). 'Elder abuse in the Latin American countries'. In *A survey on intercultural differences in the perceptions about future concerns, governmental functioning, and elder rights protection in five countries*. Tokyo: T. Tatara, ch. 5 (Published in Japanese).

Daichman, L., Wolf, R., and G. Bennett (2002). *Abuse of the elderly in the world: report on violence and health*. Geneva: WHO, ch. 5, pp. 125–45.

Gorman, M., and T. Peterson (1999). *Violence against older people and its health consequences: experience from Africa and Asia*. London: HelpAge International.

REFERENCES

Action on Elder Abuse (1995). 'Action on Elder Abuse's definition of elder abuse' (London), *Bulletin*, May/June.

Aguas, S., Lew, N., Guido, P., and M. Bertone (1996). 'Elders' perceptions of elder abuse', *Latin American Journal of Gerontology,* third year, 1: 2–7.

Aguas, S., Acanfora, M., Bertone, M., Lew, N., Guido, P., and L. Daichman (1997). 'Elders' perceptions of and to elder abuse'. Paper presented (Poster Session) at the International Congress of Gerontology, Adelaide, Australia.

Apt, N. (1997). *Ageing in Africa*. Report prepared for the World Health Organization, Geneva.

Bennett, G., Kingston, P., and B. Penhale (1997). *The dimensions of elder abuse: perspectives for the practitioner*. London: Macmillan Press.

Clark, F., and C. Till (2000). 'Taking gender into account in violence and abuse', *Age Ways: Practical Issues in Ageing and Development*, 59: 13–14.

Clough, R. (1999). 'Scandalous care: interpreting public enquiry reports of scandals in residential care'. In F. Glendenning and P. Kingston, eds., *Elder abuse and neglect in residential settings*. Binghamton, N.Y.: Haworth Press, pp. 13–27.

Daichman, L. (2002). 'Elder abuse in the Latin American countries'. In T. Tatara, ed., 'A survey on intercultural differences in the perceptions about future concerns, governmental functioning, and elder rights protection in five countries' (unpublished). Tokyo.

Daichman, L., Wolf, R., and G. Bennett (2002). *Abuse of the elderly in the world: report on violence and health*. Geneva: WHO, ch. 5, pp. 125–45.

García, A. N. (2001). 'Urban elders' perceptions of elder abuse in Chillan and Ñuble'. In *Cuadernos from the International Congress of Elder Mistreatment*. Chillan, Chile, University of Bio-Bio (Spanish).

Gilliand, N., and L. Picado (2000). 'Elder abuse in Costa Rica', *Journal of Elder Abuse & Neglect*, 12: 73–87.

Gorman, M., and T. Peterson (1999). *Violence against older people and its health consequences: experience from Africa and Asia*. London: HelpAge International.

Hudson, M., *et al.* (1998). 'Elder abuse: two Native American views', *Gerontologist*, 38 (5): 538–48.

INPEA Newsletter (2002). 9 (February) – www.inpea.net.

Keikelame, J., and M. Ferreira (2000 (March)). *Mpathekombi, ya Bantu abadala: Elder abuse in black townships on The Cape Flats*. HSRC/UCT Center for Gerontology.

Lachs, M. S., Williams, E., O'Brien, S., Hurst, L., Pillemer, K., and M. Charlson (1998). 'The mortality of elder mistreatment', *Journal of the American Medical Association*, 280: 428–32.

Machado, L., Queiroz, Z., Figueredo, S., and C. Guelman (1997). 'Elder abuse: a new challenge in Brazil.' Paper presented at an Invited Symposium on Action on Elder Abuse and Neglect at the International Congress on Gerontology (IAG) in Adelaide, Australia.

Pillemer, K., and D. W. Moore (1989). 'Abuse of patients in nursing homes: findings from a survey of staff', *Gerontologist*, 29: 314–20.

Quiroga, P., Alarcon, M., and H. Wageman (1999). 'Typology and prevalence of mistreatment on urban elders in two different regions in Chile'. Paper presented at the Sixth International Congress of Gerontology, Santiago de Chile, and published (2001) in *Cuadernos Médicos Sociales de Chile* (Spanish).

Quiroga, P., Wageman, H., and G. Torres (2002). 'Prevalence of mistreatment in elders in the city of Concepción', *Cuadernos Médicos Sociales de Chile*, 42 (1–2, 2001); (30–35, 2002) (Spanish).

Schaumburg, L. B., and D. Gans (1999). 'An ecological framework for contextualizing risk factors in elder abuse by adult children', *Journal of Elder Abuse & Neglect*, 11: 79–103.

Second Assembly on Ageing (2002). Plan of action and political declaration. A/CONF. 197/9: adopted Plenary Meeting 12 April 2002. Madrid, Spain.

Toronto Declaration on the global prevention of elder abuse, (2002) by WHO, University of Toronto and Ryerson University, Ontario, Canada, INPEA, and the Ontario Government, Toronto, Canada. Geneva: WHO.

UN (2001). *World Population Prospects*: The 2000 Revision. *Ageing and Development:* Issue 59–6–9.

Valencia Forum (2002). Conclusions presented following an Invited Symposium on Elder Abuse, Valencia, Spain, April.

Whittaker, T. (1997). 'Rethinking elder abuse: towards an age and gender integrated theory of elder abuse'. In P. Decalmer and G. Glendenning, eds., *The mistreatment of elderly people*, 2nd edn. Thousand Oaks, Calif.: Sage Publications, Inc., pp. 116–28.

WHO/INPEA (2001a). Daichman, L., Guido, O., Aguas, S., and M. Bertone, *National report on elder abuse in Argentina*. Geneva: WHO.

   (2001b). L. Machado, *National report on elder abuse in Brazil*. Geneva: WHO.

   (2002a). *Active ageing, a policy framework*. Geneva: WHO's Ageing and Health programme.

   (2002b). *Missing voices: views of older persons on elder abuse*. WHO/NMH/NPH/02.2. Geneva: WHO.

Wolf, R., Bennett, G., and L. Daichman (2003). 'Abuse of the elderly'. In Bonnie Green *et al.*, eds., *Trauma interventions in war and peace, prevention practice and policy*, by invitation and in collaboration with the United Nations. Special Consultant, Yael Danieli (UN). New York, Boston, Dordrecht, London, Moscow: Kluwer Academic/Plenum Publishers, ch. 6.

The Self in Dementia

STEVEN R. SABAT

Among the most devastating problems of ageing is that generally known as dementia, the leading cause of which is Alzheimer's disease (AD). At present, more than 4 million people have been diagnosed with probable AD in the United States alone, and 19 million family members work as carers. Recent projections indicate that, by the middle of this century, barring a cure or preventive measures, the incidence will more than triple, owing to the growing proportion of those in the "baby boom" generation who will become senior citizens, and the costs involved in caring for people with AD will reach $375 billion in the US alone (Alzheimer's Disease Association, 2000). The disease is a progressive, irreversible neuropathological disorder that destroys brain cells, depletes neurotransmitter systems (Sabat, 2001), and reduces life expectancy by 50% (Katzman, 1976). Of all forms of "dementing" illnesses, AD is the most common in older adults (Breteler *et al.*, 1992), more common in men than in women (Gurland *et al.*, 1983), and its prevalence in the population increases with advancing age (Evans *et al.*, 1989). The disease disrupts the ability to employ explicit memory (especially the ability to recall recent events), coherent and skilled movement (praxis), and selective attention, affects emotion, and many researchers have concluded that language disturbances are an "almost universal finding" among dementia sufferers (Appell *et al.*, 1982).

Although it is clear that AD can create a variety of deficits in the particular cognitive abilities mentioned above, what is less clear is the extent to which AD and other similar illnesses can affect the selfhood of the person afflicted. Given that people with AD live in a social milieu, in this chapter I should like to explore the possible effects of AD on selfhood by using Social Constructionist Theory as a heuristic device. The beliefs held by carers about the degree to which the person with AD has or has not lost his or her self can have a profound impact upon their behavior towards that person and, by extension, upon the ways in which the person with AD behaves in reaction. That is to say, if one assumes that the person with AD has no sense of self and proceeds to treat the person accordingly, and if the person with AD then reacts negatively to such treatment, it is likely that such negative behavior will be attributed to the disease as opposed to the "malignant social psychology" to which the person with AD has been exposed (Kitwood, 1988, 1990, 1998; Kitwood and Bredin, 1992). For example, if carers assume that the person with AD has no "self," they may talk about the person with AD in derogatory ways even though the person with AD is present. Thus, if the person with AD is positioned (Harré and van Langenhove, 1992) in a negative way, the negative reactions of persons with AD under these conditions are misattributed in such a way that the threat of premature institutionalization grows ever greater and the quality of life experienced by such persons will become impoverished to an indeterminate degree.

Thus, issues surrounding the integrity of the selfhood of persons with AD extend well beyond philosophical discourse and enter quite directly into the everyday world of persons with AD, and the informal and formal carers with whom they interact, as well as those involved with forging public policy and social support systems.

SOCIAL CONSTRUCTION THEORY AND ASPECTS OF SELFHOOD

Among the various approaches which have been aligned with Social Construction Theory, the one upon which I will draw in this chapter is that partly inspired by Vygotsky (1965) and Wittgenstein (1953) and offered by Rom Harré (1991), who offers a tripartite account of selfhood. I will summarize this account first and then show how the different aspects of selfhood can be shown to exist in persons with AD in the moderate to severe stages of the disease. The tripartite conception of selfhood includes Self 1, Self 2, and Self 3.

The first of these, Self 1, the self of personal identity, can be understood from two points of view: as it is expressed and as it is experienced. As expressed, Self 1 is evidenced through the use of first person indexicals such as "I," "me," "my," "mine," "myself," "our" (yours and mine), "let's" (let us – you and I), and "us" (you and me). Through the use of these terms, the speaker locates (or indexes) for others in the social world the source of beliefs, attitudes, wishes, emotions, and the like. If a person says, "I wish I could go home," the speaker is locating for others the source of the wish. In principle, a person might not be able to recall his or her name or date of birth, but still express, via the use of indexicals, an intact Self 1. If a person experiences him or herself as a singularity – as one individual (as opposed to having multiple personalities) who has a single point of view in the world – who has a continuous experience of that single point of view, he or she is experiencing an intact Self 1.

The second aspect of selfhood is Self 2, which includes the person's physical and mental attributes, past and present. Mental attributes include the person's beliefs (religious, political, social), his or her sense of humor, as well the person's beliefs about his or her attributes. Thus, a person might take pride in having been an accomplished professional in years past, might be appalled and saddened by the effects of AD upon his or her present abilities to navigate independently in the social world, might hold college and advanced degrees, and all of these attributes would be part of Self 2. It is clear that some Self 2 attributes remain intact (being a college graduate), whereas others might change (not being able to perform routine calculations due to AD) and still others might be relatively new (being diagnosed with probable AD).

The third and final aspect of selfhood is Self 3, one's social identity, which is comprised of multiple personae and which requires, for its existence, the cooperation of others. One may be at once a loving parent, a devoted child, a dedicated teacher, a caring spouse, a loyal friend, and each of these personae involve particular behavioral displays. One behaves differently towards a friend than one does towards a spouse, for example, but in each case in order for a person to construct a Self 3 persona of one or another type, one must enjoy the cooperation of another person. To wit, one cannot construct the persona of "loving parent" if one's child does not recognize one as being his or her parent, nor can one construct the persona of "dedicated teacher" if one's students do not take one as being their teacher. In this domain of social identity, we will appreciate that the person with AD is especially vulnerable, for if the focus of others is principally on the person's defects due to AD (Self 2 attributes), the person's social identity may be confined increasingly to the "burdensome patient." In such cases, a loss of Self 3 personae would hardly be a direct result of the disease, but rather a result of the lack of cooperation from others in the face of the attempts by the person with AD to construct more valued, worthy social personae.

With this as background, let us now explore the various aspects of selfhood as they may or may not be affected by AD.

SELFHOOD AND THE PERSON WITH ALZHEIMER'S DISEASE

In this section, I will refer to particular persons with AD not to imply any generalizations, but rather to illuminate the ways in which Social Construction Theory can provide a means to assess the existence of various aspects of selfhood in people with AD in the moderate to severe stages of the disease. The individuals to whom I refer herein can be seen as examples of a phenomenon whose generality is in the process of being investigated. A more detailed presentation of these individuals, as well as others who demonstrate various aspects of intact selfhood can be found elsewhere (Sabat, 1991a, 1991b, 2001; Sabat and Harré, 1992, 1994). In each case, my relationships with the people with AD were long term, lasting a minimum of one and one-half years, during which time I recorded and transcribed conversations that occurred at least once a week for more than an hour at a time. The relationships were not of the "researcher–patient" or "neuropsychologist–client" variety, but of the "person to person" variety, so that the social dynamics were such that trust and openness were developed and enduring.

The Case of Dr. M.

Dr. M. was 75 years old at the beginning of my two-year association with her, had been diagnosed with probable AD according to NINCDS-ADRDA criteria (McKhann *et al.*, 1984) four years earlier, but had experienced memory problems five years prior to the diagnosis and was considered to be in the moderate to severe stage of the disease. She evidenced severe word-finding problems, could not sign her name, was unable to perform simple calculations, copy a design, or recall the date, month, or year. She was unable to use eating utensils, and had striking difficulties with dressing and grooming. She held two advanced degrees (Ph.D. and MSW) and had spent decades of her vocational life as a professor. One and one-half years before our association began, her performance on standard neuropsychological tests was said to indicate decrements in memory, abstraction, concept formation, and word-finding that were consistent with dementia.

During our two-year association, Dr. M. gave evidence of her continuing intact Self 1 (of personal identity) through her indexing her experiences and beliefs as being her own. An extract of conversation about her word-finding problems and reactions to them is illustrative:

SRS: You're not just any ordinary person who has some problems finding words. You're a person for whom words, words to you are kind of like a musical instrument.
Dr. M.: Um hum, um hum. That's exactly right.
SRS: And so the kind of frustration you feel would be greater than for a person whose focus in life was not so literary. That could give you cause for a lot of grief.

Dr. M.: I think the issue is, that is, for me maybe especially this day for some reason or other, but for last, maybe four years, that I am not satisfied with myself because what I want isn't here. I've, uh, thinking of it and it makes me angry as well as, that is part of the . . . and I guess that is what is happening now. Don't you think?

In the above extract, Dr. M. uses first person indexicals to locate as hers the feelings that she is not satisfied with herself due to the fact that she cannot do what she would like to do and that this itself is due to AD. She also indexes as her own her feeling of being angry with herself as a result of her word-finding problems, because to her as I put it, "words are kind of like a musical instrument." In addition to revealing an intact Self 1 (the self of personal identity), she is also revealing intact Self 2 attributes and beliefs about those attributes, for it makes her "angry as well" as being "not satisfied with myself." Her beliefs about her relatively new, dysfunctional attributes which have come in the wake of AD are very clearly seen, for example, when she commented about her initial reluctance to tell her friends and family about her diagnosis: "Why this reluctance to name my malady? Can it be that the term, Alzheimer's has a connotation similar to the 'Scarlet Letter' or the 'Black Plague'? Is it even more embarrassing than a sexual disease?"

Self 2 attributes can include those which the individual has enjoyed for extended periods of time in the past, as well as those that have evolved recently, along with the related beliefs about those attributes. In the case of the person with AD, there can often exist a clash between the two, for the person can be very well aware of the deficiencies that have occurred as a result of the disease. This was quite evident in the following extract, in which Dr. M. discussed the effect of her word-finding problems:

Dr. M.: I don't know how you go through the various steps, but I want to have a, a feel that when I talk, that when I caw, talk, I, I can talk.
SRS: Um hum.
Dr. M.: I can't always do that.
SRS: Um hum, well, you're doing it pretty well right now.
Dr. M.: No, but when I haven't, we're just talking uh,
SRS: Light

Dr. M.: Light, light stuff, and even light sa stuff are problems because I miss and word and I can't find it.

SRS: Um hum.

Dr. M.: And I'm probably able to do it as other people can, but uh, not it that good, it's not good enough for me.

In order for her to say, "it's not good enough for me," Dr. M. had to make a comparison between some criterion, perhaps her past facility with language, and her present ability, recognizing that her present ability does not measure up to her personal standards. In so doing, she provides evidence of the existence of Self 2 attributes, both past and present, along with her beliefs about them. She is also using first person pronouns to index, as being her own, her experience of her present abilities as well as her beliefs about them.

Recall that one's ability to construct and manifest a variety of Self 3 personae depends upon the cooperation the individual receives from others. In this respect, the person with AD is extremely vulnerable, because, to the extent that healthy others focus upon the Self 2 attribute of AD and its deleterious effects upon other valued Self 2 attributes, while simultaneously paying less heed to those attributes which the person with AD values, he or she will encounter great difficulty in obtaining the cooperation required in order to construct Self 3 personae which reflect qualities in which he or she takes pride. If the person with AD is seen as being defective and incompetent, it will be extremely difficult for him or her to construct a Self 3 persona other than that of "The Burdensome, Dysfunctional Patient." Under such conditions, healthy others can easily conclude that this is all the person *can be*, which often turns out to be a radical misunderstanding of the person's abilities. The acid test of the belief that the person with AD is nothing more than the "dysfunctional patient" involves giving that person just the sort of cooperation he or she needs to construct worthy Self 3 personae in which he or she may take pride, and then observing the effects.

In conversations we had about events transpiring at her support group meetings, Dr. M. was able, with my cooperation, to construct a Self 3 of "colleague/mentor." After my first meeting with her support group, we discussed my reactions to having been invited to return to speak with the support group. The following extract is part of that conversation and is revealing of the Self 3 that Dr. M. was able to construct in that context:

SRS: That's how I felt when the group leader asked me if I would come back. Inside my head I was saying, "Would I? Are you kidding? I would love to!"

Dr. M.: I knew that! I knew that, I knew that it gives you just what you're looking for. So uh, and I think it gives, gives the group some. You repeated, I mean I repeated what you had said in a sense.

SRS: Yes indeed! I think we learn more about what people *can* do (when we observe them) in very rich social settings.

Dr. M.: Um hum, and you can have it for the next uh . . . paper.

SRS: That's right!

In this extract, Dr. M. (a) reveals that she understands the important connection between what transpired in the support group meeting and my own research interests, and (b) shares, in a way consistent with the role of a senior colleague or mentor, that what had transpired in that meeting constituted material which I could use for my "next . . . paper."

Herein, she is behaving in ways that are utterly inconsistent with the Self 3 of "burdensome AD patient." If she had been restricted to constructing such a Self 3, she would neither have been given the opportunity to comment about such connections, nor have been engaged in such a way so as to feel free enough to encourage a younger academic.

Even though Dr. M. could be categorized as being in the moderate to severe stages of AD, she was able, nevertheless, to construct valued and worthy Self 3 personae with the cooperation of another person. In practical terms, such findings can be seen as indicating that the factors that are used as defining points of the stages of severity of AD are distinct from the factors that can contribute to the existence and maintenance of different aspects of selfhood. That the conversations between Dr. M. and myself were, in fact, a source of great satisfaction to her and enhanced her quality of life can be inferred from what she said to me when her medical appointments precluded one or another of our meetings: "I missed you."

Interim Summary

Despite her diagnosis of AD in the moderate to severe stages, Dr. M., through her use of first person pronouns in conversational discourse, showed that she possessed an intact Self 1, or self of personal identity; she likewise demonstrated an intact Self 2, the self of mental and physical attributes and beliefs about her attributes, including her beliefs about the meaning of the disease in her life; finally, she was able to construct, with the requisite cooperation, a valued, worthy social persona (Self 3 of "mentor/colleague"). Without my cooperation, she would not have been able to construct this particular social persona. Thus, being in the moderate to severe stage of AD did not, in itself, preclude her from constructing a social persona in which she could take proper pride, nor did it prevent her from experiencing and expressing other aspects of selfhood.

The Case of Mrs. D.

Mrs. D. was seventy years old and had been diagnosed with probable AD five years before we first met. According to standard tests, she was moderately to severely afflicted. Unlike Dr. M., Mrs. D. was a high school graduate, never having attended college. When tested, she could not name (via recall) the day of the week, the month, the season, year, the city and county she was in, or the date. She had sensorimotor problems such as difficulties in picking up eating utensils when sitting at the lunch table, getting food to her mouth, and imitating the movements of the instructor during exercises, all of which may have resulted to some extent from the fact that she had difficulties in distinguishing right from left. Her ability to use spoken language was not as compromised as were her recall and her sensorimotor skills, although she did experience frequent word-finding problems and uttered unintended words and syllables at times. She had been raised in a show-business family and loved to sing and tell jokes. At the time of our association, she was living at home with her husband and attended a daycare center during the week. I met with her 2 to 3 hours per week at her home and at the daycare center for approximately one and one-half years.

Her use of first person pronouns to index her experiences and beliefs as being her own was evident throughout our association and is exemplified in her stated reason for volunteering to be a subject in studies done at the National Institutes of Health: "That was the nicety of it, cause I could have said, 'no' but believe me, if I can help me and my fe [fellow] man, I would do it." In this comment, we see evidence not only of her intact Self 1, but also of her ability to construct, with the help of research scientists, the Self 3 social persona of "research volunteer" whose purpose was to be of potential help to others.

In other conversations, Mrs. D. provided similar reasons for her "work" at the daycare center she attended. Owing to her outgoing, warm, personality and her vibrant sense of humor, the staff at the day center enlisted her help in integrating new participants into the group. As a result, Mrs. D. was able to construct the Self 3 persona of "liaison between staff and participants" and "life of the party," for she often inspired spirited laughter among other participants as a result of her ability to tell jokes and sing old songs. When asked about this "work" she did (she referred to it as her "work"), she commented:

Some of them are in bad shape, you know, that they couldn't remember a thing. I would try to help them. That's what you have to do, almost, if you want to get along . . . I think it's a nice thing to do. Instead of me sitting down with the little I have gone, a little bit, a little higher, and not trying my fellow person . . . as things went by, I would work, you know, with somebody just to keep them happy.

In the environment of the daycare center, Mrs. D. was able to construct a healthy, valued social persona (Self 3) beyond that of "AD patient." She clearly demonstrated in her conversational discourse that she possessed an intact Self 1 as well as intact Self 2 attributes such as extroversion, a warm personality, a wonderful sense of humor, sympathy for the plight of others, a fine singing voice, as well as beliefs about what she did ("I think it's a nice thing to do"), in addition to the relatively new and troublesome attributes associated with AD.

CONCLUSION

The cases of the two people with AD reported herein indicate that, despite striking losses in some cognitive abilities as a result of AD, various aspects of selfhood, as understood in terms of Social Construction

Theory, can persist nonetheless. Self 1, the self of personal identity, and Self 2, the self of physical and mental attributes past and present, likewise persist. Self 3, the multiplicity of social personae that require the cooperation of others in order to be manifested, is especially vulnerable in people with AD, but this vulnerability is not a direct result of the disease itself. Rather, it is a result of the lack of cooperation given by others in response to the person with AD. All too often, the only way in which the person with AD is seen is as the "dysfunctional, burdensome patient," which itself is anathema to the person in question. Rather than having his or her selfhood defined solely in terms of the ability to recall events, Social Construction Theory offers the possibility of understanding that the person with AD is indeed very much still a person with a self and is still deserving of the requisite respect and deference he or she would receive without question in the absence of the diagnosis.

FURTHER READING

Harris, P. B., ed. (2002). *The person with Alzheimer's disease: pathways to understanding the experience*. Baltimore, Md.: Johns Hopkins University Press.

Kitwood, T. (1998). *Dementia reconsidered: the person comes first*. Buckingham: Open University Press.

Snyder, L. (1999). *Speaking our minds: personal reflections from individuals with Alzheimer's*. New York: W. H. Freeman & Co.

REFERENCES

Alzheimer's and Related Disorders Association (2000). *A race against time*. Hondulu: 2000.

Appell, J., Kertesz, A., and M. Fisman (1982). "A study of language functioning in Alzheimer patients," *Brain and Language*, 17: 73–91.

Breteler, M. M. B., Claus, J. J., Van Duijn, C. M., Launer, L. J., and A. Hofman (1992). "Epidemiology of Alzheimer's disease," *Epidemiology Reviews*, 14: 59–82.

Evans, D. A., Funkenstein, H., Albert, M. S., Sherr, P. A., Cook, N. R., Chown, N. J., Hebert, L. E., Hennekens, C. H., and J. O. Taylor (1989). "Prevalence of Alzheimer's disease in a community population of older persons," *Journal of the American Medical Association*, 262: 2551–6.

Gurland, B., Copeland, J., Kuriansky, J., Kellever, M., Sharpe, L., and L. L. Dean (1983). *The mind and mood of aging*. Beckenham: Croom Helm.

Harré, R. (1991). "The discursive production of selves," *Theory and Psychology*, 1: 51–63.

Harré, R., and L. van Langenhove (1992). "Varieties of positioning," *Journal for the Theory of Social Behavior*, 20: 393–407.

Katzman, R. (1976). "The prevalence and malignancy of Alzheimer's disease: a major killer," *Archives of Neurology*, 33: 217–18.

Kitwood, T. (1988). "The technical, the personal, and the framing of dementia," *Social Behaviour*, 3: 161–79.

(1990). "The dialectics of dementia: with particular reference to Alzheimer's disease," *Ageing and Society*, 10: 177–96.

(1998). "Toward a theory of dementia care: ethics and interaction," *Journal of Clinical Ethics*, 9: 23–34.

Kitwood, T., and K. Bredin (1992). "Towards a theory of dementia care: personhood and well being," *Ageing and Society*, 12: 269–87.

McKhann, G., Drachman, D., Folstein, M., Katzman, R., Price, D., and E. M. Stadlan (1984). "Clinical diagnosis of Alzheimer's disease: report of the NINCDS-ADRDA work group under the auspices of the Department of Health and Human Services task force on Alzheimer's disease," *Neurology*, 34: 939–44.

Sabat, S. R. (1991a). "Facilitating conversation via indirect repair: a case study of Alzheimer's disease," *Georgetown Journal of Languages and Linguistics*, 2: 284–96.

(1991b). "Turn-taking, turn-giving, and Alzheimer's disease: a case study of conversation," *Georgetown Journal of Languages and Linguistics*, 2: 167–81.

(2001). *The experience of Alzheimer's disease: life through a tangled veil*. Oxford: Blackwell.

Sabat, S. R., and R. Harre (1992). "The construction and deconstruction of self in Alzheimer's disease," *Ageing and Society*, 12: 443–61.

(1994). "The Alzheimer's disease sufferer as a semiotic subject," *Philosophy, Psychiatry, Psychology*, 1: 145–60.

Vygotsky, L. (1965). *Thought and language*. Cambridge, Mass.: MIT Press.

Wittgenstein, L. (1953). *Philosophical investigations*. Oxford: Blackwell.

CHAPTER 4.8

Ageism

BILL BYTHEWAY

A NARROW DEFINITION

Ageism can be defined broadly or narrowly. The narrow definition is straightforward: ageism is discrimination against older people on grounds of age. Just as women are disadvantaged and oppressed as a result of sexism, just as black people and other minority ethnic groups are oppressed by racism, so older people suffer from discrimination as a result of ageism.

Action against sexism and racism has a dramatic history that, arguably, has radically changed the dominant social order of many contemporary societies. There is legislation in many countries intended to ensure 'equal opportunities' regardless of gender or ethnicity. Older people might wish for the same: there is plenty of evidence to support the case against ageism.

The classic formulation of the narrow definition, one that has been widely quoted, is:

Ageism can be seen as a process of systematic stereotyping of and discrimination against people because they are old, just as racism and sexism accomplish this for skin colour and gender. Old people are categorized as senile, rigid in thought and manner, old-fashioned in morality and skills . . . Ageism allows the younger generations to see older people as different from themselves, thus they subtly cease to identify with their elders as human beings. (Butler, 1975: 35)

It is important to appreciate that this definition is built upon actions taken within social relations. Two distinct kinds of actions are identified: *discrimination* whereby people are denied opportunities and resources on account of their age, and *prejudice*

whereby people who are perceived to be old are viewed stereotypically and negatively. There are two triggers to such actions: evidence of chronological age, and the sight of the older person. These distinctions suggest the following taxonomy of how ageism is made manifest:

	Discrimination	Prejudice
Chronological age	*Age bars* (e.g. insurance available only to adults aged under 65 years)	*Statistical weighting* (e.g. by including age in the calculation of priorities)
The older body	Formal rejection (e.g. of older people as advertising models)	Evasion (e.g. avoiding contact with older people at social events)

THE BROADER DEFINITION

In contrast, the broader definition of ageism is much more complicated. Here ageism is *not* equivalent to sexism and racism. There is no one group discriminating against another. Younger people can be discriminated against as well as older people. Indeed we are all, throughout our lives, oppressed by ageism, by dominant expectations about age, expectations that dictate how we behave and relate to each other.

Within this broader context, ageism has been defined as a set of beliefs about how people vary biologically as a result of the ageing process (Bytheway and Johnson, 1990). These beliefs underpin the actions of organisations and individuals. They generate and reinforce a lifelong fear of the ageing process, and they underpin presumed associations between age and competence and the need for protection: being 'too' young and being 'too' old. They legitimate the use of chronological age to mark out classes of people (i) who are systematically denied resources and opportunities that others enjoy and, conversely, (ii) who are granted concessions for services and benefits they are assumed to need.

Most people of course would not dispute the need for infants and extremely old people to be protected and cared for, and would not consider such persons able to manage independent living. Similarly the provision of education for children and pensions for people over a certain age, sometimes described as 'positive ageism' (Palmore, 1999), is thought to be necessary and desirable for a well-ordered society. The important point to appreciate is that education and pensions policies have used chronological age to rigidly mark out categories of people. As a consequence one's legal status is transformed upon reaching certain birthdays. Regardless of whether such change is welcomed, this is ageism made manifest.

A BRIEF HISTORY OF THE CONCEPT

Arguably, ageism has existed since time immemorial. As a *word*, however, it has a much more recent history, one largely based in the USA. Cohen (2001) argues that Lerner (1957) provided one of the earliest expressions of ageism when he wrote: 'The most flattering thing you can say to an older American is that he "doesn't look his age" and "doesn't act his age" – as if it were the most damning thing in the world to look old' (Lerner, 1957: 613). The word itself was coined in 1969 by the psychiatrist Robert Butler. At that time, he was involved in a controversy over the use of a high-rise block in Washington DC. The local authorities had proposed that it be used as public housing for people, many of whom would be old, poor and black. For Butler, the angry debates that followed echoed the generational conflict that had characterised the student–police battles of the previous year. 'Is this negativism a function of racism?'

asked the *Washington Post* reporter. 'No', said Butler, 'I think it is more a function of ageism' (Butler, 1989).

So the concept of ageism did not emerge out of academic gerontology: it originated in community action against the NIMBY tendency – 'Old people? Not in my backyard!' – a prejudice that still taxes many societies over 30 years later. It is significant that it arose out of a conflict over housing. Housing policies have often been the context in which prejudice against excluded groups has been most vehemently expressed: against poor people, single women, ethnic and religious minorities, people with disabilities, and young people. Cynthia Rich, for example, describes a similar crisis in which a group of black older women living in a 'housing tower for the elderly' demanded a meeting with the Boston Housing Authority in 1982 to protest that their lives were 'in continual danger' (Macdonald and Rich, 1983: 76).

It was perhaps inevitable, following the extensive media attention given to sexism and racism during and since the 1960s, that the word 'ageism' would be coined. That said, there had been extensive research prior to this, deploring the position of older people in what were perceived to be modern, developed and civilised societies. In the USA, for example, there was Jules Henry's famous study *Culture against man* (1965) and in the UK, Peter Townsend's *The last refuge* (1962) and Barbara Robb's *Sans everything* (1967). Similarly, in France, Simone de Beauvoir had been working on her classic 1970 study *Old age* (de Beauvoir, 1977). These and many similar studies ensured that 'the launch' of ageism was waiting to happen.

Almost immediately, Butler's initiative was matched by that of the other great age protagonist of the 1970s and 1980s, Maggie Kuhn. Following compulsory retirement, she and five others decided in 1970 to launch an intergenerational campaign against the Vietnam war. She saw this as an opportunity to forge an alliance of young and old people that would challenge ageism (Kuhn, 1977). Following media acclaim, the alliance developed into the Gray Panthers with the slogan 'age and youth in action'. Although many successful campaigns followed which challenged discrimination against older people, the Gray Panthers had a much broader mission, one that was committed to sustaining inclusion rather than deploring exclusion. For example, possibly Kuhn's most famous message was to condemn retirement communities as 'playpens': 'They're very safe. Playpens are meant to be safe and comfortable. The people are out of the way of the rest of society' (Kuhn, 1977: 43).

Despite its political timeliness, the concept of ageism was not readily incorporated into the gerontologist's toolbag. Butler became Director of the National Institute on Aging in 1974 and the following year published *Why Survive?*, a Pulitzer Prize-winning critique of ageism (Butler, 1975). Despite this, there was a growing scepticism among social scientists. Kalish (1979), for example, argued that Butler was promoting a 'new ageism' based on the model of the 'incompetent failure'.

In the 1980s, a new development arose. Alarmed by forecasts of the impact of demographic change on the US economy, Governor Richard D. Lamm of Colorado argued that sick old people should 'die and get out of the way' (Cole, 1992: 169). Americans for Generational Equity (AGE) was formed to question policies which prioritised the old at the expense of the young: 'something is wrong with a society that is willing to drain itself to foster such an unproductive section of its population' (Fairlie, 1988: 13). The campaign drew upon the work of Daniel Callahan whose *Setting limits* (1987) advocated that chronological age should be used to weight the allocation of healthcare resources against older people. AGE used the term 'new ageism' to refer to prejudice against the young.

As is apparent from this summary, the concept and study of ageism has developed primarily in the USA and, to a large extent, the agenda has been set by the popular media. In 1992, the historian Thomas Cole (1992: 228) argued that the attack on ageism 'originated in the same chorus of cultural values that gave rise to ageism in the first place'. In his view, ageism was a conceptual tool that was 'neither informed by broader social or psychological theory nor grounded in historical specificity' (p. 229). This may, however, be due to the problems that gerontologists have had in establishing a clear identity for the discipline. Achenbaum (1995: 256–7), for example, argues that it has been 'outsiders' such as Butler who have done most to popularise the subject, and he sees Butler's coining of the term 'ageism' as one important aspect of this process.

INDIVIDUAL AGEISM

We all have anxieties about the future. When we express concerns about what age will bring or a wish that we could avoid growing older, then this can be described as evidence of a fear of ageing. Underpinning this fear are the beliefs that ageing is inevitable, that the chances of illness and impairment increase with age, and that no one survives old age. An important complication is the recognition that we do not age alone, that we are all ageing, and that ageing leads to bereavement. As we grow older, we lose not only those who are closest but those with whom we can share past experiences. There is a particularly strong fear of deep old age, of being the last survivor, coping – we imagine – with failing faculties and an increasing dependence on others for assistance with the most basic routines of daily life.

This fear of ageing rubs off on relations between young and old. Levy and Banaji define ageism as 'an alteration in feeling, belief, or behaviour in response to an individual's or group's perceived chronological age' (Levy and Banaji, 2002: 50). Note how their focus is on a change of attitude: when we obtain some perception of a person's age, then our feelings towards them change. They argue that *implicit ageism* is the basis of most interactions with older people and that this emerges in cultural settings where, rather than strong and explicit hatred towards older people, there is a widespread acceptance of negative feelings and beliefs: 'The research on implicit ageism and ageing self-stereotypes suggests a need to be concerned about the multiple ways in which negative ageism infiltrates into our own thinking and behaviours' (Levy, 2001: 579). The relationship between this psychological perspective on ageist interactions and political concerns with intergenerational equity is clearly apparent. The first executive director of AGE, for example, proclaimed that 'We were formed to promote stewardship in the name of younger and future generations' (Achenbaum, 1989: 113), and it is not difficult to picture the steward looking unfavourably at older people whilst smiling benevolently upon the coming generation of grandchildren.

In the UK this issue came to a head briefly in 1989 with the publication of *Workers versus pensioners* (Johnson *et al.*, 1989). A flurry of debate and research ensued that was focused on the concept of generational equity. It is painfully apparent in this literature that complex issues of inheritance and succession were compounded with ageism in the backdrop to intergenerational conflict (Phillipson, 1998: 90–103). The important point to note is that the relations between generations are touched by ageism *only* when the age of either generation is invoked. Rather than current age, however, what is at stake in debates over generational equity is equity in the context of lifelong perspectives: pasts and futures rather than the present.

INSTITUTIONALISED AGEISM

It is easier to demonstrate ageism in the practices of institutions than in individual actions. An obvious example of institutionalised ageism is the age bar: 'How old are you? Sorry, you're too old' (or too young). Such questions and responses are easily articulated. Also, the institution expects a straightforward answer: if in doubt, your age can be deduced from your birth certificate. No problem. Except of course, that age might bar you or prejudice your chances and you might be tempted to lie. Many of us have memories of lying in our youth in order to obtain what was only available to adults: to gain admission to the cinema or to purchase cigarettes, for example. With each birthday, some regulatory doors open and others close and a new set of claims and counter-claims comes to colour our exchanges across the bureaucratic desk. In later life, questions of age re-emerge at key moments. Whether it is the driving licence or the cardiology clinic, the temptation to lie returns. Language is a powerful medium for ageism (Palmore, 2000).

Feminists have long recognised the importance of visual images in sustaining sexism. Just as the anonymous fashion model represents a fantasy of 'womanhood', so her youth is perceived to be the ideal. Nevertheless, images of older people fascinate the viewer. Whether it is a grandmother begging in a third world city or the self-portraits of Rembrandt, the viewer is drawn by the portrayal of old age, sometimes appalled. Kathleen Woodward begins *Aging and its discontents* with a telling anecdote about an exhibition that included a portrait of 'a thin old man . . . sitting on the side of his bed, his knees wide apart, his body naked except for the shuffling slippers on his feet' (Woodward, 1991: 1). She

viewed the exhibition with other conference participants and describes and discusses their reactions. For some, the portrait of the anonymous older person confirmed and consolidated their ageist prejudice: the naked man was made the object of ageist humour. Others, however, were forced to address their reaction to the sight of age. Thomas Cole might argue that such exhibitions simultaneously sustain ageism and question it.

Another way in which ageism draws upon the visual image of older people is in advertising. Increasingly, for example, anti-ageing products are being marketed through images of an older person looking depressed and decrepit 'before' treatment and happier and more youthful afterwards (Binstock, 2003). Conversely, when the product is 'new' and the target younger people, the image of their elders may be the butt of alleged humour. A particularly choice example of this was a full-page advertisement that appeared in 1993 in the national UK newspaper the *Guardian*. A woman – an old-fashioned dress, gloves, handbag, wrinkled stockings – is sitting with her back to a blank wall, looking alarmed. Next to her is a side table on which there is a small decorated box. Below is the slogan: 'This Christmas, shoot Granny and put her in a box.' Sarcastically witty small-print text follows, promoting the product – a range of cameras packaged in gift sets. There is only one further reference to 'Granny': 'She won't even have time to put her teeth in.' The *Guardian* subsequently published two complaints about this advertisement (Bytheway, 1995: 65).

There are many sources of statistics that can be used to illustrate the social and economic inequalities that result from institutional ageism. Consider, for example, Table 1, based on a UK government-sponsored survey of the income and expenditure of households (Office of National Statistics, 2001). Although it demonstrates a strong association between age and household finance, the most striking contrasts are between the three oldest age groups. Those aged 75 or more have an average disposable income that is less than half that of those aged 50 to 64. The main sources of income of the 50–64 group are wages and salaries. For the 75-plus group they are predominantly pensions and related sources. Whereas 33% of the spending of the 50–64 group goes on household essentials, this statistic rises to 44% for the oldest group.

TABLE 1. Income and expenditure by age, UK 1999–2000

Age of head of household	Under 30	30 and under 50	50 and under 65	65 and under 75	75 or over
Average disposable income	£322	£476	£452	£274	£198
Income:			%		
from wages, salaries or self-employment	88	90	77	19	6
from annuities, pensions and social security benefits	7	6	18	70	81
from other sources	5	4	6	12	13
Expenditure:			%		
spent on housing, fuel, power, food and non-alcoholic drink	38	36	33	35	44
Total number of households in sample (= 100%)	808	2,828	1,653	968	840

Based on weighted data.
Source: Down (2000), Tables 2.2 and 8.2.

The explanation for these striking contrasts rests primarily with legislation and regulation regarding employment and income. The outcome is that the oldest households have substantially less flexibility in their expenditure patterns. As a result, they are less able to cope with unexpected bills. In this way institutional ageism constrains the financial resources of older people. In regard to consumer activities, many have significantly less freedom than they had enjoyed previously and less than that of younger generations.

ANTI-AGEIST ACTION

One area of policy where action on ageism has been taken by several governments is that of employment legislation (Glover and Branine, 2001). In seven countries there is extensive age discrimination legislation: the US, Canada, Australia, New Zealand, Spain, Finland and the Republic of Ireland (Hornstein *et al.*, 2001). It has been calculated that the cost of age discrimination to the UK economy is £31 billion in lost production (Rickards, 2001). Since 1997, the UK government has introduced a number of measures aimed at tackling age discrimination in employment. These include a voluntary code on age

diversity which sets a standard of non-ageist practice regarding recruitment, selection, training, promotion and redundancy. This code anticipates the European Union's Directive on Equal Treatment in Employment (Article 13) which will outlaw age discrimination at work and which will be implemented by December 2006.

In recent years the United Nations has undertaken a number of initiatives on age, most recently the Madrid International Plan of Action on Ageing (2002). These have tended to promote human rights, social participation and positive images of age, rather than to challenge ageist policies and practices. This approach is associated with the promotion of employment in later life. For example, Paragraph 24 of the Plan notes how, in developing countries and countries with economies in transition, older people are often working in poor conditions, without the benefits that result from employment in the formal sector and often subject to age discrimination. Anticipating labour shortages, it then comments: 'In this context, policies to extend employability, such as flexible retirement, new work arrangements, adaptive work environments and vocational rehabilitation for older persons with disabilities are essential and allow older persons to combine paid employment with other activities.' This approach to the development of non-discriminatory employment, assuming uncritically that older people want paid employment, contrasts with that of NGOs such as HelpAge International. In introducing 'ten actions to end age discrimination', it comments: 'Age discrimination is our core concern. All societies discriminate against people on grounds of age. Ageism and stereotyping influence attitudes, which in turn affect the way decisions are taken and resources allocated at household, community, national and international level.' The ten actions include proposals that challenge age bars and prejudice: for example, 'make credit, employment, training and education schemes available to people regardless of age'. In short, it is important that a clear distinction is maintained between anti-ageist action which directly challenges age bars and age prejudice, and policies which promote positive images based on assumptions about what older people want or what is good for them.

GERONTOLOGISTS AND AGEISM

What should gerontologists make of ageism? Gerontology is a broad umbrella under which many aspects of age are studied from many perspectives. Despite the rather austere image created by the word itself, gerontologists are employed in many varied positions: as well as teachers and researchers in gerontology, there are professional practitioners, industrial managers, campaigners, service providers, adult educationalists, religious leaders, retired people and many others. However, although the boundaries of gerontology are only loosely demarcated, the aims are simple and unambiguous. For example, the objectives of the International Association of Gerontology are to promote gerontological research, training in the field of ageing, and the interests of gerontological organisations in international affairs. How, we might ask, does the concept of ageism assist the pursuit of these objectives?

As gerontologists, a key issue that we have to address is whether we see ageism as:

- part of a conceptual framework that we use to account for empirical evidence of inequality and discrimination in the wider world, or as
- a political or cultural phenomenon located in that wider world.

If the first, then as gerontologists we should debate the details of how we define and study it. For example, we might take a lead from Erdman Palmore, and refine his Facts of Ageing Quiz for use in countries other than the USA (Palmore, 2000). We could then conceptualise ageism as something that includes 'erroneous' beliefs about the 'facts' of age. Our aim would be to 'overcome' or 'eradicate' ageism through knowledge and education.

If we adopt the second strategy, however, we would have to accept that anyone and any organisation might take action against ageism. In this context we would not claim any particular authority in deciding what ageism is and how it should be defined or challenged. In participating in open debates about age discrimination, we might be faced with definitions that we consider bizarre. In particular, we might find that groups led by older people use an 'out-dated' vocabulary: they appear out of touch with contemporary discussions about discrimination. Or, reflecting Cole's observation, we may encounter definitions of ageism which, paradoxically, seem positively ageist. Accepting that this was how discussion of ageism has developed in the wider world, as gerontologists, we would not seek to challenge this 'mistaken' view of ageism. Rather, we would attempt to account for its emergence and distinctive construction.

It is helpful at this point to return to precedents relating to sexism and racism. In both, the lead has been taken by members of those groups that suffer the consequences. So campaigns against sexism have been led by women in a wide variety of contexts: ideological, academic, cultural, political, economic. Arguably men aligned to such campaigns have occasionally played a part (e.g. through nineteenth-century philanthropy), but it would be absurd to suggest that men have ever led, or should aspire to lead, such campaigns. Similarly, those who have led campaigns against racism have, with few exceptions, been members of oppressed racial groups. So the fight against ageism defined in the narrow sense as discrimination and prejudice against older people must be led by older people: people who have first-hand experience of the consequences.

It seems reasonable to claim that most gerontologists become so in early middle adulthood as a result of being employed in research, teaching, training or service provision. Regardless of precisely how one might define a population of gerontologists and study its demographic characteristics, the almost inevitable outcome is that the large majority are of 'working age'. There will be exceptions and it may be that the population of gerontologists is ageing. Even so, opportunities for people 'of retirement age' to occupy leading positions in education and research are limited. As with any academic discipline, gerontology continues to be led by people in the later stages of their careers, typically employed by universities and aged between 50 and 65 years. They may have relevant first-hand experience of ageism in the broader sense, but they are in a particularly weak position to claim leadership in campaigns against ageism defined more narrowly.

So the conclusion might be that, in regard to ageism defined in the broad sense, we all have experience of the fear of ageing and the oppressive use of chronological age, and it is in this context that gerontologists can play a leading role in the continuing struggle against ageism. To this end, in Bytheway (2002) I have proposed the following three shifts in the priorities of gerontological research:

- away from a focus on 'the elderly' and towards (i) ageing in general and (ii) extreme age in particular;
- away from the planning, management and delivery of age-specific services and towards the detail and routines of everyday (and every-year) life;
- away from idealised models and processes of ageing and towards an interest in how people talk about and act upon their age.

FURTHER READING

Bytheway, B. (1995). *Ageism*. Buckingham: Open University Press.
Macdonald, B., and C. Rich (1983). *Look me in the eye: old women, aging and ageism*. London: The Women's Press.
Nelson, T., ed. (2002). *Ageism: stereotyping and prejudice against older persons*, A Bradford Book. Cambridge, Mass.: MIT Press.
Palmore, E. (1999). *Ageism: negative and positive*. New York: Springer Publishing Company.

REFERENCES

Achenbaum, W. A. (1989). 'Public pensions as intergenerational transfers in the United States'. In P. Johnson, C. Conrad and D. Thomson, eds., *Workers versus pensioners: intergenerational justice in an ageing world*. Manchester: Manchester University Press, pp. 113–36.
(1995). *Crossing frontiers: gerontology emerges as a science*. Cambridge: Cambridge University Press.
Binstock, R. H. (2003). 'The war on "anti-aging medicine"', *Gerontologist*, 43 (1): 4–14.
Butler, R. N. (1975). *Why survive? Being old in America*. New York: Harper and Row.
(1989). 'Dispelling ageism: the cross-cutting intervention', *Annals of the American Academy of Political and Social Science*, 503: 138–47.
Bytheway, B. (1995). *Ageism*. Buckingham: Open University Press.
(2002). 'Positioning gerontology in an ageist world'. In L. Andersson, ed., *Cultural gerontology*. Westport, Conn.: Greenwood Publishing Group, pp. 59–76.
Bytheway, B., and J. Johnson (1990). 'On defining ageism', *Critical Social Policy*, 27: 27–39.
Callahan, D. (1987). *Setting limits: medical goals in an aging society*. New York: Simon and Schuster.
Cohen, E. S. (2001). 'The complex nature of ageism: What is it? Who does it? Who perceives it?' *Gerontologist*, 41 (5): 576–7.
Cole, T. R. (1992). *The journey of life: a cultural history of aging in America*. Cambridge: Cambridge University Press.
de Beauvoir, S. (1979). *Old age*. Harmondsworth: Penguin.
Down, D., ed. (2000). *Family spending: a report on the 1999–2000 Family Expenditure Survey*. London: The Statistics Office.
Fairlie, H. (1988). 'Greedy geezers', *New Republic*, 28 March, p. 19.
Glover, I., and M. Branine, eds. (2001). *Ageism in work and employment*. Aldershot: Ashgate.
Henry, J. (1965). *Culture against man*. New York: Random House.
Hornstein, Z., Encel, S., Gunderson, M., and D. Neumark (2001). *Outlawing age discrimination*. Bristol: The Policy Press.
Johnson, P., Conrad, C., and D. Thomson, eds. (1989). *Workers versus pensioners: intergenerational justice in an ageing world*. Manchester: Manchester University Press.
Kalish, R. (1979). 'The new ageism and the failure models: a polemic', *Gerontologist*, 19 (4): 398–402.
Kuhn, M. (1977). *Maggie Kuhn on aging: a dialogue edited by Dieter Hessel*. Philadelphia: The Westminster Press.
Lerner, M. (1957). *America as a civilization: life and thought in the United States today*. New York: Simon and Schuster.
Levy, B. R. (2001). 'Eradication of ageism requires addressing the enemy within', *Gerontologist*, 41 (5): 578–9.
Levy, B. R., and M. R. Banaji (2002). 'Implicit ageism'. In T. Nelson, ed., *Ageism: stereotyping and prejudice against older persons*, A Bradford Book. Cambridge, Mass.: MIT Press.
Macdonald, B., and C. Rich (1983). *Look me in the eye: old women, aging and ageism*. London: The Women's Press.

Palmore, E. (1999). *Ageism: negative and positive*. New York: Springer Publishing Company.

—— (2000). 'The ageism survey: first findings', *Gerontologist*, 41 (5): 572–5.

Phillipson, C. (1998). *Reconstructing old age*. London: Sage Publications.

Rickards, S. (2001). *Ageism – too costly to ignore*. London: Employers' Forum on Age.

Robb, B. (1967). *Sans everything: a case to answer*. London: Nelson.

Townsend, P. (1962). *The last refuge: a survey of residential institutions and homes for the aged in England and Wales*. London: Routledge and Kegan Paul.

Woodward, K. (1991). *Aging and its discontents: Freud and other fictions*. Indianapolis: Indiana University Press.

CHAPTER 4.9

Profiles of the Oldest-Old

LEONARD W. POON, YURI JANG, SANDRA G. REYNOLDS, AND ERICK McCARTHY

The age group 85 and older, commonly referred to as the "oldest-old," is the fastest-growing segment of the population in most if not all industrialized countries. The main reasons for their exponential growth are the steady increase in the average lifespan along with a decline in the birth rate. A dramatic example of this population growth is Japan whose population's average lifespan doubled in only 50 years from an average of 42 years in the Second World War to over 80 in the new millennium. This dramatic increase made Japan's population one of the top two most long-lived nations in the world; the other is Sweden.

Despite the remarkable growth of the oldest-old, little attention has been paid to this segment of the population as extant knowledge on ageing has focused on the 65 and older age group. This simple integration of older adults, however, conceals diverse characteristics spanning over 40 years of life. Given the ageing of the older population itself and increased heterogeneity within the group with age, more information is needed on the oldest-old. Further, the oldest-old are by definition the survivors of the human species. Assessment of the characteristics and survival skills of the oldest-old will be useful to understand this unique population better and to prepare for the future of ageing societies.

In such assessment, it would be important to note the continuity and discontinuity of the ageing processes from 65 to 85 years and beyond. Do health and abilities continue on the same trajectory after 85? Or, do the oldest-old, by virtue of being survivors, maintain special characteristics and skills that differentiated them from those with a normal lifespan? These and other questions are waiting to be explored.

INTERNATIONAL DEMOGRAPHIC TRENDS

Population ageing and the dramatic growth in the number of the oldest-old is a global phenomenon. The oldest-old currently constitute about 1% of the total human population and 17% of the older population worldwide. In developed countries, the oldest-old constitute a higher proportion (22%) of the older population, compared to 13% in less developed countries. More than half of the current oldest-old population is from six countries (China, United States of America, India, Japan, Germany, and Russian Federation). The worldwide number of the oldest-old is projected to increase fivefold by the year 2050. The most notable increase in the oldest-old is expected to take place in Japan where more than 1 in every 3 older adults will be 85 years and older in 2050.

US PERSPECTIVE

According to the 2000 US census, the number of the oldest-old in the United States of America currently numbers 4.2 million comprising 1.5% of the total population. This group is estimated to reach 6.9 million in 2020 and 18 million in 2050 when the youngest survivors of the "baby boom" generation join the group. Among the oldest-old, centenarians will show remarkable increases with the current number of 50,404 projected to increase to

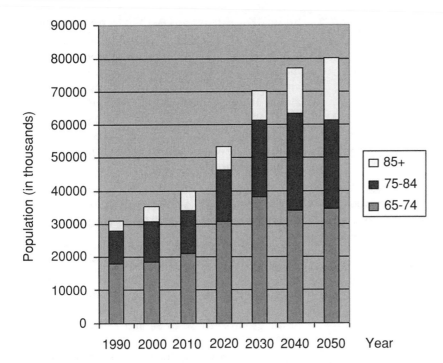

Figure 1. Older population by age group in the Unites States: 1990-2050.

214,000 in 2020 and 834,000 in 2050. The pattern of growth in the older population in the US by age group is illustrated in Figure 1. The dramatic growth in the oldest-old has great implications for our society including reconceptualization of age and ageing and modification of social policies and services.

One of the most striking characteristics of the oldest-old group is their gender distribution. The gender ratio among adults in their 60s is 8.5 males per 10 females, while this ratio is reduced to 4.2 males per 10 females among the oldest-old. The imbalance in gender ratio becomes more salient with advancing age: 8 out of 10 centenarians are female. Due to longer life expectancies of females and their tendency to have older spouses, a majority of the oldest-old is comprised of unmarried females.

There are several other sociodemographic characteristics that differentiate the oldest-old from the young-old (65–74). The likelihood of living alone increases with age, especially for females. The percentage of women living alone for the young-old is 32% while that in the oldest-old is 57%; for males, the corresponding proportions are 13% and 29%. Only a small portion (1.56 million) of the older population was institutionalized in 2000; the percentage increases dramatically with age, ranging from 1.1% for young-old to 18.2% for the oldest-old. Also, the

oldest-old were shown to have lower levels of education and higher poverty rates compared to the younger-old. Particularly, the oldest-old who were non-White and female were more disadvantaged in socioeconomic status.

Another important characteristic in the oldest-old is increased racial and ethnic diversity. In the next few decades, the racial and ethnic components of the oldest-old are predicted to change profoundly with a remarkable increase in the number of minority elders. It is projected that more than one-third of the oldest-old will be non-Whites in 2050. This projection suggests the importance of understanding cultural and ethnic characteristics of older minority populations to meet their needs properly.

CHANGES IN HEALTH AND FUNCTION

Physical and functional health in the oldest-old are generally associated with the physiological capacity to carry out both basic and instrumental activities of daily living (B/IADLs) independently. A wide range of individual differences in health and function are apparent in the oldest-old population, where

TABLE 1. Distribution of disability and institutionalization in the oldest-old

Age group	Disability (%)	Nursing home (%)
85–89	55	17
90–94	65	32
95–99	80	42
100+	82	48

individuals can vary from being extremely mobile and functionally independent, to those experiencing comorbidity resulting in frailty and dependency. It is estimated that approximately one-third of the oldest-old are healthy enough to live independently in the community, one-third are functionally impaired, and one-third are extremely frail and disabled. Table 1 further illustrates the extent of disabilities and institutionalization estimated in different segments of the oldest-old (Kramarow *et al.*, 1999). The high incidence of comorbidity, including heart, lung, and circulatory ailments, osteoporosis, osteoarthritis, dementia, and visual and/or hearing impairments, are all tangible reasons for the high incidence of frailty and dependency in the oldest-old.

LEADING CAUSES OF DEATH

The most prevalent cause of death in the oldest-old in the United States, regardless of ethnic heritage or gender, is cardiovascular disease (including both heart and cerebrovascular diseases). Cancer is a distant second, followed by chronic respiratory diseases, pneumonia/influenza, and Alzheimer's disease. Although the cause of death for a majority of the oldest-old is due to comorbidity, worldwide mortality statistics are prone to biases due to the practice of listing only one specific health condition as the cause of death (Kinsella and Velkoff, 2001).

DIET AND NUTRITION

Several dietary intake factors have been found to be associated with positive physical and functional health outcomes in the oldest-old, including a diet high in fiber, calcium, and vitamin A, consumption of certain fruits and vegetables, and eating

breakfast on a daily basis (M. A. Johnson *et al.*, 1992). It has been reported that nutritional supplementation use in the oldest-old ranges from approximately 30% to 70% depending on age, activity level, and frequency of supplement use, and women are almost twice as likely to use a vitamin or mineral supplement compared to men. The most common supplements consumed by the oldest-old include multivitamins/minerals, vitamin C, calcium, and vitamin E (Daniel *et al.*, 1996).

HIGHER RATES OF DEPRESSIVE SYMPTOMS AMONG THE OLDEST-OLD

Research on depression from lifespan perspectives has shown that depression has a curvilinear relation to age with high symptoms in young adulthood, lower in middle age, and then increases from the 60s on. Statistical reports have shown that 21% of the group aged 80 to 84 and 23% of the group aged 85 and older had severe depressive symptoms, compared with 15% in the younger-old groups. The greater levels of disability, comorbidity, and various social losses commonly experienced in later years of life may have attributed to the higher depressive symptoms observed among the oldest-old.

PROTECTIVE FACTORS FOR LATE-LIFE DEPRESSION

Late-life depression is not inevitable and there are many older adults who enjoy a high quality of life in their 80s, 90s, and 100s. Also, an increasing number of studies have shown promising findings that mental health of the oldest-old can be protected and even enhanced. Researchers have found that the negative effects of late-life stressors on depression can be attenuated through older persons' psychological characteristics such as sense of control or mastery, self-esteem, and adaptive personality traits (Dunkle *et al.*, 2001; Zarit *et al.*, 1999). These studies highlight potential roles of psychological characteristics in protecting older adults from negative consequences of life challenges in later years. Given these findings, the mental health of older adults can be recovered and promoted through interventions that reinforce positive psychological characteristics. It is particularly important for the oldest-old to have psychological strategies to accept some of the adverse changes and make positive adjustments in their later years of life.

SIGNIFICANCE OF SUBJECTIVE PERCEPTIONS VERSUS OBJECTIVE HEALTH INDICATORS

Along the same line, subjective perception plays an essential role in the lives of the oldest-old. Researchers have found that self-perceived health is more important than objective health indicators in predicting long-term health and wellbeing (Borawski et al., 1996). Also, positive attitude towards ageing was even found to increase longevity (Levy et al., 2002). These findings are consistent with the concept of "mind over matter," which implies the significance of subjective appraisal over objective situations. Positive perceptions and optimistic attitudes seem to be a key for better physical and mental outcomes among the oldest-old.

UNIQUE STRENGTHS OF THE OLDEST-OLD

Most studies have generally focused on adverse and vulnerable characteristics of the oldest-old. However, the unique strengths of the oldest-old need to be acknowledged. Since ageing itself is an adaptational process, the oldest-old have advantages in dealing with stresses and developing efficient personal coping strategies through lifetime experiences. It is also suggested that the oldest-old have differential expectations and perspectives of life and lowered reference points based on realities in advanced old age (C. L. Johnson and Barer, 1997). An example would be that the oldest-old are more likely to consider disease and disability as changes with ageing rather than health problems. Finally, the oldest-old may benefit from selective survivorship. The special status as survivors beyond the expected lifespan may bolster psychological states of the oldest-old and help them make positive evaluations of themselves (Martin et al., 2000; Poon et al., 1992b).

PREVALENCE OF DEMENTIA AMONG THE VERY OLD

It is known that the prevalence of dementia increases with age. The prevalence rate was shown to be about 5% at age 65, and the rates for each successive age group after 60 are estimated to double every five years. A summary of eight European studies (Hofman et al., 1991) showed an increase of prevalence rate from 40% to 70% between the ages of 90 and 95.

Empirical data is available on estimates of prevalence rate of dementia among centenarians from three different countries (Hagberg et al., 2001). A Hungarian study showed a prevalence rate of 43% for men and 63% for women. A Japanese study found a prevalence rate of approximately 63% and about 15% of the centenarians were found to be very cognitively intact. A Swedish study reported a prevalence rate of 30% to 50%. The variation of prevalence reported from these three countries could be due to differences in sampling methods, criteria for dementia, and measurement instruments.

INTELLECTUAL ABILITIES AMONG COGNITIVELY INTACT OLDEST-OLD

In a study comparing cognitive functions among community-dwelling and non-demented adults in their 60s, 80s, and 100s, Poon and his colleagues (1992a) found that centenarians on an average performed significantly worse compared to octogenarians and sexagenarians in learning new information and retrieval of familiar information, as well as in tests of intelligence such as vocabulary, block design, arithmetic, and picture arrangement. The exception was in everyday problem solving in that centenarians performed as well as the younger groups. In general, the magnitudes of age differences were smaller in crystallized intelligence (e.g. information contained in the lexicon, such as vocabulary) compared to fluid intelligence (e.g. learning new information, such as paired associate learning). Education was found to have a profound positive effect in mitigating the level of performance differences between subjects, especially centenarians.

INTERINDIVIDUAL DIFFERENCES

As noted earlier, centenarians on the average perform at a significantly lower level in cognitive tasks. The average was, however, a poor predictor of individual abilities among the oldest-old. In a comparison of similar cognitive tests performed by centenarians and younger comparison groups in the Georgia and Swedish centenarian studies (Hagberg *et al.*, 2001) the range and interindividual variability of cognitive performances was the largest for centenarians, compared to their younger cohorts. The large diversity was due to some centenarians who could maintain their high level of performance over their lifespan. Some centenarians performed at levels similar to younger cohorts, and some performed similarly to college students.

The above findings question the relative importance of chronological age as a predictor of cognitive functions. Chronological age is an excellent predictor of cognition when minimal information is provided. However, when physical health, pathology (dementia), mental health (depression), education, social and economic support, personality, lifestyle, and other concomitant factors are brought to bear, chronological age exerts relatively little influence.

DECREASE IN SIZE OF SOCIAL NETWORK

Most older adults maintain social networks into later years, but the size and nature of the networks change as they face declining health and re-constriction of networks due to outliving spouse and other relatives. The social networks of older adults generally contain fewer peripheral social partners than those of their younger counterparts (Fung *et al.*, 2001). Those who remain more engaged in social networks are more likely to live with others, to have a child, and to have a child living nearby. Those who are less engaged in large social networks are generally in poorer health and may reject norms which place social expectations on them incongruent with their capacities.

INNER CIRCLE TIES REMAIN STRONG

Research consistently confirms that a strong majority of the oldest-old still maintain a confidant and also name more than five people in their inner circle of social networks (Martin *et al.*, 1996). Frequently, this inner circle includes a child. In fact, these oldest-old are more likely to have a son or daughter living locally than the younger-old, probably reflecting an increased likelihood of moving towards relatives as a greater need, or potential need, for support in old age becomes more pressing. Additionally, most of the oldest-old who have children see, or have contact with, children on a daily to weekly basis.

DIVERSE SOCIAL SUPPORT

When older adults need care, it is overwhelmingly family that provides help, but the type and intensity of this help varies greatly within family units. Although shared living arrangements are largely a function of the poor health status of older adults, living with someone who is within one's age cohort does not guarantee a caregiving resource due to functional frailties in this population. If children provide assistance, it may not be necessarily "hands on" assistance. Children may help with instrumental activities of daily living such as shopping and running errands, but an older adult may hire help for household assistance with cleaning and laundry. Multigenerational households reflect cultural norms; although these households are in the minority in the United States, multigenerational households are not uncommon in Eastern societies (Yi *et al.*, 2002).

CHILDLESS RECEIVE LESS HELP FROM RELATIVES

For those elders without children, fewer receive help from relatives than those with children, and significantly fewer childless have weekly contact with any relative. Additionally, a small minority of those who are unmarried and childless report receiving instrumental help from close relatives. In spite of receiving less assistance from relatives than those with children, however, almost half of childless older people say they receive emotional benefits from kin, attesting to the importance of social ties throughout the lifespan.

DEPENDENCE MAY DECREASE SOCIAL ISOLATION

Although need for assistance with daily activities of living increases, those who are dependent on help report less social isolation, possibly because they are brought into regular social contact with caregivers (Bondevik and Skogstad, 1998). Adaptations to changing dependencies are a reflection of how the oldest-old modify their world both psychologically

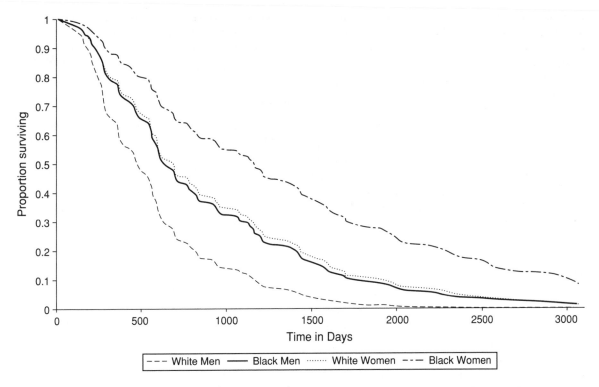

Figure 2. Survival of centenarian by sex and race.

and socially based on the realities of ageing, and redefine normative social expectations.

CONTRIBUTION OF GENDER AND RACE TO SURVIVAL

Figure 2 shows the survival functions of four groups of centenarians by gender (male or female) and race (African- or Caucasian-American). It charts the number of days of survival after reaching the age of 100 among 137 centenarians who participated in the Georgia Centenarian Study (Poon *et al.*, 2000). The majority (75.9%) of the centenarians were females and Caucasians (71.5%). At the time of initial participation in the study, the participants had a mean age of 100.8 years.

The champion survivors were the African-American females, followed by both the Caucasian-American females and African-American males. Women on the average survived 1,020 days after attaining 100 years. Men, on the other hand, survived an average of 781 days. The gender difference in survival in the first two years was not significant; however, the difference was significantly pronounced after three years in favor of females.

Gender and race were both associated with survivorship, with African Americans showing longer survival times than Caucasian Americans. At any given time, the risk of death for women was only 54% that of men. Likewise, risk of death for African Americans was 57% that of Caucasian Americans at any given time.

BEYOND GENDER AND RACE

Simple correlations among characteristics of centenarians and number of days of survival showed four other significant relationships: (1) Father's age at death was found to exert a positive effect on number of days of survival. No effect was found for mother's age at death; (2) Three variables associated with social support were also found to be related to survival. They were: talking on the phone, having some-one to help, and having a caregiver; (3) Anthropometric variables that are related to dietary sufficiency were found to relate to survival. They were: triceps skinfold (an index of body fat), body mass index, and waist to hip ratio; and (4)

Higher cognitive performance in problem solving, learning and memory, and intelligence measures in picture arrangement and block design were found to relate positively to survival.

Finally, regression modeling was employed to examine the unique and joint contribution to survival in six areas (Martin *et al.*, 2000). These areas are: health and health habits, dietary habits, cognition and intelligence, personality and coping styles, support systems, and mental health. Five factors were found to significantly predict days of survival after age 100. The significant predictors were gender, race, physical activity of daily living, verbal intelligence, and triceps skinfold.

SUMMARY AND CONCLUSION

A popular and much-discussed question is whether there is a secret of living to be the oldest-old. If there is one secret, it has not been discovered yet. Rather, the profiles of the oldest-old show significant individual diversities and paradoxes. On the one hand, there are individuals over 85 years of age who are independent and perform intellectually and physically at the same or higher levels, compared to their younger cohorts. On the other hand, frailty, dependence, and intellectual decline, even without dementia, are seen as benchmarks of the oldest-old.

While the profiles of the oldest-old show general pictures and averages, owing to the significant amount of individual diversity in this population the profiles may not be predictive of any one individual in that age range. The diversities reflected the simple fact that there are many paths to living beyond the average lifespan. At the beginning of this chapter, we inquired about the continuity and discontinuity of the ageing processes from 65 to 85 years and beyond. The profiles of the oldest-old show both continuity and discontinuity. Perhaps the diversities and paradoxes of living to be the oldest-old demonstrate a resiliency of the human spirit, and much of that resiliency remains to be understood.

FURTHER READING

Dunkle, R., Roberts, B., and M. Haug (2001). *The oldest old in everyday life: self-perceptions, coping with change, and stress*. New York: Springer.

Johnson, C. L., and B. M. Barer (1997). *Life beyond 85 years: the aura of survivorships*. New York: Springer.

Martin, P., Rott, C., Hagberg, B., and K. Morgan, eds. (2000). *Centenarians: autonomy versus dependence in the oldest old*. New York: Springer.

REFERENCES

Bondevik, M., and A. Skogstad (1998). "The oldest-old, ADL, social network, and loneliness," *Western Journal of Nursing Research*, 20: 325–43.

Borawski, E. A., Kinney, J. M., and E. Kahana (1996). "The meaning of older adults' health appraisals: congruence with health status and determinant of mortality," *Journal of Gerontology: Social Science*, 51B: S157–S170.

Daniel, T., Houston, D. K., and M. A. Johnson (1996). "Vitamin and mineral supplement use among the elderly." In B. Vella, ed., *Facts and research in gerontology*. New York: Springer, pp. 163–79.

Dunkle, R., Roberts, B., and M. Haug (2001). *The oldest-old in everyday life: self-perceptions, coping with change, and stress*. New York: Springer.

Fung, H. H., Carstensen, L. L., and F. R. Lang (2001). "Age-related patterns in social networks among European Americans and African Americans: implications for socioemotional selectivity across the lifespan," *International Journal of Aging and Human Development*, 52: 185–206.

Hagberg, B., Alfredson, B. B., Poon, L. W., and A. Homma (2001). "Cognitive functioning in centenarians: a coordinated analysis of results from three countries," *Journal of Gerontology: Psychological Sciences*, 56B: 141–51.

Hofman, A., Rocca, W., Brayne, C., Breteler, M. B. B., Clarke, M., Cooper, B., Copeland, J. R. M., Dartigues, J. F., Da Silva Droux, A., Hagnell, D., Heeran, T. J., Engedal, K., Jonker, C., Lindesay, J., Lobo, A., Mann, A. H., Molsa, P. K., Morgan, K., O'Connor, D. W., Sulkava, R., Kay, D. W. K., and L. Amaducci (1991). "The prevalence of dementia in Europe: a collaborative study of 1980–1990 findings," *International Journal of Epidemiology*, 20: 736–48.

Johnson, C. L., and B. M. Barer (1997). *Life beyond 85 years: the aura of survivorships*. New York: Springer.

Johnson, M. A., Brown, M. A., Poon, L. W., Martin, P., and G. M. Clayton (1992). "Nutritional patterns of centenarians," *International Journal of Aging and Human Development*, 34: 57–76.

Kinsella, K., and V. A. Velkoff (2001). *An aging world*, US Census Bureau, Series P95/01–1. Washington, D.C.: US Government Printing Office.

Kramarow, E., Lentzer, H., Rooks, R., Weeks, J., and S. Saydah (1999). *Health and aging chart book, Health, United States*. Hyattsville, Md.: National Center for Health Statistics.

Levy, B. R., Slade, M. D., Kunkel, S. R., and S. V. Kasl (2002). "Longevity increased by positive self-perception of aging," *Journal of Personality and Social Psychology*, 83: 261–70.

Martin, P., Poon, L. W., Kim, E., and M. A. Johnson (1996). "Social and psychological resources in the oldest-old," *Experimental Aging Research*, 22: 121–39.

Martin, P., Rott, C., Hagberg, B., and K. Morgan, eds. (2000). *Centenarians: autonomy versus dependence in the oldest-old*. New York: Springer.

Poon, L. W., Martin, P., Clayton, G. M., Messner, S., and C. A. Noble (1992a). "The influences of cognitive resources on adaptation and old age," *International Journal of Aging and Human Development*, 34: 31–46.

Poon, L. W., Sweaney, A. L., Clayton, G. M., Merriam, S. B., Martin, P., Pless, B. S., Johnson, M. A., Thielman, S. B., and B. C. Courtenay (1992b). "The Georgia Centenar-ian Study," *International Journal of Aging and Human Development*, 34: 1–17.

Poon, L. W., Johnson, M. A., Davey, A., Dawson, D. V., Siegler, I. C., and P. Martin (2000). "Psychosocial predictors of survival among centenarians." In P. Martin, C. Rott, B. Hagberg and K. Morgan, eds., *Centenarians: autonomy versus dependence in the oldest old*. New York: Springer.

Yi, Z., Vaupel, J. W., Zhenyu, X., Chunyuan, Z., and L. Yuzhi (2002). "Sociodemographic and health profiles of the oldest-old in China," *Population and Development Review*, 28: 251–73.

Zarit, S. H., Femia, E. E., Gatz, M., and B. Johansson (1999). "Prevalence, incidence and correlates of depression in the oldest-old: the OCTO study," *Aging and Mental Health*, 3: 119–28.

CHAPTER 4.10

Images of Ageing: Cultural Representations of Later Life

MIKE FEATHERSTONE AND MIKE HEPWORTH

INTRODUCTION: GLOBAL IMAGES

Why do we need to study images of ageing? In part it is a result of living in societies in which images can be readily reproduced to circulate in public and private life. In many areas of the contemporary world, it is hard to avoid images of youthful, fit and beautiful bodies often associated with idealized representations of a consumer lifestyle. These images are now global as even a cursory glance at the Internet quickly reveals. At the same time these consumer lifestyle ideals are accompanied by negative images of overweight and sickly bodies, those people we encounter in public spaces in the mall and street whose bodies have somehow betrayed them. Older people are often included in the latter category and in ageist stereotypes are caricatured as frail, forgetful, shabby, out-of-date and on the edge of senility and death. In a number of countries, campaigns have recently been mounted to counteract such negative images of older people; in Denmark, for example, explicit efforts are being made to confront the caricature of older people as negative and outdated. In Australia, the government of Victoria has provided $50,000 to promote positive images of older men and women not in terms of the youthfulness of their external appearance but in celebration of their continuing contribution to social life – one billboard in Melbourne, Australia, urged readers to 'Look past the wrinkles.' The Madrid International Plan of Action on Ageing (2002) included images of ageing as part of the promotion of a new plan of action to promote more positive attitudes towards older people.

Such counter images of positive ageing are increasingly evident and it is also clear that the various attempts to redefine the meaning of old age over the last twenty years occur within a changing social context. We all live in a world growing older: in the United States it is expected that the proportion of people over 65 will double to 70 million by 2030 (Seabrook, 2004: 7). In Britain the visibility of old people increased dramatically with the number of pensioners rising from 6 per cent to 18 per cent over the course of the twentieth century. Yet if we consider the question of ageing on a global level, it is clear that globalization and the expansion of the neo-liberal market economy is producing a range of differential effects. We cannot assume that all countries and governments will have the resources to follow the same solutions proposed in the West. Will the image of the pensioner or senior citizen able to look forward to a consumer lifestyle retirement apply around the world? Images of ageing cannot be easily detached from the politics and economics of ageing.

SOCIAL GERONTOLOGY

In this changing and diverse social context there is an increasing tendency in gerontology to acknowledge the importance of images of ageing. An indication of broader changes in the interpretation of the ageing process can be found in Blaikie's analysis of representations of ageing in popular culture (1999). In this text the author shows how evidence of significant transformations in social attitudes towards ageing and retirement can be found in images of age-ing in photographs, films, popular fiction and the media.

It is therefore not surprising that the study of images of ageing has gradually moved from a marginal position in social gerontology to occupy a more central position in the discipline. Several examples can be cited: Shuichi Wada's study of the image and status of older people in Japan (1995); the analysis by Hummel *et al.* (1995) of the images produced by children in an international competi-tion, 'Draw your grandma', which involved children aged 6–14 years in thirty-three different countries; and Kaid and Garner's work (2004) on the portrayal of older adults in political advertising in America. In the UK, one of the key textbooks on ageing by Bond, Coleman and Peace, includes a chapter by the authors of this article on 'Images of ageing' (1993).

This tendency reflects the contemporary global understanding that the ageing process cannot be adequately explained solely in biological and med-ical terms but is an interactive process involving social and cultural factors. From a biomedical per-spective the ageing process after midlife is seen to be one of decline into a dependent old age but the alternative view of ageing as a complex process of interaction between biological, psychological and social factors has resulted in a more sustained inter-rogation of medical and policy-based models of age-ing, calling for an enlarged awareness of the ageing process as lived experience which individuals and groups endow with specific meanings. If the qual-ity of later life is to be improved, it is argued, not only are medical improvements necessary but peo-ple's attitudes towards the ageing process and old age must be changed. This concern, as the examples briefly quoted above show, has directed attention to images used to represent the process of ageing into old age.

WHAT ARE IMAGES?

How do we understand images? Who produces images and how are they disseminated? What is the relationship between images and the everyday world of lived experience? And how do we evalu-ate the potential for the reform of images in a more positive anti-ageist direction? What are the main directions of global flows of images around the world today?

On its most basic level an image is seen as a rep-resentation or copy of the original reality, as found, for example, in certain types of paintings, statues and photographs which aim to present an accurate likeness or 'living image' of the human models. The impetus here is to produce valid documentary evi-dence of the person, as, for example, in a photograph of Queen Victoria in later life. Yet, as this reference to a royal and remote personage suggests, an image can also mean not so much an accurate copy or imi-tation of the actual individual but rather an impres-sion, or incomplete rendition governed by interpre-tive and imaginative framing – something intended to reveal essential features of the persona, which are not evident in a superficial glance, or the preoccupa-tion with an accurate recording of external appear-ance. A photograph of a famous older person may therefore be seen as an interpretation of the essen-tial inner character of an individual which has been artfully constructed for public display. Other exam-ples of such images of historical celebrities in later life include Ghandi, Albert Schweitzer, Einstein and Mother Theresa. It is the interplay between these two interpretations of the term 'image' (copy and impression) which leads to disputes over the distor-tion of an image in which the accuracy, imaginative input and representativeness are subjected to close scrutiny as in the question: 'what was Queen Victoria "really" like in old age?' (Rennell, 2001). A fur-ther interpretation of an image as a mental impres-sion refers to a representation deriving from any of the senses, including sound impressions, touch and smell. But it is the impact of the visual which the phrase 'images of ageing' most frequently connotes, and in the discussion in this chapter 'images of age-ing' refers to the public representations of older peo-ple in a visually and age-conscious society.

IMAGES, THE BODY AND THE SELF

Behind the public images of ageing are, of course, the 'lived bodies', of individuals who carry embodied memories. As Rennell (2001) shows, the widely pub-licized image of Queen Victoria as the grandmother of her people was in sharp contrast to the lived reality of her later life where not even her closest physician was allowed access to her ageing body. A similar example can be found in the concealment of the paralysis of the American President Franklin D. Roosevelt. The 'lived body' of ageing points to the way in which our identities are embodied and formed not just through internal biological and psychological changes, but through encounters with other bodies in direct face-to-face communication, or perceived more indirectly as when we look at someone across the street. As human beings, we experience a double aspect to our existence: our embodied identities work through both seeing (subjective perception) and also being seen by others.

In contemporary Western culture the dominant message is that a positive perception of the body is central to the way the body functions and performs. The perception of the body's functioning, health and outer appearance is formed in a social and cultural context which has two dimensions. It is firstly, predominantly, governed by the visual: a medium in which judgements (both positive and negative) are constantly made in the daily social interactions with others who can feedback positive and negative evaluations of the body. Secondly, it is a context in which we not only look at and are looked at by others, but in which we are confronted in our daily lives by countless images of the human body in the media and elsewhere.

In addition to the multitude of human images which can be found in paintings, drawings, statues, photographs, television, the cinema and the new digital media, there is the more fluid notion of body self-image (Ferguson, 1997). This double sense of image – the images depicted and recorded in various visual media and the notion that our self-image is linked to our body images – suggests that the formation of our own body image and self-image take place in a cultural context in which images cannot be seen as transparent and neutral. Our perception of our own bodies is mediated by the direct and tacit judgements of others in interactions and our own reflexive judgements of their view, compounded by what we think we see in the mirror. Through this reflexive process we are guided by our culture to react emotionally and evaluate the relationship between public and self-images in ways which become habitual and taken for granted. In this way we learn different ways of seeing and assessing the repertoire of positive and negative body images and ways of looking at bodies in different cultures. Every image of a human being is effectively an image of ageing, given that it provides a representation of the face and body which is of a person at a particular point on a chronological time scale and therefore immediately marked in terms of linear age. But our bodies do not just age in time, in tune with the mechanisms of some inner biological clock, but are 'aged by culture' (Gullette, 2004). The fact that we have 'cultured bodies', therefore, suggests that our bodies are never just biomedical entities but are perceived through a cultural matrix in which the visible signs of the ageing of the body are not only externally displayed but have become regarded as manifestations of what is regarded in the Western tradition as a process of decline and loss.

IMAGES OF AGEING IN SOCIAL GERONTOLOGY

Visual representations of later life occur widely in the history of Western art. David Lowenthal's study of memory, history and changing attitudes towards the past (1985) includes a chapter on 'The look of age' where he discusses the tendency in Western culture to value the appearance of ageing in objects (antique buildings, furniture, etc.) much more highly than the appearance of age in human beings. Antique objects age 'gracefully' whilst human beings pass into a state of 'decline'. The idea that many people in Western culture find the external signs of human ageing displeasing or a source of disgust (Elias, 1985) is persistent and well documented, but it is not simply a question of the disgust provoked by the external appearance of age as such – negative attitudes towards ageing extend beyond surface appearances to include attitudes towards the basic fact of chronological age. A good example is the celebration of the birthday in cards and other numerical markers of time passing.

As noted above, one of the central themes in the gerontological analysis of images of ageing Western culture is the pervasive nature of negative or ageist images and the importance of replacing this ageist tradition with more positive images celebrating old age as a valued period of the lifecourse. As Bytheway (1995) shows, ageism is closely associated with a particular form of collective social imagery which ignores the diversity of individual experiences of ageing and lumps all older people together under a limited range of social categories. In his book, he compiles a record of visual and verbal images of ageism in order to show how deeply embedded they are in popular culture and their influence over our attitudes towards older people. His examples include advertisements, cartoons, photographs, greetings cards and photographs of older people in care. Another striking example of the analysis of ageist imagery is the detailed research by Warnes (1993) into the origins of the word 'burden' and the ways in which it has become negatively associated with later life in the popular media and in political pronouncements about the 'burden of old age' in contemporary society. As Warnes shows, this dismissive interpretation of old age is a social construction, reflecting negative beliefs and attitudes about old age rather than any valid objective evidence concerning the quality of life of older people or their ability to make a positive contribution to society. The experience of old age is thus shaped not simply by processes of biological change but through the power of the image of 'burden' to shape our perceptions of growing older.

Ageism, then, refers to a process of collective stereotyping which emphasizes the negative features of ageing which are ultimately traced back to biomedical 'decline', rather than the culturally determined value placed on later life. This interpretation of growing older has been described by Gullette (1997), who has carried out extensive research into images of ageing in fiction, as the 'decline narrative'. The 'decline narrative' defines middle age (a period which begins around the age of 50) as the point of 'entrance' into a physical decline which continues relentlessly into old age and death. Gullette (1985) shows, in her detailed analysis of cultural intersections between fictional and non-fictional literature on ageing, how this idea has become firmly fixed in the social imagination of later life.

Whilst the central concern of gerontologists with images of ageing continues to involve a critical engagement with evidence of ageism, a number of recent developments have added a layer of theoretical sophistication to this area of study. These are:

(1) social constructionism;
(2) the sociology of consumer culture, the sociology of the body and gendered gerontology.

SOCIAL CONSTRUCTIONISM

Social constructionism provides a critique of the 'decline narrative' and the ways in which old age is 'naturalized' and fixed, by conceptualizing ageing as a cultural category (Hockey and James, 2003). It argues that the prejudice against later life, which the existing power balances operating in social and cultural life have helped to construct, can always be progressively reconstructed. A good example of this process is the effort which has been made to create active images of retirement as a dynamic phase of the lifecourse, in contrast to traditional images of retirement as a passive disengagement from social life and removal into a world represented by the 'retirement uniform' prescribed for both women and men (Featherstone and Hepworth, 1995).

Another example of the influence of images of ageing on our interpretation of biomedical change is found in Gubrium's (1986) analysis of the processes involved in the social construction of Alzheimer's disease in America. In this research into the difficult issue of determining the origins of signs of confusion in older people, Gubrium shows how images of Alzheimer's disease in, for example, poetry written by caregivers (a popular image is that of Alzheimer's as a 'thief' who steals the self) are used by carers to make sense of the identity changes that have taken place in suffering relatives. The changes in social and verbal competence resulting from the biomedical changes associated with Alzheimer's disease have to be given meaning through the use of culturally prescribed imagery. On the level of everyday lived experience, Alzheimer's disease is not only a biomedical problem: it challenges the meaning of the self and of life. The problem is that Alzheimer's disease as a biomedical category is still imprecisely defined and there are serious gaps in the diagnosis of the origins of mental confusion in later life. Gubrium argues that, faced with these problems, non-sufferers draw on visual and verbal images such as that of Alzheimer's as a 'thief' to fill the knowledge vacuum. In this process 'Alzheimer's disease' becomes a generalized label for all kinds of confusion associated with ageing.

Hockey and James (1993) adopt a similar analytical perspective when they examine the role of images in the construction of old age as a process of infantilization. Older people are not, of course, children, but there is strong evidence that when in residential care they are often treated *as if* they are. Older people who have become dependent in some way on their carers are treated as having reduced claims on conventional adult status. Thus, when addressed by carers, they may lose the adult title 'Miss', 'Mrs' or 'Mr' and be summoned like children by their Christian names or given anonymous diminutive titles like 'dear' or 'love'. The use of the metaphor of old age as a childlike state or 'second childhood' therefore justifies and supports certain forms of care in which older people are denied the status of being fully adult, and Hockey and James' analysis provides persuasive evidence of the power of images to influence the ways in which carers relate to older people.

Infantilization is, of course, regarded as a prime example of ageism and as such damaging to the elderly's self-esteem. Self-esteem is regarded as a key factor in positive ageing, and a crucial factor in the cultivation and maintenance of self-esteem is awareness of the approval of others. Self-esteem involves an affirmative interplay between the self and the external world; as described by Coleman (1993) it has two components: 'self evaluation' (a comparative exercise) and 'self worth' (1993: 128). Self-worth arises out of positive interaction with others who perceive our value, and, if such positive evaluations are absent, then those older people who are directly affected are likely to experience a diminished sense of social worth (Coleman, 1993: 129).

The role of the approval of others in the maintenance of personal self-esteem raises another significant question concerning the influence of images of ageing on the subjective experience of growing older. Images of ageing create expectations in both younger and older people about how older people should speak and act. An important issue here is the discrepancy revealed in research between the subjective experience of ageing and the attitudes and expectations of others towards those they perceive as older. A useful way of conceptualizing the distance that may exist in the everyday experience of ageing between public images of ageing and private experience is to think of ageing as a kind of mask (Biggs, 1993; Featherstone and Hepworth, 1991, 1993). The image of ageing as a mask is most commonly expressed in the words 'I don't feel old.' In this image, the body and the self do not closely correspond and the outward appearance and

functioning of the ageing body do not adequately represent the subjective experience of the inner self. The self, or the 'I', in this model is usually experienced as 'younger' than the body. The mask, as a sense of discrepancy between a 'younger' subjective self and the outward appearance of the social category of 'old person', is closely associated with ageist images. When images of old age are perceived to be negative then it is not surprising that older people may not wish to be identified as 'old' or, as suggested above, may reluctantly enter into a collaborative performance with others, during which they present themselves as old according to the conventional stereotypes. Old age thus becomes the performance of an ageist stereotype and thereby perpetuates negative images of later life. As Coleman has indicated, a 'culture's expectations of older people's roles within society have a vital place in encouraging or inhibiting personality change in later life' (Coleman, 1993: 96) – a judgement also supported in Kitwood's (1997) sociological analysis of the treatment of persons suffering from Alzheimer's disease. The difficulties in organizing speech and thought caused by neuropathology are aggravated by social interaction with those carers who refuse or are unable to help the sufferer maintain his or her former self. The self of the sufferer is thus masked not only by the disease but also by the social interaction of others. Negative and misleading images of Alzheimer's disease as 'loss of self' thereby contribute reflexively towards the social construction of dementia.

CONSUMER CULTURE, POSTMODERN TENDENCIES AND GLOBALIZATION

It has frequently been argued that a significant factor in the formation of cultural expectations of older people in society is the rapid expansion of consumer culture. This social development has played a crucial role in changing public attitudes towards ageing and the experience of growing older. Not only does a greater part of social life revolve around leisure and the purchase and utilization of commodities, but the culture of consumption suggests a world of new opportunities for self-improvement, fulfilment and expanded possibilities as more and more activities are mediated through images of the good life (Featherstone, 1991, 2001; Featherstone and Hepworth, 1982). The imagery of consumer culture places a strong emphasis upon the body and body maintenance and the active cultivation of youthful lifestyles, including the potential to renew and transform the body through new technologies, and the integration into machinic systems which makes possible cyborg and 'posthuman' bodies. All of these present the body as renewable, and ageing as something which can be held at bay and even 'defeated' through purchase, hard work, dedication and purchase (Featherstone, 1982).

The high value placed in consumer culture on visual imagery has been regarded as particularly influential by gerontologists, who are now beginning to explore the implications of consumer culture for the future of ageing (Gilleard and Higgs, 2000). But this is not to suggest that consumer culture only works through general stereotypes of idealized images of ageing which everyone is persuaded to follow. Rather, consumer culture cannot today be seen as producing a unified dominant culture in which everyone follows the same pattern of behaviour. Studies of media usage by older people and portrayals of older people in the media in America conclude that older people are 'a diverse, heterogeneous group' (Robinson *et al.*, 2004). In addition, what have been referred to as 'postmodern' tendencies within consumer culture have become more evident since the 1980s, and are manifest in greater product differentiation and the exercise of personal choice, which can include the rejection of ageist imagery. As was noted in the anti-ageist examples from Australia, Denmark and Madrid (above), the struggle to promote alternative images of ageing works directly against the youthful stereotyping of later life in consumer culture.

Consumer culture includes an expansion in the range of alternative and bohemian lifestyles, along with the growth of urban spaces for experimentation and identity exploration, especially in large cities. The traditional age-stereotypical dress styles are less in evidence and there has been a migration of more youthful and casual styles across the lifecourse. More positive images of ageing and later life are evident, especially in retirement and self-help literature which seeks to blur the boundaries between middle and later life (Featherstone and Hepworth, 1995), leading towards a less regulated and socially sanctioned 'postmodern' lifecourse (Hockey and James, 2003).

Under the impact of globalization, Western metropolises have become more diverse and multicultural with a wide range of ethnic styles and cultural forms evident. We are confronted by an expanding range of styles of dress, modes of adornment, body shapes and sizes and modes of self-presentation, which are more difficult 'to read'. There are therefore more varied and conflicting models of ageing and later life in circulation, along with a diversity of family and lifestyle forms, ranging from traditional to extended families in which the grandparent role still operates, to single households in which older people have chosen to explore single lifestyles.

The direction of this change also has implications for gender distinctions in experiences of ageing, which have also recently come to the forefront of gerontology. The emergence of feminist gerontology has focused attention on the important question of the difference gender makes to the process of ageing (Arber and Ginn, 1995; Bernard, 2001; Woodward, 1999). Feminist theorization of the body and ageing has resulted in a number of studies of images of ageing women, including representations of ageing women examined in a historical context (Gullette, 1985; Harper, 1997; Mangum, 1999; Woodward, 1999). Since Sontag's pioneering article (1978), the negative impact of images has been seen to be greater on men than on women because of the relative importance of the appearance of women in a world divided into public and private spheres and with a gendered division of labour. But the global impact of consumer culture and the 'postmodern turn' have, it is argued, destabilized the division of labour along lines of gender and this development has significant implications, at least as far as future generations of older people are concerned, for the experience of ageing. As Fairhurst (1998) shows, men are now facing similar problems to women as far as the appearance of ageing is concerned. Gullette (2004), too, has noted the merging of gender issues with regard to ageing in response to changes in the occupational structuring of society.

While consumer culture offers body maintenance and fitness routines along with a more positive active energetic image of later life, it also provides fast food and the pleasures of the inactive life of the television viewer. Currently over 60 per cent of people living in the United States are overweight, with around 20 per cent of these defined as obese (Critser, 2003). For the legions of 'failed' dieters and gym-goers who cannot attain the body image ideals of consumer culture, there is the hope of the technological fix. The assumption of technological solutions to the problems of the ageing process is also found in the treatment offered to women for the menopause, with hormone replacement therapy (HRT) widely advocated and used, despite evidence of cancer risk. The image of a 'youth pill', of the desire to avoid the negative consequences of ageing, is very much part of the publicity surrounding HRT. This now applies to men as well as women. While the male menopause is clearly not a medical condition, the term has continued to resurface regularly in the media over the last 30 years, featuring a discourse of loss and decline with the usual consumer culture medical and fitness remedies offered (Featherstone and Hepworth, 1995; Hepworth and Featherstone, 1982; Marshall and Katz, 2002). With the help of the new 'love drugs' such as Viagra, and a growing army of imitators (similar drugs are being designed for women), men are told they will be able to 'enjoy sex forever'. The problems of ageing may well be featured negatively and ageist discourses may dominate, yet consumer culture always holds out new positive images of ageing, exemplary profiles of the 'heroes of ageing' who fight decline, along with the 'quick fix' solutions which are there to be purchased.

DIRECTIONS FOR FUTURE RESEARCH

As we have indicated, images are now accepted as an integral feature of the process of defining ageing and old age which is the very basis of the discipline of social gerontology. Images shape and constitute both professional and lay conceptions of what it means to grow older, and therefore the treatment that older people receive. Not surprisingly, the study of the history of images of ageing is the study of the history of our ideas about ageing. And, on the level of practical everyday experience, the analysis of the care of older people and of patterns of social interaction in later life shows that verbal and visual images are regularly deployed and manipulated to produce ageing and old age as a social activity. We cannot therefore escape the process through which images shape these definitions, but we can understand the context within which they constitute lived

experience and enhance our awareness of the possibility of change. Images are always historical and therefore never eternally fixed. Nor are images neutral, they always carry a moral and a political message concerning the value we place on older people and the distinctions we make between acceptable and unacceptable forms of ageing (Hepworth, 1995).

And yet serious gaps in our knowledge of images of ageing remain. On the level of culture and history, we have only recently begun to collect and analyse the range of images available. On the level of lived experience, the sociological understanding of ageing as a process of interaction through which older people compare themselves with others requires a great deal more research into how people perceive and respond to images – the role played by images in interpersonal relationships through which individuals make sense of growing older. There is also a significant gap in our knowledge of ethnic variations in images of ageing (Wray, 2003).

One of the most significant pointers to future research is a more nuanced sense of the process of globalization as generating both uniformities and differences. The global postmodern, then, does not point to a new universal stage of postmodernity which supplants modernity, which everyone will have to go through; rather, it suggests a world of expanding differences which are also transmitted through the global media. The various economic, social and cultural power struggles evident globally open up the possibility that no single model of ageing, such as the Westernized consumer culture image, will prevail. This possibility goes beyond recent gerontological concern with postmodern flexibility within a Western context (Gilleard and Higgs, 2000) to prompt us to look more closely at alternative images of ageing, for example in Chinese and Indian cultures, in the Middle East and Eastern Europe. Thus the study of images of ageing opens prospect of greater diversity in the future images of ageing, reflecting wider shifts in the global distribution of power than have tended to predominate in the gerontological imagination.

FURTHER READING

Featherstone, M., and M. Hepworth (1993). 'Images of ageing'. In J. Bond, P. Coleman and S. Peace, eds., *Ageing in society: an introduction to social gerontology*. London: Sage.

Featherstone, M., and A. Wernick, eds. (1995). *Images of ageing*. London: Sage.

Gulette, M. M. (2004). *Aged By culture*. Chicago and London: University of Chicago Press.

Hepworth, M., and M. Featherstone (1982). *Surviving middle age*. Oxford: Basil Blackwell.

Hockey, J., and A. James (2003). *Social identities across the life course*. London: Palgrave.

Woodward, K., ed. (1999). *Figuring age: women, bodies, generations*. Bloomington: Indiana University Press.

REFERENCES

Arber, S., and J. Ginn (1995). *Connecting gender and ageing: a sociological approach*. Buckingham: Open University Press.

Bernard, M. (2001). 'Women ageing: old lives, new challenges', *Education and Ageing*, 16 (2): 333–52.

Biggs, S. (1993). *Understanding ageing: images, attitudes and professional practice*. Buckingham: Open University Press.

Blaikie, A. (1999). *Ageing and popular culture*. Cambridge: Cambridge University Press.

Bury, M. (1982). 'Chronic illness as biographical disruption', *Sociology of Health and Illness*, 4 (2): 167–95.

Bytheway, B. (1995). *Ageism*. Buckingham: Open University Press.

Cole, T. R. (1992). *The journey of life: a cultural history of ageing in America*. Cambridge: Cambridge University Press.

Coleman, P. (1993). 'Adjustment in later life'. In J. Bond, P. Coleman and S. Peace, eds., *Ageing in society: an introduction to social gerontology*. London: Sage.

Critser, G. (2003). *Fatland: how Americans became the fattest people in the world*. London: Penguin.

Denzin, N. (1995). 'Chan is missing'. In M. Featherstone and A. Wernick, eds., *Images of ageing: cultural representations of later life*. London: Sage.

Elias, N. (1985). *The loneliness of the dying*. Oxford: Basil Blackwell.

Fairhurst, E. (1998). "Growing old gracefully" as opposed to "mutton dressed as lamb": the social construction of recognising older women'. In S. Nettleton and J. Watson, eds., *The body in everyday life*. London and New York: Routledge.

Featherstone, M. (1982). 'The body in consumer culture', *Theory, Culture & Society*, 1 (2): 18–33. Reprinted in M. Featherstone, M. Hepworth and B. S. Turner, eds. *The body*. London: Sage, 1991.

(1991). *Postmodernism and consumer culture*. London: Sage.

(2001). 'Consumer culture'. In *International Encyclopaedia of the Social and Behavioral Sciences*. Oxford: Elsevier.

Featherstone, M., and M. Hepworth (1982). 'Ageing and inequality: consumer culture and the new middle age'.

In D. Robins *et al.*, eds., *Rethinking inequality*. Aldershot: Gower Press.

(1985a). 'The male menopause: lifestyle and sexuality', *Maturitas*, 7: 235–46.

(1985b). 'The history of the male menopause 1848–1936', *Maturitas*, 7: 249–57.

(1991). 'The mask of ageing and the postmodern life course'. In M. Featherstone, M. Hepworth and B. S. Turner, eds. *The body: social process and cultural theory*. London: Sage.

(1993). 'Images of ageing'. In J. Bond, P. Coleman and S. Peace, eds. *Ageing in society: an introduction to social gerontology*. London: Sage.

(1995). 'Images of positive ageing: a case study of *Retirement Choice* magazine'. In M. Featherstone and A. Wernick, eds., *Images of ageing*. London: Sage.

Featherstone, M., and A. Wernick, eds. (1995). *Images of ageing*. London: Sage.

Ferguson, H. (1997). 'Me and my shadows: on the accumulation of body images in Western society, Parts 1 and 2', *Body & Society*, 2 (3): 1–32; and 2 (4): 1–32.

Gilleard, C., and P. Higgs (2000). *Cultures of ageing: Self, citizen and the body*. London: Prentice Hall.

Gubrium, J. F. (1986). *Oldtimer's and Alzheimer's: the descriptive organisation of senility*. Greenwich, Conn.: JAI Press.

Gullette, M. M. (1985). 'Creativity, ageing, gender: a study of their intersections, 1910–1935'. In A. M. Wyatt-Brown and J. Rossen, eds., *Ageing and gender in literature: studies in creativity*. Charlottesville and London: University Press of Virginia.

(1997). *Declining to decline: cultural combat and the politics of the midlife*. Charlottesville and London: University Press of Virginia.

(2004). *Aged by culture*. Chicago and London: University of Chicago Press.

Harper, S. (1997). 'Constructing later life / constructing the body: some thoughts from feminist theory'. In A. Jamieson, S. Harper and C. Victor, eds., *Critical approaches to ageing and later life*. Buckingham: Open University Press.

Hepworth, M. (1995). '"Wrinkles of vice and wrinkles of virtue": the moral interpretation of the ageing body'. In C. Hummel and C. J. Lalive D'Epinay, eds., *Images of ageing in Western societies*. Geneva: University of Geneva, Centre for Interdisciplinary Gerontology.

Hepworth, M., and M. Featherstone (1982). *Surviving middle age*. Oxford: Basil Blackwell.

Hockey, J., and A. James (1993). *Growing up and growing old: ageing and dependency in the life course*. London: Sage.

(2003). *Social identities across the life course*. London: Palgrave.

Hummel, C., Rey, J.-C., and C. J. Lalive D'Epinay (1995). 'Children's drawings of grandparents: a quantitative analysis of images'. In M. Featherstone and A. Wernick, eds., *Images of ageing: cultural representations of later life*. London and New York: Routledge.

Kaid, L. L., and J. Garner (2004). 'The portrayal of older adults in political advertising'. In J. F. Nussbaum and J. Coupland, eds., *Handbook of communication and ageing research*, 2nd edn. Mahwah, N.J., and London: Lawrence Erlbaum Associates.

Kitwood, T. (1997). *Dementia reconsidered: the person comes first*. Buckingham: Open University Press.

Lowenthal, D. (1985). *The past is a foreign country*. Cambridge: Cambridge University Press.

Mangum, T. (1999). 'Little Women: the ageing female character in nineteenth-century British children's literature'. In K. Woodward, ed., *Figuring age: women, bodies, generations*. Bloomington and Indianapolis: Indiana University Press.

Marshall, B., and S. Katz (2002). 'Forever functional: sexual fitness and the ageing male body', *Body & Society*, 8: 43–70.

Rennell, T. (2001). *The death of Queen Victoria: last days of glory*. London: Penguin.

Robinson, J. D., Skill, T., and J. W. Turner (2004). 'Media useage patterns and portrayals of seniors'. In J. F. Nussbaum and J. Coupland, eds., *Handbook of communication and ageing research*, 2nd edn. Mahwah, N.J., and London: Lawrence Erlbaum Associates.

Seabrook, J. (2004). *A world grown old*. London: Pluto Press.

Sontag, S. (1978). 'The double standard of ageing'. In V. Carver and P. Liddiard, eds., *An ageing population*. Milton Keynes: Open University Press.

Wada, S. (1995). 'The status and image of the elderly in Japan: understanding the paternalistic ideology'. In M. Featherstone and A. Wernick, eds., *Images of ageing: cultural representations of later life*. London and New York: Routledge.

Warnes, A. (1993). 'Being old, old people and the burdens of burden', *Ageing and Society*, 13: 297–338.

Woodward, K., ed. (1999). *Figuring age: women, bodies, generations*. Bloomington: Indiana University Press.

Wray, S. (2003). 'Women growing older: agency, ethnicity and culture', *Sociology*, 37 (3): 511–27.

Religion, Spirituality, and Older People

ALFONS MARCOEN

INTRODUCTION

For many men and women worldwide, religion provides a source of coping techniques, social support in times of crisis and hardship, and a frame of reference for interpreting one's life experiences. Most of the elderly of today have been educated in a religious atmosphere. More than half a century later some of them adhere to their faith, others became very critical or lost their faith, and still others sought and found solace in one of the many new spiritual movements. Before exploring the literature on the role religion and spirituality may play in the lives of elderly people, let us bring to mind a few examples of older persons and their religious or spiritual views (Van Ranst, 1995).

Jane is a Catholic 84-year-old widow. She is deeply faithful and finds support in her faith. She is very happy that her parents gave her a religious education. She prays every day and goes to the mass whenever she can. She commits her pain to the Lord. She never feels lonely. Every night she prays and asks forgiveness for all the wrongdoings in her life. She asks for God's blessing for herself and for all the persons she loves. She hopes to enter into heaven after her death. Carol is a 64-year-old widow without children. About her religious views, she said the following:

I have not been religiously educated by my parents. I was the only one in my school. That was not an easy position. I always had to seal the counter-current. I find comfort in nature. Somehow I experience a presence, a kind of consolation, which for me has not to be defined as God. I cannot put into words what I feel. But there is

something that brings me into a spiritual contact. Some people say that there exists nothing, but I would not say that. It seems as if I am in need of something. But I am not able to convey in language what it is that I feel, see or think.

Maria is 61 years old. She considers religious feelings as a universal phenomenon that gave rise to many different religions. She stated: "I have strong religious feelings. I feel connected to the cosmos, to life and to God. God cannot be captured by just one church. He is much too big for that." Oscar is a 72-year-old self-made man. He said: "Faith is very important in life. It constitutes the deeper meaning of life. For me it has always been the source of what I considered to be the mission of life, namely, to be there not only for oneself but also, and in the first place, to be there for others." In one way or another, all these elderly persons experienced a relationship with something that transcended them and that gave them a spiritual anchorage in face of a growing vulnerability in old age.

Recently, Crowther and her colleagues (2002) proposed to strengthen the existing successful ageing model, introduced by Rowe and Kahn (1997), through the addition of positive spirituality as a health-promoting component. Successful and productive ageing not only implies engagement in an active life, minimizing risks and disabilities and maximizing physical and mental abilities, but also maximizing positive spirituality. Indeed, it has been frequently observed that successfully ageing adults enjoy a relatively stable state of wellbeing even when, sooner or later, they face irreversible physical decline and social isolation. In these elderly, successful ageing, according to the norm of maintained middle-adulthood vitality, developed into a state of living meaningfully, when disabilities and contextual restrictions began to arise. To maintain an optimal level of wellbeing, the ageing individual frames inevitable losses in a workable meaning system. It is precisely in the acquirement and development of such a strong and flexible meaning system that religion and spirituality may play a prominent role. They provide the ageing person with resources to optimize the process of change and eventually to accept irreversible decline and its consequences.

In the last decades religion and spirituality, as well as meaning-making, became fashionable topics of research in the social and behavioral sciences. In the domain of care of the elderly, professional workers (re)discovered the importance of religion and spirituality in the lives of many elderly people. Sociologists and psychologists started to investigate the health- and life-enhancing potential of a religious or spiritual outlook on life. Several reviews of recent research and books focusing on the themes of religion, spirituality, existential meaning, and ageing have been published (Koenig, 1994; McFadden, 1996; Reker and Chamberlain, 1999; Seeber, 1990; Sinnott, 2001, 2002; Thomas and Eisenhandler, 1994, 1999; Thorson, 2000). In this chapter we focus on some definitional issues, describe dimensions and processes of both religious and secular spirituality, deal with the development of spirituality in the second half of life, and finally discuss elements of research into the contribution of spirituality to positive ageing and wellbeing.

RELIGION, SPIRITUALITY, AND MEANING-MAKING

Religion and spirituality are related constructs. There is no unanimity about their definition. Some scholars consider religion as the more comprehensive construct; others see spirituality as the broader one. Religion is a multifaceted, more or less institutionalized, system, that brings, or tries to bring, people in contact with the transcendent and sacred dimensions of the reality in which they live. This system consists of a whole range of beliefs and symbols, it provides public worship opportunities and guidelines for private religious practices (rites and prayers), and stimulates and enhances community life among the faithful. Religions also supply to persons who search for meaning in their lives a historically grown diversity of spiritual insights and rules for a meaningful life in relation to a transcendent reality.

The great institutionalized religions are rooted in the transmission and elaboration of the deep existential experiences that shaped their founders' views on the ideal human being, his origin, and his future, and on the path that leads to his completion. Based on these founders' experiences and teachings, different spiritual insights and guidelines have been offered to, or imposed upon, millions of worshippers throughout the ages. Confronted with challenging cultural and societal changes, religiously talented individuals introduced new variants of spirituality, rooted in their own existential experiences of the ultimate reality and meaning in life.

A religiously anchored spirituality that assumes an unconditional corroboration of the existence of God is a theistic spirituality. In the depth, which may be experienced in human life and in everything it implies, God's presence is recognized. However, existential depth-experiences may also originate outside the context of an institutionalized religion or one or another religious framework. These warm feelings of relatedness to something greater than oneself then ground the emergence of a nontheistic, humanistic, or secular spirituality. If, above it, this spiritual outlook on the human existence is attended with a radical negation of the existence of God, it may even be called an a-theistic spirituality (Apostel, 1998). Spirituality is essentially a response to the search of the human being for meaning in his or her life. The search for meaning is a personal quest for which the religions offer cognitive, social, and ritual frameworks. Persons not involved in any religious tradition, who – from a psychological perspective – have identical experiences of existential depth and connection, have to create for themselves verbal and non-verbal expressions to preserve, on the level of representation, the truth they discovered about a meaningful human life.

Scientific research on the influence of religion and spirituality on ageing and being old may focus on different facets of the phenomenon. Among the aspects of religious involvement that may be focused upon are: church membership; attending religious meetings; religious beliefs and convictions;

religious or spiritual practices such as scriptural reading, prayer, meditation, and contemplation; living meaningfully inspired by one's faith; and, last but not least, personal experiences of transcendent and sacred dimensions of life. The positive impact of all these aspects of religious or secular spirituality on the ageing process, and on the life structure and self-concept of the elderly, deserves to be carefully explored. The positive character of the effect is stressed here, but it has rightly been stated that there also exists a negative spirituality that does not lead to liberation and the joy of life, and may induce hate, prejudices, ignorance, and blind compliance to a misleading egocentric guru. Mostly, however, spirituality is typically considered as a positive strength, the dimensions of which we will describe in the next section.

DIMENSIONS AND PROCESSES OF SPIRITUALITY

Based on an investigation into the meaning of the term "spirituality" among professionals from the five big religious traditions, Rose (2001) distinguished three defining characteristics. Spirituality is typically characterized by "some form of continuous religious or comparable experience, particular maintained effort or practice, and the experience of love" (Rose, 2001: 193). The basic spiritual experiences were represented with the concepts of connection and awareness. The concept of connection stands for "keeping in touch with, moving towards, and union with the Divine," considered in a theistic or non-theistic sense. The concept of awareness was used in reference to: "another dimension, deeper issues, a divine being, the full dimension of humanity, the eternal within us, God's presence, the world as a unity of God" (Rose, 2001: 198). The respondents also referred to the importance of practices and rites, which may help the person to yield, preserve, and elaborate the experience of the transcendent reality. All respondents in Rose's research also agreed that a spiritual life is normally characterized by a loving involvement in the relationship with other people.

Based on the literature, Elkins and his colleagues (1988) described nine components of spirituality. The experientially based belief in a transcendent dimension to life is the core component of which

the other dimensions are extensions. The experience of an invisible presence of "something more" that occasionally invades or permanently inhabits the person's consciousness gives rise to deeply felt convictions, such as: one's life has meaning and purpose; one has a mission to accomplish; human life is sacred not only as a whole but also in the small things and events of every day; and material goods such as money and possessions eventually do not provide ultimate satisfaction. The experience of the transcendent is also the root of empathic compassion and altruism, idealistic commitment to the betterment of the world, and the awareness of the tragic character of human existence. All these aspects of the spiritual outlook on life and the involvement in one's fate bear fruit in the lifecourse of the person.

In an attempt to define contemporary spirituality outside of any religious context, Young-Eisendrath and Miller (2000) invited several professionals and scientists to explore the meaning of what to them seemed a "mature" spirituality. A triad of concepts was proposed to reflect its components: integrity, wisdom, and transcendence. The spiritually mature and ethically committed person has integrated diverse visions of life and humanity into a complex system of meaning in which there is tolerance for ambiguity and paradox. He or she shows wisdom that may be achieved by contemporary means that are not tributary to a particular religious tradition. Transcendence (of ordinary consciousness, the self, and usual habits) in one form or another is always a component of a spiritual orientation to life. This conception of spirituality implies the emergence of a self-sustaining individual, emancipated from whatever protecting powerful Otherness (God, Goddess, and divinities), but deeply engaged with a larger meaning.

From this short overview of a few attempts to define dimensions of spirituality it becomes clear that embodied spirituality is a multifaceted phenomenon of personality development. This development is primarily a process of private experiences and internal changes on two fundamental ontogenetic trajectories, namely, individuation and attachment. The individual is actively committed to him- or herself, the others, and the world, from the perspective of a vividly experienced depth in their own existence, whether or not religiously interpreted. It is also clear that a spiritual life involves cognitive, emotional, and motivational processes. Spirituality consists of one or more cognitions or insights, isolated or integrated in traditional or non-traditional wholes of teaching, metaphors, stories, and symbols. These cognitions provide anchor points for the person's view of themself as a developing human being in relation to the transcendent reality. Religious beliefs, books, texts, and symbols are inexhaustible sources of spiritual cognitions that at particular moments in life may touch a responsive chord in a person's psyche. At that very moment, this cognition or set of cognitions becomes a deeply felt truth imbued with positive emotions of relatedness and self-confidence. This emotional response may not be enduring, but the memory of it may continue to frame the spiritual cognitions and ground the strivings and the way of life that originate from the life-giving insight into one's existence. Positive emotions of trust, joy, security, responsibility, compassion, hope, and love instigate the person to strive for the attainment of goals in accordance with one's spiritual convictions.

A spiritually living person experiences the lifelong processes of individuation and attachment, the search for the realization of oneself and the connectedness to the non-self, in the context of a sensitive openness to the transcendent reality that encompasses all existence (God, the Divine, the Ultimate Reality, Nature, the Cosmos). An authentic spiritual life is grounded in a rich interior life where the person meets him- or herself, the others, and the Other, in a multivoiced dialogue. This internal dialogue as the motivational source of visible action in the outside world needs to be maintained, in one way or another, through rituals, prayers, meditation, and contemplation.

SPIRITUAL DEVELOPMENT IN THE SECOND HALF OF LIFE

An innovative spiritual outlook on life emerges spontaneously on the path of life of some persons or is searched for and found in existing religious belief systems and practices by other persons. Once recognized, the core spiritual truth must be elaborated in order to maintain its life-enhancing quality. The emergence, elaboration, conservation, and contemplation of central spiritual views and related ethical commitments are developmental components of a spiritual life.

Optimal spiritual development is typically a process of emerging and maintained decentration (Apostel, 1998). The person's ego as conscious agent of one's lifecourse looses its centrality through the connection with the transcendent that guides and inspires the individual in his or her commitment to their true self, loving relationships with others, and care for life's environmental context.

Although spirituality may pervade an adult's life at any age, some age periods may be more receptive to spiritual cognitions and the renewal of withered visions on life. It has frequently been suggested that an authentic spirituality develops in the middle of life. Jung was one of the first to describe the essentially spiritual character of the development of self in the second half of life. After the fulfilment of the tasks of the first half of life, which are primarily focused on integration in the society as a productive and dependable member in a diversity of roles, the need for individuation may originate from the unconscious. The individuation process essentially implies the fulfilment of one's duties towards the self, and eventually leads to a state of self-realization. Through a critical confrontation with one's mainly socially determined accomplishment of roles, the dark side of one's personality, and the image and tendencies of the other gender in oneself, the person proceeds to the discovery of his or her inexhaustible and comprehensive self. A careful analysis of Jung's pioneering contributions reveals the following characteristics of the individuated person (Marcoen, 1973). He or she is a decentered individual connected to the ego-transcendent unconscious self, which is experienced as what is bearing and anchoring him or her. The individuated person is a complete person in equilibrium between the opposite dimensions that inhere the human psyche: light and shadow, good and evil, the rational and the irrational. This individual lives as an ethically autonomous person deliberately complying with the deep-seeded tendencies to self-realization and completion. He or she is an inspired person, in whom sparkles of age-old wisdom met creative receptivity and caused warm commitment to one's destiny, simply living in agreement with one's uniqueness. The ageing person who went through an individuation process developed an individual culture based on an internalization process that contrasts with the search for meaning and fulfilment in the external world that characterizes development in the first half of life. Through a journey into the unconscious territory of the psyche, the person became an internally cultivated individual who finds new meaning in life even with increasing awareness of the finitude of life. This cultivated person is also able to give himself away unconditionally to others, precisely because he owns himself. He or she gives without expecting any repayment, reward, or gratitude. All these characteristics constitute the never totally completed mature personality. Jung considers the few individuals who went through the individuation process as personalities of a future era and a community of the future. In the difficult process of individuation or self-realization, the person not only realizes his own individual destiny but also feels united with all human beings that are grounded in the common collective unconscious. Really liberated and autonomous individuals may build a conscious community of free citizens. Not everybody is called to go the lonely way into the unknown territory of the unconscious to find meaning in life.

Traditional religions provide views, individual and collective practices to keep in touch with the transcendent, and the relational warmth of communities of like-minded worshippers. However, religious believers too may develop. From a constructivistic perspective, Fowler (1976) studied human development as a quest for meaning and described six stages of faith. The first four stages typically fit into the development in the first half of life. They are labeled: intuitive–projective, mythic–literal, synthetic–conventional, and individualistic–reflective. If constructed at all, the latter of these stages is realized in late adolescence or even later, in the mid-thirties and forties. It typically consists of well-defined views on oneself and the world, expressed in clear distinctions and abstract concepts. Gnawing dissatisfaction with the lack of scope, depth, and warmth in one's way of believing and being religious may mark the readiness for a transition to the stage of conjunctive faith. Faith at this level

involves the integration of self and outlook of much that was suppressed or unrecognized in the interest of . . . self-certainty and conscious cognitive and affec-

tive adaptation to reality. This stage develops a "second naïveté" (Ricoeur) in which symbolic power is reunited with conceptual meanings. Here there must also be a new reclaiming and reworking of one's past. There must be an opening to the voices of one's "deeper self." Importantly, this involves a critical recognition of one's social unconscious – the myths, ideal images and prejudices built deeply into the self-system by virtue of one's nurture within a particular social class, religious tradition, ethnic group or the like. (Fowler, 1976: 197–8)

This description partly echoes Jung's view on the completed personality emerging from the achieved individuation process. The sixth stage of so-called "universalizing faith" also reflects some characteristics of achieved individuation.

Spiritual development within a traditional Judeo-Christian religious context always implies processes of transformation in the way one finds personal meaning in the Holy Scriptures. Individuals in the advanced stages of faith development do not understand the scriptures literally anymore, they move into a stance of symbolic interpretation of the holy books and the rites of their tradition. Based on the dimensions of literal versus symbolic interpretation of religious beliefs, images, and rituals, and on inclusion versus exclusion of participation in a transcendent reality through objects of religious interest, Wulff (1997) distinguished four basic attitudes towards religion, including four positions of belief or unbelief. The orthodox believer interprets the scriptures literally, and also literally affirms the existence of religious objects referring to a transcendent reality. The fundamentalist disbeliever assumes that religious stories and rituals are to be understood literally, but rejects them, and denies the existence of a transcendent realm. In the disbeliever's position of reductive interpretation, religious cognitions, objects, and rituals are considered as symbolic representations of a non-existent outer-worldly transcendent reality. Finally, in the restorative interpretation position, the believer reengages with the objects of religious faith symbolically interpreted and referring to a transcendent reality. This is a position of second naïveté. The empirical elaboration of this attitudinal typology led Hutsebaut (1996) to distinguish four components of attitudes towards religion and religious objects and contents, namely, orthodoxy, symbolic belief, relativism, and external critique. Connections that may be found in empirical research between these attitudes and the age of the respondents may reflect cohort differences more than developmental trends.

A recent theory that links spiritual development to the ageing process is Tornstam's gerotranscendence theory (Tornstam, 1996, 1997). This theory is a reformulation of the disengagement theory and echoes aspects of theories of Jung, Erikson, and others. Gerotranscendence is supposed to constitute a late stage in a natural process towards maturation and wisdom. The gerotranscendent individual "experiences a redefinition of time, space, life and death, and the self . . . Gerotranscendence is a shift in metaperspective, from a midlife materialistic and rational vision to a more cosmic and transcendent one, accompanied by an increase in life satisfaction" (Tornstam, 1996: 42).

From the above it may be clear that not everybody develops a relationship with a transcendent reality. Those who, through meditation and other spiritual practices, connect themselves to a transcendent realm may interpret the ultimate reality differently. Some interpret it in the light of the religious tradition in which they stand, and call it "God" or "the Divine." Others adhere to non-theistic and a-theistic interpretations and consider the unknowable transcendent realm, for example, as the totality of all that exists. The different types of religious and secular spirituality bear fruit in the lives of these individuals in that they increasingly embrace with caring concern all humans and the earth on which they live.

SPIRITUALITY AND WELLBEING IN OLD AGE: RESEARCH NEEDED

It is difficult to describe and explain the contribution of religion and spirituality to optimal living in (advanced) old age in general. Indeed, elderly research participants may belong to different generations and different (sub)cultures. The old-old and very old in Western countries today are socialized in a historical period in which religion had a strong impact on the beliefs and lives of the majority of the citizens. After the Second World War the influences of traditional religions waned – especially in Europe – but the search for meaning and spirituality remained. In the last decades, aspects of religiousness and spirituality became noticeable

variables in empirical research in the behavioral sciences. In gerontology too, interest in the topic is growing. Religiosity and spirituality measures have been developed and used in research, mainly with samples of convenience which may be biased in favor of certain religious traditions, geographical locations, social class, and gender (McFadden, 1996). These studies are still today largely cross-sectional but are now growing in methodological complexity.

Many studies have demonstrated positive associations between religiosity/spirituality, wellbeing, and physical and mental health indicators. Religiosity variables ranged from denominational membership and attending divine services, to prayer and the use of other religious coping strategies. Wellbeing, and the related construct "quality of life," have been measured with a diversity of scales. Health variables comprise mental health conditions such as depression, the confrontation with difficult life circumstances, and chronic illness, and more general and biological health indicators such as cardiovascular mortality, survival, immune system functioning, physical functioning, and use of health services. Through what kind of mechanisms religious faith and (religious or secular) spirituality affect health, constructive coping with health problems, and wellbeing in older persons will remain a central topic in future research. Some hypotheses have been put forward (Koenig, 2000). With regard to constructive coping with acute and/or chronic medical illness, religion/spirituality may provide a world view in which suffering has meaning and purpose, or provide an indirect form of control over circumstances. Physical health in the elderly may benefit by the social support that religious people experience in their communities, the healthy lifestyle they tend to cultivate, and their ability to cope with stress. These and other explanations need to be further explored in empirical research.

In order to discover what particular aspects of religiosity and spirituality have positive effects on what aspects of the lives of elderly people, further dimensionalization of the variables involved will be needed. Firstly, religiosity and spirituality as characteristics of the developing person must be differentiated into (theistic) religious, non-theistic, and a-theistic humanistic types of spirituality or ways of believing, depending on whether religious

TABLE 1. Heuristic model of the religion/spirituality, health, and wellbeing research domain

Types of spirituality	Religion and spirituality aspects	Domains of effects and consequences
Theistic religious	Beliefs	Objective
Orthodoxy		Physical health
Symbolic	Rules	Physical system functioning
Relativistic		Global daily functioning
External critique	Practices	Mental health
	Divine services	
Secular	Worshipping	Subjective health
Non-theistic	Scriptural reading	
A-theistic	Prayer	Wellbeing
	Meditation	
	Contemplation	Quality of life
	Social integration activities	Accomplishment of developmental tasks
		Coping with stress

Ontogenetic perspective:
development and changes of spirituality type and spirituality aspects, and their associations with health and wellbeing.

objects are literally or symbolically understood. Secondly, in the religion/spirituality phenomenon itself, as a lived reality, different beliefs and practices, and social integration dimensions, are to be distinguished. Thirdly, with regard to the possible life-enhancing consequences, differentiation of variables is as badly needed. Objective and subjective physical and mental health indicators are manifold, wellbeing is a multidimensional phenomenon, and the global developmental task of (successful, positive, constructive, optimal, graceful) ageing is actually composed of different subtasks. Among these tasks, the final task of dying is the core of a number of other end-of-life themes that also deserve to be studied from a spirituality perspective (Koenig, 2002; Sulmasy, 2002).

The three briefly sketched global research variables constitute a three-dimensional heuristic model of the religion/spirituality – old age research domain, that can help to order the available literature and detect blind spots of research topics which are not covered. A cube might represent this three-dimensional model of the associations between: spirituality type, religion and spirituality aspects, and (possible) effects on a person's health and wellbeing. In Table 1 the three dimensions of the heuristic model and the ontogenetic time dimension are presented. Research in this domain may not only focus on the association between the relevant variables but also on the emergence and the development of spirituality and its expressions, and the age-linked changes in its impact on health and wellbeing. Parallel to the quantitative research within this scheme, qualitative research is needed to detect and explain different trajectories that elderly people may follow in their search for individuation and attachment against a background of the awareness of an out-worldly or in-worldly transcendent reality.

FURTHER READING

MacKinlay, E. (2001). *The spiritual dimension of ageing.* London: Jessica Kingsley Publishers.

Moberg, D. O., ed. (2001). *Aging and spirituality: spiritual dimensions of aging theory, research, practice, and policy.* New York: The Haworth Pastoral Press.

REFERENCES

Apostel, L. (1998). *Atheïstische spiritualiteit.* Brussels: VUB Press.

Crowther, M. R., Parker, M. W., Achenbaum, W. A., Larimore, W. L., and H. G. Koenig (2002). "Rowe and Kahn's model of successful aging revisited: positive spirituality – the forgotten factor," *Gerontologist*, 42: 613–20.

Elkins, D. N., Hughes, J. L., Leaf, L. L., and J. A. Saunders (1988). "Toward a humanistic–phenomenological spirituality: definition, description, and measurement," *Journal of Humanistic Psychology*, 28: 5–18.

Fowler, J. W. (1976). *Stages of faith: the psychology of human development and the quest for meaning*. Cambridge: Harper & Row.

Hutsebaut, D. (1996). "Post critical belief: a new approach to the religious attitude problem," *Journal of Empirical Theology*, 9: 48–66.

Koenig, H. G. (1994). *Aging and God: spiritual pathways to mental health in midlife and later years*. Binghamton, N.Y.: The Haworth Pastoral Press.

(2000). "Religion, well-being, and health in the elderly: the scientific evidence for an association." In J. A. Thorson, ed., *Perspectives on spiritual well-being and aging*. Springfield, Ill.: Thomas, pp. 84–97.

(2002). "A commentary: the role of religion and spirituality at the end of life," *Gerontologist*, 42, special issue III: 20–3.

Marcoen, A. (1973). "Het einddoel van het individuatieproces volgens C. G. Jung," *Tijdschrift voor Opvoedkunde*, 19: 348–61 and 445–65.

McFadden, S. H. (1996). "Religion, spirituality, and aging." In J. E. Birren and K. W. Schaie, eds., *Handbook of the psychology of aging*. San Diego, Calif.: Academic Press, pp. 162–77.

Reker, G. T., and K. Chamberlain, eds. (1999). *Exploring existential meaning: optimizing human development across the life span*. Thousand Oaks, Calif.: Sage.

Rose, S. (2001). "Is the term 'spirituality' a word that everyone uses but nobody knows what anyone means by it?" *Journal of Contemporary Religion*, 16: 193–207.

Rowe, J. W., and R. L. Kahn (1997). "Successful aging," *Gerontologist*, 37: 433–40.

Seeber, J. J., ed. (1990). *Spiritual maturity in the later years*. New York: The Haworth Press.

Sinnott, J. D., ed. (2001). "Special issue on spirituality and adult development, Part I," *Journal of Adult Development*, 8: 199–257.

(2002). "Special issue on spirituality and adult development, Parts II and III," *Journal of Adult Development*, 9: 1–154.

Sulmasy, D. P. (2002). "A biopsychosocial–spiritual model for the care of patients at the end of life," *Gerontologist*, 42, special issue III: 24–33.

Thomas, L. E., and S. A. Eisenhandler, eds. (1994). *Aging and the religious dimension*. Westport, Conn.: Auburn House.

(1999). *Religion, belief and spirituality in late life*. New York: Springer.

Thorson, J. A., ed. (2000). *Perspectives on spiritual well-being and aging*. Springfield, Ill.: Thomas.

Tornstam, L. (1996). "Gerotranscendence: a theory about maturing in old age," *Journal of Aging and Identity*, 1: 37–50.

(1997). "Gerotranscendence: the contemplative dimensions of aging," *Journal of Aging Studies*, 11: 143–54.

Van Ranst, N. (1995). "Zingeving in de Ouderdom." Ph.D. thesis, Department of Psychology, Catholic University Leuven, Belgium.

Wulff, D. M. (1997). *Psychology of religion: classic and contemporary*. New York: Wiley.

Young-Eisendrath, P., and M. E. Miller, eds. (2000). *The psychology of mature spirituality: integrity, wisdom, transcendence*. London: Routledge.

CHAPTER 4.12

Quality of Life and Ageing

SVEIN OLAV DAATLAND

RESEARCH TRADITIONS

Quality of life is an ambition for all of us, and a source of dispute for philosophers from ancient times: what is a good life, and a good society? However, as a theme and construct for social research it is rather new, and has come to be associated mainly with the subjective sides of welfare. It is this perspective which is adopted in the present chapter, which will hence focus mainly on quality of life as subjective wellbeing.

This is, however, only part of the story. 'Quality of life' covers a multidimensional ground and is an amorphous construct that need be specified in order to be researchable. Two traditions have dominated the field. The first originated in economics and focused on living standards as measured by access to income and material goods. But living conditions are more than a matter of money. Sociologists added a number of social indicators that were assumed to be important for a good life, like housing, health, education, and social integration and supports. The common feature for both is a focus on (more or less) objective *living conditions* that may enable a good life. Quality of life is then studied *indirectly*. In fact, focus is most often on the constraining conditions for a good life in order to avoid paternalistically imposed norms about what the good life is, and in order to translate findings into policy and practice. Research and policy should, according to this tradition, be concerned about unjust and unreasonable constraints, and should aim to enable people to follow their own dreams, not impose a politically correct dream upon them.

The second tradition aims at quality of life *directly*, and focuses on the personal *experience of life* – on subjective and psychological wellbeing. This is a perspective taken primarily by psychologists, but includes also branches of sociology and the health sciences. Among the motivations for the subjective approach are: to take a bottom-up perspective, to avoid paternalism, and to highlight people's own conceptions of what they consider important in life – if we are concerned about people's welfare, why not ask them?

A third line is to build bridges and to integrate the two traditions by studying how wellbeing is influenced by living conditions. Campbell *et al.* (1976) have for example suggested that objective living conditions are mainly impacting on wellbeing via how the person perceives and evaluates these conditions. Actual living conditions have, according to this model, mainly an indirect effect on wellbeing. This may explain the often moderate correlations between actual and perceived living conditions. The perceived (relative) deprivation may be a better indicator for subjective wellbeing than the actual deprivation. The poorer are satisfied with less than the richer, and the older with less than the younger?

THE FOUR QUALITIES OF LIFE

Veenhoven (2000) integrates the two traditions in his classification of 'the four qualities of life'. This conceptualization of the quality-of-life field separates the opportunities for a good life from the good life itself, and refers to these two aspects as life chances and life results. A second dimension is

TABLE 1. The four qualities of life

	External qualities	Internal qualities
Life chances (opportunities)	Livability of environment	Life-ability of person
Life results (outcomes)	Utility of life	Appreciation of life

Adapted from Veenhoven (2000).

that between external and internal qualities, which Veenhoven sees as a better distinction than that between objective and subjective indicators. External qualities are located in the environment, internal qualities in the individual. The two dimensions are combined in a fourfold matrix (Table 1).

The two sectors in the upper half represent opportunities for a good life. They indicate the access to resources in the environment ('livability of the environment') and in the individual ('life-ability of the person'). The lower two sectors represent quality of life as an outcome for others ('utility of life') and for oneself ('appreciation of life'). The latter is what is more often labelled as subjective wellbeing, life satisfaction, happiness, and similar. The lower left cell is included by Veenhoven in response to criticism of the subjective wellbeing tradition for being too individualistic. In the utility to others lies the notion that a good life must be good for something more than itself, and hence be related to some higher value, and have some meaning beyond personal pleasure. The personal awareness of such value, via the appreciation one receives (or does not receive) from others, may be seen as part of subjective wellbeing in the form of self-esteem. But self-esteem may also be taken as a personal resource, and as such be placed in the upper right cell. Hence the distinction between these cells and categories is somewhat fluid. The model may still serve its function, for example by helping us clarify how the different elements over time may influence each other.

The living conditions approach belongs in the upper half of the model, mainly in the upper left cell with its focus on external conditions, the role of economy, environment and policies. More recent advances of this tradition include also individual resources and the interaction between the two. The so-called 'Scandinavian' welfare research tradition (Erikson, 1993), for example, maps not only external resources, but also the social arenas and the personal competence that are needed in order to convert resources into welfare. The capability approach of Sen (1993) does likewise, and emphasizes how both external *and* internal resources are necessary for welfare – here taken as the power (autonomy) to pursue and reach goals that one finds important.

The two traditions – the living conditions approach and the wellbeing approach – need not therefore be incompatible. The first may be seen to map out factors and processes that are influencing the latter. We may illustrate this with arrows from each cell towards the appreciation of life cell in the lower right corner of Table 1. Hence, when we focus here primarily on subjective wellbeing, we do so within the context of the opportunities and constraints represented by individual and societal resources.

SCALES AND MEASUREMENTS

Subjective wellbeing is in itself multidimensional, but, although a lot of operationalizations and measures have been suggested, there is hardly any consensus yet about what the essence of wellbeing is. Taken as an attitude, wellbeing may be seen to have cognitive, emotional, and motivational aspects (Andrews and Robinson, 1991). The motivational side lies in a tendency to seek pleasure and to avoid distress. The very rationality for the wellbeing approach lies in fact in the idea of wellbeing as a central human goal resulting from the satisfaction of basic human needs. Lacking or negative wellbeing are indicators of suffering when such needs are not met.

As for the operationalization of the concept, there has gradually developed a consensus that (subjective) wellbeing should at least include both a cognitive and an emotional dimension. The latter is usually divided into positive (happiness) and negative (suffering) affect as two more-or-less independent dimensions. The cognitive component refers to rational evaluations of how satisfied one is with life as a whole (global life satisfaction) or with different aspects (domains) of life, like family, work, income and oneself.

Evaluations are in most cases based on both rational considerations and emotional attraction. The salience of one over the other depends partly on the person, and partly on the object. Social and personal matters are probably more subject to emotional appraisal than are income and material goods. The affective system may be the dominant, as it is the older in evolutionary terms, and then more directly signals the extent to which basic needs are met.

Subjective wellbeing may be assessed by a number of methods – direct and indirect, via observations, self-reports and a variety of scales. This is a playground for psychometrics. More energy and sophistication have been invested in measurements and reliability than in theory development and validation.

Some of the larger international studies like the World Value Survey and Eurobarometer employ single-item measurements of global life satisfaction and happiness ('On the whole, are you very satisfied, fairly satisfied . . . with the life you lead?'). A number of multi-item scales exist, and may offer scores for separate domains (health, work, family, etc.) and a profile score across domains. Questions may refer to a specified time interval (last week, last year) or more generally to the present, past or future. Response scales also vary from Likert-type scales to Cantrill-ladders and graphical face scales, which are presumably more visual and less ethnocentrically biased. The different scales are often rooted in specific disciplines and aspects of quality of life, like Short Form 36 (SF36), and the shorter variant SF12, which are measuring health-related quality of life. The same goes for the WHO Quality of Life scale, which has a long (100 items) and a short (30 items) variant, and is now in the process of being standardized for special subgroups like older people. For more details about scales and measurements, see Robinson *et al.* (1991).

Level of living – or the livability of the environment to stay within the labels of Table 1 – is normally a field for sociologists and economists, and maps the access to resources and arenas that may impact on wellbeing. These scales and measurements usually find their unique form in each study, but often include a number of indices developed for comparative purposes, like indicators for class, income and purchasing power. Among such measures are also indices on the *population level*, like the Human Development Index, which was developed for the United Nations Development Program. The basic variant includes three items: public wealth as indicated by purchasing power per head, education as indicated by literacy and schooling, and life expectancy at birth. The first (public wealth) is indicating external qualities as in the upper left cell of Table 1. The second (education) may refer to both external and internal qualities, and then to any of the two upper cells that represent life chances (opportunity). The third indicator (life expectancy) is a more direct measure (outcome) of wellbeing, belonging in the lower right cell of Table 1.

Subjective wellbeing is measured partly through single-item scales of overall happiness or life satisfaction, but more usual is to employ multi-item scales for life satisfaction and positive and negative affect (or affect balance). A number of scales are available and include more-or-less similar items and procedures. Some address the negative sides of wellbeing more directly via depression or anxiety scales. Some find the tripartite division into life satisfaction and positive and negative emotions too narrow, and a poor representation of the complexities of subjective wellbeing. They therefore add other aspects or dimensions like self-acceptance and perceived purpose in life (Ryff and Keyes, 1995). Others see these characteristics as influencing factors that should be separated from the experience of wellbeing in itself.

INFLUENCES ON SUBJECTIVE WELLBEING

How is subjective wellbeing related to other factors, like demographic variables, personality traits and the life chances represented by environmental and individual resources? And what about the role of age and ageing for wellbeing?

For one thing, wellbeing seems to be only weakly related to demographic variables like age, sex, marital status and ethnicity. Such variables explain less than 10 per cent of the variance in global happiness and life satisfaction, according to a review of earlier studies by Andrews and Robinson (1991). This finding should perhaps primarily be taken as a validity test of the measurements themselves. If wellbeing scales had indeed produced different levels for men and women, old and young, Black and White, when other factors are controlled for, they could arguably be considered as biased. Valid and ethically sound measurements of wellbeing should not give preference to some population groups over others. Even seriously disadvantaged persons may enjoy and find meaning in life, and sound tests and measurements should respect that.

Subjective wellbeing is responding to the actual conditions of living, but is not a direct reflection of it. The economically well-off are, for example, normally more content with their material living conditions than are the poor, and persons in good health are more satisfied with their health than those in poor health. Such relationships have also been documented on the population level in the form of higher happiness levels in populations of wealthy nations compared to those of poor nations (Diener and Suh, 1999). There is, however, no one-to-one relationship between the actual and experienced levels; the correlation is in fact moderate.

The external conditions – the so-called 'bottom–up' influences – explain only a smaller part of the variance in subjective wellbeing according to Diener et al. (1999). The top-down influences of temperament (personality), cognitions (attributional styles) and coping styles explain far more. Several studies have found personality characteristics to be among the major predictors of emotional wellbeing. Positive affect tends to be positively related to extroversion, and negative affect to neuroticism (Diener and Lucas, 1999). So also with control beliefs: greater personal control – be it measured as internal control, self-efficacy, primary control or mastery – is associated with both cognitive and emotional wellbeing (Peterson, 1999), but may have less impact on wellbeing in old age, when accommodation and secondary control may become a better strategy (Lang and Heckhausen, 2001). Internal factors like these belong to the upper right cell of the Veenhoven matrix (Table 1), but although they are conceptually distinct from subjective wellbeing, they may in some cases be hard to separate from wellbeing and may then be seen as two sides of the same coin.

AGEING AND WELLBEING

Zapf (1984) has illustrated the relationship between actual (objective) and experienced (subjective) welfare levels in a fourfold classification of 'welfare positions'. When conditions are objectively well and subjectively appreciated, he talks about 'wellbeing'. When both are negative, he talks about 'deprivation'. Dissatisfaction despite good living conditions is taken as a case of 'dissonance', while satisfaction with poor living conditions is labelled 'adaptation'. The latter is often seen as a prototypical response in older years.

The maintaining of high subjective wellbeing in older years, despite a loss of resources (healthwise, social and economical), is by some interpreted as evidence of resilience and adaptive capacity among elders, and as a strategy to maintain self-esteem when autonomy is threatened (Baltes and Baltes, 1990). Psychoanalysts may take it as a self-defensive strategy (rationalisation, resignation). Sociologists would more likely seek the explanation in relative deprivation and reference group theory. George et al. (1985) belong to this tradition, and have suggested that the level of life satisfaction is based on an assessment of actual to expected conditions. Deviations from the expected age norm represent a relative deprivation that threatens wellbeing. This mechanism is elaborated in more detail by Michalos (1985) in the form of Multiple Discrepancies Theory, in which it is the gap between aspirations and achievements that explains the subjective experiences, not the actual level of living in itself. If older people are more satisfied than they 'ought to' be, it may hence be explained by their low expectations.

Some have a more positive interpretation of such mechanisms, for example as accommodative coping strategies in response to non-responsive environments (Brandstädter and Renner, 1990). We may also take the comparatively high levels of wellbeing among elders literally and on face value. Maybe it isn't so bad to be 60, 70 or even 80 as people in more or less ageist cultures often think, at least not in welfare states that offer a decent level of living in retirement. Poverty rates among elders have been radically reduced over the last decades in most modern welfare states, and quite a few pensioners are rather well situated. Their daily concerns over family problems may be more or less over, and the joys of the Third Age in the form of travelling, adult education or simply relaxation, may add to these benefits as long as the health is still good. For old people, life may be better than expected; for the young, worse than they hoped for. The costs of ageing become evident primarily when health seriously declines (for oneself and significant others) and dependency threatens.

Diener & Suh (1997) have, in a review of international studies, suggested that the association between age and wellbeing varies across dimensions of wellbeing. *Life satisfaction* is usually found to be stable across age groups; the so-called 'adjusted life satisfaction' (when age-related losses are controlled for) is even found to increase with age in quite a few studies. Selective mortality may be part of the explanation of these trends, as the less fortunate tend to die earlier. *Negative affect* also seems rather stable with age, while *positive affect* tends to decline slightly. The higher sensitivity of positive affect to age is often attributed to it having a more situational (mood) character, while negative affect owes its stability to being of a more dispositional nature.

Hence, the high levels of subjective wellbeing in old age, despite the age-related losses and constraints, need not be so paradoxical (Kunzmann *et al.*, 2000). wellbeing may change in character more than in levels, and may do so differently for women and men. Social support from a partner adds to emotional wellbeing for both sexes (Myers, 1999), but possibly more so for older men than for older women, who may find marriage a burden in old age (Mastekaasa, 1995). When older people in some studies are found to have higher levels of life satisfaction than the younger, but lower levels of happiness, this may indicate that people grow less emotional or at least less intense in their emotionality in old age. The relative absence of emotional excitement, which would be a source of tragedy for the young, may be a relief in old age, as suggested already by the philosophers Plato and Cicero some 2,000 years ago. Whether true or not, findings like these challenge our conceptions of what quality of life indeed is, and point to the need for further theorizing and research. More longitudinal studies in particular are called for, as the cross-sectional studies are unable to separate cohort and age effects. Younger cohorts may be more postmaterialistic and individualistically oriented and place more emphasis on their personal wellbeing, but they may then also be subject to a higher risk for disappointments.

There is also a need for more research on wellbeing in the Fourth Age. The very old have more limited adaptive capacities, and are found to have lower levels of wellbeing than the less old, in particular lower positive affect. This may be a feature of poorer health more than of age as such (Smith *et al.*, 1999; Isaacowitz, and Smith, 2003). As for Alzheimer's patients and those with other dementia syndromes, we are only starting to address what a qualitatively good life could be for such groups.

SUCCESSFUL AGEING AND QUALITY OF LIFE

Gerontology focused extensively on how people adapted to the stressors and constraints of ageing during the 1960s and 1970s, via labels like life satisfaction, morale and mental health. High levels on these dimensions were taken as indication of good adaptability and 'successful ageing'. The implicit metaphor for successful ageing is the lifecourse as a competition with winners and losers. The successful agers are those in good health, with high levels of physical and mental functioning, and active engagement in the environment (Rowe and Kahn, 1997). Criteria like these are found in several definitions of successful ageing since the 1950s, and indeed as a definition of good mental health (Jahoda, 1958). But labels have changed – healthy ageing, vital ageing, optimal ageing, active ageing, productive ageing, and positive ageing are added to the original formulation.

Most of these definitions and labels are indebted to activity theory. Disengagement has low status in these models, but so also has the ego-integrity of Erik Erikson, the mature wisdom of Carl Gustav Jung, or the acceptance of weakness as described by Charlotte Bühler. Whether true or false, these suggestions by central personalities in early psychology searched below the often trivial surface of the later successful ageing models. They also indicated that old age may have distinct qualities from other phases of life, and not simply be a bleak and outdated version of middle age. By doing so, they included also the very old in their models. They were, on the other hand, often victims of the same universalistic bias as most other models, but 'the good life', and 'to age with grace', need, however, not be the same in all cultures.

The traditional gerontological paradigm was criticised by some for being individualistic. The role of structural constraints and 'structured dependency' (Townsend, 1981) were downplayed. Others criticized it for being normative and concerned with outcomes more than agency. Successful ageing, and indeed quality of life, has to do with the road (process) more than the destination (end state) – to have goals and a motivation to try and reach them. Successful ageing is, for example, for Baltes and Carstensen (1996), a meta-theory of welfare. It implies a sense of direction in life, and capabilities and agency to follow this direction. In this directionality lies a sense of self-esteem and a purpose of living.

Quality of life is hard to comprehend, and so also is the role of age and ageing for quality of life. It may be better than expected to grow old, but most people would probably find it strange to learn that (subjective) wellbeing may increase with age at least up through the 70s, and, if so, they (the younger) would hardly call it life satisfaction, but rather resignation. We need to confront these attitudes, and to develop further our theories and measurements of quality of life and what indeed age and ageing has to do with it.

Age is a complex category, but far from empty. Although chronological age can hardly be an explanation for anything in itself, age as a phase of life, as a source of identification or as a normative category certainly can. We should therefore not aim to reduce age to an empty category by controlling for age-related and 'real' factors. The challenge is to stop before total reductionism, and to find what age-related entity gives meaning for whatever analysis we are performing.

The final test of a qualitatively good life may not be clear to us until we reach the very end of life ourselves, if at all. The larger turning points and crossroads of life tend to help us separate the important from the trivial, to extract what really counts from things of minor importance. The important may then be to feel at home in oneself and among significant others, and not be a stranger in life and society. If this is the case, then this wisdom cannot be reaped in advance. We live in the present; indeed this presence may be an essential aspect of quality of life in itself.

GUIDELINES FOR POLICY AND PRACTICE

However important subjective wellbeing is, it can hardly guide our policies directly. We need more external and objective measures for policy purposes.

Policy and practice should respect that people have different preferences and priorities, but not that their aspirations and expectations differ. If people's subjective aspirations guided our policies, then we would have to give priority to the rich and healthy rather than the poor and sick, because the former have learned to expect more, while the latter have lower aspirations (Ringen, 1995).

Purely subjective measures may therefore be misused as legitimation of unjust differences. Hence, policy needs to be informed by the actual distribution of resources and opportunities. Subjective measures may also guide us in these deliberations, as can be illustrated by the diminishing marginal utility of income for happiness. The practical implication of this finding is that policy may produce greater satisfaction for a larger number of people if priority is given to the less fortunate when scarce resources are distributed. More is not always better; there may be critical levels of resources and only minor additional benefits beyond such levels. If so, this is an argument for redistribution from the fortunate to the less fortunate, who may have far better use – and enjoyment – of the extra resources.

FURTHER READING

Kahneman, D., Diener, E., and N. Schwarz, eds. (1999). *Well-being: the foundations of hedonic psychology*. New York: Russel Sage Foundation.

Nussbaum, M., and A. Sen, eds. (1995). *The quality of life*. Oxford: Clarendon Press.

Robinson, J. P., Shaver, P. R., and L. S. Wrigtsman, eds. (1991). *Measures of personality and social psychological attitudes*. San Diego, Calif.: Academic Press.

Veenhoven, R. (2000). 'The four qualities of life. Ordering concepts and measures of the good life', *Journal of Happiness Studies*, 1: 1–39.

REFERENCES

Andrews, F. M., and J. P. Robinson, (1991). 'Measures of subjective well-being'. In J. P. Robinson, P. R. Shaver and L. S. Wrigtsman, eds., *Measures of personality and social psychological attitudes*. San Diego, Calif.: Academic Press, pp. 61–114.

Baltes, P. B., and M. M. Baltes (1990). 'Psychological perspectives on successful aging: the model of selective optimization with compensation'. In P. B. Baltes and M. M. Baltes, eds., *Successful aging. Perspectives from the behavioural sciences*. Cambridge: Cambridge University Press, pp. 1–34.

Baltes, M. M., and L. L. Carstensen (1996). 'The process of successful aging', *Ageing and Society*, 16: 397–422.

Brandstädter, J., and G. Renner (1990). 'Tenacious goal pursuit and flexible goal adjustment: explication and age-related analysis of assimilative and accommodative strategies of coping', *Psychology and Aging*, 5 (1): 58–67.

Campbell, A., Converse, P. E., and W. L. Rodgers (1976). *The quality of American life: perceptions, evaluations, and satisfactions*. New York: Russel Sage Foundation.

Diener, E., and R. E. Lucas (1999). 'Personality and subjective well-being'. In D. Kahneman, E. Diener and N. Schwarz, eds., *Well-being: the foundations of hedonic psychology*. New York: Russel Sage Foundation, pp. 213–29.

Diener, E., and M. E. Suh (1997). 'Subjective well-being and age: an international analysis', *Annual Review of Gerontology and Geriatrics*, 17: 304–24.

(1999). 'National differences in subjective well-being'. In D. Kahneman, E. Diener and N. Schwarz, eds., *Well-being: the foundations of hedonic psychology*. New York: Russel Sage Foundation, pp. 434–50.

Diener, E., Suh, E. M., Lucas, R. E., and H. L. Smith (1999). 'Subjective well-being: three decades of progress', *Psychological Bulletin*, 125 (2): 276–302.

Erikson, R. E. (1993). 'Description of inequality: the Swedish approach to welfare research'. In M. Nussbaum and A. Sen, eds., *The quality of life*. Oxford: Clarendon Press, pp. 67–83.

George, L. K., Okun, M. A., and R. Landerman (1985). 'Age as a moderator of the determinants of life satisfaction', *Research on Aging*, 7: 209–33.

Isaacowitz, D. M., and J. Smith (2003). 'Positive and negative affect in very old age', *Journal of Gerontology, Psychological Sciences*, 58B (3): P143–P152.

Jahoda, M. (1958). *Current concepts of positive mental health*. New York: Basic Books.

Kunzmann, U., Little, T. D., and J. Smith (2000). 'Is age-related stability of subjective well-being a paradox? Cross-sectional and longitudinal evidence from the Berlin Aging Study', *Psychology and Aging*, 15 (3): 511–26.

Lang, F. R., and J. H. Heckhausen (2001). 'Perceived control over development and subjective well-being: differential benefits across adulthood', *Journal of Personality and Social Psychology*, 81 (3): 509–23.

Mastekaasa, A. (1995). 'Age variations in the suicide rates and self-reported subjective well-being of married and never married persons', *Journal of Community and Applied Social Psychology*, 5: 21–39.

Michalos, A. C. (1985). 'Mulitple discrepancies theory (MDT)', *Social Indicators Research*, 16 (4): 347–414.

Myers, D. G. (1999). 'Close relationships and quality of life'. In D. Kahneman, E. Diener and N. Schwarz, eds., *Well-being: the foundations of hedonic psychology*. New York: Russel Sage Foundation, pp. 374–91.

Peterson, C. (1999). 'Personal control and well-being'. In D. Kahneman, E. Diener and N. Schwarz, eds., *Well-being: the foundations of hedonic psychology*. New York: Russel Sage Foundation, pp. 288–301.

Ringen, S. (1995). 'Well-being, measurement and preferences', *Acta Sociologica*, 38: 3–15.

Robinson, J. P., Shaver, P. R. and L.S. Wrigtsman, eds. (1991). *Measures of personality and social psychological attitudes*. San Diego, Calif.: Academic Press.

Rowe, J., and R. Kahn (1997). 'Successful aging', *Gerontologist*, 37 (4): 433–40.

Ryff, C. D., and C. L. M. Keyes (1995). 'The structure of psychological well-being revisited', *Journal of Personality and Social Psychology*, 69 (4): 719–27.

Sen, A. (1993). 'Capability and well-being'. In M. Nussbaum and A. Sen, eds., *The quality of life*. Oxford: Clarendon Press, pp. 30–53.

Smith, J., Fleeson, W., Geiselmann, B., Settersten, R. A., Jr, and U. Kunzmann (1999). 'Sources of well-being in very old age'. In P. B. Baltes and K. U. Mayer, eds., *The Berlin Ageing Study*. Cambridge: Cambridge University Press, pp. 450–71.

Townsend, P. (1981). 'The structured dependency of the elderly: a creation of social policy in the twentieth century', *Ageing and Society*, 1: 5–28.

Veenhoven, R. (2000). 'The four qualities of life. Ordering concepts and measures of the good life', *Journal of Happiness Studies*, 1: 1–39.

Zapf, W. (1984). 'Individuelle Wohlfart: Lebensbedingungen und wahrgenommene Lebensqualität'. In W. Glatzer and W. Zapf, eds., *Lebensqualität in der Bundesrepublik Deutschland. Objective Lebensbedingungen und subjectives Wohlbefinden*. Frankfurt/Main: Campus.

The Transformation of Dying in Old Societies

CLIVE SEALE

INTRODUCTION

A great deal of attention has been given by demographers, gerontologists and others (as is amply testified in other parts of this volume) to the spectacular increases in expectation of life over the past hundred years, but far less attention has been given to the way these changes have affected experiences of death and dying. In the developed world, death is now very largely in the province of old age and this in turn has changed, in an equally dramatic way, the ways in which societies provide for and attach meanings to the end of life.

The statistical distribution of mortality varies considerably, both historically and across regions of the world. Most obviously, life expectancy has risen over time, yet people in some countries can expect much longer lives than those in others. Within countries there are marked differences in the age distribution of death for different groups, for example being influenced by gender and socioeconomic differences. Additionally, variability arises between regions of the world in different causes of death, and there are great differences between countries in the availability of formal healthcare. When combined with cultural variations that affect matters as diverse as family size, gender and filial roles, beliefs about how health professionals should behave and religious customs, it will be seen that there is potentially much variation in people's experience of dying and of care before death.

The author expresses his thanks to Professor Malcolm Johnson for assistance in preparing this chapter.

The purpose of this chapter will be to map out some of this variation, initially by reviewing available statistical data about the matters I have mentioned, before turning to the consequences of these patterns for the experience of dying in different parts of the world. I shall also draw on some qualitative data about the experience of dying. Towards the end of the chapter I shall consider future prospects, given the continuation of present trends.

DYING TRAJECTORIES AND NEEDS

It is sometimes stated (for example Lofland, 1978; Hull and Jones, 1986) that the shift from infectious to degenerative disease involves a lengthening of dying trajectories. Coupled with advances in the medical capacity to predict death at an early stage in some diseases, this has led to the emergence of a particular category of experience, that of 'terminal illness', around which has developed the expertise of hospice and palliative care in some developed countries. This simple story requires some modification, which can begin with an assessment of what is known about the prevalence of disability and symptoms, as well as the length of dying trajectories, in the time before death.

Surveys of nationally representative samples of elderly people and of people in the last year of life in the UK are a useful starting point. British government surveys have shown, broadly speaking, that the prevalence of disability reflects the ageing of the population over time. Since the General Household Survey (GHS) began in 1972, the proportions of adults reporting a longstanding illness that limited daily activities rose from 15 per cent of people living in private households to 22 per cent in 1996. Women at each time-point are somewhat more likely to report this than men, and the prevalence of limiting longstanding illness, unsurprisingly, shows a sharp rise with age, so that amongst people aged 75 and over, 52 per cent report such illness (ONS, 1998a). Studies in the USA show similar patterns (Feldman, 1986).

The perception that increased life expectancy may bring with it a greater burden of disability towards the end of life led some researchers to calculate a new statistic of 'healthy life expectancy' (HLE) to modify the traditional life expectancy statistic. This showed that between 1976 and 1994 in the UK, when life expectancy rose by over 4 years for males and more than 3 for females, healthy life expectancy showed almost no change (ONS, 1998b). As a result of this increased level of disability, 30 per cent of people aged 85 or more surveyed in the 1996 GHS needed help at home in climbing the stairs, 24 per cent needed help with bathing or showering, 8 per cent with dressing and undressing, as well as smaller proportions needing assistance with other self-care activities (ONS, 1998a).

The World Health Organization (2000) reported on world rates of healthy life expectancy (or Disability Adjusted Life Expectancy – DALE) in 1999, showing that people in poorer countries 'lost' some 14 per cent of their lives to disability, compared with 9 per cent in richer countries. Japan (74.5 years), Australia (73.2), France (73.1), Sweden (73.0) and Spain (72.8) were the top five nations. The United States rated twenty-fourth (70.0 years) for a variety of reasons, including the poor health of some minorities and high levels of violence. All of the bottom ten countries were in sub-Saharan Africa, reflecting the effect of HIV-AIDS.

The symptoms and restrictions experienced by people in the last year of life have been recorded in three UK surveys, describing people dying in 1969, 1987 and 1990 by means of interviews with surviving relatives and others who knew the deceased. The first two of these (Cartwright et al., 1973; Seale and Cartwright, 1994) were from nationally representative samples, permitting a comparison over time. On both occasions respondents were asked to say which of a number of areas of restriction had been experienced by the people who died. These included such

activities as getting in and out of the bath, dressing and undressing, and washing. The major changes concerned the length of time that such restrictions were experienced. In 1969 30 per cent had needed help with at least one of these for a year or more. By 1987 this had risen to 52 per cent. In this respect, the figures support those from the GHS.

Respondents were also asked, on both occasions, to report whether certain symptoms were experienced at all during the last twelve months of life and, for symptoms reported at this stage, how long they had been experienced by the person who died. The major changes since 1969 again concerned the duration of some of the symptoms: mental confusion, depression and incontinence were all experienced over a longer time period by people in the later study. Controlling for age showed that these increases were all related to the greater proportion of people aged 75 or more in the 1987 study.

Recalling that cancer, heart disease and stroke have become increasingly prevalent as causes of death as infectious diseases have declined in importance, the analyses conducted for these separate groups in the 1990 survey (Addington-Hall, 1996) are of interest. This survey, the Regional Study of Care for the Dying (RSCD) (Addington-Hall and McCarthy, 1995), was not nationally representative, but its large size permits comparison of these different leading causes of death. This is shown in Table 1. Pain, nausea and vomiting, difficulty swallowing,

TABLE 1. Symptoms experienced in the last year of life in Britain, 1990

	Cancer %	Heart disease %	Stroke %
Pain	88	77	66
Breathlessness	54	60	37
Nausea and vomiting	59	32	23
Difficulty swallowing	41	16	23
Constipation	63	38	45
Mental confusion	41	32	50
Pressure sores	28	11	20
Urinary incontinence	40	30	56
Bowel incontinence	32	17	37
N=	2063	683	229

(*Source:* Addington-Hall, 1996.)

constipation and pressure sores are more prevalent amongst people dying from cancer. Breathlessness is a particular problem for people with heart disease; mental confusion and incontinence affect a high proportion of people dying from strokes. Overall, cancer caused, on average, a larger number of symptoms and a larger proportion of these were considered by respondents to have been 'very distressing' for the dying person. However, the duration of symptoms in cancer was less than for other conditions (Addington-Hall *et al.*, 1998). This pattern was also found in the earlier study of deaths in 1986 (Seale and Cartwright, 1994), which suggested that an experience of longer term disability was more typical in people not dying from cancer, who also tended to be a little older, on average, than those dying from cancer.

There have been other studies of dependency, symptoms and needs for care in the period before death, in the USA (M. W. Hunt, 1991; Kai *et al.*, 1993; Dudgeon and Kristjanson, 1995; Andershed and Ternestedt, 1997), Germany (Bickel, 1998), Finland (R. Hunt *et al.*, 1993) and Australia (Karlsen and Addington-Hall, 1998). Equivalent information is lacking, however, for patterns of dying in countries at earlier stages of the epidemiological transition. This means that death from infectious diseases and other causes prevalent in developing countries, and death in younger groups, are not well described. An exception is AIDS, where there are descriptions of Western populations before the advent of effective anti-retroviral therapies (Sims and Moss, 1991). However, it is likely that these Western AIDS deaths were dissimilar from typical patterns in, say, African countries, where people progress more rapidly to death due to the presence of other uncontrolled diseases such as TB, pneumonia and salmonellosis infections, without living long enough to experience the pattern of co-infections experienced in the West (Gilks *et al.*, 1998; UNAIDS, 1998; Nunn *et al.*, 1997). It is also possible that in the future an increased availability of life-preserving drugs will change the experience of this disease in poorer countries, though there remain a variety of obstacles to this. Additionally, studies of populations in developed countries rely on a contrast being made with the average, healthy adulthood that is the norm in richer countries. Morbidity data, reflecting the prevalence of debilitating but not life-threatening disease or malnutrition, which is the norm for many in developing countries (Hull and Jones, 1986), might reduce this sense of contrast between states of health and illness.

Finally, the assumption that degenerative disease creates longer dying trajectories might be questioned were comparative data available. This may be obviously true if the point of comparison is with cholera, pneumonia or trauma, but tuberculosis and AIDS both cause considerable long term debilitation, dependency and symptoms, even in an environment that precipitates an earlier death from these causes in some countries. For example, Gilks *et al.* (1998) report a World Bank estimate that Tanzanian adults with AIDS have 17 episodes of illness requiring over 280 days of care, pointing out the particular strain that such chronic illness places on poor families when the sufferer may be a parent with dependent children or other relatives.

CARE OF DYING PEOPLE

Households and family structure

On the whole, sick people turn first to their families for help, so it is important to know about any factors that change the availability of such informal care. In developed countries, the ageing of populations is generally accompanied by decreasing family size and a growing propensity for elderly people to live in households separate from their children. Because of gender differences in longevity and marriage patterns, this pattern of events commonly leaves many elderly widows living alone towards the end of life, dependent on non-resident carers for assistance if they get sick. A notable exception to the trend towards living alone in old age is Japan where, in spite of containing a high proportion of elderly people, the proportion living alone is small. In the 1980s, for example, only 10% of Japanese aged 65 and older lived alone in private households, compared with 30% in the UK, 31% in the USA and 40% in Sweden (US Congress, 1993). Cultural preferences regarding appropriate family relationships lie behind the Japanese pattern and may well apply also in many less developed countries.

On the whole, data on the household structure of elderly people is unavailable for developing countries, but data on the extent of single-person households, which is a rough proxy indicator of the proportion of elderly living alone, is available for some. In Bangladesh, the Philippines and Thailand, for example, single-person households are rare (generally less than 3 per cent of all households) and have not increased over time (Young, 1986). It should be remembered, however, that in developing countries death is less confined to older years, so a profile of elderly households is relevant to a smaller proportion of those needing care when dying. Here, concerns about family care for the dying may be offset by concerns about care for the dependents of people who have died, something that has become less relevant in developed countries because of the demographic factors outlined, but also because of relatively sophisticated systems of social insurance that are unaffordable in developing countries. With the pattern of mortality from AIDS in Africa, this has been a particularly pressing concern as the numbers of orphans increase, experiencing various forms of social and educational deprivation and abuse as a result of the lack of caretakers (UNAIDS, 1998).

UK data on elderly households shows trends over time that follow a pattern similar to that in the few other countries where this is fully documented (for example, Australia, Canada, Japan and the USA – see Young, 1986). In 1996–7 15% of households in the UK consisted of a single person above pensionable age living alone; in 1961 this figure had been only 7% (ONS, 1998b). At the more recent date, approximately four times as many elderly women as men lived alone. The 1996 GHS showed 87% of people aged 65 and over living either alone or with only a spouse (ONS, 1998a), a figure that has also been steadily increasing over time (Grundy, 1996). Grundy (1996) also reports surveys showing reductions since 1962 in the proportion of elderly parents with at least one child living within 10–15 minutes travel. The consequences of these changes for the sources of informal help and care that people could draw upon as they approached death were described in a 1987 survey of the last year of life (Seale and Cartwright, 1994). People living alone in the 1987 sample were in a particularly unfortunate situation for potential sources of help. They were the least likely to have any children or siblings alive and were most likely to be widowed or divorced and old. They were also the group most likely to progress to institutional care.

Institutional care and place of death

Widespread institutional care for elderly people is very much a phenomenon of developed countries, adopted as a solution to the shortage of informal care in families available to elderly people. This in turn is caused both by demographic factors and features of the social organisation of advanced industrialised societies that often separate elderly people from mainstream social and family life. The Japanese example suggests that the demographic pressures alone are inadequate to explain the growth of institutional care, for in Japan there are relatively low proportions in institutions in spite of there being large numbers of elderly people. In the early 1980s, for example, 4% of the Japanese population aged 65 and over lived in an institution, compared with 6% in the USA and 11% in the Netherlands (US Congress, 1993). Data from Australia, Canada, the UK and USA show that the elderly living in institutions are predominantly female (Arber and Ginn, 1991; Young, 1986).

Although most people who enter a residential institution for the elderly will eventually die there, these are not generally perceived as places primarily devoted to the care of 'dying' people. This is more normally the perception of hospices, although caring for 'the dying' is also seen as a legitimate part of general hospital care. A large proportion of people in developed societies die in hospitals, rather than at home or indeed in hospices. This is shown internationally for selected countries in Table 2.

TABLE 2. Proportion of deaths occurring in hospital for selected countries (1996; percentages of all deaths in each country)

Romania	18	France	50
Republic of Korea	23	USA	60
USSR*	24	United Kingdom	66
Spain	30	Japan	67
Italy	37	Canada	73
Poland	47	Sweden	79

*=1988 data.
(*Source:* WHO, 1988, 1998b.)

Data on place of death are only available for countries where statistical surveillance is well developed, which means countries with a high proportion of such deaths tend to enter the figures. Nationally representative figures for African countries, for example, are unavailable. Such countries are likely to show a marked rural/urban difference in the proportion of hospital deaths, and overall the proportion is likely to be low.

In countries with high rates of death occurring in hospitals, these have been rising steadily for many years. In 1960, for example, only 50% of people in England and Wales died in hospitals (General Register Office, 1962), compared with the 66% shown in Table 2 for the UK as a whole in 1996. However, there are indications that the trend towards hospital deaths tends to level off once figures of 60–70% are reached (Brameld et al., 1998; M. W. Hunt, 1991). This is partly because there is a residual core of sudden deaths, but also because deaths in other institutions such as residential homes and hospices increase, as well as successful provision of supportive community care for those who wish to die at home, something which in some countries may be determined by the ability to pay for this (Dudgeon and Kristjanson, 1995).

It has become part of the professional ethic of specialists in terminal care that a supported death at home is generally preferable to a death in hospital and much of the effort of community hospice services is devoted to achieving this outcome. The effect of community care and specialist hospice provision on place of death figures has been noted in the USA (Pritchard et al., 1998) and, in that country, specifically in relation to AIDS deaths, where hospital deaths have declined for Whites, gay men and men in general, though not for injecting drug users or children. Studies in Sweden (Andershed and Ternestedt, 1997) and Australia (R. Hunt et al., 1993; R. Hunt and McCaul, 1998) record shifts towards hospices as a place of death in recent years. Studies in the USA (Stearns et al., 1996) and Australia (Brameld et al., 1998; R. Hunt et al., 1993) report that people in their 80s and above have lower rates of hospital care, or of death in hospital, than the 'younger' elderly. This is largely due to alternative institutional provision in these countries rather than a greater proportion of home deaths. A pattern of frequent, short, non-terminal stays in hospital in the last year of life

may also develop in such countries (Brameld et al., 1998).

A review article (Grande et al., 1998) notes many of these features, making the additional point that gender makes a difference in all of this since, for the reasons outlined earlier, women in these countries tend to be disadvantaged in their ability to draw on informal family care as they approach death, therefore being less likely to die at home. Significantly, this review article covered 12 US papers, 14 Australian, 10 Italian, 3 Swedish and 1 each from Switzerland, Israel and Canada. Place of death is not a topic that has been studied systematically outside developed countries.

In several Anglophone countries, but particularly the UK and USA, a critique of the quality of care for the terminally ill arose in the 1950s and 1960s, fuelled by a more general readiness to question scientific and professional authority, and widespread concerns about rights to individual autonomy in the face of institutional power (reflected also in critiques of institutions for the mentally ill, for example). The institutionalisation and apparent medicalisation of care for the dying were criticised for their dehumanising emphasis on curative efforts at the expense of palliative care, and place of death statistics became a symbol around which these dissatisfactions coalesced.

Healthcare systems

Care specifically aimed at dying people and their families in developed countries has been marked in recent decades by the rise of the hospice movement and, latterly, the development of palliative care as a medical and nursing speciality. Details of the spread and character of this movement can be found in Seale (1998) and Clark et al. (1997). As well as imparting a new vigour to strictly medical efforts to palliate the symptoms of terminal illnesses (chiefly cancer, but also motor neuron disease and AIDS), a concern with the psychosocial wellbeing of patients and their families has meant an extension of traditional medical expertise. Nurses, by successfully claiming particular psychosocial skills, have gained a significant degree of autonomy from medical dominance in this arena of healthcare, assisted also by the formation of community support teams to advise lay carers in their homes. More recently, claims that the palliative care approach is relevant to pre-terminal phases of terminal disease (Doyle, 1997), or to additional diseases such as stroke, heart disease and dementia, or that it could be applied in the context of nursing-home care, have been heard (Field and Addington-Hall, 1999; Clark *et al.*, 1997). Such ambitions, however, should not underestimate the palliative components that already exist in the healthcare specialities that serve these groups.

The appeal of hospice and palliative care in developed countries can be understood within a broader cultural context. The tendency to plan for and control major life events is already an important feature of self-identity in late modern societies (Giddens, 1991), though it is particularly concentrated amongst more educated groups and may be more strong in Anglophone countries than elsewhere (Seale, 1998). Life planning, saving, taking out insurance against sickness as well as death and investing in schooling or training can all be engaged in with more confidence if mortality is more predictably placed at the end of the lifecourse. Gradually, dying too becomes subject to this wish for control, and hospice and palliative care practitioners provide a relevant expertise to assist this. Comparison of cancer deaths in hospital and hospice has revealed the relative success of hospice patients in planning the manner of their deaths, with hospitals picking up a higher proportion of deaths resulting from unplanned, emergency admissions (Seale and Kelly, 1997). The shift in professional attitudes and practices towards open disclosure of prognosis that has occurred in developed Anglophone countries (Novack *et al.*, 1979; Seale and Cartwright, 1994) is designed to promote patients' control while additionally opening up a new arena for psychosocial expertise (Kubler-Ross, 1969).

Rising support for euthanasia in many developed countries as an alternative means to relieve suffering and dependency towards the end of life, and to control the manner and timing of death, is a reflection of similar forces (see Seale, 1997, for a review of literature). Although the hospice and euthanasia movements clash at the level of public debate because of religious differences, in the experience of individual patients they offer very similar opportunities for control and self-direction near death (Seale *et al.*, 1997). Significantly, calls for medically assisted euthanasia are not heard in developing countries,

where the suffering of dying people is of a different nature, but nevertheless considerable, and in some cases occurs over lengthy periods (see earlier). The desire for medical assistance in this may also, paradoxically, reflect a general dependency on medically delivered solutions to suffering, which are not shared in developing countries. Justice (1995), for example, describes a culturally sanctioned method of fasting to death in Banares, India, where there is no medical involvement.

There is evidence to suggest that the largely Anglophone phenomena of hospice or palliative care and support for euthanasia are somewhat alien to the cultures of some developed countries. The case of Japan and, to a lesser extent, Italy are relevant here. Respect for the traditional authority of the medical profession coupled with relatively strong religious observance, as well as a lesser emphasis on individual autonomy and greater reliance on intra-familial support during disruptive life events, seem to be important underlying factors. Studies suggest that, in such countries, the Anglo-American practices of informing most patients with cancer of their disease, or stressing the benefits and opportunities of open awareness of dying, or involving patients rather than families in decision making, are culturally inappropriate (Long and Long, 1982; Kai *et al.*, 1993; Surbone, 1992; Gordon, 1990). Japanese prohibitions against organ transplantation (Lock, 1995) arise from religious considerations that may also explain the absence of a significant movement to support euthanasia. Nevertheless, Anglophone models of palliative care are increasingly spreading to European and other non-Anglophone developed countries. This is particularly marked in Eastern Europe, where the changes of political climate have led to a host of initiatives to relieve terminal suffering (Luczak, 1997).

Where resources support the provision of specialist services for dying people, then, awareness of cultural differences is of assistance in determining their appropriate form. In developing countries there is the additional factor of scarce resources to consider. In practice, most debate about healthcare in developing countries is confined to getting a better balance between prevention and cure, or between hospital and community services (Okolski, 1986; Northrup, 1986; Hull and Jones, 1986), without considering issues of palliation or terminal care, which might be considered luxuries affordable by richer countries. The involvement of religious authorities rather than health services in issues of dying may be seen as more appropriate. Nevertheless, examples do exist. Western-style hospice care has developed in certain cities in India, for example, though access to this tends to be confined to wealthier clients and such initiatives have had to struggle against entrenched professional attitudes and working practices that are reminiscent of the situation 50 years ago in UK and US healthcare (Burn, 1997). The eleven cancer centres in India reach less than 10 per cent of terminally ill cancer patients and only 16,000 of the estimated 350,000 people with cancer pain are treated for this each year (Stjernsward, 1997). Medical initiatives co-exist with models of palliative care for the poor that draw more on religious than on medical traditions, as is seen in Mother Theresa's work.

Community palliative care initiatives in developing countries are likely to be funded at a low level and may focus on relieving the social care needs that arise from extreme poverty exacerbated by illness rather than relief of medical conditions. This is the experience of community initiatives in relation to AIDS care in some African countries (World Health Organization, 1994) and particularly Uganda (Gilks et al., 1998), which have attended to medical and nursing aspects of terminal AIDS care only in so far as this has been affordable. In relation to palliative cancer care, sub-Saharan Africa 'remains isolated from hospice knowledge' according to Hockley (1997), with the exception of South Africa and Zimbabwe where there are nascent hospice movements. Where palliative care initiatives exist in developing countries, these must deal with a variety of problems, including 'an inadequate public health infrastructure, poor administrative systems, the lack of oral morphine and restrictions on opioid prescribing, the general poverty of patients, and poor educational opportunities for health professionals'.

The World Health Organization's Cancer Pain and Palliative Care Programme represents a pragmatic approach to the difficulties of providing palliative care in developing countries where a combination of poverty and cultural differences militate against the wholesale application of Western models. By prioritising pain relief as an essential core component of a global campaign, WHO initiatives are able to concentrate on removing obstacles to the availability of opioids and promoting a low-cost approach to relieving this core distressing symptom of terminal disease (Stjernsward, 1997).

CONCLUSION

A number of issues arise from this review, of importance if we are to understand the implications of changing causes of death and life expectancies for the future experience of dying. I have described the ageing of populations worldwide, and pointed out the consequences this can have for availability of care for elderly people towards the end of life, in both developed and developing countries. Gender differences in longevity, social status and living arrangements have implications for the experience of old age and the availability of care towards the end of life, and this differs internationally. The experiences of dying people merge with the more general experience of old age in countries that have experienced the demographic transition. This may have consequences for the relationship between services specialising in the care of dying people and services specialising in the care of elderly people.

Internationally different patterns of life expectancy and disease burden require us, too, to question the extent to which Western models of terminal or palliative care are applicable in developing countries. The care needs and dying trajectories of diseases commonly causing death in developing countries may be rare in other countries and may not be of the sort that are appropriately met by existing models of palliative care. Even if applicable, should such services attract resources in poorer countries with high levels of preventable disease? Considering richer, developed countries, there is evidence that in some there are cultures and communication practices between health carers and their clients that are at variance with those in which palliative care originally developed.

The sudden, perhaps temporary, declines in life expectancy in some Eastern European countries suggest caution in assuming that in the future there will be a general passage of all countries through the demographic and epidemiological transitions experienced by richer countries of the world. In particular, the spread of AIDS, and its impact on populations in Africa and some other regions where governments have been slow to implement preventive measures and too poor to afford drug therapies, will continue for some decades to come. This disease has a somewhat unpredictable future trajectory, but it is already clear that it has a very considerable impact both on the experience of dying, on the lives of survivors and on the economies of the countries worst affected.

FURTHER READING

de Fries, B. (1999). *End of life issues: interdisciplinary and multidimensional perspectives*. New York: Springer.

Dickenson, D., Johnson, M., and J. Katz, eds. (2000). *Death, dying and bereavement*, 2nd edn. London: Sage.

Seale, C. F. (1998). *Constructing death: the sociology of dying and bereavement*. Cambridge: Cambridge University Press.

REFERENCES

Addington-Hall, J. (1996). 'Heart disease and stroke: lessons from cancer care'. In G. Ford and I. Lewin, eds., *Managing terminal illness*. London: Royal College of Physicians, pp. 25–32.

Addington-Hall, J., and M. McCarthy (1995). 'Dying from cancer: results of a national population-based investigation', *Palliative Medicine*, 9: 295–305.

Addington-Hall, J., Altmann, D., and M. McCarthy (1998). 'Variations by age in symptoms and dependency levels experienced by people in the last year of life, as reported by surviving family, friends and officials', *Age and Ageing*, 27: 129–36.

Andershed, B., and B. M. Ternestedt (1997). 'Patterns of care for patients with cancer before and after the establishment of a hospice ward', *Scandinavian Journal of Caring Sciences*, 11 (1): 42–50.

Arber, S., and J. Ginn (1991). *Gender and later life: a sociological analysis of resources and constraints*. London: Sage.

Bickel, H. (1998). 'The last year of life: a population-based study of decedents. Living arrangements, place of death, and utilization of care', *Zeitschrift fur Gerontologie und Geriatrie*, 31 (3): 193–204.

Brameld, K. J., D'Arcy, C., Holman, C. D. J., Bass, A. J., Codde, J. P., and I. L. Rouse (1998). 'Hospitalisation of the elderly during the last year of life: an application of record linkage in Western Australia 1985–1994', *Journal of Epidemiology and Community Health*, 52 (11): 740–4.

Burn, J. (1997). 'Palliative care in India'. In D. Clark, J. Hockley and S. Ahmedzai, eds., *New themes in palliative care*. Buckingham: Open University, pp. 116–28.

Cartwright, A., Hockey, L., and J. L. Anderson (1973). *Life before death*. London: Routledge and Kegan Paul.

Clark, D., Hockley, J., and S. Ahmedzai, eds. (1997). *New themes in palliative care*. Buckingham: Open University.

Doyle, D. (1997). *Dilemmas and directions: the future of specialist palliative care*. London: National Council for Hospice and Palliative Care Services.

Dudgeon, D. G., and L. Kristjanson (1995). 'Home versus hospital death: assessment of preferences and clinical challenges', *Canadian Medical Association Journal*, 152 (3): 337–40.

Feldman, J. J. (1986). 'Work ability of the aged under conditions of improving mortality'. In United Nations, ed., *Consequences of mortality trends and differentials*. New York: United Nations, pp. 185–91.

Field, D., and J. Addington-Hall (1999). 'Extending specialist palliative care to all?' *Social Science and Medicine*, 48: 1271–80.

General Register Office (1962). *The Registrar General's statistical review of England and Wales for the Year 1960: Part III, Commentary*. London: HMSO.

Giddens, A. (1991). *Modernity and self-identity: self and society in the late modern age*. Cambridge: Polity Press.

Gilks, C., Floyd, K., Haran, D., Kemp, J., Squire, B., and D. Wilkinson (1998). *Sexual health and health care: care and support for people with HIV/AIDS in resource-poor settings*, Health and Population Occasional Paper. London: Department for International Development.

Gordon, D. R. (1990). 'Embodying illness, embodying cancer', *Culture, Medicine and Psychiatry*, 14: 275–97.

Grande, G. E., Addington-Hall, J. M., and C. J. Todd (1998). 'Place of death and access to home care services: are certain patient groups at a disadvantage?' *Social Science and Medicine*, 47 (5): 565–79.

Grundy, E. (1996). 'Population review: (5) the population aged 60 and over', *Population Trends*, 84: 14–20.

Hockley, J. (1997). 'The evolution of the hospice approach'. In D. Clark, J. Hockley, and S. Ahmedzai, eds., *New themes in palliative care*. Buckingham: Open University, pp. 84–100.

Hull, T. H., and G. W. Jones (1986). 'Introduction: international mortality trends and differentials'. In United Nations, ed., *Consequences of mortality trends and differentials*. New York: United Nations, pp. 1–9.

Hunt, M. W. (1991). 'The identification and provision of care for the terminally ill by "family members"', *Sociology of Health and Illness*, 13 (3): 375–95.

Hunt, R., and K. McCaul (1998). 'Coverage of cancer patients by hospice services, South Australia, 1990 to 1993', *Australian and New Zealand Journal of Public Health*, 22 (1): 45–8.

Hunt, R., Bonett, A., and D. Roder (1993). 'Trends in the terminal care of cancer patients: South Australia, 1981–1990', *Australian and New Zealand Journal of Medicine*, 23 (3): 245–51.

Justice, C. (1995). 'The "natural" death while not eating: a type of palliative care', In *Banaras, India, Journal of Palliative Care*, 11 (1): 38–42.

Kai, I., Ohi, G., Yano, E., Kobayashi, Y., Miyama, T., Niino, N., and K. Naka (1993). 'Communication between patients and physicians about terminal care: a survey in Japan', *Social Science and Medicine*, 36 (9): 1151–9.

Karlsen, S., and J. Addington-Hall (1998). 'How do cancer patients who die at home differ from those who die elsewhere?' *Palliative Medicine*, 12 (4): 279–86.

Kubler-Ross, E. (1969). *On death and dying*. New York: Macmillan.

Lock, M. (1995). 'Contesting the natural in Japan: moral dilemmas and technologies of dying', *Culture, Medicine and Psychiatry*, 19: 1–38.

Lofland, L. H. (1978). *The craft of dying: the modern face of death*. Beverley Hills: Sage.

Long, S. O., and B. D. Long (1982). 'Curable cancers and fatal ulcers: attitudes toward cancer in Japan', *Social Science and Medicine*, 16: 2101–08.

Luczak, J. (1997). 'Palliative care in Eastern Europe'. In D. Clark, J. Hockley, and S. Ahmedzai, eds., *New themes in palliative care*. Buckingham: Open University, pp. 170–94.

Northrup, R. S. (1986). 'Decision making for health care in developing countries'. In United Nations, ed., *Consequences of mortality trends and differentials*. New York: United Nations, pp. 135–49.

Novack, D. H., Plumer, R., Smith, R. L., Ochitill, H., Morrow, G. R., and J. M. Bennett (1979). 'Changes in physicians' attitudes toward telling the cancer patient', *Journal of the American Medical Association*, 241: 897–900.

Nunn, A. J., Mulder, D. W., Kamali, A., Ruberantwari, A., Kengeya-Kayondo, J.-F., and J. Whitworth (1997). 'Mortality associated with HIV-1 infection over five years in a rural Ugandan population: cohort study', *British Medical Journal*, 315: 767–71.

ONS (Office for National Statistics) (1998a). *Living in Britain: results from the 1996 General Household Survey*. London: The Stationery Office.

(1998b). *Social trends 28*. London: The Stationery Office.

Okolski, M. (1986). 'Relationship between mortality and morbidity levels according to age and sex and their implications for organizing health care systems in developed countries'. In United Nations, ed., *Consequences of mortality trends and differentials*. New York: United Nations, pp. 150–64.

Pritchard, R. S., Fisher, E. S., Teno, J. M., Sharp, S. M., Reding, D. J., Knaus, W. A., Wennberg, J. E., and J. Lynn (1998). 'Influence of patient preferences and local health system characteristics on the place of death', *Journal of the American Geriatrics Society*, 46 (10): 1242–50.

Seale, C. F. (1997). 'Social and ethical aspects of euthanasia: a review', *Progress in Palliative Care*, 5: 141–6.

(1998). *Constructing death: the sociology of dying and bereavement*. Cambridge: Cambridge University Press.

Seale, C. F., and J. Addington-Hall (1995). 'Dying at the best time', *Social Science and Medicine*, 40 (5): 589–95.

Seale, C. F., and A. Cartwright (1994). *The year before death*. Aldershot: Avebury.

Seale, C. F., and M. Kelly (1997). 'A comparison of hospice and hospital care for people who die: views of surviving spouse', *Palliative Medicine*, 11: 93–100.

Seale, C. F., Addington-Hall, J., and M. McCarthy (1997). 'Awareness of dying: prevalence, causes and consequences', *Social Science and Medicine*, 45: 477–84.

Sims, R., and V. Moss (1991). *Terminal care for people with AIDS*. London: Edward Arnold.

Stearns, S. C., Kovar, M. G., Hayes, K., and G. G. Koch (1996). 'Risk indicators for hospitalization during the last year of life', *Health Services Research*, 31 (1): 49–69.

Stjernsward, J. (1997). 'The WHO cancer pain and palliative care programme'. In D. Clark, J. Hockley, and S. Ahmedzai, eds., *New themes in palliative care*. Buckingham: Open University, pp. 203–12.

Surbone, A. (1992). 'Truth telling to the patient'. *Journal of the American Medical Association*, 268: 1661–2.

UNAIDS (1998). *HIV-related opportunistic diseases*, UNAIDS Technical Update. Geneva: UNAIDS.

US Congress, Office of Technology Assessment (1993). *International health statistics: what the numbers mean for the United States*. Washington, D.C.: US Government Printing Office.

World Health Organization (1988). *World Health Statistics*. Geneva: World Health Organization.

(1994). *AIDS: images of the epidemic*. Geneva: World Health Organization.

(1998). *World health statistics*. Geneva: World Health Organization.

(2000). *WHO issues new healthy life expectancy rankings*. www.who.int/inf-pr-2000/en/pr2000-life.html. Geneva: World Health Organization.

Young, C. M. (1986). 'The residential life-cycle: mortality and morbidity effects on living arrangements'. In United Nations, ed., *Consequences of mortality trends and differentials*. New York: United Nations, pp. 101–12.

The Psychology of Death

ROBERT A. NEIMEYER AND JAMES L. WERTH, JR.

In some respects, attempting to summarize the complex area of "the psychology of death" is a daunting task, whose difficulty is revealed by comparing it with writing a hypothetical summary of "the psychology of life." Clearly, the scope of the latter would be vast, encompassing psychological development from infancy through later life; emotional and motivational considerations; cognitive and decision making processes under favorable and unfavorable circumstances; clinically significant disorders and their assessment and treatment; social and interpersonal processes that call for their own level of analysis; and human coping, resilience, and personal growth, to name just a few topics of relevance. Viewed broadly, the psychology of death is equally variegated as a discipline or field of study, spanning research on the maturation of the concept of death throughout childhood; death anxiety, fear, threat, and avoidance; cognitive impairment at the end-of-life and its implications for decision making regarding life-sustaining treatment options; the refinement of assessment and diagnostic protocols for such disorders as complicated grief; family and caregiver dynamics in anticipation of or in the wake of death and loss; and the emergence of personal hardiness and meaning-making as a function of grappling with mortality. This chapter provides an orientation to many of these topics, concentrating on three major domains of research that have a substantial empirical base: the study of death anxiety and related emotions and motives, the end-of-life arena, and the experience of grief and loss. In each instance we will focus special attention on issues and findings of particular relevance to the readers of this handbook, namely those that concern older adults and those who care for them.

DEATH ATTITUDES

Although the capacity of *Homo sapiens* to contemplate their own mortality might be considered a defining characteristic of our species, it is clearly one that has evolved across historical time, yielding a rich spectrum of cosmologies, religions, philosophies, and folk beliefs that attempt to interpret the place of death in human life. Likewise, recent psychological research indicates that conceptions of death evolve across the course of development, perhaps beginning with the young child's germinal sense of self as distinct from his or her caretaker, and finding expression in predictable forms of separation protest and grief when bonds to the attachment figure are threatened (Bowlby, 1980). By middle childhood most children have begun to master the rudiments of an abstract "adult" death concept – the idea that death involves a cessation of bodily and sensory function, is irreversible (at least at a physical level), and perhaps most threateningly, is universal, in the sense that it inevitably applies to them and those they love (Speece and Brent, 1992). Although cultural variations exist in the specific content of death beliefs (e.g., whether it is envisioned as an entry to an afterlife, to a cycle of death and rebirth, or simply to a state of non-being), children of diverse cultures show parallels in conceiving of death in increasingly abstract and psychologically sophisticated terms as they mature (Tamm and Granqvist, 1995). The acquisition of this basic suite of subcomponents of a mature death concept permits the contemplation of mortality in adolescence and young adulthood, both as an existential theme encountered across the course of development, and as a specific challenge as people encounter the reality of death in the form of illness, accidents, homicide, and suicide of known and unknown persons.

Death anxiety

Literally thousands of studies have been performed on the attitudes people report in response to the contemplation of personal death, concentrating mainly on their experience of death anxiety, fear, threat, and avoidance. Although terminological distinctions are sometimes made between these attitudes, in fact most measures used to gauge their intensity in different groups have in common a focus on negative affect, dread, and terror in the face of personal death. As such measures have been refined across a period of nearly 50 years (Neimeyer, 1994, 1998), they have begun to yield a clearer picture of conditions under which the contemplation of or confrontation with death triggers substantial anxiety and often avoidance, and the various facets of fear of death that trigger special concern for some people.

Although contemporary Western society has been widely described as "death denying," segregating death in institutional settings where it becomes the province of specialists, in fact ample evidence suggests that people acknowledge thinking of death commonly, and that they typically do so with some measure of apprehension. Here, too, developmental trends can be observed, such that anxieties about personal death begin to climb in adolescence, reach their peak in middle adulthood, and, at least in some studies, wane in the closing years of life (Wong *et al.*, 1994). Not surprisingly, however, these gross trends disguise a wide variation in the degree to which focusing on one's eventual death triggers despair, paralysis, or defensive avoidance, on the one hand, or some form of acceptance, affirmation, or even meaning on the other. Indeed, more recent multidimensional assessments of death attitudes even suggest that such contradictory states can co-exist within a given person, necessitating a more fine-grained approach to assessment of death concerns than has historically been the case in this broad literature.

Death concerns in older adults

Quantitative reviews of research on death attitudes among older adults shed light on factors associated with heightened apprehension regarding personal mortality as one ages. Not surprisingly, anxieties about dying are exacerbated by deteriorating physical health, and are especially prominent for seniors struggling with issues of "ego integrity," or a sense of having lived fully and well. More generally, fear of death covaries with other indices of psychological distress, such that a general disposition towards depressive rumination or anxious anticipation of an uncertain future tends to find expression in or reinforce death-related apprehensions, per se. Environmental factors also seem to predict greater death anxiety, such as living in an institutional rather than community setting. But perhaps surprisingly, religious belief, which has generally been associated with lower fears of death, seems substantially unrelated to death anxiety in later years, perhaps as a function of range restriction in religiosity in the older population (Fortner *et al.*, 2000).

As research on death attitudes has become more sophisticated, investigators have begun to focus attention on more specific foci of death concern, and a wider range of death-related attitudes beyond death anxiety and similar negative emotional responses. The former, more differentiating focus has highlighted particular apprehensions that vary by ethnicity, and that are associated with negative attitudes towards ageing. For example, research suggests that older White Americans express greater concerns about the dying process (dying alone, in uncontrolled pain, etc.), perhaps reflecting their greater likelihood to spend the final weeks and months of their lives in institutional settings that compromise their personal sense of control and isolate them from family. Older African Americans, on the other hand, report greater fear of the state of death, as they struggle more commonly with apprehension regarding the unknown, and an afterlife of punishment or reward. For both groups, however, it is striking that death anxiety is a significant predictor of their negative attitudes towards ageing, as well as the negative stereotypes they hold towards their older peers (DePaola *et al.*, 2003). Essentially the same finding emerges for professional caregivers, such that those with more negative attitudes towards death acknowledge devaluing and disliking those older adults with whom they work, as well as reporting greater apprehension about their own ageing process. Conversely, many caregivers report substantial death acceptance, and comfort and competence in dealing with the realities of mortality and loss, an orientation that seems to be reinforced by training in hospice and palliative care.

THE END OF LIFE

The contents of this book demonstrate that significant attention has been given to the process and implications of ageing. Similarly, vast amounts of human and financial resources have been focused on delaying the actual moment of death. However, comparatively little emphasis has been placed on how people actually experience the dying process, and the work that has been done in this area has centered around the physical and medical aspects of dying and death, to the relative exclusion of psychological, spiritual, interpersonal, and cultural/societal (i.e., "psychosocial") aspects of the end of life. Of the non-medical topics associated with the dying process and eventual death, religious/spiritual issues have probably been discussed most often. In this section, we focus on psychosocial issues near the end of life. For more detailed discussions of this topic, see Chochinov and Breitbart (2000), Lawton (2000), and Werth et al. (2002).

Need for Attention to Psychosocial Issues Near the End of Life

As discussions of the end of life progress from being focused solely on physical aspects of the dying process to a more holistic consideration of the person who is dying and her or his support system, the need for attention to psychosocial issues becomes clear. In fact, recent research on the factors dying individuals believe are primary contributors to their quality of life demonstrates the central nature of issues such as freedom from psychological suffering, ability to interact with loved ones, and connection with one's higher power (Steinhauser et al., 2000).

Both research and clinical experience indicate that, although psychological factors such as mood and anxiety disorders or a sense of hopelessness may be present for some people as they approach death, they should not be considered normal or expected and therefore should not be accepted, because they

are treatable in the vast majority of cases (Block, 2001). Such mental health conditions can severely impair quality of life and affect decision making, both for the dying person and for her or his loved ones. Similarly, tension or "unfinished business" between the dying person and significant others can interfere with achieving a peaceful death of the dying person and can complicate the grieving process of the survivors, especially if there are disagreements over treatment decisions. Another key consideration is the cultural belief system(s) of the dying person and loved ones (Irish et al., 1993), especially if the perspective of these individuals differs from the views of the healthcare team.

Typical Concerns of Patients and Their Loved Ones Near the End of Life

As death approaches, people naturally may be concerned about whether their own, or their loved one's, suffering will be treated efficiently and effectively. Fortunately, most physical aspects of suffering, such as pain and breathlessness, can be effectively ameliorated for nearly everyone, although a small percentage of people may need to be sedated to unconsciousness in order for them not to suffer physically.

Once physical symptoms are palliated, attention often turns to psychosocial matters (Werth et al., 2002). Some people, depending on their cultural beliefs, may be concerned about losing autonomy, especially if control has been important to them prior to the dying process. Fear of the loss of dignity, a construct that is very individualized, can lead to significant distress. Many people may have existential concerns (e.g. the meaning of one's life) that may or may not be related to spiritual or religious beliefs (e.g. the purpose of suffering).

Some people may be afraid of losing mental acuity (e.g. through dementia or the effects of medication), perhaps because this would mean losing the ability to make their own decisions; in addition, the possibility of losing capacity may be perceived as a loss of self and, further, incapacity would interfere with the ability to interact and communicate meaningfully with loved ones. Another interpersonal concern of individuals nearing the end of life is being a physical, emotional, and financial burden on loved ones; meanwhile, significant others may be worried about not being able to provide proper care for the dying person.

Decision Processes Regarding End-of-Life Treatment Options

Regardless of whether a person knows she or he is dying, there are many end-of-life decisions that need to be made. Different countries and regions within countries have very different laws, rules/regulations, and norms in terms of accepted/acceptable options near the end of life. However, through much of the developed world, the following decisions will need to be made (either explicitly or by default): whether to draft a last will and testament and what it should say; whether to prepare an advance care directive (e.g. a living will or durable power of attorney for healthcare) and the particulars of the document; whether and how to talk to loved ones and healthcare providers about one's pending death; whether to try to die at home, in a care facility, or in hospital; whether to receive hospice care; and whether to try to live as long as possible or consider hastening death in some way (e.g. withholding or withdrawing life-sustaining treatment, asking a physician for medication that could be used to end one's life). The last option – hastening death – will be discussed in the next section.

Communication is an important aspect of many end-of-life decisions; however, open discussion of relevant considerations may not take place for any number of factors related to the dying person, loved ones, healthcare providers, and the intersection of these individuals (Quill, 2000). Cultural beliefs may preclude talking about death by anyone or among certain members of these three groups. In addition, psychological factors such as diagnosable depression or anxiety may interfere with conversation and interpersonal dynamics, while concerns surrounding issues such as perceptions of "being a burden" may prevent open discussion.

As a result of these psychosocial issues, people may not be ready when they or their loved ones are nearing death. Important decisions may not have been made or even considered. This, then, may lead to misunderstandings and misperceptions about what should happen as the person moves through the dying process. In fact, research has demonstrated that neither physicians nor loved ones can accu-

rately predict the dying person's treatment preferences, possibly leading to decisions for care that are consistent with the loved one's or physician's desires and beliefs but not those of the person who is dying. This research indicates that there is a need for culturally respectful dialogue about end-of-life decisions in order to maximize the appropriateness of care.

Hastening Death

Probably the most discussed and debated aspects of end-of-life care are when (if ever) a person should be allowed to implement a decision that could affect the manner and timing of death and what actions are acceptable in such situations. Assisted suicide and voluntary active euthanasia have been the most controversial end-of-life decisions in most countries, but in many parts of the world there is also active debate about other interventions such as withholding or withdrawing life-sustaining treatment (e.g. do-not-resuscitate orders, not starting or stopping ventilators), terminal sedation (purposefully sedating a person to unconsciousness and withholding treatment, including nutrition and hydration, until the person dies), and futility policies (where the healthcare team decides not to continue treatment in spite of the requests of the dying person and/or loved ones) (Kleespies, 2003).

Although some have stated that these actions are different for a variety of reasons based on moral, ethical, or legal reasoning, from a psychosocial perspective, the motivating factors for them are often similar. Just as clinical depression and/or hopelessness may affect a decision regarding assisted suicide, it is possible that they may also lead to a request for terminal sedation. Similarly, a person may be coerced to "request" that a ventilator be turned off or "request" active euthanasia. Research on the desire for death (which does not specify the mode of death) demonstrates the importance of these psychosocial issues. In addition, research on why people have requested and received assisted suicide and euthanasia indicates that control and dignity are also important factors.

Conclusion

Although psychosocial issues near the end of life have been receiving attention only relatively recently, their importance in the quality of life experienced by the person approaching death and her or his loved ones cannot be overstated. Both research and practice demonstrate that psychological, spiritual, interpersonal, and cultural/societal issues can have a profound impact on end-of-life care and decisions. These factors also affect loved ones' experiences of grief and bereavement after the person dies.

GRIEF AND BEREAVEMENT

In the broad context of end-of-life care, it is important to bear in mind that the ending of the life of the patient marks the beginning of a changed life for bereaved survivors. Although the majority of bereaved persons respond to loss by drawing on characteristic human capacities for coping and resilience, such favorable outcomes are by no means assured. It is therefore important to recognize the biopsychosocial impact of bereavement, to be alert to the signs of complications in the grieving process, and to assist more profoundly distressed survivors in adapting to a world in which their loved one is absent.

Symptoms of Separation

The impact of bereavement can be observed on even the most basic physiological levels. Existing research documents predictable clusters of symptoms associated with intense grief, including shortness of breath, tachycardia, dry mouth, sweating, frequent urination, digestive disturbance, and choking sensations. Taken together with other symptoms such as restlessness, increased muscular tension, and insomnia, these responses can be understood as part of a broader pattern of sympathetic arousal in response to the stress of separation (Parkes, 1996). At a more psychological level, the acute pangs of grief that peak in the early weeks following loss are associated with heightened anxiety, depression, and keen yearning for the deceased, as well as characteristic behaviors that suggest "searching" for the lost loved one, all of which is consonant with a deeply rooted evolutionary response to threats to primary attachment bonds.

Although large-scale longitudinal research has documented that the majority of bereaved men and women cope effectively with bereavement, eventu-

ally overcoming the acute symptoms noted above, this is by no means always the case. Indeed, bereavement has been associated with serious neuroendocrine disturbance and sleep disruption, as well as evidence of generalized anxiety or panic syndromes in over 40 percent of spouses some time during the first year of bereavement. Perhaps most worrisome is the accumulating evidence that the stress of bereavement is associated with a 40 to 70 percent increase in mortality among surviving spouses in the first six months following loss. Numerous investigators, for example, have long linked bereavement with cardiovascular disease, including heightened risk of myocardial infarction and congestive heart failure (Osterweis et al., 1984). Evidence is also accumulating that loss undermines the functioning of the immune system, providing an instigating context for the onset of infectious diseases and cancer. Other contributors to mortality risk are clearly behaviorally mediated, such as an increased incidence of alcohol abuse and consequent cirrhosis of the liver, as well as increased risk of suicide. Such statistics argue persuasively that the many stresses associated with profound loss can have a serious, and even lethal, impact on a sizable minority of bereaved persons. It is also likely that these risks are magnified for an older bereaved population, which could be especially susceptible to the effects of social isolation and failing health as they contend with the biopsychosocial impact of loss.

Complicated Grief

In view of these findings, psychologists have attempted to determine factors that identify persons at risk for negative outcomes associated with protracted and intense grief. Some of these risk factors can be objectively assessed through a review of the circumstances surrounding the death, as more chronic and unremitting grief is typically associated with sudden, unexpected, and traumatic death and closeness of the kinship tie to the decedent. Others, however, call for clinical judgment, such as an evaluation of the level of conflict or ambivalence in the premorbid relationship with the decedent, or assessments of mourner liabilities (such as a history of depression) that impede adaptation to loss (Worden, 1996). Particularly promising have been efforts to conceptualize complications in the grieving process itself that are distinct from major depression, panic disorder, and post traumatic stress disorder. For example, investigators have recently garnered empirical support for a set of diagnostic criteria for complicated grief, marked by efforts to avoid reminders of the deceased, purposelessness and futility, a shattered world view, and clinically significant disruption in life functioning (Prigerson and Jacobs, 2001). Moreover, diagnosis of traumatic grief six months following the loss has been associated with deleterious long term outcomes, in terms of a range of both psychological and medical outcomes.

Grief Counseling and Therapy

In addition to identifying persons at risk, helping professionals can assist the bereaved in coping with both the short term and long term challenges of loss. In the immediate aftermath of the death, for example, the bereaved may benefit from coaching in symptom management techniques, such as relaxation skills and thought-stopping to interrupt distressing intrusive imagery. In the longer run, however, what seems called for are opportunities for emotional self-expression and a deeper processing of the significance of the loss for their ongoing lives. Fortunately, contemporary grief theory and research are expanding to provide guidance in these therapeutic efforts (Stroebe *et al.*, 2001). As a result, the helping professions are developing a subtler appreciation of the ways in which loss, especially of a more traumatic kind, can shake the assumptive foundations of bereaved persons' lives, undermining their sense of security, predictability, and worth. If, as recent research suggests, the attempt to reaffirm or reconstruct a world of meaning that has been challenged by loss is a core process in grieving (Neimeyer, 2001), then it follows that interventions to assist survivors in making sense of the loss and perhaps even eventually finding a "silver lining" in it could be especially helpful to troubled survivors. Indeed, current data suggest that many bereaved people find new and sustaining meanings in their lives and losses, experiencing "post-traumatic growth" (Tedeschi *et al.*, 1998) with or without professional help. Although a small but growing literature has begun to demonstrate that grief therapy can make a positive contribution to these outcomes

(Allumbaugh and Hoyt, 1999), such results are by no means universal, with some evidence suggesting that older adults are served least well by existing forms of treatment (Neimeyer, 2000). Thus, the equivocal outcomes of much of grief counseling and therapy suggest that more research is needed into how and whether various forms of therapy assist grieving persons in integrating the loss experience into their lives and moving forward towards a more hopeful future.

CONCLUSION

Despite the daunting complexity of comprehending the role of death in human life, researchers have made substantial headway in investigating the psychology of death, concentrating especially on the causes, correlates, and consequences of various death attitudes, the special challenges faced by individuals and families at the end of life, and the subsequent adaptation of survivors to bereavement. Each of these areas has special relevance to the understanding of older adults, for whom such attitudes, (inter)personal decision making, and post-loss adaptation become compellingly important.

FURTHER READING

Chochinov, H. M., and W. Breitbart, eds. (2000). *Handbook of psychiatry in palliative medicine.* New York: Oxford University Press.
Cicirelli, V. G. (2002). *Older adults' views on death.* New York: Springer.
Kastenbaum, R. (2000). *The psychology of death*, 3rd edn. New York: Springer.
Lawton, M. P., ed. (2000). *Annual Review of Gerontology and Geriatrics (Vol. 20). Focus on the end of life: scientific and social issues.* New York: Springer.
Stroebe, M. S., Hansson, R. O., Stroebe, W., and H. Schut, eds. (2001). *Handbook of bereavement research.* Washington, D.C.: American Psychological Association.
Werth, J. L., Jr., ed. (2002). "End-of-life care and decisions," *American Behavioral Scientist*, 46 (2 and 3).

REFERENCES

Allumbaugh, D. L., and W. T. Hoyt (1999). "'Effectiveness of grief therapy: a meta-analysis," *Journal of Counseling Psychology*, 46: 370–80.
Block, S. D. (2001). "Psychological considerations, growth, and transcendence at the end of life: The art of the

possible," *Journal of the American Medical Association*, 285: 2898–905.

Bowlby, J. (1980). *Attachment and loss*, Vol. III. New York: Basic.

Chochinov, H. M., and W. Breitbart, eds. (2000). *Handbook of psychiatry in palliative medicine*. New York: Oxford University Press.

DePaola, S. J., Neimeyer, R. A., Griffin, M., and J. Young (2003). "Death anxiety and attitudes toward the elderly among older adults: the role of gender and ethnicity," *Death Studies*, 27: 335–54.

Fortner, B. V., Neimeyer, R. A., and B. Rybarczeck (2000). "Correlates of death anxiety in older adults: a comprehensive review." In Tomer, ed., *Death attitudes and the older adult*. Philadelphia: Brunner Routledge, pp. 95–108.

Irish, D. P., Lundquist, K. F., and V. J. Nelsen, eds. (1993). *Ethnic variations in dying, death, and grief*. Washington, D.C.: Taylor & Francis.

Kleespies, P. M. (2003). *Life and death decisions: psychological and ethical considerations in end-of-life care*. Washington, D.C.: American Psychological Association.

Lawton, M. P., ed. (2000). *Annual review of gerontology and geriatrics (vol. 20). Focus on the end of life: scientific and social issues*. New York: Springer, 2000.

Neimeyer, R. A. (1994). *Death anxiety handbook*. Philadelphia: Taylor & Francis.

(1998). "Death anxiety research: the state of the art," *Omega: Journal of Death and Dying*, 36: 97–120.

(2000). "Searching for the meaning of meaning," *Death Studies*, 24: 541–58.

ed. (2001). *Meaning reconstruction and the experience of loss*. Washington, D.C.: American Psychological Association.

Osterweis, M., Solomon, F., and M. Green, eds. (1984). *Bereavement*. Washington, D.C.: National Academy Press.

Parkes, C. M. (1996). *Bereavement*, 2nd edn. London: Routledge.

Prigerson, H. G., and S. C. Jacobs (2001). "Diagnostic criteria for traumatic grief." In M. S. Stroebe, R. O. Hansson, W. Stroebe, and H. Schut, eds., *Handbook of bereavement research*. Washington, D.C.: American Psychological Association, pp. 614–46.

Quill, T. E. (2000). "Initiating end-of-life discussions with seriously ill patients: Addressing the 'elephant in the room,'" *Journal of the American Medical Association*, 284: 2502–7.

Speece, M. W., and S. B. Brent (1992). "The acquisition of a mature understanding of three components of the concept of death," *Death Studies*, 16: 211–29.

Steinhauser, K. E., Clipp, E. C., McNeilly, M., Christakis, N. A., McIntyre, L. M., and J. A. Tulsky (2000). "In search of a good death: observations of patients, families, and providers," *Annals of Internal Medicine*, 132: 825–32.

Stroebe, M. S., Hansson, R. O., Stroebe, W., and H. Schut, eds. (2001). *Handbook of bereavement research*. Washington, D.C.: American Psychological Association.

Tamm, M., and A. Granqvist (1995). "The meaning of death for children and adolescents: a phenomenographic study of drawings," *Death Studies*, 19: 203–22.

Tedeschi, R., Park, C., and L. Calhoun, eds. (1998). *Posttraumatic growth*. Mahwah, N.J.: Erlbaum.

Werth, J. L., Jr., Gordon, J. R., and R. Johnson (2002). "Psychosocial issues near the end of life," *Ageing and Mental Health*, 6: 406–16.

Wong, P. T., Reker, G. T., and G. Gesser (1994). "Death attitude profile – revised: a multidimensional measure of attitudes toward death." In Neimeyer (2001: 121–48).

Worden, J. W. (1996). *Grief counseling and grief therapy*. New York: Springer.

Death and Spirituality

ELIZABETH MacKINLAY

INTRODUCTION

Heinz (1994) has described dying as the last life-career. This is a career much neglected during recent decades as death has become remote, most often occurring within hospitals and aged care facilities rather than at home. Medicalisation of the dying process and death in Western societies over the last century has resulted in fear and denial of death. Kimble (2003) writes that we might speculate that the basis of fear of ageing 'is the fear of the ultimate life event, namely, death'. Medicine has seemed to promise at least a delay, if not the elimination, of the ageing process and death itself. The experience of increasing longevity and a falling infant mortality rate mean that many people have no personal experience of death until late in life, consequently being out of touch with the process of dying. There is need for both society and individuals to re-learn how to make the final career of life.

Death and spirituality

In recent years much has been done to improve care in the physical process of dying; the palliative care movement has been important in this development. It has gone further than the obvious issues of pain management and symptom relief to embrace psychosocial and emotional issues as well. Principles of palliative care are now being taken up within aged care. However, still more is required in research and change of practice to enable truly holistic care that includes the spiritual dimension in end-of-life care.

In a study of independent-living older people that examined the spiritual dimension in the context of meaning in life, response to meaning and wellbeing in later life (MacKinlay, 1998, 2001a), fear of the process of dying (but not fear of death) was common; all participants in this study expressed fears or concerns about future vulnerability and/or the process of dying. These fears were often related to pain – not physical pain alone, but also existential pain. Although it was found in a subsequent study (MacKinlay, 2001c) that a lower percentage (45 per cent) of frail but cognitively intact elderly nursing-home residents expressed some fears of future vulnerability, including the process of dying, this is still an issue of concern for frail older people. Death brings each person to a point of fear of non-existence (Tillich, 1963). This is in essence a spiritual question, as it asks, 'What is / has been the meaning of my life?' Kimble echoes this (2003: 454) as he writes: 'Death figures in our lives as the earthly endings of our possibilities, our aspirations, and our relationships.' There is a sense in which people need to find meaning in the process of dying, as well as in the process of living.

Religion and spirituality

Although dying has been studied from a religious perspective, the spiritual perspective has received little attention. One major study (Idler *et al.*, 2001), from the New Haven site of the Established Populations for Epidemiologic Studies of the Elderly (n = 2,812), examined both cross-sectional and longitudinal self-reports of attendance at services, self-ratings of religiousness, and strength and comfort felt from religion for respondents who did and did not die within 12 months following an interview. Data were collected in four waves over a 12-year period in this prospective study. The study found that, while attendance at religious services declined among the near-deceased, this group showed either stability or a small increase in feelings of religiousness and strength/comfort received from religion.

There has been much debate as to whether religion, religiosity and spirituality are the same. At the outset it is important to attempt to clarify these terms. It is argued that religion is part of the spiritual dimension, but that the spiritual dimension is not synonymous with religion (Ellor and Bracki, 1995; MacKinlay, 2001a). Religiosity is seen as the practice of a religion. It is contended that the spiritual dimension is part of being human; just as we each have a physical body, and a psychosocial dimension, so we also have a spiritual dimension. As some people train and become high-performing athletes, so some may choose to concentrate more on spiritual development and may become 'spiritual athletes'. In the same way, it is contended that, for each individual, the spiritual dimension has the potential to continue to develop throughout the lifespan.

Most research until the 1980s focused on study of religiosity rather than spirituality; it may be suggested this was so because of the relative ease of measuring the practice of religion. Data from surveys of church attendance and other 'organisational' religious activities could be easily obtained (Harris, 1990; Kaldor, 1987, 1994). On the other hand, measures of spirituality are much more difficult to obtain. In the first place, there has been little agreement on what 'spirituality' actually is. That researchers still admit to this was evident among the keynote presentations at an international conference on ageing and spirituality in 2002.[1] However, if this important dimension of ageing is to be studied, it is evident that attempts must be made to move towards definitions that will be usable in the practice of gerontology. It is contended further research is needed to learn more of this aspect of ageing and its implications for wellbeing in later life.

This is especially so in the final career, as the individual moves towards death.

Numbers of definitions of spirituality have been developed and critiqued. Swinton (2001) notes that while the 'spirit is the essential life-force that undergirds, motivates and vitalises human existence, spirituality is the way in which individuals and communities respond to the experience of the spirit'. Other authors describe spirituality as the deepest dimension of all human life (Fischer, 1985; Armatowski, 2001; MacKinlay, 2001a). Features of von Balthasar's (1965: 5) definition include a habitual way of being and practice and it is derived from a world view: 'This world view is based on ultimate meanings that the individual holds. It is wider than the understanding of a practice of religion, and indeed can be applied to people who do not exhibit a religious faith. This definition suggests, but does not make explicit, the possibility of changing spirituality through the life span' (MacKinlay, 2001a).

Holmes (1985) has outlined a five-point definition of spirituality: 'a human capacity for relationship with that which "transcends sense phenomena"; the subject perceives this relationship as an expanded or heightened consciousness, independent of the subject's efforts. This is grounded in the historical setting and exhibits itself in creative actions in the world' (p. 54).

Although Holmes' definition is rich, an important aspect of spirituality, perhaps implicit within the definition, is relationship with other human beings. Thus, this definition lacks that further aspect that is needed to describe the fullness of human spirituality. Holmes' definition also lacks a clear indication of the habitual nature of human spirituality (MacKinlay, 2001a). On the other hand, Labun (1988) emphasises relationship as being part of spirituality. Carson (1989) goes further and writes of relationship not only with other people, but with the transcendent. Thibault (1995) writes, of spiritual style, that each person seeks to work out their sense of meaning and relationship.

Still a further definition, this time of spiritual wellbeing, was developed by the National Interfaith Coalition on Aging (NICA) in North America, 1972, at a special workshop to reach a consensus on the meaning of 'spiritual wellbeing'. This states: 'Spiritual wellbeing is the affirmation of life in a relationship with God, self, community and environment

[1] Second International Conference on Ageing, Spirituality and Well being, Durham, UK, 5–9 July 2002.

that nurtures and celebrates wholeness.' In spite of the dynamic and inclusive nature of this definition, and its allowance for a process of development in later-life spirituality, Moberg (1990) remarked this definition had failed to make a significant impact on the field of gerontology and geriatrics. A decade further on and into the twenty-first century, there may now be moves to accept definitions of this type.

In this chapter, spirituality draws on several of the definitions above, recognising:

first, the human need for ultimate meaning in each person, whether this is fulfilled through relationship with God, or some sense of another; or whether some other sense of meaning becomes the guiding force within the individual's life. Human spirituality must also involve relationship with other people. Spirituality is a part of every human being, it is what differentiates humans from other animal species. There is a real need to have a definition of spirituality that is inclusive of all religious groups and of the secular. (MacKinlay, 2001a: 51)

It is also appropriate to consider spirituality as being dynamic, with the potential to continue to change and develop throughout the person's lifetime. The spiritual dimension is what lies at the core of each person's being. It is that which searches and yearns for relationship in life and for meaning in existence. If it is considered to be a part of what it is to be human, then this can be described as a generic spirituality. Individual humans may find this need addressed in all sorts of situations and varieties of ways in life, in love, in joy, in suffering and in pain and loss (MacKinlay, 2001a: 51). A person's specific spirituality may be worked out through religion, and/or through relationship and through various other centre/s of meaning. Ashbrook (1996: 76) says that 'Beyond the self of culture lies the soul in God, the core of each person's being.'

Drawing on the literature described and recent research, in this chapter, spirituality is defined generically, as:

that which lies at the core of each person's being, an essential dimension which brings meaning to life. It is acknowledged that spirituality is not constituted only by religious practices, but must be understood more broadly, as relationship with God, however God or ultimate meaning is perceived by the person, and in relationship with other people. (MacKinlay, 2001a: 52)

Dying as the last career

Heinz (MacKinlay, 2001a: 184), in describing the final part of the lifespan as the last career of the human being, urges us to take up our last career. Heinz (1994: 5) describes this career as 'the great imaginal task of aging, laden with spiritual possibility. This is the time for the successful negotiation of a final identity that gives retrospective meaning to life and prospective meaning to death.' Heinz suggests that Western society has lost the ability and the framework needed to really develop the last career. He sees this loss as detrimental to succeeding generations.

If the challenge to develop the last career is taken up, Heinz says, the possibilities, for both individuals and the community, could be to produce over time: 'a culture of aging, last career, and death, a network of symbols, rituals, and meanings through which to mediate and express life and death, youth and age within a larger system of meaning' (1994: 7).

An important component of this final stage of life is to be willing to allow ourselves to be called into question. Heinz asks a vital question of our ageing: 'Will our dying be clothed in the metaphor of self-transcendence or of the ultimate protest of complete autonomy?' (1994: 16). We are only now beginning to re-recognise and acknowledge the importance of this spiritual lifelong journey in our sophisticated Western societies. We need to re-learn the ways of bringing this last career to fulfilment in appropriate ways: that is, we need to stop denying that we all must face our dying, and to take up the challenge of the last career. Heinz ends by saying that this is work no culture can afford to leave undone.

If we consider dying as the last career in a long life, this has important implications for people approaching the end of life. Just as other taboo topics like sex and cancer have come into the open in recent decades, it is now time for death to be openly acknowledged and prepared for. A central component of the process of dying is the spiritual dimension. The importance to at least some older people of religion is highlighted by the fact that religion was the preferred topic of geriatric patients in group therapy sessions at a state hospital in the USA (Moberg, 1968: 504). This has not changed during the intervening decades, although many people seem to find it difficult to talk about death and dying. For example, registered nurses in a course in gerontology (MacKinlay, 2001b) did not think they could raise issues around dying and death with the residents in nursing homes where they worked. When these same nurses interviewed the older people they cared for, they found that for some of the older people 'it was like opening the flood gates'.

The nurses found that many of these older people did want to speak of their fears about dying. There were comments such as, for example, 'no one has ever asked me questions like this before'; 'it's good to be able to talk about these things' (death and other fears). In a subsequent study only two nursing-home residents (in twenty interviews) did not want to talk about death and said they were afraid of death; all twenty feared a painful and protracted dying.[2] In a recent in-depth interview with a woman who has dementia, I asked where she found meaning in life. She began with these words: 'I've had a good life, I love this world and all creation, and I can feel God's presence so much more lately, (she paused) I think it won't be long before I die.'[3] These responses suggest that questions surrounding the topic of death are on the minds of elderly residents. Unless staff working with elderly people are comfortable discussing these issues and can affirm the possibility of raising such sensitive issues with those they care for, then the questions may go unasked and, of course, unexplored (MacKinlay, 2001a).

These questions go to the heart or core of life-meaning and the spiritual dimension

Nursing homes are sometimes called 'God's waiting room' and in at least some aged care facilities, diversional therapy focuses on providing interesting activities and ways of passing the time for residents. Perhaps it could be said these activities divert residents from thinking about their own approaching end of life and the last career (Fleming, 2002).

Dying and spirituality: the experiences of some older people

This chapter draws mainly on in-depth interviews of older people (MacKinlay, 2001a, 2001c) using Grounded theory and spiritual reminiscence as vehicles for examining their stories. Grounded theory was used to allow the participants to explore and express freely their spiritual life journey, avoiding foreclosure on issues that may be important to them, issues that might not be elicited through the use of questionnaires.

The first study was completed in 1997; these independent-living older people (65 years or older) spoke of their spiritual journey into later life, where they found meaning, their response to meaning, how they transcended disabilities and loss, their experience of relationship, joy, grief, fear and hope. A model of spiritual tasks and processes of ageing was constructed (Table 1) based on the stories of these older adults, using Grounded theory to identify the themes from the tape-recorded and transcribed in-depth interviews. The spiritual tasks identified were: finding ultimate meaning, responding to meaning, transcendence, moving from provisional to final meanings, finding intimacy with God and/or others, and finding hope. The findings of that study were compared with those of a subsequent study comprised of interviews with frail, cognitively intact older people who were residents of nursing homes. Further studies add to the material presented.[4] In each subsequent study until now the model of spiritual tasks and processes of ageing has been tested and affirmed. At this stage, 96 in-depth interviews have been conducted, including 28 in the present study.

Finding ultimate meaning – finding meaning in the process of dying and in grief Kimble, reflecting on life both as a pastoral theologian and from a personal perspective of three-quarters of a century of living, writes: 'Temporality and mortality do not take away the meaning that is found in human

---

[2] E. B. MacKinlay, 'Meaning in life: spirituality in older nursing home residents' (funded by a University of Canberra research grant), unpublished study 1999–2000.

[3] E. B. MacKinlay, C. Trevitt and M. Coady, 'Finding meaning in the experience of dementia: the place of spiritual reminiscence work'. Australian Research Council Linkage Grant 2002–4.

[4] E. B. MacKinlay, C. Trevitt and S. Hobart, 'The search for meaning: quality of life for the person with dementia'. University of Canberra Collaborative Research Grant 2000; and E. B. MacKinlay, C. Trevitt and M. Coady, 'Finding meaning in the experience of dementia: the place of spiritual reminiscence work'. Australian Research Council Linkage Grant 2002–4.

TABLE 1. Spiritual themes and tasks of ageing: each theme has an associated task and process

Themes identified from data	Corresponding spiritual tasks
Ultimate meaning in life	To identify what brings ultimate meaning
Response to meaning in life	To find appropriate ways to respond
Self-sufficiency/vulnerability	To transcend disabilities, loss
Wisdom/provisional to final meanings	To search for final meanings
Relationship/isolation	To find intimacy with God and/or others
Hope/fear	To find hope

(*Source:* MacKinlay, 2001a: 223.)

living, but rather propel the person to find and create meaning in the midst of transitoriness and the finiteness of human existence' (Kimble, 2003: 454). As a person becomes aware of their approaching death, so, often, comes the desire to search for the true meaning of one's life, to reflect and reminisce. According to Frankl (1984), individuals assign transitional meanings earlier in life, coming to ultimate meanings in later life and as they perceive their approaching death. Butler (1968) also noted that the stimulus to increased use of reminiscence could well be a time shift, a growing perception of shortness of time until death. Reminiscence or life review may for some include the desire for confession and forgiveness and sometimes also for reconciliation (Coleman, 1986; MacKinlay, 2001a).

Story telling is important both for the person coming to the end of their life and for those who will grieve the loss of relationship. Issues of approaching death often raise questions of life meaning. Now, as the person's life is completed, for the first time their whole life story can be told and perhaps meanings can be seen in context for the first time. Deepest meaning for humans lies within the spiritual dimension. For those who are coming to the end of their lives an awareness of their approaching death may stimulate this search for meaning, while for those bereaved, the story helps to focus the grief, the loss, and affirm the relationship of which they had been part. A number of women in one study found their greatest sense of meaning through their spouse (MacKinlay, 2001a). Telling the story and use of appropriate symbols and rituals form a vital part of the process of dying and following death, at funerals and memorial services, as well as in the continuing process of grieving.

Meaning is closely tied to a sense of hope. The loss of a long term relationship presents a major shift in meaning; if the person's whole reason for being was related to their partner, then the loss is truly devastating, and goes to the very core of their being. Doris expressed her profound grief over the death of her husband, some nine years before I had interviewed her, and she said:

I think, the grief, when one loses one's husband, is something that once again, rocks your life to its very foundations, doesn't it, because it's something, that you sort of foresee it a little, but you don't anything like foresee the way that grief's going to affect you, in all the different ways it's going to affect you, I don't think. Don't know of any other big griefs like that. (MacKinlay, 2001a: 185)

Yet, in the intervening years, Doris had rebuilt her life and established new long term relationships, particularly with members of a small group from her faith community.

Finding intimacy with others: facing loss

Elaine was one of the frail nursing-home residents (MacKinlay, 2001c); she had established a relationship with the other woman she shared her nursing-home room with. Elaine had been widowed some 15 years before; at the time of my visit, her roommate had died the week before, and she said: 'That put me back this last week, you know: I'm starting to get over that again now.' She paused and reflected about the former roommate:

Oh she was a good roommate you know, we got along so well together, and she was so crook the last few days . . . That was hard the last night, the poor thing, she was trying to tell me something, but I couldn't catch it, and that sort of got me down, you know, what was she trying to tell me, and I couldn't hear it, you know. As I say I'm over that now and every day I'm getting better. (MacKinlay, 2001c: 27–8)

After the interview I pondered on her reflections. First, this widow had experienced yet another loss of relationship, there would be grief over the loss of her roommate, and the need to establish relationship with another new roommate. Establishing new relationships for people who are already frail, with lowered energy levels and physical disabilities, is difficult, and there is always the fear that the next roommate may not be easy to get on with. At yet another level, I wondered, what was it the roommate had been trying to say – maybe she needed help in the last stages of her life. We cannot tell what it might have been. Perhaps there was some unfinished business, perhaps the dying woman wanted emotional and spiritual support, perhaps a question answered, or an assurance that she was not alone as she died. I can only make assumptions (MacKinlay, 2001c: 27–8). I wondered, too, how Elaine would cope with this experience; what might her fears of dying and death be? Perhaps for Elaine the fear may be of dying alone, even in a nursing home. Eva (MacKinlay, 2001a: 195), one of the independent older women, remembered how a friend had died alone and had not been found for a week. Eva expressed her shock at first hearing this news, but then she paused, and said with the humour that was characteristic for her: 'Oh, the two cats, you know, they'd eat me.' Eva had a great attachment to her cats and a concern for them if anything should happen to her.

Intimacies in later life, as at any time across the lifespan, are important, yet for frail older people, close relationships are more likely to become fragile and uncertain. Another woman, Wyn, told of the last time she visited a dear friend in a nursing home; her friend was very frail, and they spent time together:

I'd had the thought to go over and see her that afternoon, and oh I thought, oh dear it's too hot, don't know whether I'll bother, and then I thought, no I will (go and visit her) I'm halfway there. I'll go up and see her. And so we had a wonderful talk about death and dying and she said 'I don't think I'll see my 95th birthday' or something like that, she said and I could tell she was,

(she paused). She said her legs were aching so I said 'Well shall I rub your legs?' so I rubbed her legs and the next day I heard that she'd died, and I thought well you know, obey, obeying the whisper of guidance really was the thing that you know. I felt sad that she had died but I felt so grateful that I'd had that time with her before she died. (MacKinlay, 2001a: 213)

It seemed natural that these two friends should talk about death, on that last day before one of them died. It seems there was a deep connecting, perhaps a sharing of sacred space between these two women during that visit. The following day Wyn heard that her friend had died, and she expressed both a sense of loss and also gratitude at being there. Wyn had a deep sense of spirituality and abundant spiritual strategies in a close relationship with her God; she actively engaged in study, prayer and Christian meditation. Wyn was open to spiritual matters and able to be present to others in the deeper issues of life.

CONCLUSION

To die is not only a biological process, but, for each person, death is also a unique and a spiritual journey. Medicalisation of the dying process has largely removed death from the intimacy of family and friends; there is a need to re-claim the spiritual dimension so that people are not isolated in their dying.

Humans are by nature meaning makers, and core meaning is a spiritual concept. Using data from several studies and a model of spiritual tasks of ageing, this chapter has explored a spiritual perspective of death and dying. The importance of finding meaning in the last career of life has been acknowledged. Walking this final journey in life with the one dying is a special position for those privileged to be a part of this journey.

FURTHER READING

Cobb, M. (2001). *The dying soul: spiritual care at the end of life*. Buckingham: Open University Press.

Kimble, M. A., and S. H. McFadden, eds. (2003). *Aging, spirituality and religion: a handbook*, Vol. II. Minneapolis: Fortress Press.

Moberg, D. O., ed. (2001). *Aging and spirituality: spiritual dimensions of aging, theory, research, practice and policy*. New York: The Haworth Pastoral Press.

REFERENCES

Armatowski, J. (2001). 'Attitudes toward death and dying among persons in the fourth quarter of life'. In D. O. Moberg, ed., *Aging and spirituality: spiritual dimensions of aging theory, research, practice, and policy*. New York: The Haworth Pastoral Press.

Ashbrook, J. B. (1996). *Minding the soul: pastoral counseling as remembering*. Minneapolis: Fortress Press.

Butler, R. N. (1968). 'The life review: an interpretation of reminiscence in the aged'. In B. L. Neugarten, ed., *Middle age and aging: a reader in social psychology*. Chicago: The University of Chicago Press.

Carson, V. B. (1989). *Spiritual dimensions of nursing practice*. Philadelphia: W. B. Saunders Co.

Coleman, P. G. (1986). *Ageing and reminiscence processes: social and clinical implications*. Chichester: John Wiley & Sons.

Ellor, J. W., and M. A. Bracki (1995). 'Assessment, referral, and networking'. In M. A. Kimble, S. H. McFadden, J. W. Ellor and J. J. Seeber, eds., *Aging, spirituality, and religion: a handbook*. Minneapolis: Augsburg Fortress Press.

Fischer, K. (1985). *Winter grace: spirituality for the later years*. New York: Paulist Press.

Fleming, R. (2002). 'Depression and spirituality in Australian aged care homes', *Journal of Religious Gerontology*, 13 (3/4): 107–16.

Frankl, V. E. (1984). *Man's search for meaning*. New York: Washington Square Press.

Harris, D. K. (1990). *Sociology of aging*. New York: Harper and Rowe.

Heinz, D. (1994). 'Finishing the story: aging, spirituality and the work of culture', *Journal of Religious Gerontology*, 9 (1): 3–19.

Holmes, U. T. (1985). 'Spirituality for ministry'. In N. S. T. Thayer, *Spirituality and pastoral care*. Philadelphia: Fortress Press.

Idler, E. L., Stanislav, V., Kasl, S. V., and J. C. Hays (2001). 'Patterns of religious practice in belief in the last year of life', *Journal of Gerontology, Psychological Sciences and Social Sciences*, series 56 B, 6 (Nov.): S326–S334.

Kaldor, P. (1987). *Who goes where? Who doesn't care?* Homebush West: Lancer Books.

(1994). *Winds of change: the experience of church in a changing australia*, National Church Life Survey. Homebush West: Lancer Books.

Kimble, M. A. (2003). 'Final time: coming to the end'. In M. A. Kimble and S. H. McFadden, eds., *Aging, spirituality, and religion: a handbook*, Vol. II. Minneapolis: Fortress Press, pp. 449–59.

Labun, E. (1988). 'Spiritual care: an element in nursing care planning'. *Journal of Advanced Nursing*, 13: 314–20.

MacKinlay, E. B. (1998). 'The spiritual dimension of ageing: meaning in life, response to meaning and well being in ageing'. Unpublished doctoral thesis, La Trobe University, Melbourne.

(2001a). *The Spiritual dimension of ageing*. London: Jessica Kingsley Publishers.

(2001b). 'Understanding the ageing process: a developmental perspective of the psychosocial and spiritual dimensions', *Journal of Religious Gerontology*, 12 (3/4): 111–22.

(2001c). 'Health, healing and wholeness in frail elderly people', *Journal of Religious Gerontology*, 13 (2): 25–34.

Moberg, D. O. 1968, 'Religiosity in old age'. In B. L. Neugarten, ed., *Middle age and aging: a reader in social psychology*. Chicago: The University of Chicago Press.

(1990). 'Spiritual maturity and wholeness in the later years'. In J. J. Seeber, ed., *Spiritual maturity in the later years*. New York: The Haworth Pastoral Press.

Swinton, J. (2001). *Spirituality and mental health care: rediscovering a 'forgotten' dimension*. London: Jessica Kingsley Publishers.

Thibault, J. M. (1995). 'Congregation as a spiritual care community'. In M. A. Kimble, S. H. McFadden, J. W. Ellor and J. J. Seeber, eds., *Aging, spirituality, and religion: a handbook*. Minneapolis: Augsburg Fortress Press.

Tillich, P. (1963). *Systemic theology*, Vol. III. Chicago: The University of Chicago Press.

von Balthasar, H. U. (1965). 'The Gospel as norm or test of all spirituality in the church', *Concilium*, 9 (1).

PART FIVE

THE AGEING OF RELATIONSHIPS

CHAPTER 5.1

Global Ageing and Challenges to Families

ARIELA LOWENSTEIN

INTRODUCTION

The International Action Plan on Ageing, adopted by member states of the UN (April, 2002), calls on governments to improve elders' quality of life. On May 15, 2002 – the International Day of Families – the UN announced: "older people strengthen cohesion in families." Thus, the family must be seen as the point of departure in light of changing demographics, familial and social structures and social policies.

Modernization during the twentieth century had produced two notable changes: mastering mortality and decline in fertility. Inevitably these lead to ageing in a double way: to individual ageing and population ageing. Population ageing is caused by three factors with implications for families (Bengtson *et al.*, 2003): (1) a growth in the proportion of the 65+; (2) an increase in the absolute number of older people; and (3) improvement of life expectancy at birth. Estimated life expectancy in Europe, for 2020, ranges from 81.7 years to 85.1 for women and 75.3 to 80.2 for men (Eurostat, 1996). Another development has been the "second demographic transition" which reflects a sharp decline in fertility in most developed countries (e.g. Van Imhoff *et al.*, 1995). In the EU, fertility rates declined from 1.96 in 1975 to 1.45 in 1994, the lowest in Italy and Spain – 1.22 (Eurostat, 1996). Greater longevity causes also an increase in the number of disabled elderly (WHO, 2002). The phenomenon of an ageing population is, thus, a global one (Kinsella, 2000),

even if its pace is different in various countries. It challenges the individual, family, and societal life.

Parallel to population ageing, marked changes occurred in families: in timing of family transitions; in family structures; in patterns of family formation and dissolution; ensuing diversification of families and household forms. The diversity is related to what Stacey (1990) has labeled the postmodern family, characterized by "structural fragility" and a greater dependence on the voluntary commitment of its members. It creates uncertainty in intergenerational relations and affects lifecourse role transitions (e.g. retirement, grandparenthood). Additional structural changes include: growing number of elderly single households; increase in the proportion of childless women; and increased mobility of adult children. Other trends are changing employment patterns, especially of women, that impact family relations and caregiving. All these contribute to a shrinking pool of family support (Wolf, 2001). We also witness the impact of broader societal and technological changes, internal and external migration, shifts in social policies, and changing trends in families' preferences for care. These changes raise fundamental questions about the definition of old age, the micro experiences of elders and their families and the macro responses of societies to their needs. Important to the following discussions in this section are the questions: how is the phenomenon of global ageing reflected at the family level; and, what are the challenges to families? This chapter will address these questions by discussing similarities and differences between cultures and social structures.

FAMILY RELATIONS IN THE CONTEXT OF GLOBAL AGEING

Population projections for 2020, for Western Europe and the US, show that the 65+ will constitute 17–18 percent of the population, and the 80+ will make up about 4 percent (OECD, 1996; Treas, 1995). In Japan, which is one of the most rapidly ageing societies, it is projected for 2050 that the 65+ will be about a third and the 75+ close to 19 percent of the total population (Kojima, 2000).

These changing demographic maps cause the "transition to the ageing family," whereby families are involved in a "quiet revolution" that is transforming multiple facets of family life, as follows:

(1) There is a shift from a vertical to a more horizontal structure, with a larger number of living generations (sometimes even five living generations), but with fewer members in each generation – the beanpole or the top-heavy family (Bengtson and Harootyan, 1994; Knipscheer, 1988). Thus, today, adults can have more parents than children – resulting from increased longevity and decreased fertility, and further exacerbated by divorce and remarriage. This process alters the length of time spent in specific family roles and leads to the emergence of adult children as the generational bridge between grandchildren and grandparents.

(2) There are difficulties predicting the timing of transitions, like marriage, parenthood, and grandparenthood. The results are two distinct family types, based on timing of fertility: age-condensed and age-gapped structures (Bengtson *et al.*, 1995). Bengtson and Harootyan (1994) discuss the blurring of boundaries between generations in age-condensed families, especially when early fertility occurs across multiple generations, as among many Black families in American society. In contrast, age-gapped families result from delayed childbearing, with the first child born at age 30 or later – a growing phenomenon witnessed since the 1970s (George and Gold, 1991). Such families are characterized by increased generational age differences and clear-cut boundaries that may hinder the development of affective bonds and value congruence across generations (Rossi, 1987). In addition, the pool of poten-

tial caregivers is likely to be smaller and restricted to the middle generation.

(3) There is increasing diversity of family formats: (a) the truncated family structure, with an increase in the proportion of childless adults (e.g., about 30 percent of elderly in the UK). For such families, generational ties among siblings, extended kin, and non-kin age peers might be important. Caregiving may be problematic for ageing members of these families (Connidis, 2001). (b) Increase in the number of reconstituted families, as rates of divorce increase. These families are at considerable risk of disruption and strain in intergenerational bonds (Hagestad, 1988; Ganong and Coleman, 1998). (c) An increase in the rates of single-parent families, illegitimacy, and cohabitation before marriage.

(4) Changing labor force participation, as more women (the traditional caregivers) enter the workplace. This forces us to examine more traditional patterns of living arrangements and family relations (Lowenstein, 2000).

Some scholars argued that a decline of the traditional family is an unavoidable outcome of modern economy, reflected in the above changes (Popenoe, 1993; Sussman, 1991). Studies of intergenerational family relationships revealed, however, that these reports had been premature (Silverstein and Bengtson, 1997), that adult children were not isolated from their parents but frequently interacted with them and exchanged assistance, even when separated by geographic distances (Lin and Rogerson, 1995). Data also reveal that the extended family maintains cross-generational cohesion (Bengtson, 2000) and the nuclear family had retained most of its functions, in partnership with formal organizations (Litwak, 1985; Litwak *et al.*, 2003). Moreover, in light of changing demographics and family forms, intergenerational bonds among adult family members may be even more important today because individuals live longer and share more years and experiences with other generations (Antonucci *et al.*, 1996; Bengtson *et al.*, 2000; Lowenstein *et al.*, 2003). However, some basic questions must be addressed: (1) How much help and support is really exchanged between generations? (2) How strong are the bonds of obligations and expectations between generations? (3) What accounts for differences in contact, closeness, and similarity of opinions, expectations, and exchange of help? (4) Is there a potential for intergenerational family ambivalence? (5) What is the economic value of the intergenerational transfers within families? (6) What is the role of society, through its service system, towards enhancement of family relations? (Lowenstein, 2000).

Intergenerational family bonds reflect a diversity of forms related to individual, familial, and social structural characteristics. These serve as markers for differences in socialization, roles, culture, values, and access to resources, thereby shaping family relations. On the individual level, two variables are especially important: age and gender. The age of family members is important because age causes changes in roles and responsibilities. Gender is important because women and men undergo different socialization processes, and women tend more to maintain social relations between family members and act as primary caregivers (Connidis, 2001; Lowenstein, 1999). Family characteristics refer to positions that members hold within the family – are they married, divorced, widowed?

A third level includes social structural characteristics like race and ethnicity, as different ethnic/racial groups have been found to differently adopt various family roles. Ethnic groups hold distinct cultural beliefs, values, and norms that can influence an ageing society, determine ways in which individuals are expected to age, their status, caregiving, and other roles (Burr and Mutchler, 1999). The extent to which race and culture influence intergenerational relationships, though, is unclear. Moreover, some scholars have argued that the role of the extended family is over-exaggerated in studies of ethnic minorities, and that the strength of ties in such families is more heterogeneous than has been noted (Bengtson, 1996).

Based on the theoretical perspectives of family intergenerational solidarity/conflict and intergenerational ambivalence, the focus of this chapter is on challenges, from the above changes – in demography and family structures and behaviors – for elders and families. Several key themes are discussed: first, the continued importance of the family and the strength of intergenerational solidarity (Bengtson, 2000; Bengtson *et al.*, 1995); second, the potential conflicts between generations in caregiving situations, or in cases of divorce and remarriage

(Connidis, 2001; Kaufman and Uhlenberg, 1998; Lowenstein and Ron, 1999); third, the interrelations between the micro and macro systems – family solidarity versus state solidarity (Sgritta, 1997).

THEORETICAL PERSPECTIVES

We are able to observe only what the mores permit us to see. At any given period sociological writings on the family reflect the moral problems of the time, and this is as true today as it ever was. (Komarovsky and Waller, 1945: 443)

This notion reflects the importance of the historical and social circumstances – as well as social change – that impact the use of a particular conceptual/theoretical perspective. A theoretical framework "may provide conceptual tools to interpret complex events and critically evaluate the current state of aging" (Biggs *et al.*, 2003: 16). The theoretical paradigms presented deal with complex processes and interactions between micro-interpersonal and small-group dynamics and multiple levels of social macro-forces. Moreover, studying the private spheres of personal–family life is where we encounter the greatest complexity.

Meso level: intergenerational solidarity, conflict and ambivalence

Solidarity between generations has been in the forefront as an enduring characteristic of families (Brubaker, 1990). It has been considered an important component of family relations, particularly in successful coping and social integration in old age (Silverstein and Bengtson, 1991). The attempt to understand and analyze parent – adult-child relations in later life is often based on the Intergenerational Solidarity Model, which perceived parent–child relations as a primary source of mutual emotional and instrumental support (McChesney and Bengtson, 1988).

The term "solidarity" reflects various theoretical traditions: (1) classical theories of social organization; (2) social psychology of group dynamics; and (3) family developmental theory (Bengtson and Roberts, 1991). For an extensive review, see Roberts *et al.* (1991) and Lowenstein *et al.* (2001). Since the early seventies, Bengtson and colleagues have continued to develop and expand the model within the Longitudinal Study of Generations (LSOG) – (Bengtson *et al.*, 1975; Bengtson and Schrader, 1982; Bengtson and Harootyan, 1994; Roberts *et al.*, 1991; Silverstein and Bengtson, 1997). The model conceptualizes intergenerational solidarity as a multi-dimensional phenomenon with six components, expressing the behavioral, emotional, cognitive, and structural aspects of family relations including: structural solidarity, contact, affect, consensus, functional transfers/help and normative solidarity (Roberts *et al.*, 1991).

Research in this tradition has tended to emphasize shared values across generations, normative obligations to provide care, and enduring ties between parents and children. Empirical data, though, do not show equivocal results of the costs and benefits of intergenerational solidarity to different generations. Some studies indicate the contribution of the exchange to adult children (Barnett *et al.*, 1992), while others show the contribution to elderly parents (Kauh, 1997; Yoo and Sung, 1997). Data in still others present the "rewards" which both generations (and even three generations) incur (Bengtson and Mangen, 1988; Walker *et al.*, 1992). Such studies and others suggest that, for both generations, giving is no less important than receiving as it impacts continued interaction and wellbeing of the partners (Ishii-Kuntz, 1990; Katz and Lowenstein, 1999).

Findings on the impact of receiving support in later life on wellbeing are mixed. Some show that it improves it or serves as a buffer for stressful events (Antonucci *et al.*, 1996; Silverstein and Bengtson, 1994). Others found that support from adult children is psychologically beneficial at moderate levels and harmful at high levels (Silverstein *et al.*, 1996). Some found no impact (Umberson, 1992) while several studies found that it increased distress among older people (Ingersoll-Dayton *et al.*, 1997; Lee *et al.*, 1995). On the other hand, providing support was generally found to improve emotional states in later life (Krause *et al.*, 1992; Silverstein *et al.*, 1996). Further, studies of the effect of family solidarity on coping with crisis situations revealed that higher solidarity contributes to better adjustment in crises like widowhood or immigration (Katz and Lowenstein, 1999; Silverstein and Bengtson, 1991).

Some scholars have criticized the overly positive bias of the solidarity paradigm. Research within this

framework assumes that the individuals' personal feelings such as affection, attraction, and warmth serve to maintain family cohesion (Sprey, 1991). The very term "solidarity" implies an emphasis on consensus among family members (Marshall *et al.*, 1993). Negative aspects of family life are interpreted, in this view, as absence of solidarity. Thus, the concept of intergenerational solidarity has been criticized because of normative interpretations that easily lend themselves to idealization (Luescher, 1999). Based on empirical findings and changes in family relations and structures in different cultures, scholars have recently emphasized additional aspects: conflictual relationships, and relations that reflect ambivalence, as in caregiving.

From the early 1970s onward, studies have presented a consistent picture of continued high involvement by families in caregiving, with an explosion of literature on the topic. Data revealed that the input of caring for frail elderly from anyone outside the family is marginal, in terms of the total volume of informal care. For example, UK data estimated that close to 6 million adults (about 15 percent of the adult population) provided some regular service for an older person. The equivalent cost of this care in formal services could be estimated at £2.4 billion (Sinclair *et al.*, 1990). Even in the Nordic social welfare countries, like Sweden, where a relatively larger percentage of women are in the labor force and where over 40 percent of elders live alone, family support is still central to elder care (Tornstam, 1992; Sundstrom, 1994). Several studies, though, show that the ability of the family to cope with conflicts arising from caregiving responsibilities affect the quality of care, and the relations between caregiver and care receiver (Lieberman and Fisher, 1999; Merrill, 1996). Studies on family relations, caregiving, and wellbeing of family members living in shared households also present family conflicts (Brody *et al.*, 1995; Lowenstein & Katz, 2000; Pruchno *et al.*, 1997).

Thus, in recent years, Bengtson and others have incorporated conflict into the study of family relations, arguing that as a normal expectable aspect of these relations it is likely to impact their perception, and the willingness of members to assist each other. Conflict, though, also allows for resolving issues, thereby enhancing the overall quality of the relationship rather than harming it, and should be integrated into the solidarity paradigm (Parrott and Bengtson, 1999). However, the two dimensions of solidarity and conflict do not represent a single continuum, from high solidarity to high conflict. Rather, family solidarity can exhibit both high solidarity and high conflict, or low solidarity and low conflict, depending on family dynamics and circumstances (Bengtson *et al.*, 2000). This relates to the basic assumption of conflict theory, that conflict is natural and inevitable to human life. Social interaction, as experienced within families, always involves both harmony and conflict (Sprey, 1969); groups, like the family, cannot exist in total harmony or they would be completely static (Klein and White, 1996).

Intergenerational ambivalence has recently been proposed as an alternative to solidarity, especially in situations of elder care (Luescher and Pillemer, 1998; Luescher, 1999, 2000). Based on postmodernist and feminist conceptualizations of the family, this approach contends that family life today is characterized by plurality and a multiplicity of forms, such as divorce, remarriage, or "blended" families, that impact family relationships. It is proposed that the term "intergenerational ambivalence" reflects contradictions in parents – adult offspring relations on two dimensions: (1) at the macro-social structure in roles and norms; and (2) at the subjective level, in terms of cognitions, emotions, and motivations. Three aspects of family life might generate ambivalence (Luescher and Pillemer, 1998: 417): (1) ambivalence between dependence and autonomy – in adulthood the desire of parents and children for help and support and the countervailing pressures for freedom; (2) ambivalence resulting from conflicting norms regarding family relations, like reciprocity and solidarity in caregiving, which become problematic in situations of chronic stress; and (3) ambivalence resulting from solidarity – the "web of mutual dependency," revealed in elder abuse studies. Hence, the importance of studying intergenerational solidarity versus ambivalence for caregiving behaviors and quality of life of elders and family caregivers. This was one of the major goals of the OASIS project – "Old Age and Autonomy: The Role of Service Systems and Intergenerational Solidarity" – a cross-national five countries study (Daatland and Herlofson, 2001; Lowenstein *et al.*, 2001, 2002).

Other research that attempts to operationalize ambivalence has focused on the interplay between structural and individual ambivalence and the negotiation between them. Connidis and McMullin (2001) propose that ambivalence can be viewed as a brokering concept between the solidarity model and problematic family relations, and offer a critical perspective through their work on divorce and intergenerational relations.

Family solidarity can, therefore, hardly be a constant today in a society changing rapidly in nearly all respects (Bengtson, 1996; Katz and Lowenstein, 1999). In many families, confusion on intergenerational relations exists, after rapid changes in the context of family life, and family members have to re-negotiate new ways of solidarity (Clarke *et al.*, 1999). Recently, the theoretical debate on solidarity, conflict, and ambivalence received greater visibility in articles in the *Journal of Marriage and Family* (August, 2002). In this issue, Connidis and McMullin's discussion of "sociological ambivalence and family ties" and Luescher in his essay on "intergenerational ambivalence" argue that the ambivalence perspective links social structure and individual action. Bengtson *et al.* (2002), in responding, discuss the multidimensional nature of family solidarity. They point out that these conceptual paradigms are not competing, but complementing. They suggest that in close relationships, such as the family, first comes solidarity, then conflict, and "from the intersection of solidarity and conflict comes ambivalence" (p. 575).

Macro level: family solidarity versus state solidarity

Part of the equation in retaining autonomy in old age is the relationship between family networks and the service system, and particularly the extent to which families are supported. Data show that aged care is a public/private mix, with the exact amount varying according to country. The specific mix is related to three factors: (1) family norms and care preferences; (2) family culture that guides the level of readiness to use public services; and (3) availability, accessibility, quality, and cost of services. It is established that family care is substantial and that collective responsibility through available public services has not discouraged family care, but also that there is more willingness by elders and families to use services when dependency starts (Daatland, 1997; Katan and Lowenstein, 1999).

Although the family still accomplishes a broad series of care tasks, some responsibility for care of elders is now entrusted to the welfare state. This applies in particular to duties of children towards elderly parents (Sgritta, 1997). Social care has come to mean both formal and informal care networks existing side by side (Cantor, 1991). One of the basic policy debates in this regard is whether formal services will substitute informal family care or complement it. Ageing policies of most countries, though, regard families and service systems as alternatives that tend to counteract (substitute), not complement (Hooyman, 1992). Public opinion also tends to support the substitution idea (Daatland, 1990), while most research supports complementarity (Chappell & Blandford, 1991; Lingsom, 1997; Litwak, 1985; Litwak et al., 2003).

Welfare regimes adopting the substitution approach, like Scandinavian societies, favor more direct governmental involvement, supplying rather generous services that are predominantly public, and base their social policies on individual rights, without imposing any legal obligations on adult children towards older parents. Other welfare regimes like the conservative model of continental Europe lean heavily on insurance-based arrangements, whereas the liberal regime of the US is characterized by a limited residual state responsibility. On the other hand, countries with a more "traditional-familial" perspective and a family-based social policy hold the complementary approach whereby responsibility is shared, and services are developed to assist families in care provision. However, as the global political and economic climate seems to point towards less government responsibility for elder care and increased pressure on families, and in light of rising costs of welfare and health services, a balance should be found between these two perspectives.

CONCLUSIONS

The focus of this chapter was on the outcomes of global ageing and changing familial and social structures that impact family relations. Several key themes emerged: in the future, the family, especially the extended multigenerational family, will continue to be strong. The institution of marriage and the family will continue to be popular, together with divorce and remarriage that might restrict access to grandchildren by grandparents, leading to further developments in intergenerational ties and caregiving patterns. These social trends will challenge ageing families. The challenges on the micro-level are: continued coping with caregiving situations, and finding the balance between independence and the need for support. On the meso-level, they are: building new relations within multigenerational families, strengthening solidarity, and resolving conflicts and ambivalence. On the macro-level, they are: strengthening social integration and developing new social policies.

A starting point can be that the family unit has its own impact on the behavior and subsequently the wellbeing of individual members. Thus, the family can be considered a cultural entity that establishes a common ground for interaction and exchange and defines a family style of dealing with family issues, like caregiving or grandparenthood. As new generations of elders will be better educated with higher incomes, and as most families will be composed of four and five generations, care demands in the twenty-first century will differ. On one hand, there will be more elders and very old people – the "two-generation geriatric family" – who might need care and assistance. On the other hand, they will demand better care and will be able to purchase many services. There is, thus, a need to develop new caregiving models to deal with conflicts and ambivalence, as it evolves into a type of "caregiving careers" (Aneshensel et al., 1995).

Another theme was the similarities and differences in norms, expectations, and relations across and within societies and cultures, and the diversity in intergenerational family relations. Thus, each family – and country – may be expected to place their idiosyncratic mark on their solutions. The more we know about the extent and nature of cultural diversity in relation to these issues, the better society can respond to changing contexts and needs of older and younger generations. To borrow a phrase from Inglehart and Baker (2000) – "the broad cultural heritage of a society . . . leaves an imprint on values that endure despite modernization" (p. 19).

The last theme addressed was the interrelations between family solidarity and state solidarity. Data show that the needs and interests of family caregivers should be incorporated into policy debate and service development. The rising levels of affluence and state welfare provisions will allow the operation of choice in family relationships. Thus, sentiment rather than obligation might increasingly govern ties between older parents and younger generations. Population ageing and changes in family norms and female roles represent fundamental challenges to social integration and social policies. Innovative responses are needed on both the individual and societal levels. To help families cope with the challenges of global ageing, it is important to study further the relationships between family networks and family policy. Longitudinal research might provide a useful framework.

In this chapter an attempt has been made to address basic issues related to the impact of global ageing on family relations in the twenty-first century. The centrality of the family as the anchor for dealing with demographic, familial, and social changes was outlined, showing that responses of both families and welfare states will be vitally important in coping with future challenges to family life and fabric.

FURTHER READING

Katz, R., Lowenstein, A., Phillips, J., and S. O. Daatland (2005). "Theorizing intergenerational family relations: solidarity, conflict and ambivalence in cross-national contexts." In V. L. Bengtson, A. C. Acock, K. R. Allen, P. Dilworth-Andersen, and D. M. Klein, eds., *Sourcebook on family theory and research*. Thousand Oaks, Calif.: Sage Publications, pp. 393–402.

Kohli, M., and H. Kunemund (2003). "Intergenerational transfers in the family: what motivates giving?" In V. L. Bengtson and A. Lowenstein, eds., *Global aging and challenges to families*. New York: Aldine De Gruyter, pp. 123–42.

Litwin, H. (2004). "Intergenerational exchange patterns and their correlates in an aging Israeli cohort," *Research on Aging*, 26 (2): 202–23.

Lowenstein, A. (2003). "Contemporary later-life family transitions: revisiting theoretical perspectives on aging and the family – toward a family identity model." In S. Biggs, A. Lowenstein, and J. Hendricks, eds., *The need for theory: critical approaches to social gerontology*. Amityville, N.Y.: Baywood Publishing Co., pp. 105–26.

REFERENCES

Aneshensel, C. S., Pearlin, L. I., Mullan, J. T., Zarit, S. H., and C. J. Whitlatch (1995). *Profiles in caregiving: the unexpected career*. San Diego, Calif.: Academic Press.

Antonucci, T. C., Sherman, A. M., and H. Akiyama (1996). "Social networks, support and integration." In J. E. Birren, ed., *Encyclopedia of gerontology*, 41: 408–16.

Barnett, R. C., Marshall, N. L., and J. H. Pleck (1992). "Adult son – parent relationships and their associations with sons' psychological distress," *Journal of Family Issues*, 13 (4): 505–25.

Bengtson, V. L. (1996). "Continuities and discontinuities in intergenerational relationships over time." In V. L. Bengtson, ed., *Adulthood and aging: research on continuities and discontinuities*. New York: Springer, p. 271–303.

(2000). "Beyond the nuclear family: the increasing importance of multigenerational bonds," *Journal of Marriage and the Family*, 63: 1–16.

Bengtson, V. L., and R. A. Harootyan (1994). *Intergenerational linkages*. New York: Springer.

Bengtson, V. L., and D. J. Mangen (1988). "Family intergenerational solidarity revised: suggestions for future management." In D. J. Mangen, V. L. Bengston, and P. H. Landry, Jr., eds., *Measurement of intergenerational relations*. Beverly Hills: Sage, pp. 222–38.

Bengtson, V. L., and R. Roberts (1991). "Intergenerational solidarity in aging families: an example of formal theory construction," *Journal of Marriage and the Family*, 53: 856–70.

Bengtson, V. L., and S. Schrader (1982). "Parent–child relations." In D. Mangen and W. A. Peterson, eds., *Research instruments in social gerontology*, Vol. II. Minneapolis: University of Minnesota Press, pp. 115–86.

Bengtson, V. L., Olander, H., and A. Haddad (1976). "The 'generation gap' and aging family members: toward a conceptual model." In J. E. Gubrium, ed., *Time, roles and self in old age*. New York: Human Science Press, pp. 273–63.

Bengtson, V. L., Rosenthal, C. J., and L. M. Burton (1995). "Paradoxes of families and aging." In R. H. Binstock and L. K. George, eds., *Handbook of aging and the social sciences*, 4th edn. San Diego, Calif.: Academic Press, pp. 253–82.

Bengtson, V. L., Giarrusso, R., Silverstein, M., and H. Wang (2000). "Families and intergenerational relationships in aging societies," *Hallym International Journal of Aging*, 2 (1): 3–10.

Bengtson, V. L., Giarrusso, R., Mabry, J. B., and M. Silverstein (2002). "Solidarity, conflict and ambivalence: complementary or competing perspectives on intergenerational relationships?" *Journal of Marriage and the Family*, 64: 568–76.

Bengtson, V. L., Lowenstein, A., and N. Putney (2003). "Global aging and its challenges to families."

In V. L. Bengtson and A. Lowenstein, eds., *Global aging and challenges to families*. New York: Aldine de Gruyter, Ch. 1.

Biggs, S., Lowenstein, A., and J. Hendricks (2003). "Introduction." In S. Biggs, A. Lowenstein, and J. Hendricks, eds., *The need for theory: critical approaches to social gerontology*. Amityville, N.Y.: Baywood Publishing Co., pp. 1–14.

Brody, E. M., Litvin, S. J., Hoffman, C., and M. H. Kleban (1995). "Marital status of caregiving daughters and co-residence with dependent parents," *Gerontologist*, 35: 75–85.

Brubaker, T. H. (1990). "Families in later life: a burgeoning research area," *Journal of Marriage and the Family*, 52: 959–81.

Burr, J. A., and J. E. Mutchler (1999). "Race and ethnic variation in norms of filial responsibility among older persons," *Journal of Marriage and the Family*, 61: 674–87.

Cantor, M. H. (1991). "Family and community: changing roles in an aging society," *Gerontologist*, 31: 337–46.

Chappell, N., and A. Blandford (1991). "Informal and formal care: exploring the complementarity," *Ageing and Society*, 11: 299–317.

Clarke, E. J., Preston, M., Raksin, J., and V. L. Bengtson (1999). "Types of conflicts and tensions between older parents and adult children," *Gerontologist*, 39 (3): 261–70.

Connidis, I. A. (2001). *Family ties and aging*. Thousand Oaks, Calif.: Sage.

Connidis, I. A., and J. McMullin (2001). "Negotiating family ties over three generations: the impact of divorce." Paper presented at the 17th World Congress of Gerontology, Vancouver.

Daatland, S. O. (1990). "What are families for? On family solidarity and preferences for help," *Ageing and Society*, 10: 1–15.

(1997). "Family solidarity, popular opinions and the elderly: perspective from Norway," *Ageing International*, 1: 51–62.

Daatland, S. O., and K. Herlofson, eds. (2001). *Ageing, intergenerational relations, care systems and quality of life – an introduction to the OASIS project*. Oslo, Norway: Norwegian Social Research, NOVA Rapport 14/01.

Eurostat (1996). *Demographic statistics 1996*. Luxembourg: Office for Official Publications of the European Communities.

Ganong, L. H., and M. Coleman (1998). "Attitudes regarding filial responsibilities to help elderly divorced parents and stepparents," *Journal of Aging Studies*, 12 (3): 271–90.

George, L. K., and D. T. Gold (1991). "Life course perspectives on intergenerational and generational connections," *Marriage and Family Review*, 16: 67–88.

Hagestad, G. O. (1988). "Demographic change and the life course: some emerging trends in the family realm," *Family Relations*, 37: 405–10.

Hooyman, N. R. (1992). "Social policy and gender inequities in caregiving." In J. W. Dwyer and R. T. Coward, eds., *Gender, families, and elder care*. Newbury Park: Sage.

Ingersoll-Dayton, B., Morgan, D., and T. C. Antonucci (1997). "The effects of positive and negative social exchanges on aging adults," *Journal of Gerontology*, *52B*: S190–S199.

Inglehart, R., and W. E. Baker (2000). "Modernization, cultural change, and the persistence of traditional values," *American Sociological Review*, 65: 19–51.

Ishii-Kuntz, M. (1990). "Social interaction and psychological well-being comparison across stages of adulthood," *International Journal of Aging and Human Development*, 30 (1): 15–36.

Katan, J., and A. Lowenstein (1999). *A decade of implementation of the Long-Term Care Insurance Law – meanings and implications*. Jerusalem: The Center for Social and Policy Planning in Israel. (Hebrew.)

Katz, R., and A. Lowenstein (1999). "Adjustment of older Soviet immigrant parents and their adult children residing in shared households: an intergenerational comparison," *Family Relations*, 48 (1): 43–50.

Kaufman, G., and P. Uhlenberg (1998). "Effects of life course transitions on quality of relationships between adult children and their parents," *Journal of Marriage and the Family*, 60: 924–38.

Kauh, T. O. (1997). "Intergenerational relations: older Korean-Americans' experiences," *Journal of Cross-Cultural Gerontology*, 12: 245–71.

Kinsella, K. (2000). "Demographic dimensions of global aging," *Journal of Family Issues*, 21 (5): 541–58.

Klein, D. M., and J. M. White (1996). *Family theories*. Thousand Oaks, Calif.: Sage.

Knipscheer, C. P. M. (1988). "Temporal embeddedness and aging within the multi-generational family: the case of grandparenting." In J. E. Birren and V. L. Bengston, eds., *Emergent theories of aging*. New York: Springer, pp. 426–46.

Kojima, H. (2000). "Japan: hyper-aging and its policy implications." In V. L. Bengtson, K. D. Kim, G. C. Myers, and K. S. Eun, eds., *Aging in East and West: families, states and the elderly*. New York: Springer, pp. 95–120.

Komarovsky, M. and W. Waller (1945). "Studies of the family," *American Journal of Sociology*, 50: 443–51.

Krause, N. A., Herzog, R. and E. Baker (1992). "Providing support to others and well-being in later life," *Journal of Gerontology: Psychological Science*, 47: P300–P311.

Lee, G. R., Netzer, J. K., and R. T. Coward (1995). "Depression among older parents: the role of intergenerational exchange," *Journal of Marriage and the Family*, 57: 823–33.

Lieberman, M. A., and L. Fisher (1999). "The effects of family conflict resolution and decision making on the provision of help for an elder with Alzheimer's disease," *Gerontologist*, 39 (2): 159–66.

Lin, G., and P. A. Rogerson (1995). "Elderly parents and geographic availability of their adult children," *Research on Aging*, 17: 303–31.

Lingsom, S. (1997). *The substitution issue: care policies and their consequences for family care*. Oslo: NOVA, report 6/97.

Litwak, E. (1985). *Helping the elderly: the complementary roles of informal networks and formal systems*. New York: Guilford Press.

Litwak, E., Silverstein, M., Bengtson, V. L., and Y. W. Hirst (2003). "Theories about families, organizations and social supports." In V. L. Bengtson and A. Lowenstein, eds., *Global aging and challenges to families*. New York: Aldine de Gruyther.

Lowenstein, A. (1999). "Children caring for Alzheimer's parents – comparing perceptions of physical and mental health in the Jewish and Arab sectors in Israel," *Journal of Cross-Cultural Gerontology*, 14: 65–76.

(2000). "Intergenerational family relations and social support," *German Journal of Geriatrics and Gerontology*, 32: 202–10.

Lowenstein, A., and R. Katz (2000). "Coping with caregiving in the rural Arab family in Israel," *Marriage and Family Review*, 30 (1): 179–97.

Lowenstein, A., and P. Ron (1999). "Tension and conflict factors in spousal abuse in second marriages of the widowed elderly," *Journal of Elder Abuse and Neglect*, 11 (1): 23–45.

Lowenstein, A., Katz, R., Prilutzky, D., and D. Mehlhausen-Hassoen (2001). "The intergenerational solidarity paradigm." In S. O. Daatland and K. Herlofson, eds., *Ageing, intergenerational relations, care systems, and quality of life – an introduction to the Oasis project*. Oslo: Norway, Norwegian Social Research, NOVA Rapport 14/01.

Lowenstein, A., Katz, R., Mehlhausen-Hassoen, D., and D. Prilutzky (2002). *The research instruments in the Oasis project: old age and autonomy, the role of service systems and intergenerational family solidarity*. Haifa, Israel: The Center for Research and Study of Aging, The University of Haifa.

Lowenstein, A., Katz, R., Mehlhausen-Hassoen, D., and D. Prilutzky (2003). "A comparative cross-national perspective on intergenerational solidarity," *Retraite et Société*, 38: 52–80.

Luescher, K. (1999). "Ambivalence: a key concept for the study of intergenerational relationships." In S. Trnka, ed., *Family issues between gender and generations*. Vienna: European Observatory on Family Matters, seminar report.

(2000). *A heuristic model for the study of intergenerational ambivalence*. Arbeitspapier Nr 29. Universitat Konstanz, Sozialwissenschaftliche Fakultat.

Luescher, K., and K. Pillemer (1998). "Intergenerational ambivalence: a new approach to the study of parent–child relations in later life," *Journal of Marriage and the Family*, 60: 413–25.

Marshall, V. W., Matthews, S. H., and C. J. Rosenthal (1993). "Elusiveness of family life: a challenge for the sociology of aging." In G. L. Maddox and M. Powell Lawton, eds., *Annual Review of Gerontology and Geriatrics*, 13. New York: Springer, pp. 39–72.

McChesney, K. Y., and V. L. Bengtson (1988). "Solidarity, integration and cohesion in families: concepts and theories." In D. J. Mangen, V. L. Bengston, and P. H. Landry, Jr., eds., *Measurement of intergenerational relations*. Beverly Hills: Sage, pp. 15–30.

Merrill, D. M. (1996). "Conflict and cooperation among adult siblings during the transition to the role of filial caregiver," *Journal of Social and Personal Relationships*, 13 (3): 399–413.

OECD: Social Policy Studies (1996). *Caring for frail elderly people. Policies in evolution*, No. 19. Paris: OECD.

Parrott, T. M., and V. L. Bengtson (1999). "The effects of earlier intergenerational affection, normative expectations and family conflict on contemporary exchange of help and support," *Research on Aging*, 21 (1): 73–105.

Popenoe, D. (1993). "American family decline, 1960–1990: a review and appraisal," *Journal of Marriage and the Family*, 55: 527–55.

Pruchno, R. A., Burant, C. J., and N.D. Peters (1997). "Coping strategies of people living in multigenerational households: effects on well-being," *Psychology and Aging*, 12: 115–24.

Roberts, R. E. L., Richards, L. N., and V. L. Bengtson (1991). "Intergenerational solidarity in families," *Marriage and Family Review*, 16: 11–46.

Rossi, A. S. (1987). "Parenthood in transition: from lineage to child to self-orientation" In J. Lancaster, J. Altman, A. Rossi, and L. Sherrod, eds., *Parenting across the life span: biosocial dimensions*. Hawthorne, N.Y.: Aldine de Gruyter, pp. 435–56.

Sgritta, G. B. (1997). "The generation question: state solidarity versus family solidarity" In J. Commaille and F. de Singly, *The European family*. Dordrecht, Netherlands: Kluwer Academic Publishers, pp. 151–66.

Silverstein, M., and V. L. Bengtson (1991). "Do close parent–child relations reduce the mortality risk of older parents?" *Journal of Health and Social Behavior*, 32: 382–95.

(1994). "Does intergenerational social support influence the psychological well-being of older parents? The contingencies of declining health and widowhood," *Social Science and Medicine*, 38 (7): 943–57.

(1997). "Intergenerational family solidarity and the structure of adult child – parent relationships in American families," *American Journal of Sociology*, 103 (2): 429–60.

Silverstein, M., Chen, X., and K. Heller (1996). "Too much of a good thing? Intergenerational social support and the psychological well-being of older parents," *Journal of Marriage and the Family*, 58: 970–82.

Sinclair, I., Parker, R., Leat, J., and J. Williams (1990). *The kaleidoscope of care: a review of research and welfare provision for elderly people*. London: HMSO.

Sprey, J. (1969). "The family as a system in conflict," *Journal of Marriage and the Family*, 44: 699–706.

—— (1991). "Studying adult children and their parents." In S. K. Pfeifer and M. B. Sussman, eds., *Families: intergenerational and generational connections*. Binghamton, N.Y.: The Haworth Pastoral Press, pp. 221–35.

Stacey, J. (1990). *Brave new families*. New York: Basic Books.

Sundstrom, G. (1994). "Care by families: an overview of trends," *Caring for frail elderly people – new orientations*. Paris: OECD.

Sussman, M. B. (1991). "Reflections on intergenerational and kin connections." In S. P. Pfeifer and M. B. Sussman, eds., *Families, intergenerational and generational connections*. New York: The Haworth Pastoral Press.

Tornstam, L. (1992). "Formal and informal support to the elderly in Sweden." In H. L. Kendig, A. Hashimoto and L. C. Coppard, *Family support for the elderly: the international experience*. Oxford: Oxford University Press, pp. 138–46.

Treas, J. (1995). "Older Americans in the 1990s and beyond," *Population Bulletin*, 50 (2).

Umberson, D. (1992). "Relationships between adult children and their parents: psychological consequences for both generations," *Journal of Marriage and the Family*, 64: 664–74.

Van Imhoff, E., Kuijsten, A., Hooimeijer, P., and L. Van Wissen, eds. (1995). *Household demography and household modeling*. New York: Plenum Press.

Walker, A. J., Pratt, C. C., and N. C. Oppy (1992). "Perceived reciprocity in family caregiving," *Family Relations*, 41: 82–5.

Wolf, D. A. (2001). "Population change: friend or foe of the chronic care system," *Health Affairs*, 20 (6): 28–42.

WHO (World Health Organization) (2002). *Active ageing – a policy framework*. Madrid: Second United National World Assembly on Ageing.

Yoo, S. H., and K. T. Sung (1997). "Elderly Koreans' tendency to live independently from their adult children: adaptation to cultural differences in America," *Journal of Cross Cultural Gerontology*, 12: 225–44.

CHAPTER 5.2

Ageing Parents and Adult Children: New Perspectives on Intergenerational Relationships

ROSEANN GIARRUSSO, MERRIL SILVERSTEIN, DAPHNA GANS
AND VERN L. BENGTSON

INTRODUCTION

The Intergenerational Solidarity Paradigm has guided much of the research studying adult intergenerational relationships over the past quarter-century (e.g. Atkinson *et al.*, 1986; Lee *et al.*, 1995; Markides and Krause, 1985; Rossi and Rossi, 1990; Starrels *et al.*, 1995; Rosenthal, 1987). As we will describe below, this model has not been static; it has adapted to innovations in methods and challenges to its dominance and universality over the last decade (Bengtson *et al.*, 2002). This chapter will describe the solidarity model and will discuss the theoretical evolution of this model to include the concept of conflict, which led to the introduction of the solidarity–conflict model. The chapter also will reveal the ability of the solidarity–conflict model to incorporate ambivalence – a concept that has become the center of an enthusiastic scientific debate.

Recent theoretical, empirical, and epistemological advances in family sociology have provided the impetus for advancing knowledge concerning the concept of ambivalence – the attraction–repulsion dynamic in intergenerational relationships. It is our view that the solidarity–conflict model continues to provide a valuable paradigm for the study of intergenerational relations because it is able to encompass and explain the dualistic or ambivalent nature of intergenerational relationships. Clustering approaches have provided a promising way to represent dualism in relationships by forming typological profiles based on the solidarity theoretical framework (Silverstein and Bengtson, 1997).

The purpose of this chapter is to present our view of ambivalence and to provide empirical evidence of this concept through the application of clustering techniques to the solidarity–conflict model. Specifically, we explore how affection, a key dimension of the solidarity model, can be cross-classified with conflict to develop a typology of intergenerational relationships that allows for the possibility of ambivalence or "mixed feelings" on the part of elderly and non-elderly parents of adult children.

THEORETICAL BACKGROUND

The solidarity model

The solidarity model is a comprehensive scheme for describing sentiments, behaviors, and attitudes in parent–child and other family relationships (see Roberts *et al.*, 1991). Building on theoretical and empirical advances in the social psychology of small group and family cohesion (Hechter, 1987; Homans, 1950; Heider, 1958; Jansen, 1952; Rogers and Sebald, 1962; Hill and Hansen, 1960; Nye and Rushing, 1969), Bengtson and colleagues (Bengtson and Schrader, 1982) codified the following six principal dimensions of solidarity between generations.

(1) Affectual solidarity: emotional closeness or the sentiments and evaluations family members express about their relationships with other members.
(2) Functional solidarity (help and support): the giving and receiving of support across generations including instrumental and emotional support.

413

(3) Structural solidarity: the geographic proximity between family members as affecting their opportunities for intergenerational interactions.

(4) Consensual solidarity: agreement in opinions, values, and orientations between generations.

(5) Normative solidarity: norms and expectations regarding familistic values, and filial and parental expectations.

(6) Associational solidarity: the frequency of contact between intergenerational family members.

The theoretical debate regarding the ambivalence concept

Until recently, empirical studies of intergenerational relations could be separated into two camps: (1) the dominant solidarity camp that focused on the glue that held families together, and (2) the smaller conflict camp that focused on the tensions that broke families apart. Despite empirical advancements by Bengtson and colleagues who began in the early '90s to expand analyses of intergenerational relations to include feelings of conflict (Parrott *et al.*, 1994), and even the simultaneous feelings of conflict *and* affection (Giarrusso *et al.*, 1990), theoretical expansion of the solidarity model lagged behind.

Then in the late '90s Luescher and Pillemer introduced the theoretical concept of ambivalence that suggested the co-existence of both positive and negative elements in intergenerational relations. According to Luescher and Pillemer (1998), intergenerational ambivalence refers to "contradictions in relationships between parents and adult offspring that cannot be reconciled" (p. 416). Although an interesting theoretical development, Luescher and Pillemer failed to provide an empirical test of their ideas.

In an attempt to extend Luescher and Pillemer's theoretical work, Connidis and McMullin (2002) argued for the need to go beyond subjective feelings of ambivalence to something that they called structural ambivalence. However, Bengtson and colleagues (2002) disagreed that Connidis and McMullin's work represented a theoretical advancement, arguing instead that structural ambivalence was nothing more than role-set conflict – a concept introduced by Merton almost fifty years before (Merton, 1957). Therefore, in this chapter we focus our efforts on empirically testing the concept of ambivalence as put forth by Luescher and Pillemer.

The solidarity–conflict model

Bengtson and colleagues (2002) argued that Luescher and Pillemer's concept of ambivalence could be accounted for by revising the solidarity model to include a seventh dimension – conflict. Conflict refers to tension or disagreement, even if not openly expressed, between family members. The addition of conflict to the solidarity paradigm – resulting in the solidarity–conflict model – provided a dimension that captured negative aspects of family life and emergent constructs such as intergenerational ambivalence. In this chapter, we argue that a view of family relations as positive, negative, or ambivalent depends on a family's unique constellation on two dimensions of the solidarity–conflict model: affection and conflict. That is, we contend that ambivalence can be operationally defined as the intersection of affection and conflict. Below we reveal how classification analysis can be used to discover the unique constellations of these two dimensions in intergenerational relations.

AMBIVALENCE AS AN EMBEDDED CONCEPT WITHIN THE SOLIDARITY–CONFLICT MODEL: CLASSIFICATION ANALYSIS AND TYPOLOGIES

Despite findings showing the measures of the dimensions of the solidarity model to be valid and reliable tools for assessing the strength of intergenerational family bonds (Mangen *et al.*, 1988; Bengtson and Roberts, 1991), other work has also shown that the component dimensions of solidarity are not additive and do not form a unitary construct (Atkinson *et al.*, 1986; Roberts and Bengtson, 1990). We suggest that classification analysis – or typologies – provide a strategy that captures the complexity and contradictions of family life such as feelings of ambivalence. By cross-classifying affection and conflict, we can discover whether these two elements in conjunction with one another meaningfully describe types of parent – adult child relationships.

Classification schemes for describing diversity in the structures and functions of family relationships are not new, and have been developed with respect to nuclear families (McCubbin and

McCubbin, 1988), sibling relations in later life (Gold *et al.*, 1990), transfers of support between parents and adult children (Eggebeen and Hogan, 1990; Hogan *et al.*, 1993; Silverstein and Litwak, 1993; Marshall *et al.*, 1987) and grandparent–grandchild relations (Cherlin and Furstenberg 1986).

EMPIRICAL ILLUSTRATION OF AMBIVALENCE AS AN EMBEDDED CONCEPT WITHIN THE SOLIDARITY–CONFLICT MODEL

The development of the solidarity model was based on data from the Longitudinal Study of Generations (LSOG). This study began in 1971 with 2,044 original respondents who were members of three-generation families. Grandparents were selected via a multistage stratified random sampling procedure from a population of 840,000 individuals enrolled in southern California's first large Health Maintenance Organization (HMO) (see Bengtson, 1975, for further details). The adult children, adult grandchildren, and young adult great-grandchildren of the grandparents were also invited to participate in the survey. Follow-up surveys were administered to respondents in 1985, 1988, 1991, 1994, 1997, and 2000. We are currently completing the eighth wave of data collection. All data have been collected by mail-back surveys. The study reported in this chapter is based on a subsample of the LSOG, as will be described in more detail later in this section.

Research questions

In the study reported in this chapter, we address four questions with respect to classifying parent – adult child relationships based on affection and conflict.

(1) How many classes are needed to describe adequately the patterns formed by affection and conflict in intergenerational relations?
(2) Are the profiles of the classes in the best-fitting model meaningful?
(3) Can intergenerational relations be described by the same class-types across two different parent age groups?
(4) If so, are these class-types distributed in the same way across the parent age groups?

The importance of considering age of parents

Before addressing the specific design of the study and the results, it is important to note that even among parents with adult children, patterns formed by affection and conflict may not be the same at all stages of the family lifecycle. For instance, some evidence shows that younger adult children have greater relationship strain with their mothers and fathers than do older adult children (Umberson, 1992). There are two reasons why younger parents – adult child dyads will more likely be typified by conflict or ambivalence than their older counterparts. Adult children of younger parents are more likely to be undergoing stressful lifecourse transitions such as divorce that lead to strain in parent – adult child relationships (Kaufman and Uhlenberg, 1998). In addition, younger adult children are more likely than older adult children to be engaged in pursuits that are common sources of parent – adult child conflict: child-rearing practices, lifestyle choices, and work habits (Clarke *et al.*, 1999). Therefore, we conduct classification analysis separately for parents under 65 years of age and those 65 years of age or over.

Methods

SAMPLE. For this analysis a sample of the LSOG was selected. We use data from the survey conducted in 2000 and focus on two parent age groups: (a) those under 65 years of age (N = 496), and (b) those 65 years of age and older (N = 465).

MEASURES. Continuing efforts at refining the measurement properties of solidarity and conflict items (Bengtson and Roberts, 1991; Roberts and Bengtson, 1990; Silverstein and Bengtson, 1997; Silverstein *et al.*, 1995) have made this protocol the "gold standard" in assessing intergenerational relations. The key measures in this analysis capture affectual and conflict dimensions of the solidarity–conflict construct. Affectual solidarity was measured using the following questions: *How close* do you feel to (this child)? How well do you and (this child) *get along together?* How is *communication* between yourself and (this child)? Conflict was measured using the following questions: How much *conflict* *or tension* do you feel there is between you and (this child)? How much do you feel (this child) is *critical* of you, or what you do? How much does (this child) *argue* with you?

Parents were asked to answer these questions about their relationship with a single randomly chosen child. Each of the affectual and conflict questions was answered on a six-point Likert-type scale ranging from a minimum (e.g. "not at all") to a maximum (e.g. "extremely"). Since the distributions of the six items departed substantially from normality, dichotomous variables were formed, each divided roughly at the median. Affectual solidarity items were dichotomized by assigning the strongest positive response to a "higher affection" category, and weaker responses to a "lower affection" category. Conflict items were dichotomized by assigning responses indicating at least some conflict to a "higher conflict" category, and the absence of conflict to a "lower conflict" category.

STATISTICAL PROCEDURES. Since we are proposing that intergenerational family relations can be characterized as a circumscribed set of "ideal" types that are empirically manifested by combinations of observed variables, we use latent class analysis (LCA) to examine the typological structure underlying intergenerational solidarity. LCA is a statistical method that allows researchers to posit that a set of unobserved, or latent, classes account for the association among cross-classified categorical variables (Clogg and Goodman, 1984; Lazarsfeld and Henry, 1968; McCutcheon, 1987). A key assumption of LCA is that membership in a latent class is the true source of covariation among measured variables. Thus, a given set of latent classes is acceptable to the extent that it minimizes the *within-class* association among observed indicators – the assumption of local or conditional independence. This property underlies a statistical test of whether a theoretical model adequately describes the observed data.

The cross-classification table of the six dichotomous indicators of affection–conflict results in 64 response patterns which are analyzed for latent class structure using LatentGold (Vermunt and Magidson, 2000). Two kinds of parameters are estimated for each model tested: conditional probabilities and latent class probabilities. Conditional probabilities reflect the distribution of observed indicators for members of each latent class. These estimates are analogous to factor loadings in that they represent the association between observed and latent variables, and are useful for characterizing the nature of the latent classes. Latent class probabilities signify the distribution of members *across* types, making it useful for describing the prevalence of types within a population and for comparing prevalence between populations.

The adequacy of each model tested is assessed using several goodness-of-fit measures: the likelihood ratio chi-square test statistic (L^2) and the Baysian Informal Criterion (BIC) statistic. The L^2 tests for statistically significant discrepancies between a theoretical model and the observed data, providing a basis for judging the adequacy of a given specification through statistical inference. The BIC statistic (Raftery, 1986) is useful when selecting the best-fitting model *among* competing models, especially when choosing among non-nested models and where large sample size causes otherwise acceptable models to be rejected based on the L^2. The most desirable property of the BIC is that, compared to the L^2, it is less likely to disadvantage more parsimonious models – those that have fewer latent classes and estimate fewer parameters – in the model selection process (Clogg, 1995).

We note that the most useful typologies represent a limited number of configurations that reflect the contours of social life, without being overwhelmed by its complexity. Thus, a goal of this analysis is to identify patterns formed by affection and conflict that are meaningful as well as empirically manageable.

Results

Characteristics of the two parent age groups are described in Table 1. Parents in the younger age group are an average of 49 years of age compared to 73 years of age for those in the older age group. Children of younger parents are an average of 25 years old; children of older parents are an average of 49 years old. In both parent age groups, a greater percentage is made up of mothers than fathers (61% versus 39%). Although the majority of parents in both groups are married, somewhat fewer of those in the older group are married due to widowhood. In both parent age groups, slightly more than half

TABLE 1. Characteristics of parents under 65 years of age, and 65 years and over

Characteristic	Age group	
	Under 65	65 and over
Parent female (%)	61.1	61.4
Parent married (%)	81.6	70
Parent age (mean)	49.2	73.4
Child female (%)	51.9	57.3
Child married (%)	34.5	71.6
Child age (mean)	24.9	49.4

(52% versus 57%) talk about their relationship with a daughter. Children in the older parent group are about twice as likely as those in the younger parent group to be married.

Developing the typology

The first task in developing a framework for comparing affect and conflict across the two subsamples is to determine whether the same model can be reasonably applied to each age group of parents. We do this by first finding whether the same model adequately describes the data from each group, and then determining whether the measurement parameters of this model produce an interpretable set of types. We do this by identifying whether the best-fitting model (1) has measurement properties that

are consistent, and (2) similarly describes the types across each age group of parents.

We first tested a series of latent class structures in each parent age group by successively adding an additional class and observing the change in the BIC value for each successive model. For both groups, the BIC value shows precipitous drops (indicating a better fit) with the introduction of each additional class up to the four-class model, after which it appears to reach an asymptote and negligible improvements are attained. Thus, the four-class model was the preferred choice for both the younger and older parent groups. Further, the goodness-of-fit statistics (L^2) of the four-class model were not statistically significant ($p > .05$), revealing that this model not only provided the best fit to the data, it also provided a *good* fit to the data in each parent age group.

The conditional and latent class probabilities of the four-class model are reported for parents under 65 years of age in Table 2. The conditional probabilities describe the profile of each class, and the latent class probabilities describe the class distribution. These are presented ordered by size from the largest to the smallest class. The first class has high conditional probabilities on all affection and conflict items, suggesting an *ambivalent* type of relationship. The second type is characterized by low affection and high conflict probabilities, a type we label as *disharmonious*. The third type reveals high probability scores on affection and low scores on conflict, suggesting an *amicable* type of relationship. Finally,

TABLE 2. Latent class probabilities and latent class distributions for constrained four-class model for parents under 65

Measure	Latent class probabilities for four classes			
	Ambivalent	Disharmonious	Amicable	Civil
Closeness	**0.89**	0.19	**0.86**	0.00
Getting along	**0.97**	0.15	**0.99**	0.41
Communication	**0.79**	0.07	**0.86**	0.08
Tension	**0.74**	**0.96**	0.08	0.50
Criticalness	**0.74**	**0.90**	0.27	0.47
Arguing	**0.77**	**0.98**	0.17	0.08
Class distribution	0.34	0.26	0.23	0.17

Note. Probabilities above 0.6 are considered "high" and are shown in bold.

TABLE 3. Latent class probabilities and latent class distributions for constrained four-class model for parents 65 and over

Measure	Latent class probabilities for four classes			
	Amicable	Ambivalent	Disharmonious	Civil
Closeness	**0.94**	**0.83**	0.06	0.07
Getting along	**0.99**	**0.93**	0.07	0.55
Communication	**0.95**	**0.64**	0.04	0.04
Tension	0.01	**0.74**	**0.99**	0.15
Criticalness	0.23	**0.77**	**0.91**	0.39
Arguing	0.08	**0.70**	**0.69**	0.01
Class distribution	0.37	0.28	0.21	0.14

Note: Probabilities above 0.6 are considered "high" and are shown in bold.

the fourth type is somewhat less obvious, with moderately high probability scores on one affection item and two conflict items. It consists of those who are less close, communicate less well, and experience some tension in the relationship; however, these parents get along moderately well and do not argue with their children. This pattern of emotional strain and behavioral cordiality suggests a *civil* type of relationship.

Also in Table 2 is shown the distribution of latent classes for the younger parent sample. The largest proportion (about one-third) has relationships with adult children that are *ambivalent*. The next largest percentage of these parents has parent – adult child relationships that are either *disharmonious* (one quarter) or *amicable* (one quarter). Only 17 percent of the parents under 65 years of age had relationships with their adult children that were *civil*.

The probabilities for the four-class constrained model for parents 65 years of age and over are reported in Table 3. Observing the conditional latent class probabilities in this age group revealed remarkable consistency in these estimates compared to those in the younger group of parents. This signifies that the four types of relationships can be similarly defined in each subsample. Table 3 also shows the distribution of latent classes for parents 65 years of age and over. The largest proportion (over one-third) has relationships with adult children that are *amicable*. The next largest percentage of parents has parent – adult child relationships that are *ambivalent* (over one quarter) or *disharmonious* (about one

fifth). Only 14 percent of the parents 65 years of age or over had relationships with their adult children that were *civil*.

DISCUSSION: AMBIVALENCE AS EMBEDDED WITHIN THE SOLIDARITY–CONFLICT MODEL

Emergent theories about intergenerational relations in ageing families, such as those recently developed around the concept of ambivalence, challenge more established theories to adapt or risk being superseded. Two ways an older theory adapts is by recasting its original concepts so that they incorporate the new phenomenon. Often, in doing this, novel methods are applied to reveal new patterns in existing data. In this chapter, we apply a clustering method to two key dimensions of the intergenerational solidarity model in order to understand better the complexities of ageing parent–child relationships. Notably, an ambivalent type emerges as both a discernable and sizable category for parents in both age groups. That this type would not have been detectable using more conventional linear analyses speaks to the importance of allowing the central theoretical concepts to drive which empirical method is applied. In general, we suggest that our typological approach is a useful tool for gaining a more nuanced understanding of the quality of parent–child relations in adulthood.

Overall, the profiles of the four derived classes were similar across elderly and non-elderly parents, suggesting that the underlying model – the meaning or interpretation of the types – is invariant across two broad stages of the family lifecycle. However, differences emerged in the prevalence of each type across the parent age groups. Intergenerational relations were more amicable between older parents and adult children than between middle-aged parents and their young adult children. A greater proportion of relations in the latter group fell into the ambivalent category, a sign that young adult children are in an unsettled stage of life where they are rapidly achieving independence from their parents, but perhaps not establishing full autonomy.

In terms of theory, we note that the solidarity–conflict model is well suited to investigating mixed and contradictory feelings such as those suggested in our ambivalent type. Apparent paradoxes in the simultaneous presence of positive sentiment and conflict in intergenerational relations of this type reflect the emotional complexities of family life. Our results show that solidarity and conflict are not well represented as polar opposites on a single dimension, but can be captured more informatively through the development of typologies that allow natural discrepancies to emerge.

New directions in the application of our clustering approach abound. For instance, the question of whether coherent family forms observed in our US sample can be generalized to other countries has yet to be established. While the intergenerational solidarity constructs have been tested in several countries and cultures (Marshall, 1995; Koyano, 1996; Burholt *et al.*, 1996), cross-national comparisons of the solidarity–conflict paradigm have been rare. Recently, however, measures deriving from the solidarity–conflict model have proven to have substantial explanatory power across five nations – Germany, Israel, Norway, Spain, and England (Lowenstein *et al.*, 2001). This multinational project provides the opportunity to test our typological scheme directly in those nations.

Future research should also investigate whether patterns of affection and conflict for adult children conform to those found for parents. Based on the intergenerational stake phenomenon (Giarrusso *et al.*, 1995), parents tend to view parent–child relationships more favorably than do their children. Thus, when the adult child's perspective is taken, it is likely that a greater proportion of parent – adult child relationships will be typified as disharmonious or ambivalent, relative to the parents' perspective. Another question that should be addressed in future research is the extent to which parents or children *perceive* feelings of ambivalence. It is possible that some family members compartmentalize inconsistent feelings more than others and do not acknowledge these inconsistencies, while others are better at tolerating and expressing the existence of opposing feelings.

Reframing the solidarity model to account for conflict and the existence of ambivalence in intergenerational relations opens the door to answering research questions that are at the leading edge of family sociology. A promising application will be to study patterns of transitions from one type to another over the lifecourse of the family, and identify whether transitions come in response to life events such as widowhood and frailty in the older generation, and divorce and family formation in the younger generation. Such an approach may help map the complex emotional terrain of families, when, for instance, adult children with families of their own evolve into caregivers for their ageing parents. Taken together, these new avenues for research outline a very exciting agenda for the next decade of research on adult intergenerational relationships.

This research was funded by grants #R01AG07977 and #T32-AG00037 from the National Institute on Aging.

FURTHER READING

Bengtson, V. L. (2001). "Beyond the nuclear family: the increasing importance of multigenerational relationships in American society; The 1998 Burgess Award Lecture," *Journal of Marriage and the Family*, 63: 1–16.

Bengtson, V. L., Biblarz, T. J., and R. E. L. Roberts (2002). *How families still matter: a longitudinal study of youth in two generations*. New York: Cambridge University Press.

Bengtson, V. L., Giarrusso, R., Mabry, J. B., and M. Silverstein (2002). "Solidarity, conflict, and ambivalence: complementary or competing perspectives on intergenerational relationships?" *Journal of Marriage and the Family*, 64: 568–76.

Silverstein, M., and V. L. Bengtson (1997). "Intergenerational solidarity and the structure of adult child – parent relationships in American families," *American Journal of Sociology*, 103: 429–60.

REFERENCES

Atkinson, M. P., Kivett, V. R., and R. T. Campbell (1986). "Intergenerational solidarity: an examination of a theoretical model," *Journal of Gerontology*, 41: 408–16.

Bengtson, V. L. (1975). "Generation and family effects in value socialization," *American Sociological Review*, 40: 358–71.

Bengtson, V. L., and R. E. L. Roberts (1991). "Intergenerational solidarity in aging families: an example of formal theory construction," *Journal of Marriage and the Family*, 53: 856–70.

Bengtson, V. L., and S. S. Schrader (1982). "Parent–child relations." In D. J. Mangen and W. A. Peterson, eds., *Handbook of research instruments in social gerontology*, Vol. II. Minneapolis: University of Minnesota Press, pp. 115–85.

Bengtson, V. L., Giarrusso, R., Mabry, J. B., and M. Silverstein (2002). "Solidarity, conflict, and ambivalence: complementary or competing perspectives on intergenerational relationships?" *Journal of Marriage and the Family*, 64: 568–76.

Burholt, V., Wenger, G. C., and M. Silverstein (1996). "The structure of parent–child relations among very old parents in Wales and the United States: a cross-national comparison." Paper presented at the annual meeting of the Gerontological Society of America, Washington, D.C.

Cherlin, A., and F. Furstenberg (1986). *The new American grandparent: a place in the family, a life apart.* New York: Basic Books.

Clarke, E. J., Preston, M., Raksin, J., and V. L. Bengtson (1999). "Types of conflicts and tensions between older parents and adult children," *The Gerontologist*, 39: 261–70.

Clogg, C. C. (1995). "Latent class models." In G. Arminger, C. C. Clogg, and M. E. Sobel, eds., *Handbook of statistical modeling for the social and behavioral sciences.* New York: Plenum Press, pp. 311–60.

Clogg, C. C., and L. A. Goodman (1984). "Latent structure analysis of a set of multidimensional contingency tables," *Journal of the American Statistical Association*, 79: 762–71.

Connidis, I., and J. McMullin (2002). "Sociological ambivalence and family ties: a critical perspective," *Journal of Marriage and the Family*, 64: 558–67.

Eggebeen, D. J., and D. P. Hogan (1990). "Giving between generations in American families," *Human Nature*, 1: 211–32.

Giarruso, R., Silverstein, M., and V. L. Bengtson (1990). "Affect and conflict between middle-aged parents and adult children." Paper presented at the annual meeting of the Gerontological Society of America, Boston, Mass.

Giarruso, R., Stallings, M., and V. L. Bengtson (1995). "The 'intergenerational stake' hypothesis revisited: parent–child differences in perceptions of relationships 20 years later." In V. L. Bengtson, K. W. Schaie, and L. M. Burton, eds., *Adult intergenerational relations: effects of societal change.* New York: Springer, pp. 227–63.

Gold, D. T., Woodbury, M. A., and L. K. George (1990). "Relationship classification using grade of membership analysis: a typology of sibling relationships in later life," *Journal of Gerontology: Social Sciences*, 45: S43–S51.

Hechter, M. (1987). *Principles of group solidarity.* Berkeley and Los Angeles: University of California Press.

Heider, F. (1958). *The psychology of interpersonal relations.* New York: John Wiley.

Hill, R., and D. A. Hansen (1960). "The identification of conceptual frameworks utilized in family study," *Marriage and Family Living*, 12: 299–311.

Hogan, D. P., Eggebeen, D. J., and C. C. Clogg (1993). "The structure of intergenerational exchanges in American families," *American Journal of Sociology*, 98: 1428–58.

Homans, G. F. (1950). *The human group.* New York: Harcourt, Brace, & World.

Jansen, L. T. (1952). "Measuring family solidarity," *American Sociological Review*, 17: 727–33.

Kaufman, G., and P. Uhlenberg (1998). "Effects of life course transitions on the quality of relationships between adult children and their parents," *Journal of Marriage and the Family*, 60: 924–38.

Koyano, W. (1996). "Filial piety and intergenerational solidarity in Japan," *Australian Journal on Ageing*, 15: 51–56.

Lazarsfeld, P. F., and N. W. Henry (1968). "The logical and mathematical foundation of latent structure analysis." In E. A. Suchman, P. F. Lazarsfeld, S. A. Starr, and J. A. Clausen, eds., *Studies in social psychology in World War II*, Vol. IV: *Measurement and prediction.* Princeton, N.J.: Princeton University Press, pp. 362–412.

Lee, G. R., Netzer, J. K., and R. T. Coward (1995). "Depression among older parents – the role of intergenerational exchange," *Journal of Marriage and the Family*, 57: 823–33.

Lowenstein, A., Katz, R., Prilutzky, D., and D. Mehlhausen-Hassoen (2001). "The intergenerational solidarity paradigm." In S. O. Daatland and K. Herlofson, eds., *Ageing, intergenerational relations, care systems and quality of life: an introduction to the OASIS project.* Oslo, Norway: Norwegian Social Research, NOVA Rapport 14/01, pp. 11–30.

Luescher, K., and Pillemer, K. (1998). "Intergenerational ambivalence: a new approach to the study of parent–child relations in later life," *Journal of Marriage and the Family*, 60: 413–25.

Mangen, D. J., Bengtson, V. L., and P. H. Landry, Jr., eds. (1988). *The measurement of intergenerational relations.* Beverly Hills, Calif.: Sage Publications.

Markides, K. S., and N. Krause (1985). "Intergenerational solidarity and psychological well-being among older

Mexican Americans: a three-generation study," *Journal of Gerontology*, 40: 506–11.

Marshall, V. W. (1995). "Commentary: a finding in search of an interpretation. Discussion of 'the intergenerational stake' hypothesis revisited." In V. L. Bengtson, K. W. Schaie, and L. M. Burton, eds., *Adult intergenerational relations: effects of societal change*. New York: Springer, pp. 277–82.

Marshall, V. W., Rosenthal, C. J., and J. Daciuk (1987). "Older parents' expectations for filial support," *Social Justice Research*, 1: 405–25.

McCubbin, H. I., and M. A. McCubbin (1988). "Typologies of resilient families: emerging roles of social class and ethnicity," *Family Relations*, 37: 247–54.

McCutcheon, A. L. (1987). *Latent Class Analysis*. Newbury Park, Calif.: Sage.

Merton, R. K. (1957). "The role set: problems in sociological theory," *British Journal of Sociology*, 8: 106–20.

Nye, F. I., and W. Rushing (1969). "Toward family measurement research." In J. Hadden and E. Borgatta, eds., *Marriage and family*. Itasca, Ill.: Peacock.

Parrott, T. M., Giarrusso, R., and V. L. Bengtson (1994). "What predicts conflict in parent – adult child relationships?" Paper presented at the annual meeting of the American Sociological Association, Los Angeles, Calif.

Raftery, A. E. (1986). "Choosing models for cross-classifications," *American Sociological Review*, 51: 145–6.

Roberts, R. E. L., and V. L. Bengtson (1990). "Is intergenerational solidarity a unidimensional construct?: a second test of a formal model," *Journal of Gerontology: Social Sciences*, 45: S12–S20.

Roberts, R. E. L., Richards, L. N., and V. L. Bengtson (1991). "Intergenerational solidarity in families: untangling the ties that bind," *Marriage and Family Review*, 16: 11–46.

Rogers, E. M., and H. Sebald (1962). "Familism, family integration, and kinship orientation," *Marriage and Family Living*, 24: 25–30.

Rosenthal, C. J. (1987). "Aging and intergenerational relations in Canada." In V. W. Marshall, ed., *Aging in Canada: social perspectives*. Toronto: Fitzhenry & Whiteside.

Rossi, A. S., and P. H. Rossi (1990). *Of human bonding: parent–child relationships across the life course*. New York: Aldine de Gruyter.

Silverstein, M., and V. L. Bengtson (1997). "Intergenerational solidarity and the structure of adult child – parent relationships in American families," *American Journal of Sociology*, 103: 429–60.

Silverstein, M., and E. Litwak (1993). "A task-specific typology of intergenerational family structure in later life," *Gerontologist*, 33: 258–64.

Silverstein, M., Parrott, T. M., and V. L. Bengtson (1995). "Factors that predispose middle-aged sons and daughters to provide social support to older parents," *Journal of Marriage and the Family*, 57: 465–76.

Starrels, M. E., Ingersoll-Dayton, B., Neal, M. B., and H. Yamada (1995). "Intergenerational solidarity and the workplace: employees caregiving for their parents," *Journal of Marriage and the Family*, 57: 751–62.

Umberson, D. (1992). "Relationships between adult children and their parents: psychological consequences for both generations," *Journal of Marriage and the Family*, 54: 664–74.

Vermunt, J. K., and J. Magidson (2000). *Latent Gold Users Guide*. Belmont, Mass.: Statistical Innovations Inc.

CHAPTER 5.3

Grandparenthood

S A R A H   H A R P E R

INTRODUCTION

Life expectancy has risen steadily throughout the developed world, and this, combined with falling fertility rates, has led to the ageing of societies. Such demographic ageing has significant implications for kinship structures and roles. In particular, the shift from a high-mortality/high-fertility society to a low-mortality/low-fertility society results in an increase in the number of living generations, or *intergenerational extension*, and a decrease in the number of living relatives within each generations: *intragenerational contraction* (Bengtson *et al.*, 1996). These families thus have increasingly fewer members and longer gaps between the generations (Hagestad, 1988). Modern European families are more likely than before to be both multigenerational and slim. Termed the 'beanpole' family after Bengtson *et al.* (1990), various studies have now identified this family form as emergent in most Western industrial societies (Harper, 2003; Hagestad, 1986).

Looking at this from the perspective of the individual, increased longevity may increase the duration spent in certain kinship roles, such as spouse, parent of non-dependent child, grandparent or sibling. A decrease in fertility may reduce the duration of others, such as parent of dependent child, or even the opportunity for some roles, such as sibling. The number of individuals who will live for part of their lives as members of three- and four-generation families is thus increasing, as is the proportion of grandparents among Western populations. Individuals will thus grow older having more vertical than horizontal linkages in the family and will also spend a longer time occupying intergenerational family roles than before. For example, vertically, a four-generation family structure has three tiers of parent–child relationships, two sets of grandparent–grandchild ties and one great-grandparent–grandchild linkage. Within generations of this same family, horizontally, ageing individuals will have fewer brothers and sisters. In addition, at the level of extended kin, family members will have fewer cousins, aunts, uncles, nieces and nephews. However, while the number of living generations will increase, the absolute number of living relatives will decrease. As a consequence, grandparenthood and its associated roles and relationships are achieving a growing prominence in contemporary Western society.

DEMOGRAPHICS OF GRANDPARENTHOOD

Data from the US – the Health and Retirement Survey, and the AARP Intergenerational Linkages survey – reveal that more than half of the respondents were members of four-generation families. Three-quarters of adults will become grandparents, with one survey reporting that a fifth of all women who die after 80 will spend some time in a five-generation family as great-great-grandmothers (Hagestad, 1988). Indeed Szinovacz (1997) suggests that almost one-third of grandparents will go on to experience great-grandparenthood and be part of four-generation families A similar picture may be found in the UK. Here, estimates by Age Concern

TABLE 1. Multigenerational families by age. Percentages

	18–24	25–44	45–64	65+	Total
One generation	0.6	5.6	9.3	15.9	7.4
Two generation – Youngest	27.4	52.1	8.3	1.2	29.1
Two generation – Oldest	0.1	2.6	41.9	31.7	17.4
Three generation – Youngest	69.7	28.5	0.3	0.1	22.3
Three generation – Middle	0.6	9.4	29.1	1.9	12.7
Three generation – Oldest	0.0	0.1	7.3	46.8	8.7
Four generation	1.6	1.8	3.7	2.4	2.4

Absolute number of respondents 10,131.
Source: International Social Survey Program (ISSP) covering the US, Australia, Austria, West Germany, Great Britain, Hungary and Italy; adapted from Farkas and Hogan (1995).

England indicate that 29% of the adult population of Great Britain are grandparents, with approximately 10% of all adults under 56 years, 66% of those aged 56 to 65 years and over three-quarters of those over 66 years of age. Other estimates suggest that currently just under a third of the UK's population are grandparents, a role they will hold on average for 25 years, with some forecasts suggesting that up to three-quarters of the population will attain grandparenthood (Dench *et al.*, 1999).

Not only are families now more likely to span multiple generations, but, as a result of earlier demographic trends when people married earlier and had more closely spaced children, individuals are currently experiencing the transition to grandparenthood at younger ages. They are therefore likely to occupy the position for a longer proportion of their lives, indeed it has been estimated that some people may be grandparents for over half their lifetimes (Kornhaber, 1996). Hence, grandparents occupy what has been referred to as an 'expanding' position within the family (Roberto and Stroes, 1995). As Uhlenberg (1996) notes for the US, whereas nearly one-fifth of all children born in 1900 would be orphaned before reaching 18, more than two-thirds of those born in 2000 will still have both sets of grandparents alive when they reach 18. Similarly, by the age of 30, one-fifth of the 1900 cohort had a living grandparent, compared with three-quarters of those born in 2000.

We must be careful not to assume however, that the multigenerational family will be the norm for most families throughout an individual's life.

Analysis of cross-sectional data from the International Social Survey Program (ISSP) covering the US, Australia, Austria, West Germany, Great Britain, Hungary and Italy revealed that, at least at the end of the 1980s, a very small percentage of individuals were living in a complex multigenerational family. Just under half of the 10,000 respondents lived in a two-generation family, 43% had three living generations, but under 3% were part of a four-generation family (Table 1). There was also considerable difference between the countries, particularly with respect to the US and Europe, with an individual's chances of being a member of a particular type of multi- or single-generation family, and the position within this, varying significantly. An individual in the US was more likely to have both a surviving child and surviving parent than in any of the European countries. In conclusion, while it is likely that during an individual's lifetime, he or she will experience a period of complex, possibly four- or even five-generational living, even if for only a short portion of the lifecourse, at any one time the percentage of such long-chain multigenerational families is still low, though likely to increase over the coming decades.

However, there are studies of grandparenting from across the world.

THEORETICAL UNDERSTANDING

During the mid to late twentieth century there were a variety of ad hoc studies which included grandparenthood. The 1980s saw renewed and consolidated theoretical interest, with academic contributions in particular from psychology (Kivnick, 1983), evolutionary biology (Hrdy, 1981) and sociology (Bengtson, 1985).

The *grandmother hypothesis* has emerged from evolutionary theory. The proximity of the age of menopause and/or reproductive cessation in adult women to that of attaining grandparenthood leads to the argument that there is a trade-off between the reproductive value of existing kin, and the production of additional descendants. By ceasing to reproduce, older people can bring benefits, by investing in the reproduction of their offspring and other kin. This relies on the assumption that the children of older women will be of a lower reproductive value, due to the increased chance of less viable children, following from genetic abnormalities, or due to the higher probability of the parents dying while the children are still young and vulnerable. As Carey and Grunfelder (1997) point out, there is clearly some association between extended longevity of a species and complex social structures, and elderly group members appear to play an important role in sustaining the latter. Postreproductive female life appears common among most primate species, particularly chimpanzees and gorillas. Thus both male and female older primates take on leadership of their troops, with the specific gender varying between primate species. In addition, elderly females play an important role in caregiving, with evidence from vervets that the presence of grandmothers can more than halve infant mortality (Carey and Grunfelder, 1997). In addition, in some species, the rank of the older females is passed onto their daughters, thus carrying on into subsequent generations all the advantages or disadvantages that the rank may hold, and some older female primates play an altruistic role in risking their own lives to defend the troop (Hrdy, 1981). A similar, apparently altruistic role is also found in female black bears, who frequently shift their territories away from areas overlapping with their daughters, thereby reducing their own foraging area in favour of their offspring. It does thus appear that there is considerable evidence from the non-human species that elderly members of the population, and in particular grandparents, play an important role in the success of the society, and possibly in ensuring genetic success. *Drive theory* links the biological and psychological approaches

together, with its hypothesis that there exists a biological rather than learnt drive for grandparenthood (Kornhaber, 1996).

While there has been some psychoanalytical theory applied to grandparenthood, for example the analysis of grandparenthood and the Oedipus collection, most theoretical development has emerged from the lifecycle approaches within developmental psychology (Smith, 1995). Grandparenthood has been studied as a stage in lifespan development (Kivnick, 1983), where caring for the next generation has been perceived as being an important component for achieving late-life personal integrity. As Kornhaber (1996) argues, conceptualizing grandparenthood as a developmental process is helpful in understanding its many complexities and variations, the factors which promote successful grandparenting and the conflicts which lead to dysfunctional grandparenting. In particular, how an individual proceeds from parenthood to grandparenthood, and even great-grandparenthood, determines both their self-identity and their roles and functions as a grandparent. A different perspective is taken by King and Elder (1998) who point out that the experience of the relationship the grandchild has with his grandparent earlier will partially determine the way he takes on the role and relates to his own grandchildren later on in life. Interaction between family members therefore becomes an important determinant of family life in later years, as does this impact of family culture.

Another body of research has focused on the meaning of grandparenthood. One approach has been to explore the meaning of grandparenthood to grandchildren (Robertson, 1976; Kornhaber and Woodward, 1997), with the latter authors drawing on Piaget's developmental perspective to explore the way the grandparenthood style changes with the developmental level of the grandchild. Others have explored the meaning of grandparenthood from the perspective of the grandparents themselves (Neugarten and Weinstein, 1964; Kivnick, 1983; Wood and Robertson, 1976).

Our understanding of grandparent relationships has drawn on concepts from family sociology. The work of Bengtson on solidarity within multigenerational families is of importance here; Bengtson also emphasises a lifecourse perspective and the inclusion of cohort and period effects into our understanding (Bengtson *et al.*, 1996). This perspective is clearly also described by Szinovacz (1997), who argues that grandparents whose cohort values an active and companionate relationship with grandchildren, and whose lifestage and that of their grandchildren is unencumbered with other commitments, will have higher role involvement than others in the role. Other sociological theories which have been applied to the study of grandparenthood include *role theory*, which has been adopted to suggest that a successful transition to grandparenthood requires some socialization to the role and appropriate lifecourse timing (Szinovacz, 1997), and *social stress theory*, which is used to argue that stress associated with transition to grandparenthood is related to the *number, type and context of the transitions and moderated by gender, education, income and race* (Szinovacz, 1997).

INTERGENERATIONAL CONTACT AND RELATIONSHIPS

The opportunity for greater interaction across generations has increased because of the increase in the number of living grandparents (Uhlenberg, 1980). The length of healthy old age has increased, and with that the grandparent is more likely to be able to build a relationship with their grandchild into their adulthood (Hagestad, 1988). Most surveys report a relatively high degree of contact between grandparents and grandchildren, with average physical contact occurring at least once a month, supplemented by other forms of communication (Cherlin and Furstenberg, 1986; Dench *et al.*, 1999; Leeson, forthcoming; Harper *et al.*, 2004). However, the nature of the relationship supported by such contact varies widely across a spectrum from sharing occasional interests and leisure activities to providing regular intimate personal care. Cherlin and Furstenberg (1986), for example, identified a spectrum from detached, infrequent, ritualistic contact between family members, to frequent, close, spontaneous companionship. Interestingly, Leeson (forthcoming) reports from a longitudinal study that contact between the generations in Scandinavia both increased and intensified in the last decade of the century.

Research has also highlighted the importance of gender, age, health, proximity and family line in determining the strength and type of these relationships. Some researchers have suggested grandmothers to have a warmer, more involved relationship with their grandchildren (Cherlin and Furstenberg, 1986), while others have found grandmothers were more likely than grandfathers to have frequent contact with, and thus presumably involvement with, their grandchildren. As a consequence, research into the role of grandfathers has been limited (Kivett, 1991; Radin *et al.*, 1991; Waldrop and Weber, 1999). The overt neglect of grandfathers is most evident in US research which primarily focuses upon grandparents who provide some form of care or who co-reside with their grandchildren. Even when caregiving is not considered, grandmothers are repeatedly attributed with having more influence in almost every value domain over their grandchildren, with whom they also have stronger relationships (Roberto and Stroes, 1995). British research has tended to follow US trends in stressing the importance of grandmothers. Thus, Cunningham-Burley (1986) notes that grandparenthood is an especially desirable status for grandmothers, and Thompson *et al.* (1990) and Dench *et al.* (1999) both identify grandmothers as the 'central' grandparent. Thompson *et al.* (1990) in their study found grandchildren only ever mentioned grandmothers, implying that they are regarded as the single real grandparents. One obvious reason for this is that child rearing has been a culturally encouraged area of competence for women throughout their lifecourse, thus grandmothers are most often drawn into caring for their grandchildren. This is connected with the familiar notion of women as 'kin-keepers', who, as 'ministers of the interior' (Hagestad, 1985, 1986), place a lot of emphasis on maintaining interpersonal and family ties.

From the perspective of grandfathers therefore, it has been conjectured that men become more nurturant as they get older (Radin *et al.*, 1991) and it could be hypothesized that these qualities might be expressed in relationships with their grandchildren (Dench *et al.*, 1999). Similarly, the need to consider grandfathers as important resources for teenage mothers who are rearing their children has been stressed (Radin *et al.*, 1991).

Another important aspect of gender in grandparenting is lineage. Maternal grandmothers are consistently noted as having the most contact and closest relationship with their grandchildren (Smith, 1995). Findings show that maternal grandparents are more likely to have frequent contact with grandchildren and that grandchildren tend to have a stronger bond with maternal grandparents (Chan and Elder, 2000; Harper *et al.*, 2004). However, paternal grandparents play an important role and this is evident especially where grandsons are concerned (Barranti, 1985). Emphasis on maternal grandmothers has perpetuated the matrifocal tilt in grandparent research, supporting the notion that familial continuity is most likely to persist through women, and that women of all ages are likely to retain the closest links with their child and grandchild (Matthews and Sprey, 1984; Hagestad, 1985). Maternal grandmothers are also considered more influential than paternal grandparents in terms of promoting 'closeness' and a 'sense of security' (Hyde and Gibbs, 1993).

Looking at the degree of grandparent involvement, proximity is also a relevant factor in the extent of involvement. Those who live in closer proximity to their grandchildren have greater contact with them than if they lived further away. Another measure of diversity in the grandparent role has been between older and younger grandparents. Early work by Neugarten and Weinstein (1964) differentiate between older grandparents, who are said to be the embodiment of the formal role, whereas younger grandparents were said to enact a fun-seeking role.

Thus, grandmothers through the maternal line generally hold the strongest involvement with grandchildren, though this is mediated by the grandmother's age, health and proximity to her grandchildren (Harper *et al.*, 2004).

ROLES AND STYLES

Various roles of grandparenthood have been identified. Bengtson (1985), for example, identifies what he refers to as five separate symbolic functions of grandparents: being there; grandparents as national guard; family watchdog; arbiters who perform negotiations between members; and participants in the social construction of family history. Harper *et al.*'s (2004) study of grandmothers identifies grandmother as carer, replacement partner (confidante, guide and facilitator), replacement parent (listener,

teacher and disciplinarian) and as family anchor (transferring values, attitudes and history).

CONTEMPORARY ISSUES

Step-grandparents: divorce and reconstituted families

The experience of grandparenthood and the role of the grandparent is affected by family dynamics not necessarily under the control of the grandparents themselves. The rising incidence of divorce and the emergence of complex reconstituted families is one example. The impact of this upon the grandparent and the resultant grandparent–grandchild relationship is mediated by a variety of factors, most significant of these being the dynamics of the grandparent–parent relationship prior to the marital breakdown and the gender of the link parent with grandparents.

Within close supportive relationships the grandparents can provide considerable stability and emotional and practical support to their children and grandchildren (Kornhaber and Woodward, 1997). Alternatively, a prior disjointed grandparent–parent relationship may be unable to sustain the subsequent disruption of parental divorce, leading to a complete breakdown in grandparent–grandchild interaction (Rossi and Rossi, 1990). Given the strength of the maternal grandmother link with the grandchildren relative to paternal line and grandfather relationships, and that custody in many countries is usually with the mother, paternal grandparents are at higher risk of losing contact with their grandchildren. Work on single parent and reconstituted families (Harper *et al.*, 2004; Dimmock *et al.*, 2004) reports strong contact following divorce through the maternal grandmother line, and limited contact via the paternal grandparent line.

Extensive work by Drew and Smith (1999) has highlighted the deleterious impact on the physical and psychological morbidity of the grandparents from loss of contact with grandchildren. However, grandparents in both the US and UK have limited legal rights in terms of access and custody over their grandchildren (Kornhaber, 1996).

The limited work on the *role* of the grandparent within reconstituted or step-families (Dimmock *et al.*, 2004) serves to illustrate the complexity and range of such new family forms, which range from long-term marital-based unions, where the step-parent (and thus step-grandparents) have been in these roles since the grandchildren were very young, to brief cohabiting unions in which the grandparents have little opportunity to establish a relationship with new step-grandchildren.

Custodian grandparents

The issue of custodian grandparents has been particularly noted in the US (Burton, 1992; Fuller-Thomson *et al.*, 1997; Minkler and Roe, 1996). Some 3.7 million grandparents are currently helping to raise 3.9 million children in the US. The number of grandparent-headed households rose over the past decade by more than 50% with 1.3 million children now being raised solely by grandparents (Beltran, 2000). As Beltran points out, data from the US Census Bureau dispels the myth that grandparent-headed households are predominantly headed by Black single women (Hunter and Taylor, 1998). Of these households, 51% are headed by married couples, 44% are White, 36% Black and 18% Hispanic. Parental substance abuse, prison, mental illness and HIV/AIDS are all contributing to the rise in such households (Burton, 1992; Fuller-Thomson *et al.*, 1997; Hunter and Taylor, 1998). These custodian grandparents not only face unexpected financial responsibilities, in the US they may be unable to place these children on their health insurance policies, enrol them in neighbourhood schools or afford suitable accommodation within which to bring up their second, or even, in some cases, third family.

Intergenerational equity

Finally, recent work by Harper (2004) has introduced the notion of grandparenthood into the intergenerational contract debate. The expected age wars over public programmes supporting increasing numbers of older people have not erupted, younger cohorts have not risen up to protest against policies which benefit older adults, policies which may seem to operate against the interests of younger and midlife people. As Harper argues, key here is the importance of the relationship between the micro and macro experience of social relationship. While public programmes operate at the national level, most people nowadays actually experience intergenerational relationships at the micro-level, through interactions with family members, in this case primarily grandparents and great-grandparents. Younger people thus have first-hand experience of older people as kin rather than the public *other* and see their own families benefit from macro-level policies, even if they do not.

FURTHER READING

Arthur, S., Snape, D., and G. Dench (2003). *The moral economy of grandparenting.* London: National Centre for Social Research.

Bengtson, V., and J. Robertson, eds. (1985). *Grandparenthood.* Beverly Hills: Sage.

Smith, P., ed. (1991). *The psychology of grandparenthood.* London: Routledge.

Szinovacz, M. (1998). *Handbook on grandparenthood.* Westport, Conn.: Greenwood Press.

REFERENCES

Barranti, C. (1985). 'The grandparent/grandchild relationship: family resources in an era of revolutionary bonds', *Family Relationships*, 34 (3): 343–52.

Beltran, A. (2000). *Grandparent and other relatives raising children: supportive public policies.* Public Policy and Aging Report, 11:1. Washington: The Policy Institute of the Gerontological Society of America.

Bengtson, V. L. (1985). 'Diversity and symbolism in grandparental roles'. In V. Bengtson and J. Robertson, eds., *Grandparenthood.* Beverly Hills, Calif.: Sage, pp. 11–25.

Bengtson, V. L., Rosenthal, C., and L. Burton (1996). 'Paradoxes of families and aging'. In R. Binstock and L. George, eds., *Handbook of aging and the social sciences.* San Diego, Calif.: Academic Press, pp. 254–82.

Burton, L. (1992). 'Black grandmothers rearing children of drug-addicted parents', *The Gerontologist*, 32 (6): 744–51.

Carey, J., and C. Grunfelder (1997). 'Population biology of the elderly'. In National Research Council, *Between Zeus and the Salmon.* Washington, D.C.: National Academy Press.

Chan, C., and G. Elder (2000). 'Matrilineal advantage in grandchildren–grandparents relations', *The Gerontologist*, 40: 179–90.

Cherlin, A., and F. Furstenberg (1986). *The new American grandparent.* Cambridge, Mass.: Harvard University Press.

Cunningham-Burley, S. (1986). 'Becoming a grandparent', *Ageing and Society*, 6 (4): 453–71.

Dench, G., Ogg, J., and K. Thomson (1999). 'The role of grandparents'. In R. Jowell *et al.*, eds., *British social attitudes.* Aldershot: Ashgate, ch. 7.

Dimmock, B., Bornat, J., Peace, S., and D. Jones (2004). 'Intergenerational relationships among UK stepfamilies'. In S. Harper, *Families in ageing societies*. Oxford: Oxford University Press.

Drew, L. M., and P. K. Smith (1999). 'The impact of parental separation/divorce on grandparent–grandchild relationships', *International Journal of Aging and Human Development*, 48: 191–215.

Fuller-Thomson, E., Minkler, M., and D. Driver (1997). 'A profile of grandparents raising grandchildren in the US', *The Gerontologist*, 37 (3): 406–11.

Hagestad, G. O. (1985). 'Continuity and connectedness'. In V. Bengtson and J. Robertson, eds. (1985). *Grandparenthood*. Beverley Hills: Sage, pp. 31–49.

(1986). 'The family: women and grandparents as kinkeepers'. In A. Pifer and L. Bronte, eds. *Our aging society: paradox and promise*. New York: W. W. Norton & Company, pp. 141–61.

(1988). 'Demographic change and the life course: some emerging trends in the family realm', *Family Relations*, 37 (4): 405–10.

Harper, S. (2003). 'Changing European families as populations age', *European Journal of Sociology*, 5 (44) 2: 155–84.

'The challenge for families of demographic ageing'. In S. Harper, *Families in ageing societies*. Oxford: Oxford University Press.

(2005). *Ageing societies: myths, challenges and opportunities*. London: Hodder Arnold.

Harper, S., Smith, T., Lechtman, Z., Ruchiva, I., and H. Zeilig (2004). *Grandmother care in lone parent families*. Oxford: Oxford Institute of Ageing, Research Report.

Hrdy, S. (1981). 'Nepotists and altruists: the behaviour of old females among macaques and languor monkeys'. In P. Amoss and S. Harrell, *Other ways of growing old: anthropological perspectives*. Stanford, Calif.; Stanford University Press.

Hunter, A., and R. Taylor (1998). 'Grandparenthood in African American families'. In M. Szinovacz, ed., *Handbook on grandparenthood*. Westport, Conn.: Greenwood Press.

Hyde, V., and I. Gibbs (1993). 'A very special relationship: granddaughters' perceptions of grandmothers', *Ageing and Society*, 13: 83–96.

King, V., and G. E. Elder (1998). 'Perceived self-efficacy and grandparenting', *Journal of Gerontology*, 53B, S249–S257.

Kivett, V. R. (1991). 'Centrality of the grandfather role among rural Black and White men', *Journal of Gerontology*, 46 (5): 250–8.

Kivnick, H. Q. (1983). 'Dimensions of grandparenthood meaning: deductive conceptualization and empirical derivation', *Journal of Personality and Social Psychology*, 44 (5): 1056–68.

Kornhaber, A. (1996). *Contemporary grandparenting*. USA: Sage Publications.

Kornhaber, A., and K. Woodward (1997). 'Grandparents/grandchildren: the vital connection'. Transaction Publishers.

Leeson, G. (forthcoming). 'Changing patterns of contact with and attitudes to the family in Denmark, *Ageing and Society*.

Matthews, S. H., and J. Sprey (1984). 'The impact of divorce on grandparenthood: an exploratory study', *The Gerontologist*, 24 (1): 41–6.

Minkler, M., and K. Roe (1996). 'Grandparents as surrogate parents', *Generations*, 20: 34–8.

Neugarten, B. L., and K. Weinstein (1964). 'The changing American grandparent', *Journal of Marriage and the Family*, 26 (2): 199–204.

Radin, N., Oyserman, D., and R. Benn (1991). 'Grandfathers, teen mothers and children under two'. In P. K. Smith, ed., *The psychology of grandparenthood, an international perpsective*. London: Routledge.

Roberto, K., and J. Stroes (1995). 'Grandchildren and grandparents: roles, influences and relationships'. In J. Hendricks, ed., *The ties of later life*. New York: Baywood Publishing Company Inc., pp. 141–53.

Robertson, J. F. (1976). 'Significance of grandparents: perceptions of young adult grandchildren', *The Gerontologist*, 16 (2): 137–40.

Rossi, A., and P. Rossi (1990). *Of Human bondage: parent–child relationships across the life course*. New York: Aldine de Gruyter.

Smith, P. K. (1995). 'Grandparenthood'. In M. Bomthesn, ed., *Handbook of parenting*, Vol. III. USA: Erlbaum, pp. 89–108.

Szinovacz, M. (1997). 'Grandparents today: a demographic profile', *The Gerontologist*, 38: 37–52.

Thompson, P., Itzin, C., and M. Abendstern (1990). 'Grandparenthood'. In P. Thompson, C. Itzin and M. Abendstern, *I Don't Feel Old, The Experiences of Later Life*. Oxford: Oxford University Press, pp. 174–213.

Uhlenberg, P. (1980). 'Death and the family', *Journal of Family History*, 5 (3): 313–20.

(1996). 'Mutual attraction: demography and life-course analysis', *The Gerontologist*, 36: 226–9.

Waldrop, D., and J. Weber (1999). 'Wisdom and life experiences: how grandfathers mentor their grandchildren', *Journal of Aging and Identity*, 22 (4): 407–26.

Wood, V., and J. F. Robertson (1976). 'The significance of grandparenthood'. In J. Gubrim, ed., *Time, roles and self in Old Age*. New York: Human Sciences Press, pp. 278–304.

CHAPTER 5.4

Sibling Ties Across Time: The Middle and Later Years

INGRID ARNET CONNIDIS

Whether our siblings are thorns in our side or balm for our wounds, they are fellow travellers who have witnessed our journey, living bridges between who we once were and who we have become.

(Markowitz, 1994)

The fact that our relationships with brothers and sisters usually last longer than other family ties means that we will experience many transitions over the lifecourse that will provide an ongoing opportunity and, sometimes, imperative to negotiate and renegotiate our bonds with siblings. Despite a growing appreciation for the potential significance of siblings over the lifecourse, sibling relationships remain relatively unexplored. One reason for this is a continuing tendency to attend to ties with a spouse and children as the *sine qua non* of family life for middle-aged and older adults. This both excludes the substantial number of older persons who do not have a spouse or children and ignores a relationship that most adults have: that with one or more siblings.

Living longer; more divorces, remarriages and alternative unions; and growing gender egalitarianism – all may heighten the potential significance of sibling ties in middle and old age. They certainly will add to their diversity, with growing numbers of step- and half-siblings and ties that extend across a significantly longer and more varied lifecourse. This chapter reviews the available research and theorising about sibling ties over the middle and later years. Given variations across nations and cultures in life expectancy and in definitions and meanings of sibling ties (Cicirelli, 1995), this discussion applies to the advanced capitalist nations typically referred to as 'the West'.

THEORETICAL PERSPECTIVES

The paucity of research on siblings is matched by relatively little attention to conceptualising adult sibling relationships. One earlier attempt applied a developmental approach and associated specific developmental tasks of sibling relationships to particular life stages (Goetting, 1986). Although laudable in its attention to sibling ties across the lifecourse, this approach tends to be too rigid to capture the combination of enduring features in a relationship *and* the changing nature of that relationship over time *and* variability in how different groups might negotiate particular ties. Relationships are likely to take different forms, based on varying circumstances.

A systems perspective's attention to interdependence, selective boundary maintenance, modification of interaction network structures, and task performance potentially highlights both continuity and change in family relations, including sibling ties (Aldous, 1996). Within families, a *systems* view of sibling ties can underscore the unique features of this particular group of relationships – referred to as a subsystem – in the larger constellation of family ties, helping to reveal the cultural and social assumptions about obligation hierarchies regarding sibling versus other family relations. Early work on sibling dynamics proposed that the sibling group 'has a communication network, shares power and affective relations with clique alignments, operates

429

in accord with norms, roles, and functions, and generates cooperation and conflict' (Schvaneveldt and Ihinger, 1979). The dynamic and contradictory nature of sibling ties that this view of the sibling subsystem suggests is furthered by exploring sibling coalitions. Persisting into adulthood, coalitions may be formed as a consequence of conflict or solidarity and may have a disruptive or integrative effect on family relations (Schvaneveldt and Ihinger, 1979). Is exploring these aspects of sibling ties in middle and later life best achieved through a systems perspective?

The systems view of families has been criticised by feminists for implicitly supporting a traditional view of family life and failing to examine fundamental social forces and structures as other than given (Cheal, 1991). This association of a systems perspective with normative assumptions about the family and about society hinders its utility for exploring sibling relationships. As well, separating families into subsystems creates artificial boundaries around particular sets of relationships, often based on traditional notions of family roles. This shortcoming is especially problematic when family relationships extend beyond the nuclear unit, as in the case of adult siblings.

How can the dynamics of sibling relations, captured in the dialectics of continuity and change, cooperation and conflict, affection and power, be incorporated within a theoretical framework that includes social structure? The lifecourse perspective (Elder, Jr, 1991) applies well to the continuity and change of family relations over time, including sibling ties. Drawing attention to transitions that mark significant changes in individual lives, the lifecourse perspective encourages an examination of fluctuating points in family relationships and the ongoing negotiations and renegotiations that characterise all relationships as situations and conditions change. However, additional conceptualisation is needed to strengthen the proposed links among interdependent lives, social structure, situational imperatives and control cycles that are part of the lifecourse model (Elder, Jr, 1991).

A feminist perspective encourages a focus on socially structured relations and is evident in research regarding the division of labour among siblings when providing support to their parents (see below). Extending the concept of ambivalence to

intra-generational as well as intergenerational relations provides another vehicle for linking individual action in family relations to social structural arrangements, including gendered social relations, and emphasises the co-existence of harmony and conflict in family ties (Connidis and McMullin, 2002a, 2002b).

The popular emphasis on sibling rivalry rather than co-operation makes sibling ties a promising venue for further developing theoretical concepts that explore the complex interweaving of contradictory emotions, loyalties and demands in family relations. The more voluntary nature of adult sibling ties than of those to a spouse, parent or child makes negotiating contradictions and paradoxes more transparent because we are more likely to define our encounters with siblings as a choice. The ambiguity of cultural expectations regarding sibling ties creates another basis for ambivalence; we are expected to be involved and to be friends; to feel a sense of family commitment and to limit demands. Thus, we can learn more about negotiating ambivalence in all family ties by studying sibling relationships.

The compatibility of the lifecourse perspective with feminist approaches (Cheal, 1991) and the concept of ambivalence suggests a working perspective on sibling ties in which socially structured relations based on gender, class, race, age and sexual orientation shape the interdependent lifecourse trajectories of siblings who engage in relationships characterised by ambivalence. Conceptualised at both the psychological and sociological levels (Leuscher and Pillemer, 1998), ambivalence captures the mixed emotions and socially structured contradictions that typify sibling relations. The imperative to negotiate relationships that is created by ambivalence and situational imperatives (e.g. a parent's need for support) across the lifecourse, coupled with the assumption that all social actors attempt to exercise agency, that is, to exert some control over their own lives, form the basis for a dynamic perspective on sibling relationships over time.

THE AVAILABILITY OF SIBLING TIES

Most adults in Western countries have at least one living sibling in old age, making sibling ties a potential source of support and responsibility throughout the lifecourse. For example, even among those aged 85 years and more, 75 per cent of Canadians have at least one surviving sibling (Connidis, 2001).

The implications of declining birth rates for the future availability of biological siblings requires focusing on the distribution of family size and not birth rates alone. In many Western countries, including Canada and the United States, most of those who have had children have had two or three of them (Connidis, 2001). Longer life expectancy increases the probability of sibling survival, helping to offset the impact of fewer large families. Living longer also increases the number of overlapping years and the number of significant transitions in their parents' and their own lives that siblings will share. Only in countries like Italy, where lower birth rates reflect a substantial growth in the proportion of women having only one child, will declining birth rates mean a significant drop in the prospects of having a sibling in middle and old age. In the shorter term, those countries that experienced the baby boom – the large cohort born over a 15-year period starting in the late 1940s – will soon have an older generation that enjoys an unprecedented level of sibling availability.

WHO 'COUNTS'? LAW AND THE SIBLING TIE

Discussions of sibling availability focus implicitly on biological siblings, reflecting traditional cultural and legal definitions of family membership. Although the sibling tie is not formalised in legislation in a way that parallels the rights and duties of marital partners, or of parents and children, laws that restrict who can be legal parents do bear upon siblings. For example, in England, despite growing acceptance of a range of *social* parents, including step-parents, *legal* parents are related to their children either genetically or through adoption (Bainham, 1999). Basic to British legal definitions of parenthood is the notion that there can be only two parents, a mother and a father, excluding a biological parent's gay or lesbian partner altogether.

Unless they adopt their step-children, step-parents may assume parental responsibility but not the status of legal parent. In most of the United States and Canada, as well as Britain, in order for step-parents to obtain legal standing as a parent through adop-

tion, both the step-parent's spouse (the child's custodial parent) and the non-custodial parent must consent (National Adoption Information Clearinghouse, 2000; Edwards *et al.*, 1999). A parent who consents to adoption by a former spouse's partner must relinquish the status of legal parent. The restriction of legal parenthood to two parents has longer-term implications for parent–child relations, and, hence, sibling ties, in those countries where it is only legal parents to whom adult children bear any responsibility under law (Bainham, 1999). By virtue of differentiating among parents, based on the nature of their ties to their children, the law also differentiates among siblings. In the case of step-ties, ambiguous legal standing creates an ambivalent situation in which step-relations are to act like family while not receiving sanctioning as full family members.

THE SIBLING RELATIONSHIP OVER TIME

The simple availability of siblings does not ensure their active involvement in our adult lives. Sibling ties are comparatively elusive, existing primarily in the private realm and without the institutional girders given to marriage and parent–child relations in law (Mauthner, 2000). Their relatively voluntary nature leaves sibling ties vulnerable to the cultural priority placed on obligations to other family members, particularly a spouse, parents and children (Matthews, 1994; Rossi and Rossi, 1990). Consequently, the significance of siblings to one another is variable, depending upon the web of relationships each has spun.

There is also variability over time, as the extent of commitment to particular family members ebbs and flows. As children grow up and form their own attachments, and when partners are lost through divorce or death, older persons may both want and need to re-invest in other relationships, including those with siblings. For those who have not had long-term partners and/or children, siblings, nieces and nephews may have been higher priorities throughout their lives as both recipients of and providers of support. In later life, then, siblings may be particularly significant family members, for some as a lifelong pattern of commitment and, for others, as relationships of renewed commitment.

Many older persons live fairly near to and maintain regular contact with at least one sibling (Connidis, 2001). Contact with brothers and sisters goes down when children arrive but goes up again when they grow up and leave home (White and Reidmann, 1992). In middle and old age, siblings tend to have emotionally close bonds (Connidis, 2001). Ageing diminishes the rivalry that may have characterised childhood relations because ties with siblings are more voluntary in later life and are less subject to the effects of age differences and of attempts to assert individuality. However, poor relations with siblings in childhood are unlikely to become good ones simply by virtue of growing old (Cicirelli, 1995).

Gender, marital status and parent status all influence how often middle-aged and older persons see their siblings; women, those who are single, and those who are childless have the greatest contact (Connidis, 2001). This greater involvement produces sibling relations in middle and later life that are more likely to involve companionship and confiding among women, those who have never married, and those who are child-free. Sisters, and those who are widowed, single, and childless tend to enjoy particularly close sibling ties.

Despite limited reliance on siblings in mid- and late life, siblings do regard one another as potential sources of support should it be needed (Connidis, 1994; Gold, 1987). Such support is often forthcoming following the transitions set in motion by a family member's declining health, separation, divorce or widowhood (Connidis, 1992). One aftermath of separation and divorce is increased interaction and support between a divorced adult and his or her siblings. At the same time, both the children and parents of the divorced couple are likely to experience changes in their relationships with their respective siblings (Connidis, 2003). Thus, one divorce may have immediate and long-term effects on three generations of sibling ties. Even when there is minimal direct involvement with a sibling, adult brothers and sisters tend to remain vicariously connected through other family members, especially parents and other siblings (Matthews, 1994).

SHARING SUPPORT

The link of siblings to one another through their parents may bring them together in acts of joint filial responsibility, such as caring for a parent in need (Matthews, 2002), a case of a situational imperative. When negotiating who will provide what support to parents, siblings vary in their ability to negotiate a particular outcome based on such socially structured relations as gender and class. The gendered nature of family and paid work is highlighted in those families where both men and women (brothers and sisters) are potentially available to help parents. In such families, sisters will generally experience greater pressure to provide hands-on care to parents. Brothers, in turn, may be more pressured to provide 'male' forms of support such as yard work, household maintenance and financial advice.

Studies of support to older parents indeed document the gendered nature of such support (see Connidis, 2001, for review). Daughters (sisters) are more likely to be primary caregivers; to give extensive personal, hands-on care; and to make sacrifices at work that jeopardise their advancement. Sons (brothers) tend to be primary caregivers only when a sister is not available and are more likely to be helpers to the primary caregiver, engaged in support traditionally defined as masculine (transportation, home repairs and financial management). Class cross-cuts gender so that both brothers and sisters are more involved in personally supporting their parents when they have fewer resources.

The significance of gender extends beyond individual differences to the gender composition of sibling networks; caring styles are affected by the combination of brothers and sisters in a family (Matthews, 2002). Men who only have brothers tend to engage in reactive and direct communication with their parents about their parents' needs. In contrast, sisters communicate with one another about the proactive and reactive strategies they will employ to care for their parents. These distinctly gendered approaches to family relationships are each likely to carry their own virtues and costs. Dealing directly with parents may soften ambivalence in relations between brothers. Alternatively, advance consultations between sisters may mean confronting ambivalence in the short term but fewer surprises in the longer term regarding who is doing what for their parents. Ambivalence is likely to be greatest and more challenging to resolve when mixed-gender dyads negotiate care for parents. Indeed, discord among siblings over care for parents is greatest in mixed-gender sibling groups with a lone sister (Matthews, 2002). Such lone sisters have no one with whom to form a coalition based on a commitment to familial rather than filial responsibility in which co-ordination of efforts among siblings is assumed.

SOCIAL CHANGE AND SIBLING TIES

Families live in different historical contexts, but they seem remarkably the same over time. Siblings in the past expressed love and anger, jealousy and empathy; they complained about parents and each other; they gossiped; they told secrets and kept them... [D]espite enormous changes in the United States from 1850–1920 – urbanization, industrialization, internationalization – families' internal lives did not change much.

(Atkins, 2001)

Attending to historical perspective is a good antidote to exaggerating assumed differences over time. As we explore social change and its apparent impact on sibling ties, the critical question is whether shifting circumstances have fundamentally altered how siblings negotiate their relationships with one another and the outcomes of these negotiations over time. Matthews (2002) argues that we have difficulty assessing the significance of change for sibling ties 'without adequate appreciation of how actual families are affected by more obdurate features such as their size and gender composition... [T]here is no reason to assume that formal structural properties will have radically different effects when they are more or less common.' Following this argument, those social changes that affect the formal structural features of families are likely to have a more substantial impact on how sibling relationships are negotiated than those changes that affect the number of families in various circumstances.

Most research on adult brothers and sisters focuses on full siblings, that is, those who share a biological mother and father, although adopted siblings are usually included in attempts to count siblings. More divorces, remarriages, cohabiting in first or subsequent unions, and births beyond the first union have increased the number of half- (one shared biological parent), step- and step-like (through parent's cohabiting partner) siblings, creating more complex family histories and more diverse sibling relations.

To date, information about the extent of half- and step-sibling relationships is limited. French survey data from 1994 show that, of the nearly one-quarter of children aged 13–17 years who live with only one biological parent (primarily due to divorce), 42 per cent have at least one step-sibling, 40 per cent have one or more half-siblings, and 25 per cent co-reside with at least one half-sibling (Villeneuve-Gokalp, 2000). Thus, the future holds many more adult step- and half-sibling relations. The critical question is whether the increased diversity of sibling ties will have effects into adulthood beyond mere numbers. Will ties between siblings be negotiated differently based on variations in types of relatedness?

STEP- AND HALF-SIBLINGS

Step-ties are not a new phenomenon, but the fact that they are usually the outcome of partnering after divorce rather than widowhood is. This creates a new structural dimension to families and is the basis for a quite different dynamic in which the negotiation of step-ties coincides with renegotiating ongoing family ties that occupy parallel positions, such as father and stepfather, child and stepchild. From the vantage point of siblings, the potential unification of a family unit that follows remarriage of a widowed parent is complicated when it follows divorce by the fact that step-siblings are likely to have at least one other birth parent and, possibly, an additional stepparent. This particular complication is compounded by whether step-siblings co-reside or live in different households.

The co-existence of family members in parallel positions due to divorce and remarriage (e.g. mother and stepmother) is the basis for a unique tension in both step and non-step ties that is likely to increase ambivalence in these relationships. The socially structured assumptions of loyalty and privacy in family life co-exist with their regular violation among those engaged as either parents to both non-step- and stepchildren, or children of both non-step- and stepparents. The age at which step-relations are acquired is likely to influence both the degree of ambivalence in the relationship and the ways in which the relationship is negotiated. In the short run, living together may heighten ambivalence by forcing unwanted or challenging interaction. In the long run, the pressure to resolve ambivalence and the opportunity for contact created by co-residence may mean less ambivalence than is true for those who live apart and are less likely to personalise their ties with a step- or half-sibling.

To date, little is known about the long-term negotiations of half- and step- versus full-sibling ties. Research on younger adults suggests that, although step-ties are generally positive, they are not as close as those between birth siblings (Ganong and Coleman, 1993) and they may threaten the strength of ties between biological siblings (White and Reidmann, 1992). When a child's co-resident parent and stepparent have a baby, the new half-sibling is usually treated as a full sibling (Crosbie-Burnett and McClintic, 2000). Looking at inheritance is one way of assessing the relative position of siblings in mid- and later life.

INHERITANCE AND SIBLING TIES

Inheritance law is a good example of how legal assumptions about familial relations help to define sibling relationships and may have important implications for their negotiation. Such potential effects are usually felt in late middle age, the time in life when most adults become 'orphans'. What does the available evidence regarding inheritance decisions indicate about various forms of relatedness (full and half biological, step, adoptive) and what are the implications for sibling ties in middle and later life?

Ideas of fairness are central to inheritance decisions, outcomes and their effects. Treating everyone equally is the most common rule of fairness but siblings may consider unequal distributions of property and personal effects to be fair if they are equitable, based on relative need of the siblings or contribution to their parents (Stum, 1999). This parallels views of relative contribution to parental care, when siblings may consider an inequitable division of labour to be fair because there are acceptable reasons for some siblings to contribute more and others less to the care of their parents (Matthews, 2002). In both cases, judgements about the relative contribution of siblings and their relative rewards through inheritance are tempered by how siblings feel about one another. Emotionally close ties may supersede strict rules of fairness because maintaining good relations is con-

sidered more important (Matthews, 2002). Thus, siblings who are close to one another are more inclined to focus on maintaining good relations over receiving desired goods from a parent's estate: 'All of us kids knew that anything our parents had was not as valuable as our family relationships' (Stum, 1999).

Variations in views regarding who decides and who gets what after parents die reflect variations in the assumed rights of particular family ties and of particular family members (Stum, 1999). Among siblings, differences regarding the right to lay claim or assume entitlement to a parent's effects may be drawn between biological and step-siblings or be based on gender or birth order. In the United States, the actual distribution of inherited resources among biological and stepchildren and, hence, among full, half-, and step-siblings, is unknown but the law clearly differentiates among them in excluding stepchildren as children when there is not a will (Crosbie-Burnett and McClintic, 2000).

In part because of their tenuous legal standing, step-relationships have an added burden of proof that does not apply to more traditional family ties, especially blood ties (Connidis, 2001). Both attitudes and practices regarding inheritance and of caring for older parents show a preference for biological over step-kin as beneficiaries, unless step-ties are particularly close (Bornat *et al.*, 1999; Ganong and Coleman, 1998; Ganong *et al.*, 1998; Rossi and Rossi, 1990). Thus, in order to approximate the assumed commitments of blood ties, step-ties must be unusually involved, creating an additional basis for ambivalence between siblings based on whether they are full, half-, or step-siblings.

SUMMARY AND CONCLUSIONS

A lifecourse view of sibling ties indicates that relationships with brothers and sisters are possible sources of support into old age for most individuals. In practice, siblings are not regularly tapped for extensive support but their potential for providing help if needed is assumed by many adults. Most older persons are in regular contact with at least one fairly proximate sibling, and emotionally close bonds with a sibling are common. The intensity of ties with brothers and sisters in childhood is rarely rivalled in adulthood but, once the diversions of other family commitments and paid work are behind them, older adults usually experience a resurgence of involvement with their brothers and sisters. Throughout middle and later life, women, those who never marry or are widowed, and the childless have more involved ties with their siblings. We have also seen that sisters are more implicated than brothers in caring for parents. Yet, especially in the absence of sisters, brothers do help their parents but use a different model of responsibility when they do so.

The combination of longer lives, less permanent intimate relationships, and more half- and step-sibling relationships is likely to heighten both the significance and ambivalence of sibling ties in middle and later life. The formation of step- and half-sibling ties following the dissolution of cohabiting or spousal relationships represents a key change in family structure and requires particular research attention. As well, there is a continuing need to know more about how the socially structured relations of race, class, and sexual orientation affect the negotiation of adult sibling ties.

The egalitarian and voluntary nature of sibling ties does not relieve them of ambivalence. Indeed, the fact that the apparent equality and choice of sibling ties are embedded in an extended network of family ties, and in a set of socially structured relations, may actually accentuate ambivalence and complicate its negotiation. The considerable variation among adults in their involvement with siblings as confidants, companions, providers and recipients of emotional and instrumental support, and as possible team players in helping their parents, illustrates the impact of different life histories and larger social forces in shaping the outcome of negotiated sibling ties.

FURTHER READING

Connidis, Ingrid Arnet (2001). *Family ties and aging*. Thousand Oaks, Calif.: Sage.

Matthews, Sarah H. (2002). *Sisters and brothers / daughters and sons: meeting the needs of old parents*. Bloomington: Unlimited Publishing.

Walker, Alexis J., Allen, Katherine R., and Connidis, Ingrid Arnet (2004). 'Theorizing sibling ties in adulthood'. In Vern L. Bengtson, Alan C. Acock, Katherine R. Allen, Peggye Dilworth-Anderson and David M. Klein, eds., *Sourcebook on family theory and research*. Thousand Oaks, Calif.: Sage.

REFERENCES

Aldous, Joan (1996). *Family careers: rethinking the developmental perspective*. Thousand Oaks, Calif.: Sage.

Atkins, Annette (2001). *We grew up together: brothers and sisters in nineteenth-century America*. Chicago: University of Illinois Press.

Bainham, Andrew (1999). 'Parentage, parenthood and parental responsibility: subtle, elusive yet important distinctions'. In *What is a parent: a socio-legal analysis*. Oxford – Portland Oregon: Hart Publishing, pp. 25–46.

Bornat, Joanna, Dimmock, Brian, Jones, David, and Sheila Peace (1999). 'The impact of family change on older people: the case of stepfamilies'. In *Changing Britain: families and households in the 1990s*. New York: Oxford University Press, pp. 248–62.

Cheal, David (1991). *Family and the state of theory*. Toronto: University of Toronto Press.

Cicirelli, Victor G. (1995). *Sibling relationships across the lifespan*. New York: Plenum Press.

Connidis, Ingrid A. (1992). 'Life transitions and adult sibling ties: a qualitative study', *Journal of Marriage and the Family*, 54: 972–82.

(1994). 'Sibling support in older age', *Journal of Gerontology: Social sciences*, 49 (6): S309–S317.

(2001). *Family ties and aging*. Thousand Oaks, Calif.: Sage.

(2003). 'Divorce and union dissolution: reverberations over three generations,' *Canadian Journal on Aging*, 22: 353–68.

Connidis, Ingrid A., and Julie A. McMullin (2002a). 'Sociological ambivalence and family ties: a critical perspective', *Journal of Marriage and Family*, 64: 558–67.

(2002b). 'Ambivalence, family ties and doing sociology', *Journal of Marriage and the Family*, 64: 594–601.

Crosbie-Burnett, Margaret, and Katrina McClintic (2000). 'Remarried families over the life course'. In *Families across time: a life course perspective*. Los Angeles: Roxbury Publishing Co., pp. 37–50.

Edwards, Rosalind, Gillies, Val, and Jane Ribbens McCarthy (1999). 'Biological parents and social families: legal discourses and everyday understandings of the position of step-parents', *International Journal of the Law, Policy, and the Family*, 13: 78–105.

Elder, Jr, Glen H. (1991). 'Lives and social change'. In *Theoretical advances in life course research*. Weinham: Deutscher Studies Verlag, pp. 58–85.

Ganong, Lawrence H., and Marilyn Coleman (1993). 'An exploratory study of stepsibling relationships', *Journal of Divorce and Remarriage*, 19: 125–41.

(1998). 'Attitudes regarding filial responsibilities to help elderly divorced parents and stepparents', *Journal of Aging Studies*, 12 (3): 271–90.

Ganong, Lawrence H., Coleman, Marilyn, McDaniel, Annette Kusgen, and Tim Killian (1998). 'Attitudes regarding obligations to assist an older parent or stepparent following later-life remarriage', *Journal of Marriage and the Family*, 52: 287–97.

Goetting, Ann (1986). 'The developmental tasks of siblingship over the life cycle', *Journal of Marriage and the Family*, November: 703–14.

Gold, Deborah T. (1987). 'Sibling relations in old age: something special', *Canadian Journal on Aging*, 6 (3): 199–215.

Luescher, Kurt, and Karl Pillemer (1998). 'Intergenerational ambivalence: a new approach to the study of parent–child relations in later life', *Journal of Marriage and the Family*, 60 (2): 413–25.

Markowitz, Laura M. (1994). 'Sibling connections', *Utne Reader*, May/June.

Matthews, Sarah H. (1994). 'Men's ties to siblings in old age: contributing factors to availability and quality'. In *Older men's lives*. Thousand Oaks, Calif.: Sage, pp. 178–96.

—— (2002). *Sisters and brothers / daughters and sons: meeting the needs of old parents*. Bloomington: Unlimited Publishing.

Mauthner, Melanie (2000). 'Bringing silent voices into a public discourse: researching accounts of sister relationships'. In *Feminist dilemmas in qualitative research: public knowledge and private lives*. Thousand Oaks, Calif.: Sage, pp. 78–105.

National Adoption Information Clearinghouse (2000). *Stepparent adoptions*. www.calib.com/naic/pubs/r_step.htm.

Rossi, Alice S., and Peter H. Rossi (1990). *Of human bonding: parent–child relations across the life course*. New York: Aldine de Gruyter.

Schvaneveldt, Jay D., and Marilyn Ihinger (1979). 'Sibling relationships in the family'. In *Contemporary theories about the family*. New York: The Free Press, Vol. I, pp. 453–67.

Stum, Marlene S. (1999). 'I just want to be fair: interpersonal justice in intergenerational transfers of non-titled property', *Family Relations*, 48 (2): 159–66.

Villeneuve-Gokalp, Catherine (2000). 'The double families of children of separated parents', *Population: An English Selection*, 12: 111–38.

White, Lynn K., and Agnes Reidmann (1992). 'When the Brady bunch grows up: step/half- and full-sibling relationships in adulthood', *Journal of Marriage and the Family*, 54: 197–208.

Filial Piety in Changing Asian Societies

AKIKO HASHIMOTO AND CHARLOTTE IKELS

OVERVIEW

Filial piety refers to the practice of respecting and caring for one's parents in old age, based on a moral obligation that children owe their parents. This practice is not unique to Asia, as virtually all world religions recognize filial obligations of some form as an important moral value. From Judaism and Christianity, to Islam, Buddhism, and Hinduism, no religion fails to point to the moral value of filial duty as one of the principal tenets of family and social organization. In these teachings, children owe their parents care and respect as a matter of duty, to a greater or lesser degree. Filial obligation therefore constitutes a basis for cultural ideals and legal stipulations in many societies to ensure that children are responsible for the wellbeing of aging parents.

The practice of filial piety is often associated with East Asian societies, however, especially because of the strong historical influence of Confucianism which articulated the doctrine of filial obligation very explicitly as the centerpiece of the moral order of society. In this chapter we will address the patterns of filial piety in contemporary China and Japan where the practice has been salient. Both societies use terms for filial piety that derive from the same Chinese character 孝, called *xiao* in Chinese and *kō* in Japanese; both terms encompass a similar meaning to the Confucian attitude of obedience, devotion, and care towards one's parents and elder family members. In both Chinese and Japanese societies, Confucian principles of filial piety have been used recurrently in history as a basis of social order, spiritual anchoring, moral conduct, and social control.

At the same time, filial piety today is not merely a historical vestige of the "traditional" family, but an ongoing practice of belonging, security, and surveillance. As we will show, it is a complex negotiation of parent–child relations that embraces both a cultural ideal and contested ideology, a loving family practice and legal stipulation, and a system of regulating power in the hierarchical relations between generations. There are also considerable differences between the two nations today. We will focus on three key dimensions of contemporary practices of filial piety in Japan and China: (i) patterns of co-residence and family support, (ii) the legal framework, and (iii) public discourse and family policy.

HISTORICAL ROOTS: FAMILY AND FILIAL PIETY IN EAST ASIA

Historically, respect for elders has been an integral part of the practice of ancestor reverence in the traditional family systems in East Asia. In the moral order of the "traditional" family, the elderly held higher spiritual status with advancing age. Children, in turn, were to fulfill their duties properly – providing care to elders, continuing the family line by bearing sons, and bringing prosperity and prestige to the family through hard work – which also affected the spiritual reward given to the ancestors. In this sense, the fulfillment of family obligations, or compliance with this order of serial hierarchy, could bring about an enriched sense of belonging and ontological security.

The patriarchal family systems in East Asia practiced filial piety by reinforcing the formal Confucian hierarchies of age and gender. In these patriarchal systems, absolute authority rested with the head of the household, and that was normally passed on to the eldest son in turn. Filial order was crucial for ensuring succession, inheritance, and continuity of the family line and name, especially in Japan where it was important for the family to pool its physical and material resources, and remain a viable economic unit for agricultural production.

At different historical times, some Asian societies have also resisted the social order of filial piety, as "traditional" families proved to be oppressive and authoritarian for many. This is especially the case in China, which has experienced several anti-filial-piety social movements in its history. On the other hand, filial piety as an ideology has in the past also been used to serve state interests, whether to forge a disciplined military and diligent workforce (Japan), or to discredit previous political regimes (China).

CHANGING PRACTICES IN JAPAN

Stories of filial virtues are common in Japanese historical chronicles, both as mundane accounts and as morality tales that promote piety as a virtue. Examining the evidence, historians have noted a critical shift in the piety practices of the Japanese family around the eleventh century, when parent–child relations were transformed from one emphasizing the absolute power of parents over the lives of their children, to one emphasizing the child's absolute obligation towards parents. When the patriarchal stem family was formally established, primogeniture (family succession through a single, usually eldest, male heir) became prevalent, especially among the elite samurai (military) class (Miyagawa, 1973).

The values of obedience and deference towards parents, kō, that have currency in contemporary Japan as "long-standing" traditional virtues, owe their deep-rooted existence especially to the Confucian moral education of Tokugawa Japan, and, later, to the nationalist education of late Meiji through early Showa Japan. The influence of these once state-sponsored values is apparent when one recognizes that the last state promulgations expressing the ideology of sacrifice for the family and nation were issued in 1942 and 1943, which is within the lifetime of the older generations now alive (Sekiguchi et al., 2000).

In the decades since the stem family system ie was formally abolished after the Second World War, the Japanese family experienced major changes which had consequences for the practice of filial piety. The Family Law of 1947, enacted during the American Occupation after the military defeat, formally eliminated male and birth-order privileges in inheritance and succession, which until then comprised the economic and political backbone of the piety practice. When the Japanese family discarded the ie family and primogeniture, it effectively remade itself in a new image modeled largely on the "Western" ideal of the nuclear family. The new postwar family was represented in the language of equality, individual rights, freedom of choice, and voluntary unions – civic principles derived from a Euro-American paradigm that was entirely distinct from the preceding Confucian patriarchy. The prewar authoritarian way of life, the "feudal" way of life, was seemingly cast aside, discredited, and consigned to history, as the new family promoted relations based on democratic and individualistic rules of engagement.

Despite these institutional reforms, however, the cultural ideals about the good behavior of obedient children towards their parents met few serious challenges. The very ideal of piety, expressed as oyakōkō, for the most part remained relatively unscathed even as families began to shrink in size, and move with some frequency from one urban location to another. Although the postwar expression of piety shifted its emphasis from the child's obligation to serve parents to the child's gratitude to the parents, the discourse of oyakōkō itself continued to command cultural legitimacy. This robustness of the piety discourse is evident in the prescription to care for the elderly, privileging parents' needs, especially in old age, over those of the adult children.

In many ways, the generational dynamics of the postwar family, while ostensibly transformed, is embedded in the sentiment of piety discourses from the past. The continuity between prewar and postwar Japanese family is due in no small measure to intangible and tangible reinforcements, especially in emotional and moral socialization. The making of the filial child in contemporary practice draws on traditional cultural resources for emotional socialization, adapted to the realities of the new nuclear family.

Patterns of co-residence and family support

The practice of filial piety is often illustrated today in the prevalence of multigenerational co-residence. With much geographic mobility, social mobility and urbanization occurring in the past several decades, Japan has seen an upsurge of nuclear families and freer patterns of mate selection and marriage. Changes have also taken place in the life-course of the family, ranging from rising ages of marriage and childbirth, to higher divorce rates, lower birth rates, and longer life expectancy. As the demographic profile of the Japanese family transformed dramatically, it had inevitable consequences for the co-residence of ageing parents with children.

Accordingly, the proportion of Japanese elderly living with their adult children has declined in the past several decades at the rate of about one percent per year. Filial co-residence nevertheless remains the most prevalent living arrangement among the Japanese elderly, and the absolute number of elderly who live with children has also increased as the elderly population grew rapidly as a whole. Current trends point to a gradual shift towards delayed co-residence (tochūdōkyo) in which the Japanese old-olds move in with their adult children after a period of living independently as young-olds (Naoi, 1993). The declining co-residence in Japan does not therefore mean that cultural assumptions of need and security are converging towards the "West," but indicate that past practices are modified to suit new structural conditions. In this sense, delayed co-residence is a variant of the filial piety practice adapted to late modernity.

In the past decades, attitudes of adult children regarding the desirability of care for elderly parents have also changed. Surveys show that the number of those who feel that filial care is a duty of children has remained relatively constant; however, those who feel it is a "good custom" have declined, and those who feel that it is "unavoidable" have increased concomitantly (Miura, 2001.)

Legal framework

Contemporary family law and welfare law in Japan still bear some Confucian influence as a legal framework built on the expectation of filial obligation. The Family Law of 1947 established the equal rights and responsibilities of all adult children regardless of gender and birth order; however, in practice, those who care for the ageing parents often receive a greater share of the estate and the recognition. Filial responsibility law in Japan also applies to a wide category of family members: lineal relatives and siblings, and, under special circumstances, all other relatives within the third degree. Disputed cases brought to the Family Court are usually limited.

Family status can be applied as a criterion for social service provisions in welfare laws. The principle of private initiatives (shiteki fuyo no gensoku) refers to the notion that private, family support takes precedence over public support, that is, individuals must exhaust private resources before resorting to public funds (Hashimoto, 1996). Underlying this practice are the assumptions that social services presuppose the primacy of family support and that the social unit of self-sufficiency is the family, not the individual.

Public discourse and family policy

As the demographic profile and the legal framework of the Japanese family changed, the discourse on the ideal Japanese family also became modified. It was also subject to change as pension and health-care systems became more widely available, according the elderly more affluence and health, and, along with it, the possibility of living independently. At the same time, filial piety as a public discourse today continues to be an articulation of power in intergenerational family relations as well as state interest in reproducing gendered family support. The piety discourse recycles in today's society as a social agenda to reinforce family values and policies, legitimating children's dedicated caregiving (Hashimoto, 1997).

CHANGING PRACTICES IN CHINA

Although the historical homeland of Confucius, China has also been the East Asian country in which the Confucian values of hierarchy and obedience that nurtured the practice of filial piety have been most strongly attacked. During the New Culture and May Fourth Movements of the second decade of the twentieth century the attack was led by young writers bent on reforming a system perceived as oppressive to the young and to females of any age (Chow, 1967). The focus of these attacks was the family system and especially the parental right to arrange marriages for children. This movement was limited in impact to a small segment of the urban educated elite. More than thirty years later a much broader attack on Confucianism was launched by the Communists under Mao Zedong (Mao Tse-tung) following their victory over the Nationalists under Jiang Jieshi (Chiang Kai-shek) in 1949.

With the revolutionary aim of overturning the old society, the Communists presented major challenges to the social institutions that had undergirded Confucianism. First, the traditional rural elite were re-labeled "landlords" and largely expropriated as their land was re-distributed to poorer villagers. Second, their moral authority was destroyed as villagers were encouraged to re-analyze traditional wealth and power inequalities as the result of "exploitation." Third, the Communists passed a new marriage law in 1950 intent on destroying the "feudal" family and replacing it with monogamy, freedom of marital choice (and divorce), and gender equality. The new law did retain one important Confucian element – the reciprocal responsibilities of parents to rear and educate their children and of adult children (both male and female) to support and assist their parents. In the middle and late 1950s the Communists instituted the collectivization of productive property. Villagers became the collective owners of their farmlands while owners of small businesses and workshops were forced to pool their assets and labor. Large businesses were taken over by the state. At the same time the household registration system which tied individuals to the immediate locale of their birth went into effect. By the 1960s the parental generation no longer had the exclusive right to determine the labor or the marital prospects of the young. Similarly the old, in many cases, were no longer so dependent upon the young as, in urban areas, pensions were becoming available, and in rural areas the collective handed a family's income to the official head of household, usually a member of the senior generation.

Beginning in the 1970s the state threatened another of the key tenets of filial piety – the responsibility to continue the family line by producing a son. Along with late marriage, couples were encouraged to have no more than two children spaced at least four years apart, but generally these limitations were only modestly successful. In 1979 the state announced the one child family policy whereby a couple was (and remains) limited to producing only a single child. Though there are many exemptions to this rule, e.g. national minorities, families in hardship occupations, families whose first child is handicapped, the policy was initially implemented very harshly, and, in urban areas at least, families have had to accept the Communist ideal of gender equality. In rural areas, however, the policy has run into stiff opposition. Traditional practices of surname and, often, village exogamy have required daughters to move to their husbands' households upon marriage. Parents without sons were left with no labor power and no one to support or look after them in old age. Consequently, rural families braved sanctions until they could produce a son, and the urban one child policy has become a de facto two child policy in the countryside.

By the mid-1980s both rural and urban China had left most of the Mao-era institutions behind. Villages had de-collectivized, a private economy was operating legally right beside the state sector, and young people from rural areas were migrating into the cities in search of employment. By the 1990s the state was withdrawing from many spheres of influence – no longer guaranteeing lifetime employment to its urban workers, allowing people to find their own jobs, reducing its role in the provision of welfare benefits such as housing and healthcare (Ikels, 1996). While the overall rise in the standard of living has been beneficial to most families, its impact on the practice of filial piety is less clear.

Patterns of co-residence and family support

The rising standard of living has been most noticeable in its impact on housing and living arrangements. The traditional ideal family form was the joint family, i.e., all sons married and brought their brides into their natal household and remained together as a single economy so long as the senior male (their father) lived. Upon his death the family "divided," splitting into separate economic units even as they frequently continued living in the same dwelling. Productive property, furniture, kitchen utensils, and even living space were distributed on a more or less equal basis among the sons, though it was customary for the oldest son, who alone had the responsibility of caring for the ancestors, to get a slightly larger share. As many observers have noted, this ideal was seldom achieved. While patrilocal residence was the norm, sons seldom stayed together until their father's death. More commonly, not long after the second son married, one or the other of the brothers would seek to divide from the parental household (Cohen, 1976). Division entailed signing a document that, among other provisions, laid out the brothers' collective responsibility for the surviving parents.

Under Mao, a lack of investment in housing and prohibitions on migration had kept young people in joint families longer than they would have preferred. Under the post-1978 economic reforms, the building of new housing became one of the highest priorities. In rural areas, new housing was a necessary investment for obtaining a bride. In urban areas, workplaces used their new fiscal freedom to build modern apartment blocks for their employees. The period of co-residence became shorter and shorter – in some cases no more than a symbolic few days. Parents are ambivalent about this change in co-residence, sometimes grateful for the reduction in intergenerational friction and sometimes worried about how they will manage as widowhood and frail health become realities. These problems are especially worrisome for the rural elderly whose children have migrated. As elsewhere in the world, the elderly in China have the highest suicide in the population, with the rural rate far surpassing the urban.

In addition, the economic reforms have led to greater inequalities among regions in China, including among villages. One of the unanticipated consequences of these local inequalities has been a decline in exogamy and a rise in uxorilocal marriage (co-residence with or near the bride's natal family) in relatively wealthier villages, as potential brides with incomes of their own resist moving out of their natal villages (Chan *et al.*, 1992). Thus, in these villages, families with daughters but no sons are privileged over families in poorer villages whose daughters marry out but whose sons cannot easily obtain brides.

Legal framework

In 1980 the Chinese government passed a new marriage law which raised the minimum age for marriage and added requirements for family plan-

ning. In addition the new law, unlike the 1950 one, includes two references to older people suggesting that they are a population newly at risk. For example, whereas the earlier law emphasized the special protection of "women and children," the later law protects the "rights and interests of women, children, and the aged." Furthermore intergenerational obligations have been extended to encompass three generations, i.e., in the absence of the middle generation, grandparents (including maternal grandparents) and grandchildren (including the children of daughters) have the duty to support each other. (A 2001 revision of the 1980 law did not directly address issues related to support of the elderly, but dealt instead with bigamy, concubinage, and spouse abuse.)

In 1985, in order to take into account the changed economic context, the Chinese government passed an inheritance law that protects the rights of surviving spouses. Whereas formerly all property of the deceased father was nominally divided among the children (in reality among the sons), under the new law only half of the community property was subject to such division – the surviving spouse retained not only her half but also shared along with her children in her husband's half. The law also explicitly attempts to enforce norms of filial support stating, for example, that "a larger share may be allocated to heirs who either have fulfilled the principal obligation to support the decedent or have lived with the decedent" and "either no share or a smaller share should be allocated to heirs who had the ability and the means to provide support" but did not live up to their obligations.

Public discourse and family policy

As a result of both improvements in life expectancy and the impact of the one child family policy, the Chinese population has been ageing rapidly. In the early 1980s huge cohorts of elderly began entering retirement and became eligible for pensions at the same time that their needs for healthcare began to increase. The state and collective sectors of the economy have been hardpressed to meet their obligations to these retirees. The legislation described above makes very clear the state's position on filial piety, i.e., that it means family members bear the responsibility of providing support and care to the elderly. Filial piety does not mean subordination to the elderly nor does it mean producing a son to carry on the family name. (In fact the marriage law explicitly states that children may take the mother's or the father's surname.) To reinforce family responsibility the state initially limited access to certain kinds of welfare benefits and to state-run homes for the aged to the childless elderly. Only as these homes ran into financial problems did the state open them up – for a price – to elderly with children.

A note on filial piety in other Chinese communities

The People's Republic of China is unusual in its sustained but carefully delimited attack on filial piety. Other Chinese communities, such as Hong Kong and Taiwan, have never had to deal with such a direct campaign to eradicate traditional values. As a British colony until 1997, Hong Kong was left relatively free to maintain or change its customary practices so long as they did not interfere with trade or threaten the British administration. The British were happy to support the notion that the family was the best setting for Chinese elderly and used it to justify the policy of "care in the community" while long failing to develop support services for these caring families. The situation in Taiwan is more complex. For decades the Nationalist government presented itself as the defender of Confucian values including filial piety. Yet during these same decades Taiwan experienced high rates of internal and international migration, industrialization, and the spread of literacy, that according to some theorists should have threatened the circumstances of the elderly. Finally there is Singapore which, under Lee Kuan Yew, not only retained an emphasis on Confucianism but attempted to de-ethnicize it by claiming universal applicability. Despite these very different attitudes towards Confucianism in all of the sites under discussion, including China, a similar pattern is seen. With each passing decade a smaller proportion of the elderly lives in extended families, co-residence continues to be primarily with a son, and daughters are increasingly involved in offering various kinds of support.

CONCLUSION

Although filial piety remains an integral part of cultural identity today in East Asia, the actual practice varies from one nation to another, to a greater or lesser degree. Given the enormous social and legal changes discussed, the future of filial piety as a social practice remains somewhat uncertain in both Japan and China. The practice is also subject to global pressures today, and will likely be influenced by the global discourse of individual rights and autonomy, making for a possible gradual trend towards individualizing families in the future.

FURTHER READING

Hashimoto, Akiko (1996). *The gift of generations: Japanese and American perspectives on aging and the social contract.* Cambridge: Cambridge University Press.

Ikels, Charlotte, ed. (2004). *Filial piety: practice and discourse in contemporary East Asia.* Stanford: Stanford University Press.

Slote, Walter S., and George A. De Vos, eds. (1998). *Confucianism and the family.* Albany: State University of New York Press.

REFERENCES

Chan, Anita, Madsen, Richard, and Jonathan Unger (1992). *Chen village under Mao and Deng*, 2nd edn. Berkeley: University of California Press.

Chow, Tse-tsung (1967). *The May Fourth Movement: intellectual revolution in modern China.* Stanford: Stanford University Press.

Cohen, Myron (1976). *House united, house divided: the Chinese family in Taiwan.* New York: Columbia University Press.

Hashimoto, Akiko (1996). *The gift of generations: Japanese and American perspectives on aging and the social contract.* Cambridge: Cambridge University Press.

(1997). "Designing family values: cultural assumptions of an aging society," *Japan Quarterly*, 44 (4): 59–65.

Ikels, Charlotte (1996). *The return of the god of wealth: the transition to a market economy in urban China.* Stanford: Stanford University Press.

Miura, Fumio, ed. (2001). *Zusetsu kōreisha hakusho [Illustrated age and ageing White Paper].* Tokyo: Zenkoku Shakai Fukushi Kyōgikai.

Miyagawa, Mitsuru (1973). "Kindai izen no kazoku: Chūsei [The premodern family: the medieval period]." In Michio Aoyama *et al.*, eds., *Kōza kazoku: Kazoku no rekishi [Lectures on the family: the history of the family].* Tokyo: Kōbundō, pp. 46–75.

Naoi, Michiko (1993). *Kōreisha to kazoku: Atarashii tsunagari o motomete [Aging and the family: the search for new relationships.]* Tokyo: Saiensusha.

Sekiguchi, Yūko, Fukutō, Sanae, Nagashima, Atsuko, Hayakawa, Noriyo, and Fumie Asano (2000). *Kazoku to kekkon no rekishi [The history of family and marriage].* Tokyo: Shinwasha.

CHAPTER 5.6

Generational Memory and Family Relationships

CLAUDINE ATTIAS-DONFUT AND FRANÇOIS-CHARLES WOLFF

INTRODUCTION

The elderly are laden with an individual, family and social memory, which they pass on to the younger generations. This process is evident and accepted as universal common sense. Family intergenerational interactions play a fundamental role in psychosocial identity development and continuity in the socialisation of family members (see Bengtson and Black, 1973). In this chapter, we will examine to what extent intergenerational exchanges also contribute to the shaping of the memory of historical events and social changes that have marked each family generation, i.e. their social-historical consciousness. As stated by the pioneering works of Maurice Halbwachs on collective memory, an individual's memory is made up of interactions between the numerous collective memories of the groups to which he or she belongs (Halbwachs, 1997). We assume that individual perception of one's generational history lies at the intersection of family memory and historical peer group memory.

According to Mannheim (1952), the emergence of a new generation is produced by major events and social changes experienced during the formative years of the individuals involved. In the literature on generations produced since Mannheim's essay, and until recently, it has been commonplace to identify a generation with a founding political event that it experienced during its youth, such as the generation of 1914 (Wohl, 1979) or the ''68 generation' (Hamon and Rottman, 1984). Whatever the controversy about which time interval specifies the formative years (see Becker, 1992; Schuman and

Scott, 1989), it is now well established that the marks imprinted during the early stages of life are deep and lasting. However, the possibility of ongoing influences of historical events throughout a life must not be excluded (Attias-Donfut, 1988).

An individual's feeling of belonging to a generation, namely their generation identity and consciousness, is expressed in many ways. Mannheim (1952) pointed out the influence of historical time – in social movements and the political domain – through the 'entelechy' of a generation, its viewpoints ('Weltanschauung'), and the actions or political involvement of its members. Inglehart (1977) defined generations through the values 'materialistic' and 'post-materialistic', depending on the kind of socialisation of the individuals involved and on their level of need. Recent works have stressed how economic changes produce distinct generations in respect to their relationship to work and the welfare state (see Kohli, 1999; Becker, 2000; Attias-Donfut and Wolff, 2000).

We will not deal with the effects of social and economic changes on the lifecourse of successive birth cohorts in this chapter, nor on their values and socialisation, but we will focus on their specific memory of what are perceived as marking events. This type of memory belongs to what we call 'generational memory', even if it is only one of its aspects.[1] Our purpose is to investigate the interplay between

---

[1] Generational memory is not restricted to major events. It also includes all kinds of detailed recollection of one's lifetime, such as music, fashion, TV or movie stars, sport games and other minor things occurring during youth. It also includes

intergenerational relations, personal lives and generational memories among family generations. The underlying idea is to capture some of the processes of transmission and continuity of 'living history', i.e. experienced and embodied history, through social and family interactions. Specifically, we intend to examine the following three issues.

First, we will explore results from a cross-sectional data set at a macro social level. Considering French society, we will empirically differentiate successive family generations and cohorts with their respective memories. Also, we will briefly refer to comparable analyses done in other countries in order to point out the determinant effect of societal and historical context on each generation's memories.

Second, we will explore at a micro-social level intra-generational variations and, more specifically, the gender differences in the perception of history and social changes and the impact of personal life events on this perception. We assume that memories are gendered. Men and women do not have the same perceptions of the marking history of their generation, whether relating to the same events or emphasising different events. We will also examine the influence of variables such as education, social mobility, and urban or rural settings on an individual's selection of marking events.

Third, we will focus on family intergenerational relations and their effect on each generation's memory. Influences between generations are mutual, which means that they can be either downward, upward or both directions. These influences impact directly the time interval of generation memory since they can lead to identification with a parent's or child's cohort time. Within the family, life histories of successive generations are interpenetrated, as shown by Hagestad (1986). This interpenetration also influences generational consciousness and results in an overlapping of generational memories. This phenomenon argues in favour of taking into account every stage of life, even if youth is the most significant, as shown by Schuman and Scott

(1989). They concluded from their empirical study that political events or major changes that have been experienced by the age 20 or before are especially important in the structuring of generational imprinting.

Unlike the dominant trend in generation studies, we are also interested in detecting marks from historical experiences that occur throughout life. We will observe how far generational memory runs beyond the limits of adolescence and early adulthood. We will also examine under which circumstances adulthood and even old age are susceptible to being affected by important and marking events.

The remainder of this chapter is organised as follows. We will begin by describing the French data on which our analyses are grounded and discuss the operationality of the concept of generation defined through the sampling method of the survey. When analysing the results, we will first compare the three generations as they are empirically defined by the main marking events. We will also look at their gender differences. Then, we will explore intragenerational differences according to personal life events and different variables. Finally, we will examine the possible interactions between generational memory and intergenerational relations.

THE TRIGENERATIONAL QUANTITATIVE AND QUALITATIVE SURVEYS

Our empirical analysis is grounded in two trigenerational studies, one quantitative and the other qualitative, conducted in France in 1992 and 1996 respectively, which deal with the various forms of intergenerational solidarity.

The first survey was focused on families comprised of at least three adult generations, anchored in the middle generation, subsequently referred to as the 'pivots' (G2), aged 49 to 53. Their parents (G1) and their adult children (G3) were also interviewed.[2] It

---

unconscious memory or involuntary memory, in the meaning given by Proust (1954). In a previous work (Attias-Donfut, 1988), the notion of generation was defined as a social construct, part of the social imagery and having a function of organising 'social time' in Durkheim's sense of time shared by a group (Durkheim, 1915).

[2] A random sample of people aged 49 to 53 years was drawn from the population census in France. A preliminary telephone survey of 10,000 individuals belonging to this cohort aimed at identifying those who had at least one adult child and one living parent in order to constitute the final sample. It revealed that 67 per cent had at least one living parent and 60 per cent were members of a three-adult-generation family. Respondents provided the addresses of one of their parents and one of their adult children, who were then interviewed.

was a national study involving all the territories of France on a final sample of approximately 5,000 people belonging to 2,000 families composed of three adult generations, not necessarily living in the same household. Each questionnaire lasted about an hour and a half. The second study, a qualitative one, was carried out on a subsample of thirty trigenerational families, ninety people having been interviewed, by way of deep semi-directed interviews lasting about two and a half hours.

The same question was posed in both surveys: *'What are the historical events or social changes which have marked your generation?'* The questionnaires gave each respondent the possibility of naming three different events. This question refers to one's perceptions of lived history and one's identification to generational memory. It can be a matter of either historical events unrelated to private life or historical events impacting directly on one's private life. In order to distinguish between the two possibilities, another question was posed in the quantitative survey: *'Have you been personally affected by historical events during your life?'*, and if so, *'Which events?'*, again with the possibility of naming three different events. Importantly, the sample has a feature that is crucial to the theoretical import and objectives of the research, namely a method for delimiting and defining the observed generations, which makes it possible to operationalise the notion of generation in its various meanings.

At the crossroads of cohorts and family generations

Individuals each have several, simultaneous generational identities: in reference to their position in the family, to their relationship to work and to the welfare state, and to their historical situation. These affiliations make up a significant whole that has to be considered in all of its dimensions when examining intergenerational relations. This was made possible by the procedure used in this survey to isolate the three generations. By starting with the middle generation, selected from a cohort with a limited age variation, two other generations, the parents and the

In the end, about 5,000 individuals were interviewed. For further details on the two data sources, see Attias-Donfut (1995) and Attias-Donfut *et al.* (2002).

children, were defined within a relatively restricted age range. The pivots' parents, making up the older generation, are an average age of 77 and over 60% of them were 72 to 82. The younger respondents were even more strongly concentrated within an age span: 80% were 19 to 29. Of their children, i.e. the pivots' grandchildren, 80% were under 6 years of age.

Each of these three generations has specific, identifiable historical experiences, clearly differentiated from one generation to the next. They form three distinct cohorts in the meaning given by Ryder (1965: 845, quoted by Schuman and Scott, 1989: 359) of 'individuals having experienced the same event within the same interval of time'. The combination of the birth-reference cohort and the filiations proceeding from this cohort makes it possible to isolate within the population three generations that can be simultaneously defined, each in their position to the other two, in terms of the family, the socio-historical context and also the public-solidarity point of reference. On the basis of this construction, generational processes may therefore be studied in several interrelated dimensions, and particularly in an analysis of social and historical change interacting with family relations. We apply in this chapter the word 'generation' to both meanings, cohorts and family generation, thus enriching the symbolic import of the notion.

TRAVERSING THE THREE GENERATIONS

The contrasts between the respective experiences of the three generations are striking: G1 went through wars and economic crises, G2 benefited from the era of affluence, and G3 is coping with uncertainty while entering adult life. We examine the imprinting perceived by each of the three generations based mainly on the analysis of the quantitative survey, with a few references to the qualitative survey.

G1, the war and reconstruction generation

The history of the elderly (G1) coincides with the greater part of the century. Born during the First World War, they had their children during the Second World War and, less than two decades later, their sons were sent to the Algerian War. Wars are a part of

TABLE 1. The distribution of main historical events by generation and gender

Generation	G1			G2			G3		
	All	Men	Women	All	Men	Women	All	Men	Women
Event									
World War I	7.3	7.4	7.2	0.1	0.1	0.1	0.1	0.1	0.1
World War II	33.4	35.0	32.8	2.6	2.7	2.5	0.3	0.2	0.4
Algerian War	5.6	6.1	5.5	13.5	16.8	10.7	0.3	0.2	0.4
1968 Movement	2.1	2.1	2.0	15.9	17.8	14.4	2.6	2.9	2.3
Election of Mitterand	0.9	1.2	0.8	4.4	5.6	3.4	4.9	5.5	4.4
End of Communism	0.7	1.2	0.5	3.6	4.3	3.0	8.4	10.4	6.7
German reunification	0.4	0.3	0.5	3.0	2.9	3.2	10.1	10.1	10.0
Gulf War	0.5	0.5	0.5	3.5	3.1	3.8	9.3	9.0	9.5
Construction of Europe	0.6	0.9	0.5	1.6	2.3	0.9	5.4	5.2	5.5
Technological progress	5.2	5.0	5.3	3.0	2.5	3.4	2.9	2.9	2.9
Development of social security	6.1	6.4	6.0	1.8	1.4	2.2	0.5	0.5	0.5
Unemployment, poverty	4.2	3.9	4.1	8.2	8.1	8.4	11.6	11.1	11.9
Advancement of women	3.9	1.5	4.7	9.0	4.1	13.2	4.0	1.7	6.0
Evolution of social mores	3.6	4.1	3.4	3.3	2.4	4.1	2.7	3.3	2.3
Societal problems	2.0	1.2	2.3	3.2	2.7	3.6	4.9	4.1	5.5
AIDS	1.9	1.2	2.1	3.3	2.4	4.1	12.8	10.9	14.5
Ecological and nuclear dangers	0.4	0.5	0.4	0.9	0.8	1.0	1.8	1.9	1.8

Source: Survey, Cnav, 1992, 'Trois générations'.

all of their memories and represent the main marking events, as related by Edith, a retired farmer, 82 years old:

It was in 1915 when my father died. I remember the end of the war. I was in the garden with my mother and I saw my mother crying. I asked her 'Why are you crying?' She says 'Listen to the bells. The war is over, the Dads are coming home.' You know, this gives you a shock, too. I remember during the war a boy named Maurice, in the farm next ours. He was 2 years older than me. His father went to war, then he died too. One day, when I had the mumps with my sister, my mother wore her Sunday suit; I asked her 'Mam, it is not Sunday. Why do you go out today?' She said, 'listen my little girl, you know the little Maurice, his father is dead, like yours, and his mother has just died from the flu.' I can tell you that the following night I could not sleep: if I would lose Mother it would be so awful. I saw my grandmother and grandfather, they were unable to stand upright ... Three years after my marriage, my husband went to war. He was lucky, he was not made captive . . . but he nearly got taken . . . Twenty years later my son went to Algeria. Then I said: It's too much! I was so frightened! It's not possible! I can tell you 'The wars, don't tell me anything about! For those who suffered them, this marks for life.'

The Second World War is by far the most striking event, mentioned by three out of four respondents, whether in first, second or third position.[3] The First World War is mentioned by 15.4% and the Algerian War by 12%. Later events, like May '68 (4%), are more rarely considered as a generation marker (see Table 1 and Figure 1). Among the three choices, an important minority also refers to recent changes and events in which they recognise the time of their generation, although war has a crushing weight. These social changes include technological progress (30%), the improving of women's rights (10% of women and 3% of men), new lifestyles (sexual freedom, divorce) and AIDS (4%).

Among those who answered positively to the second question dealing with the events that directly affected their personal life, more than 90% of the respondents named the Second World War, 23% the First World War, 7% the Algerian War, and less than

---

[3] These percentages are calculated on the number of respondents, so that the proportions are much higher than in Table 1, where percentages are calculated on the total number of answers.

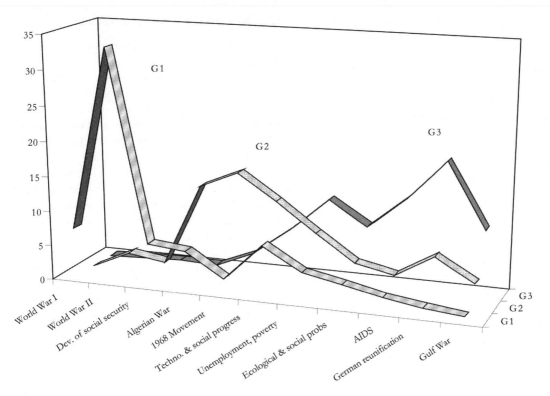

Figure 1. Generations and historical events.
Source: Survey, Cnav, 1992, 'Trois générations'.

3% the 1968 Movement. Though a small minority give the latter events, they are a sign of generation interdependency. For instance, one respondent explains that his daughter was in jail during the "68 student movement". Those whose sons went to Algeria as soldiers during the war were directly affected by this conflict. There is a correlation between the answers of the elderly and their children. When children (G2) say that they were affected by the Algerian War, their parents (G1) mention this war three times more often than other members of their generation.

Differences according to gender do not appear so clearly in the statistical data, although the qualitative interviews show that men and women do not have the same approach to the same event. Among the elderly, men and women on the whole quote the events in comparable proportions with two exceptions, the improvement in the conditions for women quoted more often by women and the Second World War cited slightly more by men. Qualitative interviews reveal that the experience of the same events is dissimilar. Women relate to life during the war while men more often focus on the political and military aspects of the war in a quite traditional division of gender territories. War memories are family memory as well, when family relations are foremost, as in the story related by Edith above. Family bonds form the social framework of women's memories, built around the notion of family, as analysed by Halbwachs (1997).

G2, the affluent generation

Born during the war of 1939–45, the 'pivots' share with their parents the memory of this historical period, though many do not have precise memories of it. They are mainly identified with two events, the 1968 Movement and the Algerian War. The former seems of greater importance though they were a little older than the leading initiators and actors of this movement (they were 25 to 29 years old). Pivots express a strong and quite coherent generation consciousness, feeling that they have personally participated in the strong social and cultural changes which characterise the '68 Movement, such as the new patterns in couple relations and in styles of childhood education. G2 members have experienced a dramatic rise in the level of education, full employment, and consumption. They have benefited from favourable conditions of access to ownership, but they now have to cope at the end of their careers with a reversal in economic trends, encountering employment difficulties and, at least for some of them, unemployment.

The mention of their history by men and women has a different tonality. While in the previous generation women inscribed their history in specifically female territories, their daughters, on the contrary, challenge the traditional gender division, whether they express feminist involvement or not. Men and women are not equally affected by great events. This is obvious in the case of wars, which are more frequently mentioned by men than by women. The Algerian War is evoked by 41% of men and 27% of women, the '68 Movement by 43% of men and 34% of women. More recent events are evoked, such as the fall of the Berlin wall and the collapse of Communist societies (by 17% of men and 15% of women).

In this generation, and more often than their mothers, we observe that women emphasise the improving female condition (25% compared to 10% of their mothers). In their generation, only 9% of the men name the improving female conditions as a marking event. There is a huge difference between men and women regarding the importance given to the changes in the conditions for women. For women of this generation, these changes come in second position, just after the Movement of '68 and before the Algerian War. For men, the women's movement comes in sixth position, just after German reunification.

Concerning what has affected private life, there are also important differences between men and women. For instance, the Algerian War is named by 44% of men and 12% of women, the '68 Movement is quoted by 16% of men and 10% of women. Despite the importance of these two major events (Algeria and '68), many other social, political or cultural facts having occurred at different periods of their lives are mentioned. This is a sign that generational memory does not stop at the border of youth, but rather goes on and accumulates its marks with the passing of time.

G3, the disenchanted generation

The youngest generation, born between 1960 and the beginning of 1970, has grown up in an affluent society, has been brought up according to liberal patterns of education and has a higher level of education than the previous generations. However, confronted with workplace difficulties (see Baudelot and Establet, 2000), young adults are disappointed. Much more than their parents and grandparents, they express a kind of disillusion. Two scourges have affected their generation, namely unemployment and AIDS. Unlike the previous generations, they do not centre their generation identity on one or two major events, but they refer instead to a set of phenomena that they are currently experiencing.

The main political event mentioned is the fall of the Berlin wall and a related one, the end of the Communist regime. Besides these two linked major historical changes, men and women mainly mention societal problems. Their view of their world seems particularly gloomy, since they evoke drugs, pollution, the nuclear threat, and famines in the Third World.

Among the young, more importance is still given to the women's movement by women than by men, but the gender differences are less marked. There is still more emphasis given by women to issue such as AIDS and societal problems, while men put more emphasis on the fall of Communism. The vision of the world by the two genders in this generation is more similar than in the two previous generations.

Some comparison with other countries

The notion that major events have a deep and lasting effect on collective memory has been supported by other studies, such as the ones carried out in the Netherlands (Becker, 1992) and in the US (Schuman and Scott, 1989). The characteristics of generations in terms of culture seem to follow the same basic trends in Western countries and particularly in Western Europe. Major political and economic events such as the great 1929 depression, the Second World War, the glorious postwar economic growth or the sixties youth protest were common to Western societies. This globalisation of political and economic changes results somehow in comparable ways of shaping memories in the societies involved. The 'four-generation model' proposed by

Becker (1992) – i.e. pre-war, silent, protest and lost generations – largely overlaps the three-generation figures found in the French survey except for a difference due to methodology. We only consider families with three generations and not the whole range of birth cohorts, as in Becker's analysis. The 'silent generation', born between 1930 and 1940, is not part of our sample.

Within this global framework, there are national differences due to specific historical evolutions. This is obvious in contemporary Germany where East and West are still two different societies in terms of collective memory, as shown by Martin Kohli in his 1996 survey.[4] Concerning the question on historical events or changes that have marked one's life, the change in 1989/90 is affirmed by almost all East Germans aged 40–54, and close to half of those aged 70–85, while in the West among the 40- to 54-year-olds it is somewhat more than half, and among the 70- to 85-year-olds, only 5 per cent. The events of '1968' have been important only for the 40- to 54-year-olds, but again in very unequal shares: 9 per cent for Westerners, 1 per cent for Easterners (Kohli, 2003). German reunification, a major event thoroughly impacting their personal lives, has replaced the dominant position of the previous major event experienced in their youth. Germans are different in terms of collective memory from the French generations of the same age, for the elderly and the middle generation (G1 and G2) in our survey. In France, the Second World War is much more salient for the younger generation than the older.

INTRAGENERATIONAL DIFFERENCES

The memory of historical events differs according to the characteristics of the respondents. We consider first some of the main social stratification variables, urban versus rural, level of education, and social mobility, and then we turn to the influence of personal life experience on the perception of historical events.

Urban versus rural area of residency

Among the youngest generation, the fall of the Iron Curtain is more important for people living

[4] We thank Martin Kohli for having kindly sent us information from his own work on this topic.

in urban areas than for those living in rural areas. For the former, the three most important events are 'AIDS', 'unemployment and poverty' and the 'fall of the Iron Curtain'. In rural areas, the three most important events are 'AIDS', the 'Gulf War' and 'unemployment and poverty'.

In the middle generation, the advancement of women is more often cited by people living in urban areas than by those living in rural areas. Among the eldest generation, there are no differences between people living in urban and rural areas regarding the first two events cited, i.e. the Second World War and the First World War. These events are so massive that they pervade all parts of society. In third position, improvement in social security is cited by countryfolk and the 1936 movement (Front Populaire) by citydwellers.

Level of Education

Among the youngest generation, the most educated level is the only group to cite the fall of Communism in the first position. The two middle levels of education cite German reunification in second position, while the two lowest levels do not cite these two events in the first three positions. Indeed, for the less educated young adults, the fall of the Iron Curtain is ranked fourth. The results are rather different when merging the fall of the Iron Curtain and the end of Communism. In that case, the ranking of this subgroup is one for all the educational levels, with the exception of the second lowest (for whom the rank is 2, after AIDS).

Among the middle generation, the two most important events, the Algerian War and the Movement of 1968, whether in first or second position, are cited by all levels of education. The lowest level cites the Algerian War in first position, while all of the others cite the Movement of 1968 in first position. Differences according to the level of education occur at the third position, where the most educated individuals cite the improvement in the conditions for women while the least educated cite the economic crisis with unemployment and poverty and place in fourth position the improvement of women.

Among the eldest generation, the event cited in third position varies according to the level of

TABLE 2. The influence of individual characteristics on memory of historical events

			Most quoted events		
			Rank 1	Rank 2	Rank 3
G3	Location	Rural	AIDS	Gulf War	Unemployment, poverty
		Urban	AIDS	Unemployment, poverty	German reunification
	Education	Bepc or less	AIDS	Unemployment, poverty	Gulf War
		Cap, Bep	AIDS	Gulf War	Unemployment, poverty
		Baccalaureate	AIDS	German reunification	Unemployment, poverty
		Graduate	AIDS	German reunification	Unemployment, poverty
		Postgraduate	End of Communism	Unemployment, poverty	AIDS
	Subjective social mobility	Ascending	AIDS	Unemployment, poverty	German reunification
		Descending	AIDS	Unemployment, poverty	Gulf War
		Unchanged	AIDS	Unemployment, poverty	German reunification
		Unknown	AIDS	Unemployment, poverty	German reunification
G2	Location	Rural	1968 Movement	Algerian War	Unemployment, poverty
		Urban	1968 Movement	Algerian War	Advancement of women
	Education	Bepc or less	Algerian War	1968 Movement	Unemployment, poverty
		Cap, Bep	1968 Movement	Algerian War	Advancement of women
		Baccalaureate	1968 Movement	Algerian War	Advancement of women
		Graduate	1968 Movement	Algerian War	Advancement of women
		Postgraduate	1968 Movement	Algerian War	Advancement of women
	Subjective social mobility	Ascending	1968 Movement	Algerian War	Advancement of women
		Descending	1968 Movement	Algerian War	Unemployment, poverty
		Unchanged	1968 Movement	Algerian War	Advancement of women
		Unknown	1968 Movement	Algerian War	Advancement of women
	Personal events	Yes	Algerian War	1968 Movement	Advancement of women
		No	1968 Movement	Algerian War	Advancement of women
G1	Location	Rural	World War II	World War I	Dev. of social security
		Urban	World War II	World War I	1936 movement
	Education	No education	World War II	World War I	Algerian War
		Cep	World War II	World War I	Dev. of social security
		Bepc, Cap, Bep	World War II	1936 movement	World War I
		Bac or more	World War II	World War I	Advancement of women
	Subjective social mobility	Ascending	World War II	Dev. of social security	World War I
		Descending	World War II	World War I	Unemployment, poverty
		Unchanged	World War II	World War I	Technological progress
		Unknown	World War II	World War I	Algerian War
	Personal events	Yes	World War II	World War I	Dev. of social security
		No	World War II	Technological progress	Dev. of social security

Source: Survey, Cnav, 1992, 'Trois générations'.

education. The most educated cite the advancement of women, while the introduction of social security is mentioned both by those having the lowest level or a middle level. The Movement of 1968 comes in fourth position among the most educated, in ninth among the following level and only fifteenth among the least educated. Even though they are the parents of the main actors in the movement, some of the oldest generation members among the most educated

identify and feel involved with these social and cultural events.

Social mobility

For the different generations, subjective social mobility influences the perception of historical events. In particular, those who feel that their social position is in decline compared to their parents are more likely to point to social problems as the marking events of their generation. This is clearly observed both for the pivot and elderly generations, where unemployment and poverty is more often cited by people in descending mobility. At first sight, there is no difference among young adults since unemployment and poverty is the second reported event regardless of the social position. However, when aggregating the different events, those who feel that their social position is in decline compared to their parents are more likely to point to social problems as the marking events of their generation. The development of social security is most often cited by those who feel that they have achieved a better social position with respect to their parents.

The influences of personal life on the historical consciousness of generations

In the qualitative survey, all the interviewees seemed personally involved in their answers to this question, and associated their own personal history with the social history. Speaking about one's generation is also, to a certain extent, speaking about oneself.

The pertinence of linking history and lives has been well established (Elder *et al.*, 1991). There is a close bond between personal life and historical events memory, as empirically shown by Schuman and Scott (1989). The analysis of our data set shows a very strong correlation between the two questions, the one related to the events in which people were directly concerned in their own life, the other concerning the perception of the historical events or changes that have marked their generation. Among the elderly, those whose lives were personally affected by the First World War more often cite the war as the marking event of their generation (22% versus 7.3%). In the same generation, 29% of those personally touched by the Algerian War cite it as the marking event of their generation (instead of 5.6% for the whole generation). Interestingly, we note that within the same generation events separated by 50 years are seen as the most important marking event of their generation.[5]

[5] Among G1, the average age of those quoting the First World War is 83.2, while it is 77.8 years old for the Second World War, and the average age is very close for those quoting the Algerian War (78.3).

In the middle generation, those personally affected by the Second World War cite it three times more often than the average as the most important marking event of their generation (their responses on that event represent 8.5% versus 2.6%). There are also big differences regarding those personally concerned by the Algerian War (22.6% versus 13.5%) and the Movement of 1968 (20.3% versus 15.9%).

Among the young, those who experienced in their youth difficulties resulting from political troubles or wars (which could be the Algerian War or other aspects of decolonisation, or as children of immigrants fleeing other countries) are more sensitive to the political events of their time between 1980 and 1992 than others.

TRANSMISSION BETWEEN GENERATIONS

Each generation is sensitive to the lifetime of their parents and the lifetime of their children. Sometimes they identify their own generation with the lifetime they share with their parents or the lifetime they share with their children. The intensity of this identification depends on the level and quality of communication with either generation. The great majority of families do communicate on these questions. Among G1, 73% of respondents speak about the events which have marked their generation with their children and 53% with their grandchildren. Among G2, 84% speak about their own marking events with their children and 56.5% with their parents. And among the young (G3), 84% speak with their parents about what have marked their own generation and 40% with their grandparents. The greatest level of reciprocal communication is between the young and their parents. The stories are more often told from one generation to the next. The 'generation stake' described in Bengtson and Kuypers (1971) is at work here. This suggests that close generational relationships correlate to a high level of historical transmission.

This is especially true among the middle generation (see Table 3). Those who report communication with their parents more often cite events belonging to their parents' period as marking events in their lives. The same trend appears concerning their communication with their children. They more often quote historical events having occurred after 1980. They also much more often cite current social

TABLE 3. Historical events and transmission between generations

Distribution		Historical 1914–1945	Historical 1946–1979	Historical 1980–1992	Societal progress	Societal problems	Other
				G1			
G1 talk to G2	No	47.7	8.7	2.3	27.9	7.0	6.4
	Yes	47.7	9.4	4.0	27.8	9.9	1.2
				G2			
G2 talk to G1	No	4.0	35.2	16.8	24.7	15.8	3.5
	Yes	5.0	33.1	16.8	27.0	17.2	0.9
G1 talk to G2	No	3.4	36.8	15.7	27.7	14.4	2.2
	Yes	4.7	33.9	16.8	26.0	16.8	1.8
G2 talk to G3	No	4.4	43.6	13.6	20.3	9.2	8.9
	Yes	4.6	32.5	17.3	27.0	17.8	0.9
G3 talk to G2	No	4.3	31.0	19.2	26.1	16.5	2.9
	Yes	4.6	35.2	15.6	25.8	16.0	2.8
G1	Historical 1914–1945	4.7	40.3	15.9	23.9	13.2	2.0
	Historical 1946–1979	2.9	33.0	15.0	26.7	20.5	1.8
	Historical 1980–1992	3.6	37.3	19.1	18.2	20.0	1.8
	Societal progress	4.2	29.3	17.6	30.7	16.4	1.8
	Societal problems	1.9	23.6	16.0	31.2	26.6	0.8
				G3			
G3 talk to G2	No	4.3	5.1	34.6	19.6	26.9	9.6
	Yes	3.9	3.5	42.1	15.3	34.7	0.5
G2 talk to G3	No	3.4	3.4	40.6	15.1	33.1	4.4
	Yes	4.1	3.9	40.8	15.7	33.1	2.5
G2	Historical 1914–1945	3.2	2.7	42.2	17.3	31.9	2.7
	Historical 1946–1979	4.0	3.9	45.6	15.3	28.4	2.9
	Historical 1980–1992	4.4	2.9	41.0	15.2	32.8	3.7
	Societal progress	3.5	4.8	36.6	16.0	37.3	1.8
	Societal problems	3.7	3.1	37.2	16.2	37.5	2.3

Source: Survey, Cnav, 1992, 'Trois générations'.

problems such as AIDS or unemployment. This pivot generation has been especially marked by the Movement of 1968 and it seems that those who were most involved in the movement discuss it less often with their parents (14.9% versus 17.4%).[6] This is the sign of the leftover social rupture and generational conflict of that era. Those who identify with the sixties are more distant from their parents and closer to their children. This is confirmed by the following additional result. On average, 58.8% of the pivots feel closer to the generation of their children than to that of their parents, compared to 60.9% among those who cite May '68.

Direct transmission also exists between the two extreme generations, though to a lesser extent than between successive generations. The qualitative survey reveals that, while the elderly fear boring their grandchildren by telling them 'old things', the young are interested in the history of their grandparents, and are even longing for it. A young woman, speaking about her grandparents said that they are 'historiens à demeure' [permanent historians at home].

[6] The proportion of respondents from the pivot generation discussing with their parents on the marking historical events is 59.7%, and it decreases to 55.6% for those quoting May 1968.

CONCLUSION

Collective memory is subject to personal interpretations by the individuals involved. Our analysis show that these interpretations are influenced by their social and familial positions. As we know, generations are gendered. According to our data, this holds true with respect to collective memory as well. Changes in gender relations also result in changes in collective memory of both genders, as we observed by comparing successive generations. Therefore, when distinguishing between different historical generations, one should also take into account gender differences.

Historical generations are also shaped by family generations and by intergenerational relations. A French nineteenth-century philosopher, A. Cournot, considered one century as a 'natural' pace of historical change, arguing that it represents three consecutive generations. During the socialisation of the new generation by the preceding one, they both receive influences from the oldest generation still living. According to Cournot (1973: 88–9), the young keep more than they imagine the tracks of the conversation they had with the elderly during their childhood. If we no longer concur with the nineteenth-century notion that there is a regular and 'natural' rhythm of change, our results support the idea of a strong influence of all the living generations on the recollection of history. Today, with a longer life, the influence of the elderly on successive generations is even more evident and is extended to four generations, including the great-grandchildren.

The stories of the successive generations reveal how the historical generations overlap. What has been lived by one's parents can also be part of one's life since it has become part of family memory. For each generation, the historical inheritance from the previous generation is added to the objective current conditions. The infant years, where the impressions are strong and durable, coincide with the youthful years of parents, which is a significant and decisive period in their lifecourse. Within the family, the lifetimes of the generations are not watertight. On the contrary, there are many gateways between them. Each generation has one foot in the history which formed its predecessor and one in its own history and time.

The knowledge of history transmitted through the family has a special tone, as distinct from history learned through the media, books or at school. It is a vivid history, embodied in family members and ancestors. The family circle is a 'memory milieu', which plays a central role in the continuity of History.

FURTHER READING

Halbwachs, M. (1997). *La Mémoire collective*. Paris: Albin Michel (first pub. posthumously 1950).

Mannheim, K. (1952). 'The problem of generations'. In K. Mannheim, *Essays on the sociology of knowledge*. London: Routledge and Kegan Paul, pp. 276–322.

Schuman, H., and J. Scott (1989). 'Generations and collective memories', *American Sociological Review*, 54: 359–81.

REFERENCES

Attias-Donfut C. (1988). *Sociologie des générations. L'Empreinte du temps*. Paris: Puf.

ed. (1995). *Les Solidarités entre générations. Vieillesse, familles, état*. Paris: Nathan.

Attias-Donfut, C., and F. C. Wolff (2000). 'Complementarity between private and public transfers'. In S. Arber and C. Attias-Donfut, eds., *The myth of generational conflict: the family and state in ageing societies*. London: Routledge, pp. 47–68.

Attias-Donfut, C., Lapierre, N., and M. Segalen (2002). *Le Nouvel Esprit de famille*. Paris: Odile Jacob.

Baudelot, C., and R. Establet (2000). *Avoir trente ans en 68 et 98*. Paris: Le Seuil.

Becker, H. A. (1992). 'A pattern of generations and its consequences'. In H. A. Becker, ed., *Dynamics of cohort and generations research*. Amsterdam: Thesis Publishers, pp. 219–48.

(2000). 'Discontinuous change and generational contracts'. In S. Arber and C. Attias-Donfut, eds., *The myth of generational conflict: the family and state in ageing societies*. London: Routledge, pp. 114–32.

Bengtson, V. L., and K. D. Black (1973). 'Intergenerational relations and continuities in socialization'. In P. Baltes and K. W. Schaie, eds., *Life span developmental psychology: personnality and socialization*. New York: Academic Press, pp. 208–34.

Bengtson, V. L., and J. A. Kuypers (1971). 'Generational difference and the developmental stake', *Aging and Human Development*. 2: 249–60.

Cournot, A. A. (1973). *Œuvres complètes*, Vol. I: *Considérations sur la marche des idées et des événements dans le monde moderne*. Paris: Vrin (first pub. 1872).

Durkheim, E. (1915). *Les Formes élémentaires de la vie religieuse*. Paris: Presses Universitaires de France.

Elder, G., Pavalko, E. K., and T. J. Hastings (1991). 'Talent, history and the fulfillment of promise', *Psychiatry*, 54: 251–67.

Hagestad, G. O. (1986). 'Dimension of time and the family', *American Behavioral Scientist*, 29: 679–94.

Halbwachs, M. (1997). *La Mémoire collective*. Paris: Albin Michel (first pub. posthumeously: 1950).

Hamon, H., and R. Rottman (1984). *Génération. Les Années de rêve*. Paris: Seuil.

Inglehart, R. (1977). *The silent revolution. Changing values and political styles among Western publics*. Princeton: Princeton University Press.

Kohli, M. (1999). 'Private and public transfers between generations: linking the family and the state', *European Societies*, 1: 81–104.

(2003). 'Generationen in der Gesellschaft. Forschungsgruppe Altern und Lebenslauf'. Mimeographed. Berlin: Freie Universität Berlin.

Mannheim, K. (1952). 'The problem of generations'. In K. Mannheim, *Essays on the sociology of knowledge*. London: Routledge and Kegan Paul, pp. 276–322.

Proust, M. (1954). *A la recherche du temps perdu*. Paris: Gallimard La Pleiade.

Ryder, N. B. (1965). *'The cohort as a concept in the study of social change'*, *American Sociological Review*, 30: 843–61.

Schuman, H., and J. Scott (1989). 'Generations and collective memories', *American Sociological Review*, 54: 359–81.

Wohl, R. (1979). *The generation of 1914*. Cambridge, Mass.: Harvard University Press.

CHAPTER 5.7

Family Caregivers: Increasing Demands in the Context of 21st-century Globalization?

NEENA L. CHAPPELL AND MARGARET J. PENNING

INTRODUCTION

Traditionally, academic and policy-relevant literature on ageing and health has conceptualized family caregiving in the context of demographic transitions and changes to family structure. It has focused on the implications of these changes for the availability of care and the physical and psychological wellbeing of individual care providers or receivers. Rarely, however, has caregiving been examined in relation to broader social, economic, and political structures and to changes such as globalization of the economy and associated restructuring of systems of national health insurance and healthcare. Yet, it can be argued that the broader economic, political, and social changes currently underway have much to do with how caregiving is practiced and experienced in individual lives. In particular, these changes can be viewed as reintroducing a traditional model of care – one that emphasizes private (paid and unpaid) responsibilities for care.

This chapter draws on a political economy framework to examine globalization, healthcare, and familial caregiving. Political economists assert that the economic mode of production (e.g., capitalism) pursued by a given society shapes social conditions and relations within it: "[t]he search for profit influences what is done in and out of markets . . . what is sold and what is paid for, what is commodified and what is not" (Armstrong *et al.*, 2001: viii). The form and character of the mode of production will vary across contexts and change over time. In Canada and elsewhere, there has been a gradual transition over time from competitive to monopoly to global capitalism, a transition brought about by increased competition for ownership of and control over the means of production. This includes healthcare. As noted by Coburn (2001: 48), for example, capitalism's efforts to treat products and services as commodities that can be sold generates considerable pressure to privatize healthcare and pursue profit. The state, through its policies and programs, therefore supports these efforts.

This has implications for class and other inequalities within as well as between countries. A structurally oriented class-based perspective predominates within political economy, based on the view of an inherent division between those who own or control the means of production and those who do not. Nevertheless, there is increasing recognition that class differences are themselves complex and intersect in many ways with gender, race, ethnic, and other factors (Calasanti and Zajicek, 1993; Coburn, 2001; McMullin, 2000). The need to incorporate both paid and unpaid work is also acknowledged: the structuring of economic and political conditions around capitalist goals (e.g., the search for profit) not only has a profound influence on the conditions and relations of work but, also, creates the conditions under which informal and unpaid caring occurs. Thus, "in order to analyse paid work, it is necessary also to analyse unpaid work . . . Neither can be understood without reference to the other . . . And that whole is gendered. It is also divided by class, race, ethnicity" (Armstrong, 2001: 124–5).

Overall, political economy theorizing draws our attention to broader structural forces within society that have an impact on caregivers. In this chapter, we address the relevance of globalization and neo-liberal political discourse and policies for the welfare state in general and for healthcare services (private, public) in particular. We examine how these broader economic and political conditions together inform caregiving and discuss differential implications associated with class, gender, ethnic, and racial inequalities. Doing so reveals similarities of experience across domains and the need to consider interactions among them. Here we suggest that recent trends are likely to further disadvantage women, lower social classes, and ethnic and racial minorities. We conclude that a comprehensive understanding of caregiving requires linking the macro structural level with individual caregiving experiences.

GLOBALIZATION AND HEALTHCARE REFORM

Globalization has been described as the most immediate legacy of transition from the twentieth to the twenty-first century (Therborn, 2000). The growth of transnational networks of investment, finance, advertising and consumption markets, and sophisticated information and communications technologies, are all part of the trend towards globalization of the economy. The global economy is widely considered the solution to every country's economic and financial crises. As reported in Navarro (2002b), for example, a 1998 World Health Organization document argues that countries resisting globalization "will find themselves marginalized in the world community and in the world economy."

In the current context, economic globalization can also be attached to a political agenda (neoliberalism); one in which the structural power and mobility of capital in production and financial markets seek to promote privatization, deregulation, and significant structural changes in national bureaucracies, decreases in welfare programs and public services, as well as liberalization of trade and monetary policies. The latter are designed to support market interests, favoring high income business sectors which will then be able to save and invest, creating benefits that will trickle down from the top to the rest of the population. Navarro (2002a) characterizes the neo-liberal position in terms of four beliefs: public deficits are intrinsically negative; state regulation of the labor market is also intrinsically

negative; social protection guaranteed by the welfare state and its redistributive policies hinders economic growth; and the state should not intervene in regulating foreign trade or international financial markets. Consistent with this perspective, government policy statements during the 1980s frequently endorsed limits to government interference, reframing its role from one of provider to one of partner or facilitator to other sectors (OECD, 1992). Increasingly, the state viewed its role as complementary to and supportive of the private sector, rather than setting limits to it, as typified the welfare state (Meyer, 2000).

Importantly, recent evidence suggests that shifts towards global capitalism are not producing the type of economic prosperity that has been predicted (see Navarro, 2002a). Where such policies have been successful in increasing profit shares and rates, this appears to be largely the result of declines in wages rather than increases in investment. Instead, implementation of the capitalist economic agenda has been accompanied by increased unemployment in all OECD countries and increased salary differentials in most, as well as by a decrease in social expenditures and a transfer of income from labor to capital. Part-time work, home-based work, self-employment, contracting out and temporary work are also increasing, while working-class rights and unions are being undermined (Coburn, 2004). Of note, countries with more re-distributive public policies and high trade union density evidenced lesser wage and income inequalities than countries without such agreements.

It is within the context of the globalization of capitalism that healthcare reform is now taking place. Interestingly, by the early 1990s, governments in most Western industrialized countries were embracing a vision of reform that called for expansion of a welfare model of healthcare. This followed two decades of economic recession together with continually escalating healthcare costs with no stabilization in sight. Governments were ready for a change. The vision that emerged was consistent with cumulative research evidence indicating that universal systems of care that had been established in most industrialized countries of the world (with the United States which lacked such a universal program being the major exception), and that primarily funded physician and acute hospital services, were expensive and, in many ways, inappropriate healthcare systems for their now ageing populations (Segall and Chappell, 2000). It embraced a broad definition of health, de-institutionalization and enhanced community-based care, movement away from fee-for-service payment for physicians, greater participation in healthcare by service users, and evidence-based decision-making (Mhatre and Deber, 1992). A revitalized system, founded on this vision and expanded to recognize multiple determinants and dimensions of health and multiple providers of healthcare, was considered both more appropriate for an ageing society and more cost-effective than systems narrowly focused on physician- and hospital-based medical care.

Prior to the 1990s, informal caregivers had silently adapted themselves to the advantages and constraints of the welfare state in which public policy operated largely in ignorance of informal care despite the fact that informal networks and, especially, family members had always contributed the vast majority of caregiving. While the old vision did not deny the role of families, it did place major emphasis on government responsibility through democratic accountability (Chappell and Prince, 1994). In contrast, the new rhetoric specifically acknowledged the contributions of families and other informal networks, as part of a broader awareness that multiple sectors (including voluntary and private sectors) contribute to health and healthcare and that the state is not and should not be considered the sole provider of care. However, it did not clearly differentiate family care from other aspects of community care. Yet this distinction is crucial. Community care requires that resources be committed to building community infrastructure. De-institutionalization of the ill without enhanced formal community care translates into greater demands on family caregivers at a time when unemployment is increasing and gaps between rich and poor are widening. Blurring the distinction between community care and family care therefore results in governments downsizing medical and hospital care, increasingly shifting the burden of care to families, while claiming to be fulfilling the vision of health reform by de-institutionalizing care.

While the vision that gradually emerged suggests an expanded role for the state in community-based health care, current reforms appear to be following the global economic agenda noted above. The 1990s have seen decreased growth in social spending in developed capitalist countries, a decrease that began in the 1980s. For example, Canadian research points to a decreasing supply of acute and extended care beds, decreases in hospital admissions and lengths of stay, and shifts of surgical treatment to outpatient settings (Brownell et al., 2001; Carrierre et al., 2000). Yet, despite increased budgets, community-based home care services also appear to be declining, with fewer people receiving such services (Penning et al., 2002). The intensity of service has increased, however, with those considered in greater need (as measured by ADL impairment and requiring personal care assistance) receiving services. This suggests a redirection of services away from clients with needs for supportive (social, instrumental) care and, therefore, those who may have the greatest potential for prevention, to those with needs for more intensive medically focused post-acute care (Deber et al., 1998). Home care is providing more medical support and less social care. This is similar to earlier transitions in the United States towards diagnostic-related groups (DRGs) for hospital funding; these were found to result in earlier discharges and increased demand for intensive post-acute care with subsequent restriction of social services and of long-term chronic care available through home care (Estes and Wood, 1986).

The endorsement of short-term post-hospital home care can be seen as a reflection of existing powerful interests within the system. As medicine has shifted its arena from inpatient to outpatient care, medical support within the community is required for this shift to be viable. The call for greater short-term post-hospital home care therefore suggests reinforcement of a narrow medical model of care and lack of support for a broader social model of care. At the same time, the pressure in an era of the globalization of capitalism is towards the commodification and privatization of healthcare services. In Canada, the welfare state is relatively well established. Yet, its universal Medicare system protects only physician and hospital services. As a result, moves to take care outside of hospital settings also open up possibilities that such services will not be covered by universal public health insurance and that, increasingly, care will be provided by private, for-profit corporations that form part of multinationals headquartered outside the country (Williams et al., 2001). Significantly, the proportion of private funding in Canada's healthcare system increased from 23.6 percent in 1975 to 25.4 percent in 1990 and an estimated 30.4 percent in 1999 (Armstrong *et al.*, 2001).

GLOBALIZATION, INEQUALITIES, AND THE PROVISION OF CARE

The economic and political changes associated with globalization (including deregulation, fiscal policies that nurture economic opportunities for higher income sectors, structural changes to welfare state policies and programs in the direction of privatization together with reductions in public and social expenditures) promise major implications for the informal care sector. These include increased demands for the provision of long-term care to older adults, accompanied by reduced access to the resources, both private (e.g. economic, social) and public (e.g. supportive services), that might help facilitate such care. As unemployment, poverty, and inequality increase, population health can be expected to decline and needs for care to increase. If, at the same time, access to public resources for meeting these needs declines, an even greater burden of care is placed on individuals themselves and on their informal networks.

Moreover, research evidence reveals these implications are not uniformly experienced but, rather, vary systematically in conjunction with class, gender, race, and ethnic inequalities. To date, limited attention has been directed towards class differences in informal caregiving. Yet, available findings suggest social class and economic position influence all aspects of care provision, including needs for care to be provided, access to informal and formal resources for securing such care, the settings within which care is made available, the types and levels of care provided, as well as the implications of care provision (Arber and Ginn, 1993; Glaser and Grundy, 2002).

The prevalence of chronic illness and disability consistently emerges as being greater among lower-class groups (Tennstedt and Chang, 1998; Williams *et al.*, 2001). Members tend to encounter long-term illness and disability earlier in life and, as a result, experience more severe problems in later life. Class inequalities in health influence not only the number of surviving kin who may need care and the extent, timing, and duration of the care

involved, but also access to informal care resources. Several researchers report findings indicating that older adults with lower incomes are more likely to be living with adult children or other relatives than those with higher incomes (Tennstedt and Chang, 1998). As well, manual workers appear more likely to provide co-resident care while non-manual workers provide extra-resident care. Arber and Ginn (1993) note that the resources possessed by the middle class enable them to care "at a distance" while working-class people, with fewer available options, are more likely to provide informal care within the household. Research evidence indicating that those with higher socioeconomic status tend to assume a care management role and purchase services but provide lower levels of direct physical care suggests a similar trend (Bengtson, Lawton, and Silverstein, 1994).

Financial resources can be used to adapt or purchase suitable housing, assistive aids and devices, or to pay privately for formal care to be provided. However, middle-class care providers are also reported to have more leverage when it comes to negotiating access to state supportive services or residential care (Arber and Ginn, 1993). Differential access to work-related resources may also come into play. For example, Neal *et al.* (1993) report finding that professionals and managers were more likely to arrive late to, or leave early from, work as a result of family care responsibilities. Similarly, Stone *et al.* (1987) found clerical workers were more likely to have to reduce their work hours to provide elder care and blue-collar workers were most likely to take unpaid time off from work, whereas professionals and managers were more likely to rearrange their work schedules to accommodate care provision.

The implications of gender inequalities also appear to extend from differential needs for care through to differential obligations and resources for providing such care. Needs for long-term care are widely documented as being greater among older women, given their higher levels of chronic illness and disability as well as greater longevity (Chappell *et al.*, 2003). Yet, women not only tend to lack access to social resources required for their own care, but also tend to be called upon to provide care to others. Thus, research findings reveal that a higher proportion of women than men, with long-term health problems, receive no assistance, suggesting that women may be at greater risk of having unmet care needs (Keating *et al.*, 1999). As well, older women tend to be institutionalized at higher rates than men and, like those facing class and economic inequalities, are more likely to be living with adult children or other relatives than are older men when in need of care.

The care of older adults with chronic illness is an important issue for women not only because the recipients of this care are overwhelmingly female, but also because this work remains largely the unpaid and unsupported care of women. While families predominate in the care of older members, within families a gendered division of labor is evident with women representing the primary sources of care (Hooyman and Gonyea, 1995). It has been well established that approximately three-quarters of all caregivers to older adults with long-term illness and disability are female and that most women can expect to provide care to older adults at some point in their lives (Keating *et al.*, 1999). While wives provide care for ailing husbands, adult daughters predominate in the care of older widowed mothers. Whereas men account for approximately three-quarters of seniors cared for by a spouse, from seventy to ninety percent of parents cared for by adult children are widowed women (Sanborn and Bould, 1991). Moreover, other family members rarely share the work of caring. Even when work is shared, the network of neighbors, friends, and extended kin appear to help only sporadically and irregularly.

The type and amount of care provided is also different. Gender is noted to be the single most important predictor of total hours spent providing care (Keating *et al.*, 1999). Women tend to carry responsibility for more intensive and time-consuming forms of care including personal care, meal preparation, laundry, and other household activities while men are more likely to assist with financial matters, heavy chores, yard work, and transportation needs. Men also appear to be more likely to assume an advisory or care management role.

While findings reveal that women who are employed are less likely to be involved in caregiving and provide fewer hours of care than those who are not employed (Penrod *et al.*, 1995), women are reportedly more likely to combine caregiving and employment and, consequently, to experience implications for their employment than are men (Gignac *et al.*, 1996). Women are also more likely to

adjust their work schedules to caregiving activities, draw on vacation time and sick days, and forgo promotions and work-related social activities due to the demands associated with care provision (Neal *et al.*, 1993). Yet, they are disproportionately employed in occupations that offer limited flexibility with respect to such arrangements. Finally, given the magnitude and consistency of gender-differentiated patterns of care, it is perhaps not too surprising that caregiving is widely noted to hold negative implications for individual health, wellbeing, employment, and associated earnings (Keating *et al.*, 1999). In general, researchers report that women engaged in caregiving experience more negative consequences than men engaged in such activities.

The nature and extent of ethnic, racial, and minority group differences in caregiving in later life remain somewhat less clearly articulated than those associated with either class or gender inequalities. As well, debate persists regarding the relative import of structural (racism, class, and economic) inequalities and cultural diversity in accounting for these differences. Contradictory findings are also in evidence, perhaps in part reflecting the number and diversity of ethnic groups studied.

Yet, findings in many ways parallel those reported in relation to class and gender inequalities. For example, research indicates that needs for care and responsibilities for its provision tend to be differentially distributed across groups: poorer health, including higher levels of chronic illness and disability, are widely reported among older adults within ethnic and racial minority groups (Dilworth-Anderson *et al.*, 2002; Tennstedt and Chang, 1998). Although some findings suggest little difference in the prevalence of disability among older Blacks and Whites in the United States, particularly among the oldest-old (Mendes de Leon *et al.*, 1995), most studies indicate higher prevalence among older Black, Puerto Rican, and Mexican American adults than other non-minority groups (Markides and Mindel, 1987). Similarly, in the Canadian context, Wister and Moore (1998) report that whereas two-thirds (66.5 percent) of all aboriginal adults aged 55 and over report disability, this is the case for just over one-third (37.4 percent) of non-aboriginal persons of similar age. As well, while recent immigrants report better health following arrival in Canada than do native-born Canadians, these differences seem to decline over time (Chen, Ng and Wilkins, 1996), suggesting a "healthy immigrant effect" that dissipates with increasing time spent in the country.

The differential prevalence of long-term illness and disability once again carries with it the likelihood of differential responsibilities for care. In Canada, as elsewhere, aboriginal Canadian, visible minority, and immigrant elders are more likely to report co-residential living arrangements and larger households, in part as a result of lower incomes and ineligibility for government transfer payments (Chappell *et al.*, 2003). Illustrating this trend, rates of co-residence are reported to be relatively high among Asian American (Markides and Black, 1996), French Canadian, and Italian elders (Merrill and Dill, 1990; Payne and Strain, 1990).

Ethnic and racial inequalities also emerge with respect to the various resources that facilitate care. For example, Hinrichsen and Ramirez (1992) report the context of caregiving for Blacks and Whites to be quite different; Black elders were poorer, occupied a lower social class position, and were more likely to be unmarried than White elders. As a result, whereas White caregivers were fairly evenly distributed between spouses and adult children, Black caregivers were predominantly adult children and, consequently, the burden of care seemed to be placed disproportionately on middle-aged women who were less likely than their White counterparts to have spousal and financial resources available to them.

Finally, differential access to formal services has also been well documented (Montgomery, 1999). Consequently, formal services are rarely used by caregivers to older ethnic minority group members (see Dilworth-Anderson *et al.*, 2002).

CONCLUSION

In sum, despite rhetoric of a reformed healthcare system throughout industrialized countries during the 1990s that called for an expanded role for the state in a more social model of care, evidence suggests that recent reforms are more compatible with a trend towards global capitalism. Data were drawn primarily from Canada, as a conservative example of this trend, to the extent that it represents a country with a relatively well-established welfare state. Even here, it would appear that class interests and existing

gender and racial/ethnic inequalities are protected and strengthened as health reform is, at least to date, attacking gains made to social programs in the 1970s and 1980s, including long-term care in the community, that most benefit seniors and their caregivers. Arguments that favored broadening the healthcare system to incorporate services more appropriate for an ageing society appear to have been used to effect change that shrinks public involvement in this arena and opens more opportunities to profitization. This is happening at a time of documented increases in inequality and therefore at a time of increased need for publicly provided health services. According to Coburn (2001: 55):

[w]hile markets produce inequalities, these may be prevented (through labour market policies of full employment, retraining programs, etc.) or ameliorated (through social welfare measures or the decommodification of education, health, and welfare). Decommodification meant that access to social resources was not completely determined by market criteria (i.e., income or wealth) or by power in the market . . . Both health, through the effects of the welfare state on the determinants of health, and health care, through various forms of national health-care systems, are tied to the fate of the welfare state.

Economic and political changes that signal the decline of the welfare state and the accompanying recommodification of healthcare and other social programs have major consequences for caregivers and the seniors who rely on their care. Moreover, research evidence suggests that these consequences will be differentially experienced. Changes to trade and monetary policies that generate increases in unemployment and poverty levels can be expected to increase further the health needs of those negatively affected by these changes, thereby increasing demands for healthcare to respond to these needs.

To the extent that the greater needs of those within these populations are accompanied by continued commodification of the social resources for care (including community-based care), the results can easily be predicted and include disproportionate increases in unmet needs, spending down of private economic resources, and intensification of personal and familial responsibilities for care provision. This, in turn, can be expected to generate repercussions for the employment, income, health, and wellbeing of those assuming such responsibilities. Ultimately, therefore, one can expect such trends not only to reinforce, but also to amplify, existing structural inequalities of gender, ethnicity, race, and class.

To understand adequately the experience of caregiving in the lives of individuals and families requires attention be focused on the sources of these inequalities, including their implications with regard to intersecting inequalities of class, gender, race, and ethnicity.

FURTHER READING

Coburn, D. (2001). "Health, health care, and neoliberalism." In P. Armstrong, H. Armstrong, and D. Coburn, eds., *Unhealthy times: political economy perspectives on health and care in Canada*. Don Mills, Ontario: Oxford University Press, pp. 45–65.

Navarro, V. (2002a). "Neoliberalism, 'globalization,' unemployment, inequalities and the welfare state." In V. Navarro, ed., *The political economy of social inequalities: consequences for health and quality of life*. Amityville, N.Y.: Baywood Publishing Company, pp. 33–107.

Williams, A. P., Deber, R., Baranek, P., and A. Gildiner (2001). "From medicare to home care: globalization, state retrenchment, and the profitization of Canada's health-care system." In P. Armstrong, H. Armstrong, and D. Coburn, eds., *Unhealthy times: political economy perspectives on health and health care in Canada*. Don Mills, Ontario: Oxford University Press, pp. 423–545.

REFERENCES

Arber, S., and J. Ginn (1993). "Class, caring and the life course. In S. Arber and M. Evandrou, eds., *Aging, independence and the life course*. London: Jessica Kingsley Publishers, pp. 149–68.

Armstrong, P. (2001). "Evidence-based health-care reform: women's issues." In P. Armstrong, H. Armstrong, and D. Coburn, eds., *Unhealthy times: political economy perspectives on health and health care in Canada*. Don Mills, Ontario: Oxford University Press, pp. 121–45.

Armstrong, P., Armstrong, H., and D. Coburn (2001). "Introduction: the political economy of health and care." In P. Armstrong, H. Armstrong, and D. Coburn, eds., *Unhealthy times: political economy perspectives on health and health care in Canada*. Don Mills, Ontario: Oxford University Press, pp. vii–x.

Bengtson, V., Lawton, L., and M. Silverstein (1994). "Affection, social contact and geographic distance between adult children and their parents," *Journal of Marriage and the Family*, 56 (1): 57–68.

Brownell, M. D., Roos, N. P., and L. L. Roos (2001). "Monitoring health reform: a report card approach," *Social Science and Medicine*, 52: 657–70.

Calasanti, T. M., and A. M. Zajicek (1993). "A socialist-feminist approach to aging: embracing diversity," *Journal of Aging Studies*, 7: 117–31.

Carrierre, K. C., Roos, L. L., and D. C. Dover (2000). "Across time and space: variations in hospital use during Canadian health reform," *HSR: Health Services Research*, 35 (2): 467–87.

Chappell, N. L., and M. J. Prince (1994). *Social support among today's seniors*. Ottawa: Health and Welfare Canada.

Chappell, N. L., Gee, E., McDonald, L., and M. Stones (2003). *Aging in contemporary Canada*. Toronto: Pearson.

Chen, J., Ng, E., and R. Wilkins (1996). "The health of Canada's immigrants in 1994–95," *Health Reports*, 74: 33–45.

Coburn, D. (2001). "Health, health care, and neoliberalism." In P. Armstrong, H. Armstrong, and D. Coburn, eds., *Unhealthy times: political economy perspectives on health and health care in Canada*. Don Mills, Ontario: Oxford University Press, pp. 45–65.

(2004). "Beyond the income inequality hypothesis: globalization, neo-liberalism, and health inequalities," *Social Science and Medicine*, 58: 41–56.

Deber, R., Narine, L., Baranek, P., Sharpe, N., Duvalko, K. K., Zlotnik-Shaul, R., Coyte, P., Pink, G., and A. P. Williams (1998). "The public–private mix in health care." In *Striking a balance, health care systems in Canada and elsewhere*, Vol. IV. Commissioned by the National Forum on Health. Quebec: Editions MultiMondes, pp. 423–545.

Dilworth-Anderson, P., Williams, I., and B. E. Gibson (2002). "Issues of race, ethnicity, and culture in caregiving research: a 20-year review (1980–2000)," *Gerontologist*, 42 (2): 237–72.

Estes, C. L., and J. B. Wood (1986). "The non-profit sector and community-based care for the elderly in the US: a disappearing resource?" *Social Science and Medicine*, 23: 1261–6.

Gignac, M. A. M., Kelloway, E. K., and B. H. Gottlieb (1996). "The impact of caregiving on employment: a mediational model of work–family conflict," *Canadian Journal on Aging*, 15 (4): 525–42.

Glaser, K., and E. Grundy (2002). "Class, caring and disability: evidence from the British Retirement Survey," *Ageing and Society*, 22: 325–42.

Hinrichsen, G. A., and M. Ramirez (1992). "Black and white dementia caregivers: a comparison of their adaptation, adjustment, and service utilization," *Gerontologist*, 32 (3): 375–81.

Hooyman, N., and J. Gonyea (1995). *Feminist perspectives on family care: policies for gender justice*. London: Sage.

Keating, N., Fast, J., Frederick, J., Cranswick, K., and C. Perrier (1999). *Eldercare in Canada: context, content and consequences*. Ottawa: Statistics Canada (catalogue no. 89–570-XPE).

Markides, K., and S. Black (1996). "Race, ethnicity and aging: the impact of inequality." In R. H. Binstock and L. George, eds., *Handbook of aging and the social sciences*. San Diego, Calif.: Academic Press, pp. 153–70.

Markides, K. S., and C. H. Mindel (1987). *Aging and ethnicity*. Newbury Park, Calif.: Sage Publications.

McMullin, J. A. (2000). "Diversity and the state of sociological aging theory," *Gerontologist*, 40 (5): 517–30.

Mendes de Leon, C. F., Fillenbaum, G. G., Williams, C. S., Brock, D. B., Beckett, L. A., and L. F. Berkman (1995). "Functional disability among elderly Blacks and Whites in two diverse areas: the New Haven and North Carolina EPESE," *American Journal of Public Health*, 85: 994–8.

Merrill, D., and A. Dill (1990). "Ethnic differences in older mother – daughter co-residence," *Ethnic Groups*, 8 (3): 201–14.

Meyer, J. W. (2000). "Globalization – sources and effects on national states and societies," *International Sociology*, 15 (2): 233–48.

Mhatre, S. L., and R. B. Deber (1992). "From equal access to health care to equitable access to health: a review of Canadian provincial health commissions and reports," *International Journal of Health Services*, 22 (4): 645–68.

Montgomery, R. J. V. (1999). "The family role in the context of long-term care," *Journal of Aging and Health*, 11 (3): 383–416.

Navarro, V. (2002a). "Neoliberalism, 'globalization', unemployment, inequalities and the welfare state." In V. Navarro, ed., *The political economy of social inequalities: consequences for health and quality of life*. Amityville, N.Y.: Baywood Publishing Company, pp. 33–107.

(2002b). "The political economy of the welfare state in developed capitalist countries." In V. Navarro, ed., *The political economy of social inequalities: consequences for health and quality of life*. Amityville, N.Y.: Baywood Publishing Company, pp. 121–69.

Neal, M. B., Chapman, N. J., Ingersoll-Dayton, B., and A. C. Emlen (1993). "Absenteeism and stress among employed caregivers of the elderly, disabled adults and children." In D. E. Biegel and A. Blum, eds., *Aging and caregiving*. London: Sage.

OECD (1992). *New orientations for social policy*. (Note by the Secretary General.) Paris, France: Directorate for Education, Employment, Labour and Social Affairs.

Payne, B. J., and L. A. Strain (1990). "Family support in later life: ethnic group variations," *Canadian Ethnic Studies*, 22 (2): 99–110.

Penning, M. J., Allan, D. E., Roos, L. L., Chappell, N. L., Roos, N. P., and G. Lin (2002). *Health care restructuring and community-based care: three regions in British Columbia*. Victoria, BC: Centre on Aging, University of Victoria.

Penrod, J. D., Kane, R. A., Kane, R. L., and M. D. Finch (1995). "Who cares? The size, scope and composition of the caregiver support system," *Gerontologist*, 35: 489–97.

Sanborn, B., and S. Bould (1991). "Intergenerational caregivers of the oldest old," *Marriage and Family Review*, 16 (1–2): 125–42.

Segall, A., and N. L. Chappell (2000). *Health and health care in Canada*. Toronto, Ontario: Prentice-Hall.

Stone, R., Cafferata, G. L., and J. Sangl (1987). "Caregivers of the frail elderly: a national profile," *Gerontologist*, 27: 616–26.

Tennstedt, S., and B. Chang (1998). "The relative contribution of ethnicity versus socioeconomic status in explaining differences in disability and receipt of informal care," *Journal of Gerontology: Social Sciences*, 53B (2): S61–S70.

Therborn, G. (2000). "Introduction: from the universal to the global," *International Sociology*, 15 (2): 149–50.

Williams, A. P., Deber, R., Baranek, P., and A. Gildiner (2001). "From medicare to home care: globalization, state retrenchment, and the profitization of Canada's health-care system." In P. Armstrong, H. Armstrong, and D. Coburn, eds., *Unhealthy times: political economy perspectives on health and health care in Canada*. Don Mills, Ontario: Oxford University Press, pp. 423–545.

Wister, A. V., and C. Moore (1998). "First Nations elders in Canada: issues, problems and successes in health care policy." In A. V. Wister and G. M. Gutman, eds., *Health systems and aging in Pacific Rim countries: ethnic diversity and change*. Vancouver, British Columbia: Gerontology Research Centre, pp. 103–24.

CHAPTER 5.8

Network Dynamics in Later Life

FLEUR THOMÉSE, THEO VAN TILBURG, MARJOLEIN BROESE
VAN GROENOU, AND KEES KNIPSCHEER

This chapter describes recent developments in gerontological network research. After a brief introduction, we distinguish three main theoretical approaches: convoy, social exchange, and individual choice. Each of these approaches addresses networks from a dynamic perspective, explaining changes in network size and composition. We discuss recent findings in the light of the three approaches, which can be seen as focusing at a different analytical level. Finally, we consider issues that remain unresolved.

Network research in gerontology mainly developed in the 1980s, in the wake of findings showing the importance of social support for several physical and mental health measures (Berkman and Syme, 1979; Caplan, 1974). The term "social networks" was used earlier in gerontology to describe groups of people interacting in face-to-face situations (Lowenthal and Robinson, 1976: 444), focusing on the older adults' ties to society through participation in networks and social roles (Rosow, 1967). The central issues and concepts in subsequent gerontological network research increasingly reflect the social support approach, which links personal relationships to health and wellbeing. Networks are considered a source of social support, and the focus is on disentangling the ways in which networks, relationships, and support are beneficial to ageing individuals. House and Kahn (1985) were among the first to conceptually distinguish social networks and social relationships from social support, thus separating the structural properties of networks and relationships from their content and functions. "Social networks" refers to the availability of relationships in terms of opportunities and constraints in the rela-

tionship structure (e.g., size, stability). As the network mainly involves personal relationships, we prefer to speak of "personal networks." "Social support" indicates the helpful content of relationships (e.g., type, quantity). Most commonly, instrumental types of support are distinguished from emotional and expressive supports. Both network and support can affect wellbeing and health in several ways, which we will not discuss here. The distinction between network and support resolved much discussion, although there remain diverging approaches to the concept of social support and its relation to personal networks. Rather than reiterate this well-documented debate (Antonucci, 1990), we want to focus on recent advances in network theory and research.

We distinguish three theoretical approaches to personal networks in later life. The convoy approach deals with the antecedents and consequences of life-course changes at the network level. Social exchange involves a group of theories stating that the continuation of relationships requires some kind of reciprocity. Individual choice pertains to theories focusing on the individual level of choices and strategies regarding one's personal network. Each approach focuses on dynamic aspects of networks, proposing mechanisms to explain network change. This makes them well suited for addressing network changes involved in the ageing process. Advances in longitudinal data collection increasingly allow for empirical evaluation of the theoretical propositions. In the following sections, each of the approaches is described in more detail, and confronted with research outcomes on changes in network size and composition.

As with any classification, we had to make simplifications that do not always do full justice to the original works. We hope this is outweighed by the new perspective on network dynamics in later life.

THE CONVOY MODEL

The convoy model is a lifespan developmental model of social networks and social support, based on role and attachment theories (Antonucci and Akiyama, 1987; Kahn and Antonucci, 1980). Each person is thought of as moving through life surrounded by a convoy: a set of people to whom he or she is related through the exchange of support. The convoy is conceived as three concentric circles, representing different levels of closeness to the focal person. The closer relationships are determined more by attachment, the relationships in the outer circle are determined most by role requirements. Role-guided relationships, such as with co-workers, can be important and affectionate, but they are primarily tied to the role setting, which generally limits them in duration and support content. The closer relationships – which can also be role relationships – usually are more stable, and include the exchange of many types of support. The convoy is evaluated theoretically in terms of adequacy of support, individual performance and wellbeing (Kahn and Antonucci, 1980; Antonucci, 2001). For the purpose of this chapter, we limit ourselves to the convoy and its determinants.

The model distinguishes convoy structure, which we call network, and convoy functions, which we call support. The lifecourse is a basic determinant of convoy structure, and encompasses changes in both personal properties (individual needs and assets) and situational characteristics (role change) (Antonucci and Akiyama, 1987). This finds expression in two general theoretical propositions on network change in later life. First, networks in late life reflect both the role changes and changes in personal properties associated with growing old, and the roles and personal properties associated with earlier life stages. Second, role changes have a stronger effect on role relationships than on the closer relationships. The general expectation is that role loss in later life leads to a decrease in role relationships, and a growing importance of family relationships in the network (Antonucci and Akiyama, 1987).

Longitudinal research generally confirms that older adults focus on their closer relationships with time (Morgan *et al.*, 1997; van Tilburg, 1998), although cross-cultural comparisons yield mixed results (Antonucci *et al.*, 2001; Wenger, 1997). There is strong turnover among the less close relationships. Research among siblings suggests that there is no substitution between relationship types (White, 2001), e.g. lost friends are only replaced by new friends or not replaced at all (Jerrome and Wenger, 1999). A general decline in total network size has not been demonstrated. Networks only get smaller at very old age (Baltes and Mayer, 1999), mainly due to health changes.

Effects of specific role changes on network size and composition are sparingly researched longitudinally. Retirement results in a decrease in relationships with co-workers, while the total network size remains equal (van Tilburg, 2003), which supports the convoy model. The recently widowed appear to focus on their closest relationships, and make new friends after a few years (Ferraro *et al.*, 1984), thus responding to changes in needs. Network effects of new roles, like grandparenthood or volunteering, have not been researched.

Roles and changes earlier in life also affect the size and composition of the network in later adulthood. The childless (Dykstra and Hagestad, 2004) have slightly smaller networks than people with adult children, but they also have more friends and other non-kin relationships throughout old age. A long-term follow up on divorce suggests that people who remain single and those with a negative evaluation of the divorce retain smaller networks after the divorce than the other divorcees (Terhell *et al.*, in press). These long-term effects corroborate the importance of the lifespan perspective of the convoy model.

THE EXCHANGE APPROACH

Social exchange theory (Blau, 1964) assumes that people constantly evaluate their relationships, based on the comparability of their support exchanges. People prefer balanced support, i.e. they give support with the expectation of receiving something in return at some time. Once a return is received, the balance of the relationship is restored. This balance is classified as reciprocity (Gouldner, 1960). The principle of balanced exchanges underlies all relationships, whether between close friends or acquaintances, and kin or non-kin (Uehara, 1995).

Direct reciprocity refers to returning the same type of support within a limited period of time, guided by the economic principle of fair trade. Other types of reciprocity may exist. First, *type-crosswise reciprocity* pertains to exchanges across support types: a relationship in which the older adult is over-benefited, i.e., receives more than (s)he gives, with instrumental support may be balanced by over-benefiting the other with emotional support. Second, *time-delayed reciprocity* covers a larger time span, and might be extended over the lifecourse. Third, more people might be involved in the exchanges. *Indirect reciprocity* occurs when support is returned through an intermediate party. When network members give support without expecting it to be necessarily returned in the same proportion and from the same people, one speaks of *generalized reciprocity* (Wentowski, 1981).

Reciprocity is a factor in the continuation of relationships. If the receiving party is not able to return the support and it is clear that this will not change in the future, the exchange of support may decline. For the under-benefited person it is more rewarding to give support in a balanced relationship where a return can be expected if it is needed. The over-benefited party might view the imbalance as an unwanted situation of dependence. The latter may occur when poor health limits older adults in returning support, either immediately or in the long run. At the end, unbalanced relationships might be terminated. However, over-benefiting of needy older adults can be normatively accepted and even desirable (Gouldner, 1960).

Various studies have shown a strong and positive correlation between giving and receiving support (Liang *et al.*, 2001; Litwin, 1998; Morgan *et al.*, 1991; van Tilburg and Broese van Groenou, 2002). In contrast to a study by Klein Ikkink and van Tilburg (1998), Boerner and Reinhardt (2003) observed type-crosswise reciprocity: the level of instrumental support provided was contingent on both instrumental and affective support received. Van Tilburg (1998) observed an age differential effect: there was balance in instrumental support given and received among younger adults, whereas older adults counterbalanced the receipt of instrumental support by giving

emotional support. This trend might be related to decreasing physical capacities and worsening health among the oldest: these changes limit the capacities to give instrumental support, but not the provision of emotional support, while increasing the need for instrumental support.

Imbalance results in the decline of supportive exchanges with older adults, in particular within less close relationships, but not in the termination of a relationship (Klein Ikkink and van Tilburg, 1998). Klein Ikkink and van Tilburg (1999) found that the chance of a relationship continuing decreased when older adults are over-benefited with emotional support. However, relationships where older adults are over-benefited with instrumental support had a higher chance of being continued. Among neighbors, direct reciprocity in instrumental support exchange partly explained continuation of the relationships (Thomése *et al.*, 2003).

Within all forms of reciprocity, support investments can be viewed as an act of self-interest since the provider will receive support from other network members whenever he needs it (Uehara, 1995). The evidence outlined above supports the idea that the dynamic in receiving and providing support ensures continuity in social interactions. However, exchanges among people cannot be seen exclusively as self-interested behavior. Mills and Clark (1982) distinguished exchange relationships from communal relationships, in which exchanges are driven by the partners' need for support, and continuation of the relationship depends on mutual concern for each other's wellbeing. In a long-term study on older parent – adult child relationships (Silverstein *et al.*, 2002), both relationship types were found. We assume that a mix of exchange and communal orientation characterizes personal relationships.

INDIVIDUAL CHOICE APPROACH

Several theories view changes in personal networks as a result of individuals' choices and strategies. In these theories the personal network is usually perceived as a means to reach highly valued goals, such as social status or wellbeing. We discuss two of these theories: the socio-emotional selectivity theory, and the notion of networks as "social capital." Both theories consider the individual as a proactive manager of the social world, but differ with respect to what "drives" the individual: emotional engagement or rational choice.

Socio-emotional selectivity theory

The socio-emotional selectivity theory (Carstensen, 1992; Carstensen *et al.*, 1999; Lang, 2001) addresses age-related decrease in social interaction in later life. Social interaction is theoretically motivated by two goals: information seeking and emotional regulation. Perceived time horizon differentiates the importance attached to both goals; when the time horizon is limited (as in old age), the short-term goal (emotional regulation) becomes more important than the long-term goal (information seeking). As a result, older people disengage from peripheral relationships, as the emotional engagement with core network relationships is more rewarding.

Longitudinal studies confirm the selective decrease in network size over a period of four to five years (Lang, 2000; Lansford *et al.*, 1998). However, this selective withdrawal did not differ by age group. More important than age per se is the time perspective: those who perceived their future time as limited were more likely to prioritize emotionally meaningful goals, and this was, in turn, associated with greater satisfaction and support from the network (Lang and Carstensen, 2002). Lang (2000) showed that people feeling near to death deliberately discontinued their less close relationships, reduced the emotional closeness with many others, and increased the emotional closeness with core network members like kin and friends.

Social capital

Where socio-emotional selectivity focuses on individual motivations, emotional regulations, and perceptions of individual time, theories of social capital focus on structural opportunities and relationship specific investments as guiding the selection of network relationships. The notion of social capital is applied at both the individual level (Bourdieu, 1986) and the community level (Putnam, 2000). At the individual level, of most interest in this chapter, the network serves as a resource to the individual (Lin, 2001).

Comparable to exchange theory, the central notion is that people invest in others to gain future access to different resources. Personal networks of friends, kin, and neighbors may provide support, whereas relationships within formal networks, such as voluntary organizations, may provide useful information, or access to jobs and other networks (Baum and Ziersch, 2003). Different from exchange theory, the whole network is taken into account. The decision to (dis)invest in a relationship is theoretically based on present costs and expected (future) benefits, the availability of high-quality alternative relationships in the network, and on the connectedness of the relationship to the network (Rusbult, 1983). Several Dutch studies used this investment-model to explain changes in personal networks following important life events, including retirement (Van Duijn *et al.*, 1999). The results show that people are more likely to discontinue relationships with high costs (e.g., long traveling time) and low benefits (e.g., little received support), in particular when they have a large network and the relationship is not strongly connected to other relationships. It was also evident that these relationship and network characteristics are better predictors of relationship change than the structural opportunities or personality characteristics of the individual.

CONCLUSION

There are clearly interrelations between the three approaches to network change in later life we have discussed. The theory of socio-emotional selectivity fits in with the convoy model, as it specifies how ageing people respond to changes in their needs and opportunities. And the same economic principles underlie investment models and exchange theory. However, the approaches should not be seen as interchangeable. Research that addresses network dynamics shows the importance of distinguishing between analytical levels. Mechanisms at the network level do not automatically apply to changes at the relationship or individual levels. Late life changes in network size clearly demonstrate this. At the relationship level there are considerable changes, especially among the more role-based relationships, but total network size remains relatively stable until very old age. Role changes, personal changes, and socio-emotional considerations can predict shifts in the composition and size of the network, but which relationship will remain and which not is explained better by the reciprocity in each relationship separately, and the individual's investment considerations. Reciprocity explains relationship dynamics, whereas individual considerations are important in predicting how much effort older adults will put into specific relationships, which leads to changes at the relationship and network levels. For a full understanding of network change it is necessary to obtain information at each of the levels.

To complete the picture, a sociological analysis of network dynamics implies a fourth level, that of the broader social context. The focus on the personal network as a potential for social support tends to overlook the place of the network as an intermediate between individual and societal processes. The availability of and need for personal relationships at different life stages is linked to the ordering of the lifecourse and the organization of modern societies at large. This is most clear in discussions on the availability of informal care in relation to welfare state changes: what people need from their personal relationships is in part determined by what they get from societal sources. The notion of role change also reminds us that important late life changes, such as retirement or emptying the nest, reflect institutional and cultural formations of later life. Shifts in gender roles and destandardization of the lifecourse have an impact on changes in later life and their consequences for personal networks (Bernard *et al.*, 2001). Although there is a long-standing debate on the consequences of modernization for personal networks (Allan, 2001; Wellman, 1979), societal dynamics are seldom addressed in gerontological network research. In addition to the growing body of longitudinal network research, more comparison of cohorts and societies can give insight into the interdependence of personal networks and their social context.

FURTHER READING

Antonucci, T. C., and H. Akiyama (1987). "An examination of sex differences in social support among older men and women," *Sex Roles*, 17: 737–49.

Lang, F. R. (2001). "Regulation of social relationships in later adulthood," *Journal of Gerontology: Psychological Sciences*, 56B, P321–P326.

Phillipson, C., Allan, G., and A. Morgan (2004). *Social networks and social exclusion: sociological and policy perspectives*. Aldershot: Ashgate.

Uehara, E. S. (1995). "Reciprocity reconsidered: Gouldner's 'moral norm of reciprocity' and social support," *Journal of Social and Personal Relationships*, 12: 483–502.

REFERENCES

Allan, G. (2001). "Personal relationships in late modernity," *Personal Relationships*, 8: 325–39.

Antonucci, T. C. (1990). "Social supports and social relationships." In R. Binstock and E. Shanas, eds., *Handbook of aging and the social sciences*. New York: Academic, pp. 205–26.

 (2001). "Social relations: an examination of social networks, social support, and sense of control." In J. E. Birren and K. W. Schaie, eds., *Handbook of the psychology of aging*, 5th edn. New York: Academic, pp. 247–453.

Antonucci, T. C., and H. Akiyama (1987). "An examination of sex differences in social support among older men and women," *Sex Roles*, 17: 737–49.

Antonucci, T. C., Lansford, J. E., Smith, J., Baltes, M., Akiyama, H., Takahashi, K., Fuhrer, R., and J. F. Dartigues (2001). "Widowhood and illness: a comparison of social network characteristics in France, Germany, Japan, and the United States," *Psychology and Aging*, 16: 655–65.

Baltes, P., and K. Mayer, eds. (1999). *The Berlin Aging Study: aging from 70 to 100*. New York: Cambridge University Press.

Baum, F. E., and A. M. Ziersch (2003). "Social capital," *Journal of Epidemiology and Community Health*, 57: 320–3.

Berkman, L. F., and S. L. Syme (1979). "Social networks, host resistance, and mortality: a nine-year follow-up study of Aladema County residents," *American Journal of Epidemiology*, 109: 186–204.

Bernard, M., Phillipson, C., Phillips, J., and J. Ogg (2001). "Continuity and change in the family and community life of older people," *Journal of Applied Gerontology*, 20: 259–78.

Blau, P. M. (1964). *Exchange and power in social life*. New York: Wiley.

Boerner, K., and J. P. Reinhardt (2003). "Giving while in need: support provided by disabled older adults," *Journal of Gerontology*, 58B: S297–S304.

Bourdieu, P. (1986). "The forms of capital." In J. G. Richardson, ed., *The handbook of theory and research for the sociology of education*. New York: Greenwood, pp. 241–58.

Caplan, G. (1974). *Support systems and community mental health*. New York: Behavioral Publications.

Carstensen, L. L. (1992). "Social and emotional patterns in adulthood: support for socioemotional selectivity theory," *Psychology and Aging*, 7: 331–8.

Carstensen, L. L., Isaacowitz, D. M., and S. T. Charles (1999). "Taking time seriously: a theory of socioemotional selectivity," *American Psychologist*, 54: 165–81.

Dykstra, P. A., and G. O. Hagestad (forthcoming). *Aging without children: a cross-national handbook on childlessness in later life*. New York: Greenwood.

Ferraro, K. F., Mutran, E., and C. M. Barresi (1984). "Widowhood, health, and friendship support in later life," *Journal of Health and Social Behavior*, 25: 246–59.

Gouldner, A. W. (1960). "The norm of reciprocity: a preliminary statement," *American Sociological Review*, 25: 161–79.

House, J. S., and R. C. Kahn (1985). "Measures and concepts of social support." In S. Cohen and S. L. Syme, eds., *Social support and health*. Orlando: Academic, pp. 83–108.

Jerrome, D., and G. C. Wenger (1999). "Stability and change in late-life friendships," *Ageing and Society*, 19: 661–76.

Kahn, R. L., and T. A. Antonucci (1980). "Convoys over the life course: attachment, roles, and social support," *Life Span Development*, 3: 235–86.

Klein Ikkink, C. E., and T. G. van Tilburg (1998). "Do older adults' network members continue to provide instrumental support in unbalanced relationships?" *Journal of Social and Personal Relationships*, 15: 59–75.

(1999). "Broken ties: reciprocity and other effects on the ending of older adults' relationships," *Social Networks*, 21: 131–46.

Lang, F. R. (2000). "Endings and continuity of social relationships: maximizing intrinsic benefits within personal networks when feeling near to death," *Journal of Social and Personal Relationships*, 17: 155–82.

(2001). "Regulation of social relationships in later adulthood," *Journal of Gerontology: Psychological Sciences*, 56B: P321–P326.

Lang, F. R., and L. L. Carstensen (2002). "Close emotional relationships in late life: further support for proactive aging in the social domain," *Psychology and Aging*, 9: 315–24.

Lansford, J. E., Sherman, A. M., and T. C. Antonucci (1998). "Satisfaction with social networks: an examination of socioemotional selectivity theory across cohorts," *Psychology and Aging*, 13: 544–52.

Liang, J., Krause, N. M., and J. M. Bennett (2001). "Social exchange and well-being: is giving better than receiving?" *Psychology and Aging*, 16: 511–23.

Lin, N. (2001). *Social capital. A theory of social structure and action*. Cambridge: Cambridge University Press.

Litwin, H. (1998). "The provision of informal support by elderly people residing in assisted living facilities," *Gerontologist*, 38: 239–46.

Lowenthal, M. F., and B. Robinson (1976). "Social networks and isolation." In R. Binstock and E. Shanas, eds., *Handbook of aging and the social sciences*, 1st edn. New York: Van Nostrand Reinhold, pp. 432–56.

Mills, J., and M. S. Clark (1982). "Exchange and communal relationships." In L. Wheeler, ed., *Review of personality and social psychology*, Vol. III. Beverly Hills: Sage, pp. 121–45.

Morgan, D. L., Schuster, T. L., and E. W. Butler (1991). "Role reversals in the exchange of social support," *Journal of Gerontology*, 46: S278–S287.

Morgan, D. L., Neal, M. B., and P. Carder (1997). "The stability of core and peripheral networks over time," *Social Networks*, 19: 9–25.

Putnam, R. D. (2000). *Bowling alone: the collapse and revival of American community*. New York: Simon & Schuster.

Rosow, I. (1967). *Social integration of the aged*. New York: Free Press.

Rusbult, C. E. (1983). "A longitudinal test of the investment model: the development (and deterioration) of satisfaction and commitment in heterosexual involvements," *Journal of Personality and Social Psychology*, 45: 101–17.

Silverstein, M., Conroy, S. J., Wang, H., Giarrusso, R., and V. L. Bengtson (2002). "Reciprocity in parent–child relations over the adult life course," *Journal of Gerontology*, 57B: S3–S13.

Terhell, E. L., Broese van Groenou, M. I., and T. G. van Tilburg (2004). "Network dynamics in the long term period after divorce," *Journal of Social and Personal Relationships*, 21: 719–38.

Thomése, F., van Tilburg, T. G., and C. P. M. Knipscheer (2003). "Continuation of exchange with neighbors in later life: the importance of the neighborhood context," *Personal Relationships*, 10: 535–50.

Uehara, E. S. (1995). "Reciprocity reconsidered: Gouldner's 'moral norm of reciprocity' and social support," *Journal of Social and Personal Relationships*, 12: 483–502.

van Duijn, M. A. J., Van Busschbach, J. T., and T. A. B. Snijders (1999). "Multilevel analysis of personal networks as dependent variables," *Social Networks*, 21: 187–209.

van Tilburg, T. G. (1998). "Losing and gaining in old age: changes in personal network size and social support in a four-year longitudinal study," *Journal of Gerontology*, 53B: S313–S323.

(2003). "Consequences of men's retirement for the continuation of work-related personal relationships," *Ageing International*, 28: 345–58.

van Tilburg, T. G., and Broese van Groenou, M. I. (2002). "Network and health changes among older Dutch adults," *Journal of Social Issues*, 58: 697–713.

Wellman, B. (1979). "The community question: the intimate networks of East Yorkers," *American Journal of Sociology*, 84: 1201–31.

Wenger, G. C. (1997). "Review findings on networks of older Europeans," *Journal of Cross-Cultural Gerontology*, 12: 1–21.

Wentowski, G. J. (1981). "Reciprocity and the coping strategies of older people: cultural dimensions of network building," *Gerontologist*, 21: 600–9.

White, L. (2001). "Sibling relationships over the life course: a panel analysis," *Journal of Marriage and the Family*, 63: 555–68.

Changing Family Relationships in Developing Nations

ISABELLA ABODERIN

INTRODUCTION

A discussion of family trends in developing nations must begin with a word of caution. This regards the danger of treating the 'developing world' as a homogenous entity, defined by its difference from the 'Western' industrialised world, and thus ignoring the tremendous cultural, social, economic and demographic differences and the great diversity in family functions, forms and relationships that exist between regions, countries and societies. An awareness of this diversity is essential. Nonetheless, there clearly are broad, common themes and perspectives that run through, and have shaped the debates on family change in all parts of the developing world, be they in Africa, Asia, Latin America, the Caribbean or Western Pacific. This short chapter sets out these common perspectives, discusses key gaps in our understanding so far of how or why family relationships have changed and, finally, outlines analytical perspectives and methodological approaches necessary for future research and debate.

CHANGING FAMILY RELATIONSHIPS IN THE DEVELOPING WORLD AGEING DEBATE

The issue of changing family relationships of older people has stood at the centre of the developing world debate on ageing since its emergence in the early 1980s. Beginning essentially as a United Nations (UN)-led initiative, the debate was effectively launched with the first UN World Assembly on Ageing in Vienna in 1982, and the ensuing first

International Plan of Action on Ageing (IPAA) (United Nations, 1982). The central importance carried by the issue of family change in this emerging discourse (which echoed its importance in the emergent Western social gerontological debate several decades earlier (Shanas *et al.*, 1968)) was due to its inextricable link with the major concern that originally underpinned and fuelled the debate. This was a 'humanitarian' concern about an expected rapid erosion of 'traditional' family support for older people, as developing nations became progressively 'westernised'. Given the absence of any formal support structures in most nations, the fear was that older people would be left destitute, vulnerable and in need. Underlying this fear was an assumption, based on modernisation theory notions, that family support was high in traditional, pre-industrial developing societies but would, as in Western societies, erode with progressive industrialisation and urbanisation, leaving older people abandoned and dependent on the state (Burgess, 1960; Cowgill, 1972, 1974). That this very assumption had been solidly refuted in the West – by historical and contemporary empirical evidence as well as theoretical critiques accumulating over the 1960s, '70s and '80s – was seemingly overlooked in the emerging developing world debate. (The reasons for this remain an interesting subject for research (Aboderin, 2004a).) The UN's humanitarian concern was further heightened, meanwhile, by demographic projections which predicted sharp rises in the numbers and proportion of older people in developing nations, as a result of growing life expectancy and falling fertility levels. The numbers of those aged 60 years or over were projected to increase almost eightfold, from 205 million in 1980 to almost 1.6 billion in 2050, while their proportion in the population was expected to rise from 6.2 per cent to 21 per cent. Thus, at the same time as old age family support was expected to be eroded, the need and demand for such support were predicted to rise. What ultimately motivated the emergent developing world debate, therefore, was a policy challenge: how, in view of the expected trends and limited public resources and infrastructure, to ensure the continued welfare of older people in developing nations? This question has, since then, explicitly or implicitly, fuelled most of the developing world gerontological research to date. Aiming to provide base-line information for policy development, the majority of this research has focused on establishing the economic, health, social and family status, support situation and needs of older people (Aboderin, 2004a). The body of evidence accumulating from this developing world research reveals an ambiguous picture of change and continuity in family support. On the one hand, it indicates the persistence of family ties and support, showing the majority of older people to live with their younger kin in households of two or more generations, to maintain close relations with their families, and to draw on their families as the primary source of support. On the other hand, the evidence also clearly documents the lack or increasing inadequacy of family support in many countries, exposing older people to vulnerability and need. In some countries, for example in East Asia, governments have responded to these changes by beginning to formulate public policies to replace some of the traditional support functions of the family (Hashimoto, 1993; Malhotra and Kabeer, 2002; Hermalin, 2003; Randel *et al.*, 1999; Aboderin, 2004b; International Association of Gerontology, 2002; Kendig *et al.*, 1992).

What to make of this evidence? To what extent and how have older people's family arrangements and support changed? And why? In other words, how have the underlying family systems, norms and intergenerational relationships evolved and how do they operate today? These questions have become crucial ones in the contemporary developing world ageing debate, largely because of their policy relevance. International discussions in recent years, especially around the second UN World Assembly on Ageing in 2002, have increasingly emphasised

the need for policies – if they are to be effective – to build on indigenous systems and values of informal family support (United Nations, 2002). Understanding how these family systems have evolved has thus become a requisite for policy development and a core challenge for research. The research agenda is thus set to broaden: from a rather narrow focus on whether or not, or to what extent, family support has declined, to wider questions of how family relationships and support norms have changed and why. So far, whilst empirical evidence is still extremely sparse, discussions have centred on four broad processes thought of as major contributors to changes in family systems and support.

CURRENT PERSPECTIVES ON DRIVERS OF CHANGE IN FAMILY SYSTEMS AND SUPPORT

Demographic and labour market trends

First, there are demographic and labour market trends affecting the *composition* and *structural arrangements* of families and households. These have been discussed mainly in terms of their effect on the availability of younger kin to provide support to older people and include:

a) the demographic transition – falling mortality and fertility rates;
b) migration, residential and labour market trends.

Second, there are macro perspectives on the drivers of change in family arrangements and support, including:

a) modernisation theory perspectives;
b) political economy perspectives.

THE DEMOGRAPHIC TRANSITION. The unprecedented demographic transition currently underway in developing countries is widely seen as the most significant contributor to changes in the structure and composition of families. The revolution in longevity and the steadily declining fertility rates, due to twentieth-century advances in the prevention of infectious, perinatal and infant mortality and the use of effective contraceptives, will dramatically raise the numbers and proportion of older people over the coming decades (Sen, 1994)

TABLE 1. Demographic transition and population ageing in developing world regions

Region	Life Expectancy at Birth			Total Fertility Rate (children per woman)			Older people (60+) as % of total population		
	1960–5	1980–5	2000–5	1960–5	1980–5	2000–5	1980	2000	2050
Africa	42.6	50.3	49.1	6.86	6.45	4.97	5.0	5.1	10.0
Asia	48.5	60.4	67.3	5.64	3.67	2.57	6.9	8.8	25.6
Latin America & Caribbean	56.8	64.9	71.5	5.97	3.93	2.55	6.6	8.1	24.1

Source: United Nations Population Division, 2003.

(Table 1). At the family level, these trends are expected to lead to a decline in the pool of younger kin potentially available to provide support to older individuals – an impact seen most dramatically in the case of China as a result of the one-child policy there. As Table 1 indicates, individual regions (as well as countries and population groups) vary greatly in terms of the stage of the demographic transition they are at, and the speed at which it is occurring. Populations in Asia (especially East Asia) and Latin America, which have seen the largest drops in mortality and fertility, are generally in a sustained process of ageing. In sub-Saharan Africa, where mortality and fertility remain high, population ageing remains slow, although a surge in premature ageing may occur as a result of the HIV/AIDS epidemic. In all regions, however, the transition will occur at a rate unparalleled in history: whereas it took countries like France, for example, 115 years to increase its older population from 7 to 14 per cent, it will take most developing nations 20 years or less (Randel *et al.*, 1999).

MIGRATION, RESIDENTIAL AND LABOUR MARKET TRENDS. In addition to the demographic transition, most developing world societies are experiencing rapid rates of rural–urban migration and urbanisation (United Nations Population Division, 2003). Their impacts on family arrangements and support are seen as twofold.

First, age-selective out-migration, predominantly of younger people from rural to urban areas or abroad, has in many cases led to older people being left behind alone, without younger adult kin living close by and available to provide care or assistance if needed.

Second, and vice versa, older people, especially migrants in the urban setting, are often said to face the loss of their traditional family support network. While it is generally recognised that the impact of city living on family support is not clear-cut but depends on individuals' family and migration histories and contexts, there is a perception that the urban context is 'less conducive' to sustaining traditional family support networks (United Nations, 2002: 13). Two factors specifically are seen as militating against the availability of younger kin to provide old age support. One is the dispersion and increasing residential separation of older people from their children or other younger-generation kin, as seen in some countries such as, for example, South Korea (Hermalin, 2003). The other is the increasing participation of women in the labour force, evident in most developing country contexts. Due to increasing competing demands on their time, women are assumed to be less able to fulfil their 'traditional role' as caregivers to older parents or relatives (Malhotra and Kabeer, 2002).

Whilst reduced physical presence or competing demands of kin will undoubtedly impact on family support arrangements, straightforward inferences to the availability of family support must be treated with caution. Whether reductions in the numbers of children per older person will mean a reduced supply of support, for example, will depend on the ability of the fewer existing children to provide adequate support and the degree to which all children in the past indeed contributed to support of parents. Similarly, the impact of women's increased labour force participation on the availability of support will depend on the priorities set when a need for care arises, as well as on the type of employment taken. Living arrangements alone, too, reveal little about the supply of support to older people. Residential separation may obscure the proximity and availability of younger kin who live close. Conversely, co-residence tells us little about the ability or willingness of co-resident younger kin to provide support or the adequacy of such assistance (Hermalin, 2003). Moreover, inferences become tenuous if distinctions are made between the different dimensions of family support. For example, whilst reduced physical presence or competing time demands may indeed affect the availability of kin to provide caregiving or domestic help, they may have no bearing, or even positive effects, on other support dimensions such as material or emotional support. These caveats illustrate the very limited extent, generally, to which inferences can be made from trends in family structures or arrangements to the nature and causes of changes in the qualitative content of family relationships and behaviours.

Macro perspectives on drivers of change in family arrangements and support

The two broad macro perspectives put forward in current discussions begin to bear on these questions. Both are concerned with explicating societal level causes of changes in family arrangements and support, and they do so based on inferences or assumptions about changes in the qualitative basis of family relationships: i.e., in individuals' conceptions and expectations of intergenerational roles and relations.

MODERNISATION THEORY PERSPECTIVES. Drawing on modernisation theory notions (Burgess, 1960; Cowgill, 1972, 1974), these perspectives emphasise the central role of 'Western' values of individualism and secularisation in underpinning shifts in family arrangements and support in developing nations. These values (promulgated through formal education and the media), together with the demise of the family as the main unit of production and social mobility (due to industrialisation, urbanisation, technological progress), are said to foster an emergence of the nuclear, conjugal family at the expense of extended family bonds. The rising emphasis on the emotional bond between spouses, and parents and their young children, is seen as underlying the migration and residential separation of adult children from their parents. Similarly, it is

seen as underpinning the reductions in fertility – by making wealth flow from old (parents) to young (children), thus making high fertility a net lifetime burden (Caldwell, 1982).

The extended family's demise is also seen as undermining family support for older people directly. Traditional values of familism and filial obligation per se are weakened by rising individualism and secularisation. In addition, the loss of older people's traditional extended family status and roles erodes their powers to enforce children's conformity with customary filial obligation norms, and their resources to offer their children in exchange for support. As a result, support in modernised societies is no longer compelled by the force of custom but depends increasingly on young people's level of sympathy or affection for, and thus *wish* to support, their older parents or relatives. The decline in old age family support is thus ultimately seen as being caused by an increasing *unwillingness* of the young to provide for the old. Underpinning this perspective are three sets of assumptions.

First, classical structural-functionalist interpretations of family support in traditional pre-industrial society, which hold that support was adequately provided because it was not dependent on the affective relationship between parents and children. Rather, it was compelled by binding norms of *filial obligation* and enforced by powerful social, economic and religious sanctions, which were wielded by older people themselves. Additionally, filial support was driven by an element of *exchange*, with aged parents providing advice, education, childcare or domestic help in return for support from their children.

Underlying these interpretations are structuralist, a-priori theory-based (rather than empirically grounded), assumptions about the nature of family relationships and behaviours in pre-industrialised societies. These stress the role of rules, specified duties and obligations with repressive sanctions ('mechanical solidarity'), and emphasise the power and authority of the aged. In contrast, relationships in modern 'advanced' societies are seen as being driven by 'organic solidarity', i.e. an emphasis on individual initiative and dignity, voluntary solidarity and interdependence.

Finally, modernisation perspectives implicitly assume a linear, uniform mode of development, which equates contemporary 'development' in developing societies with the historical processes of industrialisation and 'development' in the West. In this view, 'development' is assumed to go hand in hand with economic progress and growing prosperity (Aboderin, 2004a).

POLITICAL ECONOMY PERSPECTIVES. Political economy perspectives emphasise the central role of structural constraints, rather than weakening values or beliefs, in changing family arrangements and support in developing nations.

Though less elaborate than modernisation theory, these views highlight the reality of economic 'development' for many developing countries, which is characterised not by growing prosperity, but by poverty and rising inequality. These trends are seen as the result of national and international policies and, ultimately, countries' position in the global economy. The ensuing economic constraints faced by large parts of populations are seen as crucial factors undermining old age family support. Younger people are said to have insufficient means to cater adequately for themselves and their children as well as older parents or relatives. Faced with decisions on how to allocate their scarce resources, they must give priority to their immediate family (i.e. self, spouse and children) at the expense of the old (Treas and Logue, 1986; Goldstein *et al.*, 1983; Aboderin, 2004a). Declining family support is thus caused by a growing incapacity (rather than unwillingness) on the part of the young. Similarly, economic constraints or necessity, rather than emerging preferences, may be seen as underlying emerging migration and residence patterns or even fertility reduction.

Unlike modernisation theory, the political economy approach is not necessarily predicated upon any assumptions about the past or present basis of family relationships or behaviours. Their emphasis on the continuity of filial obligation norms, however, suggests that, at least in terms of family support, they work on the assumption that this was 'traditionally' compelled by obligation norms and remains so, where it is provided today (Aboderin, 2004a).

CHANGE IN FAMILY RELATIONSHIPS: GAPS IN UNDERSTANDING

Modernisation and political economy perspectives, as well as descriptions of demographic trends in family structures or arrangements, undoubtedly highlight some of the important factors and processes involved in changing the nature and content of family relationships and behaviours. Yet, they provide little by way of an analytical understanding of how, why, and to what extent the qualitative content of family relationships of older people in developing nations has changed over recent decades. This is due, above all, to their failure to illuminate individuals' intentions, meanings and motives. Any meaningful understanding of social phenomena or change must be grounded in an appreciation, at micro level, of individuals' perspectives and purposes and their recursive relationship with the wider structural macro context (Giddens, 1991). A solid understanding of changing family relationships, specifically, needs to focus on the shifts that have taken place in the expectations, meanings and sentiments that older people and their younger kin bring to their relationships with, and behaviours (e.g. support) to, each other (Anderson, 1995). Efforts to analyse the causes of any such shifts must consider three levels.

a) Individuals' lifecourses: how shifts in family relationships and behaviours relate to changes in the circumstances and exposures experienced by older people and their younger kin throughout their life (including experiences with each other) and the conditions in which they consequently arrive at adulthood and old age.

b) Micro and macro structural influences on individuals' lifecourse: how changes in individuals' lifecourse relate to changes in (i) the micro structural family context in which their relationships unfold, and (ii) the national and global macro structural social, economic, policy, environmental and cultural context in which they, and their families, find themselves.

c) How changes in lifecourse and relationships, in turn, shape the micro and macro structural contexts in which future expectations and behaviours unfold.

PERSPECTIVES FOR FUTURE RESEARCH

The challenge to illuminate the interplay between changes in personal biographies, family structures and the macro historical context, in causing changes in family relationships, can be seen as reflecting the central premises of the lifecourse perspective. In the West, this perspective is increasingly used as a strategic context and framework for sociological research and debate on ageing and families (Bengtson and Allen, 1993; Elder *et al.*, 2003). It should serve as a conceptual and methodological framework also for developing world research on family change. Such research should aim to capture changes that have taken place up to the present, and to trace unfolding developments into the future. Cohort analyses – comparisons between past, present and future cohorts of older people – provide the basic methodological approach for such investigations. Whilst this may involve studying population-based cohort samples at particular time intervals, deeper insights may be gained through family-based, multi-generational studies in which comparisons are made between successive 'generations' of older people within a family lineage. Such a generational sequential approach enables taking account of individual family contexts and generational transmission. Whilst a prospective, longitudinal design should be a key feature of such studies (including analyses of unfolding macro context developments), they should also involve an element of retrospective data collection.

Life or oral history approaches, as well as analysis of available historical records or survey data, are particularly important (i) to gain an understanding of the lifecourses and past contexts of the present cohorts of older people, and (ii) to provide, as far as it is possible, an interpretively grounded picture of the reality of family life for previous cohorts of older people. Such historical inquiry must critically examine, as others have done, the accuracy of the often theory-based ethnographic interpretations of the nature of family relationships in 'traditional' non-Western societies (Logue, 1990; Nydegger, 1983; Aboderin, 2004b).

Lastly, future research should observe two key principles. It should take a dynamic view of old age, distinguishing between early and later stages, and must take account of diversity: between individual developing regions and nations, and between different population groups within societies. Findings from such research will provide not only crucial information for old age policy in developing nations, but also valuable data for cross-national analyses with evidence from Western societies. Such comparison may generate further, critical insights on the nature and determinants of social change.

FURTHER READING

Aboderin, I. (2004a). 'Modernisation and ageing theory revisited: current explanations of recent developing world and historical Western shifts in material family support for older people', *Ageing and Society*, 24: 29–50.
  (2004b). 'Decline in material family support for older people in urban Ghana, Africa: understanding processes and causes of change', *Journal of Gerontology: Psychological Sciences, Social Sciences*, 59: S128–S137.
Hermalin, A. I., ed. (2003). *The well-being of the elderly in Asia. A four-country comparative study.* Ann Arbor, Mich.: University of Michigan Press.
Kendig, H. L., Hashimoto, A., and L. C. Coppard, eds. (1992). *Family support for the elderly. The international experience.* Oxford: Oxford University Press.
Nydegger, C. N. (1983). 'Family ties of the aged in cross-cultural perspective', *Gerontologist*, 23: 26–32.
Treas, J., and B. Logue (1986). 'Economic development and the older population', *Population and Development Review*, 12: 655–73.

REFERENCES

Aboderin, I. (2004a). 'Modernisation and ageing theory revisited: current explanations of recent developing world and historical Western shifts in material family support for older people', *Ageing and Society*, 24: 29–50.
  (2004b). 'Decline in material family support for older people in urban Ghana, Africa: understanding processes and causes of change', *Journal of Gerontology: Psychological Sciences, Social Sciences*, 59: S128–S137.
Anderson, M. (1995). *Approaches to the history of the Western family 1500–1914.* Cambridge: Cambridge University Press.
Bengtson, V. L., and K. R. Allen (1993). 'The life course perspective applied to families over time'. In P. Boss, W. Doherty, R. LaRossa, W. Schumm and S. Steinmetz, eds., *Sourcebook of family theories and methods: a contextual approach.* New York: Plenum Press, pp. 469–98.
Burgess, E. W., ed. (1960). *Ageing in Western societies.* Chicago: University of Chicago Press.
Caldwell, J. C. (1982). *The theory of fertility decline.* London: Academic Press, Inc.
Cowgill, D. O. (1972). 'A theory of aging in cross-cultural perspective'. In D. O. Cowgill and L. D. Holmes, eds., *Ageing and modernization.* New York: Appleton-Century-Crofts, pp. 1–14.
  (1974). 'Aging and modernization: a revision of the theory'. In J. F. Gubrium, ed., *Late life.* Springfield, Ill.: Thomas, pp. 123–45.
Elder, G. H. Jr, Kirkpatrick Johnson, M., and R. Crosnoe (2003). 'The emergence and development of the life course theory'. In J. T. Mortimer and M. J. Shanahan, eds., *Handbook of the life course.* New York: Kluwer Academic Publishers, pp. 3–19.

Giddens, A. (1991). *Modernity and self identity*. Oxford: Polity Press.

Goldstein, M. C., Schuler, S., and J. L. Ross (1983). 'Social and economic forces affecting intergenerational relations in a third world country: a cautionary tale from South Asia'. *Journal of Gerontology*, 38: 716–24.

Hashimoto, A. (1993). 'Family relations in later life: a cross cultural perspective', *Generations*, 17: 24–6.

Hermalin, A. I., ed. (2003). *The well-being of the elderly in Asia. A four-country comparative study*. Ann Arbor, Mich.: University of Michigan Press.

International Association of Gerontology (IAG) (2002). *The Valencia report 2002. A report on the outcomes of a meeting of gerontological researchers, educators and providers*. Vancouver: IAG.

Kendig, H. L., Hashimoto, A., and L. C. Coppard, eds. (1992). *Family support for the elderly. The international experience*. Oxford: Oxford University Press.

Logue, B. J. (1990). 'Modernization and the status of the frail elderly: perspectives on continuity and change', *Journal of Cross-Cultural Gerontology*, 5: 345–74.

Malhotra, R., and N. Kabeer (2002). *Demographic transition, inter-generational contracts and old age security: an emerging challenge for social policy in developing countries*, Working Paper No. 157. Brighton: Institute for Development Studies.

Nydegger, C. N. (1983). 'Family ties of the aged in cross-cultural perspective', *Gerontologist*, 23: 26–32.

Randel, J., German, T., and D. Ewing, eds. (1999). *The ageing and development report: poverty, independence and the world's older people*. london: HelpAge International, Earthscan.

Sen, K. (1994). *Ageing. Debates on demographic transition and social policy*. London: Zed Books.

Shanas, E., Townsend, P., Wedderburn, D., Friis, H., Milhoj, P., and J. Stehouwer (1968). *Old people in three industrial societies*. New York: Atherton Press.

Treas, J., and B. Logue (1986). 'Economic development and the older population', *Population and Development Review*, 12: 655–73.

United Nations (1982). *Report of the World Assembly on Aging, Vienna, 26 July to 6 August*. New York: United Nations.

(2002). *Report of the Second World Assembly on Aging*. New York: United Nations.

United Nations Population Division (2005). *World population prospects: the 2004 Revision*; http://esa.un.org/unpp.

Ethnic Diversity in Ageing, Multicultural Societies

JAMES S. JACKSON, EDNA BROWN, TONI C. ANTONUCCI, AND SVEIN OLAV DAATLAND

INTRODUCTION

In this chapter we consider the implications of age and ethnic changes in the demography of the world's populations, and the implications of these changes for the care of the elderly. We begin with a brief review of generational structure, relations, and population ageing to set the context for understanding ethnic diversity in ageing, multicultural societies. We then turn to data from the Eurobarometer studies to provide evidence concerning host nation attitudes about immigrants. Finally, we provide data from a recently completed study of five European nations and the United States identifying generational differences concerning attitudes and orientations towards care of the elderly.

GENERATIONAL STRUCTURE AND RELATIONS

Research on family life and relationships indicates that the lives of family members are interdependent and that individuals continually interact with significant family members (Riley and Riley, 1983). At the same time the structure of contemporary American families is clearly changing as a result of divorce, single parent families, and increased lifespans. These changes have made multigenerational family units an important influence on family members of all generations (Bengtson, 2001). The traditional family consisting of two parents, one person (the father) employed outside the home, and two children, while once the norm, now represents only 6 percent of the US population. On the other hand,

two-earner families, single adult-parent households, and increased life expectancies are much more common, with the complementary development that grandparents can and often do play a more active role in the lives of their grandchildren (Caldwell *et al.*, 1998). Although older people are spending many more years as active, healthy older adults, it is also the case that the oldest-old are the fastest growing portion of the ageing population (Myers, 1990). With greater age, the probability of health problems and of needing care is significantly increased.

In most cases families are accepting the increased burden of caring both for their oldest-old and for the children of working parents. The nature and quality of these relationships have important implications for the wellbeing of all generational members. Most close relationships are with spouse, children and parents, thus intergenerational relationships are critical. Changing demographics, including both increased life expectancy and decreased fertility, have changed the very structure of generational linkages. At the beginning of the twentieth century, family structure in most societies resembled that of a pyramid, with a large base consisting of children under the age of 5, and many fewer individuals over the age of 65. Treas (1995) and others (e.g. Farkas and Hogan, 1995) have argued that by 2030, this pyramid will lose its significant base, and will "even out" to look like a beanpole, with fairly equal numbers of individuals in each generation, and with more family generations alive than a century ago. This translates into fewer younger people available to take care of an increasing number of older people. In these circumstances the nature of intergeneration intra-family relations will have important implications for the wellbeing of all family members.

Another important consideration is the average distance in age between generations. When people are marrying early and having children at relatively young ages, the average age distance between generations will be short, about 15 to 20 years, but when marriage and childbearing is delayed, the distance between generations can be much longer, about 30 to 40 years. Ethnic groups vary considerably in the average age distance between generations and in the number of children born, with some ethnic groups and immigrants often having less distance between generations and more children than other ethnic groups or non-immigrants.

These differences change the nature of the family structure and can potentially change the relationship between generations. A grandparent at 35 years of age has very different expectations and abilities than a grandparent at 80. Studies of intergenerational family relations indicate that families are involved in shared kinship activities, have frequent contact with each other, and are engaged in networks of mutual assistance, both within and between generations (Hill *et al.*, 1970; Bengtson and Cutler, 1976; Markides *et al.*, 1986). Rossi and Rossi (1990) reported a high degree of familial proximity, interaction, and kinship exchanges among three-generation families. Both parents and grandparents reported being involved in giving and receiving aid, and a high degree of satisfaction with the amount of contact they had with kin. Roberts and Bengtson (1996) report that findings from their Longitudinal Study of Generations (LSOG) suggest that intergenerational relations remain stable over several decades, and that positive relations are beneficial to family members. Specifically, levels of affection remain high for members of each generation over the years and this has the effect of providing positive long-term psychological benefits for both sons and daughters into adulthood. Moreover, when improvements in parent–child relationships occur, self-esteem increases (Giarrusso *et al.*, 2001).

Changing family demographics and family structure have implications for socialization, parenting, and social support. For example, with people living longer, children are more likely to have significant interactions with grandparents as they grow older (Uhlenberg, 1996), and both ageing parents and grandparents have the opportunity to provide family continuity, stability, and support (Giarrusso *et al.*, 1996). Negative consequences of this phenomenon could also potentially emerge. Antonucci (1985) has suggested that people conceptualize their long-term support exchanges as support bank, an accounting system something like a savings bank. Deposits made early, e.g. through the provision of support to others, have direct implications for withdrawals that will be available later, e.g. when support is needed. Thus, grandparents who provide child care to their grandchildren may expect to, and be more likely to, receive care when they become dependent. Similarly, a lifetime of conflict is likely to have opposite implications when affection and care are needed by the elder.

CARE NEEDS

With the changing demographics, i.e. increases in the number of older people and decreases in the number of younger people, a critical concern is how to meet the needs of older people. Since government and other formal services are exhibiting a parallel decrease in the resources available, service needs and expectations concerning the elderly are an increasingly urgent set of issues. An ongoing concern in the literature is whether families, feeling burdened by other responsibilities, will decrease the level of care they expect to provide to family elders. Available evidence is inconclusive. Walker (1993) found that European Union countries with the highest levels of formal services tended to report the lowest levels of family care, although Lingsom (1997) reported that in Norway, where formal services were greatly expanded in the 1960s and '70s and then declined in the 1990s, there was, in fact, no parallel decline or increase in family care. While Cantor and Little (1985) suggested a hierarchical compensatory model indicating that the elderly prefer help from informal family providers over formal non-family providers, more recent evidence suggests that there are circumstances under which people actually prefer help from social services (Daatland, 1990). Our own work in the 1980s (Kahn and Antonucci, 1984) indicated that older people expected less care from their family members than their family members expected to and were prepared to provide. In this chapter we provide an overview of the most current data available on this topic, including expectations of care from both formal and informal providers among people of all ages across both European and American populations. But first we briefly consider geographical differences in population ageing.

POPULATION AGEING

While it is generally true that the world population is ageing, this is not true in all parts of the world. The United Nations Population Division and the US Census Bureau provide useful information concerning world ageing. Differences are apparent in Europe, the United States, and Africa. For example, approximately 20% of the European population will be over 60 years of age in 2005 and fully 30% will be over 60 in 2030. The changes are almost as dramatic in North America where 17% of the population will be over 60 in 2005 and approximately 25% will be that age in 2030. On the other hand, there will be hardly any noticeable change in the very small percentage of older people in Africa, where 5% of the population will be over 60 in 2005 and only 7% in 2030. Nevertheless, the role of grandparents is also changing in Africa, with many older people having to take an active role in rearing their grandchildren, because of either the death or geographic mobility of their adult children. Another important influence on the demography of ageing experience is immigration. Data from the US Census indicate that approximately 84% of older people who were foreign-born in 1970 were born in Europe, in comparison with only 4% of those older foreign-born in the United States after 1970. By contrast the comparable figures for older Asian-born people are 25% before 1970 and 75% after that year. It is clear that the ethnic face of immigration, both young and old, is changing in the United States, from a European to an Asian background.

ATTITUDES TOWARDS IMMIGRANTS

The literature on immigration is relevant because some old people immigrated when they were younger, while other older people immigrate later, to age near their children who had previously immigrated. In a recent paper, Jackson and Antonucci (2004) examined attitudes towards immigrants as

reported in fifteen European countries and the United States. In 1997, 45% of the fifteen countries of the Eurobarometer studies (Austria, Belgium, Denmark, Finland, France, Germany, Greece, Ireland, Italy, Luxembourg, The Netherlands, Portugal, Spain, Sweden, United Kingdom) felt that there were a lot, but not too many, immigrants in their country, while 40% felt there were too many immigrants. Only 14% of these European respondents felt that there were not many immigrants in their country. Of these same respondents, 65% felt their country had already reached the limits of the number of immigrants they could absorb and that more immigrants would be problematic, even though it was clear these countries were still accepting immigrants. It is highly possible that these new immigrants are not being warmly accepted.

Turning to the life circumstances and living situations of older immigrants in the United States, census data reveal that older immigrants are a third more likely than older native born older adults to be living in poverty, while older non-citizens are twice as likely (20%) as older citizens (9%) to be living in poverty. Immigrants are also more likely to have less than a high school education (29% vs. 44%). Reflecting similar gender differences among older US native-born groups, foreign-born older men are much more likely (79%) to be married than foreign-born older women (46%), but native-born older people are much more likely to live alone (men: 18%; women: 41%) than foreign-born older people (men: 10%; women: 25%). In brief, it is clear that immigrants, especially older immigrants, are facing the challenges of age with fewer resources than native-born older adults. Although the data we report are predominantly from the US, data available from the European Union suggest that these findings are also true in Europe. We next consider whether there are differences in the US and in five specific European countries which inform the situation of elders, in terms of their need for, and expectations of, care.

NORMS AND EXPECTATIONS REGARDING ELDER CARE

The Old Age and Autonomy: Service Systems and Intergenerational Family Solidarity (OASIS) study was recently completed and provides data from approximately 1,200 respondents from each of the five participating countries (N = 6,106 from England, Germany, Norway, Israel, and Spain) (Lowenstein and Ogg, 2003) on a variety of questions concerning norms and expectations regarding care of the elderly. Complementary data are provided by the 2003 National Survey of American Life (NSAL) study with 3,511 respondents, including representative samples of three major subgroups in the United States: Whites, African American Blacks, and Caribbean Blacks (Jackson *et al.*, in press). In this section we summarize the similarities and differences across countries and US subgroups.

When respondents aged 25 to 75+ in the five OASIS countries, and 18 to 65+ in the United States, were asked "Should elders depend on their children for help when they need it?", over half the respondents in all countries (with the exception of England) agreed that they should. What is impressive is the range of responses. Over 90% of the American respondents agreed with this statement while only 41% of the English respondents did so. People from Spain (60%), Norway (58%), Germany (55%) and Israel (51%) were about equally likely to agree with this statement.

We have additional information concerning age, gender, and race differences over filial norms and attitudes in general. Younger people (aged 25–49) in England and Israel report stronger filial norms than older people (aged 75+) in these countries. At the same time older people in Spain and Germany report slightly stronger filial norms, while in Norway no age differences emerged. In the United States younger people were consistently more likely to agree that elders should depend on their children for help than were older people. Although the differences across most of the adult age groups in the European countries were not large, it is impressive that older people were much less likely to agree with this statement.

An examination of gender differences was equally interesting. Contrary to expectations, men in Norway and England were more likely to agree to filial norms than women. There were no gender differences in Germany, Spain, and Israel or in the United States, with the majority of both men and women agreeing to filial obligations.

And finally, it was possible to examine ethnic/racial differences in the United States, but not for any of the five European nations. The results are interesting and can be summarized succinctly. African American Blacks are more likely than Caribbean Blacks and Whites to endorse the concept of filial obligation. These findings reveal that there are differences between Whites and Blacks, but that these can be further differentiated between Caribbean and African American Blacks. It is not clear whether history, current geographical mobility patterns, cultural variations, or socioeconomic status accounts for these differences – although it should be noted that the differences are relatively small.

COVERING THE COST OF ELDER CARE

Another set of issues involves who should pay for the increased need for care of older people in the coming years. Government policies of respective countries appear to have the largest influence on individual attitudes and beliefs. When asked if they felt the state was either totally or mainly responsible for the care of the elderly, country differences emerged that directly paralleled the current welfare policies of the country in which the respondent lived. Thus, in the United States, which has the poorest public healthcare coverage of the countries under consideration, only 23% of the population felt that providing financial support to needy elders was the responsibility of the state. By contrast, fully 79% of the respondents from Norway, with its considerable welfare benefits, agreed with this statement. Israel (50%) and Spain (40%) were in relative agreement, whereas England (35%) and Germany (34%) were the least likely to agree. In the United States, an examination of age differences indicated that younger people (18–34) were least likely to agree with this statement, whereas older age groups were more likely to agree with this statement (responses ranging from 26% to 31%). Older people generally agreed that the state should be responsible for the needs of their elders in all of the five European countries, except Spain. In the United States, Whites were slightly less likely to agree that the state should provide for the financial needs of the elderly (22%) while Blacks (29%) and Caribbeans (30%) were slightly more likely to agree with this statement. There were hardly any gender differences in response to this question in the United States. Across the five European countries there were few gender differences, although women were more likely than men to endorse the responsibility of the government in Norway, while the reverse was true in Spain.

One final area of focus is people's views about who should pay for the increased costs in the years ahead for the care of the elderly. Americans were most likely to say the private sector / volunteers should pay (66%), but were also likely to endorse the need for higher taxes (50%). They were somewhat less likely to feel that adult children should pay (35%) and least likely to feel that elderly users should pay (12%). Germans were less likely (29%) to feel that the private sector / volunteers should pay for the increased cost, while the Spaniards (19%), Norwegians and Israelis (both 16%) and English (15%) were least likely to agree. Turning to higher taxes as the best way to pay for increased needs and costs of the elderly, the British were even more likely than Americans to agree with this statement (75%), while respondents from the other four countries were considerably less in agreement (Norway: 29%; Israel: 22%; Spain: 20%; and Germany: 15%). A great many (43%) British respondents felt that it was the adult children's financial responsibility, although this was much less true in Germany (16%), Spain (14%), Israel (13%), and Norway (9%). Americans were intermediate in terms of their beliefs that the elder user should be responsible to pay for his or her care, with Germans (21%), Norwegians (17%), and English (16%) agreeing with this policy, but Israelis (8%) and Spaniards (7%) somewhat less likely to agree.

Age differences were not as great as one might have predicted. Younger people in the United States agreed (73%) that the private sector and volunteers should be responsible but older people were much less likely to feel this way (58%). The middle-aged groups were less likely than younger people but more likely than older people to agree with this statement (age 35–49: 68% agree; age 50–64, 61% agree). Older and younger people were about equally likely (~47%) to agree that collecting higher taxes was the way to pay for this expense, with middle-aged people slightly more likely to agree with this point of view. Approximately a third of the people in each age group felt that the adult children should pay for the care of their elders, while very few people felt that older people should be required to pay – older people were considerably more likely to feel this way (19%) than younger people (10%–14%). In the United States there were relatively few race or gender differences.

SUMMARY AND CONCLUSIONS

Reflecting on the well-documented changes in population ageing, the focus of this chapter was to consider how well the needs of our future elderly will be met and to consider the degree to which this will be affected by race, ethnicity, and cultural differences in the United States. We have drawn on a broad array of findings indicating similarities and differences, hopes and concerns, directions and possibilities regarding the care of older people. As we consider population data, it is critical to recognize the role that race, ethnicity, and culture will play in the ageing experience of older people. Longstanding ethnic diversity, as well as recent immigration patterns, indicates that special attention needs to be paid to these differences. Data from the Eurobarometer studies suggest that Europeans have some serious concerns about the immigration patterns they have been experiencing. On the other hand, OASIS data, also from Europe, indicate that most young people expect and plan to provide care to their ageing relatives – above and beyond the expectations of older people themselves.

We suggest that these two bodies of data provide an appropriate backdrop for ageing in the future. While there are and will continue to be important ethnic and cultural differences, there are some universal beliefs about elder care. However, these are clearly influenced to a lesser or greater degree by the policies and the immigration experiences of the countries concerned. At the same time, although people worry about their own resources, they are almost unanimous in their belief that all people should have the same rights and privileges. Clearly this is an area of paradox and contradiction.

The data presented above suggest that, while there are some universal similarities, e.g. younger people having higher expectations of care for their elders than the elders themselves, it is also clear that government policies fundamentally influence these attitudes. We should take advantage of the potential to influence attitudes and behaviors, recognizing that we must not only attend to the needs of our elders, but also shape the views of our citizens to create societies for all ages, societies that care for all of its citizens.

FURTHER READING

Antonucci, T. C., Akiyama, H., and K. Birditt (2005). "Intergenerational exchange in the United States and Japan." In M. Silverstein, R. Giarrusso, and V. L. Bengtson, eds., *Intergenerational relations across time and place. Springer annual review of gerontology and geriatrics*, Vol. XXIV. New York: Springer.

Jackson, J. S., and T. C. Antonucci (2004). "Western European attitudes about immigration: possible influences on the life experiences of aging-in-place and late-life immigrants," unpublished MS.

Jackson, J. S., Brown, E., and T. C. Antonucci (2004). "A cultural lens on biopsychosocial models of aging," *Advances in Cell Aging and Gerontology*, 15: 221–41.

Lowenstein, A., and J. Ogg, eds. (2003). *OASIS – old age and autonomy: The role of service systems and intergenerational family solidarity. Final Report.* Haifa, Israel: The University of Haifa, Center for Research and Study of Aging.

REFERENCES

Antonucci, T. C. (1985). "Personal characteristics, social support, and social behavior." In R. H. Binstock and E. Shanas, eds., *Handbook of aging and the social sciences*, 2nd edn. New York: Van Nostrand Reinhold, pp. 94–128.

Bengtson, V. L. (2001). "Beyond the nuclear family: the increasing importance of multigenerational bonds (The Burgess Award Lecture)," *Journal of Marriage and the Family*, 63 (1): 1–16.

Bengtson, V. L., and N. E. Cutler (1976). "Generations and inter-generational relations: perspectives on age-groups and social change." In R. H. Binstock and E. Shanas, eds., *The handbook of aging and the social sciences*. New York: Van Nostrand Reinhold, pp. 130–59.

Caldwell, C. H., Antonucci, T. C., and J. S. Jackson (1998). "Supportive/conflictual family relations and depressive symptomatology: teenage mother and grandmother perspectives," *Family Relations: Interdisciplinary Journal of Applied Family Studies*, special issue: *The family as a context for health and well-being*, 47 (4): 395–402.

Cantor, M. H., and V. Little (1985). "Aging and social care." In R. H. Binstock and E. Shanas, eds., *Handbook of aging and the social sciences*. New York: Van Nostrand Reinhold, pp. 745–81.

Daatland, S. O. (1990). "What are families for? On family solidarity and preferences for help," *Ageing and Society*, 1: 1–15.

Farkas, J., and D. Hogan (1995). "The demography of changing intergenerational relationships." In J. Farkas and D. Hogan, eds., *Adult intergenerational relations: effects of societal change*. New York: Springer Publishing Co., pp. 1–29.

Giarrusso, R., Silverstein, M., and V. L. Bengtson (1996). "Family complexities and the grandparent role," *Generations*, 22 (1, Spring): 17–23.

Giarrusso, R., Feng, D., Silverstein, M., and V. L. Bengtson (2001). "Grandparent – adult grandchild affection and consensus: crossgenerational and cross-ethnic comparisons," *Journal of Family Issues*, 22 (4): 456–77.

Hill, R., Foote, N., Aldous, J., Carlson, R., and R. MacDonald (1970). *Family development in three generations*. Cambridge, Mass.: Schenkman.

Jackson, J. S., and T. C. Antonucci (2002). "Environmental factors, life events and coping abilities." In J. R. M. Copeland, M. T. Abou-Saleh, and D. G. Blazer, eds., *The psychiatry of old age: an international textbook*, 2nd edn. Sussex: John Wiley & Sons, pp. 70.1–70.4.

Jackson, J. S., Torres, M., Caldwell, C. H., Neighbors, H. W., Nesse, R. M., Taylor, R. J., Trierweiler, S. J., and D. R. Williams (2004). "The National Survey of American Life: a study of racial, ethnic and cultural influences on mental disorders and mental health," *International Journal of Methods in Psychiatric Research*.

Kahn, R. L., and T. C. Antonucci (1984). *Supports of the elderly: family/friends/professionals*. Washington, D.C.: Final report to the National Institute on Aging.

Lingsom, S. (1997). *The substitution issue. Care policies and their consequences for family care*, NOVA-rapport 6/97. Oslo: NOVA (akad avh).

Lowenstein, A., and J. Ogg, eds. (2003). *OASIS – old age and autonomy: the role of service systems and intergenerational family solidarity. Final Report.* Haifa, Israel: The University of Haifa, Center for Research and Study of Aging.

Markides, K. S., Boldt, J. S., and L. A. Ray (1986). "Sources of helping and intergenerational solidarity: a three generations study of Mexican Americans," *Journal of Gerontology*, 41: 506–11.

Myers, C. G. (1990). "Demography of aging." In R. H. Binstock and L. K. George, eds., *Handbook of aging and the social sciences*, 3rd edn. San Diego, Calif.: Academic Press, pp. 19–44.

Riley, M. A., and J. W. Riley (1993). "Connections: kin and cohort." In V. L. Bengtson and W. A. Achenbaum, eds., *The changing contract across nations*. New York: Aldine de Gruyter, pp. 169–89.

Roberts, R. E. L., and V. L. Bengtson (1996). "Affective ties to parents in early adulthood and self-esteem across 20 years," *Social Psychology Quarterly*, 59 (1): 96–106.

Rossi, A. S., and P. H. Rossi (1990). *Of human bonding: parent–child relations across the life-course*. New York: Aldine de Gruyter.

Treas, J. (1995). "Older Americans in the 1990s and beyond," *Population Bulletin*, 50: 2–46.

Uhlenberg, P. (1996). "Mortality decline in the twentieth century and supply of kin over the life course," *Gerontologist*, 38: 681–5.

Walker, R. (1993). "Language shift in Europe and Irian Jaya, Indonesia: toward the heart of the matter." In Kees de Bot, ed., *Case studies in minority languages*. AILA Review, 10. Amsterdam: Association Internationale de Linguistique Appliqueé, pp. 71–87.

CHAPTER 5.11

Gay and Lesbian Elders

KATHERINE R. ALLEN

The lives of gay and lesbian elders provide a dramatic opportunity to consider very diverse people from all walks of life who have experienced particular kinds of adversity and resilience. In no way do older gay men and lesbians comprise a monolithic group, as both in-depth narratives and case studies of gay men and lesbians (e.g., Adelman *et al.*, 1993; Cohler and Hostetler, 2002; Peacock, 2000; Rosenfeld, 1999; Shenk and Fullmer, 1996), as well as surveys and mixed method studies indicate (e.g., Adelman, 1990; Berger, 1984; Kehoe, 1986; Kelly, 1977; Whitford, 1997). Given the social-historical transformations that occurred in the twentieth century, contemporary elders have experienced both extreme prejudice and unprecedented liberalization in attitudes and practices regarding sexual orientation diversity (Brotman *et al.*, 2003; D'Emilio and Freedman, 1997; Lee, 1989; Oswald, 2002). During the last third of the twentieth century, a time when contemporary gay and lesbian elders were middle-aged and ageing, the dominant discourse about homosexuality as stigma has been challenged, and, for many, replaced with a more positive political identity imbued with status and pride (Rosenfeld, 1999). Now, sexual identities are experienced as far more fluid than they were when today's elders came of age, signaling a host of new issues for scholars and practitioners to investigate and understand (DeAngelis, 2002; Klein 1990). From a lifecourse perspective, the lives of older gay men and lesbians reveal dramatic upheavals in biography, interpersonal processes, and social change.

CHALLENGING HETEROSEXISM AND AGEISM IN THE STUDY OF GAY AND LESBIAN ELDERS

With such a rich history to explore, it is curious that scholars in both ageing studies and in gay and lesbian studies have all but ignored gay and lesbian elders (Pugh, 2002). Calasanti and Slevin (2001) observe that scholars in ageing have paid even less attention to the complexity of experiences that relate to sexual orientation diversity than they have to race and ethnic diversity. Most of what is known about gay family ties is focused on gay and lesbian couples and the relationships between gay and lesbian parents and their dependent children (Allen and Demo, 1995). Little attention has been given to their adult family relationships, such as sibling ties in later life (Connidis, 2001). While there is an abundant ageing literature in general, and we know increasingly more about what it means to be a gay, lesbian, bisexual, or transgender (GLBT) individual, the intersection of being gay or lesbian with being old is relatively unexplored, compared to being old and a woman, or being old and poor, for example. Thus, the literature in gerontology lacks a focus on sexual orientation diversity, and the sexual orientation literature lacks a focus on ageing (Calasanti and Slevin, 2001).

Most of what we know about gay and lesbian elders is pieced together from empirical studies and theories designed with heterosexuals as the standard in gerontology, or younger people (especially younger gay men) as the standard in gay and lesbian studies (Jacobson and Grossman, 1996). Pugh (2002) observed that the study of gay and lesbian elders is one that has yet to blossom fully since its discovery in 1969 with the publication of Weinberg's investigation of older male homosexuals. The emerging academic arena of gay and lesbian studies has promoted an esoteric "queering" of the scientific and literary canon (Chauncey, 2000), in which mainstream theories are critiqued and prevailing scientific assumptions are transgressed. The emphasis in queer theory leaves little room for cross fertilization between such postmodern scholars and more empirically oriented scholars who conduct research and publish in gerontology.

Perhaps because the social forces of heterosexism and ageism, like sexism, racism, and classism, are so resistant to change, the scientific study of gay and lesbian elders has yet to mature. Heterosexism is a bias reflecting widespread cultural ignorance about sexuality and relationships, conceptualizing "human experience in strictly heterosexual terms and consequently ignoring, invalidating, or derogating homosexual behaviors and sexual orientation, and lesbian, gay, and bisexual relationships and lifestyles" (Herek *et al.*, 1991: 958). Related to heterosexism is another form of prejudice – homophobia, which is an irrational fear and hatred of GLBT people. Heterosexism and homophobia are publicly supported by laws and de facto discrimination, thereby influencing professional gate keeping practices that continue to exclude sexual orientation diversity as an acceptable topic of study (Allen and Demo, 1995). As well, ageism in the gay community, whereby beauty and youthfulness render older gays and lesbians invisible and forgotten, is another form of prejudice impeding the accumulation of knowledge about gay and lesbian elders (Brotman *et al.*, 2003; Pugh 2002). Particularly for gay men, age 35 may mark the beginning of old (DeAngelis, 2002).

Although disciplines change slowly, evidence from Allen *et al.*'s (2000) meta-analysis of 908 family gerontology articles published from 1990 to 1999 reveal five conceptual advances in the literature. First, more interest is being given to families in the middle and later years, rather than a near exclusive focus on ageing individuals. Second, a more sophisticated emphasis is being given to diversity, by gender, race, class, and other stratifications. Third, a feminist approach to gender relations, rather than a dichotomous approach to gender difference, is evident in the literature. Fourth, gerontologists are paying more attention to formerly ignored or stigmatized relationships. Although only 3 of the 908 articles in the decade of the 1990s focused on sexual orientation diversity, compared to one-third of the articles being about family caregiving, for example, sexual orientation was a non-existent topic in the previous decade. Finally, the literature reveals a turn from a deficit approach in ageing studies to a strengths and resilience approach. Taken together, these trends demonstrate greater appreciation of the diversity and complexity of older adult lives, and set the stage for making it possible for studies of GLBT elders to occur.

DEMOGRAPHICS AND DIVERSITY AMONG OLDER GAY MEN AND LESBIANS

Precise estimates of the number of older gay and lesbian adults are impossible to attain, due to the invisibility and anonymity of this population (Lipman, 1984). As Allen and Demo (1995) explain, it is impossible to know how many gay and lesbian individuals there are in the general population, given difficulties in varying definitions of sexual orientation, the ongoing exclusion of lesbian and gay people from research investigations, and the further exclusion of bisexuality as a type of sexual orientation diversity.

In lieu of precise population estimates, commentators frequently refer to an extrapolation from Kinsey and associates' data that approximately 10 percent of the population in the United States defines itself as predominantly lesbian or gay, although these figures have been widely criticized on methodological grounds (Allen and Demo, 1995). Lipman (1984), for example, observed that the "proportion of the aged who are homosexuals is probably as high or higher than the proportion of the aged who are nursing home residents" (p. 325). The National Gay and Lesbian Task Force estimated that there are 2.8 million gay men and lesbians in America over age 65 (Abraham, 2003).

In an important demographic analysis of the gay and lesbian population of the United States, Black *et al.*, (2000) developed a statistical portrait from three large data sets: the General Social Survey (GSS), the National Health and Social Life

Survey (NHSLS), and the US Census. This investigation addressed conceptual problems evident in earlier analyses of population estimates that took for granted the Kinsey data, by attempting to resolve two important problems: the importance of sampling from a known population and the ambiguity of the very definition of homosexuality across studies.

Findings relevant for the study of gay and lesbian elders concern geographic distribution, military service, and educational and economic attainment. Black *et al.* (2000) found that older gay men were just as likely to have served in the military during the Second World War and the Korean War as other men, compared to younger gay men today who are far less likely than other men to serve in the military. Lesbians, on the other hand, have always been more likely to serve in the military than other women with a much less pronounced decline in the second half of the twentieth century. Regarding the gay and lesbian population in general, Black *et al.* found that 60 percent of partnered gay men in the US live in only twenty cities (primarily San Francisco, Washington D.C., Los Angeles, Atlanta, and New York), whereas partnered lesbians were somewhat more geographically dispersed. Gay men and lesbians have higher educational levels than other men and women. Although gay men have lower earnings than other men, lesbians earn more than other women. These findings are among the first analyses of large-scale probability samples on a population that has received little systematic attention.

METHODOLOGICAL AND THEORETICAL ISSUES

Methodological issues abound in trying to study gay and lesbian elders. Given the relative invisibility of this population, gaining access to an appropriate sample is difficult. Until questions about sexual orientation diversity are actually included on general probability surveys, we will continue to see more descriptive studies on gay and lesbian elders and the kinds of sampling biases that mar almost every national survey, including the National Survey of Families and Households in the US (Allen and Demo, 1995). There is no known national probability sample of gay and lesbian elders, although Black *et al.*'s (2000) work with the GSS, NHSLS, and US Census is a needed beginning.

The bulk of the empirical literature on gay and lesbian individuals and families to date is based on small samples of mostly White, urban, middle-class, highly educated respondents, recruited from within the gay community (Allen and Demo, 1995; Black *et al.*, 2000). The same is true for most studies of gay and lesbian elders, in that they, too, consist of convenience samples that are small, descriptive, and typically from large urban centers where affluent gay men and lesbians tend to live (Lipman, 1984). A review of the empirical studies on gay and lesbian elders published in key gerontological journals as of this writing reveals that participants in all of these studies were located through gay-affirmative organizations (see Brotman *et al.*, 2003; Kelly, 1977; Lee, 1989; Quam and Whitford, 1992; Rosenfeld, 1999). As a result, our research into gay and lesbian elders has over sampled those who are affirmative or out about their sexual orientation or have access to a known part of the gay community (Friend, 1990; Jacobson and Grossman, 1996).

The empirical literature on gay and lesbian ageing is also gendered. We know more about gay male ageing, according to Pugh (2002), because more of that research contains both quantitative and qualitative information. The literature on older lesbians relies more exclusively on a narrative life history approach. Quantitatively orientated data are easier to summarize and extract than the richer narrative and biographical material generated about older lesbians, rendering their experiences even more invisible in the literature than that of gay men.

In terms of theoretical applications, gerontological theory has been expanded by the challenges of applying the experiences of gay and lesbian elders. Typically, a developmental framework organized around stages in Erikson's psychosocial theory has been applied to the lives of older gay men (Kimmel, 1978; Peacock, 2000). Recognizing the diversity of experiences among gay and lesbian elders, however, Rosenfeld (1999) demonstrated the use of an interactionist framework for understanding various meanings of identity cohorts of thirty-seven gay men and lesbians, aged 65 to 89. She found four distinct ways in which these elders constructed and managed their homosexual identities in relation to when in their lives they came out as gay or lesbian. Their experiences differed depending on the social-historical context of whether homosexuality itself was stigmatized (prior to the time of gay liberation) or more celebrated as it is today.

By applying a feminist lifecourse perspective, gerontologists can acknowledge the diversity among older gays and lesbians without ignoring the very real differences and discrimination that older gays and lesbians have faced (Allen *et al.*, 2000). It is important to keep in mind that both negative stereotypes and positive images are competing for public attention. One way to view the lives of gay and lesbian elders is to see the innovation and resilience that comes from confronting and overcoming a lifetime of marginalization and discrimination (Brotman *et al.*, 2003; Oswald, 2002). Many studies reveal ways in which older gay men and lesbians provide important role models for surviving adversity and creating community despite hostile social and legal barriers, without the benefit of the cushion that heterosexual privilege provides (e.g. Kehoe, 1986; Kimmel, 1978; Quam and Whitford, 1992). Just as African American families have created fictive kin ties to buffer the relatively few resources available to them in the wider society, gays and lesbians have created flourishing family ties out of friendships when their own kin have rejected them (Greene, 2002; Kimmel, 1992). They have formed support groups even in the most restrictive political climates, for example the McCarthy era of the 1950s (Jacobson and Grossman, 1996). They have utilized these chosen kin ties not just as intimate family relationships, but also as launching pads for political action, in terms of publicizing and fighting for research and education about the AIDS pandemic (Altman, 1995) and collectively advocating the rights of ageing gay and lesbian clients (Berger, 1984).

At the same time, Brotman *et al.* (2003) caution that, despite this resilience, gay and lesbian elders may be more at risk than others, given a lifetime of stigma and the lack of structural supports for people who are not heterosexual. They arrive at old age vulnerable to the heterosexism and homophobia in the elder care community, without the concomitant social buffers available to more privileged members of ageing society. Efforts to ameliorate this problem include the need for a new openness about the issue of sexuality in general in elder care, as well as the particular needs of gay and lesbian elders in formal care settings.

SOCIAL-HISTORICAL CONTEXT OF GAY AND LESBIAN AGEING

Older cohorts of gay men and lesbians have faced a lifetime of discrimination and social rejection in a variety of forms, from internalized homophobia to institutionalized heterosexism. For the first half of their lifecourse, the kind of love and sexual desire they felt was unspeakable because it was labeled deviant, a crime, and a sickness (D'Emilio and Freedman, 1997; Faderman, 1991). To identify openly as a gay man or lesbian was to invite social ostracism and financial poverty, in that prevailing medical, religious, legal, and popular opinion condemned homosexual identity and practice. In short, to be "out of the closet" would surely mean to be out of a job, a family, and an identity as a productive, healthy, and worthy citizen.

As their adult years progressed, contemporary gay and lesbian elders have witnessed, participated in, or led an array of efforts that comprise the movement for equal recognition of civil rights for gay and lesbian people. Indeed, the early years of the twenty-first century herald a cultural shift so pronounced that many gay and lesbian elders find they have little in common with the youthful "queers" who bend and blend gender categories in today's liberated GLBT communities (DeAngelis, 2002; Lee, 1989; Stein, 1993). Older gays and lesbians did not have the kind of choices about coming out in young adulthood that many gay, lesbian, bisexual, and transgender individuals do today. Like the Civil Rights movement for African Americans or the women's liberation movement for international women's rights, the contemporary gay liberation movement is unprecedented in human history. This diverse collection of efforts for gay rights has local, regional, national, and global manifestations. So too have the AIDS pandemic (Altman, 1995), legal rights for GLBT family members (Weeks *et al.*, 2001), the plethora of sexual lifeways around the globe (Herdt, 1997), and, now, the rights, protection, and recognition of older gay and lesbian adults (Brotman *et al.*, 2003; Quam and Whitford, 1992).

Sexual orientation diversity, e.g., homosexuality, heterosexuality, bisexuality, and transgenderism, then, is no longer the taboo topic it was when current gay and lesbian elders were growing up and coming of age. They have witnessed profound changes in their individual, social, and historical circumstances. The watershed moment of the contemporary gay liberation movement in the United States occurred on June 27, 1969, at the Stonewall Inn, a gay bar, in the mournful days following the burial of gay icon Judy Garland (Editors of the *Harvard Law Review*, 1990). Mid-century America was a particularly punishing time and place for sexual difference; one of the only cultural places for homosexuals to gather was the gay bar or club. Such spaces were routinely subject to arbitrary police harassment, but in the aftermath of the revered entertainer's death, drag performers and bar patrons spontaneously fought back against the police, thereby igniting a riot. Born between the two world wars, contemporary older gays and lesbians were entering middle age (Cohler and Hostetler, 2002) when this moment introduced a new generation of *proud* gay men and lesbians into the wider culture (Herrell, 1992). Surely, there were differential effects of the Stonewall revolution on their lives, as Cohler and Hostetler (2002) demonstrate in the detailed life histories of ageing gay men they collected.

After years of invisibility, retrenchment, or, at best, quiet activism among older homosexuals of all social classes in the repressive decades of the 1930s, '40s, and '50s, the "Stonewall generation" set the stage for increasing visibility and demand for civil rights for GLBT people that influences public and private discourse about sexual orientation today (D'Emilio and Freedman, 1997). For example, the 1970s brought about several important changes that made it increasingly possible to live an openly gay life. The American Psychiatric Association removed homosexuality from its list of mental disorders in 1974; the American Psychological Association removed it in 1975; the US Civil Service Commission ended the ban against employing gay men and lesbians in 1975; and Harvey Milk became the first openly gay elected supervisor of a major US city (San Francisco) in 1977 (D'Emilio and Freedman, 1997; Herek *et al.*, 1991). The 1980s and 1990s brought more focused concern on healthcare issues linked to AIDS. Today, issues of marital and parental rights for gay and lesbian families are in the forefront of public attention. The social and political climate in which gay men and lesbians claim their identity has been radically transformed from one of

shame and stigma to one of pride and empowerment (Rosenfeld, 1999).

ADAPTATIONS IN LATER LIFE FOR GAY AND LESBIAN ELDERS

A major theme in the literature on gay and lesbian ageing concerns the challenges and possibilities resulting from this legacy of marginalization, stigma, and discrimination. Older gay, lesbian, bisexual, and transgender individuals intersect with at least two social locations of minority status: nonheterosexual orientation and older age. Those who are women (Kehoe, 1986), members of racial–ethnic minority groups (Greene, 2002), have lower socioeconomic status (Quam and Whitford, 1992), or developmental disabilities (Allen, 2003), face these problems exponentially. Evidence from national health surveys, such as the National Lesbian Health Care Survey, in which issues relevant to gays and lesbians have been addressed, reveal that a lifetime of managing stress and stigma from a marginalized identity can result in higher risks of depression and suicide, addictions, and substance abuse (Brotman *et al.*, 2003). This problem is exacerbated when healthcare and social service professionals are insensitive to the needs of older gays and lesbians, leading them to avoid needed services altogether (Brotman *et al.*, 2003; Quam and Whitford, 1992).

On the other hand, the literature is replete with stories of how older gay men and lesbians have developed strength, wisdom, and tenacity as a result of enduring a lifetime of stigma. Often rejected from families of origin, it is well documented that older gay men and lesbians have much stronger support networks than their heterosexual peers (Kimmel, 1992; Lipman, 1984). As Pugh (2002) concludes in his literature review of the social support networks of older gay men and lesbians, they "have vibrant social lives, which involve mutual support" (p. 175). They are experts at developing social networks by drawing on a variety of community resources, resisting oppression, learning to take care of themselves, and facing change (Brotman *et al.*, 2003; Dunker, 1987; Oswald, 2002). Part of their community building includes a variety of comprehensive service models explicitly designed for their needs. One of the original programs is SAGE (Senior Action in a Gay Environment). Founded in 1977 in New York City, there are chapters in other states and Canada (Jacobson and Grossman, 1996).

The implications of spending most of their lives in a social environment that is repressive and punitive towards sexual minorities has a variety of outcomes for older gay men and lesbians. They have had to cope with the negative stereotypes and images of homosexuality, such as "pervert" and "sexual deviant" (Jacobson and Grossman, 1996: 347). For most of their lives, they have not had the social support, visibility, or legal protections that younger lesbians and gay men have today (Greene, 2002). As members of at least a triple minority, old lesbian women are "survivors" (Kehoe, 1986).

Given the heterogeneity in the gay and lesbian ageing population, it is important to recognize the diversity in adaptation strategies. Friend (1990) proposed a model of identity development based on older gays' and lesbians' responses to the prevailing heterosexist ideologies and practices that dominate society. *Stereotypic* older gays and lesbians have internalized the negative homophobic stereotypes and continue to live in secrecy about their identity and fear of discovery. *Passing* older lesbians and gay men are somewhat more comfortable with their identity, but still accept heterosexuality as the norm, forcing them to compartmentalize themselves as members of two divergent social worlds. *Affirmative* older gay men and lesbians have responded to heterosexism by reconstructing a positive and affirmative sense of self and typically engaging in personal and professional activism.

Narrative examples of a passing and an affirmative gay man, respectively, can be found in Cohler and Hostetler's (2002) life histories of two septuagenarians. Both examples of "successful ageing" as gay men, "Matthew" lived in two social worlds, one as a gay man with his lifelong partner, and the other as a man who was closeted at work. "Jeffrey" was completely out in all areas of his life and an activist for gay causes. Locating stereotypic older lesbians and gay men would be far more difficult, given that their internalized homophobia, with its corresponding feelings of distress, shame, and self-loathing, would keep them away from the organizations associated with the gay community from which most samples are currently recruited (Jacobson and Grossman, 1996).

CONCLUSIONS AND FUTURE DIRECTIONS

Gay and lesbian elders are emerging as a presence in the gerontological literature as well as in the gay, lesbian, bisexual, and transgender community (Allen *et al.*, 2000; Pugh, 2002; Rosenfeld, 1999). Given the forces of heterosexism and ageism, however, much of their story has yet to be told. To be gay and gray, or to be an old lesbian, is to be outside the youthful world of contemporary "liberated" gay communities (Lee, 1989) and the heterosexual ageing world (Calasanti and Slevin, 2001; Jacobson and Grossman, 1996). There is much to discover, explore, and explain about the experiences of gay and lesbian elders, not to mention people who consider themselves bisexual or transgender, who comprise an even more marginalized and invisible group (Brotman *et al.*, 2003).

Within the experiences of gay and lesbian elders are gems of insight about their resilience *and* vulnerability in the face of adversity. Coming out, or the disclosure of one's sexual identity, is a lifelong process – not the sole domain of the young, and never a once and for all accomplishment. Yet, coming out is just the tip of the iceberg where gay and lesbian elders are concerned. Their lives reveal complex intersections of individual biography, interpersonal processes (such as developing and maintaining chosen kin ties), and social-historical transformations of monumental proportion. Those who care about, investigate, and serve older adults would do well to learn and benefit from their experiences of marginalization *and* innovation.

FURTHER READING

Brotman, S., Ryan, B., and R. Cormier, R. (2003). "The health and social service needs of gay and lesbian elders and their families in Canada," *Gerontologist*, 43: 192–202.

Demo, D. H., and K. R. Allen (1996). "Diversity within lesbian and gay families: Challenges and implications for family theory and research," *Journal of Social and Personal Relationships*, 13: 415–34.

Pugh, S. (2002). "The forgotten: a community without a generation – older lesbians and gay men." In D.

Richardson and S. Seidman, eds., *Handbook of lesbian and gay studies*. London: Sage, pp. 161–81.

Rosenfeld, D. (1999). "Identity work among lesbian and gay elderly," *Journal of Aging Studies*, 13: 121–44.

REFERENCES

Abraham, Y. (2003). "Gay elders emerge from long isolation," *Boston Globe*, June 9, p. A1.

Adelman, M. (1990). "Stigma, gay lifestyles, and adjustment to aging: a study of later-life gay men and lesbians," *Journal of Homosexuality*, 20 (3/4): 7–32.

Adelman, J., Berger, R., Boyd, M., Doublex, V., Freedman, M., Hubbard, W. S., Kight, M., Kochman, A., Robinson Meyer, M. K., and S. M. Raphael, eds. (1993). *Lambda gray: a practical, emotional, and spiritual guide for gays and lesbians who are growing older*. North Hollywood, Calif.: Newcastle.

Allen, J. D. (2003). *Gay, lesbian, bisexual, and transgender people with developmental disabilities and mental retardation: stories of the Rainbow Support Group*. Binghamton, N.Y.: Harrington Park.

Allen, K. R., and D. H. Demo (1995). "The families of lesbians and gay men: a new frontier in family research." *Journal of Marriage and the Family*, 57: 111–27.

Allen, K. R., Blieszner, R., and K. A. Roberto (2000). "Families in the middle and later years: a review and critique of research in the 1990s." *Journal of Marriage and the Family*, 62: 911–26.

Altman, D. (1995). "Political sexualities: meanings and identities in the time of AIDS." In R. G. Parker and J. H. Gagnon, eds., *Conceiving sexuality: approaches to sex research in a postmodern world*. New York: Routledge, pp. 98–106.

Berger, R. M. (1984). "Realities of gay and lesbian aging." *Social Work*, 29: 57–62.

Black, D., Gates, G., Sanders, S., and L. Taylor (2000). "Demographics of the gay and lesbian population in the United States: evidence from available systematic data sources." *Demography*, 37: 139–54.

Brotman, S., Ryan, B., and R. Cormier (2003). "The health and social service needs of gay and lesbian elders and their families in Canada." *Gerontologist*, 43: 192–202.

Calasanti, T. M., and K. F. Slevin (2001). *Gender, social inequalities, and aging*. Walnut Creek, Calif.: AltaMira.

Chauncey, G. (2000). "The queer history and politics of lesbian and gay studies." In J. A. Boone, M. Dupuis, M. Meeker, K. Quimby, C. Sarver, D. Silverman, and R. Weatherston, eds., *Queer frontiers: millennial geographies, genders, and generations*. Madison, Wis.: University of Wisconsin Press, pp. 298–315.

Cohler, B. J., and A. J. Hostetler (2002). "Aging, intimate relationships, and life story among gay men." In R. S. Weiss and S. A. Bass, eds., *Challenges of the third age: meaning and purpose in later life*. New York: Oxford University Press, pp. 137–60.

Connidis, I. A. (2001). *Family ties & aging*. Thousand Oaks, Calif.: Sage.

DeAngelis, T. (2002). "A new generation of issues for LGBT clients," *Monitor on Psychology*, February: 42–4.

D'Emilio, J., and E. B. Freedman (1997). *Intimate matters: a history of sexuality in America*, 2nd edn. Chicago: University of Chicago Press.

Dunker, B. (1987). "Aging lesbians: observations and speculations". In Boston Lesbian Psychologies Collective, ed., *Lesbian psychologies: explorations & challenges*. Urbana, Ill: University of Illinois Press, pp. 72–82.

Editors of the *Harvard Law Review* (1990). *Sexual orientation and the law*. Cambridge, Mass.: Harvard University Press.

Faderman, L. (1991). *Odd girls and twilight lovers: a history of lesbian life in twentieth century America*. New York: Penguin.

Friend, R. A. (1990). "Older lesbian and gay people: a theory of successful aging." *Journal of Homosexuality*, 20 (3/4): 99–118.

Greene, B. (2002). "Older lesbians' concerns and psychotherapy: beyond a footnote to the footnote." In F. K. Trotman and C. M. Brody, eds., *Psychotherapy and counseling with older women: cross-cultural, family, and end-of-life issues*. New York: Springer, pp. 161–74.

Herdt, G. (1997). *Same sex, different cultures: gays and lesbians across cultures*. Boulder, Colo.: Westview.

Herek, G. M., Kimmel, D.C., Amaro, H., and G. B. Melton (1991). "Avoiding heterosexist bias in psychological research," *American Psychologist*, 46: 957–63.

Herrell, R. K. (1992). "The symbolic strategies of Chicago's Gay and Lesbian Pride Day Parade." In G. Herdt, ed., *Gay culture in America*. Boston: Beacon, pp. 225–52.

Jacobson, S., and A. H. Grossman (1996). "Older lesbians and gay men: old myths, new images, and future directions." In R. C. Savin-Williams and K. M Cohen, eds., *The lives of lesbians, gays, and bisexuals*. Fort Worth, Tex.: Harcourt Brace, pp. 345–73.

Kehoe, M. (1986). "Lesbians over 65: a triply invisible minority," *Journal of Homosexuality*, 12 (3/4): 139–52.

Kelly, J. (1977). "The aging male homosexual: myth and reality," *Gerontologist*, 17: 328–32.

Kimmel, D. C. (1978). "Adult development and aging: a gay perspective," *Journal of Social Issues*, 34: 113–30.

(1992). "The families of older gays and lesbians." *Generations*, 17: 37–8.

Klein, F. (1990). "The need to view sexual orientation as a multivariable dynamic process: a theoretical perspective." In D. P. McWhirter, S. A. Saunders, and J. M. Reinisch, eds., *Homosexuality/heterosexuality: concepts of sexual orientation*. New York: Oxford University Press, pp. 277–82.

Lee, J. A. (1989). "Invisible men: Canada's aging homosexuals. Can they be assimilated into Canada's 'liberated' gay communities?" *Canadian Journal on Aging*, 8: 79–97.

Lipman, A. (1984). "Homosexuals." In E. Palmore, ed., *Handbook on the aged in the United States*. Westport, Conn.: Greenwood, pp. 322–37.

Oswald, R. F. (2002). "Resilience within the family networks of lesbians and gay men: intentionality and redefinition," *Journal of Marriage and Family*, 64: 374–83.

Peacock, J. R. (2000). "Gay male adult development: some stage issues of an older cohort," *Journal of Homosexuality*, 40 (2): 13–29.

Pugh, S. (2002). "The forgotten: a community without a generation – older lesbians and gay men." In D. Richardson and S. Seidman, eds., *Handbook of lesbian and gay studies*. London: Sage, pp. 161–81.

Quam, J. K., and G. S. Whitford (1992). "Adaptation and age-related expectations of older gay and lesbian adults." *Gerontologist*, 32: 367–74.

Rosenfeld, D. (1999). "Identity work among lesbian and gay elderly," *Journal of Aging Studies*, 13: 121–44.

Shenk, D., and E. Fullmer (1996). "Significant relationships among older women: cultural and personal constructions of lesbianism." In K. A. Roberto, ed., *Relationships between women in later life*. New York: Harrington Park, pp. 75–89.

Stein, A., ed. (1993). *Sisters, sexperts, queers: beyond the lesbian nation*. New York: Plume.

Weeks, J., Heaphy, B., and C. Donovan (2001). *Same sex intimacies: families of choice and other life experiments*. London: Routledge.

Whitford, G. S. (1997). "Realities and hopes for older gay males," *Journal of Gay & Lesbian Social Services*, 6 (1): 79–95.

PART SIX

THE AGEING OF SOCIETIES

The Lifecourse Perspective on Ageing: Linked Lives, Timing, and History

VERN L. BENGTSON, GLEN H. ELDER, JR., AND NORELLA M. PUTNEY

Only in the last few decades have researchers in ageing recognized the importance of larger social and historical contexts for understanding the health and wellbeing of individuals across the lifespan. Prior to the mid 1960s, the study of human lives was exceedingly rare in sociology and psychology, especially in relation to sociohistorical context (Elder, 1998). Most human development research was characterized by a life cycle approach, one of the oldest accounts of how lives and families are organized over time. The life cycle provided a useful way of thinking about the intergenerational patterning of lives, and their sequence of role transitions, such as marriage and childbearing. The duration of intergenerational cycles, however, varies greatly, depending on the timing of marriage and childbearing. The greater the time spread between the generations, the more diverse the individual's historical experience. In addition the life cycle does not represent contemporary patterns of divorce and remarriage or childbearing outside of marriage. And it does not apply to the never married or non-parents. While the concept of life cycle provided an account of role sequences and linked lives, it did not locate people according to their life stage or historical context.

In the 1960s and '70s, the life cycle approach began to converge with a new awareness of the multiple meanings of age. Age orders social roles and events, but it also orders people through birth year and birth cohorts. Chronological age refers to stage in the developmental ageing process. These new ways of thinking about age included an emphasis on subjective experiences with society's age struc-tures and the individual's own construction of the lifecourse, as expressed particularly in the pioneering work of Bernice Neugarten (Neugarten and Datan, 1973). Age distinctions were required to place families in history and to mark the transitions of adult life. Since the mid 1980s, inquiry into the continuity and change of human lives in relation to interpersonal, structural, and historical forces has grown exponentially (Elder, 2003; Elder and Johnson, 2001). Lifecourse studies have become integral to social scientific research on ageing.

THE LIFECOURSE PERSPECTIVE

The lifecourse as concept and theoretical orientation

The "lifecourse" is conceptualized as a sequence of age-linked transitions that are embedded in social institutions and history. As a theoretical orientation, the lifecourse perspective sensitizes researchers to the fundamental importance of historical conditions and change for understanding individual development and family life. It establishes a common field of inquiry by defining a framework that guides research in terms of problem identification and formulation, variable selection and rationales, and strategies of design and analysis. The institutional structuring of lives is at the core of lifecourse analysis (Mortimer and Shanahan, 2003). Institutional contexts – the family, schools, work and labor markets, church, government – define both the normative pathways of social roles, including key transitions, and the psychological, behavioral, and health-related trajectories of persons as they move through them.

Age, in its various meanings, serves as the analytic link between changing lives, changing family relations, and changing historical contexts. Families are age-differentiated, especially because generational position defines an individual's place in the extended family structure and shapes identities, roles, and responsibilities. At the same time, families are age-integrated in that individuals of varying ages and cohorts are joined together and family-related roles and activities extend across life even as specific roles and activities shift up the generational ladder over time (Settersten, 2003). Within pluralistic contemporary societies, lifecourse trajectories and transitions display considerable variability. Yet despite this variability, continuity remains a predominant feature of individual psychological and behavioral trajectories. Multigenerational families as well display considerable continuity over time.

Principles of the lifecourse

Five principles define the lifecourse perspective. First is the principle of "linked lives," which emphasizes the interconnectedness of lives, particularly as linked across the generations by bonds of kinship. Lives are embedded in relationships with people and are influenced by them. They are linked over time in relation to changing times, places, and social institutions. Economic declines can have reverberating effects on the multiple and interlocking pathways of family members. For example, a mother's entry into the labor force can alleviate her family's financial troubles and contribute to her children's educational attainment, but it may also change the routines of family life or the balance of power in her marital relationship. Likewise, the plans of grandparents for retirement can be changed when adult children and grandchildren return home and need their support.

The second lifecourse principle pertains to historical time and place, emphasizing the importance of social and historical context in shaping individual lives. Large events such as depressions and wars, or the relative tranquility or turbulence of a historical period, shape individual psychology, family interactions, and world views. Such historical events and conditions create the opportunities and constraints that circumscribe choices and behaviors and can change the direction of lives. Follow-up stud-

ies of children who grew up during the Depression show that sociohistorical events (such as the Second World War and the US government's G. I. Bill) sometimes mitigated the negative effects of economic deprivation in childhood, opening up educational and career opportunities in young adulthood (Elder, 1987). Social change can also reduce options, as occurred in the economic restructuring of the 1980s and 1990s.

The third principle emphasizes the importance of transitions and their timing relative to the social contexts in which individuals make choices (Bengtson and Allen, 1993; Elder, 1995); the developmental antecedents and consequences of life transitions, events, and behavior patterns vary according to their timing in a person's life. There can be a "best fit" in the timing of individual development and family life stage, and their temporal convergence with structural and historically created opportunities (Elder *et al.*, 2003). For example, all age cohorts were confronted by the social upheavals of the late 1960s and 1970s, but at different stages in their lifecourse which presented different options and adaptive pressures. Biographical and historical timing had consequences for their demographic behavior, occupational outcomes, and psychological wellbeing (Putney and Bengtson, 2003). The pace of biographical, institutional, and historical change are characteristically asynchronous, producing structural or cultural lags. These disjunctures create tensions in individual lives, but they can also provide the impetus for change.

The fourth principle concerns agency and the idea that planfulness and effort can affect life outcomes. Lifecourse theory recognizes that individuals are active agents in the construction of their lives. They make choices within the opportunities and constraints provided by family background, stage in the lifecourse, structural arrangements, and historical conditions. Family life also has agentic aspects, as reflected in negotiation processes. For example, in a qualitative study, Pyke and Bengtson (1996) examined the differences between "individualistic" and "collectivistic" families when choices are made regarding caregiving for dependent elders.

The fifth principle centers on the idea that ageing and human development are life-long processes, and that the relationships, events, and behaviors of earlier life stages have consequences for later life relationships, statuses, and wellbeing. For example, longitudinal research has shown that the nurturing affirmation of children by parents contributes to higher self-esteem in adulthood (Roberts and Bengtson, 1996). Personal change and continuity are represented by concepts of lifespan development, such as cumulative advantage and disadvantage and self-identity.

Generations, cohorts, and social change

One advantage of multigenerational research on processes of ageing is that it represents related individuals rather than separate and unrelated birth cohorts (Alwin and McCammon, 2003). This enables the assessment of similarities and differences within families while controlling for various family-related factors. However, the effort to incorporate history into the study of lives and family relations has been difficult. The concept of "generation," most commonly used as a kinship term denoting position in the biological line of descent, does not easily index historical location or processes. This is because differences in childbearing patterns and the temporal gap between generations vary between families. In this sense, generations and age groups are not equivalent.

To understand the diverse pathways of individuals and families over the last half-century requires that they be situated in historical context. Analytically, this can be accomplished through the concept of "age cohort." Cohort implies the intersection of historical influence as indexed by birth year, and individual development or maturation. Birth cohorts share a social and cultural history, experiencing events and cultural moods when they are at the same stage of life. Characteristics of a birth cohort and events that the cohort experiences combine to affect members in distinctive ways, influencing their attitudes, behaviors, and outcomes across the entire lifecourse. Economic and political conditions leave lasting marks on those born in different historical periods. For women, the interaction of biology and biography with prevailing gender role norms and structural constraints has profoundly shaped their lives, but it has done so in historically specific ways, depending on their cohort membership. There is much variability within cohorts as well; members can be distinguished by class, gender, race, or their age when confronted by different socioeconomic events and conditions.

Cohort effects refer to the impact of historical events and structural arrangements on members of a given cohort as they grow older. However, such effects are not one-way; ageing cohorts in turn affect social structures (Riley *et al.*, 1994). The responses of one cohort to historical experiences often become normative patterns, affecting later born cohorts (Alwin and McCammon, 2003).

Age cohorts operate as forces of social change. "Generational turnover," or cohort succession, is often cited as a significant source of population change in attitudes and behaviors, as new cohorts bring their unique orientations into the population (Ryder, 1965). The cohort perspective suggests that historical conditions leave an indelible imprint on the attitudes of young adults at a time when they are most susceptible to absorbing the social values of the period, a phenomenon known as the "impressionable youth" hypothesis (Alwin *et al.*, 1991; Alwin and Krosnick, 1991; Clausen, 1993; Elder, 1994). Crucial to this argument is the way personal biography aligns with historical contingencies to produce sharp and durable variations across cohorts.

Paradoxically, societies can change both because individuals change (intracohort or aging effects) and because they remain stable or unchanged after an early period of socialization. Change occurs through cohort succession, where earlier born cohorts with certain values and characteristics are replaced by younger cohorts with different values and characteristics (Alwin and McCammon, 2003). This set of mechanisms is referred to as the Age-Period-Cohort model of social change because these mechanisms encapsulate the influence of ageing, time period and cohort membership on social change. The impact of a historical event on a cohort may be decomposed into a main effect (that which affects other cohorts similarly), and a unique effect (that which affects the cohort particularly). In addition, the strength or direction of change due to ageing may be conditioned on the unique historical location of each cohort.

De-institutionalization of the lifecourse

The structure of the lifecourse is closely linked to work life transitions. Across the first half of the twentieth century, these transitions became increasingly segmented into three distinct periods, reflecting an age-differentiated lifecourse (Riley *et al.*,

1994): preparation for work when young (education); work, during the middle years; and retirement from work in late midlife (Kohli, 1986). In the last few decades, however, there are signs that age structuring in education and work may be loosening – a de-institutionalization, or destandardization, of the lifecourse (Heinz, 2003). These changes in the "expected" lifecourse have implications for the study of lives and multigenerational families. Lifecourse patterns once thought fairly stable have become more fluid. They have shifted across different spheres – education, work, retirement, family – for successive cohorts of men and women, for subgroups (especially by race and social class), and across cultures.

Individuals can now move between areas and simultaneously pursue education, work, and leisure experiences throughout life, rather than being restricted to one or the other in different stages of life. In the area of work, there are indications that patterned "career" trajectories are giving way to increasing individualization (Heinz, 2003). Heinz argues that in postindustrial society there is an increasing emphasis upon personal decisions and responsibility in the shaping of work life, and a corresponding decline of normative age-markers for the timing and sequencing of labor market participation, and the timing of retirement. Paid work remains the foundation of the lifecourse, but continuous careers and stable employment are less certain because of more turbulent and globalized labor markets. At the beginning of the millennium, workers are increasingly "on their own," assuming greater responsibility for the timing of transitions, the time spent in school and work, the construction of their own pathways through the employment system, and ultimately the adequacy of provisions in retirement.

FOUNDATIONAL STUDIES OF THE LIFECOURSE

Lifecourse theory emerged in part out of efforts to understand the Great Depression experience in families and lives (Elder, 1974, 1999). Initially, an intergenerational framework and traditional life cycle approach seemed appropriate for investigating the process by which economic hardship affected the lives of children by altering family relations and socialization. However, the dramatic change of life experience from the 1920s into the late 1930s required the consideration of "age" as the essential link to historical change and life stage. A combination of the life cycle and age-based models, along with concepts of lifespan development, resulted in a multifaceted theoretical orientation on the lifecourse.

Children of the Great Depression

An early lifecourse study, *Children of the Great Depression* (Elder, 1974) challenged the then prevalent developmental stage theories by demonstrating the profound effects of historical events on human development, not only in youth but throughout the adult lifecourse. Premised on the idea that processes of individual and family change are inextricably linked to processes of historical change, the research strategy was to start with the historical event itself, and then track its myriad effects on family relations and individuals over time.

The socioeconomic change of families (with parents and children) is a strategic point at which to investigate the dynamics of generational change, of change between old and young in the succession of generations. The sample, derived from archival data in the Oakland Growth Study, consisted of 167 children born in 1920–1 who were intensively studied from 1932 to 1939. These children were preadolescents and adolescents during the Depression decade, and graduated from high school just before the Second World War. Three group distinctions entered into the assessment of economic change in family adaptation and life outcomes: birth cohorts; status groups within a particular cohort (those who had suffered economic deprivation and those who had not); and economic sectors of status groups (working-class and middle-class).

The study followed this group of children from their preadolescent years early in the Depression to their middle-age years, tracing step by step the ways in which deprivation left its mark on their relationships, careers, lifestyles, and personalities. Family adaptations and conditions were viewed as primary links between economic hardship and the individual – his or her behavior, personality, and lifecourse. These linkages included: (1) changes in the division of labor (the necessity for new forms of economic maintenance altered the domestic and economic roles of family members, shifting responsibilities to mother and the other children); (2) changes in family relationships (father's loss of economic status and resulting adaptations in family maintenance increased the relative power of mother, reduced the level and effectiveness of parental control, and lessened the attractiveness of father as a model); (3) social strains in the family (status ambiguity, conflicts, and emotional distress were consequences of diminished resources, loss or impairment of parents, and inconsistency in the status of the family and its members). The enduring effects of the Depression experience among the Oakland adults can be summarized by three points: the paths though which they achieved adult status; adult health and preferences in ways of responding to life's problems; and values.

Intergenerational continuity and change in rural America

The farm crisis of the 1980s, during which rural Iowa lost nearly 5 percent of its population, constituted a historical event that had major implications for family economies and intergenerational relations. How did outmigration from America's farms affect family ties, and especially relations between the generations? In the midst of this crisis, a panel study was launched to investigate the effects of socioeconomic decline in the region on parents and their children (Conger and Elder, 1994; Elder and Conger, 2000). The research strategy followed that used in the study for *Children of the Great Depression*: to trace out the effects of a major historical event on the way individuals, families, and households respond and adapt to major economic, social, or political disruptions and live out their lives. In the sample of 451 households, 30 percent of the families were involved in farming, and 13 percent had given up farming as a result of the farm crisis. The study focused on the interlocking nature of family economies, intergenerational relations, and the lifecourse of ageing. Among G2 parents who had left farming, exits occurred either at the beginning of their work career, or some years later as a result of the farm crisis. Such exits, which represent "generational breaks," can have important implications for proximity to parents, frequency of contact and the

quality of relations with parents, and caregiving. An analysis of intergenerational continuity and change (Elder *et al.*, 1995) compared farm to non-farm sons' relations with their G1 parents. Those who remained on the farm lived closer to and had more contact with parents, had more intense emotional relations with parents, and were involved in more caregiving to elderly parents. Surprisingly, loss of the family farm by sons had little impact on intergenerational relations with elderly fathers and mothers, at least in the short term.

LIFECOURSE STUDIES OF INTERGENERATIONAL RELATIONS

How are we to examine change and continuity in multigenerational families in contemporary times? As we have noted, generational role or position does not offer a precise way of connecting people's lives to the changes in society, because life cycle and age are essentially uncoupled. There is too much variation in the timing of life cycle transitions, if they occur at all, to afford intergenerational comparisons in historical time. However, this restrictive situation may be changing. With longitudinal studies of sufficient time span, age-matching across the generations becomes possible, thereby enabling the linking of age and life stage, generational placement, and intergenerational processes to historical change.

Multigenerational families in changing times

The Longitudinal Study of Generations (LSOG), begun in 1971 and now with eight waves of data, is a study of linked members from some 350 three- and four-generation families as they have grown up and grown old during a period of dramatic social and economic change. A major aim of the LSOG research program is to investigate the effects of sociohistorical change on the interactions among and ageing of successive family generations. Are intergenerational relationships changing? Have the dramatic social changes of the past four decades weakened family bonds? In what ways do strong intergenerational bonds promote individual family members' wellbeing over time? It is important to examine these issues because recent historical trends – such as population ageing, occupational restructuring, and diversifying family forms – have altered both the macro- and micro-social contexts in which individuals negotiate the challenges of adult development and ageing. These issues have important implications for healthcare and social policy in a rapidly ageing population: if the functions of the family have declined, then the burden on public services to the elderly will likely increase.

A lifecourse approach to multigenerational family research considers how family relationships change or remain stable across individual lives and family time, and how these processes are linked to multiple and evolving historical contexts. Multiple temporalities and levels of influences need to be taken into account. Recent advancements in multilevel modeling techniques coupled with the maturation of longitudinal studies are providing researchers with new opportunities to assess empirically these precepts of the lifecourse framework.

CHANGES IN PARENTAL INFLUENCE ON THE LIFECOURSE OUTCOMES OF OFFSPRING.

A recent study examined how family relationships serve as conduits by which values, resources, and behaviors are transmitted across multiple generations. Bengtson *et al.* (2002) used parent–child dyads and a generation-sequential design to investigate intergenerational influences on sons' and daughters' education and occupational aspiration, self-esteem, and values (individualism and materialism). The study also examined how transmission processes have been affected by parental divorce and maternal employment.

The analytic design was based on two research questions. First, have the aspirations, values, and self-esteem of Generation X youth (G4s, born between 1966 and 1980) been adversely affected by changing opportunity structures and rising divorce and maternal employment rates over recent decades? Second, were "baby-boom" parents (G3s) less *influential* for the development of their Generation X children's aspirations, values, and self-esteem than G2 parents had been for the development of these attributes among baby-boom youth? The study examined three linkages between family influences and young adults' outcomes: the family's socialization functions; the family's access to social resources; and the quality of parent–child emotional bonds

and their effect on intergenerational transmission processes.

Findings indicate that the patterns of parental *influences* on youth's outcomes were remarkably similar across two generations (young baby-boomers and Generation X youth) and historical time periods (growing up in the 1960s and the 1990s). This suggests that despite changes in family structure and socioeconomic context, intergenerational influences on youth's educational and occupational aspirations, self-esteem, and value orientations remain strong. When Generation X youth were compared with their baby-boom parents when they were in youth three decades earlier, Generation Xers had higher aspirations and higher self-esteem, and were more collectivistic. Across the generations, parental resources strongly affected their children's educational and occupational aspirations, suggesting the continuing importance of learning and modeling processes within families.

How important were period effects, such as the increases in marital disruption and women's labor force participation since the 1960s? Findings indicate that maternal employment did not negatively affect the aspirations, values, and self-esteem of youth across these two generations. Generation Xers whose parents divorced were slightly less advantaged in terms of educational and occupational aspirations and self-esteem than those who came from non-divorced families, but they were nevertheless higher on these measures than were their baby-boomer parents at the same age, regardless of family structure.

Among Generation Xers, parental divorce affected the influence of mothers' affirmation on their children's self-esteem. It was not that children of divorce felt less close to their mothers than children from two-parent families. Rather, in the context of divorce, closeness to mothers turned out to be a weaker determinant of the self-esteem that children ultimately developed. Consistent with other research (Amato, 1994; Amato and Sobolewski, 2001; Silverstein and Bengtson, 1997), father–child affective bonds were found to be significantly weaker for Generation Xers than they were for baby boomers in their youth, a result that can be largely attributed to the increase in parental divorce. Divorced fathers were found to have significantly weaker emotional bonds with their children than mothers, whether divorced or not. Further, parental divorce greatly reduced the ability of baby-boom fathers to *influence* their Generation X children's aspirations and self-esteem.

VALUE ORIENTATIONS OVER THE LIFE-COURSE. In a second lifecourse study using data from the LSOG, Roberts and Bengtson (1999) examined individual and social-structural factors that account for lifetime stability and change in two value orientations: individualism and materialism. They also examined how these values of individuals relate to broader sociohistorical and cultural shifts in value orientations. Are value orientations fixed dimensions of one's personality once adulthood is reached, or are they susceptible to adult socialization processes and changing cultural and social environments?

A generational-sequential design and hierarchical linear modeling techniques were used to address the temporal and structural complexities posed by these questions. With traditional linear modeling approaches it has been difficult to model accurately effects across structural levels – individual, family, and sociohistorical – in single-level predictor models. Statistical analysis of hierarchically structured data is sensitive to the nested nature of multilevel observations. In this analysis, individual and group growth curves in value orientations were estimated. Structural effects were assessed by estimating the higher order effects of generation, gender, and family on these growth curves.

Results showed both intra- and inter-cohort effects. G3 baby boomers became slightly more collectivist over time although there was also a pattern of significant differences between the older (G1 and G2) and younger (G3) generations. The endorsement of individualism declined across the generations from G1s to G3s. And while individuals tended to become more collectivistic as they aged, the sample as a whole was becoming more individualistic over time due to cohort replacement. There was a secular trend towards greater materialism, similar to the shift towards greater individualism during the period. However, this shift to greater materialism was not accounted for by developmental change. This suggests that most of the change in materialism reflects a sociohistorical trend. Interestingly, G1s exhibited the largest shift towards greater material-

ism, perhaps reflecting financial security concerns as this group grew older.

Findings illuminated bidirectional flows of influence linking individuals and their sociohistorical contexts. However, only limited information was gleaned about family-level change in response to social change, or about the effects of other meso-level contexts such as the workplace on individual outcomes or on overall societal changes. Future research will investigate how these meso-level contexts serve as "conduits" for bidirectional influences. This requires data-gathering strategies that allow assessments of stability and change across multiple dimensions of the meso- and macro-level contexts.

Methodological advances in lifecourse studies of families and ageing

Current LSOG research addresses several substantive questions. Do adult children today provide less support to their aged parents than *their* parents provided to aged parents three and a half decades earlier? Are norms of familism weakening over multiple dimensions of time as represented by ageing, historical period, and birth cohort? How are trajectories of ageing shaped by relationships between generations over time and are families able to buffer the effects of chronic and acute stressors on individuals' wellbeing? Have sociohistorical changes undermined the ability of older-generation family members to transmit their values, attitudes, and behaviors to younger-generation family members?

Maturation of the LSOG provides the opportunity not only to investigate these questions but also to develop statistical models that are capable of distinguishing the unique influences of ageing, period, cohort, and family membership on intergenerational processes. In order to assess the impact of social change on families, it is necessary to have data on the ageing of successive generations over identical age ranges. With 35 years of data, new designs can take full advantage of the cross-historical age-span match between successive generations.

A *generation-sequential design* permits adjacent generations in the same family (i.e., matched parent–child dyads) to be compared as they age over the same stage of life but during different historical time spans. This approach contextualizes ageing by allowing the examination of family development across two historical periods. Because ageing effects are held constant across generations, it is possible to isolate period/cohort effects on family development and responses, and to assess the effects of social change on the developmental trajectories of successive generations.

An *age-matched cross-generation design* reflects a cross-sectional comparison of parents to their children when those children reach the *same age* as their parents, and do so in another historical context. Key to this analytic design is that children "age-into" the same age as their parents over time. Without equating linked generations on chronological age it is impossible to assess adequately the effects of sociohistorical change on family processes across generations. The age-matched cross-generation design also allows us to address historical change in *intrafamilial* processes and to assess the strength of continuity across successive generational pairs separated by up to three and one-half decades of time.

CONCLUSION

How does one make sense of the complex connections that link the course of an individual's life within the context of broader social influences, such as family and society? What are the effects of social change on the experiences and direction of human lives, and on the processes of ageing itself? Such questions have long puzzled developmental theorists who have sought to understand the complex interplay of environmental and biological forces in human development (Baltes, 1997; Bronfenbrenner, 1979, 1989). It was not until the 1960s that family and ageing researchers interested in the study of lives began to pay heed to Mills' (1959) central insight that history shapes, and is shaped by, biography. A convergence of influences required new ways of looking at how people lived their lives – understandings that far exceeded the reach of traditional life cycle approaches. Several important trends of the twentieth century account for this dramatic change in research focus and energy: the maturation of early child development samples; the rapidity of social change; the changing age structure of society, particularly the ageing of the populations; and the dramatic growth of longitudinal research over the last few decades.

Since the 1960s, the lifecourse approach itself has been shaped by studies of the social world, its constraints, options, and social change. As a theoretical orientation, the lifecourse perspective orients research as to how lives are socially organized in biological, social, and historical time and guides explanations of how the resulting social pattern affects the way individuals think, feel, and act, as they age over time. Their proper study challenges us to take all life stages into account through linked lives across generations, from infancy to the grandparents of old age. This approach is particularly relevant today, where the rapid growth of the oldest segments of society lends greater significance to problems of the aged. Lifecourse studies are helping to locate people in a matrix of age-graded, family relationships and to place families in the social structures, cultures, and populations of time and place. These studies have brought time and temporality to an understanding of individual lives, families, and ageing.

REFERENCES

Alwin, D. F., and J. A. Krosnick (1991). "Aging, cohorts, and the stability of sociopolitical orientations over the life span," *American Journal of Sociology*, 97 (1): 169–95.

Alwin, D. F., & R. J. McCammon (2003). "Generations, cohorts and social change." In J. T. Mortimer and M. J. Shanahan, eds., *Handbook of the life course*. New York: Kluwer Academic / Plenum Press, pp. 3–19.

Alwin, D. F., Cohen, R., and T. Newcomb (1991). *Political attitudes over the life span: the Bennington women after 50 years*. Madison, Wis.: University of Wisconsin Press.

Amato, P. R. (1994). "Father–child relations, mother–child relations and psychological well-being in early adulthood," *Journal of Marriage and the Family*, 56: 1031–42.

Amato, P. R., and J. M. Sobolewski (2001). "The effects of divorce and marital discord on adult children's psychological well-being," *American Sociological Review*, 66: 900–21.

Baltes, P. B. (1997). "The role of modeling processes in personality development." In *The young child: reviews of research*. Washington, D.C.: National Association for the Education of Young Children.

Bengtson, V. L., and K. Allen (1993). "The life course perspective applied to families over time." In P. Boss, W. Doherty, R. LaRossa, W. Schumm, and S. Steinmetz, eds., *Sourcebook of family theories and methods: a contextual approach*. New York: Kluwer Academic / Plenum Press, pp. 469–98.

Bengtson, V. L., Biblarz, T. J., and R. E L. Roberts (2002). *How families still matter: a longitudinal study of youth in two generations*. New York: Cambridge University Press.

Bronfenbrenner, U. (1979). *The ecology of human development*. Cambridge, Mass.: Harvard University Press.

(1989). "Ecological systems theory." In R. Vasta, ed., *Annuals of child development*, Vol. VI. Greenwich, Conn.: JAI Press.

Clausen, J. A. (1993). *American lives*. New York: Free Press.

Conger, R. D., and G. H. Elder, eds. (1994). *Families in troubled times. Adapting to change in rural America*. New York: Aldine de Gruyter.

Elder, G. H., Jr. (1974). *Children of the Great Depression: social change in life experience*. Chicago, Ill.: University of Chicago Press.

(1987). "War mobilization and the life course: a cohort of World War II veterans," *Sociological Forum*, 2 (3): 449–72.

(1994). "Time, human agency, and social change: perspectives on the life course," *Social Psychology Quarterly*, 57: 4–15.

(1995). "The life course paradigm: social change and individual development. In P. Moen, G. H. Elder, Jr., and K. Luscher, eds., *Examining lives in context: perspectives on the ecology of human development*, pp. 101–39.

(1998). "Life course and human development." In W. Damon, ed., *Handbook of child psychology*. New York: Wiley, pp. 939–91.

(1999). *Children of the Great Depression: social change in life experience*, 25th *anniversary edition*. Boulder, Colo.: Westview Press.

(2003). "Generations and the life course: their interdependence." Keynote paper presented at the annual meeting of the International Sociological Association, Taipei, Taiwan, March.

Elder, G. H., Jr., and R. D. Conger (2000). *Children of the land: adversity and success in rural America*. Chicago: University of Chicago Press.

Elder, G. H., Jr., and M. K. Johnson (2001). "The life course and aging: challenges, lessons, and new directions." In R. A. Settersten, J., ed., *Invitation to the life course: toward new understandings of later life*. Amityville, N.Y.: Baywood, pp. 49–81.

Elder, G. H., Jr., Rudkin, L., and R. D. Conger (1995). "Intergenerational continuity and change in rural America." In V. L. Bengtson, K. W. Schaie, and L. M. Burton, eds., *Adult intergenerational relations: effects of societal change*. New York: Springer, pp. 30–60.

Elder, G. H., Jr., Johnson, M. K., and R. Crosnoe (2003). "The emergence and development of life course theory." In J. T. Mortimer and M. J. Shanahan, eds.,

Handbook of the life course. New York: Kluwer Academic / Plenum Press, pp. 3–19.

Heinz, W. R. (2003). "From work trajectories to negotiated careers: the contingent work life course." In J. T. Mortimer and M. J. Shanahan, eds., *Handbook of the life course*. New York: Kluwer Academic / Plenum Press, pp. 185–204.

Kohli, M. (1986). "The world we forgot: a historical review of the life course." In V. W. Marshall, ed., *Later life: the social psychology of aging*. Beverly Hills, Calif.: Sage, pp. 271–303.

Mills, C. W. (1959). *The sociological imagination*. New York: Oxford University Press.

Mortimer, J. T., and M. J. Shanahan, eds. (2003). "Preface." In J. T. Mortimer and M. J. Shanahan, eds., *Handbook of the life course*. New York: Kluwer Academic / Plenum Press, pp. xi–xvi.

Neugarten, B. L., and N. Datan (1973). "Sociological perspectives on the life cycle." In P. B. Baltes and K. W. Schaie, eds., *Life-span developmental psychology: personality and socialization*. New York: Academic Press, pp. 53–69.

Putney, N. M., and V. L. Bengtson (2003). "Intergenerational relations in changing times." In J. T. Mortimer and M. J. Shanahan, eds., *Handbook of the life course*. New York: Kluwer Academic / Plenum Press, pp. 149–64.

Pyke, K. D., and V. L. Bengtson (1996). "Caring more or less: individualistic and collectivist systems of family eldercare," *Journal of Marriage and the Family*, 58: 1–14.

Riley, M. W., Kahn, R. L., and A. Foner, eds. (1994). *Age and structural lag*. New York: Wiley.

Roberts, R. E. L., and V. L. Bengtson (1996). "Affective ties to parents in early adulthood and self-esteem across 20 years," *Social Psychology Quarterly*, 59: 96–106.

(1999). "The social psychology of values: effects of individual development, social change, and family transmission over the life span." In C. D. Ryff and V. W. Marshall, eds., *The self and society in aging processes*. New York: Springer, pp. 453–82.

Ryder, N. B. (1965). "The cohort as a concept in the study of social change," *American Sociological Review*, 30: 843–61.

Settersten, R. A., Jr. (2003). "Age structuring and the rhythm of the life course." In J. T. Mortimer and M. J. Shanahan, eds., *Handbook of the life course*. New York: Kluwer Academic / Plenum Press, pp. 81–98.

Silverstein, M., and V. L. Bengtson (1997). "Intergenerational solidarity and the structure of adult child–parent relationships in American families," *American Journal of Sociology*, 103: 429–60.

The Political Economy of Old Age

CHRIS PHILLIPSON

INTRODUCTION

This chapter reviews a number of arguments and issues arising from a political economy of ageing. The development of this approach reflected awareness (from the 1970s onwards) of the structural pressures and constraints affecting the lives of older people. Prior to the emergence of the political economy model, the main theoretical perspectives in social gerontology – role, disengagement, continuity, and life cycle theories – highlighted problems faced by individuals in adjusting to later life. The focus of social gerontology tended to be on issues such as the impact of role loss and reduced social status, loneliness and the effects of institutionalisation. Other concerns related to changes in family and community relationships in a context of urbanisation and industrialisation (Fennell *et al.*, 1988; Estes *et al.*, 2003).

The emphasis on individual adjustment to ageing came, however, at the expense of understanding the influence of social structures on the lives of older people. As Carroll Estes (1979) argued, in her influential study *The Aging Enterprise*, '[the] focus [of ageing studies was] on what people do rather than the social conditions and policies that cause them to act as they do'. In contrast, the main concern of the political economy of ageing has been to consider causal linkages between ageing on the one hand, and social, economic and political structures on the other.

This chapter will, first, identify the background to the political economy model; second, explore the different types of questions it has asked about the

nature of growing old; third, consider the different phases to the development of the theory over the past 30 years.

THE DEVELOPMENT OF THE POLITICAL ECONOMY OF AGEING

The political economy perspective developed in the context of the economic crisis that had emerged in Western societies, from the mid 1970s onwards. The origins of the crisis can be traced to a rise in world oil prices, the decline in economic growth and the simultaneous increase in both unemployment and inflation (Glyn and Sutcliffe, 1976). The economic collapse was soon joined by calls for substantial cuts in public spending – particularly that associated with the welfare state. Given that older people were the major beneficiaries of social expenditure, the case for the continuation of support at existing (or enhanced) levels came under intense scrutiny (Walker, 1996). More specifically, older people came to be viewed as a burden on Western societies, with demographic change (especially the declining ratio of younger to older persons) regarded as contributing to further economic decline (World Bank, 1994).

Political economy grew out of the subsequent politicisation of issues surrounding old age and the problems faced by traditional theories in developing an effective response (Estes and Associates, 2001). A major concern of work in the late 1970s and early 1980s from Estes (1979), Townsend (1981), Walker (1981), Phillipson (1982) and Myles (1984) was to challenge a view of growing old as a period of physical and mental decline (the biomedical model). This approach was criticised for its association of age with disease and senescence. Estes *et al.* (1982: 153) presented the arguments thus:

biomedical theories not only individualize and medicalize old age [they] also overlook the relationship between socio-economic status, the economy and health . . . [Such theories also] give little theoretical and empirical attention to the social creation of dependency through forced retirement and its functions for the economy, or to the production of senility and the economic, political and social control functions of such processes.

The basic tenets of the political economy model have been defined in terms of developing 'an understanding of the character and significance of variations in the treatment of the aged, and to relate these to polity, economy and society in advanced capitalism' (Estes, 1986: 121). This approach has challenged the idea of older people being viewed as a homogenous group unaffected by the major structures and processes of society. Instead, the focus is on understanding the relationship between ageing and economic life, the differential experience of ageing according to social class, gender and ethnicity, and the role social policy plays in contributing to the dependent status of older people.

Subsequently, the political economy perspective became one of a number of approaches grouped under the heading of 'critical gerontology', this drawing upon a variety of intellectual perspectives including Marxism and the Frankfurt School together with contemporary social theorists such as Anthony Giddens and Ulrich Beck (Minkler and Estes, 1999; Quadagno and Reid, 1999; Estes *et al.*, 2003). The next section of this chapter explores further the development of the political economy approach and its application to a number of substantive issues within social gerontology.

GROWING OLD: THE VIEW FROM POLITICAL ECONOMY

From its development in the late 1970s political economy has asked four types of questions about the experience of growing old:

- why is ageing experienced as a form of dependency?
- how are social divisions maintained in old age?
- what is the evidence for conflict between generations?
- how are older people affected by global change?

The critique of dependency was the first major theme developed by political economy, and was explored in a number of the texts and articles produced in the 1970s and early 1980s. Alan Walker (1981) developed this approach with his concept of the 'social creation of dependency' in old age, and Peter Townsend (1981) used a similar term when he described the 'structured dependency' of older people. Both writers attributed this dependency to what was viewed as the forced exclusion (through compulsory retirement) of older people from work, the experience of poverty, institutionalisation, and restricted domestic and community roles.

Carroll Estes (1979) introduced a variation on the dependency theme with her exploration of the 'aging enterprise' – the collection of professionals and businesses, supported by the state, servicing older people. Her concern was with the way in which people seemed to be treated as commodities within the welfare system. She criticised the 'age-segregated policies that fueled the ageing enterprise [as] socially divisive "solutions" that single-out, stigmatize and isolate the aged from the rest of society' (Estes, 1979: 2). In this context, political economy took a critical stance on the welfare state: on the one hand recognising its importance in providing security for older people; on the other hand highlighting the limitations of health and social care provision aimed at older people. It also raised questions about the relationship professionals have with elderly people: do they challenge low expectations about services? Do they contribute to the experience of old age as a period of decline and loss of control?

This initial focus on dependency broadened out in two main ways in subsequent debates during the 1980s and early 1990s: first, in examining the role of the state in the lives of older people; second, in tracing the impact of inequality within the life-course and into old age itself. The former reflected the influence of Marxism within the political economy model, this contributing to a view of the state as representing a site of struggle and the expression of dominant class interests. The study of the state was viewed as central to understanding old age and the life chances of older people since it had the power to (a) allocate and distribute scarce resources to ensure survival and growth of the economy, (b) mediate between the different segments and classes of society, and (c) ameliorate social conditions that could threaten the existing order (Estes, 1999). Political economy challenged the view that the state could be seen as entirely neutral or benign in its financing of support for older people. Instead the view was taken that it would almost certainly subordinate the requirements of groups such as elderly people to wider class interests. More generally, the competitive priorities of capitalism as a productive and social system meant that it was unlikely to meet the needs of elderly people on a long-term basis. This incompatibility was expressed in ways such as the following (Phillipson, 1982: 3–4; Vincent, 1995: 165–6):

1. *With each recurring economic recession it is the weakest sections of those who make up the workforce who are forced into redundancy or early retirement.* This has the effect of shifting the balance of power and rewards from labour to capital, with retirees losing out in respect of pensions and public resources more generally (Phillipson, 1978; Guillemard, 1983).
2. *The priority given to maximizing returns on capital produces a distortion in the socially identified needs of older people.* An example of this process lies in medicalizing elderly people's problems and presenting them as having technical responses, such as pharmaceutical interventions, from which profits can be derived (Burns and Phillipson, 1986). In this respect social solutions will always be forced into the priorities fixed by the dominance of capital and large corporations.
3. *The commodification of labour has the effect of breaking-up neighbourhoods and families through migration and urban decline.* Elderly people can find themselves caught between their own need for improved services, and the steady decline of facilities within their neighbourhood. The conditions for informal care and strong social networks may thus be undermined through community change dictated by the search for profit (Scharf *et al.*, 2002).
4. *Capitalism as a system of exploitation invariably leads to poverty among older people thus restricting their ability to lead a fulfilling life in retirement.* Deprivation can be seen to reflect both lifelong problems of low incomes and insecurities within capitalism, and the

inadequacy of state provision for old age through the pension system (Townsend, 1981).

Arguments such as these led to further work examining the social production of inequality within old age (Vincent, 1995). Social class was a major issue for those taking a political economy approach, with the view taken that older people were as deeply divided along class and other structural lines as younger and middle-aged adults. Alan Walker (1996) contrasted this approach with both functionalist and pluralist perspectives that tended to suggest a common interest among older people, with age acting as a leveller of class and status differentials. He went on to argue that:

There is no doubt that the process of retirement, not ageing, does superimpose reduced socio-economic status on a majority of older people – for example in the United Kingdom it results in an average fall in income of up to one-half – but, even so, retirement has a differential impact on older people depending on their prior socio-economic status. For example, there is unequal access to occupational pensions. Women and other groups with incomplete employment records are particularly disadvantaged . . . Moreover the size of occupational pensions differs considerably according to socio-economic grouping . . . There are also inequalities between generations of older people arising from their unequal access to improved private and occupational pension provision. (Walker, 1996: 33)

Political economy also made a substantial contribution to analysing other divisions within old age, notably those associated with gender (see Estes, Chapter 6.8 in this volume) and race (Dressel *et al.*, 1999). Minkler (1999: 1) emphasised that these were best viewed as 'interlocking systems of inequality' which determine the experience of growing old and which illustrate the construction of ageing on multiple levels. Minkler (1999: 1–2) went on to conclude that:

Critical gerontology in the tradition of political economy . . . offers a rich and multiperspectival framework within which to view and better understand old age as a "problem" for societies "characterized by major inequalities in the distribution of power and property" (Kart, 1987: 79). As such, it provides a much needed supplement to the study of the biological and psychological aspects of ageing, which, for all their contributions, reveal little about the social construction of ageing in a broader sociopolitical context.

GENERATIONS AND POLITICAL CHANGE

The third major question considered by political economy focused upon the impact of ageing populations on the economy and on relationships between generations. During the 1980s older people came to be viewed in some quarters as a 'selfish welfare generation', drawing a level of support from the state that would, it was argued, be unsustainable over the longer term (Thompson, 1989). The debate about 'intergenerational equity' was especially prominent in the USA, with pressure groups such as Americans for Generational Equity (AGE) and demographers such as Samuel Preston (1984) arguing that the flow of resources to older people was increasing every year while that going to children was decreasing.

In this scenario, workers became pitched against pensioners in what appeared as a zero sum trade off between competing age and social groups (Johnson et al., 1989). In the area of healthcare, the biomedical ethicist Daniel Callahan (1978a) sparked off a major debate with the publication of his book *Setting limits: medical goals in an ageing society*. Callahan's study identified three aspirations for an ageing society: first, that it should cease to pursue medical goals that combine the features of high costs, marginal gains, and benefits (in the main) for the old. Second, that older people shift their priorities from their own welfare to that of younger generations. Third, that older people should accept death as a condition of life at least for the sake of others. Callahan's intervention attracted considerable controversy (for a political economy critique, see Binney and Estes, 1990) but it fuelled an already highly charged debate concerning what came to be presented as the divergent interests and attainments of young and older people.

Political economy provided an influential contribution to challenging pessimistic views about the impact of population change. Essentially, it did this by developing three types of argument. In the first place, emphasising that the 'public burden' conception of old age undervalued the important role that older people play in society, notably in areas such as volunteering and informal care (Arber and Ginn, 1996). Second, stressing that the ageing of populations is not a new development but one that had been unfolding over the course of the twentieth century, and that in the case of Britain

involved relatively modest growth for at least the next 50 years (Vincent, 1996). Third, questioning evidence that generations were locked in conflict over the distribution of resources, pointing instead to evidence of reciprocity in support across different age groups (Arber and Attias-Donfut, 2000). More generally, political economy challenged what it viewed as the 'crisis construction' of ageing that was distorting and stifling a rational public debate about needs and resources to support older people. Vincent (2003: 86), in his review of pension funding, summarised this aspect as follows:

The view of population ageing as a demographic time-bomb has been constructed by those with a particular agenda and a specific way of seeing the world. The function of such arguments is to create a sense of inevitability and scientific certainty that public pension provision will fail. In so far as this strategy succeeds it creates a self-fulfilling prophecy. If people believe the 'experts' who say publicly sponsored PAYG [Pay As You Go] systems cannot be sustained, they are more likely to act in ways that mean they are unsustainable in practice. Certainly in Britain and elsewhere in Europe the state pension is an extremely popular institution. To have it removed or curtailed creates massive opposition. Only by demoralising the population with the belief that it is demographically unsustainable has room for the private financiers been created and a mass pensions market formed.

By the end of the 1990s, some of the rhetoric behind the 'generational war' debate had given way to more realistic appraisals about the nature and implications of demographic change. A larger issue for political economy became that of studying the interaction between ageing as a global phenomenon and the pressures arising from globalisation as a political, social and economic process. It is to this current phase in the development of the political economy of ageing that we now turn.

AGEING AND GLOBALISATION

For much of the period from the 1970s through to the 1990s, critical perspectives in gerontology focused upon national concerns about policies and provision for older people. Scholars essentially worked within the boundaries of the nation-state in developing perspectives around issues such as dependency and inequality in later life. The significant change since the turn of the new century, one that follows developments within core disciplines such as politics and sociology, has been the development of a link between critical gerontology and broader questions arising from the pressures and upheavals associated with living in a global world (Hutton and Giddens, 2000).

The background here concerns the move from 'organised' to 'disorganised capitalism', from 'simple' to 'reflexive modernity', or to the transformation from 'fordist' to 'post-fordist economies' (Phillipson, 1998). Essentially, this concerns the change from the mass institutions which defined the first phase of ageing, to the more individualised structures – privatised pensions, privatised health and social care, targeted forms of social protection – which increasingly inform the second. This new period of ageing is further defined by the emergence of new transnational actors and communities. In *Global transformations*, David Held *et al.* (1999: 49) describe this change as follows:

Today, virtually all nation-states have gradually become enmeshed in and functionally part of a larger pattern of global transformations and global flows . . . Transnational networks and relations have developed across virtually all areas of human activity. Goods, capital, people, knowledge, communications and weapons, as well as crime, pollutants, fashions and beliefs, rapidly move across territorial boundaries . . . Far from this being a world of 'discrete civilisations' or simply an international order of states, it has become a fundamentally interconnected global order, marked by intense patterns of exchange as well as by clear patterns of power, hierarchy and unevenness.

This transformed political economy is underscored by the emergence of a more aggressive form of capitalism, one contrasted with the more controlled and regulated capitalism of the 1950s and 1960s. Hutton describes the essential features of this 'turbo-capitalism', as follows:

Its overriding objective is to serve the interests of property owners and shareholders, and it has a firm belief, effectively an ideological one that – regulation, controls, trade unions, taxation, public ownership, etc. – are unjustified and should be removed. Its ideology is that shareholder value must be maximised, that labour markets should be 'flexible' and that capital should be free to invest and disinvest in countries at will . . . It's a very febrile capitalism, but for all that and its short-termism it has been a very effective transmission agent for the new technologies and for creating the new

global industries and markets. It's a tool both of job generation and of great inequality.

Analysis of the impact of globalisation on ageing is still at an early stage of development but three areas at least may be identified as having particular relevance for the political economy of ageing. In the first place, transnational bodies now play an important role in shaping national policies for old age (Walker, 2002). Examples here include the role of the World Bank in recommending a reduced role for state pay-as-you-go pension schemes (Holtzman, 1997), and the work of the World Trade Organization (WTO) in encouraging deregulation in the field of health and social care (Pollock and Price, 2000). Yeates (2001) concludes from her study of the impact of globalisation on social policy, that bodies such as the World Bank and the International Monetary Fund 'have been at the forefront of attempts to foster a political climate conducive to the residualization of state welfare and the promotion of private and voluntary initiatives'. This can be seen to represent a new global discourse about pension provision and retirement ages, but one appearing to exclude perspectives that might suggest an enlarged role for the state and which might question the stability and effectiveness of private schemes (Estes and Phillipson, 2002).

Secondly, globalisation is promoting greater mobility in movement through the lifecourse (Urry, 2000). Migration in later life is one such example (see Longino and Warnes, Chapter 6.6 in this volume); but there is also the more general phenomenon of transnational communities – families and social networks spread across wide geographical distances. This new political economy is creating what may be described as 'global families' – these arising from the communities that emerge from international migration. Arlie Hochschild (2000) makes the point that most writing about globalisation focuses on money, markets and labour flows, with scant attention to women, children and the care of one for the other. But older people are clearly an important group to add to this list. Elderly people are now an important part of the global flow: they grow old as migrants, and may go backwards and forwards from one home to the other, a point made by Katy Gardner (2002) in her research on migrants to the UK from Bangladesh. As a consequence, globalisation is producing a new kind of ageing in which the dynamics of family and social life may be stretched across different continents and across different types of societies.

Such developments may create forms of 'structured dependency' (Townsend, 1986) which play differently in a global as opposed to a national context. Structured dependency theory in critical gerontology has been criticised from a number of perspectives: for playing down human agency on the one hand, and for an undue emphasis on social inequality on the other. Yet in a global context it may be that a reformulated structured dependency argument has much to offer in addressing the widening inequalities between nation-states (as demonstrated by Robert Wade, 2001, among others) and the crises these generate in the communities supporting older people.

Global inequalities will be especially important to address given the pressures on the developing countries associated with greater longevity (Lloyd-Sherlock, 2004). Already the majority of the world's population of older people (61 per cent or 355 million) live in poorer countries. This proportion will increase to nearly 70 per cent by 2025. For many countries, however, population ageing has been accompanied by reductions in per capita income and declining living standards. Epstein (2001) notes that between 1950 and the late 1970s, life expectancy increased by at least 10 per cent in every developing country in the world, or on average by about 15 years. However, at the beginning of the twenty-first century, life expectancy remains below 50 in more than ten developing countries, and since 1970 has fallen or barely risen in a number of African countries (WHO, 2000). The AIDS epidemic is certainly a major factor, as has been the impact of civil war in many sub-Saharan countries. At the same time, the neo-liberal consensus operating within globalisation has undermined effective responses to many of the problems facing older people (Deacon, 2000; Scholte, 2000). Indeed, neo-liberalism, as practised by dominant organisations such as the International Monetary Fund and the World Bank have often intensified the difficulties facing elderly people: for example, with pressures to privatise core public services and reduce pensions as key elements in packages of economic restructuring (Stiglitz, 2002; Walker and Deacon, 2003).

Thirdly, a key issue arising from the globalisation of ageing concerns the extent to which older people will be a major (or even minor) voice in the new global economy, and efforts to re-shape the institution of old age and retirement that are occurring across different nation-states. So far, older people have been absent from influential debates such as those initiated by the World Bank (over pay-as-you-go pensions) or the WTO (over the commercialisation of care services). The major players in these debates have either been governments (from rich countries) wishing to deregulate state provision, or corporations wanting to expand into lucrative areas of work. But it is also the case that older people (and their organisations) have been marginalised in the various forums that are now raising concerns about globalisation – this despite what Walker and Maltby (1997) view as an upsurge of political activity among pensioners in a number of countries. From a political economy perspective, it is clear that the process of globalisation represents both a historical transition and an opportunity for the development and testing of new forms of political power – among older people themselves as well as across generations.

CONCLUSION

The aim of this chapter has been to explore some of the insights gained from use of a political economy perspective on growing old. Some of the main issues raised by this approach have been concerned with, first, exploring problems of dependency and loss of power in old age; second, inequalities associated with social class, gender and race; third, the impact of demographic change and the relationship between generations; fourth, the influence of globalisation on the lives of older people. What brings together these different elements is a broader view about growing old as a 'socially constructed' process (see Johnson, Chapter 7.1 in this volume), one though which cannot be fully understood without reference to the system of power and domination running through advanced capitalist society. Much work remains to fulfil the initial promise of the political economy model. The different ways in which the state exerts an influence on growing old have still to be clearly analysed. The complex interaction between class, gender and race, and the relationship of each to growing old, has yet to be unravelled.

And a start has only just been made on the understanding of how ageing affects globalisation and vice versa.

But accepting the above caveats, the intellectual question posed by political economy remains important: to understand the nature of ageing requires attention to the system of inequality that has affected people in their journey through the lifecourse. Exploring this theme will continue to be a major task for researchers working in the political economy tradition.

FURTHER READING

Arber, S., Davidson, K., and J. Ginn (2003). *Gender and ageing*. Buckingham: Open University Press.

Estes, C., and Associates (2001). *Social policy and aging*. Thousand Oaks, Calif.: Sage.

Estes, C., Biggs, S., and C. Phillipson (2003). *Social theory, social policy and ageing*. Buckingham: Open University Press.

Vincent, J. (2003). *Old age*. London: Routledge.

REFERENCES

Arber, G., and C. Attias-Donfut (2000). *The myth of generational conflict*. London: Routledge.

Arber, G., and J. Ginn (1996). *Connecting gender and ageing: a sociological approach*. Buckingham: Open University Press.

Binney, E., and C. Estes (1990). 'Setting the wrong limits: class biases and the biographical standard'. In P. Homer and M. Holstein, eds., *A good old age? The paradox of setting limits*. New York: Simon and Schuster, pp. 240–57.

Burns, B., and C. Phillipson (1986). *Drugs, ageing and society*. London: Croom Helm.

Callahan, D. (1987a). *Setting the limits: medical goals in an aging society*. New York: Simon and Schuster.

(1987b). 'Setting limits'. In P. Homer and M. A. Holstein, eds., *A good old age? The paradox of setting limits*. New York: Simon and Schuster.

Deacon, B. (2000). *Globalisation and social policy: the threat to equitable welfare*, Occasional Paper no. 5, Globalism and Social Policy Programme (GASPP). United Nations Research Institute for Social Development.

Dressel, P., Minkler, M., and I. Yen (1999). 'Gender, race, class and aging: advances and opportunities'. In M. Minkler and C. Estes, eds., *Critical gerontology: perspectives from political and moral economy*. New York: Baywood Press, pp. 275–95.

Epstein, J. (2001). 'Time of indifference', *New York Review of Books*, 12 April, pp. 33–8.

Estes, C. (1979). *The aging enterprise*. San Francisco: Josey-Bass.

(1986). 'The politics of aging in America', *Ageing and Society*, 6: 121–34.

(1999). 'Critical gerontology and the new political economy of aging'. In M. Minkler and C. Estes eds., *Critical gerontology: perspectives from political and moral economy*, 2nd edn. New York: Baywood Press, pp. 17–36.

Estes, C., and Associates (2001). *Social policy and aging: a critical perspective*. Thousand Oaks, Calif.: Sage.

Estes, C., and C. Phillipson (2002). 'The globalization of capital, the welfare state and old age policy', *International Journal of Health Services*, 32 (2) : 279–97.

Estes, C., Swan, J. H., and L. Gerard (1982). 'Dominant and competing paradigms: toward a political economy of ageing,' *Ageing and Society*, 2 (2): 151–64.

Estes, C., Biggs, S., and C. Phillipson (2003). *Social theory, social policy and ageing*. Buckingham: Open University Press.

Fennell, G., Phillipson, C., and H. Evers (1988). *The sociology of old age*. Buckingham: Open University Press.

Gardner, K. (2002). *Age, narrative and migration*. Oxford: Berg.

Glyn, A., and B. Sutcliffe (1976). *British capitalism, workers and the profits squeeze*. London: Penguin Books.

Guillemard, A. M. (1983). 'The making of old age policy in France: points of debate, issues at stake, underlying social relations'. In A. M. Guillemard, *Old age and the welfare state*. New York: Sage Publications.

Held, D., McGrew, A., Goldblatt, D., and J. Perraton (1999). *Global transformations*. Oxford: Polity Press.

Hochschild, A. (2000). 'Global care chains and emotional surplus value'. In W. Hutton and A. Giddens, eds., *Living on the edge*. London: Jonathan Cape, pp. 130–47.

Holtzman, R. (1997). '*A world perspective on pension reform.*' Paper prepared for the joint ILO-OECD Workshop on the Development and Reform of Pension Schemes, Paris, December.

Hutton, W., and A. Giddens (2000). *On the edge: living with global capitalism*. London: Jonathan Cape.

Johnson, P., Conrad, C., and D. Thomson, eds. (1989). *Workers versus pensioners: intergenerational justice in an ageing world*. Manchester: Manchester University Press.

Kart, C. S. (1987). 'The end of conventional gerontology', *Sociology of Health and Illness*, 9: 76–87.

Lloyd-Sherlock, P., ed. (2004). *Living longer*. London: Zed Books.

Minkler, M. (1999). 'Introduction'. In M. Minkler and C. Estes, eds., *Critical gerontology: perspectives from political and moral economy*, 2nd edn. New York: Baywood Press, pp. 1–14.

Minkler, M., and C. Estes, eds. (1999). *Critical Gerontology: perspectives from political and moral economy*, 2nd edn. New York: Baywood Press.

Myles, J. (1984). *Old age in the welfare state*. Lawrence, Kans.: University of Kansas Press.

Phillipson, C. (1978). 'The experience of retirement: a sociological analysis'. Ph.D. thesis, University of Durham.

(1982). *Capitalism and the construction of old age*. London: MacMillan.

(1998). *Reconstructing old age*. London: Sage.

Pollock, A., and D. Price (2000). 'Rewriting the regulations: how the World Trade Organisation could accelerate privatisation in health care systems', *Lancet*, 356: 1995–2000.

Preston, S. (1984). 'Children and the elderly: divergent paths for America's dependents', *Demography*, 21: 435–57.

Quadagno, J., and J. Reid (1999). 'The political economy perspective in aging'. In V. L. Bengston and K. Warner Schaie, eds. *Handbook of theories of aging*. New York: Springer Publishing.

Scharf, T., Phillipson, C., Smith, A., and P. Kingston (2000). *Growing older in socially deprived areas: social exclusion in later life*. London: Help the Aged.

Scholte, J. A. (2000). *Globalization: a critical introduction*. London: Palgrave.

Stiglitz, J. (2002). *Globalization and its discontents*. London: Allen Lane.

Thompson, D. (1989). 'The welfare state and generation conflict: winners and losers'. In P. Johnson, D. Conrad and D. Thomson, eds., *Workers versus pensioners: intergenerational justice in an ageing world*. Manchester: Manchester University Press.

Townsend, P. (1981). 'The structured dependency of the elderly: the creation of policy in the twentieth century', *Ageing and Society*, 1 (1): 5–28.

(1986). 'Ageism and social policy.' In C. Phillipson and A. Walker, eds., *Ageing and social policy*. Aldershot: Gower, pp. 15–44.

Urry, J. (2000). *Sociology beyond societies*. London: Routledge.

Vincent, J. (1995). *Inequality and old age*. London: UCL Press.

(1996). 'Who's afraid of an ageing population?' *Critical Social Policy*, 47: 3–26.

(2003). *Old age*. London: Routledge.

Wade, R. (2001). 'Winners and losers', *The Economist*, 28 April, pp. 93–7.

Walker, A. (1981). 'Towards a political economy of old age', *Ageing and Society*, 1 (1): 73–94.

(1996). *The new generational contract*. London: UCL Press.

(2002). 'Globalisation and policies on ageing'. Paper to 55th Annual Scientific Meeting, Gerontological Society of America, Boston.

Walker, A., and B. Deacon (2003). 'Economic globalization and policies on ageing', *Journal of Societal and Social Policy*, 2 (2): 1–18.

Walker, A., and T. Maltby (1997). *Ageing Europe*. Buckingham: Open University Press.

WHO (World Health Organization) (2000). *Health life expectancy rankings*, Press Release. Geneva: WHO.

World Bank (1994). *Averting the old age crisis*. London: Oxford University Press.

Yeates, N. (2001). *Globalisation and social policy*. London: Sage.

CHAPTER 6.3

Moral Economy and Ageing

JON HENDRICKS

Moral economy crossed into social gerontology from neighboring disciplines and has enriched its conceptual outlook on ageing. Current applications of the concept reflect both its origins and subsequent extension in gerontology. Political economy, as noted in the entry on that topic, concerns itself with the interrelationship between individual and structure by delineating how reciprocal influences of economics, politics, and social structure affect the distribution of goods or services and in so doing contour experiences and lifeworlds of individuals. Moral economy is a construct based on underlying notions of acceptable practices and norms of reciprocity based on shared beliefs and values about what is fair and just in a given context. In the West, principles of Christian charity underpin many prevalent beliefs and moral assumptions about relationships and obligations (Thompson, 1971) but these have been modified by economically derived principles associated with fiscal markets and, as Claeys (1987) points out, natural economies derived from social Darwinism. Attention to moral economics will help elucidate the rationale mitigating differential provisions in our thinking about appropriate provisions for the elderly. It will help in examining why communally defined legitimacy is implicitly conditioned by economically defined roles and how those characterizations are woven into the social fabric in such a way that they are granted normative status. How do decisions about what is "due" older persons replicate notions of distributive justice? Why is one or another social group, age category, or gender treated one way by policy makers, and other petitioners treated differently? How are moral pre-

cepts, social coherence, and the structure of social relations related to economic or bureaucratic definitions of what age means (Cole, 1985; Hendricks and Leedham, 1991; Minkler and Cole, 1991; Townsend, 1981; Walton, 1979)?

ORIGIN AND EVOLUTION OF MORAL ECONOMY

From the inception of the idea of the social contract as a means to explain societal evolution, commentators have been concerned with seminal questions about social coherence, about what holds societies together and provides a sense of solidarity. One prominent presumption has been that there is some kind of collective consciousness, commonweal, or shared affective mindset that motivates the behavior of individuals and serves as a moral bond nurturing communality. Congruent with a stage model of societal progression, the supposition has been that as societies or groups become more complex, rationalized, and stratified, the nature of moral consensus becomes equally complex and multifaceted. In less complex societies, religion and theology provide a unifying cosmology and moral code; with complexity, over-arching religious canons become attenuated, supplanted by civic secular principles that serve as an analogous bonding agent. Although he engaged a longstanding tradition, the French sociologist Emile Durkheim, writing late in the nineteenth century, is illustrative of those who grappled with the effects of industrialization and modernity on the nature of the social adhesive (Durkheim, 1965[1893]). Durkheim documented centrifugal tendencies in modern social organizations characterized by diversity and referred to the importance of symbolic frameworks and "the totality of beliefs and sentiments common to the average members of a society," necessary to provide a sense of commonality countering divarication. He noted that any utile communal code of beliefs is dynamic, reflecting time, place, material conditions, and division of labor.

Without delving into detail, suffice it to say that many scholars assume that pre-industrial societies sustained shared meanings in ways distinct from mechanisms promoting an attachment of individuals within larger social orders operating in industrial or postindustrial societies. At least among Western religions, figurative representations of idealized societal values were communicated, reinforced, and imbued with morally desirable status via personifications of deities and by means of religious practices and rituals. From tangible symbols and immediate needs fulfilled through primary exchanges, bases of solidarity become increasingly abstract, codified as hallowed moral precepts representing the collective *raison d'être* of the group. The bonds are affirmed and elaborated through social practices, including religion, ceremonial occasions, rituals, exchanges, and through symbols and ideologies given primacy and perceived as appropriate despite whatever social relativity might be encountered. A corresponding facet of the thinking on this issue is that societal institutions are interconnected and, in their many guises, from religion, to families, education, and state policies, reflect and restate beliefs and values necessary to espouse unifying sentiments for the "greater good" of the group.

The British historian, E. P. Thompson (1971) took up the mantle and utilized generalized notions of collective consciousness in an explication of solidarity, shared imagery, and social integration. The quest was to identify how common practices are acclaimed by consensus, regarded as legitimate, confirmed as just. In his original formulation, Thompson (1971) described moral economy as a characteristic of subsistence economies, antecedent to market economies, originated during an era when markets were largely localized, based on an ethos ensuing from face-to-face exchanges for necessities and through bartering. Thompson's idea of the societal state characterized by a moral economy paralleled Tonnies' (1957[1887]) idealized *Gemeinschaft*, a time of integrated world views predicated on consecrated cultural mandates palpable to all. As long as that remained the case, moral attachments were promulgated on a personalized basis and through experiential commonalities reinforced by religious practices, interaction, and reciprocal obligations. From their various forms of commerce, social and economic, members of a group derived ideas of unity and fairness, appropriate standards and practices, as well as an evaluative template for assessing themselves and others.

With the arrival of private property, mercantile economies, and accompanying increases in scale, specialization, secularization, and rationalization, interactions were informed not so much by all-embracing theology, proximate interests, immediacy, or affinity networks, but by complementarity, diversification, and corresponding normative beliefs. With each successive step away from overarching affective and experiential world views, abstracted principles to which all could pledge allegiance and which exert suzerainty over individual consciousness were utilized to stress commonality and social legitimacy capable of holding diverse elements in recognizable order. Eventually, secular, utilitarian conventions accompanying free markets came to occupy a privileged position and became a means of ensuring moral mandates, shaping shared norms and communal ethics. Furthermore, participation in the marketplace came to be seen as an equitable guiding principle allocating rights, resources, and responsibilities of citizenship. Determination of what constitutes just desserts also changed as moral claims were equated with material interests in the wake of the ascendancy of market-driven covenants (Kohli, 1987). Notions of distributive justice mirror the logic of distributive provisions, and establish points at which questions of fairness could be reasonably raised (Irwin, 1999: 704).

As governments coalesced and markets expanded, the two converged to cultivate a constellation of beliefs that provided a doctrinaire ideal, valuing people and participation while fostering further growth and expansion. As all hands were needed, politics, economics, and belief systems ensured a mutually supportive institutionalized foundation serving collective needs and informing individual consciousness. Weber (1958[1904]) coined the phrase "the Protestant ethic" to emphasize the interconnections between productivity and religious creeds extolling hard work as equivalent to a moral obligation. The emergent rationalized moral order supported economies of scale, mass production, and increases in productivity, while attending to requisite stability and keeping inequality within acceptable bounds. To prime the pumps of private enterprise, citizens needed to be educated if they were to be innovative, and they required incomes sufficient to continue to fuel consumption and propel further productivity. Insofar as inequality was counterproductive, equilibrium was sought and, as obtained, provided both political and economic authority. Public investments in social welfare were conceived as supportive of both ends with the difference being that, rather than adhering to altruistic Augustinian obligations to tend to need in its own right, need was addressed on the basis of instrumental principles grounded in relationships within the productive sphere – with a small residual category of outright indulgence for non-contributors. In this fashion, heterogeneous needs could be fitted into an integrative rationale granted credence by the citizenry through their communal espousal of collective beliefs. As they became tantamount to taken-for-granted assumptions about appropriate means to handle need or allocate social distributions in keeping with productive roles, these precepts also informed class relations and left room for various forms of exploitation and domination instead of comprehensive concurrence (Irwin, 1999; Wright, 2002).

SOCIAL GERONTOLOGY AND MORAL ECONOMY

By and large, the concept of moral economy is utilized as a means to consider underlying ideologies affecting experience as well as social prescriptions regarding older persons. The focus is not only on descriptive accounts of why social status makes a difference, but on what moral stipulations attach to diverse positions or to the second half of life. By bringing generalized conceptions of political and moral economy into a discussion of old age, it is possible to rebalance the idea that old age is a time of

inevitable dependency and helplessness through a recognition that much of what happens is created through societal organization and by the way material or social resources are allocated (Hendricks and Leedham, 1991: 53). An initial application of moral economy in gerontology was offered by Kohli (1987) but allusions may be found in related works addressing meanings attached to the latter years of life, the role of the world of work, bureaucracies of all stripes, and even the profession of gerontology itself (Estes, 1979, 1999; Katz, 1996; Hendricks, 1995; Phillipson, 1982; Walker, 1980, 1981).

Townsend (1981) anticipated subsequent applications by referring to the "structured dependence of the elderly" as a consequence of market forces and a person's perceived utility as producer or consumer. Walker (1980) referred to the creation of social ills and dependencies among older persons, noting they are not created *ex nihilo* or through intrinsic processes. Estes (1986) and others have highlighted the need to move beyond mere critique to an understanding of the character and significance of differential treatment of the aged in general and subcategories of the aged in particular (Hendricks and Leedham, 1991: 53). Kohli (1987) drew on Moore's (1978) conception of collectively validated beliefs of distributive justice and a commodified view of reciprocity as a framework for reviewing evolution of retirement provisions in Germany. He also noted that the institutionalization of the lifecourse as a series of socially defined phases is a reflection of the organization of work leading to the demarcation of old age as an attenuated phase of the same process. A further benefit of Kohli's account is his contention that the bureaucratic machinery of welfare is constructed from socially integrative beliefs – moral economy – resulting from the economic realm and from the division of labor (Kohli, 1987; Kohli *et al.*, 1983). A corollary is that principles of market economy are indistinguishable from moral economy insofar as they frame and sustain the ideology of a society.

Kohli *et al.* (1983) explored characteristics of the social construction of age stratification, the origin and determination of retirement age as representative of structural consequences of production processes. As they noted, the temporalization or chronologization of the lifecourse is rooted in taken-for-granted aspects of moral economy grounded in trajectories of employment. Commenting on even finer-grained outcomes stemming from the organization of work, Kohn and Slomezynski (1990: 3) asserted that occupational position and location in the stratification system (social status) affect people in manifold ways, even to the level of psychological processes, emotionality, and self-concepts.

In addressing the role of values within the gerontological enterprise, Moody (1998) drew attention to the range of principles in which covert value commitments are implicit, replicative of social relations, and generally left unexamined. Guillemard (1986: 226) observed that such seemingly impartial concepts as role and status mask social contingencies consequent to direct or indirect effects of material relations in the marketplace. Moral economy gives rise to a number of important insights in gerontology to the extent that it highlights the manner in which norms, practices, and social institutions are responsible for differences and inequalities articulated and reproduced across the lifecourse (Irwin, 1999). As claims on the system are institutionalized, embedded in social roles and expectations, and either become the basis of, or reflect what is generally deemed to be, "sensible" social policy, they are accepted and held sacrosanct by the citizenry (Irwin, 1999: 705).

EMERGING APPLICATIONS OF MORAL ECONOMY

It is not feasible to review all the ways in which moral economy has been applied in gerontology but a few examples may suffice. Calasanti and Bonanno (1986) considered the social construction and interpretation of dependency ratios, pointing out that the calculation of this widely used measure of dependency is supportive of existing social relations while masking myriad political pronouncements concerning age, gender, class, or work status. Walker (1981, 1990) made a similar point concerning the alarmist demography of despair in the UK and how the troublesome situation of the elderly is an outgrowth of the social consequences of market relations. Robertson (1991) has suggested that the apocalyptic connotations of Alzheimer's disease, not to mention other conditions, are consequences of a number of unexamined assumptions and echo political processes within the biomedical community.

Estes (1979, 1999) observed that perceptions of old age as a time of illness, economic crisis, and vulnerability underpin much of the professional community's interpretation and treatment of older persons. With many scholarly conceptions drawing from views about the opinions of other citizens, she urged thoughtful consideration prior to ordering perceptions into an array of facts, a cadre of conceptualizations, or paradigmatic proclamations. By and large, consensual assumptions and generative models are unlikely to reshape the agenda or alter the propensity to disempower older persons by asserting that most events in their lives are a result of normal ageing.

Some scientific assessments and much of the management of the lifecourse have had an unintended consequence. They have served to reinforce perceptions of abiding need, reflecting what older people have lost in terms of skills, abilities, vitality, and, therefore, in terms of the likelihood that they are capable of significant contributions to societal well-being. There are other equally distressing calculations of the worth of older people as well. Witness the estimated value of older persons affected by environmental pollution during the first term of the administration of President George W. Bush (Olson, 2003). In keeping with hazards implicit in the very notion, principally of masking lifetime inequalities, the model of marginalization reinforces the tendency to see old people as occupying what Bellah (1985) and colleagues termed therapeutic categories – those defined by the dimensions of intervention. Johnson (1999) juxtaposed the idea of a generalized reciprocity, an intergenerational gift relationship designed to foster a sense of communal sentiment, to accentuate the difference and what it portends for the creation of old age dependency.

An empowerment movement, incorporating principles of moral economy, is afoot as a way to counterpose an alternative perspective to the normatively labeled pathologies accruing among the elderly from current medical/economic/political models. In reviewing the nature of citizenship rights, Weiner (1997) utilized Marshall's (1950) discussion of civil rights, political rights, and social rights. Corresponding to Beveridge's intent for British social welfare legislation of 1948, social rights were cast as "the right to a modicum of economic welfare, security, to share to the full in the social heritage and to live the life of a civilized being according to the standards prevailing in the society" (Marshall, 1950: 171). As Weiner avers, these rights parallel Habermas' (1996) contention that social rights are "basic rights that secure the conditions of life, including social, technical and environmental protection, that are necessary under given circumstances for an equal chance to use the civil rights" due all citizens. Empowerment is a quest for "negotiated coordination" to equalize opportunities and life chances regardless of age or station; it is a call for participation and self-control as much as it is a claim for protection (Weiner, 1997: 226–7). It is a call for recognizing essential human worth in all interaction even more than a juridical allowance for goods, services, or entitlements. In other words, it is a quest for a moral code against ageism and for a meaningful place at the table. At the heart of a moral economy is examination of social rights revolving around questions of worth, control, and meaning at individual and societal levels, and assertions that these concerns should be at the forefront of any effort to theorize age relations (Calasanti, 2003; Hazan, 1994; Phillipson, 1982).

The extensive tendency towards commodification of need has affected not merely clients and services provided but the perception of those rendering services within the marketplace of misfortune. Olson (2003) offers insight into ways in which structural provisions and ideological precepts underpin definitions of options and appropriate services for marginalized persons experiencing privation of one type or another. She refers to the ascendancy of free-market liberalism as a principal push in the configuration of social, health, and supportive services for the elderly in such a way as to perpetuate and reinforce age, class, gender, and ethnic/racial hierarchies. Among other examples she refers to is the provision of long term care in the United States. For-profit and market-based purveyors have been chosen as preferred providers, eligible for reimbursement for long-term services. Paradoxically, those who actually supply hands-on care are not themselves well regarded or well rewarded. As Olson (2003) points out, it may be because the needs of those to whom they provide services are not held in high esteem in the milieu of societal values concerning frailty or dependency. Stoller (1993) made a comparable point in commenting that much of the cost of care is hidden by the low wage structure of the marketplace

that also colors, in turn, perceptions of the value of family caregivers who deliver comparable services. That is, if a task does not warrant high wages in the world of work, it must not be that valuable or important, even when done by non-paid providers, so why should any special provisions be proposed?

Others have noted ways in which similar values result in social relations that embody discrimination for women and ethic minorities. A number of factors are involved but, in most cases, the dynamics of class relations portend common lifestyles, educations, opportunities, and experiences in such a way that disadvantages accumulate over time (Ehrenreich and Ehrenreich, 1979: 11). Irwin (1999) explored gendered divisions of labor and how they are grounded in standards emanating from labor markets. She and others point to the gendered organization of care and how the predominance of women in both formal and informal caregiving roles speaks to resourcing issues and reproduction of inequalities. As Irwin and others aver, income security and wage structures characterizing any segment of the labor market are replicated in old age among workers exiting that same segment to the extent that earnings-related retirement benefits are predicated on earnings history. Benefit structures reproduce current contributions or prospective economic potential to such an extent that the relationship between poverty, inequality, and the conditions of later life are incontrovertible.

The significance of moral economy can help contextualize challenges being launched at pay-as-you-go pensions and social security programs. As several commentators have asserted, the underlying principle is one of an intergenerational compact based on idealized norms of reciprocity. To illustrate: though approximately three-quarters of the monetary benefits received by retirees in the UK are from lifetime earnings, the remainder comes from taxes withheld from wages of current workers (e.g. Ginn & Arber, 2000; Irwin, 1999). As criticisms of pay-as-you-go financing of benefits accrue in the public's mind, it is easy to question the legitimacy of the process when standards of living among the retired are not something to look forward to. Phillipson (2003) and others have recently introduced geoeconomic considerations into the discussion, as multinational corporations become more pervasive, affecting older persons in local communities and around the world. Not only does globalization exert inordinate suzerainty over indigenous circumstances but, as worldwide financial crises occur, they quickly lead to resource recisions or benefit reductions affecting the elderly and other beneficiary populations. At the same time, inequalities between countries are growing pronounced, leading to increasingly dire circumstances in those that are losing ground, in absolute or relative terms. There appears to be international diffusion of market-driven models for investments and distributions but not those providing any kind of symbolic unifying principles of societal responsibilities or obligations.

CONCLUSION

Ageing is more than an innate process; it is a reflection of patterns and choices made at individual and societal levels. It also incorporates accounts provided by professionals engaged with the elderly in asymmetrical power relationships, proclamations of beneficence notwithstanding (Estes *et al.*, 1984; Johnson, 1993; Katz, 1996; Minkler, 1996; Townsend, 1981). The merit of a moral economic perspective is in the exploration of ethics and values influencing what older people experience in the process of being and becoming old. Making use of moral economic perspectives is helpful in assessing the marketplace of misfortune surrounding the chronic conditions and medical descent characterizing the oldest-old. The admonition to see private troubles as outgrowths of public issues is not far from the heart of moral economy and is at the root of the social production of age and problems encountered there (Mills, 1959; Phillipson, 1982).

As many commentators have noted, there are inestimable and incomparable attributes that can arise with age. Until it is recognized that societal values provide the lens through which they are seen or by which actions are justified or interpreted, such attributes are unlikely to earn approbation (Estes, 2001; Christensen, 1978; Cole, 1985; Johnson, 1995, 1999; Moody, 1998; Phillips, 1981). If conventional ideology extols individualism, self-reliance, independence, and gainful productivity as the measure of worth, it is unlikely that gerontology will assume a liberating role. To the extent that public policies are informed principally by labor-market assumptions and economic priorities, slim chance exists for any

dramatic reformulation of segregative social policies or alternative old age welfare programs (Bond and Coleman, 1983; Myles, 1984; Walker, 1981). A recalibration of the moral compass may be needed to counterbalance the many roots of subjugation, the view of the elderly as marginal, or to help researchers realize the extent to which the problems of old age derive from the "social pathologies of other people's progress" (Titmuss, 1968: 134). Just as there are undeniable declines that occur with age, there are contributions to be made, yet they go quietly unrecognized when the predominant view is one-sided (Commonwealth Fund, 1993).

As problems are defined, so will they be resolved. The labeling power that accrues to political, technical, and professional decision makers may be intended to help the elderly but likely contains collateral payback for the proposers as well. In the 1950s, some commentators predicted the "end of ideology" in the aftermath of the victory of technological, scientific, and rational-pragmatic modes of dealing with emerging issues. Not only does such a prospect seem quaint in hindsight, but hegemonic, an attempt to exert jurisdiction over those who would challenge the neutrality of seemingly rational planning processes. Moral economy sees such deliberations as carrying normative components that stipulate why certain issues come to the fore and others recede (Biggs *et al.*, 2003).

Moral codes coexist with and simultaneously inform political economy. As Gramsci (1971) pointed out, the paradox implicit in value frameworks guiding decisions and behavior is that they are generally subscribed to by all participants, whether advantaged or disadvantaged. The reasons for the moral order being so readily accepted likely rest with internalizing and holding as one's own the principles proclaimed by the over-arching normative sentiments regarding perceptions of what is good, fair, or right. Despite minor divergence in definitions, the construct of moral economy informs inquiries that examine these normative assessments as mechanisms for elucidating why distributional arrangements of structural location and social relations make a difference in what it means to grow old.

Patterns of allocation and distribution are never concluded; they are continually reviewed, revised, and repeatedly warranted. By adopting a moral economic perspective, scholars may be able to understand better how claims are justified and how adjudication of those claims comes to stand as signifiers of the rights of one or another group. The decisions and responses are key elements in the organization of life and shape the circumstances in which people live. It may well be that claims to class-based continuation of relative advantage and disadvantage lie at the heart of old age and determine the benefits older people can expect. Age is not inclusive enough to explain what happens as people become old, and attention to moral economy provides additional insight into how life unfolds.

FURTHER READING

Johnson, M. (1999). "Interdependency and the generational compact." In M. Minkler and C. L. Estes, eds., *Critical gerontology: perspectives from political and moral economy*. Amityville, N.Y.: Baywood Publishing Company, Inc., pp. 55–74.

Thompson, E. P. (1971). "The moral economy of the English crowd in the eighteenth century," *Past and Present*, 50: 76–136.

Townsend, P. (1981). "The structured dependency of the elderly: a creation of social policy in the twentieth century," *Ageing and Society*, l: 5–28.

REFERENCES

Bellah, R. N. (1985). *Habits of the heart: individualism and commitment in American life*. Berkeley, Calif.: University of California Press.

Biggs, S., Hendricks, J., and A. Lowenstein (2003). "The need for theory in gerontology: what is theory and why should we care?" In S. Biggs, A. Lowenstein, and J. Hendricks, eds., *The need for theory: critical approaches to social gerontology*. Amityville, N.Y.: Baywood Publishing Company, Inc., 1–14.

Bond, J., and P. Coleman (1983). "Ageing into the twenty first century." In J. Bond, P. Coleman, and S. Peace, eds., *Ageing in society: an introduction to social gerontology*, 2nd edn. London: Sage Publications, pp. 333–50.

Calasanti, T. (2003). "Theorizing age relations." In S. Biggs, A. Lowenstein, and J. Hendricks, eds., *The need for theory: critical approaches to social gerontology*. Amityville, N.Y.: Baywood Publishing Company, Inc., pp. 199–218.

Calasanti, T. M., and A. Bonanno (1986). "The social creation of dependence, dependency ratios, and the elderly in the United States: a critical analysis," *Social Science and Medicine*, 23: 1229–36.

Christensen, D. (1978). "Aging and the aged: ethical implications in aging." In W. T. Reich, ed., *Encyclopedia of bioethics*, vol. I. New York: The Free Press.

Claeys, G. (1987). *Machinery, money and the millennium: from moral economy to socialism, 1815–1860*. Cambridge: Polity Press.

Cole, T. (1985). "Aging and meaning: our culture provides no compelling answers," *Generations*, 10: 49–52.

Commonwealth Fund (1993). *The untapped resource: the final report of the Americans over 55 at work program*. New York: Commonwealth Fund.

Durkheim, E. (1965[1893]). *The elementary forms of religious life*. New York: The Free Press.

Ehrenreich, B., and J. Ehrenreich (1979). "The professional managerial class." In P. Walker, ed., *Between labor and capital*. Boston: South End Press, pp. 5–48.

Estes, C. L. (1979). *The aging enterprise: a critical examination of social policies and services for the aged*. San Francisco: Jossey-Bass, Inc.

    (1986). "The politics of aging in America," *Ageing and Society*, 6: 121–34.

    (1999). "Critical gerontology and the new political economy of aging." In M. Minkler and C. L. Estes, eds., *Critical gerontology: perspectives from political and moral economy*. Amityville, N.Y.: Baywood Publishing Company, Inc., pp. 17–36.

    (2001). *Social policy and aging: a critical perspective*. Thousand Oaks, Calif.: Sage Publications.

Estes, C. L., Swan, J. H., and L. E. Gerard (1984). "Dominant and competing paradigms in gerontology: towards a political economy of aging." In M. Minkler and C. L. Estes, eds., *Readings in the political economy of aging*. Amityville, N.Y.: Baywood Publishing Company, Inc., pp. 25–36.

Ginn, J., and S. Arber (2000). "Gender, the generational contract and pension privatisation." In S. Arber and C. Attias-Donfut, eds., *The myth of inter-generational conflict: the family and the state in ageing societies*. London: Routledge, pp. 133–53.

Gramsci, V. (1971). *Selections from the prison notebooks*. Trans. Q. Hoare and G. Nowell-Smith. London: Lawrence and Wishart.

Guillemard, A.-M. (1986). "Social policy and ageing in France." In C. Phillipson and A. Walker, eds., *Ageing and social policy: a critical assessment*. Aldershot: Gower, pp. 263–79.

Habermas, J. (1996). *Between facts and norms: contributions to discourse theory of law and democracy*. Trans. W. Rehg. Cambridge, Mass.: MIT Press.

Hazan, H. (1994). *Old age: constructions and deconstruction*. Cambridge: Cambridge University Press.

Hendricks, J. (1995). "Social power of professional knowledge in aging," *Generations*, 19: 51–3.

Hendricks, J., and C. Leedham (1991). "Dependency or empowerment? Toward a moral and political economy of aging." In M. Minkler and C. L. Estes, eds., *Critical perspectives on aging: the political and moral economy of growing old*. Amityville, N.Y.: Baywood Publishing Company, Inc., pp. 51–66.

Irwin, S. (1999). "Later life, inequality and sociological theory," *Ageing and Society*, 19: 691–715.

Johnson, M. (1993). "Dependency and interdependency." In J. Bond, P. Coleman, and S. Peace, eds., *Ageing in society: an introduction to social gerontology,* 2nd edn. London: Sage Publications, pp. 255–79.

—— (1995). "Interdependency and generational compact," *Ageing and Society*, 15: 243–65.

—— (1999). "Interdependency and the generational compact." In M. Minkler and C. L. Estes, eds., *Critical gerontology: perspectives from political and moral economy*. Amityville, N.Y.: Baywood Publishing Company, Inc., pp. 55–74.

Katz, S. (1996). *Disciplining old age. The formation of gerontological knowledge*. Charlottesville, Va.: The University Press of Virginia.

Kohli, M. (1987). "Retirement and the moral economy: an historical interpretation of the German case," *Journal of Aging Studies*, 1: 125–44.

Kohli, M., Rosenow, J., and J. Wolf (1983). "The social construction of aging through work: economic structure and life-world," *Ageing and Society*, 3: 23–42.

Kohn, M. L., and K. M. Slomezynski (1990). *Social structure and self-direction: a comparative analysis of the United States and Poland*. Oxford: Basil Blackwell.

Marshall, T. H. (1950). *Citizenship and social class and other essays*. Cambridge: Cambridge University Press.

Mills, C. W. (1959). *The sociological imagination*. Oxford: Oxford University Press.

Minkler, M. (1996). "Critical perspectives on ageing: new challenges for gerontology," *Ageing and Society*, 16: 467–87.

Minkler, M., and T. Cole (1991). "Political and moral economy: not such strange bedfellows." In M. Minkler and C. L. Estes, eds., *Critical perspectives on aging: the political and moral economy of growing old*. Amityville, N.Y.: Baywood Publishing Company, Inc., pp. 37–50.

Moody, H. R. (1998). "Toward a critical gerontology: the contribution of the humanities to theories of aging." In J. E. Birren and V. L. Bengtson, eds., *Emergent theories of aging*. New York: Springer Publishing Company, pp. 19–40.

Moore, B. (1978). *Injustice: the social bases of obedience and revolt*. White Plains, N.Y.: M. E. Sharpe.

Myles, J. F. (1984). *Old age in the welfare state. The political economy of public pensions*. Boston: Little Brown and Company.

Olson, L. K. (2003). *The not so golden years: caring labor, the frail elderly and the long-term care business enterprise*. Blue Ridge Summit, Penn.: Rowman and Littlefield.

Phillips, D. Z. (1981). *Through a glass darkly*. Bloomington, Ind.: University of Indiana Press.

Phillipson, C. (1982). *Capitalism and the construction of old age*. London: The MacMillan Press Unlimited.

—— (2003). "Globalization and the reconstruction of old age: new challenges for critical gerontology." In S. Biggs, A. Lowenstein, and J. Hendricks, eds., *The need for theory: critical approaches to social gerontology*. Amityville, N.Y.: Baywood Publishing Company, Inc., pp. 163–79.

Robertson, A. (1991). "The politics of Alzheimer's disease: a case study in apocalyptic demography. In M. Minkler and C. L. Estes, eds., *Critical perspectives on aging: the political and moral economy of growing old*. Amityville, N.Y.: Baywood Publishing Company, Inc., pp. 135–52.

Stoller, E. (1993). "Gender and the organization of long-term care: a sociologist–feminist perspective," *Journal of Aging Studies*, 7: 151–70.

Thompson, E. P. (1971). "The moral economy of the English crowd in the eighteenth century," *Past and Present*, 50: 76–136.

Titmuss, R. M. (1968). *Commitment to welfare*. London: George Allen and Unwin.

Tonnies, F. (1957[1887]). *Community and society*. Trans. C. P. Loomis. East Lansing, Mich.: Michigan State University Press.

Townsend, P. (1981). "The structured dependency of the elderly: a creation of social policy in the twentieth century," *Ageing and Society*, l: 5–28.

Walker, A. (1980). "The social creation of poverty and dependency in old age," *Journal of Social Policy*, 9: 49–75.

—— (1981). "Toward a political economy of old age," *Ageing and Society*, 1: 73–94.

—— (1990). "The economic 'burden' of aging and the prospect of inter-generational conflict," *Ageing and Society*, 10: 377–96.

Walton, J. (1979). "Urban political economy," *Comparative Urban Research*, 7: 5–17.

Weber, M. (1958[1904]). *The Protestant ethic and the spirit of capitalism*. Trans. T. Parsons. New York: Charles Scribner's Sons.

Weiner, R. R. (1997). "Social rights and a critical sociology of law," *Current Perspectives in Social Theory*, 17: 217–57.

Wright, E. O. (2002). "The shadow of exploitation in Weber's class analysis," *American Sociological Review*, 67: 832–53.

Generational Changes and Generational Equity

MARTIN KOHLI

In the history of most Western welfare states, the key "social question" to be solved was the integration of the industrial workers – in other words, the pacification of the class conflict. This was achieved by giving workers some assurance of a stable lifecourse, including retirement as a normal life phase funded to a large extent through public pay-as-you-go contribution systems or general taxes (Kohli, 1987). In the twenty-first century, the class conflict seems to be defunct and its place taken over by the generational conflict (Bengtson, 1993; Kaufmann, 2005). The new prominence of the latter is due both to the evolved patterns of social security which have turned the elderly into the main clients of the welfare state, and to the demographic challenge of low fertility and increasing longevity. It remains essential, however, to assess the extent of the generational cleavage per se and the extent to which it masks the continued existence of the received cleavage between rich and poor – in other words, the extent to which new *intergenerational* conflicts have really crowded out traditional *intragenerational* ones.

THE CONCEPTS

The concept of *generation* can be defined with regard to society or to family – two levels which are usually analyzed separately but need to be treated in a unified framework (Kohli, 1996; Kohli and Szydlik, 2000). At the level of the family, generation refers to position in the lineage. At the societal level, it refers to the aggregate of persons born in a limited period (i.e., a birth cohort according to demographic parlance) who therefore experience historical events at similar ages and move up through the lifecourse in unison.

Under what conditions and to what extent this common sociohistorical location leads to a shared consciousness of being a generation and to a common mobilization as a societal actor has been the subject of intense argument and research. What is clear, however, is that the concept of generation is a key to the analysis of social dynamics. In the sequence of generations, families and societies create continuity and change with regard to parents and children, economic resources, political power, and cultural hegemony. In all of these spheres generations are a basic unit of social reproduction *and* social change – in other words, of stability over time as well as renewal (or sometimes revolution).

In some "simple" traditional societies without centralized political power and class-based social stratification, age and gender are the basic criteria for social organization. The most obvious type are the societies – to be found mostly in East Africa – based on formal age classes (or age-sets, as they are sometimes called) (Bernardi, 1985). A subtype of particular relevance to the present chapter are those societies in which the basis is not age but generation – that is, position in the family lineage. Here the sequence of generations in the family directly conditions the position of the individual in the economic, political, and cultural sphere (Müller, 1990). In modern societies these features of social organization have been differentiated and are now institutionalized in separate spheres. But they need to be linked at least conceptually, so that shifts in the relative importance of these spheres may be detected. There are indications, for instance, that in the West the main arena of intergenerational conflict has shifted from the political and cultural to the economic sphere. The political cleavage between generations has turned into a distributive cleavage.

This is where the term *generational equity* comes into play. It refers to "the argument that the elderly have been the recipients of an unfair distribution of public resources for income, health care, and social services" (Binstock and Quadagno, 2001: 343), and that this comes at the expense of the non-aged population, especially children. The discourse on generational equity has been grounded by analyses such as Preston's (1984) comparison of the wellbeing of children and the elderly, or Kotlikoff's (1992) model of generational accounting, and institutionalized through pressure groups such as Americans for Generational Equity (AGE) founded in 1984. From the US, the discourse has been imported to the UK and to the European continent (see Attias-Donfut and Arber, 2000) where institutionalization has been slower but with more current weight, such as with the German Stiftung für die Rechte zukünftiger Generationen [Foundation for the Rights of Future Generations] founded in 1996.

GENERATIONAL EQUITY: DISCOURSE AND INSTITUTIONS

The political consequences drawn by the proponents of generational equity go in the direction of reducing public spending for the elderly – e.g., by privatizing (parts of) old-age security, reducing the benefits, and increasing the retirement age limit. Other demands include age-based rationing for some types of medical care, and age tests for a range of issues such as driving or even voting. The demands are often grouped under the term *sustainability*, and linked to issues in the domain of ecology.

While the general idea of keeping the world intact for future generations is readily accepted, the more specific demands have drawn intense criticism. Among the scientific community of gerontology and the associational community of old age concerns, the generational equity demands have become a common rallying point for repudiation and indignation, and an easy target for claiming the scientific as well as the political and moral high ground.

The proponents of generational equity have accordingly been hit by a range of counter statements from public or scientific associations for the elderly, such as the report on intergenerational ties from the Gerontological Society of America (Kingson *et al.*, 1986), or the volume from the American Association of Retired Persons (Cohen, 1993).

These counter statements have indeed made a strong case (see Williamson *et al.*, 1999). They have pointed out that the expansion of old-age security should be seen as a success that – far from unduly privileging the elderly – has only given them their due share by finally bringing them up to par with the active population (Hudson, 1999). Improving their wellbeing does not necessarily come at the expense of other population groups. In a comparative macro-social perspective on Western societies, higher spending on the elderly is positively associated with higher spending on children as well (Pampel, 1994). Privatizing old-age security through a fully funded system will not solve the problem of lower returns since returns from private funds depend equally on the domestic economic product at the time they are cashed in (except if the funds are invested in more dynamic economies abroad). In fact, the discourse on generational equity may be seen as a veiled attack on the welfare state itself, and thus as an ideological ploy of the political right (Walker, 1996). In the US, moreover, the "entitlement crisis" of old age was debunked by the disappearance of the federal budget deficit in the late 1990s (Quadagno, 1996). That the deficit has now skyrocketed again under the combined pressure of the Bush administration's tax cuts and the costs of war cannot reasonably be attributed to social security.

European welfare states, however, have been less fortunate. Here, the issues of generational equity have become an important part of the broader efforts towards welfare retrenchment (Pierson, 2001; Esping-Andersen *et al.*, 2002). This is due to the tightening of public finances under the pressures of Europeanization and globalization, but also to the increasingly bleak demographic outlook. Demography is not destiny (and presenting it as such may be another form of ideology) – but it does create a major challenge in terms of population ageing. This challenge goes beyond the economically advanced societies of the OECD world. It is, however, largest for some of the latter that have shown a persistent pattern of low fertility. The reduction of mortality, on the other hand, is more equal among these societies. A major question here is whether we are approaching some natural limit of the human lifespan, as set forth by authors who have pointed out the "rectangularization" of the survival curve. Recent research points to the opposite direction: that the historical increase in longevity has been a strikingly regular process, so that there is good reason to assume that it will continue (Oeppen and Vaupel, 2002).

The joint impact of low fertility, increasing life expectancy, and relatively early exit from the labor force will drive up the contribution rates or drive down the income replacement level of pensions, especially (but not only) so in the "conservative" and "social-democratic" welfare states of continental Europe and Scandinavia with their extensive pay-as-you-go or tax-based pension systems. Immigration (see UN Population Division, 2000), increasing female labor force participation, and an increase in the retirement age limit will all provide some financial relief, but the demographic numbers are such that the issues will remain critical. The current conflicts over pension "reform" – or, more to the point, pension retrenchment – is taxing these societies' capacities for finding viable political compromises to their limits (see Myles, 2002).

Some proponents of generational equity argue that the window of opportunity for implementing these reforms is closing because the older population increasingly dominates the political arena by its sheer voting weight. They see a point of no return when the power of the elderly will be such that they will be able to block any attempt at reducing their benefits. In a formal analysis for Germany, Sinn and Uebelmesser (2003) have projected the median age of voters and the "indifference age" as the age of the cohort that is affected neither positively nor negatively by a pension reform. The assumption is that a reform will be feasible if and only if the median voter favors it (2003: 155). The authors conclude that until 2016 a reform can be democratically enforced because a majority of the voters will still be below the indifference age. The year 2016 is "Germany's last chance"; after that year, it will be a gerontocracy. Such a model is of course highly mechanical; it presupposes that voting shares fully translate into

specific policies, and that people's votes are based only on their current individual position – which is manifestly not the case (cf. below).

If political action is not purely interest-based, it may make sense to search for legitimate criteria for intergenerational distribution, i.e., for a conception of equity that can be reasoned to be fair, and by that virtue can muster general agreement. In an argument based on Rawls' theory of justice, Daniels (1988) has shown that intergenerational sharing of burden and rewards is just or fair to the extent that each successive generation can expect to receive the same treatment as the preceding and following ones when it moves up the through the stages of life. In such an ideal world, financing the elderly during one's earning years through a pay-as-you-go system is not problematic because one can expect to reap the same benefits in one's retirement funded by the next generation (a pattern often called "indirect" or "sequential reciprocity"). Unfortunately, the real world never quite conforms to this ideal. The most drastic departure from it may be represented by Thomson's (1989) account of the development of the welfare state in New Zealand. According to Thomson, it has been the result of the political activity of a specific generation which first created a youth-state in its favor with housing subsidies and benefits for young families, and then over its own lifecourse turned it into a welfare state for the elderly. New Zealand's welfare state thus represents one generation's success in exploiting its preceding and succeeding ones.

While such blatant political exploitation of the public "generational contract" seems to be the exception rather than the rule, there are other sources of discontinuity. As mentioned above, the most obvious one today is demography. In such a situation, it may prove fairer to fine-tune the pattern of intergenerational redistribution by adopting the fixed relative position (FRP) model (as set out by Myles, 2002:141, based on Musgrave, 1986): "Contributions and benefits are set so as to hold constant the ratio of per capita earnings of those in the working population (net of contributions) to the per capita benefits (net of taxes) of retirees." This allows for proportional risk sharing: "As the population ages, the tax rate rises but benefits also fall so that both parties 'lose' at the same rate" (Myles, 2002: 141).

TABLE 1. Relative equivalent disposable incomes, by age groups.
Average income of entire population = 100

	Children Age 0–17	Young Age 18–25	Young adults Age 26–40	Adults Age 41–50	Older adults Age 51–65	Younger senior citizens Age 65–75	Older senior citizens Age 75+
Canada, 1985	88	102	103	116	110	91	84
Canada, 1995	88	100	100	114	114	99	95
France, 1984	95	102	106	112	103	86	82
France, 1994	95	97	100	115	109	94	82
Germany, 1984	93	98	102	113	109	85	81
Germany, 1994	91	96	99	118	110	93	77
Hungary, 1991	99	109	103	119	96	81	77
Hungary, 1997	93	111	104	109	104	88	81
Italy, 1984	90	107	106	106	108	82	78
Italy, 1993	89	103	105	109	108	85	82
Sweden, 1983	101	71	105	119	119	91	70
Sweden, 1995	99	60	100	120	127	96	78
United Kingdom, 1985	90	114	105	124	105	74	72
United Kingdom, 1995	86	112	106	123	108	80	74
United States, 1985	82	99	104	118	121	99	84
United States, 1995	84	94	102	118	124	99	82

Note: For calculating relative income changes, population shares have been kept constant at the beginning of the period.
Source: Förster and Pearson (2002).

But problems of equity arise in the *intra*generational dimension as well. The relation of the "old" issues of inequitable distribution (or poverty, or exclusion) along class lines and of the "new" ones such as those based on generations remains a thorny one. The discourse on intergenerational equity may function as an ideology: as a way to divert attention away from the still existing problems of poverty and exclusion *within* generations, e.g. based on class or gender. If, as a consequence of demographic change, welfare systems are redesigned, these problems may be exacerbated in surprising ways. An example is the proposed rise in the age of retirement: given that longevity is socially stratified, a rising retirement limit would disadvantage the less well-off because an additional year of employment represents a larger proportional loss for someone with a shorter further life expectancy (Myles, 2002: 146). This may be one of the reasons why raising the retirement age proves to be so broadly unpopular (see below).

GENERATIONAL EQUITY: THE EMPIRICAL RECORD

Most of the claims of generational equity focus on the distribution of economic resources between the young and the old. As mentioned above, one line of research examines the input side: welfare state spending targeted to different population groups, among them the young and the old, and how it is brought about by welfare state institutions (e.g. Pampel, 1994). This concerns not only the large redistributive programs such as old-age security or health insurance, but also arrangements only partially organized or subsidized by the state such as care (cf. Anttonen *et al.*, 2003). But the most straightforward way of validating the claims of the generational equity debate is to assess the output side: the outcome of market distribution and state redistribution in terms of the economic wellbeing of the young and the old.

Table 1 presents the evolution of relative incomes by age groups from the mid 1980s to the mid 1990s

TABLE 2. Poverty rates (in percent) by country for total population, children, and the elderly

Country	Total population	Children (−18)	Elderly (65+)
Australia 1994	14.3	15.8	29.4
Austria 1995	10.6	15.0	10.3
Belgium 1997	8.2	7.6	12.4
Canada 1997	11.9	15.7	5.3
Denmark 1997	9.2	8.7	6.6
Finland 1995	5.1	4.2	5.2
France 1994	8.0	7.9	9.8
Germany 1994	7.5	10.6	7.0
Italy 1995	14.2	20.2	12.2
Netherlands 1994	8.1	8.1	6.4
Spain 1990	10.1	12.2	11.3
Sweden 1995	6.6	2.6	2.7
Switzerland 1992	9.3	10.0	8.4
UK 1995	13.4	19.8	13.7
United States 1997	16.9	22.3	20.7

Source: Jesuit and Smeeding (2002).

TABLE 3. Poverty rates (in percent) by age in West Germany, 1973–1998

Age	1973	1983	1998
Less than 6 years	8.0	11.5	15.9
7 to c. 13 years	7.6	9.9	15.3
c. 14 to c. 17 years	4.2	7.3	14.9
c. 18 to 24 years	4.6	12.0	13.3
25 to 54 years	4.0	5.8	9.6
55 to 64 years	6.2	4.9	7.5
65+ years	13.3	11.9	10.9
All	6.5	7.7	10.9

Source: Becker and Hauser (2003).

in selected OECD countries (Förster and Pearson, 2002).[1] It shows that children have lost ground in some of the countries, and that their income position is considerably below that of the active population. The income position of the elderly has indeed improved in most countries but also remains below that of the active population, particularly so in the UK with its "residual" welfare state. Moreover, the position of those above age 75 is clearly less favorable than that of the "young old."

Another perspective is that on poverty.[2] As shown by Table 2 (Jesuit and Smeeding, 2002), poverty rates among children and the elderly vary massively. The "liberal" cluster of welfare states (where the share of private pensions is larger) has generally higher poverty rates among both groups of dependents, with some interesting exceptions, however (Canada and Switzerland). With the evolution of poverty

[1] The table is based on a questionnaire sent out by the OECD to national representatives. The authors offer a comparison of their data with those obtained through other sources, e.g. the European Community Household Panel or the Luxembourg Income Study.
[2] Table 2 (based on the Luxembourg Income Study) refers to 50 percent of median equivalence income, Table 3 (based on the German Survey of Income and Consumption) to 50 percent of mean equivalence income.

over 25 years in West Germany (Table 3; Becker and Hauser, 2003), the elderly have improved their lot but only up to the general population level, while the situation of children has worsened to a level considerably less favorable than that of the general population. It should be noted that this may reflect some structural challenges, such as more single parents and fewer children to mothers with higher education. It is obvious from these results that in terms of generational equity (as well as of pronatalist incentives) families with young children should indeed be the target of supplementary welfare efforts. But the results give no reason to strip the elderly of (part of) their current benefits.

ATTITUDES TOWARDS THE PUBLIC GENERATIONAL CONTRACT

In addition to a range of national studies on attitudes towards welfare reform and generational equity, there are now several cross-national surveys that lend themselves to comparative studies, among them the International Social Survey Program (ISSP, e.g. Hicks, 2001; Blekesaune and Quadagno, 2003), the Eurobarometer (e.g. Kohl, 2003), and the new European Social Survey. Attitudes are important because in a democratic polity the acceptance of and compliance with taxes and contributions imposed by the state depends on their legitimacy. The studies generally show a level of acceptance of welfare policies that is much higher than the discourse on generational equity would lead us to expect, with pensions being the most popular part of the welfare state. There is some differentiation along the

TABLE 4. Views on more public retirement spending, 1996

Percentage indicating they would like to see more, or much more, government spending on retirement benefits, being asked to remember that if you say "much more," it might require a tax increase to pay for it

	Age group				
	Under 30	30–39	40–49	50–64	65+
Canada	34.8	23.4	24.6	30.5	20.5
Germany	45.5	41.6	41.6	48.4	51.7
Italy	55.8	60.4	65.8	65.8	75.6
Japan	54.6	48.0	53.9	57.9	60.9
Sweden	41.7	51.3	51.9	59.8	66.8
United Kingdom	63.3	79.2	79.7	79.8	87.1
United States	55.0	51.0	45.7	48.9	45.2

Source: Hicks (2001).

age dimension, but less than one would expect from an interest-based model of political preference.

One set of questions is about which one among the different institutional systems or "pillars" of the welfare mix should provide social security. On the issue of whose responsibility it should be to provide a decent standard of living for the old (ISSP, 1996), an overwhelming majority in all countries say that this should definitely or probably be the government's responsibility (Hicks, 2001: 19). The proportion stating that this should definitely be so increases over the lifecourse, but even among those under age 30 it ranges between 38% (in Canada) and 69% (in Italy). A second question concerns the desired extent of public spending for old age security (Hicks, 2001: 11). The question wording takes pains to avoid making the response too easy by signaling that "much more" spending might require a tax increase, but, even so, between 7% (in Canada) and 27% (in the UK) say "much more," and between 21% and 51% say "more"; the large majority of the rest opts for "same," between 1% and 8% for "less," and only between 0% and 2% for "much less." Clearly, there is little support for cutting old age benefits, and considerable support for expanding them. Table 4 presents the data according to age groups. The desire to expand government spending on pensions increases somewhat with age, but again less than expected, with the two North American countries even going in the opposite direction.

Bivariate results such as these may of course reflect compositional changes other than age. There is, for example, a gender gap (largest in Sweden, smallest in Japan – not shown in the table), with women having a higher preference for more public spending than men, which is partly behind the higher preference in the older age groups.

A special Eurobarometer module of Fall 2001 (as analyzed by Kohl, 2003) provides a more recent description of EU public opinion on these matters, with detailed indications on specific pension goals and policy options. The two most popular goals of pension systems are protection against poverty (92% agreement) and a guaranteed minimum pension (90%); but an adequate standard of living in relation to one's previous earnings (88%), larger equality among the elderly (84%), and the pay-as-you-go principle (81%) are also supported by more than four-fifths of the population. Figure 1 shows the support for three alternative proposals for balancing revenues and expenditures of public pension schemes. To raise awareness for the costs of each option, the trade-offs were explicitly mentioned in the question: (1) current benefit levels should be maintained, even if this means increasing contribution rates or taxes; (2) contributions should be maintained, even if this means lower pension benefits; (3) the age of retirement should be raised so that people work longer and spend less time in retirement. The first option, maintaining current pension levels, gains majority

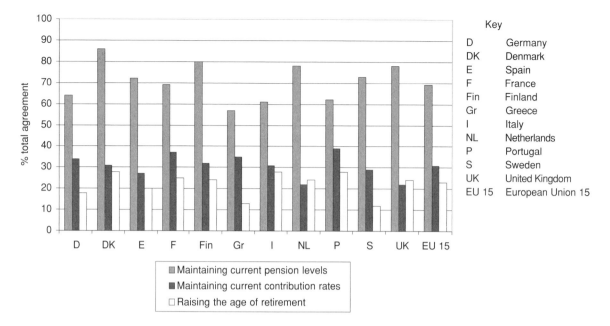

Figure 1. Support for pension policy alternatives, 2001.
Source: Kohl, 2003.

support in all EU member states. In the EU as a whole, 30% strongly agree and 38% slightly agree with this statement, while only 5% disagree strongly and an additional 15% disagree slightly. In contrast, the second option, maintaining current contribution rates, is supported by only 31% and disapproved by a majority of EU citizens (53%). The third alternative, raising the age of retirement, is generally the least popular one. If working longer turns out to be inevitable, such a policy will have to overcome considerable popular resistance.

The first option places the burden mostly on the tax-payers or the active labor force; the second, on the pensioners. But this again does not translate into massively different rates of support by age. There is some tendency for pensioners (76%) to prefer the first option more strongly than the active labor force, but, even among the latter, a strong majority (66%) support maintaining current benefit levels even at the cost of rising contributions. Raising the retirement age is rejected by 69% of the retired as well as the non-retired part of the population. Thus, the distributional conflict among generations is much less pronounced than is presumed (or advertised) by the proponents of generational equity.

THE PUBLIC AND THE PRIVATE GENERATIONAL CONTRACT

The perspective on generational equity is usually restricted to public resource flows, and neglects the private side – the transfers between family generations. The same is true for the formal generational accounting framework. For a balanced view of intergenerational exchange, this neglect needs to be redressed.

The recent research on *inter vivos* family transfers demonstrates that transfers are considerable, that they occur mostly in the generational lineage, and that they flow mostly downwards, from the older to the younger generations (Kohli, 1999). There may be expectations of reciprocity, or other strings attached, but by and large parents are motivated by altruism or feelings of unconditional obligation, and direct their gifts to situations of need. For Germany, our survey in 1996 showed that 32% of those above age 60 made a transfer to their children or grandchildren during the 12 months prior to the interview, with a mean net value of about €3,700. Thus, part of the public transfers from the active population to the elderly was handed back by the latter to their family descendants. The aggregate net *inter vivos* transfers by the elderly population amounted to about 9% of the total yearly public pension sum. This link needs to be qualified, but the overall pattern is clear: the public generational contract is partly balanced by a private one in the opposite direction. The family transfers function to some extent as an informal insurance system for periods of special needs. Even more important in monetary terms are bequests which today have also become a mass phenomenon.

In conclusion, it should be acknowledged that the potential for distributional conflicts among generations certainly exists and is fuelled by the current challenges of public finances and demography. However, the discourse of generational equity overstates the extent and inevitability of such conflicts, and sharpens them at the expense of conflicts along the more traditional cleavages of class. Survey data regularly show that the public generational contract still enjoys high legitimacy among all ages and segments of the population. Among the young, this partly depends on whether they trust in the continued viability of this contract so that they themselves will also receive its benefits. Another reason is that pensions free the young from the obligation to support their parents, and, even more importantly, that they can rely on their parents in times of need. On another level that is beyond this chapter, we would need to focus on the institutions – such as parties or unions (Kohli *et al.*, 1999) – that mediate generational conflicts by favoring or disfavoring age integration in the political arena.

FURTHER READING

Bengtson, V. L., and A. W. Achenbaum, eds. (1993). *The changing contract across generations*. New York: Aldine de Gruyter.

Johnson, P., Conrad, C. and D. Thomson, eds. (1989). *Workers versus pensioners: intergenerational justice in an ageing world*. Manchester: Manchester University Press.

Kohli, M. and M. Szydlik, eds. (2000). *Generationen in Familie und Gesellschaft*. Opladen: Leske & Budrich.

Williamson, J. B. *et al.*, eds. (1999). *The generational equity debate*. New York: Columbia University Press.

REFERENCES

Anttonen, A., Baldock, J. and J. Sipilä, eds. (2003). *The young, the old and the state: social care systems in five industrial nations*. Cheltenham: Edward Elgar.

Attias-Donfut, Claudine, and Sara Arber (2000). "Equity and solidarity across the generations." In Sara Arber and Claudine Attias-Donfut, eds., *The myth of generational conflict. The family and state in ageing societies*. London: Routledge, pp. 1–21.

Becker, I., and R. Hauser (2003). "Zur Entwicklung von Armut und Reichtum in der Bundesrepublik Deutschland – eine Bestandsaufnahme." In C. Butterwegge and M. Klundt, eds., *Kinderarmut und Generationengerechtigkeit. Familien- und Sozialpolitik im demografischen Wandel*. Opladen: Leske & Budrich, pp. 25–41.

Bengtson, V. L. (1993). "Is the 'contract across generations' changing? Effects of population aging on obligations and expectations across age groups." In V. L. Bengtson and W. A. Achenbaum, eds., *The changing contract across generations*. New York: Aldine de Gruyter, pp. 3–24.

Bernardi, B. (1985). *Age class systems*. Cambridge: Cambridge University Press.

Binstock, R. H., and J. Quadagno (2001). "Aging and politics." In R. H. Binstock and L. K. George, eds., *Handbook of aging and the social sciences*, 5th edn. San Diego, Calif.: Academic Press, pp. 333–51.

Blekesaune, M. and J. Quadagno (2003). "Public attitudes toward welfare state policies: a comparative analysis of 24 nations," *European Sociological Review*, 5 (19): 415–27.

Cohen, L. M., ed. (1993). *Justice across generations. What does it mean?* Washington: American Association of Retired Persons.

Daniels, N. (1988). *Am I my parents' keeper? An essay on justice between the old and the young*. Oxford: Oxford University Press.

Esping-Andersen, G., Gallie, D., Hemerijck, A., and J. Myles (2002). *Why we need a new welfare state*. Oxford: Oxford University Press.

Förster, M., and M. Pearson (2002). "Income distribution and poverty in the OECD area: trends and driving forces," *OECD Economic Studies*, 34, 2002/I.

Hicks, P. (2001). *Public support for retirement income reform*. OECD Labour Market and Social Policy Occasional Papers, 55. Paris: OECD.

Hudson, R. B. (1999). "Conflict in today's aging politics: new population encounters old ideology," *Social Service Review*, 73: 358–79.

Jesuit, D., and T. Smeeding (2002). *Poverty and income distribution*, LIS Working Paper 293. Luxembourg: Luxembourg Income Study.

Kaufmann, F.-X. (2005). Gibt es einen Generationenvertrag?" In. F.-X. Kaufmann, ed., *Sozialpolitik und Sozialstaat: Soziologische Analysen*. Wiesbaden: VS, pp. 161-82.

Kingson, E. R., Hirshorn, B. A., and J. M. Cornman (1986). *Ties that bind. The interdependence of generations*. Washington: Seven Locks Press.

Kohl, J. (2003). "Citizens' opinions on the transition from work to retirement." Paper presented at the ISSA 4th International Research Conference on Social Security: "Social Security is a Long-Life Society," Antwerp.

Kohli, M. (1987). "Retirement and the moral economy: an historical interpretation of the German case," *Journal of Aging Studies*, 1: 125–44.

—— (1996). *The problem of generations: family, economy, politics*, Collegium Budapest, Public Lecture Series No. 14. Budapest: Collegium Budapest.

—— (1999). "Private and public transfers between generations: linking the family and the state," *European Societies*, 1: 81–104.

Kohli, M., and M. Szydlik, eds. (2000). *Generationen in Familie und Gesellschaft*. Opladen: Leske & Budrich.

Kohli, M., Neckel, S., and J. Wolf (1999). "Krieg der Generationen? Die politische Macht der Älteren." In A. Niederfranke, G. Naegele, and E. Frahm, eds., *Funkkolleg Altern*, Vol. II. Opladen: Westdeutscher Verlag, pp. 479–514.

Kotlikoff, L. J. (1992). *Generational accounting: knowing who pays, and when, for what we spend*. New York: Free Press.

Musgrave, R. (1986). *Public finance in a democratic society*, Vol. II. New York: New York University Press.

Müller, H. K. (1990). "Wenn 'Söhne' älter als 'Väter' sind. Dynamik ostafrikanischer Generations- und Altersklassen am Beispiel der Toposa und Turkana." In G. Elwert, M. Kohli, and H. K. Müller, eds., *Im Lauf der Zeit*. Saarbrücken: Breitenbach, pp. 33–49.

Myles, J. (2002). "A new social contract for the elderly?" In G. Esping-Andersen *et al.*, eds., *Why we need a new welfare state*. Oxford: Oxford University Press, pp. 130–72.

Oeppen, J., and J. W. Vaupel (2002). "Broken limits to life expectancy," *Science*, 296: 1029–31.

Pampel, F. C. (1994). "Population aging, class context, and age inequality in public spending," *American Journal of Sociology*, 100: 153–95.

Pierson, P., ed. (2001). *The new politics of the welfare state*. Oxford: Oxford University Press.

Preston, S. H. (1984). "Children and the elderly: divergent paths for America's dependents," *Demography*, 21: 435–57.

Sinn, H.-W. and S. Uebelmesser (2003). "Pensions and the path to gerontocracy in Germany," *European Journal of Political Economy*, 1 (19): 153–58.

Thomson,, D. (1989). "The welfare state and generation conflict: winners and losers." In P. Johnson, C. Conrad, and D. Thomson, eds., *Workers versus pensioners: intergenerational justice in an ageing world*. Manchester / New York: Manchester University Press, pp. 33–56.

UN Population Division (2000). *Replacement migration: is it a solution to declining and ageing populations?* New York: UN.

Walker, A. (1996). *The new generational contract*. London: UCL Press.

Williamson, J. B., Watts-Roy, D. M., and E. R. Kingson, eds. (1999). *The generational equity debate*. New York: Columbia University Press.

CHAPTER 6.5

Gender Dimensions of the Age Shift

SARA ARBER AND JAY GINN

The worldwide trend towards ageing of societies is well documented, but there is less discussion about the changing gender composition of the older population and its implications. A related issue is gender differences in partnership status in later life, which have a profound effect on the social and economic wellbeing of older women and men but in gender differentiated ways.

The focus of this chapter is the gendered nature of later life, while other chapters have examined the growth in the ageing population. A recent groundswell of research by feminist scholars on older women has challenged earlier views of older people as homogenous, emphasising differences by gender, class and ethnicity (Arber and Ginn, 1991, 1995; Bernard and Meade, 1993; Calasanti and Slevin, 2001). Social policy makers and analysts have primarily been concerned about the 'social problems' of an ageing population. Because of the numerical predominance of women, concern has focused mainly on older women, with less attention paid to older men (Davidson *et al.*, 2003; Thompson, 1994).

This chapter examines changes in the numerical balance of the sexes in later life arising from trends in life expectancy, trends in marital status and the gendered implications of these changes. We examine two facets of life important to wellbeing for older

people – pensions and social involvement with family and friends – showing how the intersection of gender and marital status influences social advantage or disadvantage.

THE FEMINISATION OF LATER LIFE AND ITS RECENT DIMINUTION

The feminisation of later life – or the numerical predominance of women – is now diminishing. Most people in Western societies live as part of a heterosexual couple, but a numerical imbalance between the sexes means fewer people are partnered, influencing household living arrangements and potential supporters should a person become sick or disabled. The sex balance in later life has implications for the social roles and relationships of older people and the provision of services and facilities.

It is well known that the ratio of women to men increases with advancing age, but this sex ratio has varied markedly over the last fifty years. In 1961 and 1971, there were 161 women for every 100 men over the age of 65 in England and Wales, which fell to 138 women by 2001. Thus 58 per cent of people over 65 were women in 2001.

Figure 1 shows how the sex ratio has fluctuated since 1951 within the older population. Among those aged 65–74, there are now only 113 women for every 100 men, a remarkably rapid fall from a sex ratio of 156 in 1961. Above age 75, the numerical predominance of women is greater but is declining. There were twice as many women as men aged 75–84 in 1971 but only 50 per cent more by 2001,

We are grateful to the Office of National Statistics for permission to use data from the General Household Survey, and to the UK Data Archive and Manchester Computing Centre for access to the data.

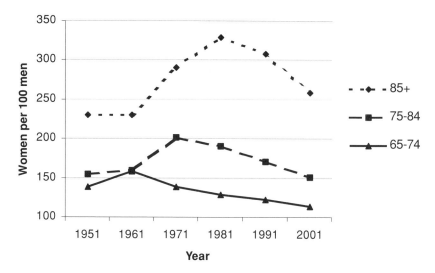

Figure 1. Sex ratios among people aged 65+ in England and Wales, 1951–2001.
Source: Population Trends 21 (Autumn 1980), derived from Table 15 for sex ratios 1951 and 1961; *Population Trends 112* (Summer 2003), derived from Table 1.4 for sex ratios 1971 to 2001.

similar to the sex ratio in 1951. The oldest-old are disproportionately women. Above age 85, there were over three times more women than men in 1981 and 1991, which fell to a sex ratio of 259 by 2001. The sex ratio is likely to fall further in the next decade, reaching its 1951 level of 230 or lower. A similar movement towards numerical convergence is occurring in many developed countries.

Two demographic factors underlie the numerical predominance of women in later life (Britton and Edison, 1986). First, those currently aged over 65 are survivors of two world wars. Deaths of young men in the First World War led to a large numerical excess of women in the cohorts aged 65–74 in 1961, who were aged 75–84 in 1971 and aged 85+ in 1981. These are the years with the highest sex ratios in Figure 1. Second, the mortality rates of men and women have changed differentially over time. Throughout the twentieth century until the 1970s, there were greater reductions in women's than men's mortality, leading to a larger proportion of women at older ages. However, since 1981 there has been a more rapid fall in male than female mortality, diminishing the sex ratio. The next section examines international trends in life expectancy, focusing particularly on the sex gap.

GENDER AND EXPECTATION OF LIFE INTERNATIONALLY

One of the main reasons for the ageing of populations is mortality reductions and consequent lengthening of average life, the other main reason is falling fertility rates. Table 1 shows gender differences in life expectancy at birth for different countries in the 1970s and late 1990s (UN 1982, 2002). In this group of developed countries, the average expectation of life increased by 4–6 years for men, and by 3–5 years for women. In most of these countries, women's life expectancy was over 80 by the late 1990s, reaching 84 years in Japan, and failed to reach 80 only in the UK and US. Singapore, a recently developed country, experienced a rapid rise in women's life expectancy from 70 to 80 between 1970 and 2000. Men's life expectancy in the late 1990s was generally around 75–76, with a high of 77.1 in Japan and Sweden, and a low of 73.8 in the US.

The greater gains in life expectancy among men than women over the last 20 years are reflected in the narrowing of the sex gap in Table 1. There was a 6–7 year sex gap in the 1970s, which fell in most of these countries by the late 1990s. Only in Japan had it increased by 1.6 years to women living 6.9 years longer than men, and in Italy by 0.4 years to a 6.4 year gap. In most other countries the sex gap fell by over a year, e.g. in the UK by 1.4 years and in the US by 2.1 years. Thus, later life is becoming disproportionately *less* feminised than in the past, with implications for marital status and living arrangements, as discussed in the next sections.

TABLE 1. Expectation of life in 1970s and late 1990s by sex and country

| | 1970s | | | Late 1990s | | | Change in |
	Male	Female	M/F gap in years	Male	Female	M/F gap in years	Sex Gap 70s–90s
France	68.5	77.1	8.6	74.8	82.4	7.6	−1.0
Italy	69.0	74.9	5.9	74.6	81.0	6.4	+0.4
Sweden	72.4	78.3	5.9	77.1	81.9	4.8	−1.1
Switzerland	70.3	76.2	5.9	76.8	82.5	5.7	−0.2
UK	70.0	76.2	6.2	75.0	79.8	4.8	−1.4
Australia	70.2	77.2	7.0	76.2	81.8	5.6	−1.4
New Zealand	69.0	75.4	6.4	75.2	80.4	5.2	−1.2
Canada	70.2	77.5	7.3	74.6	80.9	6.3	−1.0
USA	69.3	77.1	7.8	73.8	79.5	5.7	−2.1
Singapore	65.1	70.0	4.9	76.0	80.0	4.0	−0.9
Japan	73.0	78.3	5.3	77.1	84.0	6.9	+1.6

Years: France – 1978, 1998; Italy – 1970–2, 1995; Sweden – 1978, 1999; Switzerland – 1968–73, 1999; UK – 1976–8, 1999; Australia – 1978, 1997–9; New Zealand – 1975–7, 1997–9; Canada – 1975–7, 1992; USA – 1977, 1998; Singapore – 1970, 2000; Japan – 1978, 1999.
Source: UN (1982), derived from Table 34; and UN (2002), derived from Table 22.

CHANGES IN MARITAL STATUS IN LATER LIFE

Marital status is pivotal to the living arrangements, financial wellbeing and social relationships of older people, but in divergent ways for older women and men. We examine gender differences in marital status and how these are changing over time. A significant transition for many older people begins when they are widowed. Widowhood often represents the loss of a partner of 40–50 years, who may have been the main source of companionship and support, especially for men, who frequently see their wife as their primary confidante (Askham, 1994; Davidson, 1999).

Most older men are married and therefore have a partner for companionship, domestic service support and for care should they become physically disabled, whereas this is not the case for the majority of older women. Figure 2 shows that in England and Wales in 2001, 70% of older men were married compared with 40% of women. The likelihood of being married declines steeply with advancing age, more so for women than men.

Widowhood is normative for women over 65, since nearly half are widowed, reaching over four-fifths at ages 85 and over. In contrast, over three-quarters of men aged 65–9 are married (65% in first marriages and 11% remarried), still remaining at 60% in their early 80s. Even in their late 80s, almost half of men are married. Remarriage is increasingly prevalent, especially among men, with older widowed or divorced men more likely to remarry later in life than comparable older women. It is notable that more men in their late 60s are divorced (9%) than widowed (7%). Only 17% of men over 65 are widowers, increasing to 43% by their late 80s. Thus marriage is normative for older men, and most men are married when they die. However, this may blind us to issues facing the minority of older widowed men and the small but growing proportion who are divorced. Among both men and women in their late 60s, 9% are divorced or separated, compared with only 2% over 85.

The proportion of older people in each marital status shows rapid changes between 1971 and 2021 (see Table 2). A declining proportion of older men are married, due to increasing divorce (although even in 2021 two-thirds are projected to be married). This contrasts with older women, where the proportion married increases from 35% in 1971 to a projected 45% by 2021 (Shaw, 1999). This change reflects improvements in mortality at older ages, especially among men. There is a projected sharp decline in widowhood among older people between 2001 and 2021, from almost half to 35% for women and from 17% to 13% for men (Shaw, 1999).

Men

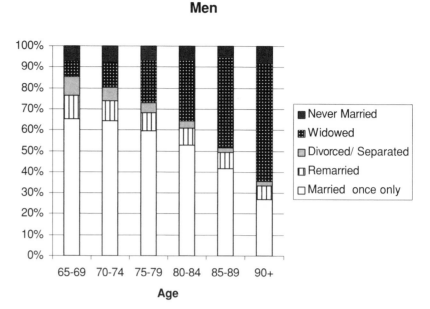

Women

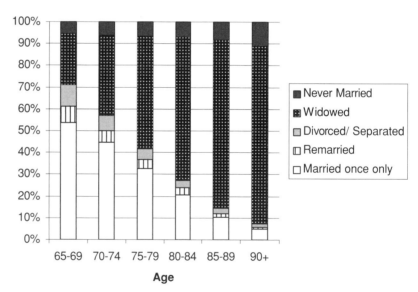

Figure 2. Marital status by gender and age, England and Wales, 2001, age 65+.
Source: ONS (2003), derived from Table S002.

The largest proportionate change between 1971 and 2021 is the increase in divorced older people, rising from 1% to 5% between 1971 and 2001, and projected to reach 13% by 2021. For every 100 widows aged over 65 there were only two divorcees in 1971 but this is projected to rise to 40 divorcees by 2021 (Table 2). Over the same period there has been a substantial fall in the proportions of never married older women from 14% to 5%. Given these marked changes in the marital status of the older population, it is timely to consider how marital status may differentiate the experiences of older men and women.

TABLE 2. Changes in marital status over time in England and Wales – 1971, 1986, 2001 and 2021, age 65 and over

(a) Men

	1971	1986	2001	2021	Change 1971–2021
Married	73	73	71	66	−7%
Widowed	19	18	17	13	−6%
Divorced	1	2	5	13	+12%
Never married	7	7	7	8	+1%
All	100%	100%	100%	100%	
N =	2.5m	3.1m	3.5m	4.8m	+92%

(b) Women

	1971	1986	2001	2021	Change 1971–2021
Married	35	37	41	45	+10%
Widowed	50	50	47	35	−15%
Divorced	1	3	5	14	+13%
Never Married	14	10	7	5	−9%
All	100%	100%	100	100%	
N =	4.1m	4.7m	4.8m	5.9m	+44%

Source: Population Trends 112 (Summer 2003), derived from Table 1.5 for 1971, 1986 and 2001; Projections for 2021 from Shaw (1999), Table 1.

GENDER DIFFERENCES IN LIVING ARRANGEMENTS

Living arrangements are linked to legal marital status but increasingly reflect newer forms of partnership such as cohabitation (or de facto partnership). Among those aged 65–74, 2.5% of men and 1.6% of women were cohabiting (including same-sex couples) in England and Wales in 2001 (Table 3). The proportion declines with advancing age, but is still 1.4% among men over age 85.

The majority of older men, 70%, live as part of a couple compared with 40% of women. A key issue for wellbeing and for service provision is the living arrangements of the remainder. The norm in England and Wales is to live alone – 22% of men and 44% of older women (Table 3). However, with advancing age, increasing proportions of older people live with a non-partnered adult child (6.7% of women and over 3.7% of men aged 85+). Similarly, the propor-

tion living with others not in a family (who may be unrelated, siblings or partnered children) increases with age, reaching 6.1% of men and 7.6% of women above age 85.

Another form of partnership – Living-Apart-Together (LAT) – is emerging and is widely found in the Nordic countries and the Netherlands. LAT refers to a stable relationship with a partner who may stay over at weekends and share leisure time and holidays but maintains a separate residence (Borell and Ghazanfareeon Karlsson 2003; de Jong Gierveld 2003). There is no national UK data on the prevalence of LAT relationships, and it is not clear to what extent LAT partners provide care for each other.

Entering a residential or nursing home represents a major threat to an older persons' autonomy and is usually resisted until there is no alternative. Older women are much more likely than men to live in such 'communal establishments', with twice as many women over 85 as men living in these

TABLE 3. Living arrangements by gender and age, England and Wales, 2001, age 65 and over (row percentages)

	Married couple family	Cohabiting couple family[1]	Lives with lone adult child(ren)	Lives with others – not in family[1]	Living alone	Lives in communal establishment[1]	Total	Thousands
Men								
65–74	73.9	2.5	1.9	3.2	17.5	1.0	100%	2,045
75–84	63.0	1.8	2.5	4.0	25.7	3.1	100%	1,168
85+	39.7	1.4	3.7	6.1	36.9	12.2	100%	281
Total 65+	67.5	2.2	2.2	3.7	21.8	2.6	100%	3,494
Women								
65–74	54.7	1.6	5.4	4.0	33.2	1.1	100%	2,322
75–84	29.6	0.8	6.2	5.7	52.5	5.2	100%	1,765
85+	7.9	0.5	6.7	7.6	54.5	22.9	100%	732
Total 65+	38.4	1.2	5.9	5.2	43.5	5.9	100%	4,819

[1] *Definitions*: 'A *cohabiting couple family* consists of two people living together as a couple but not married to each other, with or without their [unpartnered] child(ren) . . . Cohabiting couples of the same sex are included.'
Lives with others – not in family includes an older person living with unrelated others (not in a couple), siblings or a married/cohabiting child/grandchild.
'A *communal establishment* is defined as an establishment providing managed residential accommodation . . . Sheltered housing is treated as a communal establishment [only] if less than half the residents possess their own cooking facilities.' (ONS, 2003: 260–3.)
Source: ONS (2003), derived from Table T05.

settings (23% compared to 12%, Table 3). The main reason is gender differences in marital status, since the widowed and never married are far more likely to live in institutional care in later life, than those who are married, and these groups are disproportionately women (Arber and Ginn, 1991; ONS, 2003).

Living arrangements and marital status have implications for the risk of poverty in later life, but in different ways for men and women, as discussed below.

GENDER INEQUALITY IN PENSIONS

Throughout the EU and in most developed countries women have lower personal incomes than men in later life, due mainly to smaller pensions. But the magnitude of the gender gap in pensions varies across countries, due to variation in both women's employment patterns and the structure of pension systems, especially the balance between state and private pensions (Ginn *et al.*, 2001). In the 1990s older women's pension income as a proportion of men's was approximately 66% in Italy, 56% in France and 42% in Germany (Walker and Maltby, 1997). Because older women are more likely than

older men to live alone, with all the diseconomies entailed in solo living, these figures underestimate the gender difference in living standards.

Population ageing, and the controversial belief that it threatens the sustainability of state pay-as-you-go pension schemes more than that of private funded schemes, has been used in many countries to justify reducing the generosity of state pensions and increasing the role of private pensions, mainly individual defined contribution schemes. Such reforms – effectively privatisation of pensions – impact differently on men and women, reflecting women's disadvantages in the labour market, although the effects are mediated by social class, ethnicity, parental roles and partnership history (Ginn, 2003). Since pension privatisation has been taken further in the liberal Anglophone welfare states than in other types of welfare states, we examine the gender impact of this trend in Britain.

Gender inequality in later life income

In Britain, average pensioner incomes are relatively low, with about half of pensioner households qualifying for means-tested social assistance in 2003

TABLE 4. Individual income* of men and women aged 65+ by marital status. Britain, mid 1990s

| | Median income before tax in £/wk | | | | % receiving Income Support | |
	Men	N	Women	N	Men	Women
All	£118	3869	£72	5156	*	*
Married	£125	2757	£46	2180	*	*
Single	£103	228	£104	343	14%	15%
Widowed	£103	720	£85	2415	12%	24%
Divorced/separated	£101	164	£73	218	17%	37%

* For married couples Income Support is awarded jointly so statistics merely reflect which partner claimed.
Source: General Household Survey 1994–1996 (authors' analysis), published in Ginn and Price (2002.)

and at least two-thirds projected to do so by 2050 (PPI, 2003). Older women predominate among the poor, comprising three-quarters of older people living on means-tested benefits. Among those aged over 65, a quarter of widows lived on means tested Income Support in the mid 1990s and as many as 37% of divorced or separated women did so (Table 4). Older women's median personal income was about 60% of older men's in the mid 1990s. Ever-married women are considerably poorer than single (never-married) women, despite the fact that widows may inherit part of any private pension of their deceased husband. In contrast, married men had higher personal income than other men in later life.

This pattern of income inequality with gender and marital status arises mainly from differential receipt of private (occupational or personal) pensions. Low and declining state pensions in Britain mean that an adequate retirement income increasingly depends on having a substantial private pension. Only a third of older women have any private pension income, including widows' pensions based on their deceased husbands' private pensions, and the amounts are less than for men, especially among women who ever married (Ginn, 2003). For the remaining two-thirds of women, their entire pension income is through the state. In the 1990s, private pensions contributed 25% of older men's personal income but only 11% of women's (Ginn and Arber, 1999).

The gender effects of pension privatisation in Britain can be seen in the changing ratio of older women's income to older men's. In the mid 1980s

older women's median personal income was 71% of men's, declining to 60% in 1994–6 (Table 4). Since 1980, the value of the basic state pension has declined relative to national earnings while those retiring with private occupational pensions received increasingly large amounts. But women have been less able than men to compensate for declining state pensions through private sector pensions. Women's greater longevity means their pensions are more seriously eroded by inflation than men's, since pensions are, at best, only indexed to prices. The poorest pensioners are typically women in their 80s living alone.

A danger is that, as pension systems across the world are privatised, pensioners will be increasingly polarised into two groups – those with substantial private pensions (mainly men) and those disadvantaged in the labour market, whose retirement income is primarily a small state pension (mainly women). If Britain's example is followed, increased means testing will be required to alleviate pensioner poverty. Disadvantages of means testing include discouraging saving among workers and failure to reach many of the poorest pensioners. An additional drawback for married and cohabiting women is that a joint means test may render them ineligible for financial assistance despite their having a very low personal income.

Pension prospects of later cohorts

Far-reaching social changes have transformed gender relationships and norms as to partnering,

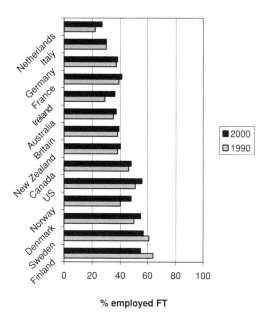

* as % of population aged 15-64 (16-64 in Britain and Sweden).
Break in series after 1990 for Sweden, Denmark, Germany and Italy
and 1999 for Norway and Finland.

Figure 3. Percentage of women employed full time*,
1990, and 2000 in 14 OECD countries.
Source: calculated from OECD (2000, 2001), Tables A and E.

parenting and breadwinning. Major changes include
growing expectations of women's equality and
financial independence irrespective of marital status. At the same time, the expectation of lifelong
marriage has declined, with increases in divorce,
cohabitation and lone parenthood as all these have
become more socially acceptable. These changes all
have profound implications for women's acquisition
of pensions.

Women's increasing participation in employment
might suggest future gender convergence in pension income. However, where pensions are closely
related to lifetime earnings, as is the case in private
pensions, it is full time employment that is crucial
for the amount of pension entitlement. The trend
in women's full time employment in OECD countries is not encouraging. Among fourteen countries,
a consistent rise since 1990 can be seen only in the
US, Norway, Ireland and the Netherlands, and the
rise is from a low base (under 30%) in these last two
countries (see Figure 3).

Family caring roles and the gender gap in hourly
earnings continue to restrict women's pension-

building. The 'family gap in pay' – or the wage loss
due to presence of dependent children – for women
varies among countries, depending on childcare services, but in Britain was 8% for one child and 24%
for two children (Harkness and Waldfogel, 1999).
For lone parents, the loss in earnings, and hence
pensions, due to motherhood is even greater (Ginn,
2003). Childlessness allows women to avoid pension poverty as individuals, yet at the level of society
this solution exacerbates the ageing of populations
(Arber and Attias-Donfut, 2000).

Unlike private pensions, state pensions that
are earnings-related or years-related often include
allowances for family caring responsibilities that
limit the pension losses, while universal citizens'
pensions tend to equalise later life income between
carers and non-carers and hence between women
and men. State pensions in all fifteen current EU
countries include some adaptation to help those
with childcare responsibilities (Leitner, 2001). Although the generosity of state pensions varies, they are
generally more women-friendly than private pensions, reducing the pension penalties of caring.

Demographic trends mean that more older
women in future, but still a minority, will have a
partner whose income they can, theoretically, share.
Yet later cohorts of married women may miss the
independent income to which they have become
accustomed. Moreover, not all husbands are willing
to share their pension equally with their wife. The
increasing proportion of divorced women, who generally have meagre pensions of their own but cannot inherit a widow's pension, is a cause for concern
(Price and Ginn, 2003).

GENDER, SOCIAL ROLES AND RELATIONSHIPS

Much research on gender in later life has taken a
political economy perspective emphasising the disadvantaged position of older women in relation
to their pensions, health status and access to care
(Arber and Ginn, 1991; Estes, 1991). There has been
less attention to older women's advantages compared to some groups of older men. For example,
older women have better social relationships with
both friends (Allan, 1985; Jerrome, 1996) and family members, with women often characterised as the

'kin-keepers' (Finch and Mason, 1993). Recent work has shown that widows often enjoy a new sense of autonomy, whereas widowers see no advantages of being widowed (Davidson, 2001). Older women may belong to the 'society of widows' (Lopata, 1973) facilitating rewarding and emotionally supportive relationships but there is no equivalent support network for widowers. We need to rebalance existing frameworks which focus on older women's disadvantages by considering the disadvantages that certain groups of older men may experience (Arber et al., 2003a).

Social contact with family members and friends is critical for health and wellbeing (Cohen, 1988; Umberson, 1992), providing emotional support in times of stress (Cooper et al., 1999). Umberson (1992) found that spouses, especially wives, had a beneficial influence on their partner's health behaviour. Phillipson et al. (2001) emphasise the increasing importance of friends for the social wellbeing of older people. De Jong Gierveld (2003) shows how older people living alone are less likely to report loneliness where they have more contact with both family and friends.

Should an older person become unable to continue their activities of daily living, such as shopping, they either require assistance from family, friends or neighbours in order to remain living in the community, or must rely on state, voluntary or privately paid support services. If support is unavailable, an older person may enter residential care at a lower threshold of disability than those who can rely on such functional support.

We examine older people who are relatively isolated, focusing on those who say they host relatives or friends in their own home, or visit relatives or friends, less than once a month (Arber et al., 2003b). The British General Household Surveys (GHS) for 1994 and 1998 are analysed, providing a nationally representative sample of over 6,500 people aged 65 and over. Logistic regression is used to compare the differential effects of marital status for women compared to men, after controlling for age in five year groups (ages 65–9, 70–4, 75–9, 80–4 and 85+). Each gender / marital status group is compared to the reference category of married men (with an odds ratio set to 1.00).

There is much greater variation in the extensiveness of social contacts according to marital status among older men than women (see Figure 4). Married men are more likely to host friends and relatives in their home than other groups of men, while married men and widowers are almost equally likely to visit others. In relation to both hosting and visiting relatives and friends, never-married men have least social contact, followed by divorced men. Never-married men have odds 5.4 times higher than married men of rarely hosting relatives and friends, and divorced men an odds ratio of 4.3 (Figure 4a). The odds of widowed men rarely hosting relatives and friends are almost twice as great as for married men. These sharp differences show that non-married men are less likely than married ones to entertain others in their home, indicating that wives facilitate home-based social interactions.

Among older men, differences in visiting relatives and friends by marital status are less marked than for hosting visits. There is almost no difference in visiting between married and widowed men, suggesting that widowers are invited to the homes of family members and friends to the same extent as married men (Figure 4b). Never-married men are least likely to visit relatives and friends, with an odds ratio of 2.3, followed by divorced men (odds ratio of 1.8). These two groups of older men appear to be relatively socially isolated from relatives and friends, which may lead to loneliness and/or lack of access to potential sources of social and instrumental support.

Married men, and older women irrespective of marital status, are more socially integrated in terms of hosting and visiting family and friends, than divorced and never-married men. The latter two groups are therefore most vulnerable to social isolation, and lack the functional social support required to remain living in the community.

CONCLUSIONS

The ageing of the population is proceeding at differential rates by gender, with recent declines in the degree of feminisation of later life. The contours of marital status are changing, with mortality gains greater for men than women and the growth in divorce and cohabitation over recent years. Partnership status is a pivotal dimension for older people, but in gender-differentiated ways.

(a) Hosts relatives or friends less than monthly

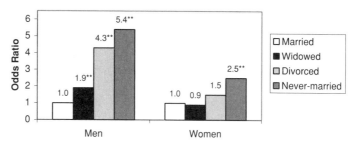

(b) Visits relatives or friends less than monthly

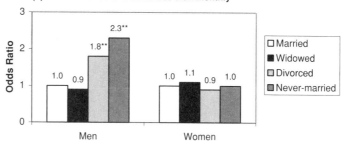

[1] Odds ratios after controlling for 5-year age groups (65-9, 70-4, 75-9, 80-4, 85+); reference category is married men with odds defined as 1.00

Significance of difference from the reference category, **p<0.01

Figure 4. Social contact with family and friends less than monthly by gender and marital status, odds ratios[1], age 65+. *Source:* General Household Survey, 1994 and 1998 (authors' analysis).

Older married men are the most advantaged group, both in terms of pensions and social contact. This advantaged position is held by the vast majority of older men, since 70% of men are married in later life, most remaining married until they die. Widowhood is the norm for women in later life. Widows have lower pensions than men and never-married women. Widows resemble married women in their level of social contacts but widowers are less likely than the married to *host* relatives or friends in their own home.

Divorced men are disadvantaged in terms of both pensions and social contacts. Divorced women, while more severely disadvantaged in terms of pension income, are equally as well integrated into social networks as other women. These findings have implications for policy on pensions and community support of older people, given the projected growth in the divorced older population.

In summary, it is important to consider the implications for policy of trends in the sex ratio and marital status in later life, if financial and social wellbeing are to be maximised.

FURTHER READING

Arber, S., and C. Attias-Donfut, eds. (2000). *The myth of generational conflict: family and state in ageing societies.* London: Routledge.

Arber, S., Davidson, K., and J. Ginn, eds. (2003). *Gender and ageing: changing roles and relationships.* Maidenhead: Open University Press.

Ginn, J. (2003). *Gender, pensions and the lifecourse.* Bristol: Policy Press.

Ginn, J., Street, D., and S. Arber (2001). *Women, work and pensions: international issues and prospects.* Buckingham: Open University Press.

REFERENCES

Allan, G. (1985). *Family life.* Oxford: Blackwell.

Arber, S., and C. Attias-Donfut, eds. (2000). *The myth of generational conflict: family and state in ageing societies.* London: Routledge.

Arber, S., and J. Ginn (1991). *Gender and later life: a sociological analysis of resources and constraints*. London: Sage.

eds. (1995). *Connecting gender and ageing: a sociological approach*. Buckingham: Open University Press.

Arber, S., Davidson, K., and J. Ginn, eds. (2003a). *Gender and ageing: changing roles and relationships*. Maidenhead: Open University Press.

Arber, S., Price, D., Davidson, K., and K. Perren (2003b). 'Re-examining gender and marital status: material well-being and social involvement'. In S. Arber, K. Davidson and J. Ginn, eds., *Gender and ageing: changing roles and relationships*. Maidenhead: Open University Press, pp. 148–67.

Askham, J. (1994). 'Marriage relationships of older people', *Reviews of Clinical Gerontology*, 4: 261–68.

Bernard, M., and K. Meade (1993). *Women come of age: perspectives on the lives of older women*. London: Edward Arnold.

Borell, K., and S. Ghazanfareeon Karlsson (2003). 'Reconceptualising intimacy and ageing: living apart together'. In S. Arber, K. Davidson and J. Ginn, eds, *Gender and ageing: changing roles and relationships*. Maidenhead: Open University Press, pp. 47–62.

Britton, M., and N. Edison (1986). 'The changing balance of the sexes in England and Wales, 1851–2001', *Population Trends*, 46: 22–5.

Calasanti, T., and K. Slevin (2001). *Gender, social inequalities and aging*. Walnut Creek, Calif.: AltaMira Press.

Cohen, S. (1988). 'Psychological models of the role of social support in the etiology of physical disease', *Health Psychology*, 7: 269–97.

Cooper, H., Arber, S., Fee, L., and J. Ginn (1999). *The influence of social support and social capital on health: a review and analysis of British data*. London: Health Education Authority.

Davidson, K. (1999). 'Marital perceptions in retrospect'. In R. Miller and S. Browning, eds., *With this ring: divorce, intimacy and cohabitation from a multicultural perspective*. Stamford, Conn.: Jai Press.

(2001). 'Late life widowhood, selfishness and new partnership choices: a gendered perspective', *Ageing and Society*, 21 (3): 279–317.

Davidson, K., Daly, T., and S. Arber (2003). 'Older men, social integration and organisational activities', *Social Policy and Society*, 2 (2): 81–9.

de Jong Gierveld, J. (2003). 'Social networks and social well-being of older men and women living alone'. In S. Arber, K. Davidson and J. Ginn, eds., *Gender and ageing: changing roles and relationships*. Maidenhead: Open University Press, pp. 95–110.

Estes, C. (1991). 'The new political economy of aging: introduction and critique'. In. M. Minkler and C. Estes, eds., *Critical perspectives on aging: the political and moral economy of growing older*. New York: Baywood.

Finch, J., and J. Mason (1993). *Negotiating family responsibilities*. London: Routledge.

Ginn, J. (2003). *Gender, pensions and the lifecourse*. Bristol: Policy Press.

Ginn, J., and S. Arber (1999). 'Changing patterns of pension inequality: the shift from state to private sources', *Ageing and Society*, 19: 319–42.

Ginn, J., and D. Price (2002). 'Can divorced women catch up in pension building?' *Child and Family Law Quarterly*, 14 (2): 157–73.

Ginn, J., Street, D., and S. Arber (2001). *Women, work and pensions: international issues and prospects*. Buckingham: Open University Press.

Harkness, S., and J. Waldfogel (1999). *The family gap in pay: evidence from seven industrialised countries*, CASE Paper 29. London: Centre for Analysis of Social Exclusion.

Jerrome, D. (1996). 'Continuity and change in the study of family relationships', *Ageing and Society*, 16 (1): 91–104.

Leitner, S. (2001). 'Sex and gender discrimination within EU pension systems', *Journal of European Social Policy*, 11 (2): 99–115.

Lopata, H. Z. (1973). *Widowhood in an American city*. Cambridge, Mass.: Schenkman.

ONS (2003). *Census 2001. National report for England and Wales*. London: The Stationery Office.

PPI (Pensions Policy Institute) (2003). *The pension credit*, PPI Briefing Note Number 1. London: Pensions Policy Institute.

Phillipson, C., Bernard, M., Phillips, J., and J. Ogg (2001). *The family and community life of older people: social support and social networks in three urban areas*. London: Routledge.

Price, D., and J. Ginn (2003). 'Sharing the crust? Gender, partnership status and pension poverty'. In S. Arber, K. Davidson and J. Ginn, eds., *Gender and ageing: changing roles and relationships*. Maidenhead: Open University Press, pp. 127–47.

Shaw, C. (1999). '1996-based population projections by legal marital status for England and Wales', *Population Trends*, 95: 23–32.

Thompson, E. (1994). 'Older men as invisible men'. In E. Thompson, ed., *Older men's lives*. Thousand Oaks, Calif.: Sage.

Umberson, D. (1992). 'Gender, marital status and the social control of behaviour', *Social Science and Medicine*, 34 (8): 907–17.

UN (United Nations) (1982). *Demographic yearbook, 1980*. New York: United Nations.

(2002). *Demographic yearbook, 2000*. New York: United Nations.

Walker, A., and T. Maltby (1997). *Ageing Europe*. Buckingham: Open University Press.

Migration and Older People

C. F. LONGINO, JR, AND A. M. WARNES

INTRODUCTION

Geographic mobility, defined as a change of house or address, occurs during the lifecourse of almost every person in the Western world, and is experienced in the United Kingdom and the United States by a majority of people after 60 years of age. Most changes of address, however, are over short distances. They are local 'housing adjustments' or, as demographers prefer, 'residential mobility'. While an unknown proportion change the co-resident household, most of these short moves have relatively little impact on the mover's activities, time use, social roles or social networks. They are, in other words, mundane, and while they contribute to socioeconomic and environmental changes, such as regional population distribution and house price trends, most have only minor consequences for older people's lives or for their health and social services.

Three other categories of mobility have more radical consequences for older people's lives, namely: moves into institutional, supported and nursing-care settings; long distance moves (across important political boundaries) which substantially alter people's daily activities, social contacts and life prospects; and international migrations from one cultural domain to another. This chapter is primarily concerned with the second category – 'retirement migration'. Recognisable flows and settlements of retired migrants have been developing for a century and are comparatively well researched and understood. Retirement migrations are of great interest to the social gerontologist, for they manifest the changing, more assertive and positive lifestyles and attitudes of older people in affluent countries. The chapter also discusses the third category, for the major flows of international and intercontinental labour migration during the second half of the last century have an important consequence: the rapid growth of minority ethnic, or culturally distinctive, older populations, many of which have combinations of disadvantage and exclusion, and present a major challenge to health and welfare services and professionals.

THE DEVELOPMENT OF RETIREMENT MIGRATION

Aside from aristocratic precursors, retirement migration first produced new concentrations of older people during the first decades of the twentieth century. By the 1930s, significant concentrations of ex-metropolitan retired people in coastal towns and adjacent rural areas had developed in several parts of Europe, particularly in England and France but also on the Belgian, northern Italian and northern Spanish coasts, and in the United States in California and Florida and, closer to the European examples, in New Jersey, Connecticut and Maine. All were relatively 'select' coastal resorts.

The principal destination areas in Great Britain were south coast resorts and a few others on the Irish and North Sea coasts, while in France hundreds of comparable settlements had a growing retired population. In the United States by the 1930s, a large concentration of white-collar retirees was found in southern California. During the 1940s, retirement migration developed vigorously in the United States but was halted in Europe by the World War. In America, Social Security pensions and the booming war economy meant that some older people could choose to leave the communities in which they had resided for 30 or 40 years and move a thousand miles or more into a strange but congenial environment. The scale of the redistribution prompted the first commercial handbook guides and substantial academic studies. By 1950, St Petersburgh on the Gulf of Mexico coast of Florida, and Miami on the Atlantic coast, were fashionable resorts and provided permanent and winter residence for rich and retired people (Vesperi, 1985). Their mild winters enabled all-year military training exercises, making them more widely known. Then after the Second World War, the development of the interstate highway system made distant locations much more accessible for vacationers and migrants alike.

In Western Europe, retirement migration revived during the 1950s and has grown strongly ever since. The 'electrification' of rural areas and mass car ownership encouraged the conversion of vacant rural dwellings and declining villages to weekend-retreat, holiday and retirement functions. Even by the 1970s, in the counties surrounding London, Paris or New York, it was difficult to distinguish part-time or second-job commuters, early retirees and full pensioners.

The enlargement and spread of the favoured British and American destinations has continued. The fastest increases of the British retirement-age population during the 1980s were in a broad band of inland English and Welsh counties to the north and west of London. Migrant retirees had also crossed the English Channel, both to adjacent Normandy and Brittany and to warmer destinations further south. By 1990, 29% of the populations of the Lot and Dordogne *départements* of France were aged 60+ years, and 0.4% of their residents were British citizens holding *cartes de séjour*, compared in all France respectively to 20% and 0.1% (Hoggart and Buller, 1993).

In the United States, the changing state destinations can be charted in detail since 1960, because the decennial census counts the number who lived at a different address five years earlier. One of the defining characteristics of interstate retirement migration is that migrants from all over the nation concentrate into only a few states. Nearly 60% (56% in 1990) of interstate migrants aged 60 or more years go to just ten of the fifty states, and in all four census decades since 1960 Florida has attracted about a quarter of the total.

A new phenomenon was observed during 1985–90, a discernible dispersal of retirement migration, that is, a small decrease in the proportion of migrants received by the major destination states, and a slight spreading of the flows. The leading four destination states, Florida, California, Arizona and Texas, all had lower percentages in 1990 than in 1980, although their ranking was unchanged (Table 1). Although the losses were initially small, the pattern has persisted and grown. Many of the newly favoured regional destinations attract migrants primarily from adjacent states, e.g. Cape Cod, Massachusetts, the New Jersey shore, the Pocono Mountains of northeastern Pennsylvania, and the Wisconsin Dells, all are outside the Sunbelt (Longino, 1995). Other locations in the southern Appalachian mountain chain and the Ozarks of Missouri and Arkansas are in the non-coastal Sunbelt (Rowles and Watkins, 1993). Southern and western Nevada and areas in the Pacific Northwest are all retirement areas of strong regional attraction, and areas frequently cited in retirement guides as good places to retire (Savageau, 2000).

A STAGE MODEL OF TYPES AND DESTINATIONS

From our knowledge of retirement migration destinations in Britain, France, America and Australia, it became possible two decades ago to formulate a stage model that still has descriptive value. In the first phase, retired migrants tend to return to dispersed regions of birth and childhood (Warnes and Law, 1982). This pattern predominates after a period of rapid urbanisation and rural–urban migration, as in France during the third quarter of the twentieth century. The phase was muted in Britain, primarily because rural–urban migration was largely completed before the First World War, and since mid-century the 'return' component of the country's retirement migrations have been less to scattered rural areas than 'down the urban hierarchy' from the South-East to provincial cities, such as Glasgow, Newcastle and Belfast. One persistent form, however, has been returns to rural areas in

TABLE 1. Ten states receiving most in-migrants age 60+ in five-year periods ending in 1960, 1970, 1980 and 1990

Rank	State	1960 #	%	State	1970 #	%	State	1980 #	%	State	1990 #	%
1	FL	208,072	22.3	FL	263,200	24.4	FL	437,040	26.3	FL	451,709	23.8
2	CA	126,883	13.6	CA	107,000	9.9	CA	144,880	8.7	CA	131,514	6.9
3	NJ	36,019	3.9	AZ	47,600	4.4	AZ	94,600	5.7	AZ	98,756	5.2
4	NY	33,794	3.6	NJ	46,000	4.3	TX	78,480	4.7	TX	78,117	4.1
5	IL	30,355	3.3	TX	39,800	3.7	NJ	49,400	3.0	NC	64,530	3.4
6	AZ	29,571	3.2	NY	32,800	3.0	PA	39,520	2.4	PA	57,538	3.0
7	OH	27,759	3.0	PA	32,300	3.0	NC	39,400	2.4	NJ	49,176	2.6
8	TX	26,770	2.9	OH	28,800	2.7	WA	35,760	2.2	WA	47,484	2.5
9	PA	25,738	2.8	IL	28,600	2.7	IL	35,720	2.1	VA	46,554	2.4
10	MO	20,308	2.2	NY	25,300	2.3	NY	34,920	2.1	GA	44,475	2.3
Total interstate migrants		931,012			1,079,200[1]			1,622,120[2]			1,901,105	
% of Total In Top 10 States		60.7			60.4			59.5			56.3	

[1] This figure was derived by extrapolating from a 1 in 100 sample. The actual census count was 1,094,014.
[2] This figure was derived by extrapolating from a 1 in 40 sample. The actual census count was 1,650,000.
Source: US Census.

the Republic of Ireland, while recently a comparable retirement stream has been established from London to the Caribbean. The equivalent pattern was hardly evident *within* the United States, and there is little information about the number of European migrants to America who in the past returned to their home countries for retirement.

The second stage in the evolution occurs when childhood connections cease to influence the location choice, and are replaced by accessibility, environmental attractiveness, housing availability and social support. The relative importance and precise effect of these four factors depend upon specific time and place conditions. In England and France, and for a brief period in Florida and on the US northeastern seaboard, retirement migration became sufficiently popular before mass car ownership to give accessibility by rail a strong influence, and retirement migrants concentrated in a few coastal towns.

The third stage sees dispersed destinations again, as a result of the increased numbers and the growing preference for attractive, 'unspoilt' landscapes. Migrants divert into smaller towns and rural areas, now with an international dimension in the Americas, in Europe, and on the western Pacific Rim from Japan to Australia. 'Concentration' and 'dispersal' are of course relative terms and their designation depends upon the spatial scale, e.g. the last thirty years have seen a considerable dispersion of favoured retirement destinations within Florida while the state's dominance of interstate retirement migration destinations has been largely maintained.

CYCLICAL FORMS OF MIGRATION IN THE UNITED STATES

Three cyclical patterns of interstate migration have been identified in the United States since the mid 1980s: seasonal, counterstream and return migration. Taking first *seasonal migration*, surveys have shown that those who go to Arizona are overwhelmingly White, retired, healthy, married couples, and that most are aged in the sixties, and have the same characteristics as amenity-motivated permanent migrants (McHugh and Mings, 1991). Those who live in the colder north are, of course, most likely to make seasonal moves in retirement. But is seasonal migration a stage or a precursor to a permanent move (Longino *et al.*, 1991; McHugh, 1990)?

The transition depends upon the balance between the migrant's ties to places and people at the origin and the destination, and upon changes in these ties over time. The vast majority do not relocate permanently, but rather extend or shorten their visits, and their repeated visits are reluctantly ended only when ill-health or reduced income forces the change. Seasonal migration generates its own lifestyle and culture, different from that of permanent migrants, but equally vulnerable.

Turning to *counterstream migration*, the term refers to the opposite or return flows that develop alongside nearly all major migration streams. In the US, counterstream interstate flows of older migrants were found to be negatively selective: the average participant was older, and more likely widowed (Litwak and Longino, 1987). These findings led to speculation that counterstreams contain a large proportion of retirees who had moved earlier to a popular retirement destination, and later returned to the state from whence they came, a speculation not verifiable with census data.

Return migration

Migration back to one's state of birth has declined since the 1970s for the retirement-age population in the US. It was never higher than that of the general population, forming about 20 per cent of the total (Serow, 1978; Rogers, 1990). Industrial states recruit workers from rural parts of the country, and over time return streams become established. It is not therefore surprising to find that a majority of African American migrants aged 60 or more years move to the southern states, nor to find that return migration rates are high among these migrants (Longino and Smith, 1991).

In Europe from the 1950s, there was large-scale labour migration into the capital and industrial cities of the north, from southern Europe, North Africa, the Caribbean, the Indian subcontinent and elsewhere. Distinctive flows included Andalucians to Switzerland, Turks to Germany, Indonesians to Holland, and Jamaicans to England. The pioneers have reached old age, and the number of 'aged labour migrants' is growing rapidly. Although only a minority return, there are now substantial flows of return migrants from northern Europe to interior Spain and Italy, Malta and the Caribbean.

A return flow to Hong Kong during the 1990s has reduced. International return migration for retirement is, however, usually problematic, because the native area has changed from the remembered conditions, family ties are characteristically weak, and entitlements to social security and health benefits are less than for lifetime residents, even for international migrants within the European Union (Ackers and Dwyer, 2002).

THE EXPERIENCE OF RETIREMENT MIGRATION

Theoretical contributions about the motivations for retirement migration have been vigorous during the past decade. These fall roughly into four model categories that deal respectively with the lifecourse, migration decision making, housing disequilibrium, and place identity.

The lifecourse model

Age and cohort are associated with migration in retirement. Increasingly, recently retired migrants tend to seek climatic and lifestyle amenities. They tend to be married, and to have higher than the average income for retired households. Most do not go back to work after a move. A caveat to this generalisation is that the destinations of the many retired migrants who move for family-oriented social reasons are widely scattered, and indeed replicate the general population distribution: these older migrants have attracted no research. A second type of family-oriented move is more for support and care than social reasons: these retirees live nearer to or with a close relative, and this type of move tends to occur when older people develop chronic disabilities that make it difficult to carry out everyday household tasks, a situation often compounded by widowhood. The third type of move is into institutional care (Litwak and Longino, 1987).

Migration decision models

Wiseman (1980) modelled the actual migration decision process, and Haas and Serow (1993) the process for amenity migrants. Their work has helped the development of predictive models of the retirement migration decision. The model components

include person–environment adjustment processes, push–pull triggers such as climate, environmental hassle and cost of living, and indigenous and exogenous controls such as personal resources or the housing market.

The housing disequilibrium model

When economic incentives related to the management of housing assets dominate the migration decision, it is often assessed independently within the context of general housing stress or disequilibrium (Steinnes and Hogan, 1992). Retirement migration often involves moves to more affordable housing.

The place identity model

Cuba (1989) argued that 'selves' as well as bodies are mobile. Moving oneself physically to another community does not necessarily mean that one also moves emotionally. There are some migrants who never put down roots but remain emotionally tied to their former communities (Cuba and Hammond, 1993). The identity transformations of northern Europeans who move to Spain are complex and receiving attention (O'Reilly, 2000), but such social psychological approaches deserve more study.

SELF-ASSESSMENTS OF MIGRATIONS

There have been many social surveys of retired migrants. Those that do more than establish the sociodemographic profile of the participants commonly ask whether the move has been successful and would be repeated. The overwhelming finding is that retired migrants make positive assessments of their own moves, the main exception being that women express a greater sense of their reduced contacts with friends, children and metropolitan facilities (Warnes *et al.*, 1999). Most moves are undertaken after careful and extended thought and planning. Often lower housing and living costs are important. Such benefits are usually realised initially. Characteristically housing and living expenses escalate in retirement boom areas, however, and with time most retired people's income falls (Walters, 2002).

TABLE 2. United Kingdom state pensions paid overseas, 1981–1999

	1981	1986	1991	1996	1999	1981–99
Number (thousands)	252	372	594	763	847	
Average annual growth[1] (%)		8.1	9.8	5.1	3.5	6.9

Notes: The figures give the number of customers of the Pensions and Overseas Directorate of the UK Department for Work and Pensions (formerly Department of Social Security). A small minority of the customers have recently returned to the United Kingdom or are resident in the Channel Islands and the Isle of Man.
[1] Average annual percentage growth since the earlier tabulated date. For further details, see Warnes (2001).

INTERNATIONAL RETIREE MIGRANTS

Since the 1960s an increasing number of affluent retired northern Europeans have taken up residence in high-amenity coastal and rural areas of southern Europe, particularly in Spain, Italy and France (King *et al.*, 2000). Every kind of 'circulation' is involved, from the extended winter holiday, through dual residence and seasonal migration, to 'total displacement' retirement migration. Consequently these displacements are exceptionally difficult to enumerate or describe, but they are not unusual: probably every British adult now knows someone who has acquired a home in or retired to Spain.

Until quite recently research has focused on the most visible types of retirement moves and those that raise demands upon welfare services and public policy or, as most often in the United States, that have impacts for regional and rural economies. International moves have only recently been systematically studied, with those from Canada to Florida (Longino and Marshall, 1990) and the similar north–south flows in Europe attracting the first studies. The increased interest in international migration is, however, drawing attention to a segment of the retired population that hitherto has been largely ignored, those that upon retirement leave the area in which they have been working for family reasons and either return to a region of childhood or early adulthood, or move to live near a child or other relative. Our understanding of their motivations and of the old age lives they pursue is rudimentary.

Data on the number of UK Social Security old age pensions that are paid overseas show, however, that this population is substantial and rapidly growing (Warnes, 2001). There were a quarter of a million recipients in 1981, and the total more than doubled during the 1980s, at an annual growth rate of 9% (Table 2). During the 1990s growth moderated, to 3.5% p.a. during 1996–9. By 1999, 798,000 British retired people received their state pensions at an overseas address, and 16,100 received widows' benefits. The total is equivalent to nearly 8% of the home population of pensioners. From the mid 1990s, several substantial original surveys of affluent northern European retirees in southern Europe, especially Spain, have been commissioned and the flow of findings is increasing (a directory is available, see Casado-Díaz *et al.*, 2002).

PROSPECTS

Most commentators suggest that retirement migration will grow in the foreseeable future, as a consequence of increased affluence and home ownership, further advances in telecommunications and transport, increased longevity, and the progressive substitution of family-oriented to individualistic lifestyles. More controversially, it can be argued that growing income inequalities, which many see as inevitable, will be an underlying stimulus for not only relocation in later life but also the choice of 'gated' or 'secure' retirement communities. Growth in the total of retirement migrations will not, however, necessarily mean increased flows into today's most popular destinations. It is clear that the locational preferences for retirement residence can change quickly, as property costs escalate in well-established locations, and entrepreneurs quickly develop alternative opportunities (McHugh, 2003). A substantial dispersal of the preferred destinations appears likely.

An alternative scenario is possible. Another fashionable prediction is that the sharp division between the 'working' and 'retirement' ages of the late twentieth century will progressively dissolve: some say that it is a prerequisite for the higher standard of living in later life that future cohorts will expect. If positive retirement must increasingly involve 'income generation', and this is to be done in rewarding and satisfying ways, then it may be important for the older person to remain in the region in which they have good employment-related connections and can elaborate 'portfolio employment'. There are also some social trends, particularly around marriage, partnering and parent–child relations, which suggest that local place ties could exert more influence in the coming cohorts than in the 'conventional' retiree households of the last half-century.

Françoise Cribier (1989) compared the retirement residence intentions of French civil servants reaching retirement in the early 1990s with those ten and more years before. She found an increase of divorce, remarriage and repartnered couples in the later cohorts, as indicated by increases in the variability of partners' ages and the number of couples with many years between their retirement ages. The consequence was that they had a lower preference for a long-distance 'clean break' retirement migration away from Paris. Social gerontologists are now avidly documenting new types of living arrangement and repartnering among the older age groups. When widowed and divorced older people repartner, they are increasingly likely to retain their independent homes. 'Living apart together' may not reduce the months spent in high-amenity retirement areas, but suggests that straightforward migrations could be replaced by seasonal, shuttling and multilocation residential strategies. It is going to be increasingly difficult to track and to describe the more complex living arrangements and lifestyles of older people.

In Europe, retirement migration to the southern littoral is probably in its infancy, while in North America, in 20 years' time, Cuba will probably be a major retirement destination, and advances in home-technologies will have encouraged further growth of retirement communities north of Toronto, and maybe in Alaska. The extent to which other parts of the Caribbean and Central America and, more speculatively, North Africa and Indian Ocean coasts, become mass rather than highly exclusive high-amenity retirement areas will depend on geopolitics and their incorporation

into the secular capitalist domain. The global dispersal of destinations is, however, well underway. Real estate companies are assiduously seeking out freehold land in the South Pacific on which to build up-market homes for buyers 'to acquire a piece of paradise' and 'a vacation or retirement property at a fraction of the cost of comparable tropical real estate in Hawaii or the Caribbean' (see www.coldwellaloha.com/international.html). In India, one Goan property developer announces that 'our developments have a vibrant, international flavour with homeowners from the UK, Germany, India, Switzerland, Holland, France and the USA. For some, this is their second (or even third) overseas hideaway. . . . Many senior citizens relocate here to enjoy the guaranteed sunshine and a comfortable, peaceful retirement' (see www.acronindia.com/buying.html). The twenty-first century is likely to see more radical developments in retirement housing location preferences and choices than we witnessed in the last.

FURTHER READING

King, R., Warnes, A. M., and A. M. Williams (2000). *Sunset lives: British retirement migration in Southern Europe.* Oxford: Berg.

Longino, C. F., Jr (1995). *Retirement migration in America.* Vacation Publications: Houston.

O'Reilly, K. (2000). *The British on the Costa del Sol: transnational identities and local communities.* London: Routledge.

REFERENCES

Ackers, L., and P. Dwyer (2002). *Senior citizenship? Retirement, migration and welfare in the European Union.* Bristol: Policy Press.

Casado-Díaz, M., Lundh, U., and A. M. Warnes, eds. (2002). *Research projects in progress or completed, and a bibliography on European retirement migration and the well being of expatriate older people.* Sheffield: Sheffield Institute for Studies on Ageing. Available online at www.shef.ac.uk/~sisa.

Cribier, F. (1989). 'Change in the life course and retirement: the example of two cohorts of Parisians'. In P. Johnson, C. Conrad and D. Thomson, eds., *Workers versus pensioners.* Manchester: Manchester University Press, pp. 181–201.

Cuba, L. J. (1989). 'Retiring from vacationland: from visitor to resident', *Generations*, 13 (2): 63–7.

Cuba, L. J., and D. M. Hammond (1993). 'A place to call home: identification with dwelling, community and religion', *Sociological Quarterly*, 34: 111–31.

Haas, W. H., III, and W. J. Serow (1993). 'Amenity retirement migration process: a model and preliminary evidence', *Gerontologist*, 33 (2): 212–20.

Hoggart, K., and H. Buller (1993). *British home owners in rural France. Property selection and characteristics*, Occasional Paper 40. London: King's College Department of Geography.

King, R., Warnes, A. M., and A. M. Williams (2000). *Sunset lives: British retirement migration in Southern Europe*. Oxford: Berg.

Litwak, E., and C. F. Longino, Jr (1987). 'Migration patterns among the elderly: a developmental perspective', *Gerontologist*, 27 (3): 266–72.

Longino, C. F., Jr (1995). *Retirement migration in America*. Houston: Vacation Publications.

Longino, C. F., Jr, and V. W. Marshall (1990). 'North American research on seasonal migration', *Ageing and Society*, 10: 229–35.

Longino, C. F., Jr, and K. J. Smith (1991). 'Black retirement migration in the United States', *Journal of Gerontology: Social Sciences*, 46: S125–S132.

Longino, C. F., Jr, Marshall, V. W., Mullins, L. C., and R. D. Tucker (1991). 'On the nesting of snowbirds', *Journal of Applied Gerontology*, 10: 157–68.

McHugh, K. E. (1990). 'Seasonal migration as a substitute for, or precursor to, permanent migration', *Research on Aging*, 12: 229–45.

—— (2003). 'Three faces of ageism: society, image and place', *Ageing and Society*, 23 (2): 165–86.

McHugh, K. E., and R. C. Mings (1991). 'On the road again: seasonal migration to a Sunbelt metropolis', *Urban Geography*, 12: 1–18.

O'Reilly, K. (2000). *The British on the Costa del Sol: transnational identities and local communities*. London: Routledge.

Rogers, A. (1990). 'Return migration to region of birth among retirement-age persons in the United States,' *Journal of Gerontology: Social Sciences*, 45: S128–S134.

Rowles, G. D., and J. F. Watkins (1993). 'Elderly migration and development in small communities', *Growth and Change*, 24: 509–38.

Savageau, D. (2000). *Retirement places rated*. New York: Macmillan.

Serow, W. J. (1978). 'Return migration of the elderly in the U.S.A.: 1955–1960 and 1965–1970,' *Journal of Gerontology*, 33: 288–95.

Steinnes, D. N., and T. D. Hogan (1992). 'Take the money and the sun: elderly migration as a consequence of gains in unaffordable housing markets,' *Journal of Gerontology: Social Sciences*, 47 (4): S197–S203.

Vesperi, M. D. (1985). *City of green benches: growing Old in a new downtown*. Ithaca, N.Y.: Cornell University Press.

Walters, W. H. (2002). 'Later-life migration in the United States: a review of recent research', *Journal of Planning Literature*, 17 (1): 37–66.

Warnes, A. M. (2001). 'The international dispersal of pensioners from affluent countries', *International Journal of Population Geography*, 7 (6): 373–88.

Warnes, A. M., and C. M. Law (1982). 'The destination decision in retirement migration'. In A. M. Warnes, ed., *Geographical perspectives on the elderly*. Chichester, Sussex: Wiley pp. 53–81.

Warnes, A. M., King, R., Williams, A. M., and G. Patterson (1999). 'The well-being of British expatriate retirees in southern Europe', *Ageing and Society*, 19 (6): 717–40.

Wiseman, R. F. (1980). 'Why older people move', *Research on Aging*, 2 (2): 141–54.

CHAPTER 6.7

Do Longevity and Health Generate Wealth?

ROBERT N. BUTLER

INTRODUCTION

Arguably, one of the few welcome advances in the bloody twentieth century was the growth of longevity, heretofore a scarce commodity (Butler, 2000). Added longevity is the singular human achievement about which public health and medicine can take pride and upon which societies can build.

It is generally accepted that wealth, herein defined as the accumulation of assets, generates health. This chapter will consider the reverse: *have health, longevity, and population ageing, in turn, engendered wealth?* Health is herein defined as a state of physical and mental wellbeing and freedom from disease such that minimal health services are required. Longevity is herein defined as both average life expectancy and any increase thereof.

THE REVOLUTION IN LONGEVITY

In the nineteenth and twentieth centuries the health of populations improved. This was due, among other things, to modern public health; the application of the germ theory of disease; the invention of vaccines and antitoxins; the greater abundance of food; and improved living arrangements that reduced overcrowding and slums. Along with workplace regulations, the treatment of disabilities, the reduction of the working week, and technological advances in factories, farms, and mines came reductions in the level of drudgery in the workplace, as well as improved safety and health.

In the twentieth century came the extraordinary unprecedented and unanticipated growth in older populations, as well as extended longevity after age 65 in the industrialized world (Butler, 2000; Porter, 1997). This led to approximately 30 additional years of life, more than had been attained during the preceding 5,000 years of human history. It is remarkable, too, how effectively society has adjusted to this historic demographic change. Social and family agencies developed special services administered to older people, private sector and public pension programs evolved, research on ageing and age-related diseases increased, special forms of medical care emerged, such as the field of geriatrics, and efforts to promote health and prevent disease moved to national, community, family, and individual levels. While these adjustments require further refinements and reforms based upon changing economic, cultural, demographic, and historical conditions, it is fair to conclude that societies have been able to adjust relatively effectively to this historic twentieth-century demographic change. In 1900 less than 3 percent of the population of industrial societies was over 65. Soon some 20 percent will be. One can only imagine what might be gained in the twenty-first century, with the applications of genomics, regenerative, and preventive medicine, as well as new medical and surgical treatments.

LONGEVITY AND WEALTH OF NATIONS

There are pundits who only emphasize the costs that arise as a result of population ageing – specifically pension and healthcare. They present disturbing actuarial studies and appeal to the political establishment to avert an "ageing crisis" by reducing public pensions and containing healthcare costs. They offer added taxation, benefit cuts, and partial or complete privatization as policy options, recommending greater individual responsibility, the competitive marketplace, and promoting pronatalism and immigration as ways to avert the "catastrophe" of ageing. Books that present this demographic shift in apocalyptic terms include the World Bank's *Averting the old age crisis* (James, 1994) and Peter Peterson's *The gray dawn* (2000).

If the growth of ageing populations and advancing longevity are indeed "failures of success" – the uncontrollable and unfortunate by-products of social-economic and medical progress – then it stands to reason that fundamental and clinical biomedical research should be halted. The medical and other helping professions as well as research institutions should instead direct their resources and imagination solely to marginal repairs of mental and physical disorders and to cost savings.

AGEISM, AND THE ECONOMICS OF AGEING

One underlying concern relating to the costs of ageing is ageism, which is the pervasive distaste for old age that, parenthetically, impels the mindless pursuit of so-called "anti-ageing" medicine, with false claims of life extension and even intimations of immortality. Ageism has never been in short supply, fueled by the ingrained fear of growing old, becoming disabled and dependent. When societies experience dangers, are nomadic, live under famine conditions, or are at war – when, in short, it is in the best interest of the group as a whole – older and disabled people of all ages have been abandoned. At such times ageism is alloyed with reality. Clearly, such abandonment is not warranted today.

Beyond ageism, another issue is ideology – the belief that people should be responsible for themselves – financing their own old age through significant investments made throughout their lives that cover both long term care and living costs of the extended life. Some people favor the concept of targeting, that is, maintaining only a minimal safety net rather than a universal pooling of risk. Some

libertarians go further, opposing any state intervention and any taxation.[1]

Another belief, often labeled as "objective reality," is that a nation simply cannot afford the costs of old age, especially in the midst of essential and competing needs – for example, the defense of the country, the needs of children, education, maintenance of the social order through police and the judiciary system, and so forth. Proponents of this belief see a "fixed pie," a "zero sum game," and may not believe economic growth will be made possible by scientific innovation and technology – or feel such progress will be too slow.

ECONOMIC ADVANTAGES OF POPULATION AEGING AND LONGEVITY

The history of the field of economics reflects ethical considerations, as exemplified by Adam Smith, a professor of moral philosophy. Since one application of economics, after all, is the reduction of poverty, and since the ultimate purposes of public health measures are the amelioration of human pain and suffering, the prevention of disease, and the extension of healthy and high-quality life, it would be prudent for both economic and public health policies to require an explicit moral context. The work of economists, including those at the universities of Chicago, Harvard, Yale, and Belfast, offer a different, compelling, and reassuring perspective on health and longevity. Here, in a nutshell, is what their work, and that of others suggests.

The underlying economic advantages of population ageing and longevity

1. Most discretionary funds are accumulated by populations aged 50 and above.
2. Most *private* intergenerational transfers go from old to young, not from young to old.
3. Healthy individuals have accumulated more savings and investments by their old age than individuals beset by illness.
4. Healthy older persons are more apt to remain productively engaged in society in their old age through continuing work or voluntary activity.
5. Healthy older persons require fewer health services.

---

[1] Adam Smith favored a role for the state in the economy for the public good and he favored progressive taxation.

6. There are growing "mature" industries including the healthcare and pharmaceutical industries, financial services, insurance – all of which profit by people's expectation and the reality that they will probably grow old. In addition housing, transportation, recreation, and travel constitute what the Japanese have called "the silver industries." In the United States these growth industries are labeled the "mature" or "senior market."

GROSS DOMESTIC PRODUCT

Canning and Bloom's work demonstrates that nations that have a five-year advantage in life expectancy show significant increases in gross domestic product, for example, from 0.3 percent to 0.5 percent GDP per year (Bloom and Canning, 2000). It is revealing to re-examine the concept of the gross domestic product and to incorporate within it the advantages of improved health, conceptualized by economist William Nordhaus, as "health income" (2003). Nordhaus measures "real output" of the healthcare industry and estimates the dollar value of the prevention of a fatality to a range of savings between $0.6 and 13.5 million. He settles on $3 million as a reasonable figure.

Currently, conventional measures of national income and output exclude the value of improvements in the health status of the population. Nordhaus developed a methodology and preliminary estimates of how standard economic measures would change if they adequately reflected improvements in health status. He discusses how the proposed measure of "health income" fits into existing theories for measuring and valuing consumption and health status, and concludes that the "value of increase in longevity in the last 100 years is about as large as the value of growth in non-health goods and services," using three forms of evaluation:

1. labor market (risk/wage tradeoff);
2. consumer purchase (price/risk tradeoff); and,
3. contingent evaluation based on preferences (Nordhaus, 2003).

There are still relatively few studies that examine the economic value of improved health. There is the life-years approach and the measure of the willingness of people to forgo health improvements or non-health improvements (Nordhaus, 2003). The

UN Human Development Index (HDI) is a relevant measure. David Cutler and Mark McClellan write, "The benefits from just lower infant mortality and better treatment of heart attacks have been sufficiently great that they alone are about equal to the entire cost of insurance for medical care over time" (2001).

PRODUCTIVE AGEING

The advantages of a productive, healthy population are obvious. The Research on Aging Act that created the US National Institute on Aging in 1974 sought to "extend the healthy middle years of life."

Some 10 percent of American older men (65 years of age and above) and a somewhat higher percentage of women continue to work in the formal sector. The percentages are growing – in part as a result of consequences of any faltering economy, any stock market losses, as well as increasing life expectancy. It also must be noted that both older men and women contribute to their families and communities in the informal sector. Millions of older people volunteer their time and donate their money in philanthropic activities that are calculated to be worth in the billions.

There is little question that, since people live longer, they will need and be expected to work longer, as long as there are jobs available and they do not face age bias in the workplace. Since societies that enjoy longer longevity tend to have lower birthrates, older workers will be needed. By living longer, there will be more contributors to social security systems.

People should be trained to work longer (International Longevity Center-USA 2001) and be otherwise productively engaged (e.g., volunteering). These are instances where the good of the individual and of the state merge.

Both superior health, savings, and investing habits as well as the expectation of later retirement should be encouraged in primary and secondary education to build greater self-responsibility and ensure improved quality of life in the later years.

"Silver Industries"

The old constitute a powerful and growing market, variously called the "silver industries," the "mature market," and the "senior market," as significant as the "youth market" of the baby-boom 1960s. Longevity affects the entire lifecourse, including what people spend on health and in the financial services industry. Optimism about the future and the sense of providence encourages people to save and invest, and life insurance and annuities illustrate the powerful spur of the future. People also seek medicines and surgical interventions to preserve their health and augment their longevity. And there is also "luxury" spending – on grandchildren, and travel and recreation. Older persons are sought by states and cities of the US South because of their value to the local economy (Greene, 2002; Sack, 1997).

THE FATHER OF GERONTOLOGY

The foregoing are not entirely new ideas: Elie Metchnikoff, the Nobel-winning scientist who introduced the word "gerontology," advanced some similar thoughts in his book *The prolongation of life: optimistic studies* (2004[1909]). This work appeared in response to a burst of ageism following France's loss in the Franco-Prussian War in 1870. As the first nation to "age," beginning in the 1800s, the French despaired and blamed the "graying" of France for its various problems and "general decline."

But Metchnikoff saw it all quite differently: "Without doubt, men say, the cost of maintaining the aged will become even heavier if the duration of life is to be prolonged. If old people are to live longer, the resources of the young will be reduced."

Although written nearly 100 years ago, these words are a striking modern forerunner of today's national alarms over rising social and healthcare costs of older persons that are being heard today throughout the developed world. Elie Metchnikoff[2] continued:

It must be understood, however, that the prolongation of life would be associated with the preservation of intelligence and of the power to work . . . When we

have reduced or abolished such causes of precocious senility as intemperance and disease, it will no longer be necessary to give pensions at the age of sixty or seventy years. The costs of supporting the old, instead of increasing, will diminish progressively . . . We must use all our endeavors to allow men to complete their normal course of life, and to make it possible for old men to play their parts as advisers and judges, endowed with their long experience of life.

In the twenty-first century we confront the question: can we afford older people (Fogel, 2000)? Elie Metchnikoff responded to the similar concern at the turn of the twentieth century. Could France support 2 million people who were over 70 years of age? It was Metchnikoff's view that society could work to prolong a healthy life, and a modified old age. Metchnikoff aptly characterized the widely held misgivings regarding the ageing of the population while considering the very real possibility for further increases in human longevity. In *The prolongation of life* he wrote, "Already it is complained that the burden of supporting old people is too heavy, and statesmen are perturbed by the enormous expense which will be entailed by State support of the aged."

Even in the 1970s Alfred Sauvy, a French demographer, still held gloomy notions of the impact of old age in France with "old people with old ideas living in old houses."

One unacceptable conclusion could be that the advances of biomedical research will result in only an increased burden of older people with frailty and dementia. Social Security, pension, and health costs will be unsustainable. Of course, these are major concerns which require special initiatives. After all, while we have the growth of healthy and productive older persons, at the same time there are increasing numbers who require costly care and both family and societal caregiving are an enormous burden.

Biomedical research ranging from "undifferentiated" basic research to translational research is of undeniable importance to delay and end dementia and frailty. So, too, it becomes essential to reform healthcare systems to make them appropriate to different age groups. Such reforms in the United States include the redesign of Medicare to be more in keeping with the needs of older persons for chronic care, geriatric training of health providers, health

[2] Metchnikoff also wrote *The nature of man: studies in optimistic philosophy* (1904) in which he formulated the concept of "orthobiosis," which signifies healthy longevity and ultimately a natural death. Metchnikoff envisioned the scientific transformation of certain "disharmonies" that occurred in the human evolutionary process into "harmonies."

TABLE 1. A glimpse into how the six billion live			
	Current life expectancy (years)	Fertility rate: average number of children per woman	Contraceptive use by currently married women (percent)
Africa	51	5.1	20
Asia	66	2.6	60
Europe	73	1.4	72
Latin America	69	2.7	66
North America	77	1.9	71

Source: United Nations Population Division.

promotion, disease prevention, community-based care (to reduce hospital care), public health and workplace initiatives, the further development of the role of the informal voluntary network, acute and chronic care including end-of-life care. (The Albert and Mary Lasker Foundation supported studies conducted by Topel and Murphy at the University of Chicago that demonstrated the economic value of medical research [Murphy and Topel, 1998].)

SHORTGEVITY

The alternative to longevity is shortgevity, which is found in most poor nations. Much is made of the globalization of the economy (and, of course, culture) but the impediments imposed by shortgevity have not been sufficiently examined. Some attention has been given to the massive diseases dominant in the developing world which cause shortgevity: tuberculosis, malaria, AIDS, and infant death from respiratory and diarrheal diseases (Murray and Lopez, 1996). Communicable diseases such as severe acute respiratory syndrome (SARS) can spread globally rapidly and severely damage economies. Development economists such as Jeffrey Sachs have articulated the economic impact of health issues in the developing world.

So long as there is shortgevity and nations have huge populations with 35 to 40 percent under 15 years of age, there will be too few healthy, productive citizens to buy, sell, and exchange goods and services with the developed world. The latter must do more about the inequalities of wealth, longevity, and health for their own self-interest. Health and

TABLE 2. Median age of population (1999)	
Oldest Countries	
Italy	40.2
Japan	40.2
Germany	39.7
Sweden	39.7
Youngest Countries	
Uganda	15.0
Niger	15.8
Yemen	15.9
Congo Republic	15.9

longevity should be critical elements in the foreign policies of nations. (See Tables 1 and 2.)

HEALTH AND CONSUMER SPENDING

Since two-thirds of economies are based upon consumer spending, it is essential to upgrade the capabilities of workers, who, after all, are also the consumers. They must be healthy and productive. But in the developing world many suffer from shortgevity! Sierra Leone, for example, has an average life expectancy of 38 years and a disability-free life expectancy of only 26 years. How can African and other nations that do not enjoy productive, healthy, and long lives be in a position to buy our goods and services and produce their own for sale and exchange? Clearly, health has become a geopolitical and geoeconomic issue. It is, important to reduce the extreme disease burden that exists in the developing world in part because of the geography of disease and the particular character of these diseases. For example, most pathogens have animal hosts, which make them, unlike smallpox and polio, ineradicable.

DO HEALTH AND LONGEVITY CREATE WEALTH?

Population health and longevity must be considered separately with regard to their possible roles in the creation of societal wealth. For example, it is possible that a population might remain healthy but collectively die at or near the time of retirement from the workforce. They would not collect pensions or require further healthcare or generate other expenses that society would have to cover. Under those circumstances, it might be easy to demonstrate that population health generates wealth.

On the other hand, the cost of longevous populations that are not productive would depend upon the degree to which health services would be required to keep this population alive, as well as upon their pensions, savings, investments, and family support.

CONCLUSION

In sum, there are myriad consequences to population ageing and longevity that affect our economy, culture, society, and personal lives. Least noted, however, has been the extent to which health and longevity have enhanced the prospects of greater riches, of the material kind. We hope that the graying of nations might also result in the maturation of humanity, given greater experience and perspective.

FURTHER READING

Bloom, D., Canning, D., and J. Sevilla (2001). *Health, human capital and economic growth*. World Health Organization Commission on Macroeconomics and Health Working Paper No. WG1:8. Geneva: WHO.

Grossman, M. (1972). "On the concept of health capital and the demand for health," *Journal of Political Economy*, 80 (2, April): 223–55.

Smith, J. (1999). "Healthy bodies and thick wallets: the dual relation between health and economic status," *Journal of Economic Perspectives*, 13 (2, Spring); 145–66.

REFERENCES

Bloom, D. E., and D. Canning (2000). "The health and wealth of nations," *Science*, 287: 1207–9.

Butler, R. N. (2000). "The revolution in longevity." In R. N. Butler and C. Jasmin, eds., *Longevity and quality of life*. New York: Kluwer Academic / Plenum Publishers, pp. 19–23.

Cutler, D. and M. McClellan (2001). "Is technological change in medicine worth it?" *Health Affairs*, 20: 11–29.

Fogel, R. W. (2000). "Can we afford longevity?" In R. N. Butler and C. Jasmin, eds., *Longevity and quality of life*. New York: Kluwer Academic / Plenum Publishers, pp. 47–59.

Greene, K. (2002). "Florida frets it doesn't have enough elderly," *The Wall Street Journal*, 15 October 2002.

International Longevity Center-USA (2001). "Lifelong learning in Norway: an experiment in progress," issue brief, December 2001. International Longevity Center.

James, E. (1994). *Averting the old age crisis: policies to protect the old and promote growth*. Washington, D.C.: World Bank.

Metchnikoff, I. I. (2004 [1909]). *The prolongation of life: optimistic studies*. New York: Springer Publishing Co.

Murphy, K. M., and R. H. Topel, eds. (1998). *Exceptional returns: the economic value of America's investment in medical research*. New York: Funding First.

Murray, C. J. L., and A. D. Lopez, eds. (1996). *The global burden of disease*. Cambridge, Mass.: Harvard School of Public Health, distributed by Harvard University Press.

Nordhaus, W. D. (2003). *The health of nations: the contribution of improved health to living standards*, Working Paper 8818. Cambridge, Mass.: National Bureau of Economic Research.

Peterson, P. (2000). *The gray dawn*. New York: Crown Publishing.

Porter, R. (1997). *The greatest benefit to mankind: a medical history of humanity*. New York: W. W. Norton.

Sack, K. (1997). "More retirees discover small towns," *New York Times*, 25 May 1997.

Women, Ageing and Inequality: A Feminist Perspective

CARROLL L. ESTES

Gender is a crucial organizing principle in the economic and power relations of the social institutions of the family, the state, and the market, shaping the experience of old age and ageing and the distribution of resources to older men and women across the lifecourse (Calasanti, 1993; Ginn and Arber, 1995; McMullin, 1995; Estes, 2000). Based on demographics alone, with older women outliving and outnumbering older men around the globe, ageing is appropriately defined as a gender issue.

Four premises undergird our approach (Estes and associates, 2001; Estes *et al.*, 2003). The *first premise* is that the experiences and situation of women are socially constructed. The predicament of older women is profoundly shaped by the division of power and labor between men and women, their respective normative proscriptions, and accompanying institutional structures.

The *second premise* is that the lived experiences and problems of older women are structurally conditioned rather than simply a product of individual behavior and choices. "Choices" and "preferences" (in economists' terms) that are available to women and other structurally disadvantaged groups are often highly constrained, if not illusory. Constraining forces reside in "gender regimes" (Connell, 1987) that are embedded and inscribed in the capitalist *state*, the *market*, and the *family*.

Gender regimes are pivotal in understanding how old age policy is constructed in ways that maintain and reproduce the relatively disadvantaged social, political, and economic status of older women and particularly of older women of color.

The *third premise* is that the disadvantages of women are cumulative across the lifespan (Crystal and Shea, 2002). The *fourth premise* is that the feminization of poverty is inextricably linked to the complex and interlocking oppressions of race, ethnicity, class, sexuality, and nation that produce the marginalization of women of all ages (Dressel, 1988; Collins, 1991). As Patricia Hill Collins' notes, these are "interrelated axes of social structure" and not "just separate features of existence."

Although variations exist within the West, US and UK welfare states are distinctly gendered and raced (J. Acker, 1988; Pateman, 1989; Orloff, 1993; Quadagno, 1994; Omi and Winant, 1994). In many European welfare regimes (e.g., Germany, Italy, France, and Ireland), laws support the authority of the husband, although policies vary and are contradictory. Even the Scandinavian welfare states of Norway, Sweden, and Denmark depend on gender-biased unpaid labor of women, raising questions about the "woman friendliness" of these states (Leira, 1993; Siim, 1993).

THE SITUATION OF OLDER WOMEN: SOCIAL AND ECONOMIC INEQUALITY

Population ageing, as defined by the increasing numbers of elderly age 60 and older, is a phenomenon in both developed and developing

Author's note: the author wishes to acknowledge the valuable assistance of Chris Phillipson and Simon Biggs in the preparation of this chapter, in the course of writing their book (Estes *et al.*, 2003).

nations. The number of elderly reached more than 600 million in 2000 and is projected to quadruple, reaching 2 billion in 2050 (WHO, 2002). The older population is growing fastest in developing countries, where currently about two-thirds of all older persons (355 million) are now living. By 2025, 75 percent of all elderly are projected to reside in the developing countries. In the developed world, the oldest-old (those aged 80 +) are growing fastest. In 1996, fully 43 percent of the world's oldest-old, aged 75+, lived in just four countries: China, the US, India, and Japan. Yet, in many developing nations, the oldest-old comprise less than 1 percent of the total population (US Department of Commerce and National Institute on Aging [NIA], 1996). And, for many countries, population ageing has been accompanied by reductions in per capita income and declining living standards. Life expectancy remains below 50 in more than ten developing countries, and since 1970 has fallen, or barely risen, in a number of African countries (WHO, 2002).

In all societies, women outlive men and, by very old age, the female/male ratio is 2:1 (WHO, 2002). Although, with the exception of infant mortality, there is a general female advantage in life expectancy, women have a proportionately *shorter* disability-free life expectancy than do men at age 65. Thus, older women bear the burden of a longer number of years with limitations of function due to one or more chronic diseases than do older men (WHO, 1995).

Women throughout the world disproportionately suffer poverty. The poorer and less developed the country, the more economically precarious the older woman is. Poverty for women is a hallmark of old age even in the most developed and wealthy nations. In the US and in other Western industrialized nations, the degree of dependency of older women upon the state grows with ageing, widowhood, divorce, and associated declines in economic and health status (Estes, 2000). Globalization further jeopardizes women in advanced old age with the growing uncertainties of state policy and diminishing or non-existent public provision.

A major source of economic despair and disparity by sex resides in the divergent gender-based caregiving and work patterns, wages and retirement benefits of men and women, and gender and racial/ethnic differences in marital status. The cumulative effects of these factors are generally negative for older women around the world. Globalization and the retraction of state supported safety nets and the threatened privatization of government guaranteed retirement and health programs (where they exist) exacerbate the difficult economic situation of older women.

Older women's economic status, even in the richest Western countries, substantiates their economic disadvantage and nation-state variations therein. With the nations in rank order, single older women's incomes fare from best to worst as follows: the Netherlands (the best), Italy, Canada, Australia, France, Germany, the UK, and the US (the worst and dead last). Single US older women have the lowest income relative to married couples of eight nations studied (Disney and Whitehouse, 2002: Fig. 4.2, p. 62). In another study of eighteen nations, Smeeding and Williamson (Disney and Whitehouse, 2002: Fig. 4.6, p. 73) found that Australia was the worst and the US was second worst of all countries studied in the "pensioner income poverty rate" (the percentage of pensioners with incomes below one-half of the population median income). Finally, pensioner income inequalities data in sixteen countries show that the US ranks second only to Greece in the ratio of 90th percentile of pensioner income to the 10th percentile (Disney and Whitehouse, 2002: Fig. 4.9, p. 78).

THE GENDERED STATE AND AGEING

Study of the state is central to understanding the situation of older women. The state has the power to: (a) allocate and distribute scarce resources to ensure the survival and growth of the economy; (b) mediate between varying needs and demands across different social groups (gender, race, ethnicity, class, and age); and (c) ameliorate social conditions that may threaten the existing order.

Feminist Theories of the State

Acker asserts that both the state and economy, among other social institutions, have been developed and dominated by men; thus, they have been "symbolically interpreted from the standpoint of men [and] defined by the absence of women" (L. Acker, 1992: 567). The power of the state extends beyond the distribution of resources to the formation and reformation of social patterns (Connell,

1987). It not only regulates institutions and relations like marriage and motherhood; it manages them. The state actually *constitutes* "the social categories of the gender order," as "patriarchy is both constructed and contested through the state" (Connell, 1987).

Patriarchy and the Sex/Gender System

Writing from the UK, Pateman (1989: 183) describes "the patriarchal welfare state" in which "since the early twentieth Century, welfare policies have reached across from the public to private and have helped uphold a patriarchal structure of family life." Ciscel and Heath contend "patriarchy is irrepressible" under globalization: "[A] new form of patriarchy has arisen with women primarily performing gendered labour in the service sector of the capitalist marketplace and the unpaid domestic labour of the home. The face of patriarchy is now that of the virtual male, where patriarchal rules and values are transmitted through the media, at home, at work, and in leisure activities" (Ciscel and Heath, 2001: 407). Women are left with whatever the market has not usurped as profitable, which boils down to "the creation of the web of relationships." This "ersatz freedom from the unfettered expansion of markets in reality represents another form of oppression, confining women and their families to lives of market supporting activities" (Ciscel and Heath, 2001: 408).

The Family and Social Reproduction

Feminists critique traditional economic theories of familism and the separate spheres which have viewed women's place in the family and their contributions to societal reproduction in ways that "privilege" relations of production that men do through paid work and "ignore . . . much of the process by which people and their labour power are reproduced" (Himmelweit, 1983: 419). Reproduction occurs on two levels: "the reproduction of labour power both in a daily and generational sense; and human and biological reproduction" (Himmelweit, 1983: 419). Women's reproduction work is informal, unpaid, invisible, and devalued. State policy blindness towards reproduction obfuscates its enormous economic and societal value. The "Care Penalty" (Folbre, 2001) describes the result of divergent male and female family roles, with the separation of care-

giving and household work, treated as private and beyond the scope of state intervention (O'Connor *et al.*, 1999: 3). This explains much about the persistent economic vulnerability of older women.

Thus, a central dynamic concerning old age and the gendered state is the contradiction between the *needs* of women throughout the lifecourse and the organization of work (e.g. capitalist modes of *production* and *social reproduction*), and the modes of *distribution* based on the recognition (and compensation) and non-recognition (and non-compensation) of "work" (J. Acker, 1988; Leira and Saraceno, 2002). "The question of what counts as work is related to who does it (men 'labour,' women 'love') and where (in the formal labour market, in the underground economy, or in the 'domestic' realm)" (Brush, 2000: 179).

Feminist Perspectives on the State and Old Age Policy

Feminists have addressed: (1) the role of the gendered wage, the family wage, and the male breadwinner model in producing the economic vulnerability of older women; (2) how older women's fate in the welfare state is predicated upon her marital status and husband's work history and how social policy in the US, the UK, and many other Western nations build upon the "Traditional gender ideology – the assumption that women are financially supported by men in the male breadwinner/ female carer model of the gender contract (Lewis 1992) – [which] bolsters exclusionary employment practices" (Ginn *et al.*, 2001: 20); and (3) the two tiers of social policy that, in capitalist countries, divide women largely by class and race: means-tested social assistance for the disadvantaged and social insurance for those workers in the formal labor market (Harrington Meyer, 1990; Estes and associates, 2001).

Women are linked to the state in three types of status that form a complex and dynamic interrelationship. Women are: (1) citizens with political rights, (2) clients and consumers of state services, and (3) employees in the state sector (Hernes, 1987; Estes and associates, 2001). These roles are neither inclusive nor mutually exclusive and their corresponding institutional structures (the family, the state, and the market) mediate between them as individual women and society.

In old age, women's status as clients or consumers (beneficiaries) of government programs is highly significant for several reasons. (1) Women's longer survival means that older women depend on state-funded health and retirement benefits for more years. (2) Because of their disadvantaged economic status, older women are more likely than older men to require government assistance. (3) Race and ethnicity contribute to the multiple jeopardy of older women of color, who are highly compromised in economic and health status and are more dependent on state programs than older White women. (4) Older women have more chronic health problems than older men, and for a longer time period (WHO, 1995). They utilize more health services, rendering them more dependent upon and needy of state-funded healthcare. (5) In the US and many other nations, there is no universal public provision of long term care (recent exceptions include Germany and Scotland). Long term care is the type of care that older women are both most likely to provide (to parents, spouses, siblings) and to need themselves, given women's longer life expectancy, widowhood, and poverty.

The Market and Older Women

Nancy Folbre (2001) and many other feminists refute Adam Smith's "Invisible Hand" theory that market-promoted selfish behavior benefits all:

The invisible hand of the market depends upon the *invisible heart of care.* [our italics] Markets cannot function effectively outside the framework of families and communities built on values of love, obligation, and reciprocity . . . The invisible hand is about achievement. The invisible heart is about care for others. The hand and the heart are interdependent, but they are also in conflict. The only way to balance them successfully is to find fair ways of rewarding those who care for other people. This is not a problem that economists or business people take seriously. (Folbre, 2001: xvi, 4).

The dilemma that women "know they can benefit economically by becoming achievers rather than caregivers" (Folbre, 2001: 4) will only grow more painful to the extent that privatized pension and health schemes take hold.

For women the "contradictory character of welfare states" (O'Connor *et al.*, 1999: 2–3) is reflected in two faces of the state: (1) the "woman friendliness" of the state (Hernes, 1987) in opening political participation, recognizing, and improving women's situation; and (2) the other less friendly side of state gender-biased retirement, non-existent long term care, and other social safety net provisions that do not redress the structurally produced economic and health dependency of older women, since they reward paid labor and discount the value of substantial unpaid caregiving that is rendered at great personal financial and health cost to women.

GLOBALIZATION, INEQUALITY AND OLDER WOMEN

Masculine domination (Bourdieu, 2001) and hegemonic masculinity are significant threads in the fabric of old age policies and their connection to the perilous state of most older women. In the West, the gender order centers on a single structural fact – "the global dominance of men over women" (Connell, 1987: 183).

Recent work on globalization and human rights draws attention to the intense and hotly contested struggles around sexism, racism, and social class that accompany global capitalism, and its attendant (and largely negative) potential outcomes for women of all ages around the world (Moghadam, 2000; Mittelman and Tambe, 2000). Rarely has this work addressed older women.

"Globalization is being used to advance a new form of ageism through the socially constructed demographic crisis of an ageing world" (Estes and Phillipson, 2002). The "apocalyptic demography" (Robertson, 1999) underlying such crisis constructions is being "used" by the World Bank (WB), the International Monetary Fund (IMF), and others as a symbolic weapon to support a privatization agenda based on the claim that welfare states cannot afford to support the ageing through publicly guaranteed retirement and health programs (Estes and Phillipson, 2002). Developing nations find their WB and IMF loans conditioned on the promise of open markets for private pensions and medical care. Vast profit incentives exist for multinational financial and insurance corporations to obtain "global custody" of the world's pensions and health insurance programs if they succeed in snuffing out public sector provision. Negative outcomes have already occurred: first, in India, where "the World Bank mandated privatisation of health care has priced medical treatment out of the reach of the poor in places where health care was once government run and free" (www.womensedge.org/events/conference2000sum;htm, 5/16/03, p. 1); and second, in Chile, where

The new privately managed pension system . . . has increased gender inequalities. Women are worse off than they were under the old pay-as-you-go system of Social Security . . . [W]omen's longer life expectancy, earlier retirement age, lower rates of labour-force participation, lower salaries, and other disadvantages in the labour market are directly affecting their accumulation of funds in individual retirement accounts, leading to lower pensions, especially for poorer women. (Arenas de Mesa and Montecinos, 1999: 3)

Globalization, marginalization, and gender form an interconnected matrix that "shape[s] patterns of poverty [and] other distributional outcomes" (Mittelman and Tambe, 2000: 88) that are devastating to women: "[E]conomic globalization marginalizes large numbers of people by reducing public spending on social services and *de-links economic reform from social policy*. This type of marginalization manifests a gendered dimension inasmuch as women constitute those principally affected by it [our italics]" (2000: 75). The forces of neo-liberal market-based globalization are heaped on top of pre-existing "rigid hierarchies of patriarchy [that] work to impoverish women." Markets further ingrain and deepen "poverty on a gendered basis" (2000: 88–9): "The twin ideologies of gender and globalization separately and in combination exacerbate the inequalities of an already-stacked deck against women, as both women's work and hardship are dramatically increased – with women pressed to take on the lowest paying jobs while continuing to care for their children, families, and elders" 2000: 76).

The loss of state protection for subsistence activities is especially harsh in developing countries where women's economic participation is so restricted. There is "gendered marginalization" in: (1) the widening of self-regulating markets and the privatization of farming land for cash crops that add new problems of food insecurity; (2) the added personal costs of public health service privatization; and (3) state spending reductions on vital services for women and children including education/teachers and local transportation (Mittelman and Tambe, 2000: 83–4).

Given that women perform most of the world's childcare and long term care work without financial remuneration ("free" labor), and at the cost of great financial, physical, and psychological hardship, the continuing and deepening themes and patterns of privatization being instituted globally are likely to jeopardize further women's lives with unpaid "overwork" over their lifetimes, and with predictably deleterious health and economic consequences.

As economic forces of globalization threaten to extinguish the welfare state role of addressing the economic and health security of the people, a central issue is the extent to which women and the elderly will assert their influence in the new global economy. Will they resist efforts to re-shape the institution of old age and retirement occurring across different nation-states (Estes and Phillipson, 2002)? Globalization represents both a historical transition and an opportunity for the development and testing of political power and strategy involving a balance between consent and coercion. "Spaces" open up for the politics of gender and of ageing amidst the complex, contradictory, and highly contingent processes that are underway (Sassoon, 2001). Navarro (2000) argues that it is erroneous to believe that globalization is inevitably antithetical to social rights and progressive welfare states with full employment. Those working on behalf of human rights must insist that nation-states do not shrink from commitment to social and human rights, full employment, and a safety net for all peoples.

Mobilization of globalization opponents exists in areas of human rights, ecology, women's rights, race and ethnic justice, and worker rights. Nevertheless, as Kuumba (2001: 91) notes, "patriarchies and sexist notions [are] . . . major impediments to the mobilization of women into gender-integrated movements."

Eastern European and Third World women are networking in struggles for "women's rights as human rights" as a defining principle of citizenship under globalization-building collaborations (e.g. Women's EDGE, the Association for Women in Development, InterAction / Commission on the Advancement of Women, and the Open Society Institute's Network Women's Program). The

Soros-funded Network has targeted problems of "Democracy with a male face," the

silencing of women's voices, and disparities between rights and practices occurring since the fall of communism in Central and Eastern Europe and the former Soviet Union. Women's absence at the leadership level in emerging democracies diminishes efforts to reform economic, social, and legal systems. Enduring gender biases explain the failure to revise outdated employment laws, modify health care fees to ensure women's equal access, and enforcement laws on gender-based violence. (Soros Foundation, 2002: p. 2)

According to the First Independent Women's Forum in 1991, "Democracy without women is no democracy."

Constituencies of older people and women are largely absent from influential debates initiated by the World Bank against public pensions or the WTO for the commercialization of care services. Key players have been governments (from rich countries) seeking to deregulate state provision, and corporations striving to expand lucrative businesses. Older people and their organizations are marginalized in these forums despite Walker and Maltby's (1997) observation of an upsurge of pensioners' political activity in a number of countries (Estes *et al.*, 2003). A starting point, therefore, must be the linkage of organizations representing women and those representing older people with the larger organizations and forums working on global social justice issues.

Without women's continuation and acceleration of their struggles, there is serious danger of the eclipse of women's rights and their further immiseration as a defining outcome of globalization. The struggle must be to ensure that developing and developed states recognize the essential contributions of women to social reproduction, via state policy that fully supports the interdependency between and among generations and women's care work.

CONCLUSION

With the development of twentieth-century capitalism and the welfare state from the 1960s through the 1980s, women's dependency gradually shifted from the family and the man to the state. In twenty-first-century hyper-capitalism and globalization, women's dependency is shifting again – this time from the state and the public realm onto the

individual backs of women and children around the globe. The struggle over the rights of citizenship is paramount.

The 1990s brought debate on citizenship and illuminating critiques of the gender bias of the "gender-neutral" conception of the "universal citizen" (Jones, 1990; Pateman, 1989; Sassoon, 1991). An alternative "feminist pluralistic notion of citizenship" builds upon the "notion of difference that includes gender as well as race, class, ethnicity, nationality, and sexual orientation [with] interest and ideology as dimensions of political mobilization and participation" (Sarvasy & Siim, 1994: 253). It is crucial to promote "a politics that, in a spirit of solidarity in the face of oppression, traverses the web of group differences but without suppressing them" (Hobson and Lister, 2002: 39). Given older women's lifetime unpaid work as carers of young and old, it is essential to incorporate "care in the definition of citizenship, so the rights to time to care and to receive care are protected as part of a more inclusive approach to citizenship" (Knijn and Kremer, 1997: 357; see Leira and Saraceno, 2002).

FURTHER READING

Estes, C. L., and associates (2001). *Social policy & aging.* Thousand Oaks, Calif.: Sage.

Ginn, J., Street, D., and S. Arber (2001). *Women, work, and pensions: international issues and prospects.* Buckingham and Philadelphia: Open University Press.

Kuumba, M. B. (2001). *Gender and social movements.* Walnut Creek, Calif.: Alta Mira Press, a division of Rowman & Littlefield.

O'Connor, J. S., Orloff, A. S., and S. Shaver (1999). *States, markets, families: gender, liberalism and social Policy in Australia, Canada, Great Britain and the United States.* Cambridge: Cambridge University Press.

REFERENCES

Acker, J. (1988). "Class, gender and the relations of distribution," *Signs*, 13: 473–93.

Acker, L. (1992). "Gendered institutions – from sex roles to gendered institutions," *Contemporary Sociology*: 565–9.

Arenas de Mesa, A. and V. Montecinos (1999). "The privatization of social security and women's welfare: gender effects of Chilean reform," *Latin American Research Review*, 34: 7–38.

Bourdieu, P. (2001). *Masculine domination.* Stanford, Calif.: Stanford University Press.

Brush, L. (2000). "Gender, work, who cares?! Production, reproduction, deindustrialization, and business as usual." In M. M. Ferree, J. Lorber, and B. B. Hess, eds., *Revisioning gender.* Walnut Creek, Calif.: a division of Rowman & Littlefield, pp. 161–89.

Calasanti, T. M. (1993). "Introduction – a socialist–feminist approach to aging," *Journal of Aging Studies*, 7: 107–9.

Ciscel, D. H., and J. A. Heath (2001). "To market, to market: imperial capitalism's destruction of social capital and the family," *Review of Radical Political Economics*, 33: 401–14.

Collins, P. H. (1991). *Black feminist thought: knowledge, consciousness, and the politics of empowerment.* New York: Routledge.

Connell, R. W. (1987). *Gender and power: society, the person, and sexual politics.* Stanford, Calif.: Stanford University Press.

Crystal, S., and D. Shea, eds. (2002). *Annual review of gerontology and geriatrics*, Vol. XXII. New York: Springer.

Disney, R., and E. Whitehouse (2002). "The economic well-being of older people in international perspective: a critical Review." In S. Crystal and D. G. Shea, eds., *Annual review of gerontology and geriatrics*, Vol. XXII. New York: Springer.

Dressel, P. L. (1988). "Gender, race, and class: beyond the feminization of poverty in later life," *Gerontologist*, 28: 177–80.

Estes, C. L. (2000). "From gender to the political economy of ageing," *European Journal of Social Quality*, 2: 28–46.

Estes, C. L., and associates (2001). *Social policy & aging.* Thousand Oaks, Calif.: Sage.

Estes, C. L., and C. Phillipson (2002). "The globalization of capital: the welfare state, and old age policy," *International Journal of Health Services*, 32: 279–97.

Estes, C. L., Biggs, S., and C. Phillipson, (2003). *Social theory, social policy and ageing: a critical introduction.* Milton Keynes: Open University Press.

Folbre, N. (2001). *The invisible heart: economics and family values.* New York: New York University Press.

Ginn, J., and S. Arber (1995). "Only connect: gender relations and aging." In S. Arber and J. Ginn, eds., *Connection gender and ageing: a sociological approach.* Buckingham and Philadelphia, Penn.: Open University Press.

Ginn, J., Street, D., and S. Arber (2001). *Women, work, and pensions: international issues and prospects.* Buckingham and Philadelphia, Penn.: Open University Press.

Harrington Meyer, M. (1990). "Family status and poverty among older women: the gendered distribution of retirement income in the US," *Social Problems*, 37: 551–63.

Hernes, H. M. (1987). *Welfare state and woman power: essays in state feminism.* Oslo and Oxford: Norwegian University Press. Distributed by Oxford University Press.

Himmelweit, S. (1983). "Reproduction." In T. Bottomore, ed., *Dictionary of Marxist thought.* Cambridge, Mass.: Harvard University Press, pp., 417–19.

Hobson, B., and R. Lister (2002). "Citizenship." In B. Hobson, J. Lewis, and B. Siim, eds., *Contested concepts in gender and social politics.* Gloucester, UK: Edgar Elgar Pub., pp. 23–54.

Jones, K. (1990). "Citizenship in a woman friendly polity," *SIGNS*, 15: 781–812.

Knijn, T., and M. Kremer (1997). "Gender and the caring dimension of welfare states: toward inclusive citizenship," *Social Politics*, 4: 328–61.

Kuumba, M. B. (2001). *Gender and social movements.* Walnut Creek, Calif.: Alta Mira Press, a division of Rowman & Littlefield.

Leira, A. (1993). "The 'woman friendly' welfare state? The case of Norway and Sweden." In J. Lewis, ed., *Women and social policies in Europe: work, family, and the state.* Aldershot: Edward Elgar Pub., pp. 49–71.

Leira, A., and C. Saraceno (2002). "Care: actors, relationships and contexts." In B. Hobson, J. Lewis, and B. Siim, eds., *Contested concepts in gender and social politics.* Gloucester: Edgar Elgar Pub.

McMullin, J. (1995). "Age and gender relations: which theoretical path is best traveled." In S. Arber and J. Ginn, eds., *Connecting gender and ageing: a sociological approach.* Buckingham and Philadelphia, Penn.: Open University Press.

Mittelman, J. H., and A. Tambe (2000). "Global poverty and gender." In J. H. Mittelman, ed., *The globalization syndrome.* Princeton, N.J.: Princeton University Press.

Moghadam, V. M. (2000). "Gender and the global economy." In M. M. Ferree, J. Lorber, and B. B. Hess, eds., *Revisioning gender.* Walnut Creek, Calif.: a division of Rowman & Littlefield, pp. 128–60.

Navarro, V. (2000). "Are pro-welfare state and full employment policies possible in the era of globalization?" *International Journal of Health Services*, 30 (2): 231–51.

O'Connor, J. S., Orloff, A. S., and S. Shaver (1999). *States, markets, families: gender, liberalism and social policy in Australia, Canada, Great Britain and the United States.* Cambridge: Cambridge University Press.

Omi, M., and H. Winant (1994). *Racial formation in the United States: from the 1960s to the 1990s.* New York: Routledge.

Orloff, A. S. (1993). "Gender and the social rights of citizenship: the comparative analysis of gender relations and welfare states," *American Sociological Review*, 58: 303–29.

Pateman, C. (1989). *The disorder of women: democracy, feminism, and political theory.* Stanford, Calif.: Stanford University Press.

Quadagno, J. S. (1994). *The color of welfare: how racism undermined the war on poverty.* New York: Oxford University Press.

Robertson, A. (1999). "Beyond apocalyptic demography: toward a moral economy of interdependence." In

M. Minkler and C. L. Estes, eds., *Critical gerontology: perspectives from political and moral economy*. Amityville, N.Y.: Baywood Publishing Company, pp. 75–90.

Sarvasy, W., and B. Siim (1994). "Gender, transitions to democracy, and citizenship," *Social Politics: International Studies in Gender, State & Society*, 1: 249–55.

Sassoon, A. S. (1991). "Equality and difference: the emergence of a new concept of citizenship." In D. McLellan and S. Sayers, eds., *Socialism and democracy*. Houndmills, Basingstoke, Hampshire: Macmillan, pp. 87–105.

(2001). "The space for politics: globalization, hegemony, and passive revolution," *New Political Economy*, 6.

Siim, B. (1993). "The gendered Scandinavian welfare states: the interplay between women's roles as mothers, workers and citizens of Denmark.' In J. Lewis, ed., *Women and social policies in Europe: work, family and the state*. Aldershot: Edward Elgar Pub., pp. 25–48.

Soros Foundation (2002). *Bending the bow: targeting women's human rights and opportunities*. New York: Soros Foundation.

US Department of Commerce and National Institute on Aging (1996). *Global Aging into the 21st Century*. Washington, D.C.: Bureau of the Census, Economics and Statistics Administration and NIA Office of the Demography of Aging, Behavioral and Social Program.

Walker, A., and T. Maltby (1997). *Ageing Europe*. Buckingham: Open University Press.

WHO (World Health Organization) (1995). *World Health Report 1995*. Geneva: WHO.

(2002). "Active ageing: a policy framework. Second UN World Assembly on Ageing." www.who.int/hpr/ageing/index.htm 10/4/03.

PART SEVEN

POLICIES AND PROVISIONS FOR OLDER PEOPLE

CHAPTER 7.1

The Social Construction of Old Age as a Problem

MALCOLM L. JOHNSON

There are two central global narratives of old age; one ancient, one modern. In their primary forms, they are almost diametrically opposite. The one over-idealised but bearing enough evidence to sustain it for many centuries. The other a mix of apocalyptic demography and politically generated generational conflict, of shifting trends and panic. In the space between is a growing body of evidence, both historical and contemporary, which is not yet capable of yielding a satisfying synthesis. But there are discernible trends and possible futures. Powerful cultural, religious, ideological and historical influences have shaped attitudes to older people and to eldership. Contrary to general view, the traditional configurations of convention, law and practice were neither universal nor unchanging over time. Similarly, there is no new global framework as an established response to the radically changed demography of the twenty-first century. The place of old age in the lifemap is still under review.

FILIAL PIETY IN THE ANCIENT WORLD

The original, long-standing account is wholly positive and benign – at least in its formulation and precepts. In the great religious and associated ethical literature of the past three millennia, old age holds a place of dignity, authority and respect. It is depicted as a repository of wisdom and the life-stage of accumulated seniority. The special status of the old is presented with great clarity in the seminal texts, which have set the moral and religious framework for the whole of the Judeo-Christian world and the world of Islam. It is represented with equal weight in the

writings of Buddhism. It is fundamental to Confucianism and the oriental secular religions, which have arisen from the teachings of Confucius. Even before religious imperialism took the seniority of eldership to Africa and South America, it was an intrinsic element in many, though not all, tribal systems.

As testimony to the primacy of the old, the legal systems which embodied cultural values, principles and practices made clear that their senior citizenship was upheld within the laws of property (the single most important signifier of status and respect). Control over property, combined with wealth succession down the male line on the principle of primogeniture, gave older men and their wives (by association) a structural salience which was amplified by moral precepts of care and respect. Inevitably these prescribed patterns were more evident where economic controls were in place and where genuine affection existed. Yet even where these factors were not present, the pressures of expectation and the harsh disapproval within local communities, made avoidance of old age deference and support an option to be avoided.

The roots of conventional historical views of old age are readily found in the key religious and philosophical texts. The Jewish writings which make up the Old Testament of the Christian Bible make many references to the need to cherish parents in old age as well as to their wisdom and honour status. For example: 'Though shalt rise up before the hoary head and honour the face of the old man; and fear thy God' (Leviticus 19:32); 'a good old age, full of days, riches and honour' (1 Chronicles 29:28); 'With the ancient is wisdom; and in length of days, understanding.' (Job 12:12); 'And King Rahoboam consulted with the old men and said. How do ye advise that I may answer this people?' (1 Kings 12:6).

In similar manner, the writings and sayings (recorded by his pupils/disciples) of Confucius provide many statements about the inescapable requirement to observe the rules of filial piety. For example:

The Master said: Now filial piety is the root of all virtue, and the stem out of which grows all moral teaching. Our bodies – to every bit of hair and skin – are received by us from our parents, and we must not presume to injure or wound them. This is the beginning of filial piety. When we have established our character by the practice of the (filial) course, so as to make our name famous in future ages and thereby glorify our parents, this is the end of filial piety. It commences with the service of parents; it proceeds to the service of the ruler; it is completed by the establishment of the character. (Shu Jing, Vol. III of *The Chinese Classics*, p. 600)

In filial piety there is nothing greater than the reverential awe of one's father . . . there is nothing greater than making him the correlate of heaven.

The son derives his life from his parents, and no greater gift could possibly be transmitted. His ruler and parent (in one), his father deals with him accordingly, and no generosity can be greater than this. Hence, he who does not love his parents, but loves other men, is called a rebel against virtue, and he who does not revere his parents, but reveres other men, is called a rebel against propriety. (from *Zuo Zhan*)

The extreme respect Chinese children are expected to give to their parents, which has been at the centre of Confucianism for over 2,500 years, was inevitably embraced by the other two main oriental religions, Buddhism and Daoism – though not to the same exacting degree, because of their monastic structures; which mean that those in holy orders were absolved from family obligations.

Islamic codes of generational relations and filial piety as articulated in the Quran, bear considerable similarities to those in the Jewish Old Testament. As the revelations of divine utterances through the prophecy and speech of the Prophet Muhammed they are regarded as the speech of Allah. The following selected verses illustrate a variety of emphases which, with many other references, place respect for

parents and the obligation to reciprocate the care they have given to their children, at the centre of Islamic conduct: 'Worship Allah and join none with Him [in worship]; and do good to parents, kinsfolk, orphans, the poor, the neighbour who is near kin, the neighbour who is a stranger' (chapter 4 verse 36); 'And your Lord has decreed that you worship none but Him. And that you be dutiful to your parents. If one or both of them attain old age in your life, say not to them a word of disrespect, nor shout at them but address them in terms of honour' (chapter 17 verse 23); 'And We have enjoined on man [to be dutiful and good] to his parents. His mother bore him in weakness and hardship, and his weaning is in two years – give thanks to Me and to your parents. Unto Me is the final destination' (chapter 31 verse 14).

But for all the moral and political power of what in later times became known as the intergenerational contract, there were always tensions and aberrations. There have been conflicts over wealth, inheritance, control, and as a result of relationship breakdowns. Intergenerational harmony did not prevail over thousands of years and then become problematic in the later decades of the twentieth century. Moses Finley (1984) in his scholarly essay on older people in classical Greece and Rome states the obligations starkly: 'Sons were held responsible for the maintenance of their parents and grandparents, and that was the end of the matter.' Contemporary ethical debates on generational relations often begin with the precepts set down by Aristotle and the reflections of Cicero on old age; so there is sound documentary evidence of a strong moral equivalence in the classical civil societies of Europe. Yet Finley goes on to say: 'And if they (the sons) were unable so to do, or if they predeceased their parents, what then? The answer is that we simply have no idea, and I see no virtue in idle guesses.' Nonetheless, he goes on to point out that there is no evidence whatever of interest in the poor or the elderly outside of the narrow kinship circle – no charities, pensions, almshouses, poorhouses or old-age homes. Even the moralists did not go beyond an appeal for decent treatment. The sophisticated world of classical scholarship, art, literature and medicine was restricted to those in the upper reaches of the class and social system. Slaves and the common people were left to the ravages of disease and poverty. Few of them are likely to have had the chance to be miserable in old age along with Cicero.

Here there may well be a divergence from ancient China, where Confucius' carefully ordered and strictly hierarchical world applied to all social levels. Filial piety, 'Xiao', was and has been central to Chinese morality. Pang (2000) points out that even before Confucius' time, about 500 BCE, it was the family, rather than a distinct powerful class, which had the authority in China. Wang (2003) adds to that view a claim that the traditional family also carried out quasi-governmental functions. So the key variables influencing a good old age in the ancient world were the stability and inclusiveness of the systems of civil society, one's position in the social and economic hierarchy (which in turn linked to expectation of life) and the presence of harmonious relations within the family: a familiar configuration.

OLD AGE IN THE POST-RENAISSANCE WORLD

More recent history, in the so-called 'developed world', is inevitably characterised by accelerating change. Since the beginnings of agricultural reform and developments in the mechanised production of food and artifacts in seventeenth- and eighteenth-century Europe, the story has been one of relentless change which disrupted long established social systems, dislodged populations into urban agglomerations, led to new forms of diseases and hazards and then into an era of public health, better living standards and medical care. During most of the intervening period, old age was an issue of no significance in the public mind. As in China today where official policy (if not always practice) remains an unreconstructed Confucian assertion that the old are the responsibility of the family, the pattern in Europe continued to be based on a similar premise until the early decades of the twentieth century. Only then did the state begin to share some of the responsibility with families and the networks of local authorities which had been required to provide for the 'indigent poor' since the middle ages.

As Peter Laslett (1984) showed two decades ago, patterns of familial support to older people, especially their living in multigenerational households,

varied considerably from country to country. He and his colleagues who founded the subdiscipline of historical demography were able to demonstrate strong patterns of co-residence in Russia and China but less intense forms across Western Europe and America. In his celebrated book *A fresh map of life* (1989), he writes 'Four generational kinship strings are known in America and Europe in the 1890s and are there quite correctly regarded as a novelty. But the members of these strings certainly never live together as family groups in Western countries today' (p. 118).

Just as living arrangements in the past varied according to political circumstances and variations in survival rates (radically changed by episodes of plague and other communicable diseases) which affect both the incidence of old age and the size of the kinship 'strings' available to offer support, so did the very notion of old age itself. The rich and powerful usually age later in all societies. Command over economic resources, superior living conditions and elevated status enable some to evade the label 'old', whilst their poorer contemporaries, disabled by harder lives, become sick and dependent – the enduring signifiers of oldness. Moreover, until the mid sixteenth century, age referred to a period of human life. Thomas Cole (1992) notes that, as age then had virtually no social significance, few people knew exactly how old they were.

The reason for the emergence of a chronologically defined lifespan lay not in any awareness of demographic change, but in a new cosmology which replaced the medieval concept of life as a cycle, with one of stages modelled on a rising and descending staircase. The journey of life had a new imagery which foreshadowed the late twentieth century theoretical construct of the lifecourse which developed as a result of the researches of Bernice Neugarten (Neugarten and Datan, 1973) and Glen Elder (1974) amongst others. The most familiar of these 'age stages' is Shakespeare's 'The Seven Ages of Man', the last of which he famously described as 'second childishness, and mere oblivion, sans teeth, sans eyes, sans taste, sans everything' (*As You Like It* Act 2 Scene 7). Here we can see the encapsulation of old age as the last decrepit stage before death, so memorably expressed that the image and indeed the words have survived to feed contemporary prejudice and ageism.

VICTORIAN REFORMULATIONS

Just as Renaissance Europe redesigned the lifepath through the creation of new understandings of age and its significance as a marker of the journey towards death, later ages have provided their own newly fashioned notions which sprang from shifts in cultural thinking and as a result of scientific – and just as often, quasi-scientific – developments. The nineteenth-century Victorian era provided a rich harvest of contrasting movements. Cole (1992) provides an extensive and compelling analysis of very different schools of thought which co-existed in Europe and North America. The 'hygiene movement', which transformed popular ideas of sickness and death, placed special value on bodily health. The reformers advocated physical perfection. Believing that disease was the price of moral transgression and ungodliness, their goal was the prolongation of life: 'The pursuit of longevity and old age as a reward for good living, combined Christian evangelism and a belief in economic progress' (p. 92).

As the century and the modern period moved on, spectacular developments in rail transport, civil engineering and manufacture created a need to replace Bunyan's notions, both of life as a pilgrimage and of the harsh trials which travellers would meet on the road, with images which reflected the rewards of doing God's work, through hard work, which formed the centrepiece of the Protestant Ethic as characterised by the German sociologist Max Weber (1930). Achenbaum and Kusnerz (1978) in their defining collection of American images of old age, selected Thomas Cole's 1842 set of four allegorical canvases which depict human lifetime as a journey down a river, representing the maintenance of faith and surviving life's trials, as a landmark in American cultural history. This less harrowing mid century perspective provided a more comfortable interpretation of old age for the industrious and prospering non-conformist middle classes. It concentrated the struggles in midlife, leaving old age as a haven. Moreover, it promised a painless and sentimentalised death – and a place in heaven as a reward for faithful endeavour. Aries (1977) calls this the Age of the Beautiful Death.

Other theologically led refinements of old age included the Romantic, which Cole (1992) tells us downplayed self-torment and aggressive or violent feelings, replacing them with a Christian piety that was more feminine. Within it, old age became more passive and nostalgic and the suffering of later life was elided. During the later part of the Victorian age, which had begun with a rationalistic Calvinism and mellowed into sentimentality, the view shifted again to encompass the individualistic and self-help philosophies which were promoted by Christian evangelicals and widely adopted by writers, artists and social commentators. Further reflections are found in hymns and popular songs which together provided a powerful medium of cultural transmission to the still largely illiterate working classes.

Yet for all the tides and fashions that rapid socioeconomic change brought, which in turn reshaped ideas about old age and the position of older people, they bore little direct application to the lives of the overwhelming majority of the populations of countries in transition. Whilst life expectation at birth rose significantly during the nineteenth century (in the UK it increased from 39 years for men and 42 for women in 1841, to 48 and 54 respectively by 1891), the common experience for the labouring classes – who represented more than four-fifths of the people in these nations – as indicated by these figures, was to continue in work until they died or became so disabled by industrial and chronic diseases that they entered a short period of dependency prior to death. So the hugely popular song 'My Grandfather's Clock', which 'stopped, short, never to go again' the day he died, aged 90, represented an aspiration most would never have seen, let alone experienced. Retirement schemes, which were first introduced in Germany around 1860 and copied across Europe, were reserved for senior civil servants. It took the greater part of another century before all categories of workers, male and female, across Western Europe, gained pension rights.

BEING OLD IN THE TWENTIETH CENTURY

Contrary to contemporary beliefs and views about old age and the place of older people in society, in earlier times there was not a single pattern of benign family-based care, reinforced by a compelling philosophy of filial obligation. But that stereotypical view does have a good deal of credence. As we have seen, religions, moral codes, legal systems and family structures did, on the whole, ensure a decently supported last stage of life for the few who were fortunate enough to live beyond their working lives. Both survival and the opportunity to benefit from it were, and to a large extent still are, highly class related. It was the educated and prosperous elites who produced the fascinating theologies, moral dialogues and cultural interpretations. Despite this, the Victorian era saw a remarkable group of mostly non-conformist Christian industrialists who developed quality work, social and housing benefits for their workers. In the UK, they included the chocolate manufacturers Rowntree, Fry and Cadbury, the woollen-mill owner Titus Salt, and the tobacco company, Wills.

The twentieth century, which saw the lead ageing countries in Europe enter a demographic explosion, soon began to see the phenomenon as a mixed blessing and then as a serious problem. In the UK the proportion of over-65s in the population in 1901 was around 5%. By the end of the century that proportion had multiplied fourfold. Moreover, the expansion of those over 75 was at an accelerating rate. In 1901 they formed 21% of the 2.4 million 'elderly' population (women over 60, men over 65). A century on, there are over 10 million in the retirement age groups, of whom 41% are over 75. To add fuel to the smouldering concerns of the anxious, amongst this older group the proportions living alone leapt from 10% to 36% – but for women the rate is 50%.

As the historian Pat Thane (2000) put it: 'Some draw gloomy conclusions from these statistics. It is suggested, as it was in the 1930s, that a population in which older age groups are growing whilst younger ones are shrinking must impose ever growing costs of pensions and medical and other forms of care upon the shrinking population of working age' (p. 479). This early expression of the unbalanced dependency ratio argument was further fuelled by the disproportionate growth of older women who live alone. It was widely believed that, with the reduction in family size, family care would dwindle as the need rose, leaving many isolated and unsupported. Indeed, old age was seen throughout the twentieth century as 'a social problem' (MacIntyre, 1977; Pratt, 1976; Estes, 1979). It was widely spoken of as 'an impending disaster', 'the burden of an ageing population', 'the rising tide'.

Governmental responses to the growing numbers of retired people varied around the developed world, but were mostly piecemeal adjustments to existing provisions. Quite early in the century it became apparent that these structures were inadequate. Public provision had historically been designed to be only a safety net. Across Western Europe the principle of subsidiarity, which grew out of Roman Catholic social doctrine in the nineteenth century, was widely adopted. It prescribed that help to individuals in need should operate at the lowest appropriate level possible. In practice this meant that the old and the sick should be cared for by the family, and only if that failed by the local parish or township. In the UK the Elizabethan Poor Law, updated in 1832, placed the same pattern of responsibility. That framework remained in place until 1948. The USA maintained the principle of individual and family responsibility well into the twentieth century. National governments avoided the creation of collectivist policies, but found themselves under increasing pressure during the first half of the century.

By the commencement of the First World War, the developed nations of Western Europe, including Scandinavia, had introduced state retirement pension schemes, but only for selected categories of worker. It was in the interwar period that the problematisation of old age began to take hold. As both Graebner (1980) and Midwinter (1997) point out, the world economy was in deep recession, with unprecedented levels of unemployment, and increases in public expenditure were unwelcome. Yet it was essential to deliver income to the very poor. Significantly, improvements to pensions occurred in the UK in 1925 as a way of taking older men out of the workforce, whilst the USA first recognised the right to a post-retirement income in the Social Security Act of 1935.

Planning for a renewed postwar society gave birth in the UK to what became the welfare state. It introduced healthcare free to all at the point of need, and state retirement pensions to all men over 65 and most women over 60. As the international economy prospered from the 1950s onwards there was something of a golden age in which the welfare state (by then adopted in different formats) appeared in other economically advanced European nations, in Australasia and Canada – but not the USA. During this time many working-class men lived for only short periods after retirement, due to a lifetime of hard and often hazardous physical labour. Michael Young and Tom Schuller (1991) expressed the position succinctly: 'The watch or clock that employers traditionally handed over to their retiring workers was a deceit. It symbolised the gift of the time that was now to be their own rather than the employers'. But the new owner was going to wear out long before the watch' (p. 18).

During this third quarter of the century, providing pensions became a recognised necessity. Less well-off countries, such as Italy (1952) and Austria (1954) introduced state pensions (Walker and Naegele, 1999). The USA, which had been encouraging and enabling the rapid spread of employment-based private pension schemes, created federal controls over the administration of private pension schemes in 1974. By this time, the greatly admired welfare state was beginning to come under criticism for undermining self-reliance – an argument advanced by right-of-centre commentators who had observed that pensions were by far the greatest cost (Thane, 2000) and that half of the beds in the hospitals were occupied by retired people.

EMERGENCE OF THE THIRD AGE AND INTERGENERATIONAL CONFLICT

A combination of general economic prosperity, relatively short lives in retirement and the evidently low levels of social engagement and life satisfaction of retired people kept the critics of older people at bay. But an inflationary world oil crisis, coinciding with the emergence of a more vocal and more active group of Third Agers, whose increased expectations were amplified by academic gerontologists, prompted a new period where older people were again seen as a problem. Townsend's (1981) allegations that older people's lives were needlessly limited by what he termed 'structured dependency', swiftly ignited a literature on the political economy of old age, which illuminated the marked social deprivations and inequalities amongst the older population. Too many, too sick, too costly, not enough family caring, was the public cry. Not enough financial and specialist services was the message of much research, whilst those who spoke for the older people themselves wanted greater access to the mainstream

arenas of social life and more control over what was done for them.

A new feature of the situation was the arrival of a well-organised group of middle-aged, middle-class Americans, who called themselves Americans for Generational Equity (AGE), who claimed the old were stealing federal dollars from their children and that budgets for Medicaid and Social Security should be cut. This very public encounter proved to be the first manifestation of a more systematic concern rising to panic, by governments all over the world, about the escalating costs of old age. In turn, attention was focused first on the undesirability of the increasing trend towards – both chosen and forced – early retirement, then on the need to extend the working life, a debate newly fuelled by the post 9/11 stock market drop and its consequences for pension funds and employers.

ISSUES FOR THE NEW MILLENNIUM

Clearly, changes to the status and value placed on old age have not yet run their course; and never will. So what are the known and likely drivers of the next generation of re-definitions?

The whole of this book was designed (by me) to help readers better understand the ways in which knowledge, ideas and practices are reshaping the landscape of age and its consequences for a globalised world. The following topics are a refined list of key developments. All are dealt with at more length in the *Handbook* by leading authors; so references to these chapters will enable detailed exploration.

Ageism was first identified and labelled by Robert Butler in 1975 and best defined by him in 1987 as 'a process of systematic stereotyping of, and discrimination against, people because they are old, just as racism and sexism accomplish this for skin colour and gender' (Butler, 1995: 22–3). Whilst the term has entered the language and there is now a presumption (and some good evidence) that structured discrimination exists against older people, Bytheway (1995), in his book *Ageism*, takes direct issue with Butler's definition, subjecting each of the key words to critical analysis. He takes his sophisticated re-evaluation further in this volume, where discrimination and the struggle against it are not denied, but argues that gerontologists and service providers should move away from their preoccupation with old age and focus on ageing in general, thus helping to remove the age/stage stigma. The prospect of his advice being heeded in the short run is slender (Minichiello *et al.*, 2000), but the notion of an all-age society is one which could emerge during this century, reducing the 'problem' of old age.

Family care and the belief that it declined markedly in the twentieth century have been the subjects of extensive research and policy analysis, world wide. Directly linked with concern about global weakening of the intergenerational contract as a result of modernisation (Cowgill and Holmes, 1972), research reviews (M. Johnson, 1995; Ter Muelen *et al.*, 2001 and others) have demonstrated that smaller families, serial marriages and geographical mobility have changed the relations between generations but have not undermined mutuality and support. Bengtson's (2002) *How families still matter* presents compelling empirical evidence of the durability of family bonds emerging out of hitherto unseen configurations of relationships – a process of social change which has continuing potential as 'a problem of old age'. See also chapters in section 5 of this volume by Lowenstein, Giarrusso *et al.*, Harper, Connidis, Hashimoto and Ikels, Attias-Donfut and Wolff, Chappell and Penning, Thomése and colleagues, and Aboderin.

Life extension which occurred at an unprecedented rate in the twentieth century, saw expectation of life at birth double. By the last decade, the fastest growing sector was in the over-80s, with more centenarians alive at the turn of the millennium than had ever lived before in all of human history. Scientific opinion consistently took the view that longevity might continue to grow modestly, but had virtually met its limit. However, the analysis of European demographic data since 1840, by Oeppen and Vaupel (2002), revealed the astonishing fact that female life expectancy (and for men equally consistently) in the lead nation, Sweden, had risen for 160 years at a steady pace of almost 3 months per year – and shows no sign of relenting. The authors conclude that there are no known limits and that the world should accustom itself to an indefinite extension of longevity. Such well-authenticated findings can only serve to amplify the 'problem' of an ageing population.

Work, retirement and income have been the subject of increasing research and governmental anguish

for the last decade, though academic commentators have been predicting the developments for more than two decades (Fogarty, 1982). Across Europe, where EU law will abolish compulsory retirement in 2006, there is a panic about people having to work longer and undertake a portfolio retirement (M. Johnson, 1997), though there is little awareness of the undramatic consequences in the USA following Senator Claude Pepper's law raising retirement age to 70 in the 1990s. The evidence base and the policy options in North America and Europe are well represented in Disney (1996) and Marshall *et al.* (2001) and by Cutler (Chapter 7.4) and Marshall and Taylor (Chapter 7.2) in this volume. Restructuring the lifecourse and reformulating retirement are set to add new dimensions to the 'problem' of old age.

Death – the province of old age

A less recognised feature of the huge demographic shifts of the twentieth century is the age of death and the way this has affected attitudes, thinking and practice. At the beginning of the century, death occurred throughout the lifespan. It happened at birth for children and their mothers. In the perinatal and childhood periods, children were lost as a result of infectious diseases, congenital abnormalities, accidents and poverty; adults, or males in particular, died as a result of hazardous and unsafe work environments and of industrial diseases. There was higher mortality among women as a result of pregnancy, childbirth and abortion. In 1901 these afflictions brought about deaths in virtually every family.

By the middle of the century, and onwards progressively, this enduring history of premature mortality showed an unprecedented marked decline. As a consequence, the twenty-first century began with a radically different mortality map, which contains lower rates of death in all age groups up to 55. Now death is, for the first time in human history, the preserve of old age. The as yet unrealised association, which brings together two twentieth-century taboos, will almost inevitably become a new part of the late life 'problematic'.

The agenda of key issues which will drive change is by no means exhausted by the above list. The special circumstances of women (see Arber and Ginn, Chapter 6.5 in this volume); ethical issues arising from care decisions / end of life / human rights (see Moody, Chapter 7.3 in this volume); Third Age identities and citizenship (Gilleard and Higgs, 2000); generational equity (see Martin Kohli, Chapter 6.4 in this volume); healthcare and long term care (see Gjonça and Marmot (Chapter 2.3), and Bowman and Kane (Chapter 7.11), in this volume). Expected breakthroughs in biology and the uses of nanotechnology could create a genuine paradigm shift, both in the extension of life and in the treatment of the disabling conditions which define old age, including Alzheimer's disease (see Kirkwood, Chapter 1.5 in this volume). Of equal magnitude is the explosion of older populations in the developing world (see Kalache *et al.*, Chapter 1.3 in this volume).

CONCLUSIONS

This brief and necessarily selective review of the life history of old age was undertaken to reveal the huge variety of attitudes to and social constructions of old age at different historical times, in different religions and cultures. What emerges from this examination is an understanding of the impact of social, economic, intellectual, political and cultural change on the places older people are ascribed within kinship systems, local communities and nation-states. In the relatively enduring belief patterns and social orders of ancient times, the evidence of a continuing place of esteem and honour within the family appears strong, though we do not know how well the lower social orders were treated or how women fared after the death of their husbands. In an ageing world, we are still going into the unknown of what I have termed 'stretching the lifespan'. The process will redefine every stage of life. If we ever reach a new equilibrium, perhaps by then old age will again find a place of honour in the human family.

FURTHER READING

Bengtson, V. (2002). *How families still matter*. Cambridge: Cambridge University Press.

Cole, T. (1992). *The journey of life: a cultural history of aging in America*. Cambridge: Cambridge University Press.

Johnson, P., Conrad, C., and D. Thomson (1989). *Workers versus pensioners: intergenerational justice in an ageing world*. Manchester: Manchester University Press.

Gilleard, C., and P. Higgs (2000). *Cultures of ageing: self, citizen and body*. London: Pearson Education Limited.

REFERENCES

Achenbaum, A., and P. Kusnerz (1978). *Images of old age in America, 1790 to the present*. Ann Arbor: Institute of Gerontology, University of Michigan.

Aries, P. (1977). *The hour of our death*. Paris: Editions du Seuil. (English edn, New York: Alfred A. Knopf Inc., 1981.)

Bengtson, V. (2002). *How families still matter: a longitudinal study of youth in two generations*. Cambridge: Cambridge University Press.

Butler, R. (1995). 'Ageism'. In G. Maddox *et al.*, eds., *The Encyclopedia of Aging*. New York: Springer.

Bytheway, B. (1995). *Ageism*. Buckingham: Open University Press.

Cole, T. (1992). *The journey of life: a cultural history of ageing in America*. Cambridge: Cambridge University Press.

Cowgill, D., and L. Holmes (1972). *Aging and modernization*. New York: Appleton Century.

Disney, R. (1996). *Can we afford to grow older?* Cambridge, Mass.: MIT Press.

Elder, G. H., Jr (1974). *Children of the Great Depression: social change in life experience*. Chicago: University of Chicago Press.

Estes, C. (1979). *The aging enterprise*. San Francisco: Jossey-Bass.

Estes, C., Biggs, S., and C. Phillipson (2003). *Social theory, social policy and ageing*. Buckingham: Open University Press.

Finley, M. I. (1984). 'The elderly in classical antiquity', *Ageing and Society*, 4 (4): 391–408.

Fogarty, M., ed. (1982). *Retirement policy: the next fifty years*. London: Heinemann.

Gilleard, C., and P. Higgs (2000). *Cultures of ageing: self, citizen and the body*. Harlow: Pearson Education Limited.

Graebner, W. (1980). *A history of retirement: the meaning and function of an American institution, 1885–1978*. New Haven and London: Yale University Press.

Ikels, C., ed. (2004). *Filial piety: practice and discourse in contemporary Asia*. Stanford, Calif.: Stanford University Press.

Johnson, M. L. (1995). 'Interdependency and the generational compact', *Ageing and Society*, 15: 243–65.

1997. 'Generational equity and the reformulation of retirement', *Scandinavian Journal of Social Welfare*, 6 (3): 162–7.

Johnson, P., Conrad, C., and D. Thomson (1989). *Workers versus pensioners: intergenerational justice in an ageing world*. Manchester: Manchester University Press.

Laslett, P. (1984). 'The significance of the past in the study of ageing', *Ageing and Society*, 4 (4): 379–89.

(1989). *A fresh map of life: the emergence of the third age*. London: Weidenfeld and Nicholson.

MacIntyre, S. (1977). 'Old age as a social problem'. In R. Dingwall, C. Heath, M. Reid and M. Stacey, eds., *Health care and health knowledge.* London: Croom Helm, pp. 41–63.

Marshall, V., *et al.*, eds. (2001). *Restructuring work and the lifecourse.* Toronto: University of Toronto Press.

Midwinter, E. (1997). *Pensioned off: retirement and income explained.* Buckingham: Open University Press.

Minichiello, V., Browne, J., and H. Kendig (2000). 'Perceptions and consequences of ageism: views of older people', *Ageing and Society*, 20: 253–78.

Neugarten, B., and N. Datan (1973). 'Sociological perspectives on the life cycle'. In P. B. Baltes and K. W. Schaie, eds., *Life-span developmental psychology: personality and socialization.* New York: Academic Press, pp. 53–69.

Oeppen, J., and J. W. Vaupel (2002). 'Enhanced demography: broken limits to life expectancy', *Science*, 296: 1029–31.

Pang, E. C. (2000). 'Filial piety in modern time: the ideal and practice of parental care.' Paper presented at the International Conference on Searching for Meaning in the new Millennium, Vancouver, B.C., Canada, 13–16 July 2000.

Phillipson, C. (1998). *Reconstructing ageing.* London: Sage.

Pratt, H. J. (1976). *The politics of old age.* Chicago: University of Chicago Press.

Ter Muelen, Ruud, Arts, Wil and Muffels, Ruud (eds) (2001). *Solidarity in Health and Social Care in Europe.* Dordrecht & Boston: Kluwer Academic Publishing.

Thane, Pat (2000). *Old Age in English History*, Oxford University Press.

Townsend, P. (1981). 'The structured dependency of the elderly: a creation of social policy in the twentieth century', *Ageing and Society*, 1: 5–28.

Walker, A., and G. Naegele, eds. (1999). *The politics of old age in Europe.* Buckingham: Open University Press.

Wang, J. (2003). 'The Confucian filial obligation and care for aged parents'. www.bu.edu/wcp/Papers/Comp/CompWang.htm.

Weber, M. (1930). *The Protestant ethic and the spirit of capitalism.* London: Allen and Unwin.

Young, M., and T. Schuller (1991). *Life after work: the arrival of the ageless society.* London: HarperCollins.

Restructuring the Lifecourse: Work and Retirement

VICTOR W. MARSHALL AND PHILIP TAYLOR

This chapter examines the relationship between work and retirement, focusing on economically developed societies of the current era, in which the complexity and ambiguity concerning this relationship is determined, in part, by the role of the state in institutionalizing retirement. At the societal level, we focus on transitions from one form of work, paid employment, into the status of recipient of a pension. The interplay of state and corporate policies about pensions and other aspects of the lifecourse influences the nature of the working lifecourse in later life and the timing of the retirement transition. Policies and practices about work and the timing of retirement are shaped by the attitudes of major stakeholders towards older workers. We therefore consider attitudes towards older workers, and the phenomenon of age discrimination in employment.

CHANGES IN THE TRANSITION FROM WORK TO RETIREMENT

The transition from work to retirement varies widely across societies and has changed dramatically since the early 1980s. In previous centuries most people did not experience a retirement transition. Retirement came to be commonly experienced in the developed world only over the course of the twentieth century (Myles, 1984). Before then, with rare exceptions, working lives ended only with death. While retirement is now virtually universal for workers in the developed world, there is great variability in its *timing*, as illustrated in Table 1, which examines relatively recent trends in economic activity rates by age group and gender, for selected developed

countries. The table illustrates only main trends for these countries. In several of these countries, *increases* in economic activity rates have occurred over the previous 5, 10, in some cases 15, years, and these are not captured by the time intervals we use. However, such reversals are small compared to the main trends since 1970 and, in any case, further support the general points we wish to make about instability in the working lifecourse. Most of the initial dynamics of activity rates were among people aged 65 or older (in some countries, 60+), in response to the introduction and maturation of state pension plans and the spread of private pension plans based on retirement at fixed ages. After the mid 1970s, economic activity rates for men aged 55–64 and, to a lesser extent, aged 45–54, began to decline in response to both corporate and public policies. Meanwhile, a trend towards increased labour force participation of women produced, in most countries, lower declines in the age 60–64 category and a convergence in labour force participation rates among workers aged 55–59. Very large differences among countries in economic activity rates for men and women are illustrated in Table 1. Japan had the highest participation of men in all three age categories in 1970 and again in 2000 and it also leads the other countries in female participation rates over age 60. Despite declines since 1970, Japan also continued to experience relatively high rates of female labour force participation in general compared to other industrialized countries. The United Kingdom and the United States have high male and female labour force participation rates relative to other countries. Variability among countries

TABLE 1. Economic activity rates for older workers in selected developed countries.

Age range		55–59(%)		60–64(%)		65+(%)	
		1970	2000	1970	2000	1970	2000
	Country						
Men	Australia	89.6	71.9	75.1	45.0	21.8	7.5
	Canada	90.5	74.0	75.0	46.7	21.7	9.4
	France	80.1	65.2	55.5	17.8	15.0	2.1
	Germany	88.7	74.5	72.9	29.8	19.3	3.9
	Japan	94.2	93.6	85.8	72.1	54.5	33.4
	United Kingdom	93.7	77.7	81.2	53.1	18.8	6.8
	United States	88.4	76.6	74.2	50.3	25.5	13.5
Women	Australia	28.8	38.1	16.2	17.3	4.6	2.1
	Canada	34.9	49.8	25.5	23.2	6.1	3.6
	France	42.6	44.3	28.4	14.5	6.3	1.2
	Germany	41.0	42.8	21.5	8.9	6.4	1.3
	Japan	50.6	57.9	38.8	37.7	15.8	13.4
	United Kingdom	45.5	51.4	21.5	21.0	4.8	2.7
	United States	48.5	59.0	35.3	33.2	9.5	7.4

Source: International Labour Office: LABORSTA.

may be attributed to a number of factors, including the nature of the economy, demography and public policy (Kinsella and Velkoff, 2001), and we examine these factors below.

EMERGENCE OF RETIREMENT AS A SOCIAL INSTITUTION IN DEVELOPED NATIONS

Retirement is a socially constructed and evolving institution, and there is no such thing as a 'normal' age for retirement. However, in all industrialized societies, a 'normative' working lifecourse ends in retirement at or around a specific age (65 in North America, earlier in many other countries). Institutionalized public and private pension provisions establish the standard against which individuals see retirement as early, on time or late.

Throughout history, many people have stopped working prior to death, because of age-related declines in health or perhaps because they no longer felt the need to 'make a living' through their work. Until quite recently, very few would have received a pension. Pensions emerged over many centuries, but until late in the nineteenth century they existed only for selected groups. Achenbaum (1996) cites as

examples bureaucrats in thirteenth-century China receiving stipends after ceasing work, and the posting to milder duties or discharge of older British and French soldiers in the eighteenth century. Titmuss (1968) notes the generation of income for one's later years in seventeenth-century England by the sale of one's office, then a new development in which pensions granted to an exiting office holder were paid by the successor, and, by 1810, introduction of the first non-contributory pension plan for civil servants. Canada implemented a pension plan for federal civil servants in 1870 (Bryden, 1974). From the last decade of the nineteenth century through the first two of the twentieth century, more groups such as teachers, police officers, railway workers and others in Great Britain, Canada, the USA and many other countries, began to receive private pensions, often at age 65 (Bryden, 1974; Quadagno and Hardy, 1996).

Government initiatives to provide retirement pensions at a defined age and as a citizen's right were the most important factors creating the social institution of retirement, and the key development in this regard was the Old Age Insurance Law adopted by the German Reichstag in 1889 as an alternative to poor-law provision for the indigent aged, which was mainly provided until that time by churches. A worker became eligible for a pension at age 71 or if permanently incapacitated. To qualify, a worker had to have contributed to the retirement fund for 30 years, or 5 years of contributions to qualify by incapacity. In 1908 a means-tested, non-contributory state pension was introduced in Great Britain, with the age of eligibility being 70 (Parker, 1982). Canada established a similar pension at age 70, in 1927 (Bryden, 1974). State pensions for those other than veterans or civil servants began in the United States only with passage of the Social Security Act in 1935, which established a contributory pension (Cain, 1974; Quadagno and Hardy, 1996). Initially, pensions were very meagre but over the decades a series of amendments to the Social Security Act increased the benefits, and a relationship of increasingly generous pension provisions to labour force participation rates has been demonstrated (Quadagno and Hardy, 1996).

Many countries have had ages other than 65 as the age of eligibility for pensions, different ages for men and women, and occasionally for different occupations. Japan has a 'normal' retirement age of 60 (currently being revised upwards) but ship workers can retire at 58 while academics have to wait until age 65 (Kimura and Oka, 2001; Moore et al., 1994). There is nothing sacred about 'retirement' starting at any specific age, but, in any country, people form a conception of a normative working lifecourse that is highly influenced by legal retirement ages.

A great deal of research, particularly European, emphasizes the role of public policies in shaping new working career patterns (Schmähl, 1989; Kohli et al., 1991). As an OECD report (1995: 9) summarizes the role of public policies: 'In many countries, early withdrawal from employment has been financed either directly or indirectly by the state: through the right to early old-age pensions, through relaxing eligibility requirements for invalidity pensions, through extending the period for which older unemployed people can claim unemployment compensation, or, less directly, by according tax privileges to employers' and private pension schemes.' North American research (e.g., Hardy and Hazelrigg, 1999; Hardy et al., 1996; Marshall, 1996; Marshall and Marshall, 1999, 2003; Quinn et al., 1990) has paid more attention to firm-based policies as motivators for early retirement. More recent European research has turned attention to corporate policies in relation to public policies (Taylor, 2003). The pattern and timing of retirement is being affected not just by public pension policies (Kohli et al., 1991; Schmähl, 1989), but by firm's policies through processes of structural adjustment (Marshall and Marshall, 2003; OECD, 1995; Quinn et al., 1990). A series of studies by the International Labour Office has 'provided ample evidence of how older workers are often used as a balancing factor to regulate labour supply' (ILO, 1995: 38), moving them in and out of retirement in response to economic pressures. Thus, the ways in which people undergo the retirement transition are shaped in part by the set of state and private sector policies, including but not restricted to pension policies, that make it more or less possible or desirable to give up paid employment.

As we have seen, the corporate world and governments, often with the active collaboration of organized labour, have created the social institution of retirement, and in so doing they have defined another key transition in the lifecourse. As this social institution developed and reached its zenith around the middle of the twentieth century, the notion that people might expect to cease working for pay at a predictable, stable age came to be shared by larger constituencies of citizens in the world's industrial societies. By the 1950s, large segments of the workforce were subject to the 'Fordist' lifecourse contract. From early in the twentieth century, employers in the United States (emulated in many other countries) sought stability in their supply of labour by emphasizing internal labour markets, in which, typically, young persons with little skill were recruited, trained within that company, and provided job security, predictable promotions and benefits that would tie them to the company (Cappelli et al., 1997). Retirement at a fixed age was both a benefit (a reward for good and faithful service) and a requirement to make the system work, since it opened up vacancies to allow promotion through the ranks in the internal labour market of the firm (Myles, 1984).

SOCIAL SCIENCE MODELS OF THE WORKING LIFECOURSE

Almost half a century ago, when the image may well have corresponded more closely to the reality of the institutionalized lifecourse, Leonard Cain described the lifecourse as having three major stages: 'during the lifecourse an individual experiences his personal division of labour, including minimally a "preparation for work" stage, a "breadwinner" stage, and a "retirement" stage' (Cain, 1964: 298). Kohli (1986: 72) subsequently described the institutionalization of the lifecourse as 'periods of preparation, "activity", and retirement'.

As the social institution of retirement consolidated following the Second World War, it did so largely in terms of men. In the United States, as late as the 1970s, few married older women experienced retirement in their own right (Hardy, 2002). The tripartite division of the lifecourse has been much criticized as a male-based model that failed to recognize the complexity of work for men and women, but it is important for two reasons. First, much of public policy concerning the lifecourse is predicated on the assumption that this simple lifecourse is normatively experienced. For example, pension entitlements in retirement are predicated to a great extent on stable labour force participation over the working years. Thus, departures from it are a cause of concern, and increasingly so as the model fails to describe contemporary realities of the lifecourse (Riley et al., 1994). Second, the tripartite framework serves as a reference point to see more clearly the complexity and variability of the working lifecourse, and to examine policy initiatives that can lead to changes in the structure of the lifecourse (Marshall et al., 2001).

Recently, scholars have argued that the lifecourse has become increasingly individualized and less structured than described by this rigid tripartite model. Large proportions of people in the developed world (with the continued exception of Japan, though some changes can be observed here) follow more individualized lifecourse trajectories with numerous job changes instead of a single 'career job', and they experience a pre-retirement transition characterized by bridge jobs, part-time work, perhaps education and retraining, and finally full retirement in the form of a permanent exit from the labour force (i.e., neither employed nor seeking work). Transitions in the latter part of the working lifecourse are less and less tied to formal government-set pension levels, and 'early exit' now often occurs prior to receipt of a full retirement pension from the state (Guillemard, 1997; Schmähl, 1989; Marshall and Mueller, 2002), while the transition to retirement is 'blurred' (Mutchler et al., 1997).

DEPARTURES FROM THE STANDARDIZED LIFECOURSE

The timing of exit from paid employment is influenced by several factors (Taylor et al., 2000). Most people wish to retire prior to state-mandated pensionable ages, provided they can afford to do so. Smaller proportions voluntarily elect to work for pay past the state pension age, and some do so from economic need. Some people exit paid employment involuntarily due to declining health or, less often, through job loss and the inability to find subsequent employment.

Since the 1970s economic and structural changes have had a major effect on the nature of employment. The decline of traditional industries such as manufacturing, mining and construction, coupled with the growth of the service sector, particularly those parts that apply new information and communication technologies, has led to a demand for entirely different skills and abilities. In the public sector, the privatization of public utilities, the tightening of public expenditure and 'value for money' approaches such as 'market testing', and, in the private sector, globalization of markets and intensive competition between domestic and overseas producers, have often led to workforce reduction, delayering of organizational hierarchies, and outsourcing of functions. These trends have had a disproportionate impact on older workers.

Governments can influence the timing of retirement by increasing or decreasing the adequacy of pension benefits, by changing the rules and discount rates concerning eligibility to receive pensions early or late, by allowing use of disability pensions as a vehicle to bridge between work and the retirement pension, and so forth. Broadly based economic policies can also influence retirement timing. Thus, the economic downturn in the US and British economies in the first three years of the current century severely reduced the anticipated retirement benefits from stocks, and led many people to delay retirement plans (Eschtruth and Gemus, 2002).

Corporations can influence exit from paid employment in a number of ways, including the nature of the retirement benefits they offer. In many countries there has been a movement away from defined benefit pensions (which encourage life-time employment and tie the individual to the firm) to defined contribution pensions, which rest with the individual alone, increase portability, and do not provide extra rewards for long service (Taylor *et al.*, 2000). Corporate behaviour has also had an impact on later life participation in paid employment because of corporate downsizing and associated layoffs. Research evidence on the impact of corporate downsizing on career stability is far from definitive, but a careful weighing of American evidence suggests that it has been associated with reductions in the proportions of people experiencing long job tenure, indexed by the percentage of employees with job durations of 8 or 10 years; and with differentiation by type of occupation and by gender (Carre *et al.*, 2000; Neumark, 2000).

Useem (1994) notes that older workers are concentrated more heavily in industrial sectors that experience certain forms of restructuring. In a study of 406 large American companies, those with older workforces were more likely to be located in manufacturing, very large companies, and twice as likely to have collective bargaining. These are all factors that can protect the older worker from the trend towards increased job instability. Yet it is precisely these types of companies that have been the most extensively restructured in the US (and probably other industrialized nations). Companies with higher proportions of workers aged 50 or older were more likely to have sold off business units, had large-scale layoffs, reduced management staff, offered early retirement, or imposed hiring freezes. Companies with younger work forces were more likely to be shutting down operations, merging units, or shifting full-time workers to part-time employment. Survey data show that early retirement was an increasingly important means that companies used to avoid simply laying off workers, whereas there were declines in the percentage of companies using hiring freezes, salary reductions, or voluntary separations to avoid layoffs (Useem, 1994).

While young workers are strongly affected by restructuring-related job loss, especially if they are in non-unionized settings that offer seniority protection, since the 1980s workers over 50 have been particularly disadvantaged (Bernhardt and Marcotte, 2000; Neumark, 2000). Having initiated their working lifecourses during a period when they might have expected to experience something close to the standardized tri-partite lifecourse, with its stable work history, predictable retirement age, and

retirement benefits, older workers may be experiencing greater difficulties with instability in the retirement transition than we might expect from younger cohorts who have not anticipated such lifecourse stability. As noted earlier, the alleged stability of the standardized lifecourse was in many respects mythological, realized primarily by males in middle-class, professional and managerial careers, and rarely by women and the working classes. Nevertheless, in the industrialized welfare states, pension systems have been organized around this model of lifecourse stability. In the past decade or so, public policy in most developed societies has been moving to disconnect later life income security from this model of the stable lifecourse.

CORPORATE BEHAVIOUR, ATTITUDES TOWARDS OLDER WORKERS, AND AGE DISCRIMINATION

Research points to widespread age discrimination in internal labour markets (Arrowsmith and McGoldrick, 1996a; Hayward *et al.*, 1997; Itzin and Phillipson, 1993; Taylor and Walker, 1994). For example, a national survey of personnel managers in the UK carried out in 1997 (Hayward *et al.*, 1997) found that older workers were regarded as being difficult to train (30%), unable to adapt to new technologies (34%) and as being too cautious (36%). At the same time, they were thought to be more reliable than younger workers (79%), as being productive employees (83%) and offering a good return on investment (84%). Similarly, research among a nationally representative sample of British employers undertaken between 1999 and 2000 (Goldstone and Jones, 2001) found that while older workers were thought to be more experienced, stable and mature, they were also thought to be slower to learn and more prone to ill-health. These findings echo those for Canada summarized in Marshall (2001).

French data for 1992 show that, regarding the perceived effects of workforce ageing, among organizations with 500 or more employees (Guillemard, Taylor and Walker 1996), 27% saw increased resistance to change as being a certainty, while 48% cent thought that this might perhaps be the case. One-fifth (22%) of respondents saw little enthusiasm for new technology as being a certainty while

48% thought that this might be the case. Also, one-fifth (21%) felt that blockages to the careers of younger workers would also occur, while 35% felt that perhaps they might occur. However, while 12% of respondents felt that workforce ageing would lead to a drop in productivity and 30% thought that this might occur, almost as many respondents (10%) were certain that a drop in productivity would not occur and 43% did not think it would occur.

Another British survey (Arrowsmith and McGoldrick, 1996b), of a major retailer, found that characteristics of a 'qualitative' or motivational nature (e.g., service, pride in job, cheerfulness, reliability) were more likely to be ascribed to older workers, whereas 'quantitative' characteristics (e.g., fast pace, trainability, handling new technology) tended to be ascribed to younger workers. This research also found that managers considered older workers to be suitable recruits, except for jobs requiring considerable investment in training or highly physical in nature. Older workers were thought to be more suitable for customer contact type roles requiring 'maturity', 'reliability' and 'conscientiousness' (e.g., service counters, packing at checkouts, replenishment) whereas younger workers were felt to be more suited to physically demanding tasks. Even though older workers' recruitment potential was recognized, traditional sources of labour, e.g. younger people, were viewed by management as the primary source when future recruitment needs were considered.

Despite the incidence of age related stereotypes among employers, their importance in influencing company policies and practices and in determining the experiences of older workers is unclear. One view (Farr et al., 1999) is that company policies are determined by norms and representations of age and stereotypes concerning younger and older workers. A related view is that attitudes and assumptions held by senior and middle managers towards older workers – as well as those of their colleagues and peers – are important in determining whether and how policies and practices are implemented (Itzin and Phillipson, 1993). An alternative view is that age 'is rarely explicitly considered by corporate management or by unions' (Marshall, 1998: 200) and that 'Corporate policies and programs have differential effects on older and younger workers, but these are largely what sociologists call "unintended

consequences"' (Marshall, 1998: 202). It has been argued that the early termination of the employment contracts of older workers is generally not the result of negative attitudes towards older workers per se, but comes from staffing calculation methods, a desire to maintain harmonious industrial relations, and the opportunity to use public or private sector early retirement mechanisms (Jolivet, 2000). It has also been argued that enterprises choose the exit of older workers more because of their economic difficulties than because of negative attitudes towards this group (Le Minez, 1995).

Several studies have investigated barriers to older workers' employment. A survey of employers (Hayward et al., 1997) found that the greatest deterrent to recruiting older workers was a low return on training investment, cited by 65% of employers questioned. Employers were also concerned about the perceived lack of appropriate skills (50%) and qualifications (46%) among older workers.

These findings of employer surveys should be treated with considerable caution. First, who was responding to the survey should be considered. There is an over-representation in such surveys of those responsible for human resource matters. Given the considerable coverage of age issues in the specialist personnel press over the last decade, awareness of age and employment issues would likely have increased among HR professionals. However, this is less likely to be so among other types of manager and supervisor. Second, there is the issue of whether the survey respondent was commenting on company *practices* or merely reporting *policies*.

THE PRACTICE OF AGE DISCRIMINATION

So far this review has concentrated on the attitudes and policies of employers. We turn now to the actual practice of age discrimination, as it is manifested in different facets of employment: recruitment and selection, performance appraisal, and training and development.

Recruitment and selection

Selectors make use of both actual information concerning applicants and that gleaned from person stereotypes based on age or other factors (Perry *et al.*, 1996). Some occupations are perceived as being mainly populated by younger people and others by older people and selectors think that such jobs can be distinguished in terms of their characteristics; e.g., 'younger' jobs are considered more likely to draw upon cognitive resources while 'older' jobs are more likely to be associated with wisdom and independence (Gordon and Arvey, 1986).

Age-related norms govern positions in organizations, but individuals who violate such norms do not automatically receive negative evaluations. Subordinate ratings by managers have been found to be lower when subordinates were older than the normative age for their career level whereas the opposite was the case when the subordinate was younger. Workers younger than the normative age for their career level were seen as on the 'fast track' whereas older workers were seen as being behind schedule (Perry *et al.*, 1996).

Job performance and performance appraisal

A large body of evidence concerning the relationship between age and job performance suggests that these variables are largely unrelated or in fact that there may be a positive relationship between them (for example, see Baugher, 1978; McEvoy and Cascio, 1989; Waldman and Avolio, 1986; Warr, 1993). However, there are difficulties in interpreting the various research studies because of methodological differences and weaknesses (Hansson *et al.*, 1997; Sterns and Miklos, 1995; Warr, 1992).

Research has also focused on the effect of age on job performance evaluations. A review of the literature (Ferris and King, 1992) concludes that there is an inverse relationship between age and job performance evaluations. When objective measures of productivity are employed, performance increases with age. However, when supervisor ratings are employed, a negative relationship is observed (Waldman and Avolio, 1986). This appears to 'highlight the ambiguous and highly subjective nature of ratings, and characterizes this process as one which provides ample opportunity for non-job-related factors to influence the evaluations' (Ferris and King, 1992; see also Liden *et al.*, 1996).

Training and learning

The British Labour Force Survey provides evidence that the key factor constraining older workers' training activities was a lack of opportunities provided by employers rather than disinterest among such workers (Taylor and Urwin, 2001). Nevertheless, there may be factors in addition to employer behaviour that reduce older workers' training activity. A study of, mainly male, manufacturing workers' participation in development activities (Warr and Birdi, 1998) found that:

- older employees were substantially less active
- education level, learning motivation and learning confidence, as well as lower age, were predictive of participation
- support from managers, co-workers and non-work sources were positively correlated with activity, while time constraints had a negative association
- controlling for other factors, age had a negative impact on activity.

RECENT POLICY SHIFTS

It has been argued by some that effects of population ageing will be to bring Social Security and health systems to the point of crisis in the near future (for example, Jackson, 2002), but this position has been rejected by other commentators who have argued, for example, 'against demographic determinism, a tendency to rely excessively on a very poor indicator, the "dependency ratio", and the crisis mentality it engenders' (Marshall, 2002; see also Working Group on the Implications of Demographic Change, 2002).

Nonetheless, the anticipated effects of the ageing of the populations of the Japanese and European economies where the effects will be felt most keenly (Auer and Fortuny, 1999) are encouraging the development of policies in the areas of health, social welfare, employment and pensions (Taylor, 2002). In Europe, in particular, where the emphasis had previously been on early retirement, a new policy consensus is emerging around the notion of 'active ageing'. European Union Member States are now committed to an employment rate of 50 per cent among older workers by 2010. Currently, only Sweden, Denmark, Portugal and the UK exceed this level and the European Union average is below 40 per cent (European Commission, Directorate – General (DG) for Economics and Social Affairs, 2001). The European Commission has set out its vision for realizing this with the following list of requirements:

- Improving the skills, motivation and mobility of older workers
- Good practice in lifelong learning is promoted and disseminated
- Adapting workplaces to workforce ageing
- Facilitating access to more suitable and flexible forms of working for ageing workers
- Removing age-discriminatory attitudes and practices. (Employment and Social Affairs, European Commission 1999: 5)

Added to this is the view that 'Successful active ageing policies involve all generations. All actors (government, firms and workers) need to adopt life-cycle strategies enabling workers of all ages to stay longer in employment' (Employment and Social Affairs, European Commission, 1999: 5). Also, Walker (1999) points to the need for a multidimensional strategy where policymakers adopt holistic and 'joined-up' approaches.

A step in the realization of these objectives is the European Union Directive for Equal Treatment in Employment, which was agreed in 2000 for implementation before December 2006. This commits Member States to outlaw age discrimination in employment. Many European countries are already implementing policies aimed at reducing age discrimination in the labour market, encouraging the recruitment of older workers, delaying early exit, encouraging the sharing of best practice among employers or helping older workers seeking guidance or training. However, the European Commission (2001) in a report to the Stockholm European Council notes that:

For older workers, despite various policy initiatives by the Member States . . . there is little evidence that these have resulted in significant increases in labour market participation among older workers. To a large extent this reflects a deep-rooted early retirement culture and the persistence of early retirement schemes (often coexisting with schemes aiming at extending older workers' working life) and negative attitudes which remain not only among employers but also trade unions and policymakers.

With the exception of Japan, which has a long history of policy making aimed at extending working life (Taylor *et al.*, 2002), among other developed countries outside the European Union there is less explicit policy involvement to alter the situation of older workers or the timing of retirement. In Canada, interest in these related areas has sparked in the past five years among academics, policy think tanks and senior government bureaucrats (Marshall and Mueller, 2002), and Canada's largest province, Ontario, now proposes joining the three existing provinces (of ten) to abolish mandatory retirement. In the United States, the age of eligibility for Social Security benefits began to rise gradually, from age 65, in 2003 (under legislation passed two decades earlier!). Rix (2001: 388) has noted that 'there is little sense of urgency in the United States about issues related to older workers', and that 'Public policymakers in the United States have yet to address in any systematic way the employment implications of an ageing America or to assess the role that public policy might play in expanding employment opportunities for, or enhancing the productivity of, older workers. Nor do these issues seem to have generated much attention in the private sector' (Rix 2001: 376). We believe, however, that as North America, Australasia and other developed nations come to experience the stronger demographic pressures that have motivated policy change in the European Union, we can expect substantial restructuring of the work situation for older workers, and their transition to retirement.

FURTHER READING

Burdetti, P. P., Burkhauser, R. V., Gregory, J. M., and H. A. Hunt, eds. (2001). *Ensuring health and income security for an ageing workforce*. Kalamazoo, Mich.: W. W. Upjohn Institute for Employment Research.

Guillemard, A.-M. (2000). *Aging and the welfare-state crisis*. Newark and London: University of Delaware Press and Associated University Presses.

Marshall, V. W., Heinz, W. R., Krueger, H., and A. Verma, eds. (2001). *Restructuring work and the lifecourse*. Toronto, Buffalo and London: University of Toronto Press.

Taylor, P. (2002). *New policies for older workers*. Bristol: The Policy Press.

REFERENCES

Achenbaum, W. A. (1996). 'Retirement before social security'. In W. H. Crown, ed., *Handbook on employment and the elderly*. Westport, Conn.: Greenwood Press, pp. 128–43.

Arrowsmith, J., and A. McGoldrick (1996a). *Breaking the barriers: a survey of managers' attitudes to age and employment*. London: Institute of Management.

—— (1996b). 'HRM service practices: flexibility, quality and employee strategy', *International Journal of Service Industry Management*, 7 (3): 46–62.

Auer, P., and M. Fortuny (1999). *Ageing of the labour force in OECD countries: economic and social consequences*. Geneva: ILO.

Baugher, D. (1978). 'Is the older worker inherently incompetent?', *Aging and Work*, Fall (1): 242–60.

Bernhardt, A., and D. E. Marcotte (2000). 'Is "standard employment" still what it used to be?' In F. Carré, M. A. Ferber, L. Golden and S. A. Herzenberg, eds., *Nonstandard work: the nature and challenges of changing employment arrangements*. Champaign, Ill.: Industrial Relations Research Association, pp. 21–40.

Bryden, K. (1974). *Old age pensions and policy-making in Canada*. Montreal and London: McGill-Queen's University Press.

Cain, L. D., Jr (1964). 'Life course and social structure'. In R. E. L. Faris, ed., *Handbook of modern sociology*. Chicago: Rand Mcnally, pp. 272–309.

—— (1974). 'The growing importance of legal age in determining the status of the elderly', *Gerontologist*, 14 (2): 167–74.

Cappelli, P., Bassi, L., Katz, H., Knoke, D., Osterman, P., and M. Useem (1997). *Change at work*. New York and Oxford: Oxford University Press.

Carré, F., Ferber, M. A., Golden, L., and S. A. Herzenberg, eds. (2000). *Nonstandard work: the nature and challenges of changing employment arrangements*. Champaign, Ill.: Industrial Relations Research Association.

Eschtruth, A. D., and J. Gemus (2002). 'Are older workers responding to the bear market?' *Just the Facts on Retirement Issues*, 5 (Bulletin of Center for Retirement Research at Boston College, Mass.). www.bc.edu/centers/crr/jtf_5.shtml.

Employment and Social Affairs, European Commission (1999). *Active ageing. Promoting a European society for all ages*. Brussels: European Communities.

European Commission (2001). *Increasing labour force participation and promoting active ageing*. Brussels: Commission of the European Communities.

European Commission, DG for Economics and Social Affairs (2001). *European economy, 2001 broad economic guidelines*, no. 72. Brussels: Commission of the European Communities.

Farr, J. L., Tesluk, P. E., and S. R. Klein (1999). 'Organizational structure of the workplace and the older worker'. In K. W. Schaie and C. Schooler, eds., *The impact of work on older adults*. New York: Springer Publishing Company, pp. 143–85.

Ferris, G. R., and T. R. King (1992). 'The politics of age discrimination in organizations', *Journal of Business Ethics*, 11: 341–50.

Goldstone, C., and D. Jones (2001). 'Evaluation of the code of practice on age diversity in employment'. In *Age diversity: summary of research findings*. Nottingham: Department for Education and Employment, DfEE Publications.

Gordon, R. A., and R. D. Arvey (1986). 'Perceived and actual ages of workers', *Journal of Vocational Behaviour*, 28: 21–8.

Guillemard, A.-M. (1997). 'Re-writing social policy and changes within the lifecourse organisation. A European perspective', *Canadian Journal on Aging*, 16 (3): 441–64.

Guillemard, A.-M., Taylor, P., and A. Walker (1996). 'Managing an ageing workforce in Britain and France', *Geneva Papers on Risk and Insurance*, 81: 478–501.

Hansson, R. O., DeKoekkoek, P. D., Neece, W. M., and D. W. Patterson (1997). 'Successful aging at work: annual review, 1992–1996: the older worker and transitions to retirement', *Journal of Vocational Behaviour*, 51: 202–33.

Hardy, M. A. (2002). 'The transformation of retirement in twentieth-century America: from discontent to satisfaction', *Generations*, 26 (2): 9–16.

Hardy, M. A., and L. E. Hazelrigg (1999). 'Changing policies on employment and pension coverage in U.S. firms', *Ageing International*, 25 (2): 24–45.

Hardy, M. A., Hazelrigg, L., and J. Quadagno (1996). *Ending a career in the auto industry: '30 and out'*. New York and London: Plenum Press.

Hayward, B., Taylor, S., Smith, N., and G. Davies (1997). *Evaluation of the campaign for older workers*. London: HMSO.

ILO (International Labour Office) (1995). *World labour report 1995*. Geneva: International Labour Office.

Itzin, C., and C. Phillipson (1993). *Age barriers at work*. Solihull: Metropolitan Authorities Recruitment Agency.

Jackson, R. (2002). 'The global retirement crisis', *Geneva Papers on Risk and Insurance*, 27 (4): 486–511.

Jolivet, A. (2000). 'Industrial relations and the ageing workforce. A review of measures to combat age discrimination in employment: the case of France', *European Industrial Relations Observatory (EIRO), EIROnline*, October. www.eiro.eurofound.ie.

Kimura, T., and M. Oka (2001). 'Japan's current policy focus on longer employment for older people'. In V. W. Marshall, W. R. Heinz, H. Krueger and A. Verma, eds., *Restructuring work and the lifecourse*. Toronto: University of Toronto Press, pp. 348–59.

Kinsella, K., and V. A. Velkoff (2001). *An aging world: 2001*. Washington D.C.: US Dept of Health and Human Services and US Dept, of Commerce. www.census.gov/prod/2001pubs/p95-01-1.pdf.

Kohli, M. (1986). 'The world we forgot: a historical review of the life course'. In V. W. Marshall, ed., *Later life: the social psychology of aging*. Beverly Hills, Calif.: Sage, pp. 271–303.

Kohli, M., Guillemard, A.-M., and H. van Gunsteren, eds. (1991). *Time for retirement: comparative studies of early exit from the labour force*. Cambridge: Cambridge University Press.

Le Minez, S. (1995). 'Les entreprises et le vieillissement de leur personnel: faits et opinions', *Travail et Emploi*, 63: 23–39.

Liden, R. C., Stilwell, D., and G. R. Ferris (1996). 'The effects of supervisor and subordinate age on objective performance and subjective performance ratings', *Human Relations*, 49 (3): 327–47.

Marshall, V. W. (1996). *Issues of an aging workforce in a changing society: cases and comparisons*. Toronto: Institute for Human Development, Life Course and Aging, University of Toronto. (Final report of the Issues of an Aging Workforce Project.) www.aging.unc.edu/infocenter/resources/1996/cases.pdf.

(1998). 'Commentary: the older worker and organizational restructuring – beyond systems theory'. In K. Warner Schaie and Carmi Schooler, eds., *Impact of work on older adults*. New York: Springer, pp. 195–206.

(2001). 'Canadian research on older workers'. Paper presented at International Association on Gerontology conference, Vancouver. www.aging.unc.edu/infocenter/resources/2001/marshallv3.pdf.

(2002). 'Perspectives on aging, work and retirement'. Panel presentation at Gerontological Society of America Annual Meeting, Boston, Mass., November.

Marshall, V. W., and J. G. Marshall (1999). 'Age and changes in work: causes and contrasts', *Ageing International*, 25 (2): 46–68.

(2003). 'Ageing and work in Canada: firm policies', *Geneva Papers on Risk and Insurance*, 38 (4): 625–39.

Marshall, V. W., and M. M. Mueller (2002). 'Rethinking social policy for an aging workforce and society: insights from the lifecourse perspective'. Discussion Paper No. W/18, Canadian Policy Research Networks. www.cprn.org.

Marshall, V. W., Heinz, W. R., Krüger, H., and A. Verma, eds. (2001). *Restructuring work and the life course*. Toronto: University of Toronto Press.

McEvoy, G. M., and W. F. Cascio (1989). 'Cumulative evidence of the relationship between employee age and job performance', *Journal of Applied Psychology*, 74 (1): pp. 11–17.

Moore, J., Tilson, B., and G. Whitting (1994). *An international overview of employment policies and practices towards older workers*. Moorfoot, Sheffield: Research Strategy Branch, Employment Department.

Mutchler, J. E., Burr, J. A., Pienta, A. M., and M. P. Massagli (1997). 'Pathways to labor force exit: work transitions and work instability', *Journal of Gerontology: Social Sciences*, 52B (1): S4–S12.

Myles, J. (1984). *Old age in the welfare state. The political economy of public pensions*. Boston: Little, Brown.

Neumark, D. (2000). *On the job: is long-term employment a thing of the past?* New York: Russell Sage Foundation.

OECD (Organization for Economic Co-Operation and Development) (1995). *The transition from work to retirement*, OECD Social Policy Studies, No. 16. Paris: OECD.

(undated). 'Training of adult workers in OECD countries: measurement and analysis', *Employment Outlook*: 149.

Parker, S. (1982). *Work and retirement*. London: George Allen & Unwin.

Perry, E. L., Kulik, C. T., and A. C. Bourhis (1996). 'Moderating effects of personal and contextual factors in age discrimination', *Journal of Applied Psychology*, 81 (6): 628–47.

Quadagno, J., and M. Hardy (1996). 'Work and retirement'. In R. H. Binstock and L. K. George and associates, eds., *Handbook of aging and the social sciences*, 4th edn. San Diego, Calif.: Academic Press, pp. 325–45.

Quinn, J. F., Burkhauser, R. W., and D. A. Myers (1990). *Passing the torch: the influence of economic incentives on work and retirement*. Kalamazoo, Mich.: W. W. Upjohn Institute for Employment Research.

Riley, M. W., Kahn, R. L., and A. Foner, eds. (1994). *Age and structural lag. Society's failure to provide meaningful opportunities in work, family, and leisure*. New York: John Wiley and Sons, Inc.

Rix, S. E. (2001). 'Restructuring work in an aging America: what role for public policy?' In V. W. Marshall, W. Heinz, H. Krueger and A. Verma, eds., *Restructuring work and the life course*. Toronto: University of Toronto Press, pp. 375–96.

Schmähl, W. (1989). *Redefining the process of retirement: an international perspective*. New York: Springer-Verlag.

Sterns, H. L., and S. M. Miklos (1995). 'The aging worker in a changing environment: organizational and individual issues', *Journal of Vocational Behaviour*, 47: 248–68.

Taylor, P. (2002). *New policies for older workers*. Bristol: The Policy Press.

Taylor, P. (2003). 'Age and employment: the firm and the state', *The Geneva Papers on Risk and Insurance*, 28 (4, October): 553–7.

Taylor, P., and P. Urwin (2001). 'Age and participation in vocational education and training', *Work, Employment and Society*, 15 (4): 763–79.

Taylor, P., and A. Walker (1994). 'The ageing workforce: employers' attitudes towards older workers', *Work, Employment and Society*, 8 (4): 569–91.

Taylor, P., Tillsley, C., Beausoleil, J., and R. Wilson (2000). *Factors affecting retirement*. London: Department for Education and Employment.

Taylor, P., Encel, S., and M. Oka (2002). 'Older workers – trends and prospects', *Geneva Papers on Risk and Insurance*, 27 (4): 512–31.

Titmuss, R. M. (1968). *Commitment to welfare*. London: Allen and Unwin.

Useem, M. (1994). 'Business restructuring and the aging workforce'. In J. A. Auerbach and J. C. Welsh, eds., *Aging and competition: rebuilding the U.S. workforce*. Washington, D.C.: National Planning Association and National Council on the Aging, pp. 33–57.

Waldman, D. A., and B. J. Avolio (1986). 'A meta-analysis of age differences in job performance', *Journal of Applied Psychology*, 71 (1): 33–8.

Walker, A. (1999). 'The principles and potential of active ageing'. Keynote Introductory Report for The European Commission Conference on Active Ageing, Brussels, 15–16 November.

Warr, P. (1992) 'Age and employment', SAPU memo, 1290, April. Social and Applied Psychology Unit, University of Sheffield.

(1993). 'In what circumstances does job performance vary with age?' *European Work and Organizational Psychologist*, 3 (3): 237–49.

Warr, P., and K. Birdi (1998). 'Employee age and voluntary development activity', *International Journal of Training and Development*, 2 (3): 190–204.

Working Group on the Implications of Demographic Change (2002). *The challenge of longer life. Economic burden or social opportunity?* London: The Catalyst Forum.

CHAPTER 7.3

Ethical Dilemmas in Old Age Care

HARRY R. MOODY

"WHO IS SYLVIA?"

Sylvia Senex, aged 80, suffers from disabling arthritis and has been living at home with her daughter for the past six years. During this period the mother's memory problems have gotten worse and her care has become more burdensome. Mrs. Senex was given tests three years ago suggesting dementia but was never told the results. Her daughter has informed her mother that she has "a neurological problem" and told her what to expect in the future but she has refused to use the word "Alzheimer's." She says that her mother would react badly to that word and her brother, despite doubts, defers to his sister as primary caregiver. Mrs. Senex has recently started receiving home care services, but the home care agency is disturbed by the fact that she has been kept in the dark about her diagnosis. What should the agency do?

This case illustrates a series of features that are common in cases of old age care that pose ethical dilemmas:

- **Dependency**. We are confronted here with a chronic, not acute, health problem: indeed, there is more than one problem with the result that activities of daily living are limited and freedom of action is diminished (Lidz *et al.*, 1992; McCullough and Wilson, 1995; Olson *et al.*, 1995).
- **Shared responsibility**. Caregiving is provided by a family member but there is some prospect of formal care with tasks shared between formal and informal sectors, raising questions of accountability.
- **Diminished mental capacity**. There is some indication of diminished mental capacity, posing questions about the patient's ability to render informed

consent concerning major life decisions (Grisso and Applebaum, 1998).
- **Trajectory of decline**. The condition of the patient, if she does in fact have Alzheimer's, is likely to deteriorate further, raising the prospect of later difficult decisions – such as whether Mrs. Senex might belong in a nursing home.

To what extent can dominant ideas of clinical bioethics guide us about what to do in a case like this? The dominant framework of contemporary bioethics – sometimes called "principlism" – is well known (Beauchamp and Childress, 2001; DuBose *et al.*, 1994). That framework might suggest that we consider broad principles – such as autonomy, beneficence, and distributive justice – and ethical rules – such as an obligation to truth-telling – that would clarify what we ought to do. Ethics is the attempt to find good reasons for acting under conditions of uncertainty, as we see in this case involving Mrs. Senex.

How would we approach the case of Mrs. Senex if we applied the perspective of principlism? We might begin by making certain assumptions about Mrs. Senex's right to informed consent and the obligation of truth-telling by professionals and family. On the other hand, we might balance these claims of autonomy by an argument that the daughter is exercising some kind of delegated consent on behalf of a relative with diminished mental capacity. We might further invoke a principle of beneficence – maximizing the welfare and happiness involved – and consider the daughter's claim that Mrs. Senex is better off not knowing. Finally, we might adopt a perspective of casuistry and ask: is it possible that Mrs. Senex knows all she needs to know; that is, the likely future course of her condition, regardless of use of the word "Alzheimer's?" The dilemma of truth-telling then would not arise because Mrs. Senex, on this account, has in fact been told the truth in everything except the use of the word "Alzheimer's."

Yet this framework of analysis, however appealing, is unlikely to be successful in this case for the following reasons:

- **Deciding for others**. The ethics of surrogate decision making has been well analyzed in the literature of bioethics (Buchanan and Brock, 1989; Cantor, 1993). There is no indication that the daughter here is acting as a formal surrogate or proxy decision maker, even if she is treated as such by the mother and the brother. Thus, the case of Mrs. Senex is *not* like cases of termination of treatment where advanced directive documents could be helpful.
- **Divided families**. There is evidence of divided opinion between family members: the brother "has doubts" about the wisdom of the decision not to tell Mrs. Senex about her diagnosis. Lack of family consensus at least calls into question the daughter's prima facie claim of substituted judgment. How do we determine who the surrogate decision maker shall be?
- **Truth-telling**. The home care agency is about to be drawn into a web of deception – not necessarily outright lying but withholding crucial information from Mrs. Senex about her condition. The division of responsibility and authority between formal and informal caregivers remains problematic in this case and similar ambiguities arise in cases of geriatric care.
- **Distributive justice**. Caregiving responsibilities are typically not shared equitably by members of the family. Does this fact argue for greater decision making authority for the family member who gives more care? What is the relationship between distributive justice and ethical decision making? It is characteristic of ethical issues in old age care that dilemmas of distributive justice are intertwined with questions about autonomy and quality of care (Gormally, 1992). Moreover, when an elderly family member happens to control substantial financial assets and caregiving becomes an element of reciprocity in considerations of inheritance, then possibilities of

financial elder abuse also become a factor to be considered (Johnson, 1995).

- **Uncertainty**. Is it possible that no one really knows what's wrong with Mrs. Senex's memory? Tests have "suggested" Alzheimer's but confirmation is elusive. If she has dementia, is it possible that her condition could be of a curable variety? What obstacles are posed by trying to find a more definitive answer to these questions (Haley and Mangum, 1999)?
- **Institutional framework**. Old age care can be provided in different institutional settings: in a hospital, a long term care institution, a community-based setting, or within the home and family. The ethical dilemmas that arise in home care (Kane and Caplan, 1993) may be different from those that arise in other community-based settings (Holstein and Mitzen, 2001). In any case, whether the setting is home healthcare, the hospital, or the nursing home, the ethics of old age care is often an "everyday ethics" that challenges us in ways not captured by the dominant model (Kane and Caplan, 1990).

We need not dismiss the dominant framework altogether. On the contrary, there are many ethical dilemmas of old age care where the dominant model of bioethics works perfectly well and provides us with analytical tools that can help in decision making. For example, a substantial literature on end-of-life choices helps us approach questions related to passive euthanasia ("allowing to die"), assisted suicide, quality of life, and decisions that must be made after a patient has lost mental capacity: for example, in a coma or in final stages of Alzheimer's (Dworkin *et al.*, 1998). The analysis of end-of-life decisions can be applied to decision making in old age care. Indeed, one might argue that old age, as such, presents nothing new here, or at least nothing that the dominant model cannot handle (Wicclair, 1993). Of course, decisions and justifications remain disputable and consensus may be hard to reach. But the categories of the dispute, one might say, remain the same.

The case of Mrs. Senex suggests that this optimistic conclusion is unwarranted. The case of Mrs. Senex is typical, like other dilemmas of old age care which present us with what some commentators might call a "blurred genre": that is, phenomena that cut across conventional boundaries – for example, medical care vs. social care, formal organizations vs. family relationships, mental competency vs.

incompetency, and so on (Geertz, 2000). It is hard to draw clean lines in such cases, harder still to apply rules and principles in any definitive way. Like geriatric medicine itself, geriatric ethics persistently crosses boundaries and demands a "multitasking" approach to ethical analysis, much different from the clean lines invoked by a rules-and-principles approach.

Is there any other feature of old age care that must be added to this portrait of ambiguity? I believe there is and it is implicit in the fact that in the case above Mrs. Senex is 80 years old. Old age care, by definition, is care arising at the end of a "natural" life-course, when there are few years ahead and many years behind. At either the clinical level or the policy level, we may wonder if this fact should entail a different perspective on ethical decisions? Recent debates about rationing healthcare on grounds of age have made this question more prominent (see Ter Meulen, Chapter 7.12 in this *Handbook*; and also Moody, 1992). Whatever we may think about the daughter's pattern of withholding the full truth from Mrs. Senex, that pattern is likely the result of a lifetime of family communication style. The ethical dilemmas of old age care, then, should never be viewed in *cross-sectional* perspective: that is, at a single point in time. Instead, we should adopt, at least implicitly, a *longitudinal perspective*, seeing the question of the moment in a longer time perspective.

Are there ethical models or methods of analysis that might better illuminate the case of Mrs. Senex? There are indeed and they have often been presented as alternatives to an ethics of rules and principles. Here we suggest a few of these approaches that help us look upon the case of Mrs. Senex in a different light.

Virtue ethics. Since the publication of *After virtue* (1981) by Alasdair MacIntyre, there has been a widespread revival of interest in ethics inspired by the ideas of Aristotle. Central to this approach is the primacy of virtue and individual character in considering problems of applied ethics. The question becomes less about *action* than about the *agent*. In the case of Mrs. Senex, the perspective of virtue ethics might raise questions about the daughter's character and intentions in choosing not to use the word "Alzheimer's" with her mother. Quality of life would be considered not only for the individual patient but for the family unit as a whole. Lastly,

there is a question of what we might call organizational virtue: what sort of organization does the home care agency become if it becomes a party to a conspiracy of silence? Whether for organizations, or professionals, or family members, there needs to be more attention to the "tyranny of small decisions": that is, the result of habits that cumulatively shape the quality and character of our lives.

Feminist ethics. Since the work of Carol Gilligan, ethicists inspired by feminism have drawn attention to elements overlooked in the mainstream models of ethics: in particular, the importance of relationships and the role of caregiving, which is a major dimension of geriatric healthcare. If only because of the primacy of caregiving in old age care, feminism is likely to have important contributions to make to ethics and ageing (Walker, 1999). For example, there is a difference, one might say, between the "ethics of intimacy" (e.g., duties that arise among family members) and the "ethics of strangers" (e.g., duties that arise in formal settings like an emergency room). In the case of Sylvia Senex, what we have is a clash between two different frames of thinking: a style of truth-telling acceptable in a family setting may not be acceptable to a formal agency like the home care service provider. A feminist approach to home care ethics would yield very different conclusions than one based on principlism (Parks, 2003). At the very least, the caregiving relationship between Mrs. Senex and her daughter demands greater legitimacy than might be given by a purely abstract analysis of rules and principles.

Narrative ethics. Narrative ethics is a perspective that insists on the priority of stories over principles in our effort to understand ethical dilemmas (Charon and Montello, 2002). But what exactly is a story or a narrative? The case of "Who Is Sylvia?" is, admittedly, a mini-case: very short on details. But even if we had lengthened it by five or ten times, it is likely to exhibit the same formalized style as a medical case history. The "voice" of the narrative is detached and impersonal; the patient and other characters in the story are rendered chiefly in terms of their immediate clinical or diagnostic significance. In short, the bioethics conversation that ensues is implicitly limited in ways that tend to submerge personal values in favor of a detached and technical tone. Finally, what we are missing in a case history, as opposed to a complex narrative, is the wider picture, the longer story of which this episode is just a small part. Even at the diagnostic level, if Sylvia Senex has Alzheimer's disease, the ethics of truth-telling might change significantly depending on what stage she was at in the course of the disease. In order to understand anything about issues of distributive justice here, we would need to know more about the history, the narrative, of Mrs. Senex in relationship to the daughter, which is a narrative that spans eight decades.

Communicative ethics. The case of "Who is Sylvia?" is prima facie a case raising questions about communication. Is it possible that Mrs. Senex and her daughter might have found a better way to communicate about her condition? Is it possible that the involvement of the home care agency could bring to the surface problems of communication that have given rise to the present impasse? One of the great organizational contributions of bioethics has been the use of ethics committees as a means of "keeping moral spaces open," in Margaret Walker's useful phrase.

In the case of "Who Is Sylvia?" as presented, we know nothing about the background of those involved, but we are unwise if we look at the present impasse in purely cross-sectional terms. Furthermore, communicative styles and practices differ significantly among members of the healthcare team (Mezey *et al.*, 2002). Habermas has defined the goal of ethical action as a condition of free and unconstrained communication among all the parties to decision making, and the touchstone could be helpful in moving Mrs. Senex and the home care agency towards some form of negotiated understanding (Moody, 1992).

Virtue ethics, feminist ethics, narrative ethics, and communicative ethics can all contribute valuable insights that could help us choose the wisest course of action for the home care agency and the family of Mrs. Senex. Further, this brief account of "alternatives to principlism" in ethics has the advantage of illuminating ethical issues in old age care easily overlooked by methods that unduly emphasize abstract or general conditions of analysis (e.g., Kantian ethics, Utilitarianism, etc.).

However, in contrast to the "rules and principles" perspective, these alternatives suffer from a common defect: namely, they too easily become a variety of merely "process ethics" with all its attendant dangers of relativism. Will a mere process yield any definitive conclusions? If "relationships," or "narratives," or "better communication" are the key to ethical action in old age care, then we may be given insight into cases, stories, and individual differences. But are we not, at the same time, likely to be deprived of any broader or deeper vantage point allowing us to justify (or condemn) particular practices in families, long term care institutions, or other settings where health and social services are provided? The great strength of ethical perspectives coming from the Enlightenment is their common rationalism and empiricism: that is, the capacity to appeal to standards by which we can appraise conduct or policy.

When we turn to differences between cultures or nations, the problem of relativism becomes more pronounced and inescapable. For example, should we refrain from telling the truth about a diagnosis to an elderly individual from East Asia because in that context truth-telling is culturally unacceptable (Moody, 1998)? Do we appeal for tolerance and respect for multicultural differences, or to universal standards of human rights (Braun *et al.*, 2000)? If we believe that failing to provide some decent minimum healthcare to individuals is a sign of unjustifiable discrimination ("ageism"), then can our ideas of the social contract somehow justify such provision of long term care (Nussbaum, 2002)? In a twenty-first-century environment of globalism, these questions about universal human rights and national policies on health care and ageing will become inescapable (Weisstub *et al.*, 2001).

Bioethics, in the last third of the twentieth century, arose under historical and institutional conditions that shaped its discourse and outlook (Jonsen, 1998). Bioethics was largely shaped and dominated in the USA, in a culture characterized by belief in individual autonomy, the pervasive influence of law and legal rules, and expanding medical technology, accompanied by an emphasis on curing rather than caring. By contrast, other countries have been much more open to acknowledging the importance of solidarity as opposed to autonomy as a fundamental principle of ethics (Ter Meulen *et al.*, 2001).

During the 1990s, there was a dramatic expansion of the literature of ethics and ageing, which took much greater account of the distinctive problems of old age care. That intellectual movement is likely to intensify still further in the first decade of the twenty-first century, as all countries become more aware of population ageing and the changes that will be necessary in health and social service systems to deal with older people. The result, we would argue, will not be simply the application of well-developed methods of bioethics to ageing, but a deeper analysis of the "blurred genre" evident in the case of Mrs. Senex. A more thorough-going analysis would combine contributions from sociology and psychology, along with hermeneutical perspectives from literature, history, and philosophy. A comprehensive approach to the ethics of old age care, therefore, will entail a widening of our interdisciplinary perspective along the lines offered by other contributions in the present handbook.

FURTHER READING

Kane, R., and A. Caplan, eds. (1990). *Everyday ethics: resolving dilemmas in nursing home life*. New York: Springer.

Mezey, M., Cassel, C., Bottreell, M., Hyer, K., Howe, J., and T. Fulmer (2002). *Ethical patient care: a casebook for geriatric health care teams*. Baltimore: Johns Hopkins University Press.

Moody, H. R. (1992). *Ethics in an aging society*. Baltimore: Johns Hopkins University Press.

Parks, J. (2003). *No place like home: feminist ethics and home health care*. Bloomington: Indiana University Press.

REFERENCES

Beauchamp, T. L., and J. F. Childress (2001). *Principles of biomedical ethics*, 5th edn. Oxford: Oxford University Press.

Braun, K., Pietsch, J. H., and P. L. Blanchette (2000). *Cultural issues in end-of-life decision making*. Thousand Oaks, Calif.: Sage Publications.

Buchanan, A., and D. W. Brock (1989). *Deciding for others: the ethics of surrogate decision making*. Cambridge: Cambridge University Press.

Cantor, N. L. (1993). *Advance directives and the pursuit of death with dignity*. Bloomington, Ind.: Indiana University Press.

Charon, R., and M. Montello (2002). *Stories matter: the role of narrative in medical ethics*. London: Routledge.

DuBose, E. R., Hamel, R. P., and L. J. O'Connell, eds. (1994). *A matter of principles? Ferment in U.S. bioethics*. Harrisburg, Penn.: Trinity Press International.

Dworkin, G., Frey, R. G., and S. Bok (1998). *Euthanasia and physician-assisted suicide: for and against*. Cambridge: Cambridge University Press.

Geertz, C. (2000). *Local knowledge: further essays in interpretive anthropology*. New York: Basic Books.

Gormally, L., ed. (1992). *Dependent elderly: autonomy, justice and quality of care*. Cambridge: Cambridge University Press.

Grisso, T., and P. S. Applebaum (1998). *Assessing competence to consent to treatment: a guide for physicians and other health professionals*. Oxford: Oxford University Press.

Haley, W. E., and W. P. Mangum (1999). "Ethical issues in geriatric assessment." In P. A. Lichtenberg, ed., *Handbook of assessment in clinical gerontology*. New York: John Wiley, pp. 606–26.

Holstein, M., and P. Mitzen, eds. (2001). *Ethics in community-based elder care*. New York: Springer.

Johnson, T. F. (1995). *Elder mistreatment: ethical issues, dilemmas, and decisions*. New York: The Haworth Pastoral Press.

Jonsen, A. R. (1998). *The birth of bioethics*. New York: Oxford University Press.

Kane, R. and A. Caplan, eds. (1990). *Everyday ethics resolving dilemmas in nursing home life*. New York: Springer.

eds. (1993). *Ethical conflicts in the management of home care: the case manager's dilemma*. New York: Springer.

Lidz, C. W., Fischer, L., and R. M. Arnold (1992). *The erosion of autonomy in long-term care*. New York: Oxford University Press.

MacIntyre, A. (1981). *After virtue: a study in moral theory*. London: Duckworth.

McCullough, L. B., and N. L. Wilson, eds. (1995). *Long-term care decisions: ethical and conceptual dimensions*. Baltimore, Md.: Johns Hopkins University Press.

Mezey, M., Cassel, C., Bottreell, M., Hyer, K., Howe, J., and T. Fulmer (2002). *Ethical patient care: a casebook for geriatric health care teams*. Baltimore, Md.: Johns Hopkins University Press.

Moody, H. (1992). *Ethics in an aging society*. Baltimore, Md.: Johns Hopkins University Press.

(1998). "Cross-cultural geriatric ethics: negotiating our differences," *Generations*, 22 (3): 32–9.

Nussbaum, M. (2002). "Long-term care and social justice: a challenge to conventional ideas of the social contract" [including replies by Norman Daniels and others]. In *Ethical choices in long-term care: what does justice require?* Geneva: World Health Organization. Available at www.who.int/chronic_conditions/ethical_choices.pdf.

Olson, E., Chichin, E., and L. S. Libow, eds. (1995). *Controversies in ethics in long-term care*. New York: Springer.

Parks, J. (2003). *No place like home? Feminist ethics and home health care*. Bloomington: Indiana University Press.

Ter Meulen, R. H. J., Arts, W., and R. Muffels, eds. (2001). *Solidarity in health and social care in Europe*. Dordrecht, Netherlands: Kluwer Academic Publishers.

Walker, M. U., ed. (1999). *Mother time: women, aging, and ethics*. Lanham, Md.: Rowman and Littlefield Publishers.

Weisstub, D. N., Thomasma, D. C., Gauthier, S., and G. F. Tomossy, eds. (2001). *Aging: caring for our elders*. Dordrecht, Netherlands: Kluwer Academic Publishers.

Wicclair, M. R. (1993). *Ethics and the elderly*. New York: Oxford University Press.

Wealth, Health, and Ageing: The Multiple Modern Complexities of Financial Gerontology

NEAL E. CUTLER

INTRODUCTION

Financial gerontology is the emerging field of inquiry that is attempting to build bridges between gerontology and finance, in both research and practice (Cutler *et al.*, 1992). As with most bridges, financial gerontology stretches in both directions – examining the impact of ageing on financial choices and planning, while also examining the impact of financial opportunities and constraints on both population ageing and individual ageing. Given the complexity of modern societies, the intersection of ageing and finance not only suggests new issues for both research and practice, but provides a lens through which the key contemporary conflicts in many societies can be viewed. This chapter offers a selective assessment of financial gerontological complexity, using examples from the general domains of wealth and health.

While our examples are drawn primarily from experience and data in the United States, the underlying gerontological and demographic dynamics are found in many economically developed countries. Similar patterns of population ageing (including middle ageing) can be seen, for example, in the United States, the United Kingdom, Australia, Hong Kong, and Japan, as illustrated in Figure 1. The general pattern is a steady increase in the percentage of "old" persons (defined here as age 65 and older) in the national population, and a noticeable upward slope in the percentages of middle-agers starting around the years 2000–5.

While analysis of the demographic history of each country's population ageing is outside the scope of this chapter, the economic implications are generally parallel as each society and economy responds to the financial effects of ageing at both the macro-societal-economic and the micro-individual-decision-making levels of analysis. As Schulz *et al.* suggest, even in countries as historically and culturally different as Australia, Japan, and the United States, the challenges and the responses that link ageing to both micro-economic and macro-economic behavior have many characteristics in common (Schulz *et al.*, 1991). Against this background, this chapter examines two dimensions of complexity:

- wealth – the complexity of the twenty-first-century "wealth span."
- health – the complex interaction of health, finance, work, and retirement.

WEALTH COMPLEXITY

The impact of population ageing and individual ageing on personal and family financial decisions can be seen by way of historical changes in the wealth span. The wealth span is a heuristic model developed to illustrate two fundamental sets of changes in how individuals (as workers, consumers, savers, investors, spenders) make financial decisions (Cutler, 2002a). One set of changes focuses on the relative *balance* in the number of years between the *accumulation stage* and the *expenditure stage* of a person's wealth span. The second set of changes focuses on the increasing *complexity* of the twenty-first-century wealth span.

A. United Kingdom

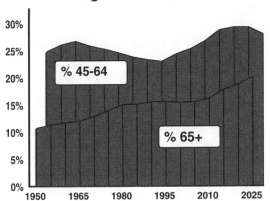

B. United States

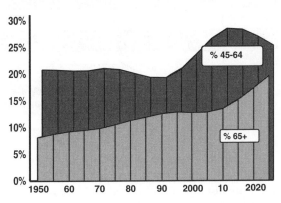

C. Australia

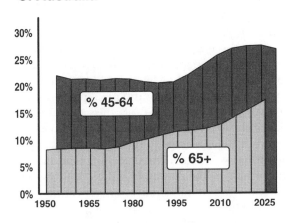

D. Hong Kong

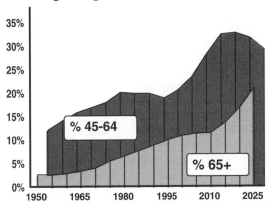

E. Japan

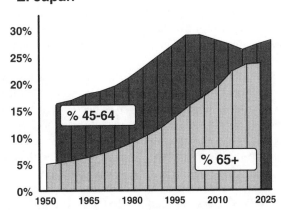

Figure 1. Cross-national comparative data showing population ageing trends.

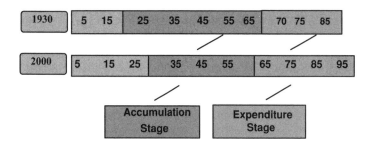

Figure 2. The wealth span in the twenty-first century.

The wealth span is graphically illustrated in Figure 2. The specific years in the model, 1930 and 2000, are not especially important. More important are the changes from "back then" to "nowadays." In this purposely simplified model of reality, we recognize that expenditures do take place in the accumulation stage, and that savings and investing continue to take place in the expenditure stage. We use these two stages primarily to focus attention on key historical changes.

Changes in Balance

The change in the relative number of years comprising each of the two stages is especially critical for financial decision making. "Back then" (c. 1930 or so), accumulation typically started when people were in their teens or early twenties, and continued to their mid-60s, symbolized by the age 65, the age of eligibility for full benefits in the US Social Security system. Nowadays (c. 2000, symbolically), however, accumulation is typically delayed as we stay in school longer. The accumulation stage ends earlier due to patterns of earlier retirement, substantially earlier than age 65 for most workers. So, nowadays, the accumulation stage (starts later, ends earlier) is noticeably shorter than it used to be.

The older, expenditure side of the wealth span model has also undergone change. Back then the expenditure stage formally started around age 65, and lasted until the mid-80s or so. Nowadays, the expenditure stage is longer: it starts earlier (early retirement), and due to increasing life expectancy it lasts longer.

The implications of this change in balance in the number of years between the two stages are manifest: compared to back then, workers (consumers, investors, etc.) nowadays have relatively fewer years to accumulate, with the critical outcome that *the wealth which is thereby accumulated must last for a longer expenditure period.*

Changes in Complexity

This change in the balance of years, however, is trumped by a second set of changes, changes in the *complexity* of the modern wealth span. For example, the biggest of these emerging complexities involves the transformation of pension systems from employer-paid (defined benefit) systems to employee-paid (defined contribution) plans (Cutler, 1996a). The implications of this fundamental change are psychological as well as micro and macro financial. Psychologically, the change focuses on the critically increased need for financial literacy on the part of the consumer. Aside from the several fiscal and administrative differences between the two kinds of pensions, the change from traditional defined benefit to defined contribution pensions is summarized by the answer to one simple question: who is responsible for the future value of my pension? It is a change from *they are* to *I am* – which in turn signals the need for substantial personal financial literacy.

Although many of the specific data examples in this chapter use the experience of the United States as a case study, the need for greater financial literacy has been identified throughout the economically developed world. In the US, research indicates that relatively low levels of financial literacy are associated not only with pension issues, but also with basic understandings of the financing of older age healthcare and long term care (Cutler, 1997; see also ASEC, 2004). In the United Kingdom, a *Report to the Secretary of State for Education and Employment* noted that, while financial education was once thought to be an issue primarily for lower-income persons, nowadays "it is a mistake to believe that only those on low incomes or in disadvantaged areas need financial literacy" (Department for Education and Skills (UK), Adult Financial Literacy Advisory Group, 2000: 17). Further, the OECD Financial Education Project highlights the need for increased financial literacy on a global level, noting that changes in pension schemes around the world are moving in multiple directions. For example, where Germany and Ireland encourage voluntary participation, "countries in Eastern Europe and in Latin America have introduced mandatory defined contribution plans" (Smith, 2003: slide 7).

Another modern complexity is linked to increased rates of female labor force participation, with the consequence of substantially greater numbers of two-worker families. In the context of pensions and related financial gerontological issues, these two-worker families can be called *DIPPIES* – "Double Income, Plural Pensions" – a phrase coined in the 1980s by Professor Richard Rose of Strathclyde University. While they are working, both members of the couple are earning not only Double Income, but also credits towards their future Plural Pensions as well. Their financial profile is not only *double* because there are two people earning, but *plural* because workers are, nowadays, likely to have more than one kind of pension accumulation.

Thus, in the United States, for example, the couple is accumulating: two Social Security pensions, two employer pensions, maybe two additional voluntary supplementary retirement accounts, other investments, and home ownership equity. The issue here is not that such a couple is necessarily rich. Rather, the DIPPIES profile emphasizes the *complexity* of contemporary family finance, and in particular how such complexity interacts with financial planning, retirement, and ageing.

To Retire or Not to Retire: An Additional Complexity

The traditional milestone event separating the accumulation stage from the expenditure stage is retirement. In the US, retirement is symbolically linked to age 65 which, since 1935, is the "retirement age" included in the public Social Security pension system. To be both more precise and more officially accurate, age 65 is not a *retirement age* but is the age of full pension benefits eligibility in the US Social Security system. Under current law, a person can collect pension benefits and continue to receive employment income. Thus, whether or not a person retires from his or her job is a different story – and, nowadays, a more complex story.[1]

A few years ago a student expressed exasperation with American social policy, with the view that US retirement policy seemed to be "schizophrenic." On the one hand, in 1978 the US Age Discrimination in Employment Act outlawed age-based mandatory retirement in most occupations, providing the legal right to work for as long as a person prefers to or is able. On the other hand, the Social Security system allows people to retire "early" at age 62 if they are willing to take a slight reduction in their monthly pension. Other elements of US pension and tax policy – such as allowing people to start withdrawing funds from their voluntary tax-deferred retirement accounts as early as age $59\frac{1}{2}$ – similarly allow, or encourage, "early" retirement. As a consequence, retirement at age 62 is more typical than retirement at age 65.

The common denominator, of course, is *choice* and not schizophrenia. Social policy has given American workers a range of employment and retirement options, at least in law – although the direction and degree to which any individual can exercise these options is dependent on a range of personal, health, financial, family, and other conditions. The complexity of the retirement decision making process is well represented in a large body of qualitative and quantitative, academic and applied research (Vitt, 2003). As is documented below, however, it is the

[1] Starting in 2003, the age of full pension benefits within the US Social Security system started to rise, such that persons born in 1938 would have to be 65 years and 2 months old to receive full benefits. This rise is scheduled to be phased in gradually; each year, from 2003 to 2027, the age of full pension benefits will rise by two months, until age 67 is reached. For example, people born in 1941 will be eligible for full Social Security benefits at age 65 years and 8 months; for those born in 1956 eligibility for full benefits will come at age 66 years and 4 months; and under current law, those born in 1960 or later will be eligible for full benefits at age 67. Under current law, workers can still choose to "retire" – that is collect benefits but at a slightly reduced rate – at age 62. The official schedule of birth years and associated year of full benefits can be seen at: www.ssa.gov/retirechartred.htm.

TABLE 1. Exercising choice: retirement behavior

age of the respondent	not retired (%)	retired and working (%)	completely retired (%)
18–34	100	0	0
35–53	95	4	1
54–64	66	14	20
65–75	21	25	54

Source: NCOA, *American perceptions of aging in the 21st century* (2000), in Cutler *et al.* (2002).

TABLE 2. Sources of health insurance (1995, adults under age 65)

	%
Private – Employer	64
Private – Not Employer	7
Public	17
Uninsured	*17*
	105% [some have multiple sources]
Insured, non-public	
Private – Employer	90
Private – Not Employer	10

Source: Employee Benefit Research Institute, *EBRI Databook*, 4th edition, 1997.

pattern of behavioral outcomes of this framework of policy choice that demonstrates the increasing complexity of the multiple relationships among finance and ageing.

Table 1 is based upon *American perceptions of aging in the 21st century*, a large national survey fielded in January 2000 by the National Council on the Ageing (NCOA; Cutler *et al.*, 2002). This study measured retirement in two ways. Early in the survey a self-identification question was asked: do you consider yourself to be retired, or not? Towards the end of the interview, when the usual personal-demographic information was collected, the traditional labor force participation question was asked: are you working, retired, student, housewife, etc.?

The study then combined responses to these two questions, yielding three categories, the age distribution of which is shown in Table 1. Not surprisingly, most younger respondents were "not retired" – meaning that they said "no" to the self-identification question, and also said "working" to the labor force participation question. The more intriguing behavioral outcome of social policy choice is seen in the 65–75 age group. To be sure, over half (54%) identified themselves as retired and also responded "retired" to the labor force participation question. However, fully 25% of this traditionally retired age group is *both retired and working*: that is, they identify themselves as retired but also are still working. (Whether they *want to work* or *have to work* is a separate question, of course.)

The bottom line continues to be *complexity*. Retirement is no longer *an event* but is *a process*, and in many cases it is a multiyear and multifactor decision

process. As such it not only illustrates but symbolizes the increasing complexity of the dynamic interactions among financial and gerontological processes.

HEALTH-FINANCE COMPLEXITY

Among the many connexions between health and ageing, one of the most challenging issues for individuals, families, and societies is how to pay for increasingly expensive healthcare services and products. In the United States consumers have a mix of public and private insurance programs through which they can pay for their healthcare. Virtually all Americans aged 65 and older are part of the national, government-administered Medicare health insurance system.[2] For people under age 65, private health insurance is the typical healthcare financing mechanism. As Table 2 reports, almost all insured Americans get their health insurance through their job, although several groups of poor, unemployed, and disabled citizens receive healthcare through a variety of public healthcare and public health insurance sources – adding additional complexities to the health-finance situation (McDonnell and Fronstin, 1999).

---

[2] For readers unfamiliar with the US Medicare system, an excellent introductory source of consumer-oriented information is the official US government Medicare handbook, *Medicare and You, 2005*: www.medicare.gov/Publications/Pubs/pdf/10050.pdf. For historical background, see Marmor (2000).

"Job Lock" Complexity

Because most American workers acquire their healthcare financing through employment, choices about seeking and changing jobs are increasingly intertwined with health-related (i.e., health insurance) financial choices. As in most countries, health insurance is no longer a "fringe benefit." To illustrate: although the number of work stoppages in the United States has declined over the past ten years, most of the nationally reported labor disputes in recent years were targeted more to health insurance issues than to traditional labor–management conflicts over wages and work rules (Ackman, 2003). Consequently, the decision to change jobs is increasingly influenced more by the comparison (including eligibility) of health insurance benefits between current and potential employer, than by such traditional reasons for changing jobs as salary, location, career advancement, or other factors.

The term "job lock" describes a situation where an employee decides not to change jobs because of health insurance benefits, "a reduction in workers' willingness to quit their jobs arising from the risk of losing health coverage" (Federal Reserve Bank of San Francisco, 1998). Job lock is relevant to workers of any age, and both anecdotal and empirical evidence suggests that it is an increasingly important aspect of employment decisions (Gruber and Madrian, 2002). In the context of financial gerontology, however, job lock adds additional layers of complexity, for at least four reasons.

1. Traditionally, retirement is a more or less permanent move out of the labor force, not simply a move to another employer and another health insurance package. While Table 1 suggests that there are changing age patterns of working vs. non-working, the number of persons who are both "retired and working" could also signal a desire to keep working in order to retain health insurance.

2. Health insurance in retirement in the US is directly connected to the national Medicare system. Consider the "cohort health psychology" of today's pre-retirees. Those who are 55 to 60 years old in 2005 (born 1945 to 1950) were 15 to 20 years old when Medicare became law in 1965. Consequently, these middle-agers spent their entire accumulation-stage years presuming that there would be a national program of health insurance for them when they got to age 65. Or so it might have appeared to them three decades ago, but the situation now is more complex.

3. When Medicare was established in 1965, eligibility for benefits was set at age 65 to correspond with what then was the normal or expected Social Security full-benefits retirement age. Nowadays, most workers retire earlier than age 65, but because Medicare eligibility remains at age 65, job lock may affect the retirement decision.

4. In previous years employers often subsidized or paid for health insurance for their younger-than-age-65 retirees. In 1990 American corporate accounting rules were changed, and now require companies to integrate their estimated accumulated *future* retiree health costs into each year's *current* accounts (Financial Accounting Standards Board, 1990). Given the large and growing size of these financial obligations, many companies either scaled back their retiree health insurance benefits or ended them altogether.

Recent research suggests that job lock is beginning to be a factor in the already complex set of factors that influence retirement and financial planning. The evidence comes from the 2002 Health Confidence Survey (HCS), developed by the Employee Benefit Research Institute (Cutler, 2002b). While the main subject of this continuing survey is American attitudes towards health plans and coverage in general, several questions were included to focus on the connection between health insurance and the retirement decision. About a fifth of the national sample of 1,000 adults said they are retired, so that the survey could ask both projective and retrospective questions about factors that influence retirement decisions.

As part of the general health–finance–retirement context, the survey asked about the overall connection between health insurance and the retirement decision. Retirees were asked: when determining what age to retire [those not retired were asked: *when you expect to retire*], how much did you think about access to health insurance benefits? The centrality of employment-related health insurance in the United States is indicated by the importance of health insurance for both groups: 54% of retirees and 48% of pre-retirees said they think about health insurance and retirement age "a lot," 25% and 26% respectively said "a little," and only 20% and 15% said "not at all."

Given the importance of job-related health insurance, the question then becomes: to what degree is it likely that workers will change their work and retirement plans because of the potential loss of their job-related insurance? The survey then asked about employee expectation of employer- or union-provided retiree health insurance.

Half of the workers in the survey said that their employer currently provides some kind of "bridge" health insurance between when they retire and when Medicare eligibility begins at age 65. The evidence of job lock comes from the following question: would you retire before you are eligible for Medicare if your employer (or union) *did not* provide health insurance benefits for retirees? Although responses to this question are in the realm of personal opinion and not behavior, the job lock consequence is reasonably clear: twice as many workers (60% said "no" and 31% said "yes") would modify their current plans to retire earlier than age 65 if health insurance was not readily available.

Elderly Parents and Long Term Care Complexity

Most of the journalistic and political discussion of ageing focuses either on the consequences of population ageing (the "crisis" caused by huge numbers of pensioners and healthcare beneficiaries) or the consequences of individual ageing (e.g., increasing number of Alzheimer's victims). Less often discussed is a third view of ageing, *family ageing*.

Family ageing refers to the changing age structure of the family. In the context of the growing complexity of financial gerontology decision making, family ageing here points to the expanding responsibilities of middle-aged children. In this financial context, family ageing focuses attention upon another aspect of "middle age." In addition to the chronological and psychological aspects of middle age, alongside such financially related elements of middle age as empty nest, retirement, and pensions, the longer our parents are alive the longer we are the generation "in the middle."

Planning for long term care thus becomes a two-(at least) factor set of decisions. Middle agers are planning both for their own future long term care and, in many instances, for the care of elderly parents. The trends in Table 3 were developed by

TABLE 3. Family ageing: increasing longevity and middle-aged "children"

	1900	1940	1990
At age 50			
at least 1 parent alive	39%	52%	80%
both alive	4%	8%	27%
At age 60			
at least 1 parent alive	7%	13%	44%

Source: Uhlenberg (1996).

demographer Peter Uhlenberg, who used historical census data on US birth rates, marriage rates, and similar data to establish rates of surviving parents of adult children (Uhlenberg, 1996). In 1900 only 39% of 50-year-old children had at least one parent alive, rising to 80% by 1990. Perhaps the more dramatic trend is for "60-year-old kids." As recently as 1940, only 13% of 60-year-olds had at least one parent alive, compared to almost half (44%) by 1990.

These historical trends in family ageing punctuate the complexity of the financial decisions facing middle-aged persons. Of course, not all of the middle agers represented in Table 3 will feel financial responsibility for their ageing parents. But what is apparent is that these additional "middle" generational pressures come at a point in the wealth span when the traditional responsibilities of middle-age decision making are already becoming increasingly complex – including, as discussed here, choices surrounding retirement and health insurance.

THE COMPLEXITY OF WEALTH AND HEALTH – A FINAL OBSERVATION

As a final observation of the increasingly complex world of finance and ageing, Table 4 offers some intriguing American evidence of the worries and concerns that middle-aged and older persons have about their financial future. The traditional goal of financial planning is to ensure that one does not outlive one's money. Calculations of replacement ratios and diversified portfolios inclusive of multiple rates of returns, alongside the choice of whether or not to annuitize an investment – are all directed to the fear of outliving one's money.

TABLE 4. "Think about your life at age 75. How worried are you about _____?"

age	% worried		
	outlive my pension	spend it all on LTC	greater LTC worry
44–53	53	58	+ 5
54–64	46	58	+12
65–75	34	49	+15

Source: NCOA, *American perceptions of aging in the 21st century* (2000), in Cutler *et al.* (2003).

The *American perceptions of aging in the 21st century* survey mentioned earlier included a set of questions to analyze worries in older age: "Think about your life at age 75. [For respondents age 71 or older: *think about what your life will be like 10 years from now.*] How worried are you about _____ – very worried, somewhat worried, or not worried at all?"

Among the possible worries included were two directly relevant to the increasing complexity of financial decisions:

- outliving your pension and savings;
- spending all your money on long term care.

Table 4 contrasts worried (somewhat + very) with not worried, and shows that in 2000, Americans were (a) worried about both, but (b) more worried about spending all their money on long term care. Interestingly, the *gap* between these two financial worries increases with age. Perhaps the most parsimonious interpretation of this worry gap focuses on the "fear of the unknown" (Cutler, 1996b) which is somewhat greater for the older respondents. For older persons, while expenditure patterns and income resources are relatively in place, both the cost and need for long term care emerge as the daunting unknowns.

Finally, the modern complexity of financial gerontology is seen most clearly in the worries of middle agers. Compared to older persons, for middle-agers both kinds of worry are greater. The portfolio of their future pension resources and the magnitude of their future expenses are unknown. As well, they face substantial uncertainties about personal health, parental health, and the future costs of healthcare and long term care. Yet it is precisely in middle age that a series of employment, investment, retirement, and related personal and financial choices must be made. In the wealth span – as in the health span – (a) what happens later is influenced by the conditions and habits of earlier years, but (b) it is never too late to begin good health (and wealth) habits (Rowe and Kahn, 1998). Given the modern complexity of financial gerontology, therefore, financial wellbeing in older age is substantially influenced by financial education received in youth and middle age. Or, to put it in the words of the UK *Report to the Secretary of State for Education and Employment*, "If adult financial literacy is to . . . empower the individual and allow them [sic] to become truly self-reliant, then financial skills and understanding need to be improved across most of the population" (Department for Education and Skills (UK), Adult Financial Literacy Advisory Group, 2000: 17).

FURTHER READING

Atchley, R. C., and A. S. Barusch (2003). *Social forces and aging.* 10th edn. Belmont, Calif.: Wadsworth.

Cutler, N. E. (2002). *Advising mature clients: the new science of wealth span planning.* New York: John Wiley & Sons.

Evensky, H. R. (1996). *Wealth management.* Columbus, Ohio: McGraw-Hill.

Haas, D. R. (2002). *Money forever: how to make your money last as long as you do.* South Boardman, Mich.: Crofton Creek Press.

Moody, H. R. (2002). *Aging: concepts and controversies*, 4th edn. Thousand Oaks, Calif.: Pine Forge Press.

REFERENCES

Ackman, D. (2003). "As GE reaches deal, strikes Are disappearing," Forbes.com, June 16, 2003. www.forbes.com/2003/06/16/cx_da_0616topnews_print.html.

ASEC (American Savings Education Council) (2004). www.asec.org.

Cutler, N. E. (1996a). "Pensions." In J. E. Birren, ed., *Encyclopedia of Gerontology.* New Academic Press, pp. 261–269.

(1996b). "Retirement planning and the cost of long-term care: battling the fear of the unknown," *Journal of the American Society of CLU & ChFC*" 50 (November): 42–8.

(1997) "The false alarms and blaring sirens of financial literacy: middle-agers' knowledge of retirement income, health finance, and long-term care," *Generations*, 21 (Summer): 34–40.

(2002a). *Advising mature clients: the new science of wealth span planning*. New York: John Wiley & Sons.

(2002b). "'Job lock' and financial planning: health insurance and the retirement decision," *Journal of Financial Service Professionals*, 56 (November): 33–6.

Cutler, N. E., Gregg, D. W., and M. P. Lawton, eds. (1992). *Aging, money, and life satisfaction: aspects of financial gerontology*. New York: Springer Publishing Company.

Cutler, N. E., Whitelaw, N. A., and B. L. Beattie (2003). *American perceptions of aging in the 21st century*. The National Council on the Aging.

Department for Education and Skills (UK), Adult Financial Literacy Advisory Group (2000). (December) *Report to the Secretary of State for Education and Employment*. www.dfes.gov.uk/adflag.

Federal Reserve Bank of San Francisco (1998). "Health insurance and the US labour market," News Release, April 13, 1998.

Financial Accounting Standards Board (1990). "Summary of Statement No. 106: employers' accounting for postretirement benefits other than pensions." www.fasb.org/st/summary/stsum106.shtml.

Gruber, J., and B. C. Madrian (2002). "Health insurance, labour supply, and job mobility: a critical review of the literature," National Bureau of Economic Research, NBER Working Paper No. W8817, February 2002.

Marmor, T. (2000). *The politics of medicare*. Aldine de Gruyter.

McDonnell, K. and P. Fronstin (1999). *EBRI health benefits databook*. Employee Benefit Research Institute. Data updates are posted almost weekly on: www.ebri.org.

Rowe, J. W., and R. L. Kahn (1998). *Successful aging*. Pantheon Books.

Schulz, J. H., Borowski, A., and W. H. Crown (1991). *Economics of population aging: the "graying" of Australia, Japan, and the United States*. Auburn House.

Smith, B. (2003). (December), "OECD's financial education project." www.ewmi.hu/file.php?id=Barbara+Smith.ppt.

Uhlenberg, P. (1996). "Mortality decline in the twentieth century and supply of kin over the life course," *Gerontologist*, 36: 681–5.

Vitt, L. A., ed. (2003). *Encyclopedia of retirement and finance*. Westport, Conn.: Greenwood Publishing.

CHAPTER 7.5

Formal and Informal Community Care for Older Adults

DEMI PATSIOS AND ADAM DAVEY

INTRODUCTION

Community-based care for older adults results from the dynamic interplay of supports from family and friends (informal), state (formal) and, to a limited extent, from voluntary sectors. The ageing of the population, along with profound changes in informal care networks due to changes in family structure and women's labour force participation, continues to raise questions among policymakers, elderly people and their families about how to care for the growing numbers of disabled elderly people. An important policy issue surrounding use of formal services by frail elderly people is the impact of formal services on the informal care provided by informal networks. Policy initiatives (e.g., National Health Service and Community Care Act 1990 in the UK) aimed at providing increased formally organised care to elderly persons in the community may not only supplement informal care provided by family and friends but may tend in some degree to replace such care. With alarmist projections of a rapidly increasing population of older people, particularly very elderly people and frail elderly people, public policy concern with increased costs of providing care now encompasses the community-based long term care system. The nature of the relationship between care provided by family members and friends and that from community-based health and personal social services has both important consequences for the wellbeing of elderly persons living in the community who receive care, and important policy implications in terms of such considerations as effectiveness, efficiency, equity and cost containment. To the extent possible, we consider commonalities and variability across Western industrialised nations.

EVOLUTION OF THEORY AND RESEARCH

Initial interest in the relationship between informal and formal support was born out of social gerontological inquiry. Cantor's (1975) *hierarchical compensatory model* (compensation model) purported that social relationships formed the basis of preferences for receipt of care; elderly individuals would prefer to be cared for first by their spouse, then children, other family members, friends and lastly formal carers (Cantor, 1975, 1980). Each group successively provides assistance when a preferred source of care is not an option, because it is either not available or unable to meet the needs of the care recipient. This model postulates the substitutability of one service for another, but within a preferred ordering. Although the literature is consistent about elderly persons' preference for caregivers, there is little evidence to support the compensatory nature of the informal care network (Denton, 1997; Penning, 2002).

Other researchers built on this substitution hypothesis by examining the extent to which families and friends would scale back their efforts in response to the availability of local authority support (formal services). In the most cited study of the *substitution model*, Greene (1983) found a tendency for formal care to substitute for informal care. He propounded that, if substitution of formal for informal support is occurring, the result would be manifest empirically in a negative relationship between level of formally provided support and informally provided support. However, despite repeated attempts to substantiate this model, the consensus among studies specifically designed to examine the substitution of formal care for the provision of informal care is that the effect is small or statistically non-significant (Hanley *et al.*, 1991). Even in longitudinal studies where there was some evidence of substitution, there was no evidence of a major or persistent trend of replacement of informal care by formal services; it was temporary and related to the lack of an available caregiver at a point in time (Tennstedt *et al.*, 1996, 1993).

Other researchers hypothesised that the specialised nature of the task and the expertise in carrying out the task are much stronger predictors of use of formal services than is the relationship to the carer and the availability of formal services (Litwak, 1985; Litwak and Szelyeni, 1969; Messeri *et al.*, 1993). The *task specificity model* emphasised how formal services and informal care complement each other by specialising the nature of their tasks. According to Noelker and Bass (1989), this 'dual specialisation' of the informal and formal system should produce the optimal care arrangement for the frail elderly person and minimise conflict that stems from contradictory group structures by clearly delineating separate responsibilities. Informal caregivers are more likely to carry out tasks (and provide emotional support) which require little skill and occur at unpredictable times, whereas formal carers are more likely to provide care which is specialised and occurs at fixed times. Past studies showed that, although there appears to be some task specificity in the informal sector, there is little evidence that there is task specificity between formal and informal care (Chappell and Blandford, 1991; Denton, 1997; Noelker and Bass, 1989). Furthermore, when formal assistance is provided, it occurs in some of the same task areas where informal care is provided (Chappell and Blandford, 1991).

Given the varied success of these initial models in adequately explaining the linkage between formal and informal care, other researchers took a closer look at the supplemental and complementary function of both types of care. There was growing consensus that formal and informal networks worked much more closely to meet the needs of elderly persons than was previously believed. Models were pro-posed which combined both the needs of the elderly person and the capacity of the informal network to meet these needs.

The *supplementation model* posited that it is more common for functionally dependent or disabled elders to receive both informal care and formal services (Soldo *et al.*, 1989; Tennstedt *et al.*, 1990), particularly if their care needs are extensive (Tennstedt *et al.*, 1990). It is clear that informal carers play a vital role in maintaining functionally dependent elders in the community (Cantor, 1980; Stoller and Earl, 1983); however, research showed also that the formal system supplements care provided by informal carers (Ginn and Arber, 1992; Davey and Patsios, 1999), particularly when the needs of the older person exceed the resources and capacity of the informal network (Edelman, 1986; Edelman and Hughes, 1990; Moscovice *et al.*, 1988; Stoller and Pugliesi, 1988). Supplementation assumes that kin caregivers are the major helpers and use service providers to augment their efforts or to provide temporary relief, i.e. respite care (Edelman and Hughes, 1990; Noelker and Bass, 1989; Stoller, 1989; Stoller and Pugliesi, 1988).

The *complementarity model* took aspects of both the compensation and supplementation models described by George (1987), Chappell (1985) and Chappell and Blandford (1991) and put forward that formal care is mobilised when crucial elements of the informal network are lacking or when there is substantial need. In short, formal services provide for those tasks which informal carers are unable to provide. Instead of informal carers providing care in isolation of formal services, there is an overall sharing of care tasks, i.e. they complement one another (George, 1987). This was supported by past research showing that both support networks provide the necessary care when elements of the informal system cannot do so alone (Chappell and Blandford, 1991; Denton, 1997).

THE POLICY ENVIRONMENT

In addition to theoretical and practical development of the various models, the dominance of particular models of the relationship between formal and informal care can be explained in part by policy debates. In the early 1980s there was a fostering of what became popularly known as 'community care', which meant shifting the balance of care from hospitals to the community where it was felt to be more appropriate. At the time (and some would argue that it remains true today), there were fears that publicly financed formal care would substitute for informal care and place unsustainable pressure on constrained public budgets (Pezzin *et al.*, 1996; Walker and Maltby, 1997). As some policymakers were concerned with controlling or even reducing public expenditure on health and personal care, the service substitution perspective was usually tested and re-tested either to confirm or to refute these claims.

With the advent and growth of community care reforms and resultant increases in the type and level of home- and community-based services, different types of models needed to be developed and tested to gauge whether and to what extent these reforms were working. In the late 1980s and early 1990s, models testing the interweaving of formal and informal systems (i.e., supplementation, complementarity) became more prominent. More recently, the emphasis has been not only on examining the impact of community care policy on meeting the needs of frail dependent elderly people (and their carers), but also on the extent to which the expansion of home- and community-based services might erode the availability and willingness of family and friends to provide care. Much of the available evidence in this regard suggests that other demographic and family trends may drive many of these changes (e.g., Davey *et al.*, 1999).

BASIC COMPONENTS OF THE MODELS

At the simplest level, each relationship of formal and informal care can be distinguished by the services/ tasks provided by each support network, the extent to which support networks provide the same or different tasks to care recipients and the statistical relationship of formal and informal care. The needs of functionally dependent elderly persons can be met by informal carers, formal service providers or a combination of both. Whereas task areas and sharing of care within task areas do not overlap in task specificity and substitution models, there is some degree of overlap in compensation, supplementation and complementary models (Denton, 1997). The statistical relationship of formal and informal

care is also paramount. Under task specificity, no relationship is assumed as each sector provides specialised task areas. For substitution and compensation models the relationship is negative as formal carers and informal carers are presumed to be substitutes for one another. Under supplementation and complementarity, a positive relationship of formal and informal care is expected as the presence of one support network denotes the presence of the other.

Furthermore, the nature of the relationship between formal care and the availability of members of the informal care network is a key feature in determining the presence of the various models (Denton, 1997). Without knowledge of the composition of the informal network, it is impossible to ascertain whether the provision of formal services indicates that informal carers have stopped providing care (substitution), have transferred their efforts to other task areas (task specificity) or whether this simply reflects local authority response to the relative unavailability or inability of the informal network to provide such care (compensation, supplementation, complementarity).

CROSS-SECTIONAL VERSUS LONGITUDINAL STUDIES

Another source of complexity as regards the interweaving of formal and informal care is that they are likely to change over time as an older person's health needs and support network change, thereby affecting access to both formal and informal sources of care. Although cross-sectional studies have the advantage of holding certain variables like disability level or caregiver availability constant, they cannot capture changes in caregiving situations over time, i.e., how formal services affect the content and level of assistance provided by the informal network (Edelman, 1986). Moreover, a family's response to the availability of formal care may develop as a long-term adjustment, particularly as older persons' functional limitations are likely to be chronic (Penrod *et al.*, 1994). Numerous studies exist which have examined changes over time in the care provided by informal and formal providers and have contributed to a fuller understanding of the dynamic relationships between and within support networks (Christianson, 1988; Diwan and Coulton, 1994;

Edelman and Hughes, 1990; Kelman *et al.*, 1994; Lyons *et al.*, 2000; Moscovice *et al.*, 1988; Stoller, 1989; Stoller and Pugliesi, 1988, 1991; Tennstedt *et al.*, 1996, 1994, 1993). Some of these studies took place over too short a period of time (Moscovice *et al.*, 1988) or too long a period of time (Stoller and Pugliesi, 1988) to capture any long- and short-run reallocation adjustments, respectively, by families in response to expanded community-based long term care services.

COMMUNITY-BASED VERSUS INSTITUTIONAL CARE

To gain a fuller picture of the interweaving of formal and informal care, the scope of past research expanded to incorporate the full continuum of care provision. Individual care systems consist of a number of different services, ranging very broadly from community- and home-based services, to various degrees of sheltered housing, nursing homes and other institutions and hospitals. The primary focus of home care studies has been on the issue of substitution, that is, on whether home care is a cheaper alternative to institutional care. Findings revealed a managed system of home and community-based services could be a cost-effective alternative to institutionalisation for chronically disabled elderly persons (for UK demonstrations, see Davies and Challis, 1986; for US demonstrations, see Christianson, 1988; Greene *et al.*, 1995). However, the ways in which these different services (community-based and institutional) substitute or complement for one another are by no means clear.

CROSS-NATIONAL APPLICABILITY

Most research in this area comes from the US and Canada (for UK studies, see Ginn and Arber, 1992, and Davey and Patsios, 1999; for Swedish studies, see Davey *et al.*, 1999, and Shea *et al.*, 2003). As Bowling *et al.* (1991) aptly point out, 'country specific studies are not necessarily applicable elsewhere in the world due to differing methods of financing and organising health care, as well as cultural differences which influence illness behaviour and predisposition to use services' (p. 689). We cannot assume that the relationship(s) between formal services and informal care, particularly as regards find-

ings from North America, can be easily applied to the British context. In each country (and this could be extended down to regions, i.e. states / provinces / local authorities), home- and community-based care and other long term care services vary in the extent to which they are part of the 'public' health service (funded), as well as in terms of accessibility, type and level of services, and user fees. There are also differences in terms of developments in the private and voluntary sectors (commonly referred to as the independent sector). Understanding these linkages is a large and important knowledge gap.

IMPLICATIONS FOR PRACTICE AND POLICY

Practice implications

ELIGIBILITY CRITERIA. Understanding typologies of care can assist care managers in distinguishing between the 'need for care' and the 'need for services'. Need for care may be measured using functional ability (ADLs), the need for services being the difference between the care required due to the functional limitations and current care resources (material and social) available to meet these needs. The literature suggests that most older people with functional limitations receive help with task areas from their family and friends. There are others, however, without available or adequate informal resources, for whom the absence of formal services may result in undermet or unmet need. It is quite possible, for example, to have a person with less severe functional limitations and no informal support to have a greater service need than someone with more severe functional limitations with adequate social and care support. In this instance, if eligibility criteria are not flexible enough to account for the heterogeneity found in the need–care paradigm, then the first person, who really needed help, would not get it, and the second person, who met the criteria but may not need the help, would be eligible.

EFFECTIVENESS OF THE VARIOUS CARE COMPOSITIONS. Understanding the interplay between the two types of care is needed to ensure both effective and efficient combinations of formal and informal care. Past research has shown that the relationship of formal and informal care very much depends on the specific needs of the elderly person, the composition of their support networks, and the likely note of change over time. Case managers can learn from these past studies by using needs-based criteria (namely ADLs) to develop and implement appropriate, individually based care plans which optimise the capacity of both support networks. Over time, these plans could be compared alongside those of more specific programmes of research, such as the community care schemes of the Personal Social Services Research Unit (PSSRU; University of Kent, Canterbury) which have been initiated to determine the best mix of care for elderly individuals who have different needs.

Policy implications

TARGET EFFECTIVENESS AND EFFICIENCY. Findings in this area can also be used as evidence of the effectiveness of service planning and delivery of community-based long term care services. Many past studies have shown that, over time, elderly people living alone and/or who had the greatest need measured in terms of functional limitations or disability were, in fact, those who were most likely to receive, and by implication, be allocated services (Bowling et al., 1991). Caution must be exercised, however, as previous studies failed to control for the potential problem that users of formal services are 'successful utilisers' (those who have applied for the service, and who have been successful in being allocated the service), and/or that non-users of formal services are 'unsuccessful utilisers' (those who either did not apply for the service or were not successful in being allocated the service).

Generally though, the policy implications of research in this area can be interpreted in different ways and depend in large part on how one defines the goals of publicly provided community care. For those who see these programmes as properly serving only those with an absolute deficit in available informal care, it is suggested that there is considerable slippage in the programmes' targeting efficiency. For those who see these programmes as also properly serving a respite function (whether in terms of overall effort by informal providers or in permitting specialisation to more satisfying areas of sup-

portive effort), it is suggested that they are doing so (Greene, 1983).

TARGET EQUITY. Findings on the importance of living arrangements (see Arber and Ginn, 1992) also raise some important equity issues about who should receive publicly funded community long term care. Those elderly persons with available and active informal networks have at their disposal a potential pool of caring that other elderly persons simply do not have. Some findings in this area, however, could be construed as contradicting informal carers' support policy. Whereas frail, elderly people who lived alone were given a range of community-based long term care, those who had functional dependencies but were living with family or friends were given very little support. Despite the rhetoric of supporting informal carers, those elderly people with access to carers were less likely to receive support from statutory (public) services (Parker and Lawton, 1994).

In addition, practitioners and policymakers need also to take into account the effect of publicly provided home care on living arrangements, as well as on the use of informal care and formal care. Analyses of the Channelling Demonstrations in the US showed not only that choices among alternative combinations depend on the type of living arrangements, but also that these living arrangements are influenced by the public provision of formal home care (Christianson, 1988). Pezzin et al. (1996) found that 'a generous home care program significantly increases the probability that unmarried persons will live independently and reduces the probability of living in shared households or in nursing or personal care homes' (p. 650).

IMPLICATIONS FOR FUTURE POLICY

Policymakers and providers face a challenging dilemma in terms of expanding publicly funded and provided community-based care. On the one hand, past findings suggest that publicly funded care could be expanded without seriously eroding the contribution of the informal sector, thereby increasing the overall amount of care provided, which in turn should continue to reduce the level of unmet need. On the other hand, one of the main rationales for expanding publicly funded care is to encourage informal support and relieve caregiver burden, but other studies have shown that increasing the amount of formal care may not dramatically reduce caregiver burden because many elders have unmet needs and most caregivers will continue to provide virtually the same amount of care (Hanley *et al.*, 1991).

IMPLICATIONS FOR FURTHER RESEARCH

Significant progress has been made in this field of inquiry over the past two decades. Several models of the relationship of formal and informal care have been developed and applied in a variety of settings. We have learned a great deal about the relationship of formal and informal care, particularly as regards home- and community-based care. Nevertheless, several issues remain outstanding and should be considered in the development of future research.

In terms of design, with very few exceptions (Christianson, 1988; Hanley *et al.*, 1991), previous research has looked at specific programmes or localities. Although these studies provide valuable information about the effectiveness or efficiency of particular services or locale, there is a need for national (and cross-national) studies that are specifically designed to capture both the context and interplay of formal and informal care. Future research should also seek to integrate spatial (setting) and temporal (time) dimensions of the caregiving situation. Care provision takes place in many settings (hospitals, at home, day centres, outpatient clinics, nursing and residential settings, and so forth) and as we have seen it changes over time.

Several measurement issues also need to be addressed in future research. As important as the cultural implications affecting interpretation of utilisation research from North America, the fundamental limitation of existing research is that it overlooks the breadth and nature of care tasks provided for elderly people over time. While it may be true that informal networks provide a vast majority of personal care and emotional support, for other care tasks, e.g., specialised household and healthcare tasks, this does not hold (see Noelker and Bass, 1989).

Moreover, an ideal examination of various models would include information on the variables affecting both the supply and demand of formal and informal care. While we do have some demand variables like the characteristics of the home care recipient, a more complete accounting would also include opportunity costs to family members and the price of formal care. Similarly, supply variables including proximity of family members or access to service providers would add important information about the trade-offs between using one type of care or the other (Hanley *et al.*, 1991; see also Trydegård and Thorslund, 2001).

In terms of analysis, researchers might examine the potential role of multilevel models for addressing questions about the relations between variability in funding levels, demographic changes, type and level of services available, and formal and informal care. Models should be fit to examine receipt of different forms of care, how these variables have changed over time within regions, and the relations between policy changes and the interplay of formal and informal care systems.

To develop theory further in this area, researchers might consider including the underlying reason for the task, i.e. the service orientation. The classic example is the grounds for bathing a client. If the bath is deemed medically necessary, then a health care worker will carry out the task. If it is not deemed a health issue, but is delivered for reasons pertaining to social care, then a care aide will help bathe the client. In previous studies, however, these two formal carers are lumped together and we are not able to tell whether the care is delivered by a health or social services person. Thus, being more specific about sources of care (i.e., distinguishing between care provided by health services and that provided by social services) would allow us to examine the relationship between health and social care, in addition to that between informal and formal care.

Closer attention could also be paid to determining the existence of the various models 'within' support networks. Most research to date has concentrated on the relationship between formal and informal care, not necessarily what interplay there is between various members of the informal support network as regards task area provision. Existing models could be used to determine whether there is substitution or complementarity, for example, between a spouse and adult child or friend.

Research into the complex and sometimes fragile relationship between formal and informal forms of elder care continues. Paramount is not only the extent to which publicly provided services act to complement, supplement or supplant informal care but the extent to which they act in the best interest of the carer and cared for.

FURTHER READING

Bauld, L., Chesterman, J., Davies, B., Judge, K., and R. Mangalore (2000). *Caring for older people: an assessment of community care in the 1990s*. Aldershot: Ashgate.

Evers, A., and I. Svetlik, eds. (1993). *Balancing pluralism: new welfare mixes in care for the elderly*. Aldershot: Avebury.

Organization for Economic Co-operation and Development (OECD) (1996). *Caring for frail elderly people. Policies in evolution*, Social Policy Studies, No. 19. Paris: OECD.

REFERENCES

Arber, S., and J. Ginn (1992). 'In sickness and in health: caregiving, gender and the independence of elderly people'. In C. Marsh and S. Arber, eds., *Families and households: divisions and change*. London: MacMillan, pp. 86–105.

Bowling, A., Farquhar, M., and E. Browne (1991). 'Use of services in old age: data from three surveys of elderly people', *Social Science & Medicine*, 33 (6): 689–900.

Cantor, M. H. (1975). 'Life space and the social support system of the inner city elderly of New York', *Gerontologist*, 15: 23–27.

(1980). 'The informal support system: its relevance in the lives of the elderly'. In E. F. Borgatta and N. McClusky, eds., *Aging and society*. Beverly Hills, Calif.: Sage.

Chappell, N. L. (1985). 'Social support and the receipt of home care services', *Gerontologist*, 25: 47–54.

Chappell, N. L., and A. Blandford (1991). 'Informal and formal care: exploring the complementarity', *Ageing and Society*, 11: 299–315.

Christianson, J. (1988). 'The effect of Channelling on informal caregiving', *Health Services Research*, 23 (1): 99–117.

Davey, A., and D. Patsios (1999). 'Formal and informal community care to older adults: comparative analysis of the United States and Great Britain', *Journal of Family and Economic Issues*, 20 (3): 271–300.

Davey, A., Femia, E. E., Shea, D. G., Zarit, S. H., Sundström, G., Berg, S., and M. A. Smyer (1999). 'How much do families help? A cross-national comparison', *Journal of Aging and Health*, 11: 199–221.

Davies, B., and D. Challis, (1986). *Matching resources to needs in community care*. Aldershot: Gower.

Denton, M. (1997). 'The linkages between informal and formal care of the elderly', *Canadian Journal On Aging – Revue Canadienne du Vieillissement*, 16 (1): 30–50.

Diwan, S., and C. Coulton (1994). 'Period effects on the mix of formal and informal in-home care used by the elderly', *Journal of Applied Gerontology*, 13 (3): 316–30.

Edelman, P. (1986). 'The impact of community care to the homebound elderly on provision of informal care', *Gerontologist*, 26: 263–74.

Edelman, P., and S. Hughes (1990). 'The impact of community care on provision of informal care to homebound elderly persons', *Journal of Gerontology B: Psychological Sciences and Social Sciences*, 45 (2): S74–S84.

George, L. K. (1987). 'Easing caregiver burden: the role of informal and formal supports'. In R. A. Ward and S. S. Tobin, eds., *Health in aging: sociological issues and policy directions*. New York: Springer, pp. 113–58.

Ginn, J., and S. Arber, (1992). 'Elderly people living at home: the relation of social and material resources to service use'. In F. Laczko and C. R. Victor, eds., *Social policy and older people: community care in the 90s*. Aldershot: Avebury, pp. 112–36.

Greene, V. L. (1983). 'Substitution between formally and informally provided care for the impaired elderly in the community', *Medical Care*, 21(6): 609–19.

Greene, V. L., Lovely, M. E., Miller, M. D., and J. I. Ondrich (1995). 'Reducing nursing-home use through community long-term-care – an optimization analysis', *Journal of Gerontology B: Psychological Sciences and Social Sciences*, 50 (4): S259–S268.

Hanley, R., Wiener, J. M., and K. M. Harris (1991). 'Will paid home care erode informal support?' *Journal of Health Politics, Policy, and Law*, 16 (3): 507–21.

Kelman, H. R., Thomas, C., and J. S. Tanaka (1994). 'Longitudinal patterns of formal and informal social support in an urban elderly population', *Social Science & Medicine*, 38 (7): 905–14.

Litwak, E. (1985). *Helping the elderly: the complementary roles of informal networks and formal systems*. New York: Guilford.

Litwak, E., and I. Szelenyi (1969). 'Primary group structures and their functions', *American Sociological Review*, 34: 465–81.

Lyons, K. S., Zarit S. H., and A. L. Townsend (2000). 'Families and formal service usage: stability and change in patterns of interface', *Aging and Mental Health*, 4 (3): 234–43.

Messeri, P., Silverstein, M., and E. Litwak (1993). 'Choosing optimal support groups: a review and formulation, *Journal of Health and Social Behaviour*, 34: 122–37.

Moscovice, I., Davidson, G., and D. McCaffrey (1988). 'Substitution of formal and informal care for the community-based elderly', *Medical Care*, 26 (10): 971–81.

Noelker, L. S. and D. M. Bass (1989). 'Home care for elderly persons: linkages between formal and informal caregivers', *Journal of Gerontology B: Social Sciences*, 44 (2): S63–S70.

Parker, G., and D. Lawton (1994). *Different types of care, different types of carer: evidence from the General Household Survey*. London: HMSO.

Penning, M. J. (2002). 'Hydra revisited: substituting formal for self- and informal in-home care among older adults with disabilities', *Gerontologist*, 42 (1): 4–16.

Penrod, J. D., Harris, K. M., and R. L. Kane (1994). 'Informal care substitution: what we don't know can hurt us'. *Journal of Aging and Social Policy*, 6 (4), 21–31.

Pezzin, L. E., Kemper, P., and J. Reschovsky (1996). 'Does publicly provided home care substitute for family care? Experimental evidence with endogenous living arrangements', *Journal of Human Resources* 31 (3): 650–76.

Shea, D. G., Davey, A., Femia, E. E., Zarit, S. H., Sundström, G., Berg, S., and M. A. Smyer (2003). 'Comparing assistance in Sweden and the United States', *Gerontologist*, 43 (5).

Soldo, B. J., Agree, E., and D. Wolf (1989). 'Balance between formal and informal care'. In M. Ory and K. Bond, eds., *Aging and health care*. New York: Routledge, pp. 193–216.

Stoller, E. P. (1989). 'Formal services and informal helping: the myth of service substitution', *Journal of Applied Gerontology*, 8 (1): 37–52.

Stoller, E. P., and L. L. Earl (1983). 'Help with activities of everyday life: sources of support for the non-institutionalized elderly', *Gerontologist*, 23: 64–70.

Stoller, E. P., and K. L. Pugliesi (1988). 'Informal networks of community based elderly: changes in composition over time', *Research on Aging*, 10 (4): 499–516.

(1991). 'Size and effectiveness of informal helping networks: a panel study of older people in the community', *Journal of Health and Social Behaviour*, 32: 180–91.

Tennstedt, S., Sullivan, L., McKinlay, J., and R. D'Agostino (1990). 'How important is functional status as a predictor of service use by older people?' *Journal of Aging and Health*, 2: 439–61.

Tennstedt, S. L., Crawford, S. L., and McKinlay, J. B. (1993). 'Is family care on the decline? A longitudinal investigation of the substitution of formal long-term care services for informal care', *Milbank Quarterly*, 71 (4): 601–24.

Tennstedt, S., McKinlay, J., and L. Kasten (1994). 'Unmet need among disabled elders: a problem in access to community long-term care?' *Social Science & Medicine*, 38 (7): 915–24.

Tennstedt, S., Harrow, B., and S. Crawford (1996). 'Informal care vs. formal services: changes in patterns of care over time', *Journal of Aging and Social Policy*, 7 (3/4): 71–91.

Trydegård, G.-B., and M. Thorslund (2001). 'Inequality in the welfare state? Local variation in care of the elderly – the case of Sweden', *International Journal of Social Welfare*, 10: 174–84.

Walker, A., and T. Maltby, (1997). *Ageing Europe*. Buckingham: Open University Press.

Health Policy and Old Age: An International Review

JILL QUADAGNO, JENNIFER REID KEENE, AND DEBRA STREET

INTRODUCTION

As people age, their healthcare needs generally increase. Whether, and under what circumstances, these needs are met, however, is as varied as are health policies throughout the world. Elderly people in most developed countries have substantial access to high-quality "Western" medicine whenever need arises. In other countries, availability of and access to even basic medical services for elderly people (or for individuals of any age) is far less predictable. This is not surprising, given the relationship between national wealth and the level of healthcare expenditures in particular countries. While the need for basic healthcare is great in countries in transition (Central and Eastern Europe) and in developing countries (mainly in Asia, Africa, and Latin America), fiscal constraints limit their capacity to deliver needed care for older people.

Central and Eastern European countries' health policies are, at best, in flux and, at worst, in disarray. The rapid collapse of state socialism and the as-yet incomplete transition to robust market economies undermined universal medical provision in most former Eastern-bloc countries. In many, healthcare infrastructures are collapsing and the cost of care is rising beyond the means of older citizens, whose incomes have been decimated in the transition.

In developing countries, where over half of all older people in the world live, extreme poverty and underdeveloped health policies result in scarce medical resources and minimal healthcare infrastructure. Even when basic medical care is available, elderly people in most developing countries face insur-

mountable barriers to receiving it. Transportation to urban centers where basic healthcare is most likely to be available is beyond the reach of many poor, rural elders. Shortages of equipment and supplies combined with high transportation and prescription costs present formidable barriers to care, even when it is nominally free (HelpAge International, 2002). In many developing countries, the only healthcare elders are able to tap are the services of traditional healers.[1]

This presents a stark contrast to developed countries where technological advances in medical care have transformed treatment of age-related acute and chronic healthcare conditions with life enhancing and life extending therapies, albeit at a price. High-tech medicine has driven up healthcare costs, at the same time as national populations are ageing. Some contend that these constitute twin pressures portending unaffordable national health policy regimes. While agreeing that technology gains contribute to rising medical costs, others argue that population ageing has minimal and manageable effects on national health accounts, which can be accommodated by tweaking health policy at the margins. This chapter describes how variations in health policies influence the provision of medical care for elderly citizens in developed countries. We consider a selection of national approaches for determining how acute and chronic care for older people

---

[1] The diversity of conditions, relative absence of health policies for the elderly, rapidity of change (countries in transition), and dearth of systematic data (developing countries) compel us to limit our discussion mainly to developed countries.

are financed and delivered, the implications of increasing medical costs in the context of ageing populations, and recent policy responses intended to resolve challenges in the provision of health services for older people.

Healthcare for Ageing Populations

Demographic trends into the foreseeable future signal that elderly people are among the fastest-growing segments of many national populations, with the most rapid growth among the oldest-old – individuals aged 85 and older (see Chapters 1.4 and 6.2 in this volume). Consequently, healthcare systems may experience unprecedented demands since older persons, on average, have more hospitalizations, more chronic disease, and use more (and more expensive) drugs and therapies than other age groups. Still, illness and disability are not inevitable – many people remain in good health into very old age (Victor, 1991). Further, early diagnoses and treatment of conditions associated with ageing, combined with healthy lifestyle choices that mitigate age-related diseases and conditions, may ease some pressures on healthcare financing related to ageing populations.

Until the twentieth century, the major causes of death for individuals of all ages were acute infectious diseases such as tuberculosis, diphtheria, gastrointestinal infections, and pneumonia. In developed countries, between 1900 and 1970, death rates from these diseases dropped dramatically due to antibiotics and immunizations and public health measures such as sanitation, purification of the water supply, etc. Still, most health policies enacted in developed countries by mid century focused on acute medical care, reflecting the most pressing healthcare needs that predominated when national health programs were implemented. Full medical coverage for acute care (illnesses or conditions with sudden onset, sharp rise, and short courses) became normative in developed countries.

ACUTE CARE IN DEVELOPED COUNTRIES. In all developed countries (with the notable exception of the United States), health policies evolved during the twentieth century to cover virtually all acute medical services for citizens of all ages. Acute healthcare is short-term, episodic care generally provided by physicians and other health professionals in institutional settings, ranging from physician practices to clinics and hospitals. In countries with universalist health policies, basic coverage of hospital and physician acute care services for aged individuals is inseparable from the healthcare benefits available to the population as a whole.

Despite the shared characteristic of universal acute care coverage for all age groups, countries typically have unique fiscal and administrative arrangements for covering such medical services. For example, the National Health Service (NHS) in Great Britain administers a national program of health services funded by compulsory contributions to a national insurance fund. Federal and provincial revenues fund medical services for Canadians, administered through provincial health ministries. Nordic countries typically operate national insurance schemes, financed by individual taxes and payments from employers. In contrast to these single-payer-type health insurance systems, Germans depend upon a multi-payer system to provide coverage to all citizens. Most German health provision is provided by more than 1,000 autonomous sickness funds (covering over 90 percent of the population), with the rest covered by private health insurance or through government employee coverage (Lassey and Lassey, 2001). Despite national variations in administrative arrangements, healthcare financing and the basket of medical services available under national health policies for older people are indistinguishable from that for other population age groups. The acute care medical needs of citizens of all ages are covered.

ACUTE CARE IN THE UNITED STATES. Among developed countries, the United States takes a unique approach to financing medical care. Instead of guaranteeing universal coverage for all citizens, the government only provides health insurance for "uninsurable" (in the private health insurance market) residual population groups – elderly and disabled people (*Medicare*) and the very poor (*Medicaid*). Most non-poor children and working aged adults are either covered by employment-based private health insurance, or lack medical insurance altogether.

Medicare is the federal health insurance program that serves people aged 65 and older who qualify for

Social Security benefits.[2] Medicare Part A, financed by payroll taxes, provides insurance for hospital care, time-limited post-hospital care in skilled nursing facilities, and outpatient diagnostic services. Medicare Part B is an optional plan covering physician services, financed by a combination of general revenue funds and monthly premiums paid by beneficiaries.

Because gaps in Medicare coverage (deductibles, co-payments, prescription drug costs, etc.) leave many acute healthcare needs unmet, beneficiaries who can afford the cost purchase private insurance to cover those needs. Two-thirds of elderly Medicare beneficiaries purchase supplemental *Medigap* policies from private insurance companies. Until 1991 the Medigap insurance market was a bewildering jumble of policies sold by insurance agents who engaged in deceptive practices, sold duplicate policies, and charged high premiums. That year, Congress enacted reforms allowing insurers to offer only nine standard Medigap options, and compelling insurance companies to pay out for services at least 65 percent of the value of premiums received over the life of a policy (Jensen and Morrisey, 1992).

Approximately one-third of retirees with Medigap benefits receive them from a former employer. Recently, employers have become increasingly unwilling to pay the cost of providing health insurance to individuals no longer employed by the firm, leading to a steady erosion of employer-provided Medigap coverage (US Census Bureau, 1998). By 2000, only 26 percent of Medicare-eligible retirees were covered by employer health benefits. Employers who continue to offer Medigap benefits have increased the retirees' share of the costs through higher co-payments and deductibles and by capping their own expenditures (US Senate, 2001). In addition to the gaps in Medicare for acute medical care, even more significant gaps in healthcare for US elders arise from the program's failure to meet chronic care needs.

CHRONIC CARE FOR ELDERLY PEOPLE.
As deaths from acute diseases declined and life expectancies increased in the latter part of the twentieth century, health policy focused on meeting health needs associated with chronic conditions in older populations. The older a person is, the more likely she or he is to have the more serious and disabling types of chronic illness. While some chronic diseases have an apparently sudden onset (e.g. heart attack), they may in fact have long latent periods before symptoms are manifested. Other conditions prevalent among older people are considered chronic regardless of the onset, including arthritis, heart conditions, osteoporosis, Alzheimer's disease, emphysema, and diabetes. Chronic care services and support often differ considerably from those required for treating acute disease, and many countries are struggling to integrate fragmented systems of treatment, care venues, and community support to provide appropriate chronic care for their ageing populations.

How well the chronic care needs of older people are met depends on many factors. The generosity of routinely provided medical benefits, particularly in relation to long-term therapies and prescription drugs, as well as treatment patterns of health professionals are part of the equation. Availability of a full range of health and social care services needed to support chronic care is another. But many researchers find that, even when coverage for acute care is adequate, in many countries chronic care for elderly people is poorly coordinated and inadequately provided.

CHRONIC CARE IN DEVELOPED COUNTRIES.
Many countries provide special care for frail elders with chronic health problems and/or disabling conditions. Chronic, long term healthcare is typically combined with social services to meet the full spectrum of care required. It is often difficult to distinguish between healthcare and social services as many of the occupations that provide services are called 'health professions' even though they address both types of needs. The general trend in Europe is to link long term care to general adult medical services either through geriatric units that are attached to hospitals or through home-based healthcare services.

There are a variety of country-specific arrangements for providing residential care. Arrangements may include domiciliary care to older people in their own residence involving assistance with household

[2] Medicare also serves disabled individuals who qualify for Social Security benefits or who have end-stage renal disease, but most beneficiaries are individuals 65 and older.

tasks, meals-on-wheels, personal care, home nursing, and remedial therapy. In all European Community (EC) and Scandinavian countries, long term care may also be provided in hospitals, nursing homes, and social care homes (Hugman, 1994). In Ireland, nurses staff care homes. In France, residential homes are registered for nursing care as well as social care, but in Germany, Italy, Spain, and the UK nursing care and social care homes are separate. However, the boundaries between nursing and social care are often unclear and there is an increasing tendency for social care facilities to cater to people with growing infirmity (Blackman, 2000).

In the UK and Australia, long term care has shifted from nursing homes and residential care as the main environments towards community-care models designed to allow elders to remain in the community as long as possible (Bernard and Phillips, 2000; Howe, 2000). Expanded domiciliary services such as home-help and meals-on-wheels allow people to stay in the community. Canada has used relatively high levels of formal home healthcare to support long term care for community-dwelling elders (Anderson and Hussey, 1999).

CHRONIC CARE IN THE UNITED STATES.

Meeting the elderly population's chronic care needs in the US depends upon navigating a patchwork of health policy initiatives, programs with different criteria for entitlement, and substantial reliance on private funding and informal care. The Medicaid program, health insurance for impoverished "medically indigent" people, covers chronic care needs selectively for some elderly people. Medicaid pays for the costs of long term custodial care in nursing homes, but only after elderly people "spend down" all income and assets to poverty level (Grogan and Patashnik, 2003). Further exacerbating the problem is that Medicaid is a joint federal/state program with eligibility rules varying from state to state. Still, in 1997 Medicaid paid for almost half of all US expenditures for nursing home care.

Introduction of the Prospective Payment System (PPS) in 1983 to contain escalating Medicare hospital benefits was a major policy change that influenced extension of Medicare into "semi-chronic" care provision. Under Medicare, PPS hospitals were reimbursed a fixed amount per patient, according to diagnosis-related groups. PPS gave hospitals incen-

tives to shorten lengths of stay and to discharge patients to post-hospital settings as soon as medically feasible. The effect was to increase rates of nursing home admissions, as hospitals discharged patients to skilled nursing facilities to recover from surgery, stroke, or other health conditions. As a result, the average length of a Medicare hospital stay declined, and skilled nursing facilities became an increasingly important site of post-hospital subacute care (Street *et al.*, 2003).

RECENT POLICY DEVELOPMENTS IN CHRONIC CARE.

Germany and Japan now have two of the most progressive and innovative models of long term care insurance in the world. Both the German and Japanese models were built on the principles of "social solidarity" and the "socialization of care" (Cuellar and Weiner, 2000; Schunk and Estes, 2001). The German model provides coverage under the general health insurance program and finances long term care through payroll taxes (Lassey and Lassey, 2001). To receive benefits, citizens must qualify based on physical need and may receive either cash or services. The program also supports home- and community-based services, and the majority of beneficiaries receive long term care services outside of nursing facilities (Cuellar and Weiner, 2000). More recently, in 2000, Japan implemented a national system of mandatory long term care insurance that covers both institutional and community-based care (Campbell and Ikegami, 2000).

Most developed countries (except Germany) require some form of means-testing or cost sharing for long term care services, in contrast to the mainly "free at point of service" approach used in acute medical provision. Some countries such as the UK and the US require that beneficiaries "spend down" their assets before receiving publicly funded services (Grogan and Patashnik, 2003). Other countries require modest income-based charges for services, while New Zealanders who are able pay the entire cost of residential care. Community-based services tend to require less cost sharing from beneficiaries in Canada, New Zealand, and Australia (Merlis, 2000).

Policymakers increasingly recognize the importance of informal caregivers in their visions of long term care and some have begun to implement services to support caregivers. Germany's system pays cash benefits to informal caregivers as a way to encourage family caregiving (Cuellar and Weiner, 2000; Schunk and Estes, 2001). Australia and Denmark pay family caregivers directly in order to compensate (although inadequately) for lost employment earnings. Yet others provide "carer credits" in Social Security systems, helping informal caregivers gain future state pension entitlements (Ginn *et al.*, 2002). Finally, many countries offer respite services to informal caregivers (Merlis, 2000).

How the prevalence of chronic disease and the level of care need among elderly people will be expressed in the future is unknown. If improved lifestyles earlier in the lifecourse and medical advances succeed in limiting or minimizing chronic conditions, there could be a compression of morbidity with people experiencing fewer years of chronic illness as they live longer, healthier lives. However, compression of morbidity may come with costs – decreased need for residential and institutional care, but increased need for technological interventions and drug therapy regimes to help sustain individuals' capacity for self-care. Alternatively, increased future longevity could be accompanied by longer periods during which disabling chronic disease processes occur, or by more people who are sick. Concern about how governments will finance both the acute and chronic care costs of ageing populations has been center stage in most recent policy debates about healthcare for elderly people.

Market Incentives in Healthcare for the Aged

In the past few decades rising public budgets, population ageing and waxing and waning enthusiasm for marketization and privatization of social services have caused many nations to reexamine the social programs they established at least half a century ago. Inadequacies and inefficiencies in existing healthcare systems have also stimulated movements for health policy reforms. Many EC countries, and others such as Australia and Canada, have shifted their emphases from exclusively state-provided care to incorporate more market-based approaches that place emphasis on increased private enterprise in healthcare. The stated goals of such reforms are to improve care while controlling health costs and expenditures (Fine and Chalmers, 2000; Lassey and Lassey, 2001).

International differences in population age groups do not account for variations in national health spending. For example, as Table 1 shows, the UK spent relatively small percentages of GDP on health in general and on healthcare for elderly people particularly, despite having nearly the "oldest" population. Routinely, per capita health expenditures for elderly people in developed countries are three to five times higher than for people younger than 65, reflecting higher levels of need in older subgroups. In absolute terms, average annual per capita health expenditures for the elderly vary substantially. As

---

TABLE 1. Health expenditures for older people, 1997

Country	Percentage of GDP on Health Expenditures	Percentage of Population Aged and Older	Percentage of GDP on Health Expenditures for People Aged 65 and Older
United States	13.6	12.5	5.0
Germany	10.4	16.8	3.5
France	9.6	16.0	3.4
Canada	9.3	12.9	3.6
Australia	8.3	12.2	3.0
New Zealand	7.6	11.7	2.5
Japan	7.3	17.5	3.4
United Kingdom	6.7	16.1	2.8

Source: Anderson and Hussey (1999:20).
Data source: OECD.

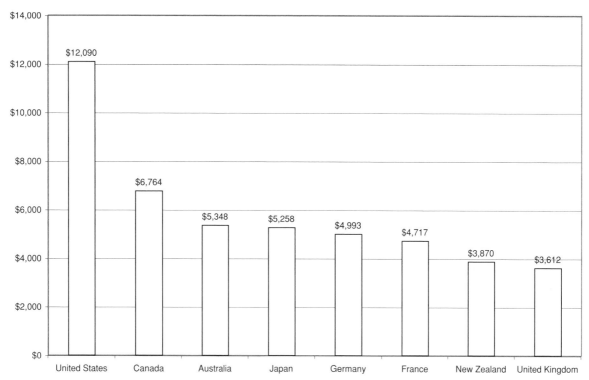

Figure 1. Per capita health expenditures for adults aged 65 and older, 1997.
Source: Anderson and Hussey (1999). Data source: OECD

Figure 1 shows, the US spends nearly twice as much annually per capita as the next highest-spending country (Canada), and more than three times the level of the more frugal nations (New Zealand, UK).

Traditionally, countries with universalist systems have sought to control health costs through rationing or global budgeting. The US has depended on market-based approaches, including co-payments, deductibles, and gaps in state coverage to rein in costs. Some EC countries, including Italy, Holland, Norway, Sweden, and the UK have enacted reforms or considered proposals to stimulate the private market and separate the roles of purchasing and providing healthcare. European countries have also sought to establish a social market in healthcare with an emphasis on local representation of consumer rights (Gilleard and Higgs, 2000).

International policies and programs designed to meet the coming challenges of health policy for ageing populations must be evaluated in terms of their impact on socioeconomic development as well as larger issues of social justice and general population wellbeing. As changes have emerged in developed countries' healthcare systems and population structures, the political rhetoric has shifted towards an economic model in which older people are defined as healthcare consumers rather than as citizens with social rights. For example, 1990s Australian health and social services reforms carried themes of deregulation, cost containment for public spending, and greater contributions for services among those who can afford to pay (Howe, 2000). In Britain, recent policy rhetoric advocating the empowerment of elderly people has emphasized "community care," but has been accompanied by steady erosion of the state's responsibility for care provision. Market-driven changes in the UK long term care system have decentralized services, increased families' responsibilities, and opened up the private sector market for those who could afford to pay for services. Indeed, as Bernard and Phillips note, in recent years there has been increased concern about intergenerational equity in the distribution of healthcare services (see Chapters 6.4 and 6.5) and an interest in shifting the balance of financing of old age care between individuals and the state (Bernard and Phillips, 2000).

The Future of Health Policy for Older People

In the context of evolving systems of healthcare provision and the changing balance of needs between chronic and acute care, inequality in access to healthcare has been exacerbated across class, race, and gender lines (Harrington Meyer *et al.*, 1994; Fine and Chalmers, 2000; Bernard and Phillips, 2000). The emerging reality of health policy for aged people in many countries is an increasingly bifurcated system, comprised of private care for those who can afford it versus means-tested and stigmatizing poverty programs for the needy (Schunk and Estes, 2001), particularly insofar as chronic care is concerned. In response to these trends, scholars in many countries have begun to argue for integrated social policies designed to address broad societal ageing rather than narrow age-based interests.

Although long term care spending in most developed countries is expected to rise in the near future, in most countries it will remain at the relatively low level of about 1 percent of the GDP (Anderson and Hussey, 1999). Internationally, long term care is usually administered through the same systems of universal medical coverage that apply to all citizens but financed separately. As rates of insitutionalization have dropped in developed countries, new debates have emerged about how to strike a balance between institutional care and community-based care (Merlis, 2000). Innovations in medical technology and pharmaceuticals will likely continue driving up costs for state-of-the-art care for older people. While these can contribute to significant gains in both the quality and quantity of life, meeting the costs of doing so will be a challenge. Although all developed countries face similar problems responding to the unique health needs of elderly people, the only predictable outcome of future health policy debates is that no single model for acute and chronic care provision will likely emerge. Governments will continue to choose a variety of country-specific means for achieving their health policy goals.

FURTHER READING

Blackman, T. (2000). "Defining responsibility for care: approaches to the care of older people in six European countries," *International Journal of Social Welfare*, 9 (3): 181–90.

Hugman, R. (1994). *Ageing and the care of older people in Europe*. New York: St. Martin's Press.

Lassey, W. R., and M. L. Lassey (2001). *Quality of life for older people: an international perspective*. New Jersey: Prentice Hall.

REFERENCES

Anderson, G. F., and P. S. Hussey (1999). *Health and population aging: a multinational comparison*. Washington, D.C.: Commonwealth Fund.

Bernard, M., and J. Phillips (2000). "The challenge of ageing in tomorrow's Britain," *Ageing and Society*, 20: 33–54.

Blackman, T. (2000). "Defining responsibility for care: approaches to the care of older people in six European countries," *International Journal of Social Welfare*, 9 (3): 181–90.

Campbell, J. C., and N. Ikegami (2000). "Long-term care insurance comes to Japan," *Health Affairs*, 19: 26–39.

Cuellar, A. E., and J. M. Weiner (2000). "Can social insurance for long-term care work? The experience of Germany," *Health Affairs*, 19: 8–25.

Fine, M., and J. Chalmers (2000). "'User pays' and other approaches to funding of long-term care for older people in Australia," *Ageing and Society*, 20: 5–32.

Gilleard, C., and P. Higgs (2000). *Cultures of ageing*. Harlow: Pearson Education Limited.

Ginn, J., Street, D., and S. Arber (2002). *Women, work and pensions: international issues and prospects*. Buckingham: Open University Press.

Grogan, C., and E. Patashnik (2003). "Between welfare medicine and mainstream entitlement: Medicaid at the political crossroads," *Journal of Health Politics, Policy and Law*, 28 (5): 821–58.

Harrington Meyer, Ma., Street, D., and J. Quadagno (1994). "The impact of family status on income security and health care in old age: a comparison of western nations," *International Journal of Sociology and Social Policy*, 14: 53–83.

HelpAge International (2002). *State of world's older people 2002*. London: HelpAge International.

Howe, A. L. (2000). "Rearranging the compartments: the financing and delivery of care for Australia's elderly," *Health Affairs*, 19: 57–71.

Hugman, R. (1994). *Ageing and the care of older people in Europe*. New York: St. Martin's Press.

Jensen, G. and M. Morrisey (1992). "Employer-sponsored postretirement health benefits: not your mother's Medigap plan," *Gerontologist*, 32 (5): 691–97.

Lassey, W. R., and M. L. Lassey (2001). *Quality of life for older people: an international perspective*. New Jersey: Prentice Hall.

Merlis, M. (2000). "Caring for the frail elderly: an international perspective," *Health Affairs*, 19: 141–9.

Schunk, M. V., and C. L. Estes (2001). "Is German long-term care insurance a model for the United States?" *International Journal of Health Services*, 31: 617–34.

Street, D., Quadagno J., Parham, L., and S. McDonald (2003). "Reinventing long term care: the effect of policy changes on trends in nursing home reimbursement and resident characteristics, Florida, 1989–1997," *Gerontologist*, 43: 118–31.

US Census Bureau (1998). *Pension receipt rate and health coverage of rates of retirees*. Washington, D.C.: US Bureau of the Census.

US Senate (2001). *Retiree health benefits: employer-sponsored benefits may be vulnerable to further erosion*. Report to the Chairman, Committee on Health, Education, Labor and Pensions. Washington, D.C.: General Accounting Office.

Victor, C. (1991). *Health and health care in later life*. Buckingham: Open University Press.

Gerontological Nursing – the State of the Art

BRENDAN McCORMACK

INTRODUCTION

Gerontological nursing has come of age, and in contemporary practice with older people nurses play an active role in meeting their care needs in a variety of settings. The term 'gerontological nursing' is relatively new and reflects the growth of a speciality that has growing confidence in its knowledge base and expertise. It has long been recognised that, whilst services for older people are often criticised for being ritualistic and unresponsive to individual need, many of the most significant developments in nursing have happened in services for older people.

This chapter will explore the development of gerontological nursing as a specialist area of practice. The development of gerontological nursing from a service dominated by custodial care to one that emphasises person-centredness in practice will be explored. The journey of gerontological nursing from routinised care, to patient-centred care, and to the current situation where there is a dominant emphasis on person-centred care, will be mapped out. Differences in the way the speciality of gerontological nursing has developed internationally will be contrasted and critiqued. The educational preparation of nurses to work with older people will be discussed and the problems associated with recognising gerontological nursing as a speciality identified. Attributes of gerontological nursing curricula that are key in order for this area of nursing to progress as a speciality in its own right will be offered. It will be concluded that, despite the challenges, gerontological nursing is a vibrant area of practice that continues to grow and develop as the healthcare needs of older people change.

THE EVOLUTION OF HUMANISTIC CARING – PARALLEL JOURNEYS OF MEDICINE AND NURSING

It is suggested that geriatrics as a medical speciality originated in the United Kingdom (UK) through the work of Marjorie Warren (Grimley-Evans, 1997), who in the 1930s introduced systematic assessment and classification of the needs of elderly and infirm residents in workhouses. She pioneered her philosophy of 'old age is not a disease' through assessment, diagnosis and rehabilitation. Through her systematic approach, many older people were discharged from the workhouse with appropriate rehabilitation and equipment to aid their independence. Dr Warren argued the case for the development of a medical speciality of geriatrics, and for the first time acute and curative aspects of care for older people began to develop. Geriatric medicine has had a turbulent history and it is only in recent years that it has achieved true recognition as a speciality in its own right, and doctors have had full access to clinical and academic career progression opportunities. The challenge for medicine and nursing has been to break away from a history of service delivery with older people that was dominated by models of institutionalisation (Goffman, 1961) and routinised care.

Routinised Care

The changing status of nursing in society is widely documented in historical and sociological nursing texts (e.g. Dingwall *et al.*, 1988). Nursing's inevitable tensions often arise as a result of its search for its autonomy in bureaucratic organisations that sometimes fail to understand the reality of nursing practice (Davies, 1976). This tension is probably most evident in the development of nursing with older people and in many respects parallels the tensions that existed in the development of geriatric medicine (Evers, 1991). The history of geriatric medicine highlights how doctors working with older people were considered inferior in status and skills, particularly as 'cure' was the ultimate goal of the medical model and there was little interest in care of people with a long-term debilitating illness where cure was not the primary goal. Historically, nursing was very much an assisting profession to medicine and was influenced by many of the same attitudes. If doctors working with older people were considered inferior to other medical specialists, then nursing with its dependency on medicine to define its identity was truly the 'Cinderella service'. The first major study of nursing older people was undertaken in 1962 by Norton *et al.* (reprinted in 1976), although Norton had been writing about nursing and older people since the 1950s (see, for example, Norton, 1954, 1965 and 1967). She and her colleagues highlighted ritualised practices, based on routine rather than need. Research following this first study continued the theme of 'routinised geriatric care' as the dominant focus of nursing practice. Norton wrote in 1954 that, in order to change the dominant routine approach, there was a need to: 're-educate those with old and established ideas that all the patient needs is toilet attention and feeding, and secondly, to educate the rising generation of nurses to the scope and interests of the work' (p. 1253). Nursing education never embraced the care of older people as an area requiring specific knowledge, skill and expertise, and thus nursing's ability to respond appropriately to an evolving rehabilitative, as opposed to a custodial, model of care was limited. Norton (1977) described this as a shift from 'bedside' to 'chairside' nursing care, but commented that nothing had really changed in the nursing approach to care as all techniques, procedures and routines had evolved from care of the patient in bed. The development of a model of 'geriatric nursing care' (Norton, 1965) that evolved from this era has largely influenced the way in which nursing

work with older people continues to be organised (McFarlane, 1976; Henderson, 1980; Nolan, 1997). The emphasis is on the assessment of individualised care needs in order to plan help and assistance that would restore self-care abilities and achieve optimal independence. The influence of American nurse theorists such as Orem (1980) and Roy (1980) is evident here. American nurse theorists continue to influence gerontological nursing theory. In addition, gerontological nursing theory is shaped by behavioural, developmental, psychosocial and coping theories, and the integration of these shapes gerontological nursing practice, education and research.

Patient-centred Care

The *traditional* style of nursing practice that dominated the majority of patient care emphasised the service of medicine as having the focus of helping patients and was essentially concerned with the dutiful completion of a hierarchy of practical tasks (Binnie and Titchen, 1999). The most appropriate and efficient work design for this style was influenced by the industrial production-line model in which the appropriately qualified nurse completed tasks in the least possible time. The lack of continuity of care however, denied patients the comfort and support of sustained, caring relationships. Nursing work with older people has now largely cast off the shackles of its legacy, has overcome many of the challenges this legacy presented and today pioneers and innovates in many aspects of nursing, such as primary nursing, rehabilitation, family caregiving, biographical assessment, dementia care and practice development, for example (Nolan and Grant, 1989; Thomas, 1992; Brooker, 2002; Dewing and Wright, 2003; McCormack, 2003). Contemporary nursing practice with older people emphasises the importance of the nurse–patient relationship. The approach emphasises the acceptance of patients as whole human beings with wants, needs and fears that need to be addressed if healthcare is going to be effective. It includes the explicit rejection of a dominant biomedical approach that is seen as unable to take account of the phenomenological aspects of ill health (Porter, 1994). It emphasises the importance of the autonomy of the nurse and supports organisational practices that encourage individual nursing decision making and the exercise of individual accountability.

This style of practice demonstrates a deep respect for the autonomy of the patient as a person. Its aim is to transform the patient's experience of illness and for nursing interventions to be therapeutic in their own right. The role of the patient-centred nurse is to *be there*, offering personal support and technical expertise, while enabling the patient to follow the path of their own choosing and in their own way. This style of nursing reflects an existentialist philosophy and has influenced many contemporary nurse theorists. At the heart of this style of nursing is the therapeutic nurse–patient relationship that requires continuity of care and the acceptance of responsibility for the outcomes of care (McCormack, 2003). Professional caring is far greater than simply providing nursing care, and involves deep emotional involvement, self-awareness, the purposeful use of self, and paying attention to the aesthetic qualities of nursing. It is this conceptualisation of care that has achieved a significant change in thinking about the moral and ethical dimension of the nurse–patient relationship.

Person-centred Care

In contemporary gerontological policy and practice, person-centredness is a key focus and it underpins key strategies such as the National Service Framework for Older People in the UK (Department of Health, 2001). Immanuel Kant (translated by Sullivan, 1990) argued for the supreme equal value of persons and their intrinsic worth. Kant's ideal of persons postulates that persons should always be treated as ends in themselves and not as a means to another's end – a principle that guides many ethical, legal and moral frameworks in Western society. The history of nursing with older people suggests that they were not treated as persons, particularly in large institutions, but instead conformed to rigid rules and boundaries that served the needs of the organisation more than the older person. The work of Tom Kitwood and the Bradford Dementia Care Group (Kitwood, 1997a, 1997b) has probably been most influential on the development of person-centred care with older people. Whilst Kitwood's work focused on people with dementia, the principles underpinning the approach have been applied

across the spectrum of gerontological nursing. Kitwood's definition of personhood is informed by the work of Swiss psychologist Paul Tournier (1999) and the philosophies of Martin Buber (1984) and Carl Rogers (1961). Thus Kitwood (1997a: 8) defines personhood as: 'a standing or status that is bestowed upon one human being, by others, in the context of relationship and social being. It implies recognition, respect and trust.' In person-centred nursing, the relationship between the nurses and the older person is paramount, and it has been argued that sustaining a relationship that is nurturing to both nurse and patient requires valuing of self, moral integrity, reflective ability, knowing of self and others, and flexibility derived from reflection on values and their place in the relationship (McCormack, 2003; Dewing, 2002). Respect for values is central to person-centred practice (Williams and Tappen, 1999; McCormack, 2001a). It is important to develop a clear picture of what the patient values about his life and how he makes sense of what is happening to him. This provides a standard against which the nurse can compare current decisions and behaviours of the patient with those values and preferences made in life in general and which form the basis of a biography (Clarke *et al.*, 2003). There is an increasing literature in gerontology on the value of biography (see, for example, Kenyon *et al.*, 2001, for an edited volume of studies in narrative geron-

the only quality assessment approaches in gerontology that formally recognises the impact of the 'milieu of care' on the care experience. Paying attention to 'place' in care relationships is increasingly recognised as important (Andrews, 2003; Luckhurst and Ray, 1999). Whilst person-centredness has been most explicitly developed in gerontological nursing, it is a principle that transcends particular nursing specialities and indeed is implicit in many models of nursing. However, following a review of the literature, Nolan *et al.* (2001) concluded that we couldn't just accept person-centredness at face value. Currently, there exists little evidence of the benefits of person-centred nursing practice and this is a clear research agenda for the future in gerontological nursing.

EDUCATIONAL PREPARATION FOR PERSON-CENTRED GERONTOLOGICAL NURSING

The standard of education for nurses working in gerontology continues to be problematic and the challenges largely arise from the lack of recognition of gerontological nursing as a speciality in its own right. In the United Kingdom, gerontological practice is a compulsory component of pre-registration/undergraduate education programmes. However, how this is translated into practice is open to interpretation and local implementation and available courses differ in structure and content (Nolan *et al.*, 2002). This lack of consistency arises from a failure by nursing regulators to recognise the need for specialist preparation to work with older people. Nay *et al.* (1999) and Wade (2003) argue that gerontological nursing education programmes need reflect the complexity of the knowledge, skill and ise needed to work effectively with older peo- of the difficulty arises from the 'invisi- much of the expertise of gerontolog- earch into expert practice demon- knowledge is embedded in the , but, when asked, nurses find knowledge underpinning hnical aspects of work his issue has plagued ifested in debates ings, i.e. what ake partic- od and

drink, dressing, for example. Such so-called 'simple tasks' in meeting the effective healthcare needs of older people are far from simple and rely on a complex relationship between:

- the particular intervention
- mood state
- attention span
- concentration
- learning ability
- memory
- orientation
- perception
- problem solving
- psychomotor ability
- reaction time
- social intactness (McDougall, 1990).

When working with older people, it is not always easy to define the 'task' in question and the observable tasks are often the least significant components of effective practice. Knowing which components of practice require the input of a registered nurse and those that can be done by a less qualified carer is crucial to effective practice. For example, distinguishing between the need for a wide and diverse range of knowledge, skills and expertise in planning and managing the overall care plan for an older person is different to identifying specific tasks that need to be performed by individuals. In older people's services, this is often *the* fundamental mistake in service delivery, i.e. services are planned on the basis of tasks rather than the overall package of care required. Additionally, because of this approach that relies on the identification of 'observable' tasks, complex aspects of care are often delegated to the least skilled and knowledgeable team members. The implications of this are significant for individual older people in terms of care outcomes and overall service delivery – for example, debates about the *actual* need for skilled, knowledgeable and expert registered nurses (RNs) when working with older people in continuing care.

Others have argued that nurses cannot use the 'invisibility' argument to defend this situation (Nolan, 1997) and that the challenge to gerontological nursing is to demonstrate the value of the knowledge, skill and expertise that they bring to a given care situation through care outcomes. Heath (1999), McCormack and Ford (1999), Nolan *et al.* (2002) and Bennett and Flaherty-Robb (2003) have all argued that measurement of outcomes in gerontology should not focus on 'health gain' as is common in health outcome measurement, but instead should focus on how nursing inputs help an individual to achieve his or her desired realistic health choices. Outcomes from gerontological nursing are based on nurses recognising their role as enablers of health, based on individual life choices and potentials. McCormack and Ford (1999) have argued that, from this perspective, outcomes from nursing care can be demonstrated, such as improvements in quality of life, increased control over life choices and improvements in physical and psychosocial functioning. Fundamentally, all of this requires recognition of the need for specialist education programmes in gerontological nursing. Whilst specialist preparation to Advanced Practice level has existed in the USA for many years, Mion (2003) argues that the reality continues that most RNs have little or no preparation in gerontological nursing as part of their education. Mion cites a survey conducted by Rosenfeld *et al.* (1999), the results of which suggest that only 23 per cent of baccalaureate nursing programmes included a course in gerontological nursing and that only 4 per cent of these met all the criteria for an exemplary geriatrics education. Additionally Bennett and Flaherty-Robb (2003) suggest that, whilst there are in the region of sixty-three Advanced Practice programmes in gerontological nursing in the USA, only a few students graduate each year. In Europe, postregistration education programmes in gerontological nursing are commonplace. However, these are at a variety of academic levels, have variable levels of practice input, adopt a variety of philosophical perspectives and none lead to a recordable qualification as a specialist role in gerontological nursing. As The National Council for the Professional Development of Nursing and Midwifery (2003) (Republic of Ireland) suggest, the reality for many nurses completing postregistration gerontological nursing specialist education programmes is that they return to their workplace and carry on as they did before.

GERONTOLOGICAL NURSING CAREER OPPORTUNITIES

The lack of recognition and value of the specialist knowledge, skills and expertise of gerontological nurses is reflected in the failure of nursing registration boards worldwide to consider gerontological nursing as a recordable qualification. Currently, a variety of roles exist that deliver aspects of gerontological practice, such as diabetes care, continence care, falls treatment and prevention programmes, health promotion, dementia care, tissue viability, mental health, stroke rehabilitation and palliative care. However, despite these roles having a dominant focus on meeting the needs of older people and many nurses who work in these roles having expert knowledge in working with older people, the specialist practice contribution of nurses to the healthcare needs of older people continues to be largely unacknowledged. Other than in the USA where the roles of Gerontological Clinical Nurse Specialist and Gerontological Nurse Practitioner have been recognised for many years, little inroad has been made in establishing gerontological nursing as a specialist area of practice. In Australia, whilst most State Nursing Boards have a recordable 'Nurse Practitioner' registration, gerontological nursing is not one of the specialist areas recognised. A similar situation exists across Europe, although in some countries, nurses do work as gerontological nurse specialists (for example, Belgium, the Netherlands and Switzerland). Whilst there is little evidence of these being 'recordable qualifications' with nursing registration boards, gerontological nurses themselves in Europe are beginning to coordinate their efforts (Milisen, personal communication) through a proposed European Nursing Academy for Care of Older Persons (ENACO). ENACO aims to enhance the outcomes from care for older persons and their caregivers through strengthening gerontological nursing education, research and health policy within an interdisciplinary context. Whilst this development is in its infancy, it potentially represents the first innovative attempt at coordinating gerontological nursing as specialist practice. Similar innovation is taking place in the Republic of Ireland. In a recent report, The National Council for the Professional Development of Nursing and Midwifery (2003) has targeted the development of Gerontological Nurse Specialists as a key priority for the future development of services for older people. An innovative, community- and population-based generic gerontological nurse specialist role is proposed, with the development taking place in partnership with university-based education providers. In the United Kingdom, gerontological nursing is not considered to be a specialist area of practice and there is no structure in place for recording nurse practitioner qualifications. The development of gerontological nurse specialist roles is slow, as identified by Schofield (1999), despite a pilot of such a role in accident and emergency services showing reduced waiting times, prevention of unnecessary hospital admissions and a greater awareness by staff of the needs of older people (Bridges *et al.*, 2000). The introduction of the 'Nurse Consultant' role in the UK has enabled the development of career opportunities in gerontological nursing that previously had not existed. As Wade (2003) argues, this has been the first opportunity for gerontological nurses to advance their careers by integrating advanced levels of clinical practice, education, practice development and research into the one clinically based role.

The global nursing shortage and the reality of fiscally driven healthcare systems mean that, increasingly, registered nursing will be targeted at the areas of greatest need (Adams and Bond, 2003; Aiken *et al.*, 2001). Gerontological nursing is thus experiencing a crucial stage of its transition. Whilst increasing research evidence suggests that there is a direct relationship between available registered nurses and patient mortality (Aiken *et al.*, 2001, 2002; Needleman *et al.*, 2002), the ratio of registered to non-registered nurses, particularly in continuing care settings, continues to decrease, with most care settings operating with minimal recommended levels of registered nursing (Scanlon, 2001; RCP/RCN/BGS, 2000). One response to this challenge is to suggest that it confirms what Armstrong-Esther *et al.* (1994) suggested, that the dominant role of gerontological nursing is 'the warehousing of elderly people until they die' and thus minimal levels of skill and expertise are required to undertake this function. On the other hand, this challenge can be seen as an opportunity for nurses to expand their role and develop specialist areas of practice. Gerontological nurses do not practice in isolation, however, and thus the specialist function of gerontological nurses can be best realised as a component of comprehensive 'population-based' services for older people. Johnson and Hoyes (1996), for example, have argued that '"Gerontological Nurse Specialists" with particular expertise in assessment and healthcare planning for older people could be employed by long-term care establishments, Primary Health Care Teams or

Community Nursing Teams'. Such nurse specialists would act as care coordinators, where specific aspects of care are delivered by other trained staff. Johnson and Hoyes (1996) argue that the 'proposed combination of Gerontological Nurse Specialists and better trained care staff would enable a more flexible and cost-effective use of nursing skills, which would be available in non-hospitalised settings to a larger proportion of the elderly population'. A similar argument has been made by the Royal College of Physicians (England), The Royal College of Nursing and the British Geriatrics Society (RCP/RCN/BGS, 2000) and the Department of Health (England) Standing Nursing and Midwifery Advisory Committee (2001). In the USA it is becoming increasingly commonplace for the role of nurse specialist and nurse practitioner in gerontology to be combined in a unified role, thus representing a shift in lines of demarcation and role boundaries. Clearly, gerontological nursing is ready to 'come of age' and develop frameworks and models of practice that look to the future of healthcare delivery and the changing nature of older peoples' needs.

BRINGING IT ALL TOGETHER – SPECIALIST PRACTICE FOR THE FUTURE

The future role of the gerontological nurse is likely to be primarily focused upon the facilitation of care plans rather than the direct delivery of care. McCormack (2001b, 2003) developed a framework for person-centred practice with older people where the key role of the gerontological nurse is that of the facilitation of the older person's authenticity (and that of others significant to them), i.e. decisions based on their beliefs, values and aspirations. Recent work by Randers and Mattiasson (2004) supports the idea of the nurse as a facilitator of older persons' decisions that are based on their authenticity. Based on this model, it is proposed here that the gerontological nurse of the future will need expertise in five functions.

1. *Informed flexibility:* facilitating decision making through information sharing and the integration of new information into established care plans.
2. *Sympathetic presence:* engaging with the older person as a unique individual and responding to their 'cues' in a way that maximises their potential.

3. *Negotiation:* facilitating patient participation through a culture of care that values the views of the patient as a legitimate basis for decision making while recognising that being the final arbiter of decisions is of secondary importance.

4. *Mutuality:* recognising the importance of the values held by all participants in decision making.

5. *Transparency:* the making explicit of intentions and motivations for action and the boundaries within which care decisions are set.

In order to operate these five functions, education curricula will need to reflect the following attributes of specialist gerontological nursing:

- Providing information in a way that is relevant to the patient's ability to understand it and in a way that is meaningful to their biography.
- Developing clear goals of care that aim to maximise the individual's potential to achieve independence.
- Facilitating knowledge and understanding of care processes, that empower the individual to gain further knowledge in the context of their life experiences and altered levels of independence.
- Reinforcement of care decisions, integration of new information and formulation of new decisions in partnership with the older person.
- Acknowledging the older person's 'emotional coping ability' and the facilitation of emotional responses to their experiences.
- Managing interactions in a way that acknowledges the centrality of the patient's life history as an expression of their values that underpin care plans.
- The recognition of the nurse's role in the prevention of constraints that negate autonomous decision making by older people.
- Facilitating patients' life reviews as a means of establishing the values that need to be held central to care decisions.
- Involving family and significant others in the provision of information necessary for negotiated decision making.
- Respecting patients' subjective view of their lives, as presented through their biographies, as central to negotiated care decisions.
- Reinforcing patients' decisions in a multidisciplinary context in order to reduce organisational constraints on autonomous decision making.
- Understanding patients' expectations of healthcare / healthcare practitioners and working with these expectations to minimise constraints on autonomous action.

- Assessing risks in decision making and the limits beyond which risks cannot be taken.
- Balancing nurses' values with those of patients and their families / significant others.
- Having technical competence in assessing, planning and delivering comprehensive care to older people.

CONCLUSIONS

Gerontological nursing has developed as a specialist field of practice. The gerontological nurse as a facilitator would appear to offer a way of regenerating gerontological nursing practice – a regeneration that identifies it as a process of dynamic caring that maintains autonomy at a time when an individual's sense of independence is under greatest threat. The importance of skilled, expert caring nursing practice can never be underestimated in the care of older people. The expert gerontological nurse tries to give the patient as many opportunities as possible to exercise freedom of choice, to express opinions, to make decisions, and to talk while the nurse really listens, and the opportunity to express their authentic self in a negotiated partnership with the nurse. The future challenge for gerontological nursing is to make this expertise explicit in the form of care outcomes that are measurable and understandable to health and social care decision makers.

FURTHER READING

Heath, H., and Schofield, I., eds. (1999). *Healthy ageing: nursing older people*. London: Mosby / Harcourt Brace and Company Limited.

Keady, J., Clarke, C., and T. Adams, eds. (2004). *Community mental health nursing and dementia care*. Buckingham: Open University Press.

McCormack, B. (2001). *Negotiating partnerships with older people – a person-centred approach*. Basingstoke: Ashgate.

Nolan, M., Davies, S., and G. Grant, eds. (2001). *Working with older people and their families*. Buckingham: Open University Press.

REFERENCES

Adams, A., and S. Bond (2003). 'Staffing in acute hospital wards: part 1. The relationship between number of nurses and ward organizational environment', *Journal of Nursing Management*, 11: 287–92.

Aiken, L. H., Clarke, S. P., Sloane, D. M., Sochalski, J. A., Busse, R., Clarke, H., Giovannetti, P., Hunt, J., Rafferty,

A. M., and J. Shamian (2001). 'Nurses' reports on hospital care in five countries', *Health Affairs*, 20 (3): 43–53.

Aiken, L. H., Clarke, S. P., Sloane, D. M., Sochalski, J., and J. H. Silber (2002). 'Hospital nurse staffing and patient mortality, nurse burnout, and job dissatisfaction', *Journal of the American Medical Association*, 288 (16): 1987–93.

Andrews, G. (2003). 'Locating a geography of nursing: space, place and the progress of geographical thought', *Nursing Philosophy*, 4 (3): 231–48.

Armstrong-Esther, C. A., Browne, K. D., and J. E. McAfee (1994). 'Elderly patients: still clean and sitting quietly', *Journal of Advanced Nursing*, 19 (2): 264–71.

Bennett, J., and M. Flaherty-Robb (2003). 'Issues affecting the health of older citizens: meeting the challenge'. *Online Journal of Issues in Nursing*, 8 (2): Manuscript 1. Available www.nursingworld.org/ojin/topic21/tpc21_1.htm.

Binnie, A., and A. Titchen (1999). *Freedom to practise: the development of patient-centred nursing*. Oxford: Butterworth-Heinemann.

Bridges J., Meyer, J., and L. Barnes (2000). 'Specialising in older people', *Nursing Times*, 96 (30): 42.

Brooker, D. (2002). 'Dementia care mapping: a look at its past, present and future', *Journal of Dementia Care*, 10 (3): 33–6.

Buber, M. (1984). *I and thou*. London: Prentice Hall.

Clarke, A., Hanson, E. J., and H. Ross (2003). 'Seeing the person behind the patient: enhancing the care of older people using a biographical approach', *Journal of Advanced Nursing*, 12: 697–706.

Davies, C. (1976). 'Experience of dependency and control in work: the case of nurses', *Journal of Advanced Nursing*, 1: 273–82.

Department of Health (2001). *National service framework for older people*. London: Department of Health.

Dewing, J. (2002). 'From ritual to relationship: a person-centred approach to consent in qualitative research with older people who have a dementia', *Dementia*, 1 (2): 157–71.

Dewing, J., and J. Wright (2003). 'A practice development project for nurses working with older people', *Practice Development in Health Care*, 2 (1): 13–28.

Dingwall, R., Rafferty, A. M., and C. Webster (1988). *An introduction to the social history of nursing*. London: Routledge.

Evers, H. (1991). 'Care of the elderly sick in the UK'. In S. J. Redfern, ed., *Nursing elderly people*. London: Churchill Livingstone.

Goffman, E. (1961). *On the characteristics of total institutions. First essay in asylums*. Harmondsworth: Penguin.

Grimley-Evans, J. (1997). 'Geriatric medicine: a brief history', *British Medical Journal*, 315: 1075–7.

Gubrium, J. F. (2001). 'Narrative, experience, and aging'. In G. Kenyon, P. Clark and B. deVries (2001). *Narrative gerontology: theory, research and practice*. New York: Springer Publishing Company.

Heath, H. B. M. (1999). 'Perspectives on ageing and older people'. In H. B. M. Heath and I. Schofield, eds., *Healthy ageing: nursing older people*. London: Mosby / Harcourt Brace and Company Limited.

Henderson, V. (1980). 'Preserving the essence of nursing in a technological age', *Journal of Advanced Nursing*, 5: 240–60.

Johnson, M., and L. Hoyes (1996). *Establishing a regulatory system for single registered care homes*. York: Joseph Rowntree Foundation, Housing Research 200.

Kenyon, G., Clark, P., and B. deVries (2001). *Narrative gerontology: theory, research and practice*. New York: Springer Publishing Company.

Kitwood, T. (1997a). 'On being a person'. In T. Kitwood, *Dementia reconsidered: the person comes first*. Milton Keynes: Open University Press.

(1997b). 'Cultures of care: tradition and change'. In T. Kitwood and S. Benson, eds., *The new culture of dementia care*. London: Hawker Publications.

Luckhurst, M., and M. Ray (1999). 'Person-centred standards of care', *Elderly Care*, 11 (6): 29–31.

Martin, G. W., and D. Younger (2001). 'Person-centred care for people with dementia: a quality audit approach', *Journal of Psychiatric and Mental Health Nursing*, 8 (5): 443–8.

Mion, L. (2003). 'Care provision for older adults: who will provide?' *Online Journal of Issues in Nursing*, 8 (2): manuscript 3. Available www.nursingworld.org/ojin/topic21/tpc21_3.htm.

McCormack, B. (2001a). 'Autonomy and the relationship between nurses and older people', *Ageing and Society*, 21: 417–46.

(2001b). *Negotiating partnerships with older people: a person-centred approach*. Aldershot: Ashgate Press.

(2003). 'A conceptual framework for person-centred practice with older people', *International Journal of Nursing Practice*, 9: 202–9.

McCormack, B., and P. Ford (1999). 'The contribution of expert gerontological nursing', *Nursing Standard*, 10 (13): 42–5.

McDougall, G. J. (1990). 'A review of screening instruments for assessing cognition and mental status in older adults', *Nurse Practitioner*, 15: 11.

McFarlane, J. (1976). 'A charter for caring', *Journal of Advanced Nursing*, 1: 187–96.

National Council for the Professional Development of Nursing and Midwifery (2003). *Agenda for the future professional development of nursing and midwifery*. Dublin, Republic of Ireland: National Council for the Professional Development of Nursing and Midwifery.

Nay, R., Garratt, S., and S. Koch (1999). 'Challenges for Australian nursing in the International Year of Older Persons', *Geriatric Nursing*, 20 (1): 14–17.

Needleman, J., Buerhaus, P., Mattke, S., Stewart, M., and K. Zelevinsky (2002). 'Nurse-staffing levels and the quality of care in hospitals', *New England Journal of Medicine*, 346 (22): 1715–22.

Nolan, M. (1997). 'Gerontological nursing: professional priority or eternal Cinderella?' *Ageing and Society*, 17 (4): 447–60.

Nolan, M., and G. Grant (1989). 'Addressing the needs of informal carers: a neglected area of nursing practice', *Journal of Advanced Nursing*, 14 (11): 950–61.

Nolan, M., Davies, S., and G. Grant (2001). 'Integrating perspectives'. In M. Nolan, S. Davies and G. Grant, *Working with older people and their families: key issues in policy and practice*. Milton Keynes: Open University Press.

Nolan, M., Brown, J., Davies, S., Keady, J., and J. Nolan (2002). *Longitudinal study of the effectiveness of educational preparation to meet the needs of older people and their carers*, The Advancing Gerontological Education in Nursing (The AGEIN) Project, report no. 48. London and Sheffield: English National Board for Nursing Midwifery and Health Visiting, and Sheffield University.

Norton, D. (1954). 'A challenge to nursing', *Nursing Times*, 50: 1253–8.

—— (1965). 'Nursing in geriatrics', *Gerontologia Clinica*, 7: 57–60.

—— (1967). *Hospitals for the long stay patients*. Oxford: Pergamon Press.

—— (1977). 'Geriatric nursing – what it is and what it is not', *Nursing Times*, 73: 1622–3.

Norton, D., McLaren, R., and A. N. Exton-Smith (1976). *An investigation of geriatric nursing problems in hospital*. Edinburgh: Churchill Livingstone.

Orem, D. E. (1980). *Nursing: concepts of practice*, 2nd edn. New York: McGraw-Hill.

Porter, S. (1994). 'New nursing: the road to freedom', *Journal of Advanced Nursing*, 20: 269–74.

Randers, I., and A. C. Mattiasson (2004). 'Autonomy and integrity: upholding older adult patients' dignity', *Journal of Advanced Nursing*, 45 (1): 63–71.

RCF/RCN/BGS (Royal College of Physicians, the Royal College of Nursing and the British Geriatrics Society) (2000). *The health and care of older people in care homes: a comprehensive interdisciplinary approach. Report of a joint working party of the Royal College of Physicians, the Royal College of Nursing and the British Geriatrics Society*. London: Royal College of Physicians.

Rogers, C. (1961). *On becoming a person*. Boston: Houghton Mifflin Co.

Rosenfeld, P., Bottrell, M., Fulmer, T., and M. Mezey (1999). 'Gerontological nursing content in baccalaureate nursing programs: findings from a national survey', *Journal of Professional Nursing*, 15 (2): 84–94.

Roy, C. (1980). 'The Roy Adaptation Model'. In J. P. Riehl and C. Roy, eds., *Conceptual models for nursing practice*, 2nd edn. New York: Appleton-Century-Crofts.

Scanlon, W. J. (2001). *Nursing workforce: recruitment and retention of nurses and nurse aides is a growing concern*, GAO-01-750T. Washington, D.C.: Government Accounting Office.

Schofield, L. (1999). 'The rise of specialist nursing roles', *Elderly Care*, 11 (8): 8–11.

Standing Nursing and Midwifery Advisory Committee (SNMAC) (2001). *Caring for older people: a nursing priority*. London: Department of Health.

Sullivan, R. J. (1990). *Immanuel Kant's moral theory*. Cambridge: Cambridge University Press.

Thomas, L. H. (1992). 'Qualified nurse and nursing auxiliary perceptions of their work environment in primary, team and functional nursing wards', *Journal of Advanced Nursing*, 17 (3): 373–82.

Tonuma, M., and M. Wimbolt (2000). 'From rituals to reason: creating an environment that allows nurses to nurse', *International Journal of Nursing Practice*, 6 (4): 214–18.

Tournier, P. (1999). *The meaning of persons*. New York: Buccaneer Books Inc.

Wade, S. (2003). 'Meeting the needs of older people'. In S. Wade, ed., *Intermediate care of older people*. London: Whurr Publishers.

Williams, C. L., and R. M. Tappen (1999). 'Can we create a therapeutic relationship with nursing home residents in the later stages of Alzheimer's disease?' *Journal of Psychosocial Nursing*, 37 (3): 28–35.

Delivering Effective Social / Long Term Care to Older People

BLEDDYN DAVIES

INTRODUCTION

This chapter is primarily about achieving efficiency in pursuing ends from means, given equity. It discusses only some themes:

- The number, variety and complexity of evaluation criteria in the context of growing resource scarcity and efforts to clarify priorities and achieve greater efficiency.

- Emphasis on flexibly matching service inputs to outcomes and user circumstances through time. Boundaries between care modes have become less distinct, though some factors have excessively slowed the process of boundary erosion. (By a care mode is meant a set of services and resources, any combination of which can be used during one stage of a journey as a periodic or continuous recipient of care; for example, care in a care home providing its own hotel and care inputs.) There has been greater awareness that the effects on outcomes depend on service mixes and levels in ways which are mediated by user risks, needs and other circumstances. The concept 'targeting' has become more important but also more sophisticated, particularly in countries in which their governments are held responsible for achieving an efficient 'system' covering a high proportion of citizens. In some countries there is evidence of quick improvements in performance in important respects, though it may be difficult to maintain the rate as more difficult problems are engaged.

- To create greater flexibility, better performance of 'care management tasks', particularly assessment, monitoring and review, is needed. There is evidence that the emphasis on care management can contribute greatly. There has been more attention to better management of transitions between and through need states and service modes. Though insufficiently, fitting care management arrangements to the circumstances of users, groups and system circumstances has occurred, with more application of concepts like 'chronic disease management' and boundary redefinition and crossing, and creation of jobs with skills better matched to needs.

- With greater explicitness and complexity of outcomes, attention to the opportunity costs of improvements in some and the form of losses in others, evidence being both from the comparison of the performance of countries and from research into the relations between service inputs and outcomes within countries. Clearer prioritisation is essential. Though relations between service inputs and outcomes can through time be improved, and there is scope for using resources more efficiently, against a background of rising demands, the main costs of improvements of one kind remain the other benefits forgone.

Entry themes – the first appearance of a new client – reflect common features in changes in care systems:

- A gestalt switch from assuming that need and user/caregiver wishes are relatively simple and uniform, and are appropriately met by a relatively narrow range of standardised services, to assumptions that needs and wishes are many, various and often complex, requiring requisite variety and complexity for a population with rising expectations. Policy values reflect ambitions of users and caregivers about autonomy and lifestyles. In consequence, there have been discussions (and in some countries the introduction) of new forms of benefit payable to persons with long term care need, and of such policy principles as 'joined-up government' across 'policy silos', 'person-led' assessment and care planning, and 'carer-blind' service allocations.

- Attempts to develop home and community care arrangements allowing higher proportions of dependent persons to be supported with care in their own homes or in homely settings in the community (OECD, 1996).

- Changes in welfare mix associated with the shift from 'unicentric welfare systems dominated by state provision to more mixed forms in which state provision is explicitly integrated and balanced with private and informal sources', involving 'alterations in dominant ideologies of welfare in which traditional social rationales are expanded to include economic and market criteria' (Baldock and Evers, 1992; Kraan *et al.*, 1991).

Space allows discussion of only some implications.

POLICY EVALUATED BY A WIDER RANGE OF MORE COMPLEX OUTCOMES

Conceptualisation of and research on the newly prioritised outcomes occurred before policy reforms gathered momentum in the US and UK, and was to varying degrees reflected in evaluations of leading experiments like the US long term care channeling demonstration and the UK Kent Community Care Project and its descendants. In contrast, the evaluative criterion primarily used by policymakers was 'cost reduction or neutrality accompanied by user/carer benefits'. Understanding the more complex outcomes made that criterion seem narrow, trapped into a discourse dominated by agency interests, distracting attention from key issues and policy possibilities.

Other developments have been to:

- Complement indicators of broad and ultimate outcomes of the whole intervention with indicators of narrow and immediate effects of each service; for instance, Geron *et al.* (2000).

- Elaborate routine systems with individualised data for users linking outcome measurement with financing, quality improvement, policy and practice analysis, and practice and practice management themselves. Perhaps the most impressive is the Minimum Data Set / Resident Assessment Instrument (RAI-MDS), the product of vast investment since the late

seventies. It does not meet all needs. It does not directly ascertain user and carer satisfaction with service, does not collect certain kinds of information affecting users' and carers' subjective perceptions of services, and it demands a high degree of investment and commitment at all levels to implement and continue to operate carefully for the data to be of high quality.

- Increasingly seek to rehabilitate and re-enable as well as partially to compensate for disability. The assumptive worlds of social and some healthcare services have been dominated by attempting to compensate for functional disabilities. For many mainstream users, the assumption dominated policy for targeting, the source and nature of information sought in assessments (within the UK, little information or input from health professions), sectoral and so professional autarchy in care planning, in the performance of service (for instance, quickly doing tasks for the users as compared with slowly teaching and helping the user to become more independent). In the UK and US, the increasing pressure on public budgets since the mid seventies was accompanied by a contraction of activity on less essential tasks, and a shift of resources away from persons at lower risk of catastrophic outcomes or admission to institutions of long term care (Davies *et al.*, 2000; Estes, 2000; Estes and Swann, 1993). The reforms made the UK system highly efficient in targeting those at high risk of admission, and effective in reducing their use of care homes by providing home care. But it had not achieved the kind of coordination, cooperation, collaboration or structural integration which would make health and social care services and other resources complementary and produce a better balance of therapeutic and compensatory needs (Davies *et al.*, 2000). From the late 1990s, however, integration has been highly prioritised and powerful incentives created to improve it (Department of Health, 1998). Despite differences in institutional context, the US also faces some of the same challenges in rebalancing and more effectively combining compensatory and therapeutic outcomes, and in integrating social and healthcare skills and resources to do so (R. A. Kane, 1995, 1999).

SERVICE INPUTS, NEEDS AND OUTCOMES

Research on the influence of variations in service quantities and mixes on outcomes has been developed to complement comparisons of the impact of models overall. Results confirm that, as with most other personal services aimed at complex outcomes, variations in user circumstances have great influence on the states which services are aimed to modify, and that the impact of similar service depends greatly on these circumstances. Therefore, matching resources, and how they are used, to user circumstances is key to equity and efficiency. For that, account must be taken of the substitutability and complementarity of services, and service *'productivities'* (the outcome produced with different service levels), specifically *'marginal* productivities' (additional benefit from additional input), for each important outcome in relation to their prices.

The earliest British productivity studies illustrated the need for better matching of resources to needs at the individual level (Davies *et al.*, 1990). Services were not matched to needs, so any marginal productivities tended to be too low to be estimable. A decade later, after five years of reform, the pattern had changed (Davies *et al.*, 2000). There were productivity effects for a wide range of outcomes: approximately 100 effects for seven broadly defined services ('home care', 'day care' and others) for seventeen benefits for users and carers of direct evaluative importance: 'final outputs'.

The productivity effects reflect the complexity which theoreticians postulate and practitioners observe:

– Many individual circumstances mediate relationships between service levels and outputs.
– The additional inputs to require increased benefits of some kinds depend on the level of other benefits achieved.
– Often, one of several services can be used instead of others to produce a benefit; that is, many are often to a substantial degree 'substitutable' for other services. It had been argued that potential substitutability is one of the most important features of the relations between ends and means in community-based care (Davies and Challis, 1986). Because of it, big gains can be made by choosing the most efficient service combinations for the circumstances. Conversely, failure to adjust service mixes to different prioritisations of benefits costs a great deal in benefits forgone by users and carers. This is shown by simulations of service mixes which by maximising one output create 'collateral' losses in the level of other benefits.

Costly also is the failure to adjust to differences in circumstances with respect to relative prices and availability of services. Some services seem under-utilised in relation to others. In particular, day and respite care appear to be under-utilised. Home care appears to be relatively over-utilised compared with newer services. Where the estimates of marginal productivities varied substantially with service levels, it was more common for higher service levels to be associated with lower marginal service productivities for home and day care – a situation described by economists as 'diminishing returns'.

The combined impact of the effects suggested that services conferred large and widespread benefits on users and informal carers. Effects are well summarised by two performance indicators for each benefit. One, the *Risk Offset of Productivity Proportion [ROPP]*, measures the degree to which the effects of risk/need factors are offset by service impacts. Its rationale is that the principal objective is to offset the consequences of risk factors. The other, the *Cover of Productivity Proportion [COPP]*, measures the proportion of the entire sample affected by the productivity effects. Service impacts in the UK estimated that ROPPs were 18 per cent or higher for seven important benefits, including the number of additional days spent at home rather than in residential homes (32 per cent); the indicator of the reduction in the felt burden of caregiving among principal informal carers (25 per cent); the indicator of users' increased sense of empowerment over daily living (24 per cent); improvements in personal care and household care due to service inputs ascribed by the user to the service impacts (22 and 23 per cent); and the degree of satisfaction of the user with the level of service being received (18 per cent). Other significant effects are for socialisation and intra-familial relationships.

Research with the same objectives has been advocated by leading scholars in the US; see, for instance, Weissert *et al.* (2003), and authors in the *Journal of Ageing and Health*, volume 11, number 3.

IMPACTS OF CARE MANAGEMENT INPUTS

Non-comparable designs usually make it difficult to infer the effects of improved care management from independent studies from periods before and after major changes in care systems. In England, the reforms announced in 1989 intended to make the better performance of care management the 'cornerstone' of a logic involving other changes radically affecting every aspect of the system (Department of Health, 1989). A study conducted from 1985 replicated after the reforms a conclusion reached by the Department of Health on the basis of its inspections and reviews of the evidence: 'this focus on individual care management, focused towards helping more people to live in their own homes, was the key change to the system' (Department of Health, 1998; Davies et al., 2000).

Most of the earlier studies were single experiments in the US, UK and Canada. The results were extensively analysed (Applebaum and Austin, 1989; Davies and Challis, 1986; Hughes, 1988; Kemper et al., 1987; Weissert, 1990; Weissert et al., 1988; Weissert and Hedrick, 1994). By the evaluative criteria set by the funding agencies, results for most of these highly diverse projects were disappointing, partly because of the designs of the collections and analyses, partly because of 'implementation gaps', partly because of weaknesses in model logics. It was difficult to infer the effects of care management itself from most of the early projects.

However there were clear lessons.

– The key mechanism, the substitution of home and community services for nursing homes, could work only for populations at high risk of substantial nursing home use, so targeting was key. Targeted users not only had to have disability-related circumstances increasing the probability of nursing home use but also be at high risk of utilisation for a range of other reasons. UK experiments focused on substituting for residential care worked better partly because targeting reflected a wider range of the predictors of admission to care homes, and partly because their logic was more systematically based on creating incentives at the field level to make support arrangements more flexible and more responsive to costs and benefits (Davies and Challis, 1986). The importance of incentives was also recognised by American analysts (Weissert, 1990). A UK study based on pooled social services and health service budgets was clearly successful because of successful targeting and its use of workers combining health and social care functions in flexible support patterns, though partly because of the high unit cost of long-stay hospitals compared

with what was shortly to become their direct equivalent, nursing homes (Challis et al., 1995).

– Care managers particularly need incentives, information, and frameworks helping to optimise the balance between service productivities and prices. For instance, reanalysis of the channelling project data suggested that the project seriously lost efficiency because its packages contained excessive quantities of social home care and insufficient inputs of home healthcare (Davies, 1992; Greene et al., 1993).

– Patterns of demand generated by care managers were more likely to provide strong incentives to providers and others to adjust their supply and other aspects of their behaviour when the care management arrangements channelled a substantial proportion of total demand, were expected to endure, and when there were mechanisms for informing managers and providing agencies about the patterns created by care-managed demand, care managers' perceptions about unmet and inefficiently or inappropriately met needs because of the absence of services, care managers' observations reflecting shortfalls in quality, and the like.

The early projects financed by the Australian Community Options Programme added other lessons, many compatible with earlier American and British experience and comparative and meta-analysis (Capitman, 1985). In particular, the Australian initiatives show the influence of project context – for instance, project 'auspices' (Department of Health, Housing and Human Services 1992).

The presence of care management arrangements is now so much part of the wallpaper that in many programmes it is the substantive innovations and general features of the setting (like the style of chronic disease management) which are emphasised, though the performance of care management tasks in ways complementing the other scheme inputs is clearly key to their success.

WITHIN-PROGRAMME MATCHING OF CARE MANAGEMENT INPUTS TO USER CIRCUMSTANCES, SYSTEM CHARACTERISTICS AND PRIORITISED OUTCOMES

Like other services, the productivity of care management is contingent on users' need-related circumstances and risks. Therefore the quantity and nature of care management must be matched to user needs, and balanced well with other inputs.

Except for relatively homogeneous caseloads and programmes whose teams face similar case mixes, there is a risk of inequity and inefficiency if the only mechanism for the matching is at the team level in the context of informal policy, without the support of an agency- and/or system-wide policy framework and mechanisms to adjust resources to enable them to be applied. Some American programmes have formal triaging mechanisms for intensive care management. Examples are programmes of care management by insurance companies for high-cost users due to chronically disabling conditions, and a few Medicaid programmes, such as Ohio's PASSPORT program (Diwan, 1999; Kunkel and Scala, 1998).

English social care management to a greater extent matches the time intensity and professional background of care managers to user circumstances. National policy guidance set out a series of 'levels' defined in these terms.

- There is great and arguably excessive local variety at the intra-authority as well as inter-authority levels (Challis *et al.*, 2002; Weiner *et al.*, 2002).
- Despite the wide area variations, the system overall is well described as providing the three levels hypothesised in reports of the Social Service Inspectorate in the late nineties (Laming, 1997): a more intensive level where the care manager is fully professionally qualified and engaged wholly on care management and complementary casework tasks; a coordinative level, providing on average fewer hours of care management input by workers who are often not fully professionally qualified and combine care management with other service-management tasks; and an 'administrative' level, in which there is virtually no face-to-face contact.
- Users are matched to level on the basis of aspects of complexity arguably associated with differences in the productivities of different levels, but the matching is loose, with great variation between teams and larger areas in the probabilities of users being matched to the higher level.
- The main effects of care management inputs are 'indirect' rather than 'direct': on what is produced from the other services, not what is directly produced by the care management itself. Indirect effects have always been argued to be the highest common factor

in the rationale for care management development (Davies, 1992).
- Care management inputs during the Set-Up phase of the care-managed career appear to be under-provided relative to services over the whole of the users' career; that is, the ratio of marginal productivities of the case-appropriate level of care management inputs during the Set-Up phase to prices is higher than the ratios of marginal productivities to prices for service inputs.
- Productivities of intensive care management are highest for more complex cases irrespective of the level of inputs. Productivities of coordinative care management are higher for other users. Greater care management inputs are associated with improved outcomes up to the average number of hours of input. Beyond that, the gains seem to be slight, and indeed may actually diminish. In contrast, the productivity curves for coordinative care management suggest increasing marginal productivities with larger inputs. Therefore, it is important to ensure that the increased resources to intensive care management should be more than matched by increased resources to coordinative care management, given the increasing marginal productivities and that the numbers receiving each level might well need to be roughly equal, though there are features of the dynamics of allocation in social services departments which might result in the opposite. (Davies and Fernandez, 2004).

The English national government have produced and are attempting to secure the local implementation of improvements in care management around a 'Single Assessment Process' in the context of a National Service Framework for elderly people. Matching care management arrangements to user circumstances is intended to become more flexible through time, reducing the effects of initial errors in allocation; and more flexible at a point in time with respect to professionals' inputs and responsibilities. (Coordination across professional and agency boundaries is much more powerfully an objective of the NSF and the SAP than it was of the reform policy of the early nineties.)

DISCUSSION

This chapter has mentioned only some strands.

- *Targeting is key.* First, good targeting requires both that those allocated resources have benefits which are great compared with the costs – 'vertical target efficiency' – and that those for whom the benefits are great compared with the costs are allocated resources – 'horizontal target efficiency' (Bebbington and Davies, 1983; Davies, 1981; Davies *et al.*, 1990). Perhaps UK reforms initially, and many US programmes, focused too little on the latter. Secondly, targeting concepts and definitions should reflect the number, variety and complexity of aims and the variety of risks and needs and service characteristics affecting the relationship between service levels and mixes and the achievement of the aims. Crude screening criteria are inadequate for the full task. Targeting criteria must make allocations reflect user variations in risks, needs, likely service effects on the risks and needs, and the relative value of the different benefits (Davies and Challis, 1986; Davies *et al.*, 2000; Weissert, 1990; Weissert *et al.*, 2003). That insight is reflected in changes in processes in, for instance, the French Allocation Personnalisée d'Autonomie and Australian assessment.

- *Adapting systems to present appropriate incentives for equity and efficiency, and provide conditions for them to work.* Despite the role of incentives argument in influential projects, English policy agencies have rarely made these logics key to what is put into effect. Incentivisation was the basis of the logic for the design of care management arrangements, some arrangements whose rationale was incentivisation were recommended in national policy guidance, but field agencies often did not introduce them. That there is much unfulfilled potential in the emphasis on care management and commissioning of services – including to at least some degree shortfalls in service supply – is to a great extent due to the absence of incentives logics of requisite sophistication for the contexts. American managed care models are based on the incentives argument. Disappointment with the performance of most programmes, including those for persons dually eligible for Medicare and Medicaid, illustrates how difficult it is to base design on realistic causal argument as well as to secure implementation of all the model features essential to make the causal processes operate (Kane *et al.*, 2003).

- *Recognising the dilemmas but potential gains from 'consumer-directed' 'direct payment' models.* In the US, important elements of their rationale are the efficiency-improving consequences of additional flexibility at the case level, together with savings on intensive care management and matching to individual needs and wishes (Doty *et al.*, 1996). Evaluations continue to show that some fears have been exaggerated and most show gains of certain kinds, implying that cash and counselling models are an important alternative for some. Evidence confirms prior expectations about the targeting patterns likely to yield the greatest gains, but actually achieving the most successful pattern of utilisation is not straightforward. The problem could be worse where a choice between a consumer-directed and a 'professional' model is stark, allowing selection of only some areas or aspects and tasks for self-direction, and where changes in the sphere of self-direction cannot be adapted flexibly through time. The very differences in perspectives between professionals and lay users which contribute to the gains illustrate differences in judgements about the consequences of alternative courses of action, and no one group has a monopoly of prescience. The effect may be a loss with respect to some benefits – for instance, less undesired use of institutions for long term care – not because the user deliberately chooses that loss, but because of misjudgements. Also many consumer-directed models around the world imply very different – and in some respects less sophisticated – equity criteria than those defined in the reform visions in countries who initially chose different financing and delivery models.

There will be immense and continually changing challenges. Studies of service productivities which simulate the consequences of alternative prioritisations of outcome illustrate that what we face are so often prioritisation dilemmas, not problems capable of solution by superior efficiency and improved technique, though it is easy to neglect the latter in the passionate advocacy of the former (Davies *et al.*, 2000). What is at first glance attractive to citizens and politicians in its beguiling simplicity may actually contribute less to welfare than a complex system balancing many criteria and using a wide repertoire of financing and delivery models.

FURTHER READING

Davies, B., Fernandez, J., with Nomer (2000). *Equity and efficiency policy in community care: needs, service productivities and their implications.* Aldershot, Hants.: Ashgate.

Doty, P., Kasper, J., and S. Litvak (1996). 'Consumer-directed models of personal care: lessons from Medicaid', *Milbank Memorial Fund Quarterly*, 74: 377–409.

Kane, R. A. (1995). 'Expanding the home care concept: blurring distinctions among home care, institutional care, and other long-term care services', *Milbank Quarterly*, 73: 161–86.

REFERENCES

Applebaum, R. A., and C. D. Austin (1989). *Long-term care case management*. New York: Springer.

Baldock, J., and A. Evers (1992). 'Innovations and care of the elderly: the cutting-edge of change for social welfare systems. Examples from Sweden, the Netherlands and the United Kingdom', *Ageing and Society*, 12: 289–313.

Bebbington, A., and B. Davies (1983). 'Equity and efficiency in the allocation of the personal social services', *Journal of Social Policy*, 12: 309–30.

Capitman, J. (1985). *Evaluation of coordinated community-oriented long-term care demonstration projects*. San Francisco, Calif.: Berkeley Planning Associates.

Challis, D., Darton, R., Hughes, J., and K. Stewart (1995). *Care management and health care of older people*. Aldershot, Hants.: Arena.

Challis, D., Weiner, K., Darton, R., Hughes, J., and K. Stewart (2002). 'Emerging patterns of care management: arrangements for older people in England', *Social Policy and Administration*, 35: 672–87.

Davies, B. (1981). 'Strategic goals and piecemeal innovations: adjusting to the new balance of needs and resources'. In E. M. Goldberg, ed., *A new look at the social services*. London: Heinemann, pp. 96–121.

—— (1992). *Care management, equity and efficiency: the international experience*. Canterbury: PSSRU.

Davies, B., and D. Challis (1986). *Matching resources to needs in community care*. Aldershot, Hants: Gower.

Davies, B., and J. Fernandez (2004). *Care management productivities in post-reform community care of older people: implications of targeting and differentiation by triaging*. London: London School of Economics PSSRU.

Davies, B., Bebbington, A., Charnley, H., Baines, B., Ferlie, E., Hughes, M., and J. Twigg (1990). *Resources, needs and outcomes in community-based care: a comparative study of the production of welfare for elderly people in ten local authorities in England and Wales*. Aldershot, Hants.: Avebury.

Davies, B., Fernandez, J., with Nomer (2000). *Equity and efficiency policy in community care: needs, service productivities and their implications*. Aldershot, Hants.: Ashgate.

Department of Health (1989). *Caring for people: community care for the next decade and beyond*. Cm 849. London: HMSO.

—— (1998). *Modernising social services*. Cm 4169. London: The Stationery Office.

Department of Health, Housing and Human Services (1992). *It's your choice: national evaluation of community options projects*. Canberra: Australian Government Publication Service.

Diwan, S. (1999). 'Allocation of case management resources in long-term care: predicting high use of case management time', *Gerontologist*, 39: 500–90.

Doty, P., Kasper, J., and S. Litvak (1996). 'Consumer-directed models of personal care: lessons from Medicaid', *Milbank Memorial Fund Quarterly*, 74: 377–409.

Estes, C. L. (2000). 'The uncertain future of home care'. In R. Binstock and L. Cluff, eds., *Home care advances: essential research and policy issues*. New York: Springer, pp. 239–57.

Estes, C. L., and J. H. Swann (1993). *The long-term care crisis: elders trapped in the no care zone*. Beverly Hills, Calif.: Sage.

Geron, S. M., Smith, K., Tennstedt, S., Jette, A., Chassler, D., and L. Kasten (2000). 'The home care satisfaction measure: a client-centered approach to assessing the satisfaction of frail older adults with home care services', *Journal of Gerontology Series B*, 55B: S259–S270.

Greene, V., Lovely, M. E., and J. I. Ondrich (1993). 'Do community-based long-term care services reduce nursing home use? A transition probability analysis', *Journal of Human Resources*, 28: 297–318.

Hughes, S. L. (1988). 'Apples and oranges: a review of evaluations of community-based long-term care', *Health Services Research*, 20: 249–59.

Kane, R. A. (1995). 'Expanding the home care concept: blurring distinctions among home care, institutional care, and other long-term care services', *Milbank Quarterly*, 73: 161–86.

—— (1999). 'Goals of home care: therapeutic, either or both? *Journal of Ageing and Health*, 11: 299–321.

Kane, R. L., Bershadsky, B., Lum, Y.-S., and M. S. Siadaty (2003). 'Outcomes of managed care of dually eligible older persons', *Gerontologist*, 43: 165–74.

Kemper, P., Applebaum, R., and M. Harrigan (1987). 'Community care demonstrations: what have we learned?' *Health Care Financing Review*, 8: 87–100.

Kraan, R. J., Baldock, J., Davies, B., Evers, A., Johansson, L., Knapen, M., Thorslund, M., and C. Tunissen (1991). *Care for the elderly: significant innovations in three European countries*. Frankfurt: Campus/Westview.

Kunkel, S., and M. Scala (1998). *Consumer direction in Ohio's PASSPORT program*. Miami, Ohio: Miami University, Scripps Gerontology Center.

Laming, H. (1997). *Facing the future: seventh annual report of the Chief Inspector of Social Services*. London: The Stationery Office.

OECD (Organisation for Economic Co-operation and Development) (1996). *Care of the frail elderly*. Paris: Organisation for Economic Co-operation and Development.

Weiner, K., Stewart, K., Hughes, J., Challis, D., and R. Darton (2002). 'Care management arrangements for older people in England: key areas of variation in a national study', *Ageing and Society*, 22: 419–39.

Weissert, W. (1990). 'Strategies for reducing home-care expenditures', *Generations*, 14: 42–4.

Weissert, W., and S. Hedrick (1994). 'Lessons learned from research on effects of community-based long-term care', *Journal of the American Geriatrics Society*, 42: 348–53.

Weissert, W., Cready, C., and J. Pawelak (1988). 'The past and future of community-based long-term care', *Milbank Quarterly*, 66: 309–88.

Weissert, W., Chernew, M., and R. Hirth (2003). 'Titrating versus targeting home care services to frail elderly clients', *Journal of Ageing and Health*, 15: 99–123.

Delivering Care to Older People at Home

KRISTINA LARSSON, MERRIL SILVERSTEIN
AND MATS THORSLUND

INTRODUCTION

Given the rapid growth in the older populations of most nations, especially among the oldest-old, it has become imperative to develop national and local policies that strategically serve the frail elderly at home without resorting to wholesale institutionalization; such policies are crucial for the wellbeing of older persons, their families, and the societies that support them. In this chapter we discuss the promise and challenges of delivering care to older people living at home in the community. We restrict our discussion to what is generally known as in-home support, focusing on formal services that allow older adults to live in their own homes for as long as possible and help them avoid institutionalization. We draw on several salient topics in this area, including: (1) challenges faced by formal in-home services in targeting older frail individuals, meeting their needs, and ensuring their independence; (2) variations in the role of the state in supporting older people at home; (3) the historical evolution of public home help services as a model for elder care, using Sweden as a case study; and (4) gendered patterns in home help services, in terms of both the recipient population and the service workforce. The limited space, however, forces us to leave out the important issue of family care and the interplay between informal caregivers and formal services when helping elderly persons to "age in place."

AGEING IN PLACE

Remaining in one's home for as long as possible is known as ageing in place. For almost all of us,

our homes have a special meaning. Perhaps this is even truer for the elderly, as homes are often the principal resources older people possess. But there is also a sentimental attachment to the place where they may have raised a family and developed ties to the community over many years of residence. The preference to remain at home is considered almost universal, shared by older people around the world. But under particular conditions, such as when it is no longer safe for them to live in their homes due to physical frailty or cognitive disorders, older people may be forced to move out involuntarily, for example to an institution or group living setting.

How prevalent is the desire to age in place? Robison and Moen (2000), in their study of expectations of ageing in place, found that slightly more than half the retirees in their US-based sample expect never to move from their current homes. Predictably, community integration was related to the desire to age in place; however, health status was not, suggesting that health-related moves are often unanticipated or involuntary. Overall, expectations of living in a highly supportive housing environment were very low, reflecting a strong desire to avoid moving to a long term care institution. The ideal of maintaining independent living in one's own home is, however, often incongruent with reality. The availability and adequacy of in-home supports are crucial for closing the gap between the residential preferences and realities of the frail older population. In-home support is thus a crucial element in fulfilling the residential choice of frail older people (and their families) to age in place, while meeting society's obligation to cost-effectively provide long term care services to those in need.

National variation in care regimes for elders at home

The allocation of formal services to dependent older persons in the community varies substantially across nations. At the macro-level, welfare state structures differ depending on the way in which welfare production is allocated among state, market, and households (Esping-Andersen, 1990, 1999). This variation ranges from the policies of the "social democratic welfare states," in which all citizens are incorporated under one universal insurance system (such as those found in the Scandinavian countries), to "liberal welfare states," where means-tested assistance and modest social-insurance plans dominate (such as those found in Australia, Canada, and the United States). A third welfare state regime is identified as the "conservative welfare state," where the state will only intervene when the family's resources are exhausted (such as Austria, France, and Germany).

The Scandinavian experience with publicly provided home help services reflects a very different set of social, political, and economic conditions compared to those of liberal welfare states, e.g. the United States. The system of old age support and care in Scandinavia is characterized by universalism and egalitarianism in allocating benefits and services to the elderly, with the goal that socioeconomic differences in access to service should be minimized (Daatland, 1997). In the United States the old age support system is guided by principles of eligibility, in which the state takes responsibility only when all else fails. The American approach to social welfare is characterized by an emphasis on private over public responsibility (Achenbaum, 1983; Cook and Barrett, 1992) and a reluctance to support those who are deemed "undeserving" (Page and Shapiro, 1992). Consequently, there has been an unwillingness to intervene in the private nature of family life, including care for elderly individuals and their families. Where community-based services for the elderly in Scandinavia are publicly delivered by social service professionals, similar services in the United States are fragmented, delivered on an ad hoc basis, and are strongly tied to economic eligibility (Parker, 2000).

International comparisons of the proportion of elderly people receiving long-term care have to be interpreted with caution, as different countries have different ways of defining care, as well as funding it. Countries like the United Kingdom and the United States, for instance, have complex forms of indirect public spending on social care that make it difficult to compare them with countries that have more universalist forms of state provision (Sipilä et al., 2003). The definition of certain key concepts may also vary among countries. "Institutional care" differs, for example, with regard to whether service-enriched housing is considered to be residential care or ordinary dwellings. The British report *With respect to old age* classifies institutional settings the following way: "If the elderly person has their own front door, bathing, toilet and kitchen facilities, however modest and possibly within a larger unit, it is not an 'institution.' If they have to go or be taken elsewhere within a building for any of these facilities then it is" (The Royal Commission on Long Term Care, 1999). In Sweden, however, this definition is too limited, as the official policy in recent years has been to bring about "home-like institutions" when building or reconstructing housing for persons with heavy care needs. It excludes, for example, "service houses" and some nursing homes where the residents have their own flats but where staff members are available in the building 24 hours a day to assist with personal care in the flat. We find the same problem when trying to define "home help" and "home care." Whereas some countries include home nursing provided by general practitioners or nurses in district health centers, others include only domestic tasks in the concept of home help.

Given these limitations, comparative statistics show that in the early 1990s more than 10 percent of the population (65/67+) received home help in Denmark, Finland, Norway, and Sweden. Between 6 and 10 percent of the population in the same age group received home help in Australia, Belgium, France, the Netherlands, and the United Kingdom. In Austria, Canada, Germany, Ireland, Italy, Japan, Portugal, Spain, and the United States, 5 percent or less of the population received home help (OECD, 1996). This comparison does not, however, take into account the number of hours of home help received.

Recently published statistics on the intensity of care show that the Scandinavian countries have developed different strategies for distributing home help services to their older populations (65/67+). Denmark, where 25 percent of the older inhabitants receive public home help an average 5.4 hours per week, is the most generous country. Sweden has reduced the coverage of home help in the general population to 8 percent, but increased the intensity of care to 6.6 hours a week. In Norway 16 percent of the older population receives an average of 2–3 hours per week, and in Finland 11 percent of the older population receives 1.5–2 hours per week (Nordic Social Statistical Committee, 2002; Szebehely, 2003). As mentioned earlier, however, the figures have to be interpreted carefully. All the Scandinavian countries, except Sweden, include persons living in service houses in the home help statistics, and in Denmark the statistics also include persons residing in certain types of nursing homes. In Norway, on the other hand, personal care is a responsibility of primary healthcare and therefore is not included in home help. In Sweden, persons who receive only meals-on-wheels are not included in the home help statistics.

THE DEVELOPMENT OF PUBLIC HOME HELP: THE CASE OF SWEDEN

As mentioned before, the definition of domiciliary care and services can vary among countries, making it difficult to make international comparisons of coverage, costs, etc. Moreover, even in countries with a long tradition of providing long term care to older adults in their own home, such as the Scandinavian countries, the concept of home help has changed over time. The boundaries between residential care facilities and home-based care have shifted over time and so has the scope of intervention. In the following sections we have tried to distinguish varying phases that can illustrate the development of home help over time using Sweden as a case study. Due to the gradual nature of change in public in-home care, dating the precise end of one phase and beginning of another was not always possible. Therefore, dates given to each phase are approximate. However, each period represents a distinct model of public in-home care with specific consequences

for care receivers, care providers, and type of care given.

The introduction phase: from the 1950s to the mid 1960s

Social care for the elderly has been a responsibility of the public sector for hundreds of years, principally as municipal poor relief, but the Swedish welfare state is mainly a post-Second-World-War phenomenon. Old age care was synonymous with institutional care until the 1950s, when the Red Cross started in-home support for elderly persons on a small scale with the help of housewives (after a British model). Following an intensive public debate on the future direction of old age care, the municipalities gradually also began to offer in-home support to dependent elderly persons, in addition to residential care in old peoples' homes (previously the poorhouses). The legal obligation of children to care for their parents was also abolished in 1956. Thus, the principles of remaining at home and receiving public help there became public goals for old age care at a relatively early date.

Municipal home help was given mainly to people who needed assistance with domestic services, such as cooking, cleaning, and doing the laundry. Persons needing more help were referred to institutional care. No particular training of the home helpers was requested. Ordinary "housewife skills" were regarded as sufficient, and women who needed some extra income were recruited. Most home helpers worked part time, assisting only a few persons. The number of hours provided to each client was fixed, but the support given during that time was largely decided by the care recipient and the home helper. The elderly person thus had a substantial possibility of influencing the type of care given and how it was carried out.

The expansion phase: mid 1960s to mid 1980s

The new services soon became very popular and their use increased rapidly after the introduction of state subsidies to the municipalities in the mid 1960s. Home help was highly subsidized and the recipients paid only a fraction of the actual costs of the services. The needs assessments focused on whether the elderly person could manage daily tasks, regardless of the existence or state of health of a spouse, or access to close kin living nearby. The rates of home help reached a peak at the end of the 1970s, when nearly a quarter of the retired elderly population in Sweden received that service in the course of a year. Most recipients received only a few hours of help per week or month, in most cases with shopping, house cleaning, or laundry. The introduction of state subsidies paved the way for the expansion of home help. It gave older people with ordinary incomes a choice. They were no longer forced to move to institutions or to be dependent on their children, but could stay in their own homes and receive assistance from the municipal home help services. This period of establishing a generous (from an international perspective) public system of in-home care of the elderly coincided with the establishment of the general welfare state in Sweden. The 1960s and the 1970s were decades during which the improving Swedish economy allowed both a wide expansion of public welfare services and room for an increasing rate of private consumption.

In the 1970s, caring for dependent elderly persons in their own homes began to be recognized as an ordinary profession rather than as a spare-time occupation for housewives. It became possible to earn one's living by working full-time as a home helper. Education was offered and the staff gradually were provided with meeting places where they could have their lunch, make phone calls to the home help recipients, etc. Being a home helper now meant that home helpers, the vast majority of whom were women, had an office to go to every morning. The home helpers' private residence was no longer the base for the job.

The 1960s and 1970s were decades when an increasing number of women entered the labor market. Housewives, a large potential workforce, made the expansion in the number of home help recipients possible, and, for many women, becoming a home helper was the start of employment outside the household. The expansion of home help enabled many middle-aged women to maintain gainful employment, rather than stay home and care for dependent parents. It can therefore be argued that the expansion of public in-home care represented a liberty of choice both for the elderly person, who no longer was totally dependent on family

care, and for next-of-kin (in most cases daughters or daughters-in-law), who were not forced to provide all care to elderly family members.

The professionalization phase: mid 1980s to 1992

The endless expansion of home help services, at a faster rate than the demographic growth in the elderly population, could not continue. A growing number of frail older people in the country put pressure on healthcare and social services, and the public eldercare system could not keep up with the growing needs among the elderly. Even though the municipalities recognized the economic advantages of supporting the home help system in order to prevent the establishment of more expensive institutions, the economic burden was seen as unacceptable. This led to stricter needs assessments, where people with less extensive needs, or the possibility of receiving help from informal sources, fell outside the realms of public concern. As a consequence, the average home help recipients had more extensive health problems, leading to new demands upon the staff and the eldercare organization. A higher proportion of elderly persons needing help several times a day and on the weekends resided in their own homes and needed assistance with both household chores and personal care. The home helpers were thus more often confronted with fragile and sick elderly persons where mere "housewife competence" was not sufficient.

During this period, the public eldercare system was reorganized to meet the shifting demands. The home helpers started to work in teams. They met every morning and divided their work according to actual needs within their group of recipients. Although the rule was that the elderly person should have a fixed home helper in order to maintain continuity, a team responsible for a geographic area could help each other with the clients. From the perspective of the staff, they now had the possibility to confer with colleagues, and sometimes with a supervisor. If several home helpers in the group had experience caring for the same elderly person, they could advise and support each other when problems arose. The consequences for the elderly recipients, however, were that the continuity of care changed for the worse. Not only could they come to meet different eldercare staff from one day to another, but even a number of different persons during the same day.

The medicalization phase: 1992 –

Under the pressure of an ageing population (Sweden currently has the oldest population in the world with 5 percent of its population 80 years of age and older), the demands on the providers of social services and healthcare increased. Criticism was directed at the existing organization of care for the elderly, particularly at the unclear demarcation lines of responsibility between providers of healthcare (the county councils) and providers of eldercare (the municipalities). The numbers of bed-blockers in acute hospital care and at geriatric clinics increased as the municipalities had difficulties providing care after discharge within institutional housing or in ordinary homes. The Swedish Parliament therefore decided on a new eldercare policy in 1992. This policy gave the municipalities responsibility for nursing homes and for patients who still needed care after discharge from hospital, in addition to the responsibility for ordinary home help services. To solve the problem with bed-blockers, the municipalities were obliged to pay for hospital care of patients whose in-patient care was considered completed.

The reform took place at the same time as budgetary reductions due to weakening economic growth in the 1990s, and resulted in a dramatic restructuring of the long term care system. In spite of the fact that the number of hospital beds was cut down and the average length of stay in acute hospital care decreased, the problem with "bed-blockers" almost disappeared. This development, however, increased the pressure on the municipal eldercare organization in terms of resources and competence. Among elderly persons living at home, the home help services were targeted to the most frail and dependent elderly with extended personal care needs. In the mid 1990s every third person with home help received help during weekends, and every fourth received help during evenings or at night (Daatland, 1997). Among married persons, the spouse (usually the wife) was frequently the only caregiver, often having little or no support from formal eldercare services (Larsson and Thorslund, 2002). Consequently, spouses, as well as persons with less extensive needs, often had to rely on family, friends, or commercial alternatives for domestic services.

During this phase, municipalities, mainly in urban areas, have started to contract out services to non-public providers, although still publicly financed and under public control. (Commercial alternatives for medical or personal care, paid out of pocket, are almost non-existent.) The competition among different providers of care has been seen as one method of stretching the public budget, and in some cases as a possibility for elderly persons to select among different providers of care, although this trend is criticized as being a departure from the Swedish model.

The increase of care-load in the eldercare system meant that the home helper's job expanded from mainly household tasks to include personal care and medical treatment. The shrinking of length of stay in hospital care means that extensive nursing and sub-acute care is transferred outside the hospitals. For many years during the twentieth century, increasing numbers of elderly people died in hospitals, rather than at home. Due to the heightened availability of home care, however, more elderly people are dying at home now than in previous decades. Even though nurse's assistants have been recruited as home helpers to take care of more complicated cases under the guidance of district nurses and general practitioners, staff members without medical training are also expected to carry out nursing tasks according to instructions, like handing over pharmaceutical preparations or applying bandages.

Changes among care receivers

The example of public home help services in Sweden shows that in-home care can represent very different types of support in different time periods even in the same country. During the "expansion phase," home help was provided to persons with smaller care needs who mainly needed support with practical chores at home. Persons with more care needs who lacked support from a spouse or next-of-kin had to move to institutions, as care was not organized to give in-home support to those needing help several times a day or on weekends. Although the principles of remaining at home and receiving help there, instead of moving to institutions, became political goals of Swedish old age care at a relatively early date, the home help services were not organized to fulfill those ambitions for the most needy. Using Peter Laslett's scheme for dividing the lifecourse (Laslett, 1987) one can say that public home help services primarily helped persons in the "Third Age" to facilitate their living, regardless of whether or not it was possible for them to receive care from children living in the vicinity. Persons in the "Fourth Age," however, an age of final dependence and decrepitude, were referred to care in nursing homes or homes for the aged.

In the present "medicalization phase," the resources are targeted at those most frail and dependent elderly, above all persons living alone, whereas persons with less extensive needs have to find other ways to get practical support or cope on their own. The economic incentive, with municipalities financially liable for "bed-blockers," in combination with reductions of beds in geriatric care, have brought about home help mainly for persons in the "Fourth Age," thereby giving them the possibility to "age in place."

Changes in type of care given

The care provided has changed from mainly assisting with household chores to also helping the elderly with personal as well as medical care in their own homes. The rapid development in medical technology and, thereby, new possibilities to treat diseased elderly persons at home, has increased the demands upon the home help services (Thorslund et al., 2001).

A consequence of the targeting of home help to persons in the "Fourth Age" is that the previous ambitions to develop more socially oriented eldercare have not been possible to maintain. In the "expansion phase," when home help was granted more generously, there was also an emphasis on preventive measures, such as help ending isolation. The rationing of help has brought about more time-effective ways of delivering care. Meals-on-wheels, for example, have replaced meals prepared in the older person's home, thereby further reducing the time for contact between the elderly person and the home helper.

Another consequence of the concentration on a smaller number of persons predominantly in the "Fourth Age" is that elderly people now have greater

trouble establishing themselves as clients in the welfare system. The effect of excluding elderly individuals with less extensive needs from public eldercare is not clear. The Swedish National Board of Health and Welfare has questioned the present strategy of prioritizing home help to the most needy. There is a risk that the policy of omitting persons with smaller care needs, as well as co-residing persons, might increase service needs in the future.

Changes among care providers

At the same time as the home help recipients have become older and frailer, the demands on the staff delivering in-home care have increased from "housewife ability" to skilled staff ability. Another consequence of targeting home help to persons in the "Fourth Age" is that the home helpers more often co-operate with members of different professions involved in the elderly person's care. By providing medical services and nursing in the homes of patients as well as adapting housing and using technical aids, it is both possible and easier for elderly and disabled people to stay in their own homes. The home helpers thus have to be prepared to work together with general practitioners, district nurses, and assistant nurses, as well as physiotherapists and occupational therapists, in the older person's home.

AGEING IN PLACE: A GENDERED QUESTION

The political consensus in favor of promoting "ageing in place" has very different implications for elderly men and elderly women. In most countries throughout the world, women live longer than men. Among those age 80 years and older, the ratio of women to men in Sweden is presently about 1.8:1. The fact that women in many countries marry men that are older than they are, and that older women have lower remarriage rates than men do, further influences the proportion of women living without a spouse in old age. In general, this also means that the probability of living alone in old age is higher for women than for men. In most Western countries the rate of intergenerational conjoint living has been decreasing, and in Sweden and Denmark only about 4 percent of the elderly live with their children or other relatives.

The demographic fact that women live longer than men has consequences for the possibility of receiving care from formal as well as informal sources. The majority of very old men live with their spouses to the end of their lives and have the possibility of receiving care from a co-residing caregiver in times of need. The majority of very old women, however, live alone and have to rely on assistance from children or other relatives outside the household or from formal sources when facing dependency. Even though the current strategy has been to give priority to the very old and frail, persons living alone, most of them women, run a higher risk of having to give up independent living.

CONCLUSION

Home care for the frail aged holds much promise as a rare convergence between the preferences of older clients and their families to age in place, and the intentions of public policy to reduce institutionalization and promote the functional and residential independence of an otherwise dependent population. Although we have focused our discussion almost exclusively on formal home care services, we recognize that the bulk of support to community-dwelling elders comes from informal, mostly family, sources in all countries (Arber and Attias-Donfut, 2000; Kohli et al., 2000).

The rapid development of housing alternatives to institutions and the rise of technological innovations have also changed the terms under which frail older people manage in their own homes. Indeed, the very notion of what it means to age in place in the community has shifted with the proliferation of alternative housing options that stand between independent and congregate living. An appropriately designed home has been found to reduce the demand for both formal and informal care in the homes of frail elders (Sanford et al., 2002). In addition, digital communication technology offers the exciting potential to augment in-home support services. Emerging technologies that allow vital health status and medication monitoring through the Internet may allow formal and informal caregivers to manage some of their duties at a distance, with greater ease, and perhaps at lower cost. The new technology may also facilitate co-operation between different formal caregivers, such as home care staff and medical service providers, as well as between formal and informal caregivers.

Our discussion of cross-national variation in the availability of home care for the aged has focused primarily on the developed world. Yet, the greatest gap in care is between developed nations and developing nations, most of which provide few, if any, formal services to older people at home. For example, frail elders in China rely almost exclusively on their children or other relatives for instrumental assistance and personal care (Li and Tracy, 1999). It is uncertain how home care will evolve in less developed nations, especially those that are achieving rapid economic growth. Hybrid models of care involving public–private partnerships, new technologies, and quasi-independent housing environments may change the landscape of in-home care in the future. What we can be sure of is that the demand for formal home care will expand as older populations swell and family size shrinks in most nations around the world. Exactly what form home help will take to best meet the needs of its expanding constituency will likely be the product of each nation's unique political structure, economic climate, and national culture.

FURTHER READING

Parker, M. G. (2000). "Sweden and the United States: is the challenge of an ageing society leading to a convergence of policy?" *Journal of Aging and Social Policy*, 12 (1): 73–90.

Sipilä, J., Anttonen, A., and J. Baldock (2003). "The importance of social care." In A. Anttonen, J. Baldock, and J. Sipilä, eds., *The young, the old and the state: social care systems in five industrial nations*. Cheltenham: Elgar, pp. 1–23.

Thorslund, M. (2004). "The Swedish model: current trends and challenges for the future." In M. Knapp, A. Netten, J.-L. Fernandez, and D. Challis, eds., *Matching resources and needs*. Aldershot: Ashgate.

REFERENCES

Achenbaum, W. A. (1983). *Shades of gray: old age, American values and federal policies since 1920*. Boston: Little Brown.

Arber, S., and C. Attias-Donfut (2000). *The myth of generational conflict: the family and state in ageing societies*. London: Routledge.

Cook, F. L., and E. J. Barrett (1992). *Support for the American welfare state: the views of Congress and the public*. New York: Columbia University Press.

Daatland, S. O., ed. (1997). *De siste årene. Eldreomsorgen i Scandinavia 1960–95 [The last years. Public elder care in Scandinavia 1960–95]*, Vol. XXII. Oslo: NOVA.

Esping-Andersen, G. (1990). *The three worlds of welfare capitalism*. Cambridge: Polity Press.

(1999). *Social foundations of postindustrial economies*. New York: Oxford University Press.

Kohli, M., Künemund, H., Motel, A., and M. Szydlik (2000). "Families apart? Intergenerational transfers in East and West Germany." In S. Arber and C. Attias-Donfut, eds., *The myth of generational conflict: the family and state in ageing societies*. London: Routledge, pp. 88–99.

Larsson, K., and M. Thorslund (2002). "Does gender matter? Differences in patterns of informal support and formal services in a Swedish urban elderly population," *Research on Aging*, 24 (3): 308–37.

Laslett, P. (1987). "The emergence of the third age," *Ageing and Society*, 7: 133–60.

Li, H., and M. B. Tracy (1999). "Family support, financial needs, and healthcare needs of rural elderly in China: a field study," *Journal of Cross-Cultural Gerontology*, 14 (4): 357–71.

Nordic Social-Statistical Committee (2002). *Social protection in the Nordic countries 2000: scope, expenditure and financing*. Copenhagen: Nordic Social-Statistical Committee.

OECD (1996). *Caring for frail elderly people. Policies in evolution*, Social Policy Studies, no. 19. Paris: OECD.

Page, B. I., and R. Y. Shapiro (1992). *The rational public: fifty years of trends in Americans' policy preferences*. Chicago: University of Chicago Press.

Parker, M. G. (2000). "Sweden and the United States: is the challenge of an aging society leading to a convergence of policy?" *Journal of Aging and Social Policy*, 12 (1): 73–90.

Robison, J. T., and P. Moen (2000). "A life-course perspective on housing expectations and shifts in late midlife," *Research on Aging*, 22 (5): 499–532.

The Royal Commission on Long Term Care, ed. (1999). *With respect to old age. Research Volume 1*. London: HMSO.

Sanford, J. A., Pynoos, J., Tejral, A., and A. Browne (2002). "Development of a comprehensive assessment for delivery of home modifications," *Physical & Occupational Therapy in Geriatrics*, 20 (2): 43–55.

Sipilä, J., Baldock, J., and A. Anttonen (2003). "The importance of social care." In A. Anttonen, J. Baldock, and J. Sipila, eds., *The young, the old and the state: social care systems in five industrial nations*. Cheltenham: Elgar.

Szebehely, M., ed. (2003). *Hemhjälp i Norden – illustrationer och reflektioner [Home help in the Nordic countries – illustrations and reflections]*. Lund: Studentlitteratur.

Thorslund, M., Bergmark, Å., and M. G. Parker (2001). "Care for elderly people in Sweden." In D. N. Weisstub, D. C. Thomasma, S. Gauthier, and G. F. Tomossy, eds., *Aging: caring for our elders*. Dordrecht: Kluwer Academic Publishers, pp. 49–63.

Long Term Care

ROBERT L. KANE AND ROSALIE A. KANE

Long term care (LTC) can be viewed as a by-product of societal ageing and chronic disease. Although not all persons with disabilities sufficient to require LTC are old, the prevalence of LTC increases dramatically with age, especially over age 85. Because LTC is closely tied to chronic illness, a continuing debate has revolved around whether it should be viewed as primarily a medical or social service. While one may argue the merits of health versus social auspices, the dominant truth is that good LTC requires attention from both sectors. LTC is often thought about as a problem associated with developed nations, but the demographic realities suggest that it poses serious challenges to all countries. (R. L. Kane *et al.*, 1990; Brodsky *et al.*, 2002; WHO, 1999). As chronic disease has become a global priority (WHO, 2001, 2002), so too has LTC.

LTC has emerged differently in the United States (US) and the United Kingdom (UK), but the programs in the two countries are coming closer together; they also face many of the same challenges and dilemmas. This chapter addresses some of the basic concepts underlying LTC and explores their policy implications.

In the absence of a universally accepted definition of LTC, a useful working definition is: "help over sustained period of time to people who are experiencing difficulties in functioning because of a disability" (R. A. Kane and Kane, 1987). This definition does not specify the type of help or who provides it. Assistance can include personal care as well as related health and social services. LTC can be provided by professionals, paraprofessionals, or friends and family. The latter are often referred to as informal caregivers in the US and carers in the UK; both countries depend on such family care as the groundwork upon which formal care is added (Arno *et al.*, 1999; R. A. Kane and Penrod, 1995; Kendig e*t al.*, 1992; Navaie-Waliser *et al.*, 2002). The usual trigger for a person to receive LTC, and consequently a frequent component of eligibility criteria for formal services covered by public or private insurance, is the inability to perform self-care and usual activities, whether this inability is because of physical impairment, cognitive impairment, or both.

This definition of LTC has a number of important implications. Functioning is the key to defining LTC needs and developing long term care services. Some would label ability to perform activities of daily living (ADLs) and other functional measures as the lingua franca of LTC to describe both the need for care and success of treatment. LTC can be provided in any location by caregiving individuals with a wide range of training and professions. Likewise, a number of different types of clients are served by LTC. They include the physically impaired, the cognitively impaired, those facing impending death who are looking for hospice-type care, and those who are in a vegetative state, minimally affected by what is going on around them. All of these client groups can be served in a variety of different settings. At present there is insufficient information to suggest with confidence just which clients do best in which settings.

The need for LTC can occur at any age. In practice, services for children with disabilities and for younger adults, especially those with lifelong developmental or intellectual disabilities, are often managed separately from those for elderly people and adults with some physical disabilities, but separate policies are not necessary. In many jurisdictions in the US people under 65 with disabilities receive different and more flexible services, and one of the important policy issues is the current inequity in how different age groups with LTC needs are treated. Elderly people are more likely to be treated in institutions or offered narrow home-health services for which they are required to remain at home, whereas younger people often receive attendant services that accompany them outside their homes and allow them to function in the community. Considerable literature now documents that paternalistic protection is more a threat to the autonomy of older LTC recipients than to that of younger ones (R. L. Kane and Kane, 2001).

The boundaries between LTC and acute care, mental health, and rehabilitation, on the health side, and housing and social services on the social side are vague. Good LTC requires a synthesis of activity from many spheres. On the one hand, LTC is often linked closely to managing chronic disease. Of the many chronic diseases associated with LTC, Alzheimer's disease looms large, and creates a challenging presence. On the other hand, LTC needs may be handled or diminished by well-designed housing and access to additional income to purchase equipment, supplies, and assistance.

There are two separate policy issues: (1) What is the most efficient way to deliver LTC? What combinations of services are most appropriate to address different people with LTC needs? (2) How should such care be financed? How much of the cost should be borne publicly and privately? These questions are conflated because the answer to the first may depend on the second. Often different decisions are made for using public and private funding.

Articulating goals for LTC, and accordingly developing accountability of LTC providers, has proven difficult. Possible goals could even seem to be in opposition. Improving or slowing the rate of deterioration of health and functional abilities may seem in conflict with a goal of meeting needs for care and assistance. The former sounds more end-results driven, whereas the latter seems compatible with simply addressing problems as they arise. Other goals, such as enhancing social and psychological wellbeing, or maximizing clients' independence and autonomy, reflect a basic commitment to encourage consumers to live in the most integrated and "normal" community settings possible and to promote a meaningful life according to the individual's own view of what that might mean.

Implementing LTC requires attention to several basic principles. The need to separate services from sites or classifications of care providers is confronted in many aspects of health and social services (R. L. Kane and Kane, 1991). The same services can be provided at different sites (e.g., in a hospital, a nursing home, a day center, a physician's office, or a patient's home) and by care organizations with different titles and regulatory authority. Hence, LTC is more rationally analyzed when the attention is focused on the user rather than on the service provider. Furthermore, because the clientele for LTC can be quite varied, it is important to recognize that different goals may apply to different people. In some cases the dominant goal involves normalization and mainstreaming, while for other groups of clients compensation and coping, or more active rehabilitation, may be most appropriate. Because most people receiving LTC, especially most older people, do so because of the toll taken by chronic disease, LTC clients have a great need for integrating ongoing outpatient and inpatient medical care with their long term care. Discussions about the conflict between the medical model and social model of care are unproductive; both camps must learn to interact for a common set of goals.

SEPARATING SERVICES AND SITE

Although services are often referred to in terms of where they are provided (e.g., nursing home (NH) care, home care), such distinctions are counterproductive and lead to great confusion and an erroneous idea that the precisely appropriate site can be identified for each client. In some cases the services provided by some LTC programs extend beyond what is usually considered LTC and this behavior adds to the general confusion. One of the most frequent areas is with acute care, particularly in the realm of post-acute care (called Intermediate Care in the UK), which is in itself the result of changing patterns of hospital care. As pressures to shorten hospital lengths of stay have increased, the demand for continuing health monitoring, management of unstable conditions, and rehabilitation that would formerly have been done in the hospital has become merged with the LTC services that the individual also needs, perhaps permanently, but certainly in the aftermath of the hospitalization. In the United States, post-acute care is typically provided by nursing homes, home healthcare agencies, and inpatient rehabilitation units. A list of LTC services regardless of venue would include nursing; physical, occupational, and speech therapy; personal care; homemaking, emergency assistance systems; telephone reassurance and monitoring services; home-delivered meals; home modification; transportation; day healthcare and social day care and equipment. Venues for the services would include nursing homes, assisted living settings, adult foster care (sometimes called family care) homes – and, of course, the consumer's own home (R. L. Kane *et al.*, 2000).

Lists of LTC services often include some that are particularly ambiguous or cross jurisdictional lines, such as respite care, family care, habilitation, and case management. Respite care, a popular service among politicians because its costs can be controlled, is not really a distinctive service. It consists of some mix of home care, day care, and short term overnight institutional care, given as a respite for family caregivers. Its distinctiveness resides in its eligibility criteria: it can be established for some subgroup of family caregivers, perhaps based on how much care they provide, or whether they live with the care receiver. Respite care is often targeted by diagnosis of the care receiver, leading to the anomalous situation that in some states respite services are available for caregivers of persons with Alzheimer's disease but not Parkinson's or stroke. Programs for families include respite care, but also may include family support groups, family caregiver education activities, and even direct mental health services for stressed families. Obviously, the boundaries of the LTC definition are stretched by these programs. Habilitation programs are a counterpart to rehabilitation (where the goal is recovering lost function) and are oriented towards building social and, if appropriate, vocational competence among people with developmental disabilities. Thus, the services are closely linked to education (especially when offered to minor children). Case management, sometimes called care management,

care coordination, or even resource coordination, is becoming the unwelcome guest at the LTC table, at least from a consumer perspective. Case management has been defined as a process of ongoing management of a group of resources on behalf of a defined clientele. It has come to be further defined by its component functions: screening, assessment, care planning, referral and service arrangement, and monitoring. Often it includes purchase of service and a modicum of fiscal responsibility for public resources. Many problems have been identified with case management as it has evolved in many industrialized countries (Challis, 1993; R. A. Kane, 2000). The litany of critiques include: it is front-loaded with attention to assessment but with poorly developed follow-up, either for managing chronic diseases or for managing everyday care; it is expensive, often accounting for an extraordinarily high proportion of the overall expenses of community LTC; it is paternalistic, unimaginative, and overprotective, thus interfering with the quality of life of the clientele; and it detracts from consumer autonomy. Yet despite all these obstacles to effective case management or care coordination, no policy makers or practitioners have suggested a better substitute. On the social side, to permit clientele to exercise expensive social benefits on their own say-so seems to invite budgetary disaster. On the health side, it is hard to imagine that vigorous, planful, long term coordination of chronic diseases would not ultimately improve the health and functioning of LTC consumers, if only it were possible to determine how to deliver such coordination.

In the US the nursing home has served as the touchstone of LTC. Policies are framed around it; other approaches are expressed as alternatives to nursing home care. The UK had relied more on a greater geriatric presence and more emphasis on community-based care. However, the pattern of care in the UK has changed. Until the mid 1980s privately operated nursing homes were rare in the UK. Clients who needed institutional care (if indeed anyone does need such care) were cared for in housing run by local social service authorities and on the long-stay wards of acute hospitals. The latter group was under the care of geriatricians whereas the former group was managed as social services charges. Ironically, the last decades have seen the growth of nursing homes in the UK just as they are gradually starting to decline in the US in the face of competition from other sources of care (Bishop, 1999).

Despite the growth in formal service providers, the bulwark of LTC has been and remains the family (Doty, 1986). Informal care, the vast majority of which is provided by spouses and daughters (and daughters-in-law) but also by many other relatives, represents over 90 percent of all the LTC provided. Indeed, that number has remained consistent, even as the role for women has changed dramatically, with more entering the labor force, and the stability of marriages has declined. It is likewise constant despite the extent of publicly supported formal care programs. While there is good reason to worry about whether this pattern will continue, and the social consequences of major deviation are enormous, there are good reasons to be optimistic that informal care will prevail, though with longer life expectancy and more serial marriage, blended families, four-generation families, and unusual family patterns, the identity of family caregivers may change. The policy question is the extent to which care from family members and friends should be supported structurally or even financially. We have already referred to the various family support and training and respite programs offered in many jurisdictions. In addition, family members are sometimes paid directly through wages or indirectly through tax relief or through cash stipends given to the person needing care, who most usually "hires" family with the stipend. Several European countries, including the UK and most famously Germany (as part of its universal LTC benefit), include an option to cash out LTC services. In the US, where only low-income citizens are eligible for most government help, a randomized controlled trial was implemented in the late 1990s to test the effects of cashing out means-tested LTC benefits. Needless to say, this demonstration was complex with a need for a great many provisos so that recipients given cash would not have their financial eligibility for services altered.

The US LTC market has seen the emergence of a new form of care, assisted living, which arose to address some of the severe social limitations of the nursing home. As enunciated in the state of Oregon, where the service component was subsidized for low-income people, assisted living was a well-understood concept: it included apartment style singly occupied accommodations (which could be shared by spouses) including full bathrooms, kitchenettes, and autonomy-enhancing features; congregate dining for three meals a day and a wide range of LTC services delivered to the tenants in their apartments; and a philosophy that emphasized choice, privacy, dignity, and normal lifestyles. It was perceived as a choice for people who would qualify functionally for nursing homes (R. A. Kane and Wilson, 1993; Wilson, 1993). However, as the concept proliferated, many providers rose up to offer these services, and the diversity of service packages marketed under this name made it hard to identify just what was really being offered in terms of either living accommodations or service packages. Moreover, various states used their licensing authority to curtail the ability of assisted living settings to service individuals with heavy care needs, either from their own conviction that they were unsafe or as a result of lobbying by nursing home providers (who wanted a niche for themselves) or consumer advocates intent on protecting frail older people. Models of assisted living now include: purpose-built apartment complexes, which may or may not serve those with heavy care needs depending on the state rules and the proprietors' wishes; assisted living as a component of a campus-based continuum of care, which includes independent housing with home care availability, assisted living, and nursing homes; and assisted living services grafted into existing low-income housing. As a result of all this confusion, consumers need a uniform classification system and a glossary so that they can make informed comparisons of price and services and also to predict whether they will be allowed to stay in a particular assisted living setting if they become confused or if their healthcare needs reach a certain threshold.

LTC POLICY ISSUES

Form

The dominant form in which LTC is delivered is fundamentally a historical artifact. The nursing home traces its parentage to the almshouse and the hospital. It is time to reappraise the situation and question whether we should preserve the distinctions among home care, nursing homes, and residential care or assisted living. One way to catalyze this decision would be to alter payment policies to pay separately for services and room and board in nursing homes, something that has already taken place for assisted living in some states. The idea of combining room and board with services in nursing home care traces back to the hospital model. Once separated, one would expect nursing homes to be under great pressure to become more livable environments in order to compete with alternative living situations where the price was less and the livability greater. Home care could be provided in older persons' own homes or in congregate housing settings where some economies of scale might allow more intensive service for the same cost.

Yet another historical accident is the use of LTC modalities to provide post-acute care. The pressures and economic opportunity presented when US hospitals were paid under a prospective system that fixed payment per episode prompted a demand for places to put former hospital patients. NHs responded to the opportunity but they were not set up to handle this type of care. Indeed, one might well ask if the same institution is well placed to deliver post-acute care and LTC. What is the rationale for combining such different care? Separating such care might entice hospitals back into the post-acute care business.

LTC reflects society's ageism. Policies that have been flatly rejected for (and by) developmentally disabled children and adults under 65 (for example, with multiple sclerosis or spinal cord injury) are still considered appropriate for older persons. The concept of the vulnerable adult makes society less willing to allow them to accept risk. Institutions that were considered inhumane for younger people are still used for older ones. Concepts like small group housing, which is a mainstay of the younger persons with disabilities, is rarely used for older ones. Part of the difference in philosophy may reflect real differences across cohorts, but much of it is due to preconceptions held by both generations.

Personnel

The big question concerning personnel is where the paid caregivers will come from. Even for informal care, there is a prospect of sharp decreases in available helpers, and in the paid sector the problem is greater. As women have more career choices, the female dominated careers such as nursing have declined greatly. Even at the level of frontline worker, such as nursing aide or home health aide, other occupational options are available that pay as well or better and are less physically and emotionally demanding. Raising wages and providing fringe benefits are necessary steps to help LTC compete for the low-wage worker, but it is unlikely that the pay could ever be high enough to serve as a major inducement. Other strategies involving reorganization of labor must be pursued. Roles must be redefined to allow less senior personnel to undertake more tasks. Nurses can deliver more primary care that is often seen as the province of physicians. Unlicensed assistive personnel can do more direct nursing tasks if they are taught to do so and a system of oversight created (Kane *et al.*, 1995; Sikma and Young, 2001). New role distributions will be greatly enhanced by information technology, which will permit offset monitoring and greater use of interactive care protocols.

Whereas more and better training is undoubtedly needed, training should not be viewed as an immunization. Staff performance is shaped at least as much by the work environment. Training should stress problem solving and comfort with information technology as much as facts. It should facilitate careful observation and provide tools to make observations and to guide behavior in response to observed changes in client status.

The grim forecasts apply to informal care as well as formal. The multiple roles of working women make caregiving even more taxing. Societies will need to think about ways to support family caregiving. Paying family members is one step, but it is unlikely that many systems can afford to take such a step, at least not beyond token payments. Other polices are needed, such as practical training in ways to cope with difficult behaviors (especially those associated with dementia) (Hepburn *et al.*, 2001). Respite services seem like a good idea, but their use has been less than expected (Kowloski and Montgomery, 1995; Montgomery *et al.*, 2002; Newcomer *et al.*, 1999).

The conceptual separation between medical and social personnel is often unproductive. Most people using LTC do so because they have serious chronic diseases, which need close medical attention. LTC workers should be trained to make meaningful observations about clients' physical status and to communicate such information effectively. New kinds of medical practitioners may be needed. Nurse practitioners have been shown to be effective primary care providers (Mundinger *et al.*, 2000) and they have increased the efficiency of nursing home residents' primary care (R. L. Kane *et al.*, 2003). Nurse practitioners may well become a major part of primary care delivery for LTC recipients in the future. If so, they should be more effective communicators with the LTC workforce and should be better positioned to overcome the dysfunctional barriers that have arisen between these two sectors.

Consumer direction

The welcome recognition that LTC involves the lives of those who need the care in intimate and detailed ways has led to an emphasis on consumer control and direction on both sides of the Atlantic. Making consumer direction operational, however, has been more difficult, especially where older clients are concerned (Simon-Rusinowitz *et al.*, 2002). One obstacle has been the protective instinct of professionals and local and national governmental authorities. In the US, concerns over litigation have made providers reluctant to allow consumers to take what they consider risks.

Another unexpected tension has developed over the movement to provide better wages, benefits, and working conditions for those who do the hands-on, frontline work in LTC, and the movement for greater consumer control. Personal attendant models of LTC, whereby the consumer or the consumer's agent (when the consumer is incapable because of dementia or intellectual disability) purchases services from self-employed individuals, weaken the protections desired for the labor force. Conversely, efforts to organize home attendants and consumer-employed workers undercut the movement towards consumer control. When large amounts of public money are involved, a "gray labor market," such as one sees in a variety of industries, is infeasible even if it were desirable. To ensure that workers maintain eligibility for retirement, disability, unemployment, and workman's compensation benefits, the employer (technically the person with the disability) needs to undertake complex paperwork. Fiscal intermediary services have arisen to perform this work

and cut checks on the part of the LTC recipient-employer. In the US, labor unions are also attempting to organize client-employed workers who serve individual LTC clients as part of a state-subsidized program. To the extent that the unionization succeeds, the conditions of labor may improve at the expense of the very flexibility for consumers that the attendant programs were meant to ensure. If the consumers are not in control of the terms and conditions of employment, such as the tasks to be done and the hours to be worked, then worker rights will have been won at the expense of consumer control.

Payment

LTC has historically been linked to residual public benefits for low-income people. Although healthcare, at least for seniors, has emerged as a universal entitlement, LTC has remained largely either privately paid for or financed through some type of scheme to subsidize those who cannot afford the care. Increasingly older persons are coming to view this form of governmental subsidy as an entitlement. They see themselves as having worked hard for many years and now entitled to some government support for their frailty. Moreover, removing the stigma of welfare from LTC will greatly help improve its image and may facilitate recruiting much-needed staff.

As with healthcare, the conceptions of LTC have been largely shaped by how it was provided. Services are defined by site of care, and so too is payment. Basing the payment on the actual needs of the client would afford more flexibility in choosing modes to provide the care. Separating room and board costs from services would be an essential step in such a scheme. Some might press for even more client-based funding by using some form of vouchers, whereby the client would retain the ability to purchase whatever from of care s/he preferred. Whereas such a plan is consistent with a marketplace view of service delivery, it has some drawbacks. Authorizing care at a high level (e.g., that needed to cover nursing homes) would inevitably induce many people who currently do not use formal services to seek vouchers, especially if they could be used widely, including paying family members. Such a step would drive up LTC costs dramatically. On the other hand, if the voucher level were set at the community service level, it might under-fund those who need institutional services, even if the room and board costs are eliminated.

In the US the government has turned to managed care as a possible means of controlling costs (or at least making them more predictable). Managed care is especially attractive in addressing those clients who are dually eligible for both Medicare (the universal non-income-tested health program for older people) and Medicaid (the health subsidy program for people in poverty). Creating a single funding stream is seen as a means of avoiding duplication and cost shifting, and thereby promoting better coordination of care. Perhaps the best example of such managed care for dual eligibles is the PACE (Program for All-inclusive Care of the Elderly) scheme. This program targets dually eligible older people who are deemed eligible for NH care by dint of their disability level but continue to reside in the community (R. L. Kane, 1999). Although it has proven effective in reducing the use of hospitals and nursing homes, its overall benefits have not yet been firmly established (Chatterji *et al.*, 1998). Other efforts to mount similar programs have shown no greater success (R. L. Kane *et al.*, 2001, 2002; Manton *et al.*, 1993).

Another potential area where payment might improve care lies in the domain of post-acute care. A bundled payment would mean that one organization was responsible for all the care a person received for a fixed period after discharge from a hospital. Bundling payments for post-acute care and hospital care, or even just bundling post-acute care payments, would encourage better choices of what types of post-acute care to use. Combining hospital and post-acute care payments would create incentives for hospital discharge planners to make more careful choices because the same organization would be fiscally and qualitatively responsible for what happens after the patient is discharged from the hospital.

Quality

It is easier to discuss quality than to define it. Likewise, it is much easier to identify egregious breaches in quality than good quality. Much progress has been made in the US towards developing quality indicators to characterize nursing homes based on aggregated data from a mandatory Minimum Data Set; these indicators identify nursing homes with greater than average rates of bedsores, weight loss, urinary catheter use, and a wide variety of other negative characteristics. The same system has been adopted voluntarily in a number of nursing homes in the UK. Much more difficult is identifying indicators of quality at the positive end of the scale: those related to identifying remediable causes of functional problems, and those related to improved quality of life.

A first step in the context of LTC is to determine the relative role of technical quality, quality of life, and satisfaction, and to decide who determines what is good quality. It is tempting to assume that the client should be the ultimate arbiter of quality, but judging such quality can require sophisticated skills. Certainly some elements of quality are firmly fixed on the client, but others require more observations or broader data systems. To the extent that the market model continues to predominate, it will be essential to provide good consumer information if consumers are to make the ultimate decisions. The current level of information falls far short of what is needed to assess performance and to choose among options. Measurement technologies, which finally have incorporated functional status as a relevant outcome for LTC, lag behind in the assessment of quality of life (R. L. Kane and Kane, 2000; R. A. Kane, 2003). In the United States, intensive work has been conducted to measure quality of life of nursing-home residents through their own self-report (R. A. Kane *et al.*, 2003), but in the community sector little has been done except to measure satisfaction.

Moving to a client-centered approach implies that the same quality standards apply to all modes of care for comparable people. It is unlikely that all of quality detection and implementation will be left to individual consumers of LTC. Some formal role for external regulators will persist. The challenge is make the regulation effective without making it burdensome. It is easier to assess quality than to assure it. The latter often entails prolonged litigation. It may be better to have fewer measures that can be more easily enforced. The measures chosen should be meaningful to a person's quality of life as well his/her quality of care.

FURTHER READING

Kane, R. A., and A. L. Caplan, eds. (1990). *Everyday ethics: solving dilemmas in nursing home life*. New York: Springer.

Kane, R. L., Kane, R., and R. Ladd (1999). *The heart of long-term care*. New York: Oxford University Press.

Wunderlich, G. S., and P. Kohler, eds. (2001). *Improving the quality of long-term care. Report of the Institute of Medicine*. Washington, D.C.: National Academy Press.

REFERENCES

Arno, P., Levine, C., and M. Memmott (1999). "The economic value of informal caregiving," *Health Affairs*, 18: 182–8.

Bishop, C. E. (1999). "Where are the missing elders? The decline in nursing home use, 1985 and 1995," *Health Affairs*, 18: 146–55.

Brodsky, J., Habib, J., and M. J. Hirschfield (2002). *Country case studies in long term care*, Vol. I: *Developing countries*. Papers presented at the World Health Organization & WHO Collaborating Center for Research on Health of the Elderly JDC-Broodale Institute. Geneva: WHO.

Challis, D. (1993). "Case management in social and health care: lessons from a UK programme," *Journal of Case Management*, 2: 79–90.

Chatterji, P., Burstein, N. R., Kidder, D., and A. J. White (1998). *Evaluation of the Program of All-inclusive Care for the Elderly (PACE)*. Cambridge, Mass.: Abt Associates Inc.

Doty, P. (1986). "Family care of the elderly: the role of public policy," *Milbank Quarterly*, 64: 34–75.

Hepburn, K. W., Tornatore, J., Center, B., and S. W. Ostwald (2001). "Dementia family caregiver training: affecting beliefs about caregiving and caregiver outcomes," *Journal of the American Geriatrics Society*, 49: 450–7.

Kane, R. A. (2000). "Long-term case management for older adults." In R. L. Kane and R. A. Kane, eds., *Assessing older persons: measures, meaning, and practical applications*. New York: Oxford University Press.

(2003). "Definition, measurement, and correlates of quality of life in nursing homes: towards a reasonable practice, research, and policy agenda," *Gerontologist*, 43: 28–36.

Kane, R. A., and R. L. Kane (1987). *Long-term care: principles, programs, and policies*. New York: Springer Publishing Company.

Kane, R. A., and J. D. Penrod, eds. (1995). *Family caregiving in an aging society: policy perspectives*. Newbury Park, Calif.: Sage Publications.

Kane, R. A., and K. B. Wilson (1993). *Assisted living in the United States: a new paradigm for residential care for frail older persons?* Washington, D.C.: American Association of Retired Persons.

Kane, R. A., Kling, K. C., Bershadsky, B., Kane, R. L., Giles, K., Degenholtz, H. B., Liu, J., and L. J. Cutler (2003). "Quality of life measures for nursing home residents," *Journal of Gerontology: Medical Sciences*, 58A: 240–8.

Kane, R. L. (1999). "Setting the PACE in chronic care," *Contemporary Gerontology*, 6: 47–50.

Kane, R. L., and R. A. Kane (1991). "A nursing home in your future?" *New England Journal of Medicine*, 324: 627–9.

(2000). *Assessing older persons: measures, meaning, and practical applications*. New York: Oxford University Press.

(2001). "What older people want from long-term care and how they can get it," *Health Affairs*, 10: 114–27.

Kane, R. L., Evans, J. G., and D. Macfadyen, eds. (1990). *Improving health in older people: a world view*. Oxford: Oxford University Press.

Kane, R. L., Weiner, A., Homyak, P., and B. Bershadsky (2001). "The Minnesota Senior Health Options program: an early effort at integrating care for the dually eligible," *Journal of Gerontology: Medical Sciences*, 56A: M559–M566.

Kane, R. L., Homyak, P., Bershadsky, B., and Y.-S. Lum (2002). "Consumer responses to the Wisconsin Partnership Program for elderly persons: a variation on the PACE model," *Journal of Gerontology: Medical Sciences*, 57A: M250–M258.

Kane, R. L., Keckhafer, G., Flood, S., Bershadsky, B., and M. S. Siadaty (2003). "The effect of Evercare on hospital use," *Journal of the American Geriatrics Society*, 51: 1427–34.

Kendig, H., Hashimoto, A., and L. C. Coppard, eds. (1992). *Family support for the elderly: the international experience*. Oxford: Oxford University Press.

Kowloski, F., and R. J. V. Montgomery (1995). "The impact of respite use on nursing home placement," *Gerontologist*, 35: 67–74.

Manton, K. G., Newcomer, R., Lowrimore, G. R., Vertrees, J. C., and C. Harrington (1993). "Social/Health Maintenance Organization and fee-for-service health outcomes over time," *Health Care Financing Review*, 15: 173–202.

Montgomery, R. J. V., Karner, T. X., and K. Kosloski (2002). "Weighing the success of a national Alzheimer's Disease service demonstration," *Journal of Aging & Social Policy*, 14: 119–39.

Mundinger, M., Kane, R., Lenz, E., Totten, A., Tsai, W.-Y., Cleary, P., et al. (2000). "Primary care outcomes in patients treated by nurse practitioners or physicians: a randomized trial," *JAMA*, 283 (1): 59–68.

Navaie-Waliser, M., Spriggs, A., and P. H. Feldman (2002). "Informal caregiving: differential experiences by gender," *Medical Care*, 40: 1249–59.

Newcomer, R., Spitalny, M., Fox, P., and C. Yordi (1999). "Effects of the Medicare Alzheimer's Disease Demonstration Evaluation on the use of community-based services," *Health Services Research*, 34: 645–67.

Sikma, S., and H. Young (2001). "Balancing freedom with risks: the experience of nursing task delegation in community based residential care settings," *Nursing Outlook*, 49: 193–201.

Simon-Rusinowitz, L., Marks, L. N., Loughlin, D. M., Desmond, S. M., Mahoney, K. J., Zacharias, B. L., Squillace, M. R., and A. M. Allison (2002). "Implementation issues for consumer-directed programs: comparing views of policy experts, consumers, and representatives," *Journal of Aging & Social Policy*, 14: 95–118.

WHO (1999). *Home-based and long term care: home care issues at the approach of the 21st century from a World Health Organization perspective*, WHO/HSC/LTH/99/1. Geneva: WHO.

——— (2001). *Innovative care for chronic conditions*, WHO/NMH/CCH/01. Geneva: Noncommunicable Diseases and Mental Health, WHO.

——— (2002). *Innovative care for chronic conditions: building blocks for action*, WHO/MNC/CCH/02/01. Geneva: WHO.

Wilson, K. B. (1993). "Assisted living: a model of supportive housing." In P. R. Katz, R. L. Kane, and M. D. Mezey, eds., *Advances in long-term care*, Vol. II. New York: Springer.

Managed Care in the United States and United Kingdom

ROBERT L. KANE AND CLIVE E. BOWMAN

WHAT IS MANAGED CARE?

The term "managed care" has become quite ubiquitous, particularly in developed countries, but has never been well defined; consequently, it has a meaning that ranges from a cynical process of rationing care through to a systematic attempt to provide integrated health and personal care aligning the most effective and efficient processes to deliver a person-centered approach. Generally, health and care delivery systems include public health programs and various means of provision that range from a wholly unlimited and free-at-the-point-of-delivery welfare state approach to entirely private care provision where everything has a direct cost. Managed care is a process that seeks to manage both the demand and supply of health and care. Enthusiasts may suggest that managed care is a well-structured amalgam of the best of a welfare state and private service.

Managed care most commonly implies a defined management strategy, usually through insurance systems of reimbursement or state welfare. Both traditional insurance, state welfare, and managed care involve some sort of capitated payment. An amount per individual subscriber (or per family) is negotiated to cover health and/or care for a specified time. Whereas traditional insurance plays a reactive role, effectively balancing subscription rates and invoices, adjusting rates as expenses increase or decline, managed care plays a more proactive role in the way care is provided, controlling costs and increasingly shaping patterns of care. In welfare state arrangements the capitation budgeting is less clear, though

limitations on levels of reimbursement are often evident. In the UK and other countries with state health and care services funded from general taxation, the principles of care management have seemed to be rooted more in rights and responsibilities than in cost and demand management.

In the US, managed care was originally associated with group practices like Kaiser Permanente, but its real growth has occurred under a model that allows managed care organizations (MCO) to contract with individual physicians or groups of physicians

The original Health Maintenance Organizations (HMOs) sought to capture a healthy market offering generous preventive services and other programs designed to attract healthy enrollees. (Some plans even offered free memberships in health clubs.) However, once enrollment was linked largely to employee benefits, the opportunities for selective marketing declined sharply. Many interventional strategies are available to MCOs to control costs:

- Prior approval requirement. A representative of the organization must first approve elective care before it will be covered. This has proven impractical with the amount of care rejected being less than the cost and intrusiveness of the process. Most companies that adopted this strategy subsequently abandoned it.
- Profiling. MCOs can review care post hoc through profiling the patterns of care among their covered providers to identify providers whose practice patterns deviate from standards (quality as well as cost). "Deviants" who do not conform may subsequently be "released" from their contracts with the company.
- Incentives. A more proactive strategy is the provision of a variety of incentives for providers to practice

more parsimoniously. MCOs may offer some form of profit sharing; providers whose direct and ancillary costs are lower than expected may receive a bonus. Alternatively, the MCO may hold back a proportion of the provider's payment to cover cost over-runs. This retained amount is released if the expenditure pattern is within an acceptable range. The most direct financial incentive is to under-capitate care wherein the provider accepts the financial risk for some portion of the subscriber's total care (e.g., ambulatory care and hospitalizations) in return for a capitated payment. In this instance, the MCO passes on all the risks and serves largely as a marketing mechanism, effectively reverting to being an insurance broker, with the care management performed by the provider.

- Cost-effective/evidence-based medicine. The initial forays into this sphere were built around the creation of practice guidelines, standards for practice that were intended to make practice more consistent, both overall and with empirical evidence of what steps had been demonstrated to be effective. The search for evidential basis for practice spawned a whole movement of evidence-based medicine (Cochrane Collaboration). It quickly became evident that the extent and presentation of scientific evidence to support the majority of practice was weak with tightly controlled evidential treatment trials being of dubious legitimacy in patients with confounding pathologies and circumstances. Practice guidelines increasingly relied on clinical consensus judgment to fill in the considerable gaps left by hard evidence. Implementing clinical guidelines has proven quite difficult (Grimshaw *et al.*, 2001; Gross *et al.*, 2001). The general resistance to changing individual practice behavior and apparent yielding of professional autonomy has been compounded by fears that guidelines were driven more by cost concerns than quality. Because so much of the guideline material was based on professional opinion, several versions of the same guidelines regularly appeared. The observation that different MCOs championed different guidelines made practice difficult and threatened their credibility.

- Disease management. This approach implies intervening more directly in the care process, generally by contacting patients directly. For example, an MCO might identify all diabetic enrollees and work with them to ensure that they follow their treatment regimens and get appropriate prophylactic care. Alternatively, they might identify subsets of diabetics who had an emergency room visit in the last year and deal with them more aggressively, inviting them to

special classes and sending a nurse to visit. In many instances of such disease management, the insurers contract with independent firms, which undertake the direct dealings with the enrollees at risk. These contracts can be independent of the patients' primary care. Alternatively, the MCO might identify patients at risk and send alert notices to their primary care physicians to perform routine tests. Some programs have developed special clinics where patients with a common problem are gathered and dealt with, first in groups and then individually. Some programs have been implemented by telephone, calling regularly to check on their enrollee's health status and compliance with their treatment regimen. Information gathered from these regular contacts is usually shared with the patient's primary care physician.

In the United Kingdom, modernization of health services has seen the establishment of a number of bodies that presage a significantly more managed approach to health and care. The National Institute of Clinical Effectiveness (NICE) provides guidance on an increasing range of interventions intended to shape patterns of treatment particularly in treatment domains where geographical variations exist (often termed the postcode lottery). National Service Frameworks for the NHS provide a series of service goals and targets enabling conformance testing and evaluation by the Healthcare Commission and The Commission for Social Care Inspection (CSCI). The Healthcare Commission and CSCI are scheduled to be combined, though the shape of the new body was still unannounced at the time of writing.

Health service delivery in England (note: Scotland and Wales have differing approaches that are not to be detailed here) is organized around various types of Trusts that take responsibility for running NHS services. A key component is the 302 Primary Care Trusts (PCTs); others include Acute Hospital Trusts, Mental Health Trusts and Ambulance Trusts. PCTs are viewed as being at the center of the NHS and receive 75 percent of the NHS budget. As local organizations, PCTs are expected to understand and respond to the needs of their community. Trusts are overseen by 28 Strategic Health Authorities (SHAs) established in 2002 to develop plans for improving health services in their local area and to make sure their local NHS organizations are performing well. The numbers of both PCTs and SHAs will likely be reduced, through mergers to improve commissioning, produce efficiencies and improve alignment to the local authorities responsible for social care (which includes personal care).

Within the Social Services Departments of Local Authorities, the directors of adult services and children's services have recently replaced a single director. For adults an aim is to improve accountability and create an integrated strategy for adult social care, both locally and nationally, and a clear focus on the holistic needs of adults. The joint working of Social Services and Health should therefore increase.

The inextricable linkage and co-dependency of health and care resources in the care and support of older people has led to various forms of pooling health and care budgets in a quest for an integrated solution. The convergence of health and care commissioning, delivery and regulation all indicate a clear direction in England.

Whilst the financial drivers for managed care in the US and care management in the UK are similar, a commonality in the themes of consistency, transparency of services, and proactive stance is increasingly apparent.

THE POTENTIAL OF MANAGED CARE AND GERIATRICS

Superficially, it would appear that managed care was made for geriatric care! Many of the concepts that have proven difficult to inculcate into traditional American fee-for-service practice for older people suddenly make more sense in the context of managed care, particularly the concept of clinical investment. Geriatric medicine is all about investing time and resources early with the expectation that this will pay off in the future. The whole concept of comprehensive geriatric assessment and its successor, geriatric evaluation and management, is based on the premise that a thorough multidimensional understanding of a patient's condition will uncover treatable, or at least correctable, problems, thus delaying functional decline and avoiding unnecessary treatment costs. Strong empirical evidence supports this belief (Stuck *et al.*, 1993). In fee-for-service medicine, few are willing to pay the up-front costs of a comprehensive evaluation, because expenditures are monitored only in the present. However, managed care sees this investment as financially justified because the firm making the investment will also recoup its ultimate benefits.

In many circumstances, specialist physicians in geriatric care are not "affordable" in traditional private practice, particularly when physicians are reluctant to use them as consultants for fear of losing control of their cases. In America, geriatrics has defined itself as a primary care service, risking overlaps with its potential referral base of primary care physicians (Burton and Solomon, 1993). People in managed care have two sets of health and care needs, care to compensate for disabilities and the management of the conditions that contribute to their condition. Older people with diseases that traditionally are managed by specialists will increasingly question why, as the complexity of their conditions progresses, their specialist needs are addressed by generic geriatric services or primary care. Under a managed care arrangement, geriatric expertise can be made available to a large number of primary care practitioners, either through general design of better clinical approaches to care or as formal consultations for difficult cases.

Geriatric care can be greatly enhanced by sophisticated information systems and, because it often implies the participation of many different disciplines, an open communication system that allows everyone to be informed about the patient's status can be a powerful care management tool. If that information can specially track relevant clinical and functional parameters, its value is even greater. Individual practitioners have not the means to develop or support the type of information system that an MCO could.

In the UK, medical care has developed in a healthcare system principally centered on chronic institutional care at its inception over 50 years ago (many hospitals emerging from "infirmaries"). New treatment services have generally been funded to the detriment of the more chronic aspects of care, particularly for older people. The reformed NHS with commissioning based at Primary Care Trust level in the context of a National Service Framework for older people has created similar potential for investment (and challenges) for elderly care to that recognized by MCOs in the US.

THE REALITY OF MANAGED CARE

The appeal of managed care was high in the United States for several reasons. It was seen as a way of controlling the rapid rise in the cost of medical care consistent with a market-driven view of the economy. Introduced into the general population, it was encouraged as an option under Medicare, the universal health insurance program for older people. Whereas the private version of managed care relied on an insurance pricing model that offered various benefit packages at different prices, the Medicare version had to conform to the overall mandates of the parent program. Hence, the benefit package was defined as including all the benefits available to Medicare beneficiaries in the fee-for-service market. The Medicare program therefore established the price. The goal was to create a price that would be attractive to MCOs but also save money for Medicare. The solution was to set the price at the average cost for Medicare beneficiaries in a county, allowing for some adjustment for case mix. In order to keep the program administration simple, the adjustments relied exclusively on administrative data (i.e., age, poverty status, and nursing residence). In effect, Medicare MCOs were paid the average cost of care.

A basic rule of capitated care is that the payment structure will affect the approach to enrollment. It was readily apparent that the best way to make a profit was to enroll patients who were healthy. MCOs receiving the average fee, for people who were healthier than average, meant that the MCO could make money if they made no changes to the system. Just as happened in the early days of HMOs, to attract a healthy clientele the MCOs might offer additional benefits, such as more comprehensive preventive services. Not surprisingly, the early enrollments were indeed healthier than average. Rather than saving money for Medicare, managed care actually cost them money because of this favorable selection (Brown *et al.*, 1993) and this approach to rate setting actually created a strong disincentive to develop assertive geriatric care. The last thing an MCO being paid the average costs wanted was to develop a reputation as an organization that was good at geriatrics! The reality of a more dependent geriatric clientele, persons whose base costs would be higher than average, would be a liability under this payment scheme. Unsurprisingly, well-proven innovations have not been implemented widely (Boult *et al.*, 2000). Population-based enrollment in the UK avoids the selection effects of US managed care.

Managed care under Medicare has evolved in a variety of ways. Traditional managed care got off to a slow start. MCOs were attracted to the areas where the base payment, which reflected prevalent practice patterns, was highest. Indeed, variation across the most and least expensive counties was over 100 percent. Moreover, the MCOs in high-paying areas could offer additional benefits at no cost, especially coverage for medications, which are not routinely covered under Medicare. As out-of-pocket costs to beneficiaries grew under the regular Medicare program, managed care became a more attractive option. Nonetheless, its popularity was limited. Its peak penetrance was about 15 percent.

Studies of the quality of care provided by managed care to Medicare beneficiaries suggest that the quality is about the same as that offered to fee-for-service recipients (Retchin and Brown, 1990, 1991; Retchin *et al.*, 1992, 1994, 1997; Retchin and Preston, 1991).

Managed care and Medicaid

Managed care was also used to address other elderly populations, especially persons who were eligible for both Medicare and Medicaid. This dually eligible group was noted as having higher costs than those in either group alone. The major goal of merging these benefits into a single managed care program was the avoidance of overlap and the ability to use the resources more flexibly. In effect, these programs combine coverage for both acute and long term care, although the extent of this coverage varies somewhat.

There is some limited data to suggest that they produce both financial and clinical benefits, but much still remains to be explored. PACE (Program for All-inclusive Care of the Elderly) stands as perhaps the best model of truly integrated care (Kane, 1999; Eleazer and Fretwell, 1999; Eng *et al.*, 1997; Wieland *et al.*, 2000; Pacala *et al.*, 2000). Developed originally to serve an elderly frail Chinese population in San Francisco, it has become a federally certified Medicare managed care program. It was designed to serve a niche market, persons eligible for both Medicare and Medicaid who were deemed eligible for nursing home care but still lived in the community. As might be expected, this is a very small target group of high-risk persons whose capitation rate is substantial. About two-thirds of the money comes from Medicaid but the Medicare rate is a generous multiple (almost two and a half times) of the base rate. This pool of resources allowed for the establishment of an integrated approach to care, which featured physicians working on salary and a clinical base healthcare. A central part of the model was the active inclusion of all those involved in any aspect of the enrollees' care as part of the core team, with regular team meetings and active information sharing. Innovative efforts were made to avoid the use of either acute or long term care institutions. Creative means were found to tap all available resources to permit housing support from other means and to integrate care into that housing. Because the medical care is provided by PACE physicians, enrollees must forsake their previous medical attendants to join; this has proved a deterrent to enrollment. Newer versions have been created that are testing the feasibility of replicating the PACE approach but employing physicians under contract. The evaluation of the original PACE demonstration project encountered logistical difficulties, but its results indicate that the program was able to reduce institutional use dramatically with no diminution in care quality (Chatterji et al., 1998).

A few states have attempted to merge the funding for these so-called "dually eligible" recipients who are covered by both Medicare and Medicaid. This population is considerably broader and more heterogeneous than the mandate for PACE, which is restricted to those eligible for nursing home care but living in the community. The dual eligible population includes people living in the community at various levels of disability and those residing in nursing homes.

Minnesota had capitated the care of all its Medicaid population some years ago, covering almost all services except nursing home care. They then took the next step of merging funding for Medicare and Medicaid. Because enrollment of Medicare recipients in a managed care program must be voluntary, enrollment in this merged entity is voluntary. In the Minnesota Senior Health Options (MSHO) program, the care is administered by health plans which subcontract with other programs to provide care elements. The main advantage of this approach is the potential flexibility obtained to develop necessary solutions unconstrained by payment regulations. To provide more coordination, the plans must employ some degree of case management for all enrollees;

the intensity corresponds to the level of impairment (Kane, Weiner, Homyak, and Bershadsky, 2001). An evaluation has thus far failed to show any major health-related benefits to this merged care (Kane et al., 2003). One of the problems may be the lack of depth of physician participation. Each physician has on average only six patients in MSHO. Such a small caseload provides an insufficient motivation to make any changes in practice patterns.

Wisconsin has developed a somewhat different approach to addressing the dual eligible population. It has implemented a variation of the PACE model. Under the Wisconsin Partnership Program (WPP), managed care programs operate PACE-like approaches with one major difference: instead of utilizing a physician hired by the program to provide primary care, the WPP model allows enrollees to use their regular primary care provider. Active case management is provided by a team of nurse, social worker, and nurse practitioner. The latter is responsible for interacting with the primary care physician to replicate the effects of the team meetings under PACE. Here too the evaluation has failed to show any substantial benefits (Kane et al., 2002a, 2002b). Once again the level of physician participation is modest.

The NHS and social services

Reconciling means-tested personal care and free-at-the-point-of-delivery healthcare has been a long-standing challenge in the UK. At the inception of the health service over 50 years ago many of the newly constituted NHS hospitals had been established and funded by municipalities or charities that had their roots in poor law institutions. Historically, poor law infirmaries had strict rules of entry (eligibility) and regime (management). They could be viewed retrospectively as early managed care organizations. Regional and local variation of these provisions, related to varying affluence, deprivation, and needs, created and perpetuated inequalities in service levels in the NHS.

Community care reforms of the early 1990s sought to bring clarity through greater distinction between health and care. However, the overlaps and gaps between health and core needs continued to undermine development, exemplified by the conundrum of whether assisted bathing or other similar care intervention should be defined as personal care or a health intervention.

At the time of writing, the UK is still best described as being in a transitional developmental stage. Older persons needing institutional nursing home care undergo a series of eligibility tests to justify full care costs being met by the NHS; if not, they are means tested for personal care whilst maintaining the principle of a health service free at the point of delivery. It is probable that this overly complex system will consolidate to an integrated solution that shares characteristics of successful US PACE schemes. The missing key is standardized assessment and information networking.

Managed long term care

The prime objective of maintaining health and personal independence has driven new investment in geriatric services both in the UK and US, with entry into long term care being variously viewed as a failure and an expensive failure. Investment in the development of long term care itself has been dismal. This is a paradox as institutional care is clearly a costly service and provides a particularly fertile setting amenable for care management. In the UK long term care has long been a poor relation within the NHS, typically using facilities and equipment discarded by an avaricious technology-driven health service. Furthermore, health and social services often had an unhelpful operational remoteness.

In the US several companies have developed special programs offering Medicare managed care to nursing home residents. The pioneer in this area was Evercare, a program operated by United Health Care (Kane and Huck, 2000). The incentives for such programs are the higher capitation rates medicare pays for nursing home residents. Although analyses indicate that nursing home residence per se is not a risk factor for higher Medicare costs (in fact, nursing home residents have lower Medicare costs than persons with the same disease and disability burden living in the community), nursing home residence has served as a convenient administrative marker for such increases in disability. The higher payment, together with a conviction that better primary care can prevent, or at least reduce, the use of hospital care, serves as the rationale for these programs.

The basic model is founded exclusively in areas of Medicare's responsibility. Payment for nursing home care is restricted to only that mandated by Medicare (i.e., skilled care after a hospitalization) and an inducement payment for extra nursing home care provided in lieu of a hospital admission.

The strategy for providing more intensive primary care relies heavily on using nurse practitioners as primary caregivers; they are paid for by Evercare but work under the supervision of private physicians with whom Evercare contracts to provide all needed primary care. The evaluation suggests that this approach to care has a marked effect on utilization. The rates of hospitalizations and emergency room visits were dramatically reduced (R. L. Kane et al., 2003). Much of this reduction is achieved by changing the locus of care by keeping the resident in the nursing home, providing treatment "in situ." Nonetheless, in the case of diagnoses deemed sensitive to primary care, the incidence of hospitalizable events was lower in the Evercare group than in the controls.

Another program that provides at least some coordination between acute and long term care is the Social HMO. Under this program, managed care organizations received the full capitated amount (instead of 95 percent), with the expectation that the additional 5 percent would be used to provide at least a modest long term care benefit. The SHMO is not targeted specifically at dually eligible persons, and only a small number of Medicaid beneficiaries are enrolled. After the initial evaluation showed little impact (Harrington et al., 1988; Manton et al., 1993; Newcomer et al., 1995), a second generation of SHMO projects was launched in the hopes of creating a model of care that emphasized more geriatrics and case management (Kane et al., 1997). Despite active efforts to adapt the SHMO model to provide a more proactive geriatric care, there is little evidence of meaningful benefit or cost-savings (Wooldridge et al., 2000).

Physicians appointed early in British geriatric medicine typically were assigned medical responsibility for Victorian institutions of containment and care. Commonly these institutions featured desperate waiting lists with little sense of rehabilitation, and rigid institutional regimes. Recognition and pursuit of the potential of assessment and rehabilitation, with trends to discharge people who previously could have expected to remain in care, made geriatric medicine successful. Recycling the dowry of resources of large-scale institutional care enabled much innovation and active treatment approaches, case finding and preventative care. Much of this inspirational practice happened in an intuitive rather than managed way and desirable outcomes were seemingly limited at times to institutional closure. The need for new investment was lacking, and there was a default approach of addressing unmet needs usually determined through scandal, rather than a proactive strategy. The primitive state of information technology and understanding of the need for care meant that the positive outcomes and value of good care went unrecorded, undermining the position of geriatric care compared with the evident value of interventions such as heart surgery and orthopaedic joint replacement.

DEVELOPING MANAGED CARE. The proposition that good managed care offers vulnerable older people greater assurance than unmanaged care is difficult to refute. Clearly, effective management is considerably dependent on information and that implies effective measurement. Even before effective management, there is a need to reconcile a number of questions and concerns that include:

1) What are the collective needs of the population for which managed care is being proposed?
2) Can the economies of scale that bring efficiencies and the potential for effective management be reconciled with individualized person-centered care?
3) Are the incentives for good practice aligned with the reasonable expectations of the service providers?
4) Does the performance and regulatory system focus on outcome satisfaction rather than merely the processes of care?

Increasing numbers of older people are enjoying improved health, independence, and fitness than ever before and most will experience short periods of illness and associated dependency prior to death. Put simply, the proposition that what is treated will lead to contained health and care needs (and costs) has unsurprisingly found favor. In the UK, Department of Health projections (at 1995/6 prices) have predicted that a fairly modest 1 percent reduction in morbidity rates each year would reduce the annual cost of publicly funded formal care by 30 percent, or

£6.3 billion, by 2030. Whilst this approach has justified much of the positive investment in the US, it has to be tempered with an appreciation of the changing population needs. An informed epidemiology of disease and disability in later life, from which clear strategies can address the significant and often quite discrete health and care issues of older people, needs to replace the outmoded concept of the "burden of ageing." A simple analogy can be drawn with the development of adult internal medicine, which has grown from general medicine to organ- or disease-specific specialty approaches. Similarly, paediatric care was initially a specialty dictated by age, but now there are clearly defined streams of specialist expertise that address diseases particular to childhood within a clinical and care culture appropriate to the population.

Managed care could address diseases more specific to later life; the diagnostic and clinical problems of older people not specifically addressed by specialty medicine include dementia, stroke, Parkinsonism, joint failure, mental illness, loss of continence, and impairment of hearing and sight. These are capable of being resolved through programs of chronic disease management. It is useful to distinguish these diagnostic groupings from common presentations and symptoms such as falls and delirium, themselves amenable to care pathways but potentially requiring specialist remedy. Whilst multiple pathology has been a driving force to keep geriatric care generalist, it is likely that the population of older people with needs outside fairly broad pathways will be the focus for specialist geriatric management.

CONCLUSION

Managed care in the US has grown from a pure fiscal framework to what is increasingly understood, when well constructed, as an efficient and effective approach to health and care. In the UK, the welfare state of health and care produced a form of care management but failure to chart its value led to poor strategic planning, with pressures (most easily seen in common mis-placement of older people in acute hospitals) to adopt managed care approaches to the health and care of older people. Whilst systems on both sides of the Atlantic started from greatly differing points, there is a convergence, and whilst the final form of services remains unclear it is possible to specify desirable features of managed care:

1) equitable and non-discriminatory access;
2) a proactive stance to care, with prevention and rehabilitation actively deployed to minimize dependence;
3) development of a range of community supports and institutions to avoid/minimize unnecessary acute hospitalization;
4) particularly careful care planning and management for people in institutional care, to maximize health and minimize acute illness episodes;
5) effectiveness measured on outcome performance and efficiency;
6) appropriate risk-adjusted capitation payment, especially if enrollment is voluntary (and thus selection bias is a real possibility).

FURTHER READING

The *Journal of the American Geriatrics Society* frequently carries insightful papers regarding managed care and older people.

Calkins, E., Boult, C., Wagner, E. H., and James T. Pacala, eds. (1999). *New ways to care for older people: building systems based on evidence.* New York: Springer Publishing Company.

Kane, R. L., Priester, R., and A. Totten (2005). *Meeting the challenge of chronic illness.* Baltimore: Johns Hopkins University Press.

REFERENCES

Boult, C., Kane, R. L., and R. Brown (2000). "Managed care of chronically ill older people: the US experience," *British Medical Journal,* 321: 1011–14.

Brown, R. S., Clement, D. G., Hill, J. W., Retchin, S. M., and J. W. Bergeron (1993). "Do health maintenance organizations work for Medicare?" *Health Care Financing Review,* 15 (1): 7–23.

Burton, J., and D. Solomon (1993). "Geriatric medicine: a true primary care discipline," *Journal of the American Geriatrics Society,* 41 (4): 459–61.

Chatterji, P., Burstein, N. R., Kidder, D., and A. J. White (1998). *Evaluation of the Program of All-Inclusive Care for the Elderly (PACE).* Cambridge, Mass.: Abt Associates Inc.

Eleazer, P., and M. Fretwell (1999). "The PACE model: a review." In P. Katz, R. L. Kane and M. Mezey, eds., *Advances in long-term care,* Vol. IV.

Eng, C., Pedulla, J., Eleazer, G. P., McCann, R., and N. Fox (1997). "Program of All-inclusive Care for the Elderly (PACE): an innovative model of integrated geriatric care and financing," *Journal of the American Geriatrics Society,* 45: 223–32.

Grimshaw, J. M., Shirran, L., Thomas, R., Mowatt, G., Fraser, C., Bero, L., Grill, R., Harvey, E., Oxman, A. D., and M. A. O'Brien (2001). "Changing provider behavior: an overview of systematic reviews of interventions," *Medical Care,* 39 (8): II-2 – II-45.

Gross, P. A., Greenfield, S., Cretin, S., Ferguson, J., Grimshaw, J., Grol, R., Klazinga, N., Lorenz, W., Meyer, G. S., Riccobono, C., Schoenbaum, S. C., Schyve, P., and C. Shaw (2001). "Optimal methods for guideline implementation: conclusions from Leeds Castle meeting," *Medical Care,* 39 (8): II-85 – II-92.

Harrington, C., Newcomer, R., and T. Moore (1988). "HMO Medicare risk contract enrollment success: an overview of contributing factors," *Inquiry,* 25 (Summer): 33–44.

Kane, R. L. (1999). "Setting the PACE in chronic care," *Contemporary Gerontology,* 6 (2): 47–50.

Kane, R. L., Kane, R. A., Finch, M., Harrington, C., Newcomer, R., Miller, N., and M. Hulbert (1997). "S/HMOs, the second generation: building on the experience of the first social health maintenance organization demonstrations," *Journal of the American Geriatrics Society,* 45 (1): 101–7.

Kane, R. L., Keckhafer, G., Flood, S., Bershadsky, B., and M. S. Siadaty (2003). "The effect of Evercare on hospital use", *Journal of the American Geriatrics Society,* 51 (10): 1427–34.

Kane, R. L., Weiner, A., Homyak, P., and B. Bershadsky (2001). "The Minnesota Senior Health Options program: an early effort at integrating care for the dually eligible," *Journal of Gerontology: Medical Sciences,* 56A (9): M559–M566.

Kane, R. L., Homyak, P., and B. Bershadsky (2002a). "Consumer reactions to the Wisconsin Partnership Program and its parent, the Program for All-inclusive Care of the Elderly (PACE)," *The Gerontologist,* 42 (3): 314–20.

Kane, R. L., Homyak, P., Bershadsky, B., and Y.-S. Lum (2002b). "Consumer responses to the Wisconsin Partnership Program for elderly persons: a variation on the PACE model," *Journals of Gerontology: Medical Sciences,* 57a (4): M250–M258.

Kane, R. L., Homyak, P., Bershadsky, B., Lum, Y.-S., and M. Siadaty (2003). "Outcomes of managed care of dually eligible older persons," *The Gerontologist,* 43 (2): 219–29.

Manton, K. G., Newcomer, R., Lowrimore, G. R., Vertrees, J. C., and C. Harrington (1993). "Social/Health Maintenance Organization and fee-for-service health outcomes over time," *Health Care Financing Review,* 15 (2): 173–202.

Newcomer, R., Manton, K., Harrington, C., Yordi, C., and J. Vertrees (1995). "Case mix controlled service use and expenditures in the social/health maintenance organization demonstration," *Journal of Gerontology: Medical Sciences*, 50A (1): M35–M44.

Pacala, J. T., Kane, R. L., Atherly, A. J., and M. A. Smith (2000). "Using structured implicit review to assess quality of care in the Program of All-inclusive Care for the Elderly (PACE)," *Journal of the American Geriatrics Society*, 48: 903–10.

Retchin, S., and B. Brown (1990). "Quality of ambulatory care in Medicare health maintenance organizations," *American Journal of Public Health*, 80 (4): 411–15.

———(1991). "Elderly patients with congestive heart failure under prepaid care," *American Journal of Medicine*, 90 (February): 236–42.

Retchin, S. M., and J. Preston (1991). "Effects of cost containment on the care of elderly diabetics," *Archives of Internal Medicine*, 151 (11): 2244–48.

Retchin, S. M., Clement, D. G., Rossiter, L. F., Brown, B., Brown, R., and L. Nelson (1992). "How the elderly fare in HMOs: outcomes from the Medicare competition demonstrations," *Health Services Research*, 27 (5): 651–69.

Retchin, S. M., Clement, D., and R. Brown (1994). "Care of patients hospitalized with strokes under the Medicare risk program." In H. Luft, ed., *HMOs and the elderly*. Ann Arbor, Mich.: Health Administration Press, pp. 167–94.

Retchin, S. M., Brown, R. S., Yeh, S. J., Chu, D., and L. Moreno (1997). "Outcomes of stroke patients in Medicare fee for service and managed care," *JAMA*, 278 (2): 119–24.

Stuck, A. E., Siu, A. L., Wieland, G. D., Adams, J., and L. Z. Rubenstein (1993). "Comprehensive geriatric assessment: a meta-analysis of controlled trials," *Lancet*, 342: 1032–6.

Wieland, D., Lamb, V. L., Sutton, S. R., Boland, R., Clark, M., Friedman, S., Brummel-Smith, K., and G. P. Eleazer (2000). "Hospitalization in the Program of All-Inclusive Care for the Elderly (PACE): rates, concomitants, and predictors," *Journal of the American Geriatrics Society*, 48 (11): 1373–80.

Wooldridge, J., Brown, R., Foster, L., Hoag, S., Irvin, C., Kane, R. L., Newcomer, R., Schneider, B., and K. D. Smith (2000). *Social health maintenance organizations: transition into Medicare + choice* submitted to *Health Care Financing Administration*. Princeton, N.J.: Mathematica Policy Research, Inc.

Healthcare Rationing: Is Age a Proper Criterion?

RUUD TER MEULEN AND JOSY UBACHS-MOUST

INTRODUCTION

The healthcare systems of all developed countries in the world are confronted with a growing demand for care resources. The main cause for this increase is the ageing of the population. Particularly, the 'double ageing' of the population – that is, the rapid increase of the proportion of the persons of 80 years old and above – will give rise to a sharp increase in the demand for care in the coming decades. Within this age group, there is an increased chance of becoming handicapped by chronic and invalidating diseases and of becoming dependent on long term care.

The growing need for care, particularly long term care for chronic diseases, poses an important problem for the allocation of healthcare resources. While the healthcare budget is not allowed to increase (that is, as part of the GNP), there is an increasing scarcity of resources for healthcare services, particularly long term care services for the elderly, like nursing homes, home care and homes for the elderly. The problem of scarce resources for the elderly cannot be addressed in economic and organisational terms only. This problem also raises fundamental ethical questions, particularly about our commitments and obligations towards our elderly family members and fellow citizens.

In this chapter we will deal with the ethical debate about the proposal to ration healthcare services for the elderly. This proposal will be discussed in the context of social and political developments like the medicalisation of old age, the individualisation of

society, the (alleged) decline of solidarity between the generations, and the social status of the elderly. In addition, there will be attention to recent political developments, like the increased emphasis on individual financial responsibility for health and the call for more evidence-based healthcare, which may affect access to care for the elderly.

LONGER LIVES

As mentioned above, the ageing and the double ageing of the population in the industrialised countries is a fact. The average life expectancy has risen significantly in the last century. This increase of average life expectancy however, cannot be called a success in all respects (Gruenberg, 1977). While individuals can enjoy themselves in a longer life, they are confronted increasingly with chronic, debilitating diseases which are typical for the later stages of life. In fact, the healthy life expectancy, that is the period of life that is free from diseases and handicaps, has remained the same, but the average life expectancy has risen. In consequence, we seem to be living in bad health for an increasing part of our lives. The increase of this age group of 80-year-olds, who suffer from these typical later stages of life-diseases, consequently leads to an increase in the demand for care from this age group, particularly on home care, nursing home care and hospital care. In view of these figures, there is a debate going on about what should be the main target of public health policies for the elderly: adding more life or more quality to our (long) lives (Légaré, 1991).

SOCIAL PROCESSES

The demand for care, however, is not only determined by the demographic process alone, but is also influenced by other social processes (Hollander and Becker, 1987). These are medicalisation, individualisation and a decline of solidarity, and the (change of the) social status of the elderly.

Medicalisation

Medicalisation can be defined as the process by which human existence is increasingly understood from the viewpoint of health and disease (Zola, 1975; Crawford, 1980). Medicalisation is characterised by an increasing utilisation of medical services. This increased utilisation will very likely continue to rise in the coming decades.

What do medicalisation and the ageing of the population have to do with scarce resources?

The scarcity of resources is in large part determined by a cultural process, in which the extension of life is made an absolute ideal. One forgets, however, that man is going to die sometime, in spite of all efforts to extend life. Life cannot be extended into eternity (Callahan, 1987). The desire for a long life goes together with a devaluation of old age as a distinct and meaningful period of life. In a society which values health and long life in a dominant way, old age can only be seen as a deviation or even as a disease which must be fought or suppressed (Cole, 1988, 1992).

The increasing medicalisation of old age is linked up with the absence of a view on the meaning of old age (Callahan, 1987). The medicalisation of old age, and thereby the over-utilisation of healthcare services, could be stopped if we recognise ourselves as fragile and mortal beings. According to Callahan (1987), fragility and mortality will only be accepted when we know how to give meaning to the last stages of our life.

Individualisation and decline of solidarity

The increase in the demand for care is also determined by the availability of informal care. This is care given by family members or neighbours. As a result of the ongoing individualisation of society and the breakdown of traditional forms of solidarity, this kind of informal care is becoming more difficult to provide. Children are moving away from their parents to other cities, having their own families or are getting divorced. They perhaps have a lifestyle with norms and values that are different from those of their elder parents. Moreover, an increasing part of the population is living in arrangements other than the traditional family.

However, living in other conditions than in the past does not prevent many children from having strong feelings of solidarity with their needy parents. It is more the ability to provide care that has become very problematic for many children, because of the geographical distance, the decreased number of brothers and sisters (who could alleviate the burden of caring), the care for their own children and the (increased) participation of women in the labour force.

Intergenerational solidarity is also increasingly coming under strain. There is a continuous change in the dependency ratio between the young and the old. A decreasing number of young people have to support financially an increasing number of older people. This is a general problem for an ageing society, which poses not only a problem for healthcare, but also for other services for the elderly, like pensioning schemes. The change in the dependency ratio results in an increase of premiums for pensioning and healthcare insurance. The young will have less to spend for themselves and for the care of their children. As a result, the tension between the young and the old might continue to rise (De Jouvenel, 1990).

The described increase of individualisation and decrease of these two types of solidarity, that is the solidarity between the young and the old in society and the solidarity between the young and the old in the family, therefore also lead to an increase in the demand for care by the elderly population from long term care services.

The social status of the elderly

The social status of the elderly is another factor that is playing a role in the demand for care. Though the elderly are very often willing to work longer and to make themselves useful for society, they are forced to leave the workforce at an age of 65 or earlier. However, when there are no opportunities for meaningful activities (study, leisure, voluntary work), this disengagement may result in feelings of superfluousness, abandonment and loneliness. It can be expected that the difference between the aspirations of the elderly on the one hand and the lack of willingness of society to respond to these aspirations will result in lower responsibility for health and a decline in subjective health status. These processes will give rise to increasing visits to general practitioners and to increasing utilisation of other medical services.

Another aspect of the social status of the elderly concerns the attitude towards the elderly. The scarcity of resources also results in a growing negative attitude towards the elderly, who might be seen as a burden for society. The elderly are occupying an increasing number of beds within hospitals, which in some cases results in waiting lists for other, younger patients. The premiums for healthcare insurance are rising, in order to pay the increasing costs of the care for the elderly. There is a growing demand, already mentioned, for informal care, which creates burdens for families and neighbours. These processes might also result in a decreasing of solidarity with the elderly, or at least to a debate about the limits of our solidarity with the older generations.

Therefore, it should be remembered that the demographic shift is only partly responsible for the growing demand for healthcare. Much more important is the impact of medicalisation and individualisation and the decreasing of solidarity between the generations. The increase in the number and proportion of the elderly is not the main cause of the growing demand for care, but the way elderly are treated by our society in general and the medical system in particular (Callahan, 1990; Clark, 1989). The alleged impact of demography on the demand for care is grossly exaggerated: focusing on the demographic process is a way of creating a myth, which hinders an insight into the real causes of the scarcity of resources. In 2001, 50 per cent of the rising healthcare costs are, according to the Dutch Central Planning Bureau, caused by technological progress. There are no unambiguous numbers on the influence of the ageing of the population on the rising costs. Therefore, the ageing of the population is not the main culprit (Van der Heijden, 2003).

Instead of being blamed, the elderly should be offered new roles and perspectives in our society, by way of retirement policies, voluntary activities and part-time work opportunities. Social attitudes towards the elderly play an important role in the demand for care: a more positive status for the elderly in our society will result in a better health status and a decrease in the demand for care.

If we really want to tackle the problem of the rising costs of healthcare and the increasing demand for care by the elderly, we need to confront the real issues that bring about this problem.

SCARCITY OF HEALTHCARE RESOURCES

The increasing demand for care is, as explained above, due to the demographic process but also to increasing medicalisation and individualisation and a worsening of the position of the elderly in our society.

Opposed to this increasing demand for care, there is a decreasing willingness of national governments to enlarge the share of healthcare in the Gross National Product (GNP). More money for healthcare results in less collective spending on other social activities and services, like education, environmental care, police protection and road construction. Some of these services are as important for good health as healthcare in itself. Besides, more money will not satisfy the demand for care. Medical technology will always produce new devices for the diagnosis or cure of diseases. These devices are immediately claimed by the patients or their doctors as a right. The scarcity of healthcare resources is a structural problem that is tightly linked to our culture and our way of life, in which health and healthcare play a dominant role (Callahan, 1990).

Solutions?

This growing need for care then, particularly long term care for chronic diseases, poses an important problem for the allocation of healthcare resources. One possible solution might be a reallocation of resources, particularly a shift from acute care to long term care. According to Callahan (1987) the increasing scarcity of long term care must be addressed by the introduction of an age limit for expensive treatments paid from collective funds. After reaching a 'natural life span' (which is not a biological, but a biographical, measure), elderly patients should not receive life-extending therapies. In exchange, the elderly should have better access to long term care facilities.

Callahan's proposal has been strongly criticised as a kind of 'ageist' discrimination (Barry and Bradley, 1991; Binstock and Post, 1991). Gerontologists and liberal ethicists, particularly, have argued that every age has its own aims and that no one can determine for another whether his life is completed or his 'natural life span' has been reached. There is no reason, they argue, why an old person would value his life less than a younger one. When one considers only years of life instead of life itself, one shows no respect for the unique value of the human person, which is the moral basis for our society.

On the other hand there is some truth in the argument that people who are 75 years old have had a 'fair share' of life, or 'fair innings' (Harris, 1985). We all have the moral intuition that to die young is a sorrow and a tragedy, but that to die at an old age is a sorrow, but no tragedy. In a situation in which treatment possibilities are limited and a choice must be made between a person who had a fair share and one who had not, it would be reasonable to choose for the latter. However, limiting of acute, life-extending care for the elderly will at this moment not solve the allocation problem. Though there may be an ethical argument in favour of setting limits on the elderly, there will probably be no financial gain. Moreover, the introduction of age criteria might reinforce the discrimination against the elderly and the process of blaming the elderly for the scarcity of healthcare resources. Besides, there will be strong resistance within the medical profession towards age limits: every physician will try to get the best treatments for his patients. Only when there are medical indications will physicians limit life-extending treatments for an elderly patient.

Not very comfortable with age limits, Cassel and Neugarten (1991) state that medicine in today's world needs to embrace the changing society in which people are living so much longer and to create a humane model of medical care that fits the new social realities. Rather than focusing on setting age limits for medical care, it should add opportunities for a continuing sense of the value of life, especially for the very old.

If one chooses to re-orientate and reallocate the healthcare resources, according to Moody, this process should not be done by way of direct and overt age limits for clinical procedures on the micro-level. It is politically more feasible to reallocate resources for the elderly by indirect means, for example by the setting of research priorities (more money for research for chronic diseases) and the allocation of resources on the macro-level (more nursing homes instead of Intensive Care Units) (Moody, 1991).

EVIDENCE-BASED HEALTHCARE

In the recent past the need for cost containment has been answered by the methods of the so-called 'evidence- based medicine' (EBM). The idea behind EBM is that doctors should only make use of therapies that have been proved to be effective, instead of making use of unproven therapies which may be ineffective or even harmful to the patient. Sackett, the founding father of EBM, defines EBM as 'the conscientious, explicit and judicious use of current best evidence in making decisions about the care of individual patients', which 'integrates the best evidence with individual clinical expertise and patients' choice' (Sackett *et al.*, 1996). Though EBM has been called to life to improve the quality of care, the principles of EBM have recently been applied to allocation decisions too. EBM stands now for a combined approach to improving the quality of clinical care as well as to controlling the costs of care by the use of the best available evidence. Information on the cost-effectiveness of scarce medical treatments plays an important role (Ter Meulen and Dickenson, 2002). Biller-Andorno *et al.* (2002) point to the fact that the introduction of empirical evidence may have the purpose of sharpening the criteria for access to scarce medical treatments by the use of cost-effectiveness analysis. Patients who are expected to benefit in a low degree from particular treatments, like the elderly and the chronically ill, may be excluded from access to scarce or expensive treatments.

On a clinical level, age itself is no contra-indication for many medical interventions, such as surgical operations on elderly people with cancer and kidney dialysis (Health Council of the Netherlands, 1998). However, the access of the elderly to these interventions will be jeopardised when access to treatment is based on cost-effectiveness analysis (or cost–utility analysis) only, as in general younger patients will have a better response to certain outcome criteria, particularly length of life (Ter Meulen and Dickenson, 2002). Because of their reduced life expectancy, elderly people will not be able to enjoy the blessings of extensive medical treatments at the same rate as younger patients (Ten Have *et al.*, 2003).

De Graeve and Adriaenssen point out that economic evaluations only look at the efficiency problem in allocating resources in terms of economic costs and investments. They do not take social acceptability or political feasibility into account, which makes them insufficient as an instrument for allocation decisions (2001).

Following the recent use of the EBM principles for making allocation decisions, there is a tendency to introduce guidelines and criteria for admission to healthcare services on the basis of evidence. Some welcome evidence-based medicine as a critical response to the inadequacies of traditional medicine (Hope, 1995). With the outcomes of systematic reviews in their hands, patients and their representatives could claim a more central role in medical decision making. However, there is a serious concern among doctors and other healthcare practitioners, that the increasing dominance of EBM might lead to a shift of power from doctors (and their patients) to managers and purchasers. Evidence-based criteria are increasingly expected to guide clinical decision making and the allocation and rationing process in European healthcare systems. However, when the values and assumptions of managed care and other evidence-based systems remain hidden and implicit, such systems can be a serious challenge to the values of European societies in respect of the quality of delivery of medical care and healthcare, as well as of access to medical and healthcare services (Ter Meulen and Dickenson, 2002).

RECENT POLITICAL DEVELOPMENTS

Welfare state governments are seeking ways to cope with the problem of how to deal with scarce resources in healthcare. The Dutch government chooses to deal with the rising healthcare costs by a combined policy of co-payments, compulsory deductibles and private additional insurance. This policy is meant to decrease the part of the collective expenditures in the Gross National Product. By keeping down the collective part, the compulsory premiums for healthcare and other social insurance are kept low and incomes (before tax) will not have to be increased. The shift from public expenditure towards private will inevitably result in a greater gap between the well-off and the lower income groups. The increased emphasis on financial responsibility of the individual will have a significant impact on the value of solidarity, which is the basis of the healthcare system. Solidarity means that the higher incomes pay for the lower income groups, as well as the people with low risks paying for the people with high risks. The already mentioned gap between the well-off and the lower income groups is reinforced by the introduction of market forces and nominal premiums in the national healthcare insurance. The elderly are affected most by this policy, because they have low incomes and are more dependent on healthcare services, particularly home care and long term care, where co-payments will be dominant. So, instead of rationing by objective criteria, most nations will address the scarcity problem by rationing by income, and thus by age (Ter Meulen, 2001).

CONCLUSIONS

In the previous sections we have tried to make clear that older people's demand for care will continue to grow. As finances are limited, there will be an increasing scarcity of resources, particularly for the elderly. Blaming the elderly for their own health problems is an easy way out, but is no solution at all. Rationing healthcare services for the elderly because of their age boils down to denying healthcare services to a growing part of the population and would mean a serious kind of discrimination.

While we cannot predict in detail what services will be required in the near future, we do know, however, what kind of services will be required to meet the needs of a predictable growing population of the elderly. We can begin today, Van den Berg Jeths and Thorslund (1995) state, to determine what priority the meeting of these needs ought to have and to design appropriate policies for allocating our resources. This policy should be combined with a policy in society aimed at improving opportunities for the elderly in society as well as strengthening their position in the healthcare system. Recognising the value of old age and reinforcing social participation by the elderly will result in better health and probably less demand for care.

FURTHER READING

Binstock, R., and S. Post, eds. (1991). *Too old for health care? Controversies in medicine, law, economics and ethics*, Baltimore: The Johns Hopkins University Press.

Callahan, D., Ter Meulen, R., and E. Topinkova, eds. (1995). *A world growing old. The coming health care challenges*. Washington, D.C.: Georgetown University Press.

Ter Meulen, R., Arts, W., and R. Muffels, eds. (2001). *Solidarity and health care in Europe*. Dordrecht / Boston, Mass.: Kluwer Academic Publishers.

Ter Meulen, R., Biller-Andorno, N., Lenk, C., and R. Lie, eds. (2005). *Ethical issues of evidence based medicine*. Heidelberg: Springer Verlag.

REFERENCES

Barry, R. L., and G. V. Bradley (1991). *Set no limits. A rebuttal to Daniel Callahan's proposal to limit health care for the elderly*. Urbana and Chicago: University of Illinois Press.

Biller-Andorno, N., Lie, R. K., and R. Ter Meulen (2002). 'Evidence based medicine as an instrument for rational health policy', *Health Care Analysis*, 10: 261–75.

Binstock, R. H., and S. G. Post, eds. (1991). *Too old for health care? Controversies in medicine, law, economics and ethics*. Baltimore: The Johns Hopkins University Press.

Callahan, D. (1987). *Setting limits. Medical goals in an aging society*. New York: Simon and Schuster.

——— (1990). *What kind of life. The limits of medical progress*. New York: Simon and Schuster.

Callahan, D., Ter Meulen, R. E., and Topinková, eds. (1995). *A world growing old. The coming health care challenges*. Washington D.C.: Georgetown University Press.

Cassel, C. K., and B. L. Neugarten (1991). 'The goals of medicine in an aging society'. In R. H. Binstock and S. G. Post, eds., *Too old for health care? Controversies in medicine, law, economics and ethics*. Baltimore: The Johns Hopkins University Press, pp. 75–91.

Clark, P. G. (1989). 'Canadian health-care policy and the elderly: will rationing rhetoric become reality in an aging society?' *Canadian Journal of Community Mental Health*, 8: 123–40.

Cole, T. R. (1988). 'Aging, history and health: progress and paradox'. In J. F. Schroots, J. E. Birren and A. Svanborg, eds., *Health and aging*. New York and Lisse: Swets.

——— (1992). *The journey of life. A cultural history of aging in America*. New York: Cambridge University Press.

Crawford, R. (1980). 'Healthism and medicalization of everyday life', *International Journal of Health Services*, 10: 365–88.

De Graeve, D., and I. Adriaenssen (2001). 'The use of economic evaluation in healthcare allocation'. In M. Parker and D. Dickenson, eds., *The Cambridge medical ethics workbook. Case Studies, commentaries and activities*. Cambridge: Cambridge University Press, pp. 251–7.

De Jouvenel, H. (1990). 'Le grand tournant démographique'. In E. Blanche, *Les conséquences médicales et socio-économiques du viellissement des populations*. Paris.

Gruenberg, E. M. (1977). 'The failures of success', *Milbank Memorial Fund Quarterly/Health and Society*: 3–24.

Harris, J. (1985). *The value of life*. London: Routledge and Kegan Paul.

Health Council of the Netherlands (1998). *President: who is old?* Rijswijk: Health Council of the Netherlands.

Hollander, C. F., and H. A. Becker, eds. (1987). *Growing old in the future. Scenarios on health and aging 1984–2000*. Dordrecht: Nijhoff.

Hope, T. (1995). 'Editorial: evidence-based medicine and ethics', *Journal of Medical Ethics*, 21: 259–60.

Légaré, J. (1991). 'Une meilleure santé ou une vie prolongée? Quelle politique de santé pour les personnes agées?' *Futuribles*, 155: 53–66.

Moody, H. (1991). 'Allocation, yes; age-based rationing, no'. In R. H. Binstock and S. G. Post, eds., *Too old for health care? Controversies in medicine, law, economics and ethics*. Baltimore: The Johns Hopkins University Press, pp. 180–203.

Sackett, D. L., Rosenberg, W. M., Gray, J. A., Haynes, R. B., and W. S. Richardson (1996). 'Evidence based medicine: what it is and what it isn't', *British Medical Journal*, 312: 71–2.

Ten Have, H. A. M. J., Ter Meulen, R. H. J., and E. Van Leeuwen, eds. (2003). *Medische ethiek [Medical ethics]*. Houten: Bohn Stafleu Van Loghum.

Ter Meulen, R. (2001). 'Care for the elderly in an era of diminishing resources'. In M. Parker and D. Dickenson, eds., *The Cambridge medical ethics workbook. Case Studies, commentaries and activities*. Cambridge: Cambridge University Press, pp. 241–9.

Ter Meulen, R., and D. Dickenson (2002). 'Into the hidden world behind evidence based medicine', *Health Care Analysis*, 10: 231–41.

Van den Berg Jeths, A. and M. Thorslund (1995). 'Will there be a scarcity of resources? The future demand for care by the elderly'. In D. Callahan, R. E. Ter Meulen, and Topinková, eds., *A world growing old. The coming health care challenges*. Washington, D.C.: Georgetown University Press, pp. 39–48.

Van der Heijden, N. L. (2003). 'Oudere is dupe op de zorgmarkt' ['Elderly are the victims on the health-market'], *De Volkskrant*, 16 September, p. 17.

Zola, I. K. (1975). *De medische macht [The medical power]*. Meppel: Boom.

CHAPTER 7.13

Adaptation to New Technologies

NEIL CHARNESS AND SARA J. CZAJA

The *Oxford English Dictionary* provides several definitions for adaptation including: "The action or process of adapting, fitting, or suiting one thing to another" and "The process of modifying a thing so as to suit new conditions." These definitions pinpoint two important dimensions of adaptation to technology: modifying people to enable them to cope with changes in their environments (e.g., through training) and modifying features of the environment to suit the capabilities of people (redesign). Both of these dimensions are essential to the older adults' successful adaptation to today's technology-driven world. The proliferation of technology across most settings implies that older adults will have to invest significant time and resources to learn to use existing and future technical systems. At the same time designers of technology need to be aware of the implications of age-related changes in abilities so that they can design systems and products that are easy to use for older adults. Unfortunately, to date, older adults have not been considered as active users of technology and the design community has largely ignored the needs and preferences of this population. The goals of this chapter are to discuss contexts in which older adults will use technology and how technology, when well designed, can promote quality of life and independence for older people.

BACKGROUND

The viewpoint we take in this chapter is that, at a first approximation, less economically developed nations can be viewed as developmentally delayed versions of today's economically advantaged nations. They will eventually face the same challenges of ageing populations and diffusion of technology. Given that the rate of adoption of technology varies widely at times between subgroups in a developed nation ("Falling through the NET II: new data on the digital divide," 1998), we would predict that both the acceptability and rate of adoption of certain technological artifacts and systems will vary across cultures.

Technology diffusion also depends on regulatory and economic circumstances. For instance, Europe generally lags behind the United States in the number of seniors who are Internet users, with a recent survey by Forrester (cited at www.nua.ie/surveys/index.cgi?f=VS&art_id=905358750&rel=true) indicating that about 20% of consumers aged 55+ were online by the end of 2002. The comparable figure for the United States for those aged 65+ was approximately 30%. The United States, as of 2002, apparently lags eleven other countries in terms of the penetration of broadband Internet connections per 100 inhabitants (ITU Internet Reports, 2003).

Two major demographic trends underscore the importance of considering adaptation to technology by older adults: the ageing of national populations (see part one of this handbook) and rapid dissemination of technological innovations. As an example, in less than 100 years, US citizens have seen a huge increase in life expectancy at birth (as have citizens in other industrialized nations). Only about 50% of the 1900 birth cohort could expect to survive until age 60, whereas 50% of the 1990 birth cohort is predicted to survive until age 80. At the same time,

Dwellings and Telephones in USA

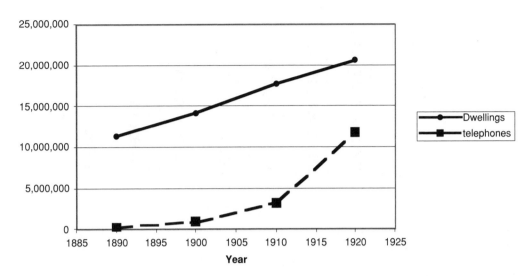

Figure 1. Dwellings and telephones in the USA. Dwelling data were gathered from http://fisher.lib.virginia.edu/census/. Phone data were gathered from www.bellsystemmemorial.com/capsule_bell_system.html#Alexander%20Graham%20Bell%20and%20the%20Invention%20of%20the%20Telephone and from www.telephonetribute.com/tribute/timeline.html.

rapid technology diffusion is particularly prominent in the economically privileged nations of the world.

A reasonable example of accelerating technology diffusion is the contrast between the diffusion of the telephone in the USA and the diffusion of access to the Internet. Bell received his first patent on the telephone in 1876. It took at least 30 years (probably closer to 50 years) for half the households in the USA to adopt telephones (Figure 1).

This estimate assumes that all phones were in dwellings and none were in businesses, which is not reasonable given their expense at that epoch. This pattern of adoption can be contrasted with the growth of Internet access in the USA. The public Internet originated in the late 1980s (the name Internet and use of TCP/IP protocol started in 1984: www.isoc.org/internet/history/), and, as shown in Figure 2, it took less than 20 years for the Internet to be widely adopted. If you use a more limited definition, World Wide Web access (initial servers were brought online between 1990 and 1991: www.w3.org/History.html), the interval for 50% household access was about 10 years.

Technology is diffusing much more rapidly now than ever before.

The digital computer is probably the archetypal technology artifact. It has progressed from being a room-sized device in the 1940s and 1950s to being a palm-sized device weighing a few hundred grams today. Microprocessor technology, invented by Intel in 1972, has become embedded in many devices to provide, in theory, greater flexibility to the user.

For flexibility to be exploited, people need to be aware of and to be

Figure 2. Commerce study of US households. Data from the USA Department of Commerce Study www.ntia.doc.gov/ntiahome/dn/anationonline2.pdf.

Commerce Study of US Households

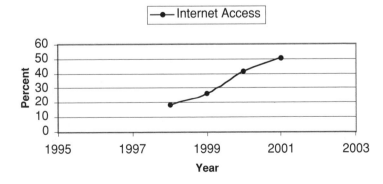

Internet Use by Age and Year

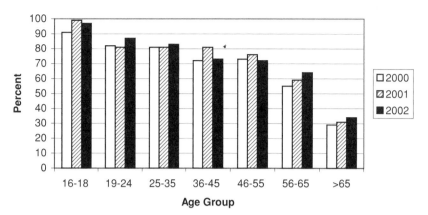

Figure 3. Internet use by age and year. Data source: the UCLA Internet Report – "Surveying the digital future," UCLA Center for Communication Policy, January, 2003.

able to use the functionality that processors provide devices. Several factors work against this process in older adults. Older adults are less likely to be in contact with new technology at home or at work. They typically live in older homes with fewer modern technology products and work in older industries and are often bypassed for training or retraining opportunities. Also, older adults are slower to learn new information than younger adults, requiring more practice and environmental support (Charness *et al.*, 2001: 110) and hence the perceived cost of learning new technology is greater for them (Melenhorst, 2002). Finally, older adults, particularly postretirement, vary enormously in wealth. Those less wealthy are less likely to purchase new technology devices. In summary, older adults are very likely to have a higher threshold for adoption of new technology (Charness and Schaie, 2003).

However, the ubiquity of computers and other forms of technology in society will necessitate use of technology by older adults. In addition, simple and familiar technologies such as the telephone are becoming more complex. Thus strategies need to be developed to ensure that older people are able to adapt to technical systems. This requires understanding factors that impact on the acceptance and use of technology among this population.

ACCEPTANCE AND USE OF TECHNOLOGY BY OLDER ADULTS

There are three primary arenas in which older adults come in contact with new technology: work, home,

and, increasingly, public venues. For example, currently more than half of the workforce in the USA uses a computer in the performance of their job (Czaja, 2001: 547). Technology is also increasingly being used in healthcare delivery for both inpatient and outpatient care, and in the performance of routine activities such as banking, shopping, and driving. A good example would be the public libraries in the USA, where manually administered card catalogues have been replaced by electronic databases, and banks where transactions are increasingly performed using technology such as automated teller machines (ATMs), automated phone menu systems, and web-based systems.

Recent data for the USA indicate that, although the use of computers and the Internet among older adults is increasing, there is still an age-based digital divide. As seen in Figure 3, in 2002 about 34% of people age 65+ accessed the Internet compared to nearly 100% of 16–18 year olds (The UCLA Internet Report – "Surveying the digital future," 2003).

A commonly held belief is that older people are resistant to change and unwilling to interact with "high tech" products such as computers. However, the available data largely dispute this stereotype and indicate that older people are receptive to using computers. However, the nature of their experience with computers, available training and support, ease of access, and the type of applications that are available are important determinants of their receptivity.

For example, Dyck and Smither (1994: 239) found that, although older adults had more positive attitudes towards computers than younger adults, they expressed less computer confidence. Their results also indicated that people who had experience with computers had more positive attitudes and greater computer confidence. Jay and Willis (1992: 250) also found that people who participated in a two-week computer-training course expressed greater computer comfort and computer efficacy. A more recent study (Czaja and Sharit, 1998: 332) examined age differences in attitudes towards computers as a function of computer experience among a community sample of 384 adults ranging in age from 20 to 75 years. The results indicated that older people perceived less comfort and efficacy using computers than younger people. However, experience with computers resulted in more positive attitudes for all participants irrespective of age. Rogers *et al.* (1996: 425) found that older adults were less likely to use ATMs than younger adults. However, the majority of the older people in their sample indicated they would be willing to use ATMs if trained to do so. In a study examining the use of e-mail among a sample of older women (Czaja *et al.*, 1993: 197), the data indicated that all participants found it valuable to have a computer in their home. However, the perceived usefulness of the system and system reliability were important factors with respect to usage.

The success of websites such as SeniorNet also points to the receptivity of older people to using computers for activities such as communication and continuing education. SeniorNet (www.seniornet.com) is a nonprofit organization whose mission is to provide people over the age of 50 with access to computer technology. Currently the organization has over 39,000 members and over 240 Learning Centers throughout the United States.

Thus, overall, it appears that older adults are receptive to using new technologies such as computers and that there are numerous factors other than age that influence the likelihood that older people will use new technology. These factors include: access to the technology, an understanding of the technology, training, technical support, and cost.

Understanding the factors that influence technology adoption is important for the development of strategies to increase the use of technology among this population.

CAN OLDER ADULTS LEARN TO USE TECHNOLOGY?

This section will review existing findings regarding the ability of older adults to learn to use technology such as computers. A number of studies (e.g. Elias *et al.*, 1987: 340; Gist *et al.*, 1988: 255; Zandri and Charness, 1989: 615; Czaja *et al.*, 1989a, 1989b: 309; Charness *et al.*, 1992: 79; Morrell *et al.*, 1995; Mead *et al.*, 1997: 152; Westerman *et al.*, 1998: 579) have examined the ability of older adults to learn to use computer technology. These studies encompass a variety of computer applications and also vary with respect to training strategies such as conceptual vs. procedural training (Morrell *et al.*, 1995) or active vs. passive learning approaches (Czaja *et al.*, 1989a). The influence of other variables, such as attitude towards computers and computer anxiety, on learning has also been examined.

Overall, the results of these studies indicate that older adults are able to use technology such as computers for a variety of tasks. However, they are typically slower to acquire new skills than younger adults and generally require more help and "hands-on" practice. Also, when compared to younger adults on performance measures, older adults often achieve lower levels of performance. However, the literature also indicates that training interventions can be successful in terms of improving performance and it points to the importance of matching training strategies with the characteristics of the learner. For example, Czaja *et al.* (1989b: 309) found that older adults benefit from using analogies to familiar concepts and from a more "active" hands-on training approach. Similarly, Mead *et al.* (1997: 152) examined the effects of type of training on efficiency in a World Wide Web search activity. The participants were trained with a hands-on Web navigation tutorial or a verbal description of available navigation tools. The hands-on training was found to be superior, especially for older adults. Older adults who received hands-on training increased the use of efficient navigation tools. Mead and Fisk (1998: 516) examined the impact of the type of information presented during training on the initial and retention performance of younger and older adults learning to use ATM technology. They found that action training – training procedures – was superior to concept training – presenting factual information – for older adults.

Generally, the literature suggests that these types of strategies are also beneficial for younger people. The literature (e.g. Czaja *et al.*, 2001: 564; Charness *et al.*, 2001: 110) also suggests that prior experience with technology is an important predictor of ability to learn to use new technology, suggesting that future cohorts of older adults may be advantaged compared to present ones. Finally, it is important to provide older people with training on the potential use of the technical system (e.g., what the Internet can be used for) as well as training on basic procedural operations (e.g., use of the mouse). As one would expect, the "usability" of the system from both a hardware and software perspective is also important (Fisk *et al.*, 2004).

TECHNOLOGY IN THE HOME: HEALTHCARE

Technology and telemedicine/e-health applications clearly hold promise in terms of increasing the physical and emotional wellbeing of older people and allowing them to remain at home longer. For example, technology can be used to monitor people with chronic illnesses such as diabetes or congestive heart failure. Patients can use technologies such as blood glucose meters to extract data on vital signs and symptoms and this information can be transmitted electronically to their physicians. Video-conferencing applications may also make it possible for physicians to "visit" or counsel patients, particularly those with mobility impairments, minimizing the need for travel. The Internet also affords patients access to a vast array of health-related information. It can also be used to facilitate communication between the patient and a provider, other family members, or people who have the same illness or disease (online support groups). Finally, reminder systems such as automated messaging can be used to remind patients of medication regimes or appointments.

Technology may also prove to be beneficial to family caregivers. Computer networks can link caregivers to each other, healthcare professionals, community services, and educational programs. Information technology can also enhance a caregiver's ability to access health-related information or information regarding community resources. Gallienne, Moore & Brenna (1993: 1) found that access to a computer network, "ComputerLink," increased the amount of psychological support provided by nurses to a group of homebound caregivers of Alzheimer's patients and enabled caregivers to access a support network that enabled them to share experiences, foster new friendships, and gather information on the symptoms of the disease. Technology can also aid caregivers' ability to manage their own healthcare needs as well as those of the patient by giving them access to information about medical problems, treatments, and prevention strategies. Software is available on several health-related topics such as stress management, caregiving strategies, and nutrition. For example, the Alzheimer's Association has a home page on the World Wide Web (www.alzheimers.com).

The Miami site of the *REACH (Resources for Enhancing Alzheimer's Caregiver Health)* program evaluated a family-therapy intervention augmented by a computer-telephone system (CTIS) for family caregivers of Alzheimer's patients. The intent of the CTIS system was to enhance the family-therapy intervention by facilitating the caregivers' ability to enable older adults to access formal and informal support services. The system enabled the caregivers to communicate with therapists, family, and friends; to participate in "online" support groups; to send and receive messages; and to access information databases such as the Alzheimer's Association Resource Guide. A respite function was also provided. In addition, the CTIS system provided the therapist with enhanced access to both the caregivers and their family members. The experience with the system was very positive with high acceptance of the system by caregivers. The majority of caregivers like the system and find it valuable and easy to use. The most common reason that caregivers used the system was to communicate with other family members, especially those who do not live nearby. The data also indicated that the system facilitated communication with other caregivers. Most caregivers reported that they found the participation in the online support groups to be very valuable (Czaja and Rubert, 2002: 469).

TECHNOLOGY IN THE WORKPLACE

Another setting where older people are likely to encounter computer technology is the workplace. Computer-interactive tasks are becoming prevalent within the service sector, office environments, and manufacturing industries. In 2001, more than half of the US labor force used a computer at work as compared to 25% in 1984 (US Department of Commerce, 2002). In addition, in 1995, at least 3 million Americans were telecommuting for purposes of work and this number is expected to increase by 20% per year over the next decade (Nickerson and Landauer, 1997: 3). The rapid introduction of computers and other forms of automated technology into occupational settings implies that most workers need to interact with computers simply to perform their jobs. This is an important issue as the number of workers age 55+ yrs is expected to increase over the next decade in most developed countries (Czaja, 2001: 547).

By 2010 the number of workers age 55+ in the United States will be about 26 million, a 46% increase since 2000, and by 2025 this number will increase to approximately 33 million. There will also be an increase in the number of workers over the age of 65 (Fullerton and Toossi, 2001: 21; United States General Accounting Office, 2001). Thus, one important issue that needs to be addressed is the adaptation of older workers to an increasingly technology-based work environment.

In general technology influences the types of jobs that are available, creating new jobs and opportunities for employment and eliminating other jobs, and creating conditions of unemployment for some classes of workers. Technology also changes the way in which jobs are performed and alters job content and job demands. Thus existing job skills and knowledge become obsolete and new knowledge and skills are required. Issues of skill obsolescence and worker retraining are highly significant for older workers as they are less likely than younger workers to have had exposure to technology such as computers (e.g. Czaja and Sharit, 1998: 332) and are often bypassed for training or retraining opportunities (Griffiths,

1997: 197). Problems with usability may also make it difficult for older workers to interact successfully with technology.

On the positive side, because in many cases technology reduces the physical demands of work, employment opportunities for older people may increase with the influx of workplace technologies. Adaptive technologies may also make continued work more viable for older people, especially those with a chronic condition or disability. The use of technology as an intervention tool for people with disabilities is expanding rapidly. For example, there are a number of technologies available that can help people with blindness or low vision problems or mobility problems to function in the workplace. Technology also makes work at home a more likely option.

In terms of actual performance, there have only been a handful of studies that have examined the ability of older people to perform computer-based tasks that are common in work settings. For example, Czaja and Sharit (1993: 59, 1998: 332) and Czaja *et al.* (2001: 564) conducted a series of studies examining age performance differences on a variety of simulated computer-based tasks (e.g. data entry, inventory management, customer service). Overall the results of these studies indicate that older adults (60–75 years) are willing and able to perform these types of tasks. However, generally, the younger adults (20–39 years) performed at higher levels than the older people. Importantly, the data also indicated that there was considerable variability in performance among the older people and that, with task experience, those in their middle years (40–59 years) performed at roughly the same levels as the young adults. In fact, task experience resulted in performance improvements for people of all ages. The results also indicated that interventions such as redesigning the screen, providing on-screen aids, and reconfiguring the timing of the computer mouse improved the performance of all participants.

To ensure that older adults are able to adapt successfully to new workplace technologies, employers need to ensure that older adults are provided with access to retraining programs and incentives to invest in learning new skills and abilities. Greater attention also needs to be given to the design of training and instructional materials for older learners. It is also important to understand how to design technology so that it is useful and usable for older adult populations, especially those with some type of impairment.

CONCLUSIONS

Computer technology holds the promise of improving the quality of life for older adults and their families. However, for the full potential of technology to be realized for these populations the needs and abilities of older adults must be considered in system design. Unfortunately, to date, designers of most systems have not considered older adults as active users of technology and thus many interfaces are designed without accommodating the needs of this population (Czaja and Lee, 2002). Usability problems relate to screen design, input device design, complex commands and operating procedures, and inadequate training and instructional support. In essence, to insure that older people are able to adapt successfully to technology we need detailed information on user preferences and needs, problems with existing systems, and the efficacy of design solutions.

FURTHER READING

Charness, N., and K. W. Schaie, eds. (2003). *Impact of technology on successful aging*. New York: Springer.

Charness, N., Park, D. C., and B. A. Sabel, eds. (2001). *Communication, technology and aging: opportunities and challenges for the future*. New York: Springer.

Fisk, A. D., Rogers, W. A., Charness, N., Czaja, S. J., and J. Sharit (2004). *Designing for older adults: principles and creative human factors approaches*. London: Taylor & Francis.

REFERENCES

Charness, N., and K. W. Schaie, eds. (2003). *Impact of technology on successful aging*. New York: Springer.

Charness, N., Schumann, C. E., and G. A. Boritz (1992). "Training older adults in word processing: effects of age, training technique and computer anxiety," *International Journal of Ageing and Technology*, 5: 79–106.

Charness, N., Kelley, C. L., Bosman, E. A., and M. Mottram (2001). "Word processing training and retraining: effects of adult age, experience, and interface," *Psychology and Aging*, 16: 110–27.

Czaja, S. J. (2001). "Technological change and the older worker." In J. E. Birren and K. W. Schaie, eds., *Handbook of the psychology of aging*. New York: Academic Press, pp. 547–68.

Czaja, S. J., and C. C. Lee (2002). "Designing computer system for older adults." In J. Jacko and A. Sears, eds., *Handbook of human–computer interaction*. New York: Lawrence Erlbaum and Associates (LEA), pp. 413–27.

Czaja, S. J., and M. Rubert (2002). "Telecommunications technology as an aid to family caregivers of persons with dementia," *Psychosomatic Medicine*, 64: 469–76.

Czaja, S. J., and J. Sharit (1993). "Age differences in the performance of computer based work as a function of pacing and task complexity," *Psychology and Aging*, 8: 59–67.

  (1998). "Ability-performance relationships as a function of age and task experience for a data entry task," *Journal of Experimental Psychology: Applied*, 4: 332–51.

Czaja, S. J., Hammond, K., and J. B. Joyce (1989a). *Word processing training for older adults*. Final report submitted to the National Institute on Ageing (Grant # 5 R4 AGO4647-03).

Czaja, S. J., Hammond, K., Blascovich, J., and H. Swede (1989b). "Age-related differences in learning to use a text-editing system," *Behavior and Information Technology*, 8: 309–19.

Czaja, S. J., Guerrier, J., Nair, S., and T. Landauer (1993). "Computer communication as an aid to independence for older adults," *Behavior and Information Technology*, 12: 197–207.

Czaja, S. J., Sharit, J., Ownby, R., Roth, D., and S. Nair (2001). "Examining age differences in performance of a complex information search and retrieval task," *Psychology and Aging*, 16: 564–79.

Dyck, J. L., and J. A. Smither (1994). "Age differences in computer anxiety: the role of computer experience, gender and education," *Journal of Educational Computing Research*, 10: 239–47.

Elias, P. K., Elias, M. F., Robbins, M. A., and P. Gage (1987). "Acquisition of word-processing skills by younger, middle-aged, and older adults," *Psychology and Aging*, 2: 340–8.

"Falling through the NET II: new data on the digital divide" (1998), www.ntia.doc.gov/ntiahome/net2/falling.html.

Fisk, A. D., Rogers, W. A., Charness, N., Czaja, S. J., and J. Sharit (2004). *Designing for older adults: principles and creative human factors approaches*. London: Taylor and Francis.

Fullerton, H. N., and M. Toossi (2001). "Labor force projections to 2010: steady growth and changing composition," *Monthly Labor Review, November*: 21–38.

Gallienne, R. L., Moore, S. M., and P. F. Brenna (1993). "Alzheimer's caregivers: psychosocial support via computer networks," *Journal of Gerontological Nursing*, 12: 1–22.

Gist, M., Rosen, B., and C. Schwoerer (1988). "The influence of training method and trainee age on the acquisition of computer skills," *Personal Psychology*, 41: 255–65.

Griffiths, A. (1997). "Aging, health, and productivity: a challenge for the new millennium," *Work and Stress*, 11: 197–214.

ITU Internet Reports (2003). "Birth of broadband: executive summary," Available from www.itu.int/osg/spu/publications/sales/birthofbroadband/BoBexecsumm.pdf.

Jay, G. M., and S. L. Willis (1992). "Influence of direct computer experience on older adults' attitudes towards computers," *Journal of Gerontology: Psychological Sciences*, 47: 250–7.

Mead, S. E., and A. D. Fisk (1998). "Measuring skill acquisition and retention with an ATM simulator: the need for age-specific training," *Human Factors*, 40: 516–23.

Mead, S. E., Spaulding, V. A., Sit, R. A., Meyer, B., and N. Walker (1997). "Effects of age and training on World Wide Web navigation strategies," *Proceedings of the Human Factors and Ergonomics Society 41st Annual Meeting*: 152–6.

Melenhorst, A.-S. (2002). "Adopting communication technology in later life: the decisive role of benefits." Doctoral dissertation, Technische Universiteit Eindhoven. ISBN 90–386–1867–0.

Morrell, R. W., Park, D. C., Mayhorn, C. B., and K. V. Echt (1995). "Older adults and electronic communication networks: learning to use ELDERCOMM." Paper presented at the 103 Annual Convention of the American Psychological Association. New York.

National Center for Health Statistics (2002). *U.S. decennial life tables for 1989–91*, Vol. I, no. 3: *Some trends and comparisons of United States life table data: 1900–91*. Hyattsville, Md.: National Center for Health Statistics 1999. www.cdc.gov/nchs/data/lifetables/life89_1_3.pdf.

Nickerson, R. S., and T. K. Landauer (1997). "Human–computer interaction: background and issues." In M. G. Helander, T. K., Landauer and P. V. Prabhu, eds., *Handbook of human–computer interaction*. Amsterdam: Elsevier, pp. 3–32.

Rogers, W. A., Fisk, A. D., Mead, S. E., Walker, N., and E. F. Cabrera (1996). "Training older adults to use automatic teller machines," *Human Factors*, 38: 425–33.

The UCLA Internet Report – "Surveying the digital future" (2003). UCLA Center for Communication Policy. Accessed from www.ccp.ucla.edu/pdf/UCLA-Internet-Report-Year-Three.pdf.

United States General Accounting Office (2001). *Older workers: demographic trends pose challenges for employers and workers*. Report to the ranking minority member, subcommittee on employer–employee relations, committee on education and the workforce, House of Representatives. Washington, D.C.: United States General Accounting Office.

US Department of Commerce (2002). *A nation online: how Americans are expanding their use of the Internet*. Washington, D.C.: Government Printing Office.

Westerman, S. J., Davies, D. R., Glendon, A. I., Stammers, R. B., and G. Matthews (1998). "Ageing and word processing competence: compensation or compilation?" *British Journal of Psychology*, 89: 579–97.

Zandri, E., and N. Charness (1989). "Training older and younger adults to use software," *Educational Gerontology*, 15: 615–31.

Ageing and Public Policy in Ethnically Diverse Societies

FERNANDO M. TORRES-GIL

This article examines the politics of ageing in diverse societies and the extent to which public policy may be influenced by the intersection of race, ethnicity, politics, and old age. The significance of these topical areas reflects the demographic trends of societal ageing, increasing diversity, immigration and migration, and the potential political activism of older persons in diverse societies. The United States is one example of a society with a history of a politics of ageing and a growing population of minority and immigrant groups who are exhibiting an interest in old age politics. What happens to public policy when race, ethnicity, and old age are politically mixed together?

Do age, ethnicity, and race matter in politics and public policy? As nations experience growing numbers of older persons and immigrant groups, will this scenario play out in their politics of ageing?

Finally, to what extent do policy makers (e.g. politicians) take into account the demands of politically active minority and immigrant elders?

This overview sets the stage for examining these multifaceted questions by assessing demographic trends that might portend a nexus between age and diversity; introducing conceptual models that may lead to a theoretical foundation; providing an overview into the politics of ageing in the United States and around the world; and using one case study where age, race, politics, and public policy come together. This approach complements other components of this handbook, including culture, ethnic diversity, political economy, generational change,and migration.

The rise of minority and immigrant elderly as political interest groups, competition between older homogeneous groups and a younger diverse population, and political organizing by older and minority individuals have received little attention. What is unique about this particular chapter is that several factors, heretofore examined separately, are brought together in an attempt to obtain insights into ageing and public policy in ethnically diverse societies. Admittedly, this is a difficult task, one constrained by the paucity of data, research, and analysis on these varied issues.

Furthermore, a focus on the United States, with isolated references to other countries, lessens the applicability and generalization to nations with different political systems, cultures, and histories. Nonetheless, this synopsis raises clues and suggestions for understanding the possibility that age, race, and diversity can complicate a politics of ageing and the public policy responses to the rise of such interest groups. The discussion and speculations about the possibility of other nations facing a politics of ageing and diversity suggest areas for future inquiry and research.

DEMOGRAPHIC TRENDS: SETTING THE STAGE

The world is ageing, albeit at varying rates, depending on the region. As societies age, the mix of age and politics can lead to a politics of ageing that influences those nations' public policies. The extent to which a politics of ageing is a major influence is debatable. As Binstock and Quadango (2001) make clear, old age political influence is "shaped fundamentally by larger societal forces" (p. 339). Nonetheless, nations around the globe must factor in the possibility that their older citizens may organize around old age interests and seek to influence how their governments respond to their concerns. Global demographic trends portend the future: the United Nations reports that about 10 percent of the world's population is now over age 60. By mid century, that percentage will double and, for the first time, older persons will outnumber children (Orme, 2002). These rates vary by country. For example, in Japan and Italy, a quarter of the populations are over 60 (and the proportion will pass 40 percent by 2050); whereas, in Africa and the Middle East, just 5 percent of the populations are over 60. Worldwide, the number of people age 60 and older will more than triple in the next 50 years, according to the United Nations' predictions.

The United States is ageing but less rapidly than Japan and Italy. Just 16 percent of the US population is over 60, and that number is expected to rise to 27 percent by 2050 (Orme, 2002). What makes the United States an important if not unique example is that its ageing is increasingly connected with its growing diversity and with a lively politics of ageing that influences public policy. The demographic nexus of ageing and diversity in the United States may serve as a scenario for what may occur in other parts of the world.

THE DEMOGRAPHIC NEXUS

The 2000 US Census Bureau data show that the median age increased from 32.9 years in 1990 to 35.3 years in 2000 and is expected to increase to 39 years or older by 2030 (US Bureau of the Census, 1990, 1996, 2000). Since 1900, life expectancy has increased by 31 years for women (from 48 to 79) and by 28 years for men (from 46 to 74). In the last century, while the total US population tripled (including those under 65 years of age), the elderly population in particular increased elevenfold (US Bureau of the Census, 1996). The elderly population is expected to grow substantially from 2010 to 2030 (US Bureau of the Census, 1996). Census 2000 found that 12.4 percent of the population was over 65, and that percentage is expected to increase to 15.7 by 2020

and to 21 by 2040 (US Bureau of the Census, 1996, 2000; Day, 1993).

Population and individual ageing are reshaping the American demographic landscape. While Census 2000 data indicate a leveling off in the growth rate of older persons (due to the lower fertility rates of the 1930s and 1940s), that will change shortly, when the baby boomers (those born between 1946 and 1964) begin to reach 65 years of age, and the projected doubling of the retiree population becomes a reality. Yet, as the society ages, the United States is witnessing a unique phenomenon: the diversification of its population.

Nearly one in every three Americans is a member of a minority group, reflecting the immigration surge of the 1990s (Rosenblatt, 2001). Not since the early 1900s have the United States seen such a dramatic growth of immigrants and minority groups. From 1990 to 2000, the nation's non-Hispanic White population dropped from 75.6% to 69.1% (US Bureau of the Census, 1990, 2000). Hispanics are now roughly equal to African Americans as two of the nation's largest minority groups. Hispanics accounted for 9% (22.4 million) of the US population in 1990 and increased to 12.5% (35.3 million) in 2000. African Americans showed a more modest increase, from 12.1% (30 million) to 12.3% (34.6 million). In the same period, the population of Asians and Pacific Islanders increased from 2.9% to 3.7%. Thus, there is greater diversity in the United States today than at any time in its recent history. About 10% (more than 25 million) of Americans today are foreign-born – a smaller proportion than the highest share last century (15% in 1910, or less than 15 million), but double the lowest share (5% in 1970, or less than 10 million) (US Bureau of the Census, 2001).

Minority populations are also ageing and becoming a larger portion of the non-Hispanic White elderly population. Williams and Wilson (2001) report that the number of ethnic minority elderly is increasing at a faster rate than that of their majority elderly counterparts. For example, the number of non-Hispanic Whites declined from 80% of the total elderly population in 1980 to 74% in 1995; and they can expect to account for 67% by 2050 (US Bureau of the Census, 1993, in Williams and Wilson, 2001). During that time, the Black elderly population will more than double, Hispanic elders will be the largest ethnic minority group of older persons, and the growth rate of older Asian / Pacific Islanders will be faster than that of any other ethnic elderly group in the United States.

These two trends – ageing and diversity – represent a demographic nexus that is shaping a new politics of ageing within a culturally diverse society. If this is the case, we can ask: are there lessons for the United States and other nations to learn as they approach this demographic intersection? Might these trends lead to an emerging politics of ageing and diversity that can influence government and public policy? To address these questions we must, conceptually at least, sort out the key elements in this equation – ageing, politics, diversity, policy – and integrate them into a usable conceptual framework.

CONCEPTUAL FRAMEWORKS

A challenge in understanding the topical question of "ageing and public policy in ethnically diverse societies" is that each of the key factors in this equation – ageing, public policy, ethnicity, and diversity – is complex and usually viewed in isolation. In addition, this equation implies that politics is another key element. The literature generally examines these factors as separate topical areas: culture and diversity, minority ageing, public policy and ageing, individual and population ageing, and the politics of ageing. To a large extent, the literature on the politics of ageing does include the elements of public policy, politics, and, in some cases, the role of minority elder groups in politics. However, involving all of the aforementioned areas in one integrated discussion and analysis is a relatively new exercise. Thus, bringing them together requires a multifaceted and multidisciplinary framework that can set the stage for a wider exploration of implications and scenarios.

One such conceptual framework is represented in Figure 1 and illustrates a nexus of ageing and diversity for 2000–10 (Torres-Gil and Moga, 2001).

The premise behind this figure is that the United States is embarking on a new period of ageing between 2000 and 2010 that will be much different than earlier periods (Torres-Gil, 1992). Between 1935 and 1990, the United States engaged in an expanding welfare state of entitlement programs and public benefits for its older population, with much of those policies predicated on reaching a specific old age. In

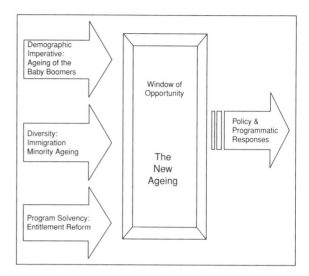

Figure 1. A nexus of ageing and diversity: 2000–10 (Torres-Gil and Moga, 2001).

addition, that period was characterized by political activism among the elderly and a sympathetic public response to their perceived needs. In the "new ageing," the policy and programmatic responses by government will be substantially different. The political and social response will be reshaped by three factors: (1) the ageing of the baby boomer population and the resulting demographic imperatives; (2) diversity, immigration, and growth of minority elders; and (3) the growing problem of maintaining fiscal solvency of large-scale entitlement programs. Taken together, these three factors may create a more robust politics of ageing buffeted by a nation becoming more ethnically diverse. This in turn may result in tensions and competition, as well as opportunities, as older Whites, older minorities, younger immigrant groups, and a younger population in general vie for scarce public resources in a time when age-based entitlement programs will lose public support.

The usefulness of this conceptual framework lies in the incorporation of diversity and ageing as a nexus for speculating on the political and public policy implications of a more heterogeneous society. But a politics of ageing in a diverse society is not a given; it may not happen simply because the demographic trends foretell more older persons and more minority and immigrant groups (and their ageing). The extent to which political action or a public

Equations

Causal Relationships

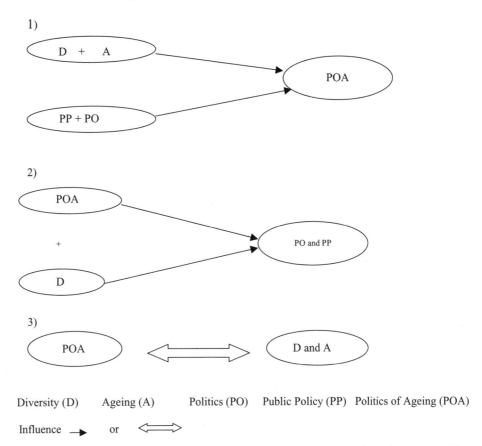

Diversity (D)   Ageing (A)   Politics (PO)   Public Policy (PP)   Politics of Ageing (POA)

Influence ➔   or   ⟺

Figure 2. Key factors in the topical equation and the fluid enfluences that may result.

policy response occurs depends on a fluid set of relationships that specify how various factors might influence each other. Figure 2 identifies key factors in the topical equation and the fluid influences that may result. This illustration isolates five factors – diversity (D), ageing (A), politics (PO), public policy (PP), and politics of ageing (PoA) – and asks, how do diversity and ageing influence politics and public policy and, conversely, to what extent do political and public policy actions cause older and more diverse populations to take an interest in a politics of ageing? The premise in this model is that increased diversity with and within an ageing population can lead to a new politics of ageing. At the same time,

attempts to reform public benefits that impact older and diverse populations can create a politics of ageing. Thus, the causal relationships can go both ways – or $D + A = PoA$ and $PP + PO = PoA$. In turn, a politics of ageing that includes dimensions of diversity and ageing can influence politics and public policy ($PoA + D = PO + PP$),while a politics of ageing that includes an older diverse population (and a younger diverse population recognizing their stake in an ageing society) can further a politics of ageing within younger and older diverse populations ($PoA = D + A$). An example of these equations is presented in the case study of "Hispanics, Social Security and Privatization in the United States." To understand how this particular example may foreshadow a nexus of ageing and diversity in public policy, we can examine the development of a politics of ageing in the United States.

THE US EXPERIENCE WITH A POLITICS OF AGEING

The United States has a storied history of interest group organizing by older persons, public policies based on age, and a politically active senior citizen electorate. Binstock and Day (1996) describe the high voting rates of older persons (while accounting for only 13 percent of the population, they account for 21 percent of those who vote in national elections) and their propensity to participate in a variety of political activities. While Binstock and Day acknowledge that the political clout of older persons may not be particularly powerful due to the heterogeneity of their views and priorities, they can be influential in causing politicians and policy makers to take note of their preferences. One manifestation of this visible politics of ageing is the proliferation of mass membership organizations, advocacy groups, and professional and trade organizations focused on old age concerns (more than 100 national organizations have focused on ageing concerns since the Second World War) (Binstock and Quadagno, 2001). The rise of old age political organizations goes back to the Great Depression of the 1930s and the resultant widespread poverty facing older persons, which in turn gave impetus to the Social Security Act of 1935. Later years saw the passage of laws providing health benefits to the elderly (e.g. Medicare, Medicaid), social supports (e.g. the Older Americans Act), a safety net for the destitute (e.g. Supplemental Security Income), and a nationwide network of state and local area agencies on ageing.

The increase of minority, racial, and immigrant groups and their ageing has also led to a politics of ageing that includes diversity. Old age organizations represent Hispanic, African American, Asian / Pacific Islander, and Native American elders. While those diverse populations are relatively young compared with the White, non-Hispanic population and have lower registration and voting rates, minority members over 65 years of age are still more likely to vote than their younger cohorts (Torres-Gil and Kuo, 1998). Thus, diverse populations in the United States are ageing and becoming a force in the politics of ageing and in public policy in general. This trend is reinforced by the demographic reality that minority groups (Hispanics and Asians / Pacific Islanders in particular) are becoming a majority population in certain regions of the United States (e.g. the South-

west), making them a potentially powerful political force. Hispanics, Asians, and African Americans are increasingly demonstrating their political clout on US domestic policy (e.g. education; social welfare; healthcare) and foreign policy (e.g. immigration; relations with Mexico, South Africa, and China) arenas. What would happen if these groups were to take an interest in ageing-related policies such as potential reforms of entitlement programs (e.g. Social Security, Medicare)? What electoral role might these voters play? To what extent will minority elders become a significant force in a politics of ageing?

Answers to these questions may depend on when the nexus of ageing and diversity is fully engaged and the direction of the causal relationships illustrated in Figure 2. What is clear is that the United States represents a political system with public policies that are increasingly influenced by ethnically diverse and older populations. But to what extent might this model be applicable to other parts of the world? What factors must be present to reflect the models in Figures 1 and 2? First, we must see whether there are indications that other nations may be witnessing old age organizing and if their political systems (hence public policies) are susceptible to a politics of ageing. Second, might the hallmarks of an ethnically diverse society – race, culture, ethnicity, immigration – be present to intersect with ageing?

SEEDS OF A GLOBAL POLITICS OF AGEING

Few countries have the open and pluralistic democratic system of the United States, a democracy that allows for many entry points to influence public policy. This form of civic culture is ideal for interest group organizing by any and all interested constituents. Most parts of the world rely on a more top-down model – whether authoritarian, parliamentary, or a limited democracy – with a populace seeking leadership or mandates from a centralized government or authority. Thus, there may be limits to a replication of the US politics of ageing. Furthermore, it is worth noting that being old is not necessarily the dominant variable in how an older person exercises his or her political choice, and old age policy issues are not always influenced by how older persons act (Binstock and Quadagno, 2001). Nonetheless, there are indications that older persons in other nations are beginning to acquire an age-consciousness and are organizing around their concerns as older persons.

For example, China is facing the seeds of rebellious activities by elderly Chinese retirees angry over unpaid or disappearing pensions and political corruption, even to the point of unprecedented public protests (Chu, 2002). The Netherlands may mirror the future for Europe in a "granny revolution" by pensioners resisting any dilution of their generous subsidies, even in the face of a declining workforce – resistance that has led to the creation of two age-based political parties (Drozdiak, 1994). Binstock and Quadagno cite the emergence of ageing-based political organizations in Australia, Canada, Japan, and Europe (2001). Thus, we are witnessing the potential emergence of varied forms of a politics of ageing in different parts of the world. And, with the continued graying of many of these nations, the high costs of social welfare programs for older persons, and declining fertility levels, we may find that old age matters in their politics, especially where fundamental changes to pensions and healthcare programs adversely affect older persons.

Given this overview of the politics of ageing in the United States and at the global level, where does diversity fit in? How is diversity linked to a politics of ageing, and what might be examples of this nexus?

THE COMING NEXUS: AGEING AND DIVERSITY

The United States today illustrates a growing intersection of ageing and diversity and its link to public policy. We see this, for example, in debates around immigration, bilingual education, and affirmative action. The large influx of undocumented persons from Latin America and the Pacific Basin create tensions and conflicts among those who feel the United States has lost control of its borders. Immigrants take jobs from native-born Americans, and states become saddled with the burden of providing education, healthcare, and social services without adequate federal reimbursements. Furthermore, fears of a dilution of the "American character," especially where native-born, non-Hispanic Whites are becoming a minority, exacerbate worries that the United States will have a growing under-class of poor, non-English-speaking, and resentful minorities and immigrants.

On the other hand, many point out the benefits of an increasingly ethnically diverse population. The bulk of both legal and undocumented immigrants are young, energetic, and aspire to the values of previous immigrants to the United States: a strong work ethic, orientation towards family and church, patriotism, an entrepreneurial spirit. This in turn has given the United States a productive and young workforce, albeit more diverse, to replace the ageing White population and to provide the productivity, entrepreneurship, and taxes to sustain old age benefits. These advantages are seen in the rejuvenation of many US cities and neighborhoods, enhanced productivity and proliferation of small businesses, and a rising middle class in these diverse areas. This resident population of culturally diverse groups gives the United States tighter bonds with countries (e.g. China, Mexico, Japan, Eastern Europe, the Philippines) important to US global trade. And, historically, immigrants acculturate to American norms (a civic culture) and move into a middle class (however poorly they started) within two to three generations.

However, debates over the ultimate benefits and consequences of America's immigration and diversification have heretofore not extended to the intersection of ageing and diversity. What are the potential challenges and dilemmas when age and minority/immigrant status is incorporated into a politics of ageing? How might it come together, and what lessons can be gleaned from this evolution in the politics of a diverse society?

A CASE STUDY: SOCIAL SECURITY AND PRIVATIZATION

The United States is in the midst of fundamental debates about the financial solvency and viability of its old age policies, which are designed to provide some form of universal health and retirement coverage for its older population. Those debates are driven, in part, by concerns that the ageing of the baby-boom population will double the over-65 population, and, with fewer workers paying into these programs, will strain the ability of the federal government to afford continuing health and retirement benefits (Torres-Gil, 1992). In addition, older persons are losing "symbolic legitimacy," their ability to rely on public sympathy and automatic political support for their demands (Binstock and Day, 1996).

The Social Security Act of 1935 represents this conundrum. This national policy is the basic federal old age benefit program for more than 46 million beneficiaries. It provides a basic social safety net with a minimum level of retirement benefits for those who qualify (old age and survivors of partnerships' insurance), as well as disability insurance coverage, survivors' benefits, and Supplemental Security Income for the poorest of the aged, blind, and disabled (Torres-Gil and Villa, 2000). Yet its funding (derived from worker and employer contributions), while currently in a large surplus, is projected to fall short of funding more than 75 percent of the future Social Security benefits for retired baby boomers sometime after 2018. Thus, proposals have been raised that would fundamentally alter the social insurance nature of this entitlement through a privatized approach.

Privatization would allow employees to take part of their Social Security payroll taxes and establish individual accounts. Thus, instead of paying into Social Security with its pay-as-you-go system (where employee contributions go to all others who qualify), they could control and invest that portion as they wish. The arguments for this approach are that individual workers have a right to their tax contributions, the rates of return in the private market are higher than the guaranteed federal interest used for current Social Security surpluses, and individuals will have an incentive to save for their retirement. Opponents argue that privatization would dilute the collective and communal nature of Social Security and leave open the question of what would happen to those who do not invest well and may still be dependent on a social safety net.

The interest group politics as to whether the United States Congress and public opinion will support this radical shift in Social Security increasingly hinges on convincing younger workers about the advantages and disadvantages of privatization. Those young workers are increasingly minority: African Americans and Hispanics. Conservative groups, who favor privatization, have astutely targeted minority and immigrant rights organizations such as the Hispanic and Black caucus of the US

Congress and advocacy groups for them. Their arguments are compelling: younger minority and immigrant employees pay a high proportion of their wages for a system of regressive payroll taxes (individuals pay up to a capped percentage of their salary [$84,900 in 2002]); they have lower life expectancies and thus may not receive a commensurate return on their contributions compared with Whites; and their entrepreneurship would have them make better use of investment devices such as individual retirement accounts. Others, especially minority ageing organizations, labor groups, and senior citizen lobbies, argue the following: older minorities rely on Social Security's myriad benefits to a greater extent than Whites; younger minorities will someday become old and need Social Security protection; and immigrant and minority family values are more conducive to the communal approach of a social insurance system.

The debates over privatization are not yet settled, and the US Congress is continuing to argue the merits of this proposal. Nonetheless, this case study for the first time highlights several features of ageing and public policy in an ethnically diverse society:

• Traditional white, elderly advocacy groups recognize that they must build coalitions with minority and immigrant rights organizations in order to draw from their political strengths and to understand the needs of younger diverse groups.
• Minority elderly advocacy groups are developing alliances with younger minority and immigrant groups to educate their youth about the stake they have in old age public policies.
• White and conservative groups see political merit in appealing to the traditional (and conservative) values of immigrant and minority groups and in appealing to the longterm concerns of these groups for a secure retirement.
• All interest groups in the Social Security debate realize that the future of old age politics and the reform of entitlement programs will increasingly depend on the political activism and preference of the growing minority and immigrant workforce in the United States.

This case study bears witness to a politics of ageing whose influence on public policy will depend in growing measure on its diverse and ageing populations. It also points out that two key factors – old age and diversity – may in fact form a basis for political mobilization among these interest groups. Although Walker (1999) states that "old-age is not a sound basis for political mobilization . . . , it is possible that future old age cohorts may be more likely to organize their political attitudes along group rather than partisan lines" (p. 7). The potential structural reforms of the Social Security Act of 1935 and other old age policies may just be the "radical policy proposals regarding old-age benefit policies" that Binstock and Quadagno (2001) feel may "engender greater age-group consciousness and voting cohesion among the elderly" (p. 345). What has not been factored into this equation, however, is the role of diversity and a politics of ageing among minority and immigrant groups.

IMPLICATIONS FOR GLOBAL AGEING

Will this case study and its lessons be replicated in other nations? Might they have the attendant circumstances to someday reach that nexus? Under what circumstances might other countries face a growing elderly population and a politics of ageing? And if others might face this situation, how might immigration and/or diversity in those countries influence their governments? Admittedly, little is known about how these trends may play out in other places. But one country, Korea, may give potential clues.

PRECONDITIONS FOR AN INCIPIENT POLITICS OF AGEING

In the midst of becoming a major industrial and technologically advanced society along Western and capitalist lines, South Korea has a homogeneous population and a traditional Confucian culture. Older South Koreans benefit from an over-riding value of filial piety – forms of respect, responsibility, affection, and repayment to the elderly – that influence cultural practice and family relationships in Korean society (Sung, 1998). Yet, while it is becoming more Westernized, Korean society is ageing (Jung-Ki and Torres-Gil, 2000). Its older population has increased from 3.2% of the total population in 1960 to 7% in 2000 and will increase to over 19% by 2030 (*Korea Statistical Yearbook*, 1997). It may only take 22 years for the proportion of Korea's elderly population (those over 65) to increase from 7% to

14% of the country's population. In comparison, it will take 85 years in Sweden and 24 years in Japan (Choi, 2001).

This rapidly ageing and changing society is creating tensions within traditional family relationships. For example, one survey shows that about two-thirds of Korean adults in their 20s to 50s would prefer to live independently of their children when they are old (Jung-Ki and Torres-Gil, 2000). In addition, the Korean government has embarked on a program to develop long term care facilities, retirement pensions, and medical and social programs for the elderly. Where these trends may eventually lead – a more Western model of individualism, ageism, isolation of elders, or maintenance of the traditional practice of filial piety – is uncertain.

On the surface, Korea may appear removed from the historical, cultural, economic, and political conditions that gave rise to a politics of ageing in the United States. But on closer examination, some of those preconditions may be unfolding in Korean society. Figure 3 provides a framework for identifying an incipient politics of ageing in societies whose political culture is unlike that of the United States (Jung-Ki and Torres-Gil, 2000).

The illustration posits that nine preconditions are necessary for a society to have a basis for a politics of ageing similar to that of the United States. They are:

1) longevity and the rise of multigenerational families;
2) a capitalist, free-market environment, the pressures of modernization, and a competitive global economy;
3) the rise of individualism, opportunity (e.g., education, professional advancement), and a move towards nuclear family households;
4) elder dissatisfaction with changes in the family and society and growing isolation from family and community;
5) an open, pluralistic democracy with an unfettered media;
6) interest group politics and the rise of advocacy and constituent-based organizations;
7) the presence of older individuals serving as advocates and spokespersons for their age cohort;
8) the adoption of Western systems of categorical programs for the elderly; and
9) the prevalence of a youth-oriented culture and of ageism.

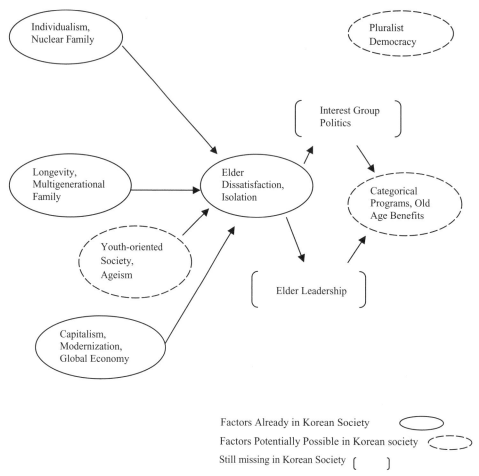

Factors Already in Korean Society

Factors Potentially Possible in Korean society

Still missing in Korean Society

Figure 3. An incipient politics of ageing leading to potential intergenerational issues (Jung-Ki and Torres-Gil, 2000).

Korean society today appears to meet four pre-conditions (represented in solid lines) and is on the verge of at least three others (represented in dotted lines): a growing youth-oriented society and signs of reticence towards care of elders in family households, categorical programs for older persons, and a budding pluralist democracy. What are still missing are two other preconditions: interest group politics among the elderly and elder leadership. Should Korean society meet at least the first seven preconditions, it may not be long before we see a visible politics of ageing.

THE ROLE OF ETHNICITY, IMMIGRATION, AND DIVERSITY

Even if a non-Western and more traditional society such as Korea moves towards a type of politics of ageing, the other key element of the nexus model, diversity, must also be present. "Diversity," as used in this chapter, refers to differences within a population and is best exemplified where the majority population is relatively homogeneous and older but must account for different cultures, races, and ethnicities in its midst that are younger. This is otherwise known as an "age–race stratified" society. The United States has a predominantly Euro-ethnic majority (e.g. Anglo, Irish, German) that is essentially Caucasian. Within such an emerging diversity are persons of color (e.g. Asian, Hispanic, Black, Native American), with a continuing mixture of other White immigrants (e.g. Armenian, Russian, Slavic). Differences in fertility rates play a key role in an age–race stratified society. In the United States, the replacement ratio of the White, non-Hispanic population is at about a 1.8. Asians and Blacks have a 2.1 ratio. The net growth of the US population is primarily Hispanic with a replacement ratio of 2.4 (US Bureau of the Census, 1999).

Other parts of the world are also facing the potential for this type of an "age–race stratified" society, wherein the older, retiree population is predominantly homogeneous, and the younger population differs by race, ethnicity, and immigration status, and serves as the workforce for an ageing society. Western Europe and its legacy of guest workers, fueled by European Union market arrangements that facilitate easy movement of labor from diverse nations and cultures, is facing similar strains. For example, the fertility rates of native Germans, Danes, and French are below replacement levels compared to their guest workers (e.g. Algerians, Turks, Arabs). This nexus of an older population of native Europeans that is increasingly reliant on diverse groups to replace its dwindling numbers may well have the potential for a politics of ageing where diversity plays a role, albeit in different ways than in the United States (e.g. religion, as witnessed by Muslim fundamentalism in secular countries such as France and Germany). Already, Europe grapples with the political controversies of politicians promoting nativist policies (to force the return of these immigrants to their native lands) and pursuing pronatalist policies (encouraging native-born people to have more children).

Japan, on the other hand, must grapple with the serious social and economic consequences of declining fertility levels and the world's highest life expectancy. With a replacement level of about 1.3 and a population of elders (age 65+) expected to be 20 percent by 2007, Japan must either encourage Japanese women to have more children, entice retirees back to the workforce, or import younger workers from other countries. The former does not appear to be working, and Japan is giving serious consideration to utilizing retirees and allowing immigration as a way to sustain its workforce (Moffett, 2003).

Israel represents a society quite close to a nexus of ageing and diversity and an age–race stratified society. Its older population is primarily of European origin, and it has a lively politics of ageing with two political parties of pensioners having run candidates for national elections (Iecovich, 2001). The declining birth rate of the population and the instability posed by its Mid-east conflicts have generated substantial immigration from Africa and the Middle East, giving it the tensions and opportunities of a younger, diverse population competing for political empowerment with a more homogeneous older society.

These examples – Korea, Japan, and Israel – indicate that other nations besides the United States may face conditions leading to a politics of ageing and diversity. Should that become the case, governments and public policy will be forced to confront a more complex dynamic of ageing and public policy in ethnically diverse societies.

CONCLUSIONS AND CLOSING COMMENTS

This chapter has attempted to outline the basis for public policy in an ageing and ethnically diverse society by presenting frameworks and illustrations of where and when this may occur. Given the newness and evolving nature of this subject (and the paucity of research), we dissect the essential elements of this multifaceted subject and present examples of what this is and where it might occur.

The United States provides the best illustration of a nation grappling with its ageing society, growing diversity, and the political implications for public policy. The nexus of ageing and diversity and its role in a politics of ageing is having a visible impact on US public policies. Other nations may find similar situations and evolving trends that may give clues to a potential politics of ageing and diversity. While we may not yet have clarity about the direction and evolution of ageing and public policy in ethnically diverse societies, the importance and relevance of this topical trend grows. A globalized world can no longer view its demographic changes in isolation from other countries. Technological flexibility in communication (Internet), common market arrangements (e.g., South and North America, Asia), trade and economic dispersion, as well as labor and workforce mobility mean that no nation is immune from the demographic pressures facing much of the world. In due course, older and developed nations (e.g. the First World) will need the youthful populations of the Third World. Maintaining expensive social programs with a declining labor and tax base will require fundamentally difficult decisions about reduction in public benefits or promoting the growth of younger immigrant and minority populations. And the aspirations of disenfranchised minorities and immigrant groups living longer will increase demands and expectations for the "good life" enjoyed by retirees in affluent nations. What is certain is that diversity will become a crucial variable in the evolution of a politics of ageing in much of the world, and, in turn, politics and public policy will influence a politics of ageing and be influenced by it. Further research and monitoring of demographic trends, politics, government responses, and immigration may reveal possibilities of this occurring.

FURTHER READING

Angel, R., and J. Angel (1997). *Who will care for us? Aging and long term care in multicultural America*. New York: New York University Press.

Hayes-Bautista, D., Schink, W., and J. Chapa (1988). *The burden of support: young Latinos in an aging society*. Stanford: Stanford University Press.

Kingson, E., Hirshorn, B., and J. Cornman (1986). *Ties that bind: the interdependence of generations*. Washington, D.C.: Seven Looks Press.

Parker, T. (2000). *What if boomers can't retire?* San Francisco: Berrett-Koehler Publishers.

REFERENCES

Binstock, R. H., and C. Day (1996). "Aging and politics." In R. H. Binstock and L. K. George, eds., *Handbook of aging and the social sciences*, 4th edn. San Diego, Calif.: Academic Press, pp. 362–87.

Binstock, R. H., and J. Quadagno (2001). "Aging and politics." In R. H. Binstock and L. K. George, eds., *Handbook of aging and the social sciences*, 5th edn. San Diego, Calif.: Academic Press, pp. 333–51.

Choi, S. J. (2001). "Economic status, work and retirement of elderly Koreans." Paper presented at Invited Symposium of the 17th Congress of Gerontology, Vancouver, Canada, July 1–6.

Chu, H. (2002). "Retirees balk at Beijing's bitter pill," *Los Angeles Times*, June 10, p. A10.

Day, J. C. (1993). *Population projection of the United States by age, sex, race, and Hispanic origin: 1993 to 2050.* US Bureau of the Census, Current Population Reports. Washington D.C.: US Government Printing Office, pp. 25–1104.

Drozdiak, W. (1994). "Elderly Dutch reach for political power in 'Granny Revolution," *Washington Post*, May 3.

Iecovich, E. (2001). "Pensioners' political parties in Israel," *Journal of Aging and Social Policy*, 12 (3): 87–107.

Jung-Ki,K., and F. Torres-Gil (2000). "Intergenerational and intragenerational equity in the United States and their implications for Korean society," *Journal of the Korea Gerontological Society*, 20 (2): 91–107.

Korea Statistical Yearbook (1997). Seoul Statistical Office.

Moffett, S. (2003). "For ailing Japan, longevity begins to take its toll," *Wall Street Journal*, February 11, pp. A11–A13.

Orme, W. (2002). "World is quickly going gray, U. N. study finds," *Los Angeles Times*, March 1, p. A3.

Rosenblatt, R. (2001). "Census illustrates diversity from sea to shining sea," *Los Angeles Times*, March 13, pp. A1–16.

Sung, K. T. (1998). "Filial piety in modern times: timely adaptation and practice patterns," *Australian Journal on Aging*, 17 (1): 88–92.

Torres-Gil, F. (1992). *The New Aging: Politics and Change in America*. Westport, CT: Auburn House.

Torres-Gil, F. and T. Kuo (1998). *Journal of Gerontological Social Work*. Vol. 30, No. 1/2, 1998, pp. 143–158.

Torres-Gil, F. and K. B. Moga (2001). Multiculturalism, Social Policy and the New Aging. *Journal of Gerontological Social Work*. Vol. 36, No. 3/4, pp. 13–32.

Torres-Gil, F. and V. Villa (2000). Social Policy and the Elderly. In J. Midgley, M. Tracey, and M. Livermore (Eds.). *The Handbook of Social Policy*, (pp. 209–220). Thousand Oaks, CA: Sage Publications.

US Bureau of the Census (1990). *Table DP-1. Profile of general demographic characteristics for the United States: 1990*. Washington, D.C.: US Bureau of the Census.

(1993). *U.S. Census of Population 1990, Social and Economic Characteristics*. Current Population Reports, Series 2–1. Washington, D.C.: Government Printing Office.

(1996). *65+ in the United States*. Current Population Reports, Special Studies. Washington, D.C.: pp. 23–190. US Government Printing Office. Retrieved from www.census.gov/pop/p23-190.html.

(1999). *Population profile of the United States 1999*. Washington, D.C.: US Government Printing Office.

(2000). "Census 2000. Table DP-1. Profile of general demographic characteristics for the United States." Retrieved from www.census.gov/Press-Release/www/2001/table/dp_us_2000.pdf.

(2001). "Adding diversity from abroad: the foreign-born population, 1999." *Population profile of the United States*

1999: America at the close of the 20th century. Current Population Reports, Special Studies Series. pp. 23–205. Washington, D.C.: US Government Printing Office, pp. 67–9.

Walker, A. (1999). "Political participation and representation of the older people." In A. Walker and G. Naegele, Eds., *The politics of old age in Europe.* Philadelphia, Penn.: Open University Press, pp. 7–24.

Williams, D. R., and C. M. Wilson (2001). "Race, ethnicity, and aging." In R. H. Binstock and L. K. George, eds., *Handbook of aging and the social sciences,* 5th edn. San Diego, Calif.: Academic Press, pp. 160–78.

Index